Europe in Our Time

Europe

1914

THIRD EDITION

IN OUR TIME

TO THE PRESENT

Robert Ergang, *Ph.D.*

D. C. HEATH AND COMPANY

MAPS BY THEODORE R. MILLER

Preface

NEVER BEFORE *in history have so many serious problems presented themselves for solution. The dominant position of our country in world affairs makes it imperative that American citizens should have clear and sound ideas concerning these problems. By providing a historical background the author hopes he will contribute in some little way toward giving the present generation a better understanding of recent events and contemporary problems. Shortly after the First World War H. G. Wells wrote: "The need for a common knowledge of the general facts of human history throughout the world has become very evident during the tragic happenings of the last few years. There can be no peace now, we realize, but a common peace in all the world; no prosperity but a general prosperity. But there can be no common peace and prosperity without common historical ideas. . . . [There must be] a sense of history as a common adventure of mankind." This is even more true today than it was at the time it was written. The international outlook must be based on appreciative understanding of the life and problems of other peoples. Only by understanding the common problems of the world can we arrive at a common peace.*

Choosing the facts and events to be included in a historical work is never easy; but when the work surveys recent or contemporary history, it is particularly difficult. The events are too near the writer to be seen in proper perspective. Some of them will soon be left behind by the march of time while others will continue to influence the destiny of man over a long period. Hence the writer makes no claim to have written a definitive history. This cannot be done until the real significance of the events has been established in the light of broader movements.

Grateful acknowledgment is made to Dr. Louis L. Snyder, Professor of History in the College of the City of New York, who gener-

ously interrupted his own work to read the first twenty chapters of the typescript and to make many excellent suggestions for their improvement. The cheerful assistance and cooperation of the editorial staff of D. C. Heath and Company is also gratefully remembered. The writer is further deeply indebted to his wife, Mildred Overbeck Ergang, for typing the manuscript, for her counsel and, above all, for her faith and encouragement.

ROBERT ERGANG

New York City

Preface to the Third Edition

THE RUSH of events since the first revision of Europe in Our Time in *1953* has necessitated the addition of two chapters in the Third Edition to cover this period. Ample bibliographies for these chapters have been provided, and important new books on the earlier periods have been added in a supplementary listing. The Third Edition, therefore, rounds off the picture of another event-filled decade of contemporary Europe to bring down to date the story of the entire period since *1914.*

R. E.

Table of Contents

WORLD WAR I

I. *The Background of World War* I   *3*

The Brewing of the Storm   3
Crises Preceding the Outbreak of Hostilities   13
The Storm Breaks   17

II. *World War* I: *The First Phase*   *24*

The Opening Campaigns   24
The Period of German Predominance   30
A Year of Hopes and Disappointments   33
New Elements in Warfare   39
Naval Warfare, 1914–1916   48

III. *World War* I: *The Second Phase*   *54*

The United States Enters the War   54
The Collapse of Russia   62
The Great German Drive   76
Allied Victory   78

IV. *The Paris Peace Conference*   *87*

Wilsonian Idealism   87
Allied Realism   92
The Treaty of Versailles   97
The Other Treaties   109

EUROPE BETWEEN TWO WARS

V. *The Weimar Republic*   *117*

The Founding of the Republic   117
Reparations and Inflation   126
The Republic at Its Height   130
The Twilight of German Democracy   140

VI. Battered and Bleeding France   *145*

The Price of Victory   145
The Road to Recovery   147
Political and Financial Difficulties   149
Depression and the Threat of Fascism   150
Foreign Policy   154
France's Uneasy Dominions   157

VII. Soviet Russia   *165*

Organizing the Revolution   165
The New Economic Policy   174
The Five-Year Plans   177
Government in the Soviet Union   189
Religion and Culture   195
Soviet Foreign Policy   202

VIII. British Economic and Imperial Problems   *206*

Britain's Government   206
Decline of British Industry and Trade   208
Cabinets and Governments   212
A King Abdicates   215
The British Commonwealth of Nations   217

IX. Fascist Italy   *227*

The Resurgence of Dictatorship   227
Postwar Italy   232
The Genesis of Fascism   235
Entrenchment in Power   238
Mussolini as Absolute Ruler of Italy   242
Fascism in Action   247
The Quest for Empire   254

X. The Succession States of the Habsburg Empire   *259*

The Collapse of the Habsburg Empire   259
Austria's Struggle for Existence   262
Hungarian Irredentism   270
The Problem of Minorities in Czechoslovakia   274
Poland Harassed by Internal and External
    Troubles   284

XI. *Turkey Faces Toward the West* 296

    The End of the Ottoman Empire 296
    Revolt Against the Treaty of Sèvres 298
    Westernization of Turkey 302
    Economic Development in Turkey 309

XII. *Nazi Germany* 313

    The Beginnings of National Socialism 313
    The Nazi Bible 317
    Nazi Technique 319
    The Nazis Consolidate Their Power 322
    Making Germany Strong 328
    Germany Prepares for War 336
    Education and Culture 344

XIII. *The Balkans* 350

    The Peninsula of Unrest 350
    Rumania 353
    Yugoslavia 361
    Greece 367
    Bulgaria 370
    Albania 373

XIV. *Spain and Portugal* 376

    Discontent among the Working Classes 376
    The Dictatorship of Primo de Rivera 378
    Republican Reform and Conservative Reaction
      382
    Civil War 388
    The Dictatorship of General Franco 396
    Dictatorship in Portugal 399

XV. *Small States of Europe* 403

    Dilemma of the Small States 403
    Belgium 404
    The Kingdom of the Netherlands 409
    The Scandinavian Countries 416
    Finland 427
    Switzerland 429

*XVI. Revolt of the East against Western Imperial-
        ism*   *432*

   Awakening of the Orient   432
   India's Struggle for Independence   435
   Strife-rent China   443
   Imperialist Japan   452

WORLD WAR II

   XVII. The Background of World War II   *465*

   Efforts to Establish Permanent Peace   465
   The Basic Causes of World War II   468
   The Road to War   481
   The Rape of Czechoslovakia   487
   The Eve of Hostilities   494

   XVIII. The Period of Axis Predominance   *499*

   From Blitzkrieg to Sitzkrieg   499
   The War at Sea   506
   The Nazi Juggernaut Crushes Five Nations   509
   The Fall of France   516
   The Battle of Britain   522
   The War in the Mediterranean Area   531

   XIX. The Turn of the Tide   *541*

   The Nazis Invade Russia   541
   The United States and the War   551
   Pearl Harbor and After   558
   Japanese Conquests   561
   Failure of the Nazis in Russia   568
   The Desert Seesaw   571
   Anglo-American Occupation of French North
      Africa   573

   XX. The Allies Triumphant   *576*

   Nazis Driven Back in Russia   576
   Destruction from the Air   579
   The Battle for Italy: The Beginning of the End
      583

D-Day: The Invasion of France 588
Climax: The Drive into Germany 593
Death Comes to Two Dictators 597
Victory in Europe 598
Victory Over Japan 600
The End of World War II 607

EUROPE SINCE WORLD WAR II

XXI. *The Preliminary Peace Conferences* *611*

The Big Three at Yalta 612
The Soviet Union and the War in the Pacific 616
Unity and Disunion 619
Potsdam, the Last Wartime Conference 622

XXII. *The Struggle for Peace* *627*

The Council of Foreign Ministers 627
The Paris Peace Conference 632
The Signing of the First Treaties 635
The German and Austrian Treaties 638
The Treaty with Japan 641

XXIII. *The United Nations* *645*

Founding the UN 645
The Organs of the UN 647
Achievements of the UN 653
The Problem of Controlling Atomic Energy 657
The Failure of Disarmament Efforts 659
The Veto in the Security Council 663
The Background of the Korean Conflict 665
The War in Korea 667

XXIV. *Western Europe after World War II* *672*

Rebuilding Western Europe 672
The Marshall Plan 673
The Schuman Plan 676
The North Atlantic Treaty Organization 679

XXV. *Postwar Germany* *686*

Germany in Defeat 686
Dividing the Country 689

Punishing the Nazis 691
Reparations and Dismantling 693
The Berlin Blockade 695
The West German Republic 698
Soviet East Germany 700
The Question of German Unity 702

XXVI. *Socialist Britain*   705

Britain's Plight 705
The Labor Government and Its Program 709
Economic Progress in Britain 712
The Return of the Conservatives 714
The King Is Dead! Long Live the Queen! 717

XXVII. *The French Dilemma*   719

The Fall of the Vichy Regime 719
The Provisional Government of General de
   Gaulle 721
The Fourth Republic 724
The French Economic Dilemma 726
Recovery and Retrogression 729

XXVIII. *Franco's Spain and the Italian Republic*   732

Franco and the Axis 732
Postwar Spain 737
Economic Conditions in Franco's Spain 742
Postwar Italian Politics 746
Establishing the Italian Republic 749
Decline of Communism in Italy 751
Economic Reconstruction in Italy 753

XXIX. *The Passing of the Old Colonial Imperialism* 758

The Resurgence of Nationalism 758
"L'Empire Est Mort!" 761
The United States of Indonesia 766
Changes in the British Commonwealth 769
Independence for India 771
The Restive Middle East 775
The Dissolution of the Italian Empire 779

XXX. *The Soviet Union since World War II*   *782*

The Soviet Union at War's End   782
The New Five-Year Plans   785
Religion and Family Life in Soviet Russia   791
Changes and Developments   794
Thought Control in the Soviet Union   796
The New Emphasis on Orthodoxy in the Arts   801

XXXI. *The New Soviet Imperialism*   *807*

The Nature of Soviet Imperialism   807
Poland and Hungary   811
Rumania, Bulgaria, and Albania   815
Yugoslavia and Titoism   818
The Sovietization of Czechoslovakia   821
China Becomes a Soviet Appendage   823

XXXII. *Recent Developments in the Soviet Sphere*   *830*

The New Soviet Leaders   830
The Downgrading of Stalin   833
The New Look   839
Soviet Economic Progress   843
The Conquest of Space   846
Unrest and Revolt in the Satellites   849
The Shift to National Leadership in Poland   851
Revolt in Hungary   853
The Reconciliation with Tito   857
The Continuing Struggle for Peace   859

XXXIII. *Recent Developments in Central and Western Europe*   *864*

Crises in France   864
The Resurgence of West Germany   871
Progress in East Germany   875
The Problem of German Reunification   878
Changes in Britain   879
Italy Moves Ahead   887
Progress in Franco's Spain   892
Dusk of Empire   895
The Suez Affair   902
The Changing UN   907
The Vicissitudes of NATO   911

APPENDIX

Bibliography   915

Supplementary Bibliography   963

Index   967

List of Illustrations

THE BRITISH AND RUSSIAN ROYAL FAMILIES AT COWES, ENGLAND, IN 1914   19

TAXICABS AND BUSES USED TO CONVEY FRENCH SOLDIERS TO THE FRONT LINES, 1914   27

A HANDLEY-PAGE BOMBING PLANE FROM THE FIRST WORLD WAR   45

AN AMERICAN SUPPLY DEPOT IN FRANCE; FIRST WORLD WAR   59

FRENCH TANKS IN ACTION; FIRST WORLD WAR   69

THE RAILWAY CAR IN WHICH THE ARMISTICE OF 1918 WAS SIGNED; IN FRONT OF LES INVALIDES, PARIS   81

PALACE OF THE LEAGUE OF NATIONS, GENEVA, SWITZERLAND   101

DR. STRESEMANN, SIR AUSTEN CHAMBERLAIN, M. BRIAND, AND DR. BENEŠ AT THE LEAGUE OF NATIONS, SEPTEMBER 22, 1926   133

ST. PIERRE, MIQUELON, THE LAST REMNANT OF THE FRENCH EMPIRE IN NORTHERN AMERICA   159

THE KREMLIN, MOSCOW   193

BOYS OF THE FASCIST YOUTH ORGANIZATIONS PARADING BEFORE IL DUCE   243

CHANCELLOR KURT SCHUSCHNIGG INSPECTING AUSTRIA'S FIGHTING PLANES; APRIL, 1936   267

PRESIDENT MASARYK OF CZECHOSLOVAKIA AND HIS SUCCESSOR, EDVARD BENEŠ   279

THE NEW AND THE OLD IN WOMEN'S CLOTHES IN TURKEY   307

AUTOMOBILE HIGHWAY NEAR BONN, GERMANY   331

A PEASANT DANCE IN YUGOSLAVIA   365

HITLER AND FRANCO SHAKE HANDS; 1940   391

QUEEN WILHELMINA OF THE NETHERLANDS; MADAME CHIANG KAI-SHEK; AND PRINCESS JULIANA   411

A LONDON MERCHANT URGES, "BUY BRITISH!" 471

PRIME MINISTER NEVILLE CHAMBERLAIN RETURNS FROM GERMANY, SEPTEMBER 30, 1938 491

A BLOCKHOUSE ON THE MAGINOT LINE 503

THE WITHDRAWAL FROM DUNKIRK, 1940; A PAINTING BY RICHARD EURICH 529

AMERICAN AND RUSSIAN SOLDIERS MEET ON THE BRIDGE AT TORGAU, GERMANY 595

THE POTSDAM CONFERENCE 623

List of Maps

CENTRAL EUROPE IN 1914   12

THE EASTERN FRONT IN WORLD WAR I   32

THE WESTERN FRONT IN WORLD WAR I   38

SUBMARINE WARFARE, 1917–1918   51

CENTRAL EUROPE IN 1924   106

GERMANY DURING THE PERIOD OF THE WEIMAR REPUBLIC   122

THE UNION OF SOVIET SOCIALIST REPUBLICS   170

THE BRITISH COMMONWEALTH OF NATIONS   216

IRELAND   221

THE NEAR EAST   224

THE PARTITION OF AFRICA IN THE NINETEENTH CENTURY   256

THE BRITISH "LIFELINE"   299

THE BALKAN STATES AND THEIR NEIGHBORS   356

THE IBERIAN PENINSULA   379

THE SCANDINAVIAN COUNTRIES   418

JAPANESE EXPANSION ON THE CONTINENT OF ASIA   444

JAPAN'S AMBITIONS IN EAST ASIA   457

THE EXPANSION OF GERMANY BEFORE THE SECOND WORLD WAR   484

THE DISMEMBERMENT OF CZECHOSLOVAKIA   488

THE INVASION OF DENMARK AND NORWAY   510

THE GERMAN INVASION OF THE LOW COUNTRIES   514

OCCUPIED AND UNOCCUPIED FRANCE   519

THE GERMAN INVASION OF RUSSIA   545

THE WAR IN THE PACIFIC   559

THE ALLIED INVASION OF SICILY AND ITALY   584

THE ALLIED INVASION OF FRANCE   590

THE ALLIED INVASION OF GERMANY   592

THE SOUTHWEST PACIFIC   602

CENTRAL AND EASTERN EUROPE AFTER WORLD WAR II   637

THE NEW INDIA   773

World War I

CHAPTER ONE

The Background of World War I

THE BREWING OF THE STORM AUSTRIA–HUNGARY'S decla-
ration of war against Serbia on July 28, 1914, precipitated the most
widespread war in human history up to that time. Before the armistice came in 1918, about 90 per cent of the world's population was
to become involved in the conflict. To put a finger on the deeper
causes of this sanguinary struggle is no easy matter, for they go far
back into the past and deep down into the subsoil of European
political, economic, ethnic, and geographical conditions. As President Wilson put it in 1917: "You can explain most wars very simply,
but the explanation of this war is not simple. Its roots run deep
into all the obscure soils of history." The factors making for war
were so complex that one historian has well described the period
preceding the world conflagration as "international anarchy." Among
the more fundamental causes of World War I the following may be
listed: (1) the system of secret alliances; (2) the armament race
among the European nations; (3) economic imperialism or the
struggle for markets, raw materials, and colonies; (4) the disruptive
force of nationalism. These and many other springs contributed their
waters to the current which swept Europe toward the abyss with
ever-quickening speed.

(1) *The system of secret alliances.* During the decades before
1914 a strong feeling of insecurity gripped the European nations.
Separated by language, by national traditions, and by peculiar ways
of thought as well as by political lines they found it difficult to
understand one another. These differences, coupled with conflicting
ambitions, soon gave rise to suspicion and mistrust which in turn
engendered exaggerated fears in the various states regarding the

3

aims and purposes of their neighbors. These fears caused the citizens of every country, great or small, to seek means of protection against the "evil designs" of other nations. Since national alliances appeared to offer security, the nations gradually entered into combinations with other states, which considered themselves threatened by the same enemies. Thus came about the alignment of the great powers into two rival groups, the Triple Alliance and the Triple Entente.

Of the two the Triple Alliance was the older. It was the handiwork of Bismarck. Having achieved his purpose of unifying Germany, a task which had necessitated the fighting of three wars, Bismarck became a man of peace. He needed peace to consolidate the new empire and to develop its resources. Keeping the peace was, however, not an easy task, for he had made a number of enemies in creating German unity. One nation alone he did not fear; what he feared was a coalition against Germany. Consequently it became the primary purpose of his diplomacy to prevent the formation of such a coalition. The nucleus of any combination of powers against Germany, he knew, would be France, for the French could not forget that Prussia had taken Alsace-Lorraine from them in 1871. Since then their one object had been to regain it. Bismarck himself had said during the Franco-Prussian war, "France will consider any peace simply as an armistice." At first he tried to make the French forget the lost provinces by encouraging them to embark on imperialist ventures, but when this failed he decided to isolate France. "So long as France has no alliances," he said, "she is not dangerous to Germany."

Believing that colonial interests would sooner or later lead to a clash between France and Great Britain, Bismarck centered his attention on drawing the other great powers close to Germany. In 1879 he concluded a defensive alliance with Austria-Hungary, known as the Dual Alliance. The main provisions of the treaty were that in case of an attack on either ally by Russia, the other was bound to come to its defense; in case of attack on either by any other power, the other was bound to maintain a benevolent neutrality.

In 1882 Bismarck expanded the Dual Alliance into a Triple Alliance which included Italy. The treaty signed by the three nations provided that if Italy were attacked by France without direct provocation, the other signatories were bound to give full assistance; Italy, in turn, was to come to Germany's aid if the latter were attacked by France; if one or two signatories were attacked by two or more great powers, all were to join against the attackers. To take such a step it was necessary for the Italians to submerge a deep-seated enmity toward Austria-Hungary, the power that had sought to thwart Italian unification. What caused them to do this was their anger over the French seizure of Tunis, which they had marked out as a suitable field for colonization.

Although the Dual Alliance was directed specifically against Russia, Bismarck did not fail to maintain cordial relations with the tsarist empire. In 1887 he negotiated with Russia a separate pact, known as the Reinsurance Treaty, in which he recognized Russian interests in the eastern part of the Balkans. Previously in 1883 Rumania had attached herself to the group of powers that had formed the Triple Alliance and later Turkey was also drawn into this circle. Thus Bismarck was successful in his plan of isolating France.

Fear of the Triple Alliance gradually resulted in the formation of the Triple Entente as a counterpoise. The way toward the formation of the Triple Entente was opened when Bismarck retired in 1890 and the young Emperor William II permitted the Reinsurance Treaty with Russia to lapse. The kaiser felt that in the contest which had developed between Austria and Russia for the control of the Balkans, Germany must needs support the former. This change of policy gave France the opportunity to build an alliance. No sooner had the treaty between Germany and Russia terminated than France began to make overtures to the latter. In 1888 France had already won the friendship of Russia by floating a loan to provide the tsarist government with funds for the building of the Siberian railway; after 1890 fear of the Triple Alliance drew the two powers together. Finally in 1894 the so-called Entente Cordiale, a military agreement the details of which were not revealed until 1918, was signed by France and Russia. The agreement stipulated that Russia would come to the assistance of France if the latter were attacked by Germany or by Italy supported by Germany, while France for her part promised to aid Russia if the latter were attacked by Germany or by Austria supported by Germany. Thus what Bismarck had feared most—a coalition against Germany—had come to pass only four years after his retirement.

Great Britain still stood apart from both groups. The British were not only imperial rivals of the French but they were also opposed to Russia's attempts to dominate the Balkans and the China trade. Gradually, however, Germany with her policy of industrial development and colonial expansion began to appear as the greater menace. The result was that Great Britain and France decided to compose their differences, and a treaty of mutual understanding between the two countries was signed in 1904. No sooner had this step been taken than Russia's unmitigated defeat in the Russo-Japanese war of 1904–1905 dissipated the British fear of the tsarist empire. In 1907 these two powers concluded agreements which practically transformed the Entente Cordiale into the Triple Entente.[1] In 1910 Japan, which had already entered into an alliance with Great Britain in 1902, came to an understanding with Russia, thereby virtually ranging herself on the side of the Triple Entente.

(2) *The armament race.* The primary purpose underlying the great alliances was undoubtedly the attainment of security, but no sooner were they founded than the mirage of security began to recede; in fact, the alliances heightened the insecurity they were intended to dissipate. On the one hand, the members of the Triple Entente did not cease to fear the Triple Alliance and, on the other, the Triple Alliance regarded the Triple Entente as a menace to its safety. The Germans, for example, saw in the Triple Entente an attempt to prevent the German Empire from achieving its "place in the sun." Thus the alliances fortified the general atmosphere of distrust, suspicion, and fear. Each group of states began to fear that the other would overreach it. This fear not only caused the groups to keep vigilant watch over each other but also to expect war.

And what was more natural than that the nations should arm for the expected fray? Moreover, the intensity of the military preparation increased as the dread of war grew. Careful, persistent preparation was regarded as essential to success. In many countries periodicals cited with relish such statements as that of Theodore Roosevelt: "Victory in any contest will go to the nation that has earned it through preparation. . . . When the day of battle comes, the difference of race will be found as nothing when compared with differences in thorough and practical training in advance."[2] Consequently all the great powers of Europe, with the exception of Great Britain remodeled their armies on the Prussian system of universal liability for service. Ever-increasing sums were lavished on things military and ever more formidable weapons were heaped up until all Europe was armed to the teeth. In time the burden of military expenditures became so heavy that it deprived the governments of the means for dealing with domestic ills. Nevertheless the armament race continued. No nation, not even the most peaceful, dared withdraw for fear of annihilation. Paradoxically, none of them wanted war. Most of them were building armaments because they

[1] The Triple Entente was never a formal alliance, but rather a "gentleman's agreement."
[2] *Quarterly Review,* vol. 207 (1907), p. 27.

believed that the maintenance of large armies and navies was the surest way of preserving peace.

Certain leaders, however, who saw that the race was inevitably leading Europe to a bloody abyss, advanced various plans for curbing the growth of armaments. The most notable was that of Tsar Nicholas II. In August, 1898, he had his foreign minister address to all powers represented at St. Petersburg a circular letter in which he expressed his anxiety over the existing state of things and urged "a reduction of the excessive armaments before they produce the very catastrophe which everyone wishes to prevent." He proposed that representatives of all powers addressed meet in conference to discuss the question. When a number of the nations received the proposition coldly, he sent out a second letter in January, 1899, which, after pointing out that the political horizon of Europe had become more clouded during the intervening months, again urged a conference for an exchange of ideas. This time the appeal was heeded. In May of the same year representatives of twenty-six powers convened at The Hague for sittings which extended over ten weeks. The assembly, known as the First Hague Conference, succeeded in establishing a permanent court to which the nations could refer their grievances for arbitration and in formulating certain laws for the conduct of warfare. But in regard to the main question, that of limiting armaments, it achieved nothing beyond stating that "the limitation of the military charges which at present oppress the world is greatly to be desired." In other words, the tsar's proposal for the limitation of armaments was given a first-class funeral. In 1907 a second congress met at The Hague. Again no agreement was reached for the reduction of armaments, and the frenzied competition continued.

A special cause of friction between Great Britain and Germany was the resolve of the German government to build a formidable fleet. The kaiser himself enthusiastically sponsored the idea by declaring that he would carry through the work of reorganizing the navy "in the same spirit in which my grandfather strengthened the army." His principal assistant in putting the idea into practice was Admiral von Tirpitz who in 1897 was placed in control of German naval policy. The first program of naval construction, enacted by the Reichstag in 1898, was followed two years later by one that was far more ambitious, and during the succeeding years other increases were voted. In the preamble of the Navy Act of 1900 it was stated that "Germany must have a fleet of such strength that a war against her would involve such risks even for the mightiest naval power as to jeopardize the supremacy of that power."

Such statements together with the continued increase in the strength of the German navy inevitably came to be regarded by the British as a challenge to their naval supremacy. It was even stated that Germany was trying to "rule the world." The British saw themselves compelled by the competition to spend large sums in maintaining a supremacy that was essential to an island power dependent upon imported food and sea-borne trade. More than this, as the successive naval programs unfolded before their gaze the British were impressed with a growing sense of danger. It was feared that if Britain should lose control of the sea it could be starved into submission in a short time. In 1912 Sir Edward Grey, the foreign minister, said in a speech: "A new situation in this country is created by the German programme, whether it is carried out quickly or slowly. When it is completed, Germany will have a fleet of thirty-three dreadnoughts—the most powerful the world has ever seen. That imposes on us the necessity, of which we are now at the beginning— except so far as we have dreadnoughts already—of rebuilding the whole of our fleet."

While the British thought themselves justified in charging the kaiser with aggressive designs, William II took great pains to deny the imputation. To King Edward VII he stated in 1905 that the German navy was "intended, equally with the German army, for the preservation of peace." Three years later he said to Lord Tweedmouth, then First Lord of the Admiralty: "It is absolutely nonsensical and untrue that the German Navy Bill is to provide a navy meant as a 'challenge to British naval supremacy'; the German fleet is built against nobody at all." It is probably true that William II had no warlike ambitions; nevertheless, the fact that he continually thought and spoke in terms of war gave rise to widespread misgivings regarding his intentions. Such provocative utterances as "our future lies upon the water," "the trident must be in our fist," and "we Germans fear God, and nothing else in the world" were certainly not calculated to allay the fears of the British. They served only to widen the breach between the two powers, to strengthen the accord between Great Britain and France, and, above all, to hasten the construction of British dreadnoughts. As one British writer put it: "Taxation proving inadequate, loans must be raised, the national debt must be increased, social legislation set back, and cultural problems postponed, in order that larger and ever larger sums may be tossed into the water. For that, in the last analysis, is what it all comes to. Germany will have it so, and whether we will or not, we must needs acquiesce, and keep abreast of the militarist powers, cost what it may." [3]

The European armament competition which culminated in a series of Army Acts during the years immediately preceding 1914 is a valuable barometer of the European war atmosphere. Early in 1913 France, for example, obtained a considerable increase in her standing army by extending military service from two years to three. Other nations followed suit. Seriously alarmed at the growing strength of the combined forces of France and Russia and thoroughly convinced that Germany's enemies were trying to encircle her with a "ring of steel," the German government voted a huge increase in the size of its standing army, raising it to almost 800,000 men. Austria-Hungary had already in the preceding year greatly increased the number of her recruits. At the same time Russia not only increased the number of her annual enlistments to 580,000 but also lengthened the period of service by six months. Thus the great nations of Europe, assembled in two groups, faced each other in full battle array. Even Belgium, Switzerland, and other countries hastily began arming in the expectation that a great European war was impending. All this moved Count Witte, the Russian statesman, to ask: "When and how will it all end? Unless the Great States which have set this hideous example agree to call a halt, so to say, and knit their subjects into a pacific, united Europe, war is the only issue I can perceive. And when I say war I mean a conflict which will surpass in horror the most brutal armed conflicts known to human history and entail distress more widespread and more terrible than living men can realise." [4]

(3) *Economic imperialism.* The unsatisfactory relations between the European states during the decades preceding 1914 were further aggravated by economic competition. This was particularly true of the relations between Germany and Great Britain. Probably the most striking feature in the history of the German Empire between 1870 and 1914 was its development from an agricultural to a manufacturing and commercial nation. Primarily an agricultural nation in 1870, it had by 1914 come to be second only to the United States of America in manufacturing and to Great Britain in shipping. During this period Germany's export trade had increased almost threefold. Some idea of her industrial development may be gained from the fact that the number of cotton spindles doubled between 1897

[3] *Contemporary Review,* vol. 99 (1911), p. 621.
[4] *Contemporary Review,* vol. 105 (March, 1914), p. 415.

and 1912, the output of coal more than doubled during the two decades before 1914, and the smelting of pig iron increased from less than four million tons in 1885 to more than fifteen million in 1913. In 1913, for example, Germany produced twice as much steel as Great Britain. But German industries not only produced goods in quantity; they also manufactured them so cheaply that German merchants were able to undersell their competitors in the world markets. While practically all the Continental nations erected tariff barriers against German goods, the British still adhered to a policy of free trade, with the result that the markets in the United Kingdom itself were soon flooded with goods bearing the legend, "Made in Germany." In other words Britain, which for decades had gloried in the title, "the workshop of the world," now saw its industrial and commercial supremacy menaced. Thus German economic rivalry, by arousing British apprehension and antagonism, became "one root of the war between the United Kingdom and Germany."

The development of industry and commerce in Germany was accompanied by a growing disposition to seek colonial adventures. While her industrialists loudly demanded colonies as a source of raw materials and an outlet for surplus products, insisting that the prosperity of the empire would not be secure without colonies, jingoists asserted that Germany was by reason of her greatness predestined to play a major role in colonial affairs.

There was nothing new in this demand for colonies. Soon after the proclamation of the German Empire in 1871 proponents of colonialism had raised the cry; Bismarck, however, discountenanced the idea, saying that "for us Germans, colonies would be exactly like the silks and sables of the Polish nobleman who had no shirt to wear under them." In the end events proved too strong for him and after 1884 he consented to the acquisition of some islands in the Pacific and some unprofitable colonies in Central Africa. A new era opened with the accession of William II (1888). Whereas Bismarck had been content to make Germany the foremost power on the Continent, the young kaiser undertook to transform Germany into a "World Power." So the Germans began to look about for undeveloped territories which might be exploited with profit. Much to their surprise they discovered that they had waited too long. Practically all the desirable colonies had been pre-empted by others. When the German government sought to share the exploitation of some of these territories, trouble ensued. In the words of an English historian, "Coming last into the field of world-policy, she could not acquire a coaling station without alarming everybody." [5] In Asia German interests clashed with those of Japan and Russia; in northern Africa German activities caused difficulties with France, Great Britain, and Spain; and when Germany turned in the direction of the Near East, both Russia and Great Britain saw their plans for the domination of that part of the globe menaced. All in all, Germany's efforts generated much friction but gained few profitable colonies.

(4) *Nationalism.* Another factor which intensified the hostility between the Triple Alliance and the Triple Entente was the spirit of nationalism, particularly that phase of it known as national self-determination. The idea that people of the same nationality should be united in one state had in the nineteenth century not only contributed to the unification of Italy and Germany but also excited political aspirations in the smaller national groups subject to other nations. Italians in the Austrian Empire and French in Alsace-Lorraine, to mention only two, wished to be united with their fellow nationals in the "mother state." *well*

In the Balkans particularly this spirit was working like a leaven. By the end of the century it had pretty well disrupted the Ottoman Empire and was threatening the Austro-Hungarian Empire with disintegration. A conglomeration of nationalities and creeds which the Habsburgs had been unable to fuse into one nation, the Austro-Hungarian Empire, also known as the Dual Monarchy, contained many ardent nationalists who were desirous of joining their brethren living in independent states. In the southern provinces of the Dual Monarchy there were, for example, more than five million Serbs who desired to be united with Serbia and whom Serbia in turn hoped to annex. When Pan-Serb propaganda was circulated in its southern provinces, the Austro-Hungarian Empire adopted all possible means to suppress it and to stop the movement which was threatening its very existence. On the other hand, the agitators were being encouraged by Russia, who posed as the "big brother" and "protector" of the Slavic peoples. Having in large part achieved its purpose of weakening the Ottoman Empire, the Russian government planned to undermine the strength of Austria-Hungary in the hope of being able to get control of Constantinople and the Straits, so that it would have a warm-water port in the south and an outlet in the Mediterranean. This was, of course, incompatible with the ambitions of Germany, which had become the most influential of the great powers at Constantinople. Thus the Balkan question was a fertile source of antagonism between the two great alliances.

[5] J. H. Rose, *Origins of the War* (1914), p. 75.

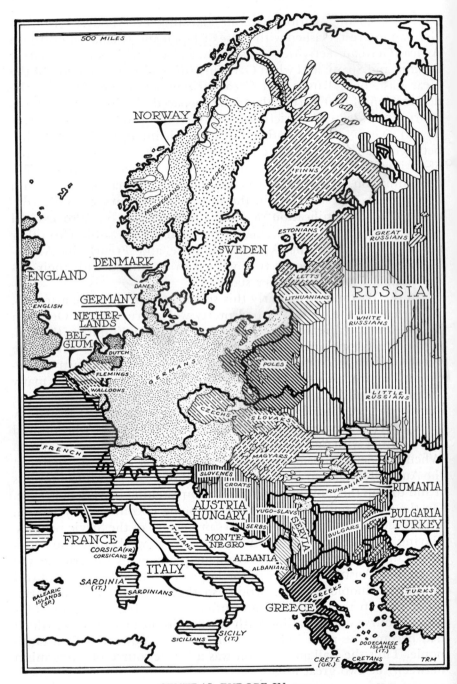

500 MILES

NORWAY

NORWEGIANS

SWEDES

FINNS

GREAT
RUSSIANS

ENGLAND

DENMARK

DANES

ESTONIANS

LETTS

LITHUANIANS

RUSSIA

ENGLISH

GERMANY

NETHER-
LANDS

BEL-
GIUM

DUTCH

FLEMINGS

WALLOONS

GERMANS

POLES

WHITE
RUSSIANS

CZECHS

SLOVAKS

LITTLE
RUSSIANS

FRENCH

MAGYARS

SLOVENES

CROATS

RUMANIANS

RUMANIA

AUSTRIA
HUNGARY

YUGO-SLAVS

SERBS

SERVIA

BULGARS

BULGARIA
TURKEY

FRANCE

ITALIANS

MONTE-
NEGRO

ALBANIA

ALBANIANS

CORSICA (FR.)
CORSICANS

ITALY

GREEKS

TURKS

SARDINIA
(IT.)

SARDINIANS

BALEARIC
ISLANDS
(SP.)

GREECE

DODECANESE
ISLANDS
(IT.)

SICILY
(IT.)

SICILIANS

CRETE
(GR.)

CRETANS

TRM

CENTRAL EUROPE IN 1914

🜍

CRISES PRECEDING THE OUTBREAK OF HOSTILITIES

The last decade before 1914 witnessed the rise of a series of international crises more serious and more alarming than any that had troubled uneasy Europe since 1870. Any one of them might have started an international conflict. Two of them developed over French attempts to establish a protectorate over Morocco. When Great Britain and France settled their long-standing differences in 1904 preliminary to concluding an alliance, the former in return for freedom of action in Egypt and elsewhere granted to France a free hand in Morocco. Thereupon Delcassé, the French foreign minister, proceeded to gain the consent of Italy and Spain to France's control of Morocco. He obtained Italian approval by recognizing Italy's pretensions in Tripoli and satisfied Spain by promising her a share of Morocco. But Germany, which like the others had been a signatory of the Madrid Convention of 1881 relating to Morocco, he completely ignored. As an English writer later stated it: "France had found it necessary to pay the British, Spanish, and Italian bills. To Britain, relief in Egypt; to Spain, almost the entire northern and part of the Atlantic coasts of Morocco, with a goodly slice of hinterland thrown in; to Italy, a free hand in Tripoli; to Germany— nothing!" [6] Delcassé, in fact, did not even take the trouble of informing the German government of the agreements.

At first German official circles seemed uninterested but as they gradually realized the full import of the agreements, disinterestedness gave way to chagrin. Not only did the fact that Germany had been treated as a "neglible quantity" hurt German pride, but the government also felt that its rights in Morocco had been flouted. To show France that she could not ignore Germany, von Bülow, the German chancellor, induced a reluctant kaiser to make a spectacular diplomatic demonstration. On March 31, 1905, William II suddenly landed at Tangier in Morocco and in a public oration declared the sultan an independent sovereign in whose territories all powers were to enjoy the same footing and exercise the same rights. This pro-

[6] E. D. Morel, in *Nineteenth Century and After*, vol. 71 (1912), p. 237.

❀❀❀

CENTRAL EUROPE IN 1914. *Note especially the overlapping of national groups and political boundaries and the conglomeration of national groups in Russia and Austria-Hungary.*

nouncement was later followed by a German proposal for a conference of the signatory powers of the Madrid treaty to discuss the Morocco question.

Although von Bülow assured the British ambassador that Germany was seeking no special privileges but only wished "to keep the door open for all nations," the Tangier incident and the request for a conference were denounced no less in Britain than in France. Edward VII, for instance, asserted that it was "the most mischievous and uncalled for event which the German emperor has ever been engaged in." Delcassé advocated resistance to the request for a conference but relented when the situation became threatening. The decision of the conference which met at Algeciras in June, 1906, was in one sense favorable to the Germans. It recognized "the sovereignty and independence of his Majesty the Sultan and the integrity of his dominions." Actually, however, the sultan was largely put under the control of France and Spain, who were given permission to police the coast towns and to establish a state bank for the purpose of managing the finances. In the latter France was to have a predominant interest.

If the Morocco crisis strained to the breaking point the relations between Germany on the one hand and Great Britain and France on the other, a new crisis was soon to do the same thing to the relations between Germany and Austria-Hungary on the one hand and Russia on the other. The cause was the annexation by Austria of the provinces of Bosnia and Herzegovina in 1908. Although these were nominally a part of the Ottoman Empire, they had been administered by the Austrian government since the Congress of Berlin in 1878. What caused the Dual Monarchy to annex them so suddenly was the attempt of the "Young Turks" to revivify the Turkish Empire so that it could reassert its authority over all parts of the Ottoman dominions. The success of this movement might have spelled the end of Austrian administration in Bosnia-Herzegovina. But the Austrians and the Young Turks were not the only ones who wanted this province. The Serbs had also been casting covetous glances at it. They hoped by annexing it to double the population of their state and at the same time secure an outlet to the sea. Consequently excitement ran high when the annexation was announced in Belgrade, the capital of Serbia. Great crowds that gathered in the streets burned the Austrian flag, smashed the windows of the Austrian embassy, and went about crying, "Down with Austria." Some of the irresponsible spirits even clamored for war.

The Serbs in themselves would not have been so serious a menace if they had not been supported by Russia. After a time the Russian government announced that the annexation of Bosnia-Herzegovina constituted a violation of the Treaty of Berlin and therefore could not be permitted. This position had the moral backing of both Great Britain and France. While the British foreign minister sent to the Austrian government a formal protest in which he urged "the necessity of reconsidering the decision to annex the two occupied provinces," the French government stated that "the Treaty of Berlin cannot be modified without an agreement between the signatory powers." In Germany the kaiser was taken aback by the bold stroke. First, it deeply hurt his feelings that the Austrian government had not taken him into its confidence while the annexation was being planned. Second, he feared that the annexation might jeopardize his influence in Turkey. "The situation presents itself," he wrote when the news was brought to him, "that after I have pursued a friendly policy for twenty years, my best ally is the first to give the signal for the partition of European Turkey." However, his ministers soon persuaded him to give his unreserved support to Austria. Would one side back down or would it be war? As the weeks passed, passions began to cool. Russia's allies, Great Britain and France, were unwilling to go to war in support of Serbian interests, and Russia herself had not yet recovered from the disastrous defeat of the Russo-Japanese War (1904–1905). So Russia gave way and the crisis passed.

In 1911 the Morocco question flared up again. During the years following the Algeciras Conference there was no improvement either in Franco-German relations or in the internal conditions of Morocco. The finances of the sultan did not improve, nor was the police force commanded by French and Spanish officers able to restore order. Finally in the summer of 1911 the French government sent an army into the interior to occupy Fez, the capital, on the ground that the sultan was unable adequately to protect the lives of foreigners. Earlier when the German chancellor learned that the French were planning this move he had warned the French ambassador, "If you go to Fez you will stay there, and then the Morocco question will be raised in its entirety, which I wish at all costs to avoid." Upon receiving the news of the march to Fez the German government at once interpreted it as a step to reduce Morocco to the status of a French protectorate, and staged another dramatic protest. On July 1 it announced that the gunboat *Panther* had been sent to the port of Agadir "to help and protect German subjects and clients in those regions." Thus another crisis had developed. This time the French, backed by the British, were determined not to yield and during the summer of 1911 many people were asking, "Will there be war?" That most of the states of Europe were expecting war can be seen from the following statement written at the time by an English historian:

"Quietly and unostentatiously Germany, France, Russia, Austria-Hungary, and Great Britain have taken all the necessary steps for an immediate mobilisation. The small neutral neighbors of Germany, which possess some of the most valuable strategic positions and harbours in the world, and which might, and very likely would, become theatres of war in a great European conflict, have strengthened in hot haste their much neglected defences. . . . The military authorities of Switzerland and Denmark also took precautions. The British fleet took up a position in the north of Scotland which it would very likely occupy in case of a war with Germany, and the German fleet took up a corresponding position in the north of the Danish peninsula. . . . Even Turkey, Spain, and the Balkan states are reported to be preparing for war. Apparently a Franco-German war might set all Europe aflame." [7]

This time Germany gave way. In November the French and German governments arrived at an agreement whereby Germany in return for a slice of the French Congo acquiesced in the occupation of Morocco by France and Spain.

In 1912 when Serbia, Montenegro, Bulgaria, and Greece combined to fall upon senile Turkey in the first of the Balkan Wars, another grave situation developed. The rapid defeat of the Turks, who lost all their European possessions except Constantinople and the adjacent districts, was a severe blow to the Austro-German policy of establishing a permanent hegemony over the Balkan Peninsula. Not only did it weaken Turkey, the ally of Germany, but it also placed a barrier of Slav and Greek states across the road to Constantinople and the Near East, thus blocking the German *Drang nach Osten* (drive to the east). For Austria the victory of Serbia was a particular menace because it raised the hopes of the Serbs within the Austro-Hungarian Empire for their eventual liberation. Gradually the tension between Austria-Hungary and Serbia grew acute. Austria began to mobilize for action, and Russia as the avowed protector of the Balkan states gathered troops behind the girdle of Polish fortresses. Again a general war was imminent. But once more the statesmen of Europe succeeded in averting it. Comparative calm settled upon Europe, but it was only the calm before the great storm.

[7] J. Ellis Barker in *Fortnightly Review*, vol. 96 (1911), pp. 590–591.

‍⟨⟩

THE STORM BREAKS

The entire European situation was distinctly critical by 1914. "The feeling that the nations are moving toward a conflict urged by an irresistible force grows from day to day," a Frenchman wrote at the close of 1913. Several months earlier an Englishman had written: "Very likely we stand close before a great war." In May, 1914, Colonel House, who had been sent to Europe to promote better relations between the European states and the United States, reported: "The situation is extraordinary. It is militarism run stark mad. The whole of Germany is charged with electricity. Everybody's nerves are tense. It only needs a spark to set the whole thing off."

The fatal spark which caused the explosion was the murder on June 28, 1914, of the Archduke Francis Ferdinand, heir apparent of the Habsburg throne, and his wife in the streets of Sarajevo, the capital of Bosnia. The actual assassin was a twenty-year-old Serbian youth named Gavrilo Princip, but the crime was instigated by the Narodna Odbrana, a powerful Pan-Serbian society whose main object was to break up the Habsburg Empire so that the Serbs under Austrian rule could be included in a Greater Serbia. The Serbs hated the archduke because he was planning to convert the Dual Monarchy into a Triple Monarchy in which the Serbs within the empire were to have self-government. It was feared that the success of this plan would make the Serbs under Habsburg rule less desirous of becoming a part of Serbia and thus frustrate the dream of a Greater Serbia. Hence, when it was announced that the archduke and his wife would attend military maneuvers at Sarajevo in June of 1914, plans were laid to assassinate him. A group of young men, inflamed by the Pan-Serbian propaganda, armed themselves with bombs and pistols. Although a number of members of the Serb cabinet, including the prime minister, knew of the plot, they made no attempt to warn the Austrian government. The archduke and his wife reached Sarajevo according to schedule and after the failure of an attempt to blow them up with a bomb, young Princip mortally wounded both of them with a pistol.

The news of the assassination shocked most of Europe, but the Austrian ministers shed few if any tears. To them the death of Francis Ferdinand not only meant the removal of a figure whose accession they had feared [8] but also offered a favorable opportunity to put an end to the anti-Austrian movement which was threatening

[8] As the Emperor Francis Joseph was in his eighty-fourth year, his days were numbered.

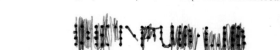

the existence of the empire. The day after the crime Count Berchtold, the foreign minister, is reported to have told the chief of the general staff that the time had come to settle the Serbian question once for all by making war on Serbia. The chief of staff eagerly supported the idea, stating that the Dual Monarchy must "choose between allowing itself to be strangled and making a last effort to prevent its destruction."

What Berchtold wanted was only a local war. Nevertheless he could not embark upon such a war unless Germany was willing to promise full support in the event of Russia's entry into the conflict on Serbia's side. So he sent a special envoy to Germany to obtain the promise of German support. The mission was successful. On July 5 the kaiser gave assurance that Austria "could depend on the complete support of Germany." As Winston Churchill put it: "The Vienna cabinet was given a blank check against the whole resources of the German Empire." At least two motives impelled William II to promise "wholehearted support." First, he was convinced that Russia was not ready for war and would back down as it had in 1908 and 1913. Second, he saw that the Habsburg Empire was Germany's one dependable ally and as such must be kept strong. Italy, it is true, was technically a member of the Triple Alliance but her interests were known to diverge from it. In the case of Austria-Hungary there was considerable chance that she would cease to be a great power unless the nationalist activities of the various groups within her borders were curbed. The latter, the kaiser believed, could be achieved by abating the rising power of Serbia.

Berchtold at once proceeded to cash the check the German government had given him. Upon the return of his envoy he told an Austrian Crown Council that "a purely diplomatic victory even if it ended with a striking humiliation of Serbia would be useless" and then drew up an ultimatum to Serbia containing terms deliberately framed to be unacceptable. Among other things the ultimatum demanded suppression of anti-Austrian publications, anti-Austrian societies, and anti-Austrian propaganda. It also demanded the removal of all Serbian officials guilty of anti-Austrian propaganda. Finally it demanded that Austrian officials be permitted to participate in the suppression of anti-Austrian propaganda in Serbia and in the proceedings against the authors of the Sarajevo crime. Having drawn up his ultimatum, Berchtold did not communicate it to Germany for modification but sent it at once to Serbia giving her forty-eight hours to accept it. When the representatives of the other European governments discovered the terms, they were amazed. The

Underwood

THE BRITISH AND RUSSIAN ROYAL FAMILIES AT COWES, ENGLAND, IN 1909

The present
Duke of Windsor

Tsar Nicholas II

King Edward VII

The Prince of Wales
(later King George V)

British foreign minister exclaimed, "C'est la guerre européenne." Just two minutes before the expiration of the time limit the Serbian answer was handed to the Austrian ambassador. Much to the surprise of the Austrian and German officials the Serbs accepted all the demands but the last two and even declared their willingness to enter into further discussion regarding these. The German emperor was highly pleased with the answer. "A great moral victory for Vienna," he said, "and with it every reason for war disappears." But the Austrian government decided that the reply was unsatisfactory and on July 28 declared war on Serbia.

Austria's declaration of war marks the beginning of the final stage of the crisis. During the next week the representatives of Germany and Great Britain made feverish attempts to avert a general war. The kaiser and his ministers made a belated but futile attempt to induce the Austrian government to accept a peaceful solution. The German chancellor, for example, wired Vienna: "We are ready, to be sure, to fulfill our obligations as an ally but must refuse to allow ourselves to be drawn by Vienna into world conflagration frivolously and in disregard of our advice." But the Austrian officials were immovable. At the same time Sir Edward Grey, the British foreign minister, was desperately seeking to restrain Russia from a mobilization which he knew would inevitably cause Germany to declare war at once. But Sazonov, the Russian foreign minister, was determined not to let Austria secure an easy victory. According to the German ambassador, he was blinded by "a hatred which is absolutely clouding more and more all judgment here." Many still hoped that the tsar would restrain his minister. Nicholas II, a weak monarch, was not equal to the task. Although he at first said to Sazonov, "Think of the responsibility you are asking me to take; think of the thousands and thousands of men who will be sent to their death," he lacked the moral courage to stand firm. After parrying the arguments of his minister for several hours he reluctantly gave his consent to general mobilization on July 29. That same evening, upon receiving a conciliatory telegram from the kaiser, he tried to countermand the order but was informed that it could not be stopped.

Germany's principal military advantage lay in the ability of her armies to move rapidly. This advantage the German general staff was determined not to sacrifice. Consequently when news of the Russian mobilization reached Berlin on the morning of July 30, the government forthwith demanded that it cease within twelve hours under threat of war. The Russian government did not answer and on August 1 Germany declared war. On the previous day Germany had also sent an ultimatum to France asking whether it would remain neutral in case of war between Russia and Germany. The French government, delaying its answer until the next day, stated that it would consult its own interests. French mobilization began the same day and on August 3 Germany declared war on France.

Although Sir Edward Grey had committed himself without the knowledge of parliament to give France naval aid, Great Britain was still a nonbelligerent. Grey could not make good his promises until parliament declared war on Germany. But he did not have to wait long for the event which convinced the British parliament as well as the British people that war was necessary. On August 2 the German government asked the Belgian government to permit an army to march through Belgium, promising "to guarantee the possessions and independence of the Belgian kingdom to the full," "to evacuate Belgian territory on the conclusion of peace," and "to pay an indemnity for any damage that may be caused by German troops." The reply was that the king of Prussia had in 1870 guaranteed the independence of Belgium and that no strategic interest would justify the violation of this agreement. It also stated that if Belgian neutrality were violated, the army would offer the most vigorous resistance to the invader. This bold defiance did not change the plans of the Germans. In their eyes the treaty was just "a scrap of paper." The early hours of August 4 saw their army invade Belgium.

It was the event which inflamed British public opinion. On the same day parliament declared war on Germany. Of the great powers Italy was the only one not in the war. The Italian government proclaimed its neutrality on the ground that its obligations to the Triple Alliance did not include support in a war of aggression. Consequently Germany and Austria, known as the Central Powers, fought alone against the Entente Allies which included Great Britain, France, Russia, Belgium, Serbia, and Montenegro.[9]

The First World War had begun, fulfilling the prophecy Bismarck had made shortly before his death to Herr Ballin, noted director-general of the Hamburg-Amerika Line, "I shall not see the world war, but you will, and it will start in the Near East." None of the powers, it seems, really wanted a European war and all made genuine though belated efforts to avert it. Nevertheless war had broken out. Why did it come? The most obvious answer is that statesmen were not ready to make the sacrifices necessary to preserve peace. They did not sufficiently foresee the consequences of their acts. In the words of Lloyd George, "The more one reads

---

[9] Japan took her place with the Allies on August 23 and Turkey entered the war on the side of the Central Powers at the beginning of November.

memoirs and books written in the various countries of what happened before August 1, 1914, the more one realizes that no one at the head of the affairs quite meant war. It was something into which they glided, or rather staggered and stumbled." The war was the fatal result of unsolved economic clashes and of the blundering incapacity of statesmen aided and abetted by the malign influence of alarmists and jingoists. For decades men on both sides had indulged in making arrogant claims, rattling the sword in its scabbard, distilling venom, piling up suspicion, fostering gigantic misunderstandings, and doing other things that created an atmosphere making for war. All countries were more or less to blame; no one nation can be saddled with the sole responsibility.

The two most potent weapons for the struggle were the German army and the British navy. Germany had trained most of her younger male citizens so that she had a reservoir of about four million to draw upon. Even more important was the quality of the training and the general organization of the German forces. In this respect Germany enjoyed a distinct advantage. The Austrian armies were inferior both in numbers and in efficiency, although they had no equal in siege artillery. However, since they were composed of so many nationalities, their special weakness was lack of homogeneity. The fighting machine which most nearly approached Germany's in size and efficiency was that of France, but its power of expansion was not so great as that of Germany whose population was larger by twenty-five millions. This difference was, however, more than offset by the French colonial levies. The country which had the largest number of trained men was Russia, with almost six millions.[10] Thus France and Russia had an enormous superiority in numbers. But the Russians were poorly equipped and their effectiveness was further limited by difficulties of transportation. As for the British army, it was well equipped and well trained but small. Since the British had not introduced universal military service, their regular army together with the reserves numbered less than 450,000 men, of which only 160,000 were ready for immediate service at the outbreak of the war. What the British did have was a navy that was second to none. A program of reform during the years before 1914 had raised the efficiency of the navy to a point unprecedented in history. Together with the French and Russian navies it constituted a force beside which the Austro-German naval combination appeared almost insignificant, although Germany had the second largest navy in the world.

[10] General Gourko (*Russia in 1914–17*, p. 75) estimates that fourteen million Russians were called to the colors up to December, 1916.

CHAPTER TWO

World War I: The First Phase

THE OPENING CAMPAIGNS

THE German plan of campaign had been carefully worked out long before the outbreak of war. It was based on a scheme originally drawn up by General von Schlieffen, chief of the German general staff from 1891 to 1896. Von Schlieffen had foreseen the possibility of Germany's being involved in a war against France, Russia, and Great Britain—in other words, in a war with one front in the east and another in the west —and had made his plan accordingly. The essence of it was to achieve a quick decision against one enemy and then settle the issue with the other. More specifically, he planned to bring France to her knees by a series of swift, overwhelming blows before Russia could mobilize her vast man power. The bulk of the army would be hurled at France and would reach Paris in two or at most three weeks. The forces would then be turned eastward against the Russians whom the Austrians, aided by a minimum German army, were to hold in check until France was crushed. The speedy execution of the plan was the key to its success. There was no time to be lost if France was to be defeated before Russia could put effective forces into the field.

The eastern boundary of France was, however, protected by a great chain of concrete forts stretching from Montmédy to Switzerland. The Germans saw that the task of piercing this powerful line would not only be difficult but could not be achieved within the required time limit. In short, it would be courting disaster to make a frontal attack. The obvious solution was to strike through Belgium and Luxemburg, where the frontier was unfortified. Only by violating the neutrality of these two countries could the army deal a swift blow at France. The Germans reckoned that the strategic benefits would more than compensate for the loss of reputation they would incur. If Belgium were held inviolable, the advantage would be with the French. On the other hand, if they could rapidly march through Belgium the advantage lay with the Germans. They could then turn the left flank of the French defense and cut the French armies from the capital.

During the night of August 1–2, before Germany had actually declared war on France, cavalry crossed the French frontier between Luxemburg and Switzerland at a number of points. These movements were, however, only in the nature of a feint to draw as many French troops as possible to the south. The main attack was directed through Luxemburg and Belgium. On the morning of August 2 the advance guard had already entered Luxemburg, which had as its sole defense a volunteer force of 150 men. The Grand Duchess made a patriotic gesture in motoring out and wheeling her car across the road on which the Germans were advancing, but the German soldiers laughingly swept by to occupy the duchy. In Belgium the Germans met a more determined and effective resistance, for the Belgians were resolved to defend their country to the utmost. Marching across the border early on the morning of August 4 the German vanguard advanced as far as Liége the same day.

It was here that the Belgians intended to make a serious stand. The defenses consisted of a ring of twelve forts regarded as the highest achievement of military science. Constructed of steel and concrete, they had turrets with walls that were twelve feet thick. But the German heavy howitzers, whose force had been underestimated, soon reduced these supposedly impregnable fortresses to a mass of wreckage. One was silenced on August 5 and three were destroyed the next day. Those to the west and north held out some days longer, but the last one fell on August 15. On August 20 the advancing Germans occupied Brussels and the same day began bombarding Namur, another ring of forts which the entente hoped would make a delaying resistance. This group was demolished even more quickly with the great guns that had eaten away the defenses of Liége. One after another the forts fell in a bombardment lasting little more than twenty-four hours. The entrance of the Germans into Namur on August 23 marked the end of the attempt to block their advance.

Although the delay amounted to only eighteen days, it was of priceless value to the French and British. During this period the British had transported all available troops, to the number of about 160,000, across the Channel and by the 21st they were in position near Mons. To their right five French armies moved into line to stay the German onset. The first engagement took place August 22 in the region of Charleroi, and the next day the British also engaged the Germans at Mons. Although both the French and the British fought with spirit and determination, they were defeated with heavy losses along the entire front. This defeat convinced General Joffre, the French commander, that any attempt to check the Germans with the men he had in his advanced position would be futile. Consequently he ordered a general retreat which would permit him to strengthen his forces for an offensive. The retreat continued until the Germans were within twenty-five miles of Paris and the fall of Paris appeared certain. Hastily the government gathered its effects and moved to Bordeaux.

Meanwhile, however, Joffre had actually strengthened his forces with fresh units, while the power of the advancing units was being greatly reduced. Furthermore, whereas the Germans had been moving farther and farther from their bases of supply, the French as they fell back came nearer to theirs. Finally Joffre decided that the time had come to take the offensive. On September 5 he addressed the following stirring appeal to his soldiers: "As we engage in the battle upon which the safety of our country depends, all must remember that the time for looking backward has passed; every effort must be devoted to attacking and driving back the enemy. Troops that can no longer advance must hold the ground won at any cost, and die in their tracks rather than retreat. In the present circumstances no weakness can be tolerated."

Early the next day the general offensive known as the battle of the Marne began. Fighting with fierce courage the French drove the Germans back across the river, retaking Châlons and Rheims, and were not halted until they reached the Aisne, where the Germans had previously prepared positions. Here began the trench warfare that was to continue for the duration. Both sides constructed lines of trenches from the Oise to the Swiss border, with the cheerless waste of no man's land in between the trenches. The defensive line was not to move so much as ten miles in either direction before March, 1917.

The battle of the Marne, in which more than two million men were engaged for a period of seven days (September 6–12), was the decisive event of the first period of the war; in fact, some students of military tactics regard it as the most significant battle of the war.[1] Although the German losses had not been overwhelming, the battle did decisively dispel the Germans' hopes for a quick victory. Their

[1] General Falkenhayn later said that the war was really lost in the battle of the Marne.

TAXICABS AND BUSES USED TO CONVEY FRENCH SOLDIERS TO THE FRONT LINES, 1914

military leaders had staked all on a speedy knockout blow and had failed. Among the factors contributing to this failure were the resistance of the Belgians, the delaying actions of the French and British troops, and the fighting qualities of the victors. The force of the German avalanche having spent itself, it was evident that instead of "a short and joyous war" the contest would be "a long and desperate struggle."

While the Germans were trying to drive through to Paris, the situation on the east front had become perilous. There the German plan failed as signally as in the west. Assuming that the Russians would not be ready to make a major move for some time, the Germans had allotted only a minimum force to the defense of East Prussia. But the assumption proved to be wrong. The Russians succeeded in mobilizing their troops much faster than the Germans had believed they could. By the middle of August a number of armies were ready to take the field. As soon as it became clear that the Germans were striking the main blow against France and were merely standing on the defensive in the east, the Russians decided to invade East Prussia. On August 17 two armies entered the province from the east and the south, flinging the inadequate German forces back upon Königsberg. Soon the province as far as the Vistula River was in Russian hands, much to the consternation of the German military leaders. On August 17 the Russians had also launched an offensive in the south which the Germans did not expect. Strong forces had invaded Silesia, had thrown back the Austrians, and were threatening Lemberg, the capital of the province. Such was the favorable situation for Russia. In France and Great Britain hopes ran high that by a continued advance the Russians would counterbalance the territorial losses in the west.

Various reasons urged the immediate deliverance of East Prussia. To abandon this province would have been disastrous from a strategic point of view, for from East Prussia the Russian armies could launch an offensive at the very heart of Germany and flank an attack on Poland. Furthermore, since East Prussia was the cradle of the Prussian monarchy, sentimental reasons demanded its deliverance. Consequently the German general staff decided that East Prussia must be cleared at once. The task was assigned to the one man who was probably best fitted to carry it out. He was Paul von Hindenburg, a retired general who from years of military duty and maneuvers in East Prussia had learned to know the terrain as well as if it had been his own estate. It had been the dream of his life to lead an army against the enemy in this region. With Ludendorff as his chief of staff and with reinforcements from the western front,[2] he proceeded at once to set a trap for the Russians, whom the weakness of the opposition had made overconfident. Moreover, dissension between the Russian generals, Rennenkampf and Samsonov, hampered the Russian effort. As the army of the left pushed forward in the district of Tannenberg, Hindenburg's troops enveloped it and destroyed most of it. Of the four and a half corps only the equivalent of one and a half escaped. It was the most complete victory the Germans won in the whole war[3] and Hindenburg became at once the great hero of the German people. His next objective was to destroy the other Russian army in East Prussia, but its commander saved it by ordering a retreat to the frontier. Thus the invasion of East Prussia came to an end.

In the meantime the Russian armies in Galicia had administered a crushing defeat to the Austrians at Lemberg in a battle that began at the end of August and lasted a week. The Austrian losses in men and materials were so heavy that they seriously crippled the army. Of the 900,000 operating in Galicia 250,000 were killed or wounded and 100,000 were taken prisoners. It was necessary for the Germans to do something to relieve the situation. The innovation of trench warfare having led to a deadlock which enabled them to maintain a defensive position with fewer men, a considerable portion of the troops were moved eastward. Thus the importance that had belonged to the west front was for a time diverted to the east. Early in October Hindenburg organized an invasion of West Poland, expecting thereby to force a retirement of the Russian armies. But the latter made an effective stand in prepared positions along the line of the Vistula. There the German attempt to take Poland came to a standstill. Gradually the situation settled down to trench warfare much as it had in the west. The end of 1914 saw the Germans and Russians facing each other in a stalemate on a front some nineteen hundred miles in length.

THE PERIOD OF GERMAN PREDOMINANCE

The fact that the plan of the Central Powers for a quick victory had failed gave the Allies time to put more trained men into the

---

[2] This diversion of troops from the western front to East Prussia at a critical time was undoubtedly a contributing factor to the defeat of the offensive in France.

[3] A notable feature of this battle was the use for reconnaissance which the Germans made of the few airplanes they had. Hindenburg paid tribute to the aid given him by the planes in these words: "Without airplanes no Tannenberg."

field and also strengthened the hope of victory in their hearts. So confident of ultimate success did they become that they divided the spoils on paper. France was to get Alsace-Lorraine and the left bank of the Rhine; Russia was allotted the Straits, Constantinople, and adjacent districts; Great Britain's reward was to be the destruction of Germany's navy, colonial empire, and merchant marine. Furthermore, in April, 1915, a secret treaty was concluded with Italy according to which Italy, in return for intervention, was to receive part of the Austrian Tyrol (the Trentino), the city of Trieste, the eastern littoral of the Adriatic, and the Dodecanese Islands. In other words, Italy was accorded the right to convert the Adriatic into an Italian lake. Having made the best possible bargain, Italy declared war on Austria, May 24, 1915.[4] Rumania, too, joined the entente upon receiving pledges of compensation.

But the hopes of the Allies were somewhat premature. They were still to experience many defeats and setbacks before victory was achieved. On the western front the whole year 1915 saw the opposing armies confronting each other from the long lines of entrenchments which stretched from the Channel to Switzerland. Occasional battles raged along this front, with enormous casualties on both sides, but the military results were not commensurate with the loss of blood. On the Italian front the results were almost equally disappointing. Fighting to wrest the Trentino from Austria, the Italian army had a superiority in numbers; but lack of proper training and especially the difficulty of the terrain prevented it from achieving military results of importance beyond diverting Austrian troops from the eastern front. In addition, 1915 witnessed the tragic failure of an attempt by the Allies to gain possession of the Straits and Constantinople. The plan for an expedition "to bombard and take the Gallipoli Peninsula, with Constantinople as its objective" was projected by Winston Churchill. It was hoped that such an expedition would relieve Turkish pressure on Russia's army in the Caucasus and open the Dardanelles as a channel through which munitions and supplies could be sent to Russia. After an English fleet, assisted by a French squadron, failed to effect a passage of the Straits in March, troops were landed on the Gallipoli Peninsula. Turkish resistance was, however, so effective that these troops were unable to advance beyond the beaches. By the end of May they had little to show for their efforts except enormous losses in men and materials. Finally heavy rains made it necessary to evacuate the expedition.

[4] Public opinion in favor of intervention was largely influenced by the fiery speeches of the poet D'Annunzio and the militant newspaper articles of one Benito Mussolini.

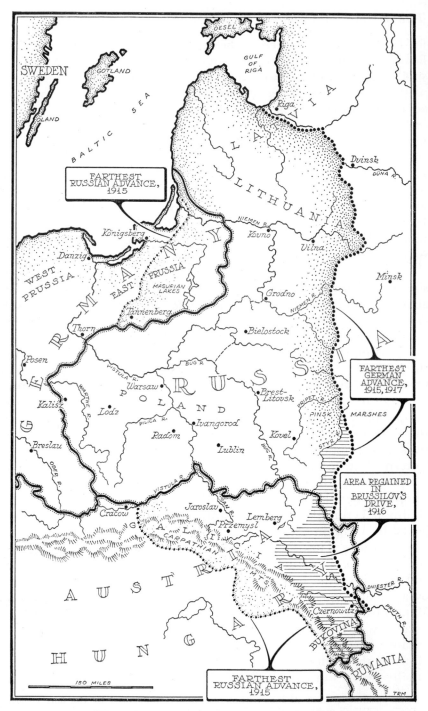

SWEDEN

GOTLAND

ÖLAND

ÖSEL

GULF
OF
RIGA

BALTIC SEA

LATVIA

Riga

Dvinsk

DÜNA R.

LITHUANIA

FARTHEST
RUSSIAN ADVANCE,
1915

Königsberg

Kovno

Niemen R.

Vilna

Danzig

WEST
PRUSSIA

EAST
PRUSSIA

MASURIAN
LAKES

GERMANY

Minsk

Grodno

Niemen R.

Tannenberg

Thorn

Bielostock

R U S S I A

FARTHEST
GERMAN
ADVANCE,
1915, 1917

Posen

VISTULA R.

BUG R.

Warsaw

Kalisz

WARTHE R.

POLAND

Lodz

PILICA R.

Ivangorod

Radom

Lublin

Brest-
Litovsk

Pripet R.

PINSK

MARSHES

BUG R.

Kovel

STYR R.

Breslau

ODER R.

VISTULA R.

AREA REGAINED
IN
BRUSSILOV'S
DRIVE,
1916

Cracow

Jaroslav

SAN R.

Przemysl

Lemberg

G A L I C I A

CARPATHIAN

MTS.

A U S T R I A - H U N G A R Y

DNIESTER R.

Czernowitz

PRUTH R.

BUKOVINA

H U N G A R Y

RUMANIA

150 MILES

FARTHEST
RUSSIAN ADVANCE,
1915

TRM

THE EASTERN FRONT IN WORLD WAR I

Not only were the British casualties of the campaign about 120,000 [5] but the failure of the undertaking encouraged the Bulgarians to join the Central Powers.

The Allies also suffered setbacks on other fronts. An offensive against the Russians in April moved into Poland with steady momentum despite counterattacks. The heavy artillery of the Germans not only quickly leveled any fort that made a show of resistance but also literally blasted the Russians out of their trenches. Although suffering from an acute shortage of munitions the Russians fought doggedly. But the odds were against them. By August their situation was so bad that they decided to evacuate Warsaw, fearing that any force which might attempt to defend it would be cut off. From Warsaw the retreat continued until almost all of Poland was in the possession of the German armies. In November, 1915, the little Serb army which had twice routed the invading Austrians was threatened on three sides by a superior force of Germans, Austro-Hungarians, and Bulgarians and was able to escape the trap only by retreating into Albania. With Serbia under their control and Bulgaria on their side, the Central Powers were now in direct contact with Turkey.

Thus at the end of 1915 they found themselves in a strong position. They had been able to hold the Allied armies in the west while achieving signal successes in the east. One of their great schemes, that of controlling the Balkan Peninsula and the Near East, appeared to be near realization. For the Allies the outlook was anything but cheerful. Joffre summarized the situation in the following words, "Our armies had everywhere been either checked or beaten." Only on the oceans and seas, with the exception of the Baltic Sea, was Allied control unchallenged.

A YEAR OF HOPES AND DISAPPOINTMENTS

The year 1916 was intended by both the Central Powers and the Allies to be a year of decision. The Germans had already begun preparations in the late fall of 1915 for delivering a blow in the west that would bring the war to a triumphant close. General von

[5] The Turkish losses were about 218,000.

THE EASTERN FRONT IN WORLD WAR I. *Since the Germans underestimated the strength of the Russians, the latter were able to penetrate deeply into Germany and Austria during August, 1914.*

Falkenhayn, chief of the general staff, outlined the plan in a report which he presented to the kaiser at Christmas. No immediate danger, he argued, threatened from Russia or Italy because a shortage of materials would prevent the former from taking the offensive and the latter was being held in check by Austria. In his estimation Great Britain constituted the worst peril. But the British were not ready to strike. Although a strong force was in the making, it would be some months before it was properly drilled. In addition, the submarine campaign which the Germans planned to launch was counted on to keep England's hands tied. Since the French, who had borne the brunt of the fighting on the western front, were believed to be at the point of exhaustion, the obvious move was to attack and annihilate their army before the British could send substantial assistance. The French, in order to meet the attack, would be forced to throw in every available man and would thus "bleed to death." More than this, by striking down France, Falkenhayn stated, "England's best sword would be knocked from her hand." It was the old strategy of Frederick the Great, that of wearing down the military power of the enemy until exhaustion induced him to surrender. On the Allied side there was equal determination to reach a decision. Joffre, convinced that the Allies could achieve victory in 1916 if their efforts were coordinated, invited representatives of the Allied powers to his headquarters to discuss plans. The representatives decided that they should seek a decision by launching simultaneous offensives on all fronts. However, it was recognized that the general offensive could not be set in motion before June because the training of the new British forces was not complete and Russia was in great need of equipment.

The Germans launched their attack first. Faced with the problem of dwindling man power, von Falkenhayn decided that only an operation on a limited front would be necessary to deal France the *coup de grâce*. An attack concentrated on one point, he argued, could inflict the greatest injury at the least cost. After surveying the possibilities, he chose the fortress of Verdun as best suited to his purposes. Not only was Verdun near the German lines but it also formed a salient in the French front which was surrounded by the Germans on three sides. Furthermore, Verdun was a famous city, the taking of which would be a success of the first order. The plan of attack was worked out meticulously. A terrific artillery barrage was to destroy all means of resistance, and the infantry was then to advance without suffering heavy losses. It was, briefly stated, the principle that "the artillery conquers, the infantry occupies." This required a tremendous concentration of artillery and troops specially trained for the attack. Soon great streams of arms and ammunition were flowing in the direction of the Verdun front. Such unexampled preparation could not, however, be completely concealed from the French. From reconnaissance reports and from information supplied by prisoners and deserters the French knew that a blow was impending. Colonel Driant, for example, wrote to a friend on February 20: "The assault of Verdun is near and the [German] Crown Prince declares, we hear from deserters, that he is going to take the town and finish the war." Nevertheless the belief persisted in the high military circles of France that the attack was merely a feint to attract French reserves while the main blow would be delivered elsewhere. Consequently, though some measures were taken to improve the defenses of Verdun and to reinforce the troops in that sector, the preparations for meeting the attack were not complete or energetic.

Toward the end of February, 1916, all was ready. The Germans were convinced that their formidable and painstaking preparations could not fail. One general even announced to his corps that it would be the last battle of the war. But once more they underestimated the fighting qualities of the French soldier. On February 21 the German artillery unleashed the most terrific bombardment ever known, after which the infantry carried the advanced French positions. On the following days progress continued so that by the 25th a German victory seemed assured. On that day the French troops were ordered to hold their positions at all costs, Joffre telegraphing that "every commander who gives an order for retreat will be tried by court-martial." The French stiffened at once. Standing firm as rocks, they rolled back attack after attack until the impetus of the German advance was broken. During the succeeding months the Germans endeavored time and again without much success to force the French positions; and on numerous occasions the French took the offensive to recapture many positions. The middle of June saw Verdun still out of German reach. On June 20 the Germans resorted to the use of a new kind of diphosgene gas against which the masks of the French artillerymen proved insufficient protection. With the artillery paralyzed the French infantry gave ground, enabling the German forces to advance to the east outwork of Verdun. The jubilation at German headquarters was tremendous. But the success had been achieved too late. The German forces lacked the strength to achieve final victory. To meet a Russian offensive that had started at the beginning of June, the German supreme command had been compelled to send seven divisions to Galicia, thereby greatly weakening its forces before Verdun. More than this, on June 24 the British opened an offensive on the Somme, to which sector more German men and materials had to be moved. Thereafter the attack on Verdun gradually came to a standstill. The second German attempt to achieve a decisive victory by a swift stroke had failed as utterly as the first. The cost in blood was frightful. No less than 315,000 Frenchmen and 281,000 Germans were devoured in the attempt.

Meanwhile the Germans had won several successes on the eastern front. The great Russian offensive which had started in June and had compelled Falkenhayn to withdraw troops from the west, at first gave every indication of being a brilliant success. It advanced with such momentum that the Austrian defenses crumbled before it and the Austro-Hungarian troops retreated in utter rout. However, the German general staff, upon seeing the plight of the Austrians, quickly sent troops who by a series of counterattacks checked the Russians all along the line from the Pripet marshes southward to the Rumanian frontier.

Furthermore, before the end of 1916 the Central Powers also dealt a decisive blow to Rumania. Long sympathetic to the entente cause, Rumania had been watching for a favorable moment to enter the fray, its primary object being the annexation of Austrian Transylvania. The early success of the Russian offensive coupled with the belief that Austria-Hungary was on the verge of collapse ended the hesitation of the Rumanian government and on August 27, 1916, it took the fateful step of declaring war on Austria-Hungary. Although the Rumanian army numbered about half a million men, they were poorly trained and poorly armed. There was a shortage not only of aircraft and artillery but also of machine guns and rifles. Some of the divisions had no machine guns whatever. What is more, there was only a six weeks' supply of ammunition for such guns as the army possessed. Nevertheless they might have placed Austria in grave peril if they had acted with dispatch. Crossing the Carpathians into Transylvania after the declaration of war, they moved so slowly that the Austro-German command was enabled to collect a picked force for a counteroffensive. Soon two strong armies were moving against the Rumanians. By a coordinated strategy these armies gradually broke the resistance and on December 6 marched into Bucharest. Before the end of the month all the province of Wallachia with its rich oil deposits and fertile grain lands was in the possession of the Central Powers.

Thus the year 1916 closed with "a gleam of triumph" for the

Central Powers. Besides eliminating Rumania as a military factor in the war, they had impaired the strength of the Russian armies to the extent that they were no longer an offensive power. But the situation of the Central Powers as a whole was not so rosy as these successes might indicate. For example, the efforts of the Austro-Hungarians against the Russians, Rumanians, and Italians had exhausted their resources and man power, the fighting against the Russians alone having cost them half a million in prisoners and dead. The Austro-Hungarian Empire was, in fact, disintegrating under the strain of war. On the western front the fighting which had ended in a stalemate had taken a terrific toll in German men, materials, and energy. Ludendorff himself later wrote: "The strain of the year 1916 had proved too great; the endurance of the army had weakened; we were completely exhausted on the western front." Within Germany the Allied naval blockade was beginning to cause widespread distress. In short, the war was gradually sapping the material, physical, and moral strength of Germany. Dissatisfaction with the achievements of the war was growing. After all the sacrifices the Germans had made and all the hardships they had endured, final victory was still out of reach.

The German government was under no illusions regarding the true state of affairs, for the danger signals were too patent to be overlooked. On the other hand, Germany would have enjoyed a great advantage if it had been able to induce the entente to accept a peace on the basis of its territorial holdings which, in addition to Belgium and northern France, included Poland, Serbia, Montenegro, half of Rumania, and much of Russia. In the hope that the entente would be willing to do this Bethmann-Hollweg, the German chancellor, on December 12 sent a note to the entente governments stating that the Central Powers "feel sure that the propositions which they would bring forward would serve as a basis for the restoration of a lasting peace." Some opposition to this offer was expected, particularly from France, but much to the surprise of the Germans it was also denounced by the British and the Italians. Lloyd George, who had just become prime minister, said emphatically, "To enter, on the invitation of Germany proclaiming herself victorious, without any knowledge of the proposals she has to make, into a conference is to put our heads into a noose." Before the end of December the Allies, believing that the peace offer was made for the purpose of creating dissension among them, sent a group reply which read in part, "The Allied governments refuse to consider a proposal which is empty and insincere. Once again the Allies de-

THE WESTERN FRONT IN WORLD WAR I

After the Germans almost reached Paris in 1914, the front was stabilized for over three years as indicated by the heavy black line on the map; the dotted line indicates the comparatively great advance of the Allies in the late summer and the autumn of 1918.

clare that no peace is possible till they have secured reparation of violated rights and recognition of the principle of nationalities and of the existence of small states."

Meanwhile President Wilson had on December 18 independently issued an invitation to the powers to state the terms on which peace might be made. It was a great opportunity for the Germans. They had in their hands a most admirable card, that is, the restoration of Belgium. A frank and unequivocal statement that Germany was prepared to restore the complete independence of Belgium and to pay the costs of the destruction caused by her armies was the *sine qua non* of any further discussions. But the Germans in their folly did not, it appears, perceive this; hence they did not play their best card. Instead they declined the President's invitation to state their terms, replying that direct discussion between representatives of the belligerent nations seemed the best road to peace. On January 10, 1917, the Allies sent their reply, which restated in more definite terms the ideas of their earlier collective statement: among other things that "the civilized world knows that they imply, necessarily and first of all, the restoration of Belgium, Serbia, and Montenegro, with the compensations due to them; the evacuation of the invaded territories in France, in Russia, in Rumania, with just reparation; the reorganization of Europe, guaranteed by a stable regime and based at once on respect for nationalities and on the right to full security and liberty of economic development . . . ; the restitution of provinces formerly torn from the Allies by force or against the wish of their inhabitants; the liberation of the Italians, as also of the Slavs, Rumanians, and Czechoslovaks from foreign domination; the setting-free of the populations subject to the bloody tyranny of the Turks." [6] It was clear that the aims of the belligerent groups were poles apart. So the war went on.

NEW ELEMENTS IN WARFARE

The First World War witnessed many important changes in the scope, methods, and instruments of warfare. One of the most striking of these was the increase in the size of the armies and in the length of the battle lines. Whereas in previous wars the soldiers had been counted by the hundreds of thousands, they were now counted by the millions. For the opening campaign the Germans assembled no less than seven armies, while the Allies collected six—five French

---

[6] *Documents and Statements Relating to Peace Proposals and War Aims,* with an introduction by G. Lowes Dickinson (1919) , pp. 12–13.

and one British. The average number of men under arms has been
estimated at twenty millions and the total number as near sixty millions, of which the Allies mobilized about forty and the Central
Powers about twenty millions. These vast numbers did not fight in
one small sector. General Joffre, the commander of the French
armies, could not, as Napoleon did at Austerlitz, survey the entire
battlefield with the aid of field glasses. At the battle of the Marne,
for example, the fighting front covered a distance of 125 miles and
when the battle lines later became stabilized they extended from the
English Channel to the frontier of Switzerland, a distance of some
six hundred miles. Only through the use of modern inventions—
the telephone and radio—did a commanding general know what
was taking place. Even a sector commander had to use these instruments in order to ascertain whether the center was holding or
the left wing was advancing according to plan.

To keep these millions of soldiers supplied with the means of
warfare was no easy task. Besides food, clothing, and medical supplies, they needed ammunition, machine guns and small arms, artillery, planes, tanks, motor trucks, radio apparatus, photographic
appliances, and innumerable other kinds of equipment. As the
arsenals could supply only a small part of the total, peacetime industries were converted to war production. Furthermore, it was often
necessary to build special railway lines to facilitate transportation
to the front, or to construct concrete roads if the transportation was
done by motor trucks. Gradually more and more civilian industries,
trades, and professions, together with all the resources of scientific
knowledge and research, were drawn into the war until the major
nations on each side became "nations of warworkers." Whereas wars
once affected merely the fighting men who comprised only a small
part of the total population, during the First World War almost the
entire populations of the belligerent nations became engaged in wartime industries, the ramifications of which were so embracing that
nearly every peacetime invention became a potential instrument
of war.

Another novelty was the entrenched lines stretching hundreds
of miles, with flanks secured by the sea at the one end and by neutral
territory at the other. After the drive on Paris had been stopped, the
fire power of the machine gun and quick-firing field gun proved too
much for the endurance of the soldiers; so they dug trenches for protection. The war became one in which the spade was as indispensable
as the rifle. There was, of course, nothing essentially new in the
simple trench. It had been used in some crude form or other almost

since the Stone Age. Caesar used it in his wars against the Gauls, and in more recent times it was used in the Crimean, American Civil, and Russo-Japanese wars. It was the use of trenches on a grand scale that was new in the First World War. Not only were they extended to a distance of six hundred miles, but in 1915 the multiple trench system appeared. When the opposing armies "dug in" after the battle of the Marne, they found that a single trench system did not offer sufficient protection against penetration. Consequently both sides constructed second and third line trenches to which the troops could retreat if they were unable to hold the first line. These various lines were connected by communication trenches through which troops and supplies could be moved without openly exposing them to enemy fire. At intervals underground dugouts were constructed in which troops could rest or find protection when they were subjected to heavy cannonading. In some places veritable underground towns were built, with first-aid stations, kitchens, storage rooms for supplies and ammunition, and sleeping quarters for officers and men. Nevertheless life in the trenches was usually anything but pleasant. Heavy rains filled them with water and mud and they were infested with vermin and swarmed with rats. Major Auld wrote: "In some parts of the line the trench rats are an absolute plague. They swarm in the dugouts and appear in all sorts of odd corners. They disturb the little rest one does get; and I have had them run all over me, even over my face, while lying in my dugout." [7]

Both sides endeavored in every possible way to make their trenches invulnerable to assault. The territory between the opposing trench systems, known as "no man's land" because it was continually swept by rifle, machine gun, and artillery fire, was covered with a maze of barbed-wire entanglements, often electrically charged. An infantry attack upon trenches protected in this way was always costly in men and material; in fact, the trinity of trench, machine gun, and barbed wire was so formidable that infantry alone was seldom able to make much headway against it. Both sides tried to blast their way through the entanglements by means of terrific artillery bombardments. Such heavy gunfire not only consumed tremendous quantities of munitions but also had two further disadvantages. It eliminated the element of surprise and tore up the ground so badly that only a short penetration was possible. Thus the opposing lines were almost impregnable against frontal or flank attacks. The fact that both sides had made their fronts equally strong brought major operations to a standstill. A stalemate termination of the war seemed

[7] *Gas and Flame* (1918), p. 95.

certain unless one side or the other could devise new offensive weapons.

The German solution for the deadlock was poison gas. Although it had been suggested as a weapon in warfare as far back as 1812, it was not actually used until April 22, 1915, when the Germans launched a gas attack in the northeastern part of the Ypres salient. Its object was to asphyxiate all the entente soldiers in the area. The gas was chlorine, a violent irritant of all mucous membranes and especially of the lungs. Since the Allied troops were without protection against it, those whom the gas cloud enveloped were suffocated. Many who were on the fringe saved themselves by burying their faces in the earth, by stuffing handkerchiefs in their mouths and noses, or by wrapping mufflers around their faces. Had the Germans waited until they had sufficient gas for an attack on a wider front, they might have inflicted irreparable losses. But before they could launch further attacks, defensive measures were devised. At first a cotton pad dipped in a chemical solution was tied over the mouth, and later each soldier was equipped with a respirator or mask which filtered the poisonous gases from the air he breathed. These masks proved effective. Because a favorable wind was necessary to propel the gas toward the opposing lines, the Germans soon had recourse to hurling shells filled with deadly phosgene gas. Later they also used mustard gas. But although they did make some advances through its use, it did not open the way to victory as they had hoped it would.

The offensive weapon devised by the British was an armor-plated, self-propelled vehicle which soon became known as a "tank." The basic idea of the tank, that of combining mobility with offensive power and armor, was not new. Centuries earlier the Chinese had used "war cars" armored against projectiles; and various kinds of "battle wagons" and "landships" had also been designed and constructed in Europe. What made the tank possible was the invention of the internal combustion engine and the caterpillar track, the former providing a compact means of propulsion and the latter enabling the vehicle to cross soft ground and trenches. But it was the necessity for overcoming the immobility of trench warfare that actually inspired the construction of the tank. As early as October, 1914, Colonel E. D. Swinton appears to have suggested the idea of an armored car on a caterpillar system, one which would be "capable of crushing down wire entanglements and crossing trenches." Winston Churchill, then First Lord of the Admiralty, thought the idea such a good one that he urged immediate action. Ultimately in

1916, after months of experiment hampered by official opposition and red tape, the first tank was brought into being. This tank, later called the *Mark I,* was the prototype of all British tanks used in the First World War. It had a maximum speed of four miles an hour and its armor was proof against ordinary .30-caliber bullets, shrapnel, and most shell splinters, but not against armor-piercing bullets.

As soon as the tanks were pronounced ready for combat they were sent to France, where they went into action for the first time on September 15, 1916, during the battle of the Somme. The Germans seem to have had no advance information concerning them; hence they were amazed when they appeared in battle. To some, the new vehicle looked like a threshing machine. One German officer later wrote: "It did look something like a threshing machine, but why should it have arrived there in the middle of a war and on a most unhealthy sector at that? We waited and watched. Then it moved. It actually started to come towards us. But that was not all. Suddenly into view came another. It joined the first one, and side by side they came on, ugly and ungainly, but terribly businesslike. Then without warning, from both of them came streams of bullets. Next they were on top of . . ." [8]

The first tank operations were not a startling success. Of the forty-nine used, only a few proved effective. Many of them either broke down from mechanical trouble or became bogged in soft ground and shell holes, while others were knocked out by the German field guns. The showing of the tank, as a whole, was so poor that it weakened the confidence of many officials in its possibilities. For a time the whole development was in danger of being snuffed out. The Germans, too, did not regard the armored Behemoth as much more than a terrible plaything and therefore made no organized attempts at defense for some time. [9] But the successes of a few of the machines did convince a number of British experts that the infant tank was a child that deserved to live. To them it had demonstrated its possibilities for crushing barbed-wire entanglements and clearing out machine gun nests. One tank had, in fact, succeeded in taking three hundred German prisoners. Consequently the development of the tank continued. Making the most of the lessons they had learned, the British produced improved tanks in quantities. It was not until the battle of Cambrai, on November 20, 1917,

[8] *Evening Standard,* September 17, 1935. Cited in Sueter, *The Evolution of the Tank,* p. 141.

[9] When later tank actions opened their eyes to the part the new weapon could play, the Germans began the construction of a type known as the "Elfriede." However, only fifteen of these machines were finished in time to see action before the end of the war.

that their value was fully demonstrated. By omitting the artillery preparation the entente forces were able to surprise the Germans, with the result that the nearly four hundred tanks used in the attack effected a penetration of 10,000 yards in twelve hours. Before the war ended the tank was to rob barbed wire of its terror completely and to reinstate mobility.

Another novelty of the First World War was extensive use of aircraft. During the decade immediately preceding the war the German government had spent much on the development of the Zeppelin, an airship with a long hull constructed of aluminum, covered with a strong weather-proof fabric, and filled with hydrogen to give it power of ascent. It was confidently believed in German military circles that the Zeppelin was for military purposes the superior of the airplane. Some even saw in it the instrument with which Germany could overcome Great Britain's insular security. In pursuance of this idea the first of a series of raids on England began in January, 1915. Of a total of forty-eight raids, twenty were directed against London. Though they caused considerable damage to life and property,[10] they did not achieve their military purpose. The aim of the crews seems to have been so poor that it is doubtful if one bomb found the target at which it was directed. Furthermore, the Zeppelins had three serious weaknesses: the bulk of their structure, the inflammability of the hydrogen gas, and lack of speed. Their huge bulk, together with the fact that they could attain a maximum speed of only 54 m.p.h., made them an easy target for airplanes and improved antiaircraft guns. So many of the "gas bags" were shot down that their use was soon discontinued in offensive tactics.

Infinitely more important than the airship was the airplane. Like the airship, the airplane had no military history; it went into the conflict as a new and untried instrument. The first ones had been slow but by the outbreak of the war the average speed of the better planes had been raised to 100 m.p.h., the maximum being 126½ miles. Both sides used this weapon in practically the same way. Its earliest use was for purposes of scouting and of regulating artillery fire. Airplanes of the Entente Powers, for example, were already active in observing and reporting the movements of the enemy at the battle of Mons. As the eyes of the army, the airplane greatly reduced the element of surprise but fell far short of eliminating it. Various factors still made accurate observation difficult. For one thing antiaircraft guns compelled the pilots to fly at an altitude

[10] 435 persons killed and 1069 injured.

A HANDLEY-PAIGE BOMBING PLANE FROM THE FIRST WORLD WAR

which blurred even photographic observations. Furthermore, troop movements were often made under cover of darkness or on cloudy and misty days. Finally, the use of the airplane for observation purposes stimulated the development of the art of camouflage, which was employed to conceal everything that was a mark for opposing guns and airplanes. Although reconnaissance and artillery control were at first regarded as the primary functions of the airplane, it was also used, usually in groups of two or three, to attack points of military importance. But since the bombs they carried were low powered and usually fell more or less at random because of faulty aim, the early raids were more spectacular than destructive. When more planes became available, raids were organized in which forty or perhaps fifty were used. Bombs, too, grew not only in size and weight but also in destructive power and, what is equally important, the pilots grew more skilled in dropping them.

The first military planes were not equipped with machine guns. At most the pilots were armed with rifles or revolvers. It even appears that the German pilots had orders to evade combat if possible so as to keep their machines intact for scouting and for directing artillery. Nevertheless there were occasional duels during the first months of the war between pilots using revolvers or rifles. The following description of such a duel was published in the *Morning Post* on August 28, 1914: "An English pilot, emerging from a cloud, found immediately beneath him a German aeroplane. Swooping down to within revolver shot, he emptied all his chambers, with an effect that he could not observe, because the cloud once more enveloped him. Later on, when he emerged from the cloud again, he saw underneath a small crowd gathered round a smashed aeroplane, and he came to the conclusion that his revolver shots had not been without effect." In another encounter a British pilot was wounded by a German pilot armed with a rifle.

Soon, however, machine guns were installed in military airplanes, but even then the pilots were still primarily scouts and range finders rather than fighters. When an aviator flew over enemy positions to direct artillery, observe troop movements, or make maps of the trenches, the enemy sought to drive him away with antiaircraft fire. This proved ineffective because the pilots could complete their reconnaissances at a height that was out of range of the guns. Consequently the commanders of the troops that were being spied upon began to send up one or more airplanes to challenge the invader and to drive him away. In this way military airplanes became fighters as well as bombers and air scouts. Thereafter when an observation plane was sent out, so-called fighter planes often accompanied it to protect it against attack. Neither side, however, succeeded in driving its enemy from the air or in establishing a definite air superiority.

ॐ

NAVAL WARFARE, 1914–1916

Even though the war on land had proved indecisive, the Allies did possess one advantage. They controlled the sea. It was this undisputed control of the sea that finally enabled them to strangle both Germany and Austria-Hungary. The British navy had been the controlling force on the sea right from the beginning. During the summer of 1914 a test mobilization had been held, after which the ships were to disperse. The First British Sea Lord, however, decided to keep the Grand Fleet concentrated because of the threatening European situation. Thus it was ready for action the moment war was declared. Its primary objective was naturally the elimination of the German High Seas Fleet and it was so located that it could strike a swift blow should the enemy seek battle. No sooner, therefore, did the war open than the question was asked, "When will the enemy come out?" But the German government decided not to risk its fleet in an all-out battle. Although the kaiser believed that ship for ship the German vessels were more than a match for the British, he felt that the numerical superiority of the latter precluded any possibility of a German victory. He wished to "keep the fleet in being," so that it could protect the coast against invasion. Hence he refused the request of the commander of the High Seas Fleet to engage the British even when "circumstances are exceptionally favorable." It was not a question for the British to seek out the enemy, for the German fleet normally lay in the Jade under the protection of the heavily fortified island of Helgoland, which was impregnable to attack from the seas.

Thus the entente navies enjoyed practically undisputed domination of the sea during the early period of the war. Only the Baltic and the Dardanelles were held by the Central Powers. Control of the Baltic was important to Germany because it kept open the supply lines from Scandinavia and thence to the outside neutral world. More than this, it enabled the Germans to cut off Russia's communication with the outer world through the Baltic. Control of the Dardanelles also put a serious check on the efforts of the Allies by keeping military supplies from Russia and thus bringing about her eventual collapse.

The fact that the German High Seas Fleet did not try conclusions with the British navy does not mean that the Germans were not active on the sea. In some way or other they were constantly threatening or impairing Allied control. For one thing, submarines made numerous attacks on English warships. That the submarine warfare was not without results can be seen from the fact that on September 22, 1914, the submarine U–9 sank three armored British cruisers off the coast of Holland. Mines were also used with good results. As early as August 5, 1914, two British cruisers were sunk by mines. Furthermore, German cruisers and armed merchantmen became actively engaged in harrying British commerce. The cruiser *Emden*, for instance, entered the Indian Ocean on August 22, 1914, and for the next eleven weeks continued to prey on commerce. Before it was destroyed by the Australian cruiser *Sidney* on November 9, it succeeded in capturing and destroying twenty-one merchant ships and their cargoes. Such commerce-destroying ships were eventually, and often quickly, captured and sunk, but others were sent out to take their places and the damage they did was considerable. The only formidable German raiding squadron was that under Admiral von Spee which sank two British armored cruisers on November 1, 1914, off the Chilean coast (battle of Coronel) but was in turn disposed of on December 8 (battle of the Falkland Islands) in an engagement which cost Germany four armored cruisers. Finally, German squadrons also made occasional raids against the British coast for the purpose of terrorizing the British into keeping a large force for home protection.

However, control of the sea was of the greatest value to the Allies, despite the menace of submarines and an occasional armed raider. It enabled them to banish German commerce from almost all the waterways of the earth and to deprive Germany of all its colonies and it also permitted British ships to use the seas for the purpose of transporting men and food supplies from remote parts of the world to Great Britain and France. Without control of the Channel, for example, it would have been most difficult to ferry troops to France and to maintain them there. To keep the Channel free of enemy raiders, submarines, and mines was no easy task. It was done through the use of nets, mine fields, and other devices. The task of maintaining these defenses was entrusted to the so-called Dover Patrol, which was ever on the lookout for enemy mines or craft. Occasionally a submarine or a raider of some sort did manage to penetrate the defenses, but on the whole the Dover Patrol maintained uninterrupted communication by water between France and Great Britain.

The primary use the Allies made of their naval superiority was to blockade the Central Powers. Before the war began, Germany had been dependent to a considerable degree on imports of foodstuffs and raw materials. In 1913 the import of foodstuffs had exceeded the export by more than $400 million and even the home production of food had been largely dependent upon imported fertilizers and fodders. In addition Germany had imported much of the raw material for its industries. From the United States, for example, it purchased nearly all the raw cotton, three fifths of the copper, and three fourths of the mineral oils used in its industries, while the Argentine supplied wool and hides. Other essential imports were rubber, manganese, and tin. Since German merchant shipping had been swept off the seas, it was but natural that the government should endeavor to import these necessities in neutral ships or through neutral ports from which the goods would subsequently be conveyed to Germany. The Allies believed that if they could cut off Germany's foreign supplies completely, the need of food-stuffs and raw materials would soon compel her to surrender. Accordingly the British proclaimed a blockade. At first only "contra-band of war" was excluded, but gradually the list was extended to include practically everything. The final stage was reached when an order in council announced on March 11, 1915, that "His Majesty has decided to adopt further measures to prevent commodities of any kind from reaching or leaving Germany." This was, of course, in violation of the rules of international law, according to which neutral countries had the right to trade with Germany. To the neutrals who presented their grievances Great Britain sought to justify its action on the ground of sheer necessity.

The German government had foreseen this blockade but had planned to end the war in triumph before it could cause serious shortages. When this plan failed, it became necessary to devise means for breaking the blockade. The weapon chosen was the submarine, and the method decided upon was unrestricted submarine warfare. At the outbreak of the war neither Germany nor Great Britain appreciated the immense potentialities of the submarine. Certainly the Germans regarded it as crude and unreliable, possessing only a certain value for purposes of observation. Accordingly it was used in the first days of the war largely for scouting in an effort to ascertain British naval dispositions. One submarine, the U–15, did fire a torpedo at the British battleship *Monarch* but without success. It was probably the first torpedo launched by a submarine with intent to kill. Before many weeks passed, the attempt to torpedo a warship did prove successful when the U–20 sank the cruiser *Pathfinder*.

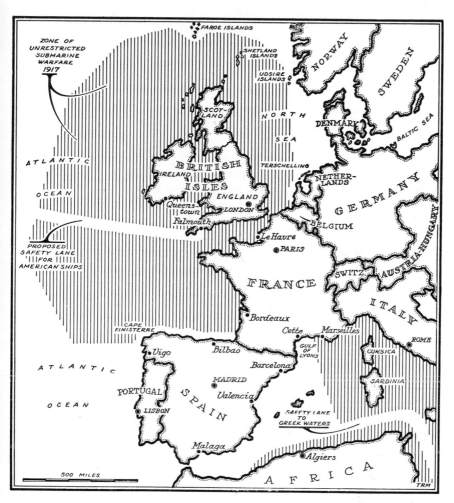

SUBMARINE WARFARE, 1917–1918

*When the Germans announced, in January, 1917, the resump-
tion of unrestricted submarine warfare, they marked out
safety lanes for the passage of American ships to England and
to the eastern Mediterranean and set forth the conditions
under which such vessels might proceed.*

Then, on September 22, as already stated, the U–9 sank three cruisers, thereby driving home to the British the menace of the submarine. This triple sinking, by demonstrating the destructive potentialities of the craft, opened a new era in naval warfare. More immediately it showed the Germans that they had in their hands a weapon "wherewith they could strike at their enemy with a freedom denied to their surface ships." Gradually the idea took shape of using the submarine to attack entente shipping.

The announcement of unrestricted submarine warfare was published on February 4, 1915, and read in part: "The waters around Great Britain and Ireland, including the whole of the English Channel, are herewith declared to be in the War Zone. From February 18 onward every merchant ship met with in this War Zone will be destroyed, nor will it always be possible to obviate the danger with which the crews and passengers are hereby threatened." This was of course no less contrary to the rules of international law than the blockade, but that fact did not deter the Germans any more than it had the British. Left and right, ships were torpedoed as the submarines went about their work. During March twenty-seven ships were sunk, and eighteen in April. However, the sinkings soon led to strained relations between Germany and the United States. On May 7, 1915, a U–boat torpedoed and sank the speedy Cunard liner *Lusitania* just off the coast of Ireland with a loss of 1198 lives of which more than a hundred were American citizens. Although the German government stated in defense of the deed that Americans had been officially warned by advertisements in the chief newspapers of the United States not to travel in entente ships and that the *Lusitania* carried munitions and other materials of war, public opinion in the United States was nevertheless outraged. Many began to insist upon an immediate declaration of war. President Wilson sent a strong protest to Germany and after a series of diplomatic notes were exchanged the German government assured the United States that henceforth "liners will not be sunk without warning and without safety of the noncombatants."

In 1916 the only great naval battle of the war was fought. Having postponed the program of unrestricted submarine warfare to avoid a break with the United States, the German admiralty decided to use the fleet more aggressively. The plan was to entice out and to destroy a part of the British Grand Fleet. To this end the German fleet left the Jade on the morning of May 30 and sailed northward. The interception of a wireless message divulged the move, and soon the Grand Fleet began steaming out of its base at

Scapa Flow toward the coast of Jutland. As a result two large fleets, the British of 150 vessels and the German of 99, were rapidly nearing each other on May 31. That afternoon the battle began and when it was over on June 1 the British had lost three battle cruisers, eight light cruisers, and eight destroyers while the Germans suffered the loss of one battleship, one battle cruiser, four light cruisers, and five destroyers. The number of killed and wounded was 6274 British and 2545 Germans. Although the German admiralty claimed a decisive victory, the fleet withdrew and thereafter clung to its base, never again seeking battle on the high seas. Actually the battle had confirmed the British mastery of the seas.

CHAPTER THREE

World War I: The Second Phase

THE UNITED STATES ENTERS
THE WAR
A T THE end of two years the war
had settled down to an indecisive struggle. Although the advantage
on land rested with the Central Powers, victory was in sight for
neither side. In 1917, however, two events took place that greatly
changed the situation: the entry of the United States on the side
of the Allies, and the withdrawal of Russia. While the first renewed
the hope of the Allies, the latter encouraged the Central Powers.

At the outbreak of the war sentiment in the United States had
been largely but not overwhelmingly pro-Ally. There was, of course,
a minority that favored the Central Powers, and there were also
large sections that were completely indifferent. Others were anti-
British but not pro-German, and still others tried to remain neutral.
In a survey "from the Atlantic to the Pacific, and from Mexico to
the Canadian border" conducted by the *Literary Digest* it was
found that of the cities surveyed 189 favored the Allies, 38 the
Germans, and 140 were neutral or divided.[1] In the East the preponderance of sentiment was pro-Ally, a fact which probably led
the British ambassador to conclude that "about 90 per cent of the
English-speaking people, and half the Irish, are on the side of the
Allies." Among the governing classes there was a distinct tradition of
friendship with England; in fact, the relations between Great Britain
and the United States had for some years amounted to almost an
entente. Most of the publicists were favorable to the Allied cause
from the beginning and this was probably true also of the leaders of
industry, commerce, and finance. The German government was

[1] November 14, 1914. Of the pro-German communities two were in the East, twenty-
nine in the Middle West, four in the South, and three in the Far West.

widely regarded as not only exceedingly militaristic but also autocratic, both distasteful to believers in democracy. Furthermore the Germans bore the odium of having started the war by invading Belgium. The blame, however, was put on the kaiser rather than on the German people as a whole. Thus one could read as early as August 4, 1914, in the *New York World:* "The kaiser plunges Europe into the most devastating conflict known to human history."

Nevertheless, even among the most ardent supporters of the Allied cause there were few if any who advocated active participation of the United States in the war. As the *Literary Digest* survey has it, "No belligerency is evident anywhere." Practically all believed that the government should adhere to its traditional policy of not meddling in European affairs. The *New York Sun,* which was soon to become openly pro-Ally, said: "There is nothing reasonable in such a war as that for which Europe has been making ready, and it would be folly for the country to sacrifice itself to the frenzy of dynastic policies and the clash of ancient hatreds which is urging the Old World to destruction." [2] Even ex-President Theodore Roosevelt, who was later to become the most ardent interventionist, at first breathed a spirit of mild neutrality. "Our country," he wrote, "stands well-nigh alone among the great civilized powers in being unshaken by the present world-wide war. For this we should be humbly and profoundly grateful. All of us on this continent ought to appreciate how fortunate we are that we of the Western world have been free from the working of the causes which have produced the bitter and vindictive hatred among the great military powers of the Old World. . . . We must profit by reading aright the lesson writ in fire and steel before our eyes, and therefore we must safeguard our future against the onfall of any similar disaster." [3]

President Wilson, whose sympathies were pro-Ally, set his heart upon keeping the United States neutral so that nothing would "stand in the way of the proper performance of our duty as the one great nation at peace, the one people holding itself ready to play a part of impartial mediation." "Every man who really loves America," he said in his appeal for neutrality, [4] "will act and speak in the true spirit of neutrality which is the spirit of impartiality and fairness and friendliness to all concerned. . . . It will be easy to excite passion and difficult to allay it. . . . I venture, therefore, my fellow countrymen, to speak a solemn word of warning to you against that

[2] Cited in Grattan, *Why We Fought,* pp. 36–37.
[3] *Outlook,* vol. 108 (1914), p. 169.
[4] August 19, 1914.

deepest, most subtle, most essential breach of neutrality which may spring out of passionately taking sides. The United States must remain neutral in fact as well as in name during these days that are to try men's souls. We must remain impartial in thought as well as in action."

Despite Wilson's effort to keep the people neutral "in thought as well as in action," the sympathy of the country became increasingly favorable to the Allies. This was in part due to the effectiveness of entente propaganda. Since both sides stood in need of loans and supplies from this country, the United States became the scene of an active contest for favors in which every known method of propaganda was employed. In this contest the Germans were not only handicapped by the fact that the tide of opinion was running against them, but their propaganda was also less adroit than that of the entente. German agents periodically released floods of pamphlets, they regularly sent translated passages from the German newspapers and magazines to something over five hundred newspapers, they circulated German moving pictures, and they subsidized periodicals. Many of these periodicals, however, reached only those who were already pro-German and much of the propaganda was directed to German newspapers which could be read only by very few. Even the Americans of German descent were largely immune to German propaganda, only the more recent immigrants proving highly susceptible. Most of them were of the second or third generation and had become so thoroughly Americanized that the ancestry of their parents or grandparents exercised little influence upon them. Thus German propaganda had little effect on opinion in the country as a whole. By the end of 1915 its blundering efforts were pretty thoroughly discredited.

Although entente efforts had little to do beyond sustaining and confirming the prevalent attitude, they were much more efficient than those of the Central Powers. The British, who enjoyed the advantage of being able to reach the public through the medium of a common language, were the most active. Before the war was many hours old the British navy cut the one cable connection the Central Powers had with the United States and thereafter all news via the cables was obliged to pass through England, where the censors naturally deleted anything unfavorable to their cause. Thus the newspapers and people of the United States saw the war largely through British eyes. But the British did not stop at censoring news dispatches; they also engaged in positive forms of propaganda. To convince the Americans that they were fighting for a righteous cause, they sent eminent men to the United States on lecture tours, sought to win the support of men and periodicals of the highest order, and supplied newspapers with releases. However, let Sir Gilbert Parker tell the story himself:

Practically since the day war broke out between England and the Central Powers I became responsible for American publicity. I need hardly say that the scope of my department was very extensive and its activities widely ranged. . . . Among other things we supplied three hundred and sixty newspapers in the smaller States of the United States with an English newspaper, which gives a weekly review and comment of the affairs of the war. We established contact with the man in the street through cinema pictures of the Army and Navy, as well as through interviews, articles, pamphlets, etc. and by letters in reply to individual American critics, which were printed in the chief newspapers of other and neighboring States. We advised and stimulated many people to write articles; we utilized the friendly services and assistance of confidential friends; we had reports from eminent Americans constantly, and established association, by personal correspondence, with influential and eminent people of every profession in the United States, beginning with university and college presidents, professors and scientific men, and running through all the ranges of the population. We asked our friends and correspondents to arrange for speeches, debates, and lectures by American citizens, but we did not encourage Britishers to go to America and preach the doctrine of entrance into the war. Besides an immense private correspondence with individuals, we had our documents and literature sent to a great number of public libraries, Y.M.C.A. societies, universities, colleges, historical societies, clubs, and newspapers.[5]

So far as propaganda goes, the United States probably would have continued nonbelligerent to the end of the war. What caused it to become an active participant was the unrestricted submarine warfare which, in addition to interfering with commerce, destroyed American property and the lives of noncombatants. It also appeared to confirm the reports regarding the inhumanity of the Germans. Thus the sinking of the *Lusitania* with the loss of 124 American lives seemed particularly brutal and senseless. Indignation ran so high that many newspapers called for war, and the Congress probably would have declared war if President Wilson had demanded it. But Wilson hoped to keep the country out of the war so that it could negotiate a peace. After receiving a number of sharp protests from the United States government the Germans decided that they did not have enough submarines to make defiance worth while and therefore abandoned unrestricted submarine warfare for a time. To

[5] *Harper's*, vol. 136 (1918), p. 522.

many it seemed that the crisis had passed and that the United States would succeed in staying out of the war. In November, 1916, Wilson was re-elected, though not by a wide margin, on the ground that "he kept us out of war" and soon after he made the peace proposals that failed. Then came the message from Germany announcing the resumption of unrestricted submarine warfare.

Having frustrated Wilson's attempts at mediation by refusing to state its terms, the German government was confronted with the necessity of ending the war by military measures. The campaigns of 1916 had convinced Hindenburg, who was now chief of staff, and Ludendorff, his principal assistant, that land armies alone could not bring the war to a successful conclusion within a short time. What they pressed for in the most urgent manner was immediate resumption of unrestricted submarine warfare, for in it they saw the means to quick victory. There were also internal reasons demanding a speedy victory. By the end of 1916 the blockade of Germany had become really stringent. The Germans, it is true, were still importing considerable food from countries within the cordon, but their supplies of fertilizer and fodder upon which the home production was dependent were now largely cut off. With fats, meats, and milk scarce, the diet was limited in the main to bread and potatoes. The summer of 1916 had also seen the potato crop fail and in the succeeding winter, known as the "turnip winter," coarse fodder-turnips became the principal fare for many. An American correspondent who was in Germany at the time wrote: [6] "No German will ever forget the terrible turnip winter of 1916–1917. . . . The writer has seen his own children come into the house from their play, hungry and asking for a slice of bread, and go back to their games with a piece of turnip because there was no bread to give them. The turnip winter was one of unusual severity, and it was marked by a serious shortage of fuel. Thus the sufferings from cold were added to the pangs of hunger. There was furthermore already an insufficiency of clothing."

The demands of the two generals for unrestricted submarine warfare were supported by many civilian leaders, who saw that if something were not done soon to bolster the morale of both soldiers and civilians it would collapse. So the program was readopted. The "unrestricted" was necessary because it had previously been demonstrated that the U-boats could not be used successfully so long as they did not sink all ships without regard for passengers and crews. As the Germans had been building submarines at top speed since

[6] S. M. Bouton, *And the Kaiser Abdicates* (1919), p. 67.

AN AMERICAN SUPPLY DEPOT IN FRANCE; FIRST WORLD WAR

the first campaign, there were many at hand and steps were taken at once to announce that in certain areas, including the waters round the British Isles, every ship, whether Allied or neutral, was liable to be sunk without notice after February 1, 1917.

Neither Hindenburg nor Ludendorff nor any other high German official seems to have been informed as to the temper and potentialities of the United States. Like most Germans they probably believed, as Mr. Gerard, the United States ambassador to Germany, stated it, that President Wilson had been elected with a mandate to keep out of the war at any cost, and that America could be insulted, flouted, and humiliated with impunity. They knew that the United States had no great standing army and they were certain that even if this country did join the Allies the submarine would obtain a victory for Germany before any sizable American force could be developed and transported to Europe. "Give us only two months of this kind of warfare," the German foreign secretary said to Ambassador Gerard, "and we shall end the war and make peace within three months." Ludendorff himself wrote afterwards: "With the help of our submarines we reckoned on a decision in our favor at the latest before America and her new armies could intervene in the war."

When Count Bernstorff, the German ambassador in Washington, received official notice from his government that unrestricted submarine warfare would begin again on February 1, he sought to have the order canceled or at least to have its inauguration postponed. But Germany had other ideas. Accordingly he informed the Department of State of the decision on the evening of January 31. "After all that had happened," he later wrote, "I could but regard this intimation as a declaration of war against the United States, and one which, in addition, put us in the wrong." A few days later, on February 3, President Wilson appeared before the Congress to announce the severance of diplomatic relations with Germany and at the same time sounded the warning that "if American ships and American lives should in fact be sacrificed by their commanders in heedless contravention of the just and reasonable understandings of international law and the obvious dictates of humanity, I shall take the liberty of coming again before the Congress, to ask that authority be given me to use any means that may be necessary for the human right, of which we are only a single champion."

The warning went unheeded. On March 12 the steamer *Algonquin* was torpedoed and sunk without warning off the English coast. Although no lives were lost, the sinking constituted an "overt act" and was followed by others in rapid succession. Public opinion became more and more hostile and from all sides came the demand for a declaration of war. Finally President Wilson, feeling that he could no longer postpone active participation, appeared before a joint meeting of both Houses to ask that the Congress "formally accept the status of belligerent which has been thrust upon it." The resolution which made the United States a belligerent was passed and was formally signed by the President on April 6.[7] To the last he had endeavored to keep the United States out of the war so that he, as the representative of a country not at war, could act as mediator in the conflict. It had been a purpose he cherished above all others, but the resumption of unrestricted submarine warfare had caused him to lose his strategic hold on the situation.

The entrance of the United States strengthened the confidence of the Allies. They did not know, however, whether this country could do more than furnish supplies and naval support. But the people were determined not to rest content with half measures. All the immense resources of the United States, man power no less than materials, were at once consecrated to the cause for which the Allies were fighting. The German army leaders who professed to have little apprehension of the effect of the United States' entry into the war were astounded at the speedy adoption of compulsory military service and at the pressure exerted to prevent supplies from reaching Germany through the Scandinavian countries and Holland. Before many months had passed they were to realize that they had blundered greatly.

THE COLLAPSE OF RUSSIA

The United States entered the war none too soon, for Russia, shaken by revolution, was about to drop out. Russia had long been ripe for revolution. Dissatisfaction with the political regime and the social order had been characteristic of the country throughout the nineteenth century. Every war in which it became involved during that period had called forth an uprising against the existing regime, the central feature of which was the autocracy of the tsar. In the early centuries when the country was exposed to invasion from all sides the people had readily submitted to the most absolute rule in return for protection. Though the need had passed, the tsars did

---

[7] In the wake of the United States other nations including Cuba, Panama, Brazil, China, Liberia, Siam, and Greece joined the Allies. Guatemala, Costa Rica, Haiti, Nicaragua, and Honduras followed in 1918.

not abdicate any of their power. Thus at the beginning of the twentieth century Russia was still ruled by an autocracy. The will of the tsar was the supreme law. He was the head of an administration composed of a group of ministers completely subordinate to him and of a huge bureaucracy that was no less corrupt than inefficient. The chief care was not the welfare of the people but the suppression of every attempt to modernize and reform the government. No means were left untried to inculcate blind submission to the tsar. Perhaps the most effective was the Holy Orthodox Church. Whereas in western Europe the church stood as an independent power, in Russia it was a kind of administrative department of the state. Since Peter the Great had replaced the patriarchate with the Holy Synod, a college of dignitaries chosen by the tsar, the latter could say not only, "I am the state" but also, "I am the church." It became the official concern of the church to invest the tsar with a sacred character by teaching the masses that he was the vicegerent of the Almighty on earth and as such must be obeyed without question. Woe to the individual or group who expressed doubts about his divine mission or who attempted to counteract it.

The government might forbid all expression of opinion upon political subjects and all free political action but it could not repress the Russian mind. No civilized people could remain content for long with a system so arbitrary, so unjust, so corrupt, so inefficient. Underneath the surface the forces of revolution, like the forces of a great volcano, were gathering for an enormous eruption. In every class except the upper clergy and the large landlords, who together formed the main prop of the throne, the leaven of revolt was working. Among the intelligentsia, which was excluded from participation in politics, there were many who had long been hatching lofty utopian schemes of revolution while others were demanding such sober reforms as civil liberties and representative government.

Even the peasants, who constituted the bulk of the people, were in a revolutionary mood. Until 1861, when they were emancipated by Tsar Alexander II, most of them had been serfs bound to the soil and subject to the arbitrary whims of their landlords, with but little opportunity to escape the blight of poverty and ignorance. Upon being freed each had received a small plot of land which he was required to redeem by annual payments extending over a period of forty-nine years.[8] This did not, however, solve the economic problem of the peasant. Many were, in fact, worse off than they had

[8] All outstanding redemption payments were canceled in 1905.

been before. Most of the plots were too small for adequate maintenance and for meeting the annual redemption payments; consequently an intense land hunger developed which vented itself in
demands for more land and in continued agrarian riots.

Equally discontented was the proletariat, which was increasing
with the growth of large-scale machine industry. The grievances of
the industrial working class were low wages, long hours, bad working and housing conditions, and the government's refusal to permit
the workers to organize trade unions. The feeling that they were
being exploited not only kindled in their minds a hatred for the
existing regime but also made them highly receptive to the Marxist
ideas that were filtering into Russia.

All the discontented parties had hoped that Nicholas II, who
became tsar in 1894, would take steps to reform the government,
establish some kind of constitution, and promulgate measures to
improve the conditions of the peasantry and the proletariat. When
he dashed this hope by declaring that he was determined to preserve
the *status quo,* various groups began to organize as a means of
achieving their demands. The strongest moderate group was the
Constitutional Democratic Party or Cadets (from the initial letters of the party's Russian name), composed of merchants, manufacturers, liberal gentry, and the professional class of the *bourgeoisie.*
This party aspired to a constitutional monarchy on the English
model. The most extreme group, excepting the anarchists, was the
Social Revolutionary Party whose basic tenet was seizure of the land
of the nobility. This, together with the destruction of the Romanov
autocracy, they hoped to achieve through such individual acts of
terror as the assassination of high government officials. The members of this party were convinced that no revolution could succeed
without peasant participation. But the group that was later to play
the major role was the left wing of the Social Democratic Party.
Marxist disciples, making the most of the discontent of the proletariat,
had worked feverishly for some years to convert the workers and
to organize them in local societies. In 1898 these societies combined
to form the Social Democratic Labor Party. Before many years passed
differences of opinion began to appear within the party. The right
wing believed that Russia was ready only for a "bourgeois" revolution and that this revolution in establishing freedom of speech
and assembly would open the way for the ultimate realization of a
socialist order. Such an attitude was too mild for the left wing led
by Vladimir Ilyich Ulyanov, better known as Lenin. He would
establish a socialist order by force at once. Because this group had

a small majority in the party at the time, it became known as the Bolsheviks (majority men), while the members of the right wing were called the Mensheviks (minority men).

Symptoms of revolution were manifest on all sides. In the words of Count Muraviev, minister of justice, "The general dissatisfaction with the existing regime has seized all sections of society. . . . Things cannot continue in this way for long." But the government took no heed of the fact that the social barometer was prophesying foul weather. Instead of trying to redress grievances, it embarked on imperialistic ventures in China and thereby became involved in war with Japan (1904). As one defeat after another both on land and on sea exposed the shameful incompetence and widespread corruption of the government, the various parties became more and more insistent for reform. The Cadets put forward their demands for freedom of speech and assembly and for representative institutions. The workers not only supported these demands but also others for higher wages and better conditions of labor. On January 22, 1905, which became known as "Red Sunday," under the leadership of Father Gapon a vast orderly procession of working people marching to present both the economic and the political demands to the tsar was brutally fired upon by the police and by troops who were loyal to the tsar. The news of the massacre spread over Russia like wildfire. Strikes broke out in many towns, railway traffic was suspended in many places, and bands of peasants burned the houses and barns and seized the lands of their landlords. Finally in October, 1905, a general strike paralyzed the industry, commerce, and transportation of most of Russia. Chaos became so general that the government was forced to give way. On October 30 the tsar issued the so-called Freedom or October Manifesto which promised that a Duma or parliament would be elected on a democratic suffrage, that "civil liberties" would be established at once, and that the new assembly would have full legislative powers. It seemed as if the people had won a complete victory. But when the more radical groups who were not satisfied with the promised reforms continued their agitation, the moderates became alarmed and hastened to make peace with the government. This move encouraged the reactionaries, who were by no means subjugated, to inaugurate a policy of repression which they tried to justify with the assertion that the weakening of the executive power was ruining the country.

Although the reactionary forces were gaining strength, the law providing for a national Duma was still in existence and it was in the meeting of this body that all the hopes of the progressives were centered. The meeting of the first Russian parliament in the spring of 1906 might, in fact, have marked the beginning of a great national transformation if the tsar had been more far sighted in his views. Unfortunately this was not the case. There were even doubts in the minds of some that he would permit the Duma to assemble. Nicholas did allow it to meet, thereby "saving his face"; but when he discovered that an overwhelming number of its members were opposition deputies, he at once took steps to circumscribe their powers. As the Duma could not see any way of reforming the government on the lines of the Freedom Manifesto so long as its legislative competency was limited, it made a fight on the question of rights and was promptly dissolved. Every possible means was employed by the government to influence the elections for the second Duma; nevertheless the voters again returned a majority of liberal members. After a session of three months this Duma was also dissolved. To make certain that the next one would be moderate and submissive, the tsar and his ministers devised a new electoral law which disfranchised most of the liberal voters and gave the large landowners a preponderance in the selection of deputies. This resulted in the election of a more submissive Duma, but it was hardly a representative assembly. Had the tsar and his ministers decided to work harmoniously with even this assembly, some progress might have been made toward a more representative government and the need for the revolution of 1917 might have been averted. But the tsar resented any interference or criticism on the part of the Duma.

Instead of becoming more liberal, Nicholas became more and more reactionary after the Revolution of 1905. It had taught him nothing whatsoever. He still failed to comprehend that there were new forces at work, that the Russia of his day could not be ruled on the same lines as the Russia of Peter the Great. In his heart he was sure that his country could be happy only under an autocrat. This conviction became even stronger after the tsarina presented him with a son and heir in 1904. Thereafter the desire to preserve the autocracy intact for his son gradually overshadowed everything else. Nevertheless it might yet have been possible to persuade Nicholas, whose great defect was a lack of will power and self-reliance, that his system was an anachronism in the twentieth century if he had not been under the domination of his consort, the Tsarina Alexandra. A woman of strong will, she was a born despot. Obsessed with the idea that only an autocratic regime could hold Russia together, she opposed all concessions to the liberals. Knowing that the tsar was often weak and vacillating she perpetually preached firmness, telling him that for the sake of Russia and their son he must be an autocrat in deed as well as in name. "Be more autocratic, my very own sweetheart, show your mind," was one of her typical admonitions. Her baneful influence over the tsar is seen particularly in the fact that she encouraged him to choose his ministers for their political opinions rather than for their qualifications for office. The British ambassador to Russia aptly characterized her in the following words: "She misjudged the situation from the first, encouraging him, when the political waters were already running dangerously high, to steer a course fraught with danger to the ship of state. A good woman bent on serving her husband's interests, she is to prove the chosen instrument of his ruin." [9]

The tsarina, in turn, was surrounded by a group of unscrupulous and self-seeking adventurers who used her as an agent to further their own ends and ambitions. The outstanding member of this group was Grigoryi Efimovich, better known as Rasputin. To him above all others the tsarina looked for guidance before giving advice to the tsar. Born in a Siberian village as the son of an illiterate moujik, he had in early manhood earned for himself the nickname Rasputin, meaning *debauchee*. About the age of thirty this half-illiterate peasant had "gotten religion" and become a roving "man of God." Despite the fact that his life was no less dissolute than before, he gradually acquired the reputation of a holy man and was credited with the gifts of healing and prophecy. In 1903 his wanderings took him to St. Petersburg, where he was soon introduced into the court circle. Later when the heir of the imperial couple was found to be afflicted with the dread disease of haemophilia, Rasputin was able to convince the tsarina that he was indispensable to her son's well-being. Whenever the tsarevich became ill, he would mumble incantations over the child and improvement would set in at once. Before long his ascendancy over the tsarina was so complete that she urged the tsar from one folly to another in order to satisfy the wishes of "the man of God," the name she used when referring to Rasputin. At first the dissolute "holy man" contented himself with securing for his friends and adherents high appointments in the Orthodox Church but later he began to take a hand in politics. Through his influence over the tsarina he was able to obtain vacant ministries for his friends and even secure the dismissal of ministers who opposed him, thereby further discrediting the Romanov rule and hastening its downfall.

When the news of Germany's declaration of war arrived on Au-

[9] Sir George Buchanan, *My Mission to Russia*, vol. 1, p. 76.

gust 1, 1914, a wave of patriotic enthusiasm swept over Russia, giving the lie to the prediction of the German ambassador that the declaration would precipitate a revolution. War against Germany was as popular as the Russo-Japanese war had been unpopular. In St. Petersburg a mob attacked the German embassy, threw the furniture into the street, and even tumbled from its pedestal the large equestrian statue on the façade. On Sunday, August 2, hundreds of thousands of Russians from all classes stood for hours in the blazing sun to catch a glimpse of the tsar, while other thousands sang "God Save the King" in front of the British embassy. Some days later in Moscow, where he went to pray in the churches of the Kremlin, Nicholas was greeted with a never-ending cheer. Many in their enthusiasm even kissed the ground over which he passed. Everywhere workmen called off strikes, and the members of the various political parties put away their differences. In the Duma, which the tsar convoked for an extraordinary session, all the deputies excepting a few of the extreme left swore an oath of loyalty to the throne and to Holy Russia. A new comradeship seemed to have sprung up between the tsar and his people, one which gave the promise of better things after a period of bitter strife. Only a few saw disaster ahead, and one of these was Rasputin. He perceived that the foundations of the imperial structure had rotted away to such an extent that any serious strain would cause it to collapse in a heap of ruins. When the order for general mobilization was given, he sent the following telegram to Madame Vyrubova, inseparable companion and confidante of the tsarina: "Let Papa (the tsar) not plan war. It will be the end of Russia and all of us. We shall be destroyed to the last man."

The military successes during the first weeks seemed to bear out the optimism with which the Russians entered the war; but when defeat followed, the weaknesses of the regime began to emerge in new proportions. It soon became clear that the government had failed to prepare properly for the war. When the troops wished to resist the German invasion they found themselves face to face with an enemy well equipped with modern machinery, guns, and artillery while they lacked some of the most essential supplies. Not only were food and medicine insufficient but there was also a shortage of armaments and munitions. The military machine was, in fact, inferior in everything but numbers and courage. From the very outset the army had only sixty batteries of artillery against Germany's 381; it had only about 12 per cent of the machine guns it needed; and before many weeks passed there was a serious shortage

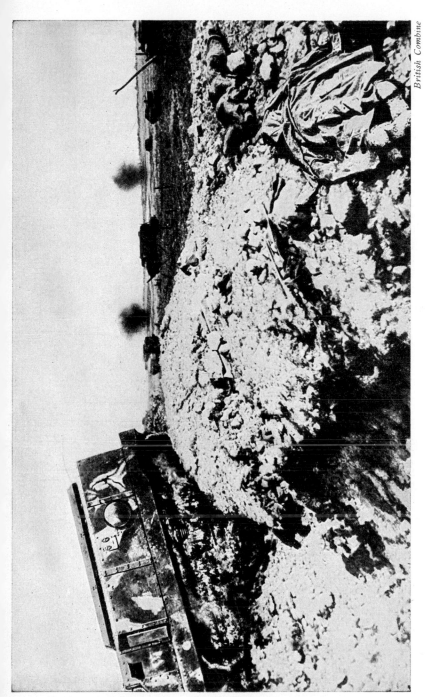

FRENCH TANKS IN ACTION: FIRST WORLD WAR

of rifles. "The shortage of rifles was so great," Sir George Buchanan wrote, "that a considerable percentage of the men had to wait unarmed till they could pick up the rifles of their fallen comrades." Even more serious was the lack of munitions. During the years before the war the government had prepared a quantity of munitions which it regarded as sufficient for a war of any length. But this stock was used up so rapidly that as early as October, 1914, a circular order called for the greatest possible economy in the use of artillery munitions. During the succeeding weeks the shortage of other kinds of munitions also became critical. Sir George Buchanan tells the story in the following words: "On September 25th General Joffre had inquired whether Russia's supply of ammunition was sufficient to meet the prevailing high rate of consumption, and had received the comforting assurance that there was no cause for anxiety on that score. Then suddenly, on December 18, the French ambassador and I were informed by the chief of staff that, though Russia had in her depots men enough and to spare to make good her colossal losses in the war, she had no rifles wherewith to arm them and that her reserves of artillery ammunition were exhausted. This announcement came as a bolt from the blue."

The problem of obtaining the necessary supplies and munitions was not easy to solve. Industries were still backward and could not fill the needs of the army. Not only did Russia not have sufficient munitions factories, the ratio being about one to every 150 operated by Great Britain, but those she had often lacked the necessary machinery and skilled labor. The military authorities had at the beginning of the war withdrawn most of the skilled laborers from the factories in order to fill the need for technical service at the front. In time refugees, prisoners of war, and women filled their places but the rate of production was very low. Nor was it easy to obtain supplies from the other entente powers because Russia was very largely blockaded. Soon after the start of the war the land frontiers toward Europe and also most of the seaways had been closed. While the German fleet dominated the Baltic, Turkey held the Dardanelles. This left Russia only three seaports—Archangel, Murmansk, and Vladivostok—each one of which had its special inconveniences. Archangel, being in the White Sea, was ice bound during much of the year; Murmansk, though an ice-free port, was without communications until the Murmansk Railway was built in 1916; and Vladivostok, on the Pacific, was separated from European Russia by the vast expanse of Siberia, traversed by only a single-track railway.

Although the Russians were still able to take the offensive on occasion, the heavy losses in battle and the confusion in internal affairs were gradually undermining the morale of the soldiers and unchaining the smoldering discontent of the civilians. Both saw what they had hoped would be a quick victory turning into a long defeat. As a result mass desertions became common in the army, and the civilian population became restive. Discouragement and discontent expressed themselves in bitter criticism of the government and, in particular, of the tsar and the tsarina. It was bruited about that the sympathies of the tsarina were with the enemy and that Rasputin was in German pay. In June, 1915, an excited mob in Red Square even insulted the portraits of the tsar and tsarina and demanded the removal of Rasputin. At the front the situation became so desperate that the tsar decided to take personal command of the army in September of the same year. After his departure for headquarters the tsarina and her group of reactionaries virtually governed Russia,[10] and Rasputin whom the tsarina consulted on all important matters exercised a greater influence than ever. "The situation," she said, "requires firmness." She would show her husband that firmness could put an end to the disorder and confusion. If a minister opposed her will, she did not rest until he was dismissed. The result was that ministers succeeded each other with startling rapidity and the confusion in the government increased. Several members of the imperial family who saw the danger of revolution tried to open her eyes to the gravity of the situation and the true character of Rasputin. But it was to no avail. Finally in December, 1916, three nobles took it upon themselves to deliver Russia from her evil genius. First they gave him poison; but when that had no effect, they shot him. Then to make sure that he would not come back to life, they put his body under the ice in the Neva River.

The news of Rasputin's assassination thrilled Russia, but his death came too late to prevent the revolution. The estrangement between the autocracy and the people was so complete that a reconciliation was no longer possible. By this time conditions were about as bad as they could be. The army was defeated and dispirited, and in the civilian population the discontent had reached the boiling point. Some were even openly proclaiming revolution to be the only cure for the political gangrene which had set in. The atmosphere was so tense that almost any cause would have been sufficient

[10] Some insight into the mind of the tsarina may be gained from reading the advice she gave her husband. "Remember to comb your hair before all difficult talks and decisions," she wrote; "the little comb [probably blessed by Rasputin] will bring its help."

) start a revolution. As it was, causes were not lacking. Poor trans-
-ortation and faulty distribution, coupled with a reduced harvest,
ad resulted in a shortage of foodstuffs in the larger cities. Those
vho wished to purchase food found it necessary to wait for hours
n long queues. In some of the working-class districts "bread was
carcely to be obtained at all."

On March 8, 1917, the discontent vented itself in a strike of
bout 90,000 workers in Petrograd,[11] followed by street demonstra-
ions and the display of banners bearing the inscription, "Down
vith Autocracy." The demonstrators were soon joined by women
demanding bread; and on each of the following days the demonstra-
ions were repeated on a larger scale. When the tsar was informed
of the growing seriousness of the situation, he made no attempt to
emove the causes but ordered the commander of the garrison to
disperse the rioters by force. Even then the revolution might have
been averted for a time if the commander had been able to carry out
he order. But the troops, sympathizing with the people, refused to
ire on the crowds. More than this, the soldiers gradually joined
hem. So the city passed completely into the hands of the revolu-
ionaries. By March 12 the tsarist rule had disintegrated so completely that the Duma appointed a provisional government to take
charge of affairs. The next day the tsar with some of his ministers
started for Petrograd in a special train, but the trainmen sidetracked
he train. Realizing that the game was played out, Nicholas abdicated his throne (March 15). Thus with but little bloodshed the
rule of the Romanovs came to an end.[12]

In the Allied countries the news of the revolution was received
with rejoicing. Previously the fact that autocratic Russia was fighting on their side had tended to weaken the effect of the statement
that they were fighting for freedom and justice. Now they could say
with greater conviction that they were fighting to "make the world
safe for democracy." Moreover, they were convinced that the elimination of the autocracy would strengthen Russia's determination and
increase her capacity for war.

But the joy of the Allies was short lived. The provisional government was unable to redeem its promise to prosecute the war
vigorously. Its members were completely out of harmony with the
desires of the people as a whole. They failed to realize that for the

---

[11] At the outbreak of the war the name of St. Petersburg had been changed to Petrograd; in 1924 it was again changed to Leningrad.
[12] Seventeen months later Nicholas and his family together with their attendants were
summarily put to death at Ekaterinburg by agents of the Bolsheviks.

peasant the revolution meant seizure of the estates of their landlord
and that the workers coveted control of the factories in which the
worked. Furthermore, the provisional government failed to realiz
that Russia was thoroughly war weary. Above everything else th
soldiers wanted to go home. Their main idea, according to Genera
Gourko, chief of the Russian staff, "was to stop the war, so that the
might the sooner benefit by the fruits of the revolution." [13] At hom
the people were equally tired of the war and wanted an end to wha
they regarded as "senseless slaughter." Drunk with the new wine o
liberty, all felt that the revolution meant they could do what the
pleased. The result was anarchy, with the workers refusing to work
the peasants to pay rent and taxes, and the soldiers to fight. Wha
the situation needed was a determined leader, but the provisiona
government did not include such a man. Being typical liberals, it
members lacked the ruthlessness necessary to win the respect of th
masses.

In an effort to win the support of the disaffected parties the
provisional government was reorganized (May, 1917) with Alex
ander Kerensky as its head. It was hoped that since he was a Socia
Revolutionary both the workers and the peasants would accept hi
leadership and that the soldiers would submit to discipline at hi
behest. The experiment failed. The more radical groups were deter
mined to be satisfied with nothing less than a thorough-going socia
revolution. When the old police ban was lifted, thousands of politica
exiles flocked back into Russia eager to play a part in political life
These were the real enemies of the provisional government. Among
them was Lenin, acknowledged leader of the Bolsheviks, who to
gether with some of his followers returned from Switzerland in the
famous "sealed train" furnished him by the German government.
No sooner did he set foot in Petrograd than he called for the overthrow of the provisional government and the establishment of working-class control. With the help of Leon Trotsky he took over the
soviets (councils of workers) and soon the streets were ringing with
the slogan, "All power to the soviets." Lenin knew exactly what he
wanted and was determined to get it at any cost. What he wanted
was to establish a soviet republic. In the words of Maxim Litvinov,[14]
"Russia must become not a bourgeois democratic but a soviet republic, that is, a commonwealth in which the central power would
belong to a central committee of all the soviets in the country, and
the local government would be carried on by the local soviets or

[13] *Memories and Impressions of War and Revolution in Russia,* p. 276.
[14] *The Bolshevik Revolution,* p. 27.

delegates from the working classes and the poorer peasantry, as the sole organs of the state." Capitalizing his knowledge of the exigencies of the situation and his understanding of the masses, Lenin was quickly able to gain support from the soldiers and peasants by promising the former peace and the latter land.

Throughout the summer and early fall of 1917 the Bolshevik cause gradually gained in strength and at the beginning of November Lenin declared that the time had come to overthrow the provisional government. The night of November 6–7 saw picked groups of Bolsheviks quietly seize the railway stations, the fortresses and military staff quarters, the central postal, telegraph, and telephone offices, and the state bank. A cruiser was also stationed on the Neva ready, if necessary, to bombard the Winter Palace, which was the headquarters of the provisional government. This was unnecessary, for the members of the government meekly submitted to arrest the next day. The provisional government was overthrown as easily as the tsarist government had been some months earlier. Russia was proclaimed a "soviet republic" and before the Congress of Soviets which assembled the same day Lenin announced, "We shall now proceed to construct the Socialist Order." A new government was set up under the title of Soviet (Council) of Peoples' Commissars, with Lenin at its head; then the congress proceeded to adopt three decrees submitted by him. First, it offered to conclude an immediate peace on the basis of "no indemnities, no annexations." Second, the lands hitherto in possession of private landlords were declared confiscated and their use transferred to the peasants. Third, control of production was vested in soviets or working-class committees. Thus a small but determined minority took over the rule of Russia.

As head of the government Lenin at once declared a cessation of hostilities, and in December opened peace negotiations with the Central Powers at Brest-Litovsk. In January the conference broke up for a time because Lenin felt that the German terms were too severe. But the Germans were determined to impose their terms, and orders were given for the army to advance toward Petrograd. Since the Russian troops were in no condition to stop the advance, there was no other course open to Lenin but to accept the German terms. On March 13, 1918, the Treaty of Brest-Litovsk was signed. It required Russia to renounce sovereignty in favor of the Central Powers over Russian Poland, Courland, Livonia, and Estonia. In addition she had to cede Ardahan, Kars, and Batum to Turkey; recognize the independence of Finland, the Ukraine, and Georgia; and agree to reparations payments in the amount of six billion marks. In short,

European Russia was completely dismembered for the benefit of the Central Powers. When Rumania also dropped out of the war early in 1918,[15] Germany's work of winning the war on the eastern front was finished. But victory on the western front was another problem.

🔥

THE GREAT GERMAN DRIVE

Meanwhile the Germans had started the unrestricted submarine campaign which, they were certain, would end the war in a few weeks. The gamble was no wild one. At first it was so successful that it really augured defeat for the Allies. During the month of April alone the U-boats sank 881,027 tons of shipping. For a time one out of every four ships leaving British ports was torpedoed. The Allies sent out many patrol boats to hunt down the submarines, and the British navy sowed mines near the submarine bases. But despite such methods of defense the campaign was proving successful. Submarines were being built several times as fast as they could be destroyed, the British mines were being swept up almost as fast as they were planted, and, worst of all, ships were being sunk several times as fast as they could be replaced. Had the Germans maintained the high rate of sinkings, Great Britain would soon have been unable to maintain its part in the war. However, the Allies did devise methods to combat the menace successfully. In May, 1917, the "convoy system" was adopted; in other words, ships went out in large fleets protected by warships. This system, together with the use of depth bombs and ship camouflage, greatly reduced losses. By the midsummer of 1917 the German leaders realized that their attempt to gain a quick victory with the submarine had failed. Thenceforth to the armistice 88,000 Allied ships were convoyed, with the loss of only 436 vessels. Perhaps even more remarkable is the fact that not one eastbound United States troopship was sunk.

By the end of 1917 the nations on both sides, excepting the United States for which the year was one of preparation, were war weary. For the Allies it had been full of disappointments. Not only had the collapse of Russia and Rumania been a severe blow to their hopes but in the fall the Italians had also suffered a serious defeat which caused a great reduction in Italian morale. Furthermore, the French attempt in the spring to smash the German line on the western front "at one blow of a gigantic fist," as General Nivelle put it, had failed. The British had made some gains on the western front but only in the Near East had they been uniformly successful.

---

[15] The treaty of Bucharest was signed on May 7, 1918.

'he news that General Allenby had entered Jerusalem in Decem-
er, 1917, caused much rejoicing in Allied circles. Among the Cen-
-al Powers the war weariness was equally widespread. While Turkey
as at the point of exhaustion, Bulgaria, having gained the terri-
>ry she wanted, was "unwilling to make further effort." In Austria-
Iungary conditions were rapidly nearing a crisis. The Austro-
Iungarian ship of state was so rotten and leaking so badly at the
:ams that it appeared unlikely to remain afloat much longer. Even
1 Germany the situation was critical. Not only had the food problem
ot been solved but the question of man power was also becoming
cute. So many men had been and were being taken into the armed
>rces that it was increasingly difficult to man the farms and the
ssential industries.

At the beginning of 1918 the German leaders tried to whip up
ie flagging energies of the people for one more great effort. They
>ld them that conditions on the Allied side were such that a deter-
iined effort would force a victory before the United States could
:ansport large numbers of troops to Europe. The offensive on the
-estern front, Ludendorff told the kaiser, "will be an immense strug-
le but it will be victorious." Indeed, conditions seemed favorable
> German success. Whereas the reserves of the French and British
/ere seriously depleted, the Germans as a result of the collapse of
Russia and Rumania were free to move to the western front most
f the troops that had previously been fighting the Russians and
Rumanians. Furthermore they had an advantage in being able to
nass their troops at those points at which they planned to break
hrough the Allied lines, while the Allies had to be prepared to
lefend their lines at all points. As early as November, 1917, the
;erman general staff had begun the transfer of troops from east to
/est and by the beginning of spring everything was ready for the
upreme effort.

The great attack was launched at dawn on March 21. Although
he Allied lines held at some points, they gave way at others. Week
.fter week the Germans made gains until at one point they were
.gain on the Marne. In advancing they had captured 225,000 pris-
>ners and inflicted almost a million casualties. From a distance of
learly seventy-five miles a small group of guns dropped shells on
'aris. Although this bombardment accomplished no results of mili-
ary importance, it did greatly alarm the people of Paris. Victory
.ppeared to be within German reach and many on the Allied side
vere beginning to believe that their efforts and sacrifices during the
our years of war would go for nothing.

But the situation was not so hopeless as some believed. In th
great drive the Germans had spent so much man power and used s
many supplies that they lacked the necessary energy to achieve th
final breakthrough. The weakening of the offensive together with th
rapid arrival of troops from the United States sustained the hope c
the Allies. At first there had been many in the United States wh
insisted upon an army of volunteers; ex-President Theodore Roos(
velt even offered his services as leader of a division which he woul(
raise. But President Wilson doubted the wisdom of sending a sma]
volunteer force. He saw that the United States must send great num
bers of troops to the front if the Allies were to defeat the German.
He appointed Major General John J. Pershing commander-in-chie
of the so-called American Expeditionary Force and on June 1
1917, Pershing and his staff reached Paris to make preparations fo
the arrival of the national army from the United States. Up t(
January 1, 1918, only small contingents arrived in France, but dur
ing the early months of 1918 troops began arriving in ever increas
ing numbers. The six months after March 21 saw no less than on
and one half million "Yanks" disembark in France.[16] Although mos
of them had had only a few months of training, they were eager an(
confident. The appearance of these troops in itself was a great mora
tonic to the weary Allies.

✎

ALLIED VICTORY

Thus the mobilized strength of the Allies was being increase(
in preparation for a counterattack. The threat of the German driv(
had finally caused the Allies to establish a unity of command unde
General Foch, who believed that "to make war is to attack." Whe
the Germans reached the Marne, he decided that the time had com(
to translate this principle into practice. In making his plans h(
hesitated to use the newly trained United States troops for purpose.
ur attack because he feared that they would not keep their organiza
tion under the strain of battle. "The prevailing opinion among th(
Allies," General Pershing wrote, "was that American units wer(
suitable only for the defensive." The need for troops was, however
so desperate that Foch finally decided to use the American soldiers
The plan was to cut off the German bulge at Château-Thierry, th(
United States attacking from one side and the French from the other
So determined was the attack that the German positions in the salien

[16] There were more than two million United States troops in France when the armi
stice was signed.

soon became untenable. Much to the surprise of the Germans as well as the Allies the "Yanks" had demonstrated their fighting abilities. A German army report of the battle states that "the qualities of the men individually may be described as remarkable. . . . They lack at present only training and experience to make formidable adversaries. The men are in fine spirits and are filled with naive assurance; the words of a prisoner are characteristic: 'We kill or get killed.' " While the success of the first operations fortified the confidence of the Allies, the unexpected strength of the attack shattered the German morale. Soon they began to withdraw all along the Marne salient. The Marne, which had been the high-water mark of German success in the drive of 1914, was also destined to be the high-water mark of their last desperate drive.

General Foch was not the man to let an opportunity slip through his hands. The first attack having proved successful, he ordered attacks at other points. When these also achieved their objectives, he decided to seek final victory that autumn instead of postponing the attempt until 1919. All the troops on the line from Verdun to the sea were to combine in a simultaneous offensive. The great assault was launched September 26. Americans, French, British, and Belgians attacked relentlessly. "Our dogged offensive," General Pershing stated, "was wearing down the enemy who continued desperately to throw his best troops against us, thus weakening his line in front of our Allies and making their advance less difficult." Each day the advance gained momentum. By September 30 the Hindenburg line was pierced to a depth of seven miles. Ludendorff, realizing that he lacked the means with which to repair the breaks, at once suggested that steps be taken to request an armistice, a suggestion which was supported by Hindenburg.

Meanwhile the first break had also occurred in the ranks of the Central Powers. Bulgaria, her armies shattered, was forced to capitulate and on September 30 concluded an armistice. The collapse of Bulgaria, together with the continued reverses, finally convinced even the kaiser that the time had come to ask for peace. On October 3 Prince Max of Baden was made Imperial Chancellor and the next day he appealed for an armistice to President Wilson, who was the Germans' hope for a tolerable peace.

Having been forced into the war against his will, Wilson endeavored to keep the war as idealistic as possible. Repeatedly he expressed the sentiment that the United States was "fighting for no advantage or selfish object of her own, but for the liberation of peoples everywhere from the aggressions of autocratic force." When the vindictive spirit of certain groups became articulate he stated that "the voices of humanity insist that the war shall not end in vindictive action of any kind; that no nation or people shall be robbed or punished because the irresponsible rulers of a single country have themselves done deep and abominable wrong" (speech of December 4, 1917). As these statements show, he made a sharp distinction between the German people and the German government. "We are not," he stated, "the enemies of the German people and . . . they are not our enemies. They did not originate or desire this hideous war or wish that we should be drawn into it; and we are vaguely conscious that we are fighting their cause, as they will some day see it, as well as our own." On the other hand, the German authorities, particularly the kaiser and the military clique, he regarded as "the ruthless masters of the German people." These masters, he said, had enslaved the German people. More than this, "the war was begun by the military masters of Germany." Against these masters the Allies must fight until a final and complete victory has been achieved. Then, when they are defeated, "the German people will thrust them aside" and a just and honorable peace will be made. In short, the President stated in unmistakable terms that peace could not be discussed until the "masters of the German people" were overthrown.

Nor did Wilson stop at stating with whom he would make peace; he also formulated the terms and principles on which the peace must be based. These were embodied in the so-called Fourteen Points which he proclaimed in his address of January 8, 1918. With the Fourteen Points he tried to show the way to a new world. First, there were to be no more secret treaties; all international agreements must be "open covenants, openly arrived at." Second, there must be "absolute freedom of navigation upon the sea, outside territorial waters, alike in peace and in war." Third, so far as possible all economic barriers to trade must be removed. Fourth, national armaments must "be reduced to the lowest point consistent with domestic safety." Fifth, all colonial claims must be adjusted on the basis of the interests of the populations involved. Other principles which the President laid down were those of "no annexations" and "national self-determination." The last of the Fourteen Points, and the greatest in the President's mind, stated that "a general association of nations must be formed under specific covenants." This League of Nations should not only prevent future conflicts but also guarantee the enforcement of the terms and principles outlined in the Fourteen Points. "The free peoples of the world," he had stated

THE RAILWAY CAR IN WHICH THE ARMISTICE OF 1918 WAS SIGNED; IN FRONT OF LES INVALIDES, PARIS

earlier, "must draw together in some common covenant, some genuine and practical cooperation that will in effect combine their forces to secure peace and justice in the dealings of nations with one another. The brotherhood of man must no longer be a fair but empty phrase; it must be given a structure of force and reality."

The Fourteen Points must be listed among the greatest pronouncements ever made by the responsible head of a great government. Outstanding leaders had in the past put forward programs for world betterment, but the central aim of all of them had been the aggrandizement of themselves, their organizations, or their countries. Not so with President Wilson. Although the idea of personal distinction undoubtedly entered into his proclamation, he was not asking anything for himself or for his country. His was a vision of a better world for mankind as a whole. There was, to be sure, no lack of adverse criticism. Some even accused him of speaking "like God Almighty," but to the peace-loving masses of the world who for years had suffered privations the pronouncement was indeed the gospel of better things to come. And by no peoples was it more gladly received than by the masses of Austria-Hungary and Germany. They believed that Wilson, as leader of the Allies, could persuade the other belligerent nations to accept his principles. That is why the German government addressed its appeal for an armistice to President Wilson.

The request which he received not only asked him "to take in hand the restoration of peace"; it also stated that "the German Government accepts the program set forth by the President of the United States in his message to Congress of January 8, 1918, and in his later pronouncements . . . as a basis for peace negotiations." In other words, the German government accepted the Fourteen Points as the basis for peace. Similar appeals were also addressed to the President by Austria-Hungary and by Turkey. In his reply Wilson requested clarification of the German note, asking whether "the Chancellor speaks" for the German people or "merely for the constituted authorities of the Empire who have so far conducted the war." When the Chancellor answered that he "speaks in the name of the German government and of the German people," the German people generally leaped to the conclusion that the offer would be accepted. As a result excitement ran high in Germany. An Amsterdam dispatch to a London paper declared: "People in Berlin are kissing one another in the streets, though they are perfect strangers, and shouting peace congratulations to each other. The only words heard anywhere in Germany are 'peace at last.'" However, the sinking of the British steamer *Leinster* with the loss of hundreds of lives of noncombatants while the negotiations were being carried on caused the President to sharpen his tone. His reply clearly stated that a change in the German government constituted "a condition precedent to peace." The answer, as Senator Reed put it, was "an unequivocal demand that the Hohenzollern shall get out."

Nevertheless, the kaiser still refused to abdicate. Although the German armies were everywhere in retreat and in danger of destruction, he did not stop trying to stir the nation to new efforts for victory in the hope of saving his throne. But the situation was beyond redemption. Mutterings of discontent were growing louder. In Berlin an enormous crowd assembled before the Reichstag building on October 25 calling for the abdication of the kaiser and the formation of a republic.

Before the end of October the second nation dropped out of the ranks of the Central Powers. It was Turkey. The capture by General Allenby of Damascus in September and of Aleppo in October had checkmated the remaining Turkish forces and rendered them helpless. There was nothing for them to do but to lay down their arms. On October 30 Turkey signed an armistice which, like that of Bulgaria, was tantamount to unconditional surrender. On October 27 Austria had also requested an armistice. In the week which followed, the Italians swept the Austrians out of northern Italy, entered Trent in the Alps and Trieste on the Adriatic, and captured 300,000 prisoners. The result was Austria-Hungary's unconditional surrender on November 3. Following this surrender the Emperor Charles abdicated and the Dual Empire disintegrated into states representing the various nationalities. Before his abdication the emperor had, in fact, appointed a liquidation ministry to hand over the imperial powers to the national governments that were taking form. Thus Germany stood alone.

Up to the end of July the majority of the German people had still been confident of victory. Then came the rude shock of discovering that their lines were crumbling. This, together with the lack of food and supplies and the collapse of Bulgaria, Turkey, and Austria-Hungary, caused a serious breakdown of morale and a growing resentment against the government that had given them false hopes. After four years of war the people wanted nothing more than peace. Although there were some among the conservatives who hoped to save the Hohenzollern rule, the majority, and particularly the parties of the left, openly demanded the kaiser's abdication when it became clear that they had to choose between the Hohenzollern and peace. One socialist deputy to the Reichstag even went so far as to voice the threat that "abdication would not save the kaiser from trial as the man who caused the war." A mutiny which broke out in the fleet at Kiel on November 3 set the spark of revolution spreading all over Germany. Four days later came the proclamation of a republic in Bavaria, followed by similar proclamations in other states. When the commanders decided against the employment of force to suppress the movement, the kaiser finally realized that he could not ride the storm. On the morning of November 9 he abdicated the throne and very prudently fled to Holland; there he took up his residence in the Chateau of Amerongen which had housed a former monarch in exile, Charles II of England.

In the meantime, as it became certain that the Germans were ready to yield, representatives of the Allies had gathered in Paris to formulate the terms for an armistice, and the German government had appointed an Armistice Commission to enter into negotiations. The German delegates were received by Marshal Foch on the morning of November 8 in a railroad car stationed in the forest of Compiègne. Reading in a loud voice and carefully dwelling upon each word, Foch presented the Allied terms to the group. They included, among other things, immediate evacuation of the invaded countries, surrender of large quantities of war materials, evacuation of the territories on the left bank of the Rhine, occupation by the Allied troops of the principal crossings of the Rhine (Mainz, Coblenz, Cologne), immediate repatriation, without reciprocity, of all Allied prisoners of war, renunciation of the treaties of Bucharest and Brest-Litovsk, surrender of all submarines with their complete armor and equipment, internment of German warships in neutral or Allied ports, and immobilization of all aircraft. Foch delivered the terms with the formal demand that they be accepted or refused within seventy-two hours. Astonished at the severity of the terms the delegates asked permission to communicate them to Berlin. A courier was dispatched to headquarters, whence the terms were telephoned to Berlin. The new government discussed them for hours before finally submitting to the inevitable and then only after instructing the delegates to protest the severity. The protests availing them nothing, the delegates signed the armistice on November 11 at 5 A.M., Paris time. Then Foch ordered the firing to cease along the entire front at 11 A.M. of the same day.

As the hands of the clock finally reached eleven, there came the sound of men cheering from the Vosges to the sea. Peace had come at last. After more than four years of suffering and bloodshed "the fires of hell had been put out." The next day a correspondent wrote from Mons: "Last night, for the first time since August in the first year of the war, there was no light of gunfire in the sky, no sudden stab of flame through the darkness, no long, spreading glow above the black trees where for four years of night human beings were being smashed to death." Released from the tension of the conflict the peoples of the Allied world gave unrestrained expression to their joy. Paris, London, Rome, and New York went wild with uncurbed enthusiasm, an example that was followed on a smaller scale in every city and village of the Allied world. The hateful accusations that had been flung at the enemy were soon forgotten, but the voids which the war left in an untold number of homes were not filled so quickly. Millions had perished in battle, while other millions were physically wrecked or at least partially incapacitated. More men were killed in the First World War than in all the European wars that had been fought since the outbreak of the French Revolution in 1789. It is estimated that of the sixty-five million who were mobilized, eight and a half million were killed or died of illness and more than twenty-one million were wounded. In addition there were nine million estimated civilian deaths from causes related to the war. In the principal European countries there was hardly a family in which some member had not been killed or maimed or was missing. As for the cost in money, the sums were so large that they become meaningless to the average mind. According to one estimate the total up to the time of the armistice was over $300 billion.

CHAPTER FOUR

The Paris Peace Conference

WILSONIAN IDEALISM WORLD WAR I had not only drained many countries of their young men and depleted their finances; it had also wrought havoc with the entire fabric of society. The old monarchies had fallen to the ground like rotten fruit, and three empires—the Austro-Hungarian, the Russian, and the Turkish—had collapsed into ruins amidst which various national groups were clamoring for independence. The new states rising on the ruins of the old empires were organizing armies in order to seize the frontiers they coveted. Consequently, although the great fire of war had been quenched, nearly a score of little fires were soon burning fiercely, adding the horrors of civil war to the desolation created by the war that had just ended. Furthermore, starvation was stalking across Europe, leaving many thousands of dead in its wake. Over the entire Continent a spirit of unrest was brooding and in some lands chaos reigned supreme.

On all sides there were problems demanding immediate adjustment. There was, for example, the stupendous task of making a new map of the world and of reducing to order a territorial chaos incomparably greater than that after the fall of Napoleon. The main issue, however, was to prevent a repetition of the great catastrophe. These were the problems confronting the Peace Conference that was scheduled to meet at Paris in January, 1919. They would have taxed to the utmost the energies and abilities of any body of men even if they had been given ample time to solve them and full authority to make any change deemed necessary. But it must be remembered that the Peace Conference had neither unlimited time nor full authority.

87

However conflicting the aims of the various belligerents may previously have been, they all appeared to be unified in the Fourteen Points which President Wilson had laid down as a basis for the settlement. Not only had the Germans accepted this program but the Allies had also consented practically without reserve to conclude peace on the principles drafted by their American associate. Thus both sides were bound by a contract and there was no outward sign of differences. A new system of international relationships in which sectional interests and discredited diplomatic traditions were to have no place had been adopted. Territorial aggrandizement, balance of power, strategic frontiers, transfers of populations against their will were all part of a past which had been formally forsworn by the Allies. For the moment the future appeared promising and Wilson's success complete. All that remained, it seemed, was to work out the application of the Fourteen Points to specific problems.

But no sooner had the thunder of the guns died away than it became evident that the European leaders had learned nothing of the new gospel and forgotten nothing of the old. They had simply paid lip service to principles which they never seriously expected to translate into concrete enactments. With the enemy prostrate in defeat the selfish national aims and ambitions began to reassert themselves and Wilson was charged with sponsoring a program of "impossible idealism." Even before the armistice was signed Lloyd George had said: "Should we not make it clear to the German government that we are not going in on the Fourteen Points of peace?" During the weeks following the armistice he repeatedly objected to some of the principles of the Wilsonian program. This gave Clemenceau courage to come out into the open with his objections. On December 30 he announced before the Chamber of Deputies that France stood for the old alliances and the old balance of power. Before long it also became clear that the French leaders were resolved to stand for a strategic frontier on the Rhine and for the annexation of peoples for the sake of minerals. Various other leaders also proclaimed the idea that Germany was solely responsible for the war and must therefore pay the costs. On December 12 Lloyd George declared in a speech that the loser pays and one of his lieutenants went so far as to announce that he would "squeeze the lemon until the pips squeak." The secret treaties which the Allies had made among themselves early in the war were also resurrected. Though the collapse of Russia and the defeat of Rumania had eliminated some of these, there still remained commitments to Italy and Japan. It was not long before it became clear that both were resolved to hold out for the full execution of the secret agreements.

President Wilson, who did not fail to perceive these changes, consoled himself with the idea that the peoples of Europe, if not their leaders, were on his side. "It is not men," he said, "that interest or disturb me primarily; it is ideas. Ideas live; men die." He believed that the great universal heart was really athirst for the new order as well as for peace, that the masses shared his hatred of war, militarism, and the old diplomacy, which bartered away peoples as chattels. In other words, he was convinced that the masses were passionately determined upon the kind of peace he himself desired, a peace in which there would be no room for the selfishness and narrow views that had characterized the proceedings of the powers in the past. Moreover he was convinced that with the masses on his side nothing on earth could successfully resist the establishment of the new order. On September 27, 1918, he had already asserted: "This is a peoples' war, not a statesmen's. Statesmen must follow the clarified common thought or be broken."

To make sure that the ideas of the people would prevail at Paris he decided to go there himself. As the spokesman of the masses he would see to it that "the moral forces that make for right and justice and liberty are united." The Paris journey was to him nothing less than an apostolic adventure, a sort of divine mission which would settle once and for all the questions which up to then had divided the peoples of the world and had formed obstacles to the dawning of an era of universal peace. No President in the history of the United States had assumed so important a role on the world's stage.

It was a proud day for Wilson when on December 4, 1918, he boarded the steamship *George Washington* in New York harbor. Although Republican leaders and a number of newspapers had expressed strong disapproval of his personal participation in the Conference, great crowds lined the waterfront to bid him success in his mission. As the ship carrying the President, his intimate advisers, and a group of experts on every country of the globe, moved toward the ocean, the craft in the harbor joined in a noisy farewell, the like of which New York had never heard. If he still entertained any doubts as to the support of the people, they were completely dispelled by the reception he was accorded in Europe. Eyewitnesses have stated that he was everywhere greeted with enthusiasm beyond description. Secretary of State Lansing who accompanied him later wrote in a critical vein: "No man ever received a more demonstrative welcome than did Mr. Wilson from the moment that the *George Washing-*

ton entered the harbor of Brest. It was a great popular ovation. His name was on every lip; throngs of admirers applauded him as he entered the special train for Paris and at the stations en route; and multitudes, delirious with enthusiasm, cheered him a welcome as he drove through the beflagged streets of the French capital in company with President Poincaré who met him at the Gare du Bois de Boulogne. It was a reception which might have turned the head of a man far less responsive than the President to public applause, and have given him an exalted opinion of his own power and accomplishment." On subsequent visits to England and Italy he was also greeted "with an emotion and delirium which only those who witnessed the progress could even imagine." It was for him the ultimate proof that the people of the three Allied nations stood unanimously in his support.

But Mr. Wilson erred in thinking that the masses of Europe shared his idealism. They did, it is true, hope that the American President might prove to be a sort of Messiah who would save them from the hard lot they had suffered in the past. But their ideas of justice were those of Old Testament vengeance and were the natural result of the sufferings they had endured during the war. For the people of the United States the war had been something distant. The American countryside was not devastated, nor were American cities destroyed. The people of the United States were well nourished and had made money as no others had. The war really came home to them only when the name of a relative or friend appeared on the casualty list. In Europe Belgians, Frenchmen, Italians, Serbs, and others had seen sections of their countries devastated and many homes destroyed. During the unrelenting struggle they had made vast sacrifices and suffered terrible hardships. In France and Belgium there was scarcely a home that had not been seared by the fires of war. Not only had millions of homes been bereft of the head of the household or of a son but many held the pitiful wreck of what once had been a sturdy man. All this had excited feelings of hatred and vengeance toward the Central Powers. These feelings had been lashed to a white heat by propagandists and the press. The people were told that the Germans were unspeakable barbarians, and in support of this statement tales of the most atrocious barbarities committed by them were circulated.

When the war suddenly came to an end, the people were expected to stifle these feelings overnight and to show a spirit of forgiveness toward the enemies they had been taught to hate. It was too much to expect of human nature. Actually the war mentality, together with the thirst for vengeance, was still uppermost. The peoples of Europe, told by the propagandists that the war had been wantonly inflicted upon them by Germany, wanted compensation for their sacrifices and sufferings. No less than their leaders they preferred a strategic frontier and a coal field here or a bit of booty there to all the faint allurements of President Wilson's ideal. Above all, they expected the Germans not only to make reparation for damages they had caused but to pay the complete costs of the war. The English, for example, gave their representatives a mandate to collect the costs "to the last shilling." Nor were the French and Italians any less eager to grind their defeated enemy in the dust. Any British, French, or Italian minister who might have tried to commit his country to an altruistic venture would have lost his place at once.

It was particularly unfortunate for the President's program that Paris was chosen as the seat of the Peace Conference. A neutral city, such as Geneva or Lausanne, would have been infinitely preferable. Wilson, in fact, had advocated holding the conference on neutral soil. But the French, who insisted that it be held on French soil, were not to be denied. They believed that France, in bearing the brunt of the attack, had earned this honor. And which place, they argued, could be more fitting to consider the future of the German Empire than Versailles, the scene of its birth in 1871? When the matter was discussed by representatives of the Allied Powers, Clemenceau was firm in the choice of Versailles and succeeded in making his will prevail. Actually not Versailles but Paris with its superior accommodations became the scene of the deliberations. A worse place could hardly have been chosen for dispassionate discussion. Paris, which for years had been under a perpetual menace of invasion, was still vibrating with the hatreds of the war. "Arriving in Paris at the beginning of February," a British correspondent wrote, "I was at once struck by the bellicose temper which seemed to pervade the entire community, and even more by the vindictive tone of the press. The phrase *Nous sommes les vainqueurs* reappeared with wearisome iteration in the leading articles and furnished the staple argument for a denial of mercy to the beaten foe." [1] Later the President and his advisers regretted the choice, the President himself going so far as to suggest the removal of the conference to another city. But nothing came of the suggestion.

[1] *Contemporary Review,* vol. 117 (1920), p. 25.

ༀ

ALLIED REALISM

By the beginning of 1919 all the hotels of Paris were crowded with delegations representing or pretending to represent almost every country of the globe. Only the defeated powers were not permitted to send delegations. Most of the delegations were large and included many experts on civil, military, and naval affairs in addition to hordes of secretaries, clerks, and typists. Those from Great Britain and the United States each comprised about four hundred members. Many of the smaller nations sent delegations of fifty or sixty.

The opening meeting, at which no less than thirty nations were represented, was an impressive scene. At three o'clock on the afternoon of January 18, 1919, President Poincaré of France said to the assembled representatives with a touch of emotion in his voice: "I leave you to your weighty deliberations. The Peace Conference is declared open." Thus the peacemakers were ready to begin formal discussions. But the real work was not done in the plenary sessions. Earlier at an informal meeting of the heads of the great powers it had been decided that in order to expedite the task the work should be done by the Council of Ten, comprised of two representatives each from Great Britain, France, Italy, Japan, and the United States and by a series of special committees constituted to deal with such matters as the League of Nations, responsibility for the war, reparation for war damage, international economic problems, and a variety of other questions.

Plenary sessions, which all accredited representatives of the Allied Powers were permitted to attend, were convoked only a few times and were largely full-dress parades at which the decisions of the Council of Ten were announced. Except for the discussion on the League the plenary conference had little voice in the settlement; in fact, it did not receive the treaty in its totality until the day before it was handed to the German delegation. "Altogether a plenary session of the conference on the preliminaries of peace," Secretary of State Lansing, who was a member of the Council of Ten, wrote, "was a farce. It was never a deliberative assembly which reached an agreement by a frank exchange of views. The delegates were called together to listen, not to criticize or object to the program of the Council of Ten. They were there to go through the formality of registering their approval, whatever their real opinions might be." Representatives of the smaller states occasionally lifted a piping treble of protest but no one paid any attention to them.

Eventually it was found more convenient that the important business of framing the conditions of the peace should be conducted by an even smaller group. So the Council of Ten was reduced to the Council of Four, composed of President Wilson, M. Clemenceau, Mr. Lloyd George, and Signor Orlando of Italy.[2] All the members of this group, popularly known as the Big Four, were men of outstanding ability. It was in Clemenceau that Wilson found his principal opponent and it was between the two that the main struggle took place. Clemenceau was cynical, witty, experienced in the ways of men, and a forceful speaker despite his seventy-seven years and his diabetes. For decades he had fought so relentlessly in the arena of French politics that he had earned the nickname "the Tiger." Becoming premier of France in the darkest hour of the war, the fierce old Tiger refused to entertain even a fleeting thought of discouragement. His was a will to victory which no reverse could shake and this will he succeeded in communicating to the army and to the nation. Wherever he went this veteran had disseminated hope and confidence. Now that the war was won, he was determined that France was not to lose the peace. Of Wilsonian idealism he was scornful. "Fourteen Points! The good Lord Himself had only Ten!" he is reported to have said. His creed was patriotism, and France was his god. Consequently he regarded everything in the light of how it would affect France. In every fibre he represented the hopes, fears, and hatreds of his countrymen.

Clemenceau knew what he wanted and was determined not to let the illusion of a better world order swerve him from his purpose an inch. "We spend a whole day arguing with Clemenceau," Wilson said, "and think we have convinced him, but find him the next morning exactly where he was before." What he wanted was indemnification for French losses and security against future German attacks. As Poincaré put it: "For the misery and sadness of yesterday the peace must be a reparation; against the dangers of tomorrow it must be a guarantee." Of the two, security was Clemenceau's chief concern. Having twice seen German armies invade and devastate France, he was determined that the danger of his country's becoming the cockpit of Europe again must be removed once and for all. "Our cities and towns," he said several weeks before the Peace Conference opened, "have been devastated. Everyone says rightly that 'it must not happen again.' I think so too." Thus he

---

[2] When the affairs of eastern Asia were under discussion, a Japanese delegate attended the meetings.

conceived the peace in terms of French military preponderance, more particularly in terms of security on France's eastern frontier. "The *idée fixe* fills his mind," a correspondent wrote, "gives it an orientation which is unfavorable to the new conception that is embodied in the League of Nations, and impels him to demand a peace treaty which will give him the kind of guarantee his military chiefs will prescribe."

Lloyd George, the prime minister of Great Britain, held something of a midway position between Wilson and Clemenceau. Possessing undeniable charm of manner, considerable brilliance of mind, and a hearty manner of address, he was a strange combination of the liberal and the reactionary. He could accept and discard political principles as easily and almost as frequently as men change their clothes. At Paris he was not so cold blooded as might appear from his promise to the British people that he would "hang the kaiser" and collect from Germany the costs of the war "shilling for shilling and ton for ton." He realized that excessive and long-term reparations could not be collected and therefore proposed that "reparations should disappear with the generation which made the war." Furthermore, he favored a minimum change of territory beyond the cession of the principal German colonies to the British Empire. In general, he advocated that the terms of the treaty be such as the German government would accept. The terms of a treaty, he stated, "may be severe . . . but at the same time they can be so just that the country on which they are imposed will feel in its heart that it has no right to complain. But injustice, arrogance, displayed in the hour of triumph will never be forgotten or forgiven." In brief, he favored more moderate terms than Clemenceau and was often chided by the latter for his moderation. But his attempts at moderation were rendered difficult by the clamors of the British jingo press which accused him of being inclined to "let the Germans off." These clamors he could never entirely ignore.

The fourth member of the Big Four, Signor Orlando, played an irritating rather than an important part. His inability to speak or understand English debarred him from participating in the discussions, which were generally conducted in that language. His aims were frankly those of an ardent Italian imperialist. Beyond these he took little interest in the discussions. France could do what she liked and Great Britain take what she wanted so long as they gave Italy what she desired. Together with the imperialist party in Italy he wanted to save the loss of thousands of emigrants who left Italy each year by securing territory in which they could settle. The lands the imperialists wanted were on the eastern coast of the Adriatic; in fact, they wished to make the Adriatic "an Italian lake." To achieve this they were ready to scrap Wilson's entire program.

The members of the Big Four conducted the business of drawing up the treaty in the best way they could discover. Discussion was quite informal and unhampered by written rules. However, the differences of opinion with which each of the four had come to the conference speedily became manifest. Each one worked for his own ends. While Wilson held out for his new order, the other three strove respectively for a French peace, a British peace, and an Italian peace. And outside the Big Four representatives of other nations were trying to achieve their selfish goals. One factor which militated against the success of Wilson's cause was his unpreparedness to submit a detailed program. Until midsummer of 1918 victory had seemed far away. The big drive that was to bring victory had been scheduled for the spring of 1919 and by that time Wilson hoped to have his detailed plans ready. But when the Central Powers suddenly collapsed like a house of cards in the autumn of 1918, he was caught unprepared. At the time of his arrival in Paris he had only a draft of a Covenant for a League of Nations and that was roughly drawn. He did, of course, have the Fourteen Points, but they were little more than general principles which were to serve as a guide in making the settlement.

The consequence of his failure to submit a concrete peace plan was that Clemenceau and Lloyd George took the initiative on most questions requiring settlement and succeeded in making their ideas prevail at least in some degree. At the very first the principle of "open covenants, openly arrived at" went by the board. Since Clemenceau, Lloyd George, and Orlando were parties to a score of secret treaties, they could hardly agree to open covenants. Once the decision in favor of closed sessions was adopted, the President's colleagues began to take exception to other principles stated in the Fourteen Points. They soon realized that Wilson, having set his heart above all on the League of Nations, was willing to make concessions in return for support of the Covenant and they were not slow to make the most of his supreme desire as a means of gaining concessions from him. He was not unaware of the fact that the ground was slipping from under him, but he clung to the consolation that the League of Nations would rectify all deviations from the Fourteen Points.

On some questions, however, he did make a resolute and successful stand. For example, he stood firm as a rock in his insistence that the Covenant of the League be included in the treaty with Germany. Neither Clemenceau nor Lloyd George desired to have the League and the peace treaty so inextricably bound together that one could not work without the other. But the President held his position until the two statesmen gave way. Furthermore, he resisted the French demand to separate the territory on the left bank of the Rhine from Germany and to create an independent Rhenish Republic as a buffer state between France and Germany. In his opposition to this demand he had the wholehearted support of Lloyd George, who saw that such an arbitrary partition would excite deep resentment in the hearts of the German people. For a time it appeared as if the peacemakers had reached an impasse. But Clemenceau was finally persuaded to accept a compromise which called for the permanent demilitarization of the Rhineland and its occupation by Allied troops for a period of fifteen years. He was also promised military help if France were to be attacked by Germany.[3]

President Wilson also stood firm on the question of Fiume. According to the secret treaty of London the Italians were to receive the whole of the Dalmatian coast of the Adriatic. But even this did not satisfy them. They laid claim also to the town of Fiume and threatened to refuse to sign the treaty unless their demands were satisfied. If they had asked only for Italia Irredenta, that is, for territory inhabited by Italians, Wilson would not have objected. As it was, their claims were clearly in violation of the principle of self-determination. When the Italian delegates referred to the secret treaty of London, the President said that he was not bound by that treaty and that furthermore Italy's acceptance of the Fourteen Points had invalidated all secret treaties. The verbal battle continued for weeks. Wilson might have been willing to make concessions in regard to the Dalmatian coast, but on the question of Fiume, which was the principal available outlet to the sea for the new state of Yugoslavia, he refused to give way.

Finally, in the hope that the Italian people would support him, the President issued a public statement of his reasons for refusing the demands of the Italian delegates. It was a kind of summons to the people to renounce the selfish nationalism of their Paris representatives. But it achieved the opposite of the result intended. Its immediate effect was to range Italian opinion almost solidly behind the demands of Orlando. The people believed no less than Orlando himself that the time for cashing in on the Allied promises had come

[3] This promise was nullified by the refusal of the United States and Great Britain to ratify the treaty of alliance.

and that it might never come again. Consequently the same masses that had hailed Wilson as a potential savior a few weeks earlier now denounced him as the archenemy of Italy. Encouraged by the support of the people, the Italian delegates temporarily left the Peace Conference in protest and a band of Italian freebooters, led by Gabriele D'Annunzio, the poet and novelist, proceeded to seize Fiume, declaring that they would hold it no matter what the Peace Conference decided. Thereupon the conference gave up the attempt to settle the question.[4]

Thus President Wilson did accomplish something of value. While it is true that he failed to hold his colleagues to their pledge, it is equally true that he kept them from running away with the treaties. Freed of his influence the Allied statesmen, having previously agreed what each country was to get, would probably have settled down to the old diplomacy of secret bargaining and quickly divided the spoils. But his influence could not be ruled out. Consequently the task of peacemaking became a struggle between the old diplomacy of force and Wilsonian idealism. If the result was not a Wilson peace, neither was it a Clemenceau peace nor an Orlando peace. It was a compromise between the old and the new. In its terms it satisfied many of the demands of the old diplomacy, particularly in regard to the transfer of territory and reparations, but on the other hand it took a long stride toward the establishment of the policy of national self-determination and it also contained provisions for a League of Nations which at least Wilson hoped would lift international relations to a higher plane. Before many months had passed, however, the bad clauses of the treaty completely overshadowed the good.

THE TREATY OF VERSAILLES

The Paris Conference produced five separate treaties, of which the Versailles document was the first and the pattern. All the treaties took their names from one of the suburbs of Paris. In addition to the Treaty of Versailles with Germany there were the Treaty of St. Germain with Austria, the Treaty of Sèvres with Turkey,[5] the Treaty of Neuilly with Bulgaria, and the Treaty of Trianon with Hungary.

[4] Ultimately Italy concluded a treaty with Yugoslavia (Treaty of Rapallo, 1920; revised in 1924) which annexed Fiume to Italy, but gave the Yugoslavs free commercial use of the port.
[5] This treaty failed and was superseded by the Treaty of Lausanne in 1923.

By the beginning of May the Treaty of Versailles was ready to be submitted to the Germans. Anyone who considers its bulk, the complexity of its problems, and its bewildering multiplicity of detail will be astonished that so gigantic a task could have been completed in so short a time. When on May 7 the treaty was handed to the German delegates, Clemenceau said to them, "The time has come when we must settle our accounts. You have asked for peace. We are ready to give you peace. We shall present to you now a book which contains our conditions." Much to its disappointment the German delegation, which was accompanied by a large number of experts on many subjects, learned that there would be no negotiations. The delegation was informed that it could present comment in writing within a maximum period of fifteen days but that oral discussion with the Allied representatives was out of question. In accepting the treaty for consideration Count Brockdorff-Rantzau, leader of the German delegation, read a long speech in which he recalled that the Allies as well as the Germans had accepted the Fourteen Points as a basis for the peace. Furthermore, while admitting that the Germans had made many grave mistakes he repudiated the accusation of Germany's sole guilt and demanded a neutral investigation of the causes of the war. However, he concluded on a hopeful note. "We shall," he said, "examine the document handed to us with good will and in the hope that the final result of our interview may be subscribed to by all of us."

Upon reading its 440 articles the delegates were unanimous in their opinion that the treaty could not be accepted unless it was fundamentally revised. Immediate departure was even suggested by some of the delegates. In Germany, where the proposed terms were soon published in the newspapers, they were denounced in unmeasured terms. Ebert, president of the German Republic, sent the delegation a telegram which declared the terms to be "unfulfillable, unbearable, and ruinous," while the president of the National Assembly at Weimar said, "Our enemies have laid before us a treaty which surpasses by far the fears of our greatest pessimists." Other leaders went so far as to state not only that the terms reduced the Germans to slavery but also that they would give rise to a war of revenge. The general feeling of the people was expressed by Erzberger, who had been chairman of the Armistice Commission, when he said, "The Treaty of Versailles is the work of the devil."

On May 29 the Germans presented their counterproposals to the Allies in a long document. After stating emphatically that the terms were inconsistent with the Fourteen Points, the text went on to attack the various items in detail and to make counterproposals. Among the things the Germans requested were oral discussion of the terms and immediate entrance of Germany into the League "as a power with equal privileges." Curiously enough, it was not Wilson but Lloyd George who was ready to yield to many of these demands. While Wilson said that the Germans could not frighten him into making changes by threats of refusal to sign the treaty, Lloyd George openly advocated modification of the terms. This exasperated Clemenceau into saying, "The task is becoming veritably impossible. For weeks and weeks I had to fight Wilson and his famous principles. Finally, with much patience, and also with much diplomacy, I came off triumphant, and in that matter Lloyd George aided me powerfully. Now it is England which is obstructing the way and changing her mind as to everything that has been decided."

Nevertheless the Allied reply of June 16 did allow the German objections to a number of points but did not appreciably narrow the gulf which separated the principles of the treaty from the Fourteen Points. Thus, for example, the reparations clauses were made a little less harsh, a plebiscite was substituted in Upper Silesia for outright annexation to Poland, and Germany was assured of membership in the League as soon as she demonstrated her willingness to observe her international obligations. The Big Four was determined that the modified terms were final. There was to be no further discussion. Either the terms were accepted unconditionally by the evening of June 23 or the armies of Marshal Foch would advance on Berlin. Everywhere in the Allied countries the people were asking: "Will the Germans sign?" For a time it seemed as if they would refuse. Premier Scheidemann and his cabinet resigned in protest and even President Ebert contemplated resignation but was dissuaded from taking the step. Other leaders stated that they would rather see Germany invaded than accept the Allied terms. An hour later the decision was telegraphed to Versailles. The final sentences of the communication read: "Yielding to overpowering might, the government of the German Republic declares itself ready to accept and to sign the peace treaty imposed by the Allied and Associated governments. But in doing so the government of the German Republic in no wise abandons its conviction that these conditions of peace represent injustice without example." [6]

The first twenty-six articles of the treaty embrace the Covenant or "written constitution" of the League of Nations. Although the name of Woodrow Wilson is closely associated with the idea of the

[6] Cited in Luckau, *The German Delegation at the Paris Peace Conference*, p. 112.

League, he was not the originator of it. It goes back at least as far as the Roman Empire. During the course of the nineteenth century peace societies had repeatedly urged the establishment of a league of states to prevent war. Nor were the details of the Covenant, as adopted, his. But it stands to his credit that he recognized the need for a league and was unwearied in advocating the establishment of one. As early as 1915 he had said that the war must not end without the organization of a league to outlaw war. During the next years the idea developed in his mind until it became the reason behind his whole program. It was the hope of realizing his plan that caused him to go to Paris. Clemenceau, who doubted the efficacy of a moral deterrent, told him that the League as he had planned it did not offer the protection France desired. "We are afraid," he said, "that your League is not strong enough. Give it an army. Give it guns and tanks and airplanes and we will consider it." In other words, he wanted the League to have at its disposal an adequate military force ready to strike at a moment's notice. To this Wilson replied, "The Covenant we offer must be based primarily upon moral sanctions with resort to force only as a last necessity." He held unalterably to his views until his colleagues agreed to the general plan and the conference voted that a League of Nations be "an integral part of the general peace treaty."

The purpose of the League, according to the Covenant, was "to promote international cooperation and to achieve international peace and security." Thus the League was to be more than a device for preventing war. It was intended to be an agency for handling affairs of common concern and for promoting the common interest. The signatories of the Covenant were to be regarded as the original members, but "any fully self-governing state, dominion, or colony . . . may become a member of the League if its admission is agreed to by two thirds of the Assembly," which was the supreme organ of the League. Geneva was selected as the meeting place of this body and English and French were adopted as the official languages. Each member was permitted to send three representatives to the Assembly, but the whole delegation had only one vote. The second principal organ of the League was the Council. Although the analogy must not be pressed, the Assembly can be likened roughly to a parliament and the Council to a cabinet. In other words, the executive functions were vested in the Council. It was composed of nine men of which five, representing Great Britain, the United States, France, Italy, and Japan, had permanent seats, while the four others were elected annually by the Assembly and represented

L'Illustration

PALACE OF THE LEAGUE OF NATIONS, GENEVA, SWITZERLAND

smaller states. At first the great powers tried to limit representation in the Council to themselves but in the end had to be satisfied with a majority representation.[7] In both Council and Assembly all decisions, excepting on minor points like questions of procedure, were required to be unanimous.

Two other organs of the League must not be overlooked. The first of these is the secretariat, a corps of some seven hundred persons of all nationalities headed by the Secretary-General. Its functions were to collect information on all subjects treated by the Council and the Assembly and to conduct the correspondence of the League. The Covenant further provided for the establishment of a Permanent Court of Justice. In 1922 this court came into formal existence in the Peace Palace at The Hague, with fifteen judges chosen for their ability rather than for their nationality. These judges were chosen by the Council and the Assembly and in no way represented the countries from which they came.[8] The business of the court included the settlement of disputes referred to it by the League Council. Such was the machinery of the League to which weary Europe looked for surcease from the periodical wars which consumed the blood and substance of mankind.

Of more direct concern to Germany were the territorial changes prescribed by the treaty. Excisions were made on every frontier. In the southwest she lost the provinces of Alsace-Lorraine, with their mineral wealth, which she had taken from France in 1871. Closely connected with Alsace-Lorraine, not only geographically but also historically, is the rich valley of the Saar, also known as the Saar Basin. Although this district was not removed permanently from German sovereignty, it was placed under the administration of the League of Nations for a period of fifteen years. At the end of this period a plebiscite was to decide under what sovereignty the inhabitants desired to be placed. The coal deposits within the area were to be "the absolute property of the French state," subject to possible redemption in 1935. On the northern frontier the two small districts of Eupen and Malmédy were assigned to Belgium, while still farther to the north a plebiscite prescribed by the treaty gave a portion of Schleswig, annexed by Prussia in 1864, to Denmark. Then there were Germany's heavy losses to a resuscitated Poland. In the reassembling, at the expense of Germany, Austria, and Rus-

[7] Even this was lost when the United States failed to ratify the treaty. In 1926 Germany took the vacant permanent seat. The same year, under the pressure of the smaller nations, the number of nonpermanent seats was increased to nine.
[8] Two eminent American jurists were members of this court at different times.

sia, of the fragments of a Poland which had been torn apart in the partitions of 1772, 1793, and 1795 Germany lost Posen, the greater part of West Prussia, and much of Upper Silesia. Furthermore East Prussia was severed from the rest of Germany by the so-called "corridor" which gave the new Poland the "free and secure access to the sea" the Allies had promised her. In giving Poland this corridor the conference found it necessary to include many Germans in the Polish state. The city of Danzig at the top of the corridor was made a free city under the rule of the League of Nations. Finally, the future of Memel, situated at the mouth of the Niemen, was left undecided, but in 1923 the League decided that it should go to Lithuania, one of the new states that were carved out of Russia. Thus the treaty deprived Germany of nearly one seventh of her European territory and about one tenth of her population. Yet the losses were not nearly so great as those imposed by the Germans upon Russia in the treaty of Brest-Litovsk, which deprived the Russians of 500,000 square miles and sixty-six million people. It may be noted, however, that the territory which Germany lost contained more than half of her iron, zinc, and lead deposits and about two fifths of her coal deposits.

In addition to much European territory the treaty took from Germany all her overseas possessions and privileges. Soon after the war started, the Allies had captured all the German colonies excepting German East Africa,[9] a task which was made easier by the inability of Germany to send them help. Having taken the colonies, the Allies decided not to return them. "In territory outside her European frontiers," the treaty states, "Germany renounces in favor of the Principal Allied and Associated Powers all her rights and titles over her overseas possessions." According to further stipulations Germany was also compelled to renounce all rights, benefits, and privileges in China, Liberia, Siam, Morocco, and Egypt and "to recognize any arrangements which the Allied and Associated Powers may make with Turkey and Bulgaria as to German rights in those countries." Finally, the treaty provided that all German movable and immovable property in the aforementioned territories was to pass without indemnification to the new governments exercising authority over them. Thus the Treaty of Versailles swept away not only the German colonial empire as such but also her spheres of influence and her commercial footholds, all of which had been a source of pride for her people.

But the task of confiscating the German colonies was easier than the task of distributing them. The division of most of them had

[9] In German East Africa the fighting continued to the end of the war.

already been arranged during the war by secret treaties, but several annoying factors, more particularly the fifth of Wilson's Fourteen Points, interfered with the outright annexation stipulated in these treaties. The Fifth Point prescribed "a free, open-minded, and absolutely impartial adjustment of all colonial claims" in which "the interests of the populations concerned must have equal weight with the equitable claims of the Government whose title is to be determined." President Wilson had stated the idea even more emphatically when he said in one of his speeches: "Every territorial settlement must be made in the interests and for the benefit of the people concerned." The Allies found the solution in the so-called mandate system under which the colonies, instead of being annexed outright, were declared the common property of the League of Nations and were then distributed to the various Allied nations to be ruled as "mandates," the distribution following fairly closely the provisions of the earlier secret treaties. The whole procedure was, in the opinion of some observers, merely "disguised annexation." The partition allocated the colonies in Africa to France, Great Britain, and the Union of South Africa. In the Far East, Australia received German New Guinea, New Zealand got German Samoa as its share of the spoils, and Japan got the German Pacific islands north of the equator (the Caroline, Marshall, Mariana, and the Palau Islands) and the rich province of Shantung.[10]

The next section of the treaty dealt with the question of disarmament. Point Four of the Fourteen Points prescribed the reduction of national armaments "to the lowest point consistent with domestic safety." The Allies did not, however, regard this in terms of disarmament for themselves. Believing that Germany was responsible for the war, they decided to disarm Germany and to keep their own armaments as a guarantee that Germany would not again endanger the peace of the world. Everything was done to make Germany helpless from a military point of view. The nation which had been the greatest military power in the world was forbidden for all time to have an army of more than 100,000 men, including officers. Precautions were also taken to prevent the building up of a large reserve force. After crushing Prussia in the battle of Jena (1806) Napoleon had limited the size of the Prussian army, but the Prussian government managed to build up a large trained reserve by giving intensive training to one levy of recruits after the other. So that the Germans would not be able to circumvent the Treaty of Versailles in the same way, it was decreed that enlistment in the *Reichs-*

[10] This was returned to China at the Washington Conference, 1921–1922.

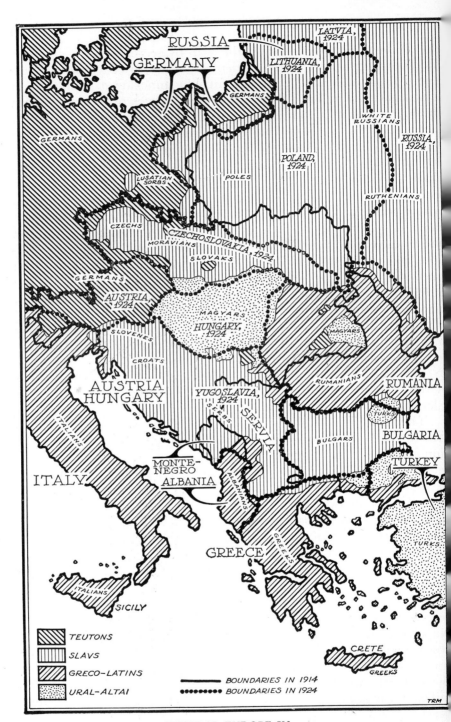

CENTRAL EUROPE IN 1924

wehr, as the army authorized by the treaty was called, must be voluntary and that "the period of enlistment for noncommissioned officers and privates must be twelve consecutive years and for commissioned officers twenty-five." Furthermore, military training under the guise of shooting, police, and athletic clubs or any other type of association was forbidden. It did not take the Germans long to find means of circumventing the restrictions.

The treaty also stated that the armed forces of Germany "must not include any military or naval air forces." In addition, the manufacture and the importation into Germany of armored cars, tanks, and all similar constructions suitable for use in war were prohibited. The navy, too, was reduced to a minimum. According to the treaty, "the German naval forces must not exceed six battleships, six light cruisers, twelve destroyers, and twelve torpedo boats," while the navy personnel was limited to 15,000. Practically all ships in excess of this number were to be surrendered to the Allies.[11] No submarines were to be included in these naval forces. "On the expiration of one month from the coming into force of the present Treaty all German submarines, submarine salvage vessels, and docks for submarines, including the tubular dock, must have been handed over to the Governments of the Principal Allied and Associated Powers."

There were many other clauses that cannot be listed here. All together they amounted to the practical disarmament of Germany. As additional security to France the treaty provided for the demilitarization of the right bank of the Rhine to a distance of fifty kilometers. All fortified works, fortresses, and field works in this zone "shall be disarmed and dismantled" and "the construction of any new fortification, whatever its nature and importance, is forbidden." The left bank together with the bridgeheads, as stated earlier, was to be occupied by Allied troops for fifteen years.

Another important section of the treaty dealt with the question of reparations. The horror and intensity of the war had given rise to the view that modern war is a crime and that responsibility for it can be expressed in terms of guilt. It led to the inclusion in the

[11] Seventy-three German ships which had been interned at Scapa Flow at the time of the armistice were scuttled by their crews just before the treaty was signed.

✿✿✿

CENTRAL EUROPE IN 1924. *Compare this map with the one on page 12 and notice particularly the changes in Austria-Hungary, Russia, and the Balkans.*

treaty of the troublesome "war-guilt clause" (Article 231), according to which Germany accepted the responsibility "for causing all the loss and damage to which the Allied and Associated Governments and their nationals have been subjected as a consequence of the war imposed upon them by the aggression of Germany and her allies." This idea that the war was a wrongful act by Germany became the basis for claiming heavy reparations. In England and France the public had been led to believe that Germany would pay the entire cost of the war. The French press, which was still dominated by war psychology and the quest for vengeance, even went so far as to demand in addition the repayment with interest of the indemnity Germany had collected from France in 1871. However, according to the pre-armistice note of November 5, 1918, which claimed compensation only "for all damage done to the civilian population of the Allies and their property," the Allies had renounced all claims to total reimbursement of their war expenses. If the French and British public was to be satisfied even in part, some way of stretching to the utmost the phrase "civilian population" had to be devised. It was General Smuts, premier of the Union of South Africa, who offered the suggestion that the words could be interpreted to include war pensions and separation allowances. This view was accepted also by President Wilson. Only Belgium was to be compensated for the entire loss to which she had been subjected as a result of the German invasion.

When it came to fixing the exact amount of Germany's debt to the Allies and the method of payment, there was less agreement. The maximum figure of $15 billion suggested by experts from the United States did not satisfy the French. They held out for a sum almost three times as large and were supported in their stand by the British prime minister, who was bound by his election pledges. Unable to compose their differences the Allied representatives decided to refer the question to a special Commission on Reparation. This Commission was to determine by May 1, 1921, not only the total amount but also the manner of payment. In the meantime Germany was required to make a payment of $5 billion in the form of gold, merchant ships, reconstruction material, coal, dyestuffs, and other commodities.

The treaty, which went into force January 10, 1920, had meanwhile become a domestic political issue in the United States. No sooner had President Wilson submitted it to the Senate for ratification than a tempest which had been gathering for some time broke loose. Some few Senators were ready to authorize ratification without material change but the majority was either opposed to ratification in any form or wanted substantial reservations. On March 19, 1920, the supporters of the treaty failed for the second time in their efforts to obtain ratification. Although the votes may in some instances have been motivated by personal enmity toward the President, the primary reason for opposition appears to have been the conviction that further participation in European affairs was not to the interest of the people of the United States. Thus the people of the United States repudiated, through the Senate, the contract Woodrow Wilson had signed at Paris in their name.[12] This repudiation seriously impaired the whole Versailles settlement. Later Lloyd George repeatedly declared that had the United States remained a party, it would have been possible, as the wartime temper cooled, to revise the treaty in Germany's favor.

THE OTHER TREATIES

Although Wilson, Lloyd George, and Orlando left Paris immediately after the Germans signed the treaty, the work of the Peace Conference was far from finished. Peace still had to be made with Austria, Hungary, Bulgaria, and Turkey. The treaty with Turkey was signed at Sèvres in August, 1920, but before it could be ratified a new Turkish leader arose in the person of Mustapha Kemal who refused to ratify it. A new one had to be worked out at Lausanne in 1923.[13] The terms of the other three are similar in many respects, and identical in some, with the Treaty of Versailles. Whole sections from this were simply incorporated in the others. Thus the Covenant of the League constitutes Part I of all. Reparation is demanded from all three states in the same terms as from Germany, and they are also required to accept the responsibility for loss and damage caused by the war. Finally, the treaties contain provisions for the reduction to a minimum of the Austrian, Hungarian, and Bulgarian armies.

After weeks of exhausting labor the Austrian peace treaty was completed and delivered to the Austrian delegation at St. Germain on July 20, 1920. The attitude of the Austrian negotiators was much more conciliatory than that of the Germans had been and as a result of an exchange of notes the Allies made some concessions. Nevertheless, when the revised text was published in the Austrian newspapers, it evoked expressions of protest and despair. The *Arbeiter Zeitung*, for example, styled it as being "bitter, spiteful, and unjust," adding that

[12] The following year the United States signed a separate treaty with Germany.
[13] See p. 302.

"the entente is using its power in the most shameful manner to ill treat and outrage a defenseless people with a peace based on might." The Austrian Assembly, being in no position to resist, voted to accept the treaty under protest, whereupon it was signed at St. Germain on September 10. The head of the delegation, Dr. Karl Renner, having done all in his power to modify the original terms laid down by the Allies, tried to look at the brighter side of the situation. "We are conquered," he said after the signing; "yet misfortune has given us liberty, freed us from the yoke of a dynasty whence for three generations no man of worth has sprung, freed us from bonds with nations which were never in understanding with us nor with themselves." But the Assembly in a spirit of bitterness drew up a resolution which opened with the words, "We raise once more our voices against a peace founded on brute force."

While the German loss of territory had been confined to fragments lopped off here and there on the periphery, the old Austria was divided in such a way that only a modest remnant remained intact. In requiring the new Austria to recognize the independence of Hungary, Poland, Czechoslovakia, and Yugoslavia the treaty reduced to its component parts the old Austro-Hungarian Empire which had been a collection of unrelated nationalities. Actually it was the war more than the peace that tore the ramshackle empire into fragments. Encouraged to revolt during the war by the promise of independence, various nationalities of the Dual Monarchy had formed republics of their own. The promise of an independent Poland had meant tearing a hole in the northeast of the Habsburg Empire, the declaration of independence by Czechoslovakia in 1918 disrupted the central part, and the new Yugoslav state took the Slav districts toward the south (Croatia, Bosnia-Herzegovina, and the Banat of Temesvár). Thus the Dual Monarchy had ceased to exist before the Peace Conference met. By and large it remained only for the peacemakers to confirm to each one of the separate states its appropriate share of territory. In addition to apportioning territory to the new states, the treaty awarded southern Tyrol (the Trentino) with its quarter of a million Germans to Italy. It had been the promise of this territory (Treaty of London) that had brought Italy into the war.

All that remained of the old Austrian Empire with its population of about twenty-eight millions and an area of about 115,000 square miles was the German-speaking central district embracing about six thousand square miles and a population of something over six millions. This was the Republic of Austria. With a third of its population living in Vienna, it was incapable of self-support. "We are independent with an independence which cannot be alienated," Dr. Renner stated; "yet we depend on the Czechs and the Poles for coal, on the Banat for cereals, on Italy for maritime commerce." Economically the situation was so desperate that the Assembly declared that ultimate union with Germany was an absolute necessity, hoping that the peacemakers would agree to the plan. The representatives of the United States approved the idea of union (*Anschluss*), but France and Italy were so strongly opposed to any strengthening of their old enemy that the plan was vetoed. This, the Austrians said, was an absolute denial of the right of self-determination. They were further displeased by the transfer of so many purely Austrian subjects to Czechoslovakia and Italy. They contended that this was in flagrant violation of the terms of the armistice. A resolution passed by the Assembly stated that "the four million Germans forced under foreign rule will for all time insist on self-determination as the only possible basis on which the modern state may be founded." The Assembly also declared that the reparation clauses of the treaty were impossible of fulfillment and that Austria would suffer economic collapse if her burden were not substantially lightened.

The Treaty of Trianon dealt as severely with Hungary as the Treaty of St. Germain did with Austria. Likewise regarded as an enemy, Hungary was carved up to the extent that it lost two thirds of its entire area and three fifths of its population. With this territory went the greater part of its natural resources in coal, iron, other minerals, and forests. What remained was an area of about 35,000 square miles and a population of about eight millions. Particularly objectionable was the transfer to Rumania of Transylvania with its three million Hungarian inhabitants. When the treaty was published in Hungary the press made such comments as: "It is annihilating," "The Treaty condemns us to ruin," and "It is an injustice that cries to Heaven." Requests for modification were presented at once, with a special request for plebiscites to settle the question of boundaries. The Allies, while acknowledging the difficulty of the ethnographic problem in their reply, unequivocally rejected the request with the statement that in Central Europe it was impossible to make the political frontiers coincide with the ethnic. There was nothing further the Hungarian delegation could do; so it signed the treaty on June 4, 1920.

The treaty with Bulgaria, though chronologically not the last, completed the immediate postwar settlement. As in the case of the other treaties a suburb of Paris—Neuilly—was chosen for the actual signing. The Bulgarian government, contrary to public sentiment, had entered the war on the side of the Central Powers in the hope that it might rectify territorial grievances left over from the Balkan Wars of 1912–1913. Having chosen the wrong side in the contest, Bulgaria was now called upon to pay the piper. Besides being required, among other things, to pay reparations and to limit her army to 20,000 volunteers, Bulgaria was mutilated by amputations of territory on the north, west, and south, in flagrant violation of the principles laid down by President Wilson and accepted by the Allied governments. On the west a series of small districts inhabited exclusively by Bulgars were given to Yugoslavia, which claimed them on "strategical grounds." More important was the loss to Greece of the Bulgarian sections of Thrace, a loss which cut Bulgaria off completely from the Aegean Sea.[14] It is estimated that no less than 1,700,000 Bulgarians were placed under alien rule by the treaty. So shocked were the Bulgarians when the provisions were announced that a day of mourning was proclaimed and Sofia, the capital, was hung in black. On November 27, 1919, the delegation signed the treaty after declaring that "all established principles of international justice and the free determination of nations are disregarded. The Bulgarian nation is punished with extreme cruelty." But the Bulgarian nation never recognized the validity of the treaty.

On April 23, 1920, Viscount Bryce said in an address before the House of Lords that in the first place the peacemakers "were bound to fulfill and carry out the purposes which they proclaimed at the time of the armistice, the purposes that were stated in the famous Fourteen Points and which were accepted and made the basis of the armistice, and upon the faith of which the armistice was accepted by the enemy powers. Those principles are briefly known as the principles of nationality and self-determination." The Balkan settlement conformed to these principles to a large extent, but in a number of instances they were completely ignored and territory was allotted on the old-fashioned principle of *vae victis, spolia victoribus* (woe to the vanquished, the spoils to the victors). Populations were moved around as if they were "mere pawns on a chessboard." It is estimated that about eight million persons were put under alien rule, creating new minorities and new irredentas. This was most deplorable because it had not only been expected but also asserted that through the Peace Conference the Balkan problem "would be solved with reference to the most equitable observation of the principle of nationality." "I think it is a misfortune," Viscount Bryce stated,

14 A clause inserted in the treaty guaranteed Bulgaria economic access to the Aegean.

"that so many provisions have been introduced into these treaties which obviously come from passion rather than from wisdom, and which are likely, therefore, to bear very unfortunate fruits in the future. . . . Peace can come only with content. If the result of these treaties is to make nations discontented, to put sections of peoples under a power which to them is alien and hostile you cannot expect them to be content, and therefore you cannot expect that there will be peace. On the contrary, you are preparing for revolts and for wars." Thus, instead of establishing a permanent peace on principles of justice and self-determination, the treaties sowed new seeds of hatred and strife in the Balkans.

On the other hand, it must be remembered that the delegates at Paris were handicapped not merely by the array on the ethnic chessboard but also by the fact that most of the new states had come into existence before the armistice. In the interval between the armistice and the meeting of the Peace Conference these states had set up their own frontiers and consolidated their positions. Any sweeping alterations of the pattern into which Europe had fallen by the time the Peace Conference started its deliberations, could have been made only through the use of force.

Europe Between Two Wars

※※

CHAPTER FIVE

The Weimar Republic

THE FOUNDING OF THE
REPUBLIC
THE so-called "revolution" which
took place in Germany in 1918 was not a spontaneous national development. Its coming was not prepared by preconceived ideologies which organized the revolutionary forces. There was no reign of terror, no guillotine, no Marat, Robespierre, or Lenin. Generally speaking, there was little bloodshed. In other words, there was no revolution in the sense that there had been a French Revolution or a Russian Revolution. It was at most a revolution without a capital R. It actually amounted to little more than a change of government. It ejected the kaiser together with the twenty-five sovereigns of the states comprising the German Empire and proclaimed Germany a republic. Beyond this it left the country cluttered with the old social and economic setup.

The change that did take place came as a result of military defeat and not because the people yearned for a republic. For more than four years they had been fighting and sacrificing in the conviction of ultimate victory. As late as September, 1918, they were still confident and optimism persisted even in the high command. Then the announcement by General Ludendorff that victory was no longer possible brought with it the vast disillusionment which defeat inevitably brings. The realization that instead of wearing the palms of victory they would have to bear the thorns of defeat, that their sacrifices and suffering had been for nothing, that millions of German lives had been lost uselessly, shook their faith in the Hohenzollern government. But, aside from a group of the more radical socialists, they did not want to abolish monarchy. What doomed the Hohenzollern rule was President Wilson's statement that the Allies would not deal with the government that had brought on the war. When the parliamentary cabinet organized by the liberal Prince Maximilian of Baden in October still proved unsatisfactory, the people decided to sacrifice the kaiser as a means of obtaining better peace terms. According to Philip Scheidemann, one of the leaders of the Social Democratic Party, "The question was: could we get better peace conditions if His Majesty abdicated and the Crown Prince renounced his rights to the throne?" Up to that time even the Majority Socialists had not demanded the abdication of the Hohenzollern and even after Wilson's statement they still tried to save the monarchy by suggesting a regency, possibly for a grandson of the kaiser.

All this time the masses, by and large, were passive, the driving force within Germany being a relatively small group of left-wing socialists. A minority group which found the Social Democratic Party too conservative had hardly seceded in 1917 to found the Independent Social Democratic Party when a split occurred within this new party. At its left there appeared a faction inspired by the success of the Bolshevik revolution in Russia. The members of this third party were called Spartacists, a name deriving from a series of subversive letters written by Karl Liebknecht and signed "Spartacus."[1] The Spartacists were the most active revolutionary party in Germany. The ideology was Bolshevist and the success of the Bolshevists in Russia was a standing summons to the Spartacists to emulate them. On the basis of Lenin's interpretation of Marx, Rosa Luxemburg, a woman of great talents, drew up a party platform prescribing a program of action which was to bring about the overthrow of the capitalist system in Germany as preliminary to world revolution. The abdication of the Hohenzollern presented the leaders with just the opportunity they had been waiting for, but it came so suddenly and unexpectedly that they were unable to make the most of it. They were almost without arms, excepting a few rifles taken from deserters.

Nevertheless they did attempt to establish a communist government. As the crisis neared at the end of October and the beginning of November, Spartacist leaders addressed gatherings in Berlin and other industrial centers urging the proletariat to rise up and establish a "free socialist republic." When it became certain that the kaiser must abdicate, self-appointed committees—the so-called workers' and soldiers' councils—formed on the model of the Russian soviets, sprang up everywhere as if by magic. On November 9 a band

[1] The Roman gladiator who proclaimed freedom for slaves.

of Spartacists, led by Karl Liebknecht, seized the royal palace and the police headquarters in Berlin. Liebknecht announced to the crowd that the proletariat was master of Germany and ordered the bells of the cathedral rung in celebration of the victory. For the moment it seemed as if the efforts of the Spartacists to establish a dictatorship on the Russian model might prove successful.

With the Spartacists taking the initiative, the old Social Democrats or Majority Socialists, the strongest party in Germany, either had to guide the revolution or find themselves treated as reactionaries. They chose the former. Even then they waited until the abdication of the kaiser had been announced and the Spartacists were marching through the streets of Berlin proclaiming the socialist republic. By this time the situation was such that Scheidemann, who was to become premier of the new republic, declared, "Now we must put ourselves at the head of the movement or there will be chaos in the Reich." On the afternoon of November 9, 1918, a delegation of Majority Socialists headed by Friedrich Ebert went to the cabinet of Prince Max and informed it that the people desired to take the controlling power into their own hands. Prince Max then turned the chancellorship over to Ebert, a leatherworker of humble background. Thus the imperial régime yielded to democracy or rather to a temporary dictatorship that was to be followed by a constitutional democracy. Ebert invited the Independent Socialists, but not the Spartacists, to cooperate in the provisional government. The Independents accepted the invitation, and a mixed committee, composed of three Majority Socialists and three Independents, took over control. The Independents soon withdrew. As assistants the Majority Socialists had the vast body of imperial officials, practically all of whom remained at their posts and continued to administer the routine of their bureaus.

The Majority Socialists were patriots and Germans first, and socialists second. They had long abandoned the Marxian theory of revolution. In 1914 their representatives in the Reichstag had voted for the war credits [2] and thereafter had continued to support the government in maintaining the war. Their purpose in seizing power after the kaiser's abdication was not to save the revolution but to save Germany. Although he was a socialist of long standing, Friedrich Ebert was determined that the Germany Bismarck had created was not to fall into ruins. When Prince Max said to him: "I commend the German Reich to your loving care," Ebert replied, "For that

---

[2] The only protest was a negative one. Karl Liebknecht left the session before the vote was taken.

Reich I have lost two sons." In inviting the cooperation of the Independent Socialists he was careful to make clear to them that there
was to be no Leninist dictatorship but that the government was to
be on constitutional lines. From the moment he took the reins in
his hands there began a noticeable tendency on his part to lean
toward the right. Even in his first proclamation there was little to
remind one of Karl Marx. "Citizens," it began, "I beg you all
urgently, leave the streets and let peace and order be your care." Nor
was he in the tradition of Marx when he announced that "human
life is sacred" and that "property is to be protected against illegal
interference." Having ordered those Germans who were marching
about the streets carrying red flags to return to their workaday tasks,
he and his colleagues took steps to create a trustworthy republican
force capable of carrying out their orders. Majority Socialists also
joined the workers' and soldiers' councils to keep the Spartacists
from gaining complete control of them.

When the councils held their first convention in Berlin on December 16, 1918, the Majority Socialists advocated the election of a
National Assembly to draw up a constitution. The Spartacists
demanded a dictatorship of the proletariat. Liebknecht himself denounced the idea of a National Assembly in an address to a gathering of striking workers, declaring that "whoever votes for the National Assembly votes for the rape of the working class!" After long
and violent debates, however, the motion for the election of a National Assembly was carried by an overwhelming majority. Thus the
German proletariat itself, much to the displeasure of the Spartacist
minority, adopted the principle of parliamentary democracy.

But the Spartacists still did not give up hope of gaining control
of the government. More peaceful means having failed, they decided
to carry out their final revolution by force before a National Assembly could be elected. They thought it would be easy to arouse
the Berlin masses against the provisional government. At a great
meeting of Spartacist workmen on January 5, 1919, a revolutionary
committee was formed and Ebert's cabinet was declared deposed.
During the next days Berlin was the scene of continued disorder.
Not only did armed groups of Spartacists seize barracks, railway stations, and the government printing offices; they also took possession
of the principal Berlin newspapers, so that the Majority Socialists
and the conservative parties had no means of appealing to the
people. These successes, achieved so easily, encouraged the Spartacist
leaders to believe that the provisional government would soon be
forced to resign.

Had the Spartacists had an able military leader, they might well have succeeded in overthrowing the government and in establishing the soviet system in Berlin. As it was, their leaders did not act with dispatch. While they were vacillating, the government appointed as Governor of Berlin one Gustav Noske, who was as severe as any Prussian general. Several German writers called him "the bloodhound of the revolution." Since about the middle of December Noske, assisted by six generals of the old army, had been busy organizing a government force out of what was left of the armies. He had succeeded in mobilizing about twenty thousand men at Dahlem, a suburb of Berlin, and this force was now moved into the city proper to put down the uprising. Supported by machine guns and howitzers, they began the attack on January 9 and continued the fight until the last Spartacist stronghold was taken. During this week they captured many prisoners, some of whom were summarily executed. On the night of January 15 Karl Liebknecht and Rosa Luxemburg, both of whom had addressed Berlin crowds with fearless vehemence, were arrested. The former was shot by his guards while he was being taken to prison, ostensibly because he tried to escape; the latter was killed with the butt end of a soldier's rifle, and her body was thrown into one of the canals. Without their leaders, the Spartacists were unable to offer effective resistance, and the attempt to establish a dictatorship of the proletariat soon collapsed completely.

The Spartacist uprising was put down on the eve of the election of the National Assembly which took place on January 19, 1919. Every person over twenty years of age was permitted to vote, one deputy to the National Assembly being allotted for every 150,000 votes. Some idea of the general interest in the election may be gained from the fact that of the thirty-five million voters on the registers more than thirty million voted. In most of the large cities the socialists not only polled the greatest number of votes but in some centers they polled more than all the other parties combined. Nevertheless the results proved disappointing to the Majority Socialists. Of the 399 deputies elected they obtained no more than 163 and the Independent Socialists only 22, the Spartacists having held aloof from the election. The results clearly showed that the bourgeois element was still the strongest and that a purely socialist regime was out of question. When it came to choosing a meeting place for the Assembly, Ebert ruled out Berlin and other large industrial cities where it might be a prey for organizers of insurrections. It was decided that the Assembly should meet on February 6, 1919, at Weimar, where

GERMANY DURING THE PERIOD OF THE WEIMAR REPUBLIC

Goethe and Schiller had written many of their masterpieces, where Herder had preached international conciliation and cooperation, and where Bach and Liszt had scored some of their greatest triumphs.

As the deputies took their seats in the National Theatre at Weimar, it became evident that although there had been some re-grouping of the old parties of the Reichstag, the general setup was much the same. While the old conservatives, who naturally sat on the right, had taken the name of the German National People's Party, the Roman Catholic (Clerical) Center remained the same. Next to the Center was a new party, the German Democratic Party which had been formed by the middle classes and avowedly favored the establishment of a republic. The left was occupied by the Ma-jority Socialists, and at the extreme left sat the Independent Social-ists. The first question to be dealt with was the question of a gov-ernment, the members of the provisional government having re-signed their self-assumed authority to the Assembly. A provisional republican constitution was drawn up, Ebert was elected the first president of the Reich (the name of the empire was retained), and Scheidemann was given the position of chancellor or premier. Ebert in assuming the presidency took this curious oath: "I swear that I will truly observe and protect the constitution of the German Reich. I desire and intend to act as the authorized representative of the en-tire German people, not as leader of a single party. But I also de-clare that I am the son of the working class, grown up in the world of ideas according to socialism, and that I have no intention of deny-ing either my origin or my convictions."

The major tasks of the Weimar Assembly were drafting a per-manent constitution and making peace with the Allies. The former was achieved in an expeditious and businesslike manner. After the subject was brought forward on February 24, the work progressed steadily until the completed document was signed on August 11. It was so long and so complex that it is possible in a brief discussion to point out only a few characteristics. The basic difference between the new constitution and the one that had been in force under the Hohen-zollern was this: whereas the old one had been essentially a treaty between the rulers of the various German states, the new one was

GERMANY DURING THE PERIOD OF THE WEIMAR REPUBLIC. *The perennial trouble centers are clearly indicated on this map—the Saar Basin, Alsace-Lorraine, and the Polish Corridor.*

the expression of the will of the sovereign German people expressed through its representatives. The new constitution began with the words, "The German state is a republic: political authority springs from the people." Many members of the Assembly hoped that it would set up complete national and political unity, a unity which would obliterate the old state frontiers and totally abrogate separate state rights. But in this they were disappointed. In the new constitution, it is true, the divisions were spoken of as *Länder* (territories), not as states. The component parts, however, still had their own constitutions and governments which exercised many powers of sovereignty independently of the central authorities. In short, Germany was still a federal state. Nevertheless, the new constitution did place the law of the empire above the law of the individual state. Thenceforth it became necessary for the states to bring their laws into accord with those of the empire.

The political system elaborated in the Weimar constitution was not borrowed from any one country. It was rather pieced together from the United States, the British, the French, and the Swiss forms of government. It provided for the election of a president as the executive head of the Republic for a term of seven years, after which he was eligible for re-election. Besides being head of the administration and commander in chief of the armed forces, he was given power to dissolve the Reichstag, appoint and receive ambassadors, and conclude treaties. He was to appoint the chancellor and the ministers, but they had to possess the confidence of the Reichstag. "Should the Reichstag by express resolution proclaim its want of confidence," the constitution declared, "the ministers concerned must resign." In brief, the president was elected for a French term of seven years, had powers like those of the president of the United States, but his ministers were responsible to the Reichstag in truly British fashion. The Reichstag was the legislative body elected for a period of four years by the suffrage of all men and women over twenty. It had the power of initiating bills, but so did the electorate if the demand for a legislative measure were supported by at least one tenth of the registered voters. Although the old upper house which represented the states as such still remained under the title of Reichsrat, it was of but secondary importance. Besides formulating bills, it could object to a bill becoming law even though it had been passed by the Reichstag. If the two houses could not reach an agreement, the president was empowered to put the question before the people for decision by a referendum on the Swiss model.

If the drafting of the constitution proceeded smoothly, the problem of concluding peace, as stated in an earlier chapter, caused many members of the National Assembly great anguish. When the terms arrived, Chancellor Scheidemann at once declared them to be "unacceptable" and resigned. The Assembly after much discussion finally decided to accept the terms subject to certain reservations. But the Allies absolutely refused to allow any reservations and demanded that the terms be accepted unconditionally. This was a terrific blow to the credit of the new government. There were in the Assembly many members, perhaps even a majority, who were monarchists at heart and had accepted the idea of a republic only because they believed that it meant a peace based on the Fourteen Points. When this belief was shattered, they came to believe that the republic had failed them; hence to many it became the symbol of humiliation. It did not occur to them that the old imperial government would have been compelled to accept more severe terms. They could not imagine any more severe terms. Hence they began to yearn for the old order, to hearken back to the old monarchy. But their hostility to the republic was negative rather than positive. Apart from a few extremists they did not actively work for the overthrow of the new government. They were not sure that the time was ripe for a change or that the Allies would permit them to make a change.

The disaffection, however, led a small group of reactionaries to believe that by a bold stroke they might succeed in overthrowing the republic. The members of this group were no less convinced than the Spartacists had been in the preceding year that once the banner of revolt was raised the nation would immediately rally around it. The moving spirit was Ludendorff, who during the revolutionary days had precipitately fled to Sweden in disguise but had later returned. He did not, however, lead the uprising in person. The leader was an obscure Prussian official named Kapp; hence the attempt is known as the Kapp Putsch. Associated with Kapp were several able soldiers of the old imperial army who had succeeded in enlisting the support of two bodies of troops that had been employed to defend the Baltic states against Russia and were about to be dismissed contrary to their wishes. Kapp issued an ultimatum to the government and when that achieved nothing the insurgents began marching on Berlin. Convinced that the defense of the capital was impossible, the Ebert cabinet fled the city on March 12, 1920, withdrawing the garrison in order to avoid unnecessary bloodshed. Early next morning the revolutionists marched into Berlin unopposed and Kapp declared himself chancellor. Ebert's government responded by calling a general strike in Berlin. As the great majority of trade union leaders were socialists, the order was readily obeyed. The effect was decisive. Without water, gas, electricity, and transportation services the life of the city was practically paralyzed and Kapp was mystified and helpless. Only two days after he entered the city he was endeavoring to come to some agreement with the Ebert government. But his proposals were flatly rejected. With Berlin threatening to succumb to chaos, Kapp lost his head and fled to Sweden. Ingloriously deserted by their leader, the troops withdrew while a jeering crowd lined the streets and the principal conspirators surrendered unconditionally. The Kapp Putsch had fizzled out.

Though this uprising had failed, the troubles of the government were far from over. It had survived only because its adversaries shrank from the responsibility of overthrowing it. The Reichstag election (June, 1920) which followed closely upon the Putsch showed that the republican minority was definitely shrinking. Not only did the total socialist vote decrease from 13.8 to 11 millions but the vote of the other parties who had openly accepted the republican form of government suffered substantial losses, while the two parties with monarchist tendencies had gained three million votes. This change was in part due to the fact that the Treaty of Versailles had come into force in January, 1920. Besides leaving the Rhine in enemy hands, it removed the German flag from Alsace-Lorraine, Flensburg, Danzig, Memel, the Polish Corridor, Upper Silesia, and the Saar. To those who had been officers in the imperial army, to the remnants of proud Junkerdom, and to many who had grown up in the glories of the Hohenzollern regime this spelled bitter humiliation. They told themselves that the kaiser's government would have fought to the last man to prevent this. Nor was the opposition to the republic confined to the older generation. Both in the universities and in the higher schools there was much monarchist sympathy. This, the republicans discovered, was due to the fact that education was almost completely in the hands of reactionaries. All over the country secret military clubs and reactionary societies were springing up, the members of which did not hesitate to resort to political assassination. Such tactics were made all the easier because the judiciary was, for the most part, antirepublican. The future of the republic looked very dark.

᠀

REPARATIONS AND INFLATION

The most serious problem of the new republic was economic. Germany, which in 1914 had been one of the three great industrial nations of the world, was in a state of economic chaos at the close of the war. By the terms of the treaty, as previously stated, she lost vast territories which contained agricultural wealth, gigantic coal, iron, and zinc mines, potash deposits, and factories of every kind. The ceded area had in 1913 produced 48.2 per cent of Germany's iron ore, 59 per cent of her zinc ore, and 15.7 per cent of her coal. The severance of these territories shattered the sensitive structure of her industries. Even without reparation payments it would have been difficult to regain her economic balance. The reparations further drained her of the materials necessary to a flourishing economic life. Under the provisions of the armistice and the peace treaty she was required to hand over to the Allies not only all materials in the war zone and all public property in the ceded territories and colonies but also all merchant ships exceeding 1600 gross tons, half of the merchant ships between 1000 and 1600 gross tons, one quarter of the fishing fleet, 5000 locomotives, 150,000 railway cars, and 5000 motor trucks. Furthermore, Germany's foreign investments in the Allied countries had been seized or surrendered and her credit in the world's capital markets had been seriously undermined. In short, Germany had not only lost a great part of her national wealth and her production facilities but her foreign trade had also been seriously disrupted.

In the first days of May, 1921, the plan which the Reparations Commission had elaborated was announced. It set Germany's debt at 132 billion gold marks, an amount which according to a number of Allied economists exceeded her ability to pay.[3] Of this sum she was to pay a billion marks during the summer of 1921 and two billion a year thereafter. The plan was handed to the Germans in the form of an ultimatum which they were to accept within six days or suffer an Allied invasion of the Ruhr, the most important industrial area in Germany. Accepting the ultimatum, the government paid the first billion marks before the end of August, 1921, and made additional payments during the early months of the next year. Meanwhile the exchange value of the mark declined steadily. It had already fallen during the war; in fact, wartime finance was largely inflationist because the government confidently believed that the Allies would have to pay the costs of the war. But the downward movement of the mark had been checked early in 1920 and a considerable recovery followed. In May, 1921, when the reparation ultimatum arrived, the rate was 62 to the dollar (4.2 to the dollar was par), but by

[3] J. M. Keynes, the English economist, believed that it was three times as much as Germany could possibly pay.

September it had dropped to 105, by October to 156, and by the end of November to 270 or 1.5 per cent of par.

By June, 1922, the economic situation had deteriorated to such an extent that the government requested a moratorium on reparation payments for two years, stating that a financial collapse was inevitable if it were not granted. At the meeting of Allied representatives in London to discuss the request the British and French showed diverging points of view. The former, fearing that the economic ruin of Germany might well involve a general ruin, were ready to agree to a moratorium to enable her to re-establish herself economically. The French took the opposite point of view. They believed that Germany, far from being ruined, was cleverly concealing her assets. In other words, they believed that the request for a moratorium was merely a trick to evade payment. M. Poincaré proposed that instead of granting the moratorium France should occupy German coal mines and forests as "productive guarantees," that Germany would make reparations deliveries, particularly of Ruhr coke upon which iron-smelting in Lorraine depended. In this he was supported by the French people, who recalled that they had paid to the last sou the indemnity imposed upon them in 1870. They had been assured that their taxes would not be raised after the war because Germany would be obliged to pay. But when their taxes mounted and the Germans began to default, their anger against the latter increased. As an American writer put it at the time: "The French peasant still has a feeling that if Foch goes into Germany with an army, he will come back with several billion dollars in his pocket."

Poincaré did not wait long before carrying out his threat to seize German mines. On January 10, 1923, France and Belgium announced that because Germany had defaulted, a Mission of Control accompanied by an adequate force would be sent into the Ruhr to supervise the activities of the coal syndicate. The next day French troops, including armored cars, infantry, cavalry, and cyclists, streamed into Essen and took possession of the railways, the post, and the telegraph service. On the following day tanks, heavy artillery, and airplanes arrived. It was a frank appeal to force and caused more bitterness between the Germans and the French than was ever produced by war. The effect upon the mark was immediate. Before the end of the month it dropped to 40,000 to the dollar.

Would the Germans resist the invasion of the Ruhr? Armed resistance was out of question, for any military campaign against the overwhelming French forces would have ended in disaster in a short time. There were, however, other means of resistance. Emphatically deprecating violence and sabotage, the German government announced a policy of "passive resistance" which was supported wholeheartedly by the people. All reparations payments, especially the deliveries of coke and coal, to France and Belgium were discontinued at once and German officials were forbidden to take orders from the occupying authorities. Gradually more and more workers withdrew from all the productive and distributive processes that might help the army of occupation, with the result that France received only those deliveries of coal and coke that her own staff could produce.

The struggle for the Ruhr was catastrophic for the mark. "Passive resistance" could be successful only if the entire population of the Ruhr, to the number of about five millions, were fed and supported. This required vast sums, which the government raised by issuing more and yet more paper. As a result the mark depreciated with cyclonic speed during the succeeding months. By the middle of June it fell to 100,000 for a dollar; by the middle of July, to 200,000; by August 8, to 5 million; by the middle of September, to 100 million; by October 9, to more than 1 trillion; and by November 15, to 4.2 trillion. Such astronomical figures were comprehensible only to addicts of higher mathematics.

This rapid fluctuation hopelessly complicated all business. Salaries in private and public enterprises had to be increased every week at first, and later every day. Toward the end, prices and wage scales were often out of date before the ink had dried upon them. Depreciation was so rapid that paper currency became worthless almost while it was being held in the hand. Wages paid on one day might the next day hardly be worth the paper they were printed on. The result was the so-called "flight from the mark," an orgy of buying to get rid of paper money. Immediately upon receiving their wages employees would rush off to buy food, clothing, anything that had an inherent value. To anticipate depreciation shopkeepers had to increase the selling price of their commodities from hour to hour. As one American observer put it, "The price of a meal often increased between soup and nuts." Finally merchants refused to sell their goods for marks, fixing the prices only in foreign currencies. In the agricultural districts primitive barter was revived when the farmers demanded clothing or hardware in exchange for produce. During the last three months before the mark collapsed completely, more than three hundred paper mills worked at top speed to manufacture notepaper, and 150 printing companies had 2000 presses running twenty-four hours a day to print enough bank notes to keep up with the inflation.

Inflation shook the social structure to its very roots. While some few accumulated vast fortunes during this chaos, many families of established wealth and position were reduced to poverty. The hardest hit of all were the lower middle classes. At one fell swoop the hard-earned savings they had invested in mortgages and government bonds or put in savings banks had been rendered practically valueless and many elderly and retired people were compelled to begin the struggle for existence anew. Inflation caused less change in the condition of the masses because they did not have so much to lose. But the annihiliation of his savings, insurance, and pension was no light blow to the worker. What pressed especially upon him was unemployment and low wages; in fact, the years from 1918 to 1924 were years of utter chaos and misery. High prices and food shortages, the latter caused in part by the Allied blockade which was continued even after the armistice, resulted in malnutrition, disease, and high mortality. Most seriously affected were the children. Dr. W. A. H. Gantt of the American Relief Administration wrote of his experiences in 1923: "I went into half a dozen children's hospitals in Cologne and Düsseldorf. The condition of the children there was really terrible and was as pitiful as anything that I have ever seen in Russia. Three fourths of the children were sick, not from any common child diseases such as measles, whooping cough, etc., but from nutritional diseases such as rickets, gastroenteritis, and malnutrition." These observations are corroborated by Dr. Haven Emerson who wrote in his *Report upon Health, Sickness and Hunger among German Children:*

> From infancy to school age marked rickets is so common, anemia, listlessness, poor muscular tone, sunken eyes, and emaciation are so generally seen that one loses a sense of proportion and is inclined to underestimate the extent of depreciation of vitality which is almost everywhere obvious among the children of the wage earners, the lesser public officials and the 20 to 40 percent of the adult population who are unemployed. Among children of school age there is a prevalence of tuberculosis not known to physicians heretofore.[4]

THE REPUBLIC AT ITS HEIGHT

Eventually the distress became so great that mutterings of revolt were heard in various parts of the country. Rather than call off its

[4] *International Conciliation* (March, 1924), p. 80.

policy the cabinet, which had inaugurated the "passive resistance," resigned. This opened the way for the appearance upon the political stage of the first great German political leader since World War I. Some historians have gone so far as to state that he was the ablest political leader since Bismarck. Gustav Stresemann, who as chancellor headed the new coalition cabinet that was formed in August, 1923, was not even a republican. Throughout his earlier life he had been a liberal monarchist and an aggressive nationalist. After the war he had opposed the acceptance of the peace treaty. In 1918 his monarchist reputation caused him to be rejected by the new Democratic Party, after which he laid the foundation of the German People's Party, collecting in it men who were willing to work in the service of the republic until such time as a restoration of the monarchy could be made by parliamentary means. Even when he became chancellor he had little enthusiasm for the Weimar constitution, but he did realize that only a republican Germany could gain from the recent foes that support and confidence without which it could not recover. Gradually, however, he appears to have undergone a change of heart. How completely he changed can be seen from the fact that while he proclaimed himself "a republican for lack of something better" in 1924, he declared in 1926 that he would "protect the republic with his life." In pursuit of his policy of saving Germany he was ready to cooperate with either the Nationalists or the socialists or with both.

Although Stresemann was not a man of great vision, he recognized that Germany must get out of the Ruhr adventure and that the only way out was unconditional surrender. He was no less eager than others to free Germany from what was termed "the shackles of Versailles," but he was convinced that this could best be accomplished by peaceful means. He felt that a disarmed Germany could not successfully resist her conquerors, that every attempt at resistance would bring only new exactions and fresh disasters. Above all else he saw that Germany and France must stop running their heads together. "Since Germany cannot fight," he said of the Ruhr struggle, "why continue the war with other weapons?" As a realist he was convinced that cooperation would achieve infinitely more than hostility and resistance. Accordingly he boldly proclaimed a policy of reconciliation with France. With feeling running high against France it took courage to make such a proposal, for Erzberger and Rathenau, his predecessors on this pathway, had only recently been assassinated. To carry out the policy he had to overcome the opposition not only of the Nationalists but also of his own party. Securing the cooperation in a grand coalition of all parties excepting the communists and extreme Nationalists, he called off the passive resistance. In November, 1923, an agreement was made with the occupation authorities according to which the Ruhr industrialists were to deliver commodities directly to the Allies.[5]

The same month also saw the stabilization of the mark through the issuance of the Rentenmark on which the old paper mark was stabilized at the rate of a trillion of the old to one Rentenmark. Although it was denominated in gold, it had no gold basis. Its sole guarantee consisted in its being exchangeable for mortgage bonds, the basis of which was a general lien on all the land and houses in Germany. Actually it rested on little more than public confidence. Stabilization on such a basis was possible only because the German people were ready and willing to accept any fixed standard of values. The history of the assignats during the French Revolution had shown how quickly a currency based on land can depreciate. But the Rentenmark by and large retained its fixed value, with an approximate exchange value of twenty-five cents or 4.2 to the dollar. As the old notes gradually disappeared from circulation, economic activities became more normal. An adding machine was no longer necessary to calculate a single purchase; nor did the worker have to rush off in great haste to convert his pay into something tangible in order to beat depreciation. It was all due to the "miracle of the Rentenmark." But this was only a temporary expedient. In November, 1924, it was supplanted by the standard Reichsmark which was, at least theoretically, put on a gold basis. Thenceforth German business in general, after an initial post-stabilization crisis, improved and expanded.

The stabilization of the currency together with the renunciation of the policy of passive resistance opened the way for a reconsideration of the reparations problem. During the occupation of the Ruhr Poincaré had blocked a request to reopen the question; but when the German government repeated the request after the Ruhr struggle had ceased, the Reparations Commission appointed two committees to make a study of Germany's economic resources and her capacity to pay. The more important of the two committees, that under the chairmanship of Charles G. Dawes, who later became Vice-President of the United States, drew up the so-called Dawes Plan. Poincaré opposed it, but in May, 1924, his government was replaced by that of Herriot, a sincere friend of conciliation. A conference of

[5] This agreement paved the way for the eventual evacuation of the Ruhr by the French forces in the summer of 1925.

DR. STRESEMANN, SIR AUSTEN CHAMBERLAIN, M. BRIAND, AND DR. BENEŠ AT THE LEAGUE OF NATIONS

SEPTEMBER 22, 1926

Allied representatives convoked in London during the summer of 1924 accepted the Dawes Plan, the Reichstag accepted it in August, and it went into effect on September 1. The outstanding features of the Plan were, first, that it reduced the astronomical figures of former plans to sums that Germany could pay and, second, it recognized that the economic rehabilitation of Germany was essential. The new schedule of payments called for one billion marks for the year 1924–1925; thereafter payments were gradually to increase to two and a half billion marks for the year 1928–1929. For the first year a virtual moratorium was granted. Of the first billion marks 800 millions were to come from the proceeds of a loan. Thus with American collaboration the demands on Germany were cut down and a foreign loan enabled her to begin meeting her obligations on an apparently reasonable basis.

In March, 1925, president Ebert suddenly died after a short illness and it became necessary to hold a presidential election. Although he had never done anything sensational, Ebert endeavored to preserve the republic against the attacks of both extremes. Standing as a bulwark of parliamentary democracy, he was hated by both the reactionaries and the communists but was esteemed by those who believed in republican democracy and in nonviolent progress toward a new social order. There was no one who seemed obviously suited to take his place. When the election was announced, all parties put forward candidates, most of whom were more or less undistinguished. As none of them secured an absolute majority, a run-off election became necessary. The Majority Socialists and the members of the Center Party, realizing that they could not win on a party basis, gave their support to Wilhelm Marx, a Rhineland capitalist. Their combined strength, it seemed, would carry the election. But the parties of the right were not ready to concede anything. In looking about for a candidate with a wide appeal they hit upon the idea of bringing Field Marshal von Hindenburg out of retirement. They believed that Hindenburg, who as the "hero of Tannenberg" had become almost a mythical figure in Germany, could rally a majority of the voters around his standard.

Since he had resigned his command of the army Hindenburg had remained aloof from politics, living quietly in Hannover. Being in his seventy-eighth year he preferred to spend his old age in peace. His mental equipment for high office was inadequate. He was not intelligent; in fact, his mental processes were as simple as those of a child. He knew nothing of economics, nothing of finance, and nothing of politics. What knowledge he possessed was largely limited to the science of warfare. He himself had confessed in his memoirs: "Since my days as a cadet I have never read a book that did not deal with military affairs." When asked to become a candidate for the presidency he protested that he was too old, but he finally surrendered to the repeated urgings of his friends. The decision to stand for election must have been a difficult one, for by birth, tradition, and calling he was bound to the old imperial order. A member of the Junker caste, he had been part of the Prussian army which besieged Paris in 1870 and had also been present in the Hall of Mirrors at Versailles when the German Empire was proclaimed early the next year. As late as 1921 he had closed a letter to the former kaiser with the words, "May I again be permitted to assure your Majesty that throughout my life my loyalty to my Kaiser, my King, and my Master has been unbounded, and that it will always be so." Convinced that it was for the good of his country, he obtained release from his vow of allegiance to the kaiser and placed himself at the service of the republic. The election was hotly contested, with the parties of the left denouncing him as "an old man without political experience" and "a puppet in the hands of his backers." But when the election returns had been tabulated, it was found that he had won over his principal opponent, Wilhelm Marx, by some 800,000 votes.

The announcement that Hindenburg had been elected caused much alarm in liberal circles and much jubilation among the reactionaries. While the former feared for the future of the republic, the latter were certain that the first step toward the restoration of the Hohenzollern had been taken. The reactionary newspaper, *Der Tag,* for example, stated: "We breathe freely once again and welcome the new light. It is as though all we had experienced since 1918 had been no more than an evil dream." [6] However, the new president was to disappoint the hopes of the reactionaries and allay the fears of the republicans for the time being. Having taken the oath to uphold the constitution, he resolved to keep it. He came more and more under the influence of the reactionaries during the later years of his presidency, but he did remain loyal to the republic until he finally yielded to Hitler. During his early years as president he gave dignity and balance to the republic, which was already gravely menaced. The result was that the years succeeding the election saw not only a consolidation of the republic but also considerable progress in other respects.

Stresemann, who had regarded the candidacy of Hindenburg

[6] Cited in Goldsmith and Voigt's *Hindenburg, the Man and the Legend* (1930), p. 290.

with much anxiety, was happy to discover that he could continue his foreign policy with the full support of the new president. What was this policy? It can probably best be summed up in the motto: "If you want peace, organize for peace." Stresemann saw that Germany's national greatness could be revived only in a peacefully organized European society and that pacification was possible only if an appeasement between France and Germany took place. So long as there existed in the French mind an acute fear of German aggression, so long as Germany was menaced by such armed French invasions as that of the Ruhr, any broad policy of pacification was impossible. Hence he began in 1925 the negotiations which led to the Treaty of Locarno which was signed in London on December 1 of the same year. By this treaty Germany and France accepted for all time the frontiers created in the west by the Treaty of Versailles. It is noteworthy that the German-French and German-Belgian frontiers were thus no longer regulated by these countries alone but that France and England became guarantors of the *status quo,* pledging themselves to give unrestricted assistance against any aggressor.

Although Germany renounced its claims to Alsace-Lorraine, there was no such renunciation of territory in the east. This left the way open for a revision by peaceful means of the frontier between Germany and Poland and between Germany and Czechoslovakia. Stresemann clearly hoped for such a revision. "It is impossible," he said in 1927 after a meeting with the Polish Marshal Pilsudski at Geneva, "to get rid of the corridor by means of a war. We must therefore examine if we can regain it in a peaceful way. This is a question which concerns the whole of Europe. A solution is only thinkable by a continuation of the policy of Locarno, that is, by close relations between Berlin, London, and Paris."

Locarno was the prelude to the entrance of Germany into the League of Nations. Once public opinion was reassured as to the danger arising from the other side of the Rhine, the more virulent war prejudices disappeared and Franco-German relations assumed a new tone almost overnight. French opposition to Germany's entry into the League melted away and in September, 1926, Germany was elected a member by unanimous vote of the forty-eight states represented and was also accorded with equal unanimity a permanent seat on the League Council. In expressing the support of his government to the ideas for which the League stood, Stresemann said: "It cannot be the purpose of the divine world order that men should direct their supreme national energies against one another, thus thrusting back the general progress of civilization. The most durable foundation of things is a policy inspired by mutual understanding and mutual respect between peoples." Aristide Briand, French foreign minister, said in reply: "Away with rifles, machine guns, cannon! Clear the way for conciliation, arbitration, peace!" Many believed that, in the words of one observer, the real end of the war had come. The entrance of Germany into the League, it is true, did serve temporarily to introduce a period of stability in European relations. But the German reactionaries were only biding their time. They regarded Germany's admission to the League as "a diplomatic defeat" and the League itself as an alliance of powers whose primary purpose was to keep Germany in bondage.

Meanwhile economic recovery was progressing by leaps and bounds. Although the weeks immediately following the stabilization of the currency in the fall of 1923 were characterized by depression in most aspects of economic activity, the upward trend began in January of 1924. A major factor in this recovery was the influx of foreign funds which relieved the desperate shortage of working capital. In fact, during the entire period up to the depression of 1929 vast sums of foreign capital continued to flow into Germany, particularly from the United States, where the postwar boom had created surplus capital looking for investment. It has been estimated that from 1924 to the end of 1928 Germany imported foreign funds to the tune of nearly nineteen billion marks (about $4 billion). Thus she was supplied with the funds necessary to launch a far-reaching program of industrial expansion.

A veritable fever of construction and replacement ensued. Many new factories were built. Machinery in the old factories was replaced with new machinery which included every modern device for economy of labor, time, and money. The result was that Germany gradually regained the leading position in those branches in which she had led before the war, more particularly in the optical, chemical, and electrical industries and in certain phases of engineering and textiles. Notwithstanding the loss of the vast coal fields and the iron and steel works of Silesia together with the ore deposits and iron works of Alsace-Lorraine, a loss that was expected to cripple the German iron and steel industry permanently, that industry again became highly prosperous.

Hand in hand with the industrial recovery came a trade boom which in turn necessitated the expansion and improvement of the means of transportation and communication. Schemes were launched for constructing or improving roads, railways, and canals, and for extending telephone and telegraph service. The fact that the Germans had been required to deliver a great quantity of rolling stock and locomotives turned out to be a blessing in disguise, for they were gradually replaced by new, modern, up-to-date materials, including more powerful locomotives and larger freight cars. In general, new materials and installations of every kind greatly increased the efficiency of the railways. The same was true of the merchant marine. The ships which had been turned over to the Allies in accordance with the peace treaties were replaced by new ones with every modern equipment. By 1930 the merchant marine had not only approached its 1914 size but since it consisted mainly of new units it was much more efficient than ever before. Nor did the Germans stop at building cargo ships. During this period they also began the construction of two giant passenger ships, the *Bremen* and the *Europa*.

By 1929 the volume of industrial production was well above the prewar level, and exports exceeded the figures of 1913 by as much as 34 per cent. In other words, Germany's industrial strength was greater than that of any other Continental country. In certain lines she had even passed Great Britain. With the growth of industry and trade had come a steady diminution of poverty and unemployment, so that by 1929 the standard of living was at least as high as it had been before the war and the number of people receiving unemployment relief was comparatively small. During the years 1924 to 1929 small depositors put no less than ten billion marks in the savings banks, and the policies issued by life insurance companies were more numerous and for larger amounts than before the war. Thus within the space of six years Germany had "climbed up from the pit of prostration and despair to an assured position of world leadership. It is one of the most spectacular recoveries in the world's entire economic history." [7]

During the years of prosperity the German government had paid the scheduled reparation annuities promptly, but the Dawes Plan was only "provisional" and there was a desire on the part of many Germans to replace this plan by one that would be "final." Prolonged discussions by a group of experts in Paris in the spring of 1929 were followed by the drawing-up of the Young Plan, so named after Owen D. Young, chairman of the General Electric Company in the United States, who headed the committee. The new plan for the first time set the total amount Germany was expected to pay and also prescribed the period during which it was to be paid. Furthermore, besides materially reducing the size of the annual payments

[7] Angell, *The Recovery of Germany*, p. 3.

it freed Germany from the humiliating foreign supervision provided by the Dawes Plan. The new payments were to begin on April 1, 1930, with the sum of 1,707,900,000 marks ($400 million). This was to increase gradually to a maximum of 2,428,800,000 marks ($570 million) in 1965–1966, after which the payments were again to decrease and finally terminate in 1988. Before the first payment was due, however, signs of the great economic crisis made their appearance.

THE TWILIGHT OF GERMAN DEMOCRACY

At the beginning of 1929 the Weimar republic seemed stable and secure. German foreign relations, particularly those with France, had improved greatly as a result of Stresemann's efforts; and economic reconstruction, aided by foreign capital, had reached a point where it promised better things to the masses. But before the year ended, a definite change for the worse set in. One of the fateful events which marked the turning point was the death of Stresemann. Prematurely worn out by his arduous labors, the noted foreign minister succumbed to a stroke in October, 1929. at the age of fifty-one. The German Republic had lost its greatest champion. To measure his achievements one needs only recall the chaos he faced when he first came into power in 1923. Not only did he play a major part in restoring order and confidence within Germany but he also restored Germany to her place as one of the most influential and respected nations of Europe. Lord D'Abernon, who as British ambassador in Berlin had worked with Stresemann, paid him the following tribute for having "raised Germany from the position of a stricken and disarmed foe to a great power": "To have accomplished this in a few years of power without the support of armed force is an achievement worthy of those who have written their names most memorably on the scroll of pacific fame." It is doubtful that he would have been able to save the republic if he had lived longer. Shortly before his death he planned to form a genuinely republican party that was to serve as the bulwark of the Weimar republic, but the plan was not carried out. With his demise sinister forces long pent beneath the surface were released. Large industrialists and great landowners whom he had compelled to put on the democratic cloak now doffed it and openly supported a dictatorship. As for the later change in foreign relations, Rudolf Olden, his biographer stated truly that with his death, "Europe lost its great chance of peace."

What really doomed the Weimar republic, however, was the world-wide economic crisis. The storm of depression, which broke in the New York stock exchange in October, 1929, and then gradually swept over the globe, hit Germany with devastating force. German prosperity, particularly vulnerable because it was based on foreign loans, collapsed like a house of cards. The crisis put a stop to the influx of foreign money and foreign creditors began to withdraw their funds, mostly borrowed on short-term credits, at an alarming rate and thereby seriously depleted the German gold reserves. As the burden of meeting these credit withdrawals fell almost exclusively upon the banks, their resources were so greatly exhausted that they were compelled to reduce their advances to trade and industry. The situation was made more serious by the fact that many Germans, fearing horrors like those of the inflation of 1923, began to withdraw their money from the banks, either to hoard it or to transfer it abroad for safety. The shortage became even more acute when it was necessary to pay reparations. All this put such a severe strain on the banks that many of them were forced to close their doors in 1931, including the third largest bank in Germany.

Lack of capital was even more fatal to German industries. Because of the shortage of working capital many industries were forced to restrict their output. Month by month, week by week, conditions grew worse and the number of bankruptcies mounted steadily. In 1931 alone there were over 17,000, a number which was exceeded in the next year. The number of unemployed grew at a terrifying rate, first by the tens of thousands and then by the hundreds of thousands. At the end of 1930 there were no less than three million unemployed in Germany, and by the early months of 1932 the number had increased to six millions. In the months of February and March, 1932, 45 per cent of the members of the Free Trade Unions were out of work; at the end of 1932 96 per cent of the members of the building trades unions were unemployed. In addition, millions of others worked only on short time. Furthermore, wages were reduced considerably. In 1931 they were cut 17 per cent, and 1932 saw further reductions. This meant serious curtailment of purchasing power, and the cumulative effect of reduced purchasing power caused a collapse of the home market. Unemployment also meant a falling off in tax receipts. As a result the government faced such a heavy deficit that it was forced to cut the unemployment dole from ten to six marks a week and to reduce war pensions by equally drastic amounts. How grave the situation was can be seen from the fact that during the early months of 1932 a quarter of the citizens of Berlin were recipients of organized charity. This was probably true in every other large city of Germany. Nor did the peasants escape the blight of depression. Compelled on the one hand to pay high taxes to the government and high rates of interest on their mortgages and debts, they did not on the other hand receive commensurate prices for their products.

The despair of the masses was all the greater because they had believed that after the terrible days of the war and of the inflation period that had followed, settled economic conditions had finally been achieved. Workers, peasants, and particularly the members of the lower middle class who had recovered a modicum of prosperity became disappointed with the republic. The feeling was shared by thousands of students who saw no hope of obtaining employment so long as conditions remained unchanged. In their bitterness many went so far as to blame the republican system. Only the more moderate socialists still retained their faith in the Weimar constitution. As unemployment increased and with it poverty and the fear of poverty, the hungry masses became revolutionary. While some went communist, others joined the National Socialist Party in which Adolf Hitler was the leading figure. The result was that these two extremist groups, both of which wanted a forcible deposition of democratic government, showed great increase of strength in the Reichstag elections of 1930. Whereas the communist vote rose from 3.25 to 4.5 millions, the Nazi vote increased from 800,000 to nearly 6.5 millions. At a single bound the number of Nazi deputies in the Reichstag rose from 12 to 107, making the party the second strongest in the country. This sudden rise of a party which had not been taken seriously into account astonished not only the Germans but the whole world; in fact, the Hitlerites themselves were astounded at the number of votes they polled.

In the new Reichstag the reactionary bloc, composed of the National Socialists and the Nationalists, had about 150 deputies; the Marxists, 220; and the government of Chancellor Brüning, only about 200. Thus the government did not have a majority. The failure to form a coalition of moderate parties left Brüning only one course to pursue and that was to rule as a minority government in the hope that the Social Democrats (socialists) would tolerate it rather than drive the chancellor into a coalition with Hitler. The Social Democrats did tolerate Brüning's government, but from that day onward the Reichstag ceased to function in a positive sense. Having no majority, Brüning ruled by means of ordinances or emergency decrees which the president was empowered to issue by Article

48 of the constitution.[8] Although the Reichstag had the right to reject such ordinances, Brüning was able to govern by this means through 1931 and into the spring of 1932 because the Reichstag did not form a majority against him. This government by ordinances was, of course, a definite step away from democratic procedure. In other words this and not Hitler's accession to power was the real beginning of dictatorship in Germany. However, the aims of the two men differed. While Brüning, it seems, was trying to save the republic, Hitler's avowed purpose was to destroy it.

The growing strength of the National Socialist Party gave Hitler confidence to stand as candidate for the presidency in the election of 1932. The opposing candidate was Hindenburg, who was supported by the Social Democrats and the Catholic Center Party. The workers and the Catholics knew that he was by sympathy a reactionary, but they put their faith in his oath to uphold the constitution. This was the decisive factor in the election, and it was proclaimed by such slogans as: "He stands by you: keep faith with him!" and "Loyalty is the essence of honor." Hitler gibed Hindenburg, who was eighty-four, about his age and boasted that he was forty years younger. It did not, however, win him the election. Although he did poll some thirteen million votes, Hindenburg carried the day with some nineteen million.

In May, 1932, Hindenburg, who was becoming increasingly susceptible to reactionary influences, dismissed Brüning as chancellor and called Franz von Papen, an out-and-out reactionary, to the helm. Although the new chancellor had only forty supporters in the Reichstag out of a total of nearly 600 deputies, he proceeded to act like a dictator. When the Reichstag opposed him, he dissolved it. But he failed to obtain the support of more than one tenth of the electorate and therefore had to relinquish the chancellorship. Hindenburg tried to save von Papen's cabinet by offering Hitler a post in it, but the future Führer asked nothing less than total power. He demanded that Hindenburg give him the same power as the King of Italy had accorded to Mussolini. The president, who disliked and distrusted Hitler, sidetracked him for the time being by appointing General von Schleicher as chancellor. But the reactionary intrigue which had destroyed Brüning after two years, destroyed Schleicher in a mere two months.

[8] Actually Article 48 applied only to cases of real emergency such as armed revolt. It does not appear to have been the intention of the framers of the constitution that the emergency decrees should supersede normal legislative procedure. This article was a weakness in an otherwise democratic constitution.

Hitler's accession to power might still have been postponed if von Papen, who hoped he might exercise some control over the Nazis, had not proposed a coalition to Hitler. Although still suspicious of coalitions, Hitler saw a chance to get control of the government if he played his cards well; so he accepted. It only remained for von Papen, who still enjoyed Hindenburg's personal confidence, to convince the president that the appointment of Hitler was the only way out of the political dilemma. Hindenburg had declared in November, 1932, that he would not appoint Hitler as chancellor because "I fear that a Presidential Cabinet led by Herr Hitler would inevitably develop into a party dictatorship. . . . I cannot answer to my oath and to my conscience for such a step." He now gave way and on January 30, 1933, gave Hitler the chancellorship. In making the appointment the president observed all the forms of democracy; nevertheless, the appointment definitely marked the end of the Weimar republic. Created by the working classes in 1918, it collapsed because the working classes did not unite to save it.

CHAPTER SIX

Battered and Bleeding France

THE PRICE OF VICTORY

THE day of armistice saw the French people intoxicated with victory. On a number of occasions during the course of the war only a hairbreadth had stood between the safety and the death of France. At such times faith in ultimate victory had burned low in the hearts of many Frenchmen. At no moment, however, did hope flicker out completely. Even when the enemy struck close to the heart of Paris, the cry "On les aura" (we shall have them) did not cease. When hope was redeemed by victory in 1918, it was natural that the French should rejoice. Not only was their country saved but their national pride was also satisfied.

Before many days passed, however, their joy was sobered by the thought of the price they had paid. France had suffered all the agonies that normally accompany defeat and had come out of the war scarred, battered, and enfeebled. The districts in which fighting had taken place presented a melancholy aspect. Cities, towns, and villages had literally been blasted off the map or converted into shapeless ruins by high explosives. Little more than heaps of rubble marked the places where once many towns had stood. Of the more than 4000 municipalities taken by the Germans, 1039 were completely demolished, over 1200 were at least half destroyed, and the rest suffered to a less extent. It has been estimated that in the occupied territory 75 per cent of the dwellings, farm buildings, and public edifices were either destroyed or seriously damaged. Of 1,090,000 buildings which once stood in the devastated area 890,000 had been destroyed. Many of the best farms were denuded of orchards, plowed into deep craters by shellfire, and covered with inextricable tangles of barbed wire.

The territory occupied by the Germans represented only a small part of the total area of France, it is true, but it contained most of the coal and iron mines and was the most highly industrialized part of the country. Before the war over 80 per cent of the iron ore and 70 per cent of the coal had come from this area. Besides this, the more advanced processes of manufacture were centered there, including about 80 per cent of the textile and steel mills. During the years of occupation practically every factory was destroyed or seriously damaged. The destruction of the buildings themselves was often only a small part of the loss. More serious was the destruction or removal of machinery, tools, and equipment of every kind, much of it difficult to replace. Equally serious was the damage to the mines. The coal mines had been the particular object of destruction because the Germans realized that the economic vitality of France depended in large measure on the coal supply. In many cases the buildings above ground, the hoists, and the ventilating systems were wrecked, and the pumps were ruined so that the mines were flooded. Other mines were dynamited or set on fire. It is estimated that in all about 220 mining operations were rendered useless.

Other losses were likewise tremendous. Agriculture suffered heavily. In the occupied regions, which included some of the best agricultural land in France, all but about 15 per cent of the cultivated soil was devastated. More than 90 per cent of the cattle disappeared, and about three quarters of the dwellings and farm buildings were destroyed or damaged. In the whole of France the number of sheep decreased by 38 per cent, the number of pigs by 40 per cent, and the production of milk by 63 per cent.

Great damage was also done to the means of transportation. Highways were torn to pieces by mines and shellfire or were deeply rutted by tanks, guns, and heavy trucks. No less than 6000 bridges were completely demolished, 700 miles of canal routes were damaged, and 1500 miles of railway wrecked.

Furthermore, foreign trade suffered grievously. By 1919 the volume of trade had decreased to a quarter of what it had been in 1913. In addition the tonnage of the merchant marine had been reduced more than a third by German submarines and by sea accidents.

The losses of capital were also great. France, which in 1913 had been a creditor nation with large investments abroad, emerged from the war with a foreign debt of nearly seven billion prewar francs. Immensely larger was the internal debt. In 1914 this had already amounted to about 12 per cent of the total national wealth, but the cost of the war and of reconstruction raised it to about 30 per cent. The value of the franc on the international exchange had dropped steadily; in fact, by 1919 it had lost 72 per cent of its purchasing power, a condition which gave rise to grave economic disorders.

Most tragic of all was the loss of human life. France had mobilized nearly eight million men or about three quarters of the males of working age. When the din of battle died away, it was found that close to a million and a half had been killed or were missing, and the number of wounded, crippled, and incapacitated was at least as high. During the war there were also 1,389,916 more civilian deaths than births, with the result that the population which, according to the census of 1911, had numbered 39.2 millions declined to about 36 millions. This loss was particularly grave for a country whose population had been almost stationary for several decades. The excess of females over males increased from 2 per cent in 1911 to 15 per cent in 1921, and the loss of so many males of working age greatly weakened the whole economic life of France.

🔥

THE ROAD TO RECOVERY

The losses in man power and material resources were so stupendous that rapid recovery in any field of activity seemed quite ruled out, but the government attacked its task boldly. In July, 1919, a vast program of reconstruction at an estimated cost of forty billion francs was announced in the Chamber of Deputies. In the devastated regions temporary shelters were hastily erected to accommodate people who yearned to return to their native towns and villages; then the work of permanent reconstruction was started. Progress was amazingly rapid. Before many months had passed new towns were rising out of the ruins. In the country districts the peasants set to work with a will. Patiently they removed the debris of battle, filled the shell holes, and leveled the stretches of battleground so that in a short time lands of chaos were transformed into smiling fields. Meanwhile industrial restoration was also proceeding rapidly. To offset the loss of man power the government opened the immigration gates and invited foreigners to take up their abode in France. So many Spaniards, Italians, Belgians, and Poles came that the number of resident aliens increased by more than 1.3 million in four years. This immigration of foreign labor had a prodigious effect on industrial restoration. "Foreigners," said a British observer, "are becoming in fact indispensable cooperators in many large and varied branches of French production." With their help the French were able to rebuild most of the demolished factories by the beginning of 1922. At the same time transportation facilities were being repaired and rebuilt so that commerce could resume. In short, before many years passed the material damages to buildings, mines, roads, bridges, canals, and railroads were repaired. So rapid was the restoration that in 1922 French foreign trade attained its prewar volume and was soon to surpass it.

An important factor in the rehabilitation of economic life was the restoration of Alsace-Lorraine, which the Germans had detached from France in 1871. The regaining of these provinces meant, first of all, that the French population was increased by 1,700,000. More specifically it meant the addition of a vigorous group of workers to the labor power of France. It further meant the recovery of the good agricultural land in the plains between the Vosges and the Rhine. But the real significance lay rather in the natural resources and the industrial equipment the two provinces contained. Thus Alsace-Lorraine brought to France the largest and richest deposits of iron ore in Europe, added about 20 per cent to the inadequate coal supply, and provided an immense store of potash. Other contributions of Alsace-Lorraine to French industry were its metallurgical works with their up-to-date furnaces and its magnificent textile industries.

During the succeeding years prosperity maintained itself on an increasing scale. Foreign trade, for example, grew from an average of 14 billion francs during the five years before the First World War to somewhat over 119 billion francs in 1926.[1] But as 1926 proceeded, ominous clouds appeared on the industrial horizon and a sudden trade reaction set in. The cause was the fall of the franc. Its value had been artificially maintained during the war;[2] then it declined after the cessation of hostilities but rose again in 1921 and 1922. It declined gradually thereafter. In 1926 it dropped at a terrifying rate until in August it reached a low of 12 per cent of its prewar value. When things were at their worst President Doumergue called upon Poincaré to find a remedy. Forming a cabinet composed of men of all parties except socialists and communists, Poincaré gave most of his attention to finances. Confidence began to return at once and by the end of the year there was, if not legal stabilization, at least *de facto* stabilization, with the Bank of France announcing its willingness to buy and sell at approximately twenty-five francs to the

[1] The increase was not so great when the inflation of the franc is taken into account.
[2] The prewar parity rate was 5.18 to the dollar.

dollar.[3] General recovery was almost immediate. French capital that had fled France returned; trade became brisk; the tourist trade, one of the most remunerative of French industries, flourished; and exports reached record figures in 1928–1929.

§

POLITICAL AND FINANCIAL DIFFICULTIES

The political picture of France during the period between two wars is one of confusion and instability. Cabinets rose and fell in rapid succession like fanciful creations of building blocks. The fundamental cause for the shortlived character of the cabinets was the multiplicity of parties and political groups in the Chamber of Deputies. In 1936, for example, they numbered no less than nineteen. Most of these did not correspond to organized parties on the outside. They were merely groups of individuals drawn together by some issue of the moment. Such groups coalesced or distintegrated according to the acceptance or rejection of the ideas they sponsored. There were no well-organized and disciplined parties except on the left or left center.[4] Moreover, in the history of the Third Republic there was never a party large enough to secure a clear majority. Consequently all cabinets were necessarily coalitions and most of them were of brief duration. A further weakness which contributed much to the instability of the government was the fact that deputies were elected for fixed four-year terms. They could vote the premier out of office at will but the latter was unable to vindicate himself by calling for a general election as in England. Once elected, the deputies lasted out their four-year term regardless of change in popular sentiment. Hence the French executive was weak, while the Chamber was strong, a situation which made for instability of leadership and great inefficiency. With a Chamber of Deputies torn by the pressure of numerous groups, each at cross-purposes with the others, it became almost impossible to pass constructive legislation.

Along broader lines the political parties and groups may be classified in three categories: the conservative right, the moderate center, and the radical left. This grouping owes its origin to the fact that the deputies to the States-General thus seated themselves on the eve of the French Revolution.[5] In France during this period the extreme right was monarchist or Fascist. In the decade of the twenties

[3] In 1928 the franc was legally stabilized at the rate of 25.52 to the dollar.
[4] Popular Democrats, Radical Socialists, United Socialists, French Socialists, and Communists.
[5] This classification has met with general adoption throughout the world.

the well-known *Ligue de l'Action Française,* whose influence was due in large part to the support of the clergy, was the most powerful group on the right. Its leaders, who insisted that the Republic was irreligious and anticlerical, identified the cause of monarchy with that of Roman Catholicism. But the *Action Française* lost much of its strength through its condemnation by the pope (1926), who wished to dissociate the church from the cause of political reaction. In the decade of the thirties another group, the *Croix de Feu,* became the dominant group on the right. The center in the main represented the *bourgeoisie,* peasant proprietors, and small businessmen. Its members were the heirs of the French Revolution and the special guardians of the republic. The left was composed largely of socialists and communists. In political doctrine these groups ranged from republicanism to full-fledged communism and anarchosyndicalism. What the leftist groups had in common was, above all, their hatred of Fascism.[6]

§

DEPRESSION AND THE THREAT OF FASCISM

During the period between the two world wars the politics of France were profoundly affected by two factors, the financial situation and the threat of Fascism. Although the years to 1929 were the most prosperous, the rising tide of economic prosperity was not reflected in improved national finances. Despite the fact that France as a country of individuals and corporations was rich, France as a government was on the verge of bankruptcy. This state of affairs resulted from the government's policy of borrowing instead of increasing taxes. During the war it had contracted a deficit of 145 billion francs but had made little effort to meet by taxation the enormous increase of expenditure. It was confidently believed that such stupendous sums would be obtained from Germany as reparations that they would free the French public from paying taxes. When there were no huge sums forthcoming immediately after the cessation of hostilities, the government further increased the public

[6] In July, 1932, the deputies were grouped as follows: RIGHT: 14 Independents; 18 Republicans and Social Group; 8 Economic, Social, and Peasant Action; and 41 Republican Federation. CENTER: 36 Republican Center; 28 Republicans of the Left; 16 Popular Democrats; 6 Republicans of the Center; 23 Independents of the Left; and 47 Radical Left. LEFT: 160 Radical Socialists; 15 Independent Left; 12 Republican Socialists; 13 French Socialists; 131 Socialists; 9 Party of Proletarian Unity; and 10 Communists. Twenty-eight deputies were unclassified. The names of many of the groups are misleading. The Radical Socialists, for example, were very much more conservative than the name indicates.

debt through large borrowings to restore the devastated areas. Consequently "balancing the budget" became one of the pressing problems of the government. The years which followed saw many ministers and cabinets rise and fall over this question. In 1925 no less than six ministers of finance and three cabinets found it an insurmountable stumbling block. During the period of Poincaré's cabinet an increase in taxation coupled with the general prosperity produced a budgetary surplus. Expenditures, however, soon increased and when, after his retirement in 1929, taxes were reduced, the budget began to show heavy deficits and the question of balancing it again came to the forefront.

When the world depression came in 1929, it affected France much more slowly than the other large countries of Europe; in fact, until 1931 it was hardly noticeable in France. But the following years were difficult. Exports declined to a tremendous extent. In 1932 they were only 65 per cent of the 1931 total and 45 per cent of the 1930 total. The tourist trade, which in the postwar decade had been an important source of income, fell off sharply. In 1934 only 700,000 tourists visited France as against 2,125,000 in 1927. Business decline and diminishing profits caused widespread failures and increased unemployment. This condition was responsible for a large-scale exodus of foreign workers. Falling prices also resulted in distress among the farmers. In other words, the disease of economic depression ate into the very vitals of France. In 1933 four prime ministers tried vainly to halt the ravages of this disease. Gradually many lost their faith in democratic government. They became convinced that the only remedy lay in a reform along Fascist lines. This conviction was strengthened by the exaggerated reports of improvements that absolutist governments were supposed to have introduced in Italy and Germany. Nor did the Fascist or semi-Fascist organizations fail to make the most of the opportunity to aggravate popular discontent with parliamentary institutions and politicians. As a result the membership of these organizations increased by leaps and bounds. In two years the *Croix de Feu* grew from a small body of distinguished war veterans into the greatest Fascist force in the country.

The rapid growth of the Fascist and semi-Fascist groups and particularly the "lightning mobilization" of the *Croix de Feu* began to alarm the left. Many of them came to believe that the Fascist movement could be stopped only through the realization of a common front against it. Discussions were soon opened to this end, but the coalition of all left parties was not finally achieved until the spring of 1936. The common program of the Popular Front (*Front*

Populaire), the name adopted for the federation of anti-Fascist parties and groups, enumerated reforms that should be accomplished in order "to defend democratic liberties, to provide bread for workers, employment for youth, and to give to the world the great human peace." The elections in the spring of 1936 resulted in a victory for the Popular Front that surpassed all expectations. When the ballots were counted, it was found that the Popular Front could command 387 votes out of 618. For the first time the socialists formed the largest group in the chamber. Accordingly their leader, Léon Blum, was invited to form a cabinet. Departing from his traditional policy of refusing to become a member of a coalition, Blum organized one in which all the major groups of the left, except the communists, were represented. The Communist Party had been invited to participate in the government but refused "in order to preserve its liberty of action." It did, however, support the new government.

Soon after it assumed the reins of government the Blum cabinet introduced a program of economic and social legislation unparalleled in the history of modern France. The first enactments were for the benefit of labor. At this time a series of formidable sit-down strikes had spread like wildfire through various branches of industry until business activity had come to a virtual standstill. As a means of placating labor the new cabinet enacted a measure (June 20, 1936) which gave employees in industry, commerce, and the liberal professions a minimum annual vacation of fifteen days with pay after one year's continuous employment in any enterprise. More leisure for employees was provided by the forty-hour-week statute which became law on June 21 and was gradually introduced into various industries, so that it was applied to 94 per cent of the workers by the beginning of May, 1937. Nor were the peasants neglected. A national wheat office was established which was to insure farmers a remunerative price and curb excessive profits of middlemen. Other legislation included the nationalization of the Bank of France; this broke the power which the "industrial and financial oligarchy" wielded over the Bank and gave twelve of the twenty-three seats on the Bank's governing board to officials appointed by the government. A further blow was dealt this same oligarchy through the conversion into state enterprises of about a dozen armament factories, while the remainder of that industry was put more definitely under state control.

The rock on which the Blum government ultimately suffered shipwreck was the financial problem. The financial situation was extremely bad, the public debt having risen 24.5 per cent from

1930 to 1935, but it soon became critical. One important reason was the necessity for spending large sums on armaments because of the threat of war posed by Hitler's accession to power in Germany (1933). The fundamental tragedy lay in the fact that France's reserves and credit were so limited that the Popular Front could not carry out its large social program in a time of intensive rearmament. The difficulty of finding the necessary funds increased year after year. At the same time both the employers and the workers remained unsatisfied. While the former complained that the forty-hour week wiped out the margin of profit, the workers insisted that rising prices were neutralizing the benefits they had gained from the new legislation. When the Popular Front took power, prices in terms of gold were generally about 25 per cent higher than British and American prices. From many sides a clamor arose for devaluation of the franc. For some months Blum resisted the demand but finally gave way. The Act which permitted a depreciation of 25.2 per cent brought only a temporary relief. Production rose but slowly, the rise being due to increased rearmament rather than to other factors. On the other hand, the condition of both the franc and the treasury were steadily deteriorating. By June, 1937, the government did not know where to turn for money. When Blum asked temporary dictatorial powers to put through a capital levy and to establish control of foreign exchange, the Chamber passed the bill. But the following day the Senate speedily gave Blum his *coup de grâce* by deciding that they would not even debate the bill. The premier's only course was to resign.

Blum's cabinet was replaced by a more conservative Popular Front government under Camille Chautemps. Although the more orthodox financial measures of the new cabinet brought temporary relief, no basic solution of the problem was forthcoming. Except in the armament industry production continued to lag, and rising prices continued to nullify the higher wages won by the workers. While capital was demanding repeal or at least modification of the Popular Front reforms, the workers were agitating for still higher pay to meet the increasing cost of living. Rising prices coupled with a rise in unemployment engendered a new wave of labor unrest, which vented itself in a renewal of strikes (December, 1937). At the same time dissension was developing in the ranks of the Popular Front between the more conservative and the more radical wings. This dissension was encouraged by the declining strength of Fascism, the threat of which had caused the formation of the Popular Front. When, like its predecessor, the Chautemps government sought to

obtain dictatorial power to prevent financial collapse, the socialists
and communists refused their approval and thereby forced Chautemps' resignation. Blum then organized a cabinet but it lasted less
than a month.

The fall of the second Blum cabinet marked the final collapse
of the Popular Front. On April 10 a new government was formed by
Edouard Daladier who belonged to the conservative wing of the
Radical Socialists. This cabinet was more representative of the
center than of the left. With the menace of the totalitarian dictatorships growing greater each day, parliament gave Daladier's government wider powers to rule by decree than those it had permitted his
predecessors. The new premier used his powers to decree a rise of
8 per cent in taxes, to unify the budget, and to modify the forty-hour-
week law. Although a forty-five-hour week was permitted for many
industries, a sixty-hour maximum was decreed for all industries contributing to the rearmament program. Rates for overtime pay were
also severely slashed. It was hoped that increased armament production would enable France to meet the growing danger from across
the Rhine.

FOREIGN POLICY

The key to French foreign policy during this period is the search
for security, more specifically for security against German aggression. The methods may have varied but the objective remained the
same. During a period of less than half a century France had twice
been invaded by huge German armies, and the last time it had taken
years of struggle to dislodge them. To prevent another such invasion
became the cardinal goal of diplomacy. At Versailles, as stated earlier,
the French representatives were occupied almost exclusively with
two aims: (1) payment by Germany; (2) security against future
aggression. When the peacemakers had finished their work, the
people were far from satisfied that security had been achieved. "It
was in this respect," Poincaré said, "that we suffered our greatest disillusionment after the signing of the Treaty of Versailles. President
Wilson and Mr. Lloyd George before leaving Paris had signed
guarantee pacts which promised France the aid of the United States
and England in case of an attack by Germany. However, these pacts
were never ratified. France remained alone in the presence of Germany." Thus the dread of a German attack continued to harass the
French like a nightmare.

During subsequent years the desire for security was so paramount that many foreigners regarded it as an obsession. While Germany was exhausted and internally disrupted, France had the strongest army in Europe and a preponderant position in the councils of Europe. In other words, France seemed to have security to spare. But the French were not concerned about the immediate future. They were looking ahead to a time when Germany would recover both her military and her industrial strength. Germany, it is true, lay prostrate at the moment, but the French realized only too well that the giant had been laid low not by their single-handed efforts but by a coalition of many nations. They knew that by themselves they would never have driven the Germans from French soil in 1918 any more than they were able to do so in 1870. They also knew that Germany retained an enormous basic superiority both in man power and in the capacity to produce war materials. Against the seventy million inhabitants of Germany, France had only forty millions and unless the birth rate rose sharply the possibility of increasing the population was anything but promising. Furthermore, the French were aware that the Germans had not accepted the Treaty of Versailles as final, that they would renounce it at the first opportunity. "The Treaty of Versailles," Briand wrote, "will always be a source of irritation. It was the fruit of war, of victory. It can be called, and is called, a treaty imposed by force, under duress, that the defeated party is morally justified in repudiating when it can do so." In short, the French, who feared the inevitable resumption of the Franco-German duel, were searching for means to prevent it.

In lieu of the Anglo-American guarantee pact France was obliged to content itself with other forms of security. One of these was to support the League of Nations as a means of preserving peace and the *status quo;* in fact, the French joined every movement and subscribed to every plan that promised to make for peace. But the plan which on the whole appealed to them as best fitted to give the security they desired was the reestablishment of the balance of power. More specifically, they aimed to build up an unquestioned preponderance of power on the side of the defenders of the established order. They made various overtures to Great Britain, but the British for the time being relapsed into their island isolationism. They were not only determined to keep clear of Continental entanglements but were opposed to having any power become too strong. By preserving a certain balance of strength between the nations Britain could continue to play the part of mediator on the Continent. Hence, although negotiations continued until 1922, the British were unwilling to offer France any further guarantee beyond the promise of aid in case the Germans should actually invade the country. Prior to World War I France had been allied to Russia but now this ally was lost by revolution. In the words of a Frenchman: "We had found in Russia a powerful ally against Germany. This asset was lost to us, though the war was won. . . . So we have to set out to find a new combination against the menace on our eastern border." Accordingly French diplomacy crisscrossed Central Europe with allies. In 1920 France concluded an alliance with Belgium and during the subsequent years also signed treaties with Poland (1921 and 1925) and Czechoslovakia (1924 and 1925). In all three cases the treaties provided for mutual military aid. It was hoped that the armies of these three countries, combined with the French army, would insure military superiority even if Germany did evade the disarmament terms of the Treaty of Versailles. Soon thereafter Rumania (1926) and Yugoslavia (1927) were added. Thus the policy of keeping Germany in a subordinate position and "encircled" was relentlessly pursued.

After the French occupation of the Ruhr in January, 1923, Franco-German relations, as previously stated, became so strained that a rapprochement between the two nations seemed out of question. The atmosphere soon cleared, however. Leading men in both nations realized that there could be no stability in Europe so long as France and Germany continued to live on past grievances, rancors, and hatreds. The Locarno Agreements, which were salve to the sore spots for a few years, were signed in 1925. Stresemann declared: "We have undertaken to initial this treaty because we believe that only on the lines of friendly neighborliness can there be a real development of states and peoples." When Germany was admitted into the League of Nations the next year, it appeared as if a spirit of international friendship would prevail.

But the hopes of those who believed that the Locarno treaties would inaugurate an era of permanent friendship were doomed to disappointment. After 1929 relations between the two nations gradually deteriorated. French fears had been temporarily relieved but Nazi militarism revived them again. Nor did the Locarno Agreements prove more satisfactory to the Germans. They had not removed such major causes of friction as the German demand for arms equality, for colonies, and for the removal of the war-guilt clause from the Treaty of Versailles. This was fuel for the Nazi Party which was vigorously fanning the flame of national sentiment in the hope of gaining enough strength to take over the government. After Hitler's accession to power. (January, 1933) French policy toward him was of necessity one of appeasement.[7] Not only did the French fear the growing German military power, but the guarantees they had established against aggression were crumbling. As Germany grew stronger and French prestige waned, the alliances France had forged lost much of their effectiveness. In 1934 Poland, one of the mainstays in the system, signed a nonaggression pact with Germany. Two years later the Belgians renounced their military agreements with France, and in 1937 Yugoslavia signed a treaty of friendship with Italy, Germany's ally. A shift from France toward Germany also took place in an economic sense. Since Germany offered a better market for agricultural products than France, which was largely self-sufficient, a number of agricultural states were drawn into the German economic sphere. It appeared as if France would have to resign herself to accepting any change in the *status quo* that Germany might make. But the situation changed in 1939 when both Britain and France openly committed themselves to defend Poland against Nazi aggression.

FRANCE'S UNEASY DOMINIONS

In addition to other difficulties France also had problems of empire. Predestined, as it were, to exploration and colonization by her geographical position and particularly her extensive seacoasts, France had been a colonizing nation since the early seventeenth century. During the first period of colonial expansion, which reached its climax in 1750, she extended her conquests over a large part of India and over the territories in North America then known as New France. But she was unable to hold the territories that had been brought under her flag by the enterprise of her explorers and fur trappers. From 1750 to 1815 a succession of wars, followed by the Revolution and the Napoleonic wars, resulted in the almost complete dismantling of the French colonial empire, with Great Britain acquiring the lion's share. At the end of the Napoleonic wars only a few fragments of the old empire remained—some islands in the West Indies, some trading factories in India, and some fishing posts off Newfoundland. All the rest had been lost except Louisiana, which Napoleon had sold to the United States. In 1830, however, the business of replacing the lost colonies with a new empire began

---

[7] The exception was the foreign ministry of M. Barthou (February to October, 1934). Barthou believed that the only way to ensure peace was to "call Hitler's bluff" at the earliest possible moment. He was unable to do so because he did not know how far he could count on British support.

again with the acquisition of Algeria. Napoleon III did little to restore France overseas, but after the establishment of the Third Republic several statesmen vigorously pushed the task of building the new empire, so that it was soon second only to that of Great Britain. In 1920 its area reached the enormous total of about four million square miles. As the area of France proper was only a little over 200,000 square miles, the foreign possessions were thus about twenty times as large as the mother country. In population, too, they outstripped the mother country, the colonies having an estimated population of sixty million whereas France in Europe could boast only some forty million.

This vast empire, comprised as it was of many races and creeds, was chaotic and far-flung. But much of it was nearer home than the old empire had been; in fact, only the blue waters of the Mediterranean separated the mother country from some of her most important colonies. Along the northern coast of Africa the tricolor waved over Algeria, Tunisia, and parts of Morocco. From the Mediterranean the colonies reached down the west coast of Africa in a magnificent sweep. With the exception of a few strips and one large block of territory, France held all the land on the west coast to a point considerably south of the equator, including Senegal, French Guinea, the Ivory Coast, Dahomey, and French Equatorial Africa. When the First World War broke out, French troops had invaded and taken possession of the German colonies of Togoland and the Cameroons. These formally passed under French control as mandates in the peace settlement. In addition to the colonies on the west coast there was French Somaliland on the east coast, and Madagascar, third largest island in the world, off the southeastern coast. To the east of Madagascar in the Indian Ocean the Reunion Islands acknowledged French suzerainty. Besides all this there were two widely separated areas in Asia, Syria in the western part and Indo-China in the Far East. While Syria was one of the mandated territories France received after World War I, French Indo-China, consisting of a number of provinces, had been acquired from 1861 to 1892. In area the latter was larger than France herself, with a population about one half that of the mother country. As reminders of the days when she fought Britain for colonial supremacy France also had a few shreds and patches of territory in India. Moreover, the Pacific Ocean was studded with microscopic islands under French rule as well as one large island, New Caledonia.

The American possessions of France were insignificant compared to the vast possessions in Asia and Africa. In the North Atlantic,

ST. PIERRE, MIQUELON, THE LAST REMNANT OF THE FRENCH EMPIRE IN NORTHERN AMERICA

the scene of their earlier colonial conquests, the French had only two small fogbound islands, St. Pierre and Miquelon, embracing an area of ninety-three square miles of rocky and barren land inhabited by less than ten thousand people whose principal industry was cod fishing. In the south the French flag still flew over the islands of Guadeloupe and Martinique. French Guiana, an immense forest watered by many rivers and situated on the continent of South America, completed the list of possessions in the new world.

The commercial promises of the colonies were almost limitless. North Africa, which had been the granary of Rome, still produced vast quantities of wheat, oats, and barley. In addition Algeria and Tunisia exported fruits, tobacco, and wool, and also marble, stone, crude metals, oils, and chemicals. Among the chief products of Morocco, besides cereals, were wool and linseed. Many thousand gallons of wine were annually shipped across the Mediterranean and blended with French wines. Equatorial Africa had vast undeveloped resources of rubber, copper, and palm oil. Madagascar was rich in forests, minerals, precious stones, and graphite. Plants for textile materials and for tanning, dyeing, and medicinal purposes were also raised in large quantities, together with such food products as rice, sugar, coffee, cocoa, and vanilla. Indo-China offered infinite possibilities for the production of rice, silk, cotton, timber, metals, and rubber. New Caledonia, one of the richest countries in the world, exported coffee, tobacco, manioc, mother of pearl, and, above all, nickel. Until the development of the Canadian nickel mines France dominated the market through her control of the New Caledonia mines. Copra, sugar, rum, and pearls were produced in quantity on the French islands of the Pacific. Upon both Martinique and Guadeloupe sugar was the staple product and other important crops included coffee, cocoa, tobacco, and cotton. Finally, there were the varied products of French Guiana including hardwood, dyes, and plants suitable for the manufacture of textiles and medicine.

Despite the prodigious wealth and resources of this empire, few Frenchmen were interested in it. Colonies were not needed to absorb the excess population of France because there was no excess. Because of the shortage of man power, colonies of Spaniards, Belgians, Poles, Swiss, Russians, and other nationals had been planted in France proper. Consequently most Frenchmen regarded their colonial empire as a sort of luxury. The expansion movement was, therefore, promoted by a handful of statesmen with "secret" funds. Whenever the people were asked for money to meet the expenses of

empire, they complained loudly. A wider colonial interest did not
develop until the Germans entered the competition for colonies.
It was German interference in Morocco, for example, that crystallized French ambitions in that colony. To those who had not been
previously interested in colonial activities World War I demonstrated that the French Empire not only offered a splendid field for
future exploitation in times of peace but also served as an invaluable
source of man power for the French forces. During the war the
colonies furnished no less than 700,000 fighting men, while more
than a million others manned war factories, ports, and means of
transportation. More than this, from the first day of the war the
colonies sent the mother country vast quantities of such essential
supplies as cereals, meats, oils, metals, and timber.

After the war when the search for security became paramount,
statesmen decided that one way to compensate for the growing shortage of men and the falling birth rate would be to make the colonies
part of a greater France. In discussing the position of France in
Europe Poincaré stated in 1923 that France was no longer a country of forty million but of a hundred million. It was a declaration
to the enemies of France that in the next war they would have to
fight not only the military contingents of forty million Frenchmen
but also the conscripts of sixty million natives of Indo-China, Madagascar, Algeria, Tunisia, Morocco, Somaliland, and other colonies.
Universal conscription became the law in the colonies as well as in
France. But the colonies were to represent an extension of France
not merely in a military sense; they were to be French in every sense.
It became the aim to assimilate rather than dominate the colonies.
Consciously, deliberately, and avowedly the colonial administrations
took up the task of gallicizing the native populations, of teaching
them to regard themselves as Frenchmen rather than as Africans,
Asians, or what not, of stimulating a French consciousness in them.
Perhaps the most vital cog in the machinery of assimilation was the
schools that were opened in the various colonies. Here children were
taught French and steeped in French traditions. French citizenship
was bestowed on natives when they were regarded as ready for it.
Participation in the government was also granted to the more adult
colonies. Thus the three departments of Algeria were permitted to
send representatives to the Chamber of Deputies to make laws that
were binding on all Frenchmen. By 1930 eight of the thirty colonies
had some sort of representation in the parliament.

Outwardly it appeared for a time as if France were meeting with
marvelous success in this program. While the anti-European move-

ment was flaring up with unexpected intensity in India, the Middle East, and even in Egypt, a comparative calm was reigning in the French colonies. The absence of open trouble made many French-men dream of a complete assimilation of the native populations into the *civilisation française*, of making all French soil one with *la Patrie*. But appearances were deceiving. Despite a certain outward ac-quiescence most natives had little appreciation of the material or intellectual benefits of Western life that were laid at their feet. Many would not even send their children to the schools the French opened. Although to superficial observers France seemed to stand secure in the loyalty of her colonial subjects, revolutionary movements were actually surging below the surface. The visions of political liberty and democratic government which motivated these movements came largely from France. Those aspects of French culture which the Arabs absorbed most readily were the nationalistic tendencies. But instead of a French nationalism either a local or an Arab na-tionalism developed. In other words, the native populations began to insist on living their own lives.

Not long after World War I North Africa was honeycombed with Moslem secret societies whose object was to liberate all Islam from the rule of the "Christian infidel." In Tunisia in 1922 the under-ground agitation for freedom culminated in the march of a dusty white-robed procession of thousands of Mohammedans to the palace of the Bey of Tunisia to lay before him a petition urging him to drive out the foreigner and resume his ancient power. With a prompt show of force the authorities dispersed the gathering and suppressed the newspapers which were the mouthpieces of the agi-tators; then to quiet the unrest the French made certain desired re-forms. It was the policy of the iron hand and the velvet glove, the former making a show of force and the latter smoothing things over by concessions to the desire for self-government. This policy settled little beyond driving the independence movements underground. Some time later the movement would break out anew and the iron-hand and velvet-glove policy would again be employed. This was true in Algeria and Morocco as well as in Tunisia. In the decade of the thirties disturbances and popular uprisings became more fre-quent. After a series of riots in Algeria an English observer wrote: "The remarkable novelty in this demonstration is the fact that there were more Europeans than natives amongst the demonstrators against French colonial rule. . . . There is the danger of natives being encouraged against the regime by Europeans."[8] Under the term

[8] *Review of Reviews* (London), vol. 86 (1935), p. 49.

"Europeans" this observer undoubtedly grouped all those who had acquired a veneer of European civilization, for the anti-French movement did draw much of its strength from younger men who had been educated in France or in the French schools of North Africa.

Nor was the unrest confined to North Africa. Everywhere in the French as in the British Empire the tide of native feeling against foreign domination was rising. The natives of Madagascar, of Syria, of the French possessions in India, and of Indo-China were all demanding freedom. There was even an organization, the *Rassemblement Coloniale,* which endeavored to coordinate the work of the various independence movements in the different parts of the empire. In the more backward regions of Africa there were no organized movements for independence, but the desire to be free was nevertheless strong and found outlet in strikes, disorders, and riots. How the colonial peoples felt can be seen from a letter written by a native of the Cameroons (after this territory was transferred to the French) to the League for the Defense of the Negro People. "We don't want the Germans, who have killed a great part of the population of our country," he wrote, "and who would do it again if they became our masters. Neither do we want the French, who are always unjust to us. We don't want anybody. We want to be independent—that is our cry. Although this cry is stifled by those who are stronger than we, it expresses our earnest desire. . . . The white man is a stranger here, and he knows it. If he does not, the day will come when he will be forced to recognize it."

CHAPTER SEVEN

Soviet Russia

ORGANIZING THE REVO-
LUTION
THE Bolshevist revolution of November, 1917, was more a revolution of theory than of occasion. The Bolsheviks raised the standard of revolt in the name of a communistic social philosophy, each item of which was built upon historical interpretation. As an ideal, communism reaches back to the very beginnings of Western political thought. Plato envisaged a communist state in his *Republic* and after him many others advocated the abolition of private property as a remedy for social injustice. But it was Karl Marx and Friedrich Engels who really organized communism into a definite philosophy in their *Communist Manifesto,* published in 1848. This pamphlet, together with the other writings of Karl Marx, supplied the basis for the philosophy of the Bolsheviks. According to it, society is made up of those who own property and those who have nothing but their ability to labor. The class which owns property molds society according to its own desires. It controls the government, makes the laws, and builds the institutions of the commonwealth. More positively, it keeps the masses of workers in subjection and exploits them for its own interests. The instrument wherewith the capitalists keep the workers in subjection is the state. The bourgeois state, Engels said, is always "a force for suppression," a method for protecting the property owners. To put an end to this suppression and exploitation the proletariat must forcibly destroy not only middle-class control of public affairs but also the bourgeois theories of life and morality. "Only a revolution," Lenin wrote, "can destroy the capitalist state. When that destruction has been accomplished, a dictatorship of the proletariat must be set up and the means of production must be nationalized." "The

proletariat," the *Communist Manifesto* states, "will use its political supremacy in order gradually to wrest the whole of capital from the capitalist class, to centralize all the instruments of production in the hands of the State, i.e., of the proletariat as the ruling class."

But the dictatorship of the proletariat is not the final goal. It is only the means to an end. The ultimate aim is the creation of a classless and stateless society. The proletarian state is needed at first because a direct transition from capitalism to communism is not possible. However, it will continue only until the last vestige of capitalism has been destroyed. Then its utility will cease and, in the phrase of Engels, it will "wither away." Having its origin and justification in the class struggle, the state can exist only so long as there are classes. In a completely communistic society there will be no classes because they are the product of economic inequality, particularly of the private ownership of the means of production. In his *State and Revolution* Lenin put his stamp of approval on Marx's statement: "The working class will," he said, "in the course of its development replace the old bourgeois society by a society which will exclude classes and their antagonisms; there will no longer be any political authority in the proper sense of the word, since political authority is the official expression of the antagonism of classes within bourgeois society." Nor will there be wages or money in the new society. All will cooperate freely for the common good on the principle "from each according to his ability; to all according to their need." This ideal of a communal society in which the necessity of a compulsive state has ceased to exist does not differ greatly from the dreams of utopians of all ages, although Marxian socialism is often termed "scientific."

The man who took the lead in attempting to translate the Marxian theories into practice was Vladimir Ilyich Ulianov, better known as Nikolai Lenin, the name he adopted to meet the needs of illegal revolutionary work under tsarism. Born at Simbirsk on the Volga on the 10th of April, 1870, he very early became a revolutionist. As a boy he read Marx and other revolutionary literature, with the result that revolution became his absorbing passion. He had a number of sisters and brothers, all of whom were also revolutionaries. In 1887 his brother Alexander, who had joined a group of terrorists aiming to end autocracy by destroying the autocrats, was apprehended in a plot to assassinate Tsar Alexander III and was hanged. Instead of stirring revenge in his heart, the death of his brother appears to have convinced young Lenin that attempts on individual autocrats, however successful they might be, were utterly futile as a means of achieving fundamental social change. It fortified his conviction of the correctness of Marx's analysis of society, particularly of the idea that a real movement of liberation can be successful only through organization of the proletariat as a class. He began at once to prepare himself for the task of overthrowing tsarism and establishing a communist order. In 1891 he entered the University of St. Petersburg and successfully passed the examinations which qualified him for the practice of law, but instead of practising law he devoted himself to revolutionary activities. He wrote articles for the subterranean press, was active in the dissemination of revolutionary literature in Russia, and carefully trained disciples in the technique of revolution. For his activities he was arrested and imprisoned or exiled a number of times, but nothing could abate his ardor or shake his faith.

Soon after the turn of the century his plan took definite shape. Like Marx he believed that history was working ceaselessly and inevitably toward the ultimate triumph of his cause, that just as certainly as feudalism had given rise to capitalism the latter would give way to the proletarian state. But he was also convinced that the capitalists who run the bourgeois state would not relinquish their privileged position voluntarily. "The substitution of a proletarian for the capitalist state," he wrote, "is impossible without a violent revolution." Hence he vehemently denounced those members of the Russian Social Democratic Party who believed that the seizure of power could be accomplished by the constitutional method of obtaining a majority in parliament. With all his inflexible resolution he threw himself into the task of organizing a select group animated by a militant revolutionary creed. This group, which became known as the Bolsheviks, he dominated by sheer moral and intellectual force, holding it uncompromisingly on the path toward revolution. During the Revolution of 1905 he continued his journalistic activities but otherwise stayed in the background because he felt that the time was not propitious for the Great Revolution. In his mind the sequence of events was crystal clear. The Revolution of 1905, he said, was the prologue to the real one, for which "we must prepare more tenaciously, more systematically, more persistently." He would freely express his conviction that a great war was brewing and that in this war Russia would go down under the weight of her infirmities. During the resulting confusion the Bolsheviks would seize the helm and establish the communist order. In short, he knew exactly what he wished to achieve and how he meant to achieve it.

When the March Revolution broke out in 1917 Lenin was living

in Switzerland as an exile, but with the assistance of the German
military authorities he was transported across Germany in the famous
"sealed car" and arrived in Petrograd the middle of April. Finding
the situation favorable to his plans he and Trotsky and the Bolsheviks began at once to prepare the overthrow of the provisional
government. Early in November he decided that the moment was
right to strike. During the night of November 6 Bolshevik troops
quietly and systematically occupied the main telephone and telegraph offices, the railway stations, and the government buildings
excepting the Winter Palace which was the seat of the provisional
government. The next day they besieged the Winter Palace. When
the members of the provisional government were informed that the
guns of a cruiser and of the Peter and Paul fortress were turned
upon them, they realized that resistance would be futile. That same
evening the all-Russian Congress of Workers' and Soldiers' Deputies
met in Petrograd. After declaring that "all local power shall be transferred to the Soviets of Workers', Soldiers', and Peasants' Deputies,"
the congress established a new government in the form of the Council of People's Commissars, with Lenin as the president of the council. Other members were Trotsky, who was given the post of Commissar of Foreign Affairs, and Stalin, who was made Commissar for
Nationalities. The former was, next to Lenin, the key man; Stalin
played a relatively unimportant role. The change of government
had been effected with but little bloodshed.[1] The bloody stage was
still to come. In some of the other cities, particularly in Moscow,
there was some street fighting but by the end of the month the soviets
held power throughout the country.

The new rulers began at once to fulfill the promises that had won
them popular support. On the evening of November 8 Lenin appeared before the Congress of Soviets and after stilling the tumultu-
ous applause said in a matter-of-fact manner: "Comrades, let us
proceed to the construction of the socialist order." The program
he presented emphasized three things: immediate peace, control of
all land by the peasants, and a "real workers' control over production." After the proposal of an immediate peace "without annexations and without indemnities" had been accepted, Lenin read a
short decree abolishing private property in land. Privately owned
land, including church and monastery land, was confiscated without indemnification, and the administration of all land was transferred to committees and soviets of peasants' deputies. These "agencies of the people" were to divide the land equally among the peasants

---

[1] The losses in taking the Winter Palace were five sailors and one soldier killed.

according to the size and labor capacity of each family. Only persons who would cultivate the land with their own labor were to be allotted holdings, the hiring of labor being expressly forbidden. This system of small holdings was in accord neither with Marxian doctrine nor with the desires of Lenin. It was the program of the Socialist Revolutionary Party, which had a strong following among the peasants.

During the months that followed, other phases of the new order were inaugurated. The banks were "nationalized," that is, they were taken over by the government. Private buying and selling was at first restricted and later prohibited under penalty of severe punishment. All debts contracted by previous governments were repudiated and all foreign investments in private industry were confiscated. To reinforce the victory of the proletariat an eight-hour day was proclaimed but cash wages were abolished. Each worker or employee was given ration cards for free food, lodging, clothing, transportation, and other necessities. Without these cards nothing could be obtained except by illegal means. All did not, however, get the same allotment. Factory workers received more food than civil servants, and the latter were allowed more than the members of the former "privileged classes." Under the slogan, "Loot the looters," apartment houses and private dwellings were expropriated by the local soviets to provide living quarters for the workers. Requisitioning committees confiscated the supplies of private stores and even compelled the *bourgeoisie* to surrender their "superfluous" food, clothing, and household articles.

The nationalization of industry, contrary to the picture conjured up by the popular imagination in the West, was not carried out in a sudden and sweeping manner. The fact is that the Soviet government proceeded somewhat cautiously in this respect. On November 14, 1917, it issued the Decree on Workers' Control which gave the workers' committee the right to be consulted "on matters of sales and purchase, of fixing the output program, and even of determining the selling price." In other words, the workers' committee was given a share in the control of an industry but it was not allowed to interfere in the executive work of running the enterprise. Article 9 specifically forbade the workers' committee "to take possession of the enterprise or to direct it," except by permission of the higher authorities. Although a number of companies passed into state ownership during the subsequent months, it was not until May, 1918, that an entire industry, that is, the sugar industry, was nationalized. The nationalization of other individual industries fol-

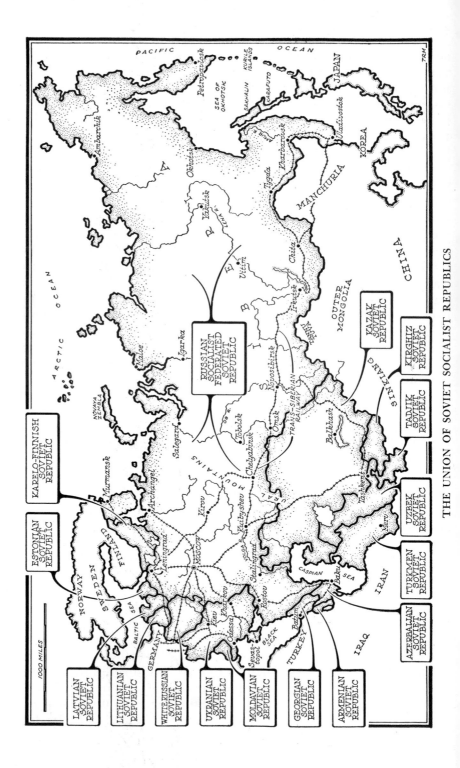

THE UNION OF SOVIET SOCIALIST REPUBLICS

lowed, but the decree which declared all industrial and commercial enterprises with a capital of a million rubles or over to be national property was not issued until June 28 of that year. Besides the large manufacturing industries, this nationalization included mining, insurance, water transport, and the few railroads that had been operated by private companies.

Since the Bolsheviks were only a minority, it was necessary for them to uphold their rule by force. "Our task now consists," Bukharin stated in *The Program of the Bolsheviks*, "in strengthening the Soviet government by all means in our power and by clearing it of various undesirable elements." [2] Like the Jacobins, the Bolsheviks used the Red Terror to achieve their ends. Not only was the former land-owning gentry which had formed the social basis of the tsarist autocracy wiped out but the *bourgeoisie*, innocent and guilty alike, were also subjected to a persecution that exceeded by far the horrors of the French Revolution. "We are not making war on individuals," wrote Latsis, one of the creators of the Red Terror; "we are exterminating the *bourgeoisie* as a class." The *Program of the Bolsheviks* stated: "We have a dictatorship of workers and peasants whose aim is to crush the *bourgeoisie*." But the so-called privileged classes were not the only ones to feel the weight of the Red Terror. All who were opposed to the Bolshevik plans either actively or passively—whether workers or peasants, Mensheviks, Social Revolutionaries, or republicans—were declared counterrevolutionaries and enemies of the people. As such they were ruthlessly destroyed or crushed into submission. To prevent any organized opposition all other political parties were forbidden and persecuted. All political meetings excepting those organized by the Bolsheviks were prohibited. As early as November 10, 1917, a decree to close all hostile newspapers was issued. Although this decree was not immediately put into effect, the government did gradually destroy such freedom of the press as had previously existed. Only the press controlled by the government authorities was allowed to exist.

The most efficient agency in the defense of the dictatorship was the All-Russian Commission for Combating Counterrevolution, Spec-

[2] *Revolutionary Radicalism,* vol. 2, p. 1701.

THE UNION OF SOVIET SOCIALIST REPUBLICS. *The region once called Russia is now a federation of republics, each of which was in 1944 accorded the theoretical right to enter into direct relations with foreign states.*

ulation, and Sabotage, better known as the Cheka, a word composed of the initial syllables of the Russian words for "Extraordinary
Commission." This commission, organized in December, 1917,
gradually increased its power to include summary arrest, trial, and
execution. Its policy was stated by the *All-Russian Cheka Daily* in
its first issue: "Let us abandon all long, fruitless, and futile speeches
about the Red Terror. The time has come, not by words, but by
deeds, to carry on the most pitiless, sternly organized mass terror."
Wholesale arrests, usually in the dead of night, were made of all
those suspected of opposition. Their families seldom heard anything
further until those who had been arrested were either condemned or
freed. Executions were carried out in secret, usually by shooting. To
the Bolsheviks the establishment of their system was so obviously
desirable that they did not count the cost in blood. How many persons the Cheka put to death cannot as yet be ascertained with any
degree of certainty. During the first phase of the terror the government, desiring to strike fear into the hearts of all opponents, published a fairly accurate list; later, however, secrecy was observed in
this regard because the frankness in reporting executions had
proved injurious to the reputation of the regime abroad. While official apologists have set the figures too low, opponents have naturally
exaggerated them. A number of writers have estimated that the
executions ran into the hundreds of thousands, and one estimate goes
as high as 1.7 million.[3]

In addition to the opposition within the territory they controlled, the Soviet government also had to meet aggression from the
outside by the so-called White armies and by foreign troops. The
first center of armed opposition was the Cossack country of the
South, especially round the Don. Having long cherished a considerable independence, the Don Cossacks did not stop at raising the
standard of revolt themselves; they also offered hospitality to all who
were opposed to Bolshevik rule. Large numbers of former imperial
officers, members of the outlawed nobility, former landowners, supporters of the church, members of the professional classes, and even
peasants flocked to the Don. Before the end of 1917 the first White
army led by former imperial officers, came into existence in the Cossack country.[4] At its greatest strength it numbered no less than
400,000 but it was poorly armed and at times short of supplies. The
formation of this anti-Bolshevik army raised echoes of revolt else-

[3] See Melgounov, *Red Terror in Russia* (1926), p. 111.
[4] It was commanded successively by Alekseev, Kornilov, Denikin, and finally Wrangel.

where. In the North another White army was organized under Admiral Kolchak. This army had the assistance of about 45,000 Czechs who having deserted from the Austrian army were on their way via Vladivostok to fight for the Allies on the western front. Nor were the Czechs the only foreign troops to oppose the Bolsheviks. The Allies, believing that the Russians would continue the war against Germany if the Bolshevik rule were terminated, sent the White armies instructors, supplies, and money and dispatched contingents of troops to various points. The British landed forces at Murmansk and Archangel; the French occupied Odessa; and contingents of British, French, Japanese, and American troops were sent to Vladivostok.[5]

All the anti-Bolshevik armies were at first successful. While the southern White army advanced as far as Orel, about 250 miles from Moscow, another was threatening Petrograd from the west. In the east the White army under Kolchak took almost all of Siberia and established a counterrevolutionary government at Omsk.[6] By the fall of 1919 the territory controlled by the Bolsheviks was reduced to the central part of European Russia. But the tide was soon to turn. The earliest Red army, a force composed of volunteers, was makeshift and ineffective. In the summer of 1918 the government decreed compulsory conscription and put upon the shoulders of Trotsky as Commissar of War the task of welding the recruits into a competent fighting force inspired with a deep hatred of the Whites. Both the Red and White armies employed a system of mass terror. Anyone suspected of aiding the enemy was summarily executed. Railroads and bridges were destroyed and roads were torn up. Ultimately the Reds won. In the spring of 1920 the White armies of the north, northwest, and Siberia either surrendered or were driven out of Russia. The White army in the south held out a little longer, but was finally thrown back upon the Black Sea and compelled to evacuate Russian soil. One of the major reasons for the defeat of the Whites was their failure to win the sympathy of the peasants, many of whom believed that they would have to give up the land they had seized during the revolution if the Whites were victorious. On the

[5] The reason some of these contingents were sent was to keep Russian military supplies from going to the Central Powers.
[6] The advance of the Czech and White armies brought death to ex-Tsar Nicholas II and his wife, his children, and a number of attendants who were living at Ekaterinburg in the foothills of the Urals. Fearing that the counterrevolutionary armies might advance far enough to liberate the imperial family, the local Soviet decided to execute the entire party. On July 18, 1918, they were shot without trial.

other hand, the Bolsheviks, like the revolutionaries of 1792 in France, were inspired by an overwhelming enthusiasm for their cause.

6

THE NEW ECONOMIC POLICY

When the last of the White armies left in November, 1920, the internal economy of the country was in a chaotic state. The attempt to inaugurate communism had failed. In industry the system of workers' control had largely broken down because the workers were unprepared to take over the management and few of the former owners were willing or able to carry on under the new system. The output of factories, mills, and mines had decreased each year until in 1920 it was only 13 per cent of the 1913 figure. The railroads, owing to deterioration of rolling stock, mismanagement, and lack of goods to be transported, were nearing a standstill. Furthermore, the fiscal machinery of the country had run down so completely that the annual deficit was more than 90 per cent of the expenditure. Above all, agricultural production had declined to 55 per cent of the prewar average. In lieu of money taxes the state had systematically confiscated the produce of the peasants and had permitted them to keep only enough for food and for the next year's sowing. For their produce the peasants received commodity cards theoretically exchangeable for manufactured goods. But, since industrial production had declined so greatly and all the goods that were being manufactured were needed for the army, the peasants got none or at best very little. Irritated by the requisitioning, many peasants decided to produce only enough food for their own needs; others resisted and promoted a series of revolts. On top of it all a severe drought in the summer of 1920 caused a failure of crops in a large part of Russia. Famine became so widespread that despite foreign help, particularly from the United States,[7] some five million persons died either from starvation or from the results of malnutrition.

With famine stalking the land, industry and transportation threatening to collapse completely, and the peasants in open hostility, the Soviet government was confronted with the choice of either changing its policy or being buried under the ruins of economic catastrophe. Lenin decided on a change of policy. In 1921 he abandoned "pure communism" and inaugurated the New Economic Policy, better known as the NEP. This new policy did not repudiate

[7] See H. H. Fisher, *The Famine in Soviet Russia* (1935).

communism, nor did it involve a fundamental change in principle or aim. It was merely a temporary concession to more moderate practices, a concession based on the principle enunciated by Lenin, "Our doctrine is not a dogma but a guide to action; not a sacred theory but a working tool." The adoption of NEP, as Lenin explained it, was taking one step backward in order to take two forward. While retaining a monopoly of foreign trade for the state, the NEP permitted private trading side by side with state retailing, granted greater freedom of management in the large industries, and allowed the existence of small private industry. For the peasants the main change was the abandonment of the policy of requisitioning surplus produce. Instead of surrendering their surpluses, the peasants paid a tax in kind. Whatever produce was left after the tax was paid they were free to sell in the open market. As an aid to the revival of economic life a regular currency system was restored and the internal stabilization of the ruble was achieved. All this, together with the cessation of war and with good harvests in 1922 and 1923, resulted in a gradual and at times energetic recovery. Private traders and shops flourished and industry and commerce generally revived to such an extent that in 1927 they surpassed the level of 1913. New life was also infused into agriculture, with the result that the tilled area reached the prewar acreage.

But Lenin did not live to see the later developments of the NEP. In 1922 a paralytic stroke laid him low and compelled him to retire from the government. He returned after a short rest but was forced to retire again and died on January 21, 1924. As the outstanding leader of the Bolshevik revolution he fundamentally affected the course of European history. A man of dominating personality, he organized a party—disciplined and utterly loyal—to serve as the spearhead of advance toward world revolution. Stalin said of him: "Lenin was born for the revolution. He was the true genius of revolutionary struggle and the greatest master of revolutionary leadership." Regarded by his colleagues with something akin to awe, he was accorded by the rank and file of the party the veneration others usually bestow on supernatural beings. He did succeed in achieving for his party the supreme power; but the world revolution he hoped for did not materialize nor did he succeed in establishing a truly communistic society in Russia. Nevertheless, as the father of Bolshevism he will remain for all time one of the key figures of European history.

Lenin's death was followed by an epic contest for his mantle between Trotsky and Stalin. The creeds of the two men did not differ substantially; both were communists and fanatical revolutionists. Their differences were of a tactical nature. Whereas Trotsky stood for uncompromising effort toward world revolution, Stalin's first concern was to establish the revolution firmly in Russia. Trotsky was unquestionably the more brilliant and picturesque personality but, as it turned out, Stalin was the better politician. He had a tremendous advantage in the fact that as secretary-general of the Communist Party he held a position of vital political importance. The most striking feature of his career is that until he was actually in the seat of power everyone, including Lenin, believed him incapable of seizing it. Lenin, it appears, had chosen him for the position of secretary-general because he believed him to be an "obedient figurehead." In this, however, he was mistaken. Moved by an intense hunger for power and possessed of a native shrewdness, Stalin at once began to make the most of his position to obtain personal control of the party by placing his henchmen in strategic positions throughout the organization. During his last illness Lenin seems to have realized that he had erred in his judgment. Demanding the removal of the secretary-general, Lenin wrote, "Otherwise his accursed pigheadedness and his unbounded egotism and stupidity will cause many splits and much strife later on within the party. He is no true communist and is full of bitter personal hatred toward Trotsky." But Stalin had already so consolidated his position that it was impossible to dislodge him. Thus the death of Lenin saw Stalin in control. Trotsky, though still the most popular living figure in Russia, was without any real political influence. He had been quietly paralyzed as a prelude to being eliminated. In 1927 he and his followers were expelled from the party and then (January, 1928) driven into exile.[8]

The new dictator was not a man of striking appearance or spectacular gifts of leadership; "not a man," one observer wrote,[9] "who appeals to the sympathies of crowds or stirs their imaginations. He is not an electric person. Let us be blunt: he is frankly unattractive." On the other hand, most observers credited him with strength of will, energy, fearlessness, and considerable shrewdness. Like Mussolini and Kemal Atatürk, he rose from the lowest grade of society. He was born in 1879 as the son of a cobbler in a small town in the Caucasus, in the state of Georgia. His real name was Josef Dzugashvili. Later as a means of covering his revolutionary activities he used various pseudonyms of which Stalin, meaning "of steel," permanently

[8] Trotsky went first to Turkey and finally to Mexico, where he was assassinated in 1940.
[9] Paul Scheffer in *Foreign Affairs*, vol. 8 (1930), p. 550.

eplaced his real name. His mother, a devout member of the Russian Orthodox Church, dreamed of making her son a priest and when young Josef was fourteen sent him to the Orthodox Seminary n Tiflis. But instead of becoming a priest he became a revolutionist. He became convinced, in his own words, that "Russian capitalism was the most atrocious and bestial in the world; the government of the tsar the most corrupt, cruel, and inefficient." In 1898 at the age of nineteen, he left the seminary, joined the Social Democratic Party, and when the split occurred in 1903 sided definitely with the Bolsheviks, working ceaselessly for the revolution during the subsequent years. For his activities he was sent to Siberia four times. Thrice he managed to escape, but upon his fourth deportation in 1913 he remained in Siberia until the March revolution of 1917. During the civil war from 1918 to 1921 he fought in the field and and when it ended began to play the political game which won for him the mantle of Lenin.

THE FIVE-YEAR PLANS

When Lenin inaugurated the NEP, many Western observers interpreted the change as the beginning of a return to full-fledged capitalism. Before many years passed, however, it was demonstrated that this view was fallacious. Not only did the government retain its hold on the base of Russian economic life; it also continued through its monopolistic control of education, the press, and other agencies of propaganda to instill communist ideas into the minds of the people. In 1922 Lenin said: "We will solve this problem, no matter what the cost: that NEP Russia shall become socialist Russia." Above all, the government soon began to eliminate the potential sources of capitalist revival. Very early the restrictions upon private traders or nepmen were increased so drastically that by the spring of 1924 more than 300,000 firms were wiped out. When certain phases of private enterprise continued to thrive despite shackles and limitations, a policy of wholesale and direct repression was adopted. Plans were also made to eliminate the "capitalist elements," particularly the kulak [10] or well-to-do peasant, from agriculture. When in 1926 and 1927 the complaints of the dyed-in-the-wool communists became especially loud because the government was permitting "capitalism" to develop unhindered in the villages, Stalin

---

[10] The kulaks were peasants who had managed through the exercise of shrewdness and thrift to acquire more land and more livestock than the other peasants. Many kulaks also had modern farm machinery and employed hired labor.

assured the communists at the fifteenth Congress of the party that the government would rid the villages of its bourgeois elements and habits of thought. Stating that police measures alone would not solve the problem, he went on to say: "The solution is to be found in the transformation of the tiny scattered peasant farms into a vast and centralized industry on the basis of cooperative farming and in the adoption of collective farming based on a new and higher technical knowledge."

In 1928 all the diversified efforts of the government were joined in a long-range plan conceived on a grand scale and known as the *Piatiletka* or Five-Year Plan. By the execution of this plan the government hoped to achieve a number of aims. First of all, there was the aim of transforming Russia from a predominantly agrarian to a predominantly industrial country. The slogan was "to overtake and to surpass the capitalist countries in production." And this was to be achieved at a rate unequaled in the history of capitalism. A second aim was to increase the productivity of agriculture which, because of the antiquated methods employed by the peasants, was very low. Thus it was hoped that the fulfillment of this plan would give Russia a high degree of self-sufficiency. A primary consideration in the attainment of this self-sufficiency was national defense. Feeling themselves isolated and disliked, the Bolsheviks not only feared an invasion but they had also not forgotten the experiences of World War I in which a nonindustrialized Russia found herself at the mercy of an industrialized enemy. But the final goal of the first and also of the Five-Year Plans that followed was the complete liquidation of capitalism in Russia and the establishment of a completely communist economy in the shortest possible time. Stalin himself said later: "The basic task of the Five-Year Plan in transforming the U.S.S.R. into an industrial country was to eliminate completely all capitalist elements; to widen the front of socialist forms of economy; and to create the economic foundation for the abolition of classes in the U.S.S.R. for the creation of a socialist society." [11]

On the industrial front the Five-Year Plan set certain definite goals. It proposed in general to increase the total value of production from 18.3 billion rubles in 1927–1928 to 43.2 billion in 1932–1933. Special emphasis was placed on heavy industry. In other words, energies were to be largely concentrated on the building of factories, the output of machinery, and the development of transportation rather than on the production of shoes, clothing, and household goods. The heavy industries were to be more than trebled. The

[11] From a speech by Stalin printed in the *New York Times*, January 29, 1933.

output of coal, for example, which was 35.4 million tons in 1927–1928 was to reach 75 million at the completion of the Plan. The production of oil was to increase from 11.8 million to 21.7 million tons. Ten million tons of pig iron were to be turned out by 1932–1933 instead of the 3.3 million tons produced in 1927–1928. Forty-two power stations were to be constructed, which would increase the annual output of electrical energy from 5 billion to 22 billion kilowatt hours. The Plan further projected the rehabilitation of old factories and the building of a number of new ones for the manufacture of steel, machinery, tractors, agricultural implements, and automobiles. The manufacture of agricultural machinery, for instance, was to increase by four times. To provide the materials for building the new plants the output of bricks was to be increased by five times and that of cement more than tripled. Finally the chemical industry, which was then in its infancy, was to be expanded to the extent of producing twenty-three times the amount of superphosphates and seven times the volume of sulphuric acid that was produced in 1927–1928.

The special emphasis put upon the development of heavy industry resulted in an extreme scarcity of consumers' goods, that is, of clothing, shoes, and household articles. In other words, the people had to forego not only comforts but also necessaries. The raw materials, machine tools, and equipment for the big steel and electrical plants could only be purchased abroad and the government had to pay for them either in foreign currency or in gold. Possessing but little gold and less foreign credit, it was obliged to cut imports to the bone even at the expense of prime necessities. Russia, for example, needed cotton from the United States but preferred to spend such credit as it had on drills, compressors, and turbines, with the result that there was a textile shortage. More than this, to get the necessary exchange values to purchase even the indispensable needs of heavy industry the government was compelled to export such things as grain and sugar which its own population needed. This was the cause of the people's hardships. As compensation for their short rations they had the conviction that more coal, cast iron, steel, locomotives, turbines, and chemicals must ultimately mean more shoes, shirts, clothing, and more food too. To spur on the undernourished workers to give their best efforts to their work the government organized so-called Socialist Competitions, one factory or shop challenging another to achieve a higher level of productivity and quality. Another means to increase the output was the introduction of the unbroken working year, that is, factories, shops, and offices operated 360 instead of 310 days a year, Sunday being abol-

ished. The rest days were staggered in such a way that only one-
fifth of the workers were absent at one time.[12]

In January, 1933, the government announced that the Plan had
been practically fulfilled in four years. "At the end of the fourth
year of the Five-Year Plan," Stalin said, "We have succeeded in
realizing 93.7 per cent of the program of general industrial production as conceived for the five years, having increased industrial production more than threefold in comparison with the prewar level
and more than twofold in comparison with 1928." To arrive at the
93.7 per cent fulfillment Stalin must have employed ingenious
statistical methods. It is true, in some branches of industry, notably
the production of oil and the manufacture of tractors and machinery,
the goal was nearly or actually attained. According to the Plan, for
example, only 825 locomotives were to be turned out in 1933, but as
early as 1931 no less than 812 came out of the factories. In a number of other respects, including the building of railroad cars, the
actual achievement exceeded the goal set by the Plan.[13] On the other
hand, in many respects attainment fell far short. This was particularly true of iron, steel, and coal. Since these are the materials
most needed in heavy industry, the failure to produce them according to the Plan caused a drop in other products. The following table
will give some idea of the achievements of the Plan:

	Planned	*Achieved*
Coal, million tons	75	65.4
Iron ore, million tons	19.4	12
Cast iron, million tons	10	6.2
Steel, million tons	10.4	5.9
Rolled steel, million tons	8	4.3
Oil, million tons	21.7	22.3
Tractors, thousands	55	50.6
Brick, million pieces	9.3	4.8
Cement, million barrels	41	22.5
Footwear, million pairs	145	84.7
Rubbers, million pairs	75	51.8
Paper, thousand tons	900	471
Sugar, thousand tons	2,600	826

Nevertheless, the fact that the goal was not reached in every
instance does not detract from the tremendous achievement of the

[12] After the outbreak of World War II the old week with Sunday as the day of rest was
restored.
[13] What the statistics do not show is that quality was often recklessly sacrificed to
quantity.

four years. The progress in almost any line appears astonishing when one considers the colossal difficulties under which the government had to work. Among these were the lack of building materials, the critical shortage of skilled labor and technicians, the comparative absence of foreign credits, the scarcity of food, and the backwardness of the people. Despite all the obstacles, mistakes, and failures Russia was during these four years transformed, as Stalin said, "from an agrarian country to an industrial country, the ratio of industrial production to agricultural production having risen from 48 per cent at the beginning of the Five-Year Plan to 70 per cent at the end of the fourth year." More than this, the Soviet Union achieved a heavy industry which ranked high for its equipment. Hundreds of old industrial plants were rebuilt or enlarged during the four years and no less than fifteen hundred new factories, many of them giant plants, were built. While the number of establishments employing 100 to 500 workers was more than doubled, establishments with more than 5000 employees were increased from 83 to 170. Never before in history had so many gigantic enterprises been constructed within so short a period. Among the more notable achievements were the mammoth steel plants of Magnitogorsk and Kuznetsk, the huge tractor plants at Kharkov and Stalingrad, the great automobile factories at Moscow and Nizhnii Novgorod, and the Dnepropetrovsk hydroelectric project.

Although the Five-Year Plan made no specific mention of agricultural collectivization, intensive efforts were made during this period to collectivize agriculture. The purpose, beyond the establishment of communism, was to increase productivity. According to the Plan, it was to be increased from 16.6 billion to 25.8 billion rubles. Such an increase was necessary if the country was to supply the growing urban population with adequate food. Any considerable increase of food production, however, was difficult if not impossible so long as the multitude of petty peasant holdings continued. In 1928 there were something like 26 million peasant holdings, many of which were tiny. Peasants with such small holdings could not profitably make use of modern machinery nor were they interested in improved agricultural methods. "The solution," Stalin said, "consists in the incorporation through example and as the result of conviction, but not of force, of the smaller and smallest farms in a great industrial organization for communal, collective, and cooperative farming, employing agricultural machinery and tractors and making use of scientific methods to intensify agricultural production. There is no other solution. Our agriculture will in no other way be able to catch up with and surpass the agricultural methods of the most highly developed capitalist countries." Theoretically the plan appeared very simple. A group of at least fifteen peasants would agree to pool their holdings and also their livestock, seeds, and agricultural implements. The large farm (kolkhoz),[14] as the collective property of the group, would be run by an elected management committee and each member would share in the proceeds according to the amount of land he contributed and the work he performed. Funds for the initial requirements and the construction of new buildings would be advanced by the government; also funds to establish stations which would rent tractors and harvester combines as they were needed.

But the first attempts to win over the peasants to collective farming did not prove very successful. They were not prepared psychologically for cooperative cultivation. For centuries they had longed to possess the land they cultivated, and their conception of revolution had been acquisition of land. Even before the Bolsheviks came to power, the peasants had started to seize and divide among themselves the land of their lords. Hence they tended to be apathetic or even hostile to the idea that they should surrender their holdings. The government succeeded in convincing many poor, landless peasants of the economic advantages of collectivization, but the more prosperous would have none of it. As a result only a small fraction of the arable area was cultivated collectively on July 15, 1929. The idea of voluntary enlistment having proved unsuccessful, vast numbers of peasants were herded into collective farms by force. Zealous communists, in fact, proceeded much faster with the process than the government had intended, much faster than it was possible to train efficient managers and produce the necessary power machinery.

A special feature of the compulsory collectivization was the "liquidation of the kulaks as a class." Many thousands of peasant households registered as kulaks were broken up, the government seizing the property and sending the personnel to Siberia for convict labor. This forced deportation and the reintroduction of the requisitioning system aroused much bad blood. Rather than surrender their livestock to the government or to a kolkhoz, or because the requisitioning did not leave enough grain for feed, many peasants slaughtered their cattle, sheep, and pigs, causing a serious shortage of meat and milk. It is estimated that during the winter of 1929–1930 alone the peasants destroyed about a quarter of their

14 There were also sovkhozy or state farms managed by government officials and worked by hired labor. Bolshevik economists called them "grain factories."

cows, a third of their sheep, and half of their pigs. Furthermore, on many of the collective farms the peasants allowed a large share of the crops to rot in the field rather than hand them over to the officials. Gradually the food situation became so critical that Stalin ordered forcible collectivization to cease, whereupon many of the collective farms that had been hastily established collapsed.

Upon the announcement of its completion the First Five-Year Plan immediately gave way to a second which was to run to the end of 1937. As in the previous Plan quotas were set for the period. The Plan was soon changed, however, because the international situation had begun to deteriorate; in January, 1933, Hitler and the Nazi Party, both openly hostile to Bolshevism, rose to power. The government was forced to revise the Second Five-Year Plan in order to make increased provision for the manufacture of war materials. Special attention was also given to a more rational distribution of industry and to the establishment of new industries. During the first period raw materials had often been transported long distances when they could have been produced near the place to which they were transported. "We are doing some quite incomprehensible things," said the commissar of heavy industry in 1933. "We carry coal all the way to Vladivostok, but half of it is consumed on the way by the engines which haul it; yet there are very good mines near Vladivostok which produce perfect coal, and this ought to be utilized for local needs." [15] Much was done to eliminate such unnecessary transportation. In general, considerable progress was made in the development of heavy industry, particularly in the production of coal, metals, and war materials. Much was also done to improve the transportation system, which was one of the weakest links in the chain of Russian economy. Two and a half times as much as in the previous period was spent on building new railways and reconstructing the old lines. Since the aims of the Second Five-Year Plan were generally less ambitious than those of the First had been, the disparity between plan and fulfillment was less at the expiration of the period.

However, in the production of consumers' goods the Plan was less successful than in the development of heavy industry. When the Plan was inaugurated, the chairman of the State Planning Commission promised the workers that "the production of consumers' goods will increase two or three times and the level of consumption . . . will establish the position of the Soviet Union in 1937 as the most advanced country in the world." But the best energies of

[15] Cited by S. P. Turin in *Slavonic Review,* vol. 11 (1933), p. 59.

the people were again given to the development of heavy industry, with special emphasis on war materials. Nevertheless production increased sufficiently to permit the government to abolish rationing for all consumers' goods at the beginning of 1936. Thereafter they could be bought without restriction. But if the quantity was sufficient, the quality was still very low. As in the manufacture of most things, quality was sacrificed to quantity.

Steps were also taken to increase the productivity of the individual worker which during the tsarist period had been so low as to become proverbial. During the confusion following the revolution it fell still lower but it began to rise with the introduction of the NEP. At the end of the First Five-Year Plan, however, it was still very low in comparison with that of the leading capitalist nations. This low productivity deprived the modern plants, which had been constructed during the period of the First Five-Year Plan at such great cost, of much of their economic value. To make the workers more efficient the government adopted a system of rewards and punishments, rewarding efficient workers with an increase of wages and punishing inefficient ones with a reduction. Whenever possible the wages were put on a piecework basis, with due regard for the skill required. Moreover a systematic effort was made to give technical training to as many workers as possible. To attract large numbers to the courses the government established a special wage scale according to which a skilled worker received two and, in some instances, three times as much as a common laborer. In other words, the scheme laid the foundations for the rise of a new working-class aristocracy.

In 1935 the appearance of Stakhanovism helped speed up the industrial output. The originator of this movement was Aleksei Stakhanov, a Donets miner who, using a pneumatic pick and aided by two timbermen, succeeded in hewing 102 tons of coal in his six-hour shift. "Such performance," Stakhanov himself naïvely stated,[16] "was absolutely unheard of; seven, eight, and nine tons had been the maximum output in our pits. This output of 102 tons was a world record." The feat was played up by the press from one end of Russia to the other, with the result that Stakhanovism spread like wildfire. Every industry soon had its Stakhanovites who set phenomenal records of individual productivity. A worker in a Leningrad shoe factory, for example, demonstrated how to speed up shoe binding from 700 pairs per day to 2500 pairs. Besides being accorded special honors, such Stakhanovites had their wages doubled

[16] *The Stakhanov Movement Explained by Its Initiator* (1939), p. 8.

or trebled and were also rewarded with special living quarters, trips to Moscow, tours in the Caucasus, or permission to buy and operate a private automobile. Their example spurred other workers on to the extent that many habitually exceeded the old standards by a considerable margin. There can be little doubt that the attempt to speed up work was not only harmful to the quality of the product but also caused considerable damage to machinery. Despite all efforts the productivity of the individual worker was in 1937 still below that in other leading industrial nations. This was admitted in the official newspaper *Pravda* on August 30, 1937; at the same time, however, it was stated that the output of the individual worker was four times as high as it had been in 1913. Actually it was not four but about two and a half times as high; nevertheless the achievement is impressive.

Above all, the government went far toward completing the collectivization of agriculture during the period of the Second Five-Year Plan. Beginning in 1933, it sought to make collective farming more attractive by endeavoring to satisfy to some extent the instinct of the Russian peasant for private enterprise. As early as January, 1933, the old system of grain procurement, according to which the peasant might sell his surplus only to authorized government agencies at a fixed price, was replaced by a new one. Thenceforth the collectives were required to deliver only a definite quota to the government at a low price. The remainder, after the tractor service had been paid in kind and the seed and fodder fund had been set aside, was to be divided among the members in proportion to the quantity and quality of work each had performed. It could then be sold in the open market for what it might bring. Furthermore, members of the collective farms were permitted to do some private farming and cattle raising. Hitherto zealots had insisted that a peasant upon joining a collective must surrender all his property, even his fowls. But in 1934 the government announced the right of the peasant family to keep certain things, and in the succeeding year a congress of delegates from the collectives that had made the best records drew up a model constitution which was ratified by the government. This constitution stated specifically that "living quarters, family cattle and fowls, and the buildings necessary for their use are not socialized but remain for the private use of the member's family." In the grain, cotton, and beet regions each peasant was allowed up to two cows, one brood sow and her brood, ten sheep and goats, twenty hives of bees, and unlimited chickens and rabbits. In regions devoted to livestock an even larger number was permitted. Beyond this, each family could also have its kitchen garden and its orchard.

The measures succeeded beyond all expectation. By 1937 the collectives and state farms included about 93 per cent of the former peasant holdings. Nor was this all. Since 1933 the standard of agriculture on the collective farms had gradually improved. An increasing number had begun to introduce scientific fertilization, a proper rotation of crops, and other fundamental measures for increasing the yield. The result was that the government was able to terminate bread rationing in 1935. In the summer of 1933, despite inadequate preparations, 89.8 million tons of grain had been harvested, probably the largest crop that had been gathered in Russia up to that time. During the next two years the harvest remained about the same; but in 1936 a new record of 107 million tons was established, nearly 20 per cent above the best previous harvest. Even then the average yield per acre was so low that a higher yield may reasonably be anticipated as more and more collectives improve their agricultural methods. In 1937 more than 98 per cent of the entire crop was gathered from collectives or state farms.

In January, 1938, Russia started a Third Five-Year Plan which was to cover the years from 1938 to 1942. In general it was a continuation of the first two Plans and aimed to "overtake and surpass the leading capitalist countries not only in technical perfection but in volume of output, that is, to have greater production per person than they do." The productivity of labor was to increase by 65 per cent and the quality of production was "to be improved in every way in all branches of industry." Like the two preceding Plans it was primarily for the development of heavy industry, the increased quotas of consumers' goods being very modest. Special emphasis was put on protection against invasion from the West by the establishment of more industries in central and eastern Russia, for despite the developments of the preceding decade in the Urals and in Siberia the western part of the country was still the great center for the manufacture of armaments and munitions. Before the Third Five-Year Plan was carried out in its entirety, the Nazi armies invaded Russia (June, 1941). By this time, the Soviet Union which in 1928 had still been primarily an agricultural nation, was one of the great industrial nations of the world. Its output was more than nine times that of 1913, and the number of workers engaged in industry had risen from eight millions in 1913 to over twenty-five millions. In respect to gross industrial output the Soviet Union had advanced to first place in Europe and second in the world.

What, it may be asked, did the worker gain from this industrial development? The gain of the industrial worker was not so great as that of the peasant; nevertheless it was considerable. First of all, wages increased. According to official statistics the average wage of the worker in Soviet industry for 1937 was about 250 rubles a month as compared with an average annual wage of 703 rubles in 1928. But the increase was not evenly distributed. While a favored few—Stakhanovites, authors, engineers, and actors—received from one to three thousand rubles a month, few workers outside of Moscow and Leningrad got as much as two hundred rubles. Second, living conditions improved greatly during the period of the Five-Year Plans. Although the primary object was the development of heavy industry, a considerable increase in the production of food and consumers' goods was achieved. Third, the worker probably paid less rent in 1937 than a low-paid worker in a capitalist country. Since the state owned the land there was no expensive ground rent to pay, but because of the urban housing shortage the Russian was living in a worse place than the average worker in capitalist countries. Fourth, in 1937 there was no unemployment problem. Everyone capable of working could get some kind of job if he was not politically suspect. Because of the rapid expansion of industry there was, in fact, a dearth of workers. Fifth, in 1937 social insurance was much broader in scope than it was in most capitalist countries. Every person working in the cities was included in the government old-age insurance and in addition there was insurance against illness, accidents, death of the breadwinner of the family, burial expenses, and other things. In short, if the condition of the worker was not so good as in most capitalist countries, it was far better than it had been under the old regime.

Perhaps the statements that follow will throw further light on the condition of the worker in 1937. A Russian historian wrote that in 1937 "the average workman had 3.6 changes of underwear, and the average workingwoman had 4.4. Of shoes they have 1.5 pairs. Of course, compared with pre-Soviet years when most workers had no city clothes and no change of underwear, the present level shows great progress; but it should not be forgotten that more than a quarter of a century has passed since then and workers' requirements have greatly increased." [17] A British correspondent reported at the beginning of 1937: "With potatoes at a ruble a kilo and rye bread a few kopeks cheaper, the Russian workingman at home lives mainly on these staple commodities, eked out perhaps by salt

[17] Yugov, *Russia's Economic Front* (1942), p. 212.

fish and vegetables in season. He rarely sees meat outside the factory dining room and never butter. . . . A poor shirt costs him a
week's pay, and a month's wages will not buy him the shoddiest
suit of clothes. Rent is low, though his whole family, including a
stray grandparent or aunt, is quite likely to be sleeping in a single
room. But the Soviet factory worker has few regrets. He is better
off than he has been. . . . He is better off—so radio, press, trade
union leader, and party official all conspire to assure him—than the
worker in any capitalist country."[18]

If the Five-Year Plans effected improvement in the condition
of both the peasant and the industrial worker, they did not tend
to bring about the establishment of a classless society. Actually the
period witnessed a marked departure from the Leninist idea that all
workers were to share equally the benefits of the proletarian state.
Industrial necessity encouraged the rise of a privileged group within
the ranks of the workers. The principle was no longer "to each according to his needs" but, as stated in the constitution of 1936, "to
each according to the work performed." The members of this
privileged group, because of the specialized nature of the work they
performed, enjoyed an income and therefore a buying power far
above that of the average manual worker. Although the contrast between the two extremes was not so great as that between the very
wealthy and the very poor in a capitalist state, it did demonstrate
that Bolshevism too has its haves and have-nots. The members of
the privileged group could either spend their excess income on luxuries, deposit it in savings banks, or invest it in state loans. Even
their children enjoyed distinct advantages over those of ordinary
workers. They had not only the right to inherit the savings and
personal property of their parents, including a house or an apartment (but no land), but they could also attend schools and universities which the children of the poor could not afford.[19] In general, the striking differentiation in earning and spending power was
on the eve of World War II creating a growing emphasis on aspects
of life which a few years earlier would have been roundly denounced as "bourgeois." Moreover, it was producing a budding
class-consciousness. It was becoming the ambition of more and more
workers to rise above the average and to enter the privileged "middle
class." The Bolsheviks, for their part, contended that the inequality
in monetary reward did not mean that classes were being formed
as in bourgeois countries. State ownership of production, they

[18] *International Conciliation*, No. 335 (1937), p. 805.
[19] After September 1, 1940, all students in the higher classes of secondary schools and
in all universities and higher educational institutions were required to pay fees.

argued, would prevent the rise of dynasties founded on the owner-ship of land, railroads, etc.

ઌ

GOVERNMENT IN THE SOVIET UNION

Anyone can remember that the Union of Soviet Socialist Republics, which straddles two continents, is the largest country in the world. Embracing no less than one sixth of the land surface of the globe, it is not only larger in Europe than any European country; it is also larger in Asia than any Asiatic country. In climate it ranges "from the Baltic to the Pacific, from the icy darkness of the Arctic Circle to the vineyards of the Crimean Riviera and the cotton plantations of sunny Turkestan." Although not so populous as China, the U.S.S.R. had a population of more that 193 millions at the end of 1940.[20] This population does not constitute one nationality in the sense the Germans or French do. It includes scores of racial stocks which speak about 250 distinct vernaculars and vary widely in their customs and beliefs. The bulk of the population is made up of those generally called Russians, including the Great Russians, the White Russians, and the Little Russians.

Besides being territorially the largest country in the world, the U.S.S.R. probably has richer natural resources than any other country. It has all the basic raw materials of modern industry except rubber. And even the lack of natural rubber is offset by the fact that it has unlimited materials for the production of synthetic rubber. It is particularly rich in water power, coal, oil, and timber. Its oil deposits are so extensive that they could supply the world for centuries, and it is one of the world's largest producers of gold.

The Union of Soviet Socialist Republics was not established immediately after the Bolsheviks rose to power in 1917. The new regime was organized in 1918 as the Russian Socialist Federated Soviet Republic, which was considerably smaller than the later U.S.S.R. because so much of the country was at the time held by anti-Bolshevik forces. But in 1922 the first All-Union Congress established the U.S.S.R., composed of four republics. Others were gradually carved out in subsequent years until the number reached sixteen in 1940.[21] The administrative system consists of soviets (or

[20] Statesman's Yearbook, 1942. According to the official census of 1939, before the addition of the five new republics (1940), the population was over 170 millions.

[21] The original four were the R.S.F.S.R. and the Ukrainian, White Russian, and Azerbaijan Republics. Gradually seven others (the Georgian, Armenian, Turkmen, Uzbek, Tadzhik, Kazakh, and Kirghiz Republics) were added, and in 1940 the Karelo-Finnish, Moldavian, Estonian, Latvian, and Lithuanian Republics were admitted to the Union.

councils elected by the "laboring masses") grouped in the form of a pyramid. The base is formed by the factory, town, and village soviets. Above these basic local authorities come the district and regional soviets; then the Supreme Soviets of the individual republics. During the early years the system rested on the principle of indirect elections, that is, the members of the higher soviets were chosen not by the electorate but by the lower soviets which had been elected by the people. But in 1936 the principle of direct election of all soviets from the highest to the lowest by secret ballot was established, and all persons over eighteen years of age were permitted to vote if they earned their living by productive labor or were not specifically disbarred.

At the apex of the pyramid stands the Supreme Soviet, which is in theory the ultimate authority over the U.S.S.R. as a whole. Elected by the people like the other soviets, it consists of two chambers, the Soviet of the Union and the Soviet of Nationalities. While the members of the former are elected from all over the U.S.S.R. in the proportion of one deputy for every 300,000 people, the members of the Soviet of Nationalities are elected to represent the various republics and autonomous territories. As the highest organ of government the Supreme Soviet, in a joint session of its two chambers, appoints the Council of People's Commissars which, as previously stated, is a kind of cabinet that exercises supreme administrative authority and actually governs the country. The Supreme Soviet also appoints the Supreme Court, which is the highest judicial organ and has supervision over all other courts. The legislative function is exercised by the Supreme Soviet itself, the two chambers forming a legislative assembly often called the "Soviet Parliament." No bill can become law unless it is approved by a simple majority of both chambers. However, since the Supreme Soviet with its more than a thousand members is an unwieldy body, it has met only at intervals of two years or longer. During the periods between sessions it is represented by a Presidium of thirty-seven members, constituting a sort of "collective presidency," which exercises many of the functions of the Supreme Soviet.

Although the state is officially, as stated in the constitution of 1936, "a socialist state of workers and peasants," hostile critics have described it as a dictatorship of the Communist Party or, more specifically, as a dictatorship of the man who stands at the head of the party. The proletariat and the peasants, it is true, have a larger share of power and opportunity than they possessed in the tsarist state, but the real power is the Communist Party, the only legally organized party in the country. Numerically it was small in comparison with the population as a whole. Numbering about 200,000 in November, 1917, it grew to about two million members and a million candidates (communists who were being tested to see if they were worthy of membership in the party) in 1932. But periodical expulsions of those whose zeal for communism had slackened or who were guilty of "heresy" decreased the membership to about a million and a half in 1939. Even when the candidates are added to this number, the total represented only about 1.5 per cent of the population. All members were carefully chosen and subjected to an iron discipline. Any lapse from this discipline was summarily punished by expulsion. The supreme organ of authority is the All-Union Party Congress which usually convenes every two years. In the intervals it is represented by the Central Committee, which in turn elects a secretariat, an Organization Bureau (Orgbureau) which carries out administrative functions, and a Political Bureau (Politbureau) which formulates the policies of the party and is the real source of authority. Theoretically the members of the Politbureau are chosen by secret ballot; actually the membership is predetermined by the Secretary General of the Party, in other words by Stalin who as the principal officer of the party is virtually its dictator.

When a new constitution, often called "Stalin's constitution," was adopted by the All-Union Congress of Soviets in 1936, the Bolsheviks proclaimed it the most democratic constitution in the world. And on paper it gives much support to this claim. According to Article 125, for example, the citizens were guaranteed "freedom of speech, freedom of the press, freedom of assembly and meetings, freedom of street processions and demonstrations." Furthermore, the new election system included all the features of constitutional democracies. Article 135 stated that "all citizens of the U.S.S.R. who have reached the age of eighteen, irrespective of race and nationality, religion, educational qualifications, residence, social origin, property status, or past activity, shall have the right to take part in the elections of deputies and to be elected, with the exception of insane persons and persons condemned by court with deprivation of electoral rights." Again, according to Article 127, "citizens of the U.S.S.R. are guaranteed inviolability of the person. No one may be subject to arrest except by an order of the court or with the sanction of a state attorney." No wonder that many foreign observers, after reading the constitution, concluded that Stalin was establishing a constitutional democracy on the Western pattern, more particularly on the pattern of the United States. Unfortunately this was not the case.

The catch is that the freedom granted by the constitution must be exercised in "the interests of the working people." And the sole judge of what constitutes the interests of the working people is the Communist Party or, in other words, the Stalin regime. Stalin himself stated before the All-Union Congress that the constitution did not alter the position of the party. "I must admit," he said, "that the draft of the new constitution actually leaves in force the regime of the dictatorship of the working class as well as it preserves unchanged the present leading position of the Communist Party." In practice the regime assumed that anyone who could not conscientiously subscribe to the teachings of the Communist Party was abnormal and therefore not fit to enjoy soviet freedom. A high official of the Commissariat for Justice explained it in the following words: "We have universal suffrage, enjoyed by all except the insane and people disfranchised by court ruling. The same applies to freedom of meeting. There can be no meetings of the insane or criminals, such as Monarchists, Mensheviki, and Social Revolutionaries." [22] Nor were the elections carried out as students of the Western democracies hoped they would be, i.e., that any number of candidates would be nominated and that election meetings would be held at which the views of the various candidates would be expounded. What actually happened was that the local committees of the party set up a single official candidate in each constituency, thereby making a farce of the idea of a "free election." In other words, the voter was free to vote for the one candidate.

According to communist theory, the state will eventually "wither away" and society will be "one gigantic cooperative running itself without supervision of officials, soldiers, police, or industrial managers." But the state, far from withering away, has grown stronger and more bureaucratic with the passing years. The Communist Party, headed by Stalin, has extended the authority of the state to a point where it regulates the life of every individual down to the last detail. In short, it has constructed one of the most powerful and most arbitrary state machines in history. The task of enforcing absolute obedience was not left to the Communist Party or even to the law courts but was entrusted to the dread GPU or secret police, which exercised practically unlimited power over the citizens. It could not only send to the state penal camps those who were suspected of being hostile but could also impose the death sentence without the

[22] Cited by W. H. Chamberlin in *American Mercury*, vol. 42 (1937), p. 181.

THE KREMLIN, MOSCOW

Sovfoto

formality of a trial.[23] It was at once the eye and the sword of the state. Its procedure was so secret and so arbitrary and its agents were so ubiquitous that a general spirit of distrust was aroused. Since no one could be sure of who might be an agent of the GPU, everyone became suspicious of everyone else. The whole nation began spying on itself. As a Soviet joke had it: "Considering that the Soviet Union has 150 million inhabitants that are being spied upon and there are 150 million spies to do the spying, the country must have at least 300 million inhabitants."

RELIGION AND CULTURE

"Revolution is a storm, sweeping aside everything that stands in its path," are the words the communists inscribed on the City Council building in Moscow. Since religion stood in the path, it too was swept aside. For the Orthodox Church, which was the official religious organization of Russia, not much can be said. Up to the eighteenth century it had been at least semiautonomous, but under Peter the Great it lost every vestige of independence. After this tsar succeeded in making his will as supreme in the church as it was in the state, the activities of the church were largely devoted to the service of the state. Its primary function was to lend its sanction to the despotism of the tsar. Accordingly it taught its members that unquestioning obedience to the tsar and contentment with one's earthly lot are the highest virtues, virtues which will be rewarded in heaven. Often the poorly paid and poorly educated clergy were compelled to act as spies for the purpose of apprehending those who entertained revolutionary ideas. More than this, the church, in regarding secular education as evil, was in large part responsible for the widespread illiteracy and general backwardness of the people. In general, the church was decidedly reactionary. It fought change with all the means at its disposal and when the revolution broke out became one of the rallying centers of the counterrevolutionary forces.

Hence the communists aimed some of their heaviest blows at the church. While affirming the right of freedom of conscience, the government decreed the separation of church and state on February 5, 1918. The priests were permitted to remain but, as one leader put it, "should be maintained by those who wish to accept their poison

---

[23] In 1934 the GPU was subordinated to the People's Commissariat of the Interior, but this did not, it seems, restrict the power of the secret police. The GPU was replaced by the NKVD, which during World War II gave way to the MVD.

from them or by those who are interested in their existence." In short, all state aid was withdrawn. Furthermore, all property owned by the church was "nationalized" and large numbers of churches were converted into clubs and antireligious museums. By permission of the local soviet a congregation could continue to use such property as church buildings, chalices, and vestments which were necessary for the performance of its rites, but all congregations were forbidden to engage in social and cultural activities. Because they were counterrevolutionary in their sympathies many priests and bishops suffered imprisonment and even death during the Red Terror. The general attitude of the party toward the church was later stated in the *Programme of the Communists:* "In nearly all capitalist countries the church is just as much a state institution as is the police; and the priest is as much a state official as is the executioner, the gendarme, or the detective. He receives a government salary for administering his poison to the masses. . . . At the time of the tsar the Russian priests not only deceived the masses but even made use of the confession to find out what ideas or intentions their victims entertained toward the government; they acted as spies whilst discharging their 'sacred duties.' "[24]

However, the communists were opposed not only to the Orthodox Church; they were uncompromisingly hostile to all religions. Judaism, Mohammedanism, and the other religions were regarded as being no less "opium for the people" than Christianity. To the communist every religion was a narcotic to dull the pains caused by capitalism and to divert the attention of the masses from the evils of the present with the promise of a reward in the hereafter. "Religion," said Lenin, "is an opiate for the people, a sort of spiritual vodka." In harmony with these sentiments the communists coined such slogans as "Religion is a deception," "Religion is the opium of the toiling people," "Religion is a weapon of reaction," and "All religions and churches, all religious organizations, are armies of bourgeois reaction serving as a defense for the exploitation of the working classes." These slogans were then used as the basis for a devastating attack against all religions. Not only was the complete renunciation of religious faith made a condition of membership in the Communist Party and its junior organization, the League of Communist Youth, but priests, monks, ministers, rabbis, and all who derived their income from religious institutions were disfranchised.[25] In addition the government eliminated religion from the

[24] *Revolutionary Radicalism*, vol. 2, pp. 1745–1746.
[25] The right of franchise was restored to them in the constitution of 1936.

schools by prohibiting the giving of any religious instruction to children under eighteen in groups of more than three. In place of the old religious orthodoxies a new orthodoxy was set up—communism. New objects of reverence were substituted for the old. The words of Marx and Lenin, and, later, Stalin, became holy writ, and the ikons were replaced with pictures of Lenin and Stalin. Communist ceremonies were even devised to replace the religious observances connected with birth, marriage, and death.

The most active antireligious group was the League of Militant Atheists, approved and partially supported by the government. While the government strictly controlled the publication of religious writings, it permitted this society to issue a flood of antireligious pamphlets and magazines. The society also sent lecturers and organizers all over the country to tell the people that "religion is a delusion and God a cosmic scarecrow, set up by rulers and *bourgeoisie,* to frighten the masses into subjection." It was also permitted to send lecturers into the schools to address the children, distribute its pamphlets, and display its posters. Such activities were in accordance with the official plans to make teaching in the schools definitely antireligious. Lunacharsky, the commissar for education, stated in an article in *Pravda* (March 26, 1929) : "Theatres, concerts, moving pictures, radio, visits to museums, richly illustrated scientific and especially antireligious lectures, well-arranged periodical and nonperiodical children's literature—all this must be set in motion, developed, completed, or created for the great objective of most quickly transforming the whole growing generation into an absolutely atheistic one." [26]

Although the crusade caused a collapse of organized religion during the period following the revolution, the decade of the thirties witnessed a revival both of religious feeling and of religious activity. The very attempt to stamp out religion had the effect, in many cases, of strengthening and driving it more deeply into the lives of the people. On the other hand, the antireligious impulse gradually lost its fervor. By 1938 the Union of the Godless had ceased to exist in sixteen provinces. The communists themselves realized their failure to destroy religion. In 1937 an article in *Izvestia* said in part: "Lately the religionists in the Soviet Union have been steadily growing in numbers and becoming increasingly active." The next year another of the official newspapers made the confession: "It is much more difficult to uproot religion from the

[26] Cited in Chamberlin, "The Struggle for the Russian Soul," *Atlantic Monthly,* vol. 144 (1929) , p. 394.

consciousness of the workers than to liberate them from the exploitation of capitalists."[27] In the same year the official attitude underwent a change. Although the antireligious propaganda did not cease, it became much milder. Moreover, Soviet agencies were directed to discontinue the closing of churches, and atheists were ordered to refrain from offending the religious sentiments of believers. After the outbreak of war in June, 1941, the League of Militant Atheists was dissolved, all antireligious publications were stopped, and a liberal attitude toward worship was adopted.

The official attitude toward literature and art was different. Instead of trying to destroy them, the communists wished to mold them to their own purposes, to create a specific soviet culture. The means employed to achieve this goal varied from time to time but the goal always remained the same. "The Bolsheviks," said one soviet critic, "are interested in such things as serve the ends of the workers and their social scheme. All else may be sifted out as worthless." Writers, for example, were expected "to express in images the new aspect of the country, the changing mode of life, the new thoughts, feelings, and aspirations of the people."[28] Each branch of creative art and thought was carefully controlled by various organized groups with the unlimited support of the Communist Party. These groups diligently scrutinized all works of creative art for heresies against the Bolshevik regime. Even the works of sympathetic writers and artists were carefully pruned of anything that was not strictly in accordance with the latest policy of the party. There was no such thing for a writer or an artist as remaining neutral. "Whoever is not with us, is against us" was the principle according to which everything was judged. As a leading member of one of the groups stated the issue: "Art will be proletarian or there will be no art." In short, there was little freedom of cultural or artistic expression except within the boundaries of communist thought. Political considerations were the dominant factors in cultural life.

The policy of the government can be seen in its attitude toward literature. During the early years it was so beset with the problem of consolidating its position and of winning the civil war that it left the task of keeping the writers in line to various proletarian groups, insisting only that the writers "go with the proletariat." The result was the rise of many schools and hues of proletarian literature. After the promulgation of the First Five-Year Plan the government began to demand that writers put greater emphasis upon the "suc-

[27] Cited in Timasheff, *Religion in Soviet Russia* (1942), p. 98.
[28] Cited in Miliukov, *Outlines of Russian Culture*, ed. by M. Karpovich, part 2, p. 118.

cesses of socialist construction." In other words, it insisted that writers devote their talents to the furtherance of the Five-Year Plan. Soviet writers, vying one with another in carrying out this prescription, produced a large crop of writings but they were, with few exceptions, low in artistic value and dull in content. This period lasted until 1932 when the Central Committee decided to abolish the various proletarian groups and to organize all writers in a single Union of Soviet Writers in an effort to make Soviet literature more homogeneous. Although more variety was permitted in regard to style and form, writers being advised to improve their style by studying the old Russian classics, all members had to subscribe to the political platform of the government. The aim of the Union as defined in its statutes was "the creation of works of high artistic significance, saturated with the heroic struggle of the international proletariat, with the grandeur of the victory of socialism, and reflecting the great wisdom and heroism of the Communist Party." [29]

Thus the new literature differed in spirit from the Russian classics. Whereas, for example, the typical hero of the old literature was a weakling who struggled vainly against his environment, the hero of the new is a supremely confident person, one who has the will to carry out his designs, to translate his ideals into everyday life. Furthermore, the new literature is characterized by a strong note of optimism in contrast to the pessimism of nineteenth-century Russian literature. Whereas the poems and novels of the earlier period often closed in a tone of hopelessness and despair, those of the new breathe an all-embracing spirit of confidence in the future.

Although Soviet literature was on the whole far behind the old Russian literature in regard to artistic mastery, some notable works did appear during the period up to the outbreak of World War II. Outstanding among these are the novels of Michael Sholokhov, a Don Cossack. Born in 1905 in the northern Caucasus, the part of Russia which forms the setting for all his works, he began writing at the age of eighteen. His fame rests on *The Silent Don,* a long epic of Cossack life published in four parts, the first in 1928 and the last in 1940. It relates in great detail the story of a group of Cossack families from the period preceding the First World War through the Russian Revolution to the year 1921. Translated into most of the civilized tongues of the globe, it appeared in the United States in two parts, *And Quiet Flows the Don* (1934) and *The Don Flows Home to the Sea* (1941). Since it presents a picture of the socialist reality, it satisfied the requirements of the censors; but there is little

[29] Cited in Struve, *Soviet Russian Literature* (1935), p. 238.

of socialist heroism in it. Its Tolstoyan realism has caused many
critics to compare Sholokhov with Tolstoy himself and with such
other giants as Dostoevski, Gogol, and Gorky. In between the publication of the parts of this work Sholokhov wrote and published
Seeds of Tomorrow (1933), translated into English as *Virgin Soil
Upturned* (1935), which deals with the building of a kolkhoz or
collective farm in a Cossack village. The composer I. Dzerzhinsky
has written operas based on *And Quiet Flows the Don* and *Seeds
of Tomorrow*. The latter was also dramatized in a four-act play.

Probably the greatest cultural achievement was in education.
When the Bolsheviks took over the reins of government, Russia was
educationally one of the most backward countries of Europe. Although educational policy varied under the different tsars, in general they did little to promote the spread of education among the
masses; in fact, some of them were openly hostile toward popular
education, believing that an educated people would not submit to
their autocratic rule. In the nineteenth century Shishkov, minister
for instruction under Alexander I, who toward the end of his reign
became reactionary, said with the approval of the tsar: "To teach
the mass of people or even the majority of them how to read will
bring more harm than good." [30] Such facilities as existed were largely
intended for the nobility and the middle classes and the educational
opportunities for even these classes were not on a level with those
of such countries as Great Britain and Germany. Consequently,
according to the census of 1897, about 78 per cent of the people
were illiterate. During the reign of Nicholas II, the last tsar, considerable progress was made in the spread of popular education,
but the legacy which the Soviet government inherited was still one
of darkness. It is estimated that in 1919 more than 60 per cent of
the population could neither read nor write, while many others
could read but not write. In some of the Asiatic provinces less than
one per cent of the inhabitants were literate.

The communists regarded the extermination of illiteracy as their
most important task in the sphere of education. "You cannot build
a communist state with an illiterate people," was a slogan which
Lenin repeated frequently. Beyond desiring to lift the people to a
higher cultural level the leaders had a more definite aim. This aim,
like that of education in any other country, was to inculcate in the
minds of the citizens the ideals of the society in which they live. In
other words, the aim of Soviet education was to create "as quickly
as possible useful fighting troops for communism." The communists

[30] Cited in Bach, *Educational Changes in Russia*, p. 4.

realized not only that youth is most susceptible to propaganda but also that the school is the best place to reach the youth of a country. Accordingly the Act on National Schools prescribed that "the whole work of the schools must aim at developing the proletarian class consciousness and the instincts proper to it in the pupils, emphasizing the solidarity of all workers against capital, and preparing the children for useful productive and social activity." Every textbook, no matter what its subject, was of necessity couched in Marxian phraseology, and every new textbook had to receive the imprimatur from a special censorship of the State Publishing Department. On the other hand, Lenin warned the officials not to make the scope of education too narrow. In a speech to a conference of the Komsomol he said: "We cannot limit ourselves to communist conclusions and learn only communist slogans. You will not build up socialism like that. You will be a communist only when you have enriched your minds with the knowledge of all that humanity has created." [31]

A further reason for the fight against illiteracy was the urgent need for skilled workers for factory and farm, particularly after the inauguration of the First Five-Year Plan, for the development of which education was essential. Lunacharsky, the commissar for education, set forth as one of the aims of education "supply of the actual needs of national economy by preparation of workers in different branches and categories of qualifications."

Within the limitations imposed on it, education made phenomenal progress. By the year 1931–1932 so many new elementary schools had been opened that compulsory education for all children between eight and eleven was proclaimed. Actually, however, the average attendance for the whole Soviet Union in that year was 67.3 per cent of all children of school age. But the government did not stop at providing schools for children. It also rapidly increased the schools for illiterate adults. Furthermore, facilities were provided for the development of skilled workers. Many apprentice schools were opened in connection with factories, and vocational schools to train specialists were established in various parts of the country. New schools of higher learning were also founded and the curricula of the old universities were revised to meet the new needs. All this resulted in a gradual decrease in the number of illiterates. It is estimated that by 1930 those who could neither read nor write numbered only 33 per cent of the population. In 1939 more than thirty million children were attending school as compared with

[31] Cited in *Slavonic Review,* vol. 17 (1939) , p. 135.

eight million in 1914. In other words, almost all the children of the U.S.S.R. were receiving free elementary education. In 1933 Stalin stated in a speech that 90 per cent of the adult population had achieved literacy, but this estimate was too optimistic; a more sober estimate has it that 81.2 per cent of the population above the age of nine could be classified as literate in 1939.[32]

SOVIET FOREIGN POLICY

When the communists seized power in 1917, their leaders were certain that the Russian Revolution was but the first step toward world revolution. They believed that this world revolution was not only inevitable but imminent, that the capitalist world would soon collapse and communist states would be set up in Europe and Asia. Even Lenin himself shared this optimism. On April 5, 1919, he stated in *Izvestia:* "We are sure of our victory over the international imperialists, and this for two reasons: first, because they have taken to fighting among themselves; and second, because the soviet movement is growing rapidly throughout the world. . . . The imperialists are digging their own graves and there are plenty of people in their own countries who will bury them and pack the ground solid over their coffins."[33] Other communist leaders also prophesied the fall of capitalism in the near future. Zinoviev, the first president of the Communist International, for example, wrote: "Old Europe is dashing at mad speed toward the proletarian revolution. . . . Separate defeats will still occur in the near future. Black will, perhaps, still win a victory here and there over red. But final victory will, nevertheless, be to the red; and this in the course of the next months, perhaps even weeks. The movement is proceeding at such terrific speed that we may say with full confidence, within a year we shall already begin to forget that there was a struggle for communism in Europe, because in a year the whole of Europe will be communist. And the struggle for communism will be transferred to America, perhaps to Asia, and to other parts of the world."[34]

In March, 1919, the communist leaders created an international organization to hasten the coming of the world revolution. It was the Third Communist International[35] or Comintern. Not that the new body was officially connected with the Soviet government it-

[32] Yugow, *Russia's Economic Front for War and Peace* (1942), p. 251.
[33] Cited in Dennis, *Foreign Policies of Soviet Russia* (1924), p. 73.
[34] Cited in Florinsky, *World Revolution and the U.S.S.R.* (1933), pp. 42–43.
[35] The First International lasted from 1864 to 1872 and the Second from 1889 to 1914.

self. The connection was indirect but nevertheless real. The Communist Party of Russia controlled both the Soviet government and the Third International. The call to the communists to assemble at Moscow was signed by Lenin and Trotsky, most of the officers elected were Russians, and Moscow was made the headquarters of the organization which directed communist parties and communist activities in all other countries. "The Communist International," its statutes stated, "has for its purpose the struggle by all available means, including armed force, for the overthrow of the international *bourgeoisie* and the creation of an international Soviet republic as a transition stage to the complete abolition of the State." The manifesto issued by the first congress read in part: "The Communist International calls on the entire proletariat of the world to take part in this last struggle. Arms against arms! Force against force! Down with the imperialistic conspiracy of capital! Long live the international republic of proletarian soviets!" To this the manifesto of the second congress added: "The international proletariat will not lay down its sword until Soviet Russia has become a link in the federation of the Soviet republics of the world."

But as the months passed, the communist leaders had to confess that they had been too optimistic. Not only had the world revolution failed to materialize but such limited communist experiments as those which had taken place in Hungary and Bavaria had proved short lived, leaving in their wake an intense hatred of Bolshevism. At the end of 1919 the Soviet government stood alone, all other European states having broken off diplomatic relations with it. When the civil wars ended and the Russo-Polish War was terminated (October, 1920) a new situation confronted the Soviet government. After years of desolating war and famine, Russia was in a state of economic collapse. What the government needed above all for the economic restoration of the country was foreign capital; but a state that was aggressively communist in its internal affairs and in its relations with other countries did not attract foreign capital. So the government decided to modify its policy. As militant communism gave way to the NEP in internal affairs, so in foreign affairs the party decided to embark on a policy of partial cooperation with the capitalist states. The new policy bore fruit almost immediately. Before the end of 1921 the Soviet Union had signed trade agreements with Persia, Afghanistan, Turkey, Poland, and, most important of all, with Great Britain, and during the succeeding years trade relations were resumed with many other countries. This resumption of trade gradually led to the recognition of the Soviet government by the other states of Europe and the world. In 1924 it was officially recognized by Great Britain, France, Italy, Norway, Sweden, Denmark, Greece, China, and Mexico. Japan fell in line the next year, and Iceland and Uruguay in 1926. [36] Thus the U.S.S.R. entered the arena of world politics.

Soviet cooperation with the capitalist states became all the more necessary after the inauguration of the First Five-Year Plan in 1928. To carry out this and the succeeding Plans, machines and equipment of all kinds were needed, and also experts, engineers, foremen, and workmen with special technical knowledge, all of which could be obtained only from the capitalist nations. Accordingly cooperation instead of world revolution was accentuated. The formula was "Friendly relations with any state irrespective of its internal regime." The first two congresses of the Communist International opened with denunciations of the capitalist system, but as early as the third congress (1921) both Lenin and Trotsky told the delegates that a revision of tactics was necessary, that they must go more slowly. The world revolution, they said, was surely coming some day but not as soon as they had expected. With Stalin emphasizing the idea of "socialism in a single state," after Lenin's death, the Comintern was naturally pushed into the background. Between 1924 and 1935 only one international congress was held (Moscow, 1928) and that for the purpose of sanctioning the First Five-Year Plan, the Plan which was temporarily shelving the idea of world revolution.

Another marked characteristic of Soviet foreign policy was its emphasis on peace; in fact, after 1928 the maintenance of peace became the main object of Soviet diplomacy. A communist leader stated the issue quite clearly when he said: "The defense of peace and of the neutrality of the Soviet Union against all attempts to drag it into the whirlwind of a world war, is the central problem of Soviet foreign policy." The government needed peace in order to proceed with the industrialization of the country. War would have interrupted the execution not only of the Five-Year Plan but also of the other constructive processes upon which the success of the regime depended. Hence the period from 1930 to 1933 saw non-aggression pacts signed with the Baltic countries, France, Finland, Poland, Turkey, Czechoslovakia, Yugoslavia, and with any other country willing to sign one. Nevertheless, no effort was spared in creating a strong Red army for defense against foreign invasion. In 1930 Stalin said in addressing the Communist Party: "Our policy is a policy of peace and strengthening of trade relations with all

[36] The United States did not accord formal recognition until 1933.

countries. . . . The result of that policy is the fact that we have succeeded in maintaining peace and have not allowed our enemies to draw us into conflict, despite a number of provocative acts and adventurist assaults by the warmongers. For the future no less we shall continue this policy of peace, with all our strength and with all our resources. We do not want a single foot of foreign territory. But we shall not give up a single inch of our own territory either, to anyone. That is our foreign policy."

Russia's diplomatic situation, however, soon began to deteriorate. In 1931 the Japanese invaded Manchuria and established a strong military force with which the Russians frequently became embroiled in border clashes. Such border incidents were embarrassing to the Soviet government whose Far Eastern army, although planned as early as 1929, still existed largely on paper. Before long the diplomatic situation also grew worse in the West. In January, 1933, the Nazis rose to power in Germany and began to rattle the swords and beat the drums of war. Both the Japanese and the Germans had definite programs of conquest. While the Japanese were taking the first steps toward what they hoped would result in their complete domination of the East, the Germans were looking eastward to the Ukraine which Hitler had said in *Mein Kampf* Germany needed for *Lebensraum*. In the face of this double threat the Soviet government felt that the nonaggression pacts alone offered insufficient assurance and it therefore decided to join the League of Nations. Although the leaders had previously denounced the League in no uncertain terms because it was upholding the Versailles settlement, they were now ready to cooperate in an attempt to stabilize existing conditions and to guarantee existing boundaries. Thus the U.S.S.R. entered the League in 1934 as a permanent member of the Council. During the ensuing years it was to play an important part in world affairs.

CHAPTER EIGHT

British Economic and Imperial Problems

BRITAIN'S GOVERNMENT DESPITE the shocks it had endured, the British government emerged from World War I but little changed. Its frame, often called a constitution, is so elastic that it can readily be stretched and contracted to meet emergencies. Consequently at the end of the war Britain was still governed by king and parliament. The hereditary monarchy remained an integral and powerful part of national life but it was a "constitutional" monarchy although the king held his position by hereditary right, and the government was a parliamentary democracy. At one time the power of the sovereign had been relatively absolute. Although he was advised by a small council of nobles, he was quite free to please himself as to the laws he made. But the legislative and much of the executive power had been gradually absorbed by parliament, more particularly by the House of Commons. In theory the king's power was still great in 1918. No law could be made without his assent; he summoned parliament to meet, he prorogued and dissolved it; justice was executed in his name and all proclamations were issued by him—in short, every formal act of government was executed in the king's name. Actually he was responsible to and dependent upon parliament. He could make few public decisions and then only with the support of a cabinet minister who if challenged had to answer to the House of Commons for his conduct.

Of the ministers who made up the cabinet the most responsible and most important was the prime minister. If any one man ruled Britain it was he. The prime minister, it is true, is nominally appointed by the king, but the choice is limited to persons who have the support of the House of Commons. Without the support of the

House the prime minister could not hold his high office for a day. He in turn selects the cabinet ministers who as a body are a sort of executive committee of parliament. One writer has stated the difference between the United States and the British cabinets as follows: "In Britain ministers are the colleagues of the premier; in America they are the servants of the President. In England they are collectively responsible for the policy of the ministry; in America they are severally responsible, each for the administration of his own department, to the President; but the policy is the President's, not theirs. In England they must, by convention, sit in parliament; in America no person holding any office in the United States shall be a member of either House during his continuance in office. In England the initiative in legislation is virtually vested in the cabinet; in America neither the President nor his ministers can initiate legislation, although by presidential messages he may recommend it." [1]

Of the two houses which compose the parliament, the House of Commons is chosen by the vote of the people while the House of Lords consists of peers who hold their titles for life. Early in the nineteenth century the right to vote in parliamentary elections was still sharply restricted, but a succession of Reform Acts in the nineteenth and early twentieth centuries gradually widened it. Progress was slow but steady so that by 1914 most men enjoyed the right to vote. A further step forward was taken in 1918 in the Representation of the People Act, which for the first time extended the vote to women. By its provisions women over thirty with certain qualifications [2] were accorded the franchise. It also widened the franchise for men so as to include all over twenty-one. Although the House of Lords still plays a part in the government, the power of imposing taxes and of raising revenue is reserved for the House of Commons. Until the eve of World War I the peers had been able to retard progressive legislation and sometimes to block it altogether. In 1911, they were deprived of this power. Thereafter money bills became law if the Lords did not assent to them within one month after they received them. Other bills the Lords may retard but cannot prevent their becoming law.

---

[1] *Fortnightly Review* (February, 1920), p. 202.

[2] Besides being thirty years of age a woman had to be either a local government elector or the wife of one. Qualification for the local government franchise was six months' ownership or tenancy of land or premises. One of the objections to the Act was that no woman would admit to being over thirty. In 1928 the age for women voters was reduced to twenty-one.

§

DECLINE OF BRITISH INDUSTRY AND TRADE

The House of Commons which was sitting at the end of the war had been elected in 1910 for a maximum period of five years. But since a political contest might have hindered the war effort, the House with the active approval of the country prolonged its own life by temporary enactments from year to year. In 1918 Britain was ruled by a coalition cabinet formed in 1916 by David Lloyd George, a Liberal. Although the prime minister and his leading colleagues were Liberals,[3] the government had gradually become more and more Conservative both in membership and in policy. As the prime minister in the crucial days of the war, Lloyd George had never faltered, never lost heart. After the armistice the belief that he had been largely instrumental in winning the war gained wide acceptance. Nor did he and his supporters miss an opportunity to cultivate this impression. In showing a newspaper reporter about his beautiful residence, known as Chequers, he pointed to a room and remarked: "This is the room where the war was won." Before the general election of December, 1918, Lloyd George skilfully appealed to the country to support "the men who had won the war." He assured the people that he would make Germany pay the cost to the last farthing, gave the impression that he was ready to hang the kaiser, and promised that he would make Britain "a fit place for heroes to live in." The people, who were just celebrating the hard-won victory, responded by returning him to Westminster with a vast majority at his back, the coalition securing 526 parliamentary seats out of a total of 707.

Having promised "a happier country for all" Lloyd George set about the task of achieving it. He called to his side men with big ideas and bade them reconstruct the national life under state direction. Little heed was paid to the cost. The idea of public thrift was to him an old-fashioned doctrine, as obsolete as mid-Victorian art. Money was spent freely on education, housing, agriculture, and other projects. And the money did not come out of German but out of British pockets. To provide the necessary funds the people were taxed and taxed. Wiser men sounded the warning that the extravagance of the government would lead to national bankruptcy, but Lloyd George and his colleagues continued merrily on their prodigal way. So that it could the more easily bear the tax burden, labor was encouraged by the coalition cabinet to be "audacious" in its de-

[3] A large section of Liberals under Mr. Asquith stood aloof.

mands upon capital. Labor needed little urging. Widespread strikes forced employers to increase wages and shorten hours. All went well while the industrial boom lasted. But in 1920 the fictitious prosperity collapsed and a trade slump came.

Previously Britain had for many decades been the workshop of the world. It was in Britain that power machinery was invented and first used. This gave the British a great advantage over other nations. They could manufacture certain articles, particularly textiles, more cheaply and efficiently, and the world was ready to consume these articles in ever increasing volume. In the textile industry no less than 75 per cent of the manufactures were exported. The demand for British goods was so great and the profits were so large that agriculture was more and more neglected. The great landowner became an industrialist, and the farm laborer became a mill worker. While receiving high prices for manufactured goods, the British could buy food cheaply from other countries. Thus Britain became more dependent on external trade than any other country in the world. British ships went forth laden with manufactured goods and coal, and returned with food and raw materials. In 1913 foreign countries supplied 73.9 per cent of the food and 67.6 per cent of the raw materials used in Britain. In other words, the use of power machinery transformed a poor country which had been an exporter of raw materials into a comparatively rich nation exporting manufactured goods and importing food and raw materials. This development, which began in the eighteenth century, continued right through the nineteenth. At the end of the century British wealth was proverbial and London was the financial center of the world. During the early years of the twentieth century foreign competition, particularly on the part of Germany, increased considerably and caused apprehension and political reactions. Nevertheless, the export trade continued to grow by leaps and bounds. During the period from 1900 to 1913 it increased by almost 80 per cent.

During World War I the situation changed. Intent upon winning the war the British concentrated their attention on the production of war materials; hence they had few manufactured products to sell abroad. Such foreign trade as continued was seriously curtailed by the German submarine campaign. Nations which had previously depended upon Britain for textiles, iron and steel products, and other manufactured goods had to go without them, buy elsewhere, or manufacture the goods themselves. At the time not much thought was given in British circles to this dislocation of trade. It was confidently believed that with the return of peace the old order would prevail. This belief was strengthened by a sudden and intensive trade boom immediately after the armistice. In the fall of 1920, however, this boom came to an end and was followed by a prolonged depression. The years after the war, instead of bringing a return to normality, raised one of the gravest problems with which a modern nation has been forced to contend.

The chronic "trade anemia" was caused by the combined operation of a number of forces. First of all, the fact that Britain produced but few civilian goods during World War I impelled its customers to develop their own industries. In other words, countries which had previously supplied their wants by importing British goods made themselves more or less industrially self-sufficient. Second, countries which had been pressing Britain in the world markets on the eve of the war became more serious competitors after its close. The end of the war saw not Britain but the United States holding first place in export trade. Nor was the United States the only serious competitor. Belgium, France, Germany, and Japan, among others, had also made serious inroads on Britain's foreign trade. In Belgium and France, for example, the factories destroyed by the Germans were replaced by modern industrial plants and the Germans themselves were not slow in scrapping antiquated machinery and obsolete methods in favor of modern equipment and improved methods. In these countries as well as in the United States mass production of standard articles was introduced as a means of producing cheaper goods.

In all this Britain lagged behind. Much of its equipment was obsolete and its organization and methods were unsuited to the new conditions. In some cases the capital requisite for purchase of new equipment was lacking; in others the unions refused to sanction the use of labor-saving machinery because they feared it would increase unemployment. Some industrialists and mine operators who could afford to do so refused to modernize their methods, preferring to retain those they had previously developed or inherited. The use of antiquated methods coupled with high wages put the British at a disadvantage in competition with other countries. Other factors helped to aggravate the depression, not the least of them being taxes. High taxes, made necessary by the war debt of thirty-five billion dollars and the severe strain the dole system put on the national treasury, severely handicapped industry and dried up much of the purchasing power of the people. Finally, in 1925 the British restored their currency to its prewar value in gold, at a time when the currencies of Germany, France, and Italy were badly depreciated.

This step, by raising the price of British goods, further handicapped the British in their race for world markets.

British manufactures consequently lost ground in foreign markets. At every turn they were met by American, German, or French goods at prices so low that they could not meet them. Since Britain's prosperity had for more than a century been largely dependent upon overseas markets, the repercussions at home were severe. More than this, since the British by and large adhered to a policy of free trade, there were few tariff barriers to keep foreign goods from flooding the home market. The resulting curtailment of both foreign and home markets checked production and threw large numbers of workers into idleness. Some industries, of course, suffered more than others. Thus textiles alone provided more than 25 per cent of the total unemployment. Previously a large volume of trade had been achieved by the sale of cheap, coarse cloths in the East, particularly in India and China, but after the war various factors contributed toward depriving the British of this market. Among them were the civil strife in China, the boycott of British goods in India, the establishment of cotton factories in India, and, above all, the competition of the Japanese, who got a firm hold on the Asiatic textile market by underselling their competitors.

Other British industries suffered even more. One of these was shipbuilding. Toward the end of the nineteenth century about 80 per cent of all ships built in the world came from British shipyards, and at the outbreak of World War I Britain's share was still 60 per cent. After the war, however, the importance of these shipyards began to decline despite the great demand for tonnage. Again the British could not meet the competition of other countries. The same was true in the iron and steel industries. In the development of the motor car, for example, the British, with their old-fashioned methods, were soon far outstripped by American manufacturers. Probably the darkest spot in the industrial picture was coal mining. Coal had, in a sense, been the very foundation of British prosperity. Not only was it used to generate the steam which turned the wheels of industry, but it had made possible the smelting of ore. Large quantities had also been exported in vessels whose furnaces were stoked with coal. During the period before World War I about two thirds of all coal exported in the world came from British mines. Among the reasons which caused the decline of British coal mining were the antiquated methods employed by the operators. So long as there was no serious competition they were able to sell their coal at a profit, but exports declined when such countries as Germany and

France modernized their methods. Moreover, the use of coal in general was decreasing because of the development of hydroelectric power on land and the increasing use of oil as the motive power in ships.

At first it was believed that the slump was a temporary result of the war and that Britain would soon recover its prosperity. But when the slump became chronic, the question of how to raise the country out of the bog of depression became the government's major problem. During the years preceding 1929 and in that year there was some degree of improvement, but after 1929 conditions took a sharp turn for the worse. In 1930 and 1931, for example, production of pig iron and steel declined to about one half the 1929 levels. Unemployment increased in the same ratio, many workers remaining totally unemployed for years. To avoid national catastrophe these people had to be supported. In 1920 Lloyd George's coalition government had extended the scope of the Unemployment Insurance Act to include most workers. The sudden upsurge of unemployment and the continued depression soon exhausted the funds allocated for this purpose and made it necessary for the government to meet the deficit by loans. The sums spent in various forms of relief up to the end of 1923 alone totaled £400 million. As the number of unemployed increased, particularly after 1929, the problem of financing the "dole," the name given to unemployment compensation, became increasingly difficult.

CABINETS AND GOVERNMENTS

Meanwhile various cabinets and administrations had failed to provide a solution for the economic depression and the resulting widespread unemployment. Lloyd George's government, which had won by a landslide in 1918, lost its support because the results of its prodigious expenditures were pathetically small. As long as the trade boom lasted, nobody cared how much public money the administration was spending to make things pleasant all around. But when the slump came and the people discovered that the national treasury was empty, their faith in the prime minister evaporated. Leading men of all parties became convinced that his continued presence at the helm would spell nothing less than complete ruin. In 1922 the Conservatives brought matters to a head by withdrawing from the coalition, a move which forced the resignation of the prime minister. Lloyd George tried to rally the country behind him with the slogan of "Retrenchment," but the jig was up. Receiving but little support in the general elections, he retired from the political scene. Thus, amid general rejoicing, the wartime coalition government came to an end.

In the general election of 1922 the Conservative Party won a clear majority of seventy, while the Labor Party increased its strength to 138. The tenure of the Conservatives was but shortlived. Regarding protective tariffs as the only remedy for the industrial slump, the cabinet precipitated a new election on the issue. Not only were both the Laborites and the Liberals opposed to protection but public opinion in general was not ready to support it. The result was a sweeping defeat for the Conservatives. Neither the Laborites nor the Liberals obtained a majority, but together they had a majority of over ninety. As the Labor Party had more members in the House than the Liberal Party, the king requested Ramsay MacDonald, leader of the Labor Party, to form a cabinet. Thus Britain received its first Labor government. The position of this government, however, was precarious, since it could be maintained only through the sufferance of the Liberals, who were of no mind to further the program of the Labor Party. Hence the government was unable to redeem the pledges it had made before the election. As early as the fall of 1924 the Liberals withdrew their support over the question of a loan to Russia. When the House of Commons voted an inquiry into the relationship of the Labor Party with the Soviet government, MacDonald, fearing that the inquiry might produce damaging revelations, asked the king to grant a dissolution.

In the ensuing election the Conservatives won a majority of two hundred over all other parties combined. The representation of the Labor Party declined and the Liberal Party, now hopelessly split into two factions, was reduced to a remnant of its former strength. For the next four and a half years the Conservatives gradually lost their popularity, partly because they failed to find a remedy for the depression and unemployment, partly because they failed to redeem their pledge of reducing public expenditures. Consequently they lost their majority in the general election of 1929. The Labor Party, which secured the largest representation, now got its second opportunity to form a government with Ramsay MacDonald as prime minister. Again Labor did not command a majority but had to rely upon Liberal support. The supreme issue was the economic situation, but the Laborites and Liberals could not agree on a bold policy for the relief of unemployment. Hardly had Labor come into power when the great Wall Street collapse took place. British foreign trade took another turn for the worse, and unemployment in Britain as in other countries increased. The figures rapidly rose from 1.1 million to 2.5 million, necessitating the borrowing of large sums to pay the dole.

Ramsay MacDonald, as the leader of the party having the largest representation in the House, remained prime minister and formed a National Government containing representatives of all parties for the single purpose of restoring the financial position of the country. By sharply curtailing expenses this government managed to balance the budget but in spite of these measures the country was driven off the gold standard. When the people were asked to express their approval or disapproval in a general election (October, 1931) they returned only fifty Laborites to the House, while the Conservatives secured 471. This acquisition of strength encouraged the Conservatives to revive the question of a protective tariff as the only way out of the slough of industrial depression. Not that there were no customs restrictions in Britain. At various times and for various reasons duties had been imposed on a number of articles, but there was no general tariff. This state of affairs satisfied neither the free traders nor the protectionists. In 1932 the Conservatives used their power to pass a number of Acts which imposed duties on most imports, excepting food and raw materials. These Acts made Britain in the inclusiveness of its tariffs, though not in their height, as protectionist as any country in the world. Imports coming from within the empire were exempted from duty. Having given the Dominions preferential treatment, Britain in turn asked the Dominions for concessions. As early as August, 1932, the so-called Ottawa agreements were signed by which all the Dominions except Ireland accepted the principle of reciprocal concessions.

As the decade of the thirties moved toward its end Britain experienced some degree of economic recovery. A comparison of 1937 with 1929, the highest previous year, shows an increase of over 20 per cent in industrial production and a commensurate increase in the number of employed. In part this revival must be ascribed to the tariff protection, which gave manufacturers most of the home market. Among the other factors were the efforts of the government to reorganize and modernize British industries, so that they could compete with those of other countries. Partly by legislation and partly by other methods much was done to bring about the amalgamation of the many individual mines and the modernization of processes. In 1937 many textile manufacturers assented to a government request to modernize their machinery. Even more important was the intervention of the government in a deliberate effort to develop and encourage heavy industry.

6.

A KING ABDICATES

On January 20, 1936, King George V, who had ruled Great Britain since 1910, passed away at the age of seventy. No British ruler had used more wisely "the right to be consulted, the right to encourage, and the right to warn." He had been a plain man doing his plain duty. His simplicity of manner and of outlook had endeared him to his people. Probably no British monarch before him was so highly respected. Whereas thrones had toppled all over Europe, the British throne had been made infinitely stronger during his reign. His death, therefore, caused genuine mourning. His son, who took the title of Edward VIII, had traveled widely in Britain and in the empire and had long been a popular figure. For forty-two years he had prepared for the throne. He had done all that the people expected of him except one thing. He had not married. He was the first bachelor to ascend the British throne since George III in 1760.

Great things were expected of the new monarch, but in less than a year he had abdicated and his brother, the Duke of York, had become king as George VI. The reason for his abdication was his desire to marry Mrs. Wallis Warfield Simpson, an American who had been divorced twice. Prime minister Stanley Baldwin, when advised of Edward VIII's intention, refused to sanction the marriage because he feared that the chain of empire, in which the king was the main link, would snap over the "scandal." The Church of England also opposed marriage to a woman twice divorced. Others who supported the opposition included the royal family, most members of the Houses of Commons and Lords, and a majority of the newspapers. For his part, the strong-willed king insisted that his marriage was a private act which did not affect his public position. When this availed him nothing, he suggested to Mr. Baldwin that he marry Mrs. Simpson without making her his queen. The answer was: "No such thing as a morganatic marriage is known to our law. . . . His Majesty's Government are not prepared to introduce such legislation." Pointing out to Edward that "in the choice of the Queen the voice of the people must be heard," he pleaded with him to sacrifice his personal interests for the good of the empire. But the fair-haired Edward stood like a rock against the wave of appeals.

Britain and the world did not have to wait long for the final decision. On December 9, a little more than a fortnight after the issue was first raised, Edward VIII notified the cabinet that he had decided to abdicate. When they urged him to reconsider, he answered: "His Majesty . . . regrets that he is unable to alter his

THE BRITISH COMMONWEALTH OF NATIONS

BRITISH EMPIRE

COMMONWEALTH OF NATIONS

decision." The next day he signed a formal abdication. In a message to the empire he said: "I have found it impossible to carry the heavy burden of responsibility and to discharge my duties as king as I would wish to do without the help and support of the woman I love." It marked the first time a British king and emperor voluntarily stepped down from his throne. On the day originally set for the coronation of Edward VIII his brother was crowned as George VI. The wife of the new sovereign, Lady Elizabeth Bowes-Lyon, daughter of a Scottish earl, became Queen Elizabeth and their ten year old daughter Elizabeth became heir apparent. George VI, who had lived a quiet life, did not at his accession enjoy his brother's popularity. Many felt that the prestige of the crown had been greatly diminished and would never be the same again. These fears were unwarranted. The storm subsided almost as quickly as it had arisen; the ship of state righted itself and sailed smoothly on.

THE BRITISH COMMONWEALTH OF NATIONS

The British monarch, in addition to being king of Great Britain, was also the sovereign head of the British Empire. This empire was an agglomeration of territories sprawling over more than a quarter of the globe. Its units were scattered so widely as to justify the statement, "The sun never sets on the British Empire." The population, representing all colors and creeds, was listed in 1922 as 440,923,000 or more than a fifth of the entire population of the earth. Of this number no less than 319 million lived in India and not more than 65 million were of European origin. The components of the empire included first of all, the Dominions of Canada, Newfoundland,[4] Australia, New Zealand, South Africa, and the Irish Free State (Eire), all of which were virtually self-governing independent nations so far as their internal affairs were concerned. India had a special status as a sort of semidominion. Next in rank were the crown colonies, which differed widely in the extent of self-government accorded them. The better known crown colonies are the Bahamas,

[4] Because of financial difficulties Newfoundland reverted to the status of a crown colony in 1933.

☼☼

THE BRITISH COMMONWEALTH OF NATIONS. *Since this map was drawn, the status of India has changed; for greater details, consult the map on* *page 773.*

Bermuda, Jamaica, Trinidad, Gibraltar, Malta, Northern and Southern Rhodesia, Ceylon, Burma, Hong Kong, and Singapore. Furthermore, there were protectorates of various kinds; in other words, native states under British rule or guidance. Most of these, e.g., Nigeria, Uganda, and the Gold Coast, were in Africa, an important exception being Sarawak in Borneo. Finally, the empire included the mandates, former German colonies or Turkish dependencies, taken over in 1919 under authorization of the League of Nations. These included Palestine, German East Africa, German Southwest Africa, Western Samoa, German New Guinea, Arab Iraq, and lesser bits. Not since Roman times has there been such a hodgepodge of territories and peoples.

When World War I broke out, there were many, including the Germans, who were certain that the imperial structure would collapse under the strain of the war. They were convinced that there would be widespread and determined revolts in Ireland, India, Egypt, and South Africa. During the course of the war there was, it is true, a rebellion in Ireland that was soon put down, and there were uprisings in South Africa and some disturbances in Egypt and India. But the trouble was insignificant in comparison with the wholehearted support the empire gave the war effort. The decision of the cabinet to plunge the empire into war was never challenged. The citizens of South Africa soon forgot their grudges, the Irish sent a large number of men into the battle against the Central Powers, and even the Moslems of India did not throw in their lot with Turkey which was the home of the head of their religion. From every land and clime the citizens of the empire, fired with a common loyalty and obligation, rallied to the flag, and all the Dominions unhesitatingly put their naval and military forces under the control of the British authorities. The war was won without the loss of an inch of territory; on the contrary, as a result of the peace settlement the empire was extended by some 800,000 square miles.

Nevertheless, a far-reaching change in the attitude of the colonies toward the mother country did take place. The war served to hasten and intensify a local national feeling in the Dominions. "The Dominions," as a citizen of one of them put it, "have reached self-consciousness in the war and a sense of national pride and nationhood." Each of the greater Dominions emerged from the war with a wholly crystallized determination to play a new role in the imperial association. As regards internal affairs the Dominions had become virtually independent in practice if not in theory.[5] On the

[5] The royal veto, though obsolete in Great Britain itself, could still be exercised on Dominion legislation but had been exercised only on rare occasions.

other hand, in foreign affairs, in the general issues of war and peace, the Dominions had been expected to accept the ruling of parliament, in which assembly they had neither voice nor vote. What they wanted was a share in making the policies from which war might flow. As early as 1915 the Canadian minister of justice stated: "Our recognition of this war as ours, our participation in it, spontaneous and voluntary as it is, determines absolutely once and for all that we have passed from the status of the protected colony to that of the participating nation." Not long thereafter a former prime minister of Australia voiced the sentiment of his country in the words: "I have been prime minister, but all the time I had no say whatever about imperial policy—no say whatever. Now that can't go on." General Smuts, prime minister of the Union of South Africa, stated emphatically that the old prewar British Empire was "gone in the sense of colonies or subordinate nations clustering around one master nation."

In 1917 the Imperial War Conference added its voice to those demanding a change. The Conference drew up a statement which asserted that its members "are of the opinion that the readjustment of the constitutional relations of the component parts of the empire is too important and intricate to be dealt with during the war. . . . They deem it their duty, however, to place on record their view that any such readjustment, while thoroughly preserving all existing powers of self-government and complete control of domestic affairs, should be based upon a full recognition of the Dominions as autonomous nations of an Imperial Commonwealth." In the years immediately following World War I no legal steps were taken to grant the demand of the Dominions, but the process of development from a colonial to an equal status continued. Thus the Dominions were separately represented at the Peace Conference and were also accorded memberships in the League of Nations. Furthermore, Canada in 1920 received the consent of the British government to the appointment of a Canadian minister at Washington. Although he was not appointed until 1926, Canada in 1922 did proceed to negotiate, without the participation of the British government, a treaty with the United States in regard to halibut fisheries.

Finally in 1926 the Balfour Committee of the Imperial Conference sought to clarify the issue. It defined the Dominions as "autonomous communities within the British Empire, in no way subordinate to one another in any respect of their domestic or external affairs, though united by a common allegiance to the crown and freely associated as members of the British Commonwealth of Nations." The definitions and statements of the Conference of 1926 constituted a body of conventions or understandings, but they were not legal rules. In law the Dominion legislatures were far from "equal in status" with the British parliament. In 1929 a technical committee was appointed to study the matter; the result was the Statute of Westminster, passed by parliament in 1931. It affirmed that "no law hereafter made by the parliament of the United Kingdom shall extend to any of the Dominions as part of the law of that Dominion otherwise than at the request and with the consent of that Dominion." In brief it made each of the Dominion parliaments equal in its sphere.

Thus the Statute of Westminster wiped out the last vestiges of the old British Empire. "The day of the centralized empire is past," said premier Bennett of Canada; "we no longer live in a political empire. . . . With the adoption of the Statute of Westminster the old empire disappears." In its place the statute constituted the British Commonwealth of Nations, an empire resting solely on voluntary cooperation. Every Dominion became master of its own destiny. The sole remaining legal tie that united the otherwise independent nations was their common allegiance to the person of the British sovereign. In other words, the king displaced parliament as the formal and actual pivot of the empire. It is one of the most remarkable changes of modern times. Although it may appear as if the Statute of Westminster weakened the ties, it actually strengthened them. As Sir Austen Chamberlain put it, "In emphasizing liberty, unity has been assured."

Meanwhile the solidarity of the empire was being put to a severe test by events in Ireland. The Home Rule Bill, about which Gladstone had thundered, was forever at the point of being passed but final action was never taken. In 1914 the Home Rule Bill was really passed and signed by the king but because the British Empire was at war with Germany the operation of the Act was suspended for the duration. This greatly displeased the people of southern Ireland. On Easter Monday, 1916, a revolt broke out, with the insurgents proclaiming Ireland a republic. The British succeeded in forcibly suppressing the uprising but did not eliminate the causes of the discontent. The hidden fires of rebellion were being stoked by the Sinn Fein Party [6] which became the dominant political factor in southern Ireland. After southern Ireland had voted Sinn Fein in the parliamentary elections, the members who had been elected to the House of Commons flatly refused to go to England, stating that

[6] The words "Sinn Fein" mean "we ourselves alone," a motto adopted by the founders of the party.

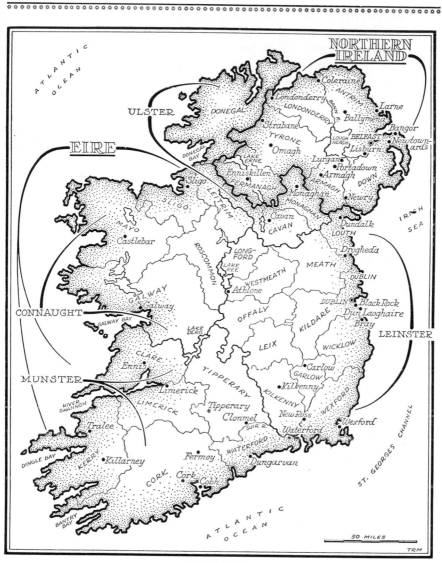

IRELAND

Eire, as the Irish Free State has been officially called since December, 1937, consists of Leinster, Munster, and Connaught provinces and three counties of the former Ulster province. Northern Ireland embraces Antrim, Armagh, Down, Fermanagh, Londonderry, and Tyrone counties of Ulster.

Ireland had never by its own consent been part of the United Kingdom. Instead they organized the Dail Eireann (Gaelic words meaning Irish Parliament) which set up a republican government to supplant the British regime.

The British government, construing this as open revolt, at once took measures to suppress the movement. A special force of ex-soldiers known from their uniforms as the Black and Tans was raised to deal with the situation. For two years a civil war raged in the unhappy island, taking its toll in lives and property. At length in 1920 the British government tried the solution of setting up two parliaments, one for the six counties of Northern Ireland (sometimes called Ulster), which are strongly Protestant, and the other for the rest of Ireland, which is Catholic. Both were to be subordinate to the British parliament in Westminster. Southern Ireland, led by the Sinn Fein Party, refused to have anything to do with the plan. The existing anarchy finally impelled the more reasonable forces in the Sinn Fein to negotiate a treaty with the British in 1921, whereby southern Ireland became the Irish Free State with a Dominion status similar to that of Canada. With the establishment of the Free State the Gaelic language was resurrected from the past and made the official tongue. This still did not satisfy the more extreme Sinn Feiners, led by Eamon De Valera, an American by birth whose American citizenship had saved him from execution at the hands of a firing squad after the Easter Rebellion of 1916. Again civil war flared up. This time Sinn Feiners were arrayed against Sinn Feiners. It was not until 1923 that the followers of De Valera decided to participate in the elections and attend meetings of the Dail. Adherents of the Irish Free State could now feel that its position was secure. In September of the same year the Free State entered the League of Nations, and the following year Irish representatives attended the Imperial Conference in London.

Although De Valera and his followers cooperated with the government, they were still not satisfied. Upon the advent of his party (Fianna Fail) to power in 1932, De Valera proceeded to introduce various political and constitutional policies aimed at diminishing British control over his people. In 1937 he capped his efforts with a new constitution which went into effect on January 1, 1938, in the twenty-six counties of southern Ireland. It was written for "the whole of Ireland," but Protestant Northern Ireland firmly refused to unite with the South. Besides changing the name of the Irish Free State to the State of Eire (pronounced Aireh), the old Irish name for Ireland, the constitution broke the last ties with Britain by abolishing the office of Governor-General. Even the name of King George VI was not mentioned except in a clause providing for cooperation with Britain in international affairs. Thus Ireland remained in the British Commonwealth of Nations. During the subsequent months the British and Irish composed, with one exception, all their outstanding differences. Only the question of Irish unity was not settled; the northern counties still remained detached from the rest. Even the election of Dr. Douglas Hyde,[7] a Protestant, as president of Eire in 1938 failed to persuade the 1,290,000 inhabitants of Northern Ireland that a political union was desirable. When World War II broke out in 1939, Eire adopted a policy of neutrality while Ulster joined Britain in the war.

Another vexing problem was that of Palestine, reverenced by Christian, Jew, and Moslem alike as the Holy Land. A narrow strip of land about the size of Vermont at the eastern end of the Mediterranean, Palestine had for years repeatedly been the scene of bitter conflict. Among the nations which contended for its possession were the Hebrews, Philistines, Babylonians, Persians, Syrians, Romans, Arabs, and Turks. The conflict in the twentieth century arose from a clash of Arab and Jewish nationalist aspirations. Toward the end of the nineteenth century a nationalist movement, generally known as Zionism, was organized for the purpose of establishing a Jewish state in Palestine where persecuted Jews could find refuge. As early as 1903 Zionist leaders appealed to Britain for aid in obtaining permission from the sultan of Turkey for such colonization. When the Turks remained cold to the proposal, Britain offered the Zionists a district in East Africa, but the offer was refused. Then came World War I. Realizing that an Arab uprising would greatly weaken Turkey, the British decided to fan the embers of Arab nationalism into a consuming flame. They made certain vague promises to the effect that Turkey's Arab provinces would be granted independence. The result was that the Arabs, interpreting the promise as including Palestine, threw in their lot with the Allies. In 1917 the Zionist leaders succeeded in obtaining from Lord Balfour, then British foreign secretary, a statement which has since become famous as the Balfour Declaration. "His Majesty's Government," it said, "view with favor the establishment in Palestine of a national home for the Jewish people, and will use their best endeavors to facilitate the achievement of this object, it being clearly understood that nothing shall be done which may prejudice the civil and religious rights of existing non-Jewish communities in Palestine."

[7] De Valera as prime minister remained the dominant power.

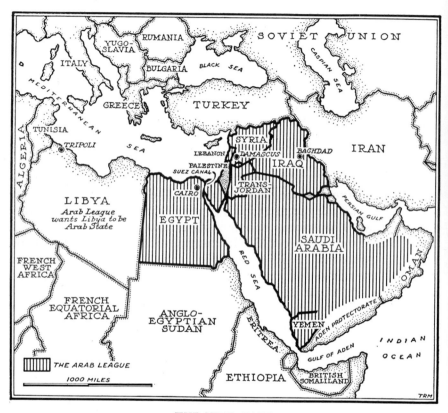

THE NEAR EAST

As a result of British efforts during the First World War, the Arab lands of the former Turkish Empire were set up into a number of states which between the two World Wars were mandates of Britain or France.

The British promises resulted quite logically in contradictory claims. On the one hand, the Zionists interpreted the Balfour Declaration as promising them a Jewish state in Palestine; on the other, the Arabs were no less emphatic in insisting that Palestine had been promised to them as an independent state. The Jews, in support of their claim, maintained that their history had been mainly the history of Palestine and that it was the country of their national literature. The Arabs for their part asked, "Under what reasonable pretext do the Jews claim Palestine, which has not been their home for more than 2000 years?" They contended that Palestine had been their home for 1300 years and that they represented the predominant element of the population. Actually about three quarters of the population was composed of Arabs, the remaining quarter being made up equally of Jews and Christians.[8]

Arabs and Jews, both being Semitic and claiming descent from Abraham, had lived in harmony and mutual tolerance under the rule of the Turks. But under British rule the flames of hatred swept over Palestine like a forest fire. Although they benefited from the new prosperity, the Arabs resented the introduction of modern machinery and improved methods, preferring to adhere to their ancient ways. The continuing Jewish immigration caused them to fear their domain would be transformed into an occidental state; hence they demanded cessation of Jewish immigration and of the sale of land to Jews. When the influx continued, the resentful Arabs launched a campaign of terrorism. Guerillas harassed the country, murdering Jews wherever they could find them. Naturally the Jews retaliated in kind, so that fear and anarchy gripped the country. After quelling serious disorders in 1920 the British hoped that the Arabs and Jews would gradually compose their differences in a common Palestinian citizenship, but the reverse was true. Feelings became more bitter with the passing years. Despite all attempts of British soldiers to suppress guerilla bands, the Arabs continued to challenge British authority. The conflict assumed the dimensions of a holy war when after 1933 larger numbers of Jews came to Palestine to escape the Nazi persecutions. By the beginning of 1936 the number of Jews had increased to 350,000, but they were still outnumbered by the Arabs more than two to one.

During the period between the two World Wars the British had proposed various solutions but to no avail. In 1922 the British High

[8] According to the official census of 1922 there were 83,000 Jews in a population of 757,000. During the succeeding years the ratio changed rapidly. In 1945 it was estimated that the Moslems numbered 472,100 and the Jews 444,912.

Commissioner sought to calm the unrest by proposing a Legislative Council in which both parties would be represented. The Arabs would have no part of it. They insisted, in turn, upon Arab independence, claiming that Palestine was the only Arab country that was not moving toward independence. In 1935 a similar plan was projected with a council of fourteen Arabs, seven Jews, and seven Britons. Both Arabs and Jews denounced the plan. While the latter feared that a council on which they were outnumbered two to one would be inimical to their interests, the Arabs continued to insist on complete self-government. In 1936 after fifteen years of bloody strife the question was turned over to a British Commission for study. The commission styled the situation "an irrepressible conflict" and proposed a plan of partition according to which Palestine was to be divided into three parts: the north and a long coastal strip was to be given to the Jews; the interior, together with a coastal strip down to Egypt, was to be joined to Arab Transjordania; and an area around the Holy Places was to be held by the British. Arabs and Jews alike violently denounced the plan. While the Jews felt that the territory allotted them would limit their expansion, the Arabs continued to stand on their demand for the whole country.

All this prompted a correspondent of the London *Times* to write that "between Jew and Arab the British official has sometimes found himself in the position of a third party whose attempts to prevent two neighbors from stoning each other merely bring him well under the fire from both."

CHAPTER NINE

Fascist Italy

THE RESURGENCE OF
DICTATORSHIP
F EW things seemed better established
at the beginning of World War I than the reign of democracy. After
the French Revolution broke the ground through the destruction
of the last relics of feudalism and by undermining the absolutist
superstructure which had been erected during the previous centuries, representative government slowly took root and was well
established in a number of states before the end of the nineteenth
century. As the years went on, more and more people shared the
conviction that it was only a question of time when free political
institutions would be the rule everywhere; in fact, to many the
triumph of political democracy seemed inevitable. Thus one may
read in a Rectorial Address of 1876 to the students of Aberdeen
University: "There is no use mincing the matter: unless the world
goes back, democracy must go forward. The will of the people must
more and more prevail." Near the turn of the century the historian
Lecky declared: "I do not think that anyone who seriously considers
the force and universality of the movement of our generation in the
direction of democracy can doubt that this conception of government
will necessarily, at least for a considerable time, dominate in all
civilized countries." [1] Just a few months before the outbreak of the
war one of Italy's distinguished historians wrote: "The fruits of the
French Revolution are still ripening. Everywhere the classes opposed
to the aristocracy—tradespeople, artisans, and peasants—are organizing and taking an interest in public affairs. They are learning to
read the papers and to make use of their political rights. They are
beginning to demand explanations, to discuss and criticize those

[1] *Democracy and Liberty,* vol. 1 (1896), p. 212.

various forms of authority which formerly they blindly obeyed."[2]

The conviction that popular government would soon be the order in all civilized countries was further fortified by World War I. The triumph of democracy throughout the world was, in fact, the moral aim of the war effort on the Allied side. As President Wilson put it in 1917: "Our object is to vindicate the principles of peace and justice in the life of the world as against selfish and autocratic power and to set up amongst the really free and self-governed peoples of the world such a concert of purpose and action as will henceforth ensure the observance of those principles." Accordingly the Allies adopted as their battle cry the slogan, "Make the world safe for democracy." And there was every indication that their efforts would be crowned with success. Not only did they win a crushing victory but the three dynasties (Romanov, Habsburg, and Hohenzollern) which had been widely regarded as bulwarks of reactionary absolutism vanished with undignified haste. It appeared as if nothing could prevent the complete triumph of democracy.

Nor did the immediate aftermath of the war arouse any fears for the future of democracy. No sooner did the war end than Europe broke into an orgy of constitution making. Among the states which adopted democratic constitutions during the years 1919 to 1922 were Germany, Austria, Poland, Czechoslovakia, Yugoslavia, Finland, Latvia, Estonia, and the Irish Free State. As late as 1920 Lord Bryce was still able to confirm his lifelong belief in popular government. "Seventy years ago," he wrote, "the word Democracy awakened dislike or fear. Now it is a word of praise. Popular power is welcomed, extolled, worshiped."[3] But he also felt bound to utter a word of warning. "If it be improbable, yet it is not unthinkable," he said, "that as in many countries impatience with tangible evils substituted democracy for monarchy or oligarchy, a like impatience might some day reverse the process."

If Lord Bryce had lived but a few years longer, he would have seen his fears realized. The "improbable" happened not only in a single instance but on a wide scale. Just at the moment when the doctrine of democratic government appeared to be on the verge of a complete triumph in Europe a widespread autocratic reaction set in. It became in fact the outstanding political phenomenon of the period between the two wars. The first dictatorship was that which emerged from the Russian Revolution of 1917. To be sure, a democratic government, often called the Kerensky government, was the

[2] Guglielmo Ferrero in *Atlantic Monthly,* vol. 111 (1913), p. 1.
[3] *Modern Democracies,* vol. 1, p. 4.

first fruit of the revolution, but its existence was brief and precarious. Hardly six months later it gave way to the "dictatorship of the proletariat" which in practice resolved itself into the dictatorship of one man. Lenin, although a vigorous advocate of the transfer of all power to the people, found it necessary to establish a personal dictatorship "as a means of preparing the people for democracy." This was followed in 1922 by the Fascist march on Rome which established Mussolini as the dictator of Italy. In 1925 Mustapha Kemal (Kemal Atatürk) secularized the Ottoman state and initiated his autocratic rule. The next year saw Pilsudski become the dictator of Poland. Three years later King Alexander established a royal dictatorship in Yugoslavia. Then, in 1933, came the strokes whereby Hitler superseded the Weimar Constitution in Germany. Besides these major instances, partial or temporary dictatorships were established in a number of other countries. By 1934 the reaction was so widespread that it covered most of the ground which had been gained in the twentieth century.

It is interesting to observe that the countries in which dictatorships were established, e.g., Russia, Italy, Germany, and Spain, were those which had no previous record of a successful liberal or democratic government. On the other hand, the idea of dictatorship gained little popular support in such countries as England, Norway, Sweden, Denmark, Holland, and Belgium where liberal or democratic governments had functioned successfully for many years prior to the First World War. In the latter states the people had learned how to exercise the sovereignty, while in the former the masses were largely unprepared to work with success the complicated mechanism of a democratic constitution. Having been subject to monarchies for centuries they had not obtained sufficient apprenticeship. Furthermore, efficient democracy requires a certain standard of popular education, and these peoples were handicapped from the start by widespread illiteracy. In addition to the unpreparedness of the people the new democracies inherited problems that severely tested the mettle of the older democracies. These problems arose largely from the disintegrating effects of the war on the social, economic, and political structure. They included stabilization of the currency, reconversion of industries to peacetime purposes, providing employment for demobilized soldiers, liquidation of huge war debts, regaining old markets and opening new ones.

In many of the new states the parliamentary system failed conspicuously in its efforts to deal with the tremendous problems of reconstruction. The system of proportional representation, adopted in most of the new monarchies, returned to the popular chamber a large number of small party groups, not one of which could hope to muster a majority. The result was an anarchy of conflicting groups and the chronic evil of ministerial instability. Cabinets were formed by coalitions, and few coalitions lasted long enough to achieve anything. Blocs, groups, and coalitions were formed and reformed like the shifting pieces of glass in a kaleidoscope. Under such conditions lawmaking degenerated into a melée of factional bickering while month after month passed with nothing achieved. Meanwhile extremists both of the right and left were busy fomenting further dissensions as a means of discrediting the existing governments. Socialists and communists, spurred on by the success of the Bolshevik Revolution, freely fed the flames of unrest by denouncing the *status quo* and offering a panacea for all the ills afflicting society. At the same time democratic government was subjected to a heavy barrage from the advocates of dictatorship on the right. More than this, they vigorously contested with clubs as well as with propaganda the claims and movements of the left. In their propaganda they played up especially the communist menace, thereby rallying large sections of the upper classes to their support. The parties of the right had been strong from the first because the revolutions had not been thoroughgoing enough in many countries to deprive the old antidemocratic forces of their former power. In Germany, Poland, and Hungary, for example, the power of the military caste, the nobility, the great landowners, and the old bureaucracy had remained practically untouched.

As confusion increased, the masses who in many countries had accepted democratic institutions with tremendous enthusiasm began to regard them with constantly diminishing respect. Democratic performance was weighed against democratic promise and found wanting. Many began to feel that democratic government had failed not only in internal affairs but also in raising their respective nations in the world's regard. This, for instance, was the feeling in Italy and Germany before dictatorship emerged. Prospective dictators were not slow to promise that this feeling would be assuaged. In general, they lavishly made extravagant promises to everybody. They appealed to mass emotions with military displays, striking uniforms, badges, and insignia. While some among the masses put faith in the promises and actively supported the autocratic movements, others supinely permitted dictators to foist an authoritarian government upon them. Thus was ushered in the day of the dictators.

The new dictatorships were of different forms; but whether they were monarchical (Yugoslavia), presidential (Turkey), military (Poland and Spain) or whether their stated philosophy was Nazi or Fascist, all showed a striking similarity in governmental technique. Whereas the inalienable rights of the individual are the guiding motives of democracy, the supremacy of the state was the basic principle of the new dictatorships. The democratic attitude toward the individual has been stated as follows: "Man is a creature of God. The state is a creature of man. It follows that the state exists for the sake of man and not man for the sake of the state. . . . The state is a means and not an end." [4] In contrast the new dictatorships asserted the Hegelian tradition that the state is an end in itself and man but a means. "The state is everything—man is nothing but an atom or a cell in this higher superhuman structure." In the latter states the ordinary citizen not only had nothing to say about the government or the laws under which he lived but he was also completely deprived of protection against acts of force by the agents of the state. Although most of the dictators, including Hitler and Mussolini, claimed that they were serving group interests and were acting as servants of the people, the state each established was little more than the apparatus of one party which comprised a minority, usually a small minority, of the nation. This minority absorbed the functions of the state and used it to achieve party ends.

For centuries it had been customary for most governments of the Western world to limit their supervision to such things as the administration of justice, police and military protection, the care of roads—in short, to the broader aspects of life. But the new dictatorships absorbed and monopolized all powers and directed all activities of individuals and groups. In other words, they were totalitarian. And the means employed by each dictator to make his state totalitarian was the party. It was this, among other things, which differentiated the new dictatorships from those of preceding periods. Neither the Roman emperors nor the dictators of the succeeding centuries up to the opening of World War I had at their command a hand-picked and highly disciplined party upon which they could rely to make their rule an all-absorbing one. Consequently Stalin and Hitler could be and were more totalitarian in their rule than the Caesars, Napoleons, Romanovs, or Hohenzollerns ever were. No sooner did one of the new dictators rise to a commanding position in the state than the dictatorial party proceeded to disband and outlaw all other parties. Gradually trade unions, industrialists, capitalists, banks, churches, education, youth organizations, the courts,

[4] Coudenhove-Kalergi, *The Totalitarian State against Man* (1938), p. 15 ff.

the cinema, broadcasting—in fact, every phase of life—were subjected to the strict control of the party. Thereafter, there was no longer anything like "private life." As the Nazi Dr. Ley put it: "There is no such thing as a private individual in National Socialist Germany." The state, for example, decided whether a citizen might marry, whom he might marry, the kind of wedding ring he might give his bride, whether he might have children, which names he might give them, and how he must bring them up. In short, the life of every individual was regulated down to the minutest detail. Anyone who refused to bend under the totalitarian yoke was speedily and remorselessly crushed.

POSTWAR ITALY

The origins of Italian Fascism were very different from those of Bolshevism. Whereas the latter gained its opportunity as the result of a series of military reverses, Fascism was the offspring of disappointed national victory. To understand the postwar state of mind in Italy one must remember that when the war broke out in 1914 and during the months that followed, the masses of Italy had no desire to fight. The old-fashioned conservatives and a majority of socialists and Catholics were at one in opposing Italy's entry and were supported in their stand by most members of the middle class and by the workers. But there was a powerful, if small, group in favor of war. This group included the army officers and those nationalists who saw in the war an opportunity for Italian expansion. Their cause was strengthened by lavish promises of territory on the part of the Allies if the Italian government would put its military strength against the Central Powers. An agreement was finally drawn up (the secret Treaty of London) and in May, 1915, a reluctant parliament declared war. The following months saw the Italians pay a heavy price. Besides disabling a large number of youths, the war claimed the lives of about 600,000 Italian soldiers. It also drained the meagre resources of the state, leaving it with a debt of over twelve billion dollars. For their sacrifices the people reaped little in the way of glory, for the defeat at Caporetto was so disastrous that it cast a shadow over the final triumph. The one thing that buoyed up Italian hope was the promise of extensive territory and of better times.

But the settlement shattered the first of these hopes. When the spoils were divided, there was deep disappointment and indignation because Italy's share was so small. While France helped herself to

253,000 square miles with more than six million inhabitants and Great Britain obtained 989,000 square miles with a population of over nine millions, Italy's share was only 23,726 square miles with 1,672,000 inhabitants. Although Italy did obtain most of her claims on the eastern shore of the Adriatic, both Dalmatia—the most important of the territories promised her—and Fiume were denied her through President Wilson's veto. Later the Italians did, it is true, obtain Fiume, but for this they were indebted rather to D'Annunzio than to their allies in the war. The fact that they did not receive all the territory they had been promised in the Treaty of London made them feel that their efforts were not appreciated by the Allies. What mattered most to the Italians was that the dream of the Adriatic as a *mare clausum* had failed to materialize. It was principally for this that they had entered the war. While the peace conference was still in session mobs milling about in the streets of Rome shouted "Death to Wilson" and demanded that he return the model of the she-wolf suckling Romulus and Remus which had been presented to him on his visit to Rome a few months previously.

The promise of better times also remained unfulfilled. At the end of the war Italy's finances were in a state of chaos, her trade was badly dislocated, and her railways in confusion. More than this, in the months that followed, conditions became progressively worse. To stimulate the fighting spirit of the troops lavish promises of economic reform had been made during the war. When the soldiers were demobilized, they demanded that the promises be fulfilled. The greatest grievance was the constant rise in the cost of living. Although prices had gone up as much as 300 to 400 per cent, wages had not risen in proportion. Such bread as the masses could buy was of the poorest quality, and other articles of everyday consumption were both high and scarce. Lodgings were practically unobtainable in many towns. In the agrarian districts discontent was as prevalent as in the towns and cities. During the war there had been much talk about expropriating the land for the peasants. Upon their return from the war they insisted on their rights to the land; and when the government did nothing, peasants in the south seized a number of estates. Thus dissatisfaction and irritation pervaded most grades of Italian society. Everyone except the profiteers and some munitions workers was worse off than before the war. On all sides the general discontent vented itself in labor strikes and agrarian uprisings.

The government, to which the people looked for relief, was so weak and disorganized that it exercised little effective authority. Having had little to do with politics the average man had not become politically conscious by 1870, when Italy was united on the basis of a monarchial constitution. In the following decades, various factors prevented the participation of the masses in politics. First, in 1871, the year of the first census after unification, the rate of illiteracy in Italy as a whole was 68.8 per cent. In Sicily and Sardinia the percentage was as high as 85. Although the government did much during the subsequent period to foster education, nearly half the population was still illiterate in 1911. Second, when the Italian state was founded, the pope ordered the Italians to ignore it. The order, it is true, was not obeyed by all, but it did exclude many from political life.[5] The result was that the whole government, national and local, was controlled by the bureaucracy and a small section of the wealthier classes, with the actual control exercised by political bosses. In the Chamber of Deputies there were no strong parties with definite principles, only small coteries whose delicate shadings of opinion were unintelligible to the man in the street. It became the goal of politics to combine enough of these groups to obtain a majority. Such coalitions usually fell apart very soon, causing ministries to rise and fall in rapid succession. During the years from 1918 to 1922 five almost equally weak cabinets were overthrown. Parliament was always starting and stopping, never arriving at a real solution of the problems confronting it. Under such conditions it was clear that the future belonged to a strong party with a remedial program.

During the months immediately after the war two parties made a bid for power, the Catholic People's Party and the socialists. As soon as fighting ceased, Don Sturzo, a Sicilian priest, recruited a large number of priests and Catholic laymen with more or less socialist leanings, as the nucleus of the People's Party. Although Catholic, it was not clerical, and it offered a program of both patriotic and radical reform. In the first election (1919) it scored a startling success in returning ninety-nine deputies to the Chamber. But its influence soon declined because of inner disagreements and its equivocal position to both nationalism and the church.

A much stronger bid for power was made by the socialists. The members of this party were recruited chiefly from the workers in factories, the railway, postal, and telegraph employees, and the agricultural laborers of the Po Valley, with a sprinkling of university

[5] In 1904 Pope Pius X decreed that Roman Catholics could vote at such elections as the bishop of the diocese considered desirable.

students and middle-class intelligentsia. Already a powerful force in politics before the war, the socialists strengthened their influence by consistently opposing Italy's entry into the war. After the war the membership of the party was reinforced by many disillusioned ex-service men. In addition, the success of the Russian Revolution stirred the party to life. As a result it was able to return 156 deputies to the Chamber in the election of 1919, but it still lacked efficient leadership and a fighting party spirit. Such leaders as it had were moderate men who accepted the monarchy and were willing to work through parliament. Seldom did a party show less sense of opportunity. Had it shown a bold front and mustered all the potential forces available in a comprehensive program of revolution, it could easily have taken over the country. Under existing conditions its propaganda met with a ready response, and even its enemies were resigned to a proletarian revolution. But the socialists were badly divided in regard to both program and tactics. More than this, many of the things they did served only to foment a conservative reaction.

In the late summer of 1920 it seemed to them that the time for action had come. Taking advantage of a lockout in the metal industries, some 600,000 workers proceeded, without striking a blow, to occupy the factories of northern Italy, principally of Lombardy and Piedmont. Helmeted and armed, they occupied the factories without the least resistance from the employers, the police, or the government. Many peasants, encouraged by the success of the workers, took it upon themselves to seize the land they were cultivating. Both steps were taken with such suddenness and ease that many unthinking partisans believed all land and industry would henceforth become the property of the workers. But the factory owners did not concur. Firmly refusing to cooperate with the movement, they left the management of the industries to the workers. In three weeks conditions reached a stage of confusion which compelled the socialists to confess failure. The workers marched out as they had marched in, and the employers again took possession. The great coup toward which all propaganda had been directed, ended in a fiasco. From that moment Italian socialism began to decline.

THE GENESIS OF FASCISM

Meanwhile, outside parliament, there had arisen a new organization, the Fascist [6] Party which was destined soon to dominate Italy.

[6] From the Latin word "fasces" which signified the bundle of rods carried by the Roman lictors. The word originally meant "banded together."

This party, in turn, became the instrument of personal power for its creator, Benito Mussolini. Born in 1883 as the son of a blacksmith in a small village of the Romagna region, Benito early absorbed many of his father's socialist ideas. His mother, who was a primary school teacher, wished her son to enter the same profession, but he did not display much interest in his studies. As he later put it: "I had no real hunger for scholastic endeavor." At the age of nineteen he did teach school for a year. Finding the work monotonous, he set out for Switzerland at the end of the term. There, in his own words, he did "whatever came to hand." He worked for some time as a casual laborer and finally obtained employment on a socialist newspaper. In Switzerland, at the time the refuge of socialist and radical leaders, he met among other outstanding personalities Nicolai Lenin who was then an exile from Russia. During this period Mussolini read, if not systematically at least cursorily, the writings of Schopenhauer, Nietzsche, Georges Sorel, and Machiavelli. In his spare time he also attended some lectures at the University of Lausanne and was particularly impressed by Pareto's lectures on political economy. But his radical opinions and revolutionary activities caused him to be banished from one canton after another. In 1905 he was back in Italy, where he began to serve the term of military training which he had previously evaded.

After this brief term Mussolini resumed his career of socialist journalist. In 1908 he went to Trent, then under Austrian rule, where he worked on the staff of several papers. However, his radical opinions and revolutionary activities soon caused his arrest and expulsion from Austria. In Italy he continued his socialist activity, eventually becoming editor of *Avanti (Forward)*, the principal organ of the Italian Socialist Party. In this paper he excoriated nationalism, militarism, war, religion, the power of the state—in short, most of the things he later exalted. His antireligious sentiment vented itself in such statements as "God does not exist." For his antimilitarist activities he was arrested in 1911 and released only after an imprisonment of five months. The crisis of his life came during the First World War. Although opposed to Italy's entrance on the side of the Central Powers, he soon began to advocate intervention on the side of the Allies. In a speech at Parma in December, 1914, he said: "It is necessary to act, to move, to fight and, if necessary, to die. Neutrals have never dominated events. They have always gone under. It is blood that moves the wheels of history." His stand evoked such a storm of socialist criticism that he resigned his editorship, after which he was expelled from the party. Undaunted, he denounced his erstwhile comrades, telling them that he would bring about a real revolution; then he founded a newspaper of his own, *Il Popolo d'Italia,*[7] which played an important role in swinging Italian opinion toward war. Late in 1915 he volunteered for active service, serving as a private until he was painfully wounded by the explosion of a trench mortar in February, 1917. Upon his recovery he was released from the army and at once resumed his turbulent part in Italian politics.

No sooner was the war over than Mussolini recognized his opportunity and threw himself into the task of founding a party which would launch him into power. The official birthday of the Fascist movement was March 23, 1919. On that day a group of about a hundred Fascists met at Milan, in answer to a summons sounded by *Il Popolo d'Italia,* to form the first of the *Fasci di Combattimento.*[8] The first Fascist program, like that of the socialists, aimed at a workers' republic and demanded such immediate measures as a tax on capital amounting to partial expropriation of all wealth and confiscation of all the possessions of religious communities. This program was, however, gradually modified until its original radical character was completely obscured. Scarcely two years after its birth Fascism underwent a whole revolution from radical to conservative. Adopting as its slogan the words, "Per l'Italia" (For Italy), it offered a mixed program in which those who were suffering from postwar discontent might find pickings to their taste. Mussolini also sought to satisfy the Italian thirst for the theatrical and spectacular by adopting a distinctive uniform and the Roman salute and by staging colorful parades. The result was that people from all sides joined the Fascist ranks. Fascism gradually pervaded the bureaucracy, the police, the courts, and the army. Meanwhile industrialists who feared the socialists and hoped the Fascists would regiment the workers, subsidized the new movement. By February, 1921, Mussolini had perhaps 100,000 followers.

Very early Mussolini organized his followers into a disciplined army of Black Shirts, with its general staff, its officers and ranks, its code of discipline, and its decorations. The first article in the code stated baldly that the Fascist Party was, above all, a "militia." This militia, putting emphasis on action rather than on ideas, at once declared war on the socialists. Groups of Fascists armed with sticks and revolvers went about destroying the printing presses of their opponents, breaking up public meetings, and beating strikers into

---

[7] This paper later became the principal organ of Fascist expression.
[8] Literally "fighting groups." The name was later applied to the local cells of the party.

submission. As early as April, 1919, hooligan bands attacked the offices of *Avanti,* the socialist daily, sacked it, and set it on fire. As the movement grew stronger, the Fascisti created a veritable terror throughout the length and breadth of Italy. The trade unions were systematically smashed and opponents of the Fascist movement were savagely beaten. Where they encountered stubborn resistance, the Fascists did not hesitate to resort to assassination. In this conflict between Fascists and socialists the total toll of human life ran into hundreds. Regarding all this the government affected an air of neutrality in which a certain leaning towards the Fascists could soon be detected. Before long they succeeded in infecting the bureaucracy, the army, and the navy to such an extent that the government did not dare to challenge their power even if it had wished to do so.

The successful skirmishes with the socialists attracted many new recruits, so that by October, 1922, the Fascisti numbered about 300,000. With socialism crushed, it remained for them to capture the state. On October 24, 1922, Mussolini before a general congress of Fascisti at Naples openly called upon the government either to settle the most urgent problems of internal and external policy or to resign and hand over the administration to the Fascist Party. "Either the government will be given to us," he stated, "or we shall seize it by marching on Rome." During the night of October 27 bands of Fascists seized public buildings and railway stations, and raided munitions depots in northern Italy; then they began the "march on Rome." On the morning of the 28th some ten thousand Fascists armed with revolvers and sticks arrived in Rome. Fascist historians later made much of this incident, but they failed to point out that Mussolini instead of "marching" rode into Rome in a railroad sleeping car. When prime minister Facta finally decided to invoke martial law, Victor Emmanuel III, among the weakest of kings, refused to sign the decree. As soon as this became known to the Fascists they hurried to Rome in larger numbers. Thoroughly frightened by this development, the king asked Mussolini to form a new ministry. Thus Mussolini became premier.

ᛕ

ENTRENCHMENT IN POWER

When the king asked Mussolini to form a new cabinet, there were only thirty-five Fascist deputies in the Chamber. It was therefore necessary for the Duce (the leader), as Mussolini was now called, to take ten non-Fascists into his cabinet as against four Fascists. The ten included representatives of the Nationalist, "Democratic," and Catholic People's parties. Only the socialists refused to collaborate. In addition to being premier, Mussolini retained in his own hands the portfolios of both Home and Foreign Offices. On November 16 he laid his program before the Chamber and asked for unlimited power until the end of 1923. He stated that if the Chamber did not grant it, he would act without regard for the constitutional power of parliament. On November 25 the Chamber voted him and the new cabinet the plenary power by a vote of 275 to 90. Only the socialists had the courage to vote against him.

Once installed in power it became the primary concern of the Fascist regime to consolidate its position and to maintain itself in office at all costs. One of Mussolini's first cares was to build up sufficient armed strength to overawe the opposition, which was by no means quiescent. To strengthen the army and also his own hold on the army, he raised its peacetime strength from 175,000 to 275,000. But knowing that many of the officers had no desire to participate in the suppression of the anti-Fascists, he organized his followers into a well-trained militia, the members of which took the oath of fidelity not to the king but to him. To this militia was intrusted the task of terrorizing the opponents of Fascism. Next Mussolini proceeded to strengthen the Fascist hold on the administration by weeding out non-Fascists. Pressure was exerted upon municipalities to dismiss mayors and councilors who were not sympathetic to the cause and to put proved Fascists in their places. With equal thoroughness all the government services, particularly the police departments, were purged and restaffed. This not only assured control of the administration to the Fascist Party but also rewarded those who had supported the cause and were now clamoring for jobs.

Meanwhile the militia or Fascist bands were ruthlessly trampling down all opposition on the principle enunciated by Mussolini, "If consent fails, there is always force." At first the full fury was turned against the socialists because they dared to oppose the Fascist rule; but when the power of the socialists was weakened, the militia turned against others who were unsympathetic. While some were forced to drink large quantities of castor oil to "purge" them of their erroneous ideas, others were beaten, had their homes wrecked, or were put to the dagger. During the period from November, 1922, to October, 1923, there were more than two thousand cases of assault, arson, and murder. Among the victims were many outstanding leaders of thought and culture. In 1923, for example, the houses of Benedetto Croce, Italy's most prominent philosopher, and Francesco Nitti, the ex-prime minister and a noted scholar, were destroyed. Non-Fascist newspapers and their representatives were the special target of the attacks. Often the correspondents of these papers were set upon in public, or the sale of the papers was prevented by force. Later newspaper buildings were stormed, printing presses were smashed, and the buildings were often set on fire. Thus Mussolini and his Fascists tried to cow their critics into silence by methods that Machiavelli would have understood and admired. It was all in accord with Mussolini's statement: "I believe that Machiavelli is still the best guide in politics."

No amount of coercion, however, could allay unsympathetic opinion, particularly in the Chamber. The hostility there was in fact growing stronger, for the representatives of the Catholic People's Party had joined the opposition in April, 1923. Since it was essential for the Fascists to control a majority in the Chamber, they devised a plan to attain it. Fascist leaders framed a new electoral law which guaranteed two thirds of the seats to the party receiving the largest number of votes. The bill encountered strong resistance but was finally passed. Before the end of the year, at which time his dictatorial power was to terminate, Mussolini obtained the king's signature to a decree which dissolved the Chamber and made a new election necessary. During the campaign, opposition parties were forbidden to hold public meetings or to distribute electioneering literature. Furthermore, Fascist organs not only stigmatized all political adversaries as traitors but also heaped scorn on Fascists who ventured to hold dissenting opinions. Despite all this, the opposition parties polled three million votes in the election held in April, 1924, against the four and one-half million cast for the Fascists. But the latter did, of course, receive a majority of the seats, a fact which enormously strengthened Mussolini's hands.

Nevertheless, Mussolini still had to face a strong minority in the Chamber. One of the most courageous of his opponents was Matteotti, a young socialist deputy. Having previously published a scathing indictment of Fascist rule, Matteotti now (May 30, 1924) made a speech in the Chamber in which he contested the validity of the Fascist majority, thereby signing, as it were, his own death warrant. A few days later he was seized in the streets of Rome, taken into the country, and murdered. The news of the murder caused great excitement, and the anti-Fascist press was not slow to state that Mussolini was the instigator of the crime. Not until nearly two years later were the murderers brought to trial and then in a small provincial town. To allay public indignation three of them were sentenced to six years of penal servitude; but they were released two months later.

During the following period the Fascists carried on a relentless campaign to prevent expression of opposition to their rule and to concentrate all power in their hands. Freedom of the press, which had already been restricted after the Matteotti murder, was now completely abrogated by the suppression of all opposition newspapers. A law promulgated in 1925 abolished elected councils in all municipalities of not more than 5000 inhabitants, entrusting their administration to officials nominated by the government. This law terminated free local government in 80.2 per cent of the municipalities. A short time later a decree supplanted municipal self-government in Rome by an administration in the hands of government appointees. In May, 1926, a law called the Legal Discipline of Collective Labor Relations Act was passed which decreed in effect that only Fascist organizations were to be recognized. Thus all anti-Fascist unions were deprived of their legal right to exist. Late in the preceding year parliament had also passed a law which greatly extended the power of the premier by prescribing that "no question can be included in the agenda of the Senate or Chamber without the consent of the premier." This meant that the Chamber could no longer even take notice of a bill introduced by one of its members unless it had Mussolini's approval. The law also gave the premier the power to have passed any law he wished, even if the opinion of the Chamber was unfavorable. Finally, this law, by making the premier responsible solely to the king, made his continuance in office independent of an adverse vote of the Chamber.

Since it was the aim of the Fascist state to be absolute master over all aspects of life, it also extended its control over economic processes. On the whole, the government abstained from a direct share in industrial enterprises, but it did make certain that all economic activities served the interests of the state. Control was achieved through the organization of associations or syndicates of employers and employees, the special purpose of which was to deal with disputes between capital and labor. The employees in every branch of industry were expected to form such an organization and if it was "recognized" by the state it could enter into collective bargaining which was binding for all engaged in that industry. Equally the employers in each industry were expected to form an association which after being "recognized" by the government could enter into agreements with the employees. In order to be recognized an organization of employees or employers had to include 10 per cent of those engaged in a specific industry. While there was no definite obligation on the part of any employee or employer to join, both, whether they joined or not, were bound to accept the agreements in regard to wages and conditions of labor which the "recognized" associations made. Furthermore, nonmembers no less than members had to pay dues. Only one "recognized" association was permitted for each trade or industry. Thus the old trade unions were outlawed. Trade-union leaders who sought to continue the old organizations were imprisoned or deported. In this way their power was gradually broken.

Both the employers' associations and employees' syndicates were directed by officers appointed by the government. The control, however, weighed more heavily on the employees because of the close relationship between many of the large employers and the Fascist hierarchy. In the syndicates only minor posts were filled by rank and file members. In other words, the role of the employees was largely restricted to paying dues and obeying orders. They could not resort to strikes or lockouts, for lockouts as well as strikes were styled "crimes against the public economy." All labor disputes had to be settled by arbitration. If the employers' and employees' associations of any industry failed to reach an agreement, the dispute was referred to an industrial court (established by law of April 3, 1926). It was the duty of the court while hearing a case to persuade the parties to come to a friendly settlement, but if they did not the court's decision was binding.

MUSSOLINI AS ABSOLUTE RULER OF ITALY

Thus the Fascist party penetrated into every crevice of the polity, absorbing all the functions of government in accordance with their slogan, "All power to Fascism." Mussolini became as nearly absolute as human ingenuity could make him. As premier of Italy, president of the Fascist Grand Council, and Leader or "Duce" of the Fascist Party, he was master of the political, economic, and social framework of the country. Few men have ever held more absolute power. His cabinet was little more than a group of officials chosen to carry out his will. He could not only prevent the Senate and Chamber from discussing laws that were not to his liking; he could also make laws on his own responsibility if circumstances implied "an urgent necessity." Furthermore, since the command of the army and navy had been transferred from the king to him, he could declare a state of siege without first getting the approval of king or Chamber. Nor

BOYS OF THE FASCIST YOUTH ORGANIZATIONS PARADING BEFORE IL DUCE

was there a constitutional organ which could limit his autocracy. The last semblance of a parliament expressive of the popular will was wiped out by a law of May 17, 1928, which made the entire kingdom a single constituency returning four hundred deputies. These were chosen in the following manner: the Corporations of Employees and Employers, presided over by Mussolini's nominees, submitted a list of candidates from which the Grand Council, composed of Mussolini's appointees and friends, chose four hundred candidates [9] whose names were then presented to the voters for approval. Since only one list was submitted, the electorate could vote either "yes" or "no" upon the ticket as a whole. And the number of those who dared invoke upon themselves the wrath of the Fascists by casting a negative vote was small.

Within the party, which was the only one permitted to exist, all power emanated either directly or indirectly from Mussolini. Every individual upon becoming a member had to take an oath which bound him "to obey without question the commands of the Duce." Next to the Duce the highest authority was the Grand Council, of which Mussolini was chairman. It included, among others, the members of the Cabinet, those who had won public recognition for their services to the revolution and any others who might be nominated to it by Mussolini. Just below the Grand Council was the National Directorate, which constituted the executive branch of the party. Each province also had a Provincial Directorate and a party secretary. Farther down were the local cells, *Fasci di Combattimento,* under the leadership of an appointed secretary and an advisory committee. The militia was composed of about 400,000 selected men who were the recipients of special favors. In 1930 the party consisted of approximately a million members out of a population of about forty-two million. At first every Italian was eligible for membership, but after 1925, with the exception of a few honorary appointments, no one was permitted to become a member unless he had worked his way up through the youth organizations, *Balilla* and *Avanguardia.* [10]

The student who looks for a constructive program or a consistent body of principles in Fascism will be disappointed. From the beginning it stressed action rather than theory. Mussolini himself stated that when he organized the first *Fascio di Combattimento*

---

[9] The Grand Council had the right to substitute candidates of its own if it so desired.
[10] The *Balilla,* composed of boys under fourteen, was a military adaptation of the Boy Scout movement. The members of the *Avanguardia* were, in turn, recruited from the *Balilla.* There were also organizations for girls.

"I had no specific doctrinal attitude in my mind. . . . My own doctrine, even in this period, had always been a doctrine of action." The simple truth is that when the opportunity presented itself for a party with a bold and determined leader to ride to power, Mussolini seized that opportunity with alacrity. Action was based on the philosophy, "Get in power and stay there." Everything else was secondary. Instead of setting any goals, the Fascists attempted to solve only specific problems. As the slogan, "Per l'Italia," shows, the primary accent was put on patriotism. Said Mussolini some months before the march on Rome, "Fascism should demand that within the frontiers there no longer be Venetians, Romagnoles, Tuscans, Sicilians, Sardinians, but Italians, only Italians." The only thing the Fascists definitely promised was to free Italy from the menace of Bolshevism.[11] Nor did the frightened industrialists, financiers, and professional people who gathered round the Fascist standard ask for more. So far as the party had principles, they were largely negative; it opposed all the basic ideas of the liberal democratic state.

It was only after the Fascists were installed in power that some of the leaders, and particularly Mussolini himself, felt the need of a philosophy to justify their actions and to create unity of thought in their ranks. Hence they set about the construction of a philosophy. The core of the Fascist myth is the Hegelian dogma of the state as the ethical whole. "Fascism conceives of the state as an absolute," Mussolini wrote, "in comparison with which all individuals or groups are relative, only to be conceived of in their relation to the state." Thus Fascism rejected individualism and regarded the individual merely as an incident in the life of the state. Like socialism it put the community before the individual. According to this doctrine the individual can attain self-realization only through subjection to authority. The duties of the individual were summed up in a slogan which was displayed everywhere in Italy, "Credere, obbedire, combattere (believe, obey, fight)." Democracy had no place in the Fascist state. In the words of Mussolini, "Fascism combats the whole complex system of democratic ideology and repudiates it. . . . Fascism denies that the majority by the simple fact that it is a majority can direct human society." The great mass of citizens, according to Fascist theory, are incapable of governing themselves; hence this task devolves on "the chosen few" who have the peculiar gift. Even this elite group needs a man who can "crystallize its ideals." This was the theoretical justification of Mussolini's rule.

Finally Fascism, as stated by Mussolini, "believes neither in the

[11] The fact is that Bolshevism was at the time no longer a menace.

possibility nor the utility of perpetual peace. It thus repudiates the doctrine of pacifism—born of renunciation of the struggle and an act of cowardice in the face of sacrifice. War alone brings up to its highest tension all human energy and puts the stamp of approval upon the peoples who have the courage to meet it. Thus a doctrine which is founded upon this harmful postulate of peace is hostile to Fascism." In other words, Fascism regarded violence as a virtue.

FASCISM IN ACTION

Under the Fascist regime there was improvement in a number of respects. For example, it made some progress in the creation of order and discipline so that there was greater safety for life and property throughout the nation. Some improvements were also made in urban cleanliness, public health, and sanitation. Since the spheres in which improvement took place were limited, foreign correspondents frequently wrote about the decrease in the number of beggars, the better service in the hotels, and the more punctual train service. A more important accomplishment was a careful survey of all the resources of the country, which led to the discovery of hitherto unknown mineral deposits and other natural wealth. The government also gave special attention to the development of water power, with the result that the manufacture and use of electricity was nearly tripled. Electric power was applied to many industries, many miles of new electric railways were constructed, and many miles of already existing railways were electrified.

The first four years of the dictatorship were a period of prosperity, but the prosperity was more apparent than real. It was a byproduct of inflation. The lira, which had stood at 21.2 to a dollar in 1922, gradually fell until in August, 1926, it reached a low point of 30.5 to a dollar. During this period foreign merchants were able to buy cheaply in the Italian market because the exchange rate favored them. As a result of increased foreign trade, employment ratios rose and wages increased. But despite the determined effort of the government to keep them down, prices rose much more than the income of the wage earner. In 1926 at the insistence of Mussolini the lira was stabilized at approximately 20 per cent above the franc. This stabilization on a high level had an unfavorable effect on foreign trade. Exports slumped badly, forcing manufacturers to curtail production, which in turn caused unemployment. Wages, which had already fallen in 1925 and 1926, were systematically forced down by the government in the succeeding period. For example, in October, 1927, a reduction of 10 per cent was imposed. Despite Mussolini's assurance that the government would permit no further reduction, the rate continued to fall.

Then toward the end of 1929 came the world economic crisis that followed upon the Wall Street crash. Mussolini's statement that "the American crisis in the fall of 1929 exploded like a bomb" was an exaggeration. The Duce was too eager to place upon it the blame for a decline which in Italy had started several years earlier. The whole machinery of Fascist propaganda worked overtime to convince the workers that if conditions were bad in Italy they were vastly worse in other countries. Actually the immediate effect of the crash was less severe than in other countries; but the longer the depression continued, the more the early advantage was swept away. Wages continued to decline and unemployment increased. It has been estimated that during the period from 1926 to 1934 wages in the main industries were reduced between 40 and 50 per cent. During the same period agricultural wages suffered a reduction of 50 to 70 per cent. Since the price level was not lowered to any corresponding degree, the result was that by 1934 purchasing power had declined by at least one third, a decline that was further aggravated by increasing taxation. At the beginning of 1935 unemployment, expressed in percentage of the population, was heavier in Italy than in most of Europe. Even the vaunted schemes of public works had slowed down. The condition of the country in general was so serious that there were ominous rumblings of revolt. In short, Fascism had not solved Italy's problem. It failed to provide the economic progress and material security which it had promised and for which it had demanded the sacrifice of individual liberties.

If the Fascist regime failed to raise living standards, it did introduce some improvements into agriculture. It continued the policy of mechanization and of making agricultural education more popular as well as more scientific. Some of the old estates were broken up into small plots which the peasants could buy through long-term payments. But the most marked achievement in agriculture was the reclamation of land. Italy had only about 120,000 square miles, on which about 40 million inhabitants lived. Of this land about one third was marsh or land otherwise unfit for cultivation. Although production had shown a steady rise as a result of the introduction of scientific agriculture, the government could not hope to become independent of foreign sources of supply unless it put more land under cultivation. To do this necessitated the draining of vast stretches of marshland. Not that there was anything new or revolutionary in such a reclamation program. Since 1860 many major tasks of reclamation had been completed by private capital and the government had also appropriated large funds for this purpose. It is estimated that between 1860 and 1922 no less than 597,000 hectares (one hectare is equivalent to 2.471 acres) had been drained. Thus the Fascist program, when viewed historically, was but an extension of one inaugurated previously.

Another achievement of Mussolini's government was the working agreement he concluded with the Roman Catholic Church. During his days as a socialist Mussolini had been an open opponent of religion. It was to him "a psychic malaise of the brain" and "an institution which strives toward political power in order to maintain the exploitation and ignorance of the people." Nor did his attitude change for some time after he stepped out of the socialist ranks. Even in his first Fascist program he proposed the nationalization of church property. It was only after he became premier that he began to adopt a milder tone toward religion. In Italy the papacy and the state had been estranged for fifty-nine years. When the Italian army formally invested the Holy City in 1870, the pope (Pius IX), as a protest against the "despoliation" of the church, voluntarily became the "Prisoner of the Vatican" and announced that neither he nor his successors would ever leave it again until Italy had repaired the wrong that had been done. He also issued the famous *Non expedit,* which forbade all good Roman Catholics to participate in Italian politics. The *Non expedit* was withdrawn early in the twentieth century, but the pope still remained the prisoner of the Vatican. Mussolini, upon becoming premier, very soon realized, as Napoleon had more than a century earlier, that the support of the church would greatly strengthen his position. Hence he began wooing the Vatican by devotion to Catholicism in public, by restoring the crucifix to the schoolrooms throughout Italy, and by introducing religious education into the schools under church supervision. In 1926 he went so far as to open secret negotiations with a view to arranging a settlement of the "Roman Question." After protracted negotiations agreement was finally reached in the Lateran treaty which was signed in February, 1929.

This treaty was actually composed of three documents: a political treaty, a financial convention, and a concordat. The political treaty set up Vatican City as a sovereign state and formally recognized the pope's exclusive jurisdiction over it, including his right to enter into direct diplomatic relations with other states. The Holy See, for its part, solemnly recognized Italy as a legitimate kingdom under the House of Savoy, with Rome as its capital. By the terms of the financial convention Italy agreed to pay the Holy See 750 million lire in 5 per cent government bonds. This was accepted as complete settlement of the obligations incurred in 1870 when the government took possession of the Papal States. The final document, the concordat, regulated the relations of church and state within the kingdom. Among other things, it made Roman Catholicism the official religion, recognized the legal existence of monastic orders and their right to own property, provided that the religious ceremony of marriage should also be binding in the eyes of the law, and made religious instruction compulsory in both elementary and secondary schools except by the express wish of the parents. On the other hand, the Vatican agreed that every new bishop would swear not to enter into any agreement or take part in any public meeting that might be in any way detrimental to the state.

The Lateran treaty, it was hoped, had removed the last misunderstandings between the papacy and the Italian government. Gratified by the accord, the clergy urged their parishioners to vote for the government list, with the result that an overwhelming number of affirmative votes were cast in the March elections (8,519,559 voted "yes" and only 135,761 "no"). In July Pope Pius XI emerged into the Square of St. Peter's. As for Mussolini himself, his personal prestige was greatly enhanced by the solution of the "insoluble Roman question."

But early hopes for cordial cooperation between the Vatican and the government were not fulfilled. The two were soon at odds over the interpretation of the agreements. The pope, for example, interpreted the marriage clause to mean that anyone who had been baptized in the Catholic faith would be required by the state to be married by the church. Mussolini, however, made it clear that any subject of the state was at liberty to adopt either the religious or the civil ceremony, according to the dictates of his conscience. Another point of disagreement arose over Mussolini's statement that freedom of discussion and conscience would be permitted in matters of religion and that all forms of worship would be freely allowed. To this the pope replied: "It is clearly and loyally understood that the Catholic religion and the Catholic religion alone is the state religion, with all the logical and juridical consequences that the state implies." In the same open letter he said in reference to Mussolini: "We certainly never expected to hear heretical and worse than heretical expressions about the very essence of Christianity and Catholicism."

One of the most serious disagreements was on the question of education. While the pope, in conformity with Catholic doctrine, maintained that the education of the young was mainly or exclusively the business of the church, Mussolini had other ideas. In presenting the Lateran treaty to the Chamber for ratification he made it quite clear that he did not propose to entrust the task of educating the children of Italy to the church. "Any other regime than ours," he declared, "may believe it useful to renounce the education of the young generations. In this field I am intractable. Education must be ours. Our children must be educated in our religious faith, but we must round out this education and we need to give our youths a sense of virility and the power of conquest." A short time later the pope seized the opportunity in addressing the pupils of a Jesuit school to state: "We can never agree to anything that compresses, decreases, or denies the rights which nature and God gave the family and the church in the field of education." During the subsequent period both sides reiterated their ideas, and the deadlock remained complete.

Another significant change brought about by the Fascist regime was that affecting the administration of education. Great progress had been made during the period from 1870 to the outbreak of World War I toward wiping out the widespread illiteracy, but much still remained to be done, particularly in southern Italy. In many of the agricultural districts of the South not only schools but also the desire for education was lacking. Many peasants, shepherds, fishermen, and the like considered reading and writing a luxury which their children could well forego. When the extent of the existing illiteracy was brought home to the government as recruits were called to service during the First World War, a commission was appointed to investigate and make recommendations. In 1920 Benedetto Croce, who was then minister of public instruction, began the task of educational reform, but the general chaos prevented the introduction of thoroughgoing measures. The Fascists, on assuming power, almost at once turned their attention to the educational system. Schools were opened in districts where they had been unknown, training facilities for teachers were improved, better discipline was established, compulsory attendance for children from six to fourteen was strictly enforced, and classes were opened in which adult illiterates could learn to read and write. To defray the cost of these reforms the appropriations for the ministry of national education were increased 47 per cent between 1922 and 1930. The result was that illiteracy, which was 27 per cent in 1923, was reduced to 21 per cent by 1927. It is estimated that by 1930 over 90 per cent of the children of school age were receiving instruction.

It was the intention of the Fascists that the educational system would be formative rather than informative. In other words, the end they had in view was not to create intelligent citizens but to make good Fascists. The lesson impressed on pupils and students from the primary school through the university was unquestioning loyalty and devotion to Fascism. This was openly admitted by Fascist writers. One of them, for instance, stated in a school calendar: "Every school, every class in every school, every subject in every class, must educate the youth of Italy to understand Fascism, to renew itself in Fascism, to live in the historical climate created by the Fascist revolution." To make sure that this was achieved, all the textbooks used in the schools were prepared by a government commission according to the prescription that "textbooks in history, geography, economics, and law and elementary school readers must be in accordance with the historical, political, juridical, and economic requirements established since October 28, 1922." Describing as they did the achievements of Fascism and exalting the greatness of its leaders, they became the means of drilling into impressionable children and adults the contention that Fascism was the country's only salvation. The primer was full of pictures of Fascists in black shirts, of Fascist symbols, and of Fascist soldiers. On the first page of the speller could be found such words as Duce, Mussolini, Fascismo. Readers for the succeeding grades were stuffed even more with propaganda. In the fourth reader the children were told how the Duce had saved Italy from Bolshevism. Thus education for Fascism was emphasized and carried through from grade to grade. It was Mussolini himself who coined the slogan, "The textbook and the musket make a perfect Fascist."

Nor was the indoctrination of the young confined to the regular school system. In the youth organizations, the *Balilla, Avanguardia,* and *Giovani Fascisti* for boys and the *Piccole Italiane* and *Giovane Italiane* for girls, veneration of the Fascist government and its leaders assumed the form of a religious cult. Instruction began with the sentence: "Let us salute the flag in the Roman fashion; hail to Italy; hail to Mussolini." Among other things the children were told over and over again that "the Duce is always right." Some idea of the influence of these organizations may be gained from the fact that in 1932 half the school children were members of either the *Balilla* or the *Piccole Italiane.* Upon entering a university former members of the youth organizations could join the *Centurie Uni-*

versitarie charged with the task of spreading propaganda among the students and of spying on professors and students suspected of opposition to Fascism.

For some time after the establishment of the regime the universities continued to be centers of liberal thought, but gradually they also lost their freedom. A decree promulgated early in 1927 stated that "professors in royal universities and instructors in secondary institutions and other professors of similar rank are to be dismissed from service when they do not give full assurance of faithful fulfillment of their duties or if they place themselves in a state of incompatibility with the general political aims of the government." A few months later the former secretary of the party said in an address: "The intellectuals above all ought to learn to trust and follow him [Mussolini], even as our soldiers do who have declared Mussolini is always right." Those holding the lesser university positions were soon regimented, but because of protests from abroad against the suppression of academic freedom the Fascists hesitated for some time before they extinguished the last sparks. In 1931, however, university employees of all ranks were called upon to take the following oath: "I swear allegiance to the King, his royal successors, and to the Fascist regime . . . to exercise the functions of teaching and to fulfill all academic duties with the purpose of forming active and regular citizens devoted to the country and to the Fascist regime." Although some of the most prominent professors forfeited their positions by refusing to take the oath, the majority submitted.

Another problem the Fascist regime tried to solve was the declining birth rate. This problem was not peculiar to Italy. The birth rate was declining in all the larger countries inhabited by people predominantly of the white race. The decline in Italy was in fact less drastic than in many other countries. Nevertheless the rate had fallen from 39.3 per thousand in 1876 to 25.6 per thousand in 1929. To check this decline was, as the Fascist Grand Council described it, "the problem of problems," for without a growing population "there is neither youth, nor military power, nor economic expansion, nor a secure future for the fatherland." "For five years," Mussolini said in 1927, "we have continued to assert that the population of Italy is like a river overflowing its banks. This is not true. The Italian nation is not growing but diminishing in size. . . . Let us be frank with ourselves: what are 40 million Italians compared with 90 million Germans and 200 million Slavs? Let us look at our western neighbors: what are 40 million Italians compared with the

40 millions of France and the 90 millions in her colonies, or with the 46 millions of England and 450 millions of inhabitants in her colonies? . . . In order to be influential Italy must begin the second half of the present century with at least 60 million inhabitants."

The Fascist regime had already taken steps to stimulate growth of the population. As a means of discouraging celibacy and childlessness it had in 1926 imposed a flat tax on all bachelors between twenty-five and sixty-five and also increased the income tax of both bachelors and the heads of small families. Stringent laws were passed to prohibit the dissemination of birth control propaganda and the practice of abortion. On the other hand, special preferences in public employment were accorded to the heads of large families in addition to important tax exemptions and special awards. Parents of large families were honored by having their photographs exhibited in public. But the results were on the whole discouraging. In 1927 the number of births increased, but in the next year a decline set in again. By 1936 the birth rate dropped to a new low of 22.4 per thousand. In 1937 marriage loans to young people were introduced in imitation of the Nazi measures. At the birth of each child a part of the loan was canceled and after the birth of the fourth child the entire loan was written off. If the marriage remained childless, the loan had to be repaid in full. Even these measures did not result in any considerable rise of the birth rate.

ら

THE QUEST FOR EMPIRE

One of the reasons why the Fascist regime was so eager to increase the birth rate was the need of a large population for the creation of a great Italian Empire. Mussolini summed up the situation in the following words: "With a declining population a country does not create an empire but becomes a colony." During his early days as a Fascist Mussolini still retained the socialist opposition to imperialism, but soon after his accession to power he experienced a change of mind. Lest he rouse the fears of other nations he stated that Fascist imperialism was a question of "peaceful expansion." Meanwhile, however, he was strengthening Italy's military forces. "The fundamental duty of Fascist Italy," he said in 1927, "is the preparation of all armed forces on land, sea, and in the air. We must be able to mobilize 5,000,000 men. . . . Then, between 1935 and 1940 will come the tragic moment in Europe's history and we can let our voice be heard." "Fascism," he wrote again, "does not think that permanent peace is possible or desirable," because "only war raises all exhibitions of human energy to their maximum tension. It puts the stamp of dignity on nations which are able to wage it openly. No other test can take its place."

Mussolini's program was an ambitious one. He was convinced that it was his destiny to become a modern Caesar who would reconstitute the greatness of ancient Rome by means of twentieth-century conquests. He would again make the Mediterranean an Italian sea. A Fascist deputy said in support of the Duce's plans, "Look at the Mediterranean, Mare Nostro, where Italians have ever been victorious. This sea has been ours and will be ours once more." Mussolini hoped that in addition to demonstrating Fascist greatness a successful imperialist war would supply Italy with sources of raw materials, for Italy possessed only scanty quantities of iron, coal, copper, and potash and had to depend entirely on foreign imports for petroleum, cotton, rubber, and phosphates. Such colonies as Italy had, which included Eritrea, Italian Somaliland, and Libya in Africa, neither provided these raw materials nor did they attract Italian colonists. Hence Mussolini demanded new colonies. "Italy," he stated, "demands the acknowledgment by other powers of her undoubted need of sun and earth. If they do not acknowledge it, Italy will be forced to take what she has a right to." By 1934 conditions were undoubtedly so critical that they encouraged him to take risks. The economic depression was still unsolved, foreign trade was still declining, and the policy of public works as a means of providing employment was beginning to lose its efficacy. The remedy, as he saw it, was a military adventure which would absorb the whole nation in its preparation and accomplishment.

As conditions in Europe became more propitious for an imperialist venture, he had to choose his objective. The obvious choice was Ethiopia, also called Abyssinia. It was the only considerable area in Africa which still maintained its independence, the rest of the continent having been divided among the powers during the scramble for colonies in the decades before World War I. The population of Ethiopia, estimated at between five and a half and seven and a half millions, was a chaotic jumble of varicolored tribes professing Christianity, Mohammedanism, Judaism, and heathenism. The country itself, embracing an area of some 350,000 square miles (about three times the size of Italy), was for the most part arid desert, uninviting and unsuited for the habitation of Europeans. The only parts where Europeans could live comfortably were the highlands, a rich agricultural country which produced barley, millet, wheat, coffee, and hides. Even so, economically the game was

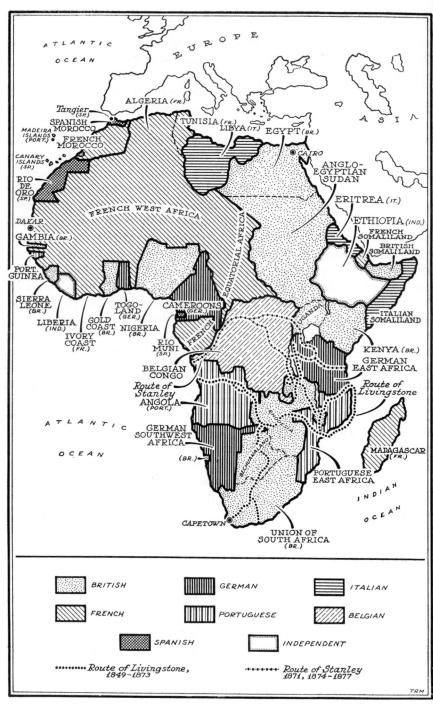

THE PARTITION OF AFRICA IN THE NINETEENTH CENTURY

not worth the candle. But the possession of Ethiopia did have strategic importance. A glance at the map will make this apparent, for without Ethiopia the provinces of Eritrea and Italian Somaliland were hemmed in and isolated. Finally, there was also the desire for revenge. As far back as 1889 Italy had claimed a protectorate over Ethiopia, but her claims had been crushed by an overwhelming defeat in the battle of Adowa (1896) at the hands of the savage tribesmen. An armed conquest of Ethiopia would wipe out the rankling memories of Adowa.

Ignoring the growing opposition to his plans in Great Britain, which saw in the move a threat to the empire's communications as well as a breach of Italy's obligations as a member of the League of Nations, Mussolini steadily pressed his preparations for war.[12] A carefully staged border clash between Ethiopian and Italian colonial troops in December, 1934, furnished the pretext for dispatching a large military force to the Italian East African colonies. In October, 1935, the invasion began with the advance of Italian troops across the border from Eritrea. The Ethiopians, with foreign military advice, offered a courageous opposition which held back the Italians for months. In the end, however, the untrained warriors with their spears, knives, obsolete rifles, and inadequate artillery could not cope with Mussolini's well trained troops equipped with airplanes, tanks, incendiary bombs, and all the other weapons of modern warfare. When the Italian troops reached a point sixty miles from Addis Ababa, the capital of Ethiopia, in May, 1936, the native defense collapsed. The emperor, Haile Selassie, fled the country and a few days later the Italians entered Addis Ababa.

In Rome Mussolini was acclaimed by enthusiastic crowds when he announced the victory. The Fascist Grand Council and the cabinet declared Ethiopia annexed to Italy as a colony, and a colonial government headed by a viceroy was established in Addis Ababa. More than this, Victor Emmanuel III assumed the title of "emperor." But the conquest was far from complete. At no time did Italian control extend beyond the areas around the towns. In

[12] The moment was propitious for the adventure because the attention of Great Britain and the other European nations was riveted on Hitler's rearmament of Germany.

THE PARTITION OF AFRICA IN THE NINETEENTH CENTURY. *The large holdings of the British, French, and Belgians contrast sharply with the territories held by the Italians.*

the rest of the country the Italians could move only in large forces accompanied by tanks and armored cars. Irregular bands of native tribesmen harassed the Italians at every turn. Probably more Italians were killed during the two years after the war than during the war itself. Even in the areas around the towns few Italians would venture out after nightfall, for, as one writer put it, "if these areas were Italy during the daytime, they were Ethiopia at night."

❋❋❋

CHAPTER TEN

The Succession States of the Habsburg Empire

**THE COLLAPSE OF THE
HABSBURG EMPIRE** SUDDENLY, or so it seemed to the outside world, in the fall of 1918 Austria-Hungary, a state of the first political and military magnitude, vanished from the map as if it had been subjected to the withering blast of some destroying angel. Actually it collapsed because it lacked a real *raison d'être*. The artificial character of this state, which corresponded to neither a nation nor a language, had become painfully apparent. Except in a bureaucratic sense this relic of earlier centuries had become almost meaningless. It was not a nation-state but a collection of ill-assorted provinces and peoples whose customs, traditions, religions, and educational and economic standards were widely divergent. Regarded from the standpoint of nationality it included no less than ten major groups and many minor ones. On the eve of the war the population was composed of the following nationalities: Germans, 12,011,081; Magyars, 10,067,917; Czechs, 6,442,577; Poles, 4,976,642; Slovaks, 1,968,452; Ukranians, 3,998,900; Slovenes, 1,256,256; Serbs and Croatians, 5,545,207; Rumanians, 3,224,728; and Italians, 771,054. The situation would have been difficult if each nationality had been a compact group within a defined area, but the contrary was largely the case. Regarded from the political standpoint it was the most complex organism of Europe, with no less than twenty-one legislative bodies of various importance and functions.

This mosaic of territories and national groups was the creation of the Habsburg dynasty. Throughout the centuries the Habsburgs had added new territories to old ones by treaties, inheritance, war, and above all by marriage. The practice of acquiring territory

259

through matrimonial ventures is expressed in the widely quoted paraphrase of Ovid:

> Bella gerant alii tu, felix Austria, nube!
> Nam quae Mars aliis, dat tibi regna Venus!
>
> Others wage war, but you, fortunate Austria, marry!
> For what Mars gives to others, Venus bestows on you!

In acquiring new territories right and left the Habsburgs paid no attention to the nationality of their new subjects. As a result they collected a conglomeration of peoples which was characterized by diversity rather than unity. In the eighteenth century a number of rulers, including Maria Theresa (1740–1780) and Joseph II (1765–1790), sought to effect the Germanization of the heterogeneous units. Generally speaking, the means they employed in the hope of securing the predominance of German culture was the inexorable suppression of the culture of the subject groups. But their efforts met with little success. After trying in vain to unify the nationalities under their rule the Habsburgs endeavored to keep their peoples in subjugation by the ancient principle of *divide et impera* (*divide and rule*). This policy was boldly announced as far back as the Congress of Vienna (1815) by the Emperor Francis II. "My peoples," he said, "are strangers to each other. That is all the better. They do not catch the same political disease at the same time. If the fever takes hold of you in France, all of you catch it. Hungary is kept in order by Italian troops, and Italy is kept down by Hungarians. Everybody keeps his neighbor in order. My people do not understand each other. Their antipathies make for security, and their mutual hatreds for the general peace."

The collapse of the Habsburg Empire had long been expected. Revolt had, in fact, been characteristic of the nation ever since the days of William Tell. So long as the spirit of nationalism was quiescent, the task of holding the component parts together was comparatively simple; but when nationalism became aggressive, the threat of dissolution became very real. Prince Metternich, during whose time (1773–1859) this spirit was awakening, compared the Habsburg state to an old, rickety, worm-eaten building. In 1867 the Habsburgs sought to bolster the shaky structure by transforming the empire into a so-called Dual Monarchy; in other words, they gave full acknowledgment to the separate existence of Hungary. The new government was a federation of two equal states under the common rule of a single sovereign who was emperor of Austria and king of Hungary. Having obtained self-government, however, the Magyars denied to the non-Magyar nationalities of Hungary that liberty, equality, and justice which they had claimed for themselves as a natural right. For another fifty years the empire continued to exist without any spirit of solidarity. During this time the various groups were growing increasingly self-conscious and restive. Two kinds of separatist movements were developing: national and irredentist. While some wished to form independent states, others had aspirations of being united to an outside neighboring state of the same blood and nationality. It was the hope of preventing its own dismemberment that impelled the Austro-Hungarian government to make the fatal decision for war against Serbia, a war which soon broadened into the First World War.

How futile the decision was! Instead of arresting dissolution, the war accelerated it. For a time, it is true, the unfortunate subject peoples were kept in awe by an army of spies, by military police, and by the unrestricted activities of the hangman and the firing squad. Thousands were imprisoned, hanged, or shot in order to strike terror into the hearts of those who were contemplating revolt. This policy, in filling the hearts of the subjects with a deep hatred of the Habsburgs, only served to hasten the final reckoning. As soon as the outcome of the war became inevitable, the bonds which held the ramshackle empire together gave way. It may be worth noting that after the death in 1916 of Francis Joseph who had ruled since 1848, his successor, the Emperor Charles, wished to reorganize his empire on a federal basis. But his advisers and the German government were not in favor of the plan and did not permit him to proclaim it until October 16, 1918. By this time it was too late to arrest or control the breakup of the empire. The door of independence had been opened and the subject peoples were rushing blindly toward liberty.

The one man outside the boundaries of Austria-Hungary who may be said to have hastened the dissolution was President Wilson, by solemnly proclaiming the right of each nationality to be the arbiter of its own destiny and to choose its own form of government. Encouraged by the President's pronouncements, the Czechs who had supplied the Habsburg armies with Skoda guns, the Slavs who had long been straining at the leash, and the Croats whose regiments formed the flower of the Austro-Hungarian army, proclaimed their independence. The actual deathblow was administered by President Wilson on October 18, 1918, when he recognized the independence of the Czechs and Yugoslavs. Emperor Charles, after trying desperately to prevent complete collapse, finally withdrew (November 11,

1918) and before many hours had passed every national group had renounced its allegiance to the Dual Monarchy. Out of the ruins new states arose at once. The Hungarians, Czechs, Poles, and Yugoslavs formed their own states, and the Austrians set up a republic in the territory that was left them. Because of the intermingling of national groups in this area, complete adherence to the principle of self-determination was impossible. Although the political boundaries were made to coincide substantially with the national majorities, there were exceptions which soon gave rise to a new irredentism.

🍂

AUSTRIA'S STRUGGLE FOR EXISTENCE

The breaking away of the Hungarian, Czechoslovak, Yugoslav, Polish, and other groups left only the small German nucleus around which the Habsburgs had originally assembled their conglomeration of nationalities. The terms of the postwar settlement pared this nucleus down still further. In the National Assembly, which adopted a provisional constitution on November 12, 1918, there had been representatives of the German South Tyrol and of German Bohemia which according to the principle of self-determination should have formed part of the new Austrian republic, but the treaty of St. Germain accorded the former to Italy and the latter to Czechoslovakia. This left Austria with a territory of 32,000 square miles and a population of 6,067,430, according to the census of January, 1920. Of this population approximately one third lived in Vienna. In other words, the Vienna which before the war had been the capital of the third largest empire of Europe became the center of a few counties whose resources were at best sufficient to support a moderate sized provincial town. The new Austria was not only a landlocked country cut off from all international trade routes but its agricultural area was so small that it was unable to produce enough food for its people. Previously the Austrians had received grain from Hungary, meat from Hungary and Galicia, and sugar, potatoes, vegetables, and beer from Bohemia. Now these commodities were excluded by tariff barriers. Austria still had iron and steel industries, but it had no coal, its most important coal districts, those of Bohemia, having been allotted to the succession states which immediately imposed hard conditions on export.

Since any attempt to preserve the economic unity of the Dual Monarchy by forming a federation of the succession states was out of question because of racial hatreds, the Austrians turned to what they regarded as the natural solution of the Austrian question—*Anschluss* (union) with Germany. Not that they wished to be absorbed by Germany; they hoped to remain a self-governing federal state within the German Republic. Such a step was regarded as being in accordance with Wilson's Fourteen Points, on the basis of which the armistice had been signed. Therefore on November 12, 1918, the National Assembly declared that "German Austria is a constituent part of the German Republic." This declaration also had widespread support outside the Assembly. Originally the monopoly of a handful of Pan-Germans, *Anschluss* became a popular cry in many other quarters. The only group that did not take it up were the (Catholic) Christian Socialists, who feared that Austria would be dominated by Protestant Prussia. On the other hand, the Social Democrats were enthusiastic in their support of the idea. But the desire for union was frustrated by the opposition of France and her satellites. Later the Treaty of St. Germain as well as the Treaty of Versailles forbade any such union without permission of the Council of the League of Nations.

To the many Austrians who favored *Anschluss* the prohibition was a sore disappointment, but the demand for it did not cease. Apart from any other consideration, the fact that it was forbidden made it desirable. There were, however, some who felt that Austria was irremediably doomed to economic collapse unless the union was effected. Dr. Karl Renner, leader of the Social Democrats, said: "You all know that German Austria has no chance of existing among the present constellations. The only thing we can do is to remain alive until the hour of liberation comes, until we as Germans can decide to join the state to which by the nature of things we belong." The reason for the other nations' opposition was simply the fear that a new German national state which included Austria would be a serious menace to the equilibrium of Europe. To what degree this fear was shared even by the Swiss may be seen from the following statement published in the *Basler Nationalzeitung:* "With a Greater Germany on the horizon, we shall witness all around us a furious nationalistic reaction. A greater German Empire reaching from Hamburg to Pressburg would push all other states to the wall by its more vital power."

As the months passed, Austria's financial position steadily deteriorated. In the words of one observer: "Some eighteen months have now elapsed since the armistice and it is no exaggeration to say that Austria is today financially, industrially, and morally in a far worse plight than she was at the cessation of hostilities. Her currency is depreciated to such a degree that it is virtually unrecognized abroad; her industries are, with few exceptions, at a standstill." [1] As the country was not able to grow sufficient food for the population, the government was forced to import foodstuffs and sell them at a loss. The result was that the budget showed an ever increasing deficit, with the national debt expanding by billions each month. Finally in February, 1922, Austria was saved from collapse by large loans from Britain, France, Italy, and Czechoslovakia. In the same year the government signed the Geneva Protocol (October 4) which guaranteed it a loan of about $130 million sponsored by the League of Nations on condition that fiscal reforms be instituted and the budget balanced. The value of exports gradually increased and agriculture developed by leaps and bounds. A new currency also helped inspire confidence. By 1926 the situation had improved so greatly that control by the League was terminated.

If the economic situation was not a happy one, neither was the political. The two major parties were the Social Democrats and the Christian Socialists. The former were moderate socialists who had wandered far from the path of strictly Marxian doctrines. Most of their strength was concentrated in Vienna, where they controlled the municipal government. In Vienna their goal was to create a model city. They provided pensions and unemployment insurance for workers, demolished old tenements and constructed modern apartment houses for workers, opened kindergartens and provided ample playgrounds for children, and set up prenatal clinics which gave free medical attention to mothers. At a time when Bolshevism was taking a temporary hold in a number of countries including Hungary, the Social Democrats prevented its establishment in Vienna. But they also resisted the pressure of the reactionary peasant provinces that was exerted through the Christian Socialist Party. Besides being composed chiefly of peasants this party was completely Catholic. This would not be unusual in a country whose population was about 93 per cent Catholic. Despite its name, the party had little about it that was socialist in the generally accepted sense of the word. As the years passed, it became more and more reactionary.

Between these two parties, and therefore between the urban and rural populations, a deep hostility developed which heavily overbalanced loyalty to the new state. While the Christian Socialists or Clericals, as they were also called, feared the socialist legislation of the Social Democrats, the latter denounced the reactionary policies of the Christian Socialists. The mutual antagonism was further

[1] *Living Age,* vol. 304 (1920), p. 381.

aggravated by the divergent economic interests of the agricultural and industrial classes. At one time the provincials went so far as to forbid the exportation of foodstuffs to Vienna. The Social Democrats, for their part, had the power to bring tremendous pressure upon their opponents by organizing strikes, demonstrations, and processions. Since both parties were returned to parliament in almost equal numbers, a strong government by one party was out of question. More than this, the fundamental opposition between a "black" countryside and a "red" Vienna obstructed all attempts at constructive national legislation. It was the tragedy of Austria that the two parties were unable to put aside their differences in order to extricate their country from the bog into which it was sinking. On the contrary, the antagonism became more bitter with the years. In the later twenties it assumed a more sinister aspect when various semimilitary organizations came into existence and were appropriated by ambitious party leaders for political purposes. These organizations defied one another and at times threatened to defy even the state. In general, they produced further restlessness, engendered suspicions, and committed various acts of violence. The two most formidable semimilitary organizations were the *Schutzbund* of the Social Democrats and the peasant *Heimwehr*, the latter organized by Prince von Starhemberg and later allied with the Christian Socialists.

During the first two years of its existence (1918–1920) the republic was governed by a coalition, but at the elections held in the autumn of 1920 the Social-Democrat representation declined and the Christian Socialists secured a majority. The latter polled some 1,198,780 votes and secured 82 seats; the Social Democrats polled only 1,037,638 and obtained 62 seats. Thenceforth until Austria was absorbed by Germany in 1938, the Christian Socialists with the help of the smaller bourgeois parties controlled the government. Both the foreign and the internal policy of this party was largely favorable to the interests of the peasants, despite the fact that the country was 60 per cent industrial. More and more the Christian Socialists lost the strong democratic influences of the early revolutionary days and became clerical and conservative. Their leader during the decade of the twenties was Monsignor Ignaz Seipel, a Catholic priest and a man of ascetic life. From 1922 to 1929 as chancellor he directed the fortunes of Austria.

Although the various loans that had been made to Austria were an invaluable aid, they did not solve the country's basic economic problems. During the years after 1922 Vienna recovered some of its former prestige as a banking and trading center, but 1929 saw the collapse of the Kredit Anstalt and the beginning of the depression. Trade withered under the blast of the depression. As always in hard times, customers for the luxury goods in which Austria specialized were scarce. The consequent drop in customs receipts was a severe blow to the national budget, which closed with a deficit amounting to more than $40 million in 1931. This decline in trade was naturally accompanied by an increase in unemployment. It is estimated that in 1932 every twelfth Austrian was unemployed. As the economic situation deteriorated, the number of Nazis increased from a mere 7000 in 1928 to no less than 100,000 in 1931, the converts having been made largely among the small *bourgeoisie* and the unemployed of all classes. The movement derived much of its strength, both moral and material, from the German Nazi movement; in fact, Hitler regarded the Austrian Nazis as a branch of his own party. The aim of the Austrian Nazis as a constituent part of Hitler's National Socialist movement was the union of Austria and Germany, and they left no stone unturned to achieve their goal. The Social Democrats, on the other hand, appalled by the terrorist methods of the Nazi regime in Germany, promptly renounced all ideas of *Anschluss*.

After 1932 economic improvement set in again but it contributed little toward mitigating the political disorders. In 1929 Chancellor Seipel had retired and, after a succession of chancellors, Dr. Engelbert Dollfuss, also a Christian Socialist, took over the office in 1932. The new chancellor was small of stature, only four feet eleven inches tall. One of his favorite statements was, "After all I am still a millimeter taller than Napoleon." The standard joke in Austria was that he could be reproduced life-size on a postage stamp. But what he lacked in size he more than made up for in determination. Insisting on the right of Austria to remain independent, he vigorously rebuffed the efforts of the German and the Austrian Nazis to seize control of the country. He responded to the Nazi terrorism and intimidation by proscribing the party. But the Nazis, as a secret organization, continued to perpetrate innumerable acts of violence. In his efforts to curb the Nazis Dollfuss frequently resorted to dictatorial methods. Finally on March 4, 1933, he suspended parliamentary government, abolished freedom of speech, press, and assemblage, and proceeded to rule as a dictator. These measures were at first regarded as temporary, but in September he announced that he had no intention of restoring parliamentary government. He was determined, he declared, to transform Austria into a corporative

CHANCELLOR KURT SCHUSCHNIGG INSPECTING AUSTRIA'S FIGHTING
PLANES; APRIL, 1936

authoritative state in accordance with the principles enunciated by Pope Pius XI in his encyclical *Quadragesimo Anno.*

To withstand the Nazi assult Dollfuss was obliged to join forces either with the *Heimwehr* or with the Social Democrats. He chose the former because the choice was more in keeping with the conservative attitude of his followers. But the price Prince Starhemberg and his *Heimwehr* asked for collaboration was the suppression of the Social-Democratic regime in Vienna. For years Starhemberg had made no secret of his determination to follow the lead of Italy and Germany and destroy the socialists by force. Now the opportunity had come. In February, 1934, the *Heimwehr* closed the Social Democrats' main organ, the *Arbeiterzeitung,* raided socialist centers, arrested Social-Democratic leaders, and sent socialists by the thousands to concentration camps established on the model of the German camps. When the Social Democrats responded by calling a general strike, martial law was declared and a bloody civil war broke out, as a result of which many hundreds of lives were lost. Later the property of the party and of the trade unions was seized, and the latter were dissolved. Dollfuss by approving the action of the *Heimwehr* again made it clear that he was not a champion of liberty.

Meanwhile Nazi hostility toward the Austrian government had become steadily more bitter. The fact that Dollfuss refused to lie down and be eaten enraged the Nazis and impelled them to attempt a daring coup. On Wednesday, July 25, 1934, hardly a month after Hitler's bloody purge, a group of 144 Nazis, disguised as regular soldiers of the Austrian army, invaded the chancellery in Vienna as part of a plan to arrest the cabinet. The conspirators shot Dollfuss, who was then allowed to bleed to death without benefit of physician or priest. But the plan to put a Nazi cabinet in power miscarried and the conspirators finally surrendered to the government.

Dollfuss' successor, Dr. Kurt Schuschnigg, who was also a member of the Christian Socialist party, took energetic steps to put down the Nazi revolts that broke out all over Austria. The ringleaders of the premature Putsch were tried and executed, many others were sentenced to long prison terms, and thousands were confined in concentration camps. For several months thereafter the Nazi agitation remained quiescent, but it was soon renewed with fervor. On top of this, dissension broke out in the cabinet. Starhemberg, who had long nourished ambitions of becoming dictator, managed to usurp power because of his *Heimwehr;* but toward the end of 1935 he was finally ousted by Schuschnigg and at the same time his *Heimwehr* was rendered innocuous. Prospects for independence appeared brighter when in 1936 an accord was signed in which Germany recognized Austria's "complete sovereignty" and adopted measures to end the trade war which had been carried on between the two countries since the attempted Putsch of July, 1934. Hitler's government even went so far as to promise to discontinue propaganda in Austria. Nevertheless, the illegal Nazi movement not only continued but actually intensified its activities. Ultimately the Nazis, despite Schuschnigg's efforts to maintain independence, were to achieve *Anschluss*.

‡

HUNGARIAN IRREDENTISM

The collapse of the Austro-Hungarian front on the Piave at the beginning of November, 1918, and the subsequent signing of an armistice precipitated a crisis in Hungary. After four years of sanguinary fighting the country emerged from the war completely defeated. Besides the economic disorganization resulting from the collapse of the Dual Monarchy, there was widespread demoralization engendered by the sudden realization of defeat. In addition the army had completely broken up after the conclusion of the armistice and hundreds of thousands of soldiers returned, not as a disciplined army but as an undisciplined mob. In some parts of Hungary chaos reigned supreme. Three governments were established in quick succession. The reason for their rapid passing was their inability to obtain better peace terms. Although they had lost the war, the Hungarians were not inclined to give up any territory. The one thing all Magyars, irrespective of party, had in common was a desire to keep prewar Hungary intact. But while the Paris Conference was deliberating, her neighbors were seizing as much territory as they could. The Czechoslovakian Republic having been proclaimed at Prague, the Czechs and Slovaks occupied those districts in which the Slovak racial element predominated. Simultaneously Croatia-Slavonia was incorporated in Yugoslavia, and Serbian troops invaded the most fertile districts of southern Hungary. At the same time Rumanian troops proceeded to occupy Transylvania, whose union with Rumania had been a definite aim for two generations. Thus the dismemberment of Hungary was a *fait accompli*.

On November 16, 1918, Hungary proclaimed herself a republic and a provisional government was formed under Count Michael Karolyi, who though an aristocrat was also a liberal and a pacifist Karolyi hoped to maintain a moderately liberal regime, but he was also determined to retain all of Hungary's prewar territory. This he hoped to do by convincing the Allies, who were soon to sit in judgment at Paris, that the Hungarians were pacifists and had been forced into the war by the Habsburgs. As proof of his pacifism he purged the government of all who had been associated with the war policy. This, however, failed to save Hungary from losing most of its territory to the subject nationalities. When in March, 1919, the Allies presented to Budapest their provisional decisions and it became clear not only that Hungary would lose its non-Magyars but that three million Hungarians would also be transferred to Rumania, Yugoslavia, and Czechoslovakia, Karolyi found himself discredited, and he resigned.

The Karolyi government was followed by four months of Bolshevist experimenting. A number of Hungarians who had been prisoners of war in Russia had organized soviets on the Russian model upon their return home. When Karolyi resigned, Béla Kun, a friend of Lenin, set up a communist regime in Budapest with the support of the soviets. This was accomplished without bloodshed and with comparatively little trouble. Only after its establishment did the Hungarian Soviet Republic resort to repressive measures. One reason for the communists' success was their promise that if Hungary turned communist, Russia would help the Hungarians hold their prewar boundaries. The new soviet republic took steps at once to put a communist program into effect. The socialization of large landholdings, mines, banks, industries, and other commercial institutions was proclaimed, all titles and ranks were abolished, separation of church and state was decreed, and taxes for church purposes were abolished. In addition, a system of education was devised to wipe out illiteracy. But as the weeks passed, the regime lost much of its support even among the workers. At no time did it control the whole country and as early as the middle of May an anti-Bolshevik government was established in Arad.

It was through his efforts to save Hungary from being dismembered that Béla Kun hoped to restore his popularity. And for a time he and his associates did succeed in securing their position by appealing to the patriotism of the Hungarians to aid in the formation of an army which he hoped would keep annexations by the succession states to a minimum. Desperately attacking the Czechs, he won several victories in June. But his successes were short lived. The Allies, who feared above all things that Bolshevism would take firm root in Central Europe, permitted the Rumanians to advance into Hungary up to a certain point. Kun rashly undertook an offensive against them and was heavily defeated. When on top of this the trade unions withdrew their support from his government, he realized that his cause was irretrievably lost. On August 1 he and his associates resigned and crossed over into Austria, leaving behind a legacy of hatred and revenge.

After various attempts to set up a stable government failed, a law of 1920 formally re-established the monarchy. But Hungary remained "a kingdom without a king." Admiral Nicholas Horthy, who had formerly commanded the Austro-Hungarian fleet, was given the supreme power with the title of "regent," but for whom he was serving as regent was not stated. Although the majority desired to see the throne once more occupied by a permanent representative, the National Assembly, while admitting the validity of King Charles' claim, felt that the time for his return had not arrived. Twice during 1921 he made unsuccessful attempts to reinstate himself on the throne. On both occasions Horthy, in view of the international situation, refused to cooperate. Charles' first attempt was largely responsible for bringing into being the Little Entente,[2] formed for the purpose of preventing the restoration of the Habsburgs. His second attempt (October, 1921) provoked the most severe protests from the Little Entente, the foreign minister of Czechoslovakia going so far as to state that the restoration of the former reigning house would mean war.

Theoretically the Horthy government was a democratic kingdom with a regularly elected upper and lower house, but this parliament served only to mask a firmly established dictatorship. The voting was minutely controlled by administrative corruption and intimidation, and every opposition was summarily suppressed. This spirit gave rise to the "White Terror" soon after the Horthy government was established in power. All radicals and even the liberals were attacked, beaten, or imprisoned. Large numbers were also put to death.[3] Since the government of Béla Kun had been composed almost exclusively of Jews, the rage of the reactionaries was vented especially on the Jews, regardless of their individual innocence. But the violence was only an incidental accompaniment of the general reaction which became the order of the day. What distinguishes the history of Hungary from the history of most other European countries was the attempt to restore the old political and social regime in its entirety, so far as that was possible. Horthy and Count

[2] Czechoslovakia, Rumania, and Yugoslavia.
[3] The spirit of vengeance and suppression remained so bitter that in August, 1932, two young Hungarian communists were executed for having returned from Moscow to Budapest to establish a communist bureau there.

Bethlen, who was prime minister from 1921 to 1931, re-established in a large degree the feudal regime of the period before 1914. Many of the estates which had been broken up were restored, so that 40 per cent of the land was held in estates of over 1400 acres. The great landlords, representing 1.3 per cent of the population, owned and controlled 50 per cent of the land, while 75 per cent of the peasants were landless. During the period that followed, the growing land hunger of an impoverished peasantry caused crisis after crisis. In the words of one observer: "Crying need and ostentatious wealth, seething unrest and smiling contentment are to be found side by side."

On June 4, 1920, the Hungarian delegation signed the Treaty of Trianon under protest. Having taken part in the war on the wrong side, Hungary had to pay the penalty. By and large the peace did little more than put its stamp of approval on the partition that had already been made. Hungary was reduced in area from 109,000 to 35,800 square miles and in population from about twenty millions to about eight. The territory it retained was a little larger than the state of Maine. In other words, Hungary forfeited approximately two thirds of its territory and considerably more than half its population. At the same time the economic resources—arable land, minerals, and forests—were reduced to a fraction of their former figures. Cut off from the sea, Hungary was almost isolated from the rest of the world by the tariff barriers of the states which surrounded it. But the most irreconcilable feature of the treaty for the Hungarians was that, the principle of self-determination notwithstanding, more than three millions of their kinsfolk were consigned to the position of national minorities in Czechoslovakia, Rumania, and Yugoslavia. No country was made to pay a larger penalty and in none did the peace engender greater bitterness. The settlement was denounced equally by all classes as an outrage against justice and humanity. Time and again Hungarian writers declared that it was to be classed with the eighteenth-century partitions of Poland.

Nor did the Hungarians become resigned to the fact that large Hungarian populations were subject to alien rule. The resentment against the treaty and the desire to regain the lost possessions run like a heavy unbroken line through Hungary's history between the two wars. Officially the government had to play the role of good boy in obediently following the dictates of the peace settlements, but unofficially plans were being laid for the recovery of the ceded Hungarians, if necessary by force of arms. Foreign policy was carefully shaped with a view to achieving this end. The question was everlastingly discussed and such discussions were an important factor in

exciting a hatred of the neighboring nationalities. During her travels in Hungary in 1925 the novelist Rebecca West reported a Hungarian she casually met as saying: " 'You see, we hate the Austrians.
And we detest the Czechs. Is it not iniquitous that a country which
fought alongside us against the Allies should be allowed to sit at the
Peace Conference and dictate terms to us and be given a slice of our
territory and a whole million of our people? Also we loathe Rumania. Seventeen hundred thousand of our people they have taken,
and the finest part of Hungary! And we detest the Serbs! And—'
'Then whom,' I asked, 'do you like?' 'No one but ourselves! And,
after all, Madam,' he added, growing philosophical, 'when one
comes to think of it, there is really no reason why one should!' " [4]

The resentment against the treaty was kept alive and even intensified by various methods. For example, statues representing
Hungaria Irredenta were erected and postcards were sold representing Hungary divided into four parts and bearing the words,
"Nem, nem, soha (No, no, never) ." Propaganda was also carried on
in other countries, particularly in England, for the revision of the
treaty. In Italy Mussolini on a number of occasions declared himself
in favor of revision of the Hungarian frontiers. In a speech at Milan
in 1936 he said: "Until justice is done to Hungary there can be no
final coordination of interests in the Danube basin. Hungary is truly
the great mutilated nation. Four millions of Hungarians live beyond her frontiers." Such statements, added to the agitation within
Hungary, kept the succession states on tenterhooks, causing them not
only to form the Little Entente for the express purpose of putting
up a solid front against Hungary but also to stand ready for any
emergency. Meanwhile Hungary, hemmed in by neighbors powerful enough to hold it in check, smoldered for twenty bitter years
The first small change in the boundaries was made when Germany,
in dismembering Czechoslovakia, tossed Ruthenia to Hungary.

THE PROBLEM OF MINORITIES IN CZECHOSLOVAKIA

The first of the new states to rise from the ruins of the Austro-
Hungarian Empire was the Czechoslovakian Republic. The Czechs,
who inhabited Bohemia, Moravia, and Silesia, had been under Habsburg rule for centuries and were particularly antipathetic to foreign
control. After the Napoleonic wars in the early nineteenth century
a vigorous nationalism developed in Bohemia, the natural accompaniment of which was a desire for complete independence. The

[4] *New Republic*, March 11, 1925. p. 64.

opportunity to achieve this desire was, however, not to come until the end of World War I. At the outbreak of the war the Czechs were placed in the embarrassing position of being called upon to fight for the Habsburg Empire. Long before the close of the war Czech soldiers openly deserted and joined the Allied army in the hope of achieving their dream of independence. But this was only one phase of the struggle. At the decisive moment the Czechs had the good fortune to have able leaders and the good sense to follow them. The man who organized the national resurrection was Dr. Thomas G. Masaryk, a coachman's son who had distinguished himself as a scholar and a college professor. Besides having a capacity for organization, Masaryk was a man of courage, tenacity, and vision.

When the war broke out, he decided that the time had come to translate the longing for independence into reality. He took into his confidence another college professor, Dr. Edvard Beneš, a man half his age, and together they formulated a program of action. Having laid their plans, they escaped from Bohemia and for the next four years traveled about ceaselessly expounding, explaining, and pleading their cause by word and pen. Besides gaining the support of the Allies, they organized an army to fight on the side of the Allies, the nucleus of this army being formed by Czech prisoners taken in battle by the Allies themselves. At the same time they also created and directed an underground movement in Prague. As the Austro-Hungarian hope for victory gradually faded, the Czech patriots became more audacious in their denunciation of the Habsburgs and more insistent in their demands for independence. The Austrian government's proposals for federalization were answered with statements like the following, made by a Czech patriot in the Austrian parliament (July 22, 1918): "We regard Austria as a century-old crime against the liberties of humanity. . . . It is our highest national duty to betray Austria whenever we can. We shall hate Austria for all eternity. We shall fight her and, God willing, shall in the end smash her to pieces."

Meanwhile the Slovaks had decided to make common cause with the Czechs, and the support of the Allied powers had been won. On August 13, 1918, Great Britain published its formal recognition of the Czechoslovak nation and the United States followed suit on September 2. A provisional Czechoslovak government, organized in Paris, formally proclaimed a Declaration of Independence on October 18. It read in part: "The Czechoslovak state shall be a republic. In constant endeavor for progress it will guarantee complete freedom of conscience, religion and science, literature and art, speech and the press, and the right of assembly and petition. The church shall be separated from the state. Our democracy shall rest on universal suffrage: women shall be placed on equal footing with men, politically, socially, and culturally. The rights of the minority shall be safeguarded by proportional representation; national minorities shall enjoy equal rights. The government shall be parliamentary in form and shall recognize the principle of initiative and referendum."

Ten days later the Czechs actually established their rule in Prague by the simple expedient of informing the Austrian government that its rule in Bohemia had come to an end. Amidst tremendous demonstrations of joy a National Assembly was summoned on the basis of the number of votes polled by the various political parties in the last election of the Austrian Reichsrat. At its first meeting (November 14, 1918) Czechoslovakia was declared an independent democratic republic, and Masaryk was enthusiastically chosen its first president. He stated his creed in the following words: "I shall defend democracy against dictatorial absolutism, whether the right to dictate be claimed by the proletariat, the state, or the church." Dr. Beneš became foreign minister, then prime minister, and in 1935 succeeded Masaryk as president. By the constitution adopted on February 29, 1920, the legislative power was vested in a National Assembly composed of two bodies, the Chamber of Representatives and the Senate, both elected by universal, compulsory, and secret voting on the basis of proportional representation. The two bodies in joint session elected the president for a term of seven years. The cabinet was formed of ministers chosen by the president on the advice of the leader of the political party in power.

The boundaries of the new state as they were definitely established by the Treaty of St. Germain (September 10, 1919) included Bohemia, Moravia, and Silesia, to which Slovakia and Carpathian Ruthenia were added. With an area of 54,877 square miles it was about the size of the state of Illinois but had a population of about fourteen millions. Despite the declaration of the Allied statesmen that self-determination would be the operative principle of the peace, the new Czechoslovakia was a miniature edition of the old Habsburg state. After abolishing German-Magyar domination over the Czechs and Slovaks, the peacemakers proceeded to establish a Czechoslovakia with large minorities. The Czechoslovaks comprised only 65 per cent of the population, the rest being made up of Magyars, Ruthenes, Poles, and Germans, with a sprinkling of Jews.

The most numerous minority group were the Germans, generally known as the Sudeten Germans, who numbered more than three millions or almost a quarter of the population, concentrated in northern and western Bohemia. They protested their inclusion in the Slav state and pleaded the right of self-determination. Furthermore, Austria asked for a plebiscite in the Sudeten districts, but this was refused.

In adding the districts inhabited by Germans to the Czech state, the peacemakers acted on a number of motives. First, there were strategic reasons. The Sudeten mountains formed a natural frontier for the protection of the new state. This was especially important because the peacemakers were intent on blocking Germany's *Drang nach dem Südosten*. Second, the separation of these districts, which were heavily industrialized, would have meant economic disaster for Czechoslovakia. The reasons are stated by one writer as follows: "The abandonment of the historic frontiers—more sharply defined by nature herself than almost any other in Europe—would have had a treble disadvantage. It would have left Czechoslovakia so entirely defenseless as to be really incapable of independent life; it would have deprived her of a large proportion of those mineral resources upon which Bohemia's prosperity has always rested; and it would have cut off the German districts themselves from their natural market." The fact still remained, however, that the inclusion of the Germans was a violation of the principle of self-determination.

President Masaryk and his government attacked the problems confronting the new state with vigor, tact, and determination. For purposes of organization the so-called National Coalition was formed by the five major Czechoslovak parties, leaving the German and Magyar parties and the communists in opposition. Notwithstanding the fact that chaos was reigning in most of central Europe, Czechoslovakia was administered with calm assurance from the very beginning. Of all the new states it was probably the only one in which reform was carried out more or less systematically. For example, at the very outset a law was passed expropriating all large estates and confiscating the Habsburg lands. As a means of making an orderly distribution, a Land Office was set up. Although much was done to satisfy the land hunger of the peasants, the execution was not so radical as the plan but what was accomplished did contribute greatly to social peace and national unity. Another achievement was the establishment of a stable currency. While other nations were issuing unlimited quantities of paper money, the Czechoslovakian government stopped printing it and several years later also balanced the budget. The price they paid was a temporary economic depression accompanied by severe unemployment; on the other hand, the currency during the period between 1920 and 1924 stood beside the Swiss franc as the only good currency of central and eastern Europe. As early as 1922, when the German mark began its dizzy slide into nothingness, the Germans and still more the Austrians began buying and hoarding Czechoslovakian currency in their flight from their own paper money.

Another sphere in which the new government achieved remarkable success was education. Although the districts inhabited largely by Czechs and Germans (Bohemia, Moravia, Silesia) had the lowest percentage of illiterates (about 3 per cent) in the old Austro-Hungarian empire, education in Slovakia and Ruthenia had been grossly neglected by their prewar masters. The few schools that the government had supported in these provinces were totally Magyarized. There was not a single state school in either Slovakia or Ruthenia in which the medium of instruction was Slovak or Ruthenian. Consequently illiteracy was widespread. To remedy this condition the government found it necessary to set up an entirely new educational system in these provinces. Since there were few teachers available to teach the Slovak and Ruthenian children in their respective mother tongues, normal schools were opened for the training of such teachers. As quickly as additional teachers were ready, new elementary schools were opened. The result was that by 1927 there were in Slovakia 2692 elementary schools using the Slovak language as a medium of instruction. During the same period other schools were also opened, including German, Ruthenian, and Magyar elementary schools and German and Czechoslovakian high schools. In 1930 the secondary schools were divided according to languages as follows: 226 were Czechoslovakian, 96 German, 10 Magyar, 2 Polish, and 8 Ruthenian. In 1922 a law was passed which made attendance compulsory for the eight years between the ages of six and fourteen. Gradually the curricula of the secondary schools were remodeled to provide technical and manual instruction for boys and domestic science for girls.

The new state had a great advantage in being well endowed with natural resources and established industries. In the extent and variety of its minerals, it ranked high among European countries. Besides possessing varying quantities of most of the metals commonly used in industry, it produced more than enough coal to meet its domestic requirements. The coal deposits and iron mines, together with excellent transportation, combined to make Bohemia, Moravia, and

PRESIDENT MASARYK OF CZECHOSLOVAKIA AND HIS SUCCESSOR, EDVARD BENEŠ

Silesia one of the most active industrial centers of Europe. Particularly noteworthy were the sugar, spirit, beer, and textile industries, but also important was the manufacture of china, machinery, hardware, furniture, and leather and paper goods. About 80 per cent of the textile industries and engineering works of the old Habsburg Empire were concentrated in Czechoslovakia. The new state was also in the enviable position of being almost self-supporting in regard to food; in fact, it was able to export many such products as oats, barley, and hops. Furthermore, most of the raw materials for the sugar, beer, spirit, and glass industries were produced within the republic. Czechoslovakia also had extensive forests which after supplying the domestic needs yielded a surplus for export. In short, the new state possessed the material foundations for prosperity and during the first decade of its existence did enjoy a large measure of prosperity.

Gradually, however, some of the problems which during the first decade had been quiescent became acute. The most serious was that of minorities. The rights which the Treaty of Versailles accorded to national minorities in all the new states were further elaborated in Czechoslovakia by a special law of February 29, 1920, which decreed that the language of the minority must be accepted by the courts and by the administrative officials in the districts in which it was spoken by 20 per cent of the inhabitants. In the districts where a minority numbered less than 20 per cent the law provided that no disadvantage was to accrue to any person through ignorance of the official language. All minorities also had proportional representation in the parliament and other bodies. There may have been some discrimination against minorities on the part of lesser officials, but denationalization was forbidden by law. During the first years, it is true, most of the administrative posts were staffed by Czechs, even in Slovakia. This was due in large degree to the scarcity of Slovaks who were qualified for such work. Thanks to the autonomous status of Bohemia and Moravia under the old monarchy, the Czechs had trained officials who stepped into the administration when it was organized. In the Slovakian districts Slovaks were substituted for Czechs as soon as they could be trained. On the whole, the minorities received better treatment than in any other of the new states.

Nevertheless, the minorities became increasingly restive, particularly during the second decade of the republic's existence. In Ruthenia, which had been granted a status of autonomy, considerable discontent was fomented by Hungarians who regarded the province as *Hungaria irredenta*. Nor were the Czechs and Slovaks as united as the name Czechoslovakia implies. Although blood relatives, they differed widely in temperament and outlook. Until they joined in the new state they had had separate histories, traditions, and institutions. The Slovaks, who were largely an agricultural people, had been isolated no less from Bohemia than from the rest of the world by the Magyar policy of repression. Consequently they had remained backward while the Czechs, who lived largely in industrial areas, were educated and progressive. A further cause of division was the religious question. Before World War I more than 90 per cent of the Czechs had been Roman Catholic; but as soon as Czechoslovakia became independent, an anti-Catholic movement was set in motion with the result that many Czechs left the Roman Catholic Church, some of them joining an independent church which used the Czech language. On the whole, the Czechs tended to be a skeptical, freethinking people. This caused offense to the Slovaks, who were mostly devout Catholics over whom the priesthood exercised a strong influence. But the main grievance of the Slovaks was the failure of the government to grant them administrative and cultural autonomy. They claimed that according to an agreement made in Pittsburgh, Pennsylvania, on May 30, 1918, Slovakia was to receive complete autonomy within a federal state, including a separate political and financial administration, a separate assembly, and separate courts of law. To this claim President Masaryk replied that in adopting the constitution the representatives of Slovakia had expressed themselves for a complete union. Whatever objections they may have had against the Prague government they could not deny that Masaryk had their interests as much at heart as those of the Czechs, for he was himself of Slovak descent. Whereas it was his purpose to forge a complete union of the two peoples, the autonomists continued their agitation for a separate administration.

By all odds the gravest problem was that of the German minority. When the new state was organized, Masaryk invited the Sudeten Germans most heartily to cooperate in the work of the administration. But instead of supporting the government, they organized separatist movements in the hope of remaining in a German Austria which they thought would become part of a federal Germany. After the Peace Conference ignored their wishes, they adopted either a hostile or a negative attitude toward the new state and often indulged in niggling criticism of its policies. Their chief complaint was that a due proportion of Sudeten Germans were not appointed as state officials. There was some justification for this complaint, but the fact that the government did not choose more of its officials from the German minority must be ascribed in part to the hostile attitude of the Sudeten Germans. The real root of this attitude was that they resented the fact that the "upstart" Czechs whom they had ruled until 1918 had gained ascendancy over them. In 1926 a beginning was made toward wider collaboration between Czechs and Germans when Masaryk succeeded in bringing two Germans into the cabinet and several years later a third member was added. Curiously enough, in the next year 80 per cent of the German members of parliament helped elect Masaryk for a second term of seven years, while many of the Slav members registered dissent. When Masaryk, who resigned in 1935, died two years later, a leader of the German Social Democrats wrote: "The German elements that remain faithful to the ideas of humanity have lost a great friend in Masaryk."

Unfortunately the foundations of German-Czech collaboration which Masaryk had laid were in an advanced stage of disintegration by this time and a little more than a year later the entire structure that had been erected under his supervision was to collapse. One factor which contributed much toward widening the breach was the world depression of 1929. Although all of Czechoslovakia was hit by the crisis, the effects were catastrophic in the area inhabited by the Sudeten Germans, the most highly industrialized district of Czechoslovakia. The entire area became, so to speak, an industrial graveyard. Factories that had once employed thousands of hands stood empty and derelict by 1930, while others employed only a small fraction of their former staffs. The unequal incidence of the effects of the depression was ascribed by the Sudeten Germans to government policy. They complained, for instance, that most of the textile contracts for the army were placed with Czech firms in the interior of the country and that, in general, the Czechs might have taken more vigorous steps toward extricating them from the slough of depression.

By 1935 it was evident that the Czechs had missed their opportunity to win over the Sudeten Germans. In May of 1935 a new party, born of economic distress and political dissatisfaction, made its appearance in parliament. It was the Sudeten Party led by Konrad Henlein. At first their demands were very moderate. Professing loyalty to the state, they demanded a greater measure of cultural autonomy, participation in the administration in proportion to their numbers, equal distribution of government contracts, and subsidies to relieve distress in the Sudeten areas. This was little more than the Sudeten Germans had previously demanded. The real difference was that the new party had the backing of Nazi Germany. While professing allegiance to the Czechoslovak government, Henlein was taking orders from Hitler. The plan of the Nazis was, of course, to foment revolt and then to intervene. Jan Masaryk, son of the founder, said at a later time regarding the problem: "Our German minority was treated far better than any other in Europe and if it had not been for the shocking propaganda from across the border we and our Sudeten Germans would have settled our differences with dignity and without bloodshed." With the support of Hitler's Nazis the Sudeten Party became the second strongest party in 1937, having forty-four seats in Parliament against the Agrarian Party's forty-five. Before many more months passed, the Sudeten Party was to become the Trojan horse which opened Czechoslovakia to German invasion.

🔊

POLAND HARASSED BY INTERNAL AND EXTERNAL TROUBLES

Poland was a succession state of the Austro-Hungarian Empire only in a limited sense, for much more of its territory had been a part of the Russian Empire than of the Dual Monarchy. As every schoolboy knows, divisions of Polish territory among Prussia, Russia, and Austria toward the end of the eighteenth century (1772, 1793, and 1795) erased Poland as a state from the map of Europe. Few events in modern history have made so ineffaceable an impression upon the mind and conscience of mankind. The extent of the Polish kingdom, the service it had rendered as a bulwark against invasion from the East, and the methods employed by Prussia, Russia, and Austria to effect its destruction made a potent appeal to generous minds everywhere. In the eyes of many, Poland became the symbol of freedom in chains. But the division of territory did not obliterate Polish nationalism. Not only did the people remain a unit in their national culture and historical memories but they also clung tenaciously to the hope of restoration. Subjection to foreign rule, in fact, served to draw them closer together than they had been before they lost their political independence. Every great European convulsion inevitably revived the Polish question. In 1807 Napoleon formed a part of the old Polish commonwealth into a semi-independent state under the title of the Duchy of Warsaw and endowed it with a liberal constitution; but this was undone after his fall. Although the Congress of Vienna (1815) again repartitioned Poland among Prussia, Russia, and Austria, Tsar Alexander I organized most of the Polish territory under his rule into a Polish kingdom. This state was also short lived. When the Poles revolted in 1830, the liberties which the tsar had granted them were withdrawn and Poland again disappeared from the map.

While they were awaiting liberation the Poles increased in number until in 1914 there were nearly three times as many on their native soil as there had been in 1795. All were impregnated with nationalism. Every attempt during the nineteenth and early twentieth centuries to Russify or Germanize them had served only to strengthen their national sentiment. When the war broke out in 1914, the Russian Poles found themselves arrayed against the Austrian and German Poles on the battlefields of eastern Europe, with both sides making a bid for their support. First the Russians announced that upon the achievement of victory the Prussian and Austrian parts of Poland would be united to Russian Poland to form a united and autonomous kingdom. Next the Central Powers, after overrunning Russian Poland, announced on November 15, 1916, that Poland "will become an independent state, with an hereditary monarchy and a constitution." As a first step they set up a Council of Regency in Warsaw to direct matters until a sovereign could be chosen. As early as the autumn of 1917 France, Great Britain, Italy, and the United States had recognized the Polish National Committee, which had been formed mainly through the efforts of Ignace Paderewski, the great Polish musician. It will be recalled that the thirteenth of President Wilson's Fourteen Points provided for the erection of an independent Polish state which should include the territories inhabited by indisputably Polish populations. The collapse of the Russian Empire in 1917 and of the Austrian and German Empires in the following year brought the long awaited opportunity to establish an independent Poland.

Although he was by no means the first to dream the new Poland, Josef Pilsudski became, as it were, the George Washington of Poland. Born in 1867 of peasant stock, he early became a socialist and a revolutionary. Above all, he became a bitter enemy of Russian domination, vowing to fight Russian oppression until Poland was free. While attending the University of Kharkov he became a member of a group that was active in the never ceasing struggle for freedom and independence. He and several of his comrades were, however, apprehended and sentenced to five years of penal servitude in Siberia. He returned a hardened conspirator. He became one of the leaders of the Polish Socialist Party and the founder and editor of a socialist newspaper dedicated to the cause of independence. In 1900 he was arrested again, but by simulating insanity he managed to have himself transferred to a military hospital, whence he escaped to Austria. From that time until the outbreak of World War I he devoted himself to the organization of rifle clubs in which young Poles were clandestinely taught the elements of military training. According to his plan the members of these clubs were to form the nucleus of an army of liberation. When the war came, he incorporated his "sharpshooters" into the Austrian army and led them into battle against the Russians. After the defeat of Russia he organized a Polish military force to fight against Germany but was arrested and incarcerated until the defeat of Germany in 1918. Upon his release he hurried to Warsaw, where the Council of Regency was happy to turn the regency over to him. Thenceforth, until his death in 1935, he remained the dominant figure in the country.

Poland was formally recognized by the United States on January 30, 1919, and by the other powers during the succeeding weeks. It still remained, however, to draw the boundaries of the new state. This was a task for the Paris Conference, which opened in January. But there was no agreement on the question as to whether the new Poland should be a large state or the small Congress Poland of 1815. While the French, who looked upon Poland as a possible future ally against Germany and a buffer against Soviet Russia, stood for a Poland that would be as large as the Allies could make it, Britain was fearful of the consequences of including large minorities. The one question upon which the Allies were agreed was that Poland should have free and unfettered access to the sea. The nearest and most convenient route being by way of Danzig, this German city was made a republic under the League of Nations, and a Corridor which separated East Prussia from the rest of Germany was cut straight across a German-speaking tract. In the Free City of Danzig the Poles were accorded certain rights with respect to access to the quays and the establishment of storehouses, but the citizens of the Free City were not pleased with this arrangement. Final delimitation of all the boundaries of the new state was a matter too difficult to be accomplished in Paris; hence the settlement of a number of questions was postponed. These questions were (1) the boundary with Russia, (2) the question of Eastern Galicia, (3) the question of Upper Silesia, (4) the boundary with Lithuania. Under Article 87 of the Versailles treaty the settlement of these questions was referred to the principal Allied Powers.

But the Poles were not content to wait for a decision by the Allied Powers. Regarding the manner in which Poland was treated by the Peace Conference as "cruel injustice," they began to clamor for territory to which they had no ethnological claim. They dreamed of a nation comparable to that of the Golden Age of the fourteenth, fifteenth, and sixteenth centuries, a Poland that had extended from the Baltic to the Black Sea. Since the Peace Conference had not restored such a Poland, the Poles decided to establish one by force of arms. Early in 1920 Pilsudski sent a military expedition against the Bolsheviks. At first the Polish efforts met with considerable success. The army advanced steadily in the direction of Kiev. As they approached, the Russian resistance stiffened but they did manage to take the city. The loss of Kiev caused the Russians to concentrate larger forces in the west, which they were able to do because they had crushed the White armies of Kolchak and Denikin. Soon they were able to launch a counteroffensive which drove the Poles back in a disorganized retreat. City after city was retaken until the Russians were almost at the gates of Warsaw. Confident that they were winning a final victory, they had advanced too fast and had become disorganized. This gave the Poles, who with the help of French officers had reorganized their army, an opportunity to deliver an effective counteroffensive which caught the Russians unawares. Carrying the Russians before them the Poles advanced until on October 3 they reached Minsk. By this time the situation looked so desperate to the Russians that they accepted the Polish terms and on October 12 a preliminary treaty was signed at Riga. The terms included Russian recognition of Polish sovereignty, renunciation of all subversive propaganda in Poland, and the abandonment of all claims to Eastern Galicia, the destiny of this region to be settled between Poland and the Allies.

According to the Treaty of St. Germain the country to the east of the River San (Eastern Galicia) with its capital of Lvov (Lemberg) was not to be added to Poland. The Allies were to be its temporary sovereigns and its permanent status was to be settled by a plebiscite to be held in 1944. This did not, however, deter the Poles from occupying it and treating its population as if they were Polish. They also decided to take matters into their own hands on the Lithuanian side. In October, 1920, a band of irregulars captured Vilna, the capital of Lithuania, and this only two days after the Poles had concluded a pact with the Lithuanians under which they recognized the sovereignty of Lithuania over Vilna. In the following year the Poles exerted strenuous efforts to acquire the whole of Upper Silesia, a highly industrialized region containing important coal fields. According to the Treaty of Versailles its fate was to be decided by a plebiscite. When the plebiscite was held (March, 1921), two thirds of the population voted to remain with

Germany, only the southeastern part voting in favor of union with Poland. This did not satisfy the Poles. After bands of irregulars tried to annex most of Upper Silesia by force, the League of Nations stepped in and divided the territory into two parts, giving Poland a large piece. But the Poles still wanted more than the allotted territory.

When the Allies finally got around to deciding the other disputed boundaries, the decisions were based on the accomplished fact. In other words, they sanctioned Poland's new boundaries which had been established by force since the conclusion of the Versailles treaty. At their meeting in Paris on March 14, 1923, the Allied Council of Ambassadors sanctioned the eastern frontier of Poland as established by the Treaty of Riga, thereby including in Poland territory that was indisputably Russian. The same Ambassadors' Conference also decided to give the whole of Eastern Galicia to Poland, despite the fact that more than 70 per cent of the inhabitants were Ruthenians (Ukrainians) and only about 14 per cent were Poles, the rest being Jews. This the conference did without in any way ascertaining the wishes of the people involved. Finally, the conference also decided to permit Poland to retain possession of Vilna and the Vilna districts despite the far stronger claim of Lithuania. In short, the dimensions of Poland that the Allies sanctioned in 1923 were twice as large as they had been when the Treaty of Versailles was concluded. In these decisions the fear of Bolshevism and France's desire to have a strong ally played an important part.

The source of future trouble lay not so much in the size of the Polish state as in the minorities which had been included in it. More than one third of the total population consisted of disaffected minorities, solid in their hatred of the Poles and in their desire to be free. The existence of so many aliens within the state was a threat to internal tranquillity and a source of external friction. To the mother countries of these groups this state of affairs was a constant challenge. Under these circumstances the creation of a strong army became the only guarantee of peace within and without. Such an army the Poles sought to create despite the fact that the national treasury was in no condition to meet the expenses.

There were other problems facing the new state, including such tasks as repairing the war devastations, building up an internal administration, and welding the Poles, to say nothing of the minorities, into a single unit. The tasks were anything but simple. By far the larger part of the territory comprising the new state had been subject to invasion. The ebbing tide of war had left behind it bleak fields and demolished factories. There was a grave food shortage, and disease was rampant everywhere. Typhus was decimating towns and villages and there were no medicaments and no physicians to fight the scourge,[5] Although many thousands were clamoring for employment, the financial means as well as the raw materials were lacking for reopening the factories that had not been destroyed. Furthermore, the new nation found itself swamped in a deluge of varying kinds of currency. There were German marks, Austrian kronen, Russian rubles, and many other kinds of paper money, but almost no gold or silver. Even among the Poles themselves there was little homogeneity. For more than a century the three fragments of the old Poland had been subjected to three quite different administrative and educational systems which left their distinctive marks on each group. When the three were reunited, they found themselves unlike in many respects.

The problems of reconstruction would have taxed to the utmost the energies of a most enlightened and experienced government, but the men who directed affairs were almost completely lacking in political experience. Marshal Pilsudski, in whose favor the Council of Regency had resigned its power, received the unanimous approval of the Constituent Assembly when it met in February, 1919, and he remained chief of state and commander in chief of the army until the autumn of 1922. Soon after he took over the reins of government, Ignace Paderewski, who had been pleading the Polish cause in western Europe and America, arrived in Warsaw. He had a long conversation with Pilsudski and, although the two men did not see eye to eye on a number of subjects, the marshal invited the musician to form a cabinet. This Paderewski did with himself as premier and foreign minister. He also became the principal Polish delegate to the Peace Conference. As such his position was difficult, for he was expected to obtain more territory than the peacemakers were willing to give. When he failed to obtain the outright possession of Eastern Galicia, he lost support at home. Realizing this, he resigned on December 9, 1919, and retired into private life. He was great as a musician, but as a politician he failed to achieve a shining success.

In March, 1921, after two years' deliberation, the Constituent Assembly finally completed and adopted the constitution. It provided for a parliament of two houses, an Assembly (Sejm) and a Senate, elected by popular vote, the right to vote being accorded to

[5] The shortage of food and medicines was temporarily relieved early in 1919 by the arrival of supplies from the United States.

every citizen who had reached the age of twenty, without distinction of sex. The executive power was vested in a president and a cabinet, the former to be elected for a term of seven years by the members of the two houses in joint session. After the constitution was framed, Pilsudski ostensibly retired to private life, although he still remained head of the General Staff. But parliamentary democracy did not give Poland a responsible and stable government. Parliament groaned under the burden of thirty parties, each of which in the words of one of its members, "was strong enough to sabotage the efforts of the others but incapable of achieving any real constructive work." The succeeding years saw a procession of unstable and short-lived ministries. No less than sixteen cabinets passed across the scene up to May, 1926. In these circumstances many eyes turned to Pilsudski, who by a bold coup gained complete control. The two houses of parliament forthwith elected him president, but the marshal to everyone's surprise declined the offer, taking instead the post of minister of war. Upon his suggestion his friend, Dr. Ignace Mościcki, was elected president but Pilsudski remained the real power behind the throne. Foreign writers often referred to him as a "dictator" but the term could be applied to him only with qualifications. He did not abrogate the constitution nor did he proceed to rule without parliament. His rule rested in the main on the support of the army, and his cabinets were composed mainly of military men. Most of the time his government had a subservient bloc in the Sejm which voted as it was told.

One of the early achievements of the republic was agrarian reform. Important in this respect was the division of the large estates. Whereas about 16,000 large landholders owned much of the land, two thirds of the agricultural population averaged less than five hectares (twelve and a half acres) to a family, which was not sufficient for subsistence. Discontent among the agricultural masses was so pronounced that reform was imperative. Division of the large estates scarcely had the consent of the landed magnates, though there were some who, being financially embarrassed, were glad to part with their holdings for a price. But the political power of the peasantry, together with the support of the left generally, was sufficient to overcome the opposition of the landowners. As early as July, 1919, a resolution was passed, and enacted as a law in the following year, which drastically limited the amount of land that could be held by any one man. The maximum varied from 60 to 100 hectares (150 to 250 acres) according to the district. During the next two decades some eight million acres were transferred to the small farmers, partly as a result of the agrarian reform laws and partly through voluntary parceling by the landlords. In 1939 Poland was no longer a country of great landlords but one in which more than 80 per cent of the land was owned by small farmers. At the same time the scattered small holdings of many peasants were consolidated. For centuries many holdings had been divided into strips that were often scattered over two or three villages. The consolidation of these strips enabled the peasants to use power machinery and, in general, to practice a more scientific agriculture.

Although Poland is endowed with all the requisites for material prosperity, economic conditions were generally bad during the period between the two wars. Thanks to the incorporation of a part of Upper Silesia, it became one of the foremost countries of Europe in mineral wealth. It had a supply of coal for centuries to come, huge resources of water power, and a great reserve store of energy in the oil fields of Galicia. Furthermore it possessed considerable quantities of zinc, lead, and silver and extensive deposits of limestone, chalk, marble, gypsum, and kaolin. It also contained some of the largest salt mines in the world. The most important industry was coal mining.

But industrial development as a whole was in the infant stage, with only about 10 per cent of the population employed in industry. Although labor was plentiful, scarcity of capital arrested industrial development. Such industry as existed, outside of mining, was largely divided between cottage industry (artisans working in their own homes) and a number of gigantic industrial enterprises created or controlled by foreign capital. When the international depression of 1929 came, it caused an outflow of foreign capital from Poland, thereby weakening private enterprise considerably. In 1937 a fifteen-year plan was initiated for the industrialization of the overpopulated district of central Poland, but before much progress could be made the country was engulfed by the tide of war.

Like most countries of eastern Europe Poland was predominantly agricultural, nearly three quarters of its population deriving a livelihood from the cultivation of the soil.[6] In the hands of the most frugal peasants in Europe the sandy soil produced large quantities of rye, barley, oats, and potatoes. As a result of the introduction of modern machinery and the wider use of fertilizer, production increased considerably during the years 1927–1929. As an exporter of rye and barley Poland held first place in Europe and its production of pota-

[6] In 1939 about 61 per cent derived a livelihood from agriculture as against 72 per cent in 1919.

toes was exceeded only by Germany and Russia. Nevertheless, since much of the produce was raised for export, the position of agriculture was precarious. Every unfavorable world trend affected it adversely. Consequently the income of the Polish farmer was much below that of most other European farmers, largely because of the low price he received for his produce. The position of the peasants became particularly difficult after 1929 when prices of agricultural products declined sharply. Having no accumulated resources to draw on, the peasants sank into a poverty that is difficult to imagine. During the decade of the thirties the government adopted various measures for relief, but financial limitations restricted the aid it could give.

Meanwhile after a decade's trial the constitution had been found wanting, largely because of the weakness of the executive branch. To remedy this a new constitution was drawn up in 1935 which increased the power of the president. The new constitution was hardly "an expression of liberalism." According to its provisions the president was to be chosen by an electoral college composed of the highest officials and seventy-five electors, two thirds of whom were selected by the Sejm and one third by the Senate. Furthermore, the president's power was strengthened in that he was given the right to issue decrees which had the force of law when the Sejm was not in session. A change was also made in the election of the members of the Senate. Two thirds were to be elected by a specially selected group of voters (the "elite") and the remaining third appointed by the president. A little more than a fortnight after the constitution was officially inaugurated Marshal Pilsudski died, leaving a political as well as a personal vacuum. One of his last acts was to appoint an old friend, General Smigly-Rydz, inspector general of the military forces, a post which carried with it supreme control of the army in both peace and war. Thus Pilsudski's cloak was bestowed on Smigly-Rydz but only in a limited sense. The latter did not wield the power the former had exercised. President Mościcki, who had been re-elected in 1933 without a dissenting vote and whose authority had been strengthened by the constitution of 1935, exercised a larger share of the power than he had while Pilsudski was living. Nevertheless the army continued to be the most important element.

One of the domestic problems for which the Poles failed to find a solution was the problem of minorities; in fact, this became more acute with the passing years. The only possible way they could have won over the minorities was by treating them with disarming liberality. This they failed to do. In general, they gave little attention to the susceptibilities of the minority groups. The Poles, it seems, had learned but little during the period they were oppressed by other nations. No sooner were they given control over large minorities than they began to treat them in the same manner they themselves had been treated by the tsar's government and this despite the treaty they had signed. The protection of the minorities was an idea which President Wilson took across the Atlantic in his "bag of good resolutions and laudable intentions" in December, 1918. It was incorporated in a Minorities' Treaty which Poland was required to sign as a necessary condition to her recognition as a sovereign independent state. In the treaty, duly signed on July 28, 1919, the government promised "to protect the interests of the inhabitants of Poland who differ from the majority of the population in race, language, or religion." In other words, the state undertook to assure the minorities complete protection of civil and religious rights. Nevertheless, a systematic policy of Polonization was carried out and those who refused to be absorbed suffered many disadvantages and were subjected to petty persecutions from small officials and from police methods. As a result they became restive and resentful, and the situation as a whole was a threat to both internal and external peace.

There was, first of all, the Jewish problem. Poland had the highest percentage of Jews among the countries of Europe. According to the census of 1931 there were no less than 3,114,000 persons of the Jewish faith in Poland. In other words, the Jews formed between 10 and 14 per cent of the total population. However, since 75 per cent of them lived in towns, they constituted more than 28 per cent of the urban population. In Warsaw, for example, there were 340,000 persons who spoke Yiddish as against a Polish population of approximately 800,000. These Jews were less inclined to be absorbed than those of any other European state. Some few, it is true, were assimilated and were styled "Poles of the Jewish faith," but a growing Jewish nationalism, stimulated in part by the attitude of the Poles, acted as a check upon even limited assimilation. When the census of 1931 was taken, only 381,000 out of a total population of more than three million Jews identified themselves as Poles. The number decreased still further by 1939. Thus, whereas the Jews of Germany represented a thoroughly German element, the Jews of Poland remained a foreign element and as such fomented a vigorous anti-Semitic movement. While Pilsudski was living he was able to hold it in check, but after his death it ran wild. Sponsored by the National Democratic Party, it gradually penetrated the ranks of the state officials. Certainly the fact that anti-Semitism was cultivated in Germany did not fail to affect the attitude of the Poles. In practice anti-Semitism took the form of an economic boycott of the Jews. As a result many were gradually driven out of the various trades, professions, and crafts in which they had taken root. Since they played such a predominant role in many spheres of economic activity, anti-Semitism served to weaken the general economic structure. Its effect upon the Jewish masses was to force them deeper into the morass of poverty and degradation.

Friction between the Poles and other minorities was equally severe. The traditional hatred of the Ukrainians and the White Russians for the Poles was further intensified by the efforts to Polonize them. There was also much racial bitterness between the Poles and the Lithuanians. But the greatest source of international friction was the German minority. With a view to Polonizing the Germans, the authorities had closed many German schools. Parents who sent their children to the German schools that remained open risked their jobs or exposed themselves to administrative chicanery. In general, those who spoke German were placed under a disadvantage. This treatment was a valuable weapon in the hands of those Germans, particularly the Nazis, who were carrying on agitation for revision of the German boundaries. The Poles retaliated by accusing the German government of even grosser mistreatment of the Polish minority in Germany. In November, 1937, Poland and Germany concluded an agreement guaranteeing just treatment for Polish and German minorities in the two countries. Thereafter the Germans complained frequently that the German minority in Poland was "being crowded to the wall, deprived of land, industry, jobs, and schools." Finally, in 1939 the treatment of the German minority in Poland became a pretext for the invasion of Poland.

But Poland's biggest worry was the fear of being crushed in the giant nutcracker of which Germany formed one arm and Russia the other. A country's foreign policy is usually determined by various elements such as its trade and commerce, its history and traditions, and other factors. In the case of Poland geographical position was most important. Situated between Germany and Russia, two vastly stronger states, her primary function was to maintain friendly relations with both and also between the two, for in a war between Russia and Germany Poland was destined to become the battleground. Thus Poland's fate was bound up in the future relations between Germany and Russia. Poland was particularly vulnerable because, apart from the Carpathians and the Pripet marshes, it had no natural frontiers, no chains of mountains, not even a rudimentary Maginot Line. Having mostly flat land frontiers, it was open to easy invasion. Hence it was Poland's further task to build up a force that would be strong enough to resist attack from whatever quarter. The budget for military matters was so large that the government was forced to neglect public education and public works. Military expenses consumed nearly half of the country's revenues during the years preceding World War II.

During the years immediately after World War I the Poles, having defeated the Russians, did not fear them too much. The great enemy was Germany. To protect themselves in this direction they concluded an alliance with France on January 9, 1921, followed by a military convention the next year. The specific sources of irritation between Poland and Germany were Upper Silesia, the Corridor, Danzig, and minorities. The Poles knew only too well that the Germans did not accept the Versailles settlement as final. Stresemann himself categorically stated in a letter to the Crown Prince (September 7, 1925) that "rectification of the eastern frontiers of the Reich, recovery of the Polish Corridor and of Danzig, and alterations in the boundary line of Upper Silesia" were included in Germany's territorial demands. Fear of Germany even increased when the Nazis began to launch a world-wide propaganda to convince neutral opinion that the Polish frontier was one of the major injustices of the Peace of Versailles. Believing that neither France nor Great Britain could be counted on to preserve the *status quo,* the Warsaw government began to cultivate friendly relations with Russia and on July 25, 1932, signed a nonaggression pact with the Soviet Union. Hitler, who before 1933 had demanded a rectification of the Polish frontier, suddenly dropped the revisionist campaign so far as Poland was concerned. Fearing a combination of Russia and Poland and desiring a free hand to accomplish the annexation of Austria, the Führer offered the Poles a ten-year nonaggression treaty. The treaty, signed January 26, 1934, stated among other things that the two governments "under no circumstances will resort to arms." This treaty led some Poles to believe that Hitler and his Nazis had abandoned the idea of revising the Polish frontier. Later when it suited his purpose Hitler denounced the treaty and sent the German Juggernaut to crush Poland.

CHAPTER ELEVEN

Turkey Faces Toward the West

THE END OF THE OTTOMAN
EMPIRE
THE Ottoman Turks, so called after Osman, their first outstanding leader, were originally an Asiatic tribe which achieved dominion over Asia Minor. About the middle of the fourteenth century they seized a foothold on the European continent and then went on to conquer the decaying Byzantine Empire. They subdued the Greeks, Serbs, Bulgarians, Albanians, and Rumanians, and finally in 1453 succeeded in taking Constantinople, which became the capital of the new empire. The empire reached its zenith in the reign of Suleiman the Magnificent (1520–1566), at which time it comprised not only Asia Minor, the Balkan Peninsula, and parts of Hungary and Russia but also Syria, Palestine, Arabia, most of the islands of the eastern Mediterranean, and even the coastlands of North Africa almost to the Strait of Gibraltar.

Thereafter the story of the Ottoman Empire is one of decline. In the seventeenth and more particularly in the eighteenth centuries it manifested unmistakable signs of decrepitude. The causes of the decline were many and complex. Outstanding among them was the fact that the string of able sultans ended with Suleiman. Under his weak successors the government soon lost whatever efficiency it had formerly possessed, and the subject peoples became more and more restless. In addition there was the coincident growth of hostile powers and the constant threat of attack from the outside, particularly from Russia and Austria-Hungary. The former, bent on securing an outlet in the Mediterranean, did not stop at casting covetous glances at Constantinople and the Dardanelles but also made the most of every opportunity to hasten the collapse of the Ottoman rule. Thus the empire was on the defensive through most of the eighteenth century. With rare exceptions every treaty of peace drove the Turks a step back toward Asia.

During the first half of the nineteenth century the disintegration which had previously set in was considerably hastened by the infiltration of Western nationalist ideas. The concept of nationalism found ready acceptance among the subject peoples and gave rise to independence movements which Russia was not slow to encourage. It appeared as if the death of the "very sick man of Europe," as Tsar Nicholas I had styled the Turkish Empire, was imminent. What saved the empire from speedy extinction was the fact that the other great powers did not wish to see Constantinople pass into Russian hands. Great Britain and France, who had previously remained in the background, now entered the picture. Seeing in Russia's plan to dominate the Dardanelles a threat to their maritime and colonial interests, they sought to revive the dying empire by artificial stimulation so that it would serve as a bulwark against Russian ambitions.[1] Although their efforts postponed final collapse, they failed to stop the disintegration. Weakness and corruption were too deep rooted to be eliminated and nationalism had achieved too great a momentum to be checked. The disintegration was particularly speedy and violent in the Balkan Peninsula, where a number of independent states including Greece, Rumania, Serbia, Bulgaria, and Montenegro came into being during the nineteenth century.

In 1914 the Ottoman government sealed its doom by deciding to stake its fortunes on the triumph of the Central Powers. The armistice, which was signed October 30, 1918, saw the Ottoman forces decisively beaten and Arabia, Syria, Mesopotamia, and Palestine in the possession of the Allies. The sultan's government had to accept the will of the Allies without question. In other words, the chronic "sick man of Europe" was officially dead and it remained only to strip the corpse completely before burying it. By the terms of the armistice the sultan's government undertook to demobilize all its military forces except such as were necessary for policing the frontiers and maintaining internal order. A few days after the signing of the armistice a powerful British fleet, accompanied by some French ships, anchored in the Golden Horn. Troops landing from these ships marched into Constantinople and occupied both shores of the Bosporus and the Dardanelles. The Treaty of Sèvres, signed on August 10, 1920, imposed the severest terms on the sultan's government.

[1] On the eve of World War I Emperor William II of Germany succeeded in effectively bringing the sultan under his control. German imperialists had a special interest in Turkey because the Bagdad railway connecting Germany with the Near East ran through it.

Although it was permitted, mainly as a concession to Mohammedan feeling, to retain the city of Constantinople, the whole of eastern Thrace together with the Gallipoli Peninsula was transferred to Greece, and the Straits were placed under the control of an Allied commission. In Asia the sultan's government agreed to surrender Syria, Palestine, Mesopotamia, and the peninsula of Arabia proper. Furthermore, the treaty provided for the creation of an independent Armenian state and for an autonomous Kurdish state to the south of it. Finally, it handed over to Greek administration the chief seaport of Asia Minor, Smyrna, with a considerable hinterland extending over one hundred miles along the coast and almost equally far into the interior.

Had the treaty stood, it would have left Turkey an insignificant, disarmed state in the interior of Anatolia. But the events of 1919 and the succeeding years changed the complexion of things. Although the sultan's government had no alternative but to accept the treaty, opposition to it soon developed in certain circles. The Turkish people, who had been engaged in almost continuous war since 1911, were dispirited and beaten, eager above all for peace and quiet, but when the Greeks sent troops to take possession of Smyrna (May, 1919) their pride was cut to the quick. In various parts of Anatolia influential Turks formed patriotic groups known as Committees for Local Defense, which attracted many embittered ex-army men who still had their arms. All that was needed for a full-fledged revolution was a leader who could rally the country.

REVOLT AGAINST THE TREATY OF SÈVRES

Such a leader was at hand in the person of Mustafa Kemal, an army officer of outstanding ability and determination who subsequently assumed the name of Kemal Atatürk. Having as a youth devoured all the revolutionary literature he could lay hands on, Mustafa Kemal during early manhood became a member of a secret revolutionary society that aimed to break the sultan's despotism and set up a constitutional government. In addition he vowed to free Turkey from the blighting influence of Western imperialist nations. Before the war broke out in 1914 he had already launched the slogan, "Turkey for the Turks." When the war was imminent he voiced his opposition to participation in it, but once the government had committed itself he devoted his every energy to the fight, his most outstanding achievement being the part he played in frustrating the British efforts to establish themselves on the Gallipoli

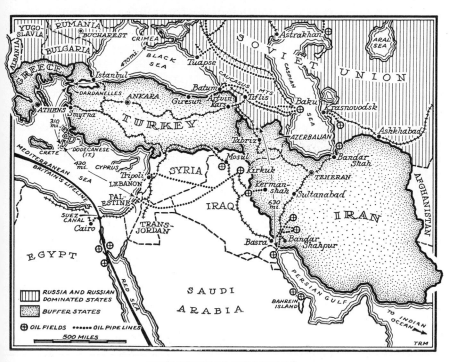

THE BRITISH "LIFELINE"

This map shows vividly the components of the struggle in western Asia—Russian pressure southward; the oil fields and pipe lines of the Arab territories; the "buffer" role of Greece, Turkey, and Iran; and Britain's "lifeline" to the Far East.

Peninsula. Thus he emerged from the war with a far-reaching military reputation. The terms of the armistice which concluded hostilities convinced him that the Allies were condemning Turkey to death. He decided that the only hope for his country lay in resistance. He tried to persuade the politicians surrounding the sultan to permit him to reorganize the army and lead it against the Greeks, but Mohammed VI and his henchmen were more interested in their own personal security than in the fate of the people. Instead of supporting his plans for resistance, they appointed him inspector general of the troops and sent him to eastern Anatolia to supervise the disarmament of the forces in that district.

But Kemal did not give up his idea of resistance. Upon arrival in eastern Anatolia he proceeded at once to reorganize the troops stationed there into an army for defense against the Greeks. More than this, he also set to work uniting the various Committees for Local Defense that were already working for the protection of Turkish rights into a nationalist party called the People's Party. In 1919 two congresses of nationalist delegates from all over the country convened in eastern Anatolia and an executive committee presided over by Mustafa Kemal was elected with headquarters at Ankara. When the sultan's government learned what was going on, it sent Kemal peremptory orders to return to Constantinople at once. Instead of complying he answered, "I shall stay in Anatolia until the nation has won its independence." Then he sent word to all towns still in Turkish hands to elect delegates to a Grand National Assembly. The assembly, composed of 350 deputies, met at Ankara on April 23, 1920, and during the succeeding days drew up a constitution and declared itself the sole lawful representative of the nation. In short, a new Turkish government came into being. Mustafa Kemal was chosen president of the Grand National Assembly, but not as yet of Turkey. Hoping to gain the support of many who were still loyal to the sultan, he declared in his speeches that a new government was necessary because the sultan was a prisoner in the hands of the Allies and therefore incapable of independent political action. Ankara was made the seat of the new government.

Meanwhile Kemal had also been organizing for national defense against Greek invasion. It was a task which would have seemed hopeless to a less determined person. Not only was the Greek army supported by the Allies, but most of the Turkish soldiers who had just returned from the front wanted anything rather than further fighting. They were utterly war weary and begged to be left in peace to till their fields. But Kemal did not permit apathy or lack of arms to deter him. Night and day he worked with fierce tenacity and indefatigable energy in assembling the remnants of the army, in finding arms for his troops, and in exciting in them the will to resist the Greeks. Finally he succeeded with the help of his close friend, Ismet Pasha, and other able assistants in creating an effective fighting force. The Greeks, after occupying Smyrna in 1919, pushed on into Anatolia the following year without suffering reverses; but in the early months of 1921 the Turkish army, led by Ismet Pasha, defeated them twice at Inönü. Upon receiving reinforcements the Greeks advanced on Ankara until they reached the Sakarya River, where they were finally stopped by the Turks under the personal command of Kemal (September, 1921). After spending some months reorganizing his forces, Mustafa Kemal decided in August, 1922, that the time had come to take the offensive. The attack caught the Greeks completely by surprise. Everywhere their lines were broken and soon their entire army was in retreat, a retreat which in its final stages became a rout. The demoralized Greeks fled helter-skelter to the coast, where they embarked for home. On September 9, 1922, the Turks reoccupied Smyrna.

Having expelled the Greeks from Anatolia, Kemal made preparations to drive them out of eastern Thrace. To do this he had to cross the Straits, which were still occupied by an Allied force. As the Turkish army approached, the French and Italian contingents withdrew but the British did not. For a time it seemed as if a clash between British and Turks would take place but they finally concluded an armistice which provided for the restoration of eastern Thrace to Turkey upon the final signing of a peace treaty. The Allies invited not only the Kemalists but also the sultan's government to the peace conference. This situation of having two recognized governments in one country moved the Grand National Assembly to take the step of abolishing the sultanate once and for all on October 1, 1922. A few days later representatives of the Ankara government took over the administration of Constantinople (called Istanbul by the Turks) and Sultan Mohammed VI fled to Malta on board a British warship.

In addition to being the secular ruler of the Ottoman Empire the sultan had also been caliph.[2] Mustafa Kemal would have liked to abolish the caliphate at the same time the sultanate was abolished, but he was not yet strong enough to risk touching the religious

---

[2] The word "caliph" means "successor to the prophet." As the successor of Mohammed the sultan was regarded not only by the Turkish Moslems but by all the Moslems of the world as their spiritual master.

sentiments of the Moslems both inside and outside Turkey. Hence the new government decided to retain the caliphate and Abdul-Medjid, another member of the house of Osman, was elected caliph with powers solely spiritual.

The peace conference opened at Lausanne in November, 1922.[3] During months of diplomatic wrangling Ismet Pasha held firmly to the demands of the Ankara government with such success that when the treaty was finally signed on July 24, 1923, it granted the Turks almost all they had demanded. Not only was eastern Thrace returned but the nationalist government also received, by and large, the boundaries it had claimed in Anatolia. Armenia was divided between Turkey and Russia. All pecuniary claims for loss and damage suffered by both sides during the period since the first of August, 1914, were reciprocally renounced. Furthermore, the capitulations, i.e., the special privileges which foreigners had previously enjoyed in Turkey, were abolished. As a step toward the achievement of racial unity in the new Turkey, provisions were made to exchange the Orthodox Greeks living in Turkish territory for the Moslem Turks living in Greece. The rest of the Christian minorities were to enjoy free exercise of their religion and the same civil and political rights as Moslems. Only in a few issues did the Turks fail to achieve their demands. Noteworthy in this respect is the provision which forbade them to fortify the Straits without the consent of the powers.[4] Thus alone among the defeated nations of World War I the Turks, after rejecting the Treaty of Sèvres, succeeded in negotiating a treaty with the Allied Powers on a footing of equality. Of all the treaties ending the war only the Treaty of Lausanne represented a genuinely negotiated treaty.

ॐ

WESTERNIZATION OF TURKEY

The treaty was the preliminary to the unconditional recognition of Mustafa Kemal and his government.[5] At the first meeting of the Grand National Assembly after the signing of the peace Kemal's status at home was also clarified. In October, 1923, the new state was officially proclaimed a republic and Kemal was chosen by the Assembly to be its first president. Although the government was

[3] It was attended by representatives of Great Britain, France, Italy, Turkey, Greece, Rumania, Yugoslavia, and the United States. While taking part in the deliberations the United States representatives did not sign any documents. A special treaty between Turkey and the United States was concluded after the signing of the treaty of Lausanne.
[4] This consent was given at the Montreux Conference in June, 1936.
[5] Soviet Russia had recognized the government as early as August, 1920.

theoretically managed by a written constitution and an elected assembly, it was not the rule of many but of one. All power in the state was concentrated in Kemal's hands. From the lowest clerk up to the prime minister every official was a member of the People's Party, the party created and controlled by him. There was no opposition party. In a country in which democratic procedure was still beyond the comprehension of the average individual a dictatorship was the only form of government possible at the moment. Halidé Edib, staunch exponent of constitutional government and leader of the feminist movement in Turkey, wrote: "In such a country a strong centralized government, if not a dictatorship, with stabilized forces backing it, is inevitable and perhaps necessary." [6] Many of Kemal's acts, it is true, were high handed and arbitrary, but in general his rule was benevolent. Kemal himself lost his temper when foreign writers called him a dictator. He liked to feel that he was exercising his authority within the limits of the constitution. Above all, he believed that he was creating a democratic tradition which would make a dictatorship impossible in the future.

With the external troubles settled and his position established, Kemal lost no time in making it clear that he intended to make Turkey a modern Westernized state. "If our bodies," he said, "are in the East, yet in spirit we look westward. We aspire to modernize our country." He had already torn up the political fabric; now he would change social ideas and habits, customs, manners, and even dress—in short, everything that bound the people to their Oriental past.

Westernization was not a new departure. It had been going on to some extent for more than a century and may be said to have begun when the first unit of Ottoman troops was equipped and drilled in the Western fashion by Sultan Selim III (1789–1807). Although some later sultans were so openly reactionary that they sought to construct bulwarks against the infiltration of Western ideas, others did endeavor to introduce changes along Western lines. Each attempt, however, to impose reforms from above was greeted by the people with reactionary demonstrations which showed how far they were from being ready to change their Oriental ways.

A more determined effort to introduce social as well as administrative reforms was made in 1908 and subsequent years by the Young Turk movement, which was supported by many young officers who had either traveled or studied in Europe. But the leaders of the movement were too much occupied with international matters and

[6] *Turkey Faces West* (1930), p. 223.

too busy maintaining their hold on the government to achieve thoroughgoing changes. Thus the end of World War I saw the Turkish
masses still clinging to their old customs. Nevertheless the Young
Turk movement was an essential preliminary to the Kemalist reforms in that it prepared the minds of many leaders for the changes
that were to come.

Whereas the Young Turk movement had been characterized by
a confusion of aims, Mustafa Kemal was sure of his own aim and
was determined to achieve it. He realized that before he could get
his people to accept Western ideas and practices he must break the
iron grip of the religion of Islam. The "good-for-nothing priests,"
Kemal said, had in the past "decided the form of the constitution,
the details of the lives of each Turk, his food, his hours of rising and
sleep, the shape of his clothes, the routine of the midwife who produced his children, what he learned in schools, his customs, his
thoughts, even his most intimate habits." [7] As the first step toward
secularization Kemal suggested the abolition of the caliphate. When
the Assembly hesitated he spurred them on by declaring that the
caliphate was "an antiquated and useless institution." As a result
the law abolishing the caliphate was passed on March 3, 1924. Next
the antiquated system of laws based on the Koran was replaced by
modern civil, penal, and commercial codes borrowed from the West,
and the religious schools and colleges were either secularized or put
under government control. The government also published decrees
dissolving the monastic orders and closing convents and monasteries
because they were centers of reaction. Finally in 1928 the Assembly
decided to make the state entirely secular by striking from the constitution the clauses which stated that Islam was the established
religion. For the official oath in the name of Allah, affirmations on
the individual's honor were substituted, a favorite form being "I
vow on my honor as a Turk."

The jettisoning of the effete ecclesiastical establishments opened
the way for other changes. One of these was putting the Turk into
European clothes. Kemal decided that if the Turks were to think
like their Western neighbors they must also look like them. Accordingly he insisted that the people cease wearing the fez, which
was the "hallmark of the Ottoman and the Moslem." "The fez,"
Kemal said, "is the sign of ignorance." First he succeeded in getting
the soldiers to wear peaked caps by showing them the practical advantages of these caps and by explaining to them that the fez was
not a Turkish but a borrowed garment; then he set out to convert

[7] Cited in Armstrong, *Grey Wolf*, p. 241.

the people to the wearing of the Western hats and caps. When many refused to give up the fez because it had a religious significance,[8] Kemal ordered the Assembly to pass a law which made the wearing of the fez a criminal offense. Those who refused to obey the law were arrested, some being given prison sentences, others bastinadoed and in extraordinary cases even hanged. This was a "language" the average Turk understood and the opposition collapsed, every Turk hurrying to find a hat, a cap, or anything with a brim. During the years that followed, other European customs and practices were gradually introduced. The international clock was adopted in place of the day which had begun at sunrise, the Gregorian was substituted for the Islamic calendar, and provisions were made for the gradual introduction of the metric system. Another noteworthy change made it obligatory for all Turks to adopt family names (1934). The use of surnames having disappeared under the influence of Islam, certain given names had become so common that in the schools it was found necessary to designate the pupils by number. As for Kemal himself, the Assembly voted to bestow on him the surname Atatürk, meaning "Father of the Turks." He in turn chose for Ismet Pasha, his prime minister, the name of Inönü, in commemoration of the victory he had won over the Greeks at the place of the same name.

A further aim of Kemal was to free his people from ignorance and to raise them to the intellectual level of the Western peoples. It is estimated that in 1927 less than 13 per cent of those over twelve years of age were literate. The widespread illiteracy was due not only to a lack of schools but also to the fact that it was difficult to use the cumbersome Arabic alphabet. To remedy this Kemal appointed a commission in 1928 to draw up a new alphabet on the Latin model, and the Assembly set a date after which the use of the old script would be illegal. Teachers were then trained to give instruction in its use, and schools were opened throughout the country to teach it to the people. Kemal himself even traveled about the country demonstrating how much easier it was to learn the new alphabet than the old one. In certain regions where the people were most apathetic the police literally dragged persons to school. As a result nearly half of the country's adult population was able to read and write after a period of ten years. The Assembly also passed a law making primary education compulsory for all children beginning at the age of seven. But because of a shortage of trained teachers the law could not be generally enforced. Nevertheless, each year

[8] The religious significance of the fez rested on the custom which required a Moslem to keep his head covered and to touch the ground with his forehead while praying.

saw an increase in the number of children attending school. It is estimated that by 1935 about 40 per cent of all children between the ages of seven and twelve were in primary school.

Nor did the efforts of the Kemalists cease with the introduction of the new alphabet and the promotion of primary education. To bring Turkey a step nearer to Europe, provisions were made for the establishment of a variety of vocational and professional schools. The best graduates of these were often sent to Europe and the United States for further study, many of them becoming leaders in the Westernization of Turkey upon their return.

Much was also done to promote interest in the fine arts. Because the Koran prohibits images or likenesses of anything in heaven, earth, or water, painting and sculpture were unknown arts in Turkey. The religion of Islam was also opposed to most forms of music as being sensual, only a simple form of folk music being permitted. But the opening of cultural centers in the larger cities, together with the relaxing of religious ties, was instrumental in arousing considerable interest in Western art and music. Kemal took the lead in violating the Islamic ban on graven images by ordering two statues of himself set up, the first in Constantinople and the second in Ankara. He further brought in music from the West, including classical compositions, Viennese waltzes, and American jazz. Dancing schools were also opened to introduce Western styles of dancing.

Finally, the government attempted to teach the masses some simple rules of hygiene and health. Little did it matter to the average Turk that his environment was filthy, his water supply polluted, and he himself disease ridden; his hour would strike only when Allah willed. It was the doctrine of kismet, a form of fatalism taught by the priests of Islam. As a means of dissipating the apathy of the masses the government instructed the priests to teach Moslems to protect themselves against bacteria and microbes as they would against vicious dogs. Measures were also taken for the protection of the water supply used for drinking purposes, the disposal of sewage, the draining of malarial swamps, the construction of sanitary outdoor toilets, vaccination against smallpox, and the prevention of other diseases.

Probably the most outstanding reform was the emancipation of women. The idea, like most of the others, did not originate with the Kemalists. A beginning had already been made in this direction during World War I. Previously Turkish women had lived the secluded life of a bygone age when the harem existed. Since prac-

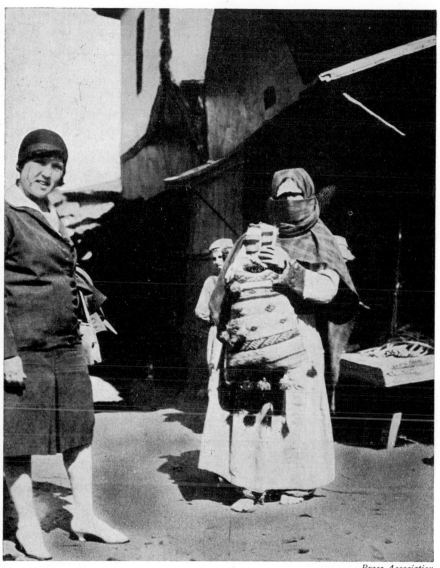

THE NEW AND THE OLD IN WOMEN'S CLOTHES IN TURKEY

tically nothing was done for the education of girls, few women were able to read or write. They were veiled at fourteen, married a year or two later, and thereafter spent most of their time in the privacy of their home. Most of them seldom went out and when they did were accompanied by members of their families or by an escort of other women. In public a woman concealed her figure in voluminous black clothes and covered her face with the exception of one or both eyes. In public conveyances there were special screened sections to protect women from the gaze of men.

During the First World War polygamy had been made subject to the agreement of the first wife, higher education had been opened to women, and in the cities many women had become clerks and civil servants to fill the places of men called to arms. It remained for the Kemalists to raise women to an equal status with men. The first change took place in women's attire. Fearing to arouse resentment, Atatürk did not attempt to achieve this change by law. He asked women schoolteachers, the wives of army officers, and other progressive women to discard the veil and adopt European styles. Soon most women who did not wish to appear old-fashioned adopted the new mode. In the agricultural districts the change was, of course, accepted much more slowly. In 1926 the Civil Code gave women equal rights with men in marriage, making it possible for a woman to divorce her husband, whereas a man could no longer divorce his wife without her consent. The same Civil Code also gave women equal rights in the ownership of property and in all legal matters. Four years later they received the right to vote in municipal elections and to hold municipal offices. In 1934 they were given equal suffrage in national elections. The next year, with women voting for the first time, seventeen women were elected to the Grand National Assembly. Business and the professions were also opened to women. Before long many were not only working in shops, banks, and business offices but also serving as teachers, physicians, lawyers, and even judges. In short, the eve of World War II saw Turkish women dressed in the latest European fashions, mingling in society, and taking part in almost every business and profession, as in any Western country.

ECONOMIC DEVELOPMENT IN TURKEY

During all this time the Kemalists did not neglect economic development. Turkey is essentially an agricultural country, its chief products being tobacco, wheat, barley, figs, and raisins. But its yield per acre was low and its agricultural techniques backward. In the years from 1923 to 1925 its agricultural yield was so poor that thousands of tons of wheat had to be imported. Such a condition was intolerable to the Kemalists and they promptly took steps to remedy it. In addition to easing the peasant's burden of taxation, the government began in 1924 to give all farm youths instruction in improved agricultural technique during the period of military training. Next the facilities for advancing credits were improved, better seeds were distributed, and cooperative marketing societies organized. The government also fostered various irrigation schemes and set up model farms on which the latest machinery was demonstrated. The result was that imports of wheat decreased rapidly after 1925 until they disappeared entirely in 1930. Thereafter Turkey began to export wheat. Furthermore, there was a large increase in the production of barley, and the production of rice was trebled in a decade. But probably the most striking agricultural success came as a result of the introduction of the sugar beet. Whereas no sugar was produced in Turkey prior to 1926 and the imports had been approximately 60,000 tons per year, production of sugar beets had by 1934 reached a volume which made the importation of sugar unnecessary.

The Kemalists also made immense strides in the direction of industrializing the country. At the time of their accession to power, industry consisted principally of foreign-owned cigarette factories, a few textile mills, and cottage industries that produced carpets and pottery. With but few industries Turkey was, so to speak, a seller of raw materials and a buyer of manufactured goods. "Industrialization," Atatürk said, "is one of our national problems. We shall create every industry, great or small, for which there are in our own land the economic conditions necessary to its work and development." To promote the establishment of large-scale industries the Assembly in 1927 offered free grants of land, to a maximum of ten hectares, for factories and railroad sidings. But as free capital for financing new industries was scarce and the government was opposed to permitting foreign concessionaries to come in, the state itself entered the industrial field. The method it employed was to establish a number of banks, each of which devoted its attention to special industries. The banks furnished funds for the building of factories and closely controlled the production of goods in the new plants. In 1934 the government embarked on an ambitious five-year plan which emphasized the production of textiles, cellulose, pottery, iron, steel, coke, coal, and chemicals. It was so successfully executed that by 1939, for example, Turkey was manufacturing about 80 per cent of its requirements of cotton yarn and cloth and almost all its requirements of woolen yarn and cloth. It is claimed that more than six hundred factories of various kinds were built between 1927 and 1939. In 1939 a second five-year plan was inaugurated aiming, above all, to increase the production of minerals and electricity and to improve harbor and shipping facilities.

Besides building many factories the Kemalists spent lavishly on railways. In 1923 Turkey had a little more than 4000 kilometers of railways, all of which were foreign owned. The Germans owned about 67 per cent and the rest was owned by British and French interests. Early in 1924 work was started on the first state-owned railways and by 1935 the government built no less than 2600 kilometers of new lines. In addition the government purchased the foreign-owned lines during the years 1934–1936. Thus by the outbreak of World War II Turkey had an extensive network of railways to serve both economic and strategic requirements. The state also owned and operated the postal and telegraph services and held a monopoly of all coastwise shipping.

Side by side with the Westernization policy the government sponsored a strong nationalistic program. Kemal Atatürk decided to make his slogan, "Turkey for the Turks," a reality and to cultivate in his people a feeling of racial pride. Many trades and professions were closed to non-Turks. Turkish goods were widely advertised, and the Turkish flag was prominently displayed in many places. After the abandonment of the Arabic script, Kemal ordained that Turkish words be substituted for the Arabic and Persian words with which the language was weighted down. The Koran was also translated into Turkish and in 1932 the suras from the Koran were recited for the first time in Turkish during prayers in a mosque at Istanbul. In the words of the patriot poet, Zia Goek Alp,

A land in which the call to prayer resounds from the mosque in the
   Turkish tongue,
Where the peasant understands the meaning of his prayers.
A land where the schoolboy reads the Koran in his mother tongue,
O son of the Turk, that is thy Fatherland.

Though the Turks became proud of their nationality, they did not become arrogant or aggressive. All dreams of Pan-Islam or of a great sphere of Turkish influence having been abandoned, the government did not have any irredentist claims. The central idea of foreign policy was peace, "peace at home and peace with the world," as Kemal put it. Peace was essential to recovery from the many years of war and to the program for the creation of a new Turkey. To insure peace, treaties were negotiated with Russia, Afghanistan, Iran, Italy, Great Britain, and other countries, and a rapprochement even took place with Greece, the hereditary enemy. In general, Turkey's relations with all the countries with which it had dealings were quite cordial. This does not mean, however, that Turkey was "a shrinking violet in the international garden." The government, having renounced imperialism itself, was determined not to let other states interfere in its affairs or take some of its territory. The idea was well summed up by Dr. Tewfik Rushdi, the foreign minister, when he said: "Turkey does not desire an inch of foreign territory, but will not give up an inch of what she holds."

Kemal Atatürk's iron physique, which for so many years had defied the laws of nature, finally crumbled and he died on November 10, 1938. Amid universal mourning the Turks laid the remains of their beloved leader to rest in the Museum of Ethnography built on a hill overlooking the city of Ankara. His real monument is the achievements of his energetic life. In the face of overwhelming odds he had the courage to defy the Greeks and the Allies at the conclusion of World War I. He emerged victorious from the bitter struggle that followed, and the Treaty of Lausanne sealed his triumph. Thenceforward he turned his energy and his genius to rebuilding the ramshackle state on new and strong foundations. Great as his achievement of establishing an independent and territorially compact state is, the fact that he gave Turkey a new soul is more important. When he began, the Turks were a backward Oriental people bound by the shackles of outworn superstitions; at his death they were well on the way toward becoming a modern progressive nation. All this he accomplished in a few years. Few if any revolutions have achieved so much in so short a time as the one he organized. Ruthless to his foes but charming to his friends, he is enshrined in the memory of his people as the "Father of the Turks."

Immediately after Kemal Atatürk's death Ismet Inönü was unanimously elected to the presidency by the Grand National Assembly. The new president had been associated with Kemal for about twenty years and had watched over the new state as prime minister for thirteen years. He was not only strong and experienced but also a man whose name carried great weight and respect throughout the country. He was deeply committed to the same ideals of Westernization and national self-sufficiency that Kemal had espoused. In foreign affairs he continued the policy of his predecessor.

CHAPTER TWELVE

Nazi Germany

THE BEGINNINGS OF
NATIONAL SOCIALISM
EW great movements in history have
attained supreme power in so short a time as did National Socialism.
In 1919 a small number of dissatisfied ex-soldiers in Munich organized a political party which for some years gave little promise of
growth; fourteen years later this party was exercising absolute authority over the lives of sixty-five million people.

No single explanation of this phenomenon can suffice. The reasons for its success are to be found in a medley of complex economic,
psychological, and political factors. Among the more important
were the defeat in World War I and the cumulative severity of the
Treaty of Versailles. While the former produced a sense of humiliation and stimulated a desire for revenge, the latter created an acute
sense of grievance. Having expected a treaty based on the Fourteen
Points, the Germans resented the loss of territory, the demand for
reparations, and the severe limitation of military power. But above
all, they resented the "war guilt" clause (Article 231), which they
interpreted as placing upon them and their allies the entire responsibility for the war. Other factors which increased their feeling of
bitterness were the French occupation of the Ruhr and the inflation
which wiped out the savings of the lower middle class.

More important in their direct bearing upon the success of the
National Socialist (Nazi) movement were the world-wide depression
and the magic of Hitler. The depression and unemployment that
followed the boom of the late twenties not only brought the war-
guilt resentment to the fore again; it also destroyed whatever respect the republic still commanded. There never had been much
zeal for the republic. The people had accepted it unenthusiastically

313

and under compulsion. From the start it had been associated in the minds of many with humiliation. It is doubtful, in fact, whether it did represent a desirable ultimate form of state for any important political group. When depression and unemployment came, public opinion was inclined to hold the republican government ultimately responsible. More than this, the great depression prepared the Germans to follow anyone who promised them bread and jobs. This gave Hitler his opportunity and he was not slow to make the most of it. By his skill in arousing popular emotion he succeeded in convincing millions that he was the Messiah they were looking for, that he could give them what they needed and desired.

To understand National Socialism it is necessary to know something about the life and ideas of its leading spirit. Adolf Hitler was born in the Austrian village of Branau on April 20, 1889, the son of a minor customs official. The elder Hitler hoped that his son would also become an Austrian official, but young Adolf showed no inclination to follow in his father's footsteps. In fact, he manifested little ambition for anything. Most of all he liked to sit by himself and dream. He was, in the opinion of his mother, "moonstruck." His only interests at school seem to have been history and geography. His history teacher at Linz, where he attended secondary school, was a Pan-Germanist, one who passionately desired the union of all people of German stock in one national state. This zeal for German nationalism the teacher was able to inculcate in his pupil. Young Adolf soon learned to regard the Habsburgs with contempt because they lacked a sense of German patriotism and to detest the Austrian Empire because it was an empire of nationalities and not a national empire. The German nationalism which was engendered in him by his teacher became the motive power of his life. It is the key to all his acts and all his ideas.

Until he was nineteen, it appears, young Hitler just loafed. But the death of his mother in 1908, preceded by the death of his father in 1903, compelled him to shift for his own living. Packing up his few belongings in a suitcase, he set out for Vienna to become "somebody," as he put it in his autobiography. He wanted to become an artist. The Academy of Art, however, refused to admit him because he could not draw. "Test drawing below standard," was the verdict of his examiners. The next five years, as he himself has described them, were "years of misery and desolation." Having no money and little talent for anything, he eked out a precarious existence by selling postcards or working at such odd jobs as a bricklayer's assistant, who carried bricks and mortar. Much of the time he had to sleep in the humblest lodging houses, commonly known as flop-houses. "That I became hard and am able to be hard," he wrote, "I owe to that period of my life."

To his Vienna experiences he also attributed many of the convictions which guided his life and the National Socialist movement. Besides deepening his sense of nationalism, they gave birth to the anti-Semitic prejudices which intensive reading later elevated into the creed that caused so much misery in Germany and other countries. The sight on a Vienna street of a Polish Jew dressed in a caftan, he asserted, convinced him that Jews could never be Germans but were a race apart. Furthermore, in Vienna he also conceived a violent animosity to Marxian socialism because he regarded its supposed internationalism, its pacifism, and its theory of class struggle as unnatural and unwholesome. When he left Vienna for Munich in 1913 he was, in his own words, "a convinced anti-Semite, a mortal enemy of Marxian philosophy, and a Pan-German."

Since the question of making a living presented the same difficulties in Munich as it had in Vienna, the outbreak of war was in one sense at least welcome to him. Instead of returning to fight with the troops of the Dual Monarchy, he joined the Bavarian army and served on the western front. During the war he was twice wounded, was promoted to the rank of corporal, and received the decoration of the Iron Cross.

The armistice again saw him confronted by the problem of earning a living. Unable to find employment he decided to become a politician. In the summer of 1919 he joined with a small group of malcontents like himself in forming the German Workers' Party, which was later reorganized as the National Socialist German Workers' Party. Almost from the beginning he seems to have become the leading figure in the movement. At the meetings of the party, usually held in the small back room of a Munich café, and at other impromptu gatherings, he discovered his talent as an orator. He himself says in his autobiography, "I could speak! After thirty minutes the people in the tiny room were electrified." Thereafter he missed no opportunity to harangue a crowd whenever he could collect one. His favorite theme, even at this time, was denunciation of the Treaty of Versailles. With his frenzied oratory he would play on the emotions of his audiences until, as he said, "I had before me a surging mass full of sacred indignation and boundless wrath."

In 1920 Gottfried Feder drew up for the party a program containing twenty-five points. Among other things it demanded "union of all Germans by the right of self-determination," "abrogation of the treaties of Versailles and St. Germain," ousting of all non-Germans from the Reich, abolition of unearned incomes and the "slavery to interest" (*Zinsknechtschaft*), nationalization of all trusts, and agrarian reform consistent with the national needs. Above all, it proclaimed the violent anti-Semitism which later became one of the main planks in the Nazi platform.

The new party aimed to be both nationalist and socialist. It was nationalist and German in that its aspirations were for Germans only; socialist, in the sense that it emphasized the obligation of the state to control everything that concerns the needs of its citizens; and a workers' party because it hoped to attract particularly the laboring classes. The organization was along military lines. In imitation of Mussolini's Black Shirts Hitler organized a party militia of Brown Shirts, called the SA (*Sturm Abteilung*) or Storm Troopers. The earliest recruits appear to have been largely unemployed veterans and ne'er-do-wells, with a sprinkling of social outcasts. Originally devised merely to maintain order at party meetings, the Storm Troopers were soon to earn a reputation for unmitigated blackguardism when Nazi leaders made terror an integral part of their system. The Storm Troopers gradually increased in number until they became a veritable army. In 1931 Hitler wrote in the *Völkischer Beobachter,* "There has grown out of a little group of all-daring fighters an army of the swastika which has already passed the second hundred thousand." In 1932 its membership rose to 300,000. When the organization of the party became nationwide in 1929, a second unit, the SS (*Schutz Staffel*) or Elite Guard, a black-garbed corps of seasoned veterans subject to duty anywhere in Germany, was organized. Nor did Hitler's indebtedness to Mussolini stop with the idea of a party militia. He also transplanted the ancient Roman salute which Mussolini had revived. As the latter adopted the *fascio* as the symbol of his party, Hitler imported the swastika from India as a symbol for his party. In addition, the Fascist anthem was imitated in a similar rhythm, and Mussolini's title of "Duce" was translated into "Führer" for Hitler.

During the first years after the party was organized, it attracted such men as Captain Roehm, Hermann Göring, and Dr. Alfred Rosenberg, but it was not widely known outside of Bavaria. It first came into the limelight in 1923 as the result of an attempted *coup d'état* or Putsch, more generally known as the "Beer-Hall Putsch" because it was plotted in the back room of a Munich café. The crisis caused by the occupation of the Ruhr convinced not only Hitler and his associates but also General Ludendorff and his nationalist followers that the moment was right for a successful Putsch. So the two men joined forces. The plan was to seize the Bavarian government as a means of liberating Bavaria from Berlin and all the "evils" of the Weimar system. But the attempt was a ludicrous failure. When the Hitler-Ludendorff followers marched into the Odeonplatz in Munich on the appointed day, a few shots fired by the police quickly scattered them and put an ignominious end to the attempt. That Hitler escaped unscathed was due to the fact that placing prudence before valor he threw himself flat upon the pavement when the firing started. Both Hitler and Ludendorff were arrested and tried for treason. The latter was acquitted because of the services he had rendered to his country during the war. Hitler was sentenced to five years' imprisonment, but a too lenient government released him before he had served a year. Meanwhile, in the general election of May, 1924, the Nazi Party succeeded in electing no less than thirty-two members to the Reichstag.

THE NAZI BIBLE

While he was confined in the fortress of Landsberg Hitler wrote the first, and after his liberation the second, volume of *Mein Kampf* which became the Bible of the National Socialist movement. In it he expounded his *Weltanschauung,* in other words, the ideas, feelings, and beliefs that would guide him if he came to power. Written in atrocious German, the work is frankly Machiavellian in its disregard of all moral considerations. The idea that the end justifies the means or, as he puts it, that "success is the only earthly judge of right and wrong" is repeated time and again. Thus he wrote: "The rightness of propaganda must be judged exclusively by its real effect." The work is not, however, a systematic exposition. Hitler's mind lacked the intellectual discipline necessary for a logical arrangement of ideas. Hence the contents are a hodgepodge of history and fiction, wisdom and folly, fantasy and statesmanship. Most of the ideas are stated over and over again. This together with the digressions makes the book uninteresting and laborious reading.

Nevertheless *Mein Kampf* is a powerful work. Politically, it is probably the most influential book that has appeared in the twentieth century. Published by the author and issued in two volumes, it did not at first gain wide circulation. It was only when it appeared in a one-volume "people's edition" at one third the original price that large numbers were sold. After Hitler's accession to power gigantic quantities were produced and it became a duty not only for the members of the party but for all civil servants to buy it. In 1939 the sales passed the five million mark, making it one of the best sellers of all time.

In *Mein Kampf* Hitler presented a creed he hoped to carry through to the end. Its central idea was that of race. Like the Frenchman Gobineau, author of the nineteenth-century essay "On the Inequality of Races," Hitler believed that "the racial question gives us the key to all problems of history." [1] He did not trouble to define race or to distinguish between "race" and "nation." All questions of definition, proof, and origins he summarily brushed aside, appealing to the reader's consciousness of the reality of race. After stating that all races are not equal, he proceeded to divide them into three groups: the culture creators, the culture bearers, and the culture destroyers. Only the Aryan or Nordic race belongs in the first category and it alone is responsible for all spiritual, cultural, and economic progress. The Germans, he asserted, are the foremost Nordic nation, the only other great European nation with any comparable claim being the British. Regarding the races to be classed as culture bearers he was purposely vague, but he did classify the Jews and the Negroes as culture destroyers. Unfortunately the Aryan race had degenerated as a result of intermarriage with inferior races. "The mixing of blood, the pollution of race," Hitler stated, "has been the sole reason why the old civilizations died out." If civilization is to be preserved and extended, the Nordics must keep their blood pure. They must be permitted to marry only Nordics. This is desirable in the interest not only of the Nordics themselves but of all humankind because they are practically the sole source of civilization and progress. "As much as we possess in the field of arts and sciences," he wrote, "almost all of it has been created by the Aryan. . . . Subdue him and darkness will sink upon the earth." [2]

Besides setting down the aims of National Socialism in regard to internal affairs Hitler also included much about the external aims of his party. If Germany is to become a world power, she must acquire more territory. The expansion of the nation necessitates such a step, for a growing nation must have *Lebensraum* (room to live). But where are the Germans to find more territory? Are they to acquire oversea colonies? Hitler vigorously opposes the acquisi-

[1] The writer to whom Hitler, either directly or indirectly, is most indebted for his race theory is Houston Stuart Chamberlain, a German of English ancestry who wrote *Die Grundlagen des Neunzehnten Jahrhunderts* (*The Foundations of the Nineteenth Century*).
[2] Hitler used the words "Nordic" and "Aryan" as interchangeable terms.

tion of colonies separated from Germany proper. The new territory much be closely connected with the fatherland so that it will never be lost. To find such land, he said, the Germans must turn their gaze to the east. Russia has vast stretches of land that would be ideally suited for German *Lebensraum*. Moreover, he was sure that the Bolshevik regime would inevitably collapse and the Germans could then win new territory through "the might of a victorious sword." "Frontiers of states," he wrote, "are made by men, and men can alter them." However, before they attack Russia the Germans must crush France, Germany's archenemy, because the French would never stand idly by and see Germany strengthen herself at the expense of Russia. To crush France and then wrest territory from Russia was, in Hitler's opinion, in accordance with the law of nature, for this is "a world of struggle where, in every part of it, one being feeds upon another and the death of the weaker is the life of the stronger." But the major war must not come until Germany is ready. To make victory certain she must not only rearm herself; she must also conclude alliances with Italy and Great Britain, one with Italy against France and another with Great Britain against Russia.

᭕

NAZI TECHNIQUE

During the period of prosperity from 1924 to 1929 the Nazi movement got nowhere, but with the onset of depression its opportunity came. The economic collapse, accompanied by a rapid rise in the number of unemployed, made Germany fertile for the Nazis. Although it is true that the cause probably would not have succeeded if the depression had not prepared the ground for it, one must not overlook the ability of the Nazis to make the most of the opportunity offered them. Essential factors in their success were their skill in yoking to their cause the forces let loose by the period of domestic disintegration and their mastery of the art of propaganda. They evolved a technique of mass propaganda and mass emotionalism which made the efforts of the other parties appear feeble and amateurish. The movement probably owes more to propaganda than did any similar movement preceding it. The Bolsheviks did not learn the uses of propaganda until they had taken over the reins of government, and the followers of Mussolini had to expose themselves to danger by fighting a real opposition; but the Nazis accomplished their rise to power largely by propaganda.

Of course the pivot about which the whole movement revolved

was Hitler himself. In guiding it he gave ample evidence of the talents he had developed during the years of his apprenticeship. The failure of the Beer-Hall Putsch in 1923 taught him that he could not gain political power by force; so he set himself to developing a technique which would win votes. He carefully studied the general theory of propaganda and, together with such associates as Dr. Goebbels, developed the specific methods employed by the party.[3] Furthermore, the personality of Hitler was an important factor. Not only was he able to instill in his associates a fanatical devotion to the cause; he was able to convince millions that he was the man of destiny. His influence over the masses was to a large extent made possible by his gift of oratory. Political oratory was something new to the Germans; in fact, Hitler was almost the only great popular speaker in modern Germany. William II had made political speeches on occasion and so had Bismarck before him, but neither of them had possessed Hitler's ability to sway the crowds. He electrified his audiences not so much with what he said as with the way he said it. He played upon the emotions of the people as a musician plays upon an instrument. By the consummate skill of his demagogy he created such an atmosphere of enthusiasm that impartial observers likened nazism to a religious revival. Certainly among party members the name of Hitler inspired all the fanatic reverence that Mohammed was accorded by his followers.

But Hitler himself was far from being the whole story of the Nazi success. The movement was worked up by an unceasing campaign in which all members participated and every possible means was employed to foster enthusiasm. Nothing that might appeal to the dramatic sense of the people was overlooked. Uniforms, flags, badges, and insignia of all kinds played their part. Banners were used to catch the eye, and patriotic music to stir the heart. Hundreds of orators were trained to carry the gospel of national regeneration into every village and hamlet. During the mass meetings, which were usually opened by a band playing stirring music, uniformed Nazis were stationed about the speaker's platform and among the crowd with instructions to punctuate the speeches with shouts of "Heil Hitler" or to applaud certain phrases. By such means the Nazis could whip up the emotions of their audiences almost at will and generate a fervor of such intensity that the imagination cannot picture it. This stagecraft was supplemented by other means of carrying the Nazi ideas to the masses. Vast quantities of printed propaganda were issued. Pamphlets by the millions were distributed

[3] The real propaganda genius of the movement was, of course, Dr. Goebbels.

from door to door or showered upon town and country from airplanes. In addition the party published more than a hundred newspapers and periodicals, the principal organ being *Der Völkische Beobachter.*

In their books, pamphlets, newspapers, and speeches the Nazis skilfully exploited the discontents of the various classes and groups. This accounts for the contradictory nature of the Nazi literature. For example, they promised work to the unemployed, and economic salvation to the white collar workers who were being forced into the ranks of the proletariat by the depression. In the hearts of many dissatisfied ex-soldiers they roused memories of prewar greatness. To the peasants who were weighed down with mortgages, debts, and taxes and to the agricultural workers who complained of low wages they promised remedies for every grievance. By advocating the abolition of unearned incomes, the nationalization of the great trusts, and the communalization of the great department stores they stirred in many socialists the hope that the party would realize the objects the Marxists had failed to achieve. They succeeded in enlisting not only the moral but the financial support of the big industrialists by their promise to crush the communist influence in Germany and to curb the power of the trade unions. Above all, by their sentimental and patriotic appeals they captured the imagination of the younger generation which because of the economic depression and the abolition of military service was for the most part unable to find anything to do.

Although the Nazis tried to cater to the specific tastes of their different audiences, they always emphasized certain stock subjects no matter what the audience. One of the most effective weapons in their armory was the denunciation of the Treaty of Versailles, particularly of the "war-guilt" clause or, as they called it, the "war-guilt lie," the disarmament clauses, and the reparations clauses. Nazi orators did not tire of repeating that the treaty had riveted the shackles of slavery on the German people and that if they would be free they must strike off these shackles "by fair means or foul." The blame for the treaty and its evils they laid at the door of the Social Democrats, who had accepted it and who had brought about the establishment of the republic which the Nazis were trying to overthrow. Moral indignation was, in fact, directed against all the parties that had supported the Weimar constitution, but in no field of propaganda were they more energetic than in their denunciation of the Jews. The Jews were declared to be the originators of Marxism, more particularly of the Social Democratic Party in Germany and of Bolshevism in Russia. They were held responsible for the occupation of the Ruhr, the inflation—in short, for all the evils of state and society. Nazi propaganda endlessly repeated such absurdities as that of a supposed international Jewish conspiracy to bleed Germany to death financially. Thus anti-Semitism was deeply sown and furiously cultivated in the minds of millions.

How much all this appealed to the Germans can be seen from the fact as stated, that the Nazis increased their vote from 800,000 in 1928 to nearly 6.5 million in 1930 and the number of their deputies in the Reichstag from 12 to 107. This made them the second strongest party in the country. In July, 1932, they carried nearly 40 per cent of the electorate, and with 230 seats in the Reichstag they were the strongest party. When they lost nearly two million votes in the election of November, 1932, Hitler declared his readiness to head a coalition cabinet as chancellor. Joining forces with von Papen and with President Hindenburg's son, he was summoned on January 30, 1933, to form a cabinet. Thus was ushered in the Third Reich.[4] Many historians doubt that senile President Hindenburg knew what he was doing.

THE NAZIS CONSOLIDATE THEIR POWER

When Hitler was appointed to the chancellorship the Nazis were not strong enough to control the state by themselves. The new cabinet was a coalition in which only three of eleven members were Nazis. The two others, beside Hitler, were Dr. Frick and Hermann Göring, the former being minister of the interior, the latter minister of aviation and Prussian minister of the interior. The vice-chancellor was Franz von Papen, who hoped that he and his Junker-Nationalists would be able to exercise a moderating influence over the Nazis. But the opposition underestimated the driving force of the Nazis, who were resolved to be satisfied with nothing less than complete control of the state. More particularly, the opposition failed to gauge Hitler's determination and political acumen. Up to January 30, 1933, he had been the leader of a political party, but having become chancellor he resolutely set himself to become the leader of the German people. The first step in this direction, as he saw it, was to increase his support in the Reichstag. His government could definitely count on only 247 deputies who, even with the support of other rightist deputies, lacked at least twenty-five

---

[4] The First Reich was the Holy Roman Empire; the Second was the German Empire which was founded in 1871 and collapsed in 1918.

votes of a majority. Hoping to gain an absolute majority he had President Hindenburg dissolve the Reichstag on February 1 and set March 5 as the day for new elections.

From the first it was obvious that the Nazis were determined to carry the elections at all costs. No sooner had they been announced than the party went to work to curb the efforts of the opposition. The task was facilitated by the fact that Göring as Prussian minister of the interior had charge of the Prussian police. In other words, he controlled the police in three fifths of Germany. He at once proceeded to convert the police into a dependable ally by "purging" it of all those who were not in sympathy with the Nazis or Nationalists. Then he issued the order to strike remorselessly at "Marxism," the word used to designate the collective opposition to Nazism. The slightest pretext sufficed to suspend opposition newspapers or to break up opposition election meetings.

As the time for polling drew near, it became evident that despite the use of repressive measures the Nazis were not gaining enough votes to obtain the desired majority. Something more was required to influence the voters. The first move came on February 24 when the police raided the Karl Liebknechthaus, communist headquarters in Berlin, and then announced the finding of documents—never made public—which were said to contain plans for a concerted communist uprising throughout Germany. Although it was stated that the signal for this uprising was to be the burning of the Reichstag building, no extra guards were placed about it. Three days later, on February 27, a fire did break out in the Reichstag building, seriously damaging it. Not a vestige of evidence was ever presented to show that the Communist Party was in any way involved in the affair; nevertheless, the government at once issued a special edict "for the protection of the Reich against communist danger." [5] It suspended all the articles of the constitution guaranteeing such fundamental liberties as freedom of speech, press, and assembly, and authorized house-searching and confiscation of property without compensation. In brief, it established dictatorial government. Communists and socialists were forbidden to hold election meetings or to employ any kind of election propaganda, communist and many socialist newspapers were suppressed, and all communist deputies that could be apprehended were placed under arrest. Storm Troopers, enrolled as auxiliary police to insure a "free" election, went

[5] At the trial Torgler, leader of the Communist Party, and four foreign communists picked at random were acquitted. The best the Nazis could do was to convict van der Lubbe, a half-wit with a dubious communist past.

about in groups tearing down the placards of the opposition and beating up communists and socialists.

Even the "red scare," the overriding of all ordinary legality, and the open use of terrorism did not stampede the masses into voting for the Nazis. The communists, it is true, lost a million votes, but nearly five million still voted for the party. When the votes were counted, it was found that the Nazi Party had polled only 43.9 per cent of the total vote and had won only 288 out of the total of 647 seats. Thus the Nazis, although they were the largest party in Germany, were still a minority. Only in conjunction with the Nationalists, who got 8 per cent of the votes and fifty-two seats, did the government have a slender majority in the Reichstag. Realizing how precarious this majority was, the Nazis lost no time in strengthening their position. They decided that if the eighty-one communists were eliminated from the Reichstag, their own party would have a clear majority over all others combined. Such a step did not appear too difficult since most of the communist deputies were already in concentration camps, in hiding, or in exile. The object was achieved by simply not "inviting" the communist deputies to attend the meeting of the Reichstag which convened on March 21. In other words, the communists were outlawed from the Reichstag.

Two days later the Reichstag passed a bill, variously called the Act of Authorization or Enabling Act (*Ermächtigungsgesetz*), which covered the Nazi despotism with a mantle of legality. At first it seemed as if they would find it difficult to obtain the two thirds majority necessary to pass the Act, but by the use of threats, promises, and cajolery Hitler managed to get the support of the Catholic Center Party. When President Hindenburg signed the bill the next day, he gave the former Austrian house painter complete dictatorial powers. Although the Act did not abolish the ordinary legislative organs provided in the constitution, it did give the cabinet power to legislate without the Reichstag and the Reichsrat. In practice the cabinet became the sole legislator. Hitler as chancellor could now even dispense with the necessity of the President's consent to legislation. "The Reich laws enacted by the Reich cabinet," the Act stated, "are drawn up by the chancellor and published in the *Reichsgesetzblatt*. They come into effect, unless otherwise specified, on the day following their publication." As the government interpreted the Act, it put no limitations on the cabinet's power to legislate by decree. For all practical purposes the constitution was dead.

Armed with such powers Hitler and his associates proceeded at once to bring everything under their control. One of the first things they did was to establish control over all the German states or, as they put it, to coordinate the states (*Gleichschaltung*). Prussia had been in Göring's hands since January 30, but in most other states the local administration was still free of Nazi control up to the election of March 5. Right after the election bands of Storm Troopers marched into a number of the state capitals, occupied the government buildings, evicted the legal governments, and installed Nazi commissioners. In other states the governments, taking warning from the fate of their sisters, resigned of their own accord and were similarly replaced. To support in theory that which had earlier been accomplished in fact, Hitler promulgated a law on April 7, 1933, which authorized him to name a regent or governor (*Statthalter*) for each of the seventeen states, with power to nominate and dismiss the members of the state cabinets and to control all officials. Thus the law disposed of the prerogatives of the separate states. Bismarck's old federal empire was gone. The new Germany was a completely unified and centralized state.

Next the Nazis in their drive for "totality of power" dissolved all political parties but their own. The goal, Dr. Goebbels announced in May, was a totalitarian state. Before the revolution was finished, he said, "People, Party, and State must become identified with the Third Reich." The Communist Party, as stated earlier, was outlawed when the Reichstag met toward the end of March. Some weeks later the Social Democratic Party was eliminated and its property confiscated. The outlawing of the "Marxist" parties was followed by the "voluntary" dissolution of the Catholic Center Party shortly afterward and at the end of June the Nationalist Party also announced its dissolution. All the remaining minor parties soon followed suit, leaving the National Socialists as the only political party in Germany. On July 14, 1933, a law was promulgated which declared the National Socialist Party to be the only legally constituted party in Germany. The creation of any new political parties was prohibited under penalty of severe prison terms and even death.

Meanwhile the Nazis had been taking steps toward achieving control of the economic as well as of the political life of Germany. The first step in this direction was to dissolve the trade unions, which had formed the backbone of the Weimar regime. Despite the fact that these unions endeavored to live in peace with the government, the Nazi leaders decided upon their dissolution. First, however, they lulled the workers into a false security by making May 1, the day the socialists and communists had set aside as a holiday on which to protest against the existing order, a national Labor Day. May 1,

1933, was celebrated with all the impressive stage settings characteristic of Nazi celebrations. On the Tempelhof parade ground near
Berlin Hitler addressed over a million workers and employees from
every factory and office in the city. Similar demonstrations were
held in other large cities. But while labor was celebrating the holiday, gangs of Storm Troopers were making ready to "liquidate"
the trade unions. On May 2, the very day after the pageantry of
Hitler's first German Labor Day, the Storm Troopers invaded all
the headquarters of the Social Democratic trade unions, took possession of the buildings, expelled the leaders or threw them into prisons
and concentration camps, and seized the union funds. Upon learning of the fate of the larger unions, the smaller Catholic trade unions
submitted unconditionally and the agricultural organizations and
cooperatives followed suit. Later, by the law of January 20, 1934, all
labor organizations were completely and finally dissolved. Thus was
demolished the autonomous organization of German labor which had
been built up over several decades. The successor was the Labor
Front, an organ of the National Socialist Party. No other labor organization was tolerated.

Nor did the Nazis stop with the dissolution of the political parties
and trade unions; they brought every phase of life under their
control. Music, theatre, cinema, and press, all were bent to Nazi
propaganda aims. "The theatre and the film," Dr. Goebbels, the
minister of propaganda, said, "must adjust themselves to the new
era. Film and theatrical producers cannot complain of lack of material; the government will, if necessary, put them on the right path.
I hope to reach the goal where the whole nation will think unitedly
and in which there will be only one public opinion." Higher as well
as lower schools were purged of all who were not sympathetic to
Nazi aims. Those who were not removed were warned that all who
refused to speak or teach in harmony with the ideals of the new Germany would be treated as "insolent slaves, who must be beaten down
with the whip." The function of the press, Goebbels stated, would
be that of "a piano on which the government can play." The number of Nazi newspapers was increased from 120 to 379 and other
newspapers were subjected to rigid control. Unfriendly or lukewarm or liberal or pacifist or "internationalist" proprietors, editors,
and correspondents were expelled and Nazi commissars were put
at the side of the journalists who remained. The slightest departure
from the prescribed path was sufficient pretext for taking control of
a newspaper. In April, 1933, for example, the *Dortmunder General
Anzeiger,* the most prosperous provincial newspaper, was taken over

by a Nazi staff because it had published a portrait of Hitler which had given him "a distorted expression suggesting vulgarity." To escape such a fate most of the great "independent" newspapers hewed closely to the line marked out for them.

No sooner did the Nazis get control of the administration, the schools and universities, and the various cultural agencies than they eliminated all Jews and persons of Jewish descent from them. The Weimar constitution had, of course, granted equal protection to all, but the Enabling Act of March 24, 1933, empowered Hitler to override the constitution. Two weeks after this Act was passed (April 7, 1933) Hitler issued a statute which removed all non-Aryans from public office. "A person," the law stated, "shall be known as a non-Aryan who has non-Aryan, in particular Jewish, grandparents. It suffices if one parent or grandparent is a non-Aryan." At first exceptions were made for non-Aryan officials who had served in World War I or who had lost fathers or sons in the war, but gradually all non-Aryans without exception were debarred from public office. Schools and universities were "cleansed" in the same way. In the universities eminent professors of Jewish descent were dismissed either by the government or more often simply by order of student committees. In many instances Nazi student boycotts forced out Jewish professors for whom the government had made exceptions because of service at the front. Books written by non-Aryans as well as by writers who entertained liberal ideas were removed from the universities and from public libraries. Sometimes they were confiscated and burned in public. Sometimes Nazi student groups staged public burnings of books.

By midsummer of 1933 the totalitarian state had been achieved. As the Nazi Party was everywhere in control, Hitler declared the revolution to be at an end. He felt that any further changes might undermine the stability of the regime. But the anticapitalist left wing was far from satisfied. Many of its members had been attracted to Hitler's party by the hope that he would establish a socialist order, but nothing had come of their hopes. No spectacular modification of the economic structure had been made. Hitler, it seemed to them, had forgotten that the name of his party was National Socialist. Some even accused him of having betrayed the revolution. In general, a struggle between the more radical and the conservative elements was impending. The struggle for power came to a head when the Storm Troopers, who were commanded by left-wingers, demanded incorporation in the *Reichswehr*. Since the Storm Troopers were numerically superior to the army such a move would have given the left wing control of the armed forces. Hitler at once opposed the move. On the pretense that a dangerous conspiracy was plotting the overthrow of the government, he instituted the purge of June 30, 1934. On this, the German St. Bartholomew's Day, many high-ranking leaders, including Ernst Roehm, the commander of the Storm Troopers, were summarily executed. Scores of actual or reputed enemies of the regime were murdered in cold blood. Among these were von Schleicher, an open enemy of Hitlerism, and Gregor Strasser, a former left-wing leader who had withdrawn from the party. It is estimated that on June 30 and the days following more than a thousand persons were put to death, most of them with little semblance of a trial.[6] Conservatism had triumphed and for the time being the fears of big business were allayed.

A few days later, on August 2, 1934, President Hindenburg died at the age of eighty-six. Even before *der alte Herr,* as the Germans affectionately called him, had breathed his last, newspapers began to speculate on his successor. Such speculation, however, was silenced by Goebbels in his role as propaganda minister with the curt remark, "All that has been taken care of." As soon as the death of Hindenburg was announced, Hitler settled the question by convoking an emergency session of the cabinet which drew up a decree merging the offices of president and chancellor. Although Hitler did not assume the title of President, contenting himself with "Leader and Chancellor," [7] he did obtain the supreme command of the army (*Reichswehr*) and the navy. Before many days passed, all the members of the *Reichswehr* were compelled to take the following oath: "I swear before God this holy oath: that I will render unconditional obedience to the Leader of the German Reich and People, Adolf Hitler, commander in chief of the forces of defense, and that as a brave soldier I will be ready at all times to pledge my life for this oath." On August 14 Hitler asked the people to uphold in a plebiscite the action of the cabinet in making him Führer and chancellor. More than 38 million cast their votes for him. The man of dreams and visions—he who had failed at everything he had previously undertaken—was now the head of the state, the head of the government, the head of the army and navy. In short, he was the nation.

MAKING GERMANY STRONG

It is impossible to give an exhaustive description of National Socialism within the limits of space available, because the move-

---

[6] See Loewenstein, *Hitler's Germany,* p. 24.
[7] In June, 1939, Hitler reduced his title to "Der Führer."

ment was so extraordinarily all-embracing. Its activities touched every phase of national life. One of the first things the Nazis did to allay discontent was to launch a "work creation" policy. Just prior to Hitler's accession to power the number of unemployed had increased to a total of about six millions. While hundreds of thousands tramped the countryside asking for work at almost any price, other thousands resorted to begging. On the outskirts of the larger industrial cities tent and shanty towns grew up and many families who could not afford the smallest rent flocked to them. So many jobless hoping for casual employment would congregate to watch construction jobs that the police ordered building plots enclosed by wooden fences. Even a great number of those who were not idle worked only part time.

The means devised to check unemployment were not necessarily novel. Some had already been initiated by earlier governments. Vast sums were spent on public works, road construction, harbor improvement, and housing. Particularly noteworthy was the improvement of the road system, which up to that time had been markedly poor. Thousands of miles of *Autobahnen* (automobile roads) consisting of two twenty-five foot lanes divided by a center strip were constructed. Besides connecting the multitudinous industrial and trading centers, these roads were important military assets.[8] Second, subsidies were given to home owners for the repair and modernization of their homes, and farm owners received subsidies to enable them to employ more farm hands. Third, tax incentives were used to produce jobs. Families, for example, who hired a new servant girl could regard her as a dependent for tax purposes. People who purchased automobiles and manufacturers who bought new machinery could deduct the amount of their purchases from their taxable incomes. Fourth, steps were taken to withdraw as many women as possible from industrial establishments. Women, the Nazis proclaimed, must busy themselves with *Kinder, Kirche, und Küche* (children, church, and kitchen). To facilitate the withdrawal of women from employment as well as to promote growth of population, marriage loans were made to women who got married, providing they gave up their jobs. Finally, the hours of work of those who were employed were reduced so as to make room for unemployed.

The net result of these measures was that the number of unemployed decreased to 2.6 millions by the end of 1936. But the problem was by no means solved. The stopgap measures, it is true, had greatly relieved the situation but they had achieved few if any long-term

[3] As it turned out, these *Autobahnen* were important military assets to the Allied armies which invaded Germany during World War II.

benefits. By this time many of the unemployment projects were running down and the number of unemployed would soon have increased had it not been for the rearmament program which was launched on a really vast scale early in 1935. The manufacture of armaments and the withdrawal of a large number of men for military service not only reduced unemployment to a minimum but soon caused a shortage of skilled labor.

As a means of controlling labor and of enforcing labor unity the government created the Labor Front, a kind of superunion, in January, 1934. The Labor Front was not a governmental department but rather an organ of the National Socialist Party. Its executive director, Dr. Robert Ley, was appointed by Hitler as head of the party, and its financial management was put under the control of the party treasurer. Its membership included employers as well as employees. Although membership was theoretically not compulsory, few workers or employers could afford to remain outside. The result was that by 1937 the Labor Front could boast more than 25 million members. When one considers the size of the population it is obvious that almost all male workers were members. In its practical working it was much like the system of workers' councils in Russian factories. Councils were organized in every industrial establishment employing twelve workers or more. In general, the Labor Front supervised everything that concerned industrial relations, with special emphasis on the promotion of "peace in industry" and the building up of "a real unity of the people in life and work." Accordingly the settlement of differences between employers and employees was one of its most important functions. Whenever possible the differences were composed by the factory council, but if neither side gave way the question was referred to special courts established for the purpose. Strikes were of course out of the question.

Another major function of the Labor Front was the organization of the workers' leisure in order to keep them in a satisfied frame of mind and to promote physical fitness. This phase of its activities, copied from the Italian *Dopolavoro,* was known as *Kraft durch Freude* (Strength through Joy). Among the things it provided for the masses were low-cost sports and sport festivals. During the years preceding World War II more than seven million workers annually participated in sports organized by Strength through Joy. It also provided music and theatrical entertainment. For example, it had its own symphony orchestra of ninety pieces that traveled all over the Reich. All the concerts and operas the workers attended, all the music they heard, and all the films and plays they saw were of course

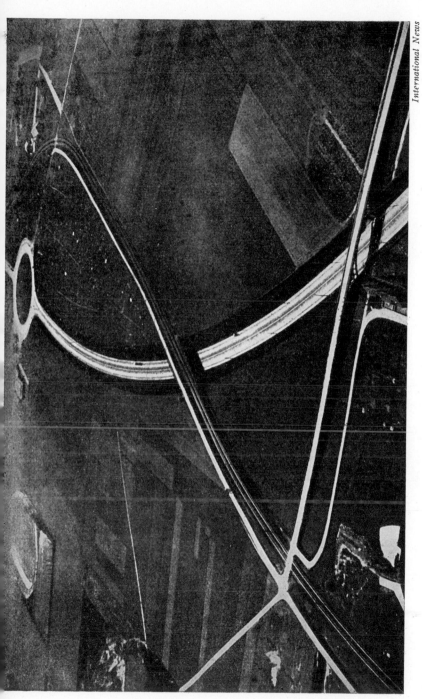

AUTOMOBILE HIGHWAY NEAR BONN, GERMANY

carefully "coordinated" with the Nazi philosophy. Often musical and dramatic activities in which they themselves could participate were organized, but the most conspicuous achievement of the movement was its work of arranging low-cost vacations for members of the Labor Front. For this purpose it purchased summer resorts at which members could spend vacations at a fraction of the usual cost. More than this, it purchased or chartered a number of steamships which until the outbreak of World War II took workers and their families on cruises to the Mediterranean, the Azores, or points in the north. Finally, an important branch of Strength through Joy, called "Beauty of Work," devoted itself to the improvement of working conditions, including such questions as better ventilation and lighting in the factories, installation of rest rooms, and protection against the harmful effects of gases, dust, and noise.

The reason so much emphasis was put on pastimes and amusement for the masses was that the Nazis failed to provide a higher standard of living; in fact, under their rule the standard of living declined by 10 per cent and probably more. Because of longer hours the average total income of wage earners did, it is true, increase by about 15 per cent, but unit wages dropped. The hourly wage of skilled workers sank from 79.2 pfennig at the beginning of 1933 to 78.3 in February, 1937, and the wage of unskilled workers declined from 62.8 to 62.3 during the same period.[9] Even the increased totals were more than offset by a rise of about 25 per cent in the cost of living. This rise, which greatly reduced the purchasing power of wages, was also accompanied by a drop in the quality of most products. Soaps, for example, contained less fat. Chocolate was adulterated with oat and acorn meal. Frequently the cheaper products were unavailable and the workers were compelled to buy more expensive products. A further shrinkage in the purchasing power of the wage earner resulted from the impounding of a considerable part of his wages by the state and party organizations. It is estimated that compulsory dues to the Labor Front and other party organizations and the "voluntary" contributions to the Winter Relief Fund and numerous collections claimed between 4.5 and 5 per cent of the workers' gross income. As compensation for all this and for the loss of political freedom, they had only the low-cost amusement provided by Strength through Joy.

Another preoccupation of the government was the question of population. The declining birth rate did not augur well for future strength. This decline was not peculiar to Germany. The annual

See *Quarterly Journal of Economics*, vol. 52 (1938), p. 416.

number of births per thousand fell from 34.3 in 1901 to 15.1 in 1932. Whereas 2,032,000 German babies had been born in 1901, the year 1932 saw the birth of only 993,000. In other words, the number of births decreased by more than 50 per cent between 1901 and 1932. The decrease was particularly rapid during the years after World War I because of the fact that approximately 1,775,000 Germans had been killed during the four years of war. Although the birth rate still exceeded the death rate in 1932, it was calculated that to maintain the population of 1932 Germany needed 1,400,000 births per year.

The decline in the birth rate caused the Nazis genuine alarm. Soon after taking over the reins of government they took energetic measures to stop the trend. They inaugurated a population policy which used all the varied resources of publicity to impress upon the people the fact that the birth rate was declining and to create a public opinion in favor of an increase in fertility. In addition bachelors were heavily taxed, thousands of small homesteads which could be paid for through small monthly rentals were constructed, and various economic inducements such as income tax reductions, rent allowances, and preference in public employment were offered to encourage large families. Probably the most effective measure was the provision of marriage loans. In August, 1933, a large sum derived from the tax on single persons was set aside for this purpose. The loans varied from a minimum of 300 to a maximum of 1000 marks and were given in coupons exchangeable at retail stores for household furnishings. No interest was asked on the loan, but it was to be repaid at the rate of 1 per cent per month over a period of eight and a half years. At the birth of each child during this period one fourth of the loan was canceled. Because unemployment was prevalent when the scheme was introduced, a loan was not granted unless the bride had been employed for at least nine months during the previous two years or unless she had been doing housework at home and was to be replaced by a domestic servant. From the time the scheme went into operation to December, 1937, loans were granted to no less than 900,000 couples.

The immediate results of the policy were substantial. Marriages increased almost at once. In 1933 the number rose 23.5 per cent over 1932, and in 1934 there was a further increase of 43.1 per cent. In 1935 a decline set in, although the rate still remained above normal until after the middle of 1936. The increase in marriages was followed in due course by an increase in births, the number rising from 971,000 in 1933 to 1,198,000 in 1934; to 1,264,000 in

1935; and to 1,279,000 in 1936. Writers pointed with pride to the fact that during the three years from 1934 to 1936 alone legitimate births were 900,000 more than they would have been if the birth rate of 1932 had remained constant.

Yet this increase cannot be entirely explained by the population policy of the Nazis. There were other influences also at work. Certainly the enormous reduction in unemployment and the resulting optimism are factors to be taken into account. However the rise of birth rate may be explained, too few babies were still being born to maintain the population at its existing level. Moreover, the rise, as has been shown, was merely temporary. Up to the outbreak of World War II the efforts of the Nazis to raise the birth rate succeeded only in postponing the numerical decline for about twenty years.[10] Nevertheless, they were more successful in raising the birth rate than any other of the Western nations.

The Nazis did not stop at trying to increase the quantity of population; they also endeavored to improve its quality. They taught that it must be the highest aim of the *Völkischer Staat* (racial state) to maintain its best elements. Accordingly new legislation was enacted to make the issuance of marriage licenses difficult. Before a couple was granted a license, they had to submit to a careful investigation which included not only a medical examination but also a study of their physical measurements and racial characteristics and a search of their family history at least as far back as their grandparents. Besides endeavoring to keep persons afflicted with certain diseases and other disabilities from having children, they wished to eliminate "alien" blood by preventing the marriage of Aryans and non-Aryans. As stated earlier, the doctrine of racial purity was a fundamental article of the Nazi faith. If the true qualities of the Aryan race are cultivated in Germany, the Nazis said, the Germans will once more become strong and powerful. Although other "alien races" were included in the prohibition, the laws were aimed particularly at the Jews. The statutes regulating the marriage of Jews and "persons of German or similar blood" varied according to the proportion of Jewish blood in each partner. For example, a person with one "alien" grandparent could by special permission marry a partner entirely of German blood, but marriage between one who was half Jewish and one of German blood was forbidden.

[10] The incorporation in the Reich of Austria and the Sudeten territories in 1938 added ten million to Germany's population. However, the birth rate in these territories was also declining. In Vienna, for example, there were 14,000 more deaths than births in 1937.

Everything possible was done to discourage the increase of the Jews. Crushing disabilities were imposed upon them in every sphere of national and social life and in every branch of cultural and economic activity. Mention has already been made of the law "for the reorganization of the civil service," promulgated in April, 1933, which retired some 12,000 Jewish officeholders. A new law of July, 1933, definitely barred all Jews and persons married to Jews from being appointed officials of the Reich, the states, municipalities, or any kind of public or legal corporation, institution, or endowment. At first exceptions were made in the case of Jewish war veterans and non-Aryans who had held office under the Hohenzollern, but later all Jewish officials were retired. Nor did the purge limit itself to the civil service; it extended to the liberal professions. Jews, with a few exceptions, were excluded from the legal profession, ousted from the practice of medicine and dentistry, and eliminated as professors in the universities. While Jewish students in the universities were limited to 1.5 per cent of the total enrollment, Jewish children, by a decree of September, 1935, were isolated in separate schools. Furthermore, Jews were forbidden to own land, were barred from the army, and denied membership in the Labor Front. Various steps were also taken to eliminate them from commerce and business. In short, Nazi legislation banned the Jew wherever it could. In September, 1935, even the last hope of the Jews was dimmed when the Reichstag decreed the so-called "Nuremberg Laws" which deprived all full-blooded Jews, even those of the Christian faith, of German citizenship.[11] It all added up to the exit of the Jew from German life. He had the choice of either migrating to another country or returning to the ghetto.

GERMANY PREPARES FOR WAR

After World War I, as stated earlier, the former imperial army was replaced by the *Reichswehr,* which was limited to 100,000 men serving twelve-year enlistments. The effective fighting power of this force was restricted by the prohibition of heavy arms and by the reduction to a minimum of lighter weapons. The air force surviving the treaty was completely obliterated, the *Reichswehr* being forbidden to possess any aircraft whatsoever. In addition heavy artillery and tank units were also outlawed. Although defeat at first caused many Germans to regard with repugnance that militarism

[11] On the other hand, these laws permitted persons of 25 and 50 per cent of "Jewish blood," formerly called "non-Aryans," to become citizens.

which had led them through four years of blood and hardships, it did not extinguish the spirit of militarism with which the people had been so deeply imbued by tradition and practice.

The military tradition was preserved in various ways. First of all, it was kept alive in the *Reichswehr*. Not only was it trained to be an army of leaders if the country should ever need to raise a large force, but the training became gradually more effective and up to date. Forbidden weapons were either imagined or represented by dummies. Outside the *Reichswehr* the military tradition was preserved in a number of ways. Associations of soldiers representing old regiments were encouraged; instruction in the "science of defense" was introduced in all the higher schools; and the glorification of former military triumphs was emphasized in elementary education. Civil aviation was developed in such a way that the transformation to military aviation could be carried out with the greatest rapidity. To promote the growth of airmindedness and to create a reserve of potential war pilots, glider clubs were organized in many parts of the country. Equally important were the many rifle, riding, and hunting clubs which featured various forms of military drill, marching with packs, and rifle practice. In addition there were numerous sports clubs which stressed *Wehrsport*, that is, sports of direct military use. Among the associations which gave military or at least semimilitary training were the *Reichsbanner, Stahlhelm, Jungdeutscher Orden, Wehrwolf,* and the *Sturm Abteilung* of the Nazi Party. The combined membership of these associations in 1932, as announced by the German press, numbered more than a million.

The question of rearming in defiance of the Treaty of Versailles was openly discussed in Germany several years before the Nazis took over the reins of government. In 1931 General von Seeckt, head of the *Reichswehr*, made a speech at Magdeburg in which he advocated increasing the force to 200,000 effectives and reducing the term of service to six years. "Even before January 30, 1933," a military historian writes,[12] "many units had been motorized and some weapons forbidden by the Treaty of Versailles, such as tanks and antitank units, began to appear in the *Reichswehr*." Thus the soil was largely prepared for the Nazis, who regarded armed strength as the one lever by which Germany could elevate herself to a position of equality among the world powers. They were certain that rearmament through its psychological effect alone would bring about a revision of the treaty. The one thing that restrained them

[12] Rosinski, *The German Army*, p. 240.

was the fear that the powers would resent too bold a progress in rearmament. Hence their first steps were taken secretly. Two months after Hitler's accession, the *Reichswehr* began to enroll volunteers in excess of the 100,000 men permitted by the treaty. On April 1, 1934, volunteers were accepted for the first time since 1920 for a training period of one year only. To aid in the development of the new army, German officers were recalled from Russia, China, and other countries where they had gone as professional military leaders and advisers. Special attention was given to the development of an air force. While military airfields were being constructed in various parts of Germany, bombers disguised as commercial planes used the commercial airfields for training purposes.

The Versailles powers did not long remain unaware of these rearmament activities. Although the discovery caused considerable alarm, particularly in France and in the small countries bordering on Germany, the powers failed to agree on a program of action. Hence they did nothing beyond making a few protests and sending a few proposals which Hitler had no need to accept. The Führer answered all protests by disclaiming any aggressive designs and by insisting that a strongly fortified Germany would be a contribution to European peace. Some, particularly among the British, accepted his statements at face value. For example, Sir John Simon, the British foreign minister, said: "We welcome the assurances of Herr Hitler that Germany's desire is for peace and that she has no aggressive designs." The French, on the other hand, took alarm to the extent that they lengthened the term of universal military service from one to two years on March 6, 1935. This caused the Nazi leaders boldly to announce their rearmament program. On March 10 General Göring proclaimed that Germany had created an air force in defiance of the treaty, and less than a week later Hitler declared that, since the various powers that had secured the disarmament of Germany at Versailles in 1919 were not carrying out their pledges to disarm themselves, Germany must reintroduce conscription. The conscription law as decreed on May 21 of the same year prescribed a year's training for all able-bodied Aryan Germans between the ages of eighteen and forty-five, the active military service beginning generally at twenty. In this way the Nazis planned to raise an army of about 500,000. When the Versailles powers again did nothing beyond offering formal protests, the Nazis realized they had won the campaign for rearmament.

Thereafter rearmament proceeded at an ever-increasing pace, so that Germany was before long living on what amounted to a wartime footing. "We are," Hitler declared in December, 1936, "already in a state of war, only the guns have not gone off." The production of airplanes was put on an assembly-line basis like that of motor cars; military reservations and airfields were constructed in many parts of Germany; and military pilots were trained as fast as the existing facilities permitted. This enabled Germany to begin the Second World War with an air fleet and a productive capacity larger than those of her opponents. Warships of all types kept the shipyards busy on twenty-four hour shifts. In 1936 the standing army was almost doubled by the extension of the training period to two years. During the succeeding years additional corps were created, so that by the end of 1938 the army had an estimated strength of about two million men. Technically it was the best equipped force in the world, with a striking power previously unknown. In all corners of Germany the people also were being trained for war. They were being drilled with gas masks and rehearsed in protection against possible air raids. In every public school the pupils were taught the use of masks and first aid against poison gas.

To the Nazis rearmament meant more than just building up the armed forces. They reasoned that if Germany was to wage a successful war it must also be ready in other respects. Above all, no efforts were spared to prepare the food supply to meet the supreme emergency of war and blockade. The leaders hoped to prevent a breakdown of food supplies like the one that had occurred during the First World War and which had been in large part responsible for the collapse in 1918. What they aimed at was "autarchy" (self-sufficiency). The idea was not their invention. Various measures designed to enhance the domestic production of food had been promulgated during the period of the Weimar Republic. It was only in 1934, however, that autarchy for military purposes became a definite goal. Although agricultural production had for some years shown a steady increase, it was not sufficient to meet the requirements. In favorable years agriculture was able to produce more than enough wheat and rye to meet domestic needs for human consumption, the surplus being used to feed livestock; and the production of potatoes, sugar, and in a large degree even of meat was sufficient for peacetime needs. But the production of other foodstuffs was less favorable. Germany produced only about 80 per cent of the cheese and eggs it consumed, and the home production of fruits and vegetables was much less. Regarding fats and oils less than half the quantity consumed was produced in Germany. Finally, the need for importing fodder protein, particularly oilseeds, was considerable.

The Four-Year Plan embraced a series of measures to render Germany independent of foreign supplies at least for the indispensible products. First of all, the government undertook a redistribution of cropping so that some of the land previously used to grow rye and potatoes would be given over to products that were being imported. Second, the government sought to extend the area of cultivation; through the draining of marshlands and the diking of lowlands along the coast no less than 1.3 million acres were added to the tillable area. Third, the new program sought to increase the yield of the poorer land by the use of fertilizers and mechanical equipment. As a result the use of artificial fertilizer increased 50 per cent from 1934 to 1937, and the number of tractors rose from 23,000 in 1933 to 57,000 by 1939. Almost 45 per cent more was spent for farm machinery in 1935 than in 1934 and the figures for the next year show a further increase of 33 per cent. Considerable effort was devoted to augmenting the yield of dairy products. Probably the most important measure to this end was the replacement of many German cows of inferior milk capacity with imported breeds of high-capacity cows.

In addition the government did a number of things to make the lot of the peasant and the farm laborer more attractive. It raised the tariffs on farm products, increased farm prices to a point far above world prices, and raised the wages of farm hands in an effort to keep them from migrating to the cities. To prevent the progressive parceling of the land and to give the peasant greater security of tenure the government issued the Farm Inheritance Act (September, 1933) which decreed that all farms up to 312 acres must pass undivided to the eldest male heir upon the owner's death, unless the heir was already the owner of such a farm (*Erbhof*). The privileged heir, who was officially designated as *Bauer* (peasant), was required to qualify for the inheritance by proving that he was a German citizen and that his ancestry was pure Aryan back to the year 1800. If he could not do this or did not wish to become the owner and operator of a farm, the next male heir received the land. An *Erbhof* could not be mortgaged, nor could it or necessary equipment be seized for debt, nor could it be sold except in very special circumstances. Since it could not be sold, mortgaged, or divided to satisfy their claims, the minor heirs were disinherited by the law. Their only claim against the heir who inherited the farm was for support until they became of age. One effect of the law was an increase in the number of landless younger sons. When many of these instead of remaining in the country as laborers drifted to the cities, a decree was published

(1934) forbidding the employment in industry of persons who within the preceding three years had been engaged in agriculture.

The government was temporarily successful in increasing agricultural production, particularly of vegetables, barley, oil-yielding plants, and forage crops. The number of livestock also increased. Furthermore, by the end of 1934 many thousands had either gone or been driven back to the soil. But in the next two years the trend reversed itself. After 1934 there was again a decline in the number of cattle, largely as a result of restrictions on the importation of fodder. When the rearmament program reached larger proportions, a larger area than had been added by the reclamation of marshes and lowlands was withdrawn from cultivation for the construction of air fields, military reservations, training camps, roads, and so on. As opportunities for employment in the armament industries increased, farm workers left the land in large numbers. The resulting scarcity of farm laborers caused the government in 1937 to lift the ban against foreign laborers during the harvest period. Storm Troopers were also sent to assist in the harvest and by an order of February, 1938, unmarried women under twenty-five were required to devote a year to agricultural labor service or to domestic service before they could take other jobs. Despite these measures agriculture continued to suffer from labor scarcity. In short, agricultural production was not substantially increased by the first Four-Year Plan. The number of hogs raised in 1938 was actually less than it had been in 1932, and a grave shortage of fats continued to exist.

Failure to attain self-sufficiency in food production was admitted by Hitler himself at the party congress of 1936. Later in the same year Göring said to a gathering at the Sport Palast in Berlin: "You know, my dear fellow Germans, and the Führer told you so at Nuremberg, that in spite of the increased security of our food supply, not all the victuals required by the population can be produced in Germany, notwithstanding all our efforts . . . My dear fellow Germans, consume the foodstuffs that our national production provides." In accordance with the last suggestion the government encouraged the people to eat more of the foodstuffs that were produced in sufficient quantities and would be available in wartime. Consequently the consumption of potatoes increased 7 per cent and that of bread 3 per cent, while the consumption of fats decreased 7 per cent and that of meat 16 per cent. Some months before the Second World War began, food rationing was instituted. A government decree issued in February, 1939, provided for the rationing of lard, butter, margarine, fish, and meat, and in August of the same year other necessaries, including clothing, were also rationed.

Realizing that Germany had been made almost as blockadeproof as possible in regard to food, the Nazis in 1936 shifted the emphasis to the achievement of self-sufficiency in raw materials needed for industrial purposes. The vast consumption of raw materials in the rearmament program was causing a growing scarcity and because of the shortage of gold it was not easy to obtain the required amounts from foreign countries. Unable to borrow from abroad, the government found it necessary to develop an intricate barter system which literally amounted to exchanging manufactured goods for raw materials. As Germany was concentrating on the manufacture of arms, it was often difficult to produce the things other countries wanted in exchange for their raw materials. Furthermore, the scarcity of raw materials recalled the experiences of World War I. Even before the blockade became effective during the First World War, Germany had suffered from a lack of supplies, a lack which, expert opinion insisted, had paralyzed the great drive on Paris in 1914. Later the blockade by causing an acute shortage of war materials had contributed greatly to defeat. To forestall a similar breakdown in another war the government decided to take energetic steps toward remedying the shortage. At the party congress in 1936 Hitler announced the plan, known as the Second Four-Year Plan, to make the Reich "within four years entirely independent of all such raw materials as can in any way be home produced by means of German ability or by means of her chemical and mechanical industries, as well as mining."

The second Four-Year Plan, as can be seen from Hitler's words, was not an absolute objective, but rather a policy of increasing the supply of home-produced materials as much as possible. Even so it was an ambitious undertaking in a country notoriously poor in most of the essential raw materials. Of the thirty-odd vital materials necessary for modern industry and modern warfare Germany had an abundance only of coal and potash. All others had to be imported entirely or in part. Thus more than 80 per cent of the mineral oil and practically all the rubber was imported. Except zinc, German mines produced only limited quantities of metal ores. German industry even had to rely to an overwhelming extent on foreign mines for iron and steel. In addition Germany had to depend on imports for practically all her nickel, chromium, mercury, and precious metals, almost all her molybdenum, about 71 per cent of her copper, and 56 per cent of her lead. As for textiles, practically all the cotton and silk and about 90 per cent of the wool came from abroad.

Finally, Germany produced only 40 per cent of the hides and skins, 15 per cent of the flax, and less than 1 per cent of the hemp, jute, and other fibers required by her industries.

In carrying out the plan Göring, who was given the title of Commissioner of the Four-Year Plan, endeavored first of all to increase the domestic production of the most necessary raw materials. Sheep-raising was energetically promoted to increase the production of both wool and meat; the cultivation of flax and hemp was extended; the mining of low grade ores, which private enterprise had found unprofitable, was undertaken by the government. Other phases of the program stressed greater economy in the use of metals and the development of substitutes. Manufacturers were not only urged to avoid unnecessary consumption of scarce materials but all scrap and waste were carefully collected. This collection did not stop with the gathering of industrial waste and empty tin cans; razor blades, bones, human hair, waste paper, garbage, sawdust, and even old coffee grounds were gathered up and put to various uses. Whenever possible a substitute (*Ersatz*) was developed for materials that had been imported. Breweries, for example, were required to use glass instead of copper pipes; water and steam pipes were made of porcelain; wires for electrical purposes were made of aluminum; and tin cigarette boxes were replaced with containers made of cardboard. Even the arms industry made cartridge cases of aluminum in order to save brass. Textile manufacturers were required to mix artificial with natural fibers. One of the first orders issued under the second Four-Year Plan was that men's clothing must contain 15 to 25 per cent of artificial wool. Later it was decreed that the various fabrics designed for civilian use must contain up to 50 per cent artificial fiber and even the fabrics of which military uniforms were made contained a considerable proportion of artificial wool.

The three most important achievements of the *Ersatz* program were cell wool, motor fuel, and rubber. As a means of meeting the shortage of wool the Nazis developed cell wool (*Zellwolle*), which is made from cellulose derived from wood and is not essentially different from rayon. In 1936 no less than 45,000 tons of this artificial wool were made in Germany, and the output for 1939 was estimated as having been four times greater. Although at first very inferior to wool, it was considerably improved by 1939. More critical than the shortage of wool was the shortage of motor fuel for the newly mechanized army. Experiments to supply motors with synthetic fuel had, in fact, been started before the First World War. During the years after the war two processes of making fuel from coal (hydro-

genation and liquefaction) were developed with such success that by
1935 Germany was producing more than a third of the motor fuel
consumed in the country. Since synthetic fuel could be made of
brown coal and Germany had large deposits of this coal, it was only
a question of building more plants. Three new ones began producing in 1937 and ten others were being built. According to a number
of estimates the production of synthetic fuel met about half the
peacetime needs during the early months of 1939. Efforts to produce
synthetic rubber were equally successful. The new product, called
buna, was made by an electrical process from coal and lime. Although buna cost about four times as much as natural rubber, it was
much more durable. The output for 1938 was estimated at 25,000 tons
or about one third of the national requirements, and the next year
saw production increase by at least 7 per cent.

EDUCATION AND CULTURE

Even before the Nazis achieved power it was clear that a political
party pretending to be the bearer of a new philosophy would seek
to control the thoughts and emotions of men. Such control, in fact,
was necessary to the continued existence of the Nazi state. Hence
they were not slow to pull down the banners of liberalism and to
hoist the swastika in the domain of education and culture as well as
in politics. They endeavored, above all, to mold the minds of the
younger generation into the Nazi pattern of thinking. "Whosoever
has the youth has the future," was one of Hitler's favorite slogans.
"In the struggles that are to come," said a Nazi leader, "we will see
to it that the youth of Germany belongs to National Socialism only,
and to Adolf Hitler." And there was no better way of perpetuating
National Socialism than through the educational system. From the
kindergarten up the school system was converted into a vast enterprise for the indoctrination of children with the Nazi philosophy.
The Nazis made no secret of their purpose. "The entire function of
all education," Dr. Rust, Hitler's minister of education, stated, "is
to create Nazis."

To make sure that the educational system would achieve the aim
they set for it, the Nazis "purified" it from top to bottom. The first
thing they did was to remove all teachers who were in any way opposed to them. The least they demanded from a teacher was outward conformity to the Nazi philosophy. Social committees examined the political records of all schools to question the teachers in
front of their pupils. All who were found unsympathetic to the

Nazi cause were either summarily dismissed or retired on pensions. Before the end of 1936 one teacher out of every five was either dismissed or retired. Those who remained were required to take the oath of loyalty to Hitler and to promise in writing that they would obey the laws of the National Socialist state. Besides eliminating all teachers who were not sympathetic to their cause, the Nazis reorganized the curriculum to suit their purposes. Old subjects were carefully colored with the Nazi *Weltanschauung,* and new ones which glorified the National Socialist movement were added. Among the new studies were race study, genetics, race hygiene, and genealogy. A decree of September 13, 1933, ordered that these studies be given special emphasis "at the expense, if necessary, of mathematics and foreign languages." The purpose, of course, was to indoctrinate every child with the Nazi philosophy of race. Hitler himself decreed in 1935 that "no boy or girl may leave school without having been brought to full appreciation of the nature and necessity of racial purity." Not only were special textbooks prescribed for all schools but school libraries were also purged of all books by Jews, books that spoke well of Jews, and books that "failed to show the proper respect" for Aryans.

But the formal school was only one of the agencies for the furtherance of the Nazi cause. Even greater reliance for inculcating the spirit of National Socialism was put on the Hitler Youth organizations. For boys there were two divisions: the *Jungvolk,* taking boys from ten to fourteen years, and the Hitler Youth proper, from fourteen to eighteen years. Paralleling these groups were similar divisions for girls, the *Jungmädel* and *Bund Deutscher Mädchen.* At first membership in the Hitler Youth was voluntary, but by a decree of December 1, 1936, it was made obligatory for all. In these organizations special emphasis was placed upon physical training. Much time, for example, was devoted to *Wehrsport* (defense sport) and to drilling according to the rhythm of marching songs. At all times military order, military discipline, and military knowledge were stressed. Even the films which were shown to the youth dealt invariably with such subjects as *Wehrsport,* aviation, and war. This was in accordance with Hitler's declaration in *Mein Kampf* that "education in a general way is to be preparation for later army service." However, the indoctrination of youth with Nazi teachings on other subjects was not neglected. Hitler Youth groups were required to attend frequent lectures on race hygiene, "history," and the various political, economic, and ethical questions of National Socialism. No Aryan German was able to escape one of the most intensive schemes of indoctrination ever devised. The general aim was stated in *Mein Kampf* when Hitler said of the German child: "His entire education and development has to be directed at giving him the conviction of being absolutely superior to the others. With this physical force and skill he has again to win the belief in the invincibility of his entire nationality." [13]

The control which the Nazis established over the universities was no less complete than their control over the lower schools. In Prussia the university professors had since 1852 been protected by law against political interference, and in other German states similar protection obtained either through law or custom. This protection, however, went by the board soon after the Nazi seizure of power. Not only academic tenure but also academic freedom, sound learning, and true scholarship became a thing of the past. As in the lower schools, non-Aryans and those who were suspected of being unsympathetic or even lukewarm to Nazi doctrines were retired on pensions, expelled without pensions, or driven into exile, the purpose being, according to the Rector of the University of Berlin, "to eliminate the dregs of a past liberal age." At first the government permitted a few non-Aryan professors to retain their positions, but this was distasteful to rabid Nazi students, who would either start riots in the classrooms of such professors or howl them down. In other cases the German Students Union, founded by the Nazis, would order the students not to attend the lectures of certain professors. Before the end of 1933 teachers' colleges were closed to students of non-Aryan descent, and in 1935 it was ordained that non-Aryans could no longer hold the title of professor. It is estimated that during the first three years of Nazi rule about 20 per cent of the university teachers were dismissed, retired, or forced into exile. Those professors who retained their positions were always under scrutiny by Nazi students or the police. Early in 1936 the minister of education declared that all professors must become Nazis and assist in the creation of a new type of National Socialist learning. To prevent "political undesirables" from becoming teachers in the universities, the administration of the universities was taken over by the government. The right of appointing the chief administrative officer of each university, whose title was "Führer" (originally Rector), and also the other university officials was vested in the minister of education. Upon the recommendation of the university officials he also appointed the teaching staff.

Equally complete was the Nazi control of the students. The Nazis decided not only who might attend a university but also what he

13 *Mein Kampf,* Reynal and Hitchcock ed., p. 618.

must study. Soon after taking office Hitler decreed that there were too many professional men in Germany and that the number of new students admitted annually should, therefore, be limited to 15,000, of whom not more than 10 per cent might be women. As a result the numbers fell from 116,154 in 1933 to 67,082 in 1937, a drop of about 42 per cent. Between 1937 and the outbreak of war in 1939 the number declined even further. The determining factor in the selection of a boy for university study was not so much his academic achievements as his record in the Hitler Youth and his zeal for Nazi ideas. Once in a university he had to join the German Students Union, a national organization under Nazi direction. In his studies he did not enjoy the freedom his predecessors had of choosing his courses. Besides being required to participate for at least three semesters in a series of compulsory sports, he had to spend a considerable part of the first two years studying such courses as eugenics, genetics, race biology, and race hygiene, the purpose of which was to indoctrinate him with Nazi racial ideas. In short, the function of guiding the intellectual life of the nation, formerly exercised by the universities, was taken over by the Nazis.

While the Nazis were applying the principle, "Whatever suits the party is right," to education, art, literature, and music, the theatre and the cinema were also bent to their aims. A work of art or a performance of any kind was good only so far as it supported their ideology. Anything that tended to diverge from the lines they laid down was styled *Kulturbolshevismus,* in other words, subversive and destructive to the state. They recognized no such thing as intellectual detachment. Whoever was not for National Socialism was against it. As Göring stated the issue, "I see only those who are for National Socialism and those who are against it, and I know how to deal with the latter."

But the fact that cultural production was subservient to Nazi interests was not enough. It was also prescribed that its creators must be Aryans. Regarding German culture as the highest expression of Aryanism, the Nazis thought it intolerable that non-Aryans should have any part in it. As early as September, 1933, a Reich Chamber of Culture was set up to supervise music, art, theatre, press, literature, radio, and the films. The statute instituting the chamber states specifically that "all creative forces in all spheres must be assembled under Reich leadership with a view to the uniform molding of the will." Membership in the chamber was compulsory for everyone active in the fields it supervised. At first the applications of non-Aryans and non-Nazis could be refused on the basis of a special regulation which read: "Admission to a Chamber may be refused, and a member may be excluded if facts justify the presumption that the person in question does not inspire the confidence or possess the ability necessary for the carrying on of his activity." Later Jews were specifically excluded from all activities supervised by the chamber.

In the field of literature, for example, Dr. Goebbels justified the suppression of all communist, socialist, liberal, and pacifist writings by declaring that the authors were not Germans and were therefore out of touch with the true life of the German people. Such authors were labeled "corrupters of the German spirit and the German soul." In other words writers who disapproved of the Nazi system had the choice of leaving the country, remaining silent, or producing inoffensive escapist literature. Most of the distinguished writers of the Weimar period chose to leave. All this explains why the literature of the Nazi era has been so mediocre and even puny. While the "new drama" attempted to glorify history as interpreted by the Nazis, lyrical poetry took the form of marching and fighting songs. As for novels and short stories, they were shallow escapist literature or Nazi heroics. In short, German literature from 1933 to 1939 was the triumph of unprincipled mediocrity and dilettantism. To prevent the reading of "obnoxious" books published before 1933 the Nazis drew up a blacklist of volumes and ordered them removed from all bookshops and public libraries. At a number of places student groups committed the works of "heretical" writers to the flames. Goebbels himself attended such a burning in the Opernplatz in Berlin and exclaimed, "What a joy to be alive!" while students threw into the fire the works of Freud, Schnitzler, Marx, Einstein, Erich Maria Remarque, Heinrich and Thomas Mann, and Emil Ludwig.

Even the great German classics of the eighteenth and nineteenth centuries were judged in the light of Nazi doctrines. While the writings of Heine and other German-Jewish writers were scored as being un-German, the works of Lessing, pioneer of the Golden Age of German literature, were ignored because he was an advocate of toleration and the friend of Moses Mendelssohn. Certain works of Goethe, Schiller, and Kleist were issued in popular editions or presented on the stage, but everything in them which might possibly conflict with Nazi teachings was deleted. Thus, for example, in Schiller's *Don Carlos* the line, "Sir! Give us liberty of thought," one of the loftiest passages in German literature, was carefully eliminated. Although the Nazis hailed Gerhardt Hauptmann as the Grand Old

Man of German literature on at least one occasion, they disapproved of his drama, *Die Weber,* because it portrays the struggle of a class and not of the entire nation *(Volk)*. Certain of the early nationalist writers were highly praised, including Fichte, author of the famous *Reden an die deutsche Nation,* and Ernst Moritz Arndt who in his poem, *Was ist des Deutschen Vaterland?* (What is the German's fatherland?), advocated that all those who speak German be included in the fatherland. Herder was lauded for his nationalism, but his cosmopolitanism was significantly overlooked. Finally, a number of minor poets who had uttered sentiments the Nazis found pleasant were resurrected. One of these was Wilhelm Raabe who had written: "If I forget you, Germany, mighty Fatherland, then I forfeit all my rights." He had also prophesied that the German oak would flourish mightily and gather all the German people under its shade.

CHAPTER THIRTEEN

The Balkans

THE PENINSULA OF
UNREST

THE Balkan [1] Peninsula is one of three peninsulas that jut southward into the Mediterranean, the other two being the Iberian in the west and the Italian in the center. Political and linguistic unity have long been established in Italy, and the Iberian Peninsula is shared by the two related nations of Spain and Portugal. There has been little unity, however, in the Balkan Peninsula. For centuries it has been inhabited by discordant peoples whose interests and ambitions clash fiercely. On this account someone has aptly called it the Peninsula of Unrest. For convenience we shall consider as the Balkans the area occupied by the states of Rumania, Yugoslavia, Greece, Bulgaria, and Albania. It is "a rough mountainous region, with fertile valleys tucked between boulder-strewn ridges and steep, wooded hills." Its mountainous nature has kept the inhabitants from any commercial development. The main occupation in all the countries has been agriculture.

There is a widespread tendency in the Western world to regard these states as insignificant. Many do not realize that from the physical viewpoint alone they are far from being so. As constituted after the First World War Rumania embraced an area of 113,889 square miles; in other words, it was only about 6000 square miles smaller than Italy. Yugoslavia, with an area of some 96,000 square miles, was nearly the size of Oregon. Greece, with about 50,000 square miles, was somewhat larger than New York. Bulgaria, with some 30,000 square miles, was about the size of Maine. Albania, the smallest of these states, encompassed an area of about 10,629 square

[1] The word "Balkan" derives from a Turkish word meaning "mountain."

miles, which is about the size of Maryland. According to the census of 1925 the total population of the five states was 42 million.

For many decades prior to the First World War the Balkan Peninsula had been the danger zone of Europe. It was the scene of plots and counterplots. Time and again upheavals in this region threatened to involve most of Europe in bloody conflict. For example, war almost broke out when Austria seized Bosnia and Herzegovina in 1908. From that time onward, students of European affairs predicted more emphatically than ever that if a great war came it would be precipitated in the Balkans.

Generally speaking, the reason for the perpetual turbulence was twofold. First, because the peninsula formed the main highway from Europe to Asia and from Russia to the Mediterranean, a number of great powers coveted control of it. This desire caused Russia and Austria to glare at one another across the chessboard of diplomacy throughout much of the nineteenth century. Toward the end of the century Germany also entered the competition. These three powers were ever ready to stir up unrest if they stood to gain thereby. In brief, live and let live was not the rule. Dealings between the nations were normally regulated in accordance with "the simple plan, that he shall take who has the power and he shall keep who can."

The second reason for the perpetual unrest was the desire for freedom and national union. Some of the nationalities in the peninsula were still subject peoples. Since freedom had been denied them so long, they put it above everything else and stopped at nothing in their efforts to attain it. On the other hand those who already had independent governments wished to include all the members of their respective nationality in one state.

The First World War, by destroying the Romanov and Habsburg empires, removed the most baleful outside influences from the lives of the Balkan peoples. But their main problem was only partially solved by the Paris Peace Conference, despite the fact that the peacemakers purported to base the settlement on such lofty principles as the right of self-determination, the right of nationality, and the right of political freedom. But the nationalities of the Balkans were so intermingled that with the best will in the world it would have been impossible for the Conference to make a cleancut division on ethnographical lines. Even when allowance is made for this fact, the settlement did not approximate the best possible achievement under the circumstances. Other motives entered into the settlement. One of these was the doctrine of punishment; many of the peacemakers were influenced by the idea that the lesser as well as the greater enemy states should pay a penalty. Then there was also the desire to block Germany's *Drang nach dem Südosten* (drive to the southeast) by strengthening the states that had been on the Allied side.

The result was a series of compromises which left much to be desired. Rumania, as one of the victors, received all of Transylvania and Bucovina, thereby more than doubling her population and becoming the largest of the Balkan states. The territory of Greece was nearly doubled. Serbia nearly quadrupled her population, Serbia and Montenegro being merged into the great commonwealth of Yugoslavia. On the other hand, Bulgaria, being on the losing side, was pared down very considerably. Once strong among her neighbors, she now became one of the smallest states in the Balkans.

The political position of these states was far from satisfactory. The victors were determined to preserve their gains, and Bulgaria was determined to recoup her losses at the first possible opportunity. The worst feature of this policy of "the spoils to the victor" was the incorporation of national minorities in states of other nationalities. Nearly 1.2 million Magyars and 600,000 Germans were, in grotesque disregard of self-determination, transferred to Rumania; nearly 300,000 Germans and a quarter million Magyars, to Yugoslavia; and about one quarter of the Bulgarians, to Greece and other states. The situation was aggravated by the fact that most of the nations did not pursue a liberal policy toward the minorities despite their promises to do so. This not only increased the discontent of the minorities but also strengthened the determination of the various national states to redeem these minorities.

During the months after the settlement of 1919 the Balkan equilibrium was so sensitive and there were so many border incidents that the word "peace" must in this connection be used only relatively. Quick to grasp the necessity of coordinating their political action, the governments of Yugoslavia, Rumania, and Czechoslovakia formed a defensive alliance as a means of frustrating the designs of the vanquished states. This alliance, known as the Little Entente, was concluded by a series of treaties in 1920 and 1921. While the general purpose was the maintenance of the *status quo,* a more specific aim was the prevention of attempts to restore the Habsburgs to power either at Budapest or at Vienna. Such a restoration, it was feared, would lead to an attempt to regain the territories which were distributed to the victorious states upon the collapse of the empire in 1918. The Little Entente, supplemented in 1929 by a tripartite treaty of arbitration, played a material role in the period between the two world wars.

But problems of territory and of national minorities were not the only ones confronting the Balkan states. In addition to the general upheaval caused by the war, the collapse of the Habsburg Empire and the creation of national states upon its ruins brought in their train such difficulties as the transfer of land to the peasantry, the advent to power of new classes, the creation of new bureaucracies, the revision of many fundamental institutions, the establishment of internal unity through the fusion of the old and the new elements in the population, and the restoration of commercial and financial stability. In most of the states, financial conditions were serious as a result of the disorganization produced by four years of war and the dislocation caused by the increase in the number of tariff walls.

There were also religious problems. Although most of the inhabitants of the peninsula were at least nominal members of the Eastern Orthodox Church, the number of Roman Catholics, particularly in Yugoslavia (Croatia), was considerable. Then there were the Mohammedans or Moslems, who were convinced of their duty to go on being loyal and consistent professors of their religion.

Another major problem was the conflict between radicalism and conservatism. Thus the difficulties facing the Balkan states were tremendous.

The discussion that follows will show briefly how the states succeeded or failed in their attempts to solve these problems, the fundamental character of which was much the same in each state. The problems included: (1) the establishment of administrative machinery, (2) the creation of commercial and financial stability, (3) the adjustment of social differences, (4) the reconciliation of racial minorities.

RUMANIA

Rumania became territorially the largest of the Balkan group as a result of the peace settlement. For fighting on the side of the Allies the peacemakers allotted to it the province of Bucovina, which had belonged to Austria; Transylvania, which had for centuries been attached to Hungary; and Bessarabia, which had been a part of the Russian Empire. In addition, the boundary between Rumania and Bulgaria was reestablished as it had been drawn in 1913, so that Dobruja became a part of Greater Rumania. Thus the area of the country was more than doubled in size, from 53,000 square miles to 113,889 square miles. Its population, which had formerly been about eight million, was also more than doubled to around eighteen million. In other words, as one result of the settlement Rumania became the sixth largest country in Europe, with an area very nearly equal to that of Italy and a population almost three fourths that of Spain.

During the period between two wars Rumania was not only the largest state of the Balkan group but it was also economically the most important. It was particularly rich in natural resources— petroleum, coal, iron, gold, manganese, copper, salt, and natural gas. The gold mines were among the richest in Europe. More important was the wealth in petroleum, which was the country's second richest source of natural wealth. In 1929 Rumania ranked seventh among the nations of the world in petroleum production, with 2.4 per cent of the world's total output. Petroleum accounted for about 40 per cent of the exports. But the richest source of natural wealth was agriculture. Almost 80 per cent of the inhabitants derived their living from the soil. Fertile fields produced great harvests of maize and wheat. Next to Argentina, Rumania exported more maize than any other country in the world. It was rich in timber, about 17.5 million acres, or one fourth of the total area, being timberland. Manufacturing was still in its infancy. During the years immediately following the termination of World War I less than one million inhabitants were employed in manufacturing establishments, but after 1935 there was a mushroom growth of industry which was largely due to the rearmament program.

The government was technically a constitutional monarchy of the normal type with a bicameral legislature but in practice it was largely absolute. King Ferdinand, who ascended the throne in October, 1914, was little more than a figurehead. The real ruler was Ion Bratianu, who dominated the political situation from 1918 until his death in 1927.[2] Through his domination of the king, Bratianu controlled the royal power to nominate and recall ministers. Once he and his nominees were in power, they proceeded to form a majority in parliament by wholesale manipulation of elections. They did not hesitate to limit the freedom of the press, to infringe upon the right of free assembly, or to resort to martial law when crises arose.

[2] The name "Bratianu" was not new in Rumanian politics. For many decades it had been closely connected with important historical events. The father of Ion Bratianu had played a primary role in winning Rumanian independence (1878).

By such means, though he was not always premier, he ruled the country for almost a decade.

The end of World War I saw the Rumanian government confronted by many knotty problems which demanded a solution. Outstanding among them was repairing the damages of war. Two thirds of old Rumania had been occupied by the Germans and systematically exploited to the point of exhaustion. At the time of the German advance into Rumania in 1917 the Rumanians had destroyed many oil wells to keep the enemy from using them. For these wells new machinery had to be purchased so that they could again be made productive. Then it was also necessary to put the finances in order. The Germans had flooded the country with German marks, which rapidly fell in value and which the Germans refused to redeem at any rate. In addition, Rumania had at the time of the German advance sent its entire gold reserve to Russia, where the Bolsheviks used it to establish their revolution. Consequently there was little or no money available for repairing the war ravages, with the result that for a time mines and industries were at a standstill and farmers could not till the fields because of a lack of fertilizers, tools, and animals. The dislocation of agriculture was such that the people, though they were an agricultural nation, were obliged to purchase food abroad to keep from starving.

Not only food but the agrarian question generally posed a serious problem. Before the war Rumania had been a country of large estates. Peasant holdings were relatively few and most of these too small to be self-supporting. During the second half of the nineteenth century uprisings impelled by land hunger were by no means uncommon. At various times the parliament did take measures toward allotting more land to the peasants, but these reforms did not settle the agrarian question. The portions of land held by the peasants were still too small to maintain the owners. In 42 per cent of the cases the allotments averaged less than five acres, while 39 per cent had no more than twelve acres and 14 per cent under twenty-five acres. Many small holders in fact were forced to sell their land and become dependent again upon the landlord. When the Bolshevik Revolution broke out, King Ferdinand in order to avert the imminent danger of a similar revolution in Rumania promised the peasants that the great estates would be split up and handed to them. The expropriation began the next year. Up to the end of 1929 nine thousand estates had been allotted to the peasants and many of the remaining large estates were divided during the succeeding years. The terms were so arranged that the

THE BALKAN STATES AND THEIR NEIGHBORS

The "peninsula of unrest," the danger zone of Europe, has never attained the unity long ago established in the other two peninsulas that jut down into the Mediterranean.

peasants paid 65 per cent of the appropriation price in forty-five annual installments, the remaining 35 per cent being borne by the state. This division changed both the status and the outlook of the peasant and gave him an incentive to plan and look forward to his own betterment.

Most persistent throughout the period was the problem of minorities. The population before the First World War had been largely, though not wholly, homogeneous. As a result of the settlement the Rumanians made up only 74.4 per cent of the population, the rest being members of other nationalities. Thus 8.4 per cent were Hungarians, 5 per cent Jews, 4.3 per cent Germans, 3.3 per cent Russians (Ukrainians), 1.5 per cent Bulgarians, 1 per cent Turks, and the rest a collection from other nationalities. The actual joining of the unredeemed provinces to the mother country was easily achieved, but the tremendous task of readjustment to new conditions and of fitting together the different parts of Greater Rumania into a harmonious whole was a task of another nature. It was not only a question of unifying the various legal systems which had previously functioned in the new provinces, but of making Rumanian nationals of the 1,500,000 Hungarians, 750,000 Germans, 500,000 Ukrainians, and 250,000 Bulgarians who inhabited these provinces. Nor were the great numbers of Magyars, Germans, Russians, and Bulgarians disposed to welcome the change of sovereignty and the efforts of the government to destroy their cultural existence. The government, it is true, had signed the Minorities' Treaty in 1919 under pressure from the Allied powers, but the Bratianu regime made no attempt to enact its provisions. On the contrary, it pursued a relentless policy of denationalization.

If it made little progress toward solving the minorities problem, it did achieve some success in other respects. Besides being directly responsible for the introduction of peasant proprietorship, it was able by a process of rigid economy coupled with a systematic readjustment of taxation to put some semblance of order into the finances. But its popularity was short lived. As the party of big business it adopted a policy which evoked widespread opposition within and sharp criticism outside Rumania. The keynote of this policy was "Rumania for Rumanians." More specifically, it advocated control of industry by Rumanians and a high tariff to protect Rumanian products. Laws were enacted to achieve both aims. Particularly noteworthy was the mining law (June 30, 1924) which aimed to give Rumanians control of the oil industry in their country. It was estimated that previously only one company out of five had been Rumanian owned and that of the capital invested no less than 80 per cent was foreign. The mining law decreed that thereafter only the state could grant oil concessions and that 55 per cent of the stock of all oil companies must be owned by Rumanian citizens. Corporations which already held concessions were given a specified time in which to sell a majority of their stock to Rumanians. Both the protective tariff and the nationalization of the subsoil aroused opposition. While the peasants contended that the tariff was prejudicial to their interests, the mining law provoked the wrath of foreign investors. When Bratianu attempted to organize Rumanian companies to develop the national resources, he could not command sufficient capital.

Meanwhile the political front had been undergoing a gradual change. Before the war there had been two important political parties, the Conservatives and the Liberals. The former represented the interests of the great landowners; the latter, the industrial and financial classes. The balance between these two was, however, upset through the introduction of universal manhood suffrage and peasant proprietorship. According to the new electoral law (1922) all male citizens, irrespective of wealth, became direct voters. Thus the landlords lost their former political privileges, which were based upon property. It was the political death warrant of the Conservative Party. While the party as such went to pieces, the former members joined the Liberal Party. Thenceforth the name "Liberal Party" was in reality a misnomer because it now became the party of the right. On the left a group of peasant parties had arisen, stimulated to life by the extension of direct suffrage to the peasants. They were the country's true liberals. In 1926 these various parties were fused into the National Peasant Party which thereafter increasingly contested the Liberal Party's control of the government. The platform of the Peasant Party was not communistic. Its basic plank was peasant prosperity through cooperatives for the marketing of agricultural produce and the buying of implements.

The downfall of the Liberal Party, which had been expected for some time, finally came in 1927. In addition to the economic decline, the death of the king and the question of the succession increased the difficulties of the ruling party and its leaders. When King Ferdinand died in July, 1927, he was not succeeded by his eldest son Carol but by Prince Michael, the son of Carol and his wife, Princess Helen of Greece. A series of youthful escapades culminating in a clash with his family and with the Bratianus caused Carol formally to renounce his right to the throne and to leave

Rumania to live in exile with his mistress, Magda Lupescu. Consequently upon Ferdinand's death, Michael, a boy of six, was declared king under a regency. Bratianu continued as the power behind the throne, but his days were numbered. Four months later he followed his royal friend to the grave. His brother, Vintila, who succeeded him as premier and as leader of the Liberal Party, sought to continue Ion's policies. He was unequal to the situation. After failing to obtain a foreign loan, the need for which had become imperative, he reached a point where he could not go on. The regency was forced to call Julius Maniu, the leader of the National Peasant Party, to the helm (1928).

The new government proceeded at once to inaugurate a program of domestic reform. It repealed the censorship of the press, eased the restrictions on racial minorities, curbed anti-Jewish demonstrations, modified the laws restricting foreign capital, reduced the tariff, lowered the cost of living, and introduced drastic economies into public administration. Nevertheless it did not produce the miraculous results the masses expected. The obstacles confronting it were too great: first, there was the inexperience of its supporters; second, the world-wide depression was making itself felt; third, the National Liberals, who still retained control of the banking institutions, bent every effort to undermine the work of the new government. When they felt the reins of government slipping through their fingers, the National Peasant leaders decided to play their last trump. They approved the return of Carol. Public opinion was not unfavorable to his return. Not only had the peasants always been fond of him, but he was also popular with the army. Hence it was not surprising that he was enthusiastically welcomed by the troops when he stepped from a military airplane at Bucharest on June 6, 1930. Two days later the two houses of parliament repealed by an almost unanimous vote the act which had excluded him from the throne and then proclaimed him king of the Rumanians. Thus the former playboy became King Carol II.

The new king was determined not to owe his crown to any party or to take orders from any group. His ambition was to eliminate factional strife and to form a national government in which all parties were represented. Personal and factional interests, he said, had ruled Rumanian politics too long and too much; henceforth national interests must be paramount. Instead of taking steps against the National Liberals who had opposed his return, he made it known that he would welcome their support. The result was that the party issued a manifesto declaring its adherence to the new ruler. With the support of the two major parties Carol settled down with a new seriousness to the business of being king. "Rumania," he said, "has vast resources and we must make them productive, thus strengthening the country economically. The army must be reorganized. Restored to a normal regime and enjoying the advantages of stability, Rumania may aspire to a high place in Europe." Carol made the development of education and the welfare of the peasants his special care and was able to achieve much in both directions. He also sought to win the support of the minorities. By his direction a statute promulgated in 1938 permitted the minorities to organize themselves into communities for the defense of their cultural, economic, and social interests.

Carol's most formidable opposition centered in the Fascist movement. The main Fascist group was the Iron Guard founded by Corneliu Codreanu. This party did not, as is often stated, originate as an offshoot of the German Nazi Party; it was an indigenous, intensely nationalistic movement which, like the Nazi Party, had an economic basis in the land hunger of the peasants and the job hunger of the middle classes. The Iron Guardists shared the anti-Semitism of the Nazis and adopted the swastika as their symbol, and parts of their platform were a literal translation of the Nazi program. In foreign politics they urged a close alliance with Germany and Italy. When they found that Carol had no intention of allying himself with them, certain sections of the party resorted to terroristic methods and political murders which included the assassination of Premier Duca in 1933. The king responded by proscribing the party, but this only served to drive it under cover. Thenceforth the Iron Guard, continuing its activities under the new name of "All-for-Country," received encouragement and subsidies from the Nazis, who were vitally interested in the priceless oil reserves and the fertile fields of Rumania and who also coveted this passageway to the Ukraine.

The internal situation gradually reached a point where the king was compelled to take drastic steps in order to save his crown and the independence of his state. He met the totalitarian challenge by an experiment in authoritarian government. In 1930 he replaced the loosely democratic constitution of 1923 by a new constitution which made the ministers responsible only to the crown. In the same year he also dissolved the old political parties and replaced them by a single legitimate organization, the Front of National Rebirth. "In difficult times," Carol said, "the labor of those at the head of the country should be strengthened by the concentrated effort of all the active and creative elements of the nation." Most of the Iron Guard leaders, including Codreanu, were sentenced to prison terms, and some two thousand members were banished to concentration camps. In November Codreanu and some of his followers were shot "while attempting to escape," as the government put it. For the time being Carol was the dictator of Rumania.

In the field of international politics events had taken a turn which augured ill for Rumania's future. Carol, whose sympathies were on the side of Great Britain and France, repeatedly refused Germany's offer to safeguard his territory because he knew that consent would mean the end of independence. He hoped the situation would develop in such a way as to make it possible for the Allied powers to come to his aid in case of necessity. By making minor revisions of the frontiers he could probably have built up a Balkan bloc that would have stood as a formidable barrier to Axis [3] ambitions. But he was determined to cling to every inch of territory that Rumania had received in 1919, and in his stand he was supported by a majority of Rumanians. In the Munich crisis of 1938 he did declare that Rumania would stand behind its treaties. Representatives even began to devise means whereby a Russian army could pass through Rumania in going to the help of Czechoslovakia, which the Nazis were about to add to the Greater Reich. As it became clear that the British and French could give him no military support, Carol tried to make the best of both worlds. While he did not repudiate his former connections, he did comply to a considerable extent with Hitler's behests because he deemed this essential for security. At the outbreak of World War II Rumania formally declared its neutrality, and none hoped more fervently than Carol II that his country would be able to adhere to it. But Rumania was inexorably sucked into the maelstrom.

🔖

YUGOSLAVIA

Yugoslavia was the second largest Balkan state, with a population of some fourteen million and an area of roughly 96,000 miles, which is over three quarters the size of the British Isles and three times that of prewar Serbia. The new kingdom began its formal existence in December, 1918, under the name, Kingdom of the Serbs, Croats, and Slovenes. Not until 1929 did it officially receive the name of Yugoslavia. Its component parts were the independent kingdoms of Serbia and Montenegro and the former Austro-Hun-

[3] Germany and Italy were the Axis powers.

garian provinces of Croatia, Slovenia, Dalmatia, and Bosnia-Herzegovina. Although the Serbs, Croats, and Slovenes constituted more
than 80 per cent of the total population, Yugoslavia, like Rumania,
had its German and Magyar minorities. Linguistically the Serbs,
Croats, and Slovenes were closely related, but in most other respects
they were far apart. Having lived apart for centuries, they had developed peculiar mental processes and psychological outlooks. They
were, for example, in different stages of development, the Croats
and Slovenes being much more advanced than the Serbians. Such
differences made them distrustful of each other. In addition to the
ethnic, historical, and economic differences, there were also religious differences which complicated the relations of the three
groups. While the Serbs belonged to the Orthodox Church and
wrote with Cyrillic characters, the Croats and Slovenes were Roman
Catholics and, though they spoke the same tongue as their Serb
kinsmen, wrote it with Latin characters. More specifically, 48 per
cent of the nation were adherents of the Orthodox faith and 37
per cent were Roman Catholics. The Moslems numbered 11 per
cent of the population.

In November, 1918, Prince Alexander, heir to the Serbian
throne, was chosen as head of the new kingdom and on December 1
began his rule as constitutional monarch. His task was far from
easy, for the internal condition of the new state was fraught with
many difficulties. Croatia and Slovenia, it is true, had hardly been
touched by the devastation of the preceding years, but Serbia had
been carrying on war for more than six years and had been held
by the enemy for four years, during which time it had been plundered of everything worth removing. Towns had been turned into
rubble heaps, roads and railroads torn up, and mines and factories
destroyed. Everything necessary for industry and agriculture had to
be procured afresh. On top of this, the national credit was low and
the rate of exchange unfavorable. Furthermore, the different provinces stood on different economic levels, had different legal systems,
and also different land systems. More than half the population was
illiterate and there was no tradition of democratic participation in
the government.

The central problem was the establishment of a system of government which could put order into the existing chaos and, above
all, command the cooperation and respect of the various groups
composing the new state. The basic issue was between what may
roughly be called "centralist" and "federalist" tendencies. Under the
stress of an acute crisis in 1918 the principle of union was accepted

on all sides, but unhappily the fundamental lines on which the union was to be worked out were not specified. In the Constituent Assembly which met in 1920 the Serbian Radical Party under the leadership of Nicholas Pashitch (1845–1926) was the most powerful group. Pashitch, who had carried Serbia through the war years and fought its battles at the Peace Conference, worked tirelessly for a highly centralized state. In other words, he wished to create a "Great Serbia," regardless of the national, cultural, and political aspirations of non-Serb peoples within the new state. Accordingly the constitution adopted at his urging was along extreme centralist lines, one which supplanted the provincial diets by one central legislative body and otherwise sought to centralize authority in Belgrade.

This constitution, promulgated in 1921, was not to the liking of the Croats, who cherished everything that marked them as distinct from other peoples. Having enjoyed a certain autonomy in the old Austro-Hungarian state they resented the attempt to shape them into the Serbian mold. They were willing to admit that the Serbs, Croats, and Slovenes must live together, but insisted that the bonds joining them must be as shadowy as possible, that each province must have the right to go its own way politically, commercially, and culturally. The chief protagonists of Croat particularism were the members of the Croat Peasant Party whose leader was Stefan Raditch, a Zagreb bookseller. The representatives of this party either refused to participate in the proceedings of the Belgrade chamber or when they were present voted against the government. Consequently there were recurrent political crises, and no cabinet was able to retain a parliamentary majority for long. Urgent legislation was far in arrears and the economic organization of the country was sadly neglected. Worst of all, the misunderstanding between Serbia and Croatia was becoming more serious. In 1928 the political strife was intensified to a point where the Croat leader, Stefan Raditch, was assassinated at a session of the Belgrade parliament.

When the Croat deputies withdrew as a result of the assassination and the very existence of the state was threatened, the demand became more and more insistent that the king take the initiative. Alexander responded by suspending parliament and abolishing the constitution of 1921 (January 6, 1929). Thereafter, with the support of the army, he carried on the government entirely on autocratic lines. The goal he set for his dictatorship was to weld the three ethnic groups into one nationality. To this end he deliberately broke with historic tradition and abolished the old names of Croatia, Bosnia, Dalmatia, etc., replacing these districts with new divisions.

He further decreed (July, 1930) the dissolution of all associations and institutions which might help preserve tribal sentiments. These measures, however, only created further grievances. Finally, in September, 1931, to allay internal discontent and to assuage foreign opinion, Alexander issued a new constitution which defined the state as a constitutional monarchy. But it restored the constitutional monarchy in appearance rather than in reality. While it contained clauses which guaranteed political liberties, inviolability of person, the right of free assembly, freedom of religion, freedom of speech, and a free press, it unfortunately nullified the rights in each instance by the addition of such phrases as "except in cases provided by the law" or "within the limits of the law," for all the laws of the dictatorship remained in force under the new constitution. There was once more a parliament, but the crown retained the right to nominate and dismiss the prime minister and all the members of the cabinet, and was able to manipulate the elections in such a way as to insure itself a majority of supporters.

King Alexander had failed to solve the basic problems of Yugoslav unity. He had merely established a police regime which, instead of breaking the passive resistance of the Croats, had made them more determined in their opposition. Everywhere there was profound discontent. In October, 1934, a turning point came as the result of the assassination of King Alexander by a Macedonian kinsman. Alexander's young son ascended the throne with the title of Peter II, but the government was carried on by a triple regency in which Prince Paul, Alexander's cousin, played the leading role. A much milder ruler than Alexander had been, Paul pursued a more conciliatory policy toward the Croats. He was still unwilling, however, to modify the constitution to the extent of granting them local autonomy. After the German designs on Czechoslovakia became patent, he changed his mind. He feared that the Nazis might make the most of the internal dissension to render the country an easy prey to Nazi domination. Thus after many years of struggle the Croat strivings for autonomy came to fruition in 1939. It was agreed that Croatia, with its 4.5 million inhabitants, should form a distinct unit under a Ban or governor, after the pattern of Croatia' previous status in the Austro-Hungarian Empire. In addition to a Ban, appointed by the crown, Croatia was to have a local diet meeting in Zagreb, and a separate budget. On the other hand, the central government retained control of foreign affairs, the army, foreign trade, transportation, religion, mining, weights and measures and the broad lines of educational policy.

A PEASANT DANCE IN YUGOSLAVIA

Under the regency of Prince Paul a change also became apparent in Yugoslavia's foreign policy. Until 1936 this was based on friendship with Great Britain and France and on adherence to the Little Entente. But in 1936 Yugoslavia began to gravitate toward the orbit of Germany and Italy, Prince Paul endeavoring at the same time to remain on good terms with Great Britain and France. The drift toward the Axis came as a result of advances made by Germany and Italy, who eagerly sought the economic resources of Yugoslavia. The regency defended its new policy by stating that it had no other choice since it could place little reliance on the guarantees of the Western democracies. It further stated that trade with Germany was more beneficial than economic relations with Great Britain and France. Finally, it also argued that Yugoslavia was only making new friends while retaining the old ones. The masses did not, however, share the opinion of the regency. Bitterly hostile to Germany and to Italy, they sharply denounced the friendship with the Axis powers.

GREECE

Greece emerged from the Balkan Wars and World War I with large acquisitions of territory. By the peace that was signed after the Balkan Wars it acquired territory in Epirus, Macedonia, Crete, and the Aegean Islands, so that it was practically doubled in size and population. When the First World War broke out, Venizelos, who had been premier most of the time since 1910, was wholeheartedly in favor of joining the Allies; but King Constantine, who was married to the sister of Kaiser William of Germany, had other ideas. Convinced of Teutonic invincibility, he tried to avoid becoming involved in the war. In 1917, after the entry of the United States, France and Great Britain put pressure on the king, who responded by abdicating in favor of Alexander, the younger of his sons (June 11, 1917). Several weeks later Venizelos formally declared war on Germany, Turkey, and Bulgaria.

The opening of the Peace Conference saw Venizelos in Paris. As the representative of Greece, he proved himself a consummate master of diplomatic technique. It is reported that at his first meeting with President Wilson the latter, wishing to end the conversation after several minutes of generalities, assured Venizelos that he would keep the Hellenic aspirations in mind. "I am grateful, Mr. President," the Greek premier responded. "What really interests me now is not Greece but your great idea of the League of Nations. To work, in the measure of my capacities, toward the realization of this great idea is my deepest desire. Consider me, please, as a soldier at your order for this task." Happy at finding a supporter of his cause, the President continued the conversation for more than an hour. Venizelos, upon returning to his hotel, said to his friends, "I think we have Smyrna." Unfortunately the Treaty of Sèvres did give the Greeks permission to occupy the Smyrna district of Asia Minor besides assigning them the greater part of Thrace. The occupation of Smyrna meant the forcible ejection of the Turks from that territory. Thus the Greeks were called upon to make a fresh military effort. But the enterprise was doomed to failure: not only was their army poorly equipped, but it was also singularly lacking in leadership. At first they made appreciable progress in their advance into Asia Minor, but with the stiffening of Turkish resistance they were gradually compelled to evacuate the district. The differences between the Greeks and Turks were composed in the Treaty of Lausanne (July 24, 1923).[4]

The new treaty left Greece with an area of about 50,000 square miles—about the size of the state of New York—and a population of about 6.5 million. Like the other Balkan nations, Greece was preeminently an agricultural state. More than 60 per cent of the population derived a living from farming. Although the land was on the whole less fertile, the momentary yield per acre was greater than in Yugoslavia, Bulgaria, Rumania, or Albania.[5] While cereals made up the greater part of the crops, considerable quantities of fruit, particularly grapes, figs, and olives, were raised. Stock raising was also an important source of income.

Commerce and industry were, however, by no means neglected. The Greeks had long been noted traders and fishermen. Nor was the industrial development as backward as in some of the other Balkan countries. Ten years after World War I Greece boasted almost 4000 large factories, and this despite a serious lack of capital and coal. Besides wines, raisins, tobacco, brandy, soap, and olive oil, the exports included yarns, carpets, and chemical fertilizers.

The political history of Greece during the period between the two great wars is the story of an almost unbroken series of political revolutions, most of which were bloodless. The changes were generally the work of resolute minorities, the public as such being completely indifferent most of the time. On October 5, 1920, King Alex-

[4] See page 302.
[5] See J. S. Roucek, "The Economic Geography of Greece," in *Economic Geography*, vol. II, pp. 91–104.

ander who had occupied the throne only a few years died of blood poisoning from the bite of a pet monkey. His death made the restoration of Constantine a real issue. Despite Venizelos' opposition, the people, who longed for a real peace and believed that Constantine would give it to them, voted overwhelmingly for his restoration. But his popularity was shortlived. When the Smyrna expedition turned out so disastrously, a large part of the defeated army held him responsible. Although there were loyal troops ready to fight for him, he abdicated to avoid civil war (September 27, 1922). The Crown Prince ascended the throne as George II, but occupied it only a few troubled months. The republicans cut short his reign by proclaiming a republic and then proceeded to secure ratification of their action in a plebiscite (April, 1924).

But the new form of government brought no more political stability than the old had. There was violent political strife, with cabinets rising and falling in rapid succession. For a considerable time there was even an actual dictatorship. In 1928 Venizelos, after an absence from political life of more than four years, returned to an active role in the government. Even his four-year rule failed to end the discord. After his retirement in 1932 the vitality of the republic gradually ebbed. Three years later (October, 1935) a group of scheming generals staged a military *coup d'état* which proclaimed Greece a monarchy. A plebiscite was staged to approve the return of George II. The exiled king announced that he would be "king of all the Greeks," not of the royalists alone. However, the political parties showed little inclination to sink their differences and to pull together for the benefit of the country as a whole. So uncompromising was the rivalry that no stable ministry could be formed. The threat of anarchy opened the way for dictatorship, and the man who seized the opportunity was General Metaxas.

Metaxas, who had the support of the army, obtained King George's signature (August 4, 1936) to decrees which suspended the articles of the constitution guaranteeing personal liberty. He then proceeded to declare martial law. Thereafter until his death (January, 1941) he ruled as dictator. Upon assuming power he at once set about reorganizing the country according to the example set by Hitler and Mussolini. In harmony with both he defined liberty as a "nineteenth-century illusion" and acted accordingly. Thus, for example, the press was muzzled and many opponents were subjected to the "castor oil treatment." But there were also reforms; among others, a minimum wage was established, an eight-hour day was declared, some of the debts of the small landowners were canceled, and workers were given health protection. Nevertheless, the Metaxas government gained little popular support until the Italian occupation of Albania (April, 1939). Fearing that Greece might be next on the schedule, the people rallied behind Metaxas, who tried to maintain a strict neutrality when World War II broke out. It was all to no avail, for the Italians coveted the Greek harbors which were important strategic points. In 1940 Mussolini's government tried to pick a quarrel with Greece. When this maneuver failed, Italy presented a crude ultimatum and then launched an unprovoked invasion of Greek territory.

BULGARIA

While Rumania, Yugoslavia, and Greece gained territory as a result of the settlement in 1919, Bulgaria was reduced to a population of something less than five million and an area of some 39,000 square miles. In other words, it was a third larger than the state of Maine and its population seven times as large. From the time of its liberation from Turkish rule in 1878 until 1913 Bulgaria had become more successful and important. But a turning point came in the second Balkan War. In the first Balkan War the Serbs, Greeks, and Bulgarians had been allies against Turkey, but no sooner was it over than the Serbs and Greeks (subsequently joined by the Rumanians) attacked Bulgaria in a war over the division of the spoils. In the settlement Bulgaria lost most of Macedonia and Dobruja. When the First World War broke out, most of the Bulgarians wished to remain neutral; but as it progressed, neutrality became increasingly difficult. In the spring of 1915, after the Dardanelles failure, King Ferdinand decided that the Central Powers must win and he therefore cast Bulgaria's lot with them. Thus the end of the war found Bulgaria on the losing side. At Paris the Bulgarian nation was reduced from a position of importance to one of comparative insignificance. Besides having its boundaries further reduced in favor of Yugoslavia and Greece, it lost its access to the Aegean. Furthermore, its finances were dealt a fatal blow by the imposition of an indemnity of 2.25 billion francs in gold. In 1923, it is true, the amount of the indemnity was reduced to 550 million gold francs which were to be paid over a period of sixty years, but the burden was still a crushing one for the impoverished nation.

The feeling of resentment over the war, the defeat, and the dismemberment which cut off a million Bulgarians from their homeland was so strong that those who had been instrumental in taking the country into the war fell out of favor with the masses. King Ferdinand fled the country in the autumn of 1918 and was succeeded by his son, Boris III. With the departure of Ferdinand the atmosphere of the court became less autocratic. The young sovereign made no attempt to control the government, which in form was a constitutional monarchy. His position was, however, no sinecure. Postwar restlessness produced class hatreds and strife which at times assumed the dimensions of civil war.

The feeling was especially tense between the townspeople on the one hand and the peasants on the other. The word "Bulgarian" derives from "Bolalagar," meaning plowman or peasant. The name was appropriate since more than four fifths of the population were peasants. Only 10 per cent were employed in industry, commerce, and transportation. The contrast between town and country was very sharp. Sofia, the capital, was well equipped with hospitals, a municipal water system, electric lights, street cars, and taxis. There were also other towns and cities with up-to-date conveniences. But the inhabitants of the villages had only the barest necessities. The average holding, which had been twenty-five acres in 1900, decreased to only fifteen in 1926. The methods of agriculture employed by most of the peasants were still primitive. As late as 1936 there were almost twice as many wooden plows as iron plows. Consequently crop yield was decidedly lower than in many European countries.

During the period preceding the First World War the administration had been in the hands of the townspeople, but early in the twentieth century a reaction against bourgeois domination began to take form. An Agrarian League was organized and gradually grew stronger until by 1919 it was the most powerful party. When it obtained a majority of the seats in the National Assembly as a result of the elections of 1919, King Boris entrusted the government to Alexander Stambolisky, the leader of the party. The son of poor parents and a man of Herculean stature and a forceful eloquence, Stambolisky was deeply venerated by the peasants. With their support he began to crush the opposition and to inaugurate sweeping agrarian reforms. For example, he expropriated large tracts of church, government, and private land which he then broke up into small farms and gave to landless peasants. In his foreign policy he bowed to the wishes of the victorious powers, accepting the Treaty of Neuilly and endeavoring to carry out its provisions.

Stambolisky's policies soon aroused bitter resentment among the urban, military, and professional classes. While his iron rule which favored the peasants created ill feeling among the townspeople generally, the military and nationalist leaders opposed his policy of friendship with the other Balkan states. Furthermore, his subordinates brought discredit upon the administration by frequently falling short in the performance of their duties. All this caused a combination of army officers, intellectuals, and the chieftains of the Macedonian Revolutionary Organization [6] to stage a *coup d'état*. In June, 1923, Stambolisky was murdered and a bourgeois government was established. For the next eleven years coalitions, most of which represented only a small minority of the people, ruled the country. In May, 1934, the parliamentary form of government was terminated completely by a Fascist group supported by the Officers' League. The new government abolished all political parties, dissolved the Macedonian terrorist organization, and entered into collaboration with the Agrarians. They made a serious mistake, however, in restricting the role of King Boris. Boris, by patient planning and guileful manipulation, succeeded in causing division within the group that had staged the coup. Having weakened the power of this group, the king proclaimed a royal dictatorship in April, 1935. After two years of personal rule he decided to recreate parliament. The new parliament, elected in March, 1938, had no actual power. In general, the royal dictatorship was no more successful than preceding governments in solving the social and economic crisis of Bulgaria.

Throughout this period the Treaty of Neuilly and its results were a major problem. Although the government continued to fulfill its treaty obligations, the fact that about a million Bulgarians were under Greek, Yugoslav, and Rumanian rule engendered a keen sense of injustice. As in Germany and Hungary the injustice of the peace provided fuel for a revisionist movement. After Hitler reorganized the German army, many discontented intellectuals openly advocated close ties with Germany in the hope that Bulgaria might with its help regain the territories lost in 1918. The king also seemed to favor such cooperation but in general there was no love lost between the Bulgarians and the Germans. On the other hand, Bulgaria's trade was largely dependent on the Axis. In 1938–1939, for example, 63.4 per cent of the exports went to Greater Germany and 57.8 per cent of its imports came from Greater Germany. This

[6] An organization which by means of terrorist methods waged a ceaseless fight to set up Macedonia, which had been apportioned to Bulgaria, Yugoslavia, and Greece, as an autonomous state.

foreign trade, supported by intensified Nazi propaganda, gradually drew Bulgaria into the orbit of Axis influence.

ぐ

ALBANIA

Albania was the smallest of the Balkan states, with a population of less than a million and an area of 10,629 square miles, which is about the size of the state of Maryland. This tiny land of rugged mountains, fertile valleys, and swampy coastal plains had been under Turkish rule for five centuries. It was only in 1913, at the close of the Balkan Wars, that its independence was recognized. During the First World War the fighting front cut Albania almost in two, the Central Powers holding the north and the Allied forces the south. At the Paris Conference there was much discussion as to what should be done with Albania. While the representatives of Greece, Yugoslavia, and Italy contended that the country was incapable of self-government, others wished to preserve it as an independent state. Italy, in particular, had long been interested in Albania, which lies at the bottleneck entrance to the Adriatic Sea and is only forty-seven miles from the Italian coast at the nearest point. At this point there is the Bay of Valona from which a hostile fleet might control the entrance to the Adriatic and seriously threaten Italy's exposed eastern coastline. On the other hand, possession of Valona would have given the Italians complete control of the gateway to the Adriatic. During World War I the Italians had, in fact, used Valona as a naval and air base. While the fate of Albania was being discussed in Paris, the Albanians took matters into their own hands. After organizing their own government, they rose against the Italians, drove them into Valona, and besieged them until they agreed to withdraw (August, 1920). In December, 1920, Albania was admitted into the League of Nations.

Albania was not only the smallest but also the most backward of the Balkan states. The Albanian proverb, "If God came to visit Albania, He would find it just as he made it," contains a considerable element of truth, for conditions in the country were still very primitive. During the centuries of Turkish rule instruction in the Albanian language was prohibited. The few Albanian children who attended the Moslem schools benefited only to the extent of learning some verses of the Koran. Consequently most of the Albanians remained grossly ignorant. Most of the inhabitants had also found it expedient to renounce Christianity. It was only in the more isolated mountain regions which the Turks were never able to administer that Christianity survived.[7] As a whole the Albanians were a sturdy race of mountaineers who carried on little or no industry, growing only enough food to exist upon and spinning enough wool to clothe themselves. They did, however, raise many cattle on the mountains, this being the country's most important industry. There were also considerable deposits of coal, iron, copper, oil, and asphalt. Near Valona there is one of the best asphalt deposits in the world. But probably the greatest asset was water power.

In 1925, after a period during which the functions of sovereignty were exercised by a council of four regents, a Constituent Assembly proclaimed a republic and elected Ahmed Zogu to the post of president. Three years later the government was changed to a monarchy, and Ahmed Zogu became Zog I, King of the Albanians. Whatever his weaknesses, Zog was a man of action who immediately bent his energies to the task of organizing and developing his country. Tremendous odds notwithstanding, he made considerable progress towards stability and civilization. For example, a law of June, 1928, made primary education obligatory for both sexes between the ages of six and thirteen. Although the law could not be strictly enforced because of the lack of schools, teachers, and textbooks, the number of children attending school increased rapidly. Zog also endeavored to improve the means of communication and travel and to develop natural resources. For this task he needed financial aid from the outside. Unable to obtain it from any other country, he accepted a loan of 50 million lire from Italy, pledging the customs receipts as a guarantee. The Italian government founded the Albanian National Bank, sent technicians to build roads and bridges, and established advisers in the various state departments.

King Zog tried on a number of occasions to limit the gradual Italian penetration. In 1933, for instance, he rejected a customs union with Italy. In the same year the Italian schools in Albania were closed. The next year he endeavored to limit the increasing Italian control over his government, but an Italian naval demonstration forced him to give way. For the next few years the relations between the two governments appeared outwardly friendly. Then, in April, 1939, in total disregard of all his pledges, Mussolini sent troops, supported by airplanes and warships, to seize control of the country. The Albanians were able to offer but little resistance. In two days the Italians occupied all the important points with a loss of only twenty-one lives. King Zog, who had vainly hoped to rally the

[7] About two thirds of the Albanians were Mohammedans and the remaining third were adherents of the Greek Orthodox and Roman Catholic faiths.

country and to obtain outside help, was forced to flee to Greece with his queen and their two-day-old son. A new government was constituted to rule under an Italian Governor-General. In Italy the *Giornale d'Italia* announced that "Italy by her intervention has restored to Albania peace and order and the liberty of civil workers which was being seriously compromised."

CHAPTER FOURTEEN

Spain and Portugal

DISCONTENT AMONG THE
WORKING CLASSES
SPAIN was one of the few European countries which did not become involved in World War I. While opinion within Spain was divided, the government remained neutral. But the war did have a tremendous influence on the country. When the naval blockade shut off the foreign supply of manufactured goods, Spaniards began to establish industries to supply the home market. This tendency toward industrialization received a further impetus from the demands of the belligerents for both foodstuffs and manufactured products. Before long the peninsula was literally humming with industry. Certain districts were industrialized almost overnight. The report of the British Overseas Trade Department for 1920 commented on the development of industry during the war years as follows: "The textile industry was so strongly established as to be in a position even to export to South America and compete with Manchester goods there. Electrical goods of quality were being made at Zaragoza. Much progress was achieved in the manufacture of glass and china ware. Shipbuilding improved. The national coal and iron industries were developed to a notable degree." Not only did France and England purchase heavily in the Spanish market during the war years but the exports to Italy also more than doubled. As a result Spain experienced a period of prosperity. Gold flowed into the country faster than at any time since the days when the Spanish galleons brought in the treasure of the Incas and the Aztecs. From being a debtor nation Spain became a creditor nation which made considerable loans to other nations.

The wave of prosperity, instead of bringing contentment, only increased the dissatisfaction of the masses. Since the prosperity rarely extended below the middle class, the peasants and industrial workers saw little improvement in their lot. Conditions among those engaged in agriculture—and Spain was predominantly agricultural with only a small percentage of the population employed in industrial establishments—were generally bad. The general situation might be summed up briefly in the words: too few landowners, too numerous and too poor tenants and agricultural laborers. About 50,000 landlords who constituted about one five-hundredth of the population owned more than half of the land. The actual management of the land was most often left to agents and middlemen whose one interest was to make the largest profit. Actual cultivation was done either by tenants who leased part of an estate or by hired laborers. Both were ruthlessly exploited. In Catalonia, for example, many winegrowers were required to give their landlords as much as two thirds of the crop. As most tenants were too poor to introduce machinery and better methods of cultivation, the yield was very low. France produced almost twice the wine from an area of about the same size. As for wheat, eleven bushels to the acre was the average yield. Agricultural laborers were paid wages barely sufficient to maintain a miserable undernourished existence. No wonder that the nationalization of land in Russia made a deep impression on the Spanish masses. In certain districts one phrase was on many lips—distribution of the land.

The industrial workers were equally dissatisfied. Although the cost of living rose sharply after 1914, most industrial workers succeeded in wringing higher wages from their employers only during the last years of the war. With the return of peace Spain found herself confronted by a decreasing demand for her goods. Exports fell off considerably and foreign manufactures again invaded the market. As a result thousands of workers were thrown out of employment and the wages of those who kept their jobs dropped, bringing acute distress to many. In short, a general depression made itself felt. One observer described the situation as follows: "There cannot be any other civilized country in the world where the laboring classes have as much to complain of their lot in life, and to rebel against it by every means in their power, as they have in Spain."[1] Workers staged repeated strikes in an attempt to restore the former scale of wages; in fact, the early postwar period was but a succession of strikes. More than this, discontented workers became easy converts to socialism and revolutionary anarchism, more to the latter than to the former. Although there was a small Socialist Labor Party,

[1] Deakin, *Spain Today* (1924), p. 11.

anarchism was a much stronger movement, particularly in Barcelona where about one third of Spain's industries were located. The anarcho-syndicalists did not hesitate to use violence in their attempt to change existing conditions.

There was among the masses a widespread dissatisfaction not only with economic conditions but also with a government that was utterly indifferent to chaos. For many decades Spain had been struggling to build a government along constitutional lines. The reigning king, Alfonso XIII, who had come to the throne in 1902, had been more successful than his predecessors, but the government was still inefficient. According to law Spain was a constitutional monarchy, with a constitution that dated from 1876. This guaranteed freedom from arbitrary arrest and provided that no tax be imposed and no law passed without the consent of the Cortes, a parliament of two chambers. But in practice the constitution was largely circumvented. The real government was known in the political slang of the country as *El Caciquismo* or the rule of the *caciques*.[2] The rule of the *caciques* was the same whether the dominant party was conservative or liberal in name. It was, in brief, a political machine. The supreme *cacique* was the prime minister and directly under him there were a dozen leading politicians each of whom had his own district over which he ruled as master. The rule of the provincial *cacique* was exercised in every town and village through local *caciques* without whose consent nothing could be done and whose allegiance was due only the higher *cacique* whom they served. Most often the local *caciques* were employers of labor or money lenders to whom the working population of the district looked for employment or in whose debt they were. Thus the *caciques* had the majority of the constituency under their collective thumb.

§

THE DICTATORSHIP OF PRIMO DE RIVERA

At the opening of 1923 two serious situations faced the government. On the one hand, there was the separatist movement in Catalonia and, on the other, the Riff uprising in Morocco. In Catalonia a group of separatists had formed a movement which wished to separate Catalonia entirely from the rest of Spain and to establish it as an independent nation. Not regarded too seriously by the government at first, Catalan separatism had grown to the point where it constituted a grave menace to Spanish unity. But it was the

[2] The word *cacique* was introduced into the language by the early explorers, it being the name of the despots they found among the tribes of the New World.

THE IBERIAN PENINSULA

The separatist movement in Catalonia and the Riff rebellion in Morocco precipitated the chain of events that led to the dictatorship of Primo de Rivera, the abdication of Alfonso XIII, the establishment of the Spanish Republic, the civil war, and the dictatorship of Franco.

Moroccan situation—more specifically, the series of disastrous defeats sustained by the army in attempting to quell an uprising of Riff tribesmen—which precipitated a change in the government. The struggle between the tribesmen and the Spaniards started as far back as 1909 when the former attacked Spanish soldiers and workers who were building a railroad in Morocco. From that time onward various attempts had been made to solve "the problem of Morocco" but without success. The summer of 1921 saw another such attempt. General Silvestre, a court favorite, marching against the Riff chieftain, Abd-el-Krim, with a force of about 20,000, suffered a disastrous defeat at Annual in Morocco. Attacked by a very inferior force, the Spaniards broke and ran. In the rout more than 10,000 were massacred and large stores of artillery and ammunition were lost. It was the worst defeat for the Spanish forces since the Spanish-American War.

At home the news gave rise to an energetic demand from one end of the country to the other for an inquiry to assign the responsibility for what had taken place. This demand finally became so insistent that the Cortes appointed a Committee of Inquiry. The evidence revealed widespread disobedience, disorder, and corruption in the army, including wholesale graft in the purchase of supplies, illicit trafficking in arms, and the pocketing of payrolls by officers while soldiers were starving and in rags. Among those implicated by the report were not only high military and government officials but Alfonso XIII himself. The report was to have been made public on September 20, 1923; but a group of officers, seeing the position of the army in jeopardy, decided to take over the government itself before the findings could reach the people. The leader was General Primo de Rivera. He carefully laid plans for a *coup d'état,* which was executed on September 13 without the firing of a shot. Whether or not the king personally helped to plan the coup, is still a moot question. With many writers Rivera's emphatic assurances that the king was not privy to the plans have carried great weight. On the other hand, Alfonso did nothing to prevent their execution. When the Marquis de Alhucemas, who was prime minister at the time, realized what was going on, he proposed the immediate arrest of the rebellious generals, but the king replied that such a grave proposal required reflection. Thereupon the prime minister resigned. Within twenty-four hours General de Rivera was ruling the country at the head of a military cabinet called the Directory.

Although he was officially only the president of the Directory, he was actually the absolute ruler of Spain. He was, it is true, subject to the king in theory and had to have his decrees countersigned by the latter before they could become law, but Alfonso could hardly refuse his signature since the very existence of the monarchy was at stake. Soon after the coup the Cortes was dissolved. When the constitutional period of three months passed without new elections, it was realized that the constitution was for all practical purposes dead. Anyone who tried to lift a finger in its behalf was at once suppressed. Martial law became the law of the country. Free speech and assembly were suspended, the press was subjected to a strict censorship, and meetings for the discussion of political matters were forbidden. In order to escape imprisonment many critics of the government became refugees in foreign lands, among them the popular novelist, Blasco Ibáñez. One move which brought joy to many who had suffered at the hands of the petty tyrants in town and country was the uprooting of the *caciques*. Proclaiming that "boss rule must be torn up by the roots," military governors took over the power previously exercised by the *caciques*. Nor did the destruction stop there. The municipal councils were also unceremoniously dissolved and their functions taken over by the military authorities. The new government further struck harshly at the separatist movement in Catalonia. The Catalan language was put under the ban, newspapers published in Catalan being obliged to appear in Castilian; Catalan festivals were prohibited; and even the typical dress of the region was ordered modified. But in spite of the official notes stating that the separatist movement had been crushed, it had only been forced underground.

Upon assuming the dictatorship General de Rivera announced that his tenure of power was purely a temporary expedient. He would, he stated, soon take steps toward re-establishing constitutional government and then retire. He did not, however, translate his words into action. In December, 1925, the military directory, it is true, was replaced by a civil directory, composed largely of civilians; but Rivera retained his powers. His dictatorship was to last more than six years. During this time he did accomplish a number of things. Pushing the war against the Riffs more vigorously, he compelled Abd-el-Krim to surrender to a combined force of Spanish and French troops in 1926. He also worked hard to promote the material well-being of the people. To stimulate the development of industry he raised the tariffs on imported manufactures and subsidized new industries. Companies from which foreigners derived profits were either confiscated or turned over to Spanish ownership. He improved transportation by fusing existing railway companies, constructing new lines, and electrifying some old ones. In the field of agrarian reform he issued legislation which created a special fund from which tenants of estates could borrow if they wished to purchase the land they were working. In general, economic conditions did improve during the first years of his rule. But the world economic crisis of 1929 undid much of his work.

After the first three or four years the pendulum of public opinion began to swing more and more against him. The liberals completely lost faith in his promises to establish constitutional government and the monarchists began to accuse him of seeking to make his dictatorship permanent. Meanwhile his efforts to found a party like that of Mussolini in Italy met with no real success. When the depression came in 1929, the regime lost its popularity even with the bankers, merchants, and industrialists. His only support came from certain sections of the army and from the old conservative Roman Catholics. Perceiving that even the king was alarmed and on the point of deserting him, Rivera resigned in January, 1930, and retired to France, where he died a few weeks later.

Alfonso, in a last effort to save his throne, entrusted the government in succession to two other dictators whose policies were somewhat more liberal. But popular feeling against the continued suppression of personal liberties and the refusal to restore the Cortes was by this time thoroughly aroused. When the government held municipal elections on April 12, 1931, thereby giving the people the first opportunity in eight years to express their feelings, the vote was overwhelmingly republican. The Spanish people did not want the monarchy, and in particular they did not want the king. The cabinet read the handwriting on the wall and resigned at once, leaving the king the choice of either ruling by force or abdicating. He chose the latter. On April 14 Alfonso XIII fled the country and republican leaders set up a provisional government with Señor Alcalá Zamora as president. Thus the abolition of the monarchy was achieved without bloodshed.

REPUBLICAN REFORM AND CONSERVATIVE REACTION

The proclamation of the republic was received with widespread rejoicing. The people felt that freedom had arrived at last, and the fiesta spirit reigned throughout the land. In the cities the streets were filled with singing and dancing throngs, and in the cafés repeated toasts were drunk to the republic. One of the first tasks of the provisional government was to arrange for the election of a constitutional Cortes. When the election returns came in, it was found that the socialists and republicans together had won a majority of the deputies. The right opposition gained only sixty deputies of a total of 470. The Cortes met in July, 1931, and turned at once to its assigned task. As finally adopted, the constitution was a document of progressive democratic government. "Spain," Article I stated, "is a democratic republic of workers of all classes, united under a regime of liberty and justice. The powers of all its organs derive from the people." All Spaniards were declared equal before the law, and the rights of freedom of speech, press, and assemblage were guaranteed. The framework of the government, as prescribed by the constitution, was simple. It was to consist of a one-chamber parliament or Cortes, elected by vote of all citizens, regardless of sex, who had reached the age of twenty-three. There was also to be a president, elected for six years by the Cortes in joint session with an equal number of popularly elected delegates. The president, in turn, was given the right to choose the prime minister and the cabinet, but the men chosen had to have the confidence of the Cortes. The constitution was proclaimed on December 10, 1931, with Alcalá Zamora as the first president.

Besides establishing a democratic government, the new constitution broke sharply with the past in various other respects. Particularly noteworthy are the provisions for the complete separation of church and state. The relation between the two had probably been closer in Spain than in any other nation of modern Europe. It was indeed so close that to many Spaniards they were practically identical. Not only had the state taken strong steps to safeguard the privileges of the Spanish Catholic Church but all secular priests had received a stipend from the government. Moreover, only the Catholic Church had been recognized by the state. But according to the new constitution, "the Spanish state has no official religion." All religious sects were placed on the same footing. "A special law," the constitution stated, "shall provide for the total extinction, within a period not exceeding two years, of state grants to the church." Education, which had been largely in the hands of the church, was secularized. Divorce by mutual consent or by either party, upon the presentation of due cause, was permitted. Furthermore, as stated in Article 26, "those religious orders the rule of which requires in addition to the three canonical vows a special vow of obedience to an authority other than that of the state are declared dissolved. Their property shall be nationalized and used for charitable and educational purposes." This Article was, of course, aimed at the Jesuits. The other orders were to be put under rigid governmental control and were forbidden to teach or to engage in commerce and industry. There was little new in this, for either repression of the religious orders or at least restriction in numbers had been one of the planks of the revolutionary program of liberal and radical parties for more than a century.

After the new constitution went into force, the government with a coalition ministry of socialists and republicans headed by premier Azaña proceeded to carry out the changes. Among the first were those regarding religious orders, church property, marriage, and divorce. In January, 1932, the Cortes passed a law dissolving the Jesuit order and confiscating its property. A few weeks later a law recognizing divorce was passed, and in June of the same year another law decreed that thenceforth the state would recognize only civil marriage. Later in the same year the Cortes enacted another bill, corresponding to the French anticlerical law of 1902, which gave the government the right to veto appointments of heads of religious associations and declared that all heads of religious associations must be Spaniards. In March, 1933, a bill was approved which provided for the "nationalization," i.e., seizure by the state, of "churches of all classes, episcopal palaces, rectories, seminaries, and other buildings of the Catholic cult." Finally, in June, 1933, a law prescribed that religious orders cease all primary teaching by December 31, 1933, and all other nonreligious instruction by October, 1933.

By its anticlerical decrees the government sought to placate the extremists and put an end to the attacks on church property. On May 11, 1931, soon after the republic had been declared, revolutionary elements in Madrid, Malaga, and other important centers had burned a large number of churches and convents. In Malaga twenty-two of the twenty-five churches had been destroyed. Sporadic burnings continued until the bill nationalizing church property was passed. When the burning of a monastery at Antequara during Holy Week of 1932 was characterized as an act of "extreme cruelty" before the Cortes, a socialist Deputy retorted that "the populace there is 85 per cent illiterate, although there are twenty rich monasteries in the vicinity. While I regret the incident, the feeling among such people is understandable." [3]

Nor were the changes introduced by the Cortes limited to the sphere of religion. A far-reaching reorganization of the army was carried out. The officer personnel was drastically reduced, the equipment was modernized, and a law was passed which based promotion to the rank of commissioned officer on rigid examinations and upon

[3] Cited in *Current History*, vol. 36 (1932), p. 236.

study at the military academy. As a result the efficiency of the army increased to a point theretofore unknown in Spain. In the field of social legislation the Cortes drew up a code which gave the worker social insurance benefits and guaranteed the right of collective bargaining. Furthermore, in 1932 the Cortes approved a bill which settled the Catalan question for the time being by granting Catalonia a substantial measure of autonomy. The Catalans were given permission to use their own flag, national anthem, and language, Catalan and Castilian being made the official languages. In addition to all this the government took measures to wipe out illiteracy. Although Alfonso's government had done much to improve educational facilities, schools were still insufficient in number and the training they offered was superficial. At the time the republic was established, about half the people were still unable to read and write. It was estimated that at least 27,000 new schools would have to be opened if all children were to have the opportunity to attend school. The government took a long step toward meeting this deficiency by establishing some nine thousand schools during the first years of its existence. It further raised the pay of most teachers, made provisions to give them better training, and established almost 1500 libraries to encourage reading and education outside the schools. But the lack of money somewhat limited the initial impulse. In April, 1934, no less than 1.7 million Spanish children were still unable to attend because of an insufficient number of schools.

Probably the most important problem confronting the government was the improvement of the extremely low economic and social condition of the peasants and farm laborers. But because of the powerful opposition of the landed interests the Cortes failed to enact remedial legislation until a year and a half after the republic was established. In September, 1932, it passed the Land Reform Bill, which gave the government the right to expropriate large estates.[4] All owners, except those of feudal estates, were to be compensated on the basis of the values declared for taxation. The task of distributing the land to landless agricultural workers and to peasants having only small plots was delegated to the Institute of Agrarian Reform, created by the same bill. Ownership of the land, however, was vested in the state. Provisions were also made to finance the purchase of seed, fertilizer, and tools, and the construction of farm buildings. This Land Reform Bill, if it had been carried out, would have started the peasant on the way to greater independence and prosperity. Up to the end of 1933, however, only about five thousand

[4] At first only in the districts around Madrid; later in all of Spain.

peasants and agricultural workers had benefited from it. The rest, estimated at 2.5 million, remained land hungry, with the result that many were being converted to extremism.

The reconstruction of the semifeudal conditions of Spanish life proved to be no easy task. Changes were carried out only by overcoming the bitter opposition of both the left and the right. On the one hand, the anarcho-syndicalists and communists took an irreconcilable position because the reforms were not radical enough; workers of the leftist persuasion waged unceasing war against the government through strikes, riots, and disorders; and on a number of occasions the more radical elements made serious attempts to overthrow the republic. On the other hand, the groups on the right felt that the reforms had gone too far. These groups included the monarchists, who were naturally opposed to the republic; a newly formed Fascist movement organized by José Primo de Rivera, son of the former dictator; merchants, manufacturers, and landlords who were antagonized by the government's pro-labor policies; and reactionary army officers.

But the most determined opposition on the right came from the Roman Catholics. The anticlerical laws angered a great body of them, including many who were genuine republicans. Some even interpreted the measures of the government and the burning of churches and convents by revolutionary mobs as a persecution of Christianity. From many sides came a demand for repeal of the anticlerical laws, a demand which was vigorously supported by the officials of the church. When the law was passed which excluded the religious orders from all except religious education, the bishops issued a pastoral letter forbidding parents to send their children to the state schools. Pope Pius XI himself condemned the legislation in an encyclical addressed to the clergy and the people, urging the Spaniards to stand up for the faith.

The first indication of the rising tide of opposition to the republican-socialist alliance was the municipal elections held in April, 1933. Despite all its efforts the cabinet secured only about 5000 seats in the municipal councils as against more than 10,000 for the opposition. Various cabinet changes took place during the succeeding months. In September Manuel Azaña finally resigned his premiership, and the republican-socialist coalition came to an end.

The general elections, held in November and December, resulted in a sweeping victory for the right and right center. Of the 472 seats in the Cortes, the right captured 212 and the center 162, leaving the left only 98. The new cabinet, consisting largely of representatives of the right and right center, showed a decided swing in the direction of conservatism. Early in 1934 it announced a program designed to modify some of the laws the earlier Cortes had passed. It called for a revision of the agrarian law of 1932, state aid to rural priests left without a means of livelihood by the anticlerical legislation, and general amnesty for political offenders. It also stated that there would be no more closing of schools conducted by religious orders.

This program did not go far enough to please the right and it excited the bitter hostility of the left. The socialists, in fact, went so far as to announce that any attempt of the right to wreck the republic would be met by armed force. When it was announced that three more members of the right would be added to the cabinet, the parties of the left on October 5 issued a call for a general strike. This was immediately followed by uprisings in the northern and central parts of the country. Desperate street fighting took place in Madrid and many other cities. For days the fate of the government hung in the balance, but because the army had remained loyal the government was finally able to crush the revolts. The issue was, however, by no means settled.

During the period that followed, as the parties of the left saw the conservative government gradually nullify the economic and social reforms that had been enacted during the first years of the republic, they became more bitter and relentless in their opposition. Nor was the discontent limited to the left parties as such. When the Agrarian Reform was amended in 1935, large numbers of peasants began to fear the return of the "old slavery." There was also widespread discontent among the workers because wages had fallen considerably. What is more, the leaders of the left parties began to realize that in unity there is strength. When the government drafted proposals for amending the constitution so that the church schools could be reopened, the Jesuits could return, and Roman Catholicism could again be made the state religion, many leftists decided that it was time to terminate the hair-splitting over political questions and to form a united front against the reactionaries. But the union was not achieved until a month before the general elections of 1936 when the so-called Popular Front comprising the left republicans, socialists, communists, and anarcho-syndicalists was organized. On the other side, the right and center formed an anti-Marxist alliance. Both now girded for the showdown. It came in the general elections of February and March, 1936, elections in which the communists and syndicalists for the first time put aside their opposition to the use of the ballot. When the votes were tabulated it was found that the Popular Front was victorious. Although the left totaled only a plurality of the votes, it managed to return a majority of its candidates to the Cortes. In the new Cortes, as it was finally constituted, the Popular Front held 266 seats as against 217 for the right and center.

§

CIVIL WAR

As soon as the results of the election became known, the cabinet resigned and Manuel Azaña, the leader of the Popular Front, formed a new ministry. It is noteworthy that this cabinet was composed entirely of middle class representatives, the socialists and the more radical groups remaining outside the government. The cabinet began at once to carry out the program the parties of the Popular Front had adopted. Political prisoners held in confinement since the uprising of October, 1934, were released, and workers whose political sympathies had cost them their jobs were reinstated. But the extremists among the masses were impatient. Feeling that the hour had struck, many became dangerously active. Every day there were acts of violence. Churches and convents were burned, the political headquarters and newspaper offices of the Fascists and monarchists were pillaged, and in the country districts impatient peasants seized large estates. Such activities by leftist groups called forth retaliation by rightist groups, with the result that murder, arson, and anarchy reigned virtually uncontrolled. Except in a few instances the government seemed unable to assert itself. President Zamora, who had been trying to steer a middle course, called down upon himself the denunciation of both parties and was expelled from the presidency by a vote of the Cortes. On May 10, 1936, Manuel Azaña, leader of the Popular Front, was elected president. Nevertheless the violence and unrest continued.

Meanwhile the members of a secret society of military officers, the Union Militar Española, fearing that the army would lose its privileges and power, had laid plans for a military uprising. A number of garrisons were to stage simultaneous insurrections and then march on Madrid. On March 15, 1936, the army chiefs even warned the government that they would act if order were not restored. The government answered by either dismissing or transferring to other posts a number of high-ranking officers suspected of reactionary sympathies. Among those transferred was General Francisco Franco, who for a time had been chief of staff and had also commanded the

Foreign Legion in Morocco. The place to which he was transferred was the Canary Islands. But he did not remain there long. He escaped to Spanish Morocco and raised the standard of revolt on July 17. Supported by the Foreign Legion, Moorish contingents, and regiments of the regular army, he quickly succeeded in making himself master of Spanish Morocco. The next day the rebellion spread to Spain itself. One after another, garrisons of various cities revolted. It is estimated that about 90 per cent of the officers and two thirds of the enlisted men joined the rebels. In other words, the Insurgents controlled most of the trained land forces. But in two of the country's defense divisions they found only small support. Most of the air force and the navy remained loyal to the government. Certain naval officers did endeavor to turn their vessels over to the Insurgents, but the attempt was frustrated by the *coup d'état,* as they had expected. The uprising developed into a prolonged civil war lasting until March, 1939.

The Spanish civil war has often been referred to as a war of Fascism against communism and vice versa. Such an explanation is, however, too simple to fit the facts. The avowed supporters of the two ideologies formed only a minority on both sides. The ranks of the Insurgents were filled with members of all the right groups, including monarchists, antimonarchical falangists, adherents of the Roman Catholic Church, and members of the class of large land-owners and of the propertied classes generally. The composition of the other side was equally heterogeneous. Drawing its support largely from the laboring masses, the Loyalist side included not only so-cialists, syndicalists, and communists but also moderate republicans and liberals of all shades. Nor did the radical element prevail. When the rebellion began, there was among those in power not a single communist or even an extreme socialist. In addition to the various reformist groups, the Loyalist cause had the support of the Cata-lonian and Basque separatists, actuated by motives of independence. Among them were many who were strongly Catholic. The supporters of each side were drawn together not so much by a common ideal as by a common fear. While the Insurgents feared a "Marxist revolu-tion," the Loyalists feared the re-establishment of the old order which would again reduce them to virtual slavery. Only in the external, non-Spanish sense did it become a battle between Fascism and com-munism, with the Insurgents getting support from the Fascist na-tions and the Loyalists from communist Russia.

The Insurgents had planned for a quick victory, but their hopes were soon blasted. Although the government had few trained troops, it hastily organized a volunteer militia which succeeded in quelling the insurrection in eastern and central Spain. In Barcelona the uprising was suppressed after three days of severe fighting; and in Madrid, the capital, the revolution was also abortive. When several garrisons in Madrid and vicinity mutinied, the militia, the civil guards, and the police captured the barracks after a sharp struggle and suppressed the mutiny. The Insurgents now began to march on Madrid from the north and from the south. In the north General Mola collected an army of about 10,000 at Burgos, but his advance was checked in the Guadarama mountains northwest of Madrid. Meanwhile General Franco had crossed from Morocco to Spain to assume the direction of the movement against the government. Because the Loyalists had naval control of the Straits of Gibraltar, he was compelled to transport his troops largely by airplane. The force he finally collected at Seville numbered only about 15,000 effective troops but was well trained. Working his way northward with this army, Franco took Badajoz on August 14 and then marched up the valley of the Tagus, arriving in the vicinity of Madrid early in November. On September 30 General Mola had set up a directory under the name of Junta de Defensa Nacional at Burgos and had proclaimed General Franco "Chief of the Government of the Spanish State." After the establishment of this government the Insurgents gradually became known as the Nationalists.

During the civil war hostilities were conducted with extreme ruthlessness. Both sides neither asked nor gave any quarter, with the result that Spain was truly a land drenched in blood. Both sides frequently executed prisoners of war, particularly if they were not members of the regularly trained army. As one Nationalist general put it: "I take no prisoners. Anybody other than uniformed soldiers of the Spanish army caught by me carrying arms finds the death he deserves." Both sides also revived the old practice of holding hostages and of slaughtering them in retaliation for raids or attacks by the other side. Above all, each side ruthlessly exterminated in the territory it held all those who sympathized with the other side. Thus in the territory under Loyalist control thousands of landowners, priests, and others were shot either without trial or after what amounted to a mock trial. In many districts self-organized bands took it upon themselves to "cleanse" the population of all whose sympathies were on the Nationalist side. The Nationalists likewise carried out wholesale executions of Loyalists and their sympathizers. All Loyalist leaders were summarily executed as soon as the Nationalist forces captured a town or village; later all sym-

HITLER AND FRANCO SHAKE HANDS; 1940

pathizers were systematically rounded up and often shot in batches of twenty or more. It is estimated that up to the end of 1936 about 500,000 persons lost their lives in the sanguinary struggle, most of them being massacred or executed behind the line of battle.

In November of 1936 the Nationalist forces attacked Madrid. They had the advantage in modern machines of warfare, including tanks, artillery, and airplanes, many of which had been sent in by the Italian and German governments. The defense of Madrid, on the other hand, was at first largely in the hands of unorganized masses. For some time President Azaña had resisted the demands of those who advocated distribution of arms to the people but had finally acceded when he saw the seriousness of the struggle. While some of the defenders had rifles and revolvers obtained from government arsenals, others had only knives, paving stones, or their bare hands. At the end of October the Loyalist cause was strengthened by the arrival of supplies, including machine guns and some planes and tanks, from Russia and of volunteers from a number of countries. When the Nationalists launched their attack against Madrid, they were met by a most determined, if not a well-armed, resistance. After bitter fighting they were able to gain a precarious foothold in University City on the outskirts of the capital, but they failed to take Madrid itself. By beating off the first assaults, the defenders gained time to organize. Military leaders soon molded the hodge-podge of men into companies and modern battalions, defense works were constructed, and most noncombatants were evacuated from the city, President Azaña and the cabinet withdrawing to Valencia. Madrid, which could have been captured rather easily at first, soon became a strong fortress. Hence the opening of 1937 saw the rival forces tightly deadlocked before the city. On the other fronts the war also appeared to be approaching a stalemate, but foreign intervention was gradually to change the picture.

The civil war in Spain had been a matter of great concern to all the great powers right from the start. While some governments were apprehensive that the struggle might involve all of Europe, others saw in it an opportunity to advance their respective ambitions and ideologies. Prominent among the latter were Portugal, Italy, and Germany. Not long after the war broke out it became clear that Franco's forces were receiving both men and supplies from Italy and Germany; in fact, Franco probably had the promise of aid before he raised the standard of revolt. In France and Great Britain statesmen feared that if this aid and intervention continued, the conflagration might spread until it engulfed the entire continent. To offset this danger the two governments at the beginning of August proposed a general nonintervention agreement and invited all the other states to adhere. The Fascist states were anything but enthusiastic over the proposal. Although they did finally subscribe, this did not stop them from continuing to extend clandestine aid to the Nationalists. In October, 1936, the Soviet government not only charged Italy, Germany, and Portugal with "systematic violation" of the agreement, but used the violation of the agreement as an excuse to send aid to the Loyalists. When France and Great Britain established a joint naval patrol of Spanish waters, the Loyalist government complained that the blockade was operating "to the exclusive advantage of the Insurgents" since a steady stream of supplies was reaching them by way of Portugal, the air, and Franco-controlled ports.

By the beginning of 1937 the sending of men and supplies by Italy and Germany had become more or less open. In March, the Loyalist government protested that four regular divisions of the Italian army were being used by the Nationalists in the Guadalajara offensive. Shortly thereafter the Italian government went so far as to give notice that not a single Italian "volunteer" would be withdrawn until the victory of General Franco was assured. Further proposals were made by France and Great Britain and further pacts were even signed but, on the whole, little headway was made toward nonintervention. In September, 1938, Loyalist prime minister Negrín announced the "immediate and complete withdrawal of all non-Spanish combatants taking part in the struggle in Spain on the government side." This caused the Italians to make a gesture at withdrawing some of their troops, but not long thereafter fresh Italian troops arrived to take the places of those that had been withdrawn. Thus what had at the outbreak been purely a civil war was soon converted into a clash of rival ideologies of the great European powers. The war, in fact, became so largely an international affair that the Spaniards, as it were, served only as auxiliaries.

Early in 1937 the Nationalists launched a fierce drive aimed at cutting the highway communications between Madrid and Barcelona, but the Loyalists, who expected the move, repulsed it after severe fighting. Next Franco turned to the Basque provinces. Although the Loyalists offered a stiff resistance, he blasted his way through to Bilbao (June 19), then pushed on to take Santander (August 25), and finally Gijón (October 21), the last Loyalist stronghold in that region. Thus all of northwest Spain was added to the territory held by the Nationalists.

Having completed the conquest of the northwest, Franco returned to his plan of driving a wedge between Madrid and Barcelona. This time he succeeded. After capturing Teruel (February, 1938) he pressed on down the Ebro valley and reached the Mediterranean by the middle of April. With the Loyalist territory split into two parts and over two thirds of the country in his hands, he announced that the war was over. The Loyalists, however, were far from ready to give up. When he realized this, he prepared a campaign directed at the conquest of Catalonia. For this purpose he collected a powerful force of more than 200,000, including six Italian army corps, fully equipped with the most modern instruments of war. The Loyalists had more men, but better fighting equipment gave Franco's forces an overwhelming superiority. German and Italian artillery, tanks, and airplanes enabled them to take town after town until the road to Barcelona was open. It was clear that the city was doomed unless substantial foreign help came quickly. No foreign help arrived and on January 26, 1939, the Nationalists occupied Barcelona. Within a fortnight the demoralized Loyalist army was driven from the rest of Catalonia, the soldiers either crossing into France or surrendering. All the territory that now remained under Loyalist control was central Spain with the two important cities of Madrid and Valencia.

The cause of the Loyalists was becoming more and more desperate. Their last hopes were blasted when France and Great Britain granted Franco's government recognition toward the end of February. Seeing that further resistance was useless, President Azaña and some of his cabinet were ready to make peace, but prime minister Negrín was determined to carry on to the bitter end. The result was that President Azaña resigned and went to France, leaving the government in the hands of Negrín. On March 5 a group of generals who favored making peace on the best possible terms ousted the prime minister and established a National Defense Council. The change, however, provoked a series of communist uprisings which were put down only with machine guns, tanks, artillery, and bombing planes. It is estimated that this civil war within a civil war brought 9000 casualties. Having quelled the uprisings, the Council opened negotiations with Franco. The latter stood fast on his demand for unconditional surrender. With the supply of munitions low and the population of Madrid on the point of starvation, the National Defense Council had no alternative but to accept the terms and surrender the city. Valencia had previously capitulated and all other armed resistance collapsed within the next few weeks. The war,

which besides costing a million lives and doing untold damage in
Spain had threatened to engulf Europe, was over (March 29, 1939).

THE DICTATORSHIP OF GENERAL FRANCO

Thoughout the war Franco had been laying the foundations for
a totalitarian state on Italian and German models. "The regime I
shall establish," he had said, "will be based on a corporative system
analogous to that of Italy and Germany but safeguarding the characteristics of Spanish traditionalism." In an effort to end the bitter
rivalry on the Nationalist side he had in April, 1937, merged all
political groups in one party called *Falange Española Tradicionalista*
(Spanish Traditionalist Phalanx).[5] This Falange, recognized as the
only legal party in Spain, became the basis of the new government.
Like the National Socialist Party in Germany and the Fascist Party
in Italy it directed the affairs of the nation. But the keystone of the
whole political structure was Franco himself. He was the head of
the state, the Caudillo (leader or chief), analogous to Duce or
Führer. He assumed authority to issue laws without consulting his
ministers; he claimed the right to appoint his successor; and he was
also the Generalissimo of the army. As a means of strengthening his
dictatorship he incorporated the army in the Falange. Having
achieved virtually absolute power, he declared himself to be "responsible only to God and to history." Certain powers, it is true,
were delegated to a National Falangist Council composed of seventy-
five representatives of the various political interests in the Falange,
and to a political junta of nineteen members, but both were made
directly responsible to Franco and charged with unquestioning
obedience.

Following the collapse of Loyalist resistance, Franco inaugurated
a systematic purge of all who had been either actively hostile or
passively indifferent to his cause. Even before the war ended, the
Nationalists had drawn up a list of more than two million persons
who were to be punished. The Law of Political Responsibilities
promulgated in February, 1939, was couched in such elastic terms
that anyone who had not been active on the Nationalist side could
be brought up for trial. Those who had either participated in or
abetted executions of Nationalists and their sympathizers or who
had attacked churches, priests, or nuns were subject to the death
penalty. Those guilty of lesser "crimes" were given long prison sentences. Hundreds of thousands of others who had been sympathetic

[5] Before the civil war the *Falange* had been a small but enthusiastic Fascist party.

to the Loyalist cause were imprisoned, exiled, or had their property confiscated. To make sure that no republican sympathizers escaped, the government instituted house to house searches, and the daily press urged citizens to denounce one another. No accurate list of those executed or imprisoned has been made public. A dispatch from Vatican City early in 1940 estimated the number of those held in prison at half a million.[6] But most journalists and observers who had visited Spain placed the total much higher, usually exceeding a million, and many placed it between two and three millions. The men and women in the prisons and concentration camps were subjected to a process of "regeneration" in which enforced fasting and the club were employed to exorcise "the baleful effects of 'red' sorcery."

Meanwhile Franco's government was also undoing many changes that had been made under the republic. Particularly noteworthy in this respect is the restoration to the Catholic Church of many privileges it had lost. Catholicism was re-established as the official state religion; religious instruction was reintroduced into every public school, college, and university; and civil marriage and divorce were prohibited. Furthermore, the property which the republic had taken from the Jesuits was restored; the reconstruction of all cathedrals, churches, and religious monuments that had been destroyed or damaged was ordered; and the annual payment of 62 million pesetas ($6.2 million) to the clergy, as stipulated in the concordat of 1851, was resumed. Franco insisted that the concordat be carried out in other respects also. First of all, he sought re-enactment of the provisions which gave the ruler the right to appoint and control the bishops of the Spanish church. Second, he wished to enforce the provisions which stated that all religious disputes were to be settled by a Spanish court of the Rota rather than by the Vatican tribunal in Rome. The Pope's reply to these claims was that the concordat of 1851 was abrogated with the fall of the monarchy. Another change which the government introduced was the termination of the autonomy exercised by Catalonia and the Basque provinces under the republic. In addition Catalonians and Basques were forbidden to speak their regional languages.

The real job of Franco's regime was to repair the damages of war and to raise the living standard of an impoverished nation. When the war ended, much of Spain lay in ruins, some by gunfire and bombs, some by deliberate wreckage. The devastation was so nearly universal that hardly a city or town had escaped. In Madrid

[6] *New York Times,* January 26, 1940.

about a third of the city had been destroyed and another third damaged by gunfire. Barcelona had suffered less damage to its buildings, but its port had been completely destroyed. The greatest damage had been done to means of transportation. Roads were in disrepair, many bridges had been destroyed, and railroads and harbors needed new equipment. Of the 3000 locomotives which Spain possessed in 1936 only about 1000 were actually usable when the war ended. Industry was in a sad state of disorganization. Many of the factories had been completely destroyed or the machinery in them had been replaced by machinery for the manufacture of war materials. Hunger was the dominant feature of the whole scene. After a visit to Spain in the summer of 1939 Professor Samuel Eliot Morison wrote: "The state of Spain is pitiable. No eggs, milk, meat, or oil is available. In Seville, once the mart of the New World, there is no coffee and sugar. Whenever the *Capitana*[7] lay alongside a dock, a breadline of hungry children waited for our leavings."

Soon after the end of the war the new government announced a great program of public works, including the re-equipment of harbors, the replacement of rolling stock on the railways, the building of new roads, the repair of old roads, and the construction of irrigation works. The slogan, as stated by Franco, was "Produce, produce, produce!" To hasten the work the government employed the men and women in the concentration camps on many of its projects. As a result some progress was made with towns, buildings, and roads, and also in increasing the output of certain mines and industries. The production of iron and steel in the Basque country, for example, was greatly expanded. The improvement, however, was limited to specific industries. Small progress was made during 1939 and 1940 toward the reconstruction of Spanish economy as a whole. Industrial recovery was retarded by a lack of raw materials and machinery, by inadequate inland transportation, and by a shortage of skilled workers. Since a large percentage of technicians and trained workers had during the war sided with the Loyalists, they were either in prison or unable to obtain employment because they were politically suspect. Foreign trade was also in a bad way. The war having dissipated Spain's gold reserves and undermined its foreign credit, the new regime could purchase goods abroad only on a barter basis. This was made difficult by the fact that goods formerly produced for export were hardly adequate for home requirements.

The condition of agriculture was equally bad at the end of 1940.

[7] The 140-foot ketch in which Professor Morison retraced the voyage of Columbus.

Before the war Spain had been self-sufficient in the principal food-stuffs and had even exported large quantities. But in 1940 shortages of farm equipment and fertilizers, scarcity and poor quality of seeds, and adverse weather conditions all contributed to a disappointing yield. The wheat crop was about half the average of the years 1931 to 1935; supplementary foods such as barley, rye, and oats were also short; and harvests of lentils, beans, and peas were very small. Olive oil, an essential ingredient of Spanish cooking, was so scarce as to become a luxury. Even the price of potatoes was three times that of the prewar period. Meanwhile wages had not risen and in many industries had been cut. The declining purchasing power of income combined with the shortage of necessary foodstuffs caused widespread undernourishment, and in some sections there were cases of actual starvation.

Nor was the Franco government successful in winning the favor or confidence of the people and in preserving unity within its own ranks. The various component groups had merged their interests during the war, but the merger did not produce an ideological fusion. No sooner did the war end than political intrigues were resumed, with each group striving for increased power. The monarchists and clergy, for example, regained a share of their former prestige but not the extensive powers they had anticipated. More than this, neither group desired the imposition of the economic and political structure of Fascism. The landlords and certain Catholic groups were seeking the restoration of the semifeudal regime, and businessmen were irritated by the endless restrictions placed upon them by the government. Many members of the military clique were jealous of the influence wielded by the civilians in the government. Thus the claims that a compromise had been reached among the monarchists, Fascists, traditionalists, and other components of the Falange were mere pretense. General Franco may have placed the lid on the Spanish cauldron but its contents were still seething.

DICTATORSHIP IN PORTUGAL

Portugal, the westernmost of the European states, comprised an area of some 35,000 square miles with a population of about six and a half millions when World War I broke out in 1914. Despite its small size it ranked fourth among colonial powers, with colonies scattered over three continents and many seas. Its island possessions in the Atlantic included the Azores and the Madeira, Cape Verde, and Principe Islands. Its colonies on the continent of Africa included

Portuguese Guinea, São Thomé, Angola, and Mozambique. In addition it had extensive possessions in the East, including Diu, Damão, and Goa in India, Macao in China, and Timor in Oceania.

Down to 1910 Portugal was a monarchy which was nominally constitutional but absolute in practice. In that year a revolution drove King Manuel II of the house of Braganza into exile, and a republic was proclaimed. Not that there was a strong demand for a republic; the fall of the monarchy was due to the conviction in the minds of the more influential citizens that the political system was so corrupt that the only remedy lay in a complete change to popular control. A new constitution, adopted the following year, vested the executive power in a president elected by the legislature for four years and the legislative power in two chambers of which the lower was elected by direct suffrage and the upper was chosen by the municipal councils.

Although the great majority of Portuguese were Roman Catholic, the republican government reduced the power of the Catholic Church by decreeing the separation of church and state. Thus Roman Catholicism ceased to be the official religion of the state and all creeds were given equal recognition. The teaching of religion in the primary schools was forbidden and many religious orders were expelled from the country. But the republican government did little to improve the economic condition of the peasants and workers or to promote education, despite the fact that more than 60 per cent of persons ten years of age and over were unable to read and write.

In general, the sixteen years of the republic's existence were characterized by extreme political instability. Right from the beginning it had to fight for its existence against monarchist attempts to overthrow it. During the subsequent years presidents and ministries followed each other in rapid succession. Hardly a year passed without a revolution and in some years there were more than one. Political conditions were unstable because not one among the half dozen parties possessed an absolute majority. Unable to rise to power through the ballot, certain groups had recourse to violence. The record was no less than a score of revolutions and forty-three new cabinets. World War I, it is true, brought some degree of internal peace to the harassed country. On August 7, 1914, the parliament proclaimed that Portugal would remain loyal to the British alliance concluded as far back as the fourteenth century, and on November 23 it formally committed Portugal to participate in military operations. Most of the factions, burying their differences for the time being, joined in prosecuting the war. As a result there was only one serious revolution during the war years. But once the war was over, the old rivalries flared up anew. More than this, they were intensified by economic conditions. Owing to the war expenditures and the financial disturbances of the postwar period, the budget deficit, which had been chronic for many decades, became serious. At the same time the currency became greatly depreciated. The escudo, which had had a par value of $1.08, fell to three cents. All this brought disillusionment to those who had greeted the advent of the republic with a Messianic faith. The most active opposition came from the working classes who, desperate from poverty, saw in a revolution like that which had taken place in Russia the only remedy for their misfortunes.

Early in 1926 the various heads of the army and navy agreed on a program to establish a military dictatorship. After practically all the military elements had aligned themselves with the movement, troops were concentrated near Lisbon. On June 6 they marched into the city and took charge of the government offices. Parliament was disbanded, the press was muzzled, all political and trade union organizations were dissolved, and those who raised their voices in protest were imprisoned, banished, or deported to the colonies. General Carmona, elected president without opposition, ruled as dictator. Some semblance of constitutional government was established in 1933 when a new constitution was framed providing for a legislative assembly of one chamber, half of whose members were elected by "educated heads of families" and half appointed by economic bodies. But the president still had the power to select and dismiss the cabinet, which was not responsible to the legislature.

With the country rapidly drifting toward economic ruin, General Carmona soon after his election began to search for a financial savior. In 1928 he summoned to Lisbon Dr. Oliveira Salazar, professor of economics at the University of Coimbra. The new minister of finance attacked his problems with determination. He increased the taxes, overhauled the machinery for the collection of taxes, eliminated much of the graft, and within a year succeeded in achieving a budget surplus. The last previous year which had seen a surplus was 1914. Gradually Dr. Salazar became the leading spirit of the dictatorship. In 1932 he assumed the additional portfolio of premier and later also became minister of war and foreign affairs. In other words, he became the dictator, even though General Carmona remained president.[8] His dictatorship, however, was not based on the

[8] General Carmona was re-elected in 1935 and in 1942.

ambition and self-glorification which characterized Mussolini and Hitler. He seldom appeared in public and when he did his appearances were not dramatic. Nor did he play on the emotions of the masses. In the words of one writer: "His style is terse and bare, and his appeal intellectual rather than sentimental. . . . He has no desire for power, nor could he derive pleasure from domination of the masses. . . . Salazar's rise to power was purely circumstantial and did not follow any direct action on his part. To quote his own words, he accepted the responsibilities, the dangers, and the crushing work that go with absolute power 'because it was an experiment necessary to try for the good of the country.' " [9]

[9] E. A. C. Ballard, "Salazar of Portugal," *Contemporary Review*, vol. 158 (1940), p. 321.

ᘐ
ᘐ
ᘐ

CHAPTER FIFTEEN

❋❋

Small States of Europe

DILEMMA OF THE
SMALL STATES

THROUGHOUT history small states have sought means of remaining outside the quarrels among the great powers. In 1815, for example, Switzerland endeavored to set up a new defense by declaring herself "eternally neutral." Such a neutrality was possible at the time of flintlocks and when the largest cannon had a range of less than a mile. But the technique of modern warfare reduced the possibility of this kind of national defense to a mere illusion. Belgium, declared "eternally neutral" in 1831, became an active participant in World War I when the Germans decided that the route through that country was the shortest way to Paris. President Wilson, who realized that in a world capable of hurling millions of men with giant armaments into battle there was little protection for weak nations, heralded the League of Nations as "the first serious and systematic attempt made in the world to put nations on a footing of equality with each other." The smaller nations did not, however, share Wilson's faith in the League. While some sought protection in clinging to the skirts of great powers and in constructing networks of treaties in the form of neutrality, nonaggression, mutual assistance, and friendship pacts, others either resorted to rearmament or merely hoped they could avoid involvement in the next conflict. All such devices were largely futile. When World War II broke out, most of the smaller nations were inexorably sucked into the maelstrom. As in World War I, the Germans did not hesitate to violate the neutrality of the smaller nations if it suited their purpose.

ᘓ

BELGIUM

Belgium is a small rectangle of 11,755 square miles on the North Sea, wedged in between Germany and Luxemburg on the east, France on the south, and Holland on the north. Its population of about eight million during the period between the two World Wars was about a million larger than that of New York City. The ratio of about seven hundred persons per square mile made it the most densely populated country in the world.

As one of the most progressive of the smaller European states, it exerts a greater influence than its size would indicate. After the revolution of 1830, which ended in separation from Holland, it experienced a rapid economic expansion. Steam and, later, electrical machinery was introduced into its industries with the result that it ranked fifth among the great trading nations of the world in 1914. Agriculture, although insufficient because of limited acreage to produce enough food for the Belgians, led all other European countries in the yield of crops per acre.

In addition to its European possessions Belgium has extensive colonial possessions in Central Africa, comprising the Ruanda-Urundi provinces, taken from Germany at the end of World War I, and the Congo Free State. The latter alone has an area of almost a million square miles and a population of some ten million.

Belgium emerged from the war with the same government it had in 1914. The Constitution of 1831 described it as "a constitutional, representative, and hereditary monarchy." The king could appoint the burgomasters of the communes, initiate legislation, and dissolve parliament under certain circumstances. Beyond this he exercised executive power through a ministry responsible to parliament. Parliament consisted of a Senate and a Chamber of Representatives, the members of the former elected in part by direct suffrage and in part by the provincial councils, the representatives elected by universal male suffrage.[1] The three great political parties were the Catholic, Liberal, and Socialist. After the German retreat in the fall of 1918, King Albert re-entered Brussels on November 22 to take up the work of restoring the devastated regions and re-establishing normal life. In February, 1934, Albert accidentally lost his life in a fall while climbing a mountain peak near Namur. He was succeeded by his son, who was crowned as Leopold III.

Situated in the most exposed corner of Europe, Belgium has been

[1] The right of suffrage was extended to include women during subsequent years.

a battleground through the centuries. On no less than nine occasions since the Germanic migrations of the fourth century has the country been ravaged. In consequence the Belgians have developed extraordinary powers of recuperation. These powers were never more in evidence than after World War I. So far as man power was concerned, Belgian losses were proportionately not so great as those of France, the ratio being 4.6 per cent of the French population in 1913 and 2.6 per cent for Belgium. The number of Belgian soldiers and civilians who lost their lives was about 46,000 and about 50,000 had been invalided. As the scene of much of the fighting, Belgium suffered great material losses. Means of communication were damaged so badly that there seemed little prospect of the resumption of normal trade in the near future. Nearly 2500 miles of tracks were demolished, many railway bridges were wrecked, and much equipment destroyed or removed. There were only 81 out of 3470 locomotives left. Furthermore, canals were blocked with the wreckage of bridges and discarded implements of warfare. Destruction in the area through which the Germans passed necessitated the rebuilding of about 100,000 houses and 1200 public buildings. Much of the land had been rendered unfit for cultivation. Before it could be used for agricultural purposes the shell craters had to be filled in, the barbed-wire entanglements removed, and the unexploded shells collected. But it was Belgian industry which suffered most. Not one factory in the war area had been left untouched. Much of the machinery had been removed to Germany and the buildings wantonly destroyed by the retreating armies.

The rapidity with which the Belgians succeeded in obliterating the traces of war was remarkable. By the beginning of 1921 the roads had been rebuilt, most of the bridges had been replaced, all canals had been cleared, and some of them had even been widened. The railway system had been re-established so that it was functioning with an activity equal to that of prewar days. More than this, industrial production had reached an average of 86 per cent of the production of prewar days, while the yield of the mines was 98 per cent. Above all, towns like Ypres, Dixmude, and Nieuport, which had been razed to the ground and which were believed blotted out forever, rose from their ruins as if by magic. The rebuilding of towns, in general, proceeded so rapidly that by the end of 1923 normal conditions seemed again to prevail with but few exceptions. Agriculture, aided by the importation of agricultural machinery, recovered so speedily that in 1921 all but a small part of the devastated land was under cultivation. This reconstruction, however, was an enormous drain on the country's treasury. The national budget increased from 830 million francs in 1914 to 2310 million in 1921, raising the public debt to nearly 40 billion francs. As the sums received as reparation from Germany did not wipe out the deficit, it became necessary to increase taxes. By 1924 they were six or seven times higher than before the war. Despite the high taxes the government did not succeed in balancing the budget until 1927.

The Versailles settlement allotted to Belgium the small districts of Eupen and Malmédy on condition that the inhabitants approve the transfer. But the desire of most of the 65,000 inhabitants to remain under German rule was so obvious that the Belgians, supported by the French, were afraid to risk a plebiscite. Finally by permission of the League of Nations the plebiscite was curtailed into the right of dissenters to register a protest. Despite all this the district was not a tremendous asset. Several times the Germans attempted to purchase the ceded territory and the Belgians did not seem unwilling to sell. In 1926, in fact, the Belgians, who were badly in need of financial help, had virtually come to terms with the Germans; but French diplomats brought pressure to bear on the government, insisting that the sale would be a breach not only of the Treaty of Versailles but also of the Locarno agreements which guaranteed the *status quo* established by the Versailles treaty. "It is very disappointing," the *Kölnische Zeitung* stated, "to think that the opportunity has been frustrated to remove an injustice inserted in the Treaty of Versailles only for the purpose of continually spoiling the relations between two countries. Of these two countries it is undoubtedly Belgium that will suffer most. The impossibility of taking advantage of the financial help which was offered to it by Germany will be felt by the whole Belgian people during a period of financial and economic difficulties."

Among the more vexing problems with which the government had to deal during the period between the two wars was that of language. There is, of course, no such thing as a Belgian language. The southern half of the population, adjoining France, speak French; the northern half, bordering on Holland, speak Flemish, which is closely related to Dutch. The men who had initiated and conducted the revolution of 1830 which severed the ties joining Belgium and Holland had been French speaking and had achieved success with the help of French bayonets. It was therefore natural that they would favor French as the official language for all administrative, religious, and educational activities. Gradually, however, a movement took form in support of the Flemish language and culture. Up to 1914 the leaders of this movement had made only mild demands, but after the war the demands became more robust. During the four years the Germans occupied Belgium they attempted to exploit the latent discontent for their own ends. They promised the Flemings cultural autonomy, made the University of Ghent exclusively Flemish, and tried in every way to persuade the Flemings that they belonged to the German race and ought to separate from the Walloons, as the French-speaking Belgians are known. But all attempts to win over the Flemings as a body proved unsuccessful.

Although King Albert, upon his triumphal return to Brussels in November, 1918, promised the Flemings equality of language and the creation of a Flemish University of Ghent, little was done during the years immediately following toward fulfilling the promise; in fact, a step backward was taken when the university was returned to its former linguistic status. The result was a widespread agitation on the part of the Flemings. Finally in the summer of 1921 a law was passed dividing Belgium into two parts in each of which all administrative matters were to be conducted in a single language, Flemish in the northern part and French in the southern. This law still left the Flemish unsatisfied. After that the question of a Flemish university became a special point of dissension. In 1922 a law was carried through parliament by a margin of only twelve votes decreeing that Flemish should be the official language of the University of Ghent but that certain courses should still be given in French. This settlement satisfied neither side. While the Walloons boycotted the university, the Flemings continued their agitation to make the university completely Flemish. The latter ultimately achieved their goal in 1930 when a new law was passed stipulating that beginning with the academic year 1930–1931 instruction in the University of Ghent was to be in Flemish only. During the decade of the thirties other laws removed other grievances. Thus, for example, in 1938 a Flemish Scientific Academy was created and two councils were established, one to foster the advancement of Flemish culture, another for French culture.

In 1930 the world depression made itself felt in Belgium. In one year foreign trade was cut in half, and during the years 1930–1935 unemployment rose steadily. As in other countries, the depression gave rise to Fascist movements, the supporters of which believed that only an authoritarian government could pull the country out of the slough. One of these movements was the Flemish Fascist movement, organized in 1931 upon the Nazi pattern and reputedly subsidized by the Nazis. But the party which achieved the greatest temporary strength was the Rexists, led by Leon Degrelle, a mystic who took the name of his party from Christus Rex. In the elections of 1936 this party succeeded in obtaining twenty-one seats in the Chamber of Representatives. However, the party's tactics of parliamentary obstruction alienated so many of its followers that the Rexists lost all but four seats in the elections of 1939.

For many years after the First World War fear and hatred of the Germans remained a strong feature of Belgium's foreign policy. The Belgians could not forget how much they had suffered at the hands of the invaders. As the policy of neutrality had not prevented the Germans from marching through the country, the Belgians were faced with the duty of finding a new basis of security. This time they turned to collective security. They sincerely hoped to reach a military agreement with Britain, but the British were in no mood to enter into any alliance whatsoever. A military agreement was, however, signed with France in 1921, the details of which were not revealed. This was fortified by a further agreement in 1926. In addition the Belgians relied on the protection of the League of Nations.

But they gradually came to the conclusion that their commitments did not afford them security. They saw the Germans defy the Versailles treaty by rearming and by scrapping the Locarno Pacts which guaranteed the postwar frontiers and the demilitarization of the Rhineland. They saw, in general, that the European powers instead of disarming were abandoning the ideals of Geneva and building up mighty war machines. Moreover, the agreement with France had become distasteful to many. While the Flemings, opposed as they were to French influence in Belgian life, denounced the agreement as likely to commit the country to an unnecessary war, the bourgeois Belgians disliked the growth of the French Communist Party, and the powerful Catholic Party resented the anticlerical attitude of the Popular Front government.

Opposition to the defensive alliance with France soon grew so strong that the government decided to sever the ties between the two nations. On October 14, 1936, King Leopold III summoned his ministers to a cabinet council and announced that Belgium had decided to abandon its military obligations and was reverting to its prewar status of neutrality. "Any bilateral policy," the king stated, "weakens our position abroad . . . excites division at home. . . . An alliance even if it is purely defensive does not achieve its purpose, because however prompt might be the aid from our ally it would come only after an onslaught by an invading army which would be devastating." In the war of 1914, he said, "our moral position would have been much weaker if the invader had been able to advance as an argument an alliance between Belgium and one of its neighbors." Belgium must henceforth, the monarch declared, take care of its own defense. "Our geographical position enjoins us to maintain a military establishment . . . to dissuade . . . neighbors from borrowing our territory for use in attacking another state." In short, it was the king's aim to avert the danger of war. As a means of better defense the throne had previously approved the strengthening of the border fortifications, the extension of compulsory military service, and the creation of a motorized army. As Europe moved rapidly toward war, Leopold bent every effort to keeping his country out of the holocaust. But his efforts availed him nothing. Belgium was to become a victim of German aggression for the second time in a quarter of a century.

THE KINGDOM OF THE NETHERLANDS

The Kingdom of the Netherlands, so called because of the depressed geographical position of the territories embraced by this state, is a small but densely populated country situated at the mouths of the Rhine, Maas, and Scheldt Rivers. In the area of a little over 12,000 square miles, which is one third larger than the state of Maryland, nearly eight million Dutchmen lived in 1920. Much of the land along the seashore had been wrested from the sea through the building of dikes, an achievement that is proudly expressed in the saying, "Deus mare, Batavus litora fecit (God made the sea, the Dutchman made the shore)."

The situation of the Netherlands at an important crossing of some of the principal highways of international commerce has for centuries made this country a natural center of trade to which merchants of the north and south have brought their wares for sale or exchange. Although at the beginning of the twentieth century the little state no longer occupied the prominent place among the nations that it held in the seventeenth, it did not live merely on the memories of a glorious past. Its merchant marine was one of the largest in the world; its industry was flourishing; and its agriculture and horticulture, raised to a high pitch of efficiency, produced a large surplus for export.

Furthermore, the Dutch managed to retain the great empire they had won in the seventeenth century. They controlled the third largest colonial empire of the world, less extensive and important only than the empires of Britain and France. It included Dutch Guiana on the continent of South America, the island of Curaçao in the West Indies, and a cluster of islands in the Pacific with a population of about fifty millions belonging to nearly forty races and tribes with different languages and varying degrees of civilization and culture. Among these islands were Sumatra, Java, the Celebes, the Moluccas, Borneo, and New Guinea. From them came a great variety of products which figured conspicuously in the world markets— sugar, spices, cinchona, copra, coffee, tea, rubber, petroleum, palm oil, tobacco, dyes, tin, gold, silver, and other metals in addition to an enormous list of minor commodities.

The government of the Netherlands is a constitutional monarchy based on the constitution of 1814 which has been revised from time to time. While the executive power of the state is vested exclusively in the sovereign, the legislative authority is exercised jointly by the sovereign and by a parliament (States-General) composed of two chambers, the Upper or First Chamber of fifty members elected by direct vote for a period of six years and a Lower Chamber of one hundred deputies elected by direct vote for a period of four years. Although appointed by the sovereign the cabinet is accountable to and dependent upon the support of the States-General. The prime minister, as in Britain, can continue in office only as long as he commands a parliamentary majority.

The ruler of the Netherlands during the period between the two World Wars was Queen Wilhelmina. Born in 1880 she succeeded to the throne at the death of her father, King William II, when she was only ten. Her mother, Queen Emma, acted as regent during her minority. Upon reaching the age of eighteen Wilhelmina was crowned in Amsterdam. It is reported that happy Hollanders celebrated the occasion by braiding the tails of their cows with gay ribbons in honor of the "lily among the tulips," as the plump girl was called by a contemporary phrasemaker. The next year she offered her palace at The Hague to the diplomats of the world for a disarmament conference known as the First Hague Conference. Thereafter the Dutch queen could be found in the vanguard of every movement making for world peace. As she was the last of her line, the question of her marriage and the birth of an heir was an urgent necessity of state. In 1901 she married Henry, Duke of Mecklenburg-Schwerin, who received the title of Prince of the Netherlands. Eight years later Princess Juliana was born of this union. Wilhelmina, who combined tact with firmness, took her posi-

QUEEN WILHELMINA OF THE NETHERLANDS; MADAME CHIANG KAI-SHEK; PRINCESS JULIANA

tion as queen seriously from the start, working hard to understand her people and their needs. Save for contact with her ministers and a few old friends, she led a quiet life. Once a year she would appear before the people on her ride to open the session of the States-General. Her courts, held only infrequently, were stiff and formal affairs. At such functions the queen indulged her one weakness, the display of costly jewels.

When the First World War broke out, she stood by the dikes, like the Dutch boy in the familiar story, holding back the waves of propaganda that would have swept her people into the conflict. Nevertheless the Netherlands, although they were spared the devastation of war, suffered economic losses in all directions. Of all the neutral states, the Netherlands probably suffered most through the dislocation of trade and industry. As a result of the blockades set up by Germany and Britain, the shipping trade dwindled to less than a tenth of its former proportions. Many factories were forced to close because of the lack of raw materials and coal. Unemployment prevailed among the working classes. The shortage of some kinds of food and the faulty distribution of the existing supply resulted in widespread undernourishment. Moreover, the necessity of having the army in a state of readiness for more than four years to defend the borders against aggression drained the Dutch coffers and made high taxes necessary. At the end of the war unemployment was rife and the country was hungry and discontented. It seemed as if the stage were set for revolution. For the first time groups of workers did demonstrate against the queen. The leader of the Socialist Party even went so far as to make a formal demand that "a republic be instituted." The queen's ministers, who feared for her safety, cautioned her not to leave her guarded palace. But Wilhelmina was not one to be frightened. Summoning her open carriage, she drove through the crowded streets of The Hague almost unattended. Her fearlessness won her instant acclaim. The crowd surged about her and cheered their *Landsmoeder* (Mother of the Land). The younger men even unhitched the horses so they might pull the coach themselves.

During the succeeding years the Dutch recovered their former prosperity. The period from 1924 to 1929 was, in fact, one of unusual economic activity. After that Dutch trade, industry, and agriculture began to wither under the blighting winds of world depression. Exports to Britain and Germany, which were by far the best customers, fell off alarmingly. Exports to Britain, for example, declined from £36 million in 1928 to £10 million in 1933, and exports to Germany from £38.5 million in 1928 to £13 million in 1933. Translated into the realities of everyday life these figures mean that by 1933 a large portion of the merchant marine was lying idle, that farmers were in distress, and that unemployment was increasing by leaps and bounds. The year 1934 saw serious riots break out in the working-class quarter of Amsterdam over the reduction of unemployment benefits. Public offices were stoned, barricades erected in the streets, and a number of lives were lost before police and soldiers could restore order. At the beginning of 1936 the country had the largest percentage of unemployed in western Europe, with more than 400,000 families being supported by the state or local communities. Economic recovery began only in the autumn of 1936 after the government, which for five years had struggled to maintain the gold standard, decided to devaluate the guilder. This devaluation, added to the revival of business all over the world, stimulated renewed activity in industry, trade, and agriculture.

By this time the government had other troubles that were giving it great concern. After Hitler's accession to power in 1933 the dark cloud of nazism spread its first shadow over the Netherlands. A Nazi party was organized and was reported to be receiving financial aid from Germany. It adopted a program that incorporated many ideas borrowed from the German Nazis, including anti-Semitism. For a time the movement spread quickly. Before many months passed, the Dutch Nazis achieved sufficient importance to cause the Roman Catholic clergy to deny the sacraments of the church to all members of the party. In the 1935 elections for the First Chamber they managed to obtain representation for the first time by gaining two seats, and in the provincial elections they polled the unexpected number of 300,000 votes or 8 per cent of the total. In imitation of the Nazi tactics in Germany before 1933 the Dutch Nazis staged street brawls against their opponents, until the government in 1936 passed a law forbidding the formation of private armies and the wearing of party uniforms. But in 1937 they saw their following reduced by half as compared with 1935, although they did obtain four of the fifty seats in the First Chamber. It was, of course, Hitler's plan to draw the Netherlands into the orbit of the Axis powers. When in 1937 the Princess Juliana married Count Bernhard zu Lippe-Biesterfeld, member of a family of minor German nobility, Hitler interpreted this step to mean closer cooperation between the two countries. But Queen Wilhelmina, known for her directness, disillusioned him with the following statement: "This is the marriage of my daughter to the man whom she loves and whom I found worthy of her love; it is not the marriage of Holland to Germany."

Since the Netherlands refused to be dominated by Germany, it was feared that Hitler might use force to achieve his ends. Hence the rearming of Germany caused great apprehension among the Dutch. As early as 1935 the government took up in earnest the problem of defending both the mother country and the overseas territories. The necessity for this was so obvious that even the extreme leftists voted for the establishment of a defense fund for antiaircraft batteries, modern airplanes, mechanized equipment for the army, new fighting ships, frontier fortifications, and coastal defense equipment. Relations with Germany grew more tense after a series of unauthorized flights of German aircraft over Dutch territory in 1937 and 1938. The Munich triumph caused the German press to assume a more menacing tone toward the Netherlands. It went so far as to suggest that it would be wise for the Dutch to cooperate with Germany in both economic and political affairs. Instead of complying with these demands they took further steps to strengthen their defenses against invasion by calling up more men and lengthening the period of their training. As the war clouds gathered, the foreign minister reaffirmed the policy of armed neutrality in case of war but added that his government would resist any army that attempted to enter Dutch territory.

As the decade of the thirties progressed, there were rumblings of trouble in the colonial possessions as well as in the mother country. The black and the brown races alike were beginning to feel conscious of their position. Although the relations between the Dutch and their subject peoples were on the whole friendly, this did not prevent the latter from demanding independence. This dissatisfaction made it necessary for the Dutch to supervise their colonies more closely and that was a strain on the national budget. At one time the government had derived a handsome surplus through the sale of products from government-owned industries in the colonies, but after the withdrawal of the government from business, this income had ceased; yet the government had to continue to defray the cost of public works in the colonies, of educating the natives, and of keeping order among them. In other words, colonial administration was becoming a financial burden to the mother country. By maintaining the policy of the open door in their colonies the Dutch had facilitated the exploitation of the natives by other nations. In 1928 the Dutch had, for example, supplied 26 per cent of the textiles purchased by the natives of the Dutch East Indies, but during the succeeding years the Japanese had seized the lion's share of the market (76 per cent), while the share of the mother country had been reduced to 6 per cent. In general, Japan's share of imports into the Dutch

East Indies increased from 10 per cent in 1928 to 31 per cent in 1935, but that of the Netherlands slumped from 20 to 12 per cent.

This decline was accompanied by a drop in tax receipts which caused the Dutch to curtail the expense of government in an effort to balance the budget. The first thing that suffered was the higher schools for the natives. This caused the natives to go to Japan for their education. And the Japanese were not slow to make the most of the opportunity to inculcate in the minds of the Indonesians a hatred for European rule. Soon the slogan "Indonesia for Indonesians" was heard far and wide in the Dutch East Indies.

The eve of World War II saw doughty Queen Wilhelmina still ruling the Netherlands in her characteristic manner. By this time all those who were occupying thrones at the time of her accession had departed from the scene. In Britain, Queen Victoria's fourth successor was wearing the crown. In the Netherlands, communists went so far as to heckle Wilhelmina during her addresses to the States-General and the Nazis infuriated her in the streets by giving the Nazi salute. But the average burgher and his wife still regarded their queen with typical Dutch affection.

THE SCANDINAVIAN COUNTRIES

Denmark, Norway, and Sweden, the three countries which make up Scandinavia, are in many respects closely related. Most of the inhabitants are of the same anthropological type and the languages they speak are so similar that members of one can understand the two others without an interpreter. In addition, the peoples have many tastes and customs in common. Nevertheless one must not take Scandinavian unity for granted; a closer examination will reveal many dissimilarities. There are differences in economic interests no less than in geographical positions. Each country possesses a somewhat different political and social organization. Each insists on particularism in language and culture: the vocabulary and, above all, the pronunciation of each language is different. Swedes insist on being Swedes no less than Danes and Norwegians are proud of their nationality. In each country strong nationalist tendencies had made their appearance before World War I and had grown stronger in the years that followed.

During the Middle Ages and far into the modern period the Scandinavians had been an adventurous, warlike people. For centuries the Vikings had harried the coasts of France and Britain, and long before Columbus touched the shores of America the Vikings had been here. Later the Swedes produced the great military leader, Gustavus Adolphus (d. 1632), and some decades later Charles XII (d. 1718). But during more recent centuries these countries turned their backs firmly upon war and the quest of martial glory. "And we Norwegians of today," the distinguished author, Sigrid Undset, wrote, "are proud, not that our forefathers were Vikings, but that these same forefathers outgrew the Viking mentality so rapidly, so that less than two hundred years after the battle of Stiklestad we were already in many ways far ahead of many older nations on the road that ultimately has led to present-day ideas about humaneness, justice, respect of the rights of personal freedom, and just treatment of individuals, poor and rich." [2] When World War I broke out, all three countries remained neutral. During the war years they experienced a certain prosperity despite the blockade and the restrictions on their domestic activities as well as on their foreign trade. They did not, however, entirely escape the destruction of war. Mines and German submarines took a large toll of their shipping. Norway, which was hardest hit, lost 1162 seamen and half of her prewar merchant marine, which had boasted a tonnage exceeding three million.

Scandinavian philosophy may be summed up in the words "peace," "freedom," "democracy," and "progress." In all these countries suffrage during the period between the two wars was probably as free as anywhere in the world, with women enjoying full political rights with men. A writer on Scandinavia says, "Here democracy is full of vitality; it acts instead of merely talking and criticizing; it is constructive, cautious, and in the widest sense of the word conservatively progressive. Furthermore, in this respect Sweden is not alone; in Denmark the position is almost identical, and Norway seems to be gravitating to a similar state of affairs. In fact, the development and consolidation of democracy in Scandinavian countries is striking and undeniable. And it is essential to realize that the bearers of democratic ideas are no longer the bourgeois liberals, or a radical intelligentsia, but primarily workmen, peasants, and the lower middle classes. This makes it particularly interesting and original." [3]

Denmark, with an area of 16,571 square miles is about one third the size of New York state and had a population of about three millions in 1918. Of this number nearly a third lived in Copenhagen, the one really large city. According to the constitution the legislative power is vested jointly in the king and the Diet (*Rigsdag*).

[2] *Free World*, vol. 5 (1943), p. 211.
[3] *Contemporary Review*, vol. 147 (1935), p. 46.

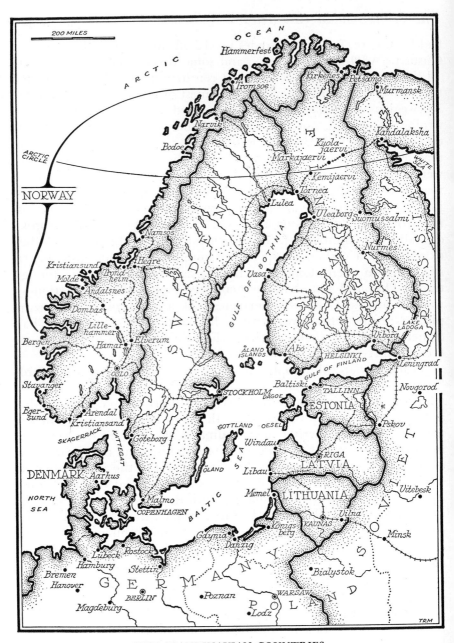

THE SCANDINAVIAN COUNTRIES

The king during the period between the two wars was Christian X (1870–1947), whose character and statesmanship made him popular with his subjects. On his daily horseback rides through Copenhagen, the tall monarch (he was six feet, six inches tall) would salute the ladies, nod to groups, chat with small boys or truck drivers, and carefully obey the traffic lights. Everywhere he was regarded with love and respect. During World War I the government had mobilized an emergency army of 70,000 but quickly demobilized them at the time of the armistice. Although a nonparticipant in the fighting, Denmark gained Northern Schleswig which had been annexed by Germany in 1864. There was a movement to return all of Schleswig-Holstein to Denmark, but Christian X, eager to eliminate the possibility of future international complications, firmly stated that he wished "to see Denmark go only as far south in Schleswig as Danish hearts beat." As a result of the plebiscite stipulated in the Treaty of Versailles Denmark was given possession of a strip of land where the inhabitants even under German rule had remained Danish in language, customs, and culture. Thus was added to Denmark an area of 1507 square miles with a population of nearly 200,000. The return of North Schleswig after fifty-four years under the German flag was an occasion for great jubilation. Many hailed it as the greatest event in a century of Danish history.

Although Copenhagen is a port and shipbuilding center of the first importance, with the largest ice-free harbor in northern Europe, the Danish people are largely devoted to agriculture. Denmark is, in a sense, a country of farmers in which most of the agencies of the state and also a vast number of cooperative enterprises are consciously devoted to the promotion of the well-being of the farmers. About 250,000 farmers are members of some 4000 cooperative societies which control the machinery for buying all the farmer produces beyond his own needs. The cooperative movement began with dairying early in the eighties and proved so successful that it was soon extended to pork packing, the export of butter, and other phases of economic activity. By the thirties more than 90 per cent of all Danish farmers were members of a cooperative dairy. The secret of the success of the movement in Denmark is that it has

THE SCANDINAVIAN COUNTRIES. *Note the boundaries of Sweden, Finland, Russia, and Germany, and the position of such cities as Leningrad, Danzig, Berlin, and Hamburg.*

enabled the small farmer to place his output as advantageously as the large-scale farmer. Besides insuring to the individual producer the best prices for his products, the movement has made for progress and efficiency. To promote agriculture and stock-raising, the cooperative societies employ agricultural advisers, arrange agricultural shows, and conduct experiments of many kinds. The farmers also have cooperative associations for buying fertilizers, feeds, and supplies. The cooperatives even charter ships to carry away the exports and to bring back the imports, such as cottonseed from the United States and soy beans from the East.

It is estimated that Danish agriculture is able to feed some twelve million people in addition to the inhabitants of Denmark. The country supplies others with great quantities of butter, eggs, bacon, and hams. No less than 50 per cent of the butter, 53 per cent of the ham, 64 per cent of the bacon, and 75 per cent of the eggs were sold abroad during the decade of the thirties. One of the best customers was England, and Germany was another. During World War I Denmark lost the British market to the United States and Canada. Nevertheless, Denmark, as one writer put it, was "the one European country that during the war literally flowed with milk and honey. It alone had an ample supply of food." Prices were so high that huge fortunes were made. But as prices fell off, the fortunes melted away. Bankruptcies and foreclosure sales became everyday affairs. Gradually, however, conditions improved. British markets were again open and Germany also consumed large quantities of Danish products.

When Hitler rose to power, the Nazis made no issue of the Schleswig territory that had been returned to Denmark. They even seemed satisfied with the treatment of the German minority in that country. Nevertheless, the long shadow of Nazi Germany fell ominously upon Denmark, whose only land frontier bordered the Reich and was unfortified. It was feared that the productive capacity of Danish agriculture might tempt a country that could not raise enough food to supply its needs. In May, 1939, Hitler sought to allay these fears by concluding with Denmark a nonaggression treaty in which both promised that they would "in no circumstances resort to war or any other form of violence against each other." But this promise was no more sacred to Hitler than any other. Before World War II was a year old, Nazi legions overran King Christian's country.

Norway, which forms the northern and western part of the Scandinavian Peninsula, has an extreme length of 1100 miles and an extreme width of 250 miles, with an estimated area of 124,555 square miles, which is about five times the combined areas of New Hampshire, Vermont, and Massachusetts. In 1918 it had an estimated population of 2,632,010. The government during the period between the two wars was a constitutional and hereditary monarchy, and the ruler was King Haakon VII, second son of Frederick VIII of Denmark, who had been elected when Norway severed its connection with Sweden in 1905. The constitution vested the legislative power in the Storting, elected by universal suffrage without distinction of sex. The king was accorded a veto, but the constitution provides that a bill becomes law without his assent if it is passed by three Stortings formed by separate and subsequent elections.

Norway is on the whole a barren and mountainous country. In 1919 it was estimated that 71 per cent was unproductive from the agricultural standpoint. Almost a quarter of the total area is covered with forest, and only 3.7 per cent is under cultivation. Nevertheless, agriculture is one of the foremost industries. The other two are fisheries and shipping, as one would expect from the fact that the coastline is more than a thousand miles long. No other country has proportionately so much tonnage in ships or so many seamen. It has been calculated that during the decade of the thirties every twenty-fifth ship on the seas of the world was Norwegian and 17 per cent of the adult male population followed the sea for a livelihood. In 1935 the foreign trade per inhabitant was five times that of the United States. Fishing has been an important industry since the earliest days of recorded history. During the period between the wars Norwegian fish products were sold in many countries. Besides cod and herring fisheries, whaling has occupied an important place in the economic life of Norway. As an industry whaling is so important that a jest states, "The whale is one of Norway's domestic animals." The other important domestic animal is the silver fox. In 1935 there were nearly 20,000 fox farms, and a large number of pelts were being exported. Another important source of natural wealth is the forests. During the two decades after 1919 woodpulp and wood products formed about 25 per cent of the total exports. Industry as a whole is based on raw materials from the forests and fisheries.

During the years of World War I the shipowners and exporters of Norway enjoyed a high degree of prosperity, but this was followed by a slump in the early twenties accompanied by a thoroughgoing deflation. As a result very many banks became insolvent and unemployment reached high figures. By 1928 Norway had to a large extent overcome the effects of the slump and was looking forward to a period of economic growth and prosperity. About the middle of 1930, however, the effects of the world depression began to make themselves felt. There followed a period of falling prices, reduced exports, and growing unemployment. But thanks to the deflation of the early years of the decade depression was not so severe as in other countries. In 1935 production reached 111 per cent of the production of 1928, while that of the United States was only 72 per cent. Moreover, whereas Norway had ranked eighth among the seafaring nations in 1923, the outbreak of World War II saw her in fourth place.

When in 1814 Norway was separated from Denmark and put under Swedish rule, the population preserved Danish as the literary language. The great Norwegian writer, Henrik Ibsen (1828–1906), wrote his works in Danish. After a few decades a movement was started to advance Norway's claim for a literary language by using Norwegian words for all things and ideas characteristic of Norwegian life, but most of the vocabulary of abstract words remained Danish. Two Norwegian writers of the period between the two wars whose works were and still are read in many countries are Knut Hamsun (1859–   ) and Sigrid Undset (1882–   ). The former's *Growth of the Soil* is often referred to as "the great Norwegian prose epic." Published in 1917, it won instantaneous success in Norway and during the subsequent years was translated into nearly every major language, winning the Nobel prize for its author in 1920. Mrs. Undset's great work of the period was *Kristin Lavransdatter* (1920–1922), a trilogy composed of *The Bridal Wreath, The Mistress of Husaby,* and *The Cross.* This great historical novel, the scene of which is laid in fourteenth-century Norway, is an ambitious attempt to sum up the meaning of life from the viewpoint of religious experience.

The voice of Norway in music was Edvard Grieg, who died in 1904 but whose music was popular during the decades of the twenties and thirties. More than any other composer Grieg embodied in his music the national spirit and folklore of Norway and the voices of the Norwegian forest.

Sweden with an area of 158,450 square miles is the largest of the Scandinavian states. The population at the beginning of 1919 was 5,813,850. The government, like those of Denmark and Norway, is a constitutional monarchy. Executive power is vested in the king, who acts with the advice of the council of state. The legislative power is exercised by an elected Diet of two chambers.

The king during the period between the two wars was Gustav V (1858–   ), great-grandson of Marshal Bernadotte, the founder of the Royal House of Sweden. King Gustav, affectionately known to his subjects as "Papa Gustav," ascended the throne in 1907. Aside from his democratic tastes and fine gifts of statesmanship, this tall ruler possesses considerable athletic ability. He is an uncommonly good horseman, an excellent marksman, an agile oarsman, and a skillful tennis player. Besides popularizing tennis in his own country, he also entered the Riviera tennis tournaments in France under the name of "Mr. G." It was King Gustav who in 1914 invited the sovereigns of Denmark and Norway to meet with him at Malmö, where it was agreed that the Scandinavian countries would try to stay out of the war. At the end of the war a contest arose between Sweden and Finland for the possession of the Åland Islands, which were regarded by the Swedes as the naval key to Stockholm. Although Finland exercised sovereignty over the islands after the fall of the Russian imperial government, the inhabitants demanded annexation to Sweden in the name of self-determination. It was finally agreed to accept the intervention of the League of Nations for the settlement of the dispute. The League adjudicated the islands to Finland.

Although Sweden had few manufactures in the middle of the nineteenth century, succeeding decades saw the development of a number of industries, particularly during the early years of the present century. Once industrialization had begun, it became clear that the nation possessed a certain talent for technical matters. The things the Swedes invented or discovered range from dynamite to steam turbines. Above all, their high-grade iron and steel enjoy an international reputation. The other pillar of their industry is wood. Notable among the exports during the period between the two wars were ball bearings, electrical machinery, calculating machines, measuring instruments, refrigerators, matches, paper, and pulp and wood products of many kinds. With the largest timber resources in western Europe, Sweden became one of the world's largest exporters of woodpulp and newsprint paper. Despite rapid industrialization, agriculture still remained the most important branch of activity. In 1935 two thirds of the population lived in the country, and as far as foodstuffs were concerned there was more than enough for the inhabitants. Many of those who pursued agriculture also devoted a great deal of time to handicrafts. Some of the textiles, toys, and woodwork made by the villagers enjoyed a world-wide reputation.

Like the other Scandinavian countries Sweden had her economic life violently dislocated by the war and its aftermath. A period of prosperity with rising prices was followed by deflation; in fact, the dislocation was probably more violent than in any other nonbel-

ligerent country. In June, 1920, the wholesale price index stood at
366 compared with 100 for the year preceding the outbreak of the
war. In September, 1920, prices began to decline, and a year later
the index had fallen to 182. This drop within a brief space of time
put a severe strain on the economic structure. The sale of goods declined both at home and abroad, and unemployment became extensive. But conditions gradually improved during the succeeding
years. In 1929 the volume of production was more than double that
of 1921.

Sweden did not feel the force of the world depression of 1929
until 1931, but its consequences for a country so dependent on
foreign trade were serious. In 1932, which saw a deepening of the
depression, the volume of production fell to 79 per cent of the 1929
level, and the proportion of unemployed trade-union members
reached 31 per cent. From the second quarter of 1934 the recovery
was rapid. As far as manufactures are concerned, the situation in
1935 was more favorable than that of other industrialized countries.
While the United States in 1935 was still about 26 per cent below
the peak-year production of 1929, Sweden was 10 per cent above it.
Unemployment at the end of 1935 was less than 1 per cent. An important factor in this recovery was a strong home market. Furthermore, the Swedish government had succeeded in keeping the krona
both stable and low abroad, thus making money cheap and plentiful
at home. This enabled private industry to expand and to re-employ
thousands of workers.

The Nazi triumph in Germany gave a strong stimulus to the antidemocratic forces in Sweden. Three Nazi groups sprang into existence and made a spectacular bid for support. If a dominating personality had arisen to unite these groups, Sweden might have been
confronted with a major political crisis. As it was, the oldest party,
after a rapid rise, discredited itself by an organized attempt on the
life of one of its members in an effort to create a Swedish Horst
Wessel. Moreover, the improvement of economic conditions in
1934 robbed the Nazis of much of their ammunition and also contributed a great deal toward reviving the faith of the masses in
democratic institutions. In any case, Hitler's bloody purge of July,
1934, dealt the final blow to the Nazi menace in Sweden.

The European arms race which began soon after Hitler's accession to power turned the eyes of Europe toward Sweden by creating
an unprecedented demand for iron and steel. In northern Lapland
Sweden possessed more than two billion tons of high-grade ore, much
of which could simply be stripped from the mountain sides. Thus

Sweden,[4] was in a position to aid any country in the development of an arms program. For many years Sweden shipped about 75 per cent of her total iron ore exports to Germany, the rest going to Britain, Belgium, and the United States. Although Germany's share decreased somewhat during the years immediately preceding World War II, Swedish iron still remained the very backbone of Germany's armament industries because of its high grade. Nor did Sweden's part in the armaments race stop with the export of ore. The Bofors plant ranked as one of the foremost munitions factories in the world. Bofors antiaircraft guns were considered equal if not indeed superior to any. Other nations were ready to buy antiaircraft guns and artillery generally as fast as Bofors could make them. Orders in 1937 amounted to $37.5 million with capacity production contracted for three years in advance.

The names of many distinguished persons of Swedish birth are familiar to educated persons the world over. In the field of literature the culture of Sweden has reached us chiefly in the writings of Strindberg and in the stories and novels of Selma Lagerlöf. There was hardly a phase of Swedish literature that Strindberg (1849–1912) did not dominate, including the drama, the novel, and the short story. His poetry was among the most beautiful in the language. Selma Lagerlöf (1858–1940) wrote with such simple charm that her works have lost little in translation. Some of her writings have been translated into thirty-five languages. Among the better known are *The Wonderful Adventures of Nils, The Legend of the Bird's Nest, The General's Ring,* and *Charlotte Lowenskold.* The acknowledged dean of Swedish poetry is Verner von Heidenstam (1859–1940), whose prose works are also of outstanding importance. His patriotic poetry is most passionate, as exemplified by the following:

> We love thee so that, if thou wert dead,
> Our love to life could awake thee.
> Though the bed is hard, though the midnight lowers,
> We'll be true while the tempest rages,
> Thou people, thou land, thou speech that is ours,
> Thou voice of our souls to the ages.

Although he did not write books or even poetry, Alfred Nobel (1833–1896) is one of the most widely known persons of Swedish birth. As the son of an inventor, Alfred Nobel spent most of his life pursuing some invention or other. Among the subjects that par-

---

[4] Only France surpassed Sweden in the quantity of iron ore exports.

ticularly occupied his attention was nitroglycerin, which had been discovered by the Italian Sobrero in 1846. It was Nobel's purpose to devise means whereby nitroglycerin could be employed without extreme danger. In 1862 he and his father erected a plant where it was manufactured on a commercial scale. After several appalling accidents, one of which claimed the life of his brother, he discovered that when nitroglycerin is absorbed in silica it loses many of its dangerous qualities. He called the new product, which was patented in 1867, "dynamite." Soon a number of plants were opened for the manufacture of it, including one in San Francisco. In 1876 he further improved it by combining nitroglycerin with guncotton. Thus was inaugurated the "Age of Dynamite" which produced new instruments of warfare, instruments which were terrible in their destructive powers. For the inventor it meant a large income from his more than twenty factories.

Alfred Nobel had a horror of war. He hoped that his product would outlaw war by making its consequences too terrible to contemplate. "Munition factories," he wrote to a friend who was an advocate of peace congresses, "will perhaps bring war to an end sooner than your conferences; on the day when two army corps are able to destroy each other in the twinkle of an eye, civilized nations will recoil with horror from a conflict and send their armies home." For years he toyed with the idea of using at least a part of his fortune to promote the cause of peace. "I should like to set a part of my property aside for a special prize," he wrote in 1892, "to be distributed every five years. The prize would be bestowed on him or her through whose efforts Europe would have been brought farthest along the way to peace." Several years later he made a will which ordained that his whole fortune be applied to the foundation of the five world prizes which now perpetuate his name. These are awarded to the person who shall have made the most important discovery or invention (1) in the domain of physics, (2) in chemistry, (3) in physiology or medicine, (4) to the person who shall have written the most distinguished work of an idealistic nature in the field of literature, (5) to the person who shall have done most to advance the cause of universal peace. While the first four are awarded by various academies and one institute in Sweden, the last is awarded by the Norwegian Storting. Among the many prize winners were Selma Lagerlöf (1909) and Verner von Heidenstam (1916).

❦

FINLAND

For centuries Finland was a buffer state between Russia and the West. Politically it was a part of Sweden but in 1809 it was added to the Russian Empire by Tsar Alexander I who took the title of Grand Duke of Finland. Although under Russian domination, the Finns enjoyed complete internal autonomy. The Diet pioneered in progressive legislation and as early as 1907 granted the right of suffrage to women. Nevertheless, the Finns were not happy under the rule of the tsars; they wanted nothing short of complete independence. When World War I broke out, the tsar deprived the Diet of most of its powers, in an effort to Russify the country. Since Finland had no army to fight for her deliverance, she could only pray.

A new era was inaugurated with the collapse of Russia in 1917. The provisional government under Kerensky hastened at once to restore autonomy. When the Bolshevik revolution made an end to the provisional government in November, 1917, the Finns embraced the opportunity to declare their independence (December 6, 1917). The first government to recognize their independence was Soviet Russia, followed by the three Scandinavian states, Germany, France, and a number of other nations. Yet Finland was not to be spared the evils and bloodshed of a revolution. A group of "Reds" identified their cause with that of the Russian revolutionists and, supplied with Russian arms, attempted to draw the country into the Bolshevik whirlpool. The Reds occupied the southern and southwestern part of Finland including the capital city of Helsinki and Finland's most prosperous port, Viipuri. In the circumstances the government found it necessary to apply to Germany for armed assistance. A sanguinary struggle followed in which the Reds were driven across the Russian frontier with heavy casualties. For a time the Finns chafed under the German rule, but the collapse of Germany in November, 1918, restored their liberty. On October 14, 1920, after many months of negotiation, a definitive treaty between Finland and Soviet Russia recognized Finnish independence.

The new republic of Finland embraced an area of 149,903 square miles, which is about the size of Montana. The population was about 3.4 million. Finnish and Swedish were adopted as the official languages, corresponding to the main elements of the population. In 1921 about 87 per cent spoke Finnish and about 12 per cent Swedish. The constitution, which was ratified in June, 1919, established a truly democratic government. "The governmental power," the constitution states, "belongs to the people, represented by the assembled Parliament." It granted free speech and free assembly under all normal conditions and guaranteed the linguistic, religious, and minority rights of all citizens. The executive power was vested in a president, elected for a term of six years; the legislative power was entrusted jointly to the president and an elected parliament.

Although it is often called the "Land of a Thousand Lakes," Finland is actually pockmarked by more than four thousand. These lakes provide fish in enormous quantities and make fishing one of the country's great industries. But the greatest industry during the period between the two wars was lumbering. More than half of Finland is covered by forest, of which about 40 per cent belongs to the state. In addition to the natural wealth in timber, Finland also has aluminum mines. There is no coal, but the system of lakes and rivers offers unlimited opportunities for the development of waterpower. Dairying and agriculture both produce exportable wealth of no mean importance. During the twentieth century industry experienced a rapid development. On the eve of World War II the linen, tobacco, and leather factories were among the most important in northern Europe. As in the Scandinavian countries, the cooperative movement has been very successful.

Finland's most distinguished world citizen during the period between the two wars was the composer Jan Sibelius (1865–   ). His popularity with his compatriots was such that they lovingly referred to him as "the uncrowned king of Finland." After studying in Helsinki and Berlin, young Sibelius in 1890 found Vienna, the home of Johann Strauss and the city that is filled with memories of Schubert, Beethoven, and Mozart. "At last," he wrote, "I have found a place that was made for me." Although enchanted by the gay city on the Danube, he followed the dictates of his own mind and instincts in his compositions. He returned to Finland in 1892 and quickly gained recognition from his countrymen. Early in his career the Diet voted him a pension so that he could devote himself exclusively to composition without being harassed by financial problems. In 1899 his *First Symphony* was received with tremendous enthusiasm; then came his *Song of the Athenians* and *Finlandia*. The latter was an expression of the surging Finnish nationalism of the time. A nationalist by temperament, he wrote a number of his early works, including *Kullervo* and the *Karelia Suite* as patriotic tributes; in fact, his music contributed much toward gaining independence for Finland. In Germany his *Finlandia* was called *Vaterland* and in Paris *La Patrie*. In Russia, so long as Finland was a part of the Russian Empire, it could not be played under any name that suggested its patriotic character.

ॶ

SWITZERLAND

Switzerland, homeland of the legendary William Tell, is a small country in the very heart of Europe. The Swiss are heterogeneous not only in their religious faith, one part being Protestant and the other Catholic, but also in ethnic origin, in speech, and in culture. In 1930 the population, numbering about four million, was divided linguistically as follows: 71 per cent German, 21 per cent French, and 6 per cent Italian. The three official languages were German, French, and Italian. None of the different ethnic or language groups could, however, claim any superiority over the others; all were definitely on the same plane. Switzerland is basically not one state, but a union of twenty-two cantons or small states, each having its local rights, customs, and government. These cantons were gradually drawn together in a voluntary union by common interests and a love of freedom. At first the bonds that held them together were loose, but as centralization became more and more necessary, unification was extended to national defense, currency, law, foreign policy, and certain phases of education and police administration.

The government is a liberal democracy established in 1848, a time when the general environment was neither liberal nor democratic. The constitution, modeled to a certain extent upon that of the United States, transformed Switzerland into a federal government. Since it was first promulgated in 1848 the constitution has been changed a number of times. All changes have been in the direction of greater participation of the people in the process of legislation. Sovereignty was vested in the people, who exercise it alike in national and cantonal affairs by means of the veto, the initiative, and, in some instances, the recall. The legislative power was lodged in a Federal Assembly consisting of a House of Representatives representing the people [5] and a Council of State which, like the United States Senate, represents the cantons or states. The right to initiate legislation was accorded equally to both houses. Provisions were made for the exercise of the executive power by a Federal Council composed of seven members elected by the Assembly. The presidency is held for twelve months only, virtually in rotation, by members of the Federal Council and has no political or adminis-

[5] Representatives, according to the act of 1930, are elected by manhood suffrage on the basis of one member for every 22,000 people.

trative significance. The president merely serves as chairman of the Federal Council.

During the early decades of the nineteenth century the population of Switzerland was made up almost entirely of peasants, but toward the end of the century and particularly in the present century manufactures developed rapidly. In 1934 nearly 46 per cent of the population was engaged in manufacturing. The country is not, however, rich in natural resources; hence it was necessary to import raw materials. To pay for such imports the Swiss had to develop export industries. Swiss watches, textiles, electrical apparatus, machinery, and chemical products were soon known in many parts of the world. During the decade of the thirties the per capita value of the foreign trade exceeded that of both Great Britain and the United States. Another important source of income during the period between the two wars was the tourist traffic. Originally isolated by high mountains, Switzerland became, with the development of modern means of transportation, a land of tourists. International expresses roared through the railway tunnels day and night. In general, the economic and social wellbeing of the Swiss was such as to evoke the envy of foreigners. The depression of 1929 naturally curtailed exports, but conditions gradually improved during the thirties.

Despite their language and cultural differences the Swiss have for centuries lived in relative peace and mutual concord while their neighbors have waged wars over the very issues which failed to disrupt the national unity of Switzerland. The Swiss demonstrated, in the words of Woodrow Wilson, "how Germans, Frenchmen, and Italians, if only they respect each other's liberties as they would have their own respected, may by mutual helpfulness and forbearance build up a union at once stable and free."

This spirit of peace and cooperation has also been characteristic of foreign policy. For more than a century Switzerland has succeeded in remaining aloof from the wars of Europe, thereby earning for herself the appellation of "Isle of Peace." During World War I her neutrality was respected by her neighbors, but during the succeeding period the effervescence of nationalism in France, of Fascism in Italy, and of National Socialism in Germany caused considerable uneasiness among the Swiss. It was, above all, the Nazis that the Swiss feared. After Hitler's accession to power Nazi newspapers, printed in Switzerland, repeatedly stated that the Swiss were "racial comrades" and even invited them to "come home to Mother Germania." A German Nazi Party was organized in Switzerland with more than forty branches, all working toward the establishment of an authoritarian state. After Germany's reoccupation of the Rhineland, the Swiss fears deepened. The Swiss believed that in case of war against France the Nazis would march through Switzerland as a means of outflanking the Maginot Line. This fear caused the minister of war to make a moving appeal to the nation to be ready "to defend its liberty by force of arms." "The moment a foreign soldier crosses our border," one of the Swiss statesmen said, "we will fight, and you may rest assured that we will fight to the last man."

CHAPTER SIXTEEN

Revolt of the East against Western Imperialism

AWAKENING OF THE ORIENT

THE contest for colonial possessions has been one of the outstanding features of European history since the time when the crusades saw the founding of the great Venetian maritime empire. During the centuries that followed, most European nations strove unceasingly to extend their influence. The object of this early imperialism was not so much possession of the territories as of the markets the territories afforded. European traders wanted to buy and sell goods at a profit in distant lands. Of special importance was the trade in precious metals, spices, and various kinds of luxuries.

With the invention of power machinery in the late eighteenth and early nineteenth centuries a new stage of imperialism began. Power machinery meant, above all, large-scale production of the necessities of life rather than the luxuries. There was every incentive, after the domestic market had been supplied, to establish political control of overseas territories as a means of monopolizing their markets. Furthermore, to keep the wheels of the machinery turning, the industrial states of Europe needed vast quantities of raw materials, many of which the backward countries of Asia and Africa could supply. More than this, profits were so large that industrialists were seeking new spheres of remunerative investment. In short, political control of backward countries to a greater or lesser extent for purposes of economic exploitation constitutes the essence of modern imperialism, however much imperialists may have tried to disguise their motives in a humanitarian garb. In addition to the seamy side there is, of course, a constructive side. Many of the benefits of Western civilization were conferred upon the backward peoples: harbors and ports were constructed in their countries, railroads were built, and steps were taken to develop natural resources.

The same general methods were employed by all imperialist powers. They simply occupied the territory whose products or markets they desired. The discoveries of science and their application to economic processes gave the Occident command of weapons that made it possible to occupy weak and backward countries with relatively small effort. In this way more than two thirds of the population of the globe became more or less subject to a few aggressive Western powers. Great Britain established political control over India and Burma; France, over Indo-China; the Netherlands, over an insular empire; and Spain, over the Philippine Islands.[1] At the outbreak of World War I Japan alone of the Asiatic nations could call herself wholly independent.

For a long time Asia was passive, even indifferent, and it seemed as if its peoples would always play a subordinate part in the political and economic development of the human race. But superiority of arms did not give the Western nations a final and lasting supremacy over the Eastern peoples. In the twentieth century the East flared into revolt and asserted its right to self-government. Many factors contributed to produce this independence movement, among them the rise of a nationalist spirit, a desire for social equality, a longing for political independence, resentment against economic exploitation by the imperialist nations, and hostility to the imposition of Western religion and culture.

The movement to free the East from European domination began to develop in the nineteenth century among those who had either been educated by teachers from the Occident or who had studied in Europe or the United States of America. Many of them had been deeply imbued with democratic ideas, and others were eager to replace the foreigners in the rule of their country. These men grasped the vision of fighting the West with its own weapons, both material and spiritual. Before the twentieth century was many years old, the victory of the Japanese in the Russo-Japanese War "sent tremors of surprise down the spine of Asia." The Orient, which had stood in awe of the white man with his engines of death, realized that he was not invincible. Lilliputian Japan, a recent convert to the ways of the West, had sent the Russian giant reeling. It generated in the hearts of the Asiatic peoples a new hope of emancipation.

[1] The United States entered the ranks of the imperialist powers when after the Spanish-American War it took over the Spanish colonial possessions.

During the next decade the Western powers were still engaged in empire making or at least in consolidating their empires. They still believed that permanent domination of the Eastern peoples was possible. Then came the First World War. During the war, it is true, the Oriental dominions of the Allies were actively loyal to the extent that Asiatic and African troops fought side by side with the English and French. However, if the war delayed the independence movement, it also served to strengthen it. While Europe was locked in bloody combat, a steady awakening was taking place among the vast populations inhabiting the territories from Egypt to the Straits of Singapore. During the war years the feeling of nationalism, which had previously been restricted to the small group of the intelligentsia, began to penetrate the masses. Not the least among the influences that awakened them from their age-old lethargy were such phrases as "self-determination" and "the rights of small nations" which were spread about the globe during and after the war. The creation of national states in eastern and central Europe at the end of the war gave point to the phrases and further whetted the appetites of the Oriental peoples for independence. Another factor which engendered discontent was the influence of Bolshevist propaganda. If the Bolsheviks did not light the fires of Eastern unrest, they did pour oil on the flames by spreading abroad the doctrines of militant proletarianism and by accusing the "imperialist powers" of "crass exploitation." The masses who had long cherished a deep hatred of the foreigner quicky absorbed these ideas.

All this strengthened the determination of the subject peoples to terminate the rule the Europeans exercised over them. Although each of the various revolts differed from the others in detail, all were formed in the same mold, all pointed toward self-government. The supporters of independence did not stop to ask whether the abolition of European political governance would throw the internal affairs of their respective countries into a state of confusion and anarchy. Their motto was: "Bad home rule is better than good foreign rule." They were determined to fight on until they were complete masters in their own house. It was the same psychology and procedure that existed in the American colonies when they were reaching out toward independence and nationhood. In the case of the Oriental peoples the aspirations for independence were reinforced by hatred of European religion and culture. The belief that theirs is a better way of life was deeply ingrained in their minds. Not that they were unwilling to accept Western science and Western technique. What they were profoundly sceptical about was Western values. Thus Rabindranath Tagore, the East Indian poet, was moved

to state that "the power by which the West thrives is an evil power."
"Christianity," said the Chinese Ku Hung-Ming, "aims to secure the
moral perfection of the individual, but Confucianism not only
makes excellent men, it makes good citizens." Hence the desire for
a combination of Western technique and Eastern values. This combination, the leaders felt, could be achieved only if the entire governmental machinery were in native hands.

During the years after World War I the independence movements
vented themselves in organized revolts, sporadic outbreaks, mass
demonstrations, and widespread disaffections. In 1927 a native of
Asia wrote: "It has dawned upon even the dullest witted person
in North America and Europe that a change has come over the
people of Asia—that they have ceased to be putty in the hands of
Occidentals—that everywhere they are challenging the right of the
Caucasians to rule and exploit them, and in some places are not
hesitating to use force to dislodge the dominant races from their
entrenched positions in the Orient." [2] The result was that Western
ascendancy was shaken to its very foundations. In Egypt, whose
civilization was Asiatic rather than African, the demand for independence was so insistent that Great Britain was forced to make
important concessions. Egypt was proclaimed independent with the
provision that British troops remain in Egypt to protect the Suez
Canal. There were formidable risings against the French in Syria,
and both Persia and Afghanistan insisted upon freedom from interference in their internal affairs. A liberation movement was also
on foot in Burma, which was one of Great Britain's richest possessions, and in the Dutch East Indies. During the same period the
Philippines asserted their right to independence in no uncertain
voice. India, which had been fairly quiet during the war, was swept
by a nationalist agitation; China, though torn by revolution, demanded restoration of its sovereignty and territorial integrity; and
Japan, the one Far Eastern country that escaped exploitation, joined
the European powers in the game of imperialism after deliberately
westernizing itself under the leadership of its feudal aristocracy. The
story of the last three nations will be told in greater detail in the
following pages.

INDIA'S STRUGGLE FOR INDEPENDENCE

In 1919 the term "India" was a geographical expression implying
the area under British rule from the eastern frontier of Persia to

---

[2] *Southern Workman*, vol. 56 (1927), p. 420.

the western frontier of the Chinese province of Yünnan. This vast territory, over twelve times the size of Great Britain, had no political unity beyond the fact that it was administered by the British sovereign as Emperor of India, through the Viceroy. Two thirds of the area was divided into provinces ruled by British governors and British councils; the remaining third consisted of Indian states, many of which were ruled by hereditary princes but all of which were under the indirect control of Britain. The population, greater than that of the two Americas, numbered more than 335 million or about one fifth of the human race. About 90 per cent were engaged in cultivating the soil. In general, it was a poverty-stricken people: about 60 per cent were either definitely undernourished or at least badly nourished. Periodic famines took a large toll in human lives.

Beyond the fact that most of the inhabitants derived their living from the soil there was little homogeneity of any kind in India. The people are in fact a most heterogeneous collection, divided by appearance, dress, ceremonial, and language. They speak no less than twelve distinct languages and over two hundred minor dialects. Moreover, they are divided by religious faiths: living side by side in different parts of the peninsula are about 240 million Hindus and about 75 million Mohammedans. So sharp are the mutual feelings that clashes between the two have been chronic. The situation is further complicated by the fact that there is little unity among the Hindus; in fact they are sharply divided into castes, of which there are between two and three thousand. Every Hindu is born into a caste and can never leave it or even marry outside it. He can eat only with members of his caste, and the food he eats is regulated by the scruples of his caste. At the top of the system stand the Brahmins or priests, who are held in reverence and commonly addressed as "Maharaj" (Your Highness). At the bottom are the so-called "untouchables," who numbered about sixty million in 1919. The name of this depressed class derives from the fact that Hindus of the higher castes believe that the touch of the members of this class pollutes food and water and that even their shadow is polluting. As outcasts, the untouchables may not draw water from the village wells, enter the temples, or live in the same section of the village as the higher castes.

This teeming continent with its conflicting religions and customs was "the brightest jewel in the British crown." Having originally entered India for trade alone, the British succeeded in establishing their sovereignty in the eighteenth and nineteenth centuries. After the development of power machinery it became Britain's greatest overseas market. More than this, it was a highly important source of products, particularly raw materials, for which Britain had a special need. The function of the British, according to Indian patriots, was primarily economic exploitation. The British in turn pointed to the fact that they had given the people many of the blessings of Western civilization, including roads, railroads, schools, better sanitation, and methods for the prevention of disease; that they had diminished child marriages and had abolished such customs as that by which widows permitted themselves to be burned alive on the funeral pyres of their husbands. Actually the British contributed but little toward raising the standard of living and not much more toward wiping out illiteracy. According to the census of 1921 only 7 per cent of the population was literate in the vernaculars and only 1 per cent was literate in English. In spite of criticism the British were determined to hold India. In 1922 Lloyd George said in the House of Commons: "One thing we must make clear, that Great Britain will in no circumstances relinquish her responsibility to India. We owe this not only to the people of this country, though they have made great sacrifices for India, but we owe it to the people of India as a whole. . . . If Great Britain withdrew her strong hand, nothing would ensue except division, strife, conflict, and anarchy." To this speech a moderate member of the Delhi Legislative Assembly replied in part: "His statement that the British came here with a view to draw Indians out of the state of anarchy is incorrect. The less said about the methods of the acquisition of India by Great Britain, the better."

Under the aegis of the British a number of steps had been taken in the direction of constitutionalism but there was no popular participation in the government. Meanwhile a sentiment of common nationality had been growing up among the members of the educated class, a class that was increasing in both numbers and influence. As early as 1885 some of their representatives had organized the Indian National Congress which stood for increasing participation of the people in the government. At first the demands of the Congress were amazingly moderate, but as a result of World War I they became more pointed and inclusive. As their part of the war effort British India and the Indian States provided a million and a half men for military service and contributed large sums toward defraying the expenses of the war which was fought "to make the world safe for democracy." This slogan, together with the Allied cry that subject nations must be free, could not fail to kindle aspirations for liberty and self-government. "Attention is repeatedly being called to the fact," the secretary of state for India reported, "that in Europe Britain is fighting on the side of liberty, and it is urged that Britain cannot deny to the people of India that for which she is herself fighting in Europe and in the fight for which she has been helped by Indian blood and treasure." In 1916 the Indian National Congress and the All-India Moslem League held a combined meeting at which the demand for home rule was proclaimed. Thus at a critical moment Great Britain was suddenly confronted by nationalist demands which threatened to interfere with the prosecution of the war. To save the situation Mr. Montagu, the secretary of state for India, formally declared in 1917 that the basic aim of British policy in India would be "the development of self-governing institutions with a view to progressive realization of responsible government."

When the war ended, the people of India believed that the time had come for them to have *Swaraj* (home rule) in fulfillment of the proclamation of 1917. This desire for home rule was strengthened by Indian soldiers returning from the front to the remotest villages with ideas of liberty and self-determination. Everywhere the educated class and the masses too were stirred by new hopes as never before. But when the months passed and nothing was done to fulfill their hopes and desires, signs of unrest began to multiply. Realizing the increasing difficulty of ruling India without support of popular opinion, the British in 1919 sought to placate Indian sentiment with the so-called Government of India Act which gave the people an increased share in the government. First of all, certain matters, including agriculture, education, public health, and public works were put under the control of Provincial Councils. On the other hand, control of finance and the police remained in the hands of the British governor of each province, thus effectually preventing the inauguration of widespread reforms. This system of divided rule was known as "dyarchy." In the second place, the Act provided for an Indian legislative assembly with power to debate but not to legislate; but the central power remained with the British. The entire scheme was designed only for British India, the Indian States remaining under the despotic rule of the native princes.

The British were certain that the Act would satisfy the people of India, but such cheerful expectations were rudely disappointed. Stirred to the depths, the Indians refused to be satisfied with anything short of complete home rule. There were some few, it is true, who urged that the reforms be accepted, but the majority in the National Congress denounced them as inadequate. It was pointed out that while native Indians were permitted to exercise minor powers of administration in the provinces, the control of all important functions of government still remained with the British. In certain parts of India disappointment was so great that it caused minor uprisings. To prevent further outbreaks the British passed the so-called Rowlatt Bill, which empowered the police to arrest and imprison without formal trial any person suspected of antigovernment activities. This law, in addition to filling the jails with thousands of Nationalists, appeared to give the lie to Mr. Montagu's proclamation of 1917. In protest the Congress called for cessation of all work for a day. This demonstration, intended to be entirely in the nature of a peaceful protest, took the form of rioting in some towns. When a large crowd which had gathered in the public square at Amritsar in the Punjab refused to disperse, General Reginald Dyer, British brigade commander, ordered his soldiers to fire on the crowd. Estimates of the number of dead and wounded vary, the more moderate being about 400 killed and 1200 wounded. Nor did General Dyer stop at this. He also issued the "crawling order" which required all Indians to pass the scene of the shooting on their hands and knees. This was deliberately devised to humiliate a proud and sensitive people.

The "Amritsar massacre" had widespread repercussions, but perhaps the most far-reaching result for the future of India was that it made a confirmed Nationalist of that strange personality, Mohandas K. Gandhi, who had previously been a loyal British subject. "In as much as one man in the Punjab was made to crawl on his belly," he stated, "the whole of India crawled on her belly, and if we are worthy sons and daughters of India we should be pledged to remove these wrongs." Born in India in 1869 as the son of a Hindu, though not of the priestly class, he went to London in 1888 to study law and while he was there spent much time studying Christianity and Western civilization. Upon his return to India in 1893 he left almost immediately for South Africa, where he worked for twenty-one years to ameliorate the conditions under which his countrymen were living in that country. When the Boer War broke out in 1899, he organized the Indian Ambulance Corps which by its service sought to demonstrate to the British the loyalty of the Indian community. He was no less active during World War I. His pacifist inclinations notwithstanding, he went so far as to participate in a recruiting campaign for the Allied cause. It was his fervent hope that the British would recognize the Indians' loyalty during the war and their very material sacrifices of men and money. But the severity with which expressions of native aspirations were repressed, caused him to cast his lot with the Nationalists. The man who had said in 1915, "The British Empire has certain ideals with which I have fallen in love," stated in 1921: "Experience has made me wiser. . . . I consider the existing system of government to be wholly bad and requiring special effort to end or amend it."

National aspirations found in Mr. Gandhi a powerful if somewhat singular champion. The austere simplicity of his life—for he lived largely on goat's milk—and his utter sincerity caused him to be revered as deity and earned for him the title of Mahatma or Great Soul. The means he advocated for attaining liberty and independence were a curious blend of religious idealism and political expediency. He would break British power in India and achieve *Swaraj* (home rule), not by force but by nonviolent means. His prescription was "passive noncooperation." In other words, what he preached with the zeal of a convert was "a peaceful general strike of the whole people." In this way, he said, "you can gain *Swaraj* in the course of a year." He cautioned, however, that the movement could be successful only if all violence and bitterness were eschewed. First of all, laborers were to refuse to work for foreign employers. British courts were to be boycotted by both lawyers and litigants. Students were to leave all schools and colleges that were owned, aided, or controlled by the British government. All honors and titles that had been conferred by the British were to be renounced. What was more important, merchants, traders, and consumers were asked to join in a boycott of British goods, particularly of cotton cloth. In place of the cotton cloth from England *khaddar* or homespun was to be used. Wearing foreign cloth was denounced as a sin, and homespun was declared the only possible dress for patriots. So that sufficient homespun would be available Gandhi sought to revive the art of spinning and weaving at home which had once been nearly universal in India. During the second year of the struggle, increased emphasis was put upon the boycott of British goods. Gandhi was convinced that if the people could make the rule of India unprofitable for the British, the latter would withdraw. Finally, he urged his followers not to pay taxes or obey the laws.

At first noncooperation was confined to only a few but it was soon adopted by the Indian National Congress as a national movement. Thereafter it spread beyond all expectations. By advocating the removal of "untouchability" Gandhi gained the support of the sixty million untouchables. He went so far as to state that India would not deserve freedom until untouchability was abolished. He even succeeded for the time being in gaining the support of the Moslems for his movement. The Moslems at first favored a resort to force but were finally persuaded to try the nonviolent method. Thus the movement became an affair of the masses rather than of a few thousand intellectuals and they responded in a manner that threw the authorities into panic. Sir Michael O'Dwyer, British governor of Bombay, said, "Our margin of safety in India was never very large and in these days . . . it has been reduced almost to the vanishing point."

As the months passed, however, the movement began to lose its nonviolent character. In some of the outlying districts various local disorders and uprisings took place. These were followed in November, 1921, by riots in Bombay in which fifty-three persons were killed and four hundred wounded. Gandhi was horrified. When other riots followed with resulting bloodshed, he denounced the violence and sought to expiate it by fasting and prayer. This apparent rift in the movement caused the British to strike hard. In March, 1922, Gandhi was arrested and sentenced to six years' imprisonment for "creating disaffection." Without the driving power of Gandhi, the movement gradually lost its force and was finally abandoned.[3]

During the succeeding years the resentment against the British continued to gain strength. In an effort to improve relations a commission, called the Simon Commission after its chairman, Sir John Simon, was appointed in 1927 to inquire into a revision of the Indian constitution. In choosing the members of the commission the British committed the blunder of not including an Indian, and this served to fan the embers of discontent to a white heat. In 1928 at the meeting of the All-Indian Congress the nationalist feeling vented itself in a demand for full Dominion status. Sweeping concessions on the part of the British might have eased the strain, but they were not ready to take such a step. At this point Gandhi, who after his release had seemingly vanished from politics, once more became the leader of his people. He introduced a resolution demanding full independence at the meeting of the All-India Congress during the last days of 1929. The Congress not only ratified his resolution but also decided to support it with an elaborate plan of "civil disobedience."

This campaign was actively launched in April of 1930 when Gandhi violated the British salt monopoly by taking salt water from the sea to his bungalow, after which he stated that workers

[3] On the advent to power of the Labor government and prime minister Ramsay MacDonald in 1924 Mahatma Gandhi, who became seriously ill in prison, was released.

should everywhere manufacture salt and boycott British goods, particularly cotton cloth. Thousands of members of the All-India Congress joined at once. As a result British imports to India declined sharply, with cotton goods registering an especially heavy drop. Gandhi had again admonished his followers that they should not resort to violence; but nevertheless there were scores of outbreaks in widely separated regions, involving heavy destruction of property and the loss of many lives.

The government responded by arresting all those who were inciting others to participate in the campaign of civil disobedience. Soon the prisons were filled to capacity. Among those arrested were two sons of the Mahatma and also Pandit Jawaharlal Nehru, the president of the All-India Congress. Finally Gandhi himself was arrested. After this the "civil disobedience" movement gradually ebbed. First of all, it lacked the cohesive strength of the earlier noncooperation movement. This time the Moslems did not give their support. Second, many of the Hindus gradually dissociated themselves from the movement for various reasons. Third, Gandhi's enthusiasm for "civil disobedience" cooled when the All-India Congress failed to support his demand that every member spin a specified amount of cotton yarn each year.

Finally in 1935 the British parliament passed the India Act, which was intended to give India political freedom. The new constitution contained two major provisions. The first granted a considerable measure of popular rule to the eleven provinces into which British India was divided; the franchise was thus extended to approximately forty million adults, including five million women. The other major part provided for the establishment of a federal or national legislature of two houses, the membership of both to be drawn from the provinces of British India and from the native states. While the British argued that the constitution represented a long step toward independence, the Nationalists regarded it as "an unwelcome British-made constitution." Jawaharlal Nehru stated that it was the primary purpose of the constitution "to keep British imperialism in India intact." On the whole, the Nationalists claimed that such concessions as the British had made were only in trivial matters. In support of this contention they pointed to the fact that such phases of government as the police and the civil service, foreign affairs, railways and defense, currency and exchange, and banking and tariffs were still in British hands. When the constitution was put in effect in 1938, the All-India Congress announced that it would have nothing to do with it. Only after much urging on the part of Gandhi did the Congress agree to accept the measures dealing with self-government of the provinces.

When World War II broke out, the All-India Congress issued a declaration which stated that "while India's sympathy is entirely on the side of democracy and freedom, she is not able to associate herself with the present war when freedom is denied her." The Congress did, however, agree to defer final decision "to allow full elucidation of the issues on the present and future position of India." It was a golden opportunity for the British to win the support of India's millions in the war effort by making concessions to nationalist feeling. The Labor and Liberal press, in fact, urged the government to declare its aims with regard to India. For years before the war the most scathing denunciations of Nazi aggression had come from India, and it would have been easy to gain her wholehearted support. But Lord Linlithgow, the Governor-General, merely reiterated previous statements that the goal of British policy was that "India may attain due place among the Dominions." Even more blunt was the Marquess of Zetland, secretary of state for India, when he declared that greater independence was not in the best interests of the people and urged them to achieve agreement among themselves before asking for full independence. Later pronouncements of the British failed to impress the Nationalists.

STRIFE-RENT CHINA

China is a geographical term which embraces a land mass of some four million square miles, an area considerably larger than Europe. Besides China proper (the eighteen provinces south of the Great Wall) it includes Manchuria, Mongolia, Sin-kiang, and Tibet. There is no accurate census of the population for the period between World War I and World War II. Competent authorities have accepted the round figure of 400 million for the years immediately following World War I. In 1929 the Chinese Maritime Customs estimated the population, including Manchuria, at 438,933,373. The fact that the Chinese form so large a part of the human race has given rise to the expression, "Of every five persons in the world one is a Chinese."

The history of China during more than half a century before World War I is largely a story of exploitation by the Western powers and Japan. From the early years of the nineteenth century when its commercial possibilities became apparent to Western traders, the governments of Europe vied with one another in entrenching themselves so that they could ruthlessly exploit the unwieldy colossus of

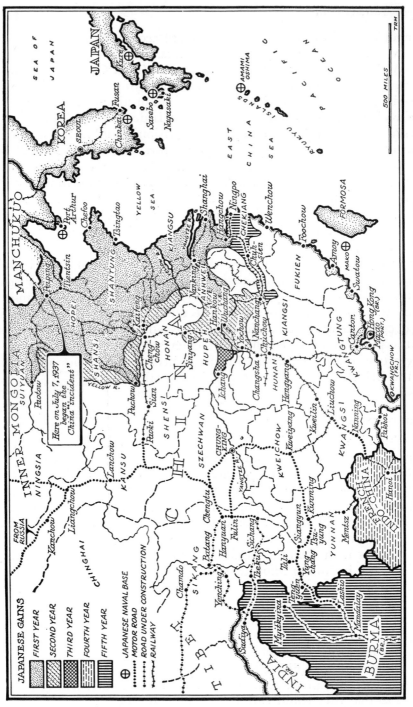

JAPANESE EXPANSION ON THE CONTINENT OF ASIA

the Orient. The method of establishing themselves on Chinese soil was to extract under various pretexts special rights and privileges from the Chinese government. This was possible because China's army was weak, the control of the government over the vast domain was loose, and the country was torn by internal dissension. Every special right or privilege which foreign governments succeeded in acquiring further limited the authority and power of the Chinese government. More than this, every concession wrung from China by one of the powers was shared by the others. Among the rights obtained by Europeans—and shared in part by citizens of the United States—were: (1) the right of extraterritoriality, i.e., of entire freedom from Chinese law; (2) the right of living in special areas reserved for foreign residents and administered by their own municipal or consular officers; (3) the right to regulate the customs duties of China and thus favor their imports into China; (4) the right to administer certain parts of China, usually lands and ports situated at strategic points along the coast, under the guise of "leasing" them; (5) the right of holding a practical monopoly of trade and the natural wealth in certain districts known as "spheres of interest" or "spheres of influence."

Until the decade of the nineties, when Japan and Germany began to extend their influence, the leaders in the acquisition of special privileges were Great Britain, France, and Russia. Britain was the first to recognize in China a vast field of opportunity for its merchants. One of the principal items in its profitable trade was Indian opium. When the Chinese emperor, alarmed at the ravages caused by the drug, tried to stop the trade about 1840, he precipitated the first Opium War,[4] which ended in the treaty of Nanking (1842) whereby the island of Hong Kong became a British Crown Colony and five Chinese ports were opened to foreign trade. In 1843 Great Britain imposed on China the General Regulations of Trade which gave the British the privilege of extraterritoriality.

Other nations were not slow to take advantage of the opportunity. In 1844 the United States and France concluded treaties with

[4] A later attempt of the Chinese to restrict the sale of opium brought on the second Opium War in 1857.

JAPANESE EXPANSION ON THE CONTINENT OF ASIA. *The map covers the period from the clash of Chinese and Japanese troops near Peiping on July 7, 1937, until the summer of 1942.*

China which conceded the right of their nationals to be tried before their own consuls. During the period from 1850 to 1864 various disturbances gave the powers a pretext for taking over the administration of the tariff system, thus further curtailing China's sovereignty. This was to be a temporary measure but it was continued indefinitely. The British collected the duties and, after the interest due on loans was deducted, turned the remainder over to the Chinese government.

Between 1860 and 1895 China was continually being forced by war or by the threat of war to surrender larger or smaller districts to the powers, who saw in their possession opportunities for trade expansion or political aggrandizement. In 1860 Russia demanded and received a strip of territory running southward toward Korea on which it built the seaport of Vladivostok, later to become the terminus of the trans-Siberian railway. In 1862 the Chinese were persuaded to renounce their rights in Burma, and it was annexed by the British in 1866. Shortly before the end of the century came the Sino-Japanese war (1894–1895), after which China was compelled to acknowledge the independence of Korea and to cede to Japan the island of Formosa. Soon afterward the scramble began to "lease" ports and strategic points along the coast. In 1898 Germany "leased" Kiaochow Bay after the murder of two German missionaries; and Great Britain, France, and Russia also managed to "lease" strategic points. Not content with the concessions they had gained, the powers began to exert pressure on the Chinese as a means of acquiring "spheres of influence," which often involved large areas with millions of inhabitants. That the acquisition of such "spheres" was highly detrimental to China's economic development, keeping it in a state of chronic insolvency, was of little concern to the imperialist powers; in fact, they derived further advantages from making loans to the government. In order to obtain the loans, China had to pledge its forests, mines, and other sources of natural wealth. This intrusion helped bring on the Boxer uprising of 1899–1900, which caused the United States, Britain, Germany, France, Russia, and Japan to send troops to China. It was another opportunity to exact further concessions.

Thus, at the opening of the twentieth century, the Chinese found themselves with their best ports "leased" to or controlled by foreigners, their coastal and inland trade dominated by foreigners, their customs duties and other revenues pledged to foreigners. Almost two thirds of their country had been marked out in "spheres of influence," and in fourteen of the principal ports foreign settlements had been established that were not subject to Chinese law. Under extraterritoriality foreigners could conduct themselves as they pleased without any recourse on the part of the Chinese government. In short, the history of China's foreign relations from 1842 to 1900 is a story of gradual loss of independence and the establishment of an increasing control over many phases of activity.

China's humiliation in the war of 1894–1895 convinced many of the educated Chinese that reform was imperative if the nation were to survive at all. The leader of the reform movement was Dr. Sun Yat-sen who earned for himself the title of "Father of the Chinese Revolution." A reformer from youth, he had when hardly more than a boy protested against child-selling, infanticide, concubinage, foot-binding, idol-worship, and other practices. Later when he realized that thorough-going reform was impossible under the Manchu dynasty, he became a revolutionary. Leaving a promising career as a surgeon, he carried on revolutionary propaganda among students and soldiers. In many parts of China he organized secret groups who worked for the overthrow of the Manchu rulers. "The Chinese have no real government," he said in *The Solution of the Chinese Question,* published in 1904; "a new government, an enlightened and progressive government, must be substituted for the old one." The result of his activities was that in 1911 antidynastic riots broke out which soon grew to the magnitude of revolution. Early in 1912 the dynasty fell and China was proclaimed a republic.[5] Chosen as first president, Dr. Sun in the interests of peace and unity yielded the presidency to Yuan Shih-kai, a well-known general who had strong forces at his disposal but who was a reactionary in politics. In 1913 Yuan Shih-kai, declaring that the people were not ready for republican government, dissolved the Assembly. For the next three years he ruled as virtual dictator until his death in 1916. During the following decade the military governors whom he had appointed administered the provinces as independent lords while affairs as a whole were in a state of chaos.

In 1917 China, upon invitation of the Allies, joined in the war against the Central Powers. Internal conditions were such that China could take no active part in the struggle, but a work force of about 175,000 was recruited for service behind the lines in France. At the end of the war delegations representing both the Peking and the Canton governments laid their grievances before the Peace Conference at Paris and asked for the abolition of extraterritoriality,

[5] In 1912 Sun Yat-sen's party adopted the name of Kuomintang or National People's Party.

cancellation of "spheres of influence," postal and tariff autonomy, and the restoration of all "leased" territories. The conference gave the delegates but little satisfaction. After permitting Japan to retain the province of Shantung, it ruled that the other questions did not fall within its jurisdiction. So great was the disappointment of the Chinese representatives that they refused to sign the Treaty of Versailles. China, did, however, succeed in making some gains. In the separate treaty between China and Germany it was specified that the German extraterritorial privileges were canceled. Further progress was made at the Washington Arms Conference (1921), at which Japan was induced to restore Shantung. It was also agreed that on January 1, 1923, foreign postal agencies in China were to be abolished. Finally, nine powers signed a treaty pledging themselves to respect the political, administrative, and territorial sovereignty of China.

Meanwhile Dr. Sun Yat-sen was not inactive. Having achieved the overthrow of the Manchus he worked for reform and the end of imperialism. Time and again he reiterated his determination to have all unequal treaties abolished. It was a bitter disappointment to him that the Peace Conference had not taken steps in this direction. "After the war," he said, "England, France, and Italy recognized that Wilson's proposals for the liberation of peoples were too much at variance with the designs of imperialism, so when it came to the time for discussing peace they used all kinds of methods to sidetrack Wilson's proposals." Far from discouraging him, however, the disappointment served to steel his will and fortify his courage. In 1918 he had founded at Canton what was to become the Nationalist government, built around the Kuomintang. He had hoped to receive the support of such western democracies as Great Britain and the United States in laying the foundations for a democratic state. When this was not forthcoming, he turned to Soviet Russia, which was regarded with favor in China because it was ready to surrender its special privileges. The Russians were delighted at having the opportunity of cooperating with China against the "imperialist nations." Early in 1923 emissaries conferred with Sun Yat-sen and in the following year a treaty was signed whereby in return for the relinquishment of extraterritorial rights Russia obtained diplomatic recognition and a renewal of trade relations. Sun Yat-sen then opened the ranks of the Kuomintang to the communists upon the promise of the Russians not to introduce the Russian brand of communism into China. The following year the Cantonese government established a military academy, staffed by Russian officers, as the first move in the building of a large Chinese army. In March, 1925, Sun Yat-sen died of cancer.

During his lifetime Dr. Sun Yat-sen had had considerable difficulty in keeping the eyes of his followers upon the goal of freedom and independence and had often found questions of practical administration very trying. But after his death men forgot his unpracticability and concentrated on his ideas and idealism. A patriotic cult, akin to a religion, grew up about his memory. He became the idealized and idolized symbol of China's freedom, his writings became the Bible of the nationalist movement, and his birthday and deathday were made patriotic holidays.

The leadership in the struggle for freedom and independence was assumed by one of his disciples, General Chiang Kai-shek. In 1926, after organizing a formidable army of soldiers and propagandists at Canton, he began a military campaign to bring all China under the control of the Kuomintang. Month after month the powerful revolutionary army marched northward, overwhelming all opposition. As the force neared the Great Wall, a rift developed in the Kuomintang between the right and the left over the role of the Russian advisers. The right, and particularly the bankers who were financing the expedition, objected to the growing influence of the communists. Chiang, who needed the support of the bankers, decided to take the middle-class road to national salvation. Halting the northern advance, he purged the Kuomintang of the radical elements and set up a conservative government at Nanking.

Once again the Chinese were split into factions. This time it was the communists against the nationalists. The communist leaders sponsored the ideals of Bolshevism but probably received no support from Russia. The seeds they sowed found fertile soil among the peasants, most of whom were staggering under a heavy burden of taxation. In some districts communist teachings provoked what was in essence a peasants' revolt, with peasant mobs terrifying the landlords and dealing summarily with some. Mounting industrial unrest also prepared the ground for the growth of communist ideas among the working classes. To both the industrial workers and the peasants the communists held out hope of a better life. Where they were weak they were regarded as "Red bandits"; but where they were strong they made a clean sweep of the old order and set up a sovietized regime backed by a Red army. Their hold on the masses increased until by 1934 it extended over about one sixth of the country, including some of the richest parts of central China. Thus the communists existed as a state within a state. Although the military equipment of the nationalist government was vastly superior to that of the proletarian bands, the latter offered stubborn resistance. Compelled to retreat in 1934 and 1935, they made a fresh stand in the mountains of the northwest.

Despite the fact that the period from 1928 to 1937 was one of civil war and internal dissension, considerable progress was made toward the establishment of a more stable regime. The central figure in this development was Chiang Kai-shek. He and his armies were the chief buttress of the nationalist government. He was variously commander in chief of the armed forces, chairman of the executive committee of the Kuomintang, and president of the government, and at times filled several cabinet posts concurrently. But whatever positions he held, he was always the dominant personality. His government was the focus around which the antipodal forces of China found some degree of stabilization. As early as 1927 he strengthened his hold on the Kuomintang by marrying Mei Ling Soong, a sister of Madame Sun Yat-sen and member of the influential Soong family. Having been educated at Wellesley College in the United States, she shared her husband's interest in Western civilization. On their wedding day Chiang declared: "From now on we two are determined to exert our utmost for the cause of the Chinese Revolution." During the succeeding years Madame Chiang did help her husband bear the tremendous responsibility of the revolution.

Such success as the nationalist government enjoyed gave its representatives courage at various international conferences to demand the abrogation of all special privileges and grants in China. The result was that China had made some progress toward emancipation by 1929. In that year the Belgians consented to the cancellation of the Tientsin concession, and the British returned their Chinkiang concession to Chinese administration and the next year surrendered Amoy. Having obtained the formal assent of most powers to the establishment of tariff autonomy, the government issued its own schedule of duties in 1929. It also took a definite step toward the abolition of extraterritoriality by issuing the following edict: "For the purpose of restoring her jurisdictional sovereignty, it is hereby decided and declared that on and after January 1, 1930, all foreign nationals in the territory of China who are now enjoying extraterritorial privileges shall abide by the laws, ordinances, and regulations duly promulgated by the central and local governments in China." For a time it appeared as if a serious crisis would develop at the opening of the year 1930, but the British Foreign Office came forward with an acceptable suggestion. In place of an immediate change they proposed a period of experimentation to find the proper substitute for the extraterritorial courts which were theoretically abolished. During the provisional period the courts were to function as before. Thus the crisis was avoided but the problem remained unsolved.

The principal aims of the government were to extend its control over larger areas, to achieve uniformity of administrative structure, and to modernize the country. The last offered unlimited opportunities. Although it is easy to exaggerate the progress that was made, there were advances in many fields. One of the more important was the improvement of transportation and communication. The government began to build railroads into the hinterland for both strategic and economic purposes. Besides increasing trade these railroads were to become important factors in resistance to Japanese invasion. At the same time, the government was instrumental in expanding both heavy and light industry.

The government also gave technical instruction to farmers for the purpose of raising the productivity of the soil, special care being given to the promotion of the cotton and silk industries. A painstaking investigation of the school situation was also made in the interests of better education, with the result that more schools were opened and those that existed were given better equipment. Some idea of the spread of primary and secondary education may be gained from the fact that the number of children attending school increased from three million in 1921 to eleven million in 1934. The government, too, did much to promote better health and sanitation. Schools of modern medicine were organized and country-wide campaigns were inaugurated for the control of disease. In short, the government greatly changed the face of China. On the other hand, there were complaints about the arbitrary methods of the government. Some writers also painted a picture of widespread graft and corruption in certain circles.

Unfortunately much that the enterprise of the government constructed was subsequently ruined by the invading hordes of Japanese. The Japanese imperialists and militarists, having long planned to dominate China, were not pleased to see her making strides in the direction of unification and modernization. They realized that if China ever attained the status of a strong, well knit nation possessing an army and navy commensurate with the size of its population and territorial greatness, Japan would have to release its hold on the continent of Asia. In 1931 the Japanese invaded Manchuria to prevent this area from being absorbed by the nationalist government.

China's stubborn resistance provoked the Japanese into acts of wanton destruction. Callously they swept aside all international rules of warfare and in their endeavor to spread terror pillaged the cities, devastated large areas of land, and deliberately slaughtered their prisoners of war. Generalissimo Chiang's appeal to the League of Nations evoked sympathy for China's sad plight but did not impel the European powers to send organized help. China had to stand alone against the barbarous aggressor. As the war rolled along its blood-drenched path, the Japanese armies captured large areas but they could not crush the indomitable spirit of the Chinese. Not until after the attack on Pearl Harbor drew the United States into World War II did China receive substantial aid. Then arms and equipment began to flow into China for the struggle against Japan.

ᛈ

IMPERIALIST JAPAN

In 1914 the Japanese Empire consisted, first of all, of Japan proper, a long chain of islands extending from northeast to southwest along the eastern coast of the continent of Asia. In this chain there are four main islands and hundreds of smaller ones. The total area of Japan proper is 147,707 square miles, somewhat less than that of California. In addition there were Korea, Formosa, the Pescadores, Japanese Sakhalin (Karafuto), and the leased Liaotung Peninsula. That Japan proper is not rich in natural resources is indicated by the fact that 55 per cent of the imports were raw materials. For instance, all the raw cotton, aluminum, wool, and rubber, and almost all the lead, zinc, iron ore, petroleum, and tin used in Japanese industry was brought in from the outside. Since the country is largely mountainous, only about 17 per cent of the land was being cultivated. The population per square mile of tillable land in 1930 was 2774 compared with 2170 in Great Britain, 806 in Germany, and 229 in the United States. Moreover, the Japanese were a prolific people, the population having increased from thirty-three million in 1872 to over sixty-four million in 1930. Though there was some emigration, the number of emigrants was not large. The proletarian found the customs and climate of his home islands so congenial that he had little desire to settle abroad.

In form the government during the period between the two Great Wars was a constitutional monarchy. The constitution, promulgated by the emperor in 1889, provided for a parliament or Imperial Diet consisting of two houses, a House of Peers and a House of Representatives. The former included, among others, the princes of the blood, marquises, counts, viscounts, and barons, persons nominated by the emperor for meritorious services to the state, and four members of the Imperial Academy of Sciences. The members of the House of Representatives were elected by a suffrage based on the payment of taxes, but in May, 1925, a law was passed which provided for general manhood suffrage.[6] In the constitution the legislative prerogatives of the Diet were carefully outlined. While the emperor convoked, opened, closed, and prorogued the Diet, his ordinances could not "alter any of the existing laws." Moreover, imperial ordinances issued by the emperor at a time when the Diet was not in session were subject to approval by it. The emperor occupied a unique position in the system. He was the head of the state in an absolutely unconditional sense. Much is made by Japanese writers of the fact that the constitution was not forced upon him but was a gift to his people. "The adoption of the constitutional system," one Japanese writer stated,[7] "should not be associated with any idea of restricting the Tennō's (emperor's) sovereignty, nor be understood as accepting the principle of limited monarchy as in the West . . . the Tennō constitutes the immovable central authority and fountainhead of all matters, political, military, economic, religious, festival, moral, etc."

Thus the emperor stood over and above the constitution as heaven is above the earth and from him all authority emanated. He did not, however, participate actively in politics. Hence Japan was ruled, not by the emperor but in the name of the emperor. His unique position derived in large part from the myths of his divine origin. These myths stated that he is descended from the sun goddess, Amaterasu-o-mikami. The first emperor was her grandson Jimmu, who is supposed to have reigned about 660 b.c. and from whom the recent emperors were said to have descended in unbroken succession. Accordingly the Japanese called their emperor "Tennō" which means "the heavenly king." Article III of the constitution declared him to be "sacred and inviolable," but the classical statement is that of Prince Ito who wrote in his *Commentaries:* "The emperor is heaven-descended, divine and sacred." This doctrine, repeated again and again in official statements, was inculcated in the minds of Japanese youth from elementary school to university. Philosophers and writers preached it as a religion, and radio, cinema, and the theater broadcast it to the people. How firmly the tradition took hold of popular imagination was demonstrated by the

[6] The law of 1925 fixed the number of representatives at 466.
[7] *Cultural Nippon,* vol. 6 (1938), p. 41.

prohibition against looking upon him from an elevated position and the refusal to permit his picture to be printed on postage stamps where ordinary fingers could pollute the divine profile.[8] The myth was also circulated that one must not look at his face lest one be blinded.

The principal religions of Japan are Shintoism and Buddhism. Christianity made steady progress during the nineteenth century, but baptized Christians of all denominations do not total 1 per cent of the population. It is Shintoism, which exists in two forms, secular and theological, that has the largest number of followers; in fact, all Japanese patriots are believers in secular Shintoism, though they are Buddhists or even Christians. Secular Shintoism was encouraged by the state as a means of cultivating patriotism through ancestor worship and the veneration of national heroes. As a cult of patriotism it emphasizes particularly the paying of homage to the former emperors of Japan and their "divine ancestress," Amaterasu. It also inculcates reverence for all soldiers killed in battle. These were periodically deified by the emperor in special ceremonies. The number of these "gods" in the Japanese pantheon was about eighty million. Since ancestor worship has a place in Buddhism, secular Shinto is a feasible arrangement for Buddhists, but for Christians it was more difficult. Nevertheless, Christians did practice it. The Reverend Shigeichi Miyazaki, former secretary of the Japan Council of Christian Churches, stated: "If Jesus, who made the pilgrimage to the Jewish temple at Jerusalem every year, had happened to live in Japan, He would have made the yearly pilgrimage to the Grand Shrine of Ise as His Heavenly Father's abode." [9] It was at Ise that Amaterasu was enshrined.

Before a United States naval squadron commanded by Commodore Perry opened the country to foreign intercourse in 1853, Japan had for more than two centuries been cut off from contact with other nations. It did not possess even the beginnings of Western science. Soon afterward the government embarked on a policy of Westernization. The decision to remake the country after the Western pattern was not adopted by the people but by a small number of statesmen who saw in this step the only means of preserving Japanese sovereignty. Almost at once after Japan was "opened," there were demands for concessions and extraterritorial rights. Recognizing that

[8] Some Japanese writers went so far as to state that the people themselves, as the descendants of Amaterasu, partook of this divinity. "From the fact of the divine descent of the Japanese people," the Japanese scholar Hirata stated, "proceeds their immeasurable superiority to the natives of other countries in courage and intelligence."
[9] *New Republic,* vol. 93 (1937), p. 39.

military and naval strength was the only evidence that would demonstrate Japan's equality with Western nations the government proceeded to build an army and a navy on the Western model. Three decades later the country possessed a powerful fleet manned by expert seamen, and a large military force equipped with the best modern weapons. In addition, it had a constitution and an administration organized on Western patterns, a postal system that reached the remotest village, a network of railway and telegraph lines, and industries and mines in which the latest Western techniques were used. Furthermore, Japan had competent representatives at foreign courts, a large merchant marine on the world's oceans, and an extensive system of education at home. Even Western styles of clothing had become the vogue in court circles. All this was achieved without violation of national feeling.

Having copied Europe in other ways, the Japanese also began to dream grandiose dreams of empire. The natural and logical outlet for their imperialist ambitions was China. Since the European powers had enriched themselves at China's expense, why should Japan not do the same thing? Moreover, the Korean Peninsula, with an area of 80,000 square miles, stretched invitingly toward Japan. It was not difficult for the Japanese to pick a quarrel with China over Korea. When the Sino-Japanese war broke out in 1894, everyone outside Japan believed that China would find little difficulty in defeating so small an antagonist. But the reverse happened. China went down like a row of ninepins, giving Japan a commanding position among the imperialist powers. In the Treaty of Shimonoseki (April 17, 1895) China recognized the full and complete independence of Korea, a euphemism for surrendering it to Japanese hegemony.[10] China further ceded the island of Formosa with its rich mineral deposits, and the Liaotung Peninsula with Port Arthur. But Japan was unable to retain this substantial footing on the mainland. Her imperialist and military surge alarmed Russia, France, and Germany and caused them to appear as the champions of China's integrity. The pressure which the three European nations exerted forced Japan to relinquish the Liaotung Peninsula. Not long thereafter the Russians, who had been seeking an ice-free port, obtained a lease of Port Arthur for twenty-five years (1898), together with a concession to build a railway through the peninsula.

The check upon Japanese ambitions, however, was only temporary. Russia's acquisition of the very territory the three powers had denied to Japan embittered the Japanese and spurred them on

[10] Korea was annexed outright by Japan in 1910.

to greater activity in the development of military and naval power. Nor did they overlook diplomacy. In 1902 they concluded an alliance with Britain which, though not specifically directed at Russia, provided for British neutrality in the event of conflict. When the Japanese were ready, it was easy to find a cause for war. This time the world took them more seriously, but the general opinion still was that an Asiatic people would stand little chance of victory in the fight against the tsarist military forces. Japanese speed and strategy, combined with Russian weakness, gave the Asiatics a quick victory. By the terms of the Treaty of Portsmouth (1905) Russia agreed to transfer to Japan "with the consent of China," the lease on the Liaotung Peninsula and Port Arthur. This consent was obtained the same year in a treaty between China and Japan. The Treaty of Portsmouth also gave Japan all the island of Sakhalin south of the 50th parallel, a land area of about 14,000 square miles. The acquisition of these large areas still did not satisfy the Japanese appetite. In 1910 the government openly annexed Korea, thus putting an end to China's hopes in that quarter.

From the time of the Russo-Japanese War the development of Japan followed an unbroken upward curve. She steadily strengthened herself not only in land and sea armaments but also by the vigor of her commercial enterprise. Although the country remained essentially agricultural, the government promoted the development of manufacturing industries, first as a means of defense against the Western nations and later as the most promising solution of the problem presented by a rapidly growing population. Such towns as Tokyo, Yokohama, Osaka, Kobe, and Nagoya became great industrial centers which by virtue of the plentiful supply of cheap labor enabled Japan to enter into the competition for certain world markets.

When the First World War opened, Japan quickly seized the opportunity to strengthen her position in the Far East. Casting her lot with Britain and France, she proceeded to drive the Germans out of Shantung and to occupy the leased territory, taking over Germany's railroads, mines, etc. against the protests of the Chinese. In 1915 she presented the famous Twenty-one Demands that would virtually have converted China into a Japanese colony. Since the Peking government was in no condition to offer resistance and the Western powers were too busy with their own affairs to give China any support, General Yuan Shih-kai was compelled to accept the demands in large part.

In general, the period of the First World War was one of growing

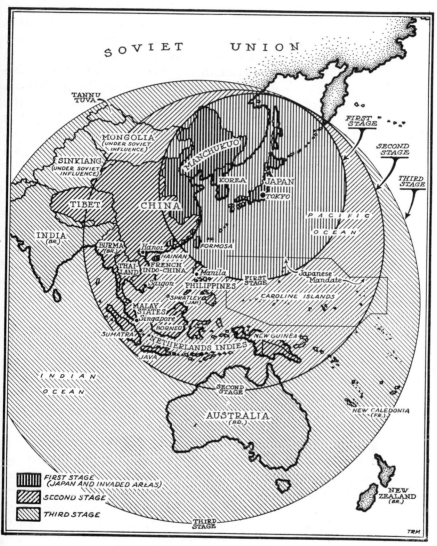

JAPAN'S AMBITIONS IN EAST ASIA

On August 1, 1940, Prince Konoye officially expressed Japan's purpose as "building Greater East Asia"; the establishment of the "co-prosperity sphere" was to go forward in three successive stages as indicated on the map.

strength. In addition to gaining territory and a preferential position in China, Japan also garnered large profits from the Asiatic trade while the European nations were locked in bloody combat. By the end of the war her prestige had increased to such an extent that she occupied a place among the Big Five who drew up the peace treaties. The Japanese delegates, however, confined their attention chiefly to securing their interests in the Far East. The result was that Japan received a considerable share of the spoils. Besides retaining possession of Shantung, she received the mandate over the Pacific islands formerly owned by the Germans comprising the Marianne, Caroline, and Marshall groups.[11] In the words of a Japanese writer: "Japan emerged from the war practically unharmed and relatively stronger. She is now the only nation in the East, Far or Near, that enjoys complete independence. She is the indisputable leader nation of the Orient. The world war offered her the opportunity of 'ten thousand' years and Japan will see to it that she will have her place in the sun. Japan will see to it that the Western nations shall not meddle in the affairs of the Far East without Japan's consent. Japan considers it her obligation to redeem the unnumbered millions of Asiatics from what might be the world's greatest tragedy—of being reduced to a perpetual servitude to the white races."[12]

Beginning with the Washington Conference (1922) Japan assumed a more peaceful and conciliatory policy. The government not only agreed to return the Shantung properties to China but during the subsequent years it showed remarkable restraint on a number of occasions when force could have been employed to the advantage of the Japanese. In 1928 Japan even became one of the original signers of the Pact of Paris for "the renunciation of war as an instrument of national policy." The building of both land and sea armaments did not, of course, cease. During the decade of the twenties the annual expenditures for armament purposes consumed from 27 to 47 per cent of the national budget. Nor was Japanese interest in China less keen. To strengthen its hold on Manchuria the government built railways, opened new industrial plants, and encouraged colonists to settle there. But the Japanese did insist that their primary interests in Manchuria were economic, not political. Soon, however, Japan's economic life was to suffer a severe blow. The crash on the New York stock exchange in the autumn of 1929 had a very serious effect

[11] The strategic value of the islands lay in their position athwart the direct sea route from the United States to the Philippines.
[12] Setsuo Uenoda, "Japan's Right to Empire," *Asia,* vol. 19 (1919), p. 1217.

because the United States had previously purchased nearly all the silk exported by Japan. During 1930 the price of raw silk dropped 50 per cent, bringing acute distress to the peasants. Export of other products also fell off sharply because of the increase of Indian, Australian, and American tariffs. As a result the export of cotton goods declined in 1930 by 34 per cent in value and 12 per cent in quantity. As a whole, export trade in 1930 was 27 per cent less than that of the preceding year.

The remedy which the Japanese adopted was a vigorous policy of imperialism. Their leaders turned to China in their search for raw materials, markets, and food supplies. The convictions of leading industrialists had been summarized some years before in the following words: "It must be remembered that Japan's material well-being is dependent upon the resources of China. Japan has no resources essential for modern industry, and China has everything that Japan needs. Japan can be a great commercial nation only by cooperation with China. Japan's commercial expansion in China, therefore, is a virtual necessity for her national existence." Consequently Manchuria took on a new importance. A land of fertile soil and excellent climate, it held out the promise of supplying Japan, among other things, with soy beans, grain, and meat. Moreover, it could furnish various raw materials, notably iron ore, coal, and petroleum, all of which were badly needed in Japan. It was also hoped that Manchuria would offer a wider market for Japanese exports. Not that the leaders had not known this earlier. What galvanized them into action was the threat to their interests in Manchuria. The rising tide of Chinese nationalism was seeking to restrict, even terminate, Japanese activities in this area. To the great annoyance of the Japanese the Nationalist government was making an effort to extend its influence in Manchuria. It was even attempting to build a railway that would compete with the Japanese railroads.

To insure an adequate supply of raw materials, to increase the export trade, to divert the attention of the hungry masses from their plight, and to prevent Manchuria from being drawn into the Chinese Nationalist orbit the government decided to send a military expedition to Manchuria. A pretext was soon established. On September 18, 1931, a small bomb exploded on or near the tracks of the Japanese-owned South Manchuria Railway near Mukden. The damage was so small that a train passed over the spot a few hours later; but on the pretext of dealing with organized groups of Chinese bandits the Japanese army began its occupation of the country. Superiority of equipment and organization made the scattered units of Chinese soldiers easy prey. Within a few days most of the cities were in Japanese hands. Early in 1932 the Japanese set up the puppet state of Manchukuo and proclaimed its independence from China. The Chinese, though unable to offer effective military resistance, did have a defensive weapon in a boycott of Japanese goods. For a time it caused a substantial reduction in Japan's trade with China, but it was gradually abandoned. When a truce, signed near Tientsin on May 31, 1933, ended the fighting, Japan had extended its control over an area more than three times as great as that of Japan proper. The new territory, which included Manchuria with Jehol, part of Inner Mongolia, and the so-called Demilitarized Zone within the Great Wall, had a population of about thirty-three million, of which less than 3 per cent was Japanese.

It soon became evident that the occupation of Manchuria was only one stage in a larger operation. The next would be the establishment of Japanese control over all of China. During the years after 1932 the Japanese Foreign Office announced in no uncertain terms that Japan had "special interests" in China, warning all other nations to keep hands off. Mr. Saito, the ambassador in Washington, explained this to mean that "Japan must act and decide alone what is good for China." But these ambitions were not restricted to China. Their ultimate aim was the hegemony of the Far East. The sponsors of this aim were the Japanese military and naval officers. In the summer of 1932 Sadao Araki, who was then minister of war, stated in the columns of *Kaikosha,* the organ of the military association: "The spirit of Japan must spread over the seven seas and the five continents. Everything that opposes its expansion must be overwhelmed, if necessary by force. The countries of eastern Asia have been oppressed by the white people. Japan will not tolerate this condition any longer." [13] This determination to assume supremacy in the Far East is visible in every major decision of Japanese policy during this period. It can be seen in the hostile reaction to any suggestion of aid to China, it accounts for Japan's official withdrawal from the League of Nations in 1935, and it explains the declaration of the Japanese government that after the end of 1936 it would no longer be bound by the naval limitations it had accepted in 1922. [14]

Plans were gradually maturing for a military expedition which would establish Japanese predominance in China so completely as to drive out all foreign competition and turn the country into a

[13] *Living Age,* vol. 346 (1934), p. 310.
[14] At the Washington Conference it was agreed to fix the ratio between the navies of Great Britain, the United States, and Japan at 5–5–3.

Japanese province. In the summer of 1937 large-scale military operations were launched, accompanied by extensive use of air bombing. The fact that war was not officially declared did not make the fighting less destructive or bloody. Judging on the basis of their previous experience, the Japanese did not expect to meet much resistance. They were convinced that the whole thing would be a minor episode in which China would receive a quick thrashing and would then see the wisdom of Japanese rule. The armies, it is true, did succeed in taking most of the chief cities including Peiping, Nanking, Shanghai, Hankow, and Canton, but they were unable to subdue the country. When the Chinese failed to lay down their arms the Japanese, determined to break the will to resist, resorted to methods of warfare that shocked the world. But such methods served only to draw the Chinese together in their stubborn resistance. Even the fact that China was losing three men to every Japanese soldier failed to discourage the Chinese. The Nationalist government continued to place fresh armies in the field to replace those that had been destroyed. "If we can keep this up," a Chinese general stated, "China can exterminate the male population of Japan while losing 105 million men; and we will still have over 300 million left." Not only did organized troops offer resistance but guerilla bands continued to harass Japanese lines of communication and to waylay small enemy detachments. Thus the fighting continued month after month with the Japanese unable to deal the final blow.

The year 1940 still saw the Japanese seeking a solution which would free their hands for the next stage in the establishment of hegemony in the Far East. Supplies from the outside were beginning to flow into China in increasing quantities, causing the Tokyo military cliques to consider the possibility of eventual defeat. Retreat was ruled out not only because it would have damaged national pride but also because of the repercussions it would have had at home. Nor was there any possibility of negotiating a satisfactory peace. Peace on terms that would have saved Japan's face was precluded by China's determination to resist until the last invader had been driven from her soil. Seeing their power and prestige in jeopardy, the army and navy cliques proposed war against the United States as a solution of the puzzle. Special point was given to this proposal because the United States, in addition to bolstering Chinese resistance, was exerting economic pressure to block Japanese expansion toward the south, particularly in Malaya, the Philippines, and the Dutch East Indies. About a year after the outbreak of World War II Japan became a partner of Germany and Italy (Tripartite Pact of September, 1940), thereby merging the Far Eastern and European issues. The Japanese were certain that the Axis would win the war and they would then share in the distribution of the booty. During the year that followed, Hitler's agents pressed for action against the United States, while within Japan the military cliques were assiduously cultivating the war fever. The result was the attack on Pearl Harbor, December 7, 1941.

World War II

CHAPTER SEVENTEEN

The Background of World War II

MILLIONS of people the world over hailed the end of the war in 1918 as the beginning of a new age, an age that was to be better in every way. Many of the nations that had participated in the long struggle emerged from it in a state of exhaustion. They had sacrificed the flower of their youth, dissipated their national wealth, and suffered social and moral injuries. But for all this many people had one consolation. They believed that the triumph of freedom was final, that the "war to end war" had really ended war. They were certain that the years of suffering had convinced mankind of the necessity not only of internal political, economic, and social reforms but also of making a settlement that would eliminate war. Such a settlement was regarded as easy of achievement. Whereas in 1914 the power had been rather evenly distributed between the Triple Alliance and the Triple Entente, in 1919 Germany and her allies were defeated, Russia was in the throes of a civil war, and the new states which had been founded were struggling to establish themselves. It was patent to even the most casual observer that the victorious Allies dominated the scene. Thus they had practically a free hand to establish a durable peace by removing the conditions that had made for war. And their representatives appear to have been convinced that the settlement they reached would, despite its weaknesses and imperfections, provide a more or less permanent arrangement. When the main lines had been drawn up, a delegate to the Paris Peace Conference congratulated one of the principal authors of the treaty in the following words: "I congratulate you upon having concluded a treaty of peace founded on a just and durable basis."

But the "new order" which had been instituted at the Paris Conference was neither new nor just nor durable. Instead of ushering in a new order, it confirmed the worst excesses of the old. More than this, no sooner had the "new order" been instituted than it began to disintegrate. If the settlement was to survive, it was necessary for the victorious powers to join in upholding it. But the unity and co-operation which had been so important in winning the war disappeared on the morrow of the peace negotiations. The enthusiasm of victory having spent itself, each turned to its own interests. Thereafter all efforts to perpetuate the alliance were of no avail. Once the war was over the people of the United States were impatient to demobilize their armies and return to "normalcy." After the Senate refused to ratify the Versailles treaty, the people of the United States eagerly embraced an isolationist policy. Upon their withdrawal the British refused to assume the obligations an Anglo-French alliance would have imposed on them. Feeling somewhat secure in their insular position, they were eager to restore their shattered commercial and financial supremacy and to return to their imperial interests. So far as they were concerned, security had been attained and a new war lay in too remote a future to be of immediate concern. They were not even opposed to the restoration of a considerable part of Germany's power as a counterbalance to French hegemony in Europe. Differences also developed between Britain and France in the affairs of the Near East, and their foreign policies began to diverge.

The French felt abandoned and almost betrayed. The guarantee they had hoped to secure was a permanent superiority of force on the part of the Allies, a superiority so great that it would be impossible for the defeated powers to attempt to overthrow the settlement. With both the United States and Britain refusing to support such an alliance, France was left facing Germany alone, a Germany with a much larger population and a much greater industrial power. Consequently the fear of a new war obsessed the French. What they sought above all was security, which, they believed, could be attained only by upholding the *status quo*, more particularly, by insisting upon the complete and lasting disarmament of Germany. Nor was France the only country to hold this opinion. A number of others had benefited territorially or otherwise as a result of the war and therefore naturally wished to maintain the *status quo*. Among these were Belgium, Poland, Czechoslovakia, Rumania, and Yugoslavia. Gradually those who were interested in upholding the Paris settlement drew together. On the other hand, not one of the defeated powers really accepted the settlement as either just or permanent. It may have been necessary for them to execute the terms but all were animated by the hope that a revision would soon be inaugurated. Thus not many years after "the war to end war" Europe was again divided into two camps.

By 1924, however, the bitterness which had followed the war began to subside. On the one hand, the Allies recognized that the return of Germany as a respectable member to the European family of nations was a prerequisite to the establishment of a more stable and tranquil order; on the other, the Germans, under the leadership of Stresemann, were ready to shelve the idea of revenge at least temporarily for a policy of reconciliation and peaceful readjustment. The general revival of trade and industry stimulated by the flow of wealth from the United States made life more pleasant for most Germans and inclined them to overlook the grievances which had caused so much hate and bitterness in the immediate postwar years. The result of this change of attitude was the Locarno treaties of 1925 in which the French, Germans, and Belgians promised to settle all differences by peaceful means instead of resorting to war.[1]

Three years later a group of American publicists led by Frank B. Kellogg, then secretary of state, joined with Briand in the initiation of the Kellogg-Briand Pact for the Renunciation of War. In this treaty most of the nations of the world, including Germany, Italy, and Japan, renounced war altogether as an instrument of national policy and agreed that the settlement of all disputes or conflicts of whatever nature among them should never be sought except by pacific means. Had this policy been carried out, it would have ushered in the millennium. But a large loophole was left for escape from its provisions. In a letter attached to the treaty, and expressly mentioned in most notes of acceptance, it was explained that the treaty neither "restricts nor impairs the right of self-defense" which is held to be "an inalienable right" of every sovereign state. What wars may not be justified on the grounds of self-defense?

In many circles it was believed that the Locarno treaties and the Kellogg-Briand Peace Pact would usher in a new era of international understanding. But before many months it became clear that this was a delusion. Actually there was no real reconciliation

---

[1] This did not mean, however, that the Germans had abandoned all hope of obtaining a revision of the Versailles settlement. In a memorandum which Stresemann wrote to the former German Crown Prince on September 7, 1925, on the eve of his departure for Locarno, he laid down as primary aims of German policy "the rectification of our eastern frontiers: the recovery of Danzig, of the Polish corridor, and a revision of the boundary in Upper Silesia."

between Germany and France because the Locarno treaties did not remove such basic causes of friction as the war-debt problem. Neither did they lead to a reduction of tariffs or to a reconsideration of the most objectionable features of the Versailles settlement. Nor did they cause the French to turn their spears into pruning hooks and their swords into plowshares. The old fear of Germany remained undispelled. Despite the Locarno treaties and the Kellogg Pact, France and her allies still preserved the military alliances against Germany. By the time the ratification of the pact was announced (July 24, 1929) the spirit that had led to the signing of the treaties had died.

After 1930 international relations in Europe, and in the world generally, deteriorated and the system of collective security was gradually undermined. Before long it became clear that the nations were again drifting toward war. Why then, it may be asked, did the efforts to establish collective security fail? What brought about the deterioration of the international system? What were the factors that gave momentum to the movement toward war? Many people would answer these questions by saying that the war was caused by the insane ambitions and wanton aggression of Hitler and the Nazis. In one sense this is true. Hitler did set off the conflagration by his invasion of Poland. He did make the crucial decision regarding war or peace. But if we would know why things happened as they did we must study not only personalities but the economic, social, political, and moral forces that produced Hitler, made possible his rise, and permitted him to do the things he did. These same forces were also responsible for the dictatorships in Italy, Japan, and other countries. In the words of a British writer: "If you want to know why things happened or why they did not happen, you must investigate not only the individuals but the forces which jerked their arms and their legs and minds in one way or another."

THE BASIC CAUSES OF WORLD WAR II

The basic causes of World War II are no less complex than those which brought about the First World War; in fact, most of the causes that had been active in producing the one helped generate the other. Among the factors which undermined the spirit of internationalism and caused Europe to move toward war were: (1) economic conflicts and grievances; (2) the League's inability to meet the heavy tasks laid upon it; (3) the unwillingness of the nations to disarm; (4) the problem of national minorities; (5) the failure of the powers to revise the Versailles settlement; (6) the revival of nationalist spirit. The last was to a greater or less extent the motive force in all the factors. As in all great political changes, some are in part cause and in part effect of the movement away from internationalism. Some caused more friction than others but all contributed to the stream of events which was gradually carrying the nations of the world toward the abyss.

(1) *Economic conflicts and grievances.* Of all the causes making for war these were certainly among the most important. The struggle for markets, raw materials, and colonies, which had been one of the major causes of World War I, did not abate during the subsequent period; it became more acute. The two countries which on the eve of World War I were struggling hardest to acquire colonies as sources of raw materials and markets for manufactured goods, were Italy and Germany. Neither was less dissatisfied after the war. Whereas the Italians felt that they should have received a larger share of the spoils, the Germans were disappointed because they had been deprived of the few colonies they had managed to acquire. The third member of the so-called "have-not" group was Japan which, like the others, was nursing imperialist ambitions. These three countries, in relation to the extent of their industrialization and rate of increase of their population, were poorest in natural resources. The bulk of the earth's surface, wealth, and population was embraced by the empires of Britain, France, the United States, Belgium, Portugal, and the Netherlands. Britain alone controlled nearly a quarter of the world's territory and population and more than a quarter of its wealth. Out of twenty-five essential raw materials and minerals there were in the British Empire adequate supplies of eighteen, while Germany had adequate supplies of only four. Italy was in a worse plight, having virtually no coal, little oil, and only small iron resources. The situation was equally bad in Japan, which had limited quantities of coal and iron, no resources in oil, and so small an area of arable land that it was difficult to supply the needs of her growing population.

During the era of prosperity the "have-not" nations found ready markets for their manufactured products and were thus able to purchase the raw materials they needed. But with the coming of the economic depression in 1930 the situation changed. Everywhere the attempt was made to reserve the home markets for home products. This aim gave rise to the "Buy-at-Home" movement. Slogans were coined to stop the purchasing of foreign goods. The British opened the drive with the cry, "Buy British," [2] but were soon imitated by other nations. In Germany the slogan was *"Kauft Deutsch!* Buy German goods and give work and bread to your fellow citizens!" Gradually most of the countries adopted such slogans as "Invest in France," "Buy American," and "Buy Japanese." Nor did the efforts stop with slogans. Most nations also resorted to tariff barriers as a means of protecting the home markets. Before 1914 most states had showed a tendency to restrict the free exchange of goods by tariffs. After the war the obstacles to international trade were made more numerous and more complicated than they had been in any previous period of human history. All the new states erected barriers high enough to compel their nationals to purchase goods manufactured within their own boundaries. The world depression caused a further increase in tariffs. In 1932 even Great Britain, which had long been the citadel of free trade, turned to protectionism. More than this, the Ottawa agreements of the same year erected around the British Commonwealth of Nations a Maginot Line bristling with tariffs. France, Italy, and Germany had even higher tariffs. Nor were these the final weapon in most countries. Various other devices such as quotas and embargoes were resorted to as a means of excluding imports. A country would inform other countries that they might send so much and no more or an embargo would be imposed on certain products.

Instead of solving economic difficulties, the erection of high tariff walls and the adoption of quotas and embargoes caused widespread distress, particularly in the countries which did not possess the raw materials that were vital to their industries. With their goods barred from foreign markets they lacked the credit to purchase raw materials. The inability to procure raw materials and to sell manufactured products caused a sense of economic suffocation. Imperialists in these nations began to ask such questions as: "Why is it that a few states should possess so large a share of the riches of the earth and the rest have so little? Why should such small countries as Hol-

---

[2] A British writer stated: "At the moment the appeal to 'Buy British' is posted everywhere to catch the Briton's eye. He is adjured to 'live British,' that is, to spend his spare money, if he has any, at home, wintering on the Cornish Riviera rather than pour more gold into already gold-filled France. Is this, it may be asked, an altruistic injunction? Is it not rather a supreme example of national selfishness? . . . we have to justify our position by asserting and maintaining that, for the time being and in the midst of a world of tariff walls, such a position is not merely justified, but is necessary if we are to live. No matter how clearly we may see that it would be greatly better for the economic welfare of mankind that all those walls should be razed to the ground, we still have to realise that practical politics require us to face the world as it is, and not as we should wish it to be."—*Quarterly Review,* vol. 258 (1932), 6–7.

A LONDON MERCHANT URGES, "BUY BRITISH!"

land, Belgium, and Portugal possess such large colonial empires? Why should a single empire control a quarter of the earth's surface?" Over and over again publicists and agitators in the "have-not" nations insisted that their respective countries were entitled to a fair share of the earth's natural wealth or, at the very least, access to the materials needed for their industries. When nothing was done to effect a more equitable distribution, the three "have-not" countries decided to get their share by force. Accordingly the Japanese marched into Manchuria, the Italians took Albania and Ethiopia, and Hitler launched Germany on a career of expansion. Such military expeditions were part of the undeclared war which preceded the major struggle.

(2) *The failure of the League of Nations.* Following the holocaust of World War I the minds of men were fascinated by the hope held out by the League that nations might live peaceably together and settle their differences at the common conference table. In other words, the League was to organize a federation of mankind in which national policies were to be voluntarily subordinated to international order. This federation would safeguard the interests of both the small and the great powers with equal zeal. There was little doubt in the minds of its proponents that it could actually achieve this. When in January, 1920, a group of seven men representing Great Britain, France, Italy, Japan, Belgium, Brazil, and Spain met in Paris to set up the Council of the League, the chairman, M. Leon Bourgeois, described the meeting as "the birth of a new world." While the United States denied the League at its birth and left it on Europe's doorstep, Germany and the other defeated nations were at first excluded from it. Consequently it was inevitable that in German eyes the League should appear as a committee of conquerors whose prime purpose it was to uphold the Paris settlement.

The first years of the League's existence were largely occupied in building up the machinery of international administration. Problems referred to it in these early years dealt largely with the delimitation of frontiers. Some of these problems were solved with considerable success. Other items on the credit side of the ledger were in the field of reconstruction and relief work. During this early period the delegates watched one another with doubt and distrust. In Lord Cecil's words, "At first things moved stickily." But in 1924 the spirit of the League changed. For the first time the offer of a seat to Germany was discussed, and in the next year Germany was admitted and the Locarno treaties were adopted. The next three years were the most flourishing period in the League's history. Not only did Britain, France, and Germany discuss international affairs on a basis of equality but the assemblies, which had previously been poorly attended, now attracted the prime ministers and foreign ministers of the whole Continent. In 1927 membership numbered no less than fifty-six nations. The future looked so promising that Lord Robert Cecil said: "The truth is that the League of Nations has become, instead of a frail experiment, an indispensable organ of cooperation for the great part of the governments of the world." [3]

But after 1929 it became increasingly apparent that the League could not cope successfully with the burdens laid upon it, that a workable system to preserve peace did not exist. It has frequently been stated that the withdrawal of the United States doomed the League from the start. As a matter of fact it did lose much of its prestige and authority as a result of the voluntary withdrawal of the United States. It meant that the one strong power which might have spoken most freely in the Council was absent, an absence which shattered the hope of a universal league. More than this it made membership somewhat more optional and encouraged various nations to use threats of resignation as a means of achieving their aims. However disastrous the effect of American abstention was, it is not easy to prove that our adherence would have made the League strong enough to enforce collective security. It had still greater weaknesses. What was lacking was the will to succeed. If the members had given the existing machinery for the peaceful settlement of international difficulties the proper support, they could have achieved a common purpose. They may have sincerely desired peace, but they were not willing to pay the price to obtain it. While some were not ready to assume the responsibility which wholehearted support involved, others were not ready to submit to the limitation of their sovereignty which the idea of internationalism implied.

When economic difficulties became grave and the general temper more warlike, the League was unable to arrest the drift toward war. The dictator nations flouted it at will. "The history of the League of Nations between World War I and World War II," Gaetano Salvemini wrote, "was the history of the devices, ruses, deceptions, frauds, tricks, and trappings by means of which the very diplomats who were pledged to operate the Covenant of the League managed to circumvent and stultify it. They were its most effective foes, since they were undermining it from within, while nationalists, militarists, and Fascists were attacking it openly from without in all lands."

[3] *Living Age*, vol. 337 (October, 1929), p. 202.

The Nazis particularly ridiculed it, calling it "a joint-stock company for the preservation of the booty won in the war." The Japanese invasion of Manchuria in 1931, which was a breach of the Covenant, dealt a staggering blow to the League's prestige. Japan was scolded but little else was done to stop its imperialist venture. When Mussolini's designs on Abyssinia became potent, the latter appealed to the League to preserve her territorial integrity and existing political independence. Half-hearted sanctions were imposed, but oil, without which Italy could not have conquered, continued to flow freely. Thus the impotence of the League was ruthlessly exposed. In 1936 Lord Queenborough wrote: "The League is dead." In 1938 prime minister Neville Chamberlain said: "If I am right, as I am confident I am, in saying that the League as constituted today is unable to provide collective security for anybody, then I say we must not try to delude small weak nations into thinking that they will be protected by the League against aggression and acting accordingly, when we know that nothing of this kind can be expected." [4]

(3) *The League's greatest failure was its inability to achieve real progress toward disarmament.* The Treaty of Versailles contained the following clause regarding this point: "In order to render possible the initiation of a general limitation of the armaments of all nations, Germany undertakes strictly to observe the military, naval, and air clauses which follow." In disarming Germany the victorious nations pledged themselves eventually to apply the same measure to themselves and the Germans believed that they would do so. Thus the German delegation to Paris (May 29, 1919) stated: "The German government is willing to consent to the abolition of compulsory military service on the condition that this will be the initiation of a general limitation of armaments of all nations." In reply Clemenceau told the delegation, "The acceptance by Germany of the conditions fixed for her disarmament will facilitate and hasten the realization of a general reduction of armaments, and it is their intention to open negotiations immediately with a view to the adoption eventually of a scheme of general reduction."

During the next twelve years there was a plethora of conversations, conferences, and agreements, but no substantial reduction emerged from the babel of talk and the mass of papers. Nothing really effective was accomplished because the nations did not want to disarm. The feeling of security was lacking. The French, with the threat of Germany on their frontier, were in no mood to disarm

[4] *Foreign Affairs,* vol. 17 (1938), p. 200.

themselves; nor were the British inclined to scrap their navy or to reduce it to a level similar to that of their defeated foes. At the invitation of the United States the powers did assemble for a Disarmament Conference at Washington in 1921. There the United States, Great Britain, and Japan, in order to forestall another race like that preceding World War I, accepted a ratio of 5:5:3 respectively for the construction of capital ships but reached no agreement on reducing the number of smaller combat ships. Moreover, although the use of poison gas was prohibited, no decision was reached regarding the size of land forces. This was the most successful of the disarmament conferences between the two wars. During this period the various German governments time and again called upon the victorious powers to apply to themselves the same measure of disarmament that had been imposed on Germany. The Germans were not ready to remain permanently the one disarmed nation in a system of armed nationalism. They pointed to the paradox of a League whose members had sworn never to go to war but were all relying on huge armaments to protect their interests. Still the great powers refused to agree. In 1927 Lloyd George himself stated that the nations which had pledged themselves to disarmament had not reduced their armaments "by a single division, flight of aeroplanes, or battery of guns."

When at last a disarmament conference, called by the League, met at Geneva in 1932, there was little disposition on the part of anyone to disarm. The Brüning government explicitly stated that Germany was willing to remain on the armament level prescribed by the Treaty of Versailles and even to accept a further reduction if the other powers were willing to reduce their forces to the same level. A conditional promise of equality was given in January, 1933, but Hitler's advent to power in the same month terrified the French. Consequently the British and French representatives announced that no practical steps in the direction of equality to Germany could be taken for four more years. This statement was interpreted by the Germans as conclusive proof that the League was completely dominated by the victors of World War I. So they withdrew from the conference and started to rearm, at first by stealth and then openly.

The refusal of the great powers became grist for the Nazi propaganda mill in Germany. It facilitated Hitler's efforts to convince the people that rearmament was the road to power and national achievement. Before the end of 1931 General von Seeckt had already made plans for a huge army, but it remained for Hitler to carry out the plans. Meanwhile Italy and Japan were busy building up their armaments. Japan had already set the precedent in the invasion of Manchuria and soon Germany and Italy were to join her in adopting force and the threat of force as a means of achieving their aims. To equal the threat, the other nations frantically turned to the building of armaments. In short, a state of affairs developed which was reminiscent of that prior to World War I when every great power endeavored to arm itself to the point at which it was stronger than its neighbors. Once more the pre-World War I faith in arms began to prevail.

(4) *The problem of national minorities.* Another fertile cause of friction and antagonism between nations was the question of minorities. The peacemakers at Paris had tried to settle such problems once and for all by adopting the Wilsonian principle of "self-determination." But they did not apply this principle in the strict sense of the word. Its application was conditioned by such factors as economic necessity, military defense, religious and political traditions, and punishment of the defeated nations. Moreover, in many areas of central Europe they were unable to apply the principles fully because the national minorities were intermixed in such a way that the drawing of clear-cut frontiers was out of question. Consequently, members of one nationality were included within the boundaries of states in which they constituted minorities. In the Soviet Union the plan of giving cultural freedom and equality to the many minorities ruled out the conflicts between the various language groups, but conditions were different in central Europe. There the national groups became hotbeds of ferment. Encouraged by propaganda from their "homeland" they demanded reunion with the "mother state" or full autonomy within the framework of the state to which they had been assigned by the peace treaties.

A number of states sought to exploit the principle of self-determination but it was the Nazis who made the most of it. At the Peace Conference in 1919 Lloyd George had warned against the inclusion of large numbers of Germans in foreign states. "I am," he said, "strongly adverse to transferring more Germans from German rule to the rule of some other nation than can possibly be helped. I cannot conceive any greater cause of future wars than that the German people . . . should be surrounded by a number of small states . . . each of them containing large masses of Germans clamoring for reunion with their native land." His warnings were not heeded. The Nazis seized upon this violation of the principle of self-determination almost at once. If it is true, they asked, that World

War I was fought for the self-determination of nationalities, why was Austria forbidden to unite with Germany and why were a large number of Germans put under foreign rule? Claiming that this wrong must be righted, the Nazis aimed, in the words of their party program, at the "unity of all Germans in a Greater Germany." They used every conceivable means to create dissatisfaction among the Germans under foreign rule. They even went so far, in their efforts to convince the world that these minorities should be incorporated into Germany, as to make extravagant claims about the mistreatment their fellow nationals were suffering. In other words, the principle of self-determination furnished them with a convenient pretext for annexing Austria and the country of the Sudeten. More than this, in 1939 they employed it as a pretext for the invasion of Poland, which kindled the fires of World War II.

(5) *Resentment against the Versailles treaty.* Even the severest critics will confess that the settlement made at Paris in 1919 removed many old injustices; but it is equally true that it also caused others. From this point of view it is regrettable that so little of President Wilson's healing message of international justice and cooperation found its way into the peace terms. While the treaty would undoubtedly have been worse except for the efforts of the British and American delegations, it still violated the whole spirit and intention of the Fourteen Points. In depriving Germany of every scrap of colonial empire, in creating the Polish Corridor which severed East Prussia from the rest of the Reich, and in cutting Danzig away from Germany the settlement created a burning sense of injustice. More than this, in including the "war-guilt" clause (Article 231) whereby Germany accepted full responsibility for the war, the peacemakers inflicted a bitter humiliation upon the German people. Signor Nitti, who was prime minister of Italy at the time the treaty was signed, said in 1922: "It will remain forever a terrible precedent in modern history that against all pledges, all precedents, and all traditions the representatives of Germany were never even heard."

The German people, although they felt duped, had no choice but to accept the treaty. But a feeling of injustice and humiliation rankled in their hearts. President Wilson had proved himself a good prophet when just before the United States entered the war he had called for "a peace without victory," saying that "victory would mean peace forced upon the loser, a victor's terms imposed upon the vanquished. It would be accepted in humiliation under duress at an intolerable sacrifice, and would leave a sting, a resentment, a bitter memory, upon which the terms of peace would rest."

The German people did not regard the settlement of its frontiers with Poland as anything more than provisional. Like President Wilson they insisted that the basis of durable peace must be justice, and for them justice was lacking so long as the treaties remained unrevised. Although Article Nineteen of the League Covenant provided for the reconsideration of treaties which had become unfair and for the adjustment of international conditions whose continuance might endanger the peace of the world, the League members never made use of this Article. The French, in fact, never ceased to declare that not a jot or tittle of the treaty could be either expunged or altered. On the other hand, there were many in Germany who regarded it as the chief cause of Germany's postwar difficulties.

It was the economic depression that again turned the attention of the Germans to the settlement and inclined them to listen to the Nazi blandishments. Economic suffering, combined with a revived consciousness of humiliation, raised their emotions to the point of explosion. Convinced that anything would be better than nothing, they called on their leaders to do something toward lifting them out of the slough of depression and despondency. This gave Hitler his long-awaited opportunity. During the years from 1930 to 1933 the Allies might still have robbed his sails of much wind by revising the treaty. But nothing was done. No sooner was he in power than he began his preparations to demolish the settlement. He did not share Stresemann's hope that the treaties might be revised by international negotiation. He was convinced that "only force counts." This is the basic idea of *Mein Kampf*. Thus he wrote: "The reconquest of lost territories cannot be achieved by solemn appeals to Almighty God or pious hopes in a League of Nations, but only by armed force."

(6) *Resurgence of the nationalist spirit.* The one factor operative in all the forces which were undermining collective security and paving the way toward war was the nationalist spirit, the same spirit which had been one of the basic causes of World War I. During the decades immediately preceding 1914 the nationalist psychology dominated every department of human life. School, press, churches, literature, art, and other influences had combined to cultivate it. But during the war it lost much of its glamor. The soldiers in the mud of Flanders as well as the civilians, under the desire to prevent another war, became lukewarm converts to international psychology. All realized that if war was to be outlawed, conflicting national ambitions would have to give way to a system of international control. This attitude was reinforced by the speeches of President Wilson

and others who advocated a pacific internationalism based upon cooperation and the promotion of common interests. But when the war ended, the spirit of nationalism dictated the peace settlement in large part, with the result that the framework of the "New Europe" was reconstructed on strictly national lines. Then the League was created as an antidote, as a focus of internationalism and international organization. In many fields, including commerce, industry, finance, the post, telegraph, and railways, a vast system of cooperation had quietly grown up during the nineteenth century. What was lacking, however, was a psychology in which the common interests of nations would be regarded as infinitely more important than the interests of any one nation. The cultivation of this psychology was to be one of the primary tasks of the League.

During the twenties important progress was made in fostering the international mind. To many it appeared as if this spirit would gradually prevail. But after 1929 a reaction set in. New emphasis was put on the things that divide nation from nation. The outstanding cause was the economic depression. So long as prosperity continued, the international spirit flourished in certain circles; but the coming of the depression led to a recrudescence of economic nationalism which, in turn, stimulated nationalism in other forms. As in the period prior to World War I nationalism became the all-pervading influence, with nations again seeking security in armaments and hostile alliances. "At a time when the need for mutual understanding is most imperative," the League of Nations World Economic Survey states,[5] "countries persist in acting as if the narrowest form of economic nationalism and the strictest isolation were the only roads to salvation." The revived nationalism was, in some of its manifestations, even more intolerant than the earlier had been. In Italy and Germany, where the spirit allied itself with Fascism and nazism, its votaries worshiped the state as an end in itself while internationalism was ridiculed as being "sickly and wishy-washy." In a number of other countries, too, dictators rode to power on a wave of popular nationalist enthusiasm. To retain their power they found it necessary to sustain this enthusiasm; and in order to do this, they resorted to aggressive measures against other nations. Thus they converted the nationalist spirit into a juggernaut of destruction.

[5] *Proceedings of the Institute of World Affairs,* vol. 10 (1932), p. 171.

🍋

THE ROAD TO WAR

From 1920 to 1932 peace rested precariously on French military predominance supplemented by the uncertain support of Great Britain. A new chapter began with the rise of Adolf Hitler to power in Germany in January, 1933. Up to that time the Germans and the peoples of Europe generally had been thinking of the problems and settlements of World War I; thereafter they thought more and more in terms of the next war. In the spring of 1933 when Hitler asked the Reichstag to give him four years to carry out the political, social, and economic reorganization of Germany, the Nazis did not divulge exactly what their plan was. But those who shared the secrets of the policymakers knew that one of its basic purposes was military. The details were worked out in a series of conferences attended by Hitler and the military and political chiefs of the National Socialist Party in consultation with the general staff.

The fact that Germany would rearm as rapidly as possible was, of course, no secret to the other European countries. Inasmuch as denunciation of the Versailles treaty was one of the cardinal doctrines of National Socialism, it was believed that the new government would challenge what remained of this treaty as soon as it had made the necessary preparations. Of all the neighbors of Germany the Poles were the most nervous. They believed that Hitler's first blow for territorial revision would be aimed at Danzig and the Corridor. This fear had impelled the Poles to sign a three-year nonaggression pact with Russia in 1932, some months before Hitler became chancellor. Russia, against whom much of *Mein Kampf* was aimed, had equal reason to distrust Nazi ambitions. Hence after Hitler's accession to power the treaty between Russia and Poland was strengthened by various additions. This pact aroused widespread fears in Nazi circles that these two countries might unite with France to crush Germany before she could rearm. As a means of preventing what the Nazis regarded as a premature war, the leaders asked party members to sound a more accommodating note; above all, to cease making references to the annexation of Danzig or the taking of the Corridor. Hitler himself tried to calm the misgivings Nazi ambitions had aroused in other countries with such statements as: "Germany will tread no other path than that laid down by the treaties. The German government will discuss all political and economic questions only within the framework of, and through, the treaties."

The Nazi strategy was successful in allaying Polish fears. Not only did tension subside but the two nations surprised the world by issuing a joint declaration of nonaggression in November, 1933. Later, in January, 1934, this declaration was supplemented by a formal treaty whereby the two nations pledged each other not to resort to war to settle differences that might arise between them. In commenting on this pact before the Reichstag Hitler said: "The attempt to settle the differences between our two countries by war would in its calamitous consequences be out of proportion to any possible gain." But if he endeavored to avoid serious embroilment until Germany was ready to fight, he did permit himself manifestations of bravado with the evident object of seeing just how far he could go. Such a step was the withdrawal of Germany from the League in October, 1933. Having taken it he immediately resorted to honeyed words of peace. "The history of the last 150 years," he said, "should, in its changing course, have taught France and Germany that essential and enduring changes are no longer to be gained by the sacrifice of blood. . . . No one could demand that millions of men in the flower of youth be annihilated for the sake of a readjustment of our frontier." Several weeks later (November 10, 1933) he again sounded the trumpet of peace. "I am not crazy enough to want a war," he said; "the German people have but one wish—to be happy in their own way and to be left in peace." More than this, in his discussions with foreign diplomats and correspondents the word "peace" was always on his lips. But his actions in frantically rearming Germany gave the lie to his statements; in fact, what he was trying to do in the first place was to deceive his prospective enemies until he was strong enough to assert himself. Later he boasted repeatedly of having secretly armed Germany to the teeth while other countries were asleep.

Hitler himself dispelled all doubts about rearmament in March, 1935, by openly restoring universal military service, a move which was contrary to the disarmament clauses of the Treaty of Versailles. Europe had a choice of two policies: either to take up arms in defense of the treaty or acquiesce quietly in its violation and revision. It chose the latter course. Nothing was done to stop Hitler from building up his army in preparation for "the day" when he would carry out his designs. Only three months later Britain openly recognized the abolition of the disarmament clauses by concluding a naval agreement with Germany. This agreement, while ostensibly limiting German naval strength to 35 per cent of the British strength, made Germany a present of naval supremacy in the Baltic and furthermore permitted her to build submarines up to 100 per cent of British strength.

All this time while Hitler was rearming Germany, the British did little or nothing to bolster their land, sea, and air forces. When information reached them regarding the alarming lengths to which German rearmament was going, it was belittled, ridiculed, or ignored. A number of leading organs of the press derided the idea that German armaments could imply any threat to the security of western Europe. There were, however, some who were alarmed, and among them Winston Churchill. In 1934 he told the British people of "the tremendous covert armaments which are proceeding" in Germany, warning them that "wars come suddenly." He told the House of Commons that "though little is said about it in public, Germany has already a powerful, well equipped army, with an excellent artillery and an immense reserve of armed, trained men. The German munitions factories are working practically under war conditions, and war material is flowing out from them, and has been for the last twelve months in an ever broadening flow."[6] Churchill also sounded other warnings during the subsequent months. For his pains he was dubbed an alarmist or his fears were characterized as "Churchillian nightmares." One writer went so far as to state that "nothing is left but to exclaim in Gilbertian phrase:

> Tale tremendous, Heaven defend us.
> What a tale of Cock and Bull."

However, not long after Hitler announced the reintroduction of conscription, a number of things happened which caused widespread alarm. Hitler's act was shortly followed by Mussolini's announcement that the 1911 class of reservists would be called up and would raise the number of men under arms to about 800,000. In Britain a real anxiety was generated by the discovery that the figures which prime minister Baldwin had given the House of Commons regarding the relative air strength of Germany and Britain were erroneous. It was found that by November of that year (1935) the German air force would be three or four times as strong as that of Britain. Moreover, the German machines were faster and of later design. The immediate result of this disclosure was that the three major parties in the House joined in supporting the policy of raising the air force to a level with that of Germany as quickly as possible. But hope of forestalling an armament race was not abandoned. Plans were made to resume negotiations for a limitation in the near future.

[6] Churchill, *While England Slept* (1938), pp. 141–142.

THE EXPANSION OF GERMANY BEFORE THE SECOND WORLD WAR

REMILITARIZED, MARCH, 1936
ANNEXED, MARCH, 1938
ANNEXED, OCTOBER, 1938
OCCUPIED, MARCH, 1939
ANNEXED, MARCH, 1939
ANNEXED, SEPTEMBER, 1939

Meanwhile Hitler was endeavoring to lull Europe into a sense of security with such statements as: "We want to be a peace-loving element among the nations. We cannot repeat that often enough." (January 30, 1936.) A few weeks later he made his next open move. On March 7, 1936, the German army reoccupied the Rhineland and denounced the Locarno treaties. Again Hitler tried to allay the fears of Germany's neighbors with such words as (March 7, 1936) : "We have no territorial demands to make in Europe," and a week later he stated (March 15, 1936) : "The German people do not wish to continue waging war to readjust frontiers. Each readjustment is bought by sacrifices out of proportion to what is gained." The Germans themselves were surprised when nothing happened. They had expected opposition to the occupation of the Rhineland. As a colonel put it, "The French can't stand provocations like that." General von Fritsch, the commander in chief, had at first opposed the march into the Rhineland because he felt that the Reichswehr was not ready for war. But Hitler assured him that there would be no war. As a guarantee he gave his generals the order to evacuate the Rhineland without firing a shot if the French should mobilize and cross the frontier. In France there was a strong desire to offer resistance because the demilitarized zone was the one remaining element of the compromise France had been induced to accept at the Paris Peace Conference in lieu of the complete separation of the Rhineland from Germany. But General Gamelin, chief of the French staff, stated that he would require 400,000 men to occupy the Rhineland. So nothing was done and Hitler again had his way.

In 1936 Hitlerite Germany took a long step toward escaping from her isolated position by drawing closer to Italy. The way for a rapprochement between Hitler and Mussolini was really opened when the former realized that he could hope for no readjustment of the territorial clauses of the Treaty of Versailles and when Il Duce became irked because sanctions were invoked against him in the Ethiopian conflict. Thereafter the dictators discovered that they had much in common, which was evident from the similarity of their methods and political ideals. When Spain's civil war flared up in July, 1936, they made that peninsula the battleground for the

THE EXPANSION OF GERMANY BEFORE THE SECOND WORLD WAR. *Here the student can trace the steps by which Germany flouted the Treaty of Versailles from the remilitarization of the Rhine to the invasion of Poland.*

struggle of dictatorship against the "red menace." It gave both the opportunity to try out new tactics and new weapons in preparation for the great struggle that was in the offing.

To the states of central Europe the failure of Britain and France to stop Germany was incomprehensible. Germany's occupation of the Rhineland, Mussolini's defiance of the League in the Ethiopian question, the rapprochement between Germany and Italy raised the stock of both countries among the Balkan peoples and caused them to grow cool toward France and Britain. Hungary and Bulgaria were of course already in the Italian bag but, encouraged by the growing might of Germany and Italy, they drew closer to the Axis powers. When nothing was done to stop Germany, the rulers of Yugoslavia became convinced that the British and French had lost their supremacy on the Continent. Furthermore, it convinced them that they could expect no help from Britain and France. Hence, early in 1937 the Yugoslav government signed pacts with both Bulgaria and Italy. The attitude of the Western powers discouraged the Greek and Turkish governments to the extent that they took a more conciliatory attitude toward Germany. Only Czechoslovakia and Rumania adhered to the old political line. Even they endeavored to show France and Britain the danger of permitting European affairs to continue in the course in which they were moving. It was to no avail.

On January 30, 1937, at the Reichstag session commemorating four years of Nazi rule Hitler formally served notice to the world that he would no longer be bound by the Treaty of Versailles. Again nothing happened. The Führer then decided that the time had come to test the inertia of the European states by a series of territorial aggrandizements. He felt that Germany for internal reasons required an ideological success. As usual he sought to mislead the European states with such statements as: "The genuineness of Germany's desire for peace and international understanding is demonstrated by her large-scale building schemes." Meanwhile he was laying plans for the incorporation of Austria in a Greater Germany. Union with Austria was a cardinal doctrine of the Nazi creed. In *Mein Kampf* Hitler had stated that it was "a life task to be achieved by any and every means." Accordingly early in 1938 he announced that Germany would no longer tolerate the persecution of ten million brethren living in "two neighboring states." Dr. Goebbels' propaganda machine had been let loose in Austria earlier but despite its apparent success Nazis were barred from the cabinet. In February Hitler forced Dr. Schuschnigg, the Austrian chancellor, under threat of invasion to admit two Nazis to his cabinet, in return for which he promised to reaffirm Austrian independence.

A few weeks later Hitler was ready to move German troops into Austria. When General von Fritsch objected, Hitler dismissed him summarily. The invasion began on the morning of March 12 and the next day Austria was formally annexed to the Reich. Less than three years earlier he had said emphatically (May 21, 1935): "Germany neither intends nor wishes to interfere in the internal affairs of Austria, to annex Austria, or to conclude an *Anschluss.*" Upon his arrival in Austria after the *Anschluss,* Hitler said: "I believe it was God's will to send this Austrian boy to the Reich and permit him to return to unite the German people. . . . Everything that has happened must have been preordained by divine will. . . . I have proved that I can do more than the dwarfs who were running the country into the ground. . . . My name will stand forever!" Thus Hitler achieved the conquest without opposition from the other European states. The possession of Austria gave him the desired pincers against Czechoslovakia, whose military position became practically untenable.

THE RAPE OF CZECHOSLOVAKIA

The annexation of Austria brought under Hitler's rule two thirds of the ten million Germans to whom he had referred in his speech of February 20. The other third were the Sudeten Germans living in Czechoslovakia. At the time of the seizure of Austria he stated that he had no designs on Czechoslovakia, but Europe did not have to wait long before his actions belied his statements. In Czechoslovakia the *Anschluss* had caused a surge of pro-Nazi sentiment among the Sudeten Germans which resulted in a rush to join Henlein's party. Hitler did not lose any time in giving the latter stronger backing and in loosing a flood of imprecations against Czech "violence." In annexing Austria he had added the state as a whole, but to "bring the Sudeten Germans home" involved the dismemberment of one of the most enlightened states of Europe. This did not deter him. On May 19 reports began to circulate regarding the concentration of troops near the borders of Czechoslovakia. Inquiries by the British elicited the reply that the troop movements were merely "routine." But a frontier incident and Henlein's refusal to continue negotiations convinced the Czechoslovak government that an invasion was imminent. After manning their frontier fortifications, they appealed to France and Britain for aid. Urging

80 MILES

GERMANY

POLAND

RUMANIA

HUNGARY

AUSTRIA

ANNEXED BY
GERMANY,
1938

ANNEXED BY
POLAND,
1938

ANNEXED BY
HUNGARY,
1938

CZECHOSLOVAKIA'S
BOUNDARIES
BEFORE MUNICH

SUDETENLAND

BOHEMIA
(GERMAN PROTECTORATE)

MORAVIA

SLOVAKIA
(GERMAN ALLY)

RUTHENIA

CARPATHIAN MOUNTAINS

SILESIA

Lublin

Radom

Lvow

Przemysl

Cracow

Czestochowa

Breslau

Glatz

Reichenberg

Dresden

ELBE R.

Eger

Pilsen

PRAGUE

Krumau

Budweis

ELBE R.

Troppau

Teschen

Brunn

Znaim

Bratislava

VIENNA

DANUBE R.

Ivice

Lucenc

Rosenau

Kaschau

Munkács

Ungvar

Huszt

BUDAPEST

DANUBE R.

THE DISMEMBERMENT OF CZECHOSLOVAKIA

the Czechs to make further concessions, the French government promised to fulfill its pledge to come to Czechoslovakia's assistance and Britain agreed to support France. This caused Hitler to realize that his aims could not be attained except by war or a serious threat of war. Hence he put an end to the crisis by denying that he had any design on Czechoslovakia.

Even though the tension had eased for the time being, the question was by no means settled. During the succeeding months Nazi aggressiveness increased despite the fact that the Czech government was making more and more concessions to the Sudetens. In September the British prime minister, Neville Chamberlain, decided to take the matter in hand. Believing that Europe was rushing headlong into war, he devoted all the energy and resources at his command to prevent it if possible; if not, to play for time in which Britain could rearm. On September 14, 1938, he sent Hitler the following telegram: "In view of the increasingly critical situation I propose to come over at once to see you with a view to trying to find a peaceful solution." Upon receiving the answer that the Führer would be glad to see him, Chamberlain boarded a plane for Berchtesgaden on September 15. During the three-hour discussion that followed, the British prime minister realized that the situation was fraught with great danger. Hitler did not mince words in stating that he was determined to incorporate the Sudeten districts into the Reich and demanded their outright surrender. To this Chamberlain replied that he would have to consult his colleagues about the matter.

When he made a report of his conversation with Hitler to the members of the British cabinet, they were anything but enthusiastic about the details. On September 18 premier Daladier of France, accompanied by foreign minister Bonnet, arrived in London for a consultation. After a long discussion the representatives of the two governments accepted Hitler's demand that the principle of self-determination be applied to the Sudeten Germans. The next day Britain and France presented a note at Prague in which the Czech government was bluntly informed that the preservation of European peace necessitated the transfer to Germany of "the districts mainly inhabited by Sudeten Germans." As Chamberlain wished to resume

THE DISMEMBERMENT OF CZECHOSLOVAKIA. *The year 1938 saw the extinction of the Czechoslovak Republic. Poland and Hungary were given small pieces but Germany appropriated the major portion.*

his conversations with Hitler, a reply was requested "at the earliest possible moment." The Czech cabinet after much discussion refused the demand, styling it "the basest betrayal in history." But this was not the final answer. When British and French authorities told the cabinet that it could not expect military aid from them if it persisted in its refusal, the Czechs decided they could do nothing but yield.

The morning of September 22 saw Chamberlain in a plane bound for Germany where he met the German dictator in the town of Godesberg on the Rhine and informed him of Czechoslovakia's agreement to cede all territories with 50 per cent or more Sudeten. The prime minister, who still labored under the delusion that Hitler like himself was working for "an orderly settlement rather than a settlement by the use of force," was convinced that his report would settle the matter in a friendly fashion. But much to his surprise he discovered that Hitler was determined to occupy the Sudeten territory with German army units no later than October 1 instead of working out the details of the transfer in a peaceful and orderly manner. When he protested, the Führer flew into one of his famous rages and stated that the situation in Czechoslovakia was becoming more and more unbearable and must be terminated. This time Chamberlain refused to capitulate. He stood firmly on the principle, "We will negotiate, but we won't bow to force!" Upon his return to England the Czechs were told that Britain and France no longer advised them not to mobilize. Mobilization followed immediately. At the same time the British began to mobilize their fleet and the French called more men to the colors. On September 28, when war seemed imminent, Hitler backed down and accepted Chamberlain's suggestion for a conference that was to include representatives of Britain, France, Germany, Italy, and Czechoslovakia. For the first time one of Hitler's lightning coups had failed to come off, but he became more determined than ever to achieve his purpose.

The conference took place at Munich on September 29. Chamberlain, Daladier, Hitler, and Mussolini were present, but the Germans saw to it that the Czechs were not represented. This time both the French and the British yielded to pressure. An American correspondent, who was present when the conference closed early the next morning and who saw the four men emerge from the conference room, wrote: "The first of the four statesmen to come out of that hall was the French premier, Edouard Daladier. If ever I have seen a man sunk in the depths of despair, I saw one that night

PRIME MINISTER NEVILLE CHAMBERLAIN RETURNS FROM GERMANY,
SEPTEMBER 30, 1938

in Daladier. . . . The British prime minister, Neville Chamberlain, is known to the correspondents as 'Poker Face.' He kept his feelings to himself, that night as always. But that was not true of the two dictators, as they came out of the conference hall almost arm in arm. Signor Mussolini wore the broad smile of a man who had just put his bank roll on the right horse. And Herr Hitler seemed to be no longer of this earth. All my life I have heard the expression 'walking on air,' but never quite realized it could have literal meaning until I saw Herr Hitler that night in Munich." [7]

Hitler had reason to feel as if he were walking on air, for Chamberlain and Daladier, who went to Munich to "try what reason and good will and discussion would do," had accepted the substance of what had been rejected at Godesberg. Hitler, it is true, had agreed to occupy the territory in five stages. Moreover, the line of occupation was to be fixed by an international committee. Essentially, however, he was given just what he said he would take.

Back in London, Chamberlain received a wild ovation. He told the people who cheered him that he had brought back "peace with honor." "I believe," he said, "it is peace for our time." The English could now put away their gas masks and enjoy the blessings of peace. In France there was similar evidence of relief that the world had been saved from war. Rues de la Paix were renamed Boulevards Neville Chamberlain in honor of the great "man of peace." In Rome and Berlin there was great enthusiasm over what was interpreted as a victory for the dictators. Only in Czechoslovakia was there an atmosphere of sadness and despair. Without giving the Czech representatives an opportunity to state their case, the four powers had partitioned the country. The Czechs had no recourse but to yield. In announcing the catastrophe to his people over the radio premier Syrovy said, "Superior force has compelled me to accept."

On Saturday, October 1, the day Hitler had originally designated, German troops marched into Zone 1, while panic-stricken groups of Czechs, Jews, and non-Nazi Germans fled in the utmost confusion. The work of the so-called international commission was farcical for it merely put a rubber stamp on the German decisions. Only where the Germans could see no military or economic advantage in departing from it did they follow the ethnical or language line. It was, indeed, a mockery to call the procedure self-determination.

[7] *Saturday Evening Post,* vol. 211 (December 3, 1938) , p. 6.

〆

THE EVE OF HOSTILITIES

At the beginning of 1939 a noted English historian wrote: "Look-ing round at our distressed continent at the opening of 1939 we seem to see the scales of war and peace hanging level in the air. Such a perilous balance is easily upset. The chief factor making for war is the land hunger of Germany, Italy, and Japan." [8] Although the Italians and Japanese had conquered territories occupied by peoples of different nationalities, Hitler up to this time seemed only to be endeavoring to unite all Germans in a greater Germany. The peaceful conclusion of the Sudetenland question at Munich led the British, French, and others to hope that his ambitions were fulfilled. He himself had stimulated this hope by saying (September 26, 1938) : "The Sudetenland is the last territorial claim I have to make in Europe. . . . I have assured Mr. Chamberlain, and I emphasize it now, that when this problem is solved, Germany has no more territorial problems in Europe." On a later occasion he said: "I shall not be interested in the Czechs any more, and I can guarantee it. We don't want any more Czechs."

But the addition of territory inhabited by ten million Germans only served to whet his appetite. He now turned from the idea of nationality and self-determination to *Lebensraum* (living space) and economic autarchy. During the first part of 1939 his propaganda machine placed less emphasis on racial doctrine and more on the "mission" of the German people. In short, the concept of nationality made way for a doctrine of naked imperialism. As usual he sought to mislead his neighbors with such statements as (January 1, 1939) : "In general we have but one wish—that in the coming year we may be able to make our contribution to the general pacification of the world." A few weeks later he said (January 30, 1939) : "Only the warmongers think there will be a war. I think there will be a long period of peace." Meanwhile he was rearming feverishly and looking about for the next victim for his aggressions. The policy of appease-ment which the British and French had adopted caused him to hold them in contempt. He was convinced that unless they were attacked Britain and France would not fight. Hence he felt he could do almost whatever he liked.

During the early weeks of 1939 Hitler was merely waiting for a favorable opportunity to deal the *coup de grâce* to the Czecho-slovakian state which since the dismemberment of the previous year

[8] G. P. Gooch in *Contemporary Review*, vol. 155 (1939) , p. 136.

had been struggling with inextricable internal difficulties. After summoning President Hacha, the successor of President Beneš, to Berlin and forcing him by a threat of aerial bombardment of Prague to surrender his country, German troops crossed the frontiers from the Sudetenland and annexed Bohemia and Moravia. Next, after recognizing the independence of Slovakia, he took it under his protection and made it virtually a part of the Third Reich. This left only the province of Ruthenia of the former Czechoslovakian state and that was overrun by Hungarian troops. Thus the Czechoslovakian republic after twenty years of freedom passed once more under alien dominance.

Still Hitler did not stop. One week after the destruction of Czechoslovakia, he demanded of Lithuania its chief city and only seaport, Memel, which prior to World War I had been a part of Germany. The Lithuanians had no choice but to surrender it. On March 23 German troops marched into the area, adding a Baltic harbor area of more than a thousand square miles to the Reich. The next move was made not by Germany but by Italy. While Hitler was adding vast territories and populations, Mussolini had succeeded only in conquering Abyssinia, a possession of doubtful value. He now felt that it was time to make further additions to the Italian Empire. On April 7 troops landed at three points on the Albanian coast and overran the country. It seemed as if the dictators were pretty much having their way about everything.

The absorption of Bohemia and Moravia convinced the British and French that Hitler's wailings about mistreated minorities were simply a smoke screen to cover expansion eastward. They realized that no small country could thenceforth consider itself safe from Nazi seizure or domination. Believing that the Nazi juggernaut would roll on toward the east, they began to consult with the countries that would be in the path of aggression. On March 31 Chamberlain stated that "in the event of any action which clearly threatened Polish independence, and which the Polish Government accordingly considered vital to resist with their national forces, His Majesty's Government would feel themselves bound at once to lend the Polish Government all support in their power." In April Britain extended her guarantee of assistance to Greece and Rumania if their independence should be threatened. The French Government immediately stepped to Britain's side with a similar declaration.

The problem of sending help to the small countries of central Europe was not easy, particularly in the case of Poland. The only way any real help could be brought to Poland was by enlisting Soviet

Russia on the side of Britain and France. There appeared to be many reasons why the Bolsheviks should join the "stop-Hitler front." Not only was much of Hitler's *Mein Kampf* aimed at Russia but the Führer had since his accession to power continued his denunciation of the Russians. Thus on January 30, 1937, he said: "We look upon Bolshevism as upon an intolerable danger to the world. . . . Any treaty links between Germany and present-day Bolshevist Russia would be without any value whatsoever." Negotiations for an alliance between the British and the French on the one hand and the Russians on the other were started, but they dragged on without producing anything definite.

Meanwhile Hitler made no secret of his intentions. Before the end of March he presented a number of proposals to the Polish government. The first demanded the return of Danzig to German control. Others proposed the cession to Germany of a route through the Polish Corridor to connect West and East Prussia with a railway line and extraterritorial status. Upon hearing of the Anglo-Polish mutual assistance agreement he chose to interpret it as an attempt to encircle Germany [9] and used it (April 28, 1939) as an excuse for tearing up the Anglo-German naval agreement of 1935 and for denouncing the nonaggression pact he had made with Poland in 1934. Less than three months earlier (January 30, 1939) he had said in a speech to the Reichstag: "We have just celebrated the fifth anniversary of the conclusion of our nonaggression pact with Poland. There can be scarcely any difference of opinion today among the true friends of peace with regard to the value of this agreement." Not long afterward he moved closer to Italy. On May 22 an Italo-German military alliance was signed providing for consultation of the two parties if the interests of either were threatened and arranging definitely for cooperation and collaboration in the event of war. Not long after this the German press and radio launched a campaign of abuse against Poland, reminiscent of the campaign that had been conducted against Czechoslovakia. The Poles were accused of mercilessly and systematically persecuting the German minority and of perpetrating against the Germans barbarian acts of every description. It all had a very familiar ring.

During the time the German propaganda machine was grinding out Polish atrocity stories, the French and British continued their

---

[9] In answer to Hitler's claim that Germany was being "encircled" Lord Halifax said in a speech to the House of Lords: "Germany is isolating herself and doing it most successfully and most completely. Our people were not backward in recognizing some of the mistakes of the Versailles treaty that required remedying, but each time during these last years that there seemed a chance of making progress in understanding, the German government has taken action which has made that progress impossible."

negotiations with Soviet Russia without reaching an agreement. While the Russians could not forget that the British and French had largely ignored them during the previous years, the British still harbored much of their old distrust of Bolshevism. Just when it appeared as if negotiations were moving toward a successful conclusion, the world was startled by the announcement from Berlin on August 19 that Germany and the Soviet Union had agreed to conclude a pact of nonaggression. Four days later the pact was signed. It pledged the two contracting parties to refrain for ten years from acts of aggression against one another and from supporting either actively or by association any other power hostile to either of the parties. Subsequently it was revealed that negotiations had been going on for months. What it all meant no one really knew. The one thing certain was that the bottom had fallen out of the Franco-British negotiations with Russia. But the Soviet-German pact did not cause the British and French to retreat. Chamberlain stated emphatically that "whatever may prove to be the nature of the German-Soviet agreement, it cannot alter Great Britain's obligations," and France stood equally firm. While the French called up fresh reserves, Chamberlain reaffirmed Britain's guarantee to Poland.

After the conclusion of the pact Hitler became bolder in his demands. On the very day on which it was signed, he told Sir Nevile Henderson, the British ambassador to Germany, that he "did not desire war but would not shrink from it if it was necessary." At their next meeting the Führer informed the ambassador that he "preferred war now to when he would be fifty-five or sixty." During the last days of August appeals for peace were made by a number of leading figures, among them President Roosevelt, the pope, the queen of Holland, and the king of Belgium, the latter speaking in the name of the ruling heads of Norway, Sweden, Denmark, Holland, Belgium, Luxemburg, and Finland. But Hitler adhered to his determination to take over Danzig and the Polish Corridor. On August 25 he summoned Sir Nevile Henderson and asked him to fly to London to offer the British government his friendship, once the Polish question was solved. If he expected another capitulation like that of Munich, he was sadly mistaken. The British ambassador told him at once that his government insisted upon settling the Polish question by free and peaceful negotiation and would keep her pledge to the Polish nation.[10] On August 28 the British government replied to Hitler's offer by suggesting direct discussion between the German and the Polish governments. The reply stated that if such direct

---

[10] On the same day the Anglo-Polish declaration of the previous May was converted into a five-year Assistance Agreement.

discussion led to a German-Polish agreement "the way would be open to the wider and more complete understanding between Great Britain and Germany which both countries desire." When Henderson delivered the answer, the German dictator said that he had to satisfy the demands of his people, his army was ready and eager for battle, his people were united behind him.

On the evening of August 29 Hitler informed the British ambassador that the German government was ready to accept the British proposal for German-Polish negotiations and would expect the arrival of a Polish plenipotentiary the next day. The British answer suggested that Hitler hand the proposals to the Polish ambassador in Berlin and explained that it was impossible to send a Polish emissary on such short notice. But the Führer continued to demand a plenipotentiary. On August 31 the Polish ambassador endeavored to obtain an interview with von Ribbentrop, the Germany foreign minister, but he was not received until evening. Then von Ribbentrop informed him that the offer to arbitrate had expired and that the refusal to send a plenipotentiary was tantamount to a rejection of the German demands. The terms were then broadcast, but the orders had already been given to the German army and air force to advance. At dawn the next day German troops crossed the frontier, and the German air force began to bomb towns and to kill civilians who did not even know war had begun. While this was taking place, Hitler said in a speech in Berlin: "I will not war against women and children. I have ordered my air force to restrict itself to attacks on military objectives."

Hitler invaded Poland believing that the democracies, unprepared and hating war, would not stand by their pledges. In this he was mistaken. On September 1 a warning was handed to von Ribbentrop that Britain and France would fulfill their pledges of support to Poland if Germany did not cease her aggression and withdraw her forces. Hitler made no reply. Early on September 3 the British ambassador delivered an ultimatum, to expire at 11 A.M., asking that Germany suspend the fighting in Poland. When the reply at 11:20 A.M. proved to be unsatisfactory, Britain issued a declaration of war. On the same day France presented a similar ultimatum, to expire at 5 P.M., after which time the French government also declared France to be at war with Germany. It was Britain as the head of an empire rather than Britain as an island state that declared war on September 3. During the first weeks of September all the Dominions also declared war. On September 2 Mussolini had declared his "neutrality"; hence Germany stood alone for the time being.

CHAPTER EIGHTEEN

The Period of Axis Predominance

FROM BLITZKRIEG TO
SITZKRIEG
THE German armies that moved against
Poland on the morning of September 1 were in a technical sense the
best equipped force in the world. Its resources included speedy
reconnaissance and fighter planes, dive bombers, tanks of various
sizes, antitank guns, antiaircraft artillery, and other modern inventions of military science. It also had facilities for moving faster than
any armies ever moved in history. In other words, the marching
power of the *Reichswehr* was measured in motors instead of legs.

Their object was to overwhelm Poland before the French and
British could launch a major offensive in the West. The Germans
were no less eager than they had been at the outbreak of World
War I to prevent a two-front war. In the First World War they had
failed to destroy the French armies before the Russians became dangerous. This time they had taken the precaution to conclude a nonaggression treaty with Russia. The Nazi leaders had hoped that the
announcement of the Soviet-German treaty would result in the
abandonment of Poland by the British and French; when it did not,
they were again faced with the possibility of waging war on two
fronts. To avoid being bogged down in Poland for any length of
time, Hitler concentrated an absolutely overwhelming force against
Poland, leaving only a minimum holding force in the West.

The German general staff had carefully laid the invasion plans
and rehearsed them in maneuvers of the preceding summer. The attack was to be launched simultaneously by two main groups, a northern group and a southern group. Upon entering Poland both were
to converge toward Warsaw. The general direction which the attack
would take was not unknown to the Polish general staff. In order to

499

prevent the Polish forces from being enveloped by the converging attack it decided that they were to fall back in a series of delaying actions to the line formed by the rivers Narew, Bug, Vistula, and San. There, reinforced by the arrival of reserves from eastern Poland, they hoped to hold out until the rainy season would make operations difficult and France and Britain could launch an attack in the West. On paper the plan of defense seemed excellent, but the general staff had failed to take into account the new German strategy known as *Blitzkrieg* (lightning war). This strategy involved the coordination of air and mechanized forces in a swift thrust to overwhelm the enemy. The formula of the *Blitzkrieg* as evolved by the Nazis included: destruction of the enemy air force in a surprise attack; bombing of all means of communication and transportation used for mobilization; dive-bombing and machine-gunning of enemy troop concentrations to open the way for the *Blitzkrieg* troops; speedy advance of the ground forces composed of motorcycle infantry, armored cars, light tanks, and light artillery carried in trucks, supported by fighter and bomber planes; subsequent advance of medium-sized tanks, antitank and antiaircraft artillery, and motorized infantry; advance of the regular infantry and heavy artillery.

This strategy was carried out with great precision and speed. In the early hours of September 1 many hundreds of German planes swooped down on various objectives. Among the first targets were the stations of the Polish air force. So successful was this stroke that almost the whole force was destroyed before it could leave the ground. On September 2 the Germans claimed its virtual elimination. Thereafter they were the undisputed masters of the air and could at leisure bomb almost any target they pleased. While some planes were attacking the airfields, others were dropping bombs on railway junctions and stations, barracks, depots, freight trains, and motor convoys—in short, on all facilities used by an army for mobilization. Special targets were the junctions of the three main north-south railways. The Poles had little defense of any kind against these attacks. Antiaircraft guns were so scarce that many antiaircraft units were equipped only with machine guns. The result was that in a few hours the railway systems practically ceased functioning. This was particularly serious because the absence of good roads forced the Polish army to depend on railroads for mobilization and troop movements. To avoid provocation the government had postponed a general mobilization until the last possible moment; in fact, the order had not been issued until August 31. Hence the attack found the Poles unready and unable to mobilize their forces.

The situation also favored the Germans in other respects. Both the terrain and the weather were "made to order" for the attack. The absence of any natural obstacles in the western part of Poland permitted the German mechanized forces to move with great speed. As the weather was dry, the advance could be made cross-country with little regard for roads. Even the rivers, which were at low level, did not stop them long. Preparedness was so thorough that engineer units arrived with pontoon bridges already cut to the measure of the destroyed bridges. In short, the Germans were able to strike with a maximum force according to a well-chosen plan under excellent weather conditions and over a terrain that was ideal for mechanized warfare.

The result was catastrophic for the Poles. Before their armies could begin either to resist or to retreat, the whole political and military organization of the country was in hopeless confusion. The troops that had been mobilized were broken up into uncoordinated groups by air attacks. These groups lacked such basic equipment as antitank guns which were necessary if they were to offer effective resistance to the German mechanized forces. Consequently the advance was so rapid that in a few days the entire industrial and mining region, situated in the southern part of the country, was at the mercy of the Germans. On September 8 the world was startled by the announcement from Berlin that the Germans had entered Warsaw. A spearhead, it is true, had entered the outskirts of the city but was compelled to retreat because it had outdistanced its supporting units. However, on the 15th the Germans did arrive before the city in force and on the next day the area was practically surrounded.

The last forlorn hope of the Poles that an effective resistance could be organized in eastern Poland was blasted on September 17 when the Russians marched in along the whole length of the undefended eastern frontier. The purpose, as announced by the Russians, was "to protect their own frontiers." Meeting with but little resistance they crossed nearly half of Poland in two days, cutting Hitler off from the rich oil fields of Galicia and blocking his direct road to Rumania. By September 20 resistance was over except for Warsaw and a few other "pockets." In Warsaw the Poles continued their resistance under intensive air attacks but were forced to capitulate on September 27 after, according to the official record, "all possibilities for further resistance had been exhausted because of lack of ammunition, the disruption of the sewer and water supply systems, and the failure of the food supply." Two days later the German Foreign Office announced the signing of a treaty with Russia

which divided Poland between the two countries. The line of division, drawn roughly north and south through Warsaw, gave Russia
substantially more than half the total area. This territory consisted
largely of farms, forests, and marshlands, while Germany got the
industrialized western part of the country. In the central part of
southern Poland a Polish state was set up under German protection,
but it was small and hopelessly landlocked. Thus in a little over a
month [1] Poland had been beaten into submission in one of the
fastest moving campaigns of military history. The collapse had been
so rapid that Britain and France did not find time to give any aid.
But the victory had not been gained without a price, for German
casualties numbered more than 91,000 killed and 98,000 wounded
in addition to heavy losses of equipment. The Polish losses in killed,
wounded, and missing were, of course, very high. But this did not
prevent the Poles from continuing their fight for liberation. While
the underground continued to be active within Poland, those who
managed to escape were organized under General Sikorski. In May,
1940, the Polish army in France numbered over 70,000. Later Polish
airmen were to render invaluable service in the battle of Britain.

The Russians did not stop after annexing the eastern half of
Poland. Foreseeing eventual war with Germany, they decided to improve their strategic position further in the West. On September 29
they signed a treaty with Estonia which yielded rights of military
garrison and naval and air bases on Estonian soil. During the succeeding weeks similar treaties were concluded with Latvia and
Lithuania. As the acquisition of bases and strategic territories had
up to that point not been too difficult, the Soviet government decided to forge an iron belt around the eastern end of the Baltic.
To this end it demanded from Finland, among other things, the
leasing of a section of territory near the mouth of the Gulf of Finland and the exchange of a strip of territory north of Leningrad
for a section of Soviet Karelia. The government was adamant in its
refusal, believing that fulfillment of the demands would gravely
jeopardize Finnish independence. When the Finns refused to yield,
the communist press inside and outside the Soviet Union launched
a campaign of abuse against them. Notwithstanding the fact that
the Russians enjoyed a potential superiority in man power of almost
50 to 1, Soviet newspapers proclaimed in screaming headlines that
the Finns were preparing to attack Russia. Such statements caused
many a wry smile around the world.

To those who had observed Nazi technique it was patent that

[1] The last battle on a major scale was fought on October 5 near Lublin.

A BLOCKHOUSE ON THE MAGINOT LINE

a Russian invasion of Finland was imminent. *Pravda,* the official organ of the Communist Party in Russia, had in fact hinted that Finland might meet the fate of Poland. On November 28 the Soviet government denounced its nonaggression treaty with Finland and two days later Red troops invaded the country at five points. It appeared as if the task of overwhelming the Finns would be easy. Much to the surprise of Moscow and of the world, the Finns, entrenched behind their Mannerheim Line, offered a very effective resistance. The Soviet forces, it is true, enjoyed a certain initial success but at the end of 1939 not one of their five separate drives had achieved success. During the next two months the Finns, under able leadership, continued to stand firmly, meanwhile exacting a high toll in Russian lives. It was only when Russia moved in her best troops and equipment at the end of February that the Finnish troops were forced to give way through sheer weight of numbers. Peace discussions began on March 6 ànd a week later a peace treaty was signed. The terms were more severe than Russia's earlier demands had been. They included the cession of the entire Karelian isthmus with Viborg (Viipuri), the second largest city of Finland; the western and northern shores of Lake Ladoga with its cities; a number of islands in the Gulf of Finland; and several other strips of territory. Furthermore, the Finns consented to the leasing of the peninsula of Hangö and gave the Russians the right to construct a railroad across Finland to Sweden. In short, Finland was placed militarily at the mercy of Russia. The Finns had no other choice than to accept the terms.

Meanwhile there was little activity on the western front. During the early days of September the French army had, after completing its mobilization, undertaken a series of minor operations which carried them a few miles into the no man's land between the Maginot and Siegfried Lines. When the main German forces returned to the West after the conclusion of the war against Poland, the French evacuated the narrow strip of territory they held and retired to prepared positions along their frontier. While these operations were in progress the first instalment of the British Expeditionary Force under General Lord Gort crossed the Channel and moved up to its allotted position on the French front. Then began that unparalleled interlude variously known as *Sitzkrieg,* Bore War, Phony War, or "War of Words." While the British camped on the frozen fields of Flanders, the French sat in the ponderous fortifications of the Maginot Line. The Germans, for their part, having almost completed their own fortified line called the Siegfried Line or

West Wall, also appeared to be watching and waiting. They seemed to have little desire to hurl themselves against the formidable Maginot Line, while the French and British were just as reluctant to charge the Siegfried Line. About all the news correspondents had to report was: "All quiet on the western front." Thus the situation remained for more than five months. All over the world many people were asking such questions as: "Will the coming spring bring a great offensive on the western front?" Others were convinced that the military situation was a stalemate. One British newspaper even suggested that a suitable new marching song for the Allied forces would be: "All dressed up and nowhere to go." As the weeks and months passed, the Nazi menace began to appear more and more remote. On April 4, 1940, Chamberlain declared that "now after seven months of war I feel ten times as confident of victory as I did at the beginning." He felt that Hitler had missed his great opportunity in not overwhelming France and Britain before they had mobilized and strengthened their forces. "One thing is certain," the British prime minister said, "he [Hitler] missed the bus."

THE WAR AT SEA

If the months after the fall of Poland were a period of inactivity on land, at sea where no fortified lines immobilized action there was considerable activity. The comparative naval strength of the belligerents was about as follows:

	Great Britain	France	Germany
Battleships	12	5	3
Battlecruisers	3	2	2
Cruisers	62	19	4
Aircraft Carriers	7	2	—
Destroyers	178	69	21
Escort Vessels	35	—	—
Submarines	56	75	55

The number of German capital ships was, of course, much too low to permit them to challenge the British fleet. The navy Hitler had inherited from the Weimar Republic was inconsequential in comparison with the navies of France and Britain. Because of the restrictions imposed by the Treaty of Versailles only five cruisers, three destroyers, and three pocket battleships of 10,000 tons [2] had been built during the period from World War I to 1933. Of submarines,

[2] The construction of pocket battleships was a method employed by the Germans to circumvent the provisions of the treaty.

the weapon that had nearly won the First World War for Germany, there were none at all when Hitler took the reins of government. During the subsequent years, however, the Germans worked almost frantically to build a fleet of submarines.

Since the German fleet was not powerful enough to challenge the British, to say nothing of the combined fleets of Britain and France, the object of sea warfare became one of blockade. While the British sought to prevent the shipping of essential war materials to Germany, the Germans attempted to "starve out" the British, as they had done in 1917. When war was declared, the British navy at once took charge of the sea and within a few days German merchant ships were largely driven off the ocean as they had been in 1914. The Germans, because of the inferiority of their war fleet in surface ships, were compelled to strike below the surface or from the air. Accordingly they began the sea war methodically with a broad scale submarine campaign. U-boats, already posted at their stations in the Atlantic along the routes usually followed by British merchant shipping, set to work immediately. The war was only nine hours old when the *Athenia*, a 13,581 ton British liner carrying 1400 passengers bound from London to Montreal, was torpedoed without any warning some two hundred miles due west of the Hebrides with the loss of ninety-three lives.

During the first week of the war no less than eleven British merchantmen were sent to their doom. British losses of the first two months were 54 ships representing a total of 236,532 tons, while the losses of British allies and neutrals totaled 91 ships or 356,273 tons. An outstanding feat of the campaign was the sinking on September 18 of the *Courageous*, a battleship of 22,500 tons that had been converted into an aircraft carrier. Even more striking was the exploit of a submarine which penetrated the harbor defenses of Scapa Flow, the British naval base in the north of Scotland, and sank the *Royal Oak*, a 29,150 ton battleship, with a loss of more than eight hundred lives. In sinking this battleship the Germans, so to speak, paid off an old score, for the eight 15-inch guns of the *Royal Oak* had sunk four German battleships at the battle of Jutland during the First World War.

The number of sinkings by submarines decreased sharply, however, after the British organized the convoy system which had been so effective in World War I. Then, too, with the development of improved methods of detection and pursuit, German losses increased. It is estimated that about twenty of the original German sea-going fleet of U-boats were sunk, captured, or badly damaged during the first two months of war. Moreover, the cruising radius of the U-boats was limited. Outside this radius British commerce moved without interference. To support the campaign the German Admiralty revived the raider activity which had taken such a large toll of Allied shipping in World War I, the *Emden* alone having sent 74,000 tons of Allied shipping to the bottom. This time, instead of using merchant cruisers, they used pocket battleships. While the *Graf Spee* pursued Allied shipping in the South Atlantic, the *Deutschland* operated in the North Atlantic. But the success of the two ships was not as spectacular as had been expected. In all the *Graf Spee* sank 50,139 tons before it was cornered by three British cruisers off the coast of Uruguay on December 13. After giving battle, she took refuge in Montevideo harbor. For some hours there was conjecture as to whether she would submit to internment or go out and do desperate battle with Allied warships. But the commander settled the issue by scuttling the ship. The *Deutschland* in the ten weeks she was at sea sank only one British steamer and an auxiliary cruiser. The reason for the comparatively poor results was that most British ships were protected by convoys.

But the Germans did not stop at sending out U-boats and pocket battleships. When the loss of British merchantmen decreased in October, the German Admiralty began to lay mine fields off the coast of Britain. The losses of British and neutral shipping were still not very high until after the middle of November when the Germans began to scatter magnetic mines in the narrow channels of the Thames estuary. These mines, filled with TNT, were detonated when a passing iron hull induced and completed an electrical circuit within the mine. They were either laid by submarine mine layers or dropped from seaplanes. In itself the magnetic mine was not new. The British had used several varieties in World War I, but the Germans had greatly improved their effectiveness. In just one week in November, twenty-four ships of all countries were sunk. The antidote developed by the British was to send out fishing trawlers, which were made of wood and could therefore pass over the mines without detonating them, to sweep the Thames estuary clean of mines at least once a day. Despite German attempts to scare off the trawlers by machine gunning and bombing them from the air, the British fleets continued to do yeoman service in clearing the inshore waters. Instead of "starving out" the British, the Germans succeeded up to the middle of March, 1940, in sinking only about 3 per cent of their shipping. Meanwhile Germany had lost 7.5 per cent of her tonnage by sinking, capture, or scuttling. The rest of her merchant fleet was lying idle with the exception of a small number of ships that moved in the Baltic or within neutral Scandinavian waters.

While the struggle was being waged on and under the sea, there was some activity in the air, but aerial warfare did not move into high gear during the early months. Both sides conducted extensive reconnaissance flights over land and sea. When such patrols met the enemy, there were occasional clashes but beyond this there was little fighting. For the bombers there was more activity. On the 4th of September the first British air attack was made by twelve bombers on Wilhelmshaven, one of the principal German naval bases. The Germans retaliated with a number of bombing attacks on Scapa Flow and Scotland's famous Firth of Forth, but they were all attacks in small force. One of the great surprises was the comparative ineffectiveness of air attacks on convoys of merchantmen and on battleships. Bombs dropped from the air did, it is true, cause considerable loss of mercantile shipping but not so much as had been expected. Against battleships planes were much less effective. The German *Luftwaffe* did not fulfill Hitler's prediction that his bombers would obliterate the British fleet. On October 9, 1939, for example, a flock of German bombers engaged a British force of cruisers which had gone into the open sea in pursuit of German battleships. The result of a five-hour battle was that one of the cruisers was damaged. According to the Nazi leaders the worst was yet to come. On November 15 Marshal Göring declared that Nazi bombing planes had not yet begun to "show the British what it means to be at war with Germany."

THE NAZI JUGGERNAUT CRUSHES FIVE NATIONS

The military inactivity of the winter of 1939–1940 came to an abrupt end on April 9. For months Hitler had been collecting ships and troops in the Baltic ports with a view to seizing both Denmark and Norway. Control of the Scandinavian Peninsula, the Nazi leaders hoped, would give Germany bases for air attacks against Britain and harbors from which her naval units could operate in the North Atlantic. Moreover, such control would mean an additional source of food supplies for Germany and less food for Britain. The Nazis further realized that control of Norway would make it difficult for Britain to interfere with their access to Swedish iron ore which was so vital to the war effort. Plans for the occupation of the two countries had been worked out to the smallest detail. But before the Nazis moved northward both verbal and actual feints were made in the

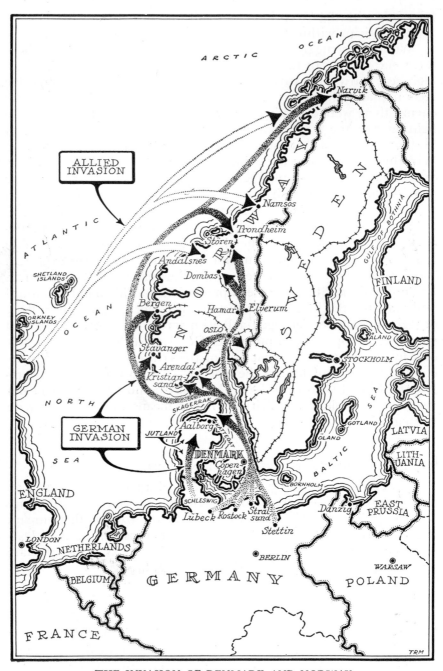

THE INVASION OF DENMARK AND NORWAY

direction of the western front. After an announcement by Marshal Göring that "a decisive blow must be struck in the West," troops were concentrated along the western front and the Swiss border. But the attack did not materialize. Early on the morning of April 9 German troops crossed the Danish border. Before many hours passed they reached Copenhagen, where the guard at the royal palace offered some resistance. But resistance was so hopeless that King Christian asked his people to accept the situation.

While Denmark was being overrun, German forces were also invading Norway, the conquest of which was more difficult than that of Denmark. For months German propaganda had been working on certain susceptible elements with the result that a group of "fifth columnists," some of them holding high positions, were waiting to aid the invaders. On April 7 naval forces were sent out to decoy the British fleet away from the coast of Norway. The next day a formidable expedition left the German Baltic ports, steamed up the Kattegat into the Skagerrak, and at dawn the next morning entered Oslo Fiord. Previously at 1:30 A.M. the commander of three warships at the naval station on the west coast of the fiord had received a telegram ostensibly from Dr. Koht, foreign minister of Norway, ordering him not to fire on the German warships that would come up the fiord. He obeyed the order unquestioningly. The conspirators did, however, overlook the mine layer *Olaf Tryggvason* which was anchored in the fiord. When the German ships arrived at 4:30 A.M., the mine layer promptly attacked them, crippling the cruiser *Bluecher* so badly that it later sank. At 5 A.M. the German minister in Oslo demanded of Dr. Koht that Norway submit to German occupation immediately. He refused. At 9 A.M. bombers swooped down on Fornebo Field, Oslo's principal airport, and battered its defenders into submission. Soon thereafter a swarm of transport planes roared into sight, bringing German troops, light guns, ammunition, and other equipment. Between the troopships and battleships, threats to bomb the city, air transports pouring men and guns onto Fornebo Field, and the activity of the fifth column, Oslo was in full surrender by 4. P.M.

❖❖

THE INVASION OF DENMARK AND NORWAY. *On April 9, 1940, the Germans invaded Denmark and Norway and obtained the surrender of both countries within a few hours.*

Simultaneously German troops landed at Christiansand, Arendal, Egersund, and Stavanger in the south, at Bergen and Trondheim in the central section, and at Narvik in the north. In all these places sheer surprise coupled in varying degrees with treachery and incompetence prevented any effective resistance. Consequently within a few hours every important harbor, all airfields, and five of the six divisional headquarters were in German hands. King Haakon and his ministers managed to escape to England, where they established a government in exile to continue the fight. In Norway the Germans set up a puppet government under a certain Major Quisling, who had previously organized a local Nazi party. As a result the name Quisling quickly became an international synonym for traitor. To strengthen their hold on the country the Germans poured a steady stream of reinforcements into Norway, so that they had a firm grip on it by the time the Allies were ready to act. On April 14 and the succeeding days two small Franco-British expeditionary forces were landed in central Norway, one northeast of Trondheim and the other southwest of the same port. But the difficulties in their path proved insuperable. From the time of their landing they were bombed almost ceaselessly by German planes. Since they had no airfield, they could not send fighter craft up to drive the bombers away. As they pushed forward, the expeditionary forces were threatened with envelopment by mechanized detachments. The situation became so hopeless that the forces re-embarked, the last troops leaving on May 2.[3]

In Paris and London Hitler's occupation of Norway and Denmark brought political crises in its wake. The French overthrew premier Daladier and replaced him with Paul Reynaud. In Britain, too, dissatisfaction with the government came into the open. Even many of Chamberlain's supporters joined with those who demanded that his government be replaced by one that was truly national in that it would include representatives of the opposition parties. In the House of Commons the attacks were particularly vehement. One member declared: "We are fighting today for our life, for our liberty, for our all; we cannot go on being led as we are." He closed his attack with Cromwell's words to the Long Parliament: "You have sat too long here for any good you have been doing. Depart, I say, and let us have done with you. In the name of God, go." Chamberlain was faced with the alternative of either forming a government which would include representatives of all parties or of stepping aside so

[3] An Allied force which had been successful in taking Narvik did not leave Norway at this time but found it necessary to evacuate the town after the fall of France.

that someone else could. He tried the former but found that the opposition would not join a government of which he was the head.
Bowing to the inevitable he resigned on May 10. Winston Churchill
succeeded him as prime minister. His government was a three-
party coalition. One of its first achievements was to set up a Ministry of Air Production to speed the output of aircraft. In an eloquent speech before the House of Commons on May 13 Churchill
did not depict the war situation in terms of an easy victory. He
stated that he had nothing to offer the country but "blood and toil
and tears and sweat." But his driving zeal and inspired oratory were
a stimulus to his countrymen.

After the fall of Denmark and Norway the other small countries
began to speculate as to which would be the next victim. They did
not have to wait long to find out. On May 10 Hitler again unleashed
his forces for a third lightning campaign that was to dwarf the
preceding ones. This time his objectives were Belgium, Luxemburg,
and the Netherlands. Possession of these three states, the Germans
believed, would not only add the industrial resources of Belgium
to Germany's war effort and replenish the German food supplies,
but would also afford them advanced bases for an attack on France
and England. Above all, possession of Belgium would enable them
to outflank the Maginot Line and invade France across the unfortified Belgian frontier. Although both the Belgians and the Dutch
were conversant with Hitler's record, they still relied upon neutrality
to keep them out of the war. Hitler had of course repeatedly stated
that he would not violate the neutrality of the three countries. The
pledge was repeated as late as the evening of May 9.

At dawn the next morning his forces swarmed into the Netherlands, Belgium, and Luxemburg. The last state, having no army,
was occupied without resistance. The other two resisted with every
means at their command. For the third time the Germans adjusted
the *Blitzkrieg* methods to fit a particular situation. While the ground
forces advanced against the vital points, the *Luftwaffe* launched a
devastating attack upon all rearward communications of France as
well as of the invaded countries, particularly upon airfields and
nodal railway junctions. A novel feature of the attack was the use
of parachute troops to capture airfields and to disrupt mobilization
facilities.

It was the Dutch who received the brunt of the opening blow.
Having neither the planes nor the tanks necessary for effective resistance, they knew they would be overwhelmed if help did not arrive quickly from France and Britain. They therefore planned to

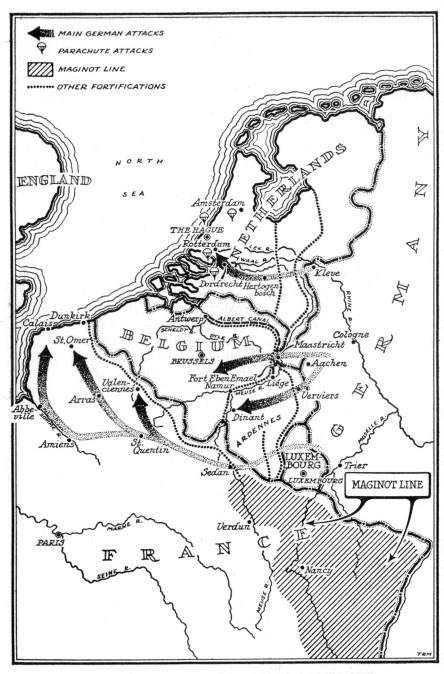

MAIN GERMAN ATTACKS

PARACHUTE ATTACKS

MAGINOT LINE

OTHER FORTIFICATIONS

THE GERMAN INVASION OF THE LOW COUNTRIES

slow down the advance until this help should arrive. Part of their plan called for the flooding of wide areas to a depth which would interfere with the progress of tanks but would not permit the use of barges. In addition they mined the important bridges, constructed pillboxes at strategic points, and made provisions to block the roads. But the German mechanized forces moved with such speed that the Dutch had no time to translate their plans into action. The invaders crossed many of the mined bridges before they could be blown up and used shallow-draft rubber boats to cross the flooded areas. As early as May 13 Queen Wilhelmina and some of her ministers found it necessary to flee to England. The next day the Dutch army was compelled to surrender. Capitulation was expedited by the bombing of Rotterdam. Flying low over the city, German planes reduced more than two square miles in the heart of the city to rubble, with a great loss of life; then the Germans threatened to repeat the procedure in other cities if the Dutch did not surrender at once. By such methods the Dutch were overwhelmed in five days.

Belgium lasted two weeks longer. No sooner had the Germans crossed the border than King Leopold asked the Allies for aid. French and British troops moved forward at once, but the German air force disrupted communications so completely that it was difficult to set up an effective defense. Meanwhile mechanized forces, including about 5000 tanks, advanced with astounding speed. This force, added to the dive bombers, parachute troops, and fifth columnists, succeeded in badly disorganizing the position of the Allies, who had neither tanks nor antitank guns that could stop the advance of the panzer units. The consequence was that the Allies had to fall back toward the Scheldt as early as May 16. By May 18 the Germans had occupied Brussels, Louvain, Malines, and Antwerp. Before another week passed, the cabinet was urging the king to leave the country. But Leopold remained with his army. The Belgian position soon became hopeless. To prevent further bloodshed the king ordered his troops to lay down their arms in unconditional surrender on May 28. Leopold himself was confined to his castle on the outskirts of Brussels.

During the campaign in Belgium a German force had driven

THE GERMAN INVASION OF THE LOW COUNTRIES. *Note the extent of the Maginot Line and the German strategy in breaking through the weaker fortifications along the Belgian border.*

rapidly across southeastern Belgium and had then turned toward Abbeville on the French channel coast. This drive had isolated the Allied forces and left them only the single port of Dunkirk as a means of escape. On the day after the Belgian surrender the official German communiqué announced that the fate of the French and British armies was sealed. By every canon of military strategy they were doomed. But they refused to accept the dictum as final. While some of them sold their lives dearly in rearguard actions which slowed up the forces that were closing in on Dunkirk, the Allies began to evacuate their troops from the bomb-shattered port. At first British and French destroyers ran directly into the canal-like docks to take aboard battalion after battalion. But within a few hours German bombers had reduced the facilities to such a shambles that this method had to be abandoned. Soon one of history's strangest armadas appeared off the beaches. It included merchantmen, passenger steamers, ferries, motor launches, private yachts, fishing smacks, and even tugs with strings of barges. While an outside ring of British and French cruisers and destroyers covered the sky with flaming curtains of antiaircraft fire and the Royal Air Force was using every available plane to drive off German bombers, British and French troops scrambled into the transports to be ferried to Britain. The evacuation continued for six days. London admitted the loss of six British and seven French destroyers, three auxiliary naval vessels, and twenty-four smaller craft out of 1500 vessels employed in the evacuation (May 30–June 4). In addition most of the military equipment the British forces had taken to the Continent was lost. But the armada did succeed in evacuating more than 330,000 soldiers. It was, as Winston Churchill said, "a miracle of deliverance." Britain had suffered a military disaster in France but the rescue of so many troops made it appear almost a victory.

THE FALL OF FRANCE

Hardly had Belgium been knocked out when Hitler launched another campaign. Speaking in the House of Commons on June 4, Winston Churchill said: "What has happened in France and Belgium is a colossal military disaster. The French army is weakened. Belgium is lost. The whole of the Channel ports are in Hitler's hands. We must expect another blow struck almost immediately at us or the French." After twenty-six days of continuous fighting in which considerable casualties were incurred, especially among aircraft and tanks, it was generally believed that the German forces would need some time to reorganize and overhaul their equipment. But they still had a number of armored divisions in reserve. These were quickly pressed into service and on the day after Churchill made his speech they opened the battle of France. The first phase of the drive began on the lower Somme and had as its aim the capture of the French ports. A further drive was launched for the purpose of taking the Maginot Line from the rear. For the first three days the French stood their ground. Several weeks previously General Gamelin had been replaced as chief of the Allied land forces by General Maxime Weygand, who at once set to work to establish a defense in depth. But the time was too short to achieve much. After the third day the superiority of the German mechanized forces began to show. On June 8 there was an ominous retirement of the French left that gave the Germans room for envelopment.

They were not slow in making the most of their opportunity. On June 9 they sent into the battle every plane and every tank they could assemble. The next day advance troops were across the lower Seine west of Paris. When another spearhead crossed the Marne at Château-Thierry on June 12, it became clear that General Weygand had lost control of the situation. The French also realized that Paris was doomed. To save the city from destruction by bombers and artillery, the Allied command decided to surrender it. The government withdrew to Tours and on June 14 the Nazi legions rolled into the city. Many Frenchmen, believing further resistance hopeless, were ready to sue for peace. Premier Reynaud had other ideas. On June 13 he had announced at Tours that France would go on fighting "even if it were in one province only; even if it were in North Africa only." But on the 16th he was forced out of office. President Lebrun at once called upon Marshal Pétain, who was a man of eighty-four, to form a government. He formed a ministry composed largely of representatives of the right, the chief figure being Pierre Laval, a friend of the Germans. The next day Pétain told the people in a broadcast that he had assumed the direction of the government and that he regarded a continuation of the struggle "against an enemy superior in numbers and in arms" as futile. He continued: "It is with a heavy heart I say we must cease the fight. I have applied to our opponent to ask him if he is ready to sign with us, as between soldiers after the fight and in honor, means to put an end to hostilities." The aged marshal imagined that Hitler would talk to him like one soldier to another; hence he surrendered before he had even inquired what the terms of an armistice would be.

In the meantime Germany had gained an ally. On June 10 dur-

ing the darkest hour in nine months of fighting against Germany
Mussolini entered the war. It was generally expected that he would
enter the minute German victory seemed certain so that he could
claim a share of the spoils. When the Germans began to move toward
Paris, he decided that the right moment had arrived. On the afternoon of June 10 he appeared on the balcony of the Palazzo di
Venezia in Rome and announced to a cheering crowd that Italy
was going to war with France and Great Britain. In announcing
Italy's entry into the war Il Duce declared that he had "done all
that was humanly possible to halt the war, but it was useless"; hence
Italy would fight "to safeguard her honor, her interests, and her
future." Italy, he said, was entering the conflict against "the pluto-
cratic, reactionary democracies of the West which at all times have
opposed the march of events and often plotted against the very
existence of the Italian people." "Italian people," he said, "rush
to arms and show your tenacity, your courage, and your valor."
That same evening President Roosevelt expressed the opinion of
many when he said: "The hand that held the dagger has struck it
into the back of its neighbor." Italy brought against the Allies a
navy of more than 700,000 tons, some 4000 planes, and an army of
about a million. The army attacked France at once, but the attack
had little effect on the general situation. Later Italy's participation
did cause the fighting to spread to the Mediterranean, Suez, and
Africa.

Upon receiving Pétain's request for an armistice, Hitler did
not reply for three days. Finally he received three French envoys on
June 21 and handed them the German terms. The next day the
terms were accepted. With his flair for the dramatic Hitler decided
that the armistice be signed at Compiègne in the same railway coach
in which General Foch had handed the German representatives the
armistice terms on November 11, 1918. The terms included: (1) cessation of hostilities six hours after the signing of the Italian armistice,
this being the same time limit as in 1918; (2) the occupation of
more than half of France, giving the Germans control of the Atlantic coast from the North Cape to the Pyrenees; (3) France was
required to pay the costs of the occupation; (4) demobilization of
the French army and surrender of its arms and of all war materials
including artillery, tanks, planes, and coast defenses at German dis-
cretion; (5) the French navy, excepting such part of it as was necessary to protect French colonial possessions, was to be turned over to
Germany and Italy for demobilization and internment, the Germans
promising not to use the ships for their own war purposes. On

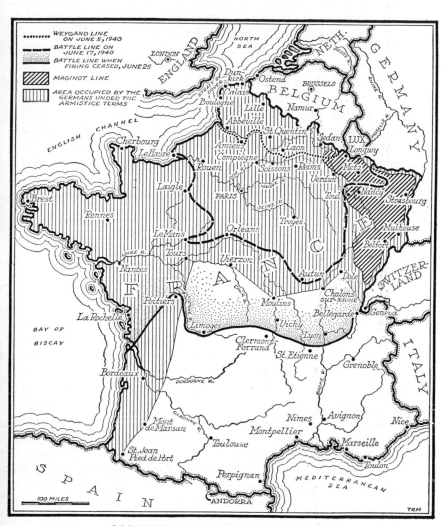

OCCUPIED AND UNOCCUPIED FRANCE

The speed of the German invasion can be seen in the position of the battle line on June 5, on June 17, and on June 25; more than half the country was overrun in less than three weeks.

June 24 the French delegates accepted Italy's armistice terms, and the fighting ceased.[4]

The deeper causes of the French collapse were many and complex. Among the more noteworthy was, first, internal dissension. Constant labor unrest, political corruption and intrigue, and factionalism of various kinds had divided France against herself. While in Germany all the forces of the nation had been working frantically to rearm the country, in France mutual hostility was poisoning the relations between workmen and employers so that production was greatly impeded. In 1936 "sit-down strikes in the factories, lack of energy on the part of the government, the red tape of bureaucracy, and the unreasonable demands of the committees on procurement reduced French production almost to zero. During the year 1937 the number of airplanes produced each month by French factories fell to the almost unbelievable figure of thirty-eight—at a time when the monthly production in Germany was exceeding a thousand planes."[5]

Second, the heart of the French people was not in the struggle. When the war broke out, there was little enthusiasm for it; in fact, considerable sections of public opinion were definitely opposed to it. In general, the French were a tired and sated nation, asking only to be left alone. Right from the start defeatism hung over the country like a thick pall. When the Germans began to invade France, many sections of the population became completely demoralized.

Third, the doctrine of defense which was advocated by many French military leaders was an important factor in bringing about the debacle. Not only had stories of the impregnability of the Maginot Line been hammered into the people day after day by a press in the service of the Daladier government, but the legend was also accepted by many high-ranking officers of the army. It was assumed that the Germans, if they ever attacked France, would batter millions of men to death against the Maginot Line. Hence the general staff prepared only for a defensive war, forgetting that successful decisions are attained by offensive action. The Maginot Line was good so far as it went, but it went only half way along the frontier. It had not been extended to protect the frontier between France and Belgium. When the Germans decided to outflank the Line, as most military experts outside France expected them to do, the French

---

[4] Italy's gains were limited to the few miles of French territory they had won before the armistice. These concessions by the Germans were so minor that many interpreted them as a gesture of contempt for Italy.

[5] André Maurois, *Why France Fell* (1941), p. 13.

were totally unprepared to defend themselves against mechanized forces in a war of movement. They did not have enough planes or enough tanks or enough antiaircraft guns. The air force, which after World War I had been one of the best in the world, had been permitted to deteriorate during the thirties. The British were, of course, in no position to furnish necessary matériel. Nor does it appear that the French general staff had learned anything from the German conquest of Poland. There is no evidence to show that they used the nine months after that event to devise methods to meet such tactics. Hence the troops, though they fought with a dogged courage, were no match for the armies of the Third Reich where an efficient militarism was reinforced and inflamed by the spirit of Nazi revolutionism.

When it became clear that the French would surrender, the thought that raced through the minds of the British people was: "What will become of the French fleet? Will Hitler use it to invade Britain?" Even after the signing of the armistice terms in which Hitler stated that he would not use the fleet, the British continued to be uneasy. Experience had taught them not to put faith in his promises. The addition of the fleet to the German and Italian navies would have given the Axis sea power of such proportions that they could have challenged British control of the sea. Fortunately for the British a large number of French warships happened to be in British ports and could therefore be brought under British control without difficulty. But in North Africa, at Oran and neighboring ports, the French naval commanders could not bring themselves to hand over their ships to the British. On July 3 the British sent a note to the French commander at Oran informing him that the British in the interests of self-defense could not permit the French ships to fall into German hands. The commander was asked either to join the British in the war or to demilitarize his ships for the duration or to scuttle them. When the commander did not reply within a given time, the British fleet opened fire and in a fierce but short naval action destroyed most of the ships. In time the British gained control of most of the French navy, excepting such ships as were scuttled, destroyed, or disabled.

In about ninety days of actual fighting the Nazi steam roller had crushed six countries, two of them with armies considered among the best in Europe. No other great power in modern history had fallen so quickly and so catastrophically as France. In 1870–1871 French resistance was stubborn and persistent compared with that of 1940. When the fall of France was announced to the German people, they staged scenes of wild rejoicing. The great triumphs which their forces had achieved strengthened their belief in the invincibility of their armed forces. Nor were they alone in this belief. Throughout the world there were many who shared it. Of all the countries attacked not one had been able to offer effective resistance. It appeared as if nothing could prevent the Nazis from dominating Europe. Only Britain stood between them and complete victory. "You have just one more battle to win," propaganda minister Goebbels told the German soldiers; "then the bells of peace will ring." The promise seemed reasonable. According to Hitler's timetable he was to dictate peace to Britain in London on August 15.

THE BATTLE OF BRITAIN

Once the Germans had occupied the northern coast of France, an invasion of Britain became a serious possibility. On June 17, the day on which the French government decided to sue for peace, Winston Churchill said in a broadcast speech: "What has happened in France makes no difference to British faith and purpose. We have become the sole champions now in arms to defend the world cause. . . . We shall defend our island and, with the British Empire around us, we shall fight on unconquerable until the curse of Hitler is lifted from the brows of men. We are sure that in the end all will be well." The next day he told the House of Commons that "the battle of Britain is about to begin." By every calculation the moment was propitious for invasion. Britain was ill prepared for resistance. Right after Dunkirk there was but a single fully equipped division available for defense. The others did not have tanks, artillery, and machine guns. They had abandoned all their heavy equipment at Dunkirk, in some cases even their rifles. There were no coastal or road defenses against invasion, such as began to appear over the whole country later.

Why, then, did not Hitler order the invasion at once? Even before the surrender of France the Nazis had proclaimed this as their intention. A number of things caused Hitler to hesitate. First, there was the desire to lay the foundations of the new Europe while the time was ripe. Peasant unrest had been growing in eastern Europe and he feared that Russia might step in before he had established Nazi influence. Second, military considerations prevented him from undertaking the invasion at once. The German forces were disorganized in the sense that they had outrun themselves. Hitler himself was as surprised as anyone over the speedy victory in France.

The battle of France ended so quickly that he and the Nazi leaders did not have a detailed strategy worked out. Nor did they have the specialized weapons that were necessary for a seaborne invasion. Above all, the evacuation at Dunkirk had proved conclusively that a landing in Britain would be possible only if the Germans could win superiority in the air and find some way of neutralizing the opposition of the British navy. Rather than risk an invasion Hitler hoped that he could propagandize Britain into peace. He believed that the people were convinced of the futility of continuing the war; therefore in a "last appeal" he called upon them to submit or be destroyed. Instead of surrendering, they worked harder than ever to produce planes and tanks and guns. The coastal defenses were also made ready, so far as that was possible.

The rejection of his appeal by the British, who were determined to carry on the fight in the face of tremendous odds, infuriated Hitler as few things had. He would show them that they had made a great mistake in deciding to continue the struggle. He would annihilate them. The German radio went into action with a series of broadcasts designed to scare the British out of their wits. London was pictured as suffering the same fate as Warsaw, and the British were told that they would soon be reduced to eating cats as the Parisians did in 1871. When the Nazis proceeded to the attack, their first aim seems to have been to establish supremacy in the air by sweeping the Royal Air Force from the skies, bombing its airfields out of existence, and blasting the plane factories to bits. Thus Hitler would open the way for an easy invasion. But he and his associates grossly underestimated the RAF. Although the *Luftwaffe* had many more planes, the British planes and pilots were better.[6] The antiaircraft gunners, too, quickly improved their marksmanship with practice. Methods of detecting enemy planes improved rapidly. When the visibility was good, the British Air Command would receive reports before the German planes reached the English coast, and at times warning of an impending air raid was given as soon as the Nazis took off from the airfields in France, Holland, or Belgium.

At first the German bombers came to Britain on their forays in mass formations of from fifty to one hundred, largely without fighter plane protection. Each group was usually preceded by dive bombers. During the first weeks the raids were generally conducted during the daylight hours, because the Nazis believed that daylight bombing was more effective. Upon being notified of the approach of enemy

[6] The numerical inferiority was gradually wiped out by increased production in Britain and the arrival of planes from the United States.

planes the RAF pursuit planes would rise and the antiaircraft guns would spray the skies with lead. This double attack often wrought havoc upon the enemy, much to the surprise of the Nazis who had not expected such efficiency. On August 15 the Germans sent a veritable armada—estimated at nearly a thousand planes—of Stuka dive bombers, heavy bombers, and fighters for an attack on southern England. The Spitfires and Hurricanes of the RAF handled them roughly. On that day alone the British shot down 180 planes. During the week ending August 17 the RAF and the antiaircraft batteries shot down no less than 492 while losing only 115 of their own, thereby dashing the Führer's hopes of a quick knockout by the *Luftwaffe*. On August 20 prime minister Churchill paid tribute to the RAF before the House of Commons in the following words: "Never in the field of human conflict was so much owed by so many to so few."

Early in September the Germans began to concentrate hundreds of self-propelled barges, speedboats, and other light craft along the coasts of Norway, the Netherlands, Belgium, and northern France. While invasion troops were being trained to embark and disembark quickly, the German radio warned the British of an invasion. The RAF replied by repeatedly dropping bombs on the concentrations of light craft. During the period of full moon Allied sympathizers were on tenterhooks wondering whether the Germans would launch their invasion before the moon waned. But October came without an attempt. With the onset of bad weather observers concluded that the battle of Britain had settled down for the winter to an air-and-sea war.

Meanwhile the *Luftwaffe* was continuing its attacks. On September 15 a second mass attack was made on southern England. This one fared even worse than that of a month earlier. Definitely confirmed losses of German aircraft on that day amounted to 185. This attack must have wrecked Marshal Göring's hopes of dealing the death blow to the RAF. But the attacks did not cease. Instead of sending large group formations of bombers, the German Air Command now sent them in small flights of from three to twelve directed at widely distributed targets. Bombs were aimed not only at London docks, power plants, gas works, railroad stations, and telephone exchanges, but also at facilities in other British ports, at industrial cities in the Midlands and north country, and even at isolated plants in the open countryside. Much destruction was, of course, wrought by these attacks, but they failed to achieve their purpose of bringing Britain to her knees. Moreover, the *Luftwaffe* paid dearly in the number of planes it lost. Between August 8 and October 31 no less than 2375 were shot down in daylight.

As daylight raiding was not achieving its object, the *Luftwaffe* turned to night bombing. This was a tacit confession of their inability to penetrate the British defenses by day. In making the forays at night the Air Command hoped both to lower the morale of the people by disturbing their sleep and to reduce plane losses. Defense against bombing attacks in darkness was more difficult than during the day.

For the Germans night bombing was facilitated by the use of radio beams to direct their pilots. This obviated the necessity of sighting the target and enabled planes to remain at high altitudes without sacrificing accuracy. Thus a bomber might "ride in" on a radio beam from northern France and when it reached the intersection of this beam with one sent out from some point in the Netherlands the bombardier would drop his bombs knowing that he was directly over his target. In the vicinity of London the principal targets were the dock areas, key points in the water supply system, and important railway junctions. But, while the bombing of London created the biggest headlines, it was not necessarily the most destructive. Intensified attacks were also launched against the great shipbuilding centers of western Britain, the textile centers of the Midlands, and the factories where Spitfire and Hurricane planes were made. Other targets were the seaports of Cardiff, Bristol, Portsmouth, Harwich, Hull, Ramsgate, Dover, and Southampton.

Besides dropping explosive bombs the Germans used incendiaries. The first large-scale incendiary raid was made on London, December 29, 1940. Before fire fighters could rush to the scene, large fires were blazing on every side. Many historic landmarks of old London suffered complete or partial destruction. During the succeeding days civilian spotters and fire fighters were organized to take charge of the situation. Thereafter most of such fires were quickly extinguished. Month after month the bombing attacks continued. From September, 1940, to May, 1941, the British suffered an intensity of air attacks then without precedent. It has been calculated that 43,667 civilians were killed and 50,387 seriously injured before the end of 1941. But the attacks failed to accomplish their aim. British docks and factories, it is true, were destroyed in addition to hundreds of thousands of civilian homes. Whatever loss in production the bombings caused was more than made up by the importation of planes, ammunition, and other military supplies from the United States and Canada. Nor did the Germans succeed in breaking British morale. The bombings made the people more determined than ever to defeat the Nazis. A British girl, living in a much bombed city, wrote in 1940: "It is nothing but Dante's Inferno, but it's marvelous what one can get used to—even bombs. We will beat them and give them their own medicine back." [7] Such statements were typical.

All this time the British did not simply remain targets of the Germans; they were striking back vigorously with their own bombers. Between the time of Hitler's invasion of Belgium and the Netherlands and the opening of the battle of Britain the RAF staged many raids on the Reich. Most of these were in small force. Germany was not exactly an unknown country to the RAF pilots. During the months of the *Sitzkrieg*, the RAF, while making reconnaissance flights, had carefully mapped future targets. Their first objective was the Ruhr Valley which with its mines, foundries, steel mills, and important railway lines was the industrial heart of Germany. Night after night bombs fell on steel works, munitions factories, power stations, oil refineries, synthetic oil plants, and railway junctions. Repeatedly such place names as Düsseldorf, Dortmund, Duisberg, Essen, Cologne, and Gelsenkirchen appeared in British air communiques. After hundreds of bomb clusters had been dropped into the Ruhr, the Germans began to shift much of their war production to remote places. Other favorite targets were plane factories. For a time the air raid sirens screamed almost nightly at the Dornier, Heinkel, Junkers, Messerschmitt, and Focke-Wulf factories. Unremitting attacks were also made on the naval dockyards and ports of Hamburg, Bremen, Wilhelmshaven, Kiel, and Cuxhaven. German airfields in Belgium, the Netherlands, and France were also subjected to heavy bombings. The RAF even ranged as far afield as the great Skoda armament works at Pilsen in Czechoslovakia and various motor, magneto, and aircraft factories in Italy.

Perhaps the most publicized raids were those which dropped bombs on military targets in the Berlin area. While the British were expecting the Germans to attack London, the Berliners lived under the illusion that Berlin would remain unscathed. Marshal Göring had on a number of occasions assured them that their defenses were impregnable, that the *Luftwaffe* and the antiaircraft guns would tear to bits any Britisher who would dare to challenge the Reich's might. Nevertheless, the rain of bombs did come. Berliners learned about air-raid casualties, sleepless nights, and haggard mornings after. It was the first time German civilians had felt the impact of war since Napoleon's day. In the wars of the nineteenth

[7] *Round Table*, vol. 31 (1940), p. 428

century and in the First World War German territory had been immune because the armies had carried the war into the surrounding countries. This time the old strategy had failed. War had come home to the Germans. One American newspaper correspondent reported that the Germans living in the bombed towns were "nervous wrecks from constant raids."

Far more important for the ultimate outcome than the bombing activities was a diplomatic victory won by the British. In March, 1941, the Congress of the United States acted upon prime minister Churchill's statement that Britain "hasn't a chance" unless it could count on unlimited war supplies from America. It passed the so-called Lend-Lease Act which, in effect, was a pledge that the industry of the United States would make up the difference between Britain's limited output of war materials and the growing output of Germany resulting from increased utilization of factories, raw materials, and labor in occupied Europe. In other words, American business entered the war on the side of Britain. From that time on, the menacing shadow of rapidly increasing production lay across Germany's path. The ink on the Act was hardly dry when the President asked the Congress for $7 billion to start the program of building and lending materials to Britain. Previously fifty of the older United States destroyers had been transferred to Britain, which needed them for convoy duty to reduce the growing losses of ships.

But all the war matériel the United States could produce was worthless unless it could be delivered, and the problem of transportation was not simple. Before President Roosevelt signed the Lend-Lease bill the so-called battle of the Atlantic had increased in fury. This time the Germans were determined to make the blockade so effective through the use of submarines, mines, and airplanes that Britain would soon be brought to her knees.

After heavy initial losses, sinkings of British ships had declined as the convoy system was perfected, and for some months it seemed as if the Royal Navy had the situation well in hand. But in the summer of 1940 there was a sharp increase in losses of merchant ships. The fundamental cause of this change was the use by the Germans of the harbors and bases along the coastline from Norway to the Pyrenees. This made the situation of Britain much more difficult and complicated than it had been during World War I when German sea power had largely been bottled up in the Baltic. After June, 1940, the Germans had easy and direct access to the trade lanes of the Atlantic. It was no longer necessary for their submarines to run the gauntlet of minefields and patrols before reaching their hunting grounds. Moreover, Italy's entrance into the war had forced Britain to send into the Mediterranean a considerable number of warships, all of which were vitally needed for antisubmarine and convoy duty in the Atlantic. Then, too, the inability of the British to make use of the bases in western Ireland, which had proved so useful in 1917 and 1918, complicated the problem of escorting merchant ships. Finally, in World War II the Germans had long-range bombers which not only bombed ships at sea but also served as scouts to locate British convoys and to notify the submarines of their course by radio. Thus the Germans could strike more quickly and effectively than ever before.

Until October, 1940, the British had been able to replace their ship losses by purchase, capture, or construction, but after this time the steady toll of sinkings was gradually whittling away the margin of safety. On the very day on which President Roosevelt signed the Lend-Lease bill the British Admiralty announced that during the week ending March 2, German submarines, bombers, and raiders had sunk twenty-nine British and Allied ships totaling 148,038 tons. It was the fourth worst week of the war for British shipping. During the two weeks after the signing of the bill the losses were 240,000 tons.

The heavy losses moved Colonel Knox, the United States secretary of the navy, to declare that the British were losing ships at the rate of three times their capacity to replace them. It is important to realize that even before the war there had existed a world-wide shipping shortage. During the decade after 1929 British tonnage had declined by two million tons and that of the United States by three million. Hence the problem of supplying Britain with the necessary materials at home and on the fighting fronts would have been a major one even if the Nazis had not sunk a single ship. As it was, Britain was doomed to fall steadily behind in the struggle to keep its commerce going unless the United States could ease the crisis by supplying ships. "In no sphere of our war efforts," prime minister Churchill stated, "is the help which the United States government can give us under lease-lend legislation more urgent than that of shipping." In short, the menace of the Nazi blockade was for Britain the most critical aspect of the war.

The construction of a merchant fleet which could assure a constantly greater flow of materials to Britain posed a grave problem for the United States, which was scheduled to produce only one million tons of merchant shipping in 1941. The first move toward keeping open the supply lines was taken by President Roosevelt late

THE WITHDRAWAL FROM DUNKIRK, 1940; A PAINTING BY RICHARD EURICH

in May when he made known a scheme to collect two million tons of existing shipping for transfer to Britain, including the vessels of Axis or Axis-controlled nations tied up in American harbors. While coast guardsmen were boarding the thirty Axis and fifty-four foreign ships to prevent the crews from scuttling them, Congress passed a bill empowering the government to take over foreign shipping immobilized in American ports by the war. Many naval experts felt, however, that aid in the form of ships was only a partial solution of the problem. They were convinced that American convoys would be the minimum of effective aid, but public opinion in general was not ready for this step. The United States neutrality patrol, which operated as far as a thousand miles off America's shores, did, however, give some aid by warning all shipping of the presence of U-boats and raiders in these waters. More than this, the fifty destroyers which the Congress permitted President Roosevelt to turn over to the British, enabled them to give their convoys better protection and to increase the toll of German submarines.

WAR IN THE MEDITERRANEAN AREA

During the first year of the war the Mediterranean basin rarely figured in the news. Although the three exits—the Straits of Gibraltar, the Suez Canal, and the Dardanelles—were of vital importance to both belligerents and neutrals, there was no major struggle for their control. But the picture changed somewhat after Italy entered the war. Mussolini was hungry for conquest. He decided after the Franco-Italian armistice to conquer for himself a great Mediterranean empire at the expense of Britain. In Fascist circles it was generally believed that the battle of Britain would necessitate the recall of the bulk of the British fleet for home duty. With France out of the war, Mussolini was certain he would have his own way in dealing with the British colonies in Africa. A desert *Blitzkrieg*, it seemed to him, would account for Egypt and the Suez Canal. One army would move northward from Italian East Africa, while the other was moving into Egypt from Libya. Gradually the two armies would draw together and finally crush the British in the vise, thus forcing them out of North Africa.

For a time it appeared as if his plans might succeed. In Italian East Africa he collected an army of about 70,000, composed largely of native troops under the command of the Duke of Aosta, a member of the Italian royal family. On August 5, 1940, this army advanced in three columns against British Somaliland, situated at the southern

entrance to the Red Sea. Since the prewar plans for the defense of
Somaliland had been based on the joint resources of France and
Britain, the small British garrison of 7000 was greatly outnumbered.
In the face of such odds it had no choice but to withdraw. The occupation of British Somaliland gave Mussolini the opportunity to
swagger and boast of "a great conquest." With much fanfare the
drive from Libya into Egypt was launched on September 14 by a
second Italian army of about 250,000 white and native troops under
the command of Marshal Graziani. Its aim was to strike across northern Egypt to the Suez Canal. Moving from its bases at Bardia and
Fort Capuzzo, Graziani's forces captured Solum and Sidi Barrani,
while the British retired to Mersa Matruh, the railhead of the line
to Alexandria. At Sidi Barrani the invading army halted to gather
supplies and reinforcements for a drive on Alexandria. But difficulty in obtaining mechanized equipment delayed the advance so
long that General Wavell, who commanded the British army in
Egypt, was able to train and strengthen his forces for a counterattack.

If the British were unable to spare men for the African battlefield, they did station a considerable part of their fleet in the Mediterranean. During the months Graziani was waiting for supplies,
they made a sweep of the eastern Mediterranean looking for the
Italians. A number of brief engagements took place, with the Italians
invariably seeking safety in their bases. The Fascist high command
was apparently trying to keep its fleet intact to defend the long
coastline of Italy in case of invasion. The British, on the other hand,
were trying to entice them into a decisive contest. Throughout this
time the main portion of the Italian fleet continued to hug the harbor of Taranto, on the heel of the Italian boot. Finally on the
evening of November 11–12 the British fleet took position off
Taranto, and during the night torpedo planes from their aircraft
carriers dealt the Italian ships a crippling blow. Three battleships
and two cruisers were severely damaged by torpedoes; this meant
temporary loss of half the Italian line of six battleships. As the rest
of the fleet was no longer safe from attack at Taranto, it sought
shelter on the western coast. This gave the British absolute naval
supremacy in the eastern Mediterranean.

Meanwhile the Axis powers were taking action to eliminate
British influence from the lands on the northern shores of the
Mediterranean. It was a phase both of Hitler's attempt to establish
his "new European order" in the Balkans and of the imperial tradition of *Drang nach Osten* (drive to the east). Forcing the British
out of the Balkans meant not only the severance of important lines of

communication but also Axis control of valuable sources of raw materials. The grain, butter, hogs, and other foodstuffs of these regions would enable the Germans and Italians better to withstand the British blockade. Thus the Balkans were caught in the middle of the contest. But the Axis powers sought to establish their control without the use of force. The means they employed were economic pressure, threats, and propaganda. So that they might exploit these countries to the utmost, Hitler and Mussolini wished to keep them from becoming embroiled with each other. Irredentist feelings were running high at the time. To eliminate one of the causes of friction the Axis powers ordered Rumania to comply with Bulgaria's claim to southern Dobruja.[8] King Carol's government yielded in the hope of obtaining protection against further encroachments by the Russians, who had already occupied the Rumanian province of Bessarabia. It was, however, only the beginning of the partition of Rumania. Before the end of August, 1940, Rumanian and Hungarian delegates were summoned to Vienna, where the foreign ministers of Germany and Italy, Herr von Ribbentrop and Count Ciano, arbitrarily forced Rumania to turn over the northern half of Transylvania to Hungary. In Rumania the Vienna award provoked violent anti-Axis demonstrations, with vigorous denunciations of King Carol for having yielded Rumanian territory. Opposition to Carol became so strong that he abdicated on September 3 in favor of his son, Prince Michael, and departed into exile.

During the succeeding weeks Hitler's "diplomatic offensive" made excellent progress in the Balkans. Pressure was put on General Antonescu, who after King Carol's abdication had become the "strong man" of Rumania, until he accepted the course dictated by the Axis. On September 30 in the Berlin chancellery he signed on the dotted line, thereby making his country a member of the new Nazi order. Soon afterward German troops occupied certain areas of Rumania "by invitation." Three days before General Antonescu capitulated, Count Csacky, foreign minister of Hungary, had signed his country's formal adhesion to the Axis alliances. On October 1 Slovakia, which since March, 1939, had been a German protectorate, was added to Hitler's concert of Europe. In Berlin there was great rejoicing over these successes. The Nazis, however, were still not satisfied. Pressure was also being exerted to force Bulgaria and Yugoslavia into camp. The only Balkan state completely on the British side was Greece. Since the Greeks were immune to diplomatic offensives, it was decided to subjugate them by force.

[8] For Hitler this was another opportunity to undo the peace treaties of 1919.

The Axis power which undertook to conquer Greece was Italy. Relations between the two had been strained since August 14, 1940, when a Greek mine layer was sunk by a submarine believed to be Italian. After much shouting and many threats in the Nazi manner, the Italian government issued a three-hour ultimatum to Greece at 3 A.M. on October 28 over an alleged "frontier incident." Before the government of premier Metaxas had an opportunity to reply, Italian troops had moved into Greece from Albania. On paper the odds against the Greeks seemed desperate. To oppose the modern mechanized forces of Italy, Greece had about two hundred obsolete planes which the Italians could have put out of action on the first day if they had followed German *Blitzkrieg* methods. For land warfare the Greek army possessed no mechanized equipment and very little heavy artillery. Another factor that seemed to be against them was that the strongest part of the so-called Metaxas line faced Bulgaria and not Albania. On the other hand, the Greek troops were hardy and well trained in mountain warfare.

The Italian army which crossed into Greece numbered about 200,000 men. It was apparently expected that at the approach of this force the Greeks would surrender with little or no resistance. For three days the army made good progress. It raced joyously down a half dozen parallel valleys while the Greek troops took to the hills. Confined within narrow valleys the Italians were unable to exploit their numbers or to make good use of their mechanized equipment. The Greeks waited until the columns were strung out and vulnerable, and then began their counterattacks with mountain artillery. "General Mud," who had failed to save the Poles and the French, came to the assistance of the Greeks. The Italians soon became so completely disorganized that the Greeks were able to pinch off the advance columns. Next a series of counterattacks caused the Italians to retreat toward Albania with the Greeks at their heels. Three weeks after they had crossed the border, the Italians were right back where they had started. But the Greek forces did not stop at expelling the enemy from Greece. Pushing on into Albania they took Koritsa (Corizza), the main Italian base, together with a large number of prisoners and much military equipment. Thereafter they continued to advance slowly, so that by the end of 1940 about a quarter of Italian Albania was in their hands.

Coming simultaneously with the naval losses, the failure of forty-three million Italians to crush seven million Greeks profoundly affected Italian morale. It was, indeed, a bitter pill for a nation that had been gulled with exaggerations of its strength in the air and its mechanized striking power on land. Signs of discontent became manifest. As a means of allaying it, Fascist publicists called for more discipline and more purges. For the blustering Mussolini the reverses were a sore blow to his prestige, the Achilles heel of any dictator. It appeared as if the Germans would have to come to Italy's aid. The Duce, however, was still determined to redeem his prestige without help. An editorial in his own paper, *Il Popolo d'Italia*, stated: "Italy will settle her business without help until Greece's back is broken."

But there were more reverses in the cards for Italy. General Wavell, taking advantage of the defeats in Albania and of the British naval supremacy in the Mediterranean, launched an offensive against Marshal Graziani's army early in December. He had been preparing for this move for months by training a heterogeneous army of British, Australian, New Zealand, Indian, Polish, and Free French troops in desert warfare. From this army he picked a striking force of about 40,000, holding the rest in reserve. Although the army he sent against the Italians was small, it was well equipped with tanks and armored cars. More than this, plans were made to coordinate the movements of the mechanized land forces, the air arm, and the British Mediterranean fleet.

Moving out from Mersa Matruh on December 7, the British struck at Sidi Barrani. It surrendered on December 11, together with the entire garrison of 30,000 white and native troops. The British continued to move westward, taking Salum and Fort Capuzzo on December 16 and driving the invader out of Egypt. The next point of attack was Bardia, which surrendered on January 5. From there Wavell advanced immediately on Tobruk, where a stiffer resistance was encountered. But on January 22 that town also fell after a terrific combined attack from land, air, and sea. Nearly 25,000 prisoners were taken. Racing his mobile troops westward, Wavell took Derna on January 30 and Bengazi on February 7. More prisoners were taken at both places. In two months the British had not only conquered the entire northern coast of Africa from Sidi Barrani to Bengazi, but they had also taken vast quantities of military booty and about 140,000 prisoners, which was many more than there were troops in the striking force. It was the first real British success in land fighting during World War II. This success, coming at a time when British morale needed a lift, did much to cheer the entire empire. Wavell moved on to capture El Agheila on February 9, but then the offensive stopped.

The military balance in Libya was changing. General Rommel,

Germany's outstanding student of mechanized warfare, now took charge of the Axis forces in North Africa and a German mechanized division and a force of fighter and bomber planes appeared on the front. British public opinion clamored for the conquest of Tripoli, but Wavell did not have the necessary equipment to achieve this. Furthermore, events in the Balkans necessitated the transfer of British troops there from North Africa. The upshot of it all was that when Rommel's force recaptured Bengazi on April 4, Wavell decided to withdraw his troops to his Egyptian bases in order to avoid encirclement. He did, however, leave a strong garrison in Tobruk, which could be supplied from the sea. The Nazi forces did not stop at Tobruk. With complete recklessness as to lines of communication they charged past the British that had been left there and forthwith took Bardia, only eight miles from the Egyptian border. Pushing on into Egypt, they also captured Salum. Thus in ten days they recovered most of North Africa. Once again the Suez Canal, keystone of all British operations in the eastern Mediterranean, was threatened. But for the time being the center of interest shifted to the Balkans. Thenceforth the North African front was to remain static until the British launched a new offensive in the following November.

While the Libyan campaign was under way, preparations were being made for the conquest of Italian East Africa. An army of 60,000 men from New Zealand, South Africa, India, and other parts of the empire was collected and when it was ready moved against the Italian East African empire from four sides. The Fascists had stationed a modern army of 200,000, including both white and native troops, in their colonies. To overcome this force the British used the strategy of a series of drives against selected points. After the Italians had been driven out of Italian and British Somaliland, the British concentrated on Eritrea and Ethiopia. In the former area, where the pick of Italian troops was concentrated, the Italians entrenched themselves in strong positions on mountain tops and stubbornly held out for many weeks. In Ethiopia the advance of the British polyglot forces was more steady. Native warriors rose against the Italians, harried them behind the lines, ambushed them in the mountains, and made life miserable for them in general. As one British column neared Addis Ababa, the capital of Ethiopia, the Italians evacuated it, and on April 6 the imperial troops marched in without encountering resistance. In Eritrea, too, the Italians were driven out or surrendered. The surrender of the Duke of Aosta and his army on May 19 virtually completed the military conquest of Italian East Africa.

In addition to losing her East African empire Italy had also suffered a naval defeat in the battle of Cape Matapan on March 27. It all started with an attempt to intercept a convoy carrying a small British force to Greece. Upon being notified that Italian ships were in the open, a British squadron at once set out in pursuit. They overtook the Italians after nightfall and by a combined air and naval attack sank three heavy cruisers and two destroyers besides inflicting damage on other ships. The British sustained no damage to their ships and lost only two naval aircraft, an almost unparalleled ratio. This defeat, together with the defeats in Libya and East Africa, left no doubt as to the weakness of the Italian forces. As a result the morale of the people fell to a low level and in Milan and other cities crowds demonstrated against continuing in the war. But the Germans at once increased the number of their army and airforce units stationed in Italy. Thus Mussolini's country became more and more the virtual prisoner of Nazi Germany.

Reinforcement of the German units in Italy was not enough; the Italians also needed help in the Balkans. Although Mussolini had decided to "break the back of Greece" without German help, he made no progress in this direction during the early months of 1941. The Greek troops continued to hold the initiative they had gained earlier in the conflict. But German military preparations as well as the continued "diplomatic offensive" foreshadowed military intervention in the Balkans. On March 1 Bulgaria signed with the Axis; and almost before the ink was dry, German troops began to enter that country through Black Sea ports or across the Danube.

By using the German troops in Bulgaria as a threat, Hitler was able to put heavy pressure on Yugoslavia. This pressure finally induced the prime minister and foreign minister to sign an agreement at Vienna on March 25, according to which Yugoslavia was also to become a part of the "new Nazi order." But the masses had other ideas. A public demonstration followed by a *coup d'état* forced Prince Paul and his ministers into exile, and young Prince Peter was proclaimed king. The new government at once took steps to repudiate the pact of March 25, but nevertheless made professions of friendship with the Axis powers. This did not satisfy Hitler, who had hoped to engulf the Balkans by sheer threat of might. Just when he seemed to be on the verge of success, the doughty Yugoslavs had reversed the position of their government.

Hitler decided to use force where "diplomacy" had failed. The German press and radio at once began to rail against the Yugoslavs, accusing them of beating German residents and burning their homes. This was followed on April 6 by a declaration of war. In Yugoslavia the Germans saw facing them nearly twenty divisions of troops or about 650,000 men, with an airforce of almost nine hundred planes. There was also a Greek army of fifteen divisions or about 300,000 men. Then, too, the British had landed some troops in Greece, including seasoned Australians, New Zealanders, and Britons, all of them eager to avenge Dunkirk. These forces if put together would have constituted an army greater in numbers, though not in training and equipment, than the German force in the Balkans. Again Hitler applied the fundamental rule of his strategy, i.e., to cut the enemy into fragments and then to destroy the fragments one by one. In general, the Nazis employed the same tactics they used in Poland and the Low Countries. The airforce led off the attack by bombing airfields, demolishing bridges, smashing communications, and disrupting vital services in the towns. An American correspondent who was an eyewitness to the first raids on the town of Skoplje reported that the German bombing was "exceedingly accurate, although most of the bombs were of small caliber. Therefore the damage was not permanently serious but of a nature to disrupt all regular services. The power station was out of order. There was neither electric light nor telephone. The radio station had ceased functioning. Army headquarters was knocked about and had been transferred. Telephone cables lay twisted in the road."

Despite the success of the bombing attacks many observers believed that the Yugoslavs would do well in the land battles. Unfortunately their army had little modern fighting equipment, such as tanks, planes, and antitank guns, but it was hoped that this shortage would be offset by the mountainous terrain which was regarded as being more or less blitzproof. The Nazis again upset all calculations. Before the Yugoslavs reached their battle stations, the Germans had virtually completed the first phase of the *Blitzkrieg*. The mountains notwithstanding, they moved almost as fast as if the terrain had been Poland, Denmark, or France. The opening thrust came from Bulgaria through four passes into southeastern Yugoslavia, where the Yugoslav high command had stationed just one division of Croat reservists. While one spearhead turned south into Greece, the rest pressed on across Yugoslavia to meet the Italians at the Albanian border. On the sixth day German patrols met the vanguard of the Italian army. En route the Nazis had taken control of the cities of Nish and Skoplje and much of the strategic Vardar Valley. Two other spearheads, one moving southward from Rumania through Dragoman Pass, entered Belgrade, the capital of Yugoslavia, on April 13. The final collapse of organized resistance was hastened by the advance of another German army from Hungary toward Zagreb, which was taken on April 11. The army moved on toward Sarajevo, the scene of the assassination which kindled the fires of World War I. The Italians also took part in the campaign by sending an army into Slovenia and Croatia. By April 15 the strategical position of the Yugoslavs was so hopeless that negotiations for surrender were opened. The actual surrender took place two days later.

While the Germans were dividing and overwhelming the Yugo-slavs, they were also moving against the Greeks. As three Nazi spear-heads were driving across Yugoslavia, a fourth, as previously stated, turned southward toward Salonika. Still another column, after fight-ing a bloody engagement with the Greek defenders of Rupel Pass, moved into the Vardar Valley. Finding this part of Greece virtually unprotected, the spearheads rolled into Salonika. Next the Germans began systematically to take the forts in the Metaxas Line, which took its place in the list of such sad names as Maginot Line, Manner-heim Line, and Albert Canal. As another Nazi force drove down into Greece from the north, the British-Greek force sought to stem the German advance, but their equipment and supplies were inade-quate and they were gradually pushed back. In the face of the Ger-man superiority the British did not permit themselves to be inveigled into another Dunkirk. They took the precaution of not losing con-tact with a suitable harbor for retreat. At Thermopylae a small force of Australians, New Zealanders, and Britons managed to hold up the Nazi advance long enough to permit the main British force to evacuate from southern Greek ports. On April 26 mechanized Ger-man forces rolled into Athens unopposed. Two days earlier the Greek army in Albania, whose retreat had been cut off, surrendered. By the end of the month the German occupation of the Greek main-land was virtually complete. *Blitzkrieg* methods, combined with air and mechanized superiority, had achieved another speedy triumph. In addition to 345,000 Yugoslavs the Germans claimed to have cap-tured 218,000 Greek and 10,000 British prisoners while suffering but a small number of casualties.

Although the Germans dominated the mainland of Greece, the British still held the island of Crete, which they had occupied with Greek approval shortly after the Italian attack on Greece in the fall of 1940. The British, of course, realized that the Germans would spare no efforts to acquire control of an island of such strategic im-portance. The contest for its possession, which began on May 19, was one of the strangest battles of the war. On the evening of May 19 waves of German bombers appeared over the three main airfields for the purpose of crippling as many RAF planes on the ground as possible and of putting the antiaircraft guns out of commission. After midnight about a hundred transport planes swept in to drop paratroopers near the airfields. Dropped from a height of only four hundred feet, these men reached the ground before many of them could be shot. Other planes dropped rifles, machine guns, light mortars, and ammunition attached to parachutes of different colors. At the first hint of dawn new transport planes came with more parachutists. Gliders, towed by other transports, severed their tow lines over the airfields and, floating gently to the ground on air currents, skidded to a stop before discharging their human cargo. By the time it was light, fighting was well under way, the primary objects of the attack being the airfields and principal roads. As the day ended, the British claimed to have killed or captured 1800 of the first 3000 Germans that landed, but German planes continued to bring more men. By the end of the third day the British had lost the key points of the island. After that it was only a question of mopping up scattered groups. In one respect the Germans failed. They had hoped to capture the Greek king, George II, who had taken refuge in Crete, but he managed to elude capture and to escape to Cairo.

ଗ
ଗ
ଗ

CHAPTER NINETEEN

❋ ❋

The Turn of the Tide

THE NAZIS INVADE
RUSSIA

THE winter of 1940–1941 saw the great German industrial machine again hard at work equipping the army for a specific campaign. In certain circles it was no secret that Hitler was preparing for a final showdown against Bolshevism. Plans to this end had been carefully elaborated by the general staff. If the Nazis were going to overwhelm Russia before armaments from the United States began to arrive in Britain in large quantities, they had to do so in one swift decisive blow; hence they summoned all their strength to deal it. The enormously powerful German army which had been made ready began its march into Russia at 4 A.M. on Sunday, June 22. An hour and a half later the German ambassador in Moscow called on foreign minister Molotov to inform him that German troops had crossed the frontier. The reason for this move, the ambassador said, was the concentration of Red army units near the German frontier. The Soviet foreign minister replied that the German government had presented no objections, that the attitude of the Soviet government was peaceful, and that Germany was consequently the aggressor. In a broadcast delivered later on the same morning Mr. Molotov labeled the attack as "perfidy unparalleled in the history of civilized nations." He further asserted that during the entire period the treaty of nonaggression was operative the Soviet government had faithfully observed its terms.

Stalin said nothing as the Red army braced itself to meet the attack. He had never had any illusions about Hitler's real intentions. Not only Hitler but also Dr. Alfred Rosenberg, the "official philosopher" of the Nazi Party, had advocated the conquest of Russia and the physical destruction of communism. Stalin therefore knew

541

that the Nazis would strike at the first good opportunity. In order to gain time to arm against this attack he had concluded the non-aggression treaty in August, 1939. More than this, he had on April 13, 1941, concluded a pact of neutrality with Japan as a means of protecting Russia's eastern flank in case of a German attack.

While foreign minister Molotov was broadcasting to the Russians, Hitler, his foreign minister Joachim von Ribbentrop, and propaganda minister Paul Goebbels were making public Germany's purported reasons for the invasion. They alleged that the German government had signed the nonaggression treaty in good faith but the Russians had not cooperated. First, Russia had in contravention of the pacts of 1939 forced Latvia, Estonia, and Lithuania to consent to the establishment of Soviet military and naval bases in those countries. Second, the Russian attack on Finland and the subsequent annexation of strategic territory and bases was beyond what Germany considered legitimate expansion of the Soviet sphere of influence. Third, instead of waiting for a peaceful adjustment, the Soviet government had insisted on forceful settlement of its claims on Rumanian territory in June, 1940. Fourth, Molotov had in November, 1940, presented an even more ambitious plan which included the complete abandonment of Finland by Germany, the establishment of Russian military and naval bases at the Straits of Constantinople, and a Soviet protectorate over Bulgaria. Fifth, the concentration of Russian troops near the German borders was a definite threat to Germany. Later, in his speech of October 3, 1941, Hitler stated that he had remained silent while the Soviet government was strangling Finland and overpowering the Baltic States. "I took decision only," he said, "when I saw that Russia had reached the hour to advance against us. . . . We gradually received proof that on our frontiers one airfield after another was set up and one division after another from the gigantic Soviet army was being assembled there."

The foregoing allegations by the Nazi bigwigs were only excuses to the German people for suddenly turning the giant military machine against the Soviet Union. The real reasons were somewhat different. Among the deciding motives was, first of all, the fact that the Nazis could not tolerate the presence of a major military power which could suddenly strike at Germany. Their leaders knew that the Soviet rearmament program was proceeding at a rapid pace. According to reports they had received, it would be completed in large part by August, 1941, after which time the Red army would be a definite menace. Hitler and his general staff realized that they did not dare to launch an all-out attack on Britain so long as the huge Soviet army could fall on Germany's flank. So they decided to strike before preparations were complete. Another factor which motivated the attack was the Nazi hatred of Bolshevism. Ever since the founding of the Nazi Party the Bolsheviks had been Enemy No. 1, and Hitler had ranted endlessly against them. Nothing would have pleased him more than to announce from the steps of Lenin's mausoleum in Moscow that Bolshevism was dead and that National Socialism would reorganize the world. In the hope that he might win the support of anticommunist elements throughout the world and particularly in Britain and the United States, he announced that the time had come "to save the entire world from the dangers of Bolshevism." Finally, the attack on Russia was one of Hitler's oldest ambitions. It was a phase of the old *Drang nach Osten* dream so passionately set forth in *Mein Kampf*. His new order would be incomplete without the inclusion of the fertile Ukrainian plains and the oilfields of the Caucasus. If the war was to last a long time, the Germans would need all the foodstuffs and raw materials they could get from Russia, and Hitler preferred to control them directly rather than depend on Stalin's promises.

Hitler with his flair for ostentation and the dramatic started his campaign on the same day on which Napoleon attacked Russia in 1812. This was, so to speak, a challenge to the achievements of the Little Corporal. He, Hitler, would show the world that he could achieve what Napoleon had failed to accomplish, i.e., to overwhelm Russia. He confidently believed that he could destroy the Red army in a few weeks. His *Blitzkrieg* against Russia would be a repetition on a grander scale of his military triumphs in western Europe. Nor was he alone in his opinion. Military "experts" in many parts of the world believed that he would quickly crush the Red army in steam roller fashion. Some even ventured the opinion that he would reach Moscow in two weeks. As already indicated, the primary aim of the offensive was the destruction of the Russian forces in the shortest possible time. As the campaign developed, it became increasingly clear that Moscow, the main center of communications of European Russia, was the principal territorial objective. A second objective was Leningrad. The German high command seems to have assumed that the fall of Moscow and Leningrad would result in the disruption of the Soviet army and that then the Germans could seize the Ukraine and the Caucasus with little effort. Moreover, Hitler had a mania for capturing capital cities.

The German forces, joined within a short time by the Hungarians, Bulgarians, Rumanians, and Finns, advanced on a front extending more or less compactly for a thousand miles. Unready to meet the attack, the Russians quickly relinquished the Baltic states and Poland and retired behind the Stalin Line, a series of fortified positions where they hoped to make a stand. Not all Russian troops, however, managed to escape. The sweep of the German armored columns surrounded two large forces in the vicinity of Bialystock and annihilated them. Then the panzers rolled on to attack the Stalin Line. Counterattacks slowed the *Blitzkrieg* somewhat, but the pressure was so terrific that the Russians were forced slowly backward. Even the Stalin Line stopped the Nazis only temporarily. By July 16 they succeeded in piercing it at a number of points.

The Nazi forces reached the outskirts of Smolensk on July 17, but resistance in this sector was so determined that the city was not entirely in German hands until about the middle of August. A Russian general described the battle for Smolensk in the following words: "Having covered every inch of ground with corpses, the Nazis broke through to Smolensk. Stubborn fighting for the town proper raged for almost a whole month. The city repeatedly passed from hand to hand. More than one German division found its last resting place on the approaches to Smolensk and in the town itself. Every street and every house was contested by severe fighting and the Nazis paid very heavy for every yard of their advance." As early as July 13 the official German News Agency had announced that "the route to Moscow is open and no further natural or artificial barriers intervene." But the announcement proved to be greatly misleading. The Russian armies still stood as a formidable barrier between the Germans and Moscow. For weeks a stubborn defense held the Nazi forces more or less stationary around Smolensk. Time and again they hurled massive formations against the Russian positions without effecting any decisive change. Even the fiercest onslaughts broke against the rocklike resistance. On September 3 the Nazis themselves admitted that their drive on the central front had been stopped.

In other sectors, however, the Nazis were vigorously driving deeper into Soviet territory. In the northwest the push was nearing Leningrad. The capture of Shlisselburg, the great railway center, on September 9 brought Leningrad within artillery range, and the German guns began a systematic bombardment of the city on the next day. As a last desperate measure to save the city Marshal Voroshilov enlisted the entire civilian and military population to raise defenses. Thereafter operations around this city assumed the character of siege warfare punctuated by occasional attempts to drive

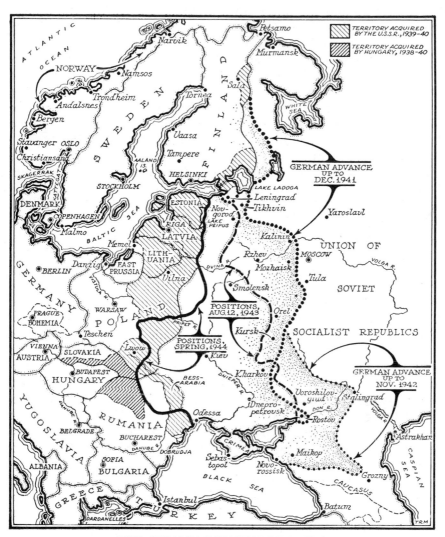

TERRITORY ACQUIRED
BY THE U.S.S.R.,1939-40

TERRITORY ACQUIRED
BY HUNGARY, 1938-40

THE GERMAN INVASION OF RUSSIA

*The grueling nature of the campaign may be inferred from
the slowness with which the German line was pushed back
from the advanced positions of December, 1941.*

back the Germans. Meanwhile the Germans were making spectacular advances in the southwest, where they reached Kiev on August 8 and Odessa on August 13. Resistance at both places was so effective that the Nazi forces did not take the former city until September 20 and the latter until October 16. During the attacks upon the two cities other German forces drove toward the Dnieper. Fearing that he could not hold Dnepropetrovsk, General Budenny ordered the destruction of the great dam near Zaporozhe which besides being the principal source of power for the industries of the Donets basin symbolized Soviet progress to the entire country. One Russian announcement read: "We blew up this dam so as not to allow this first child of the Soviet five-year plans to fall into the hands of the Hitler bandits. The Germans will get nothing."

During the month of September the Germans were busy on the central front assembling a tremendous force for a drive from Smolensk toward Moscow. The drive, designed to open the way to the Soviet capital, was launched at the beginning of October. On October 3 Hitler boasted: "We have planned ahead to such a degree that I have been able, in the midst of this gigantic war of materials, to cease production in many fields, for I know that there is not a single enemy left whom we would not be able to force down with the quantities of war material available." For a time the drive made excellent progress, enabling the Germans to take Briansk and Vyazma. By October 16 they were within sixty miles of Moscow. Inside the city preparations were being made for a street-to-street defense. The Red troops fighting, as it were, with their backs to the wall, stopped the advance for the time being by desperate counterattacks. Although their advance was stalled on the central front, the Nazis were making considerable progress in the southern sector. On October 16 they took Odessa and on the 19th Taganrog on the Sea of Azov. On the 22nd Perekop at the entrance to the Crimea fell and two days later the great industrial city of Kharkov was occupied, but not before all its industrial plants had been either removed or completely destroyed. On November 1 the German forces began an invasion of the Crimea which carried them to the approaches of Sevastopol and Kerch. The latter city was taken on November 18, but Sevastopol continued to hold out. An advance into the Donets region resulted in the capture of Rostov on the Don on November 23. In the northwest the combined Finnish-German forces had also gained ground in their drive on Leningrad. By November 22 the city was surrounded on three sides, but the final impetus to take it was lacking.

In the meantime the Germans on November 15 had started a

drive on the central front with a large force. This time they proposed to encircle Moscow and cut it off from the rest of Russia instead of trying to storm its central defenses. Advance was slow. Gradually the prongs were extended until in the north they reached Klin, where the rambling red house of Tchaikovsky that had been converted into a museum was destroyed, and in the south to Tula, the home of Tolstoy who wrote the great epic of the Napoleonic struggle, *War and Peace*. The menace of encirclement was becoming serious. Just when it seemed as if the plan would succeed, the Russians stopped the offensive by desperate resistance. The drive had reached the limits of advance at all points for the year 1941. It was on December 5, 1812, that Napoleon drew his greatcoat about him and started for France, leaving his Grande Armée behind in Russia. The greatest adventure of the Little Corporal had failed. By the same date in 1941 Adolf Hitler, another corporal, must have realized that his mighty effort to beat down Russia had failed. Three days later, on December 8, he announced: "The German army does not expect to take Moscow this winter."

During five months of fighting, the Germans had occupied about 615,000 square miles of Soviet territory, an area about three times as large as Germany before the annexation of Austria. The cost was high. Hitler himself admitted that. The losses in killed, wounded, and missing had reached a total of 673,415 up to December 1, and during the fighting in December another 300,000 were added. Thus one may conclude that the Nazi losses in man power in the Russian campaign of 1941 were at least a million, exclusive of the sick and frostbitten. In addition they had suffered tremendous losses in equipment, particularly guns, tanks, and planes. Still they had been unable to bring about a decision in their desperate attempt to destroy the Red army. The Russian forces, while sorely beset, were not only resisting bravely but also making preparation for widespread counterattacks. When Hitler underestimated Soviet strength, he made the gravest mistake of his career. Russian armaments were far larger and stronger than Nazi spies had reported. Stalin, knowing that his Nazi "friend" would surely double-cross him, had left no stone unturned in making preparation for the great assault. What Hitler had underestimated above all was the Russian spirit of resistance. The German panzer spearheads, it is true, were able to drive through the lines and take large numbers of prisoners, but the troops that were left behind the spearheads refused to surrender. They organized guerilla groups which would shoot from hidden points, attack lines of communication, or pounce upon smaller groups.

Equal disappointment awaited Hitler in regard to the large

quantities of booty he hoped to collect. Although he had gathered rich stores of all kinds during his previous conquests, his need of foodstuffs, oil, iron, steel, and other strategic metals was still urgent. Under the terms of the trade agreement concluded in August, 1939, Russia was to supply these needs. Germany did actually receive great quantities of grain and oil and much manganese, chrome, and antimony, but she needed still more. Hitler believed that if he could control the vast resources of Russia, particularly the natural wealth of the Ukraine, the danger of losing the war through lack of basic materials would be over. None of these hopes was fulfilled. Soon after the invasion started, Stalin had ordered a "scorched earth" policy like that practiced by the Chinese against the Japanese. In other words, he called for the destruction of everything in the path of the invader. This policy was very literally and efficiently carried out. In all the captured industrial cities both factories and supplies had been removed or destroyed before the Nazis succeeded in reaching them. In the invaded territory generally bridges were burned, railroads torn up, and highways mined to make the advance more difficult. Even Hitler's hopes of quickly turning the Ukraine into a great German food arsenal did not materialize. Many grain-fields which were still uncut were ruined by troops and tanks. Where they were undamaged, agricultural workers were scarce, most able-bodied men having been summoned to the armed forces. Where workers could be found, there was little field machinery for them to use, and before much could be done about it winter set in. Thus the results were picayune. Hitler was temporarily master of the most fertile soil of Europe but could not harvest its coveted fruits.

Hitler's hopes that the conquest of western Russia with its natural resources and industrial centers would paralyze the Russian war effort were doomed to disappointment. Steel production was still about 50 per cent, and coal production large. Both new mines and new armament factories were being opened in the east. While a number of these plants had been successfully transferred from the west, others were equipped with new machinery which had been made in Russia or was imported. Consequently airplane production, for example, was soon at full blast far from the battle front. More important still, Russia was accessible to imports from the outer world. Some aid was soon on the way from Britain and the United States, although neither country had much to spare for the time being. Early in September prime minister Churchill revealed that the British had sent hundreds of planes and also a unit of the Royal Air Force to Russia. Nor was the United States government inactive.

On September 16 it was announced that American technicians were already at work in Russia assembling materials sent there from the United States. The next day $100 million were made available by the Reconstruction Finance Corporation for Soviet purchases in the United States. Finally, toward the end of September delegates from Britain and the United States made arrangements with Soviet officials for supplying war materials on a large scale so that, as Mr. Churchill put it, the Soviet command would "know what monthly quotas of weapons and supplies we can send and they can count upon." Even more important than any formal agreement was the problem of opening an avenue through which the goods could be taken into Russia. As the Leningrad–Murmansk railway had been cut by enemy action, only Vladivostok and Archangel were available as ports of entry. But neither was ice free in the winter, and the hostile attitude of Japan ruled Vladivostok out completely. The best southern route ran across Iran (Persia). German agents in Iran, however, did their utmost to block the passage of materials over this route. When the Iranian government refused to expel these agents at the request of London and Moscow, British and Russian troops invaded Iran on August 26. On September 16 they occupied Teheran. Although peace was concluded after the reigning shah abdicated in favor of his son, the Allied forces continued to occupy the northern provinces.

Before the Nazis invaded Russia it was predicted in many quarters that if they did not succeed in destroying the Russian armies in six weeks they would bog down for the season. This is exactly what happened. In late September there was a light snowfall which did not interfere appreciably with the fighting but did serve as a warning that winter was approaching. Thereafter the Germans fought against time. The increased tempo of their drive betrayed their anxiety to wind up the campaign before severe weather. The advent of winter in mid-October, a month earlier than had been expected, caught them quite unprepared. They had been so certain that they would overwhelm Russia before the onset of winter that such necessities as fur coats and gloves, fur-lined jackets, and heavy footgear had either not been prepared at all or only in very inadequate quantities.[1] Nor had they assembled adequate stores of other essential materials. Moreover, their offensive weapons, particularly tanks, planes, and armored cars, had not been tested under and serviced

---

[1] Dr. Goebbels belatedly tried to solve this situation by ordering all German civilians to surrender their spare winter clothing. It was a makeshift attempt to atone for the lack of long-distance planning.

for zero conditions. Consequently the panzer divisions were largely immobilized after the beginning of December. There were, in fact, few divisions which had any training whatever in the special require- ments of winter warfare in subzero temperatures. Thus the season changed the situation on the eastern front. Whatever advantages of better organization and strategic initiative the Germans may have had in the summer campaign were to a large extent canceled by the change in conditions of warfare.

Early in December the Red army, which Nazi propaganda had repeatedly described as "destroyed," launched a major offensive along the entire front from Leningrad to the Sea of Azov. Winter having settled down in earnest, the Russians had better opportunities for a successful counterattack. For years units of their army had been systematically trained in the tactical needs of winter warfare. Special attention had been given to the training of infantry to travel and fight on skis. In addition the Red army also had many divisions of cavalry trained for winter combat and such special mechanized equipment as propellor-driven armored sleds. All these were now put to the test. In the south the Russians had already battered their way back into the great manufacturing city of Rostov on November 30, only two weeks after the Nazis had taken it. The advance did not stop until the Germans were driven back beyond Taganrog. In the north the counterattack relieved the pressure on Leningrad but failed to dislodge the Germans from Shlisselburg, possession of which severed railway communications between Lenin- grad and Moscow. On the central front the Nazis were swept out of Klin, Kalinin, and Tula. In these attacks the Cossacks, who had made Napoleon's retreat from Moscow a continuous misery, took heavy revenge upon the fleeing columns with their rifles and their glistening sabers.

On the map the Soviet gains did not loom so large as the great blocks of territory the Germans had conquered, but the Red army with the help of winter had done what no other nation succeeded in doing. It had slowed up and finally turned back the "invincible" *Wehrmacht*, inflicting upon it great losses in men and equipment. A correspondent on the central front wrote: "Never before have I seen such destruction over so many miles as that which followed in the wake of Kuznetzov's army from Klin westward. . . . There were at least a thousand military vehicles smashed and burned and destroyed in the first twenty-five miles. Tanks were on their sides, trucks overturned, windshields smashed, and engines shattered." Despite the wrecked equipment, roadside scenes were reminiscent of the familiar paintings depicting the retreat of Napoleon's army, except that the twisted figures of the dead bore swastikas on their uniforms instead of the imperial arms of France.

Besides taking a high toll in human life and in equipment, the retreat had an immense effect on Nazi morale. Soldiers captured by the Russians during the retreat lacked the swagger and bravado which had characterized earlier captives. It even had a depressing effect on the morale of the civilian population in Germany. The mounting lists of dead and the long trains of wounded pouring back into the Reich brought home to the German people the seriousness of the situation. It also effected a change in German opinion of the Russian soldier. Whereas the Nazis had previously denounced the Red troops as being scarcely human, they now began to extol their fighting qualities. Thus a German military expert stated in the *Völkischer Beobachter:* "The toughness and staying power of the Soviet soldiers are almost beyond belief. The Soviets fought for every inch of ground even when their situation was obviously completely hopeless."

THE UNITED STATES AND THE WAR

The outbreak of the Second World War in September, 1939, posed a new set of problems for the United States. From 1935 to 1937 an imposing body of neutrality legislation had been enacted to keep from getting involved in foreign wars. In 1939 the people were still deeply influenced by the isolationist tradition and there was a determination to avoid being sucked into the maelstrom. On the other hand, sentiment was sympathetic to the Allies. From the very outset of hostilities Germany had few defenders except the underground propaganda organizations. Even those sections where a large part of the population was of German extraction sympathized with France and England because they were fighting to maintain the principles of democracy. President Roosevelt made veiled reference to this sympathy when he said on the eve of September 3: "This nation will remain a neutral nation, but I cannot ask that every American remain neutral in thought as well. Even a neutral has a right to take account of the facts." [2] On September 5 the President proclaimed the neutrality of the United States and in accordance with the provisions of the Neutrality Act placed an embargo on the shipment of arms to the belligerents. A few days later he proclaimed

[2] This was in sharp contrast to President Wilson's appeal of 1914 in which he called for neutrality in thought as well as in deed.

a national emergency and issued orders for increasing the defense forces.⟩

But the currents of opinion soon shifted. What at the beginning had been passive sympathy soon became active. Before many weeks President Roosevelt took steps toward giving the Allies material aid. He summoned Congress to convene in special session on September 21 for the purpose of considering a revision of that part of the Neutrality Act which forbade the sale of arms to belligerents. In his message to Congress he styled the arms embargo as "most vitally dangerous to American neutrality, American security, and American peace." Although isolationists immediately denounced the requested revision as unneutral, sympathy for the Allies proved to be the deciding factor. On November 4, 1939, Mr. Roosevelt signed a revised Neutrality Act which permitted the Allies to purchase munitions. It did not, however, permit American shipping to enter the war zone, defined by the President as including the waters about the British Isles, the Atlantic coast of France, and the Baltic. Thus aid to Britain and France meant the right to purchase for cash and to transport the goods across the ocean in British ships. With the repeal of the embargo, large consignments of aircraft and other implements of war, much of which had been ordered by Britain and France before the combat started, could be shipped to Europe.

The events of 1940 caused a further shift in public opinion. After the attack on Norway and Denmark the isolationists lost ground rapidly. When the occupation of the two Scandinavian countries was followed by an attack on Holland, Belgium, and Luxemburg a feeling of anger and horror swept through the country, particularly as a result of such acts as the bombing of Rotterdam. The American people became passionately partisan in that they wanted Hitler defeated. Mussolini's entry into the war at the moment when victory without risk seemed certain, further strengthened the anti-Axis feeling. But it was the French debacle that caused a more violent shock than perhaps anything that had occurred in Europe since the days of George III. As the march of the Nazi legions continued across France, anger and horror gave way to apprehension. It was believed that a victory for the Axis armies in Europe not only would mean a threat to democratic principles but would inevitably lead to war between the Axis and the United States. The possible acquisition of the Allied fleets by Germany convinced most of the remaining isolationists that it was time to take stock of the military establishment. What they found was the world's second strongest navy and one of the world's smallest armies. The size of the army was increased almost at once, and on June 17 the President signed bills increasing naval tonnage by 11 per cent. The next day Admiral Stark, Chief of Naval Operations, recommended a 70 per cent increase of the navy so that the United States would be ready for every eventuality. It was the first step toward a two-ocean navy. In addition a program for an airforce of 35,000 planes and an army of millions was adopted.

When France crumpled and Britain stood alone against the control of Europe by the Axis powers, it became clear that only the United States, the one great industrial power outside Europe, could furnish Britain with the arms needed to fend off the German attack. Realizing that Britain was the last bastion of democracy, public opinion favored giving her every material aid the United States could command. In the presidential elections of 1940 support for the British cause was endorsed by the platforms of both major political parties. General John J. Pershing, who had led the United States expedition to Europe in World War I, supported the aid-to-Britain campaign with the statement: "By sending help to the British we can still hope with confidence to keep the war on the other side of the Atlantic." Even a majority of the isolationists asked only that the administration be careful not to plunge the country into actual fighting. Aid to Britain took various forms. Of the utmost importance was the increasing canalization of trade into Britain and British Commonwealth territories. During the period from September, 1939, to August, 1940, Britain, Canada, Australia, the Union of South Africa, and India received 95 per cent of all American exports of airplanes and airplane parts, and 90 per cent of the firearms, munitions, and explosives.

As the stream of materials which flowed to the British was hardly more than a trickle in comparison with their needs, used arms, ships and planes were turned over to them. Thus, to replace some of the munitions they had lost in the evacuation of Dunkirk, equipment from the United States reserve stocks of World War I was sold to them in June, 1940. Included in this equipment were 600,000 rifles, 80,000 machine guns, 316 trench mortars, and nine hundred 75 mm. field guns as well as a large supply of ammunition. In addition, 240 obsolete army and navy planes were sold. To enable them to give their convoys better protection, fifty over-age destroyers were transferred to the British navy, in return for which the United States acquired eight strategic bases on British soil in the West Atlantic and the Caribbean. Finally, during the period from September, 1939, to the end of 1940 the United States sold 132 merchant ships to Britain and 43 to Canada.

During 1941 the United States became more and more deeply

involved in World War II. On March 11, after two months of spirited debate, Congress passed the Lend-Lease Act which empowered the President to provide goods and services to those anti-Axis countries whose defense he deemed vital to the security of the United States. The next day he submitted his seven billion dollar budget. During the succeeding months large quantities of materials financed by this budget were made available to the British and to a lesser extent to the Chinese and Russians. But the problem of transporting these supplies still remained most pressing. Britain was unable to replace her sea losses despite increased production. To relieve the need for ships the United States in the same month seized two German, twenty-eight Italian, and thirty-six Danish ships anchored in American harbors. This made it possible to release a corresponding tonnage to Britain, but even this was only a temporary solution of the problem. Early in April Washington negotiated an agreement with the Danish minister which placed Greenland under American protection for the duration of the war and gave this country the right to establish naval and air bases on the island. Thus the United States was able to extend protection to merchant ships to within 1800 miles of the embattled British Isles.

Month after month the country was moving nearer to a "shooting" war. On September 1, in an address marking the second anniversary of the opening of World War II, the President uttered the following "fighting" words: "I know that I speak the conscience and determination of the American people when I say that we shall do everything in our power to crush Hitler and his Nazi forces." The *New York Times,* commenting on this speech, stated in an editorial (September 3): "The United States is no longer a neutral in this war. It is no longer on the side lines. It has made its choice. It is a belligerent today. . . . The definitive action was the passage of the Lend-Lease Act." Next day the destroyer *Greer,* en route to Iceland with mail and plainly marked with a large American flag, was attacked in full daylight by a submarine. This submarine, which the Nazis admitted to be German, deliberately fired a torpedo at the *Greer* but missed. A week later the President took another step toward war when he announced in a radio address that he had ordered the navy to shoot if necessary. This statement was amplified in an article by the President published in *Collier's* on October 11, in which he stated that this country could not afford to wait until it was physically attacked "before starting to shoot." The real commitment came in the Navy Day address of October 27 when he said: "The forward march of Hitlerism can be stopped and it will be

stopped. Very simply and very bluntly—we are pledged to pull our
own oar in the destruction of Hitlerism." Not long after, Congress
as the result of the sinking of a number of ships during September
and October repealed the remaining provisions of the Neutrality
Act (November 14), thereby permitting the arming of the United
States merchant ships and their entry into the war zones. Thus the
United States had abandoned all but formal pretenses of remaining
at peace with the Axis. The American people were now allied with
those of the British Commonwealth in everything but fighting. Many
began to wonder when the fighting would start.

The final decision was thrust upon the nation on December 7
when Japan attacked American possessions in the Pacific. After
opening a decade of aggression by the invasion of Manchuria on
September 18, 1931, Japan had joined Germany and Italy in signing the German-inspired anti-Comintern Pact in 1936 (November
25). The following summer saw the Japanese launch large-scale
military operations in China. Although they succeeded in taking
many large cities, they failed to subdue the country. By 1940 the
"undeclared war" in China had developed into what appeared to be
a stalemate, but increased aid to China from the United States
during the succeeding months raised the specter of defeat. Their
leaders began to look for an "honorable" way out of the dilemma.
The answer was provided by the militarists—expansion to the south.
In the years since Japanese troops had marched into Manchuria,
conditions had changed greatly. Britain, occupied at home in fend-
ing off Nazi attacks, was no longer able to act as policeman. Nor
could the Dutch and French do much to protect their interests so
long as they were under the Nazi heel. Moreover, the United States,
exponent of the *status quo* in the Far East, was busy aiding the
British to resist the Nazi onslaught. Thus the time appeared auspi-
cious for the Japanese to establish a "new order" in Asia, one that
would not concern itself merely with the Chinese millions. For some
years the Japanese had been enviously regarding two prizes in particular, the Dutch East Indies with their riches in rubber, oil, and
tin, and French Indo-China, with its tin and zinc mines, its coal,
and its great rice paddies.

When the Germans engaged the Russians in 1941, thereby removing another brake, the expansionists saw their way clear for a
showdown with the United States and Britain. In September, 1940,
Japan had moved completely into the Axis camp by signing the
Tripartite Pact. This enabled the militarists to dangle the threat of
a two-ocean war before the Americans. It was hoped that it would

induce the government to close its eyes to any territorial changes that might take place in the Far East. Before signing the Tripartite Pact the Japanese had insisted upon Hitler's endorsement of their plan to occupy Indo-China. The endorsement must have been given, for on September 22 the French authorities at Hanoi, the capital, announced surrender to the Japanese ultimatum, and the Japanese forces moved in. Determined that seizure of Far Eastern territory must cease, President Roosevelt on July 26 froze all Japanese assets in the United States. The nations of the British Commonwealth at once took the same step and the Dutch East Indies followed suit. A few days later President Roosevelt subjected all oil shipments to Japan to licensing and sharply restricted the shipment of scrap iron to any points outside this hemisphere.

Thus the Japanese government was harassed by economic pressure from within and without. On the outside the blockade which the so-called ABCD powers (America, Britain, China and the Dutch East Indies) established, cut off about 75 per cent of normal imports. Inside Japan the shortage of materials, added to the strain of a war economy and the needs of a growing population, caused widespread economic distress. Conditions became so bad that fear of an inner explosion gripped the leaders. Army and navy cliques who had sponsored the program of aggression that started in 1931, saw their influence on the wane and decided that action of some kind was imperative to regain their hold on the people. Meanwhile German advisers were also pressing for action. A war with the United States, the Germans hoped, would stop the flow of American materials to Britain and Russia.

Before resorting to arms, the militarists decided to see if they could not prevail upon the United States government to reverse its stand. For this purpose Mr. Saburo Kurusu was dispatched to Washington early in November of 1941. The same day on which he boarded the trans-Pacific clipper to San Francisco, the *Japan Times and Advertiser,* mouthpiece of the Japanese foreign office, stated that Japan's patience had "reached the point of exhaustion" and then proceed to set forth a list of minimum concessions that the Americans and British would have to make if they were really desirous of a peaceful settlement of affairs in Asia. Included in the list were the following: cessation of all military and economic aid to China; a policy of "hands off" in China so that the Chinese would be "free to deal with Japan"; acknowledgment of Japan's "co-prosperity sphere"; recognition of Manchukuo; and removal of all restrictions upon shipping and commerce. Envoy Kurusu arrived at San Francisco on November 14, announcing that he might make "a touchdown"; but when actual negotiations began, it became evident that the ideas of the two nations were diametrically opposed.

President Roosevelt and secretary of state Hull had few doubts regarding the ruthless temper of the Japanese, but they clung to the hope that the militarists might still come to their senses before taking an irrevocable step. Preliminary discussions began on November 17 between Mr. Hull, Mr. Kurusu, and Mr. Nomura, the Japanese ambassador. As early as the next day the Japanese representatives left with Mr. Hull the notorious memorandum which set forth as Japan's terms for the settlement a list of demands almost identical with those published twelve days earlier in the *Japan Times and Advertiser*. In presenting the memorandum to Mr. Hull, Mr. Kurusu and Ambassador Nomura asked him to bring the matter to the attention of the President at once for a final answer, adding that they could not be responsible for the conduct of their government if the answer was delayed. During the next days President Roosevelt and Mr. Hull carefully canvassed the situation in search of a formula on the basis of which the "peace conversations" could be continued. Finally on the afternoon of November 26 the secretary of state handed the Japanese ambassador a note setting forth in detail the terms upon which the government believed an amicable settlement of all the outstanding difficulties in the Pacific and eastern Asia could be achieved. The proposals included the withdrawal of all Japanese forces from China and Indo-China, recognition by Japan of the territorial and political independence of the Asiatic countries, future adherence of Japan to the rules of law and order in her relations with other countries, relinquishment of her "Greater Asia Co-prosperity Sphere," and withdrawal from her association with the Axis powers.

The Japanese preferred not to make a complete about-face. Since the final decision to go to war must have been made very soon after they received Mr. Hull's note of November 26, the final stage of the "peace negotiations" was an elaborate piece of make-believe in order to gain time so that the units could reach Pearl Harbor for the surprise attack. On December 2, when the Japanese cabinet suggested that negotiations in Washington should continue, the aircraft carriers that appeared off Pearl Harbor on the morning of December 7 must already have left port. President Roosevelt, it appears, did not expect the break to come before the receipt of the Japanese reply to the note of November 26. Evidently anticipating that it would give rise to a crisis, he dispatched a personal appeal to

Emperor Hirohito on Saturday, December 6, urging him to co-operate in the effort to maintain peace in the Pacific. The appeal closed with the words: "I address myself to Your Majesty at this moment in the fervent hope that Your Majesty may, as I am doing, give thought in this definite emergency to ways of dispelling the war clouds. I am confident that both of us, for the sake of the peoples not only of our great countries, but for the sake of humanity in neighboring territories, have a sacred duty to restore traditional amity and prevent further death and destruction in the world."

PEARL HARBOR AND AFTER

Less than twenty-four hours later the Japanese dropped bombs on the naval fortress located on the Hawaiian island of Oahu. There was no warning of any kind, not even such an ultimatum as Hitler was wont to issue before he sent his legions across the border. At 7:55 A.M. on December 7 dive-bombers, torpedo-carrying planes, and fighter planes, totaling more than a hundred, with the insignia of the Rising Sun emblazoned in red on their wings, roared over Pearl Harbor. The attack was in imitation of the Nazi *Blitzkrieg* tactics. The Japanese appeared to reason that if they could destroy the Hawaiian fleet they could proceed to the occupation of selected points in the Far East without fear of a flank attack. The time was set for Sunday morning when most of the ship and aircraft crews would be on holiday leave. Aided by the element of surprise, the Japanese succeeded in sinking or damaging severely five battleships, three destroyers, a mine layer, a target ship, and a floating drydock. In addition they damaged three battleships, three cruisers, a sea-plane tender, and a repair ship. On nearby airfields their bombs destroyed more than 240 army and navy planes. Most serious were the losses in personnel. The treacherous attack caused the death of 2343 officers and enlisted men; the number of wounded was 1272. In short, United States naval and air power in the Hawaiian Islands was paralyzed for the time being. Within the next few hours the Japanese struck in a carefully planned offensive at the islands of Wake, Midway, and Guam, the city of Manila, and the British base at Singapore. Only after these attacks did they issue a formal declaration of war.

At 2:05 P.M. Eastern Standard Time, after the bombardment of Pearl Harbor had been under way for forty-five minutes and hundreds of American soldiers and sailors had already perished, Ambassador Nomura and Envoy Kurusu walked into the State Depart-

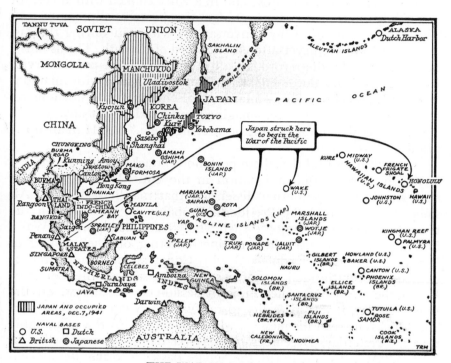

THE WAR IN THE PACIFIC

*The vast extent of the war area in the Pacific is indicated by
the fact that the approximate distance from San Francisco to
Hawaii is 2400 miles, from Honolulu to Guam 3760 miles,
from Guam to Manila 1700 miles, from Darwin to Singapore
2185 miles, from Singapore to Manila 1580 miles, and from
Manila to Tokyo 1860 miles.*

ment in Washington to deliver to Mr. Hull the Japanese answer to the note of November 26. Upon receiving the note the secretary of state proceeded to read it at once. Having finished the farrago of insults and falsehoods he arose and in a voice choked with anger, for he already knew of the attack, said to the Japanese representatives: "I must say that in all my conversations with you during the last nine months I have never uttered one word of untruth. This is borne out absolutely by the record. In all my fifty years of public service I have never seen a document that was more crowded with infamous falsehoods and distortions—infamous falsehoods and distortions on a scale so huge that I never imagined until today that any government on this planet was capable of uttering them." Mr. Hull abruptly dismissed his callers.

It was but natural that these perfidious attacks should generate a feeling of outrage and indignation in the United States, but they also wiped out any internal dissension that may have existed. All stood as one behind the President. Probably no President in the history of the country enjoyed such wholehearted support. In Washington Mr. Roosevelt held a cabinet meeting on the evening of December 7 and later conferred with Congressional leaders on arrangements for the delivery of a special message to the Congress. When the two houses met in joint session at 12:30 P.M. on the following day, it was in reality to ratify rather than to declare war. The President read his message which opened with the memorable words, "Yesterday, December 7, 1941—a date which will live in infamy." After he concluded, the Senate passed a formal declaration of war unanimously, while the House passed a declaration with only one dissenting vote.[3] The absence of any debate such as had taken place when President Wilson asked for a declaration of war in 1917 was an eloquent commentary on the feelings the Japanese attack had aroused.

Other nations quickly stepped to the side of the United States. Britain, in fulfillment of the pledge made by Winston Churchill on November 10 that he would support the United States in a war with Japan, also issued a declaration of war.[4] This example was soon followed by the other nations of the Commonwealth and by the Dutch East Indies. China, which after more than four years of fighting was resisting the Japanese more determinedly than ever, took

[3] The one negative vote was cast by Miss Jeanette Rankin of Montana, who had also voted against war in 1917.
[4] Because of the difference in time between England and the United States the British declaration actually preceded the one in Washington.

steps at once to act in close cooperation with Britain and the United States. Before many days passed, the doubts regarding relations with Germany and Italy were also resolved. On December 11 both Hitler and Mussolini announced that their countries were joining Japan. All that was left for Congress to do was to declare formally that a state of war had "been thrust upon the United States." Thus the circle of war closed around the world, almost every important nation becoming involved with the entrance of the United States and Japan.

Although the Japanese had sunk or damaged a large number of ships, wrecked a large number of planes, and taken a large toll of human life, they had failed in the primary purpose of "knocking out" the United States before the war really began. The attack, instead of discouraging the people, only strengthened their resolve to fight to a victorious conclusion. The nations aligned against the Axis had such a great preponderance of man power and such a tremendous potential of industrial power that there seemed little doubt in the Allied countries as to the outcome of the war. But the victory still had to be won; hence the people of the United States quickly set about making their war machine equal to the task. In every direction vast changes were inaugurated to transform the nation from a state of partial defense to one of total war, which demanded that every resource and device had to be organized and exploited and the energy of every individual employed in a common effort. In short, war became the major industry. Congress at once began to pass the legislation necessary to accelerate the war effort. It passed an amendment permitting the use of national guardsmen and selective service troops in countries outside the Western hemisphere, and another measure amended the Selective Service Act of 1940 by requiring the registration of all men from 18 to 64 years, inclusive. Every department and agency of the government, in fact, became busy with the new tasks. Nor was this all. Industry also speeded its output, with the result that ships, planes, tanks—all the machines of war—were soon pouring from the factories in an ever-swelling stream.

JAPANESE CONQUESTS

Japan's striking power proved to be much greater than had been thought possible. This put the Allies on the defensive throughout the broad expanse of the Pacific during the five months after Pearl Harbor. With the United States navy damaged so severely, the Japanese could have taken the Hawaiian Islands and might even have threatened invasion of the mainland, but they decided to launch a series of attacks in other directions. As a nation already mobilized, Japan was ready. The United States, Britain, and the Netherlands, on the other hand, were not prepared to send adequate supplies and reinforcements to the East. At this time the navy was not as yet a two-ocean navy. What remained of the Pacific fleet was not large enough to fight off the Japanese, who had concentrated their entire navy in this area. Moreover, the Japanese had the advantage of operating from their home bases that were thousands of miles away. In regard to land forces they had an equal initial advantage. While they had their armies ready to strike, the United States was just in the process of collecting and drilling a force. Public opinion still regarded Germany as the chief enemy. Whatever war equipment could be spared was being sent to the conflict in Europe.

The efforts of the Japanese met with speedy success on all sides. Only three days after Pearl Harbor their bombers sank with a heavy loss of life the two British battleships, *Prince of Wales* and *Repulse*, which had ventured into the Gulf of Siam without fighter escort. Their naval supremacy strengthened by this victory, they proceeded at once to attack various American, British, and Dutch possessions. Their first target was the islands of Guam, Wake, and Midway which they believed would be used as steppingstones in moving American forces to the East. Guam, for the fortification of which Congress had voted funds too late, was quickly occupied, but the subjugation of Wake was more difficult. The contingent of 378 marines stationed on this island repelled attack after attack, sank seven Japanese ships, including a cruiser, and shot down a number of enemy planes, before it was overwhelmed. Although the military installations on Midway were subjected to severe bombings, no attempts were made during the first weeks to land enemy troops on it; hence this last island continued in United States hands. But the loss of Guam and Wake made the task of sending reinforcements to the Philippines almost insuperable.

Simultaneously with these attacks the Japanese had sent larger forces against other Allied possessions, among them Hong Kong. This colony, which had been a British possession for a century, had developed into the greatest trading center of southern China. It had been expected that in case of war it would be one of the first objects of enemy attack, and preparations had been made against assault; but the man power stationed there was not sufficient to repel the Japanese. As early as December 11 it became necessary for the defenders to abandon the mainland positions and retire to the island. The rejection two days later of an ultimatum to surrender the island caused the Japanese to launch an all-out assault by land, sea, and air. The defenders still held out for almost two weeks. A particularly determined attack on December 23 and 24 with mortar fire and dive bombers caused the garrison to bow to the inevitable. The surrender came on Christmas Day.

The attack on Singapore was no less successful. This city, situated at the southern tip of the Malay Peninsula, was the great British naval base in the East. Many regarded it as the key to the defense of both British and Dutch possessions in the region. After driving down the peninsula from various points, the Japanese forces reached the "gates" of Singapore at the beginning of February. On February 8, after an intense bombardment by artillery and dive bombers, assault troops crossed the Straits of Johore in steel barges to gain footholds on the island. The garrison, hoping that help would arrive, fought back desperately. The tightening grip of the Japanese, however, forced a surrender on February 15. The loss of Singapore was a severe blow to the strategic position of the Allies in the Far East. After renaming it Shonan (Light of the South), premier Tojo told the Japanese parliament that the possession of this base would enable the Japanese to conquer all British and Dutch possessions in the Far East, including India, Australia, and New Zealand.

Although events were to prove Tojo's statement overoptimistic, success did continue for some time. Before Singapore fell, the Japanese had started a campaign to conquer the Dutch East Indies. They had advanced into Sumatra and had also taken the naval base of Amboyna, east of Celebes. After the release of the forces that had been fighting on the Malayan peninsula, they made preparations for an all-out attack. On February 21 Allied air and naval units attacked a convoy carrying Japanese troops to the Dutch East Indies and inflicted considerable damage on it. But a Japanese fleet appeared on the scene to meet the main body of the Allied Far Eastern fleet in a series of engagements which began February 27 and ended March 1. In these engagements the Japanese succeeded in badly crippling the remainder of the Allied fleet. Allied losses included five cruisers and six destroyers. It was the greatest Japanese naval victory since Pearl Harbor.

For the Allies this disaster spelled the doom of the Dutch East Indies. The Japanese, unhampered by naval threats, could now bring up reinforcements to complete the conquest. Striking at three principal points in Java, their forces moved swiftly inland. The army which the Dutch had organized in the East Indies, numbering about 130,000 men with 400 planes, fought back fiercely and took a heavy toll of men and equipment. This force, however, was not strong enough to stop the advance. On March 5 Batavia, the capital of Java, fell. The capture three days later of the Dutch headquarters at Bandung completed the campaign.[5] With the surrender of the Dutch army on March 9 all but scattered resistance ceased.

Concurrently with these campaigns the Japanese were also waging a campaign in Burma. A woefully inadequate British force of not more than 20,000 set up one defense line after the other but was pushed back again and again until the Japanese were only sixty miles from Rangoon, the capital. At the beginning of March the British, aided by American volunteer fliers, made a last desperate stand on the Sittang River. Their line held for a time, but the Japanese finally managed to breach it, thereby sealing the fate of Rangoon. On March 8 the British troops evacuated the capital and made their way as best they could to India. The possession of Burma meant that the southern terminus of the famous Burma Road, the vital gateway for war supplies to the Chinese, was in enemy hands. As a result the situation of the Chinese became most critical. To relieve it the Allies had to find other means of transporting supplies to the Chungking government. The principal means employed thereafter was air transport, more particularly planes based in India.

Some of the most bitter fighting of the early months of 1942 took place in the Philippines, which the Japanese attacked simultaneously with Hong Kong. They were determined to secure the submission of the islands for at least two reasons: first because they lay across the path of Japanese expansion, and second because of their wealth of natural resources. They were defended by a force under the command of General MacArthur consisting of 40,000 Filipino and 15,000 United States troops, with a small airforce that was no match for the Japanese. The principal target was Luzon, the main island. Through the use of their superior air and naval forces the Japanese were able to make landings at a number of places and by Christmas of 1941 had succeeded in overrunning all the island except the area around Manila Bay. On January 2, despite the determined resistance of MacArthur's men, they took both Manila and the naval station at Cavite, forcing the troops to retreat to the Bataan Peninsula and the island of Corregidor.

The Japanese were to find the reduction of Bataan a slow and costly procedure. They gradually brought up more and more rein-

5 The Dutch naval base at Surabaya on the island of Borneo fell the next day.

forcements so that about 200,000 troops were eventually engaged in the attack. Day after day they launched assaults which were repulsed with the same regularity. At times General MacArthur's men even resorted to counterattacks which forced the enemy to retreat. Nevertheless, the process of attrition was wearing down the United States-Filipino force. Malaria and dysentery were also decimating the ranks. As only a small trickle of supplies reached them, hunger and exhaustion contributed their share toward weakening the defenders. By the beginning of March the situation had become so hopeless that President Roosevelt ordered General MacArthur to escape from Bataan and to proceed to Australia to assume supreme command of the Allied forces in the southwest Pacific. This change put Lieutenant General Jonathan Wainwright at the head of the Filipino-American force in its gallant but hopeless stand. During the succeeding weeks Japan attacked the defenders with renewed intensity, bombarding them from the air, pounding them with heavy artillery, and attacking them with infantry units. Finally on April 9, after four months of valiant fighting against insuperable odds, the soldiers accepted bitter defeat. General Wainwright removed 3500 troops to the fortress of Corregidor, after which the remaining troops, numbering about 35,000 surrendered.

But the conquest of the Philippines was not yet achieved. For almost a month the guns of Corregidor and its surrounding forts continued to bark defiance despite intensified artillery and air attacks. The last phase of the battle began with the heaviest artillery and air barrage of the entire struggle. After this had continued for four days, the Japanese succeeded on May 4 in landing assault troops on the rocky shores. All the next day to the following dawn the two forces fought a savage hand-to-hand struggle over the rugged two square miles of island before the Japanese finally overpowered the weakened and half-starved defenders. Finally on May 6 the fighting ceased and terms of surrender were discussed. General Wainwright was compelled to accede to the immediate surrender not only of Corregidor and its surrounding forts but of all the scattered forces operating in various parts of the Philippine Islands. Prisoners taken by the enemy numbered about 11,500. Thus the epic fight which won wide acclaim for the Filipino-American army came to an end.

Thus far the outlook for the Allied cause in the Far East had been gloomy indeed, but in May and June the clouds were lifted for a few weeks. The domination which the Japanese navy had exercised was sharply curtailed as the result of two battles. The first was the battle of the Coral Sea, fought off the coast of Australia.

Early in May a great Japanese armada was sighted moving through the southwest Pacific for the evident purpose of cutting the United States supply lines to Australia. Naval planes from aircraft carriers tore into the Japanese force, battering it so badly that it beat a hasty retreat. At least twenty Japanese ships were sunk or disabled, including an aircraft carrier, a heavy cruiser, a light cruiser, two destroyers, and four gunboats. It was the first serious defeat of the Japanese in the south Pacific. But they quickly rallied their forces and a month later aimed a new blow at Midway Island. Once again Allied air and naval forces rose to the challenge. In the battle of Midway (June 3–7) they met and drove back a powerful concentration of some eighty ships organized on the grand scale of modern war. Land-based planes from Midway Island struck the first blow and forced the armada to turn back. The retiring Japanese were then pursued by carrier-based planes which inflicted great damage. On the third day Admiral Nimitz announced: "A momentous victory is in the making. . . . Pearl Harbor has now been partially avenged." Of the eighty ships at least twenty were sunk or damaged, among them four carriers, two heavy cruisers, and three destroyers. It was a crippling blow, one which definitely ended Japan's naval superiority in the south Pacific.

While the main Japanese fleet was battling at Midway, a smaller force was busy seizing three islands of the Aleutian chain stretching from Alaska toward Siberia. On June 3 planes from a Japanese carrier bombed Dutch Harbor and Fort Mears on Unalaska Island, and several days later landings were made on Kiska and Attu, and later on Agattu. These desolate, fog-bound islands were of strategic importance because they might have served as a base for an attack upon Tokyo or upon the Japanese Kuriles which were only eight hundred miles away. Late in August a United States task force of army troops supported by the navy occupied the Andreanof Islands, 125 miles west of Kiska. Using these as a base, planes bombarded the Japanese positions on the Aleutians and also took a heavy toll of Japanese ships. By October the Japanese had retired from two of the islands to concentrate their installations on Kiska.

Up to this time the Allied forces had been largely on the defensive. The purpose had been to check the Japanese advance while the Allied nations were gathering strength to take the offensive. The first blow in this offensive was struck on the night of August 6 when an expeditionary force made a surprise attack on the Solomons, a fringe of volcanic islands strung for six hundred miles across the northern end of the Coral Sea. Since Japanese occupation of these islands held a threat to the supply line to Australia, it was decided to dislodge the enemy. As the task force approached, General Mac-Arthur's airmen began smashing at air bases at Rabaul, Lae, and Salamaua to prevent the Japanese from using their planes against the convoy. The first objective was Tulagi Harbor on Florida Island, one of the best harbors in the South Seas. Simultaneously landings were also made on the large island of Guadalcanal and on two smaller islands. Guadalcanal was of particular importance because the Japanese were cutting a large airfield out of the jungle on this island. On the morning of August 7 United States marines established a beach head and after three days of bitter fighting succeeded in driving the Japanese off the airfield into the jungle. The Allied force was equally successful in its attack at the other three points. On the night of August 8, however, the fleet suffered a severe loss when the Japanese surprised four cruisers that had been stationed to screen landing operations and quickly sank all of them. But the Allied force managed to hold the harbor of Tulagi as a base for naval attacks, and also the airport at Guadalcanal, named Henderson Field in memory of a hero of the battle of Midway.

The Japanese militarists refused to accept the loss of the Solomons, a loss that was a sharp blow to their prestige. Time and again they made determined attempts to drive the marines from Guadalcanal. Repeatedly under cover of midnight mists they landed small bodies of troops to reinforce the guerilla bands still lurking in the black mangrove jungles of the island. Heavy air attacks were aimed at the airfield on a number of occasions. Warships also approached to pour shells into the airfield zone. On October 11 Allied warships intercepted a Japanese fleet convoying a considerable number of transports to Guadalcanal. Other engagements in which Allied sea and air forces frustrated attempts to land reinforcements took place during the subsequent weeks. In mid-November a large force of battleships, cruisers, and destroyers was sighted convoying a fleet of transports headed for Guadalcanal. Although outnumbered, the Allied fleet drove them back with the loss of two battleships and five cruisers. It was another serious blow to the Japanese navy. Their futile attempts to retake the Solomons in 1942 cost them more than sixty ships sunk and more than eighty damaged, to say nothing of the 450 planes that were shot down over Guadalcanal. The ratio of United States losses was about one to seven.

At the end of the first year, the Japanese were well entrenched in Malaya, Burma, the Dutch East Indies, and the Philippines, territories rich in materials for which they had special need. It seemed as if their plan for a Far Eastern co-prosperity sphere would be realized. In addition they possessed a chain of outposts which were advantageously placed to serve as bases for a further advance. But their successes had been largely achieved by default. The United States had been caught off guard and unprepared; British efforts had to be incidental; and the Netherlands were prostrate when the Japanese launched their attack. During this year while the Japanese were using up much equipment which they could not soon replace, the industries in the United States were outdistancing all previous production records. By the end of the year six of the eight ships that had been damaged at Pearl Harbor had not only been repaired but were back in service, and many new battleships, carriers, cruisers, and other types of ships had been added to the fleet. Planes were rolling off the assembly line in almost unbelievable numbers. What this would eventually mean was indicated when a group of army bombers operating from the U.S.S. *Hornet* carried the war to the very heart of Japan on April 18, 1942. The planes unloaded demolition and incendiary bombs on Tokyo, Yokohama, Kobe, and Nagoya.

FAILURE OF THE NAZIS IN RUSSIA

Throughout the winter of 1941–1942 the Russians continued to exert relentless pressure on the Nazis to force them westward. In the Leningrad area they slowly pushed them away from the old tsarist capital, and in the region southwest of Moscow they retook several towns. But all this did not deprive the Nazis of the initiative. It was universally expected that with the coming of spring they would reopen a major attack. In preparation, both sides were bringing up reserves of men and supplies. The primary objective of the new offensive was, however, different. In embarking upon the invasion the Germans had aimed at the annihilation of the Russian armies in a short time, but a year of fighting had convinced them that their resources were not adequate to the task. Not only the fighting qualities but also the fighting equipment of the Soviets had surprised the world. The new strategy therefore called for a major blow in one sector. The starting point was to be the Ukraine, where the Germans had made such spectacular advances in the preceding summer. A drive to the Volga and into the Caucasus would separate the Russian armies of the north from those of the south and would also cut off large areas from which they drew military supplies, food, and reinforcements. Conquest of these areas would also deprive the Russians of industrial establishments in which much of their heavy equipment was produced and thus prevent them from organizing a major offensive against the Germans. Finally, the complete mastery of the Black Sea coast would render the Black Sea fleet ineffective and put the Germans in a position to drive toward Egypt around the eastern end of the Mediterranean.

Before starting the drive the Nazis had one task to complete. In the autumn campaign they had overrun most of the Crimea but had failed to take Sevastopol. They had begun to lay siege to it in October, 1941, and had continued throughout the winter. In a few weeks dive bombers and large mortars reduced it to a mass of ruins. Nevertheless, the Russians held out until the beginning of July. On the third of July the last Russians evacuated and the next day the Russian high command announced that Sevastopol had fallen.

Meanwhile on June 28 the big drive toward the Don River had begun. For it the Germans collected an estimated sixty divisions, of which ten to twelve were armored divisions with a strength of more than a thousand tanks for the battlefront and an equal number in reserve. As for strength in the air, they had collected over 3000 first-line planes or enough to permit the use of a thousand in a single mission. The immediate objective was Voronezh, an industrial city of 325,000 inhabitants a few miles east of the Don River or about 125 miles from Kursk, the starting point of the drive. The offense was opened by the *Luftwaffe* with a fierce bombardment of the Russian positions east of Kursk. After the planes had opened a gap in the Russian defenses, tank columns pressed on rapidly. At the end of a week Berlin announced that spearheads had advanced more than a hundred miles and had reached the Don on a broad front. On July 7 powerful tank forces crossed the Don and were followed by many divisions of infantry. Not many hours later this force was attacking Voronezh. Although the Berlin radio claimed that it had been taken, the Germans never did get a secure hold on it. Russian troops fought so determinedly for the possession of the city that the battle surged back and forth in the streets. On July 16 the Russians claimed the initiative at a number of points, and four days later the Germans were driven back across the river at one or two places.

If the Germans had been able to hold Voronezh, they would, it appears, have driven directly eastward to the Volga. By a rapid fanning-out they could then have moved northward to approach Moscow from the rear and southward to cut off the route along which lend-lease supplies reached Russia via the Caspian. But the stubborn resistance at Voronezh caused them to change their strategy.

They shifted the direction of their drive southward between Kharkov and the Don toward the city of Voroshilovgrad. After taking it on July 20, they exerted their main pressure against the lower Don and the city of Rostov. Fighting in the outskirts of Rostov was fierce. Here the Russians sent into battle their giant fifty-two-ton tanks, called KV's,[6] which were equipped with a three-inch cannon in addition to machine guns and were protected by armor so heavy as to make them almost invulnerable to fire from the 77 mm. guns of the Germans. The Russians did not, however, have enough KV's to overcome the Nazi superiority in armored vehicles, tanks, and planes. Berlin claimed capture of the city as early as July 26, but not until two days later did the Russians admit being forced out.

After the fall of Rostov the German high command divided its offensive, sending part of its forces to clear the Black Sea coast and the Caucasus and part toward the Volga at Stalingrad. In the Caucasus one of the major objectives was the petroleum fields. The great fields of Baku were more than seven hundred miles to the south, but smaller oil fields, including those of Maikop and Grozny, were nearer. The northern part of the Caucasus was also a fertile area from which the Russians drew a substantial part of their food supply. For a time the Germans advanced with remarkable speed. In rapid succession they took, among other places, Maikop, Krasnodar, and Georgievsk, the last being 275 miles southeast of Rostov. On September 10 they also captured the port of Novorossiisk on the Black Sea. But they failed to penetrate the Caucasus range and reach the Baku oil fields.

In the meantime the other drive had reached Stalingrad, which was to be the scene of a long epic struggle. This modern city was one of the proudest fruits of the Soviet economy and as such held a special place in the nation's affections. More than this, its large tractor and armament plants made it an essential part of the military effort. It was not a fortress like Sevastopol, but an industrial city protected by such fortifications as could be thrown up on short notice. When the Germans approached the city toward the end of August, they admitted that it would take them two weeks to drive the Russians out of the city. The Russians, however, had different ideas. The garrison, composed of both civilians and troops, met the attacks with a do-or-die determination. Although the Nazis had a distinct superiority in tanks and planes, the defenders made up in fighting spirit what they lacked in equipment. At first the Germans achieved a series of penetrations, but their advance was gradually slowed.

[6]Named after Marshal Klementi Voroshilov.

The Russians contested not only every building but every room with their lives. Casualties were so numerous that, as almost every report stated, it was "impossible to count the corpses." German dead often numbered two thousand in a day. Despite the great sacrifice in men and materials, the Germans were unable to take the city. Vanity induced Hitler to continue the attack even after his generals advised him that further attempts were fruitless. The most determined effort was made on October 14 after Hitler demanded the occupation of Stalingrad regardless of cost. But the Russian defenses held. General Chuikov said of this attack: "I would not have believed such an inferno could open up on earth. Men died but they did not retreat."

While the Germans were battering away at Stalingrad, the Russian high command projected a plan for encircling the attacking forces. On November 19 they launched two spearheads, one from the north and the other from the south. Both were to proceed westward and then toward each other in a pincer movement. Driving rapidly toward their objectives in *Blitzkrieg* fashion, they succeeded in a short time in encircling fourteen divisions. The ordinary means of supply being cut off, the German high command had to use aerial transports to provide these troops with food and ammunition. On Christmas Day they made a desperate attempt to relieve the encircled divisions, but were unsuccessful. All that remained for them was to sell their lives as dearly as possible. At the end of the first week of January less than 200,000 Germans remained of the original force of 330,000.

When the Nazis did not reply to an ultimatum of January 8 which demanded surrender, the Russians launched a determined attack to annihilate them. On January 17 it was estimated that the German garrison had been reduced to less than 80,000. Ten days later only 12,000 remained. The decisive triumph came on January 31 when the German force in central Stalingrad, together with sixteen generals, surrendered. The last of the resisting groups was overwhelmed during the succeeding days, thus bringing the epic of Stalingrad to a close. For the Russians it was an occasion for jubilation tempered by the knowledge that a bitter struggle was still ahead. Nevertheless, Stalingrad was the definite turning point in the Russian campaign.

THE DESERT SEESAW

In North Africa the year 1942 saw the desert seesaw swing back and forth. At the opening of the year the British Eighth Army was engaged in an offensive which had started in November and by January had pushed General Rommel back to El Agheila. But the tide of battle soon began to flow against the British. While they had weakened their forces to send aid to the Far East, the Axis forces had succeeded in getting reinforcements in tanks, aircraft, and artillery. Rommel had, above all, received new 88 mm. guns which were far superior to the British 25 pounders. This gave him the necessary strength to strike back. Starting slowly, he retook Bengazi in late January. For the next few months the lines remained fairly constant, but in June Hitler's "master of desert warfare" unleashed the long-expected offensive with terrific power. On a single day (June 13) his forces destroyed 224 British tanks out of a total of 300. The British quickly retreated into Egypt after leaving a garrison of 25,000 men in Tobruk. Previously Tobruk had held out against the fiercest Axis bombardment for a period of eight months. This time General Rommel concentrated the bulk of his forces in a violent attack on the port by planes, artillery, tanks, and infantry. The next day (June 21) Tobruk surrendered with its entire garrison and large quantities of equipment, including one hundred tanks. Hitler was so jubilant that he immediately promoted Rommel to the rank of Field Marshal.

But Rommel did not stop with the capture of Tobruk. He pursued the retreating British into Egypt, where he engaged them at Mersa Matruh. The British commander, realizing that his army was in danger of being encircled, withdrew farther eastward. Rommel quickly took Mersa Matruh with six thousand prisoners and again set out in pursuit of the British. This time the British decided to make a stand at El Alamein where the desert narrows to a passage of thirty miles. Here Rommel could not employ his favorite strategy of using his tanks in wide sweeps to threaten the British with encirclement, for they were protected on the right by the Mediterranean and on the left by the swampy and impassable Qatarra Depression. On July 1 the Nazi marshal hurled his entire strength against the British, but the line held. The Axis forces had finally been stopped. As El Alamein was less than seventy-five miles from Alexandria, it was feared that Rommel might try again to smash through to Cairo and the Suez Canal. The Afrika Korps was by this time, however, not only battle weary from months of fighting but also far removed from its supply bases. In August Rommel did probe the British line for weak places, but for the time being no major offensive developed. Nevertheless, so long as Rommel remained in Egypt he constituted a menace to Alexandria and the Suez Canal.

In August General Auchinleck, who had made the successful stand at El Alamein, was replaced by General Montgomery. Preparations were soon under way for a counteroffensive. Nor was Rommel idle. He prepared a line of fortifications which he confidently believed would hold against any assault. On a visit to Berlin in early October he told reporters: "We did not advance into Egypt merely to be thrown out again. We propose to hold what we have." On the night of October 23 General Montgomery opened his offensive with a terrific artillery barrage and air bombardment. For a week he continued to attack various points of the line. Finally on November 4 he succeeded in driving two armored wedges through the defenses. Making the most of the opportunity he quickly sent three armored divisions through the gaps, with the result that Rommel was forced to a retreat which gradually became a rout. The Axis forces were mercilessly bombed by British and United States planes. Six Italian divisions, which had been abandoned by the German mechanized divisions without food and water, surrendered en masse. By November 8 the British were in possession of Mersa Matruh, and before another week passed the Axis forces had been driven out of Bardia and Tobruk. On November 4 prime minister Churchill told parliament that the forces in North Africa had suffered 75,000 casualties. After Derna and Bengazi fell to the British in quick succession, a lull of three weeks ensued during which both sides reorganized. Next the British advanced on El Agheila and forced the Germans to evacuate it. The British continued to pursue the Germans, and the end of the year saw Rommel still in full retreat toward Tripoli and the Mareth Line.

ANGLO-AMERICAN OCCUPATION OF FRENCH NORTH AFRICA

The success of the British in Libya made the Allied nations fear that the Axis leaders might decide to occupy the French North African colonies as compensation. To forestall such a move President Roosevelt and prime minister Churchill decided upon an Anglo-American expedition to occupy the colonies. Plans were laid for the greatest armada of its kind ever undertaken, one that was to include more than 500 troop and supply ships and a protecting force of more than 350 warships of all kinds. Preparations were carried out with such secrecy that the blow, when it came, was a complete tactical surprise. Gibraltar was made the rendezvous of the armada. Divided into two convoys it proceeded to establish beach head landings at a dozen points in French Morocco and

Algeria. On the night of November 7, just eleven months after the attack on Pearl Harbor, President Roosevelt surprised the world with his announcement that a powerful United States force under the command of Lieutenant General Dwight D. Eisenhower was landing on the Atlantic and Mediterranean coasts of French North Africa.[7] The element of surprise greatly reduced the opposition. Algiers, one of the three main objectives, surrendered at the end of the first day. At Oran the resistance was stiffer, but by November 10 troops gained control of the city and the nearby naval base at Mers-el-Kebir. The most determined resistance was encountered at Casablanca. Not only did the French coastal batteries fire at the assault boats but the immobilized French battleship, the *Jean Bart,* hurled 15-inch shells at the armada. Her guns were, however, soon silenced by dive bombers. A French destroyer squadron which harassed the landing forces also had to be eliminated. After the landing had been made, tanks and infantry quickly forced their way into the city, but the French commander and his forces continued to resist until November 11. On that day Admiral Darlan, commander in chief of the Vichy-French forces, ordered resistance to cease in all of French North Africa.

All in all, the occupation of this vast territory with its coast line of 1500 miles, was accomplished in less than four days and with small losses. The total casualties were 860 killed or missing and 1050 wounded. The occupation placed Marshal Rommel's army in danger of being gripped by powerful Anglo-American pincers. The drive by the United States forces from the west and the British from the east to expel the last Axis troops from North Africa was soon to begin. In Europe Hitler responded to the occupation by sending troops into unoccupied France and by permitting Italian troops to occupy Corsica and Nice. Marshal Pétain, head of the French government which had its headquarters at Vichy, protested that Hitler was violating the terms of the armistice. The Germans ignored the protest. Hitler had also promised that the French warships would not be used by Germany or Italy. This pledge was no more sacred than previous Nazi promises. On November 27 a Nazi force entered the naval base at Toulon to take over the ships that were anchored there. The plan was frustrated by the garrison. Some of the ships escaped to North Africa; the others were scuttled by their crews.

In the Atlantic the loss of shipping to U-boats continued at an alarming rate. In January, 1942, losses in United States and British

[7] Because of the difference in time the landings actually took place at 1 A.M. on November 8.

ships set a new record. As the Allied naval resources were strained almost to the limit in furnishing convoys for the main supply routes, shipping in the Caribbean and along the eastern coast of the United States was almost without protection during the early months of 1942. Hence these areas became the favorite hunting ground of the U-boats. During one week in March submarines sank twenty-two ships in the Atlantic. On June 16 the United States navy reported the sinking of ships off the Virginia coast in sight of thousands of spectators on the shore. A week later the navy announced that the system of convoys had been extended and that plans had been projected whereby lanes of coastwise shipping would be patrolled in an effort to cut down the losses. When convoys were established, the submarines went elsewhere in search of victims. Hence the losses continued. The total number of Allied ships sunk during the first six months of 1942 was set unofficially at 327. United States shipyards set a new record in June by launching sixty-six new ships, but the situation called for still more. The losses of the next six months brought the total for 1942 to well over ten million tons, while production for the year was only eight million tons. Replacement of tonnage became such an urgent problem that President Roosevelt called for sixteen million tons in 1943. But the sinkings were not all one-sided. On June 18, 1942, it was claimed in London that the RAF alone had sunk or damaged 750,000 tons of Axis shipping thus far in 1942.

CHAPTER TWENTY

The Allies Triumphant

FOR the Germans the year 1943 had
opened with the Stalingrad disaster. It was the most serious setback
they had suffered in the war. Shortly after Hitler announced that
Stalingrad was practically taken, they were told that most of the
large force had been wiped out and the rest captured. To many
the report seemed incredible. As further details arrived, however,
they realized the import of the defeat. Nor was this the only bad
news. On January 1 the Russians had taken Velikiye Luki and annihilated the entire garrison when it refused to surrender. This loss
was not acknowledged until January 25.

The Russian successes were all the more remarkable because they
had been achieved without the full use of their available power.
They had held large forces in reserve which were now ready to
undertake a widespread counterattack. During the fall and early
winter the high command had labored strenuously to replace the
heavy losses suffered during 1942. They were now, in fact, better
equipped for a counterattack than they had been in 1942. New
production centers, set up in the Urals where they were out of
bombing range, were beginning to turn out vast quantities of planes,
tanks, mines, mortars, and artillery. By the beginning of 1943 Russia was producing practically as many planes as Germany. This
production was also supplemented by lend-lease supplies from
Britain and the United States. Furthermore, the Russians had to a
large extent solved the problem of mobility under winter conditions
which had seriously hampered their efforts in the preceding winter.
The Germans, on the other hand, faced the Russians with their
lines extended. Their generals had urged withdrawal to a more

favorable position but had been overruled "by the intuition of Corporal Hitler," as Winston Churchill put it. The Führer, it appears, feared the effect of further withdrawals upon the morale of the satellite nations. Rumania was already in a state of panic and there was danger that this panic might spread to Hungary and Bulgaria, thus crumbling the whole Balkan front. The Finns, too, were so tired of the war that the Germans feared their exit from it. In any case, the German troops remained in their perilously advanced position.

In the early weeks of 1943 the Russians moved westward on a front extending from Moscow to the Caucasus and were able to wrest a number of centers of resistance from the Nazis. On February 8 they took the strongly fortified city of Kursk, which had been the main bastion of the Nazis' winter line in the Ukraine. A week later (February 16) Kharkov, which had been in German possession fifteen months, was taken. When the Red army reached the outskirts of Kharkov, the Nazis had begun a systematic demolition of the city's newest and largest buildings, many of which were the pride of the Ukraine. After the Russians occupied the city, the *Luftwaffe* caused further destruction by bombing it. On the same day on which Kharkov fell the Soviet forces also entered Rostov, the key to the entire German southern front. It was their greatest victory since the battle of Stalingrad. Nor was this all. On March 3 they regained Rzhev, a stronghold on the central front 130 miles from Moscow. Nine days later (March 12) they took Vyazma, an important point on the railway between Moscow and Smolensk. But they had gambled too boldly. In their rapid advance they had overextended their supply lines and made themselves vulnerable to counterattack; the Nazis made the most of the opportunity to retake Kharkov on March 14. When heavy rains and spring thaws at the end of March stopped major military operations, it was found that the Red army in its winter drive had reconquered 185,000 square miles of territory.

As the summer of the third year of the Russian war approached, Hitler was faced with a difficult decision. Should he launch a major offensive against Russia or not? An all-out attack offered the only chance of winning, but there were great obstacles to overcome before the Germans could be ready. At Stalingrad they had lost a large number of their best troops, and an all-out attack would have required the use of all available reserves at a time when the shortage of man power was becoming a pressing problem. Furthermore, they no longer enjoyed air superiority. Constant fighting and

Allied bombing of production centers had weakened the *Luftwaffe* to a point where they could no longer control the skies. Then, too, the Red army had found the answer to the German *Blitzkrieg*, thereby robbing the Nazis of their tactical superiority. In 1941 the Germans had attacked along a front of 1800 miles; in 1942 a 480 mile sector was chosen for the summer campaign; but in 1943 the attack was restricted to a 160 mile sector running from Orel through Kursk to Belgorod. Moreover, this time the element of surprise was completely lacking. The offensive which finally got under way on July 7 almost immediately encountered superior forces. In three days the Russians claimed to have destroyed more than two thousand tanks and nearly a thousand planes. By the end of the first week the offensive had been stopped at most points.

As early as July 12, after one of the heaviest artillery barrages in history, the Russians began their counteroffensive, which was aimed at the German fortified base at Orel. They employed enveloping movements and hoped that the Germans would endeavor to maintain their positions despite flanking. But the Germans chose to retreat after destroying everything of value and planting mines to delay pursuit. On August 5 they were defeated in an unusually heavy tank battle and evacuated Orel. On the same day Belgorod, 125 miles to the south and only less important than Orel, also fell. Thus the Russians took the last two important bases which the Germans could have used for an attack on Moscow. Farther south the offensive was equally successful. Slowly forcing the Germans back day after day, the Red army on August 24 regained Kharkov, which before the war had been the third largest Russian city. It was the fourth time Kharkov had changed hands since 1941. Early in August a third and equally heavy offensive had been launched in the sector between the German strong points of Bryansk and Smolensk. On September 7 Stalino, which had been one of Russia's important steel centers, was taken. By October 1 both Bryansk and Smolensk were in Russian hands and the reconquest of the Ukraine was in sight. They were beating the inventors of the *Blitzkrieg* at their own game. On a curving line from Smolensk to the Sea of Azov and the Caucasus the Germans were in retreat.

By the beginning of October the Russians had reached the midsections of the great Dnieper River. On the other side of the river, protected by 600-foot cliffs, stood Kiev. Crossing the river to the north and the south, the Russians employed a pincer movement which after much bloody fighting resulted in the capture of the city on November 6. Surviving citizens presented evidence of the mass slaughter of thousands of Jews and others by the Germans before they retreated. After the fall of Kiev the Russians pushed on toward Zhitomer, situated only sixty-seven miles from the old Polish border. They took the town, but lost it to the Germans a few days later. Nevertheless, they made considerable gains on the whole. It was estimated that they had retaken more than 135,000 square miles during the summer campaign, thereby raising the total territory recovered since Stalingrad to 335,000 miles. The price in blood and lives was high. In June, 1943, they stated that their losses in dead and wounded since the Germans entered Russia were 4,200,000 and estimated the German casualties at 6,400,000. The Germans responded by making extravagant claims of Russian casualties and by minimizing their own. Whatever the German losses, the Russian drive had exposed the lack of German reserves. It was clear that the Germans were near the bottom of their man power reservoir. The fighting from June to November, 1943, further drained the available supply.

DESTRUCTION FROM THE AIR

After using their bombers sparingly during the first period of the war, the British decided in 1942 that the time had come for a more intensive bombing campaign. Up to this time the scattered attacks by small numbers of planes were little more than pin pricks, and the damage they inflicted could be repaired in a short time. Repeated blows by hundreds of bombers, on the other hand, could ruin entire industrial districts so completely that it would take many months to rebuild them if they were rebuilt at all. Then, too, large-scale bombing would overwhelm the enemy defenses by the sheer weight of the attack. Mass formations sent out in the summer of 1942 devastated a large part of the old Hanseatic city of Lübeck and also of Rostock where the Nazis had built a huge plant for the manufacture of Heinkel planes. The bombings of 1942 reached a climax in the raid on Cologne, when more than a thousand planes dropped two thousand tons of explosives during a ninety-minute attack (May 30, 1942) and in the bombing three days later of Essen, the home of the Krupp munitions works, by more than one thousand planes. The British, however, sustained such heavy losses from antiaircraft guns and from the attacks of German fighter planes that for the remainder of the year they contented themselves with sending out smaller detachments.

Everything that took place in 1942 was dwarfed by what followed in 1943. First of all, the British had larger bombers which could carry eight-ton loads of bombs as compared with the two-ton loads of the earlier bombers. Second, the bombs were larger and more deadly, as the name "block busters" indicates. Third, the fact that the British made most of their raids at night greatly reduced their losses. Fourth, the efforts of the Royal Air Force were supplemented by the Eighth United States Army Air Force based in Britain. After many months of preparation, this force assayed its first raid on the Reich in January, 1943. The Flying Fortresses, with their strong defensive equipment and precision bombing sights, made high-altitude bombing possible in the daytime. Finally, the conquest of North Africa made possible a new system of "shuttle bombing." Instead of turning back over Germany where Nazi intercepters were awaiting them, the planes would fly southward to North Africa and after resting a few days would drop another load of bombs on Germany on the return trip to England.

Beginning in January, 1943, the combined Allied air force based in England dropped an ever-increasing tonnage of bombs on vital war industries, strategic railway centers, and other military objectives in both Germany and the occupied countries. Until the Allies were ready to open a second front this remained the most effective way of weakening the enemy. Good weather often enabled the Allied force to continue the "around-the-clock" bombings for days in succession. These huge loads of death repaid the Germans a thousand-fold for their attacks on London and Coventry in 1940. The once mighty *Luftwaffe,* now hopelessly outnumbered, struck back fiercely at the raiders but could not stop them. The principal target of the bombers was western Germany and particularly the Ruhr Valley, where many of the vital war industries were situated. During one period of thirty days beginning in May more than ten thousand tons of bombs were dropped in this area. Besides destroying the factories with explosive and incendiary bombs the Allies blasted the Moehne and Eder dams (May, 1943) in the Ruhr area, causing devastating floods which wrecked many industrial plants. Among the cities used as targets were Düsseldorf, Essen, Cologne, Dortmund, Stuttgart, Mülheim, Krefeld, Duisburg, and Hamm. Cologne, with its U-boat equipment plants, was bombed with monotonous regularity. On June 24 two thousand tons of bombs were dropped on this city, causing fires which could be seen a hundred miles away. On July 4 and 9 the attacks were repeated, the raid on the latter date being the 119th attack on this city since the beginning of the war. These bombings spelled the death of Cologne as an industrial city.

The destruction was, indeed, appalling, but the bombing was so accurate that the great cathedral was not leveled.

But the raids were not restricted to the vicinity of the Ruhr Valley. Bombs were dropped as far north as Trondheim in Norway and as far south as the industrial cities of Italy. Among the many objectives were the great Renault tank works near Paris, the Skoda arms plants in Czechoslovakia, the Diesel engine works at Nuremberg, the Zeiss instrument factories at Jena, the locomotive and aircraft plants at Kassel, the great Ploesti oil refineries in Rumania, and the ball-bearings works at Schweinfurt. Two of the most frequent targets were the vital submarine bases of Lorient and St. Nazaire. Other U-boat centers, shipyards, and ports that were raided included Kiel, Antwerp, Bremen, Emden, Wilhelmshaven, and Flensburg. The great summer offensive of 1943 was climaxed by raids on Hamburg, Germany's greatest seaport. During a period of six days, beginning July 24, over 8000 tons of bombs were dropped on this city. Fires that could be seen a hundred miles away caused the death of many thousands who had sought safety in air raid shelters. No less than 75 per cent of Hamburg was destroyed. As the news of the destruction spread, the citizens of Berlin became panicky, fearing that their city would be next. By this time they no longer had any faith in Göring's promise that not one enemy plane would darken the sky over Germany. Nor did they have to wait long before their fears were realized. Minor raids were, of course, no novelty. On a number of occasions speedy British Mosquito bombers which carried only small bombs had harried Berlin. But in August, 1943, a force of British and Canadian bombers dropped eighteen hundred tons on the German capital in forty-two minutes, completely devastating four square miles of the city. The raid cost the Allies fifty-eight heavy bombers.

Although the Allies often suffered heavy losses, they did succeed in greatly curtailing the production of war materials. The raid on Schweinfurt, for instance, which had cost 593 men and 60 planes had cut German production of ball bearings in half. As a result of such bombings bottlenecks developed in many industries which reduced the output of planes, tanks, and submarines. It was the destruction of submarine bases which accounted in part for the drop in shipping losses during the summer of 1943. Besides reducing production, the raids also lowered German morale. It was reported toward the end of 1943 that one million homes had been destroyed, rendering five million Germans homeless. In many of the bombed districts such bitter remarks as "For this we are indebted to the

Führer" became commonplaces. At first, propaganda minister Goebbels and his assistants sought to bolster the sagging morale with
stories of how German planes were bombing New York. These
stories found such general acceptance that when Nazi prisoners
reached New York they were amazed at not finding the city in
ruins. The official statements invariably admitted only a few casualties after a bombing raid and reported that only churches and hospitals had been hit. But in 1943 the destruction was so widespread
that Goebbels could no longer conceal the facts. He now told the
naked truth in the hope of exciting hatred and of arousing the
people to greater effort against the Allies. Thus a German radio
commentator said of the devastation in the Ruhr: "Nobody who
has not seen it with his own eyes can have the faintest notion what
it is like."

The Germans struck back as best they could with their weakened *Luftwaffe,* even to renewing the bombing attacks on England.
Meanwhile they were developing a *Vergeltungswaffe* (vengeance
weapon) in the form of a flying bomb which Hitler hoped would
wreak the same destruction on Britain which the Allies had visited
on Germany. "Our enemies," he said, "will pay in blood and lives."
The flying or robot bomb, known as the V–1, was actually a small
pilotless plane which carried in its nose an explosive equivalent to a
one-ton bomb and was capable of attaining a speed of four hundred
miles per hour. During the winter of 1943–1944 Allied reconnaissance discovered concrete installations along the French coast for
launching robot bombs. After these were destroyed by bombing
raids, the Germans developed other sites and on the night of June
12–13 began the attack on southern England. During the next
eighty days they launched approximately 8000 bombs, of which
about 2300 or 29 per cent reached their mark. Of the remaining
number, 46 per cent were shot down or brought down by balloons,
while 25 per cent were erratic in the direction of their flight. Nevertheless, those that reached their mark, most of them landing in
the London area, killed 5479 persons and injured 15,934 besides
destroying 25,000 houses, rendering 50,000 uninhabitable, and damaging almost a million.

In September the Germans began to send over the second "vengeance weapon" in the form of a rocket bomb known as the V–2.
Although considerably larger it carried only the same charge of
explosive as the V–1. It did, however, possess a number of advantages. As its speed was about 3000 miles per hour, which is many
times faster than sound, it gave no warning and therefore could not

be so easily intercepted. Furthermore, it rose into the stratosphere to a height of sixty or seventy miles, after which it would descend at a terrific rate and hit the ground with such velocity that it buried itself deeply before exploding. Hence the explosion caused earth tremors in the vicinity, but the blast effect was not nearly so great as that of the V–1. It was also more inaccurate than the V–1. Nevertheless, the damage it wrought was considerable. During the months from September to December, 1944, no less than 1425 were killed and 3134 were injured by the V–2.

Meanwhile the Allies were making excellent progress in subjugating the U-boat. Whereas in 1942 shipping was being sunk about as rapidly as it could be constructed, the situation changed in 1943. Although Atlantic shipping was at the highest level of the war thus far and although the German "wolf packs" had increased to fleets of twenty-five to thirty U-boats, the rate of sinkings declined sharply. During the month of June the losses were lower than in any previous month of the war. The total losses for the first half of 1943 were about 475,000 tons monthly. During the same six months from about 1,000,000 to 1,780,000 tons were completed monthly in United States shipyards alone, permitting the Allies to accumulate tonnage for a far-reaching offensive. A joint Anglo-American statement of January, 1944, reported: "In 1943 U-boats sank but 40 per cent of the merchant ship tonnage that they sank in 1942." A number of factors were responsible for the decrease. In addition to the reduced output of submarines one might mention the use of aircraft carriers to protect convoys. Another very important factor was the development of improved detection devices, among them sonar which forced the U-boats to proceed more cautiously. During the summer months of 1943 enemy submarines were destroyed at the rate of one a day. In the fall, speedier and more heavily armed U-boats appeared. Their new antiaircraft guns were such as to enable them to fight it out with a plane instead of submerging. But the improvement was not enough to redress the balance.

THE BATTLE FOR ITALY: THE BEGINNING OF THE END

In North Africa the year 1943 saw the continuation of the Allied drive which started in the previous year. The British pressed on from the east to force the surrender of Tripoli on January 24. By the end of the month Rommel's Afrika Korps had abandoned Tripolitania and withdrawn to Tunisia. Meanwhile United States troops had been moving eastward but were stopped at Faïd Pass

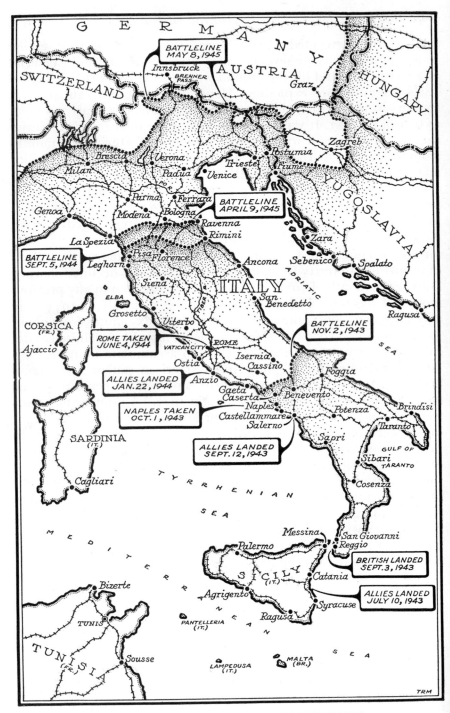

THE ALLIED INVASION OF SICILY AND ITALY

and driven back a considerable distance. Both forces, however, gradually pushed ahead. Tunis and Bizerte were captured on May 7, and during the succeeding days the remnants of the Axis force were harried from the air. Seeing that his situation was hopeless, General von Arnim, who had succeeded General Rommel as commander of the Afrika Korps, surrendered the rest of his troops. The British-American forces took 267,000 prisoners during the campaign. It was another serious blow to German morale.

Overwhelming Allied air superiority was a leading factor in the victory. No less than 1253 Axis planes were shot down during the drive. The air power which had been developed in the battle of Tunisia was at once turned on the little Italian island of Pantelleria, midway between Tunisia and Sicily. Stunned by the repeated bombings, the island surrendered as the first British troops waded ashore. It was the first step toward the invasion of Sicily. Having blasted Mussolini's dreams of empire, the Allied forces now made preparations to invade the mother country.

After extensive preparations the long-expected assault on Sicily got under way during the night of July 9–10 when large numbers of parachute troops were landed several miles behind the coast to disrupt communications and attempt to occupy the airfields. Early the next morning two thousand invasion vessels of all kinds, including warships, barges, and landing boats, arrived from North Africa to land British, Canadian, and United States troops on more than a hundred miles of the coast. As the troops landed, they met only light opposition, mostly from Italian shore units. Before the sun was high that morning, General Eisenhower reported that "the success of all landings was already assured." The British and Canadians had little trouble maintaining their beach heads, but the Americans were opposed by units of the crack Hermann Göring division. While the Germans were being pushed back, the Italians surrendered in droves. By August 17 the conquest of Sicily was complete. Besides taking quantities of undamaged war materials, the Allies captured about 130,000 prisoners. Allied casualties numbered 21,000 as against 30,000 Axis casualties. Above all, it was an important advance movement. General Eisenhower called it "the first stage in the liberation of the

❋❋

THE ALLIED INVASION OF SICILY AND ITALY. *Some of the heaviest fighting of the war raged about Cassino and along the "Gothic Line" from Pisa to Rimini.*

European continent," and President Roosevelt hailed it as "the beginning of the end."

The loss of Sicily completely disillusioned the Italian people, whose morale Mussolini had sought to bolster with empty promises. Instead of seeing the glories of the Roman Empire revived, they saw their colonies conquered, their armies destroyed, their fleet defeated, their cities devastated by bombers, and their economy wrecked. More than this, they saw the Gestapo further curtail their already restricted liberties. And the future held out no hope for better things. Even the members of the Fascist Council were anything but optimistic. They had so completely lost faith in the Duce that they demanded his resignation on July 24. When he became defiant, King Victor Emmanuel III summoned him to the palace, informed him of his dismissal, and had him taken into custody. The formation of a new government was then entrusted to General Badoglio. Within a few hours most of the Fascist leaders were either under arrest or in hiding. The rank and file of the party now melted away and Fascism vanished like a long nightmare. The Italian masses upon hearing of the change surged about the streets, giving themselves up to unbridled rejoicing and to shouting invectives against the former dictator. Almost at once socialists, communists, and other groups which had existed underground for nearly twenty-two years made their appearance with printed proclamations. Beneath the joy of being rid of Fascism there was a deep desire for peace. In a broadcast from his headquarters in North Africa on July 29 General Eisenhower praised the Italians for ridding themselves of Mussolini and Fascism and intimated that he was ready to deal with a representative of the Italian government. Marshal Badoglio opened secret negotiations for the cessation of hostilities. On September 3 the Italian government accepted "unconditional surrender."

After the conquest of Sicily the Allied force was ready to be used against the European continent itself. The first phase of the new campaign began on August 19 with a heavy air attack on various points of the Italian peninsula which continued during the succeeding weeks. The principal targets were the railroads. On one raid more than five hundred United States bombers attacked Rome's airfields and railway facilities. Just before dawn on September 3 spearheads of the British Eighth Army together with Canadian divisions moved across the Strait of Messina to establish beach heads on the toe of the Italian boot. On September 8, by which time the British had established a firm grip on the peninsula, General Eisenhower announced that the Italian government had negotiated an armistice five days previously. Hitler, however, was determined not to let the Allies occupy Italy and sent in as many divisions as he could spare to stop their progress. The day after the armistice was announced, United States troops established a beach head at Salerno within striking distance of Naples. As the Germans had prepared defensive positions for just such an attack, the fighting was bitter. For a time it seemed as if they would drive the Allied force into the sea, but the latter fought grimly and finally forced the Germans back. Thereafter the Germans employed every sort of booby trap and gunfire to retard the advance. Although considerable progress was made, the end of the year saw the Allied armies still closer to Naples than to Rome.

The early months of 1944 were marked by the failure of the Allies to achieve their immediate objectives. The terrain, the bad weather, and the determined fighting of the Germans whose forces were about equal to those of the Allies, made any kind of progress difficult. Prime minister Churchill described the situation to parliament in the following words: "Many people have been disappointed with the progress there since the capture of Naples in October. This has been due to extremely bad weather which marks the winter in a supposedly sunshiny land and which this year has been worse than usual. Secondly, it is because the Germans bit by bit have been drawn into Italy and have decided to make exertions for the retention of the city of Rome." To block the Allied drive on Rome the Germans had utilized the natural barriers to set up a defense line about eighty miles south of the city. The opposition was light at first, but the Germans quickly brought up 98,000 men to oppose the Allied force of 92,000. Thus they managed to stop the attempt to drive inland. For a time it appeared as if a stalemate had been reached. In May, however, the Allies succeeded in breaking through the line at Cassino,[1] after which the drive went forward over the rugged terrain.

After weeks of bloody fighting the Allied forces finally came within sight of Rome, the Eternal City, the city of Cicero, Caesar, and a host of emperors, popes, and kings. Since no purpose could be served by a defense which would certainly have resulted in the destruction of many priceless historical monuments, the Germans fought only rearguard actions to permit the withdrawal of their troops. On June 4 the Allies occupied the relatively unscarred city. It was the first Axis capital to capitulate to the Allies

[1] During the attack the famed monastery of Monte Cassino, original home of the Benedictine Order, was destroyed after the Germans made it an artillery post.

and the first time the city had been taken by an attack from the south. United States tanks which led the Allies into the city were greeted by cheering throngs who tossed flowers at their liberators and presented them with fruit and wine. But for the troops the grim business of war was not finished. On June 5, the day on which the inhabitants of Rome really welcomed the Anglo-American soldiers, King Victor Emmanuel III signed a decree "irrevocably" turning over his royal powers to Crown Prince Humbert, who became "Lieutenant General of the Realm." Victor Emmanuel, however, still reserved for himself the title of "King of Italy and head of the House of Savoy." When General Badoglio was unable to form a new cabinet at Prince Humbert's orders, he was succeeded by Ivanoe Bonomi, who had been prime minister in the pre-Mussolini era. Bonomi formed a cabinet of anti-Fascist patriots and in October the free government of Italy was recognized by the United Nations.

The fall of Rome was rather the beginning than the end of the Italian campaign. Without a pause the Allied troops rolled on through the city and across the Tiber. During the months that followed, they moved steadily northward through Tuscany to the Gothic Line in the northern Apennines. In his message to the Congress on January 6, 1945, President Roosevelt said of the fighting in Italy: "Over very difficult terrain and through adverse weather conditions, our Fifth Army and the British Eighth Army have in the past year pushed north through bloody Cassino and the Anzio beach head and through Rome until they now occupy heights overlooking the valley of the Po."

D-DAY: THE INVASION OF FRANCE

When President Roosevelt made a speech in Washington on the evening of June 5, 1944, to proclaim the capture of Rome to the nation he said: "Our victory comes at an excellent time . . . while our forces are poised for another strike at western Europe." The next day the long-awaited "second front" was opened in France. For many months preparations for the invasion had been under way. Large numbers of troops and vast quantities of supplies were assembled in England. After the preliminary preparations were completed General Eisenhower, fresh from his victories in North Africa, was called in to weld the diverse elements into a powerful fighting machine. It was a force composed of representatives of many peoples, the bulk being British, Canadian, and United States troops. During final inspection General Eisenhower said of his troops: "If their fighting is as good as their training, God help the Nazis!" To carry this vast army to France, thousands of transports and landing barges were collected and also combat ships to protect them. During the early hours of June 6 a thousand planes either dropped parachutists in Normandy or towed gliders there. These airborne troops landed behind enemy lines to sever communications and seize key defense posts. A thousand heavy bombers were also attacking the beach defenses along the coast of France, dropping no less than ten thousand tons of bombs on them.

Meantime between midnight and dawn a fleet of more than four thousand ships, protected by a canopy of planes, was approaching the coast of Normandy in the greatest amphibious operation of all time. Shortly after 5 A.M. the warships opened fire on the shore batteries and defense installations, and an hour later the first waves of troops began to go ashore. Although the Germans knew that an invasion attempt was in the making and also approximately when it would be launched, they did not know where the blow would fall. The feints made by the Allies at Calais and Dieppe, which were the logical points of attack, appear to have misled the Germans. Hence the choice of Normandy in preference to the so-called "invasion" coast took them by surprise and enabled General Eisenhower to establish a sixty-mile beach head between Cherbourg and Le Havre. On the whole the landings were carried out smoothly and with fewer losses than had been anticipated. Overwhelming naval and air support permitted the Allied command to land large numbers of men and much matériel on the coast to protect their beach heads. The Nazis missed their chance, first, in not attacking the invaders from the air and, second, in not launching a vigorous counterattack while they were disorganized on or near the beaches. After the beach heads had been established, General Eisenhower broadcast a message to the peoples of the Hitler-controlled continent which read in part: "People of western Europe! A landing was made this morning on the coast of France by troops of the Allied Expeditionary Force. This landing is part of the concerted United Nations plan for the liberation of Europe, made in conjunction with our great Russian allies. I have this message for all of you. Although the initial assault may not have been made in your own country, the hour of your liberation is approaching."

The nub of the immediate Allied problem was to gain a port of entry. The obvious goal was Cherbourg. With the aid of a strong airforce operating from airstrips established on the beach heads, United States troops lunged westward toward Cherbourg. German

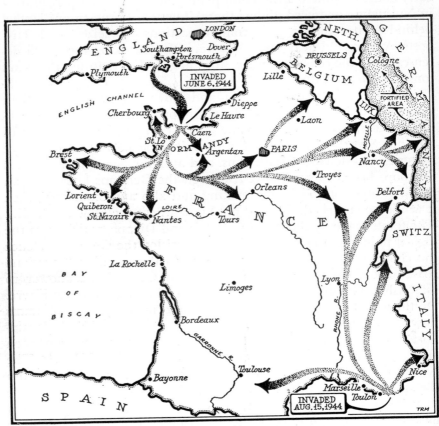

THE ALLIED INVASION OF FRANCE

Picturesque code names were given to various attacks during the Second World War, such as Operation Overlord for the cross-channel invasion of June 6, 1944; Operation Anvil for the invasion of southern France; and Operations Veritable, Grenade, and Lumberjack for the drives toward the Rhine.

resistance notwithstanding, they moved closer and closer. By July 2 the city was not only in their hands but they had also completed the mop-up of the peninsula on which it is situated. The occupation of this port blasted the German hopes of driving the Allied force into the sea. The beach heads were now secure. Progress inland, however, was very slow. At first the troops managed to move at the rate of about three miles a day. But the Germans sent in more troops and panzer divisions to localize the conflict. After being restricted for about six weeks an American armored column broke through the lines at St. Lô. This turned the tide of battle. Armored elements under the impulsive and brilliant General Patton quickly moved through the breach to strike out in two directions. While one spearhead turned into Brittany and toward the ports of Brest, St. Malo, Lorient, St. Nazaire, and Nantes, the other turned eastward toward Paris and the Seine through Tours, Orleans, and Chartres. On August 15 an army of American and French troops landed on the Mediterranean coast of France, east and west of Toulon. Without encountering much opposition they speedily took Toulon, Marseilles, and Nice. By September 3 they had also occupied Lyons.

Meanwhile in the north over a million American, British, Canadian, French, Polish, Belgian, and Dutch troops were pushing the Germans steadily eastward. Allied forces in crossing the Seine at first by-passed Paris, where French irregulars were fighting to drive out the German garrison. When the fighting continued for some days with the outcome uncertain, General Patton sent a French tank division and supporting American units to settle the issue. Two days later, on August 25, the Germans surrendered. That night Paris blazed with light. Swirling in street serpentines the Parisians went wild with joy. Their beloved city was free.

Other Allied forces joined Patton's army in the movement toward Germany, while a force of British and Canadians, with a sprinkling of other nationalities, turned toward Belgium. The advance during the last days of July and the month of August was a *Blitzkrieg* unmatched by the German drives of 1940. It not only shook the *Wehrmacht* to its foundations but was literally breaking it to pieces. In all it cost the Germans nearly a million casualties including most of their remaining armored divisions. Progress was so rapid that the middle of September saw no less than six of General Eisenhower's armies drawn up against Germany's western borders. Attempts to enter Germany, however, were halted by the Siegfried Line or West Wall. A renewed attempt about the middle of November to break through made steady if somewhat slow progress. Suddenly

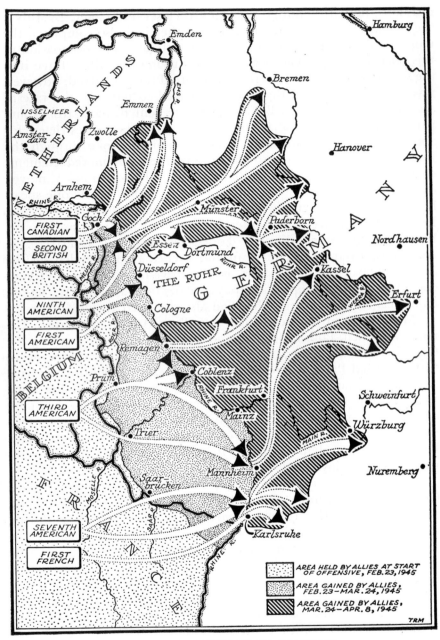

THE ALLIED INVASION OF GERMANY

on December 16 General Eisenhower's plans were disrupted by a major German counteroffensive launched by Marshal von Runstedt with great force in the Ardennes sector held mainly by United States troops. As a result of the blow the Germans were able to push toward the Meuse about fifty miles. After stopping the drive on December 25 by tenacious resistance, American troops gradually regained most of the territory. Prime minister Churchill referred to this "battle of the bulge" as "the greatest American battle of the war." It was the last great German offensive. Although it did delay the final Allied drive for a time, it also greatly weakened the German forces.

CLIMAX: THE DRIVE INTO GERMANY

Meanwhile the Russians were driving rapidly toward Germany. After capturing Sevastopol on May 12, 1944, and clearing the Germans out of the Crimea, the Red army opened a drive in June on the Finnish front which carried them to the 1940 Finnish-Soviet frontier by July. On June 22 the main summer offensive got under way on the central front with an attack on Vitebsk. Although this was the strongest sector of the German defenses, the drive quickly gathered momentum. Numerical superiority permitted the Russians to flank and surround the German strong points instead of trying to take them by frontal attacks. This strategy enabled the Red armies to take both Vitebsk and Minsk within a short time. By the middle of July Vilna in Lithuania was in Russian possession, while farther south the fighting was everywhere on Polish soil. Progress was so rapid that in August the Red armies had to stop to reorganize. Besides taking vast stretches of territory and a large toll of men, the drive also had political results. When the Soviet troops crossed the Rumanian border and began moving nearer the capital, King Michael issued an order to cease fighting the United Nations. On September 13 he signed an armistice with Russia on condition that Rumania furnish twelve divisions to fight Germany. In the north, Finland had agreed to leave the Axis camp on September 4. On October 28 Bulgaria also joined Finland and Rumania in the fight

THE ALLIED INVASION OF GERMANY. *In "one of the outstanding military successes in history" the Americans liquidated the Ruhr pocket, capturing 325,000 Germans, among whom were thirty generals (April 18, 1945).*

against Germany. Finally, by the end of October the progress of the
Red army had forced the Germans to abandon Greece. This left
Hungary as the only German satellite. Admiral Horthy, the ruler
of Hungary did, it is true, appeal for an armistice, but Fascist ele-
ments seized control of the country and continued the fight against
Russia.

After reorganizing their forces, the Russians opened their last
great offensive in January, 1945, with their main power moving
through Poland directly toward Berlin. At the same time Russian
divisions were moving through East Prussia, and in Hungary the
Soviet troops encircled Budapest. By early February they were along
the Oder in places not much more than thirty miles from Berlin.
The Germans had neither the men nor the material to stop the
advance on so wide a front. If the high command had recalled its
troops from Norway, Denmark, Italy, and other parts of Europe to
stand on the defensive behind the Siegfried Line or on the Rhine,
they might have held off the Allied forces for a long time. As it
was, the Russians swept everything before them. On April 13 they
took Vienna, and three days later the final push for Berlin was
under way. April saw the first divisions entering Berlin.

In western Europe a major Allied offensive was to have started
in January, but the Ardennes counterattack forced a postponement.
When it was finally launched on February 23, eight armies began
moving toward the Rhine. After breaching the successive defenses
of the Siegfried Line, Eisenhower's troops gradually forced the Germans back across the river. At the Rhine there occurred an historic
incident which greatly aided the crossing and thereby shortened
the war. The First United States Army succeeded in reaching a railroad bridge at Remagen before the Germans could destroy it, although they did damage it. Making the most of the opportunity, an
armored division crossed the bridge and was quickly followed by
other forces. By the time it collapsed from cumulative damage, the
Allies had a firm, deep, and wide bridgehead on the east bank. The
advance out of the bridgehead was accompanied by a general crossing along most of the river in Germany. After the crossings had been
made, one army cut off Holland while the rest gradually segregated
the Ruhr cities from the Reich. As the Allied armies deprived Germany of most of her industrial areas, her strategical position became
more and more hopeless and the *Wehrmacht* became more and more
disorganized and demoralized, permitting the Allied armies to race
across Germany with only scattered opposition. On April 26 the
Russian and Allied armies, meeting at Torgau, split Germany in two.

AMERICAN AND RUSSIAN SOLDIERS MEET ON THE BRIDGE
AT TORGAU, GERMANY

🔖

DEATH COMES TO TWO DICTATORS

During the succeeding days fate knocked at the door of two of Europe's dictators. Mussolini, since his release from arrest by German paratroopers in September, 1943, had been leading a wraith-like existence in northern Italy as a Nazi puppet ruler. When the resistance collapsed, the Nazis abandoned him and he was apprehended near Lake Como by anti-Fascists (Partisans). With him at the time was the last of a long line of mistresses, Claretta Petacci. "Let me save my life," Benito said to his captors, "and I will give you an empire!" But they made short shrift of the erstwhile dictator. The next day, April 28, he and his mistress, together with sixteen of his Black Shirt henchmen, were shot. The reputed executioner, known to the Italian underground as Colonel Valerio, reported that the man who was responsible for the death of so many thousands "died a coward." As he was about to be shot, he kept babbling: "But, but, but, but Mr. Colonel." After the execution his battered, bullet-riddled corpse and also the others were carted to the Piazza Loreto, a public square in Milan, where they were strung up by the heels. Thousands of men and women milled about the eighteen disheveled bodies in the muddy square. The crowd vented their pent-up fury by kicking Mussolini's corpse, spitting upon it, or reviling the ex-dictator. One eye-witness reported that "the mob surged and swayed around the grisly spot. One woman emptied a pistol into the Duce's body. 'Five shots!' she screamed; 'five shots for my five murdered sons.' Others cried: 'He died too quickly! He should have suffered!' But the hate of many was wordless. They could only spit." Thus ended the man who tried to be Caesar.

Two days after Mussolini's death it was announced over the German radio that Hitler had died in the Berlin chancellery then under attack by the Russians. According to Gerhard Herrgesell, stenographer to Germany's supreme headquarters staff, Hitler realizing that the cause was irretrievably lost had after the Russians began their attack on Berlin repeatedly said during a meeting in the basement of the chancellery: "I will fall here," "I will fall before the chancellery," and "I must die here in Berlin." "The Führer," Herrgesell stated, "always maintained that no force, however well trained and equipped, could fight if it lost heart, and now he felt his last reserve was gone. . . . During all this time artillery fire on the chancellery was increasing and even deep down in the cellar we could feel concussions shaking the building." After the meeting

Herrgesell left Berlin by plane. It was after his departure that Hitler died. Various reports regarding the manner of his death are extant. Herrgesell believes that Hitler went "looking for death to which he was not so completely resigned, and that he may have died by artillery fire." Others reported that Hitler and Eva Braun, his wife of a few hours, died in a suicide pact. Despite conflicting stories of his death and the absence of absolute proof that he had died, it was generally assumed in Allied countries that he was dead. With his death another attempt to dominate the continent of Europe had been blocked. Never in modern times had a man so insignificantly monstrous become the absolute head of a great nation. The ruin he caused in terms of human life alone is incalculable. The bodies of his victims were heaped across Europe from London to Stalingrad. The tragedy of his life left only one lesson: he gave terrifying evidence of the hell let loose on earth when hate becomes the motive around which men rally for action; he demonstrated that hate produces nothing but destruction and finally destroys the hater.

VICTORY IN EUROPE

In certain Allied circles it was believed that fanatical Nazis would continue to resist in scattered pockets after the armies had stopped fighting. But the announcement of Hitler's death seems to have sapped the German morale completely. Collapse was rapid during the succeeding days. On the day of Hitler's death fighting ended in Italy. After a lull of five months the Eighth Army had on April 9 launched a full-scale attack which secured a complete breakthrough in a week, causing the Germans to sign unconditional surrender terms on April 29. The next day the Russians took Berlin after a period of fierce day-and-night house-to-house fighting. On May 4 more than a million Germans surrendered to Field Marshal Montgomery's army, thus bringing the fighting in Holland and northern Germany to a close. It was the biggest mass surrender of Germans since the armistice of 1918. By this time the rest of the armies had disintegrated to such an extent that General Eisenhower declared: "On land, sea, and in the air the Germans are thoroughly whipped. Their only recourse is to surrender." By May 7 even Admiral Doenitz, who appears to have usurped the Hitlerian succession, realized that the Reich which Hitler had said would last a thousand years had fallen into ruins. On that day the surrender agreement was signed at Rheims, and on May 8 in Berlin virtually the same terms were signed in the name of the German high command. Hostilities ceased at 12:01 A.M. on May 9. So the curtain fell in Europe on the greatest tragedy in the history of that old and weary continent.

After five years, eight months, and seven days the war in Europe had come to an end. No war ever ended more decisively. The terms of surrender were explicit. "We, the undersigned," they read, "acting by authority of the German high command, hereby surrender unconditionally to the Supreme Commander, Allied Expeditionary Force, and simultaneously to the Soviet high command, all forces on land, sea, and in the air which are at this date under German control." The surrender was complete and the terms placed no obligations on the victors. Thus it could not be said, as was the case after World War I, that the German army was never beaten or that the terms of the surrender were violated. General Eisenhower's Order of the Day for May 8 read in part:

"It is my especial privilege, in the name of all nations represented in the theater of war, to commend each of you for the valiant performance of duty. . . . Your accomplishments at sea, in the air, on the ground, and in the field of supply have astonished the world. Even before the final week of the conflict you had put 5,000,000 of the enemy permanently out of the war. You have taken in stride military tasks so difficult as to be classed by many doubters as impossible. You have confused, defeated, and destroyed your savagely fighting foe. . . . Full victory in Europe has been attained. Working and fighting together in single and indestructible partnership you have achieved a perfection in the unification of air, ground, and naval power that will stand as a model in our time. . . . Let us have no part in the profitless quarrels in which other men will inevitably engage as to what country and what service won the European war. Every man and every woman of every nation here represented has served according to his or her ability and efforts and each has contributed to the outcome."

In the United States President Truman announced the Allied victory in a message which began: "This is a solemn but a glorious hour. I only wish that Franklin D. Roosevelt had lived to witness this day." President Roosevelt had seen the coming victory from a distance, but did not live to see it achieved. He passed away suddenly on April 12, 1945, less than three months after his fourth inauguration, as a result of a cerebral hemorrhage. His hold on the imagination of people everywhere was such that the shock of his death was felt as profoundly in Moscow, Paris, and Mexico City as in the United States. To millions in all parts of the earth he was the embodiment of the finer virtues of the American people, a gleaming symbol of liberty, and a tireless champion of freedom. As Stalin said of him, he was "a great organizer of the struggles of freedom-loving nations against the common enemy, and the leader in the cause of ensuring the security of the whole world." Shortly before his death, with supreme confidence that victory was in sight, he summoned the nations of the world to meet in San Francisco on April 25 to formulate a global charter as the basis for international peace and cooperation. The result was the United Nations charter. Death came to President Roosevelt so suddenly that he left a speech scheduled to be delivered the next day. Its theme was: "The only limit to our realization of tomorrow will be our doubts of today. Let us move forward with strong and active faith."

VICTORY OVER JAPAN

In the United States the joy over the result in Europe was tempered by the fact that the task of defeating the Japanese was still ahead. On V-E Day President Truman had said in his message: "Our victory is but half won. The West is free, but the East is still in bondage to the treacherous tyranny of the Japanese. When the last Japanese division has surrendered unconditionally, then only will our fighting job be done." To the Japanese the defeat of Germany was of course disappointing. They certainly would not have attacked Pearl Harbor in December, 1941, if the Germans had not seemed to be winning. But the defeat did not incline them to surrender. They continued to fight in their fierce, stubborn manner.

During the early months of 1943 there had been a lull in the fighting. This lull had been broken only by the battle of the Bismarck Sea (March 2–4, 1943), in which a Japanese convoy of ten warships and fifteen transports carrying 15,000 troops had been totally destroyed. When the Allied forces in the southwest Pacific started a new drive in early June, 1943, it was a relief to many who feared that the absorption of the United States in the European phase of the war would give the Japanese opportunity to entrench themselves so firmly in their newly acquired territories that it would be extremely difficult to dislodge them. The general goal of Allied strategy was to smash the outer defenses of the Japanese fortress. In other words, it aimed at the capture of the important bases in the south Pacific, after which the Allies planned to move gradually northward toward Japan.

The first step was to eliminate all Japanese from the Solomons and New Guinea. Allied forces under Admiral Halsey occupied

Rendova Island (June, 1943) and at the beginning of July began the attack on Munda air base, situated on nearby New Georgia Island. The pattern of the fighting closely resembled the battle of Guadalcanal. Despite stubborn resistance Allied forces moved in until they had possession of the coveted air strip. After weeks of jungle fighting the entire island was overrun (August 7, 1943). The struggle for Munda was featured by a naval battle in Kula Gulf on July 5, during which nine Japanese warships were believed to have been sunk. After the taking of New Georgia the Allies moved northward to attack Bougainville, the last Japanese stronghold in the Solomons. On October 31 a force of marines landed at Empress Augusta Bay on Bougainville Island and after a bitter struggle took possession of it. In the meantime another force under General MacArthur had moved against New Guinea, taking the important bases of Salamaua, Lae, and Finschafen before the end of November.

The success of the Allied operations in the Solomons and New Guinea opened the way for an attack farther north. The new targets were low atolls in the British Gilbert Islands which the Japanese had seized in December, 1941. Makin atoll [2] was occupied with only moderate resistance, but the attack on Tarawa was the most difficult task the marines had attempted up to that time. Before landings were made, Betio, a little island a scant square mile in size, which was the main fortification of the Tarawa atoll, was subjected to a severe aerial attack in which seven hundred tons of bombs were dropped. Warships also poured in 2900 tons of shells. It was difficult to see how any Japanese could survive this attack. But their engineers had used stonehard coconut logs, steel rails, and concrete to build pillboxes which they covered with three or four feet of sand. These fortifications were so incredibly strong that only a direct hit by heavy shells or bombs could damage them. There were five hundred of them in the small area of Betio, staggered in such a way that marines who captured one came under fire from two others. The water was so shallow near the island that the attacking marines had to debark some distance from the beach and as they waded toward the island made excellent targets for the sharpshooters. Only after three days of the bitterest fighting, in which they lost 1026 killed and 2557 wounded, did the marines succeed in occupying the atoll.

At the end of 1943 the position of the Allies was still poor

[2] The dictionary defines an atoll as "a coral island or islands consisting of a belt of coral reef surrounding a central lagoon."

THE SOUTHWEST PACIFIC

despite the fact that considerable progress had been made in breaching the outer defenses of the Japanese fortress. On the other hand, attempts of the enemy to extend his gains had been definitely blocked. Moreover, during the year supplies had been sent to the Pacific in ever-increasing quantities. Some idea of the progress made in the United States during the twenty-four months after Pearl Harbor in turning out war materials can be gained from the fact that the tonnage of warships increased from two to five millions, the number of men in the armed forces from 1.8 million to 7.7 million, and the number of planes from 12,000 to 80,000. Having received large numbers of men and great quantities of material, the Pacific commanders were now ready to begin a coordinated offensive aimed at the heart of Japan. No sooner had they gained control of the Gilberts and southeastern New Guinea than they began to build air bases, improve harbor facilities, construct barracks and supply bases—in short, they developed jumping-off places for future thrusts. Progress was in no sense easy. The Japanese clung tenaciously to the territories they had occupied.

The first great operation in 1944, designed to secure stepping-stone bases closer to the Japanese isles, was against the Marshall Islands. Soon after the occupation of the Gilberts the "softening up" process by means of air bombing had begun. Actual invasion started on January 31, when a force under Admiral Nimitz went ashore unopposed on Majuro atoll. It was the first time United States soldiers had set foot on soil that had been Japanese prior to Pearl Harbor. Next day another force landed on Kwajalein, the world's largest atoll, sixty-six miles long and eighteen miles wide. Here the fighting was bitter and it was necessary to kill more than 8000 Japanese before it could be occupied. American losses in killed were 286. On February 17 Admiral Nimitz's forces landed on Eniwetok and by February 22 control of this atoll was complete. United States losses were 169 killed, compared with Japanese losses of 2665 killed. The explanation of the small number of American dead lies in the fact that the atolls were thoroughly bombed and shelled before landings were made. The Japanese government was gravely concerned over the conquest of the Marshall Islands. Soon after the

THE SOUTHWEST PACIFIC. *The first goal of Allied strategy was to smash the outer defenses of Japan—the Solomons, New Guinea, the Gilberts, the Marshalls, and the Philippines.*

landings on Kwajalein, premier Hideki Tojo said that the war "keeps increasing in ferocity day by day and we are now being confronted with the situation where the fate of the Greater East Asia sphere and the rise and fall of Imperial Japan will be decided."

Next Admiral Nimitz took the most daring single step attempted thus far. He invaded the Marianas, some parts of which were only about 1400 miles from Tokyo. Because of the great distance from airfields the "softening-up" had to be carried out by planes from carriers. The first landing was made on Saipan (June 14) and it encountered some of the most determined opposition in the Pacific war. It required more than three weeks to overcome the organized resistance, while sniping continued for months thereafter. According to official estimates 26,571 Japanese were killed and 2099 were captured in the attack. American casualties in dead and wounded numbered about 15,000. Following the landings on Saipan, troops began the reconquest of Guam, which had been a United States possession before the outbreak of the war. When mopping-up operations had been completed, it was announced that 17,436 Japanese had been killed. In the attack on Tinian Island 6932 Japanese were killed. The conquest of the Mariana Islands was followed on September 14 by an invasion of the Palau Islands, which were so strongly defended that organized resistance was not overcome until October 12. This time the number of Japanese dead was 13,354. Simultaneously the strength of the Japanese navy was also being whittled down by repeated attacks. For example, while the land action against the Marianas was under way, planes from carriers attacked a Japanese squadron and sank two airplane carriers, two destroyers, and one tanker. Numerous other engagements took place with similar results.

In October, after weeks of preparation, General MacArthur's forces undertook the largest operation attempted up to that time. The goal was the freeing of the Philippines, partly to cut off Japanese supplies to the East Indies and partly to provide a base for an attack on Japan itself. Three great naval forces sought to frustrate these plans. On October 19 MacArthur's troops landed on the island of Leyte. During the next few days and nights the supporting fleet and airforce inflicted upon the Japanese a major defeat and compelled them to withdraw. Fifty-eight or sixty enemy warships were sunk or damaged. It was a staggering blow. The Japanese land forces, however, continued a stiff resistance, but the American invaders moved steadily forward and by Christmas Day had occupied the entire island. On December 15 landings were made on

Mindoro, where an airfield was quickly established within 155 miles of Manila. The actual invasion of Luzon, on which Manila is located, did not take place until January 9, 1945. Japanese resistance was not as heavy as expected until Manila was reached. On February 6 the capital was attacked from every direction. It was occupied only after bloody house-to-house fighting in which the Japanese destroyed much of the city. While this battle was in progress, General MacArthur's men were also fighting for Bataan and Corregidor. The attack was made both by parachute troops and by infantry landing from boats. The battle on Corregidor lasted for two weeks until the remaining Japanese were driven out of the underground passages. Thereafter General MacArthur's men went from island to island, most frequently outwitting the enemy by attacking at points where landings were not expected.

Next the Allied commanders moved to obtain island bases on the very doorstep of Japan. The first objective was the ugly volcanic island of Iwo Jima, eight square miles in size and some 400 miles from Kyushu, southernmost of the Japanese home islands. Possession of Iwo Jima was important because it was the seeing eye that warned Tokyo of the approach of bombers and also because it would be of great value in pushing the B–29 attacks against Japanese cities. Then, too, it would afford a haven for crippled or battle weary superfortresses on the return trip from Japan. The battle for the possession of Iwo Jima, defended as it was by the cream of the Japanese army, was one of the toughest and most costly of the war. Although the airforce bombed the island for fifty-four consecutive days, the defense works were constructed in such a way that the bombing did not damage them too seriously. The Japanese guns had all been trained on the only landing beach, and when the United States troops went over the sides on February 19, 1945, Japanese troops fired point blank at the landing party. Progress was difficult and costly as the Japanese had to be blasted out of the pillboxes and driven out of large fortified caves. It was not until March 15 that the United States flag was raised over the entire island.

A fortnight after the Iwo Jima battle, the United States navy had assembled for action the greatest invasion armada ever to operate in the Pacific. It was composed of 1400 ships and about 100,000 soldiers and marines. The target this time was poverty-stricken, malaria-ridden Okinawa, an island in the Ryukyus sixty miles long and from two to twenty miles wide, about 370 miles from Kyushu. After a terrific preparatory bombardment marines and soldiers

swarmed ashore on Easter Sunday morning (April 1). Japanese resistance on the beach was weak, permitting the troops to push on to
the east coast and cut the island in two. But Okinawa was far too
important a strategical prize for the Japanese to sell it cheaply. The
commander, who had about 70,000 troops and some 500 artillery
guns at his disposal, decided to make a stand at the southern end
where it would be difficult for troops to land behind them. Hence
occupation of the northern end was comparatively swift but in the
south progress was slow and the cost in blood tremendous; in fact,
Okinawa was one of the bloodiest battlefields of the war. Not until
June 22 was the hold of the United States troops on the island
secure, but resistance by small groups of Japanese continued for
some time thereafter. Japanese casualties included 101,853 killed
and 9498 captured, while American losses in killed were 7283 and in
wounded 31,398.

During the time the ground fighting was in progress, the Japanese struck repeatedly at the supporting Allied naval forces. Among
other means of attack they organized a suicide corps of flyers whose
mission it was to crash-dive their explosive-laden planes into ships.
Although most of these "kamikaze" planes were shot out of the air,
those that struck ships did considerable damage. They failed to sink
any major vessels but they did sink thirty-three destroyers and smaller
units besides damaging sixty ships. The resulting American casualties
were 4907 killed and 4824 wounded. In their attempts to destroy
the Allied naval force the Kamikaze (Divine Tempest) Corps lost
more than 4000 planes and pilots. On April 5–6 the Japanese attempted to deliver a decisive sea-air blow by sending out a naval task
force which included their last big battleship flanked by cruisers and
destroyers. But before it reached Okinawa it was sighted by patrol
flyers and quickly attacked by four hundred carrier planes which
sank most of the ships. It was the swan song of the Japanese navy.

Besides losing Iwo Jima and Okinawa the Japanese were also dis-
lodged from other bases. During April, May, and June the Philippine campaign was pressed to a relentless conclusion with the result
that General MacArthur was able to announce on July 5, 1945, that
the entire archipelago had been liberated with the exception of areas
infested by guerilla bands. Thus MacArthur and his men had erased
a tragic defeat with a remarkable victory. With the Philippines, Iwo
Jima, and Okinawa safely in their hands the Allies were in position
to move northward toward Kyushu. In the Philippines they had an
area for massing troops in preparation for a final assault; on Okinawa
they had a number of airfields only ninety minutes' flying time

from Tokyo; and the airfield on Iwo Jima had been developed as a base for superfortresses and for long-range fighter planes which accompanied the big bombers on their raids. Repeated bombing and incendiary raids by seven hundred to one thousand planes had carried destruction to the principal industrial cities. On May 31 our War Department listed a large number of war industries in Tokyo, Nagoya, Osaka, and Kobe which had been attacked, in addition to dockyards, communication centers, and transportation facilities. During the months of March, April, and May bombers had dropped approximately 58,000 tons of bombs on Japanese targets. At least a quarter of the population had felt the terror of the devastating raids, and the government officials were able to give the frightened people but scant consolation. All indications pointed to the fact that Japan's sands were running out rapidly.

THE END OF WORLD WAR II

As the Allied forces were preparing to strike at the heart of Japan, the cataclysmic bursts of two atomic bombs brought the war to a sudden end. On July 26 representatives of the United States, Britain, and China, meeting at Potsdam, had called upon Japan for unconditional surrender, stating that "the alternative for Japan is prompt and utter destruction." The Japanese government had turned down the ultimatum. Then, on August 6, as if in fulfillment of the threat, the first atomic bomb ever to be used in warfare was dropped on Hiroshima. President Truman in announcing the event said in part: "Sixteen hours ago, an American airplane dropped one bomb at Hiroshima, an important Japanese army base. That bomb had more power than 20,000 tons of TNT. It had more than 2000 times the blast power of the British 'Grand Slam,' which is the largest bomb ever used in the history of warfare." The President then went on to explain that it was an atomic bomb, "a harnessing of the basic power of the universe." Some idea of the destructive power of the bomb may be gained from the fact that it would have required two thousand bombers to carry twenty thousand tons of TNT. The force of the blast was such that three fifths of Hiroshima was blown off the face of the earth. According to a report issued by Allied headquarters some months later, 78,150 people were killed.

On August 8 Russia entered the war in fulfillment of Marshal Stalin's promise at the Yalta Conference (February, 1945) that the Soviet Union would join in the war against Japan within ninety days after the end of the European war. Russian armies at once marched into Manchuria, but it was all in the nature of an anti-climax. The position of Japan was already hopeless. The next day (August 9) a second bomb was released with even more disastrous results on Nagasaki, a shipbuilding port and industrial center. This bomb was already an improved type which made the first one obsolete. It convinced even the Japanese that their situation was hopeless. On August 10 the Tokyo radio broadcast an acceptance of the Potsdam ultimatum, asking only that Emperor Hirohito retain his sovereignty. The following day the Allies dispatched a note to Tokyo which accepted the Japanese offer with the stipulation that "from the moment of surrender the authority of the emperor and the Japanese government to rule the state shall be subject to the Supreme Commander of the Allied powers." After days of suspense the Japanese finally announced acceptance of the terms on August 14. In his rescript Emperor Hirohito stated: "The enemy has begun to employ a new and most cruel bomb, the power of which to damage is, indeed, incalculable." A continuation of the war, the emperor said, would "result in an ultimate collapse and obliteration of the Japanese nation." General MacArthur, who was appointed Supreme Commander for the Allied powers, conducted the formal surrender ceremonies on board the battleship *Missouri* in Tokyo harbor on September 2. In obedience to Emperor Hirohito's instructions, Japanese troops in China, Manchuria, Formosa, and the many islands of the Pacific laid down their arms and submitted themselves to the directions of the Allied commanders. World War II, after six years of the most bloody fighting in history, was officially ended.

Europe Since World War II

Europe in World War II

✿ ✿

CHAPTER TWENTY-ONE

The Preliminary Peace Conferences

THE curtain had fallen on the bloody battlefields. The war which to the Chinese had meant eight years of torture and destruction; which to the British signified Dunkirk, the Blitz, and a long postponed victory; which to the Russians meant a colossal casualty list and the thorough devastation of the western part of their country; which to the United States signified long rows of crosses from Belgium to Okinawa—the greatest and most terrible war of all times was over. The time for which people everywhere, victors and vanquished, had lived and died, which had been the terminus of all their thoughts, the goal of their working, fighting, and enduring, had finally arrived. All were now released from the agony of suspense regarding the outcome. While the vanquished were sad and disappointed, the peoples of the United Nations were happy over the victory they had scarcely dared hope would ever come. In thousands of cities, towns, and villages the inhabitants wildly hailed the end of armed combat. There was joy over the defeat of the forces of aggression. But the realization of the problems yet to be solved tempered the spontaneity of the joy. Although the awful heartache of the war was over, there was the headache of tomorrow in the offing. More fearful responsibilities and more crucial liabilities rested on the victors than on the vanquished.

Among the problems which confronted the Allies were the problems of forging a peace out of weariness, cynicism, inertia, and disunion, of coping with hunger, misery, and disease, of rehabilitating the economic life of both victors and vanquished—in short, of rebuilding a shattered world order. Above all, there was the problem of the atomic bomb, a problem so fraught with significance for the future that the war itself shrank to minor importance. Even a world jaded by destruction was moved by the horror of the bomb which in a split second returned so many thousand human beings to the dust from which they sprang. People everywhere realized that the discovery which had suddenly ended the war had possibilities so tremendous as to stagger the imagination. "I realize," President Truman said in the hour of victory, "the tragic significance of the atomic bomb. . . . We thank God that it has come to us, instead of to our enemies; and we pray that He may guide us to use it in His ways and for His purposes."

Among the many differences that distinguished the peacemaking of World War II from that of World War I two are outstanding. First, the peace efforts after World War II were not based on lofty principles or openly expressed idealism comparable to that which heralded the peace talks after World War I. There were no such wholesome aspirations as those embodied in President Wilson's Fourteen Points. The evident assumption was that the Big Three (the United States, Britain, and Soviet Russia) had by their power, wealth, and strategy won the war and that they could by the same token establish an enduring peace. The inclusion of China and France in the peace talks was distinctly a concession. Second, after no great war in modern times have the victors allowed so much time to pass before making a settlement with their enemies. After World War I the Allied statesmen had taken up the work of making peace almost immediately. Within three months after the armistice delegates from the nineteen victorious powers gathered in Paris to begin the work and in another three months the treaties were practically ready. After World War II it was more than eighteen months before the lesser treaties were ready for the signing.

§

THE BIG THREE AT YALTA

As the first stage in the peacemaking we may regard a number of conferences which were held while the fighting was still in progress. At these conferences representatives of the Allied Powers agreed on certain phases of the postwar settlement. The most important conference was undoubtedly the one held at Yalta (February 4–11, 1945) by the Big Three (prime minister Churchill, Marshal Stalin, and President Roosevelt). Certainly none of the other conferences has provoked more controversy. Yalta has, in fact, been blamed for much of the international friction and many of the ills of the postwar period. Some of the Yalta deals were made public at once, while others were kept secret for a time.

The Yalta meeting was called ostensibly to complete plans for the final military push against Hitler and his Nazis. Military leaders who had accompanied the Big Three to the conference busied themselves with this problem while prime minister Churchill, Marshal Stalin, and President Roosevelt discussed other questions. One of these was the division of Germany into occupation zones. The idea of zonal occupation was first suggested at Teheran (December, 1943) and was elaborated in 1944. According to Elliott Roosevelt, his father did not favor the establishment of separate zones. "Father," he wrote, "had come to the Crimea hoping to convince the other partners that control of Germany should be integrated, not divided into zones. . . . But both the British and the Soviets were lukewarm to the idea; they were able to convince Father that the zone idea should be set up." [1]

The first plan called for three zones (one each for Great Britain, Soviet Russia, and the United States) with a Central Control Commission to establish unity of administration. When the plan was discussed Churchill proposed four zones so that France could be allotted a zone of occupation. Stalin at first opposed French participation in the control of Germany, and Roosevelt was inclined to agree with him. The latter, however, was gradually won over to the idea of French participation, and Stalin, also, finally agreed on condition that the French zone be carved out of the zones allotted to Britain and the United States. Stalin shared Molotov's opinion that this should be done "only as a kindness to France and not because she was entitled to it." [2] But Stalin was still against permitting France to take part in the control machinery. Roosevelt, who for a time shared this opinion, later changed his mind and even succeeded in convincing Stalin to permit French participation in the Control Commission. Berlin, too, was divided into four zones, one for each ally. Unfortunately no final decisions were made regarding access to these zones, since Berlin would be deep in Russian territory. A secret agreement was also made between Roosevelt and Stalin which permitted the Russians to capture Berlin. Finally, it was decided that Germany be compelled to compensate to the greatest possible extent for the loss and suffering she had caused the Allied nations. There was considerable discussion regarding Russia's share of reparations, but the final details were not worked out.

[1] Elliott Roosevelt, *As He Saw It* (1946), p. 238.
[2] James F. Byrnes, *Speaking Frankly* (1947), p. 25.

Settling the problems concerning Germany did not conclude the work of the conference. President Roosevelt, at whose suggestion the conference had been held, had two other objectives. He wished, first, to gain Russia's help in the war against Japan and, second, to get Russia's cooperation in his efforts to secure a permanent world peace. Edward R. Stettinius, who as Secretary of State attended the Yalta conference, wrote: "It was President Roosevelt's belief, and he expressed it to me many times, that if he and the prime minister could sit around a conference table again with Marshal Stalin, not only would the war be brought to a speedier conclusion, but plans could also be laid to solve these problems and to create the basis for an enduring peace." [3] Nor was Mr. Roosevelt alone in this belief. In the United States there were many leaders who believed that a *modus vivendi* with Russia could be worked out, despite the fact that the Soviet government was an absolute dictatorship.[4] Public opinion in the United States generally believed cooperation between the Allies to be a practical possibility. The President and Harry Hopkins even worked out a plan which had as its object the conversion of Stalin from Soviet imperialism to democratic collaboration. The plan was one of appeasement. William C. Bullitt quotes the President as saying: "I think that if I give him everything I possibly can and ask for nothing in return, noblesse oblige, he won't try to annex anything and will work with me for a world of democracy and peace." [5] Unfortunately Mr. Roosevelt completely misjudged the Soviet leader.

Stalin also had two main objectives. First, he aimed to realize certain imperialist objectives of tsarist Russia in eastern Europe and eastern Asia. Second, he was striving to create world-wide conditions for communist revolution. Through his pact with Hitler, Stalin had planned to remain aloof from a war which would tear the capitalist world apart. Meanwhile he would build up a powerful military state in Russia as a means of promoting world revolution at the proper moment. This plan was temporarily disrupted by Hitler's invasion of Russia. During the succeeding months the Russians were engaged in a bitter struggle for existence; but after the tide definitely turned in the winter of 1942–1943, Stalin again resumed his march on the road of imperialism. Prime minister Churchill was ready to set bounds to Soviet expansion, but President Roosevelt had other ideas.

[3] *Roosevelt and the Russians: the Yalta Conference,* edited by Walter Johnson (1949), p. 25.
[4] On February 10, 1940, the President had said: "The Soviet Union, as everybody who has the courage to face the facts knows, is run by a dictatorship as absolute as any dictatorship in the world."
[5] *Life,* vol. 25 (August 30, 1948), p. 94.

After the meeting with Stalin at Teheran, he said, as quoted by his son: "The biggest thing was in making clear to Stalin that the United States and Great Britain were not allied in one common bloc against the Soviet Union. That's our big job now and it will be our big job tomorrow, too, making sure that we continue to act as referee, as intermediary between Russia and England." [6]

Marshal Stalin was ready to cooperate to a certain degree at a price. The first price he demanded was the settlement of the Polish boundary question to his liking. He demanded that the Curzon Line be made the western boundary of the U.S.S.R., a frontier that assigned to the Soviet Union almost half of Poland's prewar territory. Both Churchill and Roosevelt finally accepted Stalin's proposal, but suggested that the Soviet Union make some concessions to the Poles in drawing the line. It was also agreed that the Poles were to be compensated through the extension of the western boundary of Poland into Germany. At first Stalin recommended that Poland extend into Germany as far as the Neisse River, but Churchill, who realized that this would mean the inclusion in Poland of nine million Germans, asserted that "it would be a pity to stuff the Polish goose so full of German food that it will die of indigestion." No definite decision was reached on the question. At the end of the conference the Big Three merely announced that "Poland must receive substantial accessions of territory in the north and west." In defense of the agreement which made the Curzon Line Russia's western boundary Mr. James F. Byrnes, who was at Yalta as Director of Defense Mobilization, said in a speech delivered September 6, 1948, at Seattle, Washington:

The Russian armies were then in control of Poland. It was not a question of what we would *let* the Russians do, but what we could *get* the Russians to do. Generalissimo Stalin had previously made clear that he regarded the Curzon Line as the eastern frontier of Poland and considered the area east of that line as having been wrested from Russia by force. Churchill had already supported the Curzon Line in Parliament. . . . Roosevelt accepted a situation not of his making and one which he was powerless to alter.

Stalin further demanded the establishment of a Polish government that would be agreeable to Russia. Both President Roosevelt and prime minister Churchill, fearing the domination of eastern Europe by the Soviet Union, insisted that the Polish government must be "free and sovereign." "Britain," Mr. Churchill said, "declared war

[6] Elliott Roosevelt, *As He Saw It* (1946), p. 206.

616 The Preliminary Peace Conferences

on Germany in order that Poland should be free and sovereign." The President told Marshal Stalin that he favored a government "which would represent all the political parties." Both Churchill and Roosevelt hoped that some consideration would be given to the Polish government-in-exile in London, but the Soviet Union had already set up a provisional government at Lublin. The Western world was soon to realize that Stalin's idea of a friendly government is one completely dominated by Soviet Russia. Stalin did accept the pledge of "free and unfettered elections as soon as possible on the basis of universal suffrage and secret ballot." The pledge, however, was never carried out.

🔄

THE SOVIET UNION AND THE WAR IN THE PACIFIC

Stalin made the most of a further opportunity to gain territory when President Roosevelt asked for Russian help in the war against Japan. As events turned out, the Western Allies did not need the help of the Soviet government. By February, 1945, Japan's offensive strength had been destroyed. Only a few weeks later General Kenney announced that the Japanese air force was "no longer a threat." By this time, too, her fleet had lost its striking force, and United States naval craft were cruising at will in Japanese waters. Furthermore, in informed circles Russia's entry into the war in the Pacific was regarded as certain since it was the best way for Stalin to share in the division of the spoils. But those who realized this do not seem to have reached the President's ear. The estimate of the situation as it was presented to him was a pessimistic one. The United States War Department believed that the total strength of the Japanese army was still in the vicinity of five million men and that the Japanese government "might determine upon resistance to the end in all the areas of the Far East under its control." The plans to overcome this resistance are described by Secretary of War Stimson in his *Memoirs:*

We were planning an intensified sea and air blockade, through the summer and early fall, to be followed on November 1 by an invasion of the main island of Honshu in the spring of 1946. . . . We estimated that the major fighting would not end until the latter part of 1946 at the earliest. I was informed that such operations might be expected to cost over a million casualties, to American forces alone.[7]

7 H. L. Stimson and M. Bundy, *On Active Service in Peace and War* (1948), pp. 618–619.

This estimate appears to have made a deep impression on the President. According to Edward R. Stettinius, the President told Mr. Churchill that he thought the war might continue until 1947. Naturally he was eager to avoid a long-drawn-out war and its cost in blood. Furthermore, according to Stettinius, immense pressure was "put on the President by our military leaders to bring Russia into the Far Eastern war." [8] The joint chiefs of staff of the United States had sent to the State Department just before Yalta a document which asked "Russian entry at the earliest possible date consistent with her ability to engage in offensive operations." In October, 1943, Stalin had assured Secretary of State Hull, while the latter was in Moscow, that Russia would join in the war against Japan. Mr. Hull wrote in his *Memoirs:*

> He astonished and delighted me by saying clearly and unequivocally that, when the Allies succeeded in defeating Germany, the Soviet Union would then join in defeating Japan. Stalin had brought up this subject entirely on his own. . . . He finished by saying that I could inform President Roosevelt of this in the strictest confidence. I thanked him heartily. The Marshal's statement of his decision was forthright. He made it emphatically, it was entirely unsolicited, and he asked nothing in return.[9]

At Teheran a few weeks later Stalin assured both President Roosevelt and prime minister Churchill of his support in the Pacific war.[10] But Marshal Stalin conveniently seems to have forgotten his promises when the question was brought up at a secret meeting between him and the President. He told Mr. Roosevelt that certain concessions desired by the Russians in the Far East were essential for Russian entry into the war against Japan.

The Soviet demands were in violation of the Atlantic Charter which pledged that no nation—neither the Soviet Union nor any other country—would seek territorial aggrandizement. But the President was so eager to have Russia's help in the war that he accepted Stalin's terms. Moreover, he also consented to get Chiang Kai-shek's acceptance of the agreement. Prime minister Churchill accepted Stalin's proposition because he believed the future of the British Empire, and particularly the fate of Hong Kong, to be at stake. The terms were incorporated in a secret treaty signed by the Big Three without the participation of the United States State Department or the British Foreign Office. The full text was not released by the

8 *Roosevelt and the Russians,* p. 90.
9 *The Memoirs of Cordell Hull,* vol. II (1948), pp. 1309–1310.
10 Deane, *The Strange Alliance* (1946), p. 226.

United States State Department until March 24, 1947. Since this treaty has been the center of much controversy, it might be well to quote it in full:

The leaders of the three great powers—the Soviet Union, the United States of America, and Great Britain—have agreed that in two or three months after Germany has surrendered and the war in Europe has terminated, the Soviet Union shall enter into the war against Japan on the side of the Allies on condition that:

1. The *status quo* in Outer Mongolia (the Mongolian People's Republic) shall be preserved;

2. The former rights of Russia violated by the treacherous attack of Japan in 1904 shall be restored, viz.:

a. The southern part of Sakhalin as well as the islands adjacent to it shall be returned to the Soviet Union;

b. The commercial port of Dairen shall be internationalized, the preeminent interests of the Soviet Union in this port being safeguarded, and the lease of Port Arthur as a naval base of U.S.S.R. restored;

c. The Chinese Eastern Railroad and the South Manchurian Railroad, which provides an outlet to Dairen, shall be jointly operated by the establishment of a joint Soviet-Chinese company, it being understood that the preeminent interests of the Soviet Union shall be safeguarded and that China shall retain full sovereignty in Manchuria;

3. The Kurile Islands shall be handed over to the Soviet Union.

It is understood that the agreement concerning Outer Magnolia and the ports and railroads referred to above will require concurrence of Generalissimo Chiang Kai-shek. The President (Roosevelt) will take measures in order to obtain this concurrence on advice from Marshal Stalin.

The heads of the three great powers have agreed that these claims of the Soviet Union shall be unquestionably fulfilled after Japan has been defeated.

For its part, the Soviet Union expresses its readiness to conclude with the National Government of China a pact of friendship and alliance between the U.S.S.R. and China in order to render assistance to China with its armed forces for the purpose of liberating China from the Japanese yoke.

Joseph V. Stalin
Franklin D. Roosevelt
Winston C. Churchill

February 11, 1945.

In getting the assurance of Russia's entry into the war, President Roosevelt gained for his chiefs of staff the one and only concession they expected from Yalta. Military expedience seems to have eclipsed all other considerations. Mr. Stettinius recorded that when he asked the President whether he wanted any help from the State Department, the latter told him "it was primarily a military matter and . . . had best remain on a purely military level." In looking back to the Yalta conference at a later time, Mr. John Foster Dulles wrote: "At Yalta, Stalin won great political victories which enabled him to expand Soviet influence into the heart of Europe and throughout much of north China. He won those victories because his eye was on the political ball while we were thinking only in military terms." [11] Rear Admiral Ellis M. Zacharias wrote: "The story of Yalta is really the tragic story of the wrong estimate of a clear-cut military situation and of the accident of choosing the erroneous, timid, inaccurate estimate." [12] Mr. Sherwood's explanation in *Roosevelt and Hopkins* is that "Roosevelt would not have agreed to that firm commitment had it not been that the Yalta conference was almost at an end and he was tired and anxious to avoid further argument." It has been pointed out by a number of historians that President Roosevelt did not agree to all the Russian demands. At first the Russian delegation asked for Port Arthur and Dairen outright and also for full control of the Manchurian railways.

UNITY AND DISUNION

Stalin also quickly named his price when the President broached the question of a United Nations organization. His price was three votes in the General Assembly of the United Nations. In addition to the U.S.S.R. as such, White Russia (Byelorussia) and the Ukraine were to be listed as members of the General Assembly. President Roosevelt was at first not in favor of giving the Soviets two additional votes. "There is no doubt," Robert Sherwood wrote, "that Roosevelt had come to Yalta determined to oppose the Russian demand for the two additional votes." [13] The President had told congressional leaders before he went to Yalta that if necessary he would counter with a demand for forty-eight votes for the United States. At Yalta he found, however, that Churchill did not object to Stalin's demand. This fact, coupled with his eagerness to get the machinery of the United Nations started, inclined him to pay the price. Before leaving Yalta he did get a pledge from both Churchill and Stalin that their countries would support the demand for two additional votes for the United States if such a request were to be made. But on April 3 Secretary of

11 *U.S. State Department Bulletin*, August 7, 1950, p. 208.
12 *UN World*, vol. 3 (January, 1946), p. 16.
13 Robert Sherwood, *Roosevelt and Hopkins* (1948), p. 856.

State Stettinius announced that the United States would not ask for the additional votes at the San Francisco Conference. In general, President Roosevelt's attitude toward the United Nations was much like President Wilson's attitude toward the League. Both were convinced that their respective organization held the key to peace and both were ready to sacrifice principles to gain support for their projects.

At Yalta Roosevelt also deferred to Stalin's wishes in the question of voting procedure in the Security Council of the projected United Nations organization. It was agreed that decisions of the Security Council on all matters should be made by an affirmative vote of seven members, including the five permanent members. This procedure gave each of the permanent members of the Council an absolute veto.

The conference ended on a note of unity. At the final banquet the representatives of the three governments toasted each other liberally. Marshal Stalin in one of his happy moods led in a toast to the alliance between the three powers. Churchill and Roosevelt were also happy. According to Admiral Leahy, "the American delegation, including Roosevelt and most of his staff, was weary but in a high mood. They felt the foundations of world peace had been laid in the eight days of almost continuous meetings at this former resort of royalty beside the Black Sea." [14] Upon his return to the United States President Roosevelt told the Congress: "I come from the Crimean Conference with a firm belief that we have made a good start on the road to a world of peace. . . . Never before have the major allies been more closely united—not only in their war aims, but also in their peace aims. And they are determined to continue to be united, to be united with each other—and with all peace-loving nations—so that the ideal of lasting peace will become a reality."

Prime minister Churchill said in his report to the House of Commons: "I trust the House will feel that hope has been powerfully strengthened by our meeting in the Crimea. The ties that bind the three great powers together, and their mutual comprehension of each other, have grown." Most of the newspapers of Britain and the United States echoed these sentiments. Thus one could read in the *New York Times:* "The alliance of the Big Three stands firm. Progress has been made. The hope of further gains is high. The conference marks a milestone on the road to victory and peace."

Unfortunately it was all wishful thinking. Within two weeks after the conference adjourned, discord was rife. Instance after instance

14 *I Was There* (1950), p. 291.

arose in which Russia's interpretations of the Yalta agreements differed from those of the Western powers. Secretary Stettinius offered the following explanation of the breakdown of friendly relations: "Marshal Stalin had difficulties with the Politburo, when he returned to Moscow, for having been too friendly and for having made too many concessions to the two capitalistic nations, which could, in dogmatic Marxist eyes, never be really trusted by Communist Russia."

The premise which Stalin had accepted at Yalta that in the former Axis satellite states interim governments were to be formed which would be "broadly representative of all democratic elements in the population and pledged to the earliest possible establishment through free elections of government responsible to the will of the people" was deliberately flouted. Even before President Roosevelt reported to the Congress, deputy foreign minister Vishinsky violated this premise by intervening in Rumanian affairs to compel King Michael to oust a coalition of moderates and to replace it with a Soviet left-wing puppet regime. There was no consultation with the Western powers. When it was pointed out to him that his arbitrary political methods would not be well received in the United States and Britain, Vishinsky said sharply: "Let the sparrows twitter." The next object of strife between the Kremlin and the Western powers was Poland. A commission had been set up by the Big Three at Yalta to form a Polish "Government of National Unity." But the commission became hopelessly deadlocked over Soviet demands. The Kremlin then arbitrarily established the Lublin government as the legitimate government of Poland and proceeded to ignore the pledge of free elections at the earliest possible time. The elections which Soviet foreign minister Molotov had promised President Roosevelt would be held in a month's time were actually held twenty-three months later and were anything but "free and unfettered."

An acrimonious exchange of messages took place between Stalin and Roosevelt shortly before the latter's death. It started when Stalin falsely accused the British and Americans of promising the Germans easier peace terms if the German armies in Italy would surrender. In his reply President Roosevelt stated that no negotiations had taken place and assured Stalin that he would be fully informed of any move. The return message offended the President deeply when Stalin insisted that he had knowledge of such negotiations and "that it was evident the President had not been advised by his own military leaders." [15] Roosevelt stated in reply that he resented the "vile mis-

[15] James F. Byrnes, *Speaking Frankly* (1947), p. 57.

representations" and then told Stalin that apparently his "informants
wished to destroy the friendly relations between the two countries."
After the President's death Churchill tried his hand at winning Stalin
by a personal appeal (April 29, 1945). But it was to no avail. Stalin
was not moved one iota from his grand design of establishing Soviet
domination over eastern Europe.

When other disagreements arose to mar the relations between
Soviet Russia and the Western powers, President Truman cut off
Lend-Lease to European Russia and sent Harry Hopkins to Moscow
to explain. Mr. Hopkins told Stalin that the people in the United
States had become alarmed over Russia's failure to carry out the
Yalta agreement in Poland. Stalin replied by accusing the United
States of violating the Yalta agreement in admitting Argentina to
the UN Conference at San Francisco. He also charged that the curtailment of Lend-Lease had been abrupt and "even brutal." Hopkins,
however, did manage to iron out some of the differences. A brief
period of good will ensued during which the United Nations Charter
was ratified and the Potsdam Conference was called.

POTSDAM, THE LAST WARTIME CONFERENCE

The last wartime conference of the three great powers was held
at Potsdam, near Berlin, July 17 to August 2, 1945. Because of the
proximity of Potsdam to the German capital, the conference is often
called the Berlin Conference. Of the Big Three only Stalin was there
for the entire conference. Winston Churchill was present at the early
sessions, but was replaced by Clement R. Attlee, the new British
prime minister.[16] President Truman, who headed the United States
delegation, was bound not only by the promises President Roosevelt
had previously made but also by the exigencies of the war against
Japan. Not knowing how much more time would be required to
crush the Japanese, both the United States and British delegations
continued the policy of capitulating to Stalin's wishes.

When the conference assembled at Potsdam, the Nazis had surrendered and the four zones had been set up. Hence the principal
topic was Germany and its future. "It is not the intention of the
Allies," the three powers declared, "to destroy or enslave the German
people. It is the intention of the Allies that the German people be
given the opportunity to prepare for the eventual reconstruction of
their life on a democratic and peaceful basis. If their own efforts are

[16] Mr. Attlee became prime minister as the result of British parliamentary elections
held on July 23.

Press Association

THE POTSDAM CONFERENCE

steadily directed to this end, it will be possible for them in due course to take their place among the free and peaceful peoples of the world."

The three powers then proceeded to set down the terms for a defeated Germany. First, they decreed the complete disarmament and demilitarization of Germany, together with the elimination and control of all German industry that could be used for military production. "All German land, naval and air forces . . . together with all clubs and associations which serve to keep alive the military tradition in Germany, shall be completely and finally abolished in such manner as permanently to prevent the revival or reorganization of German militarism and nazism." Furthermore, "all arms, ammunition and implements of war and all specialized facilities for their production shall be held at the disposal of the Allies or destroyed. The maintenance and production of all aircraft and all arms, ammunition and implements of war shall be prevented." The three powers also decided that the National Socialist Party, its affiliated and supervised organizations, and all Nazi institutions be dissolved with finality and that German political life be reconstructed on a democratic basis. To make possible the successful development of democratic ideas and to eliminate Nazi and militarist doctrines completely, control over German education was decreed. It was further agreed that "war criminals and those who have participated in planning and carrying out Nazi enterprises involving or resulting in atrocities of war crimes shall be arrested and brought to judgment."

When the question of reparations was decided, the Soviet Union, which had suffered the greatest economic losses, was accorded the lion's share. It was permitted, first of all, to satisfy its claims by taking from its own zone industrial equipment and other assets. "The determination of the amount and character of the industrial capital equipment unnecessary for the German peace economy and therefore available for reparations shall be made by the Control Council under policies fixed by the Allied Commission on Reparations." In addition to reparations from its own zone, the Soviet Union was given the right to take from the western zones 25 per cent of such metallurgical, chemical, and machine-manufacturing equipment as was not needed for the new German peace economy. Ten per cent of this equipment the Soviet government was to receive "without payment or exchange of any kind in return," but for the other 15 per cent it agreed to pay "an equivalent value of food, coal, potash, zinc, timber, clay products, petroleum products and such other commodities as may be agreed upon." The Soviet Union was also given complete control over German external assets in Finland, Bulgaria, Hungary, Rumania, and Eastern Austria plus an unannounced portion of those elsewhere. While the Soviet Union agreed to settle "the reparation claims of Poland from its own share of reparations," the reparation claims of the United States, the United Kingdom, and other countries entitled to reparations from Germany "shall be met from the western zones and from appropriate German external assets."

Two further decisions of the conference incorporated the Soviet point of view. The first of these handed over provisionally to the U.S.S.R. the city of Koenigsberg and the eastern part of East Prussia. Soviet desires were also carried out in the provisional settlement of Poland's eastern boundary. The remainder of East Prussia together with the port of Danzig and an additional slice of German territory extending to the Oder and Neisse Rivers were turned over to Poland pending the final determination of the boundaries in the peace settlement.

✿ ✿

The Struggle For Peace

THE COUNCIL OF FOREIGN
MINISTERS
IN ADDITION to its other decisions
the Potsdam Conference also set up the machinery to draft the first
treaties. James F. Byrnes relates that he favored a different procedure
in drawing up the treaties than had been followed after World War I.
"If we waited until the end of the war with Japan," he wrote, "and
then held one peace conference, attended by all the states at war,
with no preliminary draft to use as a basis for the treaties, there would
be endless bickering." He therefore prepared a plan for the creation
of a Council of Foreign Ministers to which the task of preparing the
preliminary draft was to be entrusted. President Truman accepted
the plan after consideration and it was then presented to the Potsdam
Conference which quickly approved it. In the protocol made public
at the end of the conference the plan was stated in the following
words:

> The governments of the United Kingdom, the United States, and the
> U.S.S.R. consider it necessary to begin without delay the essential prepara-
> tory work upon the peace settlement in Europe. To this end they are
> agreed that there should be established a Council of the Foreign Ministers
> of the five great powers to prepare treaties of peace with the European
> enemy states, for submission to the United Nations. The Council would
> also be empowered to propose settlements of outstanding territorial ques-
> tions in Europe and to consider such other matters as member govern-
> ments might agree to refer to it.

A cordial invitation was then sent to the Chinese and French governments requesting the foreign ministers of those countries to join the
other three foreign ministers for the purpose of drawing up the

treaties. When the Soviet delegates opposed the immediate drafting
of a treaty for Germany, the Council was authorized to prepare
drafts for treaties with Italy, Rumania, Bulgaria, Hungary, and
Finland.

Since the making of the peace rested solely in the hands of a few
powers, the drawing up of the treaties appeared to present no extreme diplomatic difficulties. The one essential was agreement among
the Allies themselves. It had been a frequent experience of previous
centuries that coalitions formed against a common danger tended to
dissolve as soon as the danger was removed. Thus the concert of
powers which in 1814 had defeated Napoleon was in 1815 at the point
of dissolving into a war between Great Britain and France on the one
hand and Russia and Prussia on the other. Even in World War I the
united front gave way to disunity during the peace talks. In this respect the situation after World War II was no exception. During the
struggle to defeat the Axis there had been at least an outward semblance of unity among the Allied nations. It is, of course, easy to exaggerate the degree of unity that existed. Quite understandably Allied
propagandists did their utmost to conceal from the enemy all discord.
As an example of noncooperation one could cite the fact that the
Russians always insisted on fighting their own war in their own way.
Until late in 1944, when his armies had already crossed the German
borders, General Eisenhower had to plan his campaigns without
knowing where and when the Russians would strike. But there had
been some degree of unity and cooperation among the Allies. At least
they were united in their determination to defeat the Axis.

Whatever unity had existed during the war quickly evaporated
when peace discussions began. In place of the common objective each
of the victors substituted new objectives as varied as there were nations. Especially evident was a determination to acquire strategic
areas and to establish spheres of influence. But the fundamental
cause of the cleavage was Russia's brusque efforts to expand her
sphere of influence. The Russian leaders planned their diplomatic
campaign as carefully as they had planned their military campaigns.
Soviet expansion was at complete variance with the aims of the
United States and Great Britain and was therefore resisted by them.
Having capitulated to the wishes of Stalin and his associates at Yalta
and Potsdam, the two countries adopted a more independent and determined attitude after the defeat of Japan. The surrender of Japan
freed the Western democracies from the entanglements of war, and
the possession of the atomic bomb gave them a trump card of incalculable power. Furthermore, the death of President Roosevelt and

Mr. Churchill's retirement from Downing Street brought to the front a group of men who were not bound by personal commitments to Stalin.

The stiffening of policy became evident at the first meeting of the Council of Foreign Ministers, which opened in London on September 10, 1945. Present were United States Secretary of State James F. Byrnes, British Foreign Secretary Ernest Bevin, Soviet Foreign Commissar V. M. Molotov, French Foreign Minister Bidault, and Chinese Foreign Minister Shieh-chieh. The first task of the Council was the preparation of a treaty with Italy, and disagreement began as soon as the question was presented. The Italian colonies immediately became a bone of contention. As a solution of the problem Secretary Byrnes suggested that they be placed under the trusteeship of the United Nations and after a period of time some of them be given their independence. This was acceptable to the other foreign ministers. The parting of the ways came when they tried to agree on a method of administering the territories. While Bevin and Byrnes favored a trusteeship under the United Nations as such, Molotov proposed individual trusteeships with Russia as sole trustee for Libya. This proposal evoked the vigorous opposition of the British and United States foreign ministers, both of whom were opposed to Russia's gaining a foothold in the Mediterranean.

Nor did the differences over the treaty with Italy end with the question of the African colonies. When the question of reparations was raised, Mr. Molotov quickly demanded that Italy pay the Soviet Union $300 million. The ministers of Britain and the United States, mindful of the improbability of extracting any such payments, immediately objected. Disagreement also flared up over the question of Trieste. Whereas Russia wished to give the Adriatic port and adjacent territory to Yugoslavia, Britain and the United States wanted it to remain with Italy. When the discussion turned to the other treaties the British and United States ministers objected to Russian domination of totalitarian governments in Rumania, Bulgaria, and Hungary, stating that treaties could not be signed with the governments of these countries until free and unfettered elections were held. The result of all this was that the conference which had been expected to draw up a peace plan for Italy adjourned after twenty-two days without having reached one major agreement. The foreign ministers of the five great powers agreed only on the fact that they could not agree. They found themselves so far apart on the treaty questions that they did not even issue a final communiqué. Thus the first meeting of the Council of Foreign Ministers ended in failure. What it did demonstrate was that the task of peacemaking would be a difficult one.

The failure of the London Conference augured ill for the success of the United Nations General Assembly, which was scheduled to hold its first meeting in London on January 10, 1946. Without agreement among the great powers there was little hope that harmony would prevail in the General Assembly. The situation impelled Secretary of State Byrnes to urge a meeting of the Council of Foreign Ministers at Moscow in December, 1945, and his proposal was accepted. From December 16 to 26 the foreign ministers of Britain, the United States and the Soviet Union conferred, while the world anxiously awaited developments. The answer came in the final communiqué, issued December 27, which revealed that at least a semblance of unity had been restored. One of the major achievements was a formula for drafting the treaties. It provided that only those members of the Big Five who had signed the surrender terms with the various Axis satellites were to take part in the actual drafting of the peace treaties with those countries. More specifically, it prescribed that the peace treaty with Italy was to be drafted by Britain, the United States, Soviet Russia, and France, the last being regarded as a signer for purposes of the peace treaty. It further prescribed that the peace treaties with Rumania, Bulgaria, and Hungary be drafted by the foreign ministers of the Soviet Union, the United States, and the United Kingdom. Since the United States had not declared war on Finland, the treaty with that country was to be drawn up by the foreign ministers of the Soviet Union and the United Kingdom.

Agreement was also reached on a number of other questions. It was decided that the United States and the Soviet Union should set up a joint commission to unify Korea and to aid in forming a provisional Korean government under the control of democratic leaders. Korea as such was to be placed under the trusteeship of the United States, Britain, China, and the Soviet Union for a period "up to five years," then granted independence. The foreign ministers further agreed on "the need for a unified and democratic China under the National (Chiang Kai-shek) Government" and reaffirmed the policy of "nonintervention in the internal affairs of China." Mr. Byrnes and Mr. Molotov, according to the communiqué, were "in complete accord as to the desirability of withdrawal of Soviet and American troops" from China "at the earliest practicable moment." The British and United States ministers also agreed to recognize the Rumanian government (already recognized by the Soviet Union) as soon as they were satisfied that it had been broadened to include two representatives of democratic groups and when assurances had been given regarding free elections, freedom of speech, press, religion, and association.

The agreement which was regarded as most significant at the time concerned atomic energy. It was agreed that the United States, Britain, and the Soviet Union, together with China, France, and Canada, would jointly propose to the first meeting of the United Nations General Assembly the creation of a commission "to consider problems arising from the discovery of atomic energy and related matters."

The communiqué issued at the close of the conference was received with much rejoicing in the Soviet Union, Britain, and the United States. The Soviet press quite uniformly hailed the conference as "a big step forward." In the British and United States press, too, there was much favorable comment and the foreign ministers of the two countries also made favorable reports. Thus British Foreign Secretary Ernest Bevin said: "I do not believe in creating in the public mind the idea that one conference is going to solve all problems. But we have gone one further stage on the way." United States Secretary of State Byrnes stated that the "important thing" about the conference was "that closer relations have been established, so that the possibility of agreement has been greatly increased." A number of observers were quick to state, however, that the agreements had been achieved in large part by concessions to Soviet Russia. One correspondent summed up Mr. Byrnes' trip to Moscow in the words: "He came, he saw, he concurred."

The next meeting of the Council of Foreign Ministers was held in Paris, April 25, 1946. This time the foreign ministers of Britain, France, the Soviet Union, and the United States were present. The meeting began auspiciously. The ministers unanimously agreed to limit the future naval strength of Italy and to appoint a committee of naval experts to apportion surplus Italian craft among their countries and Greece and Yugoslavia. The southern Dobrudja was awarded to Bulgaria, Transylvania to Rumania, and the Soviet Union was permitted to retain Bessarabia and northern Bucovina. Thereafter issue followed issue across the green felt table, only to be placed in the file of unsolved problems. Instead of settling an issue when it was raised, the ministers would disagree and pass on to the next one. Finally Mr. Molotov tried some "horse trading" by offering to yield on reparations and make adjustments on the question of Italian colonies if the United States would agree to give Trieste to the Yugoslavs. But Mr. Byrnes emphatically turned down the proposition. Thus day after day passed without any agreement being reached.

By May 15 the Council had become so hopelessly deadlocked that a recess to June 15 was voted.

When the Council reconvened, some progress toward a settlement was made. M. Bidault of France suggested the setting up of a temporary international regime as a solution of the Trieste problem. The other foreign ministers finally agreed to accept the idea of an international regime, but no agreement could be reached on the method of administration. While Mr. Molotov held out for four-power rather than United Nations supervision, the other foreign ministers insisted that responsibility for supervision should lie with the Security Council rather than a four-power commission. The foreign ministers did agree, however, that the Soviet Union was to receive from Italy $100 million in reparations. Agreement was also reached on the transfer of the Dodecanese Islands to Greece and on the administration of the Italian colonies. At the Moscow meeting of the Council of Foreign Ministers it had been decided that when the treaty drafts were ready, all the members of the United Nations that had actively waged warfare against the European states would be convoked to consider them; hence the foreign ministers decided to sent out invitations for a conference of twenty-one victor nations.

THE PARIS PEACE CONFERENCE

The first peace conference resulting from the Allied victory over the Axis in World War II opened in Paris on July 29, 1946. Delegates of the Big Four powers and the "Little Seventeen" assembled in the ornate French Senate Chamber to consider the drafts of the treaties for Italy, Finland, Bulgaria, Hungary, and Rumania. Actually it was not a peace conference at all. At Vienna in 1815, at Berlin in 1878, and at Paris in 1919, peace conferences had assembled for the actual purpose of drawing up peace treaties. In 1946 the small nations were called together merely to state their views on treaties which had been drawn up by the great powers. Nor were they to change the provisions of the treaties; their official activities were limited to making "recommendations" which representatives of the Big Four would accept or reject at a subsequent meeting. Furthermore, consideration was limited to the treaties with the smaller nations. There was to be no discussion of treaties with Germany and Japan. The real settlement was, therefore, yet to come.

In one respect there was a parallel between the peace conferences of 1919 and 1946: both were dominated by the great powers. At both Paris Conferences this domination did not go unquestioned. At the first session in 1919, Clemenceau made it perfectly clear that the Big Four would dominate the meetings. Thereafter they decided all the important issues while the smaller nations looked on. In 1946 the great powers felt that their domination of the conference should not be questioned. But it was. Even before the meeting opened Dr. Herber V. Evatt, Australia's plain-speaking representative, stated that "the right of making the peace should belong to all those nations who have been partners in achieving the common victory." A fair and democratic peace, he insisted, could "be obtained only by fair and democratic procedures," and justice in the peace settlements depended to a large extent "upon the active participation of a wider group of belligerents than that of three or four or five major powers." Announcing that he did not intend to permit arbitrary rules of procedure to submerge the views of the smaller nations, he demanded that the recommendations of the conference be passed by a simple majority vote.

A week of stormy debate followed. Dr. Evatt's demand for a simple majority vote stemmed from the fact that the Big Four had previously decided that decisions on recommendations and all other questions must be passed by a two-thirds majority. At the Paris Conference the great powers held to their decision. Commissar Molotov, believing that Dr. Evatt's speech had been inspired by the British and Americans, stated that these two powers wanted the simple majority procedure since they could control thirteen votes, but not the fourteen necessary for a two-thirds majority. On the other hand, the two-thirds procedure was favorable to the Soviet Union, which when supported by its satellites could make it difficult for the small nations to get a decision. Secretary of State Byrnes' statement that "the United States will stand by its agreements in the Council" terminated the revolt of the small nations. Later (August 7) the Rules Committee presented a compromise, suggested by the British, which provided that recommendations passed by a simple majority would go on the agenda of the Big Four Council of Foreign Ministers as well as those adopted by a two-thirds majority. Greater importance would, however, be given to the latter. Two days later the compromise was adopted over the bitter opposition of the Soviet bloc.

The major struggle in the conference was between the Soviet bloc and the Western democracies. Whereas the Russians sought to consolidate, and even expand, their sphere of influence, the Western democracies sought to contain the Russians. Every possible opportunity was seized by the Russians to make demands for themselves and their satellites. Thus Mr. Molotov denounced the plea of Premier

de Gasperi of Italy for a less punitive treaty and also Finland's plea
for a reduction in the reparations it was required to pay. But when
such Soviet satellites as Bulgaria and Rumania asked for treaty
changes, the Soviet delegation vociferously supported the demands.
The result was endless debates punctuated with angry words and
bitter wrangling. Some correspondents frankly styled the conference
"the battle of Paris" as if it were an integral part of World War II.
Another commented that "the real peace we now need is between
the East and the West." Jan Christiaan Smuts, the venerable South
African statesman, said in an address to the Peace Conference: "We
seem already, in this moment of unparalleled victory, to be forming
up into new camps between East and West. . . . This fear of our
splitting up into camps transcends all other issues arising from this
conference."

For thirteen hectic weeks the conference discussed and debated
the treaties article by article. The division between the Russian bloc
and the pro-Western states was repeatedly reflected in the voting,
with the latter commanding a two-thirds majority against the six
votes of the pro-Soviet delegates. Finally on October 15 the conference
finished its work and disbanded, leaving the task of putting the finish-
ing touches on the treaties to the Big Four Council of Foreign Ministers. Prime minister Smuts made the following comment on the conference: "In view of the great differences and conflicting claims in
connection with these peace treaties, and the vigor and violence with
which they were fought in commissions, many despaired of the success of the conference. At any rate the conference has not failed and
whatever the final result the job so far has been done which the conference set out to do." What the conference did achieve was to show
the Council of Foreign Ministers the many shades of opinion on the
controversial phases of the treaties.

The Council of Foreign Ministers met in New York City on
November 4, 1946, to consider the recommendations of the Paris Conference. Present were British Foreign Minister Bevin, French Foreign
Minister Bidault, Soviet Foreign Minister Molotov, and United
States Secretary of State Byrnes. A deadlock ensued almost immediately when Mr. Molotov opposed many of the recommendations of the
Paris conference. The ministers were at odds on the question of navigation on the Danube, on the Trieste question, on the distribution
of the Italian fleet, and on a number of other issues. After a number
of fruitless meetings the attitude of the Soviet delegation finally
softened on November 27. Concessions on this and the succeeding
days hastened the completion of the final draft. The Soviet delega-

tion accepted the proposal to internationalize Trieste as a Free Territory under a governor to be appointed by the UN Security Council. While previously supporting the proposal that only the riparian states should share in the control of the Danube, it now accepted the suggestion that all nations have equal rights in the Danube trade. Other agreements followed. Finally on December 12 the Council closed its New York session with the announcement that the treaties would be signed on February 10, 1947.

🌀

THE SIGNING OF THE FIRST TREATIES

On February 10, 1947, the peace treaties ending World War II with Italy, Rumania, Bulgaria, Hungary, and Finland were signed in the historical Salle de l'Horloge of the Quai d'Orsay, the great hall in the French Foreign Office in Paris where the Kellogg-Briand Pact outlawing war was signed in 1928. Foreign Minister Georges Bidault of France stated in the opening address to the delegates that he hoped the former enemy nations would take their places in a world "forever delivered from war." After M. Bidault had opened the ceremonies, the signing proceeded with dispatch and without incident. The table upon which the actual signing took place had once been owned by Louis XV and Louis XVI. It was the table upon which the wounded Robespierre had lain before he was guillotined. The five former enemy countries and the Allied nations which had actively fought against them signed the treaties. All doubt regarding Yugoslavia's adherence to the treaties because of dissatisfaction over not receiving Trieste was dispelled when the Yugoslav foreign minister signed under protest. All five treaties contain definite provisions designed to limit armaments, prevent the recurrence of Nazism or Fascism, and guarantee civil rights.

The first treaty to be signed was that with Italy, the chief satellite of Nazi Germany. It reduced the fledgling Italian Republic to a third-rate power. First of all, Italy was shorn of her African empire—Libya, Eritrea, Italian Somaliland, and Ethiopia—which included an area of 1,240,000 square miles and a population of fifteen million. Second, Italy was compelled to cede the Dodecanese Islands to Greece, give five small Alpine boundary areas to France, transfer two-thirds of her North Adriatic province of Venezia Giulia to Yugoslavia, and surrender the port of Trieste. Third, Italy renounced all special interests in China and recognized the sovereignty and independence of the State of Albania. Fourth, Italy was required to pay reparations totaling $360 million. At Potsdam the Soviet delegation had suggested that Italy pay a total of $600 million, but the United States had opposed such a sum as tending to impoverish Italy. Eventually a compromise was reached. The final sum of $360 million, to be paid over a period of seven years, was distributed as follows: $100 million to Russia, $125 million to Yugoslavia, $105 million to Greece, $25 million to Ethiopia, and $5 million to Albania. In addition the Italian government was required to make compensation up to two-thirds of the value of Allied property damaged in Italy during the war. Fifth, Italy was deprived of the right to maintain military forces that could again threaten the peace. "The Italian army, including the Frontier Guards," the treaty states, "shall be limited to a force of 185,000 combat, service and overhead personnel and 65,000 Carabinieri (cavalrymen armed with carbines), though either of the above elements may be varied by 10,000 as long as the total ceiling does not exceed 250,-000. . . . The Italian air force including any naval air arm shall be limited to a force of 200 fighter and reconnaissance aircraft and 150 transport aircraft." The personnel of the air force was limited to 25,000 effectives, and bombers were outlawed. The Italian navy, too, was reduced to the point of virtual disbandment, it being limited to 115,000.

For the other satellites the treaties prescribed similar terms. All except Bulgaria lost territory and all were compelled to pay reparations. Rumania lost Bessarabia and part of Bucovina to Russia, and southern Dobruja to Bulgaria. On the other hand, Rumania received part of Transylvania from Hungary. As regards reparations, the Rumanians were to pay $300 million to Russia. The army was restricted to 125,-000 men, the air force to 8000 men (no bombers), and the navy to 7250 tons. While Bulgaria lost no territory, she was ordered to pay Greece $45 million and Yugoslavia $25 million. On the credit side Bulgaria gained southern Dobruja. Hungary's share of reparations totaled $300 million ($200 million to Russia, $50 million to Czechoslovakia, and an equal sum to Yugoslavia). Territorial losses consisted of a few towns to Czechoslovakia and part of Transylvania to Rumania. Last of all, Finland ceded the ice-free Arctic port of Petsamo to Russia along with the province of Petsamo, thereby giving the Soviet Union a common frontier with Norway. Her share of rep-

CENTRAL AND EASTERN EUROPE AFTER WORLD WAR II. *This map shows the four zones into which occupied Germany was divided at the end of the war. It also indicates the danger spot immediately after the war centering in Greece, the Aegean, and the Dardanelles.*

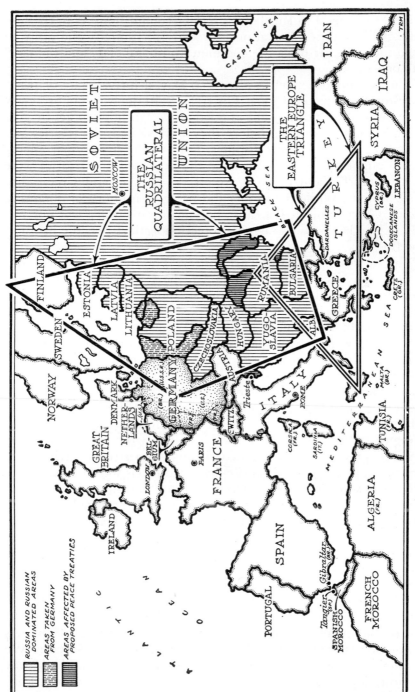

CENTRAL AND EASTERN EUROPE AFTER WORLD WAR II

arations, to be paid to Russia, was set at $300 million. As in the case of the Axis satellites, her armed forces were limited—the army to 34,000 men, the air force to 3000 men (no bombers), and the navy to 10,000 tons.

Thus twenty-one months after V-E Day, a formal state of peace was restored to part of Europe. The treaties, in the words of Secretary Byrnes, were "not perfect, but as good as we can hope to get by general agreement." But even before they were signed, the treaties had become the subject of new disputes. Four of the five former enemy states brought up the revision issue the same day the treaties were signed. Only Finland did not protest. Yugoslavia and Greece also issued protests. While the former did not give up hope of obtaining Trieste, Greece objected because her northern border was not rectified to give her better strategic protection against possible invasion from Bulgaria.

The Italians were particularly bitter. The treaty, it seemed, did not please anyone. Count Carlo Sforza, the Italian foreign minister, stated that it must be revised because an Italy stripped of its colonies and of some of its homeland "cannot possibly nourish" its 45 million inhabitants. In Rome most newspapers appeared with heavy black borders, flags were flown at half-staff over public buildings, and many houses were hung with black crepe. At 11 A.M. on the day the treaty was signed, ten minutes of silence was observed as a period of mourning. No sooner had the silence ended than crowds in Rome began to riot. The principal demonstration occurred in the Piazza Venezia, which had frequently been the site of Benito Mussolini's famous harangues. After the disturbers were driven from the square, they organized processions which filed through the streets waving flags and singing patriotic airs. Hostile demonstrations were staged before Allied offices and legations. At the tomb of the unknown soldier a United States flag was torn to bits. When the mob arrived before the Yugoslav Legation it smashed the windows, and some hoodlums entered the building to break the furniture. Some of the young men even raised the cry of "Duce! Duce!"

THE GERMAN AND AUSTRIAN TREATIES

Peace had been concluded with the smaller countries, but agreement on Germany, the key country of Europe, was still lacking. As Senator Connally said on the floor of the United States Senate: "We must never lose sight of the fact that Germany remains far and away the most important single element in the peace settlement. Thus far we have merely skirted the edges of Europe's major peace problem." Before it disbanded in New York in December of 1946 the Council of Foreign Ministers had accepted an invitation to meet in Moscow in March, 1947. The principal goals of the Moscow meeting were to be three: (1) to lay the foundation for a treaty with Germany; (2) to complete a peace treaty with Austria; (3) to conclude a four-power treaty against future German aggression.

At the time the Council was invited to meet in Moscow, its Western members interpreted the invitation to mean continued cooperation. But when the foreign ministers assembled in Moscow they were speedily disillusioned.[1] They soon discovered that the Big Four did not see eye to eye on any of the three principal issues. The foreign ministers, for example, could not agree on the future of Germany. The United States policy called for a federated Germany and for reparations which would not choke off production. This was also, in a general sense, Britain's aim. France's primary interest was again her own security, and Russia was working for a strong, centralized German government with a pro-Soviet orientation and for large reparation payments. Mr. Molotov insisted on $10 billion in reparations from German production and industrial equipment, declaring that his country had "legitimate rights" to such reparations since it suffered the greatest devastation from Hitlerian aggression. The other foreign ministers regarded this as too great a burden to impose on Germany. They also opposed his demand that Poland be permitted to retain the German territory she was occupying and turned down the Soviet proposal that German assets in Austria be paid to Russia as reparations. "We do not believe the Soviet proposal on German assets in Austria," Secretary Marshall said, "is consistent with the pledge made at Potsdam that no reparations would be taken from Austria."

After the longest session in the series, the Council finally disbanded on April 24. The final social event was a glittering banquet tendered by Premier Stalin for the Big Four foreign ministers and the high-ranking members of their delegations. Liberal toasts were drunk by both Russians and Americans. Actually, however, there were no historic accomplishments to celebrate. The session had failed to produce concrete agreements on the treaties. Certain minor accomplishments were, it is true, recorded. The ministers had laid plans for the liquidation of the Prussian state, had agreed to reduce the occupation forces in Germany, and had settled a number of con-

[1] Present were Bevin of Britain, Bidault of France, Molotov of the Soviet Union, and the new United States Secretary of State, General George Marshall.

troversial points in the Austrian treaty. On the basic issues they were more deeply divided than before they started the Moscow sessions. They had failed to agree on these major issues: (1) the amount of reparations Russia was to collect from Germany; (2) economic unification of the German occupation zones; (3) the scope and form of Germany's provisional and permanent governments; (4) the matter of Germany's final eastern frontier; (5) the future of the Ruhr; (6) the future of the Saar; (7) a United States proposal for a forty-year Big Four pact to keep the Reich militarily impotent; (8) the definition of German assets in Austria to be paid as reparations to Russia.

The mood of the participants when the Moscow conference ended was one of mingled disappointment and hope. Foreign Minister Molotov said: "Our work is not finished, but nevertheless we have done a substantial amount of preliminary work." Secretary Marshall declared upon his return to Washington: " We are naturally disappointed but I think we have a fair chance of reaching agreement on these critical matters within a reasonable time, however depressing delays may seem." But his hope was not realized. Deputies of the Big Four foreign ministers assembled in London early in November, 1947, in an effort to iron out some of the disagreements before the arrival of the foreign ministers. No progress was made. A correspondent described a session in the following words: "One after another of the subjects on the agenda was placed patiently before them by Patrick Dean, British deputy in the chair, and one by one they were put back into their folders without agreement. . . . As the Kremlin has shown in the past two years of negotiations, it will not give its deputies the authority to yield an inch or compromise in any way."

On November 25, 1947, the Big Four Council of Foreign Ministers (Bevin, Bidault, Marshall, and Molotov) met in London. The conference started off in the manner only too widely expected, with the discussions revealing fundamental disagreements. Time and again Molotov indulged in lengthy denunciations of the Western powers. It was the old technique of ascribing to them the sins the Soviet Union had committed. Secretary Bevin stated that Molotov was using the meeting "for propaganda declarations which would be pleasant to German ears." "I remain convinced," Secretary Marshall said, "that the Soviet delegate does not really believe his allegations. Let us get down to work for the good of the world instead of casting allegations for propaganda purposes." Perhaps the best description of Molotov's performance was given in a *Manchester Guard-*

ian headline which read: "Mr. Molotov's Variations on an Original Theme." "To us," Secretary Marshall reported, "it was but a dreary repetition of what had been said and resaid at the Moscow conference." After a number of sessions Foreign Minister Bidault aptly summed up the situation in these words: "We seem to be going around in circles, a process which tends to make one sick." One reporter described the conference as "four men on a merry-go-round."

Reparations gradually became the key issue. Mr. Molotov opened the question by insisting that the Soviet Union be permitted to collect $10 billion reparations from Germany, mostly from current production. The fact that the demand violated the Potsdam ban on reparations from current production did not seem to trouble the Soviet foreign minister. He said bluntly: "The Soviet Union is not asking but demanding that the question of reparations be at long last decided." This demand drew the vigorous opposition of the British and United States ministers. France's Bidault became weary and exasperated presenting a series of compromises which one after another Molotov declared unsatisfactory. Secretary Marshall later said: "Reparations from current production, that is, exports of day-to-day German production with no return, could be made only if the countries at present supplying Germany, notably the United States, foot the bill. We put in and the Russians take out." He scored "Mr. Molotov's refusal to furnish the Council of Foreign Ministers with information concerning the reparations already taken from the Eastern Zone."

It was the question of reparations from current production that largely had caused the break-up of the Moscow conference. The same question proved to be the rock on which the London Conference foundered in December, 1947. By December 15 the Council was, as Bidault put it, "at a dead end." The situation caused Secretary Marshall to say: "I reluctantly conclude that no useful purpose would be served by debate on other points of our agenda." He then suggested adjournment. No one proposed a date or place for another session. At the close of the session Ernest Bevin wondered "whether this is a body that will ever be able to settle the European and German problem."

THE TREATY WITH JAPAN

As month after month passed with no break in the deadlock over the German and Austrian questions, President Truman decided "to abandon the conference method and to seek peace through diplomatic processes." In December, 1950, he sent Mr. John Foster Dulles,

Republican adviser to the State Department, to consult with other governments about a treaty with Japan. The consensus of opinion was incorporated in the framework of the treaty which General MacArthur had prepared, and this draft was reconciled with one the British had made. The text was then circulated among the Allied powers for further suggestions and changes. Finally, on September 4, 1951, nearly six years after V-J Day, delegates of fifty-two nations assembled in the San Francisco War Memorial Opera House for the formality of signing the treaty. Not all the nations were represented. China (Nationalist or Communist) was neither consulted on the draft nor invited to San Francisco. On the other hand, Yugoslavia, India, and Burma did not send representatives.

At San Francisco Soviet Deputy Foreign Minister Gromyko proposed a series of amendments which would have changed the basic character of the treaty by making it more severe. But he received support only from Poland and Czechoslovakia. Consequently the amendments were voted down. The signing of the treaty took place on September 8, with Russia and her two satellites boycotting the ceremony. Thus only forty-eight nations and Japan signed the treaty which reestablished Japan as a sovereign nation after six years of subjection as a conquered country. It was specified that the treaty "will come into force" upon its ratification by a majority of the signatories, including Japan and the United States. With the countries that did not attend the conference or sign the treaty Japan is authorized to sign separate treaties.

The treaty with Japan is not vindictive. It is, in President Truman's words, "a treaty of reconciliation which looks to the future and not to the past." Its conciliatory spirit was widely hailed. Mr. Herbert Morrison, Britain's foreign minister, said: "Our act of signature does more than liberate Japan in international law. It does so on terms which restore her self-repect and which dignify both Japan and ourselves." Premier Yoshida of Japan, after stating that the great loss of territory "causes us pain and anxiety," nevertheless praised the treaty as "an instrument of reconciliation" and promised that his country would live at peace with the world and carry out its treaty provisions. "The Japan of today," he said, "is no longer the Japan of yesterday. We will not fail your expectations of us as a new nation, dedicated to peace, democracy, and freedom."

In its territorial aspects the treaty reduced Japan to the geographical boundaries of 1854, before it began its campaign of imperialist expansion. First, Japan renounced all right to the Kuriles and the southern half of Sakhalin Island. According to the terms of the Yalta agreement both were handed over to Russia. Second, Japan "will concur" in a trusteeship, administered by the United States, of the Bonin and Ryukyu Islands, including Okinawa, which the United States took in bitter fighting during World War II. Third, Japan renounced all right to the island of Formosa, but the treaty made no provisions for the disposition of the island. Fourth, Japan also lost the former German islands—Marianas, Marshalls, Carolines—which the Japanese had ruled under a League of Nations mandate accorded them after World War I. In short, Japan lost her entire overseas empire, which amounted to 45 per cent of the territory she held on Pearl Harbor Day. Japanese sovereignty was limited to the four main islands of Honshu, Hokkaido, Kyushu, and Shikoku, and minor adjacent islands.

One of the most controversial aspects of this, as well as of most other treaties, was the question of reparations. Although the treaty recognized Japan's responsibility, it did not set specific sums that Japan must pay. The Western nations were convinced that the Japanese economy could not stand the strain of immediate large payments. Accordingly the treaty requires Japan to negotiate reparations agreements with the various countries. One suggestion offered by the treaty is that Asian countries send Japan raw materials and receive manufactured goods in return. The fact that the treaty did not provide for immediate reparations payments evoked criticism from some of the Far Eastern countries. Those who were disappointed over the reparations provisions included the Philippines and Indonesia, both of whom had suffered much from Japanese aggression.

The Japanese treaty, unlike the first treaties signed after World War II, does not place specific restrictions on Japanese rearmament. "The Allied Powers," the treaty states, "recognize that Japan as a sovereign nation possesses the inherent right of individual or collective self-defense." Japan did, however, accept the obligations set forth in the United Nations Charter, "to refrain in its international relations from the threat or use of force." The treaty stipulates that all occupation forces of the Allied Powers shall be withdrawn from Japan not later than ninety days after the treaty goes into effect, but it does not prohibit the stationing of foreign armed forces in Japanese territory under separate agreements. Such an agreement was immediately concluded between Japan and the United States. By its terms United States forces will remain in Japan until that country is able to defend itself. The fears of such countries as Australia, New Zealand, and the Philippines over the possibility of aggression by a rearmed Japan were dispelled by the Pacific mutual defense treaties which they signed with the United States.

The treaty went into effect April 28, 1952, after it had been ratified by the nations whose representatives had previously signed it. The deposit with the Japanese government of the ratified treaty marked the end of the occupation of Japan by foreign troops. After Premier Yoshida officially made the announcement to the Japanese Parliament that the treaty had been ratified, the national flag of Japan (a red ball—the Rising Sun—on a white ground) was raised on all public buildings for the first time since the unconditional surrender in 1945. The change also inaugurated the resumption of diplomatic relations between Japan and other countries. President Truman in welcoming the first Japanese ambassador since the Pearl Harbor attack said in part: "During the past six years the Japanese people and government have worked to build a democratic and peace-loving nation with a sincerity and earnestness that has won the respect of the world. The treaty of peace affords Japan an opportunity to make a great contribution to world peace and progress." Premier Yoshida in a statement thanked the Allies for "a magnanimous peace unparalleled in history" and called upon his countrymen to follow the "broad highway of peace and democracy." On the same day on which the treaty that had been signed at San Francisco went into effect, another treaty was signed between Japan and Nationalist China. India, which had not signed the San Francisco treaty, formally announced the end of her state of war by reopening relations with Tokyo. This was not the case, however, with Russia, Poland, and Czechoslovakia. Immediately after the ceremony which restored Japan's sovereignty the Soviet Union lodged a formal protest against the peace treaty and the action of the United States in dissolving the Far Eastern Commission.

✿ ✿

CHAPTER TWENTY-THREE

The United Nations

FOUNDING THE UN

THE League of Nations was the first organization in history expressly organized for the maintenance of world peace by international cooperation. After the Napoleonic wars there had been a Holy Alliance in which all the chief powers of Europe, except Britain, had joined. But there was no serious attempt to make effective the principles that were proclaimed. Within a few years the Holy Alliance was little more than an agreement by the absolutist powers to maintain despotic government in their countries and elsewhere. Neither did the League maintain the high hopes it engendered. After holding out great promise in the decade of the twenties, it declined to impotence in the thirties. The official attitude toward the League in almost all countries might be summed up in the statement of M. Clemenceau: "I like the League, but do not believe in it." By the time World War II broke out, the League as a peace-keeping agency was dead.[1]

But the idea of an international authority for the establishment and preservation of peace did not die with the League. Planning for a new international body began early in the war. Like the League of Nations it began as a confederation of victorious allies. The first step was taken when President Roosevelt and prime minister Churchill met aboard the U.S.S. *Augusta* in the Atlantic in August, 1941, and agreed on a set of principles which soon became known as the Atlantic Charter. Among the principles embodied in the Atlantic Charter are the following:

[1] The League Assembly officially adjourned on April 18, 1946, after taking the necessary steps to terminate the existence of the League. Its properties and assets were transferred to the United Nations.

645

They [the United States and the United Kingdom] believe that all of the nations of the world, for realistic as well as spiritual reasons, must come to the abandonment of the use of force. . . .

They believe, pending the establishment of a wider and permanent system of general security, that the disarmament of . . . nations which threaten aggression outside of their frontiers . . . is essential.

On January 1, 1942, the term "United Nations" made its appearance when twenty-six nations pledged themselves to wholehearted cooperation against the Axis.[2] The agreement was published as the "Joint Declaration by United Nations." The first objective of the United Nations was, of course, to defeat the Axis, but a secondary goal was the establishment of a just and enduring peace and the elimination of war as an instrument of national policy.

During the succeeding months Allied opinion became more and more convinced of the need for an international organization to establish and preserve peace. Thus the conference of foreign ministers (the United States, U.S.S.R., Britain, and China) which met in Moscow in October, 1943, made the following declaration: "The four powers recognize the necessity of establishing at the earliest practicable date a general international organization, based on the principle of the sovereign equality of all peace-loving states, large and small, for the maintenance of international peace and security." In 1944 representatives of the same powers met from August 21 to October 7 at the Dumbarton Oaks estate near Washington for the purpose of projecting a plan for the new organization which would serve as a basis for discussion. In other words, much of the spade work for the United Nations Charter was done at Dumbarton Oaks. The representatives failed to reach agreement on the voting procedure in the Security Council, but at Yalta (February, 1945) President Roosevelt, prime minister Churchill, and Marshal Stalin did agree on a working formula.

At Yalta the Big Three also decided to hold a conference at San Francisco in April, 1945, for the purpose of preparing "a charter for a general international organization for the maintenance of international peace and security." Invitations were sent out to all nations which were at war with one or more of the Axis powers and which had adhered to the Washington Declaration of January 1, 1942. The conference opened on April 25 with delegates from forty-six nations present.[3] Some idea of the number of people involved in the con-

[2] Twenty-one other nations joined this war-time alliance before March 1, 1945.
[3] Four more nations were admitted to membership during the conference: Byelorussia (White Russia), the Ukraine, Denmark, and Argentina.

ference may be gained from the fact that the delegates and their staffs of consultants and advisers totaled 1722. In addition the secretariat numbered almost a thousand. Press representatives reached the appalling number of 2446. Thus there were more than five thousand people at the conference. The opening address was made by President Truman, who said in part:

At no time in history has there been a more important conference, nor a more necessary meeting, than this one in San Francisco which you are opening today. . . . You members of this conference are to be the architects of the better world. In your hands rests our future. By your labors at this conference we shall know if suffering humanity is to achieve a just and lasting peace. . . . We must make certain, by your work here, that another war will be impossible. We, who have lived through the torture and the tragedy of two world conflicts, must realize the magnitude of the problem before us. . . . We must provide the machinery which will make future peace not only possible but certain.

The San Francisco Conference worked hard. The delegates, organized into twelve committees, labored day and night to produce a system of collective security. Athough the basis for a charter had already been laid in the Dumbarton Oaks proposals, other nations had sent in a mass of proposed amendments. The fifty nations not only differed widely in their political traditions, economic and social systems, and in their historical backgrounds but also in their conceptions of what should be included in the UN Charter. Hence the delegates had to struggle in day and night sessions, including Sundays, to reach compromises. United States Secretary of State Edward R. Stettinius, who was the chief spokesman of his nation at San Francisco, said at the close of the conference:

If ten years hence, you should go back to the dusty files of the newspapers of the Spring of 1945, you would probably get an impression from the headlines that our proceedings at San Francisco consisted of a series of "rows," "crises," and "deadlocks," and you would probably wonder how on earth a Charter was ever created. . . . There can be no doubt that the Charter of the United Nations is a more powerful and democratic instrument for the preservation of peace and the promotion of human well-being than was outlined in the Dumbarton Oaks Proposals.

THE ORGANS OF THE UN

On June 25 the work of drafting the Charter was completed and the next day it was signed by the representatives of fifty nations. It was to come into force as soon as it had been ratified by the great powers and a majority of other signatory states. This took place on October 24, 1945. Later the General Assembly officially designated October 24 as United Nations Day. The purpose of the United Nations organization is stated in the preamble of the Charter: "We, the people of the United Nations, determined to save succeeding generations from the scourge of war, which twice in our lifetime has brought untold sorrow to mankind . . . do hereby establish an international organization to be known as the United Nations." The nations that signed the Charter agreed to "settle their international disputes by peaceful means in such a manner that international peace and security and justice are not endangered," to "refrain in their international relations from the threat or use of force against the territorial integrity or independence of any state." The states which took part in the conference were to be known as the original members, but membership was declared open to all peace-loving states which are ready to accept the obligations contained in the Charter.

Although the San Francisco Conference revised very considerably the Dumbarton Oaks text, its core was retained essentially unaltered in the UN Charter. The basic idea is that the great powers as victors in World War II assume responsibility for the maintenance of world security. Their dominating position in the UN was achieved through the Security Council, in which was vested the decisive power and therefore the primary responsibility for the maintenance of international peace and security. Gaetano Salvemini stated bluntly:

> The gist of the Charter may be summed up as follows: the small powers delegate all rights to the great powers who control the Security Council, and the great powers reserve for themselves the right to do what they please and to go to war when they please and against whomever they please. Each one of them intends to remain the law unto itself.

The Security Council, which functions continuously, consists of eleven members, five of whom—Britain, China, France, the United States, and the Soviet Union—hold permanent memberships. The other six are elected for a two-year term by the General Assembly. Each nonpermanent as well as each permanent member of the Security Council has one vote. In procedural matters a decision can be reached by the affirmative vote of any seven members, but in all other matters the seven votes must include those of the five permanent members. In other words, the negative vote of a permanent member can defeat any resolution. It was provided, however, that "a party to a dispute shall abstain from voting."

The voting procedure in the Security Council was the subject of the fiercest debates at the San Francisco Conference. Russian insistence that the veto right of any great-power member apply even to the discussions of the Security Council threatened the very existence of the conference. It was the memory of United States Secretary of State Stettinius that saved the day. With President Truman's permission he cabled Harry Hopkins, who was in Moscow at the time, asking him to remind Stalin that when the voting procedure was discussed at Yalta the Russians had agreed that the people of the United States and of the smaller nations would not accept a world organization unless the right of free discussion was guaranteed. Some days later Stalin consented to abide by the voting procedure that the Big Three had accepted at Yalta. Even after the Russian delegation abandoned its demand for a veto over discussion of international disputes, many of the other nations still protested the veto power of the Big Five. They had the choice of either accepting the veto or wrecking the entire UN project. The attitude of many of the small nations is expressed in the song which the Australian delegation sang:

> We must not alter Yalta,
> It would not please the Russ;
> We must not alter Yalta,
> For Joe would make a fuss.
> What Yalta means is doubtful,
> But Joe must have his say;
> His view must be accepted
> Or he'll take his bat away.[4]

Their desire to keep the UN ship from foundering caused the middle and small nations finally to approve the Yalta voting formula.

The Yalta formula which gave each of the five great powers the right to veto decisions on all "substantive" matters was less stringent than the voting procedure in the League Council. The Covenant of the League of Nations had prescribed that decisions in the League Council could be made only by the unanimous vote of all members. This rule made it impossible to reach decisions on most questions and difficult on almost any question. The unanimity of the Yalta formula was a qualified unanimity. Even after the great powers have achieved unanimity they still need the votes of two nonpermanent members in order to make the decision official.

The second important organ of the UN is the General Assembly. Politically it is the basis of the United Nations. As such it has been

---

[4] The reference, in the terminology of the game of cricket, is to a Russian threat to withdraw from the conference.

described as "the town meeting of the world" and "the cockpit of the nations." The General Assembly is actually the closest approach that mankind has made to a world parliament. The League of Nations, it is true, had its Assembly, but the membership of the League was not nearly so universal as that of the UN. In the General Assembly, which meets annually, all member nations have an equal vote. According to Article 10 of the Charter it "may discuss any questions or any matters within the scope of the Charter or relating to the powers and functions of any organs provided for in the Charter." Thus the range of the Assembly's "deliberative power" is wide. The General Assembly may also recommend measures for the peaceful solution of any dispute or situation which is likely to prove detrimental to the general welfare or to impair friendly relations among nations. Originally the General Assembly was planned as a place for the little nations to "let off steam" while the big powers run the world in the Security Council, but it has come to be regarded more and more as the heart of the UN, as the real arena for international action. Besides being a "deliberative organ" it exercises various other functions. It elects the six nonpermanent members of the Security Council and the members of various councils and committees that function under its supervision. It also considers and approves the budget of the UN and apportions the expenses among the member states. Thus it is much more than a "debating society." Through its various activities it wields a tremendous moral and political influence.

Among the other important organs of the UN are the Economic and Social Council, the Trusteeship Council, the International Court of Justice, and the Secretariat. The Economic and Social Council, consisting of eighteen members elected by the General Assembly for a three-year term, is responsible for promoting "higher standards of living, full employment, and conditions of economic and social progress and development," "international culture and educational cooperation," and "universal respect for, and observance of, human rights and fundamental freedoms for all without distinction as to race, sex, language, or religion." The Trusteeship Council was established to administer the "Trust Territories," including former League of Nations mandates, territories detached from enemy states as a result of World War II, and territories voluntarily placed under the system by the states responsible for their administration. The International Court of Justice, organized to supersede the World Court of the League, is the principal judicial organ of the United Nations, and as such has the function of settling disputes of an international nature. The Secretariat consists of the Secretary-General, who is the chief administrative officer of the UN, and his staff. The Secretary-General is appointed by the General Assembly, and he in turn appoints the staff under regulations established by the General Assembly.

When the League of Nations expired there was a readiness on the part of many to write it off as a failure and to adopt what they regarded as a fresh approach to the problem of peace and security. They were ready to scrap the experience and idea of the League completely. Actually, however, the UN is a continuation of the old League, stronger in some respects and weaker in others, but nevertheless a continuation. The UN, like the League, is a voluntary association of nations to establish and preserve peace, and as such it carries on the League tradition largely by the same methods employed by the League. Winston Churchill recognized the continuity between the two organizations before the UN was founded. Upon his return from Yalta he told the House of Commons:

The former League of Nations, so hardly used and found to be inadequate for the tasks it attempted, will be replaced by a far stronger body in which the United States will play a vitally important part. It will embody much of the structure and characteristics of its predecessor. All the work that was done in the past, all the experience that has been gathered by the workings of the League of Nations, will not be cast away.

Gaetano Salvemini, the Italian historian, was even more emphatic:

Telling us that in the UN we are about to embark on a new experiment in international practice is insulting human intelligence. The UN does not embark on a new experiment. This is its significance. This is the whole and naked truth.

The fact that there is a definite continuity between the League and the UN does not mean, however, that the builders of the UN did not try to improve upon the League. They broke away from League precedent in a number of respects. One of the chief criticisms launched against the organizers of the League was that the Covenant was made a part of the peace treaties at the end of World War I. The architects of the UN made the United Nations Charter an independent instrument. Furthermore, at the end of World War I the great powers drafted the League Covenant and put it into operation without consulting with the smaller nations. Although the great powers laid the basis of the UN Charter in the Dumbarton Oaks proposals, they did give the smaller nations the opportunity to discuss, criticize, and amend their work. Hence the Charter is in a wider sense the product of a general consultation of nations. But the greatest advance which the Charter made over the League Covenant is in its provision for an "international police force" to prevent aggression. It is generally agreed that the principal weakness of the League was its inability to employ armed force against aggressors. The organizers of the UN sought to eliminate this weakness by providing that when the Security Council is unable to preserve peace and to stop aggression by peaceful means it may invoke military force. This force is to be provided by all the members of the UN.

At the conclusion of the San Francisco Conference the UN still existed only on paper. No time was lost, however, in assembling the machinery blueprinted in the Charter. The first General Assembly met in London on January 10, 1946, in the blue and gold auditorium of the Central Hall of Westminster, with delegates from fifty-one countries answering at roll call. The session was confined largely to organizational matters. Trygve Lie, Norwegian foreign minister, was chosen Secretary-General of the UN and various other officials were elected, including six nonpermanent members of the Security Council and the fifteen judges of the International Court of Justice. An Atomic Energy Commission was also established, as recommended by the Council of Foreign Ministers (Moscow, 1945), to consider problems arising from the discovery of atomic energy and related matters.

A further important decision of the first session of the General Assembly was that the permanent headquarters of the UN were to be located in the United States. During the second part of the first session, which opened in New York City on October 23, 1946, the question of a specific site was settled. After the site committee had made hurried trips to points in New York state, San Francisco, Boston, and Philadelphia, an offer was received from John D. Rockefeller, Jr. who agreed to spend $8.5 million for the acquisition of a six-block area in the heart of New York City for a skyscraper UN home. The General Assembly accepted the gift "with a feeling of sincere gratitude." Demolition of the existing structures on the site began in the summer of 1947, and the excavation work was started about a year later. In the meantime a board of prominent architects and engineers from different parts of the world were busy drawing up the plans for the headquarters. They provided, among other things, for a General Assembly hall, a Secretariat office building, a conference area for Council chambers and committee rooms, and underground garages

The construction of the $65 million project proceeded rapidly. The first building to be erected was the thirty-nine-story Secretariat building, which was ready for use at the end of 1950. The General Assembly building is scheduled to be ready in time for the 1952 meeting of the Assembly.

᛫᛫

ACHIEVEMENTS OF THE UN

The story of the UN has been one of disappointments and achievements. On the credit side, it has made a number of successful attempts to persuade nations to settle their differences over the conference table instead of resorting to war. It has even made peace between nations who had started to fight. Thus, for example, peace was restored in Palestine and the new State of Israel was admitted to the UN as the fifty-ninth member. Furthermore, through the offices of the UN a cease-fire agreement was arranged between India and Pakistan, which prevented war from engulfing 400 million people. The UN was also helpful in working out a peaceful solution between the Dutch and Indonesians.

Although the first purpose of the UN, in the eyes of the founders, was the maintenance of international peace and security, it has other important purposes. These may be summed up as the promotion of economic and social well-being. It is one of the major distinctions between the UN Charter and the League of Nations Covenant that in the former the wider functions of economic and social development are separated from the function of preserving peace. In the UN these functions center largely in the Economic and Social Council (ECOSOC), composed of representatives of eighteen states who are elected by the General Assembly. Under its supervision regional commissions and specialized agencies engage in a wide variety of activities. Three regional commissions grapple with the world's economic problems, one for Europe, one for Asia, and one for Latin America. Except for Spain, all the countries of Europe have participated in the Economic Commission for Europe (ECE), which has done excellent work in allocating such natural resources as coal, ore, and timber among the member nations. It has also facilitated the efforts toward the increase of steel production by the distribution of suitable quantities of metallurgical coke. Among its other achievements are agreements to lift restrictions on the freedom of European roads, conventions on customs procedures relating to the international transportation of goods, and agreements regarding tourist traffic.

The other two regional commissions can also boast important

achievements. The Economic Commission for Asia and the Far East (ECAFE) has taken up such problems as the elimination of political and economic barriers to international trade, the promotion of trade between Europe and the Far East, the development of hydroelectric power, and the improvement of production and marketing practices in both agriculture and industry. It has also appointed a Bureau of Flood Control to undertake investigations and to recommend measures for controlling the annual floods which cause great losses of life and property. The Economic Commission for Latin America has done fruitful work on such problems as foreign trade, cyclical economic fluctuations, and the general financial, industrial, and agricultural development of Latin America. At the Havana session of the Commission in the spring of 1948 representatives of twenty-one countries devoted themselves to a task which President Socarrás of Cuba in his opening address described as "driving the shadow of hunger from the American scene" through increased production. Some of the subjects it discussed were the dissemination of scientific knowledge of agriculture, specifically with regard to fertilizers and insecticides; the improvement of agricultural equipment, implements, and machinery; and the establishment of means for granting credits for their purchase. The Commission also projected plans for the development and utilization of forest resources and the modernization of fishing fleets.

Certain other agencies associated with the UN perform more specialized and limited functions. Some of these, like the Universal Postal Union and the International Labor Organization, antedate the founding of the UN. But there are also new ones. Their number is so large, however, that only a few can be briefly discussed here. The International Refugee Organization has enabled more than a million displaced persons to find homes overseas, the Central Opium Board has been working to curb illicit traffic in drugs, and the Committee on Freedom of Information has been trying to offset the world-wide movement toward censorship. One of the most gigantic tasks has been assigned to the Food and Agriculture Organization (FAO). Its goal, in brief, is to increase the production of food to meet the demands of an increasing world population. To achieve this it must help solve the problems of the farmers who compose more than two-thirds of the world's population. In this capacity it is called upon to propose measures to meet agricultural depressions, to find remedies for the heavy losses incurred in harvesting and storing grain, to increase agricultural production through chemical control of weeds, seed-borne diseases, and insect pests, to devise means for controlling animal diseases, to project plans for mechanizing small farms, and to improvise means for a more equitable distribution of food.

Another notable agency is the United Nations Educational, Scientific, and Cultural Organization (UNESCO), whose purpose, as stated in its constitution, is to "contribute to peace and security by promoting collaboration among the nations through education, science, and culture in order to further universal respect for justice, for the rule of law, and for the human rights and fundamental freedoms of all." In its efforts to realize this puropse UNESCO has busied itself, first, with the work of rehabilitating educational facilities in twenty war-devastated countries, and, second, with a campaign to wipe out illiteracy and to raise educational standards in all member states.

The objective which the constitution of the World Health Organization (WHO) has set for this specialized UN agency is "the attainment by all peoples of the highest possible level of health." Some of its functions are: to act as coordinating authority on international health work; to stimulate and advance the work of eradicating epidemic and other diseases; to promote maternal and child health and welfare; to promote improved standards of teaching and training; to standardize diagnostic procedure; and to develop, establish, and promote international standards with respect to food, biological, and pharmaceutical products. Its activities have included effective control of malaria in Greece and Italy through the spraying of insecticides and other measures, the training of specialists to assist in malaria control programs all over the globe, and the launching of a program for the prevention of tuberculosis in various countries. WHO is also carrying out a program to eliminate venereal disease, to improve environmental sanitation, and to train sanitary workers for duty in many of the backward countries. WHO assisted in the rescue work after an earthquake killed 6,000 persons and rendered 100,000 homeless in Ecuador; it carried on research to produce an anti-scorpion serum to protect the children of Trinidad; and it established research laboratories for the study of endemic diseases in various parts of the world. Perhaps its most spectacular achievement was its work in the Egyptian cholera epidemic of 1947. Its efforts in collecting cholera vaccine and other needed supplies helped to stop this epidemic with a speed which set a record in medical history.

One of the outstanding achievements of a specialized agency was the preparation of a Universal Declaration of the Rights of Man by the Commission on Human Rights. The Declaration is part of a larger project called the Universal Bill of Human Rights. The other part is to consist of a covenant or treaty regarding the establishment of these rights. After it was decided in 1947 to divide the Universal Bill of Human Rights into two parts, the Commission devoted itself with enthusiasm to the realization of the first part. A draft of the Universal Declaration of the Rights of Man was ready in June, 1948, and after some amendment was adopted by the General Assembly (December, 1948) without a dissenting vote (48 voting, 8 abstaining). The Universal Declaration of the Rights of Man is the first attempt in history to set down the minimum rights which every person, wherever he may live, should enjoy. As such it marks an important step toward strengthening the concept of the dignity and worth of human beings. The General Assembly proclaimed it "a common standard of achievement for all peoples and nations" and urged its member nations to establish its principles. Millions of copies in many languages were scattered over the face of the globe. The first ten of its thirty articles read as follows:

Article 1. All human beings are born free and equal in dignity and rights. They are endowed with reason and conscience and should act toward one another in a spirit of brotherhood.

Article 2. 1. Everyone is entitled to all rights and freedoms set forth in this Declaration, without distinction of any kind, such as race, color, sex, language, religion, political or other opinion, national or social origin, property, birth or other status.

2. Furthermore, no distinction shall be made on the basis of the political, jurisdictional or international status of the country or territory to which a person belongs, whether this territory be an independent, Trust, Non-Self-Governing territory, or under any other limitation of sovereignty.

Article 3. Everyone has the right to life, liberty and the security of person.

Article 4. No one shall be held in slavery or servitude; slavery and the slave trade shall be prohibited in all their forms.

Article 5. No one shall be subjected to torture or to cruel inhuman or degrading treatment or punishment.

Article 6. Everyone has the right of recognition everywhere as a person before the law.

Article 7. All are equal before the law and are entitled without any discrimination to equal protection of the law. All are entitled to equal protection against any discrimination in violation of this Declaration and against any incitement to such discrimination.

Article 8. Everyone has the right to an effective remedy by the competent national tribunals for acts violating the fundamental rights granted him by the constitution or by law.

Article 9. No one shall be subjected to arbitrary arrest, detention or exile.

Article 10. Everyone is entitled in full equality to a fair and public hearing by an independent and impartial tribunal in the determination of his rights and obligations and of any criminal charge against him.

THE PROBLEM OF CONTROLLING ATOMIC ENERGY

Unfortunately the successes of the UN in some branches of endeavor are matched by failures in others. Many people believed that the very fact that more than fifty nations had voluntarily joined the organization to preserve peace signified the end of all wars. Hence there was great disappointment when wars continued as before. President Truman said in his address to the General Assembly on the fifth anniversary of the founding of the UN (October 24, 1950): "Five years ago, after the bloodshed and destruction of World War II, many of us hoped that all nations would work together to make sure that war could never happen again. We hoped that international cooperation, supported by the strength and moral authority of the United Nations, would be sufficient to prevent aggression. But this was not to be the case."

Not only did the UN fail to prevent wars, it was also unsuccessful in establishing effective control over atomic energy. It was not that the UN did not take up the problem at once. One of the first decisions made by the General Assembly at its first meeting in London was to establish the Atomic Energy Commission (January 24, 1946). All the nations represented in the Security Council were given membership in the Atomic Energy Commission. Canada was also given representation because of its contributions to the development of the atomic bomb. At the first meeting of the Commission (June, 1946) Mr. Bernard M. Baruch, the United States representative, presented a working plan which came to be called the Baruch Plan. This plan is based on the premise that atomic energy, because of the grave risks involved in its use, can be controlled only by an international authority which is not in any way subject to national rivalries. It advocates putting every phase of atomic production, including the mining of all fissionable materials, under the control of this international board. Such international control would prevent any nation or group of nations from misusing atomic energy for its own purposes. Secret production or research by any one nation would be prevented by periodic international inspection. While the plan was being set up, and until it was operating effectively, the United States would retain its secret knowledge of atomic energy as well as its atomic bombs and plants.

The essentials of the Baruch Plan were accepted as a satisfactory solution of the problem of atomic energy by all nations serving on the first Atomic Energy Commission except the Soviet Union and its satellites. More than this, they have been accepted by a majority of every Atomic Energy Commission that has since convened. Since the plan was first presented to the Atomic Energy Commission, the Russians have given way on a few minor points here and there, but the basic premises have remained unacceptable "as a whole or in their separate parts." What the Russians found most objectionable was the rigorous inspection system which was a necessary component of the idea of international ownership and management of atomic facilities. They did not wish to surrender what might be called "sovereignty" which the system of strict international inspection demanded. Hence they proposed a counterplan to offset it. Their plan proposed (1) that the atomic bomb be outlawed by simple convention; (2) that all stockpiles of bombs be destroyed simultaneously; (3) that control over atomic energy development be left to individual countries; (4) that a limited, not an unrestricted, system of inspection be established. Since this plan offered no guarantee of security, no assurance that the atomic race would not continue, it evoked no support beyond the Soviet satellite nations.

As the years passed, hope of achieving agreement on atomic control slowly withered. The question was first brought before the General Assembly during the autumn of 1948 in Paris. There the plan which a majority of the members of the Atomic Energy Commission had repeatedly endorsed was, after substantial amendment, passed by a vote of 40 to 6, with the Soviet Union and its satellites opposing. The Assembly also directed the Atomic Energy Commission to continue its work. But the deadlock looked so hopeless that the Commission despaired of finding a way out of the impasse and finally suspended its sessions indefinitely. The distrust on both sides was too deep-seated to achieve compromise on any major issue.

In November, 1947, Mr. Molotov had reported that the U.S.S.R. was in possession of the "secret of atomic energy." At the time most of the other nations dismissed the statement as a bluff. But in 1949 the announcement was made in the United States that an atomic explosion had taken place in the Soviet Union. Just how the Soviet scientists gained possession of the secrets of atomic energy was not divulged by the Soviet government. It is known that some of the "secrets" were transmitted to the Russians by British and United States citizens.

THE FAILURE OF DISARMAMENT EFFORTS

Nor was much progress made in the direction of general disarmament. The General Assembly took up the question of reducing armaments during the first year of its existence. On December 14, 1946, it passed a resolution recommending "that the Security Council give prompt consideration to formulating the practical measures . . . which are essential to provide for the general regulation and reduction of armaments and armed forces and to assure that such regulation and reduction of armaments and armed forces will be generally observed by all participants and not unilaterally by only some of the participants." The Security Council implemented the General Assembly's resolution by establishing the Committee for Conventional Armaments (February 13, 1947) as one method of studying the problem of armaments reduction. This committee was charged with the task of drawing up practical proposals for the regulation and reduction of armaments and armed forces and to submit them to the Security Council. All matters falling within the competence of the Atomic Energy Commission were expressly excluded from the jurisdiction of the Committee on Conventional Armaments. This committee, in its plan to limit armaments to those consistent with, and indispensable to, the maintenance of international peace and security, also advocated a system of international supervision. This, of course, was unacceptable to Russia and its satellites. Hence the disarmament efforts stalled at that point.

At the meeting of the General Assembly in 1948 the question of disarmament was again discussed. A number of speakers deplored the fact that after many months of work by the Commission for Conventional Armaments and the Atomic Energy Commission no positive results had been achieved. The Syrian delegate, for example, said:

Ninety-nine per cent—and perhaps more—of the world's population abhor war and military manoeuvering. They are eager to see peace established and reigning over the whole world. This overwhelming majority of mankind appeal pitifully to the leaders of the world, and to the fashioners of world policy, to have compassion on them and prevent eventual global destruction. The leaders who were able to win a tremendous war should not fail to win the peace.[5]

[5] *UN Bulletin,* vol. 5 (October 15, 1948) , p. 807.

Various plans for disarmament were suggested, but the Soviet Union found objections to each one. It refused to agree to a census of armaments and armed forces on the professed ground that the census failed to include a count of atomic weapons.

Later the Russians proposed a plan which called for a one-third reduction of armaments and armed forces in all countries. But the plan found no acceptance among the other members of the Big Five. They felt that such a reduction would solve nothing since it would not remove the fear of war. The Soviet Union would still have an arms predominance; in fact, the reduction would have increased the Soviet Union's relative military strength. Mr. Hector McNeil, representing Great Britain, said that the method of disarmament proposed gave "a premium to those who had disarmed least. Unlike the U.S.S.R., the United Kingdom, in common with most of the other countries of Western Europe, has committed itself to drastic disarmament since the last war, and its defense forces are now down to a minimum." [6] Before it disbanded the Assembly recommended by vote of 43 to 6 that the Security Council continue to pursue the study of the armaments problem through the Commission for Conventional Armaments "in order to obtain concrete results as soon as possible."

Meeting after meeting took place without any results. At the 1949 session of the General Assembly the question of a reduction of armaments was again discussed. Again the Russians objected to the disarmament plan supported by the majority and proposed a one-third reduction of armaments. M. Pierre Montel, the French representative, said in rejecting the Soviet plan that as soon as World War II was over and the UN was organized the Western allies had automatically disarmed. The Soviet Union, on the other hand, had maintained and improved its equipment and military forces instead of disarming. As a result, he said, the Russian army had reached a strength unprecedented in history. Moreover, the industries feeding this army were steadily expanded and, finally, Russia had also succeeded in adding the atomic bomb to its force.[7] During 1950 the Russians boycotted the Security Council and the Commission for Conventional Armaments, because of the dispute over Chinese representation in the UN. Consequently there could be no further consultation among the great powers over the disarmament question until the Russians returned. On April 27, 1950, the representative of the U.S.S.R. declared expressly that his delegation would not take part in the work of the Committee for Conventional Armaments so long as the rep-

6 *Ibid.,* p. 866.
7 *Ibid.,* vol. 7 (December 15, 1949), p. 724.

resentative of the "Kuomintang group" was permitted to remain; nor would it regard as valid any decision taken by the Commission with the participation of the Kuomintang representative.

Meanwhile the burden of armaments was weighing heavily on most countries. On many sides national leaders were urging that the efforts to achieve a reduction of armaments be continued. Thus President Truman said (October 24, 1950):

We must continue to strive through the United Nations to achieve international control of atomic energy and the reduction of armaments and armed forces. Cooperative and effective disarmament would make the danger of war remote. It would be a way of achieving the high purposes of the United Nations without the tremendous expenditures for armaments which conditions in the world make imperative today.

At the sixth session of the General Assembly, which convened in Paris in November, 1951, the question of armaments and the atomic bomb took precedence over all other problems. At the opening of the session United States Secretary of State Dean Acheson presented a disarmament plan jointly sponsored by Britain, France, and the United States. The plan proposed, first, a UN inventory of existing armaments, including atomic bombs. "The national inventories of all armed forces and armaments," he said, "must be checked and verified in each country by inspectors who are nationals of other countries working under the United Nations." Second, he called for the establishment "of some sort of criteria for the balanced reduction of armaments and armed forces." "These criteria, which can be worked out," he said, "would determine the exact amounts and kinds of armaments and armed forces which each country will finally be permitted to have." Third, he proposed a continuous UN inspection to make certain that each nation complies. He challenged the Soviet Union to translate "peace talk into action." "The record of the past year," he stated, "doesn't reveal a single action—and I am talking about action, not words—by the Soviet Union that indicates it is willing to cooperate with the rest of the world in abating the tensions and dangers of war." Mr. Acheson closed with a plea for cooperation. "We firmly believe," he said, "that a workable agreement is within our reach, if all nations will approach this task with good faith and a will to peace."

The delegates of many nations hailed the Big Three plan as the potential basis of a real peace and disarmament effort. Brigadier General Carlos P. Romulo of the Philippines pointed out that the plan made two significant advances over previous plans: first, the Western powers stated their willingness to include atomic weapons in an arms census; and, second, they were ready to consider reduction of both conventional and atomic armaments as a single problem.

But the Russians adopted a different attitude. Less than twelve hours after the Western powers had presented their new plan to reduce armaments, the Soviet delegates rejected it without making even a pretense of examining it or weighing its possibilities. More than this, they poured ridicule on it. Soviet Foreign Minister Vishinsky denounced it as "spurious" and styled it a "dead mouse." Indeed, the idea that it was based on a genuine desire to limit armaments and effectively eliminate the specter of atomic warfare merely excited him to laughter. As he put it: "I could hardly sleep all night last night after having read that speech. I could not sleep because I kept laughing." Even the Kremlin appears to have believed that its Foreign Minister had gone too far in his attack, for when the speech was published in the Soviet Union the remark about laughter was deleted. Mr. Anthony Eden, who had become British Foreign Secretary as the result of the Conservative victory in the British elections (November, 1951), said in a speech to the Assembly: "Mr. Vishinsky's cataract of abuse did not anger me, but it saddened me."

As a substitute for the new Western program Vishinsky offered a plan which would in effect impose disarmament on the Western powers without effective provisions for similar disarmament behind the Iron Curtain. The Soviet plan proposed: (1) a disarmament conference; (2) "prohibition" of the atomic bomb, but without inspection; (3) the old one-third reduction of armaments which the West had previously rejected since it would leave unchanged the Russian preponderance of strength over the West. The Canadian Secretary of State for External Affairs said that the Soviet plan was the "same old record as before only somewhat more scratchy this time." The permanent United States delegate commented: "Old claims, old misrepresentations, old charges and old proposals."

The conflict between the great powers saddened the other delegates to the General Assembly. Some suggested that the great powers try once more to negotiate their differences among themselves. Secretary-General Trygve Lie also called upon the Big Four foreign ministers to meet, saying, "This is the time and the place to begin." On November 26 the United States delegates expressed willingness to get together with the Soviet delegates for the purpose of trying to reconcile the Western and Russian disarmament plans. Some days later the Soviet foreign minister accepted the proposal for secret talks. Again hopes ran high that the Big Four could find common ground on the central issues of disarmament. But the differences were too deep-rooted to be overcome so long as the two sides faced each other in hostile postures. One negotiator stated at the end of the sessions: "I cannot report anything in the nature of progress."

THE VETO IN THE SECURITY COUNCIL

The great obstacle that prevented a majority in the Security Council from reaching decisions was the provision that all decisions, except those on procedural matters, must be made by a majority vote which must include the votes of the Big Five. Thus any one of the great powers can by withholding its vote veto any majority decision of the Security Council. This voting procedure was agreed upon at the Yalta meeting of President Roosevelt, prime minister Churchill, and Marshal Stalin. President Roosevelt himself appears to have proposed it. He saw in it a means of preserving unanimity among the great powers. Ironically, Stalin, too, saw the veto as an instrument of great power unity. "The danger in the future," he said, "is the possibility of conflicts among ourselves." Actually the inclusion of the veto by the great powers was motivated by the desire to avoid any commitments that would limit their freedom of action. At the San Francisco Conference, in June of 1945, the smaller nations objected vigorously that the veto would thwart the will of the majority, but when the great powers insisted on its inclusion they capitulated. A Belgian newspaper correspondent summed up the situation at San Francisco in these words:

> The smaller countries realize very well that the destiny of the world lies with the Great Powers; they have the means in men and technical material to check any aggressor at any time. . . . There is a serious chance that for some time neither Germany nor Italy nor Japan will be in a position to attack anybody. Only the present-day Big Powers will be able to do that. If they insist on complete unanimity for the decisions of the Security Council, they do so—they declare—because they realize there is no peace possible in the world when a lack of harmony prevails among the bigger nations. . . . It is the sacred duty of the smaller nations to do their utmost to prevent the big ones from growing apart: on their cooperation rests the future of the world.

Unfortunately the great powers did grow apart, despite everything the small nations could do to prevent it. When this happened the veto designed to promote unanimity became an obstacle in the path of progress. As it came to be used more and more frequently it robbed the Security Council of much of its usefulness. The veto was employed, as it suited the purposes of one of the great powers, to prevent inquiries and investigations into disputes, to bar the admission of new members into the UN, and for other purposes which frustrated the possibilities of the UN. The veto was used on occasion by most of the great powers, but the nation which used it most frequently was the Soviet Union.

On a number of occasions the question of eliminating the veto had been discussed in the General Assembly without leading to action. But the invasion of South Korea by the North Koreans (June 25, 1950) convinced most of the great powers that if a system of prompt and dependable action against aggressors was to be established means would have to be devised to enable the General Assembly to circumvent the veto. Had the Russian representative been present at the emergency meeting of the Security Council on the day South Korea was invaded he could by his veto have prevented any decision and consequently any action.

The situation called for measures which give the General Assembly the right to consider an emergency without delay if the Security Council should fail to act. Secretary of State Acheson proposed such measures in a group of resolutions entitled "United Action for Peace." The resolutions proposed, first, that if there should be a threat to or breach of the peace or an act of aggression and the Security Council fails to exercise its primary responsibility because of lack of unanimity among its permanent members the General Assembly may, by vote of any seven members of the Security Council or by a majority of the members of the UN, be summoned to an emergency special session. At this session it may make recommendations for collective measures by member states. In cases of a breach of the peace or act of aggression the recommendations may include the use of armed force. Second, the resolutions proposed the establishment of a Peace Observation Commission which is to observe and report on any area of tension where the peace is likely to be endangered. This Commission, as the eyes and ears of the UN, could not only sound a warning of developing friction or possible aggression; it could also supply the Assembly with prompt and reliable knowledge if the latter found itself obliged to act. Third, the resolutions recommended that the member states maintain elements in their national armed forces especially for UN service. Finally, they proposed the establishment of a Collective Measures Committee for the purpose of studying methods which might be used to maintain and strengthen world peace.

The proposals were presented to the Fifth General Assembly

which met at Flushing Meadows in the fall of 1950 and were approved (October 18 and 19) by an overwhelming majority. Fifty-two members voted for the adoption, with only the U.S.S.R. and its satellites opposing. Thus the machinery of the UN for preserving the peace was greatly strengthened.

§

THE BACKGROUND OF THE KOREAN CONFLICT

The North Korean invasion of South Korea inaugurated the most critical period in the history of the United Nations. Although Korea is a small mountainous country of about 85,000 square miles, it had long been a danger zone in Far Eastern politics, for it occupied the heart of a strategic triangle with Russia on one side, China on another, and Japan on the third. Rivalry over its control was a major cause of the Sino-Japanese War (1894–1895) and of the Russo-Japanese War (1904–1905). To the Japanese the control of Korea, "which points like a dagger at the heart of our country," was particularly important and after defeating the Russians in the Russo-Japanese War they received a free hand in Korea and in 1910 incorporated it in the Japanese Empire. During World War II some 10,000 Korean troops fought with the forces of Chiang Kai-shek against Japan in the hope that their country would be granted freedom and independence at the end of the war. This hope was strengthened by the Cairo Declaration, issued on December 1, 1943, by President Roosevelt, prime minister Churchill, and Generalissimo Chiang Kai-shek. It contained the following statement: "The aforesaid three great powers, mindful of the enslavement of the people of Korea, are determined that in due course Korea shall become free and independent." This pledge was reaffirmed in the Potsdam Declaration which was also signed by the Soviet Union. Few, if any, countries, therefore, celebrated V-J Day with greater enthusiasm than did Korea.

But events did not turn out as the Koreans had expected. When the Japanese accepted the terms of unconditional surrender it was agreed between the Soviet Union and the United States that the troops of the former country were to accept the surrender of the Japanese forces in Korea north of the thirty-eighth parallel, while the Japanese troops south of that line would surrender to United States troops. This line which had been established as a "temporary military expedient" gradually became a permanent division. The Council of Foreign Ministers, it is true, agreed with Chinese approval that Korea should be independent after a trusteeship period "of up to five years," but during the months that followed the Soviet Union and the

United States could not agree on a provisional government for the whole of Korea. The principal cause of the breakdown of negotiations was the Russian insistence that all Korean leaders who were not friendly to Russia be barred from consultation in the creation of the provisional government and from participation in the government. After two unsuccessful meetings the United States authorities took steps to establish a provisional government in their zone and the Russians did likewise. Thus Korea was torn between two rival powers, with each power trying to create a government friendly to itself.

Having failed in the efforts to reach an agreement the United States asked the UN General Assembly to offer a solution. On November 14, 1947, the General Assembly created the United Nations Temporary Commission on Korea charging it to hold elections in Korea and to make arrangements with the occupying powers for the complete withdrawal of all foreign armed forces from Korea. The Soviet authorities, however, refused to permit the commission to enter North Korea. In the south the elections were held (May, 1948) and resulted in the establishment of the Republic of Korea with Seoul as capital and Dr. Syngmann Rhee as president. At its next session the General Assembly declared this to be the only lawful government in Korea. Following this declaration the new government was accorded recognition by the United States and thirty-one other nations. The Soviet Union and its satellites not only did not recognize the new state, thereby preventing it from becoming a member of the UN; it also proceeded to organize a strong puppet regime in North Korea, calling it the Democratic People's Republic of Korea (September, 1948). Under the supervision of Soviet military officers this puppet government built a North Korean army of 200,000 equipped with Russian tanks, artillery, and planes. During the next years the North Koreans were subjected to a steady barrage of communist propaganda sprinkled liberally with the statement that United States imperialism was preventing the reunification of Korea. In other words, the North Korean army was indoctrinated to believe that it must fight for the reunification of the country.

The UN commission did not cease its efforts to bring about the unification of Korea, but was unable to make any progress. As the South Korean government was functioning well, the United States decided to withdraw its forces in accordance with the recommendation of the General Assembly (December 12, 1948). The evacuation was completed in June, 1949. An announcement by the Soviet government declared that the Soviet troops had been withdrawn in

December, 1948. When the UN commission sought to verify the Soviet claim, it received no response to the messages it sent to the U.S.S.R. and could therefore take no action.

A new election which was held in the Republic of South Korea (May, 1950) brought into power many of the so-called middle-of-the-roaders, men who believed that a reunification of Korea could be achieved through rapprochement with the North Koreans. This caused the North Koreans to believe that many South Koreans might even welcome a reunion with the North. Among the factors, then, that impelled the invasion of South Korea one might list the following: (1) the desire to include South Korea within the Russian sphere; (2) the great strategic value of Korea for an attack on Russia, China, or Japan; (3) the fact that the South Koreans were weak militarily, while the North Koreans were strong; (4) the conviction that the United States or the United Nations would not defend Korea.

THE WAR IN KOREA

The invasion began at 4 A.M. on Sunday morning, June 25, 1950, when a large North Korean army supported by powerful lines of Soviet tanks, Yak fighter planes, and heavy artillery crossed the thirty-eighth parallel. The precision with which the entire force moved demonstrated that the invasion had been carefully planned. To the South Korean army it came as a complete surprise. Even if it had received some advance notice it would have been able to offer only feeble resistance since it was ill-equipped to meet the invader. It did not have a single plane or tank and its artillery was hardly heavy enough to do much damage. During the period of occupation the United States, to forestall accusations of imperialism, had refrained from building a strong, well-equipped army in South Korea. It had supplied the South Korean army only with light arms of sufficient caliber to repel guerrilla attacks. The repeated pleas of President Syngmann Rhee for tanks, heavy artillery, and fighting planes were ignored. Hence the rifle-equipped army of South Korea was no match for the formidable fighting force of the North Koreans. It appeared as if the invaders would penetrate to the southern tip of the Korean peninsula in a short time.

The invasion of South Korea was a direct challenge to the principles of the United Nations and this organization accepted it as such. No sooner had the news of the attack reached the United States than a meeting of the Security Council was requested. Secretary General

Trygve Lie summoned the Council to meet on the same day (June
25) less than twenty-four hours after the attack had begun. In presenting the case to the Security Council the United States representative said in part:

A full-scale attack is now going forward in Korea. It is an invasion
upon a state which the United Nations itself, by action of its General
Assembly, has brought into being. It is armed aggression against a government elected under United Nations supervision. Such an attack openly
defies the interest and authority of the United Nations.

The Security Council responded by adopting by a vote of 9 to 0 (the
Soviet representative being absent and Yugoslavia abstaining) the following resolution:

The Security Council, noting with grave concern the armed attack
upon the Republic of Korea by forces from North Korea, determines that
this action constitutes a breach of the peace: (1) Calls for the immediate cessation of hostilities, and calls upon the authorities of North Korea
to withdraw forthwith their armed forces to the thirty-eighth parallel;
(2) Requests the United Nations Commission on Korea (a) to communicate its fully considered recommendations on the situation with the least
possible delay, (b) to observe the withdrawal of the North Korean forces
to the thirty-eighth Parallel, and (c) to keep the Security Council informed on the execution of this resolution; (3) Calls upon all members
to render every assistance to the United Nations in the execution of this
resolution and to refrain from giving assistance to the North Korean
authorities.

The North Koreans completely ignored the resolution of the Security Council to stop the fighting and to withdraw their forces north
of the thirty-eighth parallel. When the Security Council met again
on June 27 President Truman's announcement that he was sending
armed assistance to the government of South Korea was read before
it. The United States representative, after stating that "it is hard to
imagine a more glaring example of disregard for the United Nations
and for all the principles it represents" than that of which the North
Koreans were guilty, proposed a resolution calling upon the members
of the United Nations to restore peace by force in Korea. The resolution which was quickly passed recommended that member states
"furnish such assistance to the Republic as may be necessary to repel
the armed attack and to restore international peace and security in
the area." By July 4 four nations—Britain, Australia, New Zealand,
and the Netherlands—in addition to the United States, had responded by sending forces to aid the South Koreans. By July 12 forty-

seven UN members and three nonmembers (Italy, Ceylon, and Jordan) had announced their support of UN military action against North Korea. The Soviet Union, the Ukraine, and Byelorussia (White Russia) were joined by Poland, Czechoslovakia, and Yugoslavia in denouncing the UN resolution as illegal since both the Soviet Union and Red China were not represented in the Council.

The next development in the UN came on July 7 when the Security Council authorized the United States to establish a unified command of the UN forces in Korea. It further authorized the UN command to fly the UN flag in the operations against the North Koreans. President Truman acted at once upon the Security Council authorization by naming General Douglas MacArthur commander of all United Nations military forces defending South Korea.

Meanwhile the first contingent of United States forces had landed at Pusan and on July 5 had gone into action against the North Korean tank-led columns driving southward. They were, however, so inferior in numbers and so poorly equipped that their attempts to stem the Red advance were futile. The light American tanks proved to be no match for the heavier Soviet models and equipment. Consequently the UN forces had to fall back. The Red forces even stepped up their drive. By July 13 they had advanced a hundred miles and occupied nearly half of South Korea. Gradually as more UN troops were landed the Red advance was slowed; nevertheless the southward movement continued. The area held by the UN forces was gradually whittled down to an area fifty miles wide and ninety miles long in southeastern Korea about the port of Pusan, the main supply port for the UN troops. The area held by the UN troops became so small that in some circles the fear was expressed that the war might turn into another Dunkirk. Early in August, however, the UN forces made a desperate stand and in some sections even counterattacked thus administering the first setback to the Reds. But the UN forces were not as yet ready to launch a major counteroffensive. For the time being the primary purpose was to stop the Red advance while preparations for a counteroffensive were being made.

The UN offensive was launched early in September and made excellent progress. While the main drive moved northward toward Seoul, landings were also made from the sea at Inchon, twenty-two miles west of Seoul (September 15–16). By September 21, United States marines were fighting in the outskirts of Seoul. After the former capital of the South Korean government was retaken the UN forces moved northward to the thirty-eighth parallel. There was much discussion in UN circles as to whether General MacArthur should or would cross the parallel. The question was answered early in October when, with the tacit consent of forty-seven delegates to the UN General Assembly, he launched an all-out invasion of North Korea. Although the North Koreans continued to offer stiff resistance, the advance of the UN forces was steady. On October 19 UN divisions broke through to Pyongyang, the capital of North Korea, and on October 26 the South Korean Sixth Division reached the Manchurian frontier at Chosan. Things were going so well that General MacArthur announced that the war was "definitely coming to an end" and that complete UN victory was only a matter of days.

At the eleventh hour Communist China without any formal declaration of intervention sent vast unexpected strength to reinforce the North Korean forces. UN military headquarters estimated the number of Chinese who entered the fighting at 60,000, with more coming in a steady stream from Manchuria. A North Korean broadcast announced that the Chinese had permitted "volunteers" to fight in defense of the "Chinese area" bordering the Yalu River, but Chinese captives quickly gave the lie to this statement. They stated emphatically that there had been no "volunteering" for service in Korea. General MacArthur, still hoping to end the war by knocking out the Chinese communist forces with one big blow, launched an offensive against them on November 24. By this time the Red forces had more than doubled. After crushing the UN offensive the Chinese embarked on a counteroffensive with an estimated 200,000 troops. The drive quickly shattered the center of the UN line and threatened to destroy the UN forces. To keep from being cut to pieces they had to retreat rapidly. Great losses were suffered by both sides. The retreat continued until the end of the year saw the UN forces south of the thirty-eighth parallel defending the approaches to Seoul. They hoped to stop the Red advance before it again engulfed the South Korean capital. But the momentum of the drive was too great. The UN forces again pulled out of Seoul under pressure and retreated southward for some weeks while taking a heavy toll of the advancing enemy.

During the early months of 1951 the line of battle moved up and down the Korean peninsula. A counteroffensive started by the UN forces in February carried them northward again. After retaking Seoul on March 14 they forced the Reds to retreat across the thirty-eighth parallel. In April the communists collected an estimated force of 400,000 for another drive. The pressure of overwhelming numbers did cause the UN forces to retreat slowly, but they took a heavy toll of the enemy. This time they refused to surrender Seoul. The Reds after suffering heavy losses in trying to take the South

Korean capital finally gave up the attempt. Thereafter they failed to launch any major offensives.

In June the Russians excited hopes for a quick termination of hostilities when they suggested that representatives of both sides hold meetings for the purpose of arranging a ceasefire. The truce talks did not actually begin until July 8 at Kaesong and then immediately ran into difficulties. Not only could the negotiators reach no agreement on a ceasefire line, but friction also developed over the refusal of the Reds to permit newspaper correspondents to be present. The result was that week after week passed without appreciable progress. Finally the talks were interrupted and on August 23 discontinued. After a lapse of sixty-three days they were resumed on October 25 at Panmunjom. Finally on November 26 after four long months during which the fighting had continued [8] an agreement on a ceasefire line was reached. The UN and communist negotiators agreed: (1) that the existing battle line as of that day would be the final ceasefire line if the armistice were signed within thirty days; (2) that if the truce lasted longer the line would be redrawn along the battle line at that time; (3) that air, land, and sea fighting would continue until then; (4) that after the armistice was signed each side would withdraw one and a quarter miles from the ceasefire line to create a buffer zone.

One obstacle still remained. It was the question of repatriating the prisoners of war. While the communists insisted that all prisoners of war be forcibly repatriated, the UN negotiators held out for voluntary repatriation. Month after month passed without agreement. Fighting flared up anew and casualties continued to mount. Finally it was agreed (June 28, 1953) that all prisoners desiring to be repatriated would be sent home as soon as the armistice was signed. The rest were to be held for a period of about four months and then declared free civilians. On July 27, 1953, the armistice was signed and the fighting ceased 12 hours later. In the armistice agreement provision had been made for a conference to arrange Korea-wide elections and national unification. But the conference, held in Geneva, April 26 to June 15, 1954, ended in a deadlock and Korea remained divided. Since that time neither side has yielded on its position.

[8] U.S. casualties increased from 79,139 to 100,176 during this time.

Western Europe after World War II

REBUILDING WESTERN
EUROPE

WORLD WAR II left large parts of Western Europe in disorder and ruins. Not only was the loss of life much greater than it had been in World War I but the general destruction was much more widespread. Great damage had been done to harbors and transportation systems. Beyond the physical destruction there was a general dislocation of economic life. "It has become obvious in recent months," Secretary of State Marshall said in June, 1947, "that the visible destruction was probably less serious than the dislocation of the entire fabric of European economy. . . . The feverish preparation for war and the more feverish maintenance of the war effort engulfed all aspects of national economies." As a consequence industrial production in France was reduced to 30 or 40 per cent of prewar, and in Italy it fell to 20 per cent. Even the production of such a necessity of life as bread grains fell to two thirds of the prewar average. Internal and external trade were badly dislocated, prices of necessities were high, and there was a serious shortage of raw materials.

No time was lost in assuming the task of reconstruction and rehabilitation, and for a time things went well. The United States granted interim loans and extended credit to various countries of Western Europe so that they could purchase the commodities and raw materials which they needed so desperately. Recovery in the months that followed was remarkable. In Italy by the end of 1946 industrial production reached about 60 per cent of its prewar level, in France about 85 per cent. In England it was approaching the prewar level. Increased production was also evident in agriculture, although its aggregate output was still below prewar level. In 1947, however, a crisis developed. The European countries had spent so much for food, raw materials, and machinery that their gold and dollar reserves were largely depleted and they were faced with the dire prospects of being unable to buy more. Further imports were necessary in order to maintain the progress achieved and to sustain the already low standards of living, but further spending of dollar reserves threatened the countries with bankruptcy.

World War II was not the basic cause of the dollar shortage. It had set in long before the outbreak of hostilities in 1939. During the nineteenth century and the early years of the twentieth industrial Europe had found extensive markets in backward and semi-industrial regions. For decades some 250 million Western Europeans produced goods for more than a billion consumers in eastern Europe, Asia, and Africa. Vast wealth had flowed into Europe, but with the decline of imperialism in the twentieth century the stream of gold grew less and less. Countries that had formerly been backward built their own factories and began to close their home markets to European goods. Thus Japan not only supplied its own markets but also became a competitor of the European countries for the eastern markets. While the opportunities for, and gains from, exports became more limited, the demand for imports of food and raw materials expanded. The result was that some European countries began to spend more for imports than they received for exports. Before World War II they had been able to make up the difference with income from foreign investments, the shipping trade, and tourist business. During the war, however, income from exports declined to a minimum and many of the investments were liquidated or pledged as payment for critical raw materials. The tourist trade, of course, largely disappeared, and the shipping trade was but a fraction of its former volume. Thus the end of the war saw the gold and dollar resources near the vanishing point, while the demand for imports had increased. The crying need was fresh dollar resources.

THE MARSHALL PLAN

It was up to the United States to offer the European countries financial help. The offer came in June, 1947. In a commencement address at Harvard University on June 5 Secretary Marshall pointed out that a serious situation had developed. "The truth of the matter," he said, "is that Europe's requirements for the next three or four years of foreign food and other essential products—principally from

America—is so much greater than her present ability to pay that she must have additional help, or face economic, social and political deterioration of a very grave character." This help, he continued, can come only from the United States. "It is logical that the United States should do whatever it is able to do to assist in the return of normal economic health in the world, without which there can be no political stability and no assured peace. Our policy is directed not against any country or doctrine but against hunger, poverty, desperation, and chaos. Its purpose should be the revival of a working economy in the world so as to permit the emergence of political and social conditions in which free institutions can exist."

In projecting the plan to aid Europe, which was soon called the Marshall Plan, Secretary Marshall was careful to state that "the initiative must come from Europe." "It is already evident," he said, "that before the United States Government can proceed much further in its efforts to alleviate the situation and help start the European world on its way to recovery, there must be some agreement among the countries of Europe as to the requirements of the situation and the part those countries themselves will take in order to give proper effect to whatever action might be undertaken by the government." He called on the European states (1) to take inventory of their resources; (2) to make a list of their needs; (3) to draw up a program under which dollars might be best used to help Europe help itself. This having been done the United States would study the program and determine to what extent Europe's requirements could be supplied.

Secretary Marshall's speech was widely hailed as a statesmanlike step toward a long-term program in place of the piecemeal aid the United States had previously given various European states. The welcome was particularly enthusiastic on the part of Foreign Secretary Bevin of Britain and Foreign Minister Bidault of France because both countries had spent much more rapidly than originally planned the credits granted them by the United States. The former, for example, praised the United States proposals as "a real attempt by a great country . . . to make its contribution to creating a healthy world." The big question was how Soviet Russia felt about the Marshall Plan. There was optimism in the air when Mr. Molotov accepted an invitation to discuss the plan with British and French representatives. But he dashed whatever hope the world may have had for European unity when he said that the Soviet Union "rejects this plan as being altogether unsatisfactory and incapable of yielding any positive results." The Russians, it appeared, were not interested in any program that would revive the depressed economy of Europe and increase the prestige and influence of the United States. The Soviet press denounced the plan as meaning "interference in the internal affairs of other states."

The British and French ministers nevertheless decided to go ahead with the plan and sent out invitations to a conference. Besides the Soviet Union, which had turned thumbs down on the plan, two other countries were not invited. The first of these was Germany, which at the time had no government to speak for her, and the other was Spain, whose dictator was *persona non grata* with the other countries. A total of twenty-two countries were invited in addition to Britain and France. Not all accepted the invitations. The absentees, in addition to the Soviet Union, were the eight countries in the Russian sphere of influence: Albania, Bulgaria, Czechoslovakia, Finland, Hungary, Poland, Rumania, and Yugoslavia. All of these countries were in need of aid; in fact, officials of Poland and Czechoslovakia had announced that their countries would be represented. But last-minute pressure by the Kremlin caused both to decline the invitation. Hence the Marshall Plan was confined to the countries outside the Soviet sphere. The refusal of Russia to participate and also to permit the Soviet satellites to send representatives drew a sharp line between the Russian sphere and Western Europe.

When the representatives of sixteen nations [1] met in Paris on July 12 the conference proceeded to "draw up as quickly as possible a program to cover Europe's resources and Europe's needs." In its three sessions the conference set up an over-all Cooperation Committee; also four subcommittees to study such special phases of the general economic problem as food and agriculture, iron and steel, transportation, and fuel and power. On April 16, 1948, representatives of the sixteen participating countries established the Organization of European Economic Cooperation whose principal task it has been to make recommendations for the allocation of Marshall Plan aid. The work of this organization was implemented by the Economic Cooperation Administration (ECA) with headquarters in Washington. During 1948 and 1949 the ECA authorized almost $4 billion annually to Marshall Plan nations for the purchase of commodities, raw materials, machinery, and equipment.

The aid provided by the Marshall Plan was an important factor in promoting recovery in Western Europe. Results during the years that followed were impressive. Gradually Western Europe rebuilt its

[1] Austria, Belgium, Britain, Denmark, Eire, France, Greece, Iceland, Italy, Luxembourg, Netherlands, Norway, Portugal, Sweden, Switzerland, and Turkey.

plants, reopened its channels of trade, and brought its currencies back into line with reality. By the end of 1948 industrial production had in the aggregate surpassed the production of 1938. Industrial growth continued in 1949 and during the first months of 1950. By this time Western Europe's industrial production had been lifted to about 27 per cent above prewar levels. Thus five years and billions of Marshall Plan dollars after V-J Day, Western Europe was beginning to regain its economic health. As economic recovery became more clearly discernible in Britain, France, Germany, and Italy, social tension relaxed and desperate remedies proved less attractive. In other words, communist peril lost some of its terrors.

Just when Europe had sufficiently recovered to stand on its own feet with drastically reduced United States aid, the drive for Western rearmament was launched as a means of preventing World War III. Under the rearmament program, which was grudgingly undertaken as a result of United States prodding, the convalescing economy suffered a sharp setback. The setback was by no means general to Europe. West Germany, which did not adopt the rearmament program after the outbreak of war in Korea, remained strong with regard to external finances, and Italy continued to enjoy a relatively good foreign trade position. The two countries hardest hit were Britain and France. While the volume of imports increased because of the need for raw materials, the volume of exports decreased because much of the coal, steel, manpower, and raw materials was being diverted into defense production. Moreover, rising prices made the cost of rearming so high that the military budgets did not go as far as had been anticipated. The result was a new dollar shortage. The remedy which both Britain and France adopted was a curtailment of nonessential imports. This move, however, reacted on the economies of the other countries of Europe. Both Britain and France began at once to clamor for more aid from the United States and the Congress responded by granting it.

🔔

THE SCHUMAN PLAN

One of the most striking developments in Western Europe since 1945 has been the movement toward European unity. For many decades the countries of Europe had been competing with each other in intensifying trade restrictions, raising tariff barriers, and setting up import quotas to "protect" the home industries. The tariff blocks which resulted have been likened to "a crazy quilt whose varicolored squares had been cut out but not sewn togther." After World War

II wiser counsels began to prevail, supported by the awareness that a divided Europe is a weak Europe and by the belief that a united Europe could gain greater prosperity as well as greater weight and influence. The first step toward closer cooperation in Europe was the creation of a customs union called "Benelux," embracing Belgium, the Netherlands, and Luxembourg. Later sixteen countries established the Organization of Economic Cooperation to study the needs of the various nations with regard to Marshall Plan aid.

One of the major developments in the direction of European unity is the Schuman plan, conceived by the French foreign minister Robert Schuman and the economic expert Jean Monnet. It is a plan for merging the coal, iron, and steel industries of Western Europe under a supranational authority. The plan involves the resources of six nations: France, West Germany, Italy, and the Benelux countries. Britain refused to join but promised close cooperation. Under the Schuman plan the six countries would produce and market coal, iron, and steel as though they are one country. These basic industries would be administered by a new type of body, a kind of superstate having actual property and doing a $4 billion annual business. Its administrative machinery was outlined in such a way that it could eventually be the basis for a European political federation. The executive functions in this supranational government are to be exercised by the High Authority, a cabinet of nine members. The High Authority must answer to an assembly in the same way in which cabinets are responsible to national assemblies in European governments. In this assembly France, West Germany, and Italy will each have eighteen members, Belgium and the Netherlands ten each, and Luxembourg four. There will also be a High Court to settle disputes and a Council to check the activities of the administration, the Council to be composed of one cabinet member from each of the participating nations.

The architects of the Schuman plan hope that it will be a major turning point in international relations in Europe. It aims, first of all, to set up a tariff-free European market for the backbone industries. "Europe," premier Pleven of France said, "cannot maintain the towering material stature possible to its people's skills and spirit so long as it is divided by patchwork territorial fences. They foster localized instead of common interest." A second purpose is to make the coal, iron, and steel industries of the Ruhr a part of a European system, so that they can never be used again to power or promote German militarism. In general, the conception of those who devised the Schuman plan for merging Western Europe's coal and steel was to overcome the hostility between France and Germany and to achieve a reconciliation and mutual confidence through this and other economic partnerships. The authors of the plan also hope that the two countries will gradually move toward political unity.

In March, 1951, after nine months of negotiation, the foreign ministers of the six states initialed the Schuman plan treaty, but it was still necessary for the parliaments of the various countries to ratify it. The first nation to approve the plan was the Netherlands, but the big question still remained whether the governments of France and West Germany would ratify it. Participation of these two countries was regarded as essential to its success and there were some misgivings regarding opinion in these countries. In December, 1951, the question was answered in part when the French National Assembly ratified the plan by the overwhelming vote of 377 to 233, with only the Communists and Gaulists voting against it. It was the largest majority given to any bill in many months. But the tallest hurdle—ratification by West Germany—was still ahead. Debate in the German Bundestag continued for three days with the Socialists offering vigorous opposition. But on January 11, 1952, the hurdle was successfully scaled when 225 deputies voted in favor of ratification and only 144 against.

The organs of the European Coal and Steel Community outlined in the Schuman Plan quickly came into being. In August, 1952, the High Authority was set up and immediately began to function. Early in September two more organs of the Community took form. On September 8 in Luxembourg the Council of Ministers held its organizational meeting and elected West German chancellor Konrad Adenauer as its first chairman. Two days later in Strasbourg the Assembly held its organizational meeting and chose Paul-Henri Spaak, former Belgian premier, as president. Thus Europe's first supranational assembly was established with 76 parliamentarians from six countries.

At the suggestion of the Council of Ministers, the Assembly took up the task of writing a plan or constitution for a European Federation. It was hoped that this plan for European political unity would be ready for consideration by the Assembly and the governments represented in it by March, 1953. Before a European political federation can become a reality, however, a settlement will have to be reached on the Saar question which has embittered the relations between the two major European partners for more than thirty years. The Saar, a 900-square mile valley between Germany and France, belonged to the former country before the war, but is now autonomous. While its population is predominantly German, the Saar has close economic ties with France. A plan prepared by the French calls for the internationalization of the Saar. Under this plan it would become a kind of European District of Columbia and as such would be the governmental seat of a European political federation. Representatives of both Germany and France have voiced optimism regarding a settlement of the Saar issue. Thus Chancellor Adenauer said with a nod of approval from France's Robert Schuman: "We are full of hope for a settlement of this delicate question over the next few months."

THE NORTH ATLANTIC TREATY ORGANIZATION

Western Europe was also drawn together by the threat of Soviet military power. When it became evident that the Soviet Union was bent on expansion rather than cooperation, a group of European states and the United States and Canada decided to unite in order to "contain" Soviet expansion. As Secretary of State Acheson put it, "We have learned that if the free nations do not stand together they will fall one by one." "Under the ominous threat of communistic dictatorship," General Eisenhower said, "the nations of the North Atlantic area have looked at the situation and said, 'We may defend ourselves collectively, but individually we are very badly exposed.'" In short, a group of nations planned to provide collective security by voluntary cooperation. But there was no intention of getting into an armament race with Soviet Russia. "If we can make it sufficiently clear, in advance," President Truman said, "that any armed attack affecting our national security would be met with overwhelming force, the armed attack might never occur."

After preliminary discussions the North Atlantic Treaty was signed in Washington on April 4, 1949, by plenipotentiaries of twelve nations: Canada, Denmark, Portugal, Iceland, Britain, France, Italy, the Netherlands, Norway, Belgium, Luxembourg, and the United States. The purpose of the participating nations is thus stated in the preamble of the treaty: "They are determined to safeguard the freedom, common heritage, and civilization of their peoples, founded on the principles of democracy, individual liberty, and the rule of law. They seek to promote stability and well-being in the North Atlantic area. They are resolved to unite their efforts for collective defense and for the preservation of peace and security." Although negotiated outside the United Nations, the treaty was drafted in such a way as to be in harmony with United Nations principles. Secretary Acheson, one of its authors, said: "It is aimed at coordinating the exercise of the right of self-defense especially recognized in Article 51 of the United Nations Charter. It is designed to fit precisely into the framework of the United Nations and to assure practical measures for maintaining peace and security in harmony with the Charter."

The North Atlantic Treaty consists of fourteen articles. The first states that the signers will "settle any international disputes in which they may become involved by peaceful means in such a manner that international peace and security, and justice, are not endangered." Article Four states that "the parties will consult together whenever, in the opinion of any of them, the territorial integrity, political independence, or security of any of the parties is threatened." In Article Five a stern warning is sounded: "The parties agree that an armed attack against one or more of them in Europe or North America shall be considered an armed attack against all; and consequently they agree that, if such an armed attack occurs, each of them . . . will assist the party or parties so attacked by taking forthwith, individually and in concert with the other parties, such action as it deems necessary, including the use of armed force, to restore and maintain the security of the North Atlantic area." In other words, the moral obligation of each participating nation is to treat an armed attack against one or more countries in the pact as an attack against itself. The Russians, however, interpreted the North Atlantic Treaty differently. Following the publication of the text the Soviet Union sent a protest to many of the participating countries, including Britain, France, and the United States, stating that the treaty is obviously directed against the Soviet Union and is aggressive in character.

In a sense the principle behind the North Atlantic Treaty goes back to 1947. In that year President Truman announced the so-called Truman Doctrine, which promised support to "free peoples who are resisting attempted subjugation." The two nations that were in the greatest need of immediate aid were Greece and Turkey. While Greece was engaged in a civil war that was part of a communist drive to conquer the country, Turkey was menaced by demands from the Kremlin for territorial and air-base concessions, the granting of which would have terminated the country's national independence. In May, 1947, Congress voted $400 million to bolster the economies and defenses of the two countries. During the succeeding years military missions from the United States worked industriously and successfully to build up their defenses.

In September, 1951, the members of the Council of the North Atlantic Treaty Organization meeting at Ottawa decided that sub-

ject to the ratification by their governments they would extend to
Greece and Turkey an invitation to become full members of the
North Atlantic Treaty Organization. The invitation was ratified
and the number of members of NATO was increased to fourteen.
These new members, who have in readiness more than thirty divisions
of hardy, well-trained soldiers, serve as a kind of protective cover for
the Middle East. Further, the inclusion of Turkey and Greece extended the North Atlantic defense area eastward to the Black Sea and
the Caucasus.

No one at the time the treaty was signed appears to have foreseen
the formal development of what is known as the North Atlantic Treaty
Organization (NATO). There was no mention in the original treaty
of a joint military command in time of peace. What the authors of the
treaty had in mind was a simple declaration that the nations signing
the treaty would use all their resources against any nation that threatened the security of the North Atlantic area. Two momentous events
which soon occurred promoted the development of a closer organization among the treaty members. These were the atomic explosion
which was set off in Russia in September, 1949, and the outbreak of the
Korean war in June, 1950. In posing a greater threat of attack by
the communist states these two events caused the treaty nations to
accept the idea that they had to coordinate their rearmament efforts
and pool their forces. As a result, the post of North Atlantic commander in chief was created and General Dwight Eisenhower was chosen
to fill the post. (He was succeeded by another U.S. military leader,
General Matthew B. Ridgway, on June 1, 1952.) Headquarters—
known as SHAPE (Supreme Headquarters of the Atlantic Powers
in Europe)—were established in Paris. The old policy of rearming
in a leisurely way was replaced by a policy of training military forces,
manufacturing armaments, and building airfields with the greatest
possible speed. Despite many handicaps considerable progress was
made. Military budgets in the NATO countries were increased
sharply, military production was doubled and, in some cases, quadrupled, and the number of men under arms was increased.

Regarded from the American point of view, NATO is the for-
mulation of a guarantee by the United States of the security of Western Europe pending the time when Europe may be able to dispense
with that guarantee. As one of the major conditions for helping to
defend Western Europe "as far east as possible" the United States insisted that West Germany must be rearmed and brought into the
plan of defense. The proposal to rearm the Germans brought all the
latent French fear of Germany to the surface. This deep-seated fear

was aggravated by the insistence of the West German government that it be admitted to NATO on terms of absolute equality with its former enemies. Chancellor Adenauer insisted that he could not obtain ratification of the rearmament project unless his terms were accepted. The move evoked, as it were, triple fears. In addition to fearing its military power the French feared also the economic and political power of a rejuvenated Germany. They were convinced that the Germans upon achieving their freedom would go on to dominate Europe in all three ways. The French therefore demanded guarantees from Washington and London that Germany, once it was rearmed, would not be able to break away from NATO and go on another bloody nationalist rampage. Some Frenchmen, on the other hand, welcomed German rearmament, feeling that it would place upon West Germany a defense burden comparable to the one that was so oppressive to France. Among the Germans themselves there was no enthusiasm for the idea of rearming. Having been twice badly defeated the Germans were apathetic; in fact, they disliked the idea of contributing heavily for their own defense.

In spite of opposition, at the Lisbon meeting of the Council of the North Atlantic Treaty Organization (February, 1952) agreements were reached which, in the words of Secretary of State Acheson, were a "vast step forward in terms of European development." This opinion was shared by French Foreign Minister Robert Schuman who said: "One rarely attends a conference which accomplished as much as this one did." British Foreign Minister Anthony Eden declared that the Lisbon conference marked "the beginning of a new era." In the six-day meeting the NATO Council of Foreign Ministers covered a wide range of problems. The principal decisions were in regard to NATO's over-all defensive strength, West Germany's contribution to Western defense, and NATO's administration.

First, the powers set high goals for themselves in the construction of Western defenses. The aim was to build up enough strength to deter aggression by Soviet Russia and her satellites. It was therefore decided to increase General Eisenhower's NATO command from the existing strength of about thirty divisions to approximately fifty divisions. These divisions were to be either combat-ready by the end of 1952 or available for emergency use on thirty days' notice. The projected plan did not include available Greek and Turkish forces or any German units. Representatives of Britain, France, and Italy made clear, however, that they would require additional financial aid from the United States to achieve these goals, emphasizing that they would need access to sufficient stocks of raw materials at reasonable prices, and also assurance of an adequate amount of foreign exchange to avoid widening the dollar gap.

Second, the NATO Council agreed to take into the organization as an associate the state of West Germany, which was asked to contribute twelve divisions to a continental European army, while France was to furnish fourteen and Italy twelve, and the Benelux countries five. Thus NATO took steps to rearm West Germany less than seven years after the destruction of Nazi militarism. After the formation of the continental European army, West Germany would be asked to contribute $2.4 billion a year as her share of defense costs. Some time before the Lisbon meeting the foreign ministers of the six European nations had agreed that the European army would be a real internationalized one-uniform army, as the French wished, and not merely a loose coalition as desired by the Dutch and Belgians. "Through the European army," General Eisenhower said, "we can avail ourselves of German strength under conditions that are satisfactory to the people of Germany and that still do not give rise to justifiable fears in the rest of Europe."

Third, the NATO Council decided to incorporate the existing administrative organs into a permanent operating organization with established headquarters. It was agreed that high-level representatives of each nation should meet in "permanent session" and that there should be a NATO secretariat under a Secretary General somewhat like the United Nations set-up. A number of representatives also suggested that the NATO administration was becoming too unwieldy to rotate from one member capital to another. Consequently it was decided to give the NATO administration permanent headquarters. The place chosen was Paris, near the Supreme Headquarters of the Atlantic Powers in Europe (SHAPE).

The organization described developed from the provision in the North Atlantic treaty which states that the parties to the treaty "hereby establish a Council on which each of them shall be represented" and that this Council shall establish "such subsidiary bodies as may be necessary." In the fully developed organization the Council remained at the top. In this council not only foreign ministers but also defense ministers and finance ministers may sit, depending on the problems that are to be discussed. When the three ministers from each of the member countries are present the council is said to be in plenary or "full" session. This council sets the general lines of policy for the North Atlantic community in so far as the ministers have authority to do so. The next body is the Permanent Council of NATO which was agreed upon at Lisbon. Composed of men of ministerial rank it will sit continuously (in a legal, not a literal sense) at NATO headquarters in Paris. The third body is the Secretariat, headed by the Secretary General whose duties have not as yet been sharply delineated. On the military side there is the Military Committee on which all the member states are represented by responsible military leaders. A second military body is the Standing Group, staffed by British, French, and United States officers and having its headquarters in Washington. It is to the Standing Group that the Supreme Allied Commander in Europe is responsible.

Before the decisions made at Lisbon could be translated into reality many difficulties had to be overcome. All the decisions were subject to approval by the parliaments of the member states. In addition there was the big question of how the European governments would pay for the costly rearmament which had been voted. Several days after the conclusion of the Lisbon conference the French Cabinet of M. Edgar Faure fell because the National Assembly refused to vote the tax increase necessary to supply some of the funds needed for rearmament. After a number of men had failed to get sufficient support from the National Assembly to form a cabinet, M. Antoine Pinay finally succeeded in winning endorsement as premier, and on March 11, 1952, his middle-of-the-road cabinet won assembly approval by a vote of 290 to 101. M. Robert Schuman, leading exponent of European integration, remained in the cabinet as foreign minister. Premier Pinay at once assured General Eisenhower that his government would fulfill to the best of its ability France's commitments to NATO. The new premier was, however, still faced with the task of finding a solution for the economic problem. The 1952 rearmament program called for the spending of $3 billion more than current revenues provided.

Nevertheless, the leaders of NATO were confident that the Lisbon projects would be carried out. "If we act with vigor and firmness," Secretary Acheson said, "we can prove again that free people, when resolute, are unconquerable." Chancellor Adenauer of West Germany expressed confidence that his country would ratify the Lisbon decisions despite the vigorous opposition of the Socialists. He advocated that a more closely knit European Union be established and stated that West Germany would join any nation that took the initiative in drafting a constitution for a United States of Europe. "A United States of Europe," he said, "would be necessary even if there were no Soviet danger," because "no single European country can have the necessary living standard just from her own strength." General Eisenhower urged that the countries of Europe officially call a constitutional convention to study the problems of a "greater political and economic unity." "As time goes on," he said, "it seems obvious that Europe cannot gain strength and stability if it is to remain split up in a number of independent economies. There must be progress toward the unification of Western Europe if the objective of permanent security and peace in the western world is to be realized. . . . I look upon the European defense force as a step toward the political and economic union that I believe necessary."

Postwar Germany

GERMANY IN DEFEAT

T

HE Third Reich which Hitler had boasted would last a thousand years went down to defeat in 1945 after an existence of only twelve years. During its short life the Nazis had not only caused untold destruction, agony, and bloodshed, but they had paid a heavy price themselves. Seeking to conquer by the sword, they suffered the Biblical penalty of those who take up the sword. The loss of German life, to say nothing of the millions from other countries who died, was tremendous. According to the records of the German army, almost two million German soldiers were killed and a million and a half were missing up to November, 1944. Some of the bloodiest battles were fought after this time. The number of deaths among civilians was also high. Some estimates have set the number of those killed by air raids at 600,000. The number of dead was further increased by those who died in concentration camps and the refugees who perished from cold and hunger. Furthermore, the number of maimed and crippled ran into the millions. If all are included the total of killed and seriously wounded exceeds ten million.

When the Allied armies moved into Germany toward the end of World War II they expected to find a population that would defend Nazism to the last ditch. What they found was a stunned and apathetic people happy to be freed from the Nazi tyranny. Most of those who had still believed in Nazism were disillusioned in the last months of the war. As defeatism spread, the Nazis themselves, haunted by fear, endeavored to whip the German people into a frenzy of effort to ward off the inevitable. Those who were brash enough to express

686

"defeatist" sentiments were quickly rushed off to concentration camps. Little wonder that "I would rather believe in victory than walk around without my head" became a popular saying. As the Nazi forces fell back before the advancing Allied armies, they not only blew up bridges and wrecked factories but they also destroyed food warehouses and clothing stores at a time when many thousands of bombed-out Germans were living on the brink of starvation. This convinced the rank and file that the Nazi leaders cared little for them. Soon the leaders were gone but the hunger, devastation, and rubble remained. Goebbels had repeatedly stated during the last months that if the Nazis fell they would carry Germany with them. That threat was now a reality.

"Germany is a chaos," one correspondent wrote. "It is a country of crushed cities, of pomposities trampled on the ground, of frightened people and also glad people, of horrors beyond imagination." The once beautiful cities of Germany—Aachen, Berlin, Cologne, Bonn, Koblenz, Frankfurt, Mainz, Nuremberg, Würzburg, and many others—had in large part been turned into masses of ruins. Forty-nine of the largest cities of Germany were damaged to a greater or lesser extent. Only Halle on the Saale had the good fortune of emerging from the war practically untouched. If a city was not bombed or laid low by fire in air raids, it sustained damages during the ground fighting. It is estimated that 3.6 million homes were either totally destroyed or heavily damaged, leaving 7.5 million people homeless. Buildings and monuments which had been erected by generations were turned into heaps of rubble. The Ruhr, which had been the center of heavy industry in Germany, was at the end of the war largely a wasteland of weird twisted girders and jumbled masonry. Those who managed to survive the bombings lived in the cellars of what had been their homes, like frightened animals in their burrows. The middle-sized towns had not fared much better. Those that remained more or less intact were striking exceptions.

The chaos of this land of ruined cities was increased by millions of refugees and released slave laborers who were sweeping across occupied Germany. Many thousands who had fled eastward to escape the bombing of the western cities were now returning. Since the houses of many of them had been destroyed, they were homeless and destitute. In addition there were millions of peasants and workers who, together with their families, had been dispossessed and driven away by Poles and Czechs, Austrians and Hungarians, Rumanians and Yugoslavs. There were also large numbers of slave laborers, men, women, and children, who had been brought in from conquered countries to work in German war plants. This mass of humanity, officially labeled DP's or "displaced persons," clogged the roads and crowded the cities, posing an enormous problem for the Allied armies whose supply services were already heavily taxed. Those who had homes were, if possible, sent back to them. But there still remained millions who had no homes or were unwilling to return to Russian-dominated regions.

Thus there was much human wreckage in addition to the wreckage of cities. The ruins of the cities were not nearly as horrifying as the ruins of humanity, particularly those which the Allied armies found in the concentration camps. Reports on the conditions prevailing in these camps had previously reached the outside, but most people, made skeptical by the phony atrocity propaganda of World War I, refused to put much faith in the stories of inhuman treatment. But the discoveries of the advancing Allied armies shocked the world. Such names as Belsen, Buchenwald, Dachau, Erla, Gardelegen, and Nordhausen will long signify man's inhumanity to man. Those who were confined in these camps included criminals, political opponents of the Nazis, and many who merely had the misfortune of being born Jews. The political opponents included not only the communists but also members of various resistance movements and even some who had merely let slip a remark against the Nazi regime. The diet on which these people had to live was a little thin soup and a few ounces of black bread once each day. This diet was about one fourth of what is necessary to keep a person alive. Consequently many thousands died of starvation and disease. It was a way of exterminating the opponents of the Nazis. Josef Krämer, who had been commandant of Belsen, said conditions in his camp were not bad. "The death rate here," he said, "is quite small. Only about one thousand a month." Records show, however, that in March of 1945 alone many thousands died of starvation and disease in his camp.

When the Allied forces reached the camps they found stacks of emaciated corpses, the inmates having died in such numbers that the Nazis were unable to dispose of the bodies. At Dachau they found a whole trainload of corpses. Most of those who were still living were little more than skin and bones. A correspondent who accompanied the advancing Allied armies wrote: "Only a handful could stand on rickety, pipe-stem legs. Their eyes were sunk deeply into their skulls and their skins under thick dirt were a ghastly yellow. Some sobbed great dry sobs to see the Americans. Others merely wailed pitifully." Many were so weak that they died before they could be given treatment. At Buchenwald and other places the Allied troops also found whipping blocks, torture rooms, gas chambers, and crematoria. The soldiers did not see them being used, but inmates have testified to their use. A British captain who was liberated said: "They hanged; they shot; they had traps where you stood on a trap door which let off a bullet into your neck; they electrocuted; they injected with phenal; they injected air; they injected with milk." For breaches of discipline at Buchenwald prisoners were dispatched in wholesale lots. They were first strangled and then cremated in incinerators which had a capacity of 400 per ten-hour day.

The Gestapo records show that in 1944 alone more than 250,000 Germans were arrested. Beginning in 1940 large numbers of anti-Nazis from the conquered countries were sent to the Nazi concentration camps. When found by the Allied armies these camps had reached the lowest degrees of misery because of overcrowding and the hasty concentration of inmates from camps in other areas. As the Allied troops approached the camps, the Nazi SS (Schutz Staffel) guards who had charge of the camps tried to do away with as many of the prisoners as they could. Some were clubbed to death and others shot. At Gardelegen the SS guards herded 500 political prisoners into a warehouse and burned them alive. General Eisenhower was so moved by what he saw that he invited prime minister Churchill to send a delegation from the British parliament to see Buchenwald. With them came a group of United States congressmen. What they saw froze them with horror. Said one United States congressman: "This is barbarism at its worst." The members of parliament reported: "The memory of what we saw and heard will haunt us ineffaceably for many years. Such camps as this Buchenwald mark the lowest point of degradation to which humanity has yet descended."

DIVIDING THE COUNTRY

Politically as well as in other ways Germany emerged from the war in a state of utter helplessness and confusion. After the German defeat in 1918 a new government was set up almost at once, but in 1945 the situation was different. Because of President Roosevelt's insistence on unconditional surrender the armistice was followed by a complete collapse of the framework of government in Germany. Consequently the Allies had to assume supreme authority on all levels of government. The Allies quickly occupied the country and by the end of May divided it into the four zones of control. In addition the area of Greater Berlin was divided into four sectors constituting a fifth zone. On August 30 the establishment of the Allied Control Council was announced and the German people were told that this council would thenceforth be the supreme authority in Germany. The Allied Control Council, with Berlin as its seat, met on several occasions and issued important proclamations. Among these were proclamations which abolished all Nazi laws which had provided the basis of Hitler's regime.

Although the division of Germany was to be only a prelude to economic and political reunification, the demarcation lines quickly hardened into veritable frontiers. It was comparatively easy to pass from one zone to another in the zones of the western states, but passports and permits were required to cross the lines into the Russian zone and vice versa. Each zone also reflected the ideas of the power which controlled it. In all of the zones new states or provinces (Länder) were created in accordance with the Potsdam agreement to decentralize the government. Each province (Land) was permitted a certain degree of self-administration with ministries and a separate diet (Landtag). Trade unions were permitted to resume their activities and political parties were allowed to resume a restricted political life. Several old political parties reappeared very quickly. Since Nazi sympathizers, however, could not reorganize under any disguise, there were no extreme right-wing parties. Among the major parties the Christian Democratic Union (also called Christian Social Union or Christian Democrats) was one of the strongest, much of its strength being based on the vote formerly given to the Catholic Center Party and the Bavarian People's Party. Another major group was the Social Democratic Party which sponsored a program of socialism. The Communist Party was small, polling in the United States zone only about one sixth as many votes as the Social Democrats.

In their zone the Russians worked with single-mindedness and vigor to organize the government and life in general along Soviet lines. Right from the beginning they had the handicap of overcoming the ill will toward them which the conduct of the Red Army had generated. They quickly revived as many cultural activities as possible, including music and the theater, and sought in many other ways to curry favor with the German people. Big posters in the Russian zone proclaimed that " the Hitlers come and go but the German state and the German people remain." German communists, largely trained in Moscow, took over the work of molding the life of the Russian zone into a Soviet pattern. Supporting this development was the Communist Party which was numerically weak, but in 1946 a fusion of this party with the Social Democrats took place in the Russian zone. Many Social Democrats who opposed the merger were conveniently consigned to such reopened concentration camps as Buchenwald and Sachsenhausen. The first party conference of the new Socialist Unity Party (Sozialistische Einheitspartei Deutschlands or SED) was held on April 22, 1946. Elections for the local assemblies and diets took place in the fall of 1946 and resulted in the Socialist Unity Party's electing from 60 to 70 per cent of the representatives in all the provinces. The Russians had hoped that the Social Democratic Party of Germany as a whole would join at least sympathetically with the SED. In this they were disappointed.

The strategy adopted by the communists was that of trying to win over the Germans of the other zones by nationalist appeals. While accusing the Western powers of trying to prevent the unification of Germany, the SED boldly proclaimed over and over again, "We fight for Germany's unity" and "The Elbe is no boundary for our party." The communists also tried to win support by stating that it was the British and Americans and not the Russians who had bombed the German cities. But these tactics did not achieve the desired results. They failed to convince the Social Democrats of the western zones to join the SED. But the Socialist Unity Party did, by pushing into the background the international character of communism and by accentuating the nationalism which had been a part of National Socialism, succeed in enrolling many of the little Nazis in the eastern zone.

📖

PUNISHING THE NAZIS

According to the Potsdam agreement the military governments were to purge Germany of Nazis and Nazism. This denazification was carried out with varying degrees of intensity in the different zones. In the western zones a considerable number of officials were removed from office and many industrialists were removed from positions of industrial importance. More seems to have been done in this respect in the United States zone than in the others. At the end of September, 1945, General Eisenhower announced in his first report that 80,000 persons had been arrested and 70,000 removed from various positions in the United States zone. In the denazification courts attention was mainly centered on the prominent personalities. But the denazification quickly slowed down. The British and Americans soon became more interested in winning the friendship of the Germans than in punishing the Nazis. The Western Allies discovered that purging the Nazis who were industrial leaders caused a slow-down in industrial production; hence a considerable number were permitted to remain in their positions.

In the Soviet zone special emphasis was put on purging the Nazis who had been leading militarists or particular opponents of communism. Some of the Nazi industrialists who were ousted by the military governments in the western zones were given prominent positions in the Soviet zone. The small-fry Nazis were quickly forgiven and openly welcomed into the SED. Special efforts were also made to enlist former members of the Hitler youth organizations in the ranks of communist youth groups.

If most of the Nazis were pardoned, this was not the case with a small number of the top leaders of the party. When the Nazi rule collapsed, some of the top Nazi leaders went into hiding and others surrendered to the Allied commanders. No two of them stayed together and not one died in an effort to stop the Allied advance. At one of the last meetings of the Nazi leaders each one was given a glass tube filled with potassium cyanide and protected by a brass capsule. Goebbels used his to poison himself and his family in Berlin. Henlein, who had been the leader of the Sudeten Germans, died in the same way. Himmler, the leading anti-Semite, lived for some weeks in disguise, but when apprehended crushed the glass tube between his teeth and swallowed the poison. Twenty-four other leaders were indicted by the International Military Tribunal in Berlin on October 18, 1945. They were charged with (1) conspiring to commit crimes against peace; (2) committing specific crimes against peace by planning, preparing, initiating, and waging wars of aggression against a number of states; (3) committing war crimes, including murder and ill treatment, in occupied territory or on the high seas, of slave laborers and prisoners of war; killing hostages, and plundering and devastating property; (4) committing crimes against humanity, including murder, extermination, enslavement, and deportation of civilians, and political, racial, and religious persecution.

The trial, which was a landmark in international law, opened November 20, 1945, and was conducted before an inter-Allied tribunal of which Lord Justice Lawrence of Britain was chairman, the other judges being from Britain, France, Russia, and the United States. It was unfortunate indeed that at least one neutral and one German judge were not included on the tribunal. This would have convinced the world and particularly the Germans of the fairness of the trial. The trial, in which the accused were defended by German counsel, dragged on so long that the public, both in Germany and abroad, became bored with it. During the trial Robert Ley, former head of the Labor Front, committed suicide in prison. Verdicts were finally rendered at the end of August, 1946. Death sentences were imposed on twelve of the defendants, among them Hermann Goering, former head of the Luftwaffe; Joachim von Ribbentrop, Hitler's foreign minister; Wilhelm Keitel, former chief of the German High Command; Alfred Jodl, Nazi chief of staff, 1942–1945; and Arthur Seyss-Inquart, former governor of Austria and commissioner for Holland during the occupation. Martin Borman, secretary of the Nazi Party, who had not been apprehended, was condemned to death in absentia, and Hermann Goering cheated the gallows by taking poison a few hours before his scheduled execution. The ten sentences of execution were carried out on October 16, 1946. Three other defendants, including Rudolf Hess, who flew to Scotland during the war to propose peace terms, were given life sentences. Others received lesser sentences. Thus Admiral Karl Doenitz who succeeded Hitler as Fuehrer was given ten years. Both Hjalmar Schacht, former minister of economics, and Franz von Papen, former ambassador to Austria and Turkey, were acquitted, over the objections of the Russians.

REPARATIONS AND DISMANTLING

The idea of victors exacting indemnity payments from the vanquished is not new, but the manner in which the indemnities were paid has undergone innovations. At Yalta and Potsdam the Allied negotiators tried to avoid the mistake made by the Allies after World War I when they demanded impossible money tribute from Germany. This time they decided that the reparations should be paid in capital equipment instead of money. The aim of this policy was twofold: (1) to provide compensation for the equipment destroyed by the Nazi invaders; (2) to keep future German industrial production, and thus the war potential, down to a "safe" level. The latter was in harmony with the policy, publicly expressed by the Big Three after the Potsdam meeting (July, 1945), which called for the conversion of Germany from a heavy-industry state to a country of light industry and agriculture. The French, who were not represented at Potsdam, approved this policy and continued to adhere to it. They insisted that Germany must be deprived of the power to wage war, so that the invasions of the past could not be repeated. Hence the Ruhr arsenal must be taken from Germany and the productive power of German industry must be destroyed. In the United States, too, the "hard peace" policy prevailed for a time. In its most severe form it was expressed in the Morgenthau Plan, which advocated that Germany be reduced to an agrarian nation which would be powerless to wage war.

This idea continued to prevail for some months after the war, and in accordance with it the Big Four in 1946 agreed on a maximum level for Germany's industry, keyed to an annual steel production of 5.8 million tons.

The Russians approached the question of reparations with the definite intention of getting all they could. Thus they removed most of the machinery from plants in the western zones of Berlin before they turned these zones over to the western powers. The dismantling policy of the Russians in their own zone was also drastic. Many of the large industries were dismantled piece by piece and shipped to Russia. In some cases even the personnel which operated the plant was moved to the Soviet Union. How much the Russians took is not known with any degree of accuracy, since they refused to give any figures regarding the value of what they had taken. Soon, however, there was a serious drop in production in the Soviet zone, causing the Russians to slow the pace of their dismantling considerably. Instead of dismantling many plants marked for this purpose, they organized the industries into Russian limited companies, which produced for export to Russia. About 25 to 30 per cent of the industrial capacity of the zone was included in this category. Another 30 per cent of the industry in the Soviet zone was turned over to the communist-dominated state governments and reparations were extracted from current production. Such industries as remained in the hands of individual Germans were rigidly controlled. This was not particularly difficult since all allocations of raw materials and equipment were made by a central administration.

In March, 1946, it was planned that about 400 war plants should be dismantled and a few demolished as a matter of military security. In addition, about 1600 other plants not directly engaged in war production were called "surplus" and earmarked for dismantling as a curb on excess productivity. Most of the armament plants had been dismantled during the first two years of the war, but many of the "surplus" plants were still intact. Both the British and United States authorities, however, gradually slowed the dismantling pace because they realized that the "hard peace" policy which called for wholesale dismantling was serving no useful purpose and doing much harm. First, it was arousing widespread resentment among the Germans. The Germans naturally resented the dismantling of the factories which provided them with employment and also with goods for export to pay for imported food. Second, the policy of wholesale dismantling was seriously interfering with German, and therefore with West European, recovery. The Western Allies realized that a Germany held down to a low level of industry would constitute in the heart of Europe an economic slum which would depress the living standards of all European countries. Germany would be a pauperized country which would have to be supported by Britain and the United States.

To speed up German recovery the Western powers did two things. First, they raised the permitted level of steel production in West Germany to 10.7 million tons in 1947. Despite this increase the Germans still claimed that the steel capacity left to them was insufficient for Germany to become self-supporting. Second, they decided that the recovery of Europe would be furthered by not dismantling all the factories earmarked for this purpose. As early as the summer of 1946 United States authorities had declared that it was necessary to stop reparation deliveries from their zone to safeguard its economy. In June, 1947, with no prospect of Germany being treated as an economic unit, the 1946 plan was revised by the three Western Allies. The number of plants now declared surplus and available as reparations was almost halved, from 1600 to 858. It seemed ludicrous for the United States to be sending dollars into Germany at the same time that factories were being removed from that country. Finally the ECA appointed a commission to look into the matter. This commission, known as the Humphrey Commission, recommended after a careful survey that of the 381 plants it had been requested to examine 167 should be retained. The recommendation was discussed by the foreign ministers of Britain, France, and the United States at a meeting in Washington in April, 1949, and it was finally decided that of the 167 industrial plants which the Humphrey Commission recommended should be retained, 159 should be retained and only nine dismantled. The field of industries permitted to the Germans was also extended slightly. Thus, for example, the Germans were given permission to build ships up to 7200 tons instead of being limited to 1500 tons.

THE BERLIN BLOCKADE

As the months passed, the possibilities of achieving economic or political unification of Germany grew less and less. There was much talk on the part of the Russians about the restoration of German unity and the withdrawal of the occupation troops. Remembering Lenin's statement that "Who controls Germany controls Europe," the Soviet press constantly and lovingly painted the Soviet Union as the friend of the great German Reich of the future. At the same time it blatantly denounced Britain and the United States as wishing to dismember the German nation. Actually the Russians had no desire to see German unity restored without a guarantee that their ideas would prevail once they had withdrawn their troops. Each one of the great powers, in fact, envisaged a Germany rebuilt in its own image. While Russia saw Germany as a future communist state, Britain saw it as a democratic socialist state, and the United States looked ahead to a new Germany which would be a land of free enterprise. As for the French, they did not care much what kind of social and economic system was set up so long as Germany remained weak and could not again threaten invasion.

When it became clear that the Soviet Union would reject any settlement which did not concede virtual Soviet control of German economic and political life, the Western powers decided not to delay any further the measures urgently needed to end the stagnation of their occupation zones which made western Germany a heavy burden to the taxpayers of Britain and the United States. "The German stalemate," Secretary of State Acheson later stated, "heightened the general European crisis. The European recovery program could not succeed without the raw materials and finished products which only a revived German economy can contribute." The Western powers decided to coordinate and eventually to unify their zones. A step in this direction had already been taken in forming the bizonal area through an economic merger of the British and United States zones in 1947. In the spring of 1948 representatives of the three Western Allies met in London to discuss the economic merger of the French zone with the British and United States bizonal area. On June 1 it was announced that agreement had been reached on the coordination and eventual merger of the three zones. Agreements were also reached on trizonal currency reform, on an international control of the Ruhr, and on a federal constitution and government for the three western zones.

The Russian authorities immediately condemned the initiative of the Western powers in western Germany as a breach of the Potsdam and Yalta agreements. While the talks were still going on in London the Russians began to apply a series of restrictions and impediments which hampered communications between the western zones and Berlin. With only a single railway, a single auto road, and a twenty-mile-wide corridor uniting Berlin with the western zones it was within the power of the Kremlin to close the land routes at any time. And that is what the Russians did. The culmination came after the Western Allies introduced a new currency in their zones on June 18, 1948, and in the western zones of Berlin a few days later. On

June 24 the Soviet authorities, alleging "technical difficulties," stopped all railroad, auto, and barge traffic, both freight and passenger, from the western zones to Berlin. At the same time the Russian sector was cut off from the rest of the city. Power stations in the Soviet sector and Soviet zone also ceased to supply electric current to the western sectors of Berlin "because of a shortage of coal." The Kremlin was gambling on the hunger of 2,250,000 Berliners to halt the Western program of economic reform and perhaps force the Western powers out of Berlin. But the Western Allies were determined to stay in Berlin at any cost. They conceived the idea of developing a large-scale air supply system called the airlift as a means of taking supplies into Berlin. Fortunately there was an airport in the United States sector. Food, clothing, and other necessaries were loaded into large cargo planes at Frankfort and Wicsbaden and then flown into Berlin. Soon the cargo planes were landing every three minutes, day and night, at the Tempelhof Airdrome in Berlin.

The airlift was not a complete solution of the problems created by the Soviet blockade of the western zones of Berlin. To supply these zones adequately and to keep the wheels of industry turning no less than 16,000 tons of coal, food, clothing, and raw materials were required each day. The airlift moved quickly to 3,000 and gradually to 7,000 tons for a single day, but it was still a long distance from 16,000 tons. Hence the city soon began to feel the pinch. As a means of cutting down the food needs, the Western Allies evacuated 40,000 children; nevertheless, it was a winter of cold, darkness, and food shortage for those who remained in the city. A shortage of raw materials also caused industries to shut off the flow of supplies to Soviet Berlin and the Soviet zone. This counterblockade, hitting eastern Germany like a boomerang, increasingly affected the economic life of the Russian zone, which desperately needed the coal, iron, steel, and manufactures of the Ruhr and western Germany.

When the leaders of the Western Allies addressed notes to Moscow asking for an immediate end to the blockade, the Kremlin countered by demanding an assurance that they would not proceed further with the establishment of a West German government. But the worsening economic conditions gradually inclined the Russians to discuss the lifting of the blockade. A series of informal talks in the spring of 1949 resulted in an agreement between the four powers. On May 5 the following communiqué was issued:

All the restrictions imposed since March 1, 1948, by the Government of the U.S.S.R. on communications, transportation, and trade between the Eastern zone and the Western zones will be removed on May 12, 1949.

All the restrictions imposed since March 1, 1948, by the Governments of France, the United Kingdom, and the United States, or any one of them, on communications, transportation, and trade between the Western and Eastern zones of Germany will also be removed on May 12, 1949.

Thus after a blockade of 320 days during which "Operation Vittles" had moved 1,592,787 tons of supplies into western Berlin, the blockade came to an end. The Soviet government had lost a desperate effort to dislodge the Western Allies. The airlift still continued until 200,000 tons had been stockpiled in the western zones of the city. With planes, trucks, and freight cars bringing in supplies the food shops were soon bulging. Prices dropped sharply, in some cases by half, enabling the average consumer to restock his larder.

&

THE WEST GERMAN REPUBLIC

While the blockade was in effect, the foreign ministers of Britain, France, and the United States met in Washington to discuss the whole range of issues relating to Germany. A communiqué released on April 8, 1949, stated that complete agreement had been reached on the establishment of a German Federal Republic in which "the German Federal State and the participating Länder [states] will have full legislative, executive, and judicial powers, in accordance with the Basic Law and with their respective constitutions." A constitutional convention, engaged in the task of drawing up the Basic Law (Grundgesetz) or constitution, had been in session in the city of Bonn since September 1, 1948. "With the establishment of the German Federal Republic," the communiqué stated, "there will be a marked change in the organization to carry out occupation responsibilities. Military Government as such will be terminated, and the functions of the Allied authorities will become mainly supervisory. Each of the Allied establishments in Germany will come under the direction of a High Commissioner, aside from the occupation forces which will remain headed by military commanders. The Three High Commissioners together will constitute an Allied High Commission, which will be the supreme Allied agency of control."

The freedom of action of the new state was, however, still limited. According to the communiqué, there would be "certain limited fields in which the Allies will reserve the right to take direct action themselves or to direct authorities to take action." The powers retained by the occupation authorities were defined in the Occupation Statute. The fields in which the Allied powers retained authority included the following: (1) disarmament and demilitarization; (2) the Ruhr, reparations, and decartelization; (3) foreign affairs, including international agreements made by or on behalf of Germany; (4) displaced persons and admission of refugees; (5) protection, prestige, and security of Allied forces, dependents, employees, and their representatives; (6) respect for the Basic Law and the state constitutions; (7) control over foreign trade and exchange.

Control over internal action was to be limited to the minimum necessary "to ensure use of funds, food, and other supplies in such manner as to reduce to a minimum the need for external assistance to Germany." In general, the three occupation powers expressed the desire and intention that "the German people shall enjoy self-government to the maximum possible degree consistent with such occupation." Special care was taken to prevent a resurgence of German militarism by providing for a Military Security Board with powers of inspection to insure against both military and industrial rearmament.

The Basic Law (or constitution) of the German Federal Republic was adopted by the Parliamentary Council [1] on May 8, approved by the High Commissioners on May 12, 1949. The Basic Law is closely modeled on the Weimar Constitution. It provides for a federal president, chosen for a term of five years, and for two legislative chambers, the Bundestag or lower house, elected by universal suffrage for a period of four years, and the Bundesrat or upper house representing and appointed by the governments of the states. The constitution also provides for a federal chancellor (prime minister) who is elected by the lower house. The city of Bonn was chosen as the capital of the new government. Elections for the lower house took place in August, 1949, after a vigorous political campaign. The voting gave the combined Christian Democratic Union, which stood for a liberal economy, and the Christian Social Union a small but decisive lead over the Social Democrats advocating a controlled economy. Of 402 deputies returned the former gained 139, while the Social Democrats returned 131. Ten parties received representation in the new parliament, with the communists holding only fifteen seats. Dr. Konrad Adenauer, the leader of the Christian Democratic Union, was elected chancellor by a very small margin and proceeded to form a right wing coalition. Hence the Social Democrats formed the opposition.

Dr. Adenauer formed his government on September 20 and the next day the military government was dissolved, the occupation stat-

[1] Since the constitution was called "Basic Law" because it was merely intended for a period of transition, the convention could not be called "constitutional convention."

ute came into force, and the Allied High Commission became the
final authority in western Germany. The new government immediately petitioned the High Commissioners to desist from further dismantling of plants vital for German productivity. Upon receiving
definite assurance regarding disarmament from the Federal Government, the Allied powers agreed to remove a further number of industrial plants from the dismantling list. The plants that were spared
included steel, synthetic oil, and rubber works. Permission was also
given the new government to reestablish to a limited extent German consular and commercial relations abroad. A bureau was opened
in Bonn to direct these activities. This bureau was the first em-
bryonic foreign ministry of the Bonn government.

6.

SOVIET EAST GERMANY

Meanwhile the Russians had gradually been preparing the way
for the establishment of a new government in their zone. A draft constitution had already been prepared in the autumn of 1948 by the
People's Council (Volksrat), a hand-picked body, chosen largely by
the Social Unity Party (SED) from the trade unions, youth associations, and other communist-dominated organizations. On May 15–
16, 1949, an election of delegates for a People's Congress was held.
One correspondent wrote an interesting brief account of the election:

> The elections were staged by the communist-run Socialist Unity Party
> (SED) on the single-ballot totalitarian basis. To make doubly sure, the
> Communists ruled that unmarked ballots, those bearing written com-
> ments, or those entirely crossed out were to be counted as "Ja" votes.
> If a voter wrote "Nein" instead of marking the circle for the "Nein" vote,
> it was also to be counted as a "Ja" vote, because it was a double negative.
> Voting booths were inclosed on only three sides and were low enough so
> that anyone could peer over the top. The Communists had promised
> hour by hour results. But not until twenty hours after the polls closed
> did they reveal that 33.9 per cent of the 12,887,234 votes cast were
> "Nein." [2]

Of the 2,215 delegates put up for election on the single-candidate
ballots, 893 were Communists, 386 represented Communist-front organizations, and 373 were hand-picked "nonpartisan" fellow trav-
elers. The rest were chosen from tolerated minority opposition
groups in order to give the election some semblance of being free
and democratic. This congress, which had been elected for the purpose of supporting Mr. Vishinsky's demands for a unified Germany

2 *Newsweek*, vol. 33 (May 30, 1949), p. 24.

at the Paris Council of Foreign Ministers, approved the constitution, but nothing further was done for the time being.

Desiring to put the blame for the division of Germany on the Western states, the communist leaders postponed the announcement of the new state until after the Western powers had made the decision to accord a future West German regime a large degree of self-government. On October 1, 1949, the Soviet Union sent identical notes to the three Western powers protesting the formation of the West German Republic. "The Soviet Government," the note read in part, "considers it necessary to state, inasmuch as there has been formed at Bonn a separate government as indicated, a new situation has been created in Germany at the present time which renders of particularly great importance the fulfillment of the tasks for the restoration of the unity of Germany as a democratic peace-loving state." On October 7 the Soviet-sponsored people's chamber then proceeded to declare the constitution in force. At the same time the Soviet authorities announced the transfer of administrative functions theretofore exercised by the Soviet Military Administration (SMA) to the people's chamber, with the final authority vested in the Soviet Control Commission.

In its main features the new constitution resembled the constitutions which had been introduced in the Cominform countries. It provided for a parliament of two chambers, a Volkskammer (people's chamber) of 400 deputies elected by the voters and a Länderkammer (states' chamber) representing the states.[3] It also contained provisions for freedom of speech, the press, and public meeting, and it recognized private property. The provisions which promised democracy and freedom were, however, limited and conditioned by other provisions. The "freedoms" can be enjoyed only if they are exercised in the interest of "the people" or, in other words, in the interest of the communist totalitarian regime.

Herr Wilhelm Pieck, an old-time Comintern agent aged seventy-three, was elected president of the Soviet-sponsored state by unanimous vote of the states' chamber and people's chamber. In his acceptance speech the new president accented the German nationalism the Russians were sponsoring. "Never," he said, "shall the partitioning of Germany, the permanence of military occupation of western Germany by the occupation statute, the severing of the Ruhr district from the German economic body be recognized by the German Democratic Republic." The German people, he continued, must not

---

[3] The Soviet zone embraced five states: Thuringia, Saxony, Brandenburg, Pomerania, and Mecklenburg, with a total population of about seventeen millions.

rest "until the unity of Germany is restored and all the territories
are recovered." In enumerating the territories to be recovered he
carefully avoided mention of the almost 40,000 square miles of German territory extending to the Oder and Neisse Rivers which the
Poles had occupied. Herr Otto Grotewohl, the chancellor or prime
minister of the new state, also sang to Soviet accompaniment when
he stated: "Friendship with the Soviet Union is a prerequisite not
only for our future development, but even for the national existence
of the German people and state." Stalin himself hailed the establishment of the Soviet puppet state in eastern Germany as "a turning
point in the history of Europe."

THE QUESTION OF GERMAN UNITY

On March 10, 1952, the Russians delivered a note to the United
States, Britain, and France containing a proposal for German unity.
It arrived at a time when the Soviet Union was facing the disagree-
able fact of the integration of West Germany into the North Atlantic
Treaty Organization. Negotiations were being carried on toward im-
plementing the agreements reached at the Lisbon conference of
NATO for the restoration of West German sovereignty and the inclusion of German troops in a European army. Such a move on the
part of the Soviet Union was not wholly unexpected. It was widely
believed in diplomatic circles that the Kremlin would not permit the
integration of West Germany in NATO without at least trying to
prevent it. The note suggested that the Big Four meet without delay
to discuss the question of the peace treaty with Germany and to take
immediate measures for the unification of Germany and the formation of an all-German government. The note further suggested that
free all-German elections be conducted to establish a new all-German regime and that no limitations be placed on the national economy of Germany. The new Germany would also be permitted armed
forces for self-defense with a limited war economy. The frontiers of
the new state would be determined in accordance with the Potsdam
agreements of 1945. In return unified Germany must obligate herself "not to enter any kind of coalition or military alliance directed
against any power which has taken part with armed forces in the war
against Germany."

Two schools of thought regarding the Soviet note quickly developed. The first school supported the view that the offer was merely
a propaganda move to keep West Germany out of NATO. Secretary
of State Acheson called the issuance of the note the "golden apple

tactic," in reference to the mythological story of the goddess of discord who, not having been invited to a wedding, threw a golden apple over the fence to create dissension among the guests. "Germany," Acheson said, "can be united and free as a full member of the free community of Europe. But a united Germany cut off from defense with and by the West could not be a free Germany. The German people have only to look across the curtain at their brothers in East Germany to see what the Soviet Union means by freedom." A number of Western statesmen expressed grave reservations about permitting a unified and independent Germany to arm itself. They regarded such a move as a step in the wrong direction. Having German divisions as part of a European army was one thing, but an independent German army was something else.

The second school believed that the Soviet offer might be genuine and that even if it was not "the Western powers can hardly afford to dismiss it out of hand." The supporters of this school argued that the Russians might be willing to surrender their hold on East Germany in return for a unified Germany outside of the Western defense system. "We must not consider the Russian note simply an instrument of propaganda," said France's Robert Schuman; "it may mark a change of Russian policy toward Germany." The lure of the Soviet siren was at first strong in Germany, for few Germans want to see an iron curtain slammed down permanently across their country. August Euler, leader of the Free Democrats of West Germany, said: "For the first time the Soviet has come up with a proposal worth discussing." Jacob Kaiser, a member of the Adenauer cabinet, stated: "Germany and the West must consider whether or not a turning point has been reached." But Chancellor Adenauer himself was not swayed by the note. He still adhered to his determination to align West Germany with the Atlantic alliance, even though this did mean a postponement of German unification.

The Western Allies joined in drafting identical replies to the Kremlin. In doing so they were careful not to close the door to further negotiations. With so much at stake they decided to probe all possibilities. They did, however, assert in moderate tones that if the Russians were sincere they would permit a UN commission to enter the Soviet zone of Germany for the purpose of determining whether free elections could be held there. The reply also raised the question as to whether Germany would be free to conduct its own foreign policy and participate in European agencies like the Schuman Plan. Finally the note suggested that Russia was invoking the Potsdam agreement because it wishes Poland to keep the German territory east of the Oder-Neisse Rivers. In answer Soviet Foreign Minister Vishinsky telegraphed that the Soviet Union would consent to four-power supervision of Soviet zone elections, but not to UN supervision. Four-power supervision would give the Soviet Union a powerful veto.

As the weeks passed the nations of Western Europe began somewhat reluctantly to share the opinion that what was first described as a Soviet "peace offensive" was only a new attempt to sow discord among the NATO countries, that the latest diplomatic moves of the Kremlin were really efforts to disrupt rather than further the cause of peace. A *New York Times* correspondent reported from Europe at the end of March, 1952: "The suspicion is now growing, stimulated by both public and private debate, that Moscow is not only seeking merely to forestall or wreck Western rearmament by a clever verbal offensive, but is trying to create a situation in Germany favorable to future Soviet-German rapprochements like those of Rapallo and the Stalin-Hitler pact of 1939."

Meanwhile the Western powers had continued their efforts to integrate West Germany into the North Atlantic Alliance. A major step was taken in this direction on May 26, 1952, when the foreign ministers of the United States, Britain, and France, and the chancellor of West Germany, signed a "peace contract," which included the West German republic "in the community of free nations as an equal partner." This "contract" voided the Occupation Statute and abolished the Allied High Commission. It further specified that relations between the signatory powers would thenceforth be conducted through ambassadors and that foreign military forces stationed in West Germany were no longer occupation forces. "The Federal Republic," the peace contract states, "released from all control, will thus be able on its own responsibility to develop its democratic and federal institutions within the framework of its basic law." The conclusion of the peace contract did not mean, however, that all foreign troops were to be removed at once from West Germany. The Western allies reserved the right to maintain troops in West Germany for the purpose of defending the freedom of the new state, but promised to withdraw the troops as soon as the necessity of defending West German freedom no longer existed.

Socialist Britain

BRITAIN'S PLIGHT

IN TERMS of human life and human suffering other nations may have paid a greater price, but as regards national effort and the expenditure of national wealth Britain was second to none. Although a victor nation, the British emerged from the war utterly exhausted. Moreover, they faced the vast problems of propping up a crumbling empire, of converting their economy from war to peace, and of repairing the physical damages caused by German bombs. Enemy action had damaged nearly four million houses, of which several hundred thousand had been more or less destroyed. The bombings had also done extensive damage to business buildings throughout London, in Coventry, Birmingham and other midland cities, and in other parts of Britain. Clearing away the rubble of business buildings and factories and repairing and rebuilding these structures was quickly achieved. The reconstruction of dwelling houses took place much more slowly and there was a real and pressing shortage of housing. But the problem also had its bright side. Because of the poor structural quality of slum houses a large percentage of the buildings which had been knocked down by the blast of bombs were houses which should have been demolished years before. Thus the destruction provided the opportunity to rebuild communities according to modern planning principles. In town after town city planners were called in to work out long-term plans for city development.

The big question for the British at the termination of hostilities was "How can Britain pay for essential imports of food and raw materials?" Imports are not a matter of choice, but of necessity. Britain by herself can neither feed her population of about 48 millions, nor can she supply her industries with the necessary raw materials; in fact, she has not been self-sufficient since the beginning of the nineteenth century when her total population was about 12 millions. On the eve of World War II, 75 per cent of her wheat, 55 per cent of her meat, 75 per cent of her sugar, and 85 per cent of her butter came from abroad. Cocoa, coffee, and tea were entirely imported. With the exception of coal, the availability of raw materials for British industry is largely a question of imports. All the cotton, rubber, and practically all the petroleum as well as most of the timber, five sixths of the wool, and two thirds of the iron ore had to be imported from other countries. At the end of the war Britain needed essential imports in even larger quantities. The plight in which the British found themselves was that they had no money with which they could pay for these imports.

Britain's plight was not wholly the result of the war. Long before Hitler invaded Poland signs of decline were evident in Britain's economy. By 1938 Britain was annually spending £40 million more for imports than she received as income from abroad. But the war did hasten this decline. Before the war Britain was still able to maintain a standard of living that was slightly higher than that of most European countries because the country was able to pay for the things it needed—food and raw materials—and the things it wanted—tobacco and movies. The income which the British used for this purpose was derived from three sources: (1) from extensive foreign investments; (2) from the merchant marine; (3) from the sale of exports. But the war greatly reduced all of these sources of income, practically exhausting two of them. To pay for the extensive imports needed during the war the British were forced to liquidate their overseas investments. When the war ended, the British, instead of investments, had a staggering debt. From being the world's greatest creditor nation Britain had become a debtor nation. The income from the merchant marine, too, had largely disappeared. About half of the British shipping fleet was sunk during the war and much of the British carrying trade was absorbed by other countries.

Consequently there remained only the export trade as a means of acquiring sufficient income to pay for the necessary imports of food and raw materials. But the value of products being exported was far too small to pay for the imports. During the war, while the British were concentrating on arms production, the output for export had declined greatly. Foreign competitors had made the most of the opportunity to preempt the overseas markets which previously had been outlets for British goods. The loosening of the imperial ties had also caused the British to lose markets. Each time a piece, as, for example, India or Burma, was lifted out of the empire, another blow was dealt to the economic stability of Britain. Such losses were incredibly painful at the end of a war in which Britain had given everything she had. But even if Britain had retained the prewar standards of export, the income would not have been sufficient to pay for the imports. It was officially estimated that in order to reach the standards of prewar life, when one third of the nation was underprivileged, the rate of production would have to be increased to three and a half times the level to which it had been permitted to fall during the war. To achieve a higher standard Britain would have to produce still more. In short, the urgent need of the British was to produce more goods for export at a price which would enable British concerns to meet foreign competition.

A number of formidable obstacles stood in the way of attaining this goal. The two principal ones were low productivity per man-hour and obsolete methods of production. The output per man-hour varied, of course, in different industries, but in general it was much lower than in a number of other countries, particularly in the United States. The report of the British Cotton Textile Mission to the United States (April, 1944) shows that the output per man-hour in British mills was from 30 to 40 per cent less than in United States mills. Another report on the manufacture of boots and shoes shows that the output per man-hour in British factories was about one half that in the United States. This low output was in large part due to the use of obsolete machinery and adherence to antiquated methods of production. What had originally made Britain the "workshop of the world" was the realization that machinery could outproduce handicrafts. But the British carried the idea only to a certain point. They appear to have overlooked the significance of the fact that improved machinery outproduces obsolete machinery. While other nations, in order to achieve higher productivity, were ready to discard old methods and old equipment even though the latter was not worn out, the British were reluctant to scrap their obsolete machinery and to modernize their methods. Thus the machine which originally had given Britain industrial supremacy had become an industrial handicap. Low output per man-hour combined with antiquated methods of production resulted in high prices, making it difficult for the British to compete with more progressive nations.

One of the most acute problems of the British economy was in the coal industry. This industry had been sick for decades and seemed to be getting worse in 1945. Orginally the British mine owners, with a view to speeding royalty returns, had leased small tracts to a large number of coal-digging companies. The result was many small mines in which modern techniques could not be employed. Moreover, from long working the shafts had become deep and many of the remaining coal seams were thin. Because the wages were poor and the working conditions bad the working force had gradually thinned out. Those who remained were mostly worn out from hard labor and too old to seek other employment. The sons of the old miners were not attracted to the mines. In 1943 Lord Londonderry, chairman of the Londonderry Collieries, naïvely told parliament that "these young men, unlike their forefathers, are not keen to go down the pits. I do not know the reason." The low wages and bad working conditions had not only caused the younger men to turn to other employment; it had also embittered the older ones, so that they hated the mines and their owners. The operators, for their part, manifested a complete lack of sympathy with or understanding of the miners' problems.

Since the operators either could not or would not introduce modern equipment and techniques, obsolete methods continued in many mines. Improved methods were introduced into some of the mines in the years before 1939, and during the war the British mines made further progress in mechanization, but what was done was only a small percentage of what was needed. The British coal industry as a whole lagged far behind the coal industries of a number of other countries. In 1913 the British miner still produced more than the German and Dutch miner. While the British miner produced 1.016 tons per man-shift, the miner in the Ruhr produced only 0.93 and in the Netherlands only 0.807. By 1938, however, both had outstripped the British miner. Whereas by this year the output of the British miner had increased only to 1.148, the Ruhr miner's had risen to 1.523 and the Dutch miner's to 1.619. In 1938 an Englishman wrote: "The real bounty to German coal exports is that German miners turn out 40 per cent more coal per man at 25 per cent less cost than the British miner."

Such facts and figures explain the long-range decline of the British coal industry. In 1913 the industry produced 287 million tons, of which 97 million were exported. Production in 1929 was 258 million tons, of which 77 million tons were exported. By 1938 production had declined to 227 million tons and exports to 46 million. In 1945 the total output was down to 182 million tons and exports to eight million. In other words, exports in 1945 were only one twelfth of the exports in 1913. Not only was the output small but the price was high. Since the price of coal is a major factor in determining the price of most manufactured products in Britain, the coal situation was a fundamental measure of Britain's inability to compete in world markets.

The coal industry was not unique. The same backwardness and inefficiency was to be found elsewhere. Cotton manufacturing, for example, had been for many years just as sick as the coal industry. Between 1900 and 1937 there was little increase in the productivity of labor in the cotton industry. Too little attention was paid to measuring the efficiency of both labor and machinery. The steel industry, too, needed drastic overhauling and modernization. Although the industry suffered from antiquated machinery and obsolete methods, the private owners did little to correct these conditions. A considerable sum had been spent on the modernization of the steel industry in the years preceding World War II, but it had hardly made a dent.

THE LABOR GOVERNMENT AND ITS PROGRAM

The task of finding cures for the many ills afflicting the economic and social life of Britain fell to the Labor government which rose to power in July, 1945. After an existence of nine years and almost seven months, the fourth longest in British history, the parliament which had guided the destinies of the country during the war was dissolved in June, 1945, and new elections were held July 5. It was widely believed that the Conservatives would lose a number of seats to the Labor Party, but even the Laborites themselves did not expect so complete a victory. When the results of the elections were announced on July 25, it was found that the Labor Party had, at the expense of all other parties, gained more than 200 seats. The Conservatives had lost over 150, while the Liberal Party obtained only eleven seats against the eighteen they had previously held. The Labor Party had never before captured as much as 30 per cent of the votes, but in 1945 it won nearly 50 per cent of all the votes cast. The distribution of seats in the new House of Commons was Labor 394, Conservatives 216, Liberals 11.

Various factors appear to have contributed to the Labor victory. Although Churchill was admired by all Britons irrespective of party as a great war leader, he was unable to convince the people to place their fate in his hands during peacetime. The British voters turned out to cheer the man who had led them through the dark days of the war, but cast their votes for the Labor Party. Churchill, it appears, failed to convince the voters that the Conservative Party behind him had any serious intentions of carrying out the large-scale program of social reforms he announced. They preferred to stake their future on the Labor Party, which asserted that it could provide a better life for the majority of Englishmen with its program of reform on socialist lines. The promises of the Labor Party attracted many voters of the middle and lower-middle standard of living in suburban and rural areas. When these were added to the solid core of supporters in the urban areas and the coalmining districts, the consequence was an overwhelming victory for the Labor Party.

How did the Labor Party propose to achieve the task of modernizing industrial equipment and increasing output enough to bridge the deficit of dollars? The solution offered prescribed, first of all, a program of austerity. The British were asked to reduce the volume of food imports by cutting down the consumption of food. A rationing system was set up which strictly limited the quantity of meat, butter, and other food each person was entitled to purchase. There was, of course, nothing new in this. It was merely a continuation of the rationing system that had been introduced during the war. Efforts were also made to increase the production of food. Farmers were asked to sow as much grain as possible so as to make the maximum contribution to the nation's granary. Furthermore, a long-term program for the development of agriculture was drawn up for the purpose of reducing to a minimum the national dependence on imported food. In the plans to increase the production of food, provisions were also made for the expansion of the fishing industry, particularly the whale fisheries which contribute considerable quantities of fats to the British food supply.

But the Laborites realized that the curtailment of food imports and the limited expansion of food production alone would not bridge the gap. The second, and major, item in the program of the Labor Party was the nationalization of key industries. Since private enterprise had fallen down badly and had failed to effect much improvement, the Laborites insisted, nationalization or state ownership was absolutely necessary to achieve the required efficiency. They hoped to achieve through state-owned and managed monopolies the productive efficiency which in the United States was developed by competitive private enterprise. The program, however, did not call for the complete nationalization of the means of production and distribution. Eighty per cent of the industries were to remain in the hands of private enterprise. But the 20 per cent slated for nationalization included the key industries like coal, steel, transportation, and communication. The change from private to public ownership was to be not abrupt, but gradual. Moreover, it was not to be confiscatory. The owners of the industries were to be compensated. Private industry was not, however, to be completely free to do as it pleased. A development plan was projected for the 80 per cent of the industry that was left in private hands, so that its operations would conform with the plans of the central planning organization.

The first nationalization bill was laid before parliament in October, 1945. It contained provisions for ending the 261-year career of the Bank of England as a private enterprise. Public ownership of this bank had long been a cherished tenet of the Labor Party's creed. With a Labor government in power it was regarded as a necessity, so that the government could make certain that new capital could be raised for schemes to which it gave top priority. The control of credit facilities by the government was particularly necessary since the demand for capital was in excess of the supply. The bill which became law on February 14, 1946, was eminently fair in its treatment of shareholders. It provided for the issuance of government stock in exchange for that held by the 17,000 shareholders, with a guarantee, for the next twenty years, of the same income as the shareholders had received during the previous twenty-two years.

The first major industry to be nationalized was the coal industry. Government ownership of the coal mines had been one of the major planks in the election program of the Labor Party. At the second reading of the coal nationalization bill the Minister of Fuel maintained that the coal industry could be restored to a state of efficiency only through state ownership, since many of the private interests refused to do anything. Another argument put forward was that the modernization of the industry required an outlay of capital which was beyond the means of most private owners. The bill, which became law on July 12, 1946, provided for a nine-member National Coal Board with full power over the mining and distribution of coal. On August 1, 1946, the Arbitration Tribunal, which had been set up to determine how and how much the former owners of the coal mines were to be paid, fixed the sum at $667 million, to be paid in government stock. Before the end of 1946 the National Coal Board announced that a five-day week would be introduced in the industry May 1, 1947.

During the months after the nationalization of the coal industry further progress was made in carrying out the program of nationalization. Before the middle of 1947 the cable and wireless communication services, civil aviation, the electrical supply, and the gas industry were brought under public ownership. The most controversial measure was the bill which provided for the nationalization of the country's inland transportation. After a lively battle between the Labor Party and its opponents the bill was finally passed in the summer of 1947, and January 1, 1948, was set as the date of acquisition. Thus the nation's railways, ports, truck lines, and bus lines were put under public ownership. The price to be paid the former owners was set at somewhat more than $4 billion. The task of administering British transportation was vested in the British Transport Commission. After some discussion the much disputed nationalization of iron and steel was postponed because the government itself believed that action in 1947 would disturb the national economy.

The Labor government also introduced many changes in the field of social service. Under the National Insurance Act, which was passed in August, 1946, every British citizen was given social security "from the cradle to the grave." The funds for this purpose are contributed by employers, employees, and the state. Probably the most widely discussed measure was the National Health Service Act which became law in November, 1946. By its provisions medical and dental care became available without charge to anyone who desired them. For this purpose health centers or clinics were established throughout Britain at public expense. The local councils which were in charge of these centers then invited all physicians, surgeons, and dentists in the vicinity to register for service. As payment for their services they were to receive part salary and part capitation fees. They also retained the liberty to carry on private practices outside the health centers.

ECONOMIC PROGRESS IN BRITAIN

The passing of legislation to nationalize the key industries did not at once bridge the gap between imports and exports; in fact, the Laborites themselves did not expect to achieve this goal until 1951. To tide the government over until it could achieve a balance of payments in its foreign trade, dollar credit was needed. Negotiations were at once opened for a loan from the United States, and on December 7, 1945, an agreement was signed for a loan of $3.75 billion. In some respects the recovery of British exports which followed was remarkable. By the end of 1946 the volume of exports had reached and slightly exceeded the prewar level. The advance was most marked in the field of chemicals and nonferrous metals. Thus in the second quarter of 1946 the volume of exports of electrical goods was 160 per cent above the 1938 level. Exports of nonferrous metals and goods manufactured from them in general were 217 per cent above the 1938 level. But some very serious weaknesses also manifested themselves. At the end of 1946 the volume of exports of cotton goods was only 41 per cent, and the export of coal only 13 per cent, of the 1938 level. Even at home there was a serious coal shortage. During the early months of 1947 coal production was insufficient to supply the generating capacity of Britain. Consequently electricity for industry was cut off in February, 1947, causing about two thirds of the British plants to close. Unemployment reached about two and a half millions and exports to the value of over £200 million were lost.

Before the end of 1947 the upward trend was resumed again, and by December, 1948, the volume of exports rose to about 150 per cent of the prewar level, bringing it near to the level (175 per cent of prewar) regarded as sufficient to support prewar living standards. Industrial production as a whole in 1948 was 21 per cent above the level of 1946. The improvement, however, was still not sufficient to adjust the balance between imports and exports. Before the balance could be achieved a reversal, caused by a drop in exports, set in during the second quarter of 1949. A number of countries, and particularly the United States, reduced their purchases of British goods considerably. In June, for example, sales to the United States were less than three fifths of the monthy average for the first months of the year. British policy makers vainly turned to measures like currency restrictions, reduced import quotas, and foreign loans. When the gold and dollar reserves continued to dwindle, the government finally decided to devaluate the pound. In September, 1949, it was reduced in value from $4.03 to $2.80 or 30.5 per cent.

The devaluation of the pound compelled the British consumer to pay more for his bread, but by indirectly reducing export prices it did stimulate foreign trade. The most striking result was that the dollar deficit was reduced to $31 million in the last quarter of 1949, and the first quarter of 1950 showed an earned surplus. Gold and dollar resources climbed from a postwar low of $1,688 million in 1949 to $3,300 million in 1950. The situation looked so promising that Marshall Plan aid was discontinued at the end of 1950. But the Korean war, in giving rise to a vast rearmament program, undid much of the progress. While the price of raw materials rose sharply the price of exports had risen only 18 per cent. Moreover, the rearmament program absorbed many raw materials which had previously been used to manufacture exports. As a result the trade deficit in the first four months of 1951 was two and a half times as large as it had been in the same period of the previous year. In a drive to narrow the gap between imports and exports the British were asked to tighten their belts another notch, dollar imports were curtailed, price controls were tightened, and efforts were made to increase production for export. All this contributed but little toward establishing a balance between imports and exports. On the other hand, the British also failed to achieve the rearmament goals they had set.

Meanwhile the Labor government had taken a further step in the nationalization plan by nationalizing the steel industry. This industry had been one of the most efficient of the British industries. During the years after the war considerable progress had been made in modernizing it, but much still remained to be done. The act to nationalize steel, the first manufacturing industry to be put under state ownership, was passed in November, 1949, but the transfer date was not set. Nothing further was done until the government announced its intention in September, 1950, to proceed with the nationalization over the strenuous objection of the opposition led by Mr. Churchill. When a vote was taken, the government won by the slim margin of 306 to 300. It was the highest opposition vote recorded in the House since 1924. After the vote supported its plan, the government announced that the transfer of the ninety-two iron and steel companies to the Iron and Steel Corporation set up by the government would take place in February, 1951. According to the government plan, the individual companies were not to be dissolved, as had been the case in the nationalization of transport, electricity, and gas. Operation of the old companies was continued under the Iron and Steel Corporation. All stock was to be transferred to the corporation at prices fixed by the government.

THE RETURN OF THE CONSERVATIVES

By the fall of 1951 Labor had ruled Britain for more than six years and during the last months had remained in power by the slim margin of half a dozen votes. Not in a century had Parliament been so evenly divided. The margin held by the Laborites was not sufficient to give it security of tenure or the power necessary to put its program into effect. It was a situation which led prime minister Attlee to seek a new mandate. The campaign which preceded the election was by all accounts a drab one, but on election day (October 25) about 82 per cent—a very high percentage—of the electorate voted. The result was a victory for the Conservatives. The victory, however, was anything but a landslide. The Conservatives won 321 seats in the

House of Commons against 295 for Labor. As regards the popular vote the Conservatives polled slightly less than the Laborites. While the former received the support of 48.0 per cent of the voters, the Laborites polled 48.7 per cent. The nearly fourteen million votes the latter won was the largest number any party has received in the history of Britain. The explanation for the discrepancy is that in many districts the Laborites piled up huge majorities, while the Tory vote was better distributed. The key to the victory is the fact that the Liberals voted for Conservative candidates. Thus the parliament of 1951, like the preceding one, was divided almost equally between two parties.

Mr. Churchill and his party were disappointed over the closeness of the results. They had hoped for a margin of at least fifty seats. It was generally agreed that a majority of at least thirty seats was necessary for a government to carry out its program. This did not, however, discourage Winston Churchill who, nearing 77, was requested by King George to form a new government. In the new cabinet Anthony Eden was made foreign secretary and leader of the House of Commons, Richard Austen Butler became chancellor of the exchequer, and Gwilym Lloyd-George, son of the famous Welsh prime minister, was chosen as minister of food.

For a brief moment there was hope that the Churchill government, in some magic way, would usher in better times and a more abundant life. But the same conditions which had caused one economic crisis after another still prevailed. In addition, the government had the problem of rearming. Lacking the funds to make drastic changes, the Churchill government had no choice but to continue the existing controls and even tighten some of them. One of the first things it did was to curtail food imports. This meant the disappearance of most canned foods, including meat, which had filled out the meager British rations. A correspondent reported to the *New York Times* (January 5, 1952):

For those with money enough to dine in the better restaurants two or three times a week, the austerity of the diet can be relieved, for there is plenty of game and poultry to be had at staggering prices. Turkey, for instance, sells for more than seven shillings (ninety-eight cents) a pound. On the other hand, rationed foods are, thanks to the subsidy at the taxpayers' expense, extraordinarily cheap. But the catch is that the meat ration provides only about one meal a week in most families. The holder of each ration book is able to buy one shilling and five pence (twenty cents) worth of meat a week. That sum will buy two small lamb chops or about half a pound of stew beef. Meat is rationed according to price.

Eggs are distributed when they are available. Recently holders of ration books have been getting less than one egg a week.

In general, the new regime did not advocate any startling changes either in domestic or foreign policy. The welfare state of the Laborites was to remain intact, the industries that had been nationalized were to continue under public ownership, and the various controls were to continue during the crisis brought on by rearmament. The only major change that was being considered was the "denationalization" of steel. In his first move to cut government expenditure Churchill reduced his annual salary from $28,000 to $19,000 and ordered the cabinet salaries cut from $14,000 to $9,200. He further directed that in the future government cars be used only for government business. Dramatic though these moves may have been, they effected only a small saving. More drastic measures were necessary to solve Britain's problems.

In his speech to the country on December 22, 1951, Mr. Churchill disabused the British people beforehand of any undue expectations. In a cheerless message he promised them only further hardships. He told his audience that upon taking office he found the country "on the verge of insolvency." The bottom of the barrel, he said, had been scraped. "Our meat stocks were lower than they have ever been since the crunch of war and the U-boats." Britain, he continued, fell short by £500 million of paying for its imports in 1951. In October alone the British gold resources had decreased by more than £300 million. Hard measures, he said, were necessary to stop the drift toward ruin. "I am telling you beforehand it's uphill all the way. . . . You must not expect the Americans to solve our domestic problems for us."

Winston Churchill's policy of drastic economies as a means of putting Britain's listing economy back on an even keel did achieve some results. In February, 1952, the British Board of Trade announced that in the preceding month Britain's exports had achieved an all-time record of $700 billion. This slashed the adverse balance of trade by 15 per cent. Imports were estimated to have been in the vicinity of $1 billion or about the same as the monthly average of the second half of 1951. Because of higher prices, however, the volume of imports was smaller. The improvement notwithstanding, the deficit of exports over imports as a result of the month's trading was still about $300 million. On May 3, 1952, prime minister Churchill told the British people in a radio broadcast that confidence in the pound sterling was growing and that if all went well Britain should be paying her own way by the end of the year. The task of pruning the socialism that had been grafted on to the British economy, he said, was not a simple one; nor could it be done quickly. He also stated that the bill to restore the nationalized iron and steel industry to private ownership had been drafted and that it would be presented to parliament before the end of 1952.

§

THE KING IS DEAD! LONG LIVE THE QUEEN!

On the morning of February 6, 1952, Britain and the world were shocked and saddened by the announcement of the death of George VI. Some months earlier the king had undergone an operation for the removal of a cancerous lung, but appeared to be making a recovery. He had spent the last day of his life at his favorite pastime, hunting, and had planned to spend the next day in the same way. Born in 1895, second son of George V, he had neither wanted the throne nor expected to occupy it. As a youth he showed no special gifts or promise. His health was wretched, he stammered, and was shy and retiring. In the naval examinations which he took in 1913 he ranked 64th in a class of 65. He served in the navy during the early part of World War I and later became an airplane pilot on the western front. In 1923 he married Lady Elizabeth Bowes Lyon, the first commoner to become queen of England since Katherine Parr, the sixth wife of Henry VIII. A chain of unforeseen circumstances elevated George to the throne in 1936 when his brother Edward VIII abdicated to marry Mrs. Simpson.

George VI succeeded his brother at a time when the prestige and authority of the throne were seriously diminished. But he soon won the hearts of his people. Regarding himself as "a very ordinary person," he endeared himself to the British people by his devotion to his royal role, his fairness, and his rectitude. He exhausted himself by faithful performance of the tedious ceremonial rounds. He was, however, keenly aware of the limits of his royal prerogatives, and at no time did he try to overstep them. During World War II, George VI shared with unflinching courage the sweat and the tears, the bombings, fires, and destruction. Both he and the queen refused to leave London during the blitz, except to pay official visits to other bombed areas. In his personal and family life he set for his subjects a high standard of conduct. The influence of his example was particularly strong when the accepted moral codes were under heavy pressure from war and postwar strains. It is particularly noteworthy that the popularity of this monarch reached its zenith in socialist Britain.

Winston Churchill, in paying final tribute to his royal friend, acclaimed him as "so strong in his devotion to the enduring honor of our country, so self-restrained in his judgments of men and affairs; so uplifted above the clash of party politics yet so attentive to them; so wise and shrewd in judging between what matters and what does not." As a mark of esteem for the departed king many British and foreign writers referred to him as George the Good and George the Well-beloved.

The years of George VI's reign were some of the most troubled in British history; in fact, in no time during his reign were the peoples of Britain and the Commonwealth free from anxiety. They were either preparing for war, fighting a bloody struggle, or trying to recover from the devastation and destruction of war. These were years which saw the complexion of empire change considerably. When George VI ascended the throne he did so as king-emperor, but at his death he retained only the title of king. He lost the title of Emperor of India when India was granted her independence in 1947.

The successor of George VI is his daughter, who acceded to the throne at the age of 25, as Queen Elizabeth II. At the time of her father's death Princess Elizabeth was on a visit to East Africa with her husband, Prince Philip, as part of a trip George VI had originally planned to make himself. She returned at once to take the oath and to be acclaimed sovereign of Britain and the British Commonwealth. Thus she became the first woman to occupy the British throne since the passing of Queen Victoria in 1901. There is a popular conviction in England that things go well and that the country is prosperous when the throne is occupied by a woman. Accordingly the hope is widely cherished that the new queen will preside over a second Elizabethan Age.

CHAPTER TWENTY-SEVEN

The French Dilemma

THE FALL OF THE
VICHY REGIME

FROM June 16, 1940, until the invasion of the European continent by Allied forces in 1944 France was under the rule of the collaborationist Vichy government, so called because its headquarters were in the city of Vichy. At the head of this government stood Marshal Pétain, the hero of Verdun in World War I, who in 1940 had reached the age of eighty-four. The military collapse of France in June of 1940 had given the old marshal a sense of destiny. He saw himself in the role of France's savior. Having been taken into the cabinet a few days earlier as vice premier and military counselor, he threatened on June 16 to resign if the government did not sue for peace. After Premier Reynaud was forced out of office, Pétain took the helm and immediately moved to end the fighting. As he saw the situation, the Germans had already won the war and further fighting would be costly and useless. He was convinced that his personal prestige would win from Hitler every consideration and would, above all, move the Nazi leader to grant France a generous armistice. "I am making to France," Pétain said, "the gift of my person to allay her misery." Having signed a peace which would cost France very little, he, Henri-Philippe Pétain, would build a new and glorious French state. Pierre Laval, his right-hand man, had visions of setting up a government on the Nazi or Fascist model, and then entering into full collaboration with Hitler and Mussolini. This was not in accordance with the marshal's plan. The course he charted for himself and his government appears to have been one of neutrality. He would collaborate with Germany only in so far as it was necessary to save France. His guiding star would always be the welfare of France. Hitler's ruthless armistice demands soon dissipated the old marshal's illusions regarding Nazi generosity, but having drawn the wine he had to drink it.

As soon as the French people recovered from the shock of the collapse and realized what happened they became restive, causing Pétain to fear an uprising. He believed that such an eventuality could only end in disaster for France. Moreover, to build his state edifice he needed peace. Even denunciation of the Germans might call forth reprisals. To prevent this, Pétain introduced a series of restrictive measures in that part of France which was not occupied by the Germans. He imposed a strict censorship on the press, radio, and cinema; and also limited the right to hold meetings. In short, no Frenchman was permitted to write or speak openly about public affairs. Punishment for those who disobeyed was swift and certain. Anyone judged to be "a danger to the public safety or to the national defense" could be summarily imprisoned without right of appeal to a higher authority. Pétain himself stated in a broadcast of August 12, 1941, that because of divided opinion in the country he had been "compelled to double the powers of the police, whose discipline and loyalty alone can guarantee the maintenance of public order." Thus France was bound by Germany and gagged by Pétain.

At times Pétain fiercely resisted the mounting impositions and encroachments of the Germans, causing the Nazis to complain about his lack of cooperation. Their favorite nickname for him was Marschall Immer Nein (Marshal Always No). In this connection it can be stated that he permitted the fleet to scuttle itself rather than fall into German hands. On the other hand, there is the enigma as to why Marshal Pétain acquiesced when the Vichy government imposed in the nonoccupied zone many of the restrictions against Jews which had been imposed by the Nazis in the occupied zone. Jews were, for example, restricted in or excluded from many professions and activities. Thus they were excluded from the radio, theatre, and cinema and restricted to 2 per cent in the practice of law and medicine. In higher education the number of Jewish students was limited to 3 per cent. These and various other restrictions which the Vichy government imposed on the French people caused resentment and resistance. The underground press interpreted the Vichy motto of "Work, Family, and Nation" in the following way: "Work—for Germany; Family—deported; Nation—enslaved."

When the Allies invaded Italy the Vichy ringleaders saw the handwriting on the wall and tried to surrender their power to a National Assembly so that it could select a new government favorable to the Allies, but the move failed. After the invasion of France was announced by the Allies, Pétain asked the people to be neutral. The success of the Allied landings in June, 1944, caused the Vichy cabinet to vote itself out of existence. Pétain and Laval were then taken to Germany by the Nazis.

After the liberation from the Nazis the French people gave vent to the hates and fears they had stored up during the years of occupation. The widespread demand for punishment of the Vichy leaders and collaborators resulted in a frenzy of trials and purges. Particularly insistent was the demand for the punishment of Pétain. When the marshal heard that he was to be tried *in absentia,* he obtained the authorization of Hitler to go to Switzerland, and at once presented himself at the French frontier to answer in person. He never wavered in his belief in himself and in the righteousness of his cause. His defense was: "I have spent my life in the service of France. . . . I led her armies to victory in 1918; then, although I had earned peace, I never ceased to dedicate myself to her. I answered her calls, whatever my age and weariness. On the most tragic day in her history she turned once again to me. I wanted nothing, asked for nothing. I was begged to come: I came." On August 14, 1945, he was sentenced to death for collaborating with the enemy, but General de Gaulle, because of Pétain's age and distinguished career, commuted the sentence to life imprisonment.[1] In May, Pierre Laval, often referred to as "the evil genius of the Vichy government," had returned from Germany via Spain and was put on trial. He too was sentenced to death, but without recommendation of clemency. After vainly attempting to end his life by poison he was executed by a firing squad (October 14, 1945).

🔊

THE PROVISIONAL GOVERNMENT OF GENERAL DE GAULLE

In the meantime a provisional government had been set up in France, with General de Gaulle as president. At the time of the surrender in 1940, de Gaulle refused to participate in the overthrow of the Third Republic. He went to London and there organized the Free French movement, which later became known as Fighting France. The basic purpose of this movement was to free all French territories from Axis domination and to restore independent sover-

[1] Pétain was imprisoned on the Ile d'Yeu. When the ninety-five-year-old marshal became seriously ill in 1951, President Auriol commuted his sentence and ordered that he be transferred to a military hospital on the mainland as soon as his health would permit. Pétain died before he could be moved (July 23, 1951).

eignty. For the next five years Frenchmen regarded General de Gaulle as the symbol of French resistance. Even the communists gave him their support. His famous declaration of June 18, 1940, "France has lost a battle, but France has not lost the war," made him the spokesman for all the occupied countries of Europe in their resistance to Nazi domination. In 1943 de Gaulle's movement was merged with the French resistance movement in North Africa, and a Committee of National Liberation was organized. Gradually de Gaulle became the sole leader of all the political and military forces of the committee. In June of 1944 the committee adopted the title of Provisional Government of the French Republic and was accorded recognition by a number of European states. General de Gaulle as president exercised general supervision over governmental affairs, assisted by a cabinet representative of all shades of prevailing opinion.

In August the Provisional Government set October 21, 1945, as the date for electing delegates to a National Assembly, to be composed of 586 members, of which 522 represented European France and 64 overseas territories. In addition the voters were asked two questions on the ballot. The first was: "Do you want the assembly elected today to be a constituent assembly?" In other words, the voters were asked whether they wished to restore the constitution of the Third Republic or have the assembly draw up a new one. No less than 96 per cent of the voters asked for a new constitution with a resounding "Yes." The second question asked if, in case the answer to the first question was in the affirmative, the constituent assembly should exercise public authority until the new constitution was completed; that is, whether it should elect a president and choose a cabinet, the members of which would be responsible to the assembly. The voters again answered "Yes," but this time by a smaller majority.

The three important parties in the election were the Communist Party, which drew its inspiration from the Soviet Union, the Socialist Party, which had a Marxist tradition despite its middle-class membership, and MRP (Mouvement Republicain Populaire), whose support came from the Catholic trade unions and young Catholic leftists. Since the last party was strictly denominational, its influence could not extend into all circles. Of the 522 deputies chosen to represent France proper, the Communists elected 142, the MRP, 140, and the Socialists 133. The Socialists, who had been expected to emerge as the dominant party, were third in the number of seats gained. It was the first national French election in which women were accorded the right to vote. Women were also permitted to stand for election, with the result that 5 per cent of the winning candidates were women. The honor of being the largest single party went to the Communists. It was the first time they achieved this distinction. The party polled more than 26 per cent of the total vote. Many Frenchmen voted with the Communists not because they had some conception of Marxist teachings, but because they saw in the Communist Party the only organized group which held out a promise of better things. When the assembly met on November 6, de Gaulle and his cabinet submitted their resignations, but one week later de Gaulle was unanimously elected president of the Provisional Government.

As commander in chief of the resistance army General de Gaulle had enjoyed the almost solid support of the French people. They saw in him a great future leader of France. He was "le grand Charles," as the Fighting French affectionately called him. The tie that bound the various groups together was the common aim of defeating the Nazis. A large majority of these groups were leftist in their political views and looked upon de Gaulle as a democratic socialist. This was an important factor in his election as president of the Provisional Government. But he had hardly been chosen president when the solid phalanx cracked. The Communists and Socialists realized that he was not a revolutionary, but a conservative, and in some respects even a reactionary. The Provisional Government did, it is true, pass a bill which nationalized the Bank of France and credit in general, but whatever was done in the way of socialization was a deliberate sop rather than a sharing of ideas between de Gaulle and his opponents. A clash developed at once when General de Gaulle started to form a cabinet. In an effort to establish harmony between the various groups, he sought to establish the government on a nonparty basis. This meant choosing cabinet members for their ability rather than their political strength. When the Communists demanded at least one of the three key cabinet posts (armed forces, foreign affairs, or ministry of interior) he refused to accede to their demands.

Although de Gaulle was successful in resisting the Communist demands, he was no longer the leader of a united nation, but rather of a political group. A deep and abiding source of friction was his insistence upon more power for the executive, that is, for himself, and distinctly less power for the assembly. Behind his talk of "a coherent, orderly, concentrated state" many Frenchmen detected the scent of dictatorship. They saw in it an attempt to revive Bonapartism. "The de Gaulle experiment," one journalist wrote, "is a second Napoleonic adventure." Their suspicions appeared to be confirmed when de Gaulle decided to spend a large part of the national income on the armed forces. Both the Communists and the Socialists had little sympathy for such plans. Gradually the opposition of both parties became more determined. "He used to be known as le grand Charles," one opposition journalist stated, "but now he's known as la grande illusion." Of the major parties only the MRP continued to give him staunch support. During the early weeks of his presidency de Gaulle resigned twice, but still commanded enough support to get a majority vote of confidence. However, when a new crisis developed on January 20, 1946, de Gaulle strode into the room where his cabinet was gathered and brusquely told the members: "I have had enough. I do not want to assume direction of a government in which political parties or groups do not cease to attack me." He then left abruptly and drove to his home in the country to await a recall to govern on his own terms. The call did not come. The Constituent Assembly chose M. Felix Gouin, a Socialist, as his successor.

THE FOURTH REPUBLIC

During the weeks after General de Gaulle's resignation the Constituent Assembly continued its work on the new constitution and on May 5, 1946, presented the completed draft to the voters. When the votes were counted it was found that the voters had rejected it because it gave the legislature too much power. It was the first time a constitution was ever disapproved by the French voters. Early in June a new Constituent Assembly was elected to draft another constitution. The major change was the gain of nineteen seats by the MRP and the loss of an equal number by the Socialists. Thus the representation in the new assembly was MRP, 160; Communists, 146; Socialists, 115. In September, 1946, a new constitution was adopted by the assembly; it was ratified by the voters in October. Actually the new constitution differed little from the first. It provided for a bicameral parliament—a National Assembly elected by direct vote of all eligible voters and a Council of the Republic chosen by indirect elections. The power of the upper house was limited so that it could not reject, but only delay measures of the National Assembly. The president was to be elected by the two houses in joint session for a term of seven years and to be eligible for reelection only once, all members of French royal families being ineligible. The president was to designate the premier, but the latter and his ministers were to be responsible to the National Assembly. The cabinet must resign only if an absolute majority of all the deputies votes no confidence.

The first National Assembly under the constitution of the Fourth

Republic was elected on November 10, 1946. From this election the Communists emerged with 169 seats, while the MRP won 163, and the Socialists had to be satisfied with 103. Thus the Communists were again the strongest party. But the Socialists' loss of seats meant that no two of the three major parties could command a majority. On top of this the Socialists could not decide whether to support the MRP or the Communists. Consequently the task of forming a cabinet proved to be very difficult. After many candidates and combinations were vetoed, a majority of the deputies finally accepted Leon Blum, the seventy-four-year-old Socialist leader, as a compromise candidate. The new premier, with his all-Socialist cabinet, was merely a stop-gap.

During the years that followed, the old malady of short-lived cabinets reappeared to plague France. Since no party was large enough to command a parliamentary majority, coalitions were necessary in order to form a cabinet, and coalitions are usually short-lived. No cabinet enjoyed the solid support of the nation. Lacking this support, each government had to move cautiously, like an acrobat sliding along a tightrope, even though the occasion demanded prompt and vigorous action. Under such conditions no cabinet could hope to remain in office long, and the life span of the cabinets was even shorter than it had been before World War II. From the liberation in 1945 to March, 1952, France had thirteen governments. The frequent elections, in which the French people were called upon to vote on complicated national issues, kept France in a continual state of political excitement and instability. During the election campaigns the French public was literally bombarded with a series of incompatible ideas and ideals.

It is exceedingly doubtful whether definite political stability can be attained without a change in the constitution. Paul Reynaud, France's wartime premier, said early in 1952:

After the war we changed our constitution—we wanted a stronger executive power, but instead got a more feeble one than before the war. Reforms are essential. We must give the cabinet the power to dissolve parliament and call new elections. This would make the deputies much wiser and quieter. As in England, the cabinet should set the assembly agenda and restrict the opposition proposals to one afternoon weekly. More power should be given to the Council of the Republic (upper house). These reforms would not give us a two-party system as in the United States and Britain, but they would reduce the frequency of crises. Immediately, we need a national union government uniting all the parties except the Communists. Our problems are too serious for a smaller coalition.

୪

THE FRENCH ECONOMIC DILEMMA

Economic life in France, as in the other countries that had participated in the fighting, was in a state of paralysis and chaos when
World War II ended. Despite the fact that the period of fighting in
1940 was brief and the final invasion covered only a few months,
destruction was greater than it had been in World War I. According
to some estimates, the material damage was twice as great as in the
earlier World War. In the general bombing to which France was subjected one building in every twenty-two was totally demolished. Probably the most important factor in the economic breakdown was the
disruption of the transportation system. During the last year of the
war the French railroads were a primary target of the Allied bombers, with the result that railway transportation was immobilized by
the destruction of 4,000 bridges and trestles. During the five years
of war and occupation the number of locomotives was reduced from
11,000 to less than 3,000, and the number of freight cars from 457,000
to 174,000. Practically every important station, marshaling yard, and
junction point was thoroughly bombed. The breakdown of transportation prevented the distribution of vital materials needed for reconstruction and for the rehabilitation of industry. It also put difficulties in the way of the distribution of food to all parts of France.
Serious food shortages developed. In some districts there was no
bread; in others, bread was difficult to obtain. Because of a drought
during the summer of 1945 the food shortage grew much worse. By
the end of the year the bread problem had become one of the gravest
that faced the government.

The facilities for foreign trade had also suffered badly. During
the war France lost 70 per cent of her total tonnage of merchant ships;
harbor installations were destroyed by Allied bombers to the same
extent. The destruction of harbors greatly impeded the arrival of
imports necessary for relief and rehabilitation. When the French
tried to revive the luxury industries (fashions, perfumes, and cos-
metics) they found that other countries had developed their own
industries. Moreover, stocks of vital raw materials, necessary to the
rehabilitation of other peacetime industries, were exhausted. The
machinery which remained was worn out. It had been operated at
full blast, had not been properly cared for, and few repairs had been
made.

All the French economic difficulties were aggravated by an inflation of prices which had begun during the Nazi occupation. From

the beginning of the occupation until they were expelled, the Nazis had forced the French treasury to pay more that 631 billion francs in indemnities and occupation expenses. As a means of meeting these and other expenses the Vichy government had increased the money in circulation from 114 billion francs in 1939 to 620 billion in the autumn of 1944. Inflation followed. While prices soared, wages lagged far behind.

It would be a mistake to attribute the postwar difficulties of France entirely to the war. The bombing by both the Allies and the Germans, the plundering by the Nazis, and the general destruction of the war did aggravate the situation, but they did not cause it. Both French industry and French agriculture had been gradually falling behind for three decades. During the period between the two great wars the rebuilding of regions devastated in World War I and the preparations for World War II consumed the funds which might have been used to modernize French industry. Consequently French businessmen and industrialists had not kept pace with a rapidly changing world. Equipment and methods in the French coal mines were nearly as obsolete and old-fashioned as those in Britain. Those power companies which constructed generating stations built coal-generating stations instead of hydraulic ones because the power and coal-mining industries were linked financially.

In general, there appears to have been opposition both by labor and management to modernization of equipment and standardization of techniques. Although France was one of the major steel-producing countries in Europe, other countries were outdistancing her in regard to improved techniques. Even before World War II the average productivity of the French industrial workman was about one third that of a workman in the United States. Labor productivity declined further during the war as the equipment deteriorated. As a result of bombings, German requisitioning, and wear and tear the French supply of machine tools had been largely depleted during the war. Since France was dependent on foreign countries for machine tools, she was cut off from her source of supply and could not replace them. When French industrialists emerged from their five years of isolation and were able to compare their facilities with those of other countries, many of them realized that their task was not merely to bring back the conditions of 1938, but to renovate their factories from top to bottom. Their equipment was almost a quarter-century behind the times.

At the time of the liberation the French did not comprehend the economic situation. They realized that they had suffered tremendous losses, but they were so happy over their regained freedom that they were optimistic about the future. They believed that once they applied themselves to the task of rebuilding, their economy's productive capacity could be restored rapidly. Obviously they would have to prime the pump with imports. They would have to import some foodstuffs, raw materials for the industries, and new machinery for some of the factories. There seemed to be money available for these imports. The French had foreign investments to liquidate and, above all, the United States was ready with loans to encourage France in her efforts to restore her economy. In December, 1945, an agreement was signed with the United States whereby the Export-Import Bank made a loan to France of $550 million.

The recovery which took place appeared for a time to justify the optimism. Excellent progress was made in the task of restoring communications and transport facilities. Most of the bridges that had been destroyed were either temporarily or permanently rebuilt and the amount of freight carried by the railroads gradually increased. Much, too, was done to restore the merchant marine through construction and purchase of ships. The production of coal was increased and the output of factories rose considerably. Then suddenly the pace slackened. Again many thought that the slow-down was temporary and that the factors responsible for it were psychological. Inspectors sent out by the government, however, found that the cause of the slump was not psychological, but was due to worn-out or antiquated machinery, lack of coal, and lack of electricity and water power. Again it was a question of more imports.

A larger volume of imports and a lesser volume of exports spelled "budget deficit." For a time the government sought to reduce the deficit by cutting military appropriations and raising various taxes. But government leaders soon realized that such measures would not produce enough to cover the deficit. Increased industrial production came to be regarded as the real remedy. As the first step the government created a planning commission headed by M. Jean Monnet which laid the groundwork for what might be called the French five-year plan (Monnet Plan), a program for economic recovery. The Monnet Commission estimated that it would cost $30 billion, spread over five years, to reconstruct and modernize French industry. Of this sum at least $4 billion was needed for the purchase of machinery and raw materials from the United States. But France was in no position to supply such a sum, even by using its remaining gold reserves and liquidating its foreign holdings. It was plain that France needed foreign credit in order to make the necessary purchases.

The necessary credit was provided by the United States. In May,

1946, Premier Blum of France and Secretary of State Byrnes signed documents by which credits totaling $1.4 billion were extended to France. Early in 1948 the Marshall Plan gave France the first of a series of transfusions, pumping money into the economic bloodstream of France. Nearly a billion dollars was spent on France the first year and nearly $700 million in the second. Of this money about 75 per cent was spent directly in the United States. The purchases included food, raw materials (notably cotton, petroleum, and nonferrous metals), modern machinery for French industry, and machinery to mechanize French farms.

§

RECOVERY AND RETROGRESSION

It was exactly the treatment the patient needed. Gradually health and vigor began to return. By the end of 1949 the French ports were completely restored and were able to handle 10 per cent more traffic than they could take care of in 1938. By this time, too, the coal mines had been largely restored and modernized. 1949 saw France produce more coal than any previous year except 1929. As a result of the construction of new hydroelectric plants the output of electricity in 1949 was 50 per cent above the prewar level. Agricultural production was almost back to prewar levels. In other words, France was almost self-sufficient with regard to foodstuffs. The food situation was so stable that it was possible to burn the last ration books at the end of 1949. The index of production as a whole was up about 30 per cent over 1938. This gave the franc a strength that put black marketeers in francs out of business. The recovery which had been so remarkable in 1949 continued in the early months of 1950. In the first seven months of 1950, for example, 28,000 motor vehicles were manufactured as against 23,000 for the whole of 1949. Tourist trade was booming again and exports rose sharply. Recovery was so remarkable that governmental leaders hoped to balance the budget and be independent of foreign aid by 1952–1953 when the scheduled Marshall Plan aid was to be terminated.

As the recovery had progressed, the strength and prestige of the Communists had declined to some extent. They lost some of their strength in the municipal elections and their representation in the national government decreased. The greatest decline came in the national elections of 1951 when they lost 42 per cent of their parliamentary seats, although their total vote was only 8 per cent less than in 1946. They were no longer a threat to the continued existence of the republic, but were still a force of proportions.

After the outbreak of the Korean war, however, the economic sit-

uation in France began to deteriorate, and by the early months of
1952 it was critical. Among the factors which contributed to the economic decline were acute inflation, a weak tax system, the drain of
imperial war, and the cost of rearmament under the North Atlantic
Treaty. When the demand for raw materials needed for both rearmament and peacetime industries caused prices to rise, general inflation resulted, as in other countries. In March, 1952, French housewives were paying 50 francs for a loaf of bread that cost only 36
francs a year earlier. The price of coffee during the same period had
risen from 793 to 931 francs for two pounds. Sugar, which had been
103 francs for two pounds, had risen to 127. It is estimated that the
increase in the cost of most foods has been 15 per cent and of manufactured goods 25 per cent. The high prices not only handicapped
French goods in the competition for foreign markets but also wrought
hardships for the poorer classes, particularly since wages had been
falling behind prices for some time. From many sides demands were
made that wages be tied directly to the cost of living.

In addition to high prices taxes weighed heavily on the poorer
classes. Under the French tax system most of the taxes derive from
indirect levies which are most burdensome to the low-income groups.
Of the total French revenues in 1949 only 17 per cent came from income taxes on individuals and corporations as against more than 80
per cent in the United States. Even then many of the middle class
in France manage to evade income taxes by various subterfuges. But
the greatest weakness of the French tax system is that it does not produce sufficient revenue to meet the necessary expenses. Early in 1952
M. Wilfred Baumgartner, governor of the Bank of France, said: "It
is undoubtedly due in large part to the events in Korea that the currency, after achieving stability at the end of 1949, has begun again to
lose value. But there are also internal reasons. This alone explains
why price increases in France in the past eighteen months have been
much greater than in other European countries. . . . The state as
well as the people is living above its means. The state pretends
to be able to take over a whole series of burdens which it is unable
to counterbalance by taxes or loans."

One severe drain on the treasury was the cost of retaining
the French empire. Although what remained of the prewar French
empire had been largely either in a state of revolt or in a mood verg-
ing on revolt, French public opinion was not ready to grant the colonies independence. Most Frenchmen were convinced that if France
did not retain its rank among the imperial powers it would sink to
the position of a second- or third-rate nation. Hence the struggle with

the colonies continued. The greatest drain on the French treasury was the fighting in Indo-China, continuing year after year. Not only has the financial drain been great but the loss of life has also been high. But the French refuse to withdraw. They fail to realize that a nation of 40 million people with a sick economy cannot continue to hold in subjection more than 100 million people motivated by ideas of self-determination and independence.[2]

In addition to the drain of empire there was the cost of rearmament as a means of protecting Europe against communist aggression. In February, 1952, the assembly voted a budget of $4 billion for defense purposes, but failed to state how the funds were to be raised. The condition of the French treasury was so bad that during the forty days M. Edgar Faure was premier government spending exceeded revenues by approximately $2.85 million a day. Until M. Faure borrowed $70 million from the Bank of France (which insisted on repayment in three weeks) the treasury had only enough cash to pay government workers for one more month. When the premier sought to finance the rearmament program by increasing taxes 15 per cent the National Assembly voted down the proposal 309 to 283. M. Faure at once handed his resignation to M. Vincent Auriol, president of the French Republic (February 29, 1952). When several political leaders failed to get enough support from the assembly to form a cabinet, many feared that the inability of the right center to muster enough support might give General de Gaulle an opportunity to return to power. In the end, however, a number of Gaullists deserted the party to support M. Antoine Pinay, who formed a middle-of-the-road cabinet. But the French political situation was anything but stable.

While Britain was making some progress in closing the gap between imports and exports during the last months of 1951 and the early months of 1952, France was losing ground. In its trade with foreign countries France showed a deficit of $165 million in January, 1952. The rapid rise of imports over exports caused the government to reduce imports from Western Europe. This, however, was hardly a solution. The financial predicament remained a problem which future governments would have to solve.

[2] See p. 763.

CHAPTER TWENTY–EIGHT

✿✿

Franco's Spain and the Italian Republic

FRANCO AND THE AXIS
SPAIN did not join either side in the fighting during World War II. When the war broke out the Spanish government proclaimed itself neutral and Generalissimo Franco himself ordered all Spaniards to observe the strictest neutrality. Although the Caudillo (Spanish synonym for Führer) was indebted to Hitler for aid during the Civil War, the latter did not look for any help from Spain in planning the Polish campaign. On August 22, 1939, Hitler said to his commanders in chief: "Franco is a factor favorable to us. However, we can ask only benevolent neutrality from Spain. . . . we must take into consideration that Spain does not as yet have a Fascist party of our internal unity." But documents from the German Foreign Office, captured by United States forces during the invasion of Germany, show that Franco played a wary game. When the Nazi legions poured into Western Europe in the spring of 1940, he appears to have concluded that Germany would be the winning side and that if Spain was to share in the division of the spoils he would have to become an active participant soon. On June 3, 1940, he wrote to Hitler:

Dear Führer: In the moment when the German armies under your leadership are bringing the greatest battle of history victoriously to an end, I should like to deliver to you the expression of my enthusiasm and admiration as well as that of my people who with emotion have been following the course of a glorious battle which they feel as their own, and which is unfolding the hopes which already have gleamed in Spain when your soldiers shared with us the battle against the same enemies, even if then concealed. . . . I don't need to assure you how great my wish is not to be aloof from your needs and how great will be my satisfaction to perform for you . . . the services which you esteem most valuable. . . . With the best wishes for the future greatness of Germany, and with the expression of my unchangeable friendship and affection.

Just one week after the Caudillo wrote to Hitler, Italy's Benito Mussolini rushed to join Nazi Germany in the war lest he be too late for the spoils. On Italy's entry into the war General Franco changed the official status of Spain from neutrality to nonbelligerency. Nor did he stop at this. On June 14 Spanish troops occupied the international port of Tangier, which is situated just opposite Gibraltar. A short time later he also presented to the Nazi ambassador in Madrid his terms for joining the Axis in the war. On August 10 the ambassador cabled to Berlin: "The Spanish government has declared itself ready, under certain conditions, to give up its position as a nonbelligerent state and to enter the war on the side of Germany and Italy." Franco's price was Gibraltar, French Morocco, and the Oran section of Algeria plus the necessary military supplies and economic assistance needed for the war. The cable stated that "besides this military assistance economic support of Spain will also be necessary. To this belongs above all else the delivery of gasoline and, at the beginning of next year, delivery of grain for bread."

But Hitler regarded Franco's terms as too high. Having conquered much of Europe and having gained an active ally in Italy, the Führer felt that he did not need the Caudillo's help at the specified price. He even complained to Count Ciano, Italy's foreign minister, that Franco was asking too much. Meanwhile Franco was "chafing at the bit." He was eager to move into the war before Britain would fall under a Nazi attack. Unless he was in the war at the time of Britain's fall, he could not claim Gibraltar as a reward for Spain's participation. The Nazi High Command had prepared plans, known as "Operation Blitzschnell," for an invasion of the British Isles and it was generally believed that the attack would be launched soon.

Failing to get a satisfactory reply from Hitler, the Spanish ruler turned to Mussolini. On August 15, 1940, he wrote:

Dear Duce: Since the beginning of the present conflict it has been our intention to make the greatest efforts in our preparations in order to enter the foreign war at a favorable opportunity in proportion to the means at our disposal. . . . We have requested from Germany the necessities for action, while we push forward the preparations and make every effort to better the provisioning situation as far as possible. For all these reasons, you will understand the urgency in writing you, to ask your solidarity in these aspirations for the achievement of our security and greatness, while I at the same time assure you of our unconditional support for your expansion and your future. With my greatest admiration for the brave Italian comrades who are fighting so gloriously, I send you most cordial regards.

In his answer of August 25, 1940, Mussolini sought to calm Franco's fears about Spain's ability to stand the economic strain of the war. He wrote in part:

Ever since the outbreak of the war I have been constantly of the opinion that "your" Spain, the Spain of the Falange revolution, could not remain neutral until the end of the war, but at the right moment would change to nonbelligerency and finally to intervention. Should that not happen, Spain would alienate herself from European history, especially the history of the future, which the two victorious Axis powers will determine. . . . I should like to say to you, dear Franco, that I, with these my practical considerations, do not wish to hasten you in the least in the decision that you have to make, for I am sure that in your discussions you will proceed on the basis of the protection of the vital interests of your people and am just as certain that you will not let this opportunity go by of giving Spain her African Lebensraum.

In the meantime negotiations between the Franco government and the Nazis had continued. On August 21, 1940, the German ambassador in Madrid reported Franco as saying: "Spain is already half in the war anyhow and it might be better to go the whole way and be assured of Italo-German economic support than to suffer the effects of the British blockade and the American boycott of Spanish goods." On September 10 Señor Surrano Suñer, Spain's foreign minister, complained to Nazi Foreign Minister Ribbentrop that Spain's wishes regarding Gibraltar and other territories had been ignored and that nothing had been done to furnish Spain with guns for an attack on Gibraltar. Hitler, who still felt that there was plenty of time to whittle down the Spanish demands, countered with an offer which involved giving the Nazis a foothold in the Canaries and two ports in Spanish Morocco. This did not please the Caudillo at all. He realized only too well that if he were to give the Germans two ports in Spanish Morocco the economic value of the region would be lost to Spain.

The bargaining continued during the months that followed. Hitler, who was blaming the lack of German sea power and the bad flying weather for not having launched the great attack against Britain, began to show more interest in drawing Spain into the war. A meeting was arranged between the Caudillo and the Führer. It took place in a railroad car at Hendaye, France, on October 23, 1940, and was the first meeting between the two. According to notes taken at the meeting, Franco opened the conversation by telling Hitler that "Spain has always been allied with the German people spiritually without any reservation and in complete loyalty. In the same sense, Spain has in every moment felt herself at one with the Axis. In the Civil War the soldiers of the three countries fought together and a profound unity had arisen among them. Likewise, Spain will in the future attach herself closely to Germany. . . . In the present war as well, Spain will gladly fight at Germany's side." Hitler, for his part, assured Franco that everything was going well. There are strong indications that the date for Spain's entry into the war was fixed at this meeting. Documents found near the end of the war show that the date agreed upon was January 10, 1941. Both Hitler and Franco seemed to be satisfied with the results of the meeting. During the weeks that followed, a draft for a Hispano-German alliance was prepared and on November 11 the Nazi ambassador in Madrid reported that the Spanish foreign minister had accepted the terms for entering the war. The next day Hitler himself issued a directive which stated that "political steps to bring about an early Spanish entry into the war have been taken."

But as the time for Spain's entry drew nearer something went wrong. Documents available at the present time do not make clear exactly what happened. This much is definite, however: Franco was sparring for time. According to the German ambassador, Franco stated December 12, 1940, that "it is impossible for Spain to enter the war on the suggested date." As reasons for postponing Spain's entry he listed the "continued menace of the British fleet, incompleteness of Spain's own military preparations, and absolute inadequacy of Spain's provisioning." Undoubtedly the fact that Hitler had not beaten Britain to her knees, that the Italians had suffered serious reverses in Greece, and that the United States was making military preparations were influential factors. Franco's hesitation naturally did not please Hitler. In his efforts to reassure the Spanish government, the Führer summoned Suñer to Berlin, argued, shouted, and pounded on the table. When Suñer mentioned large-scale military preparations in the United States Hitler said sharply: "America's entry into the war won't change things in any way." Still Spain did not enter the war. On February 6, 1941, the Führer wrote to Franco that through the latter's refusal to enter the war two months had been lost and the opportunity to have Gibraltar safely in Axis hands had been missed. Hitler's letter read in part:

It is my most heartfelt conviction that the battle which Germany and Italy are now fighting is thus determining the future of Spain as well. Only in case of our victory will the present regime continue to exist. Should Germany and Italy lose this war, however, then any future for a really national and independent Spain would be impossible.

I have been striving to convince you, Caudillo, of the necessity in the interests of your own country and the future of the Spanish people, of uniting yourself with those countries who formerly sent soldiers to support you, and who today of necessity are battling not only for their own existence, but indirectly for the national future of Spain as well. . . .

Germany has for her part declared herself ready to deliver to Spain, immediately after undertaking entrance into the war, food—that is, grain —to as great an extent as possible. . . . This of course remains contingent upon the final decision for Spain's entry into the war. About one thing, Caudillo, there must be clarity: we are fighting a battle of life and death and cannot at this time make any gifts. If it should later be asserted that Spain could not enter the war because she received no supplies, that would not be true.

The plea of the Führer fell on deaf ears. Franco did not give the order which would have started the Spanish army moving.

The Nazi invasion of Russia first evoked considerable enthusiasm in Spain. Many rejoiced that the Germans had launched a campaign against the common communist enemy. Señor Suñer openly lauded the Germans and denounced Britain and the United States. A regiment of volunteers from the ex-combatants of the Civil War was organized to fight in Russia and a considerable number of laborers were sent to Germany. Franco himself in a speech to the Council of the Falange voiced the Spanish hatred of communism and asserted that the Allies had lost the war. But he still did not enter the war. When the Nazi armies, after failing to reach Moscow in 1941, bogged down in the snow and cold of the Russian steppes, Franco said no more about becoming an active partner of the Axis. Then came the entry of the United States, an event which exercised a profound effect on those Spaniards who were convinced of a German victory, among them Franco himself. Three days after Pearl Harbor he issued a decree which announced that Spain would maintain her status of nonbelligerency. In assessing Germany's strategic position at the end of the fifth year of war General Jodl, chief of the German General Staff, told an assembly of Gauleiter at Munich (November 7, 1943) that the "palm of victory has eluded us" because of the failure to attain three specific objectives. These were: the failure to make a landing in Britain, the failure to overwhelm Russia in 1941, and the failure to draw Spain into the fighting early in the war. In other words, he

insinuated that the German government had blundered in not paying the price Franco asked.

As Hitler's defeat became inevitable, General Franco tried to
make an about-face. The Allies became "en vogue" in the Spanish
newspapers and news favorable to the Allies was featured on the front
page. At the same time Franco sought to ingratiate himself with Britain by offering his services in the cause of "a speedy and just peace."
But the British, remembering that the conquest of Gibraltar had been
one of his primary aims, rebuffed him. Having failed in his efforts
to "appease" the British, he turned his sights in the direction of the
United States. His progaganda machine began to grind out elabora-
tions on the theme, "Spain regards herself a spiritual belligerent
against Japan." This despite the fact that Franco's consul in the Philippines had been an open collaborator with Japan. Another propaganda offensive was launched early in 1945 to get Spain invited to
the UN conference at San Francisco. Franco loudly proclaimed that
"Falangism is not Fascism," but "a special mode of life." But the efforts were futile. The collapse of the Axis finally caused Franco to
clear the autographed portraits of Hitler and Mussolini from his
desk in El Prado.

᪥

POSTWAR SPAIN

When the war ended, Spain found herself in an unfriendly world.
Many had believed that the collapse of Italy and Germany would be
the signal for Franco's exit, that he would have a plane ready to take
him to the Argentine on a one-way trip. But Franco made no move to
leave Spain or to divest himself of the power he wielded. Such conduct on his part was totally unexpected. The Spanish historian Salvador de Madariaga wrote from his exile in Britain early in 1946: "The
survival of a Fascist regime in Spain a year and a half after the Führer-
dämmerung is an oddity." Beginning in June, 1945, a series of denunciations of the Spanish government was launched, the objective
being to bring about the downfall of the Franco regime. At San
Francisco the delegates from Mexico proposed that Franco Spain be
excluded from the UN and that the proposal be included in the charter. Although the motion was defeated, the charter specifically bars
those states "whose regimes have been installed with the help of
armed forces of countries which have fought against the United Nations." At the end of the Potsdam meeting in August, 1945, the Big
Three (Britain, the United States, and the U.S.S.R.) made the following declaration:

The three governments feel bound to make it clear that they for their part would not favor any application for membership put forward by the present Spanish government, which, having been founded with the support of the Axis powers, does not in view of its origins, its nature, its record, and its close association with the aggressor states, possess the qualifications necessary to justify such membership.

Nor did the attacks on Spain stop there. On March 4, 1946, a statement prepared by representatives of Britain, France, and the United States was released. The statement read:

There is no intention of interfering in the internal affairs of Spain. The Spanish people themselves must in the long run work out their own destiny. In spite of the present regime's repressive measures against orderly efforts of the Spanish people to organize and give expression to their political aspirations, the three governments are hopeful that the Spanish people will not again be subjected to the horrors and bitterness of civil strife.

On the contrary it is hoped that leading patriotic and liberal-minded Spaniards may soon find means to bring about a peaceful withdrawal of Franco, the abolition of the Falange, and the establishment of an interim or caretaker government under which the Spanish people may have an opportunity freely to determine the type of government they wish to have and to choose their leaders. Political amnesty, return of exiled Spaniards, freedom of assembly and political association, and provision for free public elections are essential. An interim government which would be and would remain dedicated to these ends should receive the recognition and support of all freedom-loving peoples.

In 1946 the question of Franco's government was also considered by the UN. It was first taken up in the Security Council after one member declared that the Spanish situation "endangers international peace and security." No definite procedure against Spain was adopted, however. Next the question was brought before the UN Assembly (October, 1946) with Mr. Trygve Lie, the secretary general, stating that "the Franco regime would remain a constant source of mistrust" and that he hoped that "those who gave us victory and peace may also find ways and means whereby liberty and democratic government may be restored to Spain." After long debates and discussions by subcommittees the General Assembly finally passed the following motion on December 12, 1946: "That the Franco government of Spain be debarred from membership in international agencies established by, or brought into relationship with, the United Nations, and from participating in conferences, or other activities which might be arranged by the UN or these agencies, until a new and acceptable government is formed in Spain." It was further stated "that all members of the United Nations immediately recall from Madrid ambassadors and ministers plenipotentiary accredited there." At the time the resolution was passed there were hardly any ambassadors or ministers plenipotentiary accredited to Madrid. Of the fifty-five member states thirty were not in diplomatic relationship with Spain at all, and another nineteen had no ambassador or minister plenipotentiary stationed in Spain. The total result was that three members (Britain, the Netherlands, and Turkey) did recall their minister or ambassador. On the other hand, the Argentine government which had previously had no minister in Madrid immediately sent one.

Generalissimo Franco must have breathed a sigh of relief when the UN rested its case. Far from effecting his downfall the foreign opposition gave the Franco regime a new lease on life. The reaction of a proud and independent people was a wild outburst of support and loyalty. They were ready to cut each other's throat in a family quarrel, but when the other nations united against them the Spaniards rallied round the Franco government. They resented the very idea that foreign powers should decide whether Franco or someone else should be the head of the Spanish state. Even the attitude of those opposed to the Franco government was: "We want a change of regime, but we do not wish to have it done from the outside." To the Franco regime the words of condemnation were useful for propaganda purposes. While the Spanish press made the most of the idea that there was a "plot against Spain," the Cortes entered a formal protest against "foreign interference and infamous attacks," concluding with a message of homage and adherence to the Caudillo. Franco himself breathed defiance, saying that "the outside world is not important. We are looking to the inside." In general, Franco's position was stronger after the attack than it had been before.

Meanwhile Franco had been trying to win some degree of approval from foreign opinion for his government by moving in the direction of what he called "organic democracy." Many monarchists had hoped that the victory of the Allies would be the signal for a monarchist restoration and Don Juan, son of Alfonso XIII, was eagerly awaiting a summons to Madrid. Periodically Franco gave the monarchists new hope by pushing the Falange, Spain's totalitarian party, into the background. But after a time the Falange was always brought to the fore again. With a view to meeting the criticism of his regime, he had a succession law drafted which in June, 1947, was passed by the Cortes.[1] After stating that "the head of the state is Gen-

[1] The Cortes, the traditional Spanish parliament, was reestablished in Fascist form in 1943, all of its members being appointed directly or indirectly by the government.

eral Francisco Franco" the law provided that "in case of death or in-capacity the head of the state shall be succeeded by the person of royal blood who shall be chosen by the combined council of the kingdom and government and accepted by two thirds of the Cortes." After the whole government machinery of press, radio, and propaganda was brought into play in behalf of the law, an overwhelming majority of the Spanish voters approved it in a plebiscite.

The publication of the Law of Succession envisaged the possibility of Franco laying down his office. Hope stirred again in the ranks of the monarchists and Don Juan awaited momentary recall to Madrid. But the Law of Succession had no practical meaning for the near fu-ture; in fact, all the changes Franco has made since World War II have been superficial and have in no way altered the essential nature of the regime. After they were made Spain was still a police state which tolerated no real opposition. Franco, the master politician, has for purposes of political strategy permitted the press to print certain criticisms of his regime and has even permitted underground litera-ture to pass through the mails. But it is merely a pretense at tolerat-ing the opposition. Any real threat is summarily dealt with by Franco's police. No one is permitted to challenge the authority of Franco's government.

Since the Franco government has lasted longer than any Spanish government since pre-Napoleonic days one might well ask: "What are its principal props?" There is, first of all, the Falange, the Spanish totalitarian party. This party, which includes only a very small per-centage of the Spanish voters, is the natural sponsor of a Fascist re-gime. It has a firm grip on the trade unions and is linked to the police. As it suits his political purposes, Franco has pushed the party off its pedestal and then restored it to its place. When all has been said, the Falange is still the only political instrument on which he can count. Perhaps Franco's strongest prop is the army. Traditionally conserva-tive, the army has been carefully and purposefully pampered. For the 800,000 men in the armed services there were in 1948 no less than 100 generals and 25,000 officers. Of these more than 80 per cent owe their promotions to Franco and are bound to him by firm ties of loyalty and gratitude. In 1947 no less than 47 per cent of the national budget was spent on the armed forces and the secret police. Besides receiving pay checks the army officers also enjoy special privileges. The unarmed masses realize only too well that successful revolt against the army, abetted by five kinds of secret police, is out of question.

Another source of support for the Franco regime is the Spanish

Catholic Church. Although the Church has little love for the Falange, its rival in education and ideology, and although there has on occasion been much behind-the-scenes criticism of the Caudillo in ecclesiastical circles, the net moral weight of the Church has been on Franco's side. Both the clergy and the laity have not forgotten how leftist groups wrecked and burned church buildings and monasteries. To them Franco stands as the man who stopped the communists and restored order. Not only has the Franco regime given powerful aid to religious activities; the Church itself has wielded more power under Franco than it did under the Bourbons. Thus it exercises a strict censorship of books, plays, and films. It can prevent the publication of any book, the staging of any play, and the showing of any film to which it objects. What is equally important, control of secondary education is entirely in ecclesiastical hands.

Franco also receives support from other circles. Most of the important Spanish financiers and industrialists are ranged almost solidly behind him. For a time toward the end of the war the prevailing sentiment was monarchist, but when the Allied victory was followed by the establishment of socialist governments in a number of countries the upper bourgeoisie again gave its support to Franco, under whom the financiers and industrialists have fattened their wallets. In general, Franco has enjoyed the support of most Spaniards who fear either communism or another civil war or both. Although many cherish no particular love for the Franco government, they see communism as the alternative. Actually there is no such antithesis, but Franco's propaganda machine has helped to nourish the fear of communism. He himself set in circulation the slogan: "Franco, yes; communism, no." In the same way the fear of another civil war has caused many to support Franco. Many who would like to see a change of government are not ready to subject Spain to the scourge of another civil war. Thus many who fear communism and civil war support Franco as a lesser evil.

On the negative side the fact that the opposition is badly divided is a source of strength. Among the leftists there is a sharp cleavage between communists, socialists, and anarcho-syndicalist groups. The republicans, always in a small minority, are both divided and scattered, with many of the leaders in exile and those who are in Spain badly discouraged. Even among the monarchists there is no unity. Although a majority of the monarchists favor a restoration of Don Juan, they are widely divided on the question of what kind of government is to be established under him. Unless the various groups unite, they are incapable of effective opposition. The prospects for such an eventuality are not promising at the present time. It is the general opinion of foreign observers and students of foreign affairs that Franco has little to fear from any quarter. Upon his return to the United States in February, 1952, Mr. Stanton Griffis, retiring ambassador to Spain, stated that he believed Generalissimo Franco was more powerful than ever, saying "There is little or no opposition to him in Spain."

ECONOMIC CONDITIONS IN FRANCO'S SPAIN

General Franco's greatest source of weakness is the economic condition of Spain, which has gone from bad to worse. Although the Civil War left the country economically prostrate, Spain did have an opportunity during World War II to recoup some of her losses. During the war years both the Allies and Germany competed for the purchase of Spain's industrial surpluses. The export business was so good that Spain was able, for the first time in some years, to show a favorable balance of trade. The profits from the export trade enabled the country to pay some of its foreign debts and to build up the gold reserves. The profits might well have been used toward rehabilitating industry, transportation, and agriculture, but, because of the war, materials needed were not available. The Spanish government was unable to purchase fertilizer for the farms, machinery for the factories, and equipment for the transportation system.

Consequently Spain found herself at the end of the war in a worse position than in 1939. When the purchases of the belligerents ceased there was a general letdown in industry; the output in 1945 was 25 per cent below the preceding year. In the same year a drought caused a nearly complete crop failure. To maintain even a minimum diet, the government was forced to import large quantities of food. By the end of 1945 the value of imports again exceeded the value of exports by $35 million. Although the harvest was better in 1946 the crop was still insufficient to feed the growing population of Spain [2] and more food had to be imported. At the end of World War II the condition of the railways, which are mostly state-owned, was particularly bad. Little has been done since that time to improve them. A foreign correspondent wrote in 1950: "What is going on in Spain is an advanced case of hardening of the arteries. The most vivid symbol is perhaps the national railway system, which has been falling to pieces for fifteen years."

[2] The population of Spain had increased at the annual rate of about 250,000 since the war.

The real condition of the economic system did not become apparent at once. During the months immediately after World War II the economic retrogression was ascribed to the process of adjustment resulting from the war. Gradually, however, it became clear that there were other causes at work. One of these was inflation. The figures of the Spanish Chamber of Commerce show that, if 1936 is rated as 100, the cost of living had risen to 570.7 before the end of 1948, and was even higher at the end of 1951. Wages had at best risen only threefold. Actually the gap between food prices and wages was even wider, since some of the food prices had risen almost 1000 per cent. The people living on the land—about 60 per cent of the population —have managed to obtain enough food, but for the urban working-man this was more difficult. Some of the members of the white-collar class were able to augment their incomes by doing such work as bookkeeping and other odd jobs after hours, enabling them to supplement their meager rations with purchases in the black market. Most factory workers did not have this opportunity. The poor grasped at the opportunity of selling their coffee and sugar rations for money with which they could purchase bread. In Spain the chasm between the rich and the poor is wide. An observer who visited Spain in 1948 wrote:

A workingman's wage will be ten to twelve pesetas a day; in dollar terms, that's about thirty cents. What is it worth in purchasing power? Very little. . . . In San Sebastian, just below the French frontier, I hunted out a dirty one-course bar-restaurant in the worst part of the fisherman's quarter, and the price of a single dish of tasteless meat, no doubt equine, sicklied over with tomato sauce, was eleven pesetas. The Spanish bread ration is one small poor quality bun a day, which can be obtained cheaply. A black-market loaf, however, in bread-eating Spain, is seven and a half pesetas. Eggs cost a workingman one day's wages per half dozen: enough cheese to give portions for two is two-thirds of the day's pay. . . . For disorder, poverty, spiritual decay, the pauperization of children, there is perhaps little to choose from between Spain and Italy. In Rome or in Seville you can see the overdressed rich at outdoor cafe tables, while hungry children flock around them to beg, or crawl between their polished shoes for scraps of food they have discarded. In Seville I watched children scramble for cast-aside heads of crayfish and greedily lick out the brains and eyes; while young Spaniards in silk shirts smiled amusedly and sipped manzanilla.[3]

Little has been done by the Franco government toward solving the agrarian problem. Before the Civil War the country was self-

[3] *Harper's Magazine*, vol. 196 (1948) , p. 564.

sufficient in regard to basic foods and in addition exported large quantities of fruit, vegetables, and wine. The income from these exports served to pay for heavy imports in other lines. But under the Franco regime the country has been unable to produce enough to feed its population. The only crops which have maintained their earlier average are olive oil and lentils. The production of fruit has dropped considerably. Only about half as many oranges have been grown each year since World War II as under the Republic. The over-all output of cereals declined 30 per cent. While the wheat crop during the period from 1926 to 1935 averaged 41 million quintals (hundredweights), it was, according to official figures, only 24 million in 1948. The production of barley also declined from an average of 22 million quintals to 13 million, of oats from 6.3 million to 3.7, of rice from 3 to 2.2, of maize from 4.4 to 3.8, and of potatoes from 44.5 to 26.7. To feed the city population considerable quantities of food had to be imported from various sources. In paying for the imports of food and raw materials the Bank of Spain largely exhausted its gold reserve. During the years 1948 and 1949 the Argentine sent large shipments of grain to Spain, but since Spain had little more than promises with which to pay, Perón refused further credit to the Franco government. Spain did, however, manage to float several loans during 1950 and 1951 for the purchase of food.

The decline of food production is due to a number of causes. A major cause is the prolonged shortage of nitrogenous fertilizers. Before World War II these were purchased in large quantities from Germany, but since nitrates are a major war material, the Spanish government found it impossible to purchase them during the war. Ever since the war, supplies have been adequate, but such funds as the Franco government has had were used to purchase other things, including nonessentials. Some idea of how little the Franco government has spent on the improvement of agriculture can be gained from the fact that less than 1 per cent of the 1950 budget was allocated to the ministry of agriculture. A further cause of the decline in food production is the decreased acreage under cultivation. It has been estimated that since Franco rose to power no less than four million acres have been taken out of cultivation for various reasons, including lack of fertilizer and drought. The latter has been an important factor in the lower food production during the years after World War II. After the drought of 1945 Spain had only one year of adequate rainfall before there was a serious water shortage in 1948. The long-term needs of Spanish agriculture include irrigation systems to increase the amount of land under cultivation, more fertilizer, modern farm equipment, especially tractors, and better roads and improved railway service for the distribution of the crops.

Industrial self-sufficiency has been a major scheme of the Franco government since it rose to power. The promises have been lavish, but the achievements niggardly. The progress made in one line has usually been offset by deterioration in another. If the industrial production of 1940, just after the country emerged from the Civil War, is rated as 100, the index rose only to 110 by 1948, and has risen only an equal distance since that time. Apparently not satisfied with the progress that was being made under private enterprise, Franco set up a state holding company in 1941 which he called the National Institute of Industry (Instituto Nacional de Industria or INI) to promote economic development in Spain. INI, patterned on Nazi and Fascist models, was authorized to construct plants for the production of oil and lubricants from coal, of artificial textiles, of aluminum, nitrates, and paper goods, of agricultural implements and equipment, and of trucks, motor cars, and airplanes. Other projects included the construction of power plants and geological surveys for the purpose of discovering minerals. The result has been anything but phenomenal. Thus a plant which was scheduled to produce 20,000 tons of textile fiber in 1949 actually turned out less than one tenth that amount. Whereas the production of electricity was increased from 2.8 billion kilowatt hours in 1936 to a little more than 5 billion in 1949 through the construction of hydroelectric and thermal power stations, the distribution of electricity was very poor. At the end of 1950 industries in Madrid, for example, had power only nine hours a week, while elevators could run only at certain hours. In Barcelona textile mills which did not have their own generators could operate only one full day each week. According to reports from Spain the cables used in the distribution are in such bad condition that 25 per cent of the transmitted electricity is lost.

Since the close of World War II many of the factories of Spain have been operating on only a part-time basis because of lack of raw materials. The iron and steel industry, for example, operated at only 60 per cent of capacity in 1950. Even more restricted have been the operations of the cotton textile industry, which before the Civil War had produced much for export and had been the most important source of foreign exchange. The manufacture of textiles has been hampered by the shortage of raw cotton. Production in other industries showed even greater declines, among them the coal, shipbuilding, and cement industries. While certain basic industries were idle because of the lack of raw materials, a number of nonessential industries were operating at full capacity because of the favoritism of government officials.

One characteristic which distinguishes Franco's totalitarian rule from that of Hitler and Mussolini is the almost total absence of economic planning. One foreign correspondent went so far as to style Franco's rule "a dictatorship without a plan." When the government failed to project a comprehensive plan for economic recovery, the Banco Urquijo, a private institution, in 1948 published a report which estimated that to rehabilitate the Spanish economy it would require an annual minimum of about $1.5 billion over a period of four years for new industrial machinery, new agricultural equipment, and raw materials for the basic industries. These imports were to be in addition to the importation of food and fodder, and raw materials for the production of consumer goods which would have to be paid for from Spain's exports. Finally in March of 1950 Franco's minister of industry and commerce published details of a plan to construct power stations and factories which would complete the basic industrialization of Spain and make the country industrially self-sufficient. The announcement, however, was received with a great deal of skepticism both within Spain and outside. Funds were not available to carry out the plan. Such small loans as Spain managed to float were hardly sufficient to bring temporary relief to an economy on the verge of bankruptcy, to say nothing of the vast expenditures that are necessary to solve Spain's basic economic problems.

⑤

POSTWAR ITALIAN POLITICS

After the dismissal of Mussolini (July 25, 1943) Italy reverted to the status of a constitutional monarchy based on the constitution of 1848. But the overthrow of the Fascist dictatorship and the armistice with the Allies (September 3, 1943) did not bring peace to Italy. A little more than a month after the armistice the Italians joined in the war against Germany as "co-belligerents." Although that part of Italy which was under Anglo-American control was temporarily administered by AMG or AMGOT (Allied Military Government of Occupied Territories) plans were made to shift control from military to civilian authorities. Victor Emmanuel III, who had been king of Italy since 1900, decided that the burden of state was too heavy for a person of his years. He therefore issued a formal statement announcing his withdrawal from public life. He did not abdicate. What he did was to transfer all royal authority to his son, Crown Prince Umberto, who received the title of Lieutenant General of the Realm. The change became effective on June 4, 1944, the day the Allied forces entered Rome. On June 9 a coalition cabinet representing the anti-Fascist parties was formed to administer the government. After two other premiers [4] found the task too burdensome, Alcide de Gasperi formed his cabinet (November 24, 1945). Although the membership of the cabinet changed periodically, de Gasperi remained prime minister for many years.

The new government set June 2, 1946, as the day on which the voters were to express their preferences regarding the structure of the state and to elect deputies to a constituent assembly. Since the overthrow of Mussolini there had been so much agitation against the monarchy, particularly on the part of the communists, that even Prince Umberto favored a referendum. Not that he was eager to retire from public life. He hoped that the opposition would be silenced by a strong vote of confidence for the monarchy. Since it was believed that the presence of Victor Emmanuel III, who had cooperated with Mussolini, would diminish the chances of victory for the monarchy, the old king finally abdicated on May 9, 1946, and embarked for Egypt. Umberto waged a vigorous campaign in which he stressed the value of a constitutional monarchy for Italy. He also played on the fears of communism. But the opposition, too, was active in drawing attention to Umberto's pro-Fascist and pro-Axis record. Umberto II, king of Italy for only a few weeks, followed the election returns hopefully, but when the results were announced on June 10 he saw that the monarchists had lost. While over twelve million voters had declared for a republic, only something over ten million had voted to retain the monarchy. After the cabinet on June 13 transferred the authority he had previously exercised to the prime minister, Umberto went into exile.

If the monarchy lost in the elections, so did its bitterest enemy, the communists, who had hoped the elections would give them a good start on the road to power. They managed to get only about four million votes or about 18 per cent of the total. The Socialists polled four and a half million votes, while the Christian Democrats received eight million. The result was that the Christian Democrats, the middle-of-the-road party, emerged as the largest party with 207 seats. The Socialists won 115, and the Communists 104. The rest of the seats, numbering 117, were distributed among five small parties.

[4] Ivanoe Bonomi—June, 1944 to June, 1945; Ferruccio Parri—June, 1945 to November, 1945.

An interesting aspect of the election is the fact that the Unionist Party, which advocated the union of Italy with the United States, polled 68,000 votes.

The republic was officially proclaimed on June 10, 1946. When the constituent assembly met, it turned at once to the task of electing a provisional president. Two prominent candidates who had considerable support failed to gain enough votes. The first was the aged Vittorio Orlando who had been one of the Big Four at Paris in 1919. Although Orlando had the support of the Christian Democrats, he was opposed by the leftists. The other was the philosopher Benedetto Croce, who, although he was favored by the leftists, failed of election because of the opposition of the Christian Democrats. Finally Enrico de Nicola, a Socialist, was elected as a compromise candidate. As for the cabinet, the coalition cabinet, representing Communists, Socialists, and Christian Democrats, which had been formed by de Gasperi at the end of November, 1945, continued in office.

Alcide de Gasperi had first entered Italian politics shortly after World War I. In 1919 he had participated with Don Luigi Sturzo, the fiery Sicilian priest, in founding the Populist Party, the purpose of which was to give Catholicism an active voice in the affairs of Italy. As a member of this party he stood in opposition to Mussolini and his Fascists. He even called on Victor Emmanuel III in person to demand the dismissal of the Duce. Mussolini had his revenge in attacking de Gasperi in the fascist press and in suppressing the newspaper of which de Gasperi was editor. After the Populist Party was dissolved in 1926, de Gasperi obtained employment indexing books in the Papal Library at the Vatican. In his last meeting with the members of his party he told them:"Wait for the hour of justice; do not despair of liberty." He himself waited patiently for Mussolini's fall. When the time came he returned to politics as the leader of the reorganized Catholic Party, now called the Christian Democratic Party. The members of this party come from various social strata. They include large landowners, industrialists, white-collar workers, aggressive intellectuals, and just plain people. The ties that bound this varied group together were the Catholic faith and a distaste for communism.

De Gasperi himself, though a conservative by background and temperament, recognized the great need for reform. "I'm in the center," he said, "and the center is shifting to the left." He endorsed such measures as taxing the rich and breaking up some of the feudal estates in southern Italy. He refused large contributions from the large landowners because the would-be donors asked him to move slowly in introducing agrarian reforms. "Christian Democracy," he said in 1948, "is the party of the little people; it repudiates the spirit of reaction and marches toward reforms and social justice." In addition to agrarian reform he also supported measures for better housing, for the alleviation of unemployment, and for better working conditions. As a personality he is quiet and reserved, lacking the flamboyant manner of Mussolini. He has, therefore, not been a popular hero. His forte is holding together the motley interests of his own party and of the coalition supporting his cabinet; hence he is often called "the compromiser." In everything he does de Gasperi is first and foremost a member of the Catholic Church.

One of the problems confronting the new republic was the conclusion of a speedy peace with the Allies. After much delay the treaty was signed in Paris on February 10, 1947. But the Italians were very unhappy about the terms. Having joined in the war on the Allied side in 1943 against their ex-allies, the Germans, they resented the fact that Italy was ranked as an ex-enemy state. They felt that their efforts had not been appreciated, that the Allies had let them down at the peace conference. When the conditions of the treaty became known in Italy a mob staged a demonstration in Rome before the Allied Military Headquarters and in many places British and United States flags were torn down. The provisions of the treaty that evoked the most emphatic protests were those depriving Italy of her colonies and of Trieste. The members of the constituent assembly also had strong feelings about the treaty, but finally decided that Italy had more to gain by accepting than by rejecting it. Hence the treaty was ratified by a vote of 266 to 68 on July 31, 1947. All parties hoped, however, that the onerous terms would soon be revised. Having been ratified, the treaty became effective on September 14 and occupation troops were withdrawn before the end of the year.

ESTABLISHING THE ITALIAN REPUBLIC

Meanwhile the constituent assembly was making progress in drafting the new constitution. The actual work of preparing a draft was delegated to a committee of about fifty-five deputies, but the whole assembly reviewed the individual articles when they were ready. Thus on March 22 the assembly approved the first article which reads: "Italy is a democratic republic founded on labor. Sovereignty belongs to the people." An article which caused considerable debate was the one recognizing Catholicism as the sole state religion and incorporating the Concordat of 1929 into the constitution. When this article was submitted to the assembly, de Gasperi stated that the very existence of the republic depended on its acceptance, and the Christian Democrats warned that the rejection of Article Seven might provoke civil war. The opposition, of which the Republicans and old-line Socialists were the backbone, denounced the article vigorously, but lost much of its strength when Palmiro Togliatti, leader of the communists, announced that he and his followers were in favor of the article because they believed that the unity of the Italian people must be maintained. Togliatti's purpose in approving the inclusion of the Lateran Pacts in the constitution was to win votes by pretending that communism is not the enemy of religion. When a vote was taken the assembly approved the article 350 to 149. By accepting Article Seven the assembly went farther than Mussolini in making Italy a clerical state, for the article states that the Lateran Pacts can be revised only with the consent of the Vatican. Religious instruction in the elementary schools was intrusted to the teacher, but the Church has the right to supervise and to disapprove of textbooks that are not in harmony with Catholic teachings.

The completed draft, in its final form, was accepted by the assembly on December 22, 1947, with the approval of all major parties. The vote was 453 to 62. The constitution contains provisions for a bicameral legislative body consisting of a Chamber of Deputies and a Senate. The deputies are elected for a five-year term by universal direct suffrage on the part of all citizens over twenty-one (including women) . One deputy is elected for each 80,000 inhabitants. Senators are elected on a regional basis, five from each region plus one for each 200,000 inhabitants. Two thirds of the senators are elected by direct suffrage and one third by the regional councils. Meeting in joint session as the National Assembly the two bodies by a two thirds majority elect the president of the republic. Like his French counterpart, he is elected for a term of seven years, but his power is even more restricted. All presidential acts must be countersigned by his ministers. The president is accorded the right to name the premier, but the cabinet, which the latter forms, must be approved by a majority in both chambers. The constitution further provides for a Constitutional Court with powers to settle disputes between regions, to settle controversies regarding the powers of the state, to try cases of malfeasance, and to pass on the constitutionality of legislation. Noteworthy also is the fact that the constitution guarantees women equal rights in all matters.

The new constitution went into effect on January 1, 1948, necessitating the holding of elections for a parliament. The date set for the voting was April 18, 1948. The pre-election campaign was waged with vigor by all parties. The Christian Democrats stressed two points above all others, Marshall Plan aid as a means of rehabilitating the economic life of Italy and measures to prevent communist domination. The Moscow-inspired communists, of course, opposed the idea of Marshall Plan aid and hoped to prevent Italy's cooperation with the Western bloc. But their efforts did not produce satisfactory results. The election returns showed that the Christian Democrats had won a sweeping victory. They won 307 of the 574 seats in the Chamber of Deputies, while the Popular Front (the union of the communists and the left-wing socialists) gained only 182. In the Senate the Christian Democrats won 149 out of 345, against 117 for the Popular Front. For the first time in Italian politics one party had secured a parliamentary majority. In speaking to the nation on the day after the elections Premier de Gasperi ascribed the results to the "firm determination of the Italian people not to be bolshevized."

§

DECLINE OF COMMUNISM IN ITALY

Although the communists had cooperated in a fashion with the other major parties in the cabinets of Premier de Gasperi, they had by no means discarded the idea of ultimately achieving full power. In October, 1946, they had joined the left-wing socialists in forming the Popular Front for the express purpose of achieving power for the working class. After the Popular Front scored some notable gains in the municipal elections during the months that followed, the relationship between the parties in Premier de Gasperi's cabinet became more precarious. De Gasperi was urged to drop the communists from the cabinet, but refused on the basis that communist participation in the government made for stability. When the friction between the communists and Christian Democrats continued to increase he did make the change and formed a cabinet without the communists (May, 1947). It was the first time since the end of the Badoglio regime that Italy had a definitely anti-communist government. Thereafter De Gasperi centered his effort upon keeping the other parties united against the communists. The majority the Christian Democrats achieved in the elections of 1948 would have permitted them to form a cabinet composed solely of members of their party. De Gasperi chose, however, to keep his militant anti-Marxist front intact. "The way I interpret the election results," he said, "it was a victory of all forces endorsing democracy at home and abroad." He therefore invited the Republicans, the Liberals, and even the moderate Socialists to participate in the new government and the Christian Democrats had to be satisfied with eleven of the twenty cabinet posts.

The fact that the Christian Democrats had won an absolute majority did not cause the communists to relax their efforts. They tried in every way to hamper and confuse the plans of the government. Besides criticizing the government at every turn and denouncing the Marshall Plan at every opportunity, they fished diligently in the troubled waters of economic discontent. They were not slow to exploit the peasants' land hunger for political ends and were successful in fomenting strikes and unrest among the agricultural as well as among the industrial workers. As a protest against the attempted assassination of the communist leader Togliatti (July 14, 1949) by a student, the communist-dominated Labor Confederation sought to paralyze Italy with a general strike. The general strike was called after widespread demonstrations were staged throughout the country. But the government immediately applied stern measures with the result that the strike was brief. Later in the year the communists resorted to slow-down and sit-down strikes beginning in the Fiat plants and spreading to other industries. When the first shipload of weapons was sent out from the United States as part of the program to rearm the European members of the North Atlantic Treaty Organization the communists openly threatened to prevent the unloading of the ship. But the government refused to be intimidated. The minister of defense answered the threat by announcing that if necessary he would use troops to unload the ship. Although the communists did stage a local strike at Naples, the cargo of weapons was unloaded under military protection. Their efforts notwithstanding, the prestige of the communists faded noticeably, even in the trade unions. During the year which followed the elections of April, 1948, even the membership of the Communist Party declined about 20 per cent. The communists were definitely in retreat.

The decline of communist power had, in turn, a weakening effect upon the government of Premier de Gasperi. As the fear of communism receded into the background, many who had supported the Christian Democrats as a means of preventing the communists from seizing power returned to their old parties. Some, convinced that de Gasperi and his Christian Democrats were no longer needed, joined the opposition. This was the case with the Liberals (1950). Many Christian Democrats became lukewarm in their support of the party as the danger of a communist seizure of power was removed. Some went so far as to advocate reestablishment of the monarchy. De Gasperi himself excited opposition among the large landowners in the party by his advocacy of agrarian reforms. On the other hand, the premier's program of reform was too conservative for the leftist elements in the party. But, despite all opposition, de Gasperi was still premier in the fall of 1952.

ECONOMIC RECONSTRUCTION IN ITALY

The economy of Italy did suffer heavy damage from Allied bombings and from Nazi and Allied artillery fire and tanks, but the destruction of industrial plants was not as great as reported at first. The greatest damage was done in central and southern Italy. There the devastation reduced the industrial capacity by about 30 per cent. In the north, however, where most of the important plants and mills are situated, the destruction was only minor in comparison. Most of the plants, including those which produced automobiles, aluminum, textiles, and paper, were undamaged. It has been estimated that only 7 per cent of the industrial capacity was lost. In general, about 90 per cent of Italy's productive capacity was maintained intact. Nevertheless the Italian industrial machine was afflicted with a general paralysis at the end of the war and had been for some time before the fighting ceased. Thus the Fiat works which had a capacity of 5000 cars per month were producing about twenty-five. A number of factors were responsible for this, among others, the immobilization of transportation, the disappearance of raw materials, the scarcity of electric power, and the long severance of the south from the north, which prevented an exchange of goods and commodities within Italy.

If the industrial plants escaped wholesale destruction, the transportation facilities suffered severely. In the southern part of Italy 80 per cent of the bridges were wrecked by Allied bombs or by the retreating Germans. It is further estimated that 80 per cent of the locomotives, 86 per cent of the passenger coaches, and 62 per cent of the freight cars were destroyed. Furthermore, 80 per cent of the motor trucks and 72 per cent of the motor cars were destroyed or badly damaged. Even in the north much railroad equipment was destroyed by the Allied bombings, and much was taken to Germany by the Nazis. Sadder still was the condition of water transportation. During the war years about 85 per cent of the Italian merchant marine was sent to the bottom of the sea. The inability of the transportation facilities to function properly prevented the distribution not only of finished products and raw materials but also of food. This was an important cause of the serious food shortages in many parts of Italy.

At the end of the war the stock of raw materials in Italy was almost totally exhausted. Unfortunately the country lacks most of the basic resources for the extensive development of modern large-scale industry. The only raw materials that it possesses in sufficient quantities for the country's needs and a surplus for export are bauxite, mercury, zinc, sulphur, and hemp. Of the fourteen million tons of coal Italy used in 1938 only two million were produced at home. Less than half of the iron ore consumed in Italy came from domestic sources. The country is also deficient in oil, copper, chrome, tin, and nickel. Italy must also import most of the cotton and much of the wool that are needed for her industries. During the war years the stock of raw materials originally imported from abroad disappeared and few raw materials were produced at home. In comparison with 1938 the output of raw materials had declined by 65 to 90 per cent in 1945. In the northern part of the country industries were at a total standstill for lack of raw materials.

At the war's end Italy experienced a food shortage as well as a shortage of raw materials. There was basically nothing new in this. A frugal diet of bread and spaghetti has never been far above the starvation mark for a large part of the Italian population. Italy has been a poor country because the population is too large for the limited quantity and low quality of the land. At the end of the war the food situation was worse than usual. Agriculture was producing less. This was due not only to the disruption and confusion caused by the war but also to the lack of fertilizers, the disappearance of cattle, and the shortage of agricultural machinery and implements. Besides being scarce, food and clothing were also high in price. From 1938 to 1945 retail food prices in central and southern Italy had increased thirty-three times, and in northern Italy seventeen times, but wages did not rise commensurately. In the textile industry, for example, wages ranged from 12,000 to 20,000 lire per month in 1945. Women hat workers earned about 4,000 lire per week. At first glance such wages look impressive, but money had little purchasing power. A fairly good dress cost 25,000 lire. One writer made the following comparison for the year 1945:

In the United States one can obtain a good meal in a restaurant for one dollar—or 100 lire, while in Italy the cheapest meal today costs 300 lire; in the United States a sport shirt costs $2.50 or 250 lire, while in Italy it costs (if one finds it) 1,000 lire. . . . A good pair of shoes costs in the United States $8.00 or 800 lire against 3,000—5,000 lire in Italy. From these examples it follows that in Italy a worker must do thirty hours of work to pay for a meal against fifty minutes of the American worker; forty (or more) days for a pair of shoes against eight hours in America.[5]

A number of reforms were needed if the country was to produce more food for its growing population. It was widely held that a sweeping distribution of land would contribute much toward the improvement of agriculture. Actually there are not as many large estates as is generally believed. In the northern part small owners are in the majority. To break up the large farms in this part of the country might well be a calamity, since they are operated not on a feudal, but on a scientific, capitalist basis. The problem in the northern part was in 1945 largely one of wages, hours, and compensation, questions to be decided by negotiation between employers and farm unions. Even in central Italy the large estates included only a small proportion of the land. Most of the estates are organized on a share-crop basis. In comparison with conditions in the south the sharecroppers of the central regions are fairly prosperous. It is on the large estates of southern Italy that the peasants are exploited and the need for change is most urgent. While the landlord lives in luxury, his tenants live in hovels, often six to ten in one room, eking out a bare existence from badly eroded soil. This shows that division by itself will not solve the agrarian problem in Italy.

Other needs of Italian agriculture include more fertilizer, more irrigation projects, and equipment adapted to the nature of the country. Italy's land is starved for fertilizer. The only fertilizer most peasants in the south have ever heard of is manure, and many do not even use that. Even if the peasants did know about other fertilizers, they would not have the means to purchase them. Unable to afford plows, many tenants simply chop up the wretched soil with picks. It is no wonder, therefore, that the yield is low. To relieve the meat shortage in the diet of most Italians more cattle are needed. There is also a great need for better livestock. Because the Italian peasant has little knowledge of proper feeding and crossbreeding, the cattle, sheep, and goats of Italy have deteriorated badly. Further needs include better seed, crop rotation, soil conservation, and irrigation and drainage. In general, the number of people engaged in agriculture was, and still is, too large in relation to the quantity of land and capital available. It would greatly relieve the pressure of the agrarian population if several million peasants could be absorbed by industry.

The wherewithal needed to import sufficient capital goods and raw materials in order to rehabilitate agriculture and industry was

5 C. M. Franzero in *Fortnightly Review,* vol. 164 (August, 1945) , p. 95.

gold or foreign exchange credit. But neither private individuals nor the government itself had the financial resources required. Ever since 1927 the value of imports had exceeded that of exports by a considerable sum. To pay the difference the Italian government had drawn on its gold reserves and foreign exchange holdings, with the result that these had declined from $1,184 million in 1927 to $181 million in 1939. Further drains during the war years lowered the holdings to $24 million in 1945. During the same period the national debt had risen from 92 billion lire in 1922 to 405 billion in 1943. The condition was such at the end of the war that Italy had no security to offer for foreign loans.

The Italian government did obtain food and also funds with which it could make some of the most necessary purchases. Food came, first of all, from UNRRA (United Nations Relief and Rehabilitation Administration). At one time in 1945 the grain supply in the warehouses was only enough to supply the demand for two weeks. To avoid a serious shortage, UNRRA grain shipments consigned to other countries were diverted to Italy. When Premier de Gasperi visited Washington in quest of credits early in 1947, he received $50 million in payment of purchases made by United States forces in Italy, pledges for the immediate shipment of 50,000 tons of wheat, and a loan of $100 million from the Import-Export Bank. But it was Italian participation in the Marshall Plan that provided larger sums. Allocation to Italy for the first year (1948–1949) was $601 million. During the succeeding years there were further subsidies of substantial size. The total aid from April, 1948, when the ECA (European Cooperation Administration) under the Marshall Plan started, to February, 1951, amounted to $1,225 million.

The extra fillip which the Marshall Plan gave to Italy's economic life showed itself in a marked improvement in both agriculture and industry. Agricultural production gradually increased and production in many branches of industry maintained a steady increase. Toward the end of 1950 industrial production records began to exceed those of 1938. In October, 1951, Premier de Gasperi himself said: "Production is 30 per cent higher than the prewar level." A good example of rehabilitation is the Fiat plant at Turin. With a loan of $23 million obtained from the United States, sufficient machinery was purchased so that by the end of 1950 the plant was turning out passenger cars at the rate of more than 100,000 a year, in addition to busses and trucks. In general, motor vehicle production was 78 per cent higher at the end of 1950 than before the war. In the rayon industry, too, the output had increased by 60 per cent, while the annual production of electricity was 50 per cent over prewar output. Foreign trade also improved. Although Italy lost not only her colonies but also Venetia Giulia and her lucrative German market, and although the high prices of Italian products were a handicap in foreign markets, Italy's foreign trade reached 152 per cent of the prewar trade at the end of 1948.

Progress has been remarkable, but many problems still await solution. One of the major ones is that of agricultural production. Even full production is barely sufficient to provide a minimum diet for the Italian population. The problem of providing sustenance becomes increasingly more difficult because of the fact that the population is increasing at the rate of approximately 400,000 a year. The government, it is true, did propose reforms, but has carried them out only in part. And this despite the fact that the three major parties—Christian Democrats, Socialists, and Communists—were agreed on the necessity for reform. Finally in 1949 about 3.75 million acres were marked for distribution, but by the middle of 1952 only a small part had actually been turned over to the peasants.

Much also remains to be done in other respects. Italy still imports considerably more than it exports. The estimated excess of imports over exports in 1951–1952 is $450 million. For some years Marshall Plan funds have made it possible to pay the deficit. Where will Italy find the huge sums after Marshall Plan payments stop? The problem of unemployment is also a serious one. In 1950, unemployment increased to above two million. Premier de Gasperi said (October 1951): "We are striving to increase employment at home and to find new outlets for our labor abroad: an arduous task in a country which has about 2,000,000 unemployed, out of an active population of about 21,000,000." Although the rearmament program promises to wipe out unemployment temporarily, a permanent solution is still needed.

The central problem in Italy, as in other European countries, is to increase the productivity of both industry and agriculture. Only in this way can the economic life be vitalized. Such progress as has been made is only a beginning. But for further progress Italy needs more capital. Her needs have been estimated at $1 billion annually for many years to come.

❋❋❋

The Passing of the Old Colonial Imperialism

THE RESURGENCE OF NATIONALISM

HARDLY had World War II come to an end when the colonial peoples of the world began to seethe with unrest. In the Middle East as well as in the Far East political nationalism was asserting itself in the form of widespread revolts against the old imperialisms. On all sides native peoples were demanding the right to independence and self-government.

During World War I the gospel of self-determination as proclaimed by Woodrow Wilson caused a surge of nationalism the world over. At that time the European powers retained some of the imperial fruits by offering the colonial peoples autonomy within the framework of empire. In this way they managed temporarily to curb the rising tide of nationalism. This was true among other places in India, Indo-China, and Indonesia. But the concessions made by the mother countries failed to satisfy. When the end of World War II presented these countries with another opportunity, the colonial peoples quickly seized upon it to demand independence or even to proclaim their independence. This time the peoples who had previously failed were determined to submit no longer to foreign rule, to be satisfied with nothing less than complete independence. The Javanese, for example, publicized their determination by inscribing on their banners the words, "Merdeka (independence) or death."

The desires of the colonial peoples for self-government were not always accompanied by a concomitant ability to administer the affairs of their country. This did not, however, weaken their determination. They refused to accept the argument that they were not ready for self-rule or that others could rule them better than they could rule

758

themselves. They were determined on becoming their own masters whatever might be the perils of such a status. The oriental masses, one step from starvation, could picture nothing worse than the conditions under which they were living. Ho Chi-minh, leader of the revolt in Indo-China, expressed the general sentiment when he said: "We will keep on fighting and our children, if necessary, will keep on fighting. Independence is the thing. What will follow will follow, but independence must come first if anything is to follow at all."

Although conditions and backgrounds differed in the various countries, the general struggle for independence was essentially one. The basic cause—the desire to terminate the exploitation by foreigners—was everywhere the same. Various factors, however, played a part in giving impetus to the struggle for freedom. One of these was the drive of the Japanese into southeast Asia during World War II and the propaganda campaign they waged. When the Japanese demonstrated that the Europeans could be driven out of southern Asia, they robbed the white empire builders of much of the respect the colonial peoples previously had had for them. During the years in which they were able to hold their conquests the Japanese excited resentments against the French, Dutch, and British with the slogan "Asia for Asiatics." The colonial peoples did not, of course, get the freedom and independence which the Japanese promised them; but after the collapse of the Japanese empire they were nevertheless reluctant to give up the idea of freedom and return to their former status as European dependents.

The Western nations, too, were instrumental in stimulating the demand for independence by holding out promises of freedom. During World War II the principle of self-determination, which President Wilson had proclaimed so eloquently in World War I, was reemphasized as one of the primary Allied objectives. Thus in the Atlantic Charter (August 14, 1941) President Roosevelt and prime minister Churchill proclaimed that their respective countries "seek no territorial changes that do not accord with the freely expressed wishes of the peoples concerned." They further stated that "they respect the right of all peoples to choose the form of government under which they will live; and they wish to see sovereign rights and self-government restored to those who have been forcibly deprived of them." An Asiatic author wrote: "It was in their darkest hour that the Allied leaders issued one of the most stirring documents of recent times—the Atlantic Charter. For the peoples of Asia it was a symbol of a new era in the relationship between the East and the West. The political domination and economic exploitation of Asia by

Europe was to be replaced by mutual aid and cooperation between the two." [1] Equally influential was the statement in the charter of the United Nations that it is one of the purposes of the new organization to promote the development of "friendly relations among nations based on respect for the principle of equal rights and self-determination of peoples." When the United States implemented this declaration by granting independence to the Philippines (July 4, 1946) the hopes of all colonial peoples soared.

That the Eastern peoples are not unacquainted with the literature of democracy was demonstrated in Batavia at the end of World War II. Believing that the occupation troops would be Americans, certain Batavians had inscribed on the walls of houses and public buildings such phrases as "Give us freedom or give us death," "We fight for our inalienable right to life, liberty, and the pursuit of happiness," and "Government of the people, by the people, and for the people."

Other factors also played a part in stimulating the demand for independence. One of these was the weakness of the colonial powers at the end of World War II. The fact that the mother countries emerged from the war militarily, financially, and even politically weak presented the colonial peoples with an unprecedented opportunity to make demands. In addition, the pervasive influence of communism was also an important factor making for revolt. The communists were not so much the instigators as the perpetuators of the revolt. Once the revolts had broken out the communists tried to turn them to their own advantage. They did not openly peddle communism; in fact, the word "communism" was rarely mentioned. The appeal was to nationalism. Thus the communists put new life into the words "Asia for Asiatics." Their appeal to nationalism was a means of arousing opposition to the Western democracies and of influencing the peoples in favor of the Kremlin.

The revolts that broke out during the years immediately after World War II posed new problems for the imperialist powers. In the nineteenth century they had been able to suppress colonial uprisings with a small well-trained force of European soldiers. Examples of such suppression are the Sepoy Mutiny in India and the Boxer Rebellion in China. Because the development of modern arms changed the character of warfare this was no longer possible after World War II. Armed with modern weapons the colonial peoples waged warfare in the guerrilla style with the support of most of the populace. Even though the imperialist powers were able to hold some of

[1] S. Raja Ratnam in *Asia,* vol. 45 (August, 1945), p. 378.

the cities, they were unable to control the hinterland, particularly if the terrain was hilly and covered with natural thickets which gave the advantage to guerrilla fighters.

The surge of nationalism was not confined to Asia. In North Africa it was equally strong. Along the Mediterranean coast from the Atlantic to the Suez Canal the demand for independence has been loud and determined. Two countries—Egypt and Libya—have achieved independence and the others—Algeria, Tunisia, and Morocco—have become more insistent in their demands. The disintegration of European empires in North Africa and Asia has had no parallel in central Africa, the last great colonial region of the world. There the native peoples are so backward and so generally illiterate that few will insist they are ready for self-government. But even the peoples of central Africa are sputtering with nationalist ideas. Recognizing this, the British and the French have accorded them increasing participation in both regional and central administrations.

"L'EMPIRE EST MORT!"

The French empire included almost seventy million inhabitants. The hatred of France which was rampant in her empire derived in part from the fact that the mother country had at times been unduly repressive and had, in general, paid little attention to the political aspirations of the native peoples. One Frenchman after observing French colonial methods said: "The most interesting thing about the French empire is that it still exists." Actually France had lost a part of her empire during the war years. Independence was granted to the two mandates, Syria and Lebanon. As early as 1936 the French administration had proposed a treaty to give Syria and Lebanon full independence at the end of three years, but, while the Syrian Chamber of Deputies ratified the treaty, the French Chamber did not. In 1941 after the forces of Vichy France were ejected, the Free French acknowledged in principle the independence of the two "Levant states," as the French called them. When the Free French did nothing to implement the declaration, riots broke out, precipitating recognition of the independence of both states. French military units still remained in both states, but even they were finally withdrawn in 1946 after an attempt to reestablish French control had failed in the previous year.

The French realized that unless they could bank the fires of nationalism which were burning so brightly, the entire structure of empire would be consumed. Liberated France did not have the economic and military strength to suppress the nationalist strivings; consequently the French devised other means for establishing better relations with their colonies. Unlike the British, they did not talk about "dominion status" as an ultimate goal. They would replace the "French empire" with the "French Union." France would be a partner and friend. The colonial peoples were to be no longer subjects but French citizens with the right of manhood suffrage. This arrangement was foreshadowed as early as 1936 by M. Moutet, Socialist minister of colonies, when he said: "The black peasants of the millet and peanut country, the yellow man of the rice fields, we place them all on the same level of moral equality, social justice, and brotherhood as the workers and farmers of France."

The plan for the French Union was outlined in Articles 60 to 82 of the new French constitution adopted by the Nationalist Constituent Assembly on September 28, 1946. According to its provisions the French Union is made up of two component parts: the French Republic (which includes metropolitan France and the overseas departments and territories) and the Associated Territories and States (Tunisia, Morocco, and the Indo-Chinese Federation). The president of the French Republic serves as president of the union. There are also provisions for a high council and an assembly. While the former is composed of a delegation from the French government and of representatives from the various associated states, the assembly consists "half of members representing metropolitan France and half of members representing the overseas departments and territories and the associated states." The assembly cannot pass legislation. Its function is merely to consider legislative proposals submitted to it either by the French Republic or by the governments of the associated states. The new arrangement as a whole has been described as a kind of solar system, with the French Republic as the sun and the other members of the French Union revolving about it at various distances from the parent body. Whether the French will be able to allay the strong desire for independence on the part of the colonial peoples only the future can tell. That the old conception of empire has definitely been discarded was proclamed by a sign in the Paris ministry of overseas France reading: "L'Empire est mort. Vive l'Union Française."

Although the French Union received its birth certificate in the new French constitution it needed the assent of the larger colonies in order to be born. In most of the French colonies the inhabitants have since that time asserted a desire to develop their own national characteristics rather than to become mere imitation Frenchmen. Many months before the plan for a French union was incorporated in the new constitution, major hostilities broke out in Indo-China, the richest colony of the prewar empire of France. Indo-China, which as the name indicates is the age-old bridge between India and China, extends southward from communist China in much the same way as Korea extends southward from Manchuria. Before the war Indo-China was divided into five states: Tongking, Annam, Cochin-China, Cambodia, and Laos. In size it is about 275,000 square miles or more than a third larger than France. The population in 1948 was about 25 millions, of which four fifths are Annamese and the rest a mixture of Malayan-Chinese stock. Some idea of the wealth of the country may be gained from the fact that it is rich in raw materials and has some fertile agricultural districts. In 1939 almost 25 per cent of the world's exports of rice came from Indo-China. The country was also the third largest exporter of natural rubber and the largest coal exporter in the Far East. For the French it was not only a rich source of food and raw materials but also a market for French goods and an outlet for French capital.

During the seventy years they ruled the country the French did little to improve conditions. In 1945 the illiteracy rate was still almost 90 per cent. For higher education Indo-Chinese students had to go to France or some other foreign country. In France they learned of liberty, equality, and fraternity, but found little application of such ideas when they returned to their home country. Many of the foreign-trained Indo-Chinese, therefore, became leaders of the opposition to French rule. Despite the country's rich natural resources, the masses at the end of World War II were still living in primitive fashion and receiving wages that were a mere pittance. President Roosevelt regarded the French colonial government of Indo-China as the worst in the Far East. In harmony with this opinion a journalist wrote after the revolt broke out:

The press has printed ludicrous statements about German espionage specialists who allegedly organized the Viet Nam. But those really responsible for the movement are the French themselves—the chickens have come home to roost. The French regime of Indo-China was the most oppressive of all Far Eastern regimes. A distinguished French journalist, Andre Viollis, who visited Indo-China just after having published a book violently attacking the British regime in India, had to admit regretfully that conditions in Indo-China were incomparably worse.[2]

2 Louis Claire in *Forum,* vol. 105 (1946), p. 447.

The Indo-Chinese were tired of French rule, tired of being exploited and humiliated. Frequent plots had been laid and many small risings against French rule had taken place in the years prior to World War II, but the French had succeeded in suppressing them. When the Japanese after the fall of France in 1940 signed an agreement for economic collaboration with the Vichy government and then proceeded to occupy Indo-China, nationalists in the country organized the League for the Independence of Indo-China, more commonly called Viet Minh. Although the communists were the dominant element in the movement, the name "communist" was for tactical reasons never used in connection with the organization. To all intents and purposes it was merely a nationalist movement with the following aims: (1) complete and unconditional independence; (2) eviction of the French. In the same year the Free French, who hoped to keep Indo-China in the French empire, promised to introduce extensive reforms after the war, General de Gaulle himself declaring that Indo-China would be given "a new political status within the French community." In March, 1945, after the tide of the war had turned against them, the Japanese sought to frustrate any reestablishment of French rule by inducing the native Indo-Chinese rulers to issue a declaration of independence.

The defeat of the Japanese and their surrender (August 15, 1945) was the signal for the Viet Minh to act. On August 25, after forcing the abdication of the Emperor Bao Dai who had ruled as a Japanese puppet, it made the most of the period of confusion to proclaim the independent republic of Viet Nam (Viet Nam, meaning "Southland," was the ancient name of the country embracing the states of Annam, Tonking, and Cochin-China). Ho Chi-minh, a Russian-trained communist who was a bitter opponent of French rule, became the premier of the new republic. He had spent much of his life working and planning for Indo-Chinese independence and was ready to stake everything on the success of the movement. The strength of the Viet Minh movement was such that the French decided to recognize the republic of Viet Nam (March 6, 1946) as a "free state having its government, its parliament, its army, and its finances, and forming part of the Indo-Chinese Federation [3] and the French union." But a dispute soon broke out between the French and Viet Minh over the question of how much territory was to be included in the republic of Viet Nam. It was agreed that the sparsely populated kingdoms of Cambodia and Laos were to receive a degree

[3] The French hoped to organize the five states of the country into an Indo-Chinese Federation.

of local autonomy, but remain linked to France in matters of foreign policy. Regarding Cochin-China it was agreed that "the people of Cochin-China shall decide by a referendum whether they wish to join the Vietnamese republic."

No sooner had the French signed the agreement than they realized that the inclusion of Cochin-China, with its fertile agricultural areas, into the republic of Viet Nam would mean the loss of French interests in this state. They therefore encouraged a separatist movement in Cochin-China and in June, 1946, recognized it as an independent republic with a cabinet responsible to the French high commissioner. The Viet Minh group at once accused the French of betraying their promises and in December, 1946, Ho Chi-minh's troops forcibly entered Hanoi and decorated its streets with signs reading: "Down with French Imperialism" and "Death to French Domination." This move marked the beginning of full-scale colonial war. At first the French forces enjoyed considerable success. Gradually the most important cities of southern Indo-China were brought under French control. But in the long run the French operations proved relatively ineffective against the guerrilla tactics of the Viet Minh. Even in the cities and towns occupied by the French there was little security. Viet Minh agents, protected by a sympathetic population, burned warehouses, destroyed supply depots, and even threw hand grenades into theaters and restaurants frequented by French soldiers. "We will make Indo-China uninhabitable for the French," a guerrilla leader said; "we certainly do not want the war but if we have to have it, we will destroy everything there is in order to build a new life for ourselves, even if the French force us to start from the vericst beginning."

The French hoped to set up a government in which native leaders would participate, but the French would exercise the control. Such a settlement was unacceptable to the majority of the Indo-Chinese. Not that communism was the primary reason for the opposition to the French. Although Ho Chi-minh's army and government were being increasingly controlled by communists, the majority of the supporters of the Viet Minh movement were non-communists. They supported Ho Chi-minh, not because he was a communist, but because he promised national liberation from the French. The hatred of the French, arising from past indignities, was greater than the fear of communism. In 1949 the French tried to provide an effective antidote to Ho Chi-minh's leadership by recognizing Bao Dai, Western-educated ex-emperor of Annam, as the rightful ruler of Indo-China. The French hoped to convince the Indo-

Chinese that they would be better off under Bao Dai's regime, that Ho Chi-minh was a Russian puppet, and that Bao Dai could procure for them by negotiation the same independence for which the Viet Minh asked them to die. But the move was not successful. The great majority of Indo-Chinese saw in Bao Dai the tool of French colonialism.

Thus the war continued month after month and with it the drain on the French finances, the French being obliged either to abandon Indo-China to its fate or to sacrifice several thousand men and about a billion dollars a year to maintain a military stalemate. It is well established that the Chinese communists have been training and equipping the Viet Minh forces, but this fact has not permitted the latter to overwhelm the French. On the other hand, it is difficult to see how the French forces alone can win a decisive victory.

The demand for independence was not restricted to Indo-China. Nationalism asserted itself in all parts of the French empire. In many colonies unrest and agitation have erupted into scenes of violence. Although the administrations are different in Morocco, Tunis, and Algeria, the surge of nationalism is strong in each colony. In Algeria, which as a part of metropolitan France is administered by the ministry of the interior, fiery nationalists tried to excite a widespread independence movement with such speeches as: "For 116 years we have been under the French yoke. Still we sleep on the ground, we wear only a simple gandourah, we walk barefoot, and most of us go three or four days without eating a piece of cake." In Morocco and Tunisia, which as protectorates are governed through their native rulers (the Sultan of Morocco and the Bey of Tunisia), nationalist movements are also active. In Morocco the sultan himself has shown strong nationalist tendencies. Under the new French constitution Morocco and Tunisia were brought into closer union with metropolitan France; Guadelupe, Martinique, the Reunion Islands, and French Guiana have been incorporated into the French administrative system as "departments," while Madagascar, French West Africa, and French Equatorial Africa have been granted more self-government. It still remains to be seen, however, whether the new French policy will succeed in allaying the nationalist surge.

THE UNITED STATES OF INDONESIA

At the end of World War II the Dutch, too, were confronted with a rebellion in their richest colony, the Dutch East Indies, a string of islands stretching along the equator for more than a thousand miles and inhabited by more than seventy million people. The importance of these islands for the economic life of the Netherlands can be judged from the fact that about 17 per cent of the Netherlands income in prewar years was derived from the Dutch East Indies. At that time this colony produced more than 90 per cent of the world's quinine, 83 per cent of its pepper, 37 per cent of its rubber, 31 per cent of its copra, 20 per cent of its tin, and many other important materials. The Dutch East Indies were such a rich prize that the Japanese lost no time occupying the islands after Pearl Harbor. When the Japanese realized that they could not hold the East Indies, they set up an Indonesian regime before their surrender and even left arms behind for the Indonesians. With this encouragement the Indonesians refused to return to a colonial status. During the more than 300 years of colonial rule the Dutch had gained a reputation for their administration in the East Indies. This did not, however, satisfy the Indonesians. Only two days after the surrender of Japan a group of nationalists in Java, led by Achmed Soekarno, proclaimed an independent republic of Indonesia, adopted a national flag, and took steps to draw up a provisional constitution modeled on that of the United States. When British forces arrived to drive out the remaining Japanese, intermittent fighting took place. The clashes continued after Dutch troops replaced the British in 1946, with the Indonesians determined to prevent the reestablishment of the colonial status. So far as they were concerned "colonialism was dead."

The Dutch were surprised at the fierce determination of the Indonesians, but they were of no mind to let so rich a prize slip from their grasp. For almost a year they alternately fought and negotiated with the Indonesians. On November 15, 1946, an agreement was reached whereby the Dutch recognized the authority of the Indonesian Republic over Java, Sumatra, and the smaller island of Madura. A second state, East Indonesia, was organized to embrace the islands east of Java, except Borneo and New Guinea. After an interim period lasting until January 1, 1949, the new states were to become part of a Netherlands-Indonesian Union under the Dutch crown. By this arrangement the Dutch managed to salvage most of their prewar economic privileges. The agreement gave the Dutch equal footing with the Indonesians in matters of taxes and civil rights and provided for the restitution of foreign property. But differences regarding various arrangements soon arose. While the Indonesians wanted more freedom to conduct their affairs, the Dutch were reluctant to relinquish any of the authority they had previously exercised. Thus, for example, the Indonesians wanted sole control of the police during the interim period against Dutch insistence that control be held jointly.

In July, 1947, hostilities were renewed when a Dutch force of about 60,000 equipped with such weapons as tanks and rocket-firing planes marched against the Indonesians. Although the native forces were stronger in man power they lacked modern weapons and were, therefore, forced to fall back. In carrying out a scorched-earth policy they burned their towns as they retreated. It was manifestly impossible for even the well-armed Dutch forces to overcome the guerrilla warfare waged by the Indonesians with the support of millions of determined inhabitants. On August 1, 1947, the UN Security Council, deeming the hostilities a threat to world peace, called upon the Dutch and Indonesians to "cease hostilities forthwith" and "settle their disputes by arbitration or by other peaceful means." Although the Dutch questioned the authority of the Security Council to act in the matter they nevertheless abided by the orders. Negotiations were resumed, but were again broken off by a resort to force. In January, 1949, the Security Council issued another cease-fire order. Although negotiations were resumed, intermittent clashes continued.

Finally as a climax to the extended discussions the Statute of Union was signed at The Hague by the Netherlands and Indonesia on November 2, 1949. By this agreement the Dutch recognized the full independence of their former colony. Java, Sumatra, Borneo, the Celebes, and many smaller islands were recognized as parts of a federal state to be known as the United States of Indonesia.[4] United Nations commissioners who participated in the final conference were important factors in reaching a peaceful settlement of the controversy between the Dutch and the Indonesians. The new state and the Netherlands were joined in a voluntary union by the Statute of Union. Article One of the statute reads: "The Netherlands-Indonesian Union effectuates the organized cooperation between the Kingdom of the Netherlands and the Republic of the United States of Indonesia on the basis of voluntariness and equal status with equal rights; the Union does not prejudice the status of each of the two parties as an independent and sovereign state." The statute further states that the cooperation between the Netherlands and the United States of Indonesia "shall take place with respect to matters lying primarily in the field of foreign relations and defense and as far as necessary finance and also as regards matters of an economic and a cultural nature." According to Article Five, "the head of the Union shall be Her Majesty Queen Juliana, Princess of Orange-

[4] The status of New Guinea was to be decided at a later time,

Nassau, and in case of succession her lawful successors to the crown of the Netherlands."

Thus after four years of fighting and negotiation peace was established between the Dutch and the new United States of Indonesia. According to a special agreement all Dutch troops were scheduled to leave Indonesia within six months. The terms of the agreement, in recognizing the Dutch commercial interests in Indonesia, left control of the new nation's economic life largely in Dutch hands, despite the fact that the Indonesians theoretically have the final and complete authority over their economic and financial affairs. As the capital of their new government the Indonesians chose the city of Batavia, the old capital of the Netherlands Indies, which was renamed Jakarta. When the signing of the Statute of Union was announced crowds in the streets of Jakarta cheered President Soekarno, whom most Indonesians regarded as the personification of independence. Like the roll of thunder the shouts of "Merdeka, Tetap Merdeka (Freedom, Freedom Forever!)" reverberated through the city. "We are one nation," President Soekarno said, "and we pray that we may live as a single free nation. . . . We want to build a strong nation, prosperous and orderly. . . . I appeal to you all to show our hospitality to our foreign guests, including the Dutch."

CHANGES IN THE BRITISH COMMONWEALTH

The British Commonwealth, embracing the largest extent of colonial territory, has undergone the greatest change. In the Commonwealth, as in the other colonial empires, the crisis was sharpened as a result of World War II. In many parts of this far-flung empire the trends toward independence which had started earlier were accelerated by the weak condition in which Britain emerged from the war. The fact that Britain was a mere shell of her former self was bound to weaken her authority in those sections of the empire which were striving for independence. Even some of the smaller colonies believed that they could twist the tail of the wounded lion with impunity. But the British had no intention of permitting their empire to dissolve. Winston Churchill said emphatically in 1942: "I haven't become the king's first minister to preside over the liquidation of the British Empire." This feeling was shared by the Labor Party. Even the most ardent Laborites did not advocate the disruption of the empire. "I'm not prepared to sacrifice the British Empire," Foreign Secretary Bevin said in 1946, "because I know that if it fell a great collection of free nations would go into the limbo of the past and would create disaster. . . . It would mean the standard of life of our constituents would fall considerably." During the years the Labor Party was in power no measures were passed to alter radically the character or direction of colonial life.

If it was true that the British did not wish to see the collapse of their empire, it was equally true that a country that was greatly weakened by the war and that was in the throes of an economic depression could not afford to spend vast sums in military operations designed to hold the restive colonies in the empire by force. Hence the British continued the policy which had been incorporated in the Statute of Westminster (1931), which raised the overseas dominions —Australia, Canada, New Zealand, and South Africa—to an equal status with Britain. These former dominions attained full independence in every respect, but remained associated with the Commonwealth. This same policy was applied to other peoples who reached political maturity. They were treated as equals in the hope that they would want to continue their partnership in the British Commonwealth. With one exception, Burma, they did stay in the Commonwealth.

Among the peoples of the British Empire who demanded autonomy or complete independence at the end of World War II were Ceylon, Malaya, and Burma. The inhabitants of Ceylon, an island off the southern tip of India, had been promised a constitution as early as 1943. This promise was carried out when the British in 1946 promulgated a constitution which gave the inhabitants of Ceylon control over the internal affairs of the country, with only matters relating to defense, external affairs, and serious racial and religious conflicts being reserved for decision by the British government. To the Ceylonese the new arrangement was a disappointment in that it did not establish the dominion status for which many had hoped. In February, 1948, however, the island achieved full dominion status.

More complex was the problem of Malaya, which is situated at the southern tip of southeast Asia and includes the prewar base of Singapore. The situation was complicated by deep-seated racial and national animosities. In a population of 5.8 million, 43 per cent were Malayans, 45 per cent Chinese, and 10 per cent Indians, with each race disliking the other two. The antagonism between these groups has precluded the development of a nationalism comparable to that of Indonesia. Although the British accorded Malaya a considerable degree of self-government, the British remained as a stabilizing influence.

In Burma the demand for independence was one of long standing.

In 1935 the British gave the Burmese a liberal constitution and two years later separated Burma from India, constituting it a separate state. But this failed to satisfy the Burmese. They wanted complete independence. When the Japanese invaded southeast Asia during World War II the Burmese nationalists joined them in fighting the British. In 1943 the Japanese proclaimed Burma an independent state, with a government under the control of the Japanese commander in chief. Upon the collapse of the Japanese government the Burmese independence movement again asserted itself. The Anti-Fascist People's Freedom League, a powerful political organization led by U Aung San, stated that nothing short of complete independence would be acceptable to its members. In January, 1947, an agreement was reached between Britain and her former dependency which promised the latter full independence. After a constitution had been drafted the Burmese were to decide whether they wished to remain in the Commonwealth as a dominion or to sever all ties with the British Commonwealth. The Burmese chose the latter.

INDEPENDENCE FOR INDIA

Probably the most serious problem for the British was that of India. During the two decades before World War II the desire for freedom had been growing stronger and stronger. When World War II broke out the Congress Party, the largest political party in India, refused to support the war effort unless the country was granted full independence. In 1942 the British government sent Sir Stafford Cripps to India with a promise of independence at the end of the war in return for active participation in the war. But the Indian leaders doubted the sincerity of the British promises. When Mahatma Gandhi told his people not to participate in the war effort, styling the British promise "a post-dated check on a crashing bank," he was temporarily imprisoned (1942). Most of the other leaders shared his opinion. If the British, they asked, are convinced that the peoples of India are ready for freedom, why do they not grant it at once? Jawaharlal Nehru, president of the Congress Party, said: "Come what may, we will come out as a free nation or be thrown into the ashes."

When the British at the end of the war took measures toward carrying out their promises they encountered new difficulties. They had hoped to turn authority over to a single Indian government, but before they could do so an open rift developed between the Hindus and Moslems. While both opposed the British, they also opposed each other. The Moslems, who were a minority in India, opposed the establishment of a single state in which the majority would prevail. They feared that no consideration would be given to their religion and way of life. They resented, above all, the fact that they had not been consulted by the Congress Party. In 1946 the Moslems proclaimed the slogan "Pakistan (independent Moslem state) or death." Mohammed Ali Jinnah, absolute leader of the Moslem League, demanded complete separation of all regions inhabited by a Moslem majority and their organization into a separate state to be known as Pakistan. The Congress Party, which wanted a united India, opposed the demand. Feelings grew so bitter that riots broke out in various parts of India, taking a high toll in lives. It is estimated that in Calcutta alone ten to fifteen thousand people were killed.

Despite the bitterness between the Moslems and Hindus the British continued with their plans to surrender the governing authority. On February 20, 1947, prime minister Attlee proclaimed the approaching end of an epoch when he announced to the House of Commons the final stage of British authority in India. "His Majesty's Government," he said, "wish to make it clear that it is their definite intention to take necessary steps to effect the transfer of power into responsible Indian hands by a date not later than June, 1948." Subsequently, after the Hindus and Moslems succeeded in agreeing on a plan, the date was advanced. The plan called for the division of India into two or more states. The two major states were to be Pakistan of the Moslems and India of the Hindus. It was hoped that the smaller princely states would federate either with Pakistan or Hindu India and thus obviate the formation of a third state. Almost all the states ultimately joined with Hindu India. Thus Hindu India with a population of more than 300 million still surpasses the population of any other state except China. The population of Moslem Pakistan is about seventy millions. The terms of the independence of Pakistan and India, which became effective in August, 1947, provided that both should remain members of the Commonwealth for one year, after which they would be free to remain or withdraw as Burma had done.

On August 15, 1947, a new period began in the history of India. It was the day that ushered in freedom for that teeming subcontinent. All over India the British flag was hauled down after two hundred years of British rule. In place of the Union Jack there rose the orange, white, and green banner of the Indian Union or the white and green flag of Pakistan. The new India was ushered in without violence between the British and the people of India. But the bitterness between

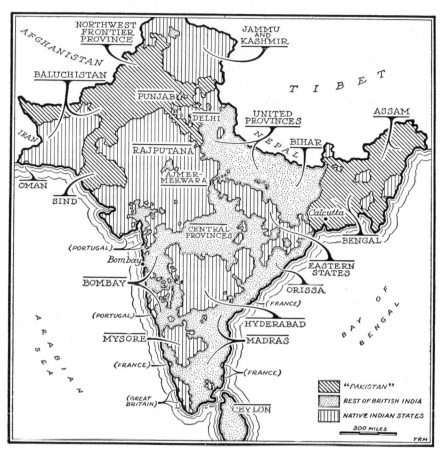

INDIA IN 1947

On August 15, 1947, the British flag was hauled down in India, and the Hindu Dominion of India and the Moslem Dominion of Pakistan entered the British Commonwealth of Nations.

the Hindus and Moslems had still not subsided despite the declaration of Jawaharlal Nehru, the first prime minister of Hindu India, who told his people that "our first and immediate objective must be to put an end to all internal strife and violence, which disfigure and degrade us and injure the cause of freedom." In Karachi, the capital of Pakistan, Mohammed Ali Jinnah, the first governor general, said: "Our object shall be peace within and peace without." Nevertheless rioting and bloodshed continued during the settlement of the boundaries and the period during which the princely states decided which of the two major states they wished to join. In at least one instance open war between India and Pakistan was averted through the offices of the United Nations.

Mahatma Gandhi, "the architect of free India," did not accept the idea of a partitioned India. The violence between the Hindu and Moslem communities grieved him greatly. He sought to encourage the different peoples to live together in harmony and good will. In his view it was time for a "reunion of hearts." On October 2, 1947, his seventy-eighth birthday, he said: "With every breath I pray God to give me strength to quench the flames or remove me from this earth. I who staked my life to gain India's independence do not wish to be a living witness to its destruction." Finally he decided to fast as a means of dispelling the clouds of bitterness that hung over India. The five-day fast was successful in that it brought solemn promises of greater consideration for the Moslem minority. But the Mahasabha Hindu faction, which was fanatically opposed to Hindu-Moslem unity, resented Gandhi's efforts. The members of this faction favored militant action against the Moslems. On January 20, 1948, soon after the frail ascetic broke his fast, an attempt was made on his life with a bomb, but failed. Although his life was in danger, the Mahatma made no effort to protect himself. He continued to walk freely among the people and to converse with everyone who approached him. But on January 30 the apostle of nonviolence fell victim to the bullets of an assassin. As he was on his way to a prayer meeting which he held daily, a member of the Mahasabha faction stepped in front of the Mahatma and fired three shots into his chest and abdomen. Gandhi breathed: "Ram! Ram! (God! God!)," touched his palm to his forehead in a gesture of forgiveness, and collapsed, dying a short time later.

Gandhi's death was a great loss not only to India and Pakistan but to the cause of peace throughout the world. Prime minister Nehru of India said of him: "Reactionary or revolutionary, he has changed the face of India, given pride and character to a cringing and demoralized people, built up strength and consciousness in the masses, and made the Indian problem a world problem." In his tribute to Gandhi Dr. Albert Einstein, the distinguished physicist, said: "Generations to come, it may be, will scarcely believe that such a one as this ever in flesh and blood walked upon the earth."

When Pakistan and India made decisions as to their future status, the former decided to remain in the Commonwealth as a dominion, while India chose to become a republic. As the time drew near for India to become a republic, the bond uniting it with the British Commonwealth appeared to be growing thinner. But the government of India finally decided not to divorce itself completely from the Commonwealth. In April, 1949, prime minister Nehru and representatives of seven other Commonwealth states met to consider the question of how an India that was determined to become a republic could remain in a Commonwealth whose only formal bond is allegiance to the king. After long deliberation the ministers found their formula in the Statute of Westminster, the constitutional foundation of the Commonwealth. The formula stated that since the member nations are "united by a common allegiance to the crown" the crown is "the symbol of the free association of the members." Hence, although India would abandon her allegiance to the crown, she could retain her membership in the Commonwealth by recognizing the symbol. It was another illustration of the elasticity of British institutions.

THE RESTIVE MIDDLE EAST

Although the surge of nationalism was greatest in the Far East, it also asserted itself in the Middle East, which is the cultural and religious center of the world's 275 million Moslems. The region is also a vital juncture between the three continents and an extremely rich source of oil, the "liquid gold" which is so essential to all the great powers. The petroleum deposits in the ground of the Middle East have been estimated at thirty billion barrels. Despite these rich resources the masses are disease-ridden and illiterate, and live in grinding poverty, wresting a bare existence from the soil by primitive agricultural methods. Many nationalist leaders asserted that there is enough natural wealth in the area to raise the abysmally low standard of living if the imperialist nations could be expelled and complete independence could be established. By the end of World War II the Arab East, including Saudi Arabia, Yemen, Egypt, Lebanon, Syria, and Iraq, had to a large extent attained its national aspirations. But the countries that were still under European domination began to demand independence, while those that were largely independent insisted on the termination of all arrangements which impinged either on the appearance or actuality of independence. Hence there has been a growing distrust of, and distaste for, British rule and for arrangements previously entered into with the British.

One of the most vexing problems for the British was undoubtedly that of Palestine. At the end of World War II the conflict between the Arabs and Jews over the future of Palestine was still as bitter as it had been before the war; in fact, the mutual hostility was intensified by the pressure of Jewish immigration during and immediately after the war. Many Jews fleeing from Nazi persecutions looked to Palestine as a refuge. Although both the Arabs and the British tried to limit the migration of more Jews to Palestine, many managed to enter illegally. As a result the Jewish population had grown to nearly 600,000 by the end of the war. Any attempt on the part of the British to placate the Zionist by permitting the admittance of more Jews to Palestine was bitterly resented by the Arabs. The unabating Arab-Jewish hostility seriously unsettled the whole Middle East. The neighboring states openly sympathized with the Palestine Arabs and even threatened to invade the Holy Land to protect the Arabs there.

Early in 1947 the British made one last attempt to find a way out of the impasse by calling a conference of Arabs and Jews from the affected areas. But the expected deadlock developed at once. Finally the British Labor Government suggested a partition of Palestine into two zones, one with a Jewish majority and the other with an Arab majority. At the end of five years, if the Jews and Arabs agreed, Palestine would become independent; if they did not agree the issue would go to the United Nations. Both Arabs and Zionists rejected the proposal. While the Arabs continued to insist on an exclusively Arab state in Palestine, the Zionists wanted Palestine as a national Jewish homeland. The British, since they were unable to reach an agreement between the contesting parties, referred the problem to the United Nations. Meanwhile fighting and violence between the Jews and Arabs continued. Jewish terrorists even attacked British personnel. In November, 1947, the UN General Assembly voted for the partitioning of Palestine into separate Jewish and Arab states. During the succeeding months the British proceeded with their plans to give up the Palestine mandate. The mandate was officially ended when the British High Commissioner left on May 15, 1948, and the country was divided in accordance with the boundaries prescribed by the General Assembly. The Zionists at once proclaimed the State of Israel which was immediately recognized by the United States of America.

Nationalism also rose to a high pitch in Egypt. After Egypt was declared "independent with reservations" by the British in 1922 various issues had arisen to disturb the relations between the two countries. Finally Mussolini's attack on Ethiopia in 1935 convinced both the British and the Egyptians of the advantages of cooperation. Consequently a treaty was signed in 1936 for a period of twenty years. Besides recognizing Egypt's complete independence the treaty provided for British control of the Suez Canal "until such time as the two parties agree that the Egyptian army is in a position to insure by its own resources the liberty and entire security of navigation of the canal." In the meantime Britain was permitted to station troops on Egyptian territory near Ismailia for the purpose of insuring the defense of the canal. Britain was also given the right to use Alexandria and Port Said as air and naval bases, and to move troops over Egyptian territory in case of war or threat of war. Furthermore, the joint rule of Britain and Egypt was to be continued in the Anglo-Egyptian Sudan. In 1946 the Egyptians demanded the replacement of the treaty of 1936 by one that would provide for the withdrawal of all foreign troops. Nationalist elements in Egypt, and particularly the members of Wafd or the Nationalist Party, staged anti-British demonstrations, with the mob shouting, "Down with the British!" In November, 1946, King Farouk of Egypt announced that the British had agreed to withdraw their troops from Cairo and Alexandria. He also expressed the hope that an agreement would be reached regarding the withdrawal of the British from the Sudan. But the negotiations that followed were unsuccessful and in October, 1948, the British announced that the international situation prevented the removal of their remaining troops.

For imperial and strategic reasons the British were determined to retain their hold on the Suez Canal, which has been called "the jugular vein of Britain's imperial communications," and on the Sudan. So the British stood on the pact. Their refusal to withdraw caused tension and terrorism to mount to a new crescendo. Students and workers staged anti-British demonstrations and Egyptian "liberation battalions" turned to sniping at British soldiers and to ambushing small groups. The British government responded by reinforcing its troops and by trying to seal off the Canal Zone from the rest of Egypt. For a time there was comparative quiet, but in January, 1952, a fierce battle developed in Ismailia between British soldiers and Egyptian nationalists in which forty-three Egyptians and three Britons were killed. The news of the battle caused violent repercussions in Cairo. Mobs set fire to British buildings and business places and in some areas were joined by police shouting "Down with the British! Long live Russia, friend of Egypt!" King Farouk finally took the matter in hand, declared martial law, effected some cabinet changes, and succeeded in restoring order. But the relations between the British and the Egyptians remained very delicate.[5]

In 1951 a crisis also developed in Iran (Persia) where Britain's most valuable foreign enterprise, the Anglo-Iranian Oil Company, was located. Although Iran was politically an independent nation, the Anglo-Iranian Oil Company had control of the oil production of the country on a royalty basis. These royalties formed approximately one-third of the total revenues of the Iranian state. For the British the Anglo-Iranian Oil Company was important because it was the chief supplier of the British navy. In 1950 the Iranian oil output amounted to 35.5 million tons or more than 6 per cent of world production. Of this total the Anglo-Iranian Oil Company's Abadan refinery, the largest in the world, produced 27 million tons. In this year, however, the Majlis (the Iranian Parliament) in a frenzy of nationalism voted unanimously to nationalize the oil industry. In 1951 the Britons who operated the Anglo-Iranian Oil Company were forced out of the country despite the fact that the Iranians lacked the technical experience to run the industry. Hence the flow of Iranian oil to world markets was cut off. To the British the nationalization of the Iranian oil industry was a severe blow, for the Anglo-Iranian Oil Company largely represented what remained of British economic and political influence in the Near East.

The many changes that have taken place in the British Commonwealth weakened it in some respects and strengthened it in others. What remained of the British Empire, as distinguished from the British Commonwealth, was largely in Africa. About four fifths of Britain's seventy million remaining colonial peoples live on the African continent. The rest of Britain's colonies consist largely of islands and coastal regions scattered far and wide over the seaways of the world. But while the British Empire was shrinking, the British Commonwealth as such was growing. Although India, Pakistan, and Ceylon dropped out of the Empire, they joined the Commonwealth, bringing more than 400 million people with them. Thus the Com-

---

5 As the result of a virtually bloodless coup d'état, staged by General Naguib with the support of the Egyptian army on July 23, 1952, King Farouk was forced to abdicate in favor of his infant son, Prince Ahmed. Naguib asserted that he would drive the British out of the Nile valley.

monwealth has grown since 1945 from 87 million to almost 500 million. The strength of the tie that unites the nations of the Commonwealth was displayed in 1949 when the representatives of the member nations, after accepting India into the Commonwealth, made the following declaration: "Accordingly the United Kingdom, Canada, Australia, New Zealand, South Africa, India, Pakistan, and Ceylon hereby declare that they remain united as free and equal members of the Commonwealth of Nations, freely cooperating in the pursuit of peace, liberty, and progress."

THE DISSOLUTION OF THE ITALIAN EMPIRE

When Mussolini took his country into the war in 1940 as an Axis partner of Nazi Germany, Italy had an empire that was more than a million and a quarter miles in extent with an estimated population of more than fourteen millions. Before the end of the war the Italian government had lost control of the entire area. In 1941 the Italians were driven out of Eritrea, Ethiopia, and Italian Somaliland by Allied forces, and during the next two years the Italians were also expelled from Libya. In 1943–1944 they lost Albania and the Italian Aegean Islands. Thus the Italians emerged from the war without an empire. Most Italians did, however, desire the return of at least a part of the old empire and the Italian government itself presented extensive arguments for the return of its pre-Fascist African colonies. They wanted these colonies back to salve their national pride, but what is more important, the Italian government desperately needed Lebensraum (living space) for some of the many millions cramped in the narrow Italian boot.

The victors, however, ultimately ruled against the Italian desires. In the peace treaty which was signed in 1947 Italy was obliged to renounce her sovereignty over her former empire. While Albania was ostensibly given her independence, and independence was restored to Ethiopia, the Dodecanese were awarded to Greece. Under Article 23 of the Italian peace treaty the final disposition of the other former Italian colonies in Africa was to be determined jointly by the Big Four (Great Britain, France, the U.S.A., and the U.S.S.R.). If these powers were unable to reach an agreement on the question within one year after the enactment of the treaty (September 15, 1948), the question was to be referred to the General Assembly of the United Nations for a decision. The territories in question were Libya, Italian Somaliland, and Eritrea, having a total area of about 890,000 square miles and a population of about two and a half millions. Much of the territory comprising these colonies consists of desert and semidesert, only small areas being favorable for human settlement. But in the Council of Foreign Ministers the question of the Italian colonies became one of the most controversial of the postwar problems. There was no agreement on any of the plans and schemes that were put forward. Even the dispatching of a commission to the territories did not result in an agreement. Finally the four powers conceded their failure to find a solution and referred the issue to the General Assembly.

After long discussions and investigations by committees the question was presented to the General Assembly which reached a decision in November, 1949. Regarding Libya the Assembly decided: " (1) that Libya, comprising Cyrenaica, Tripolitania, and the Fezzan, shall be constituted an independent and sovereign state; (2) this independence shall become effective as soon as possible and in any case not later than January 1, 1952; (3) that a constitution for Libya, including the form of government, be determined by representatives of the inhabitants of Cyrenaica, Tripolitania, and the Fezzan meeting and consulting together in a National Assembly." In the case of Italian Somaliland the Assembly recommended: " (1) that Italian Somaliland shall be an independent sovereign state; (2) this independence shall become effective at the end of ten years from the date of the approval of the Trusteeship Agreement by the General Assembly; (3) during the period mentioned in paragraph 2, Italian Somaliland shall be placed under the International Trusteeship System with Italy as the administering authority." On April 1, 1950, a provisional Italian administration replaced the British military administration as the governing authority in Italian Somaliland. In 1960, however, it is to become an independent state. A UN advisory council will aid and advise Italy in its trusteeship administration.

On the disposal of Eritrea the Assembly did not reach a final decision. It was decided that after further investigation the status of Eritrea would be determined in 1950. Haile Selassie, the emperor of Ethiopia, urged its federation with Ethiopia, maintaining that almost half of Eritrea's population desired a reunion with Ethiopia. Economically Eritrea was dependent on Ethiopia, since it derived its livelihood largely from the transit of goods to and from Ethiopia. Haile Selassie also based his claim to Eritrea on his country's need for an outlet to the sea. After sending a commission to Eritrea to ascertain more fully the wishes of its inhabitants the General Assembly decided on December 2, 1950, to federate Eritrea with Ethiopia.

After a transitional period the former Italian colony was to become an autonomous unit under the sovereignty of the Ethiopian crown not later than September 15, 1952. During the period that the country remains under British administration an Eritrean government is to be organized and a constitution drafted.

CHAPTER THIRTY

The Soviet Union Since World War II

IF the end of the war was welcome to the other Allied nations it was particularly so to the Soviet Union. No nation had paid a larger price for victory both in blood and in property. The Russians, in fact, suffered more casualties and greater devastation than all the other Allied nations combined. G. M. Malenkov, a member of the Politburo, stated in 1947 that "seven million people were killed in action, perished during the occupation, or were forcibly driven off to Germany." This figure does not include the decline in the population due to the decline of the birth rate. Besides the appalling loss of life there was a tremendous destruction of property. The report submitted to the Allied Reparations Commission in September, 1945, listed the number of buildings destroyed at six million. Even more striking was the damage suffered by the railroads. A commission appointed by the Soviet government to survey the war damage reported that 4100 stations and 13,000 bridges had been destroyed, 15,800 locomotives and 482,000 freight cars had been damaged, destroyed, or removed, and 65,000 kilometers of track had been destroyed.[1]

Equally great was the destruction of machinery and industrial plants. The Ukraine and the Don Basin which the Germans occupied and devastated had before the war been the Soviet Union's most highly developed industrial region. In their work of destruction the Nazis were very thorough. The special commission ap-

[1] These statistics are given for what they may be worth. Because of the Soviet censorship there is no way of checking their accuracy. It is possible that the damages may have been exaggerated as the basis for a claim for German reparations.

pointed by the Soviet government to survey the damages reported that a total of 31,850 industrial establishments, employing four million workers, were destroyed. In addition the Nazis either removed or rendered useless large quantities of machinery and machine tools. Particularly thorough was the destruction of the power plants in the occupied area. First of all, the Nazis dismantled many of the power plants and shipped the machinery to Germany. It is estimated that they removed 11,300 generators, 14,000 steam boilers, and 1400 turbines. Much of the equipment they did not ship to Germany was either put out of commission or short-circuited so that it would burn itself out. They blew up the Dnieper Dam so effectively that it did not begin to produce power again until 1946. In the Ukraine there is a small territory called the Donbas which was to Russia what the Ruhr was to Germany. The state of Stalino of which this district was a part produced no less than 40 per cent of Russia's entire output of coke, 30 per cent of its coal and pig iron, and 23 per cent of its steel. Nazi demolition squads performed their work with such thoroughness that when the Soviet industrial experts arrived after the Nazis had been forced out they found that 99.5 per cent of the productive capacity had been destroyed or put out of order.

The territory occupied by the Germans also embraced some of the best agricultural lands in the Soviet Union. It is estimated that from the more than seventy million acres of arable land in the occupied districts the Russians had derived 47 per cent of their agricultural produce. The War Damage Commission reported that the Nazis had in these districts destroyed or burned 98,000 collective farms, 1876 state farms, and 2890 machine and tractor stations. The losses in agricultural equipment were listed as 137,000 tractors, 49,000 harvester-thresher combines, and about four million plows, harrows, and other farm implements. High, too, were the losses of domestic animals. The Soviet authorities did manage to evacuate some of the animals before the Germans conquered the districts, but they were able to save only a small proportion. The commission listed the losses as seven million horses, seventeen million cattle, twenty million pigs, and twenty-seven million sheep and goats.

The foregoing account of the losses sustained by the Soviet Union by itself presents a one-sided picture. Actually the setback administered to Soviet industry was less than the figures indicate. By an all-out effort the Russians managed to offset the losses in both industry and agriculture. This they did, in part, by evacuating some of the plants from the occupied areas before the Nazis moved in. Reportedly 1300 large industrial plants were dismantled and transported to the eastern districts of the Soviet Union. At the same time new plants were constructed in the Ural region or beyond. As a result the industrial capacity of eastern Russia was greatly expanded. According to Soviet statistics the total output of industry in the Urals increased 260 per cent and in Siberia 180 per cent during the war years. In 1945 the output of Russian industry as a whole was only 8.3 per cent below the prewar output. The increase in the industrial capacity of the eastern districts of the Soviet Union, including Siberia, was largely limited to the heavy industries, particularly industries producing munitions. When the manufacture of munitions was curtailed at the end of the war the index of industrial production dropped sharply.

Efforts to make up for agricultural losses in the west through the expansion of production in the east met with only limited success. It is estimated that an additional twelve million hectares were brought under cultivation in the eastern districts by 1944, but the over-all agricultural output remained below the prewar level. As for consumer goods, they were neglected. By 1945 the production of such goods was still 43 per cent below the prewar level. Consequently living standards dropped to a level that was even lower than it had been before the war. It was said with considerable truth that "the people were reduced to wearing tatters and rags." Clinical thermometers, for example, were rarely to be found except in military hospitals. The average country doctor had to ascertain as best he could whether a patient's temperature was above normal. The drop in the production of consumer goods was accompanied by an increasing housing shortage. It is estimated that the Nazi destruction rendered twenty-five million people homeless. This housing shortage forced thirty people to live in the same space that in 1937 had been occupied by twenty. In addition many others were forced to live in caves, storm cellars, and abandoned army dugouts and barracks.

The Soviet government lost no time in restoring its economy. Twenty-two months, for example, after the Donbas and Stalino districts had been liberated, production had been restored to 57 per cent of the prewar level. Even the massive equipment needed for iron and steel production was in part repaired and restored so that the production was 25 per cent of prewar. Many coal mines were drained and mining operations were resumed, with the result that in these districts the coal output reached two fifths of prewar by July, 1945. By the first anniversary of V-E Day much of the damage to the Dnieper Dam had been repaired, coal production had reached 60 per cent of prewar in the liberated regions, and work had been resumed in the nickel and manganese mines.

in 1940, **26** million tons of sugar beets or an increase of 22 per cent over 1940, and 3.1 million tons of cotton or a 25 per cent increase over 1940. The rate of increase for potatoes and other vegetables was higher. In short, the total agricultural output was to be raised 27 per cent by 1950 in comparison with 1940. To aid the peasants in achieving the set goal the government proposed to supply them with the necessary farm machinery, including tractors, seeders, and combines. Accordingly the plan called for the building of twice as many tractors before the end of 1950 as there were at the tractor stations when the Nazis attacked in 1941. The improvement was to be qualitative as well as quantitative. More attention was to be paid to the use of fertilizers and to multiple-field crop rotation. Nor was animal husbandry overlooked. To replace the stock of animals depleted during the war the plan specified that by the end of 1950 the number of horses was to be increased by 46 per cent over 1945, cattle by 39 per cent, sheep and goats by 75 per cent, and pigs by 200 per cent. Finally, the plan also contained provisions for the restoration and expansion of drainage and irrigation systems and for the electrification of collective and state farms.

No great change of policy regarding consumer goods is to be found in the Fourth Five-Year Plan. Although more emphasis was put on the production of consumer goods than in previous plans, the old policy of making the consumer wait for the goods he needs until his country's industrial strength has been built up was continued. Only the most pressing consumer needs were considered. The extremely low level of 1945 was to be raised, but the scheduled improvement over the prewar standard was very limited. The objective of 240 million pairs of shoes for 1950 was very little above the goal that had been set for 1938. Moreover, it meant that home production would provide the Soviet citizen with only one pair of shoes each year. The British shoe industry in 1947 produced two pairs of leather footwear per head and in the United States the per capita output was almost three pairs. The goals for such essential goods as cotton and woolen textiles were also low. The Fourth Five-Year Plan, however, proposed to improve living conditions in one respect. It made provisions for the rehabilitation of the wrecked housing and for the construction of new houses, particularly of the one-family and two-family types. An entirely new industry was to be created for the construction of prefabricated houses. What is more, a law of 1947 permitted workers to purchase these houses and to bequeath them to their heirs.

After the plan had been announced the whole energy of the Soviet

Union was directed toward its fulfillment. Various means were employed to spur on the workers to produce more. The first of these was the wage incentive. Workers who produced more were paid more. Differentiation of wages which had been introduced by the earlier Five-Year Plans despite the equalitarianism that is deeply rooted in Marxist philosophy became more marked under the Fourth Five-Year Plan. The lure of high wages was used particularly to get workers to enter the heavy industries. Second, the government used the patriotic appeal. Propaganda releases proclaimed Russia to be the most advanced nation of the world. Other nations, and particularly the capitalist nations, were depicted as incapable of progress because they were decadent. Third, the government employed criticism, threats, and punishments. The daily press was encouraged to publish criticisms of industrial managers regarding both the quantity and quality of goods produced in their plants. Physicians, for example, could denounce the poor quality of drugs, store managers were given space in the newspapers to criticize the poor quality of shoes, clothing and furniture, and patrons were permitted to state in the press that railroad service was below standard. Condign punishments were meted out to those on whom criticism was wasted. The goal was to increase productivity in industry 36 per cent and in construction 40 per cent over the 1940 level.

In 1950 Premier Stalin announced that the Fourth Five-Year Plan had been completed in less than five years and that production under the plan had been increased by 73 per cent over 1940. The production of pig iron and steel was reported as having increased by 45 per cent instead of the planned 35 per cent. The figures are impressive. In 1913 Russia produced only 4.2 million tons of steel. This was increased to 18.3 million tons in 1940, and the goal for 1950 was 25.4 million tons. Equally impressive are the figures for the production of coal. In 1913 the coal production was 29 million tons, by 1940 it had increased to 166 million, with the goal 250 million for 1950. It was announced that this goal, too, was exceeded slightly. Production of electricity was reported as being 87 per cent above the 1940 figure and almost ten per cent higher than the goal set by the plan. Oil production has risen to a level 22 per cent above prewar, which was higher than the goal set. In terms of population the production was still far below that of Britain and the United States. For example, the production of coal was still less than one and a half tons per head against four tons produced in Great Britain or the United States. Steel production, according to Soviet figures, was less than 350 pounds per head in 1950. Great Britain and the United

States had in 1947 produced 628 pounds and 1,008 pounds, respectively. Much of the difference is accounted for by the fact that in 1949 only one of every sixteen citizens of the Soviet Union was employed in industry, while the ratio was one in eight for the United States and one in five for Great Britain.

As for consumer goods the average Russian citizen was little better off than he had previously been. The shoe output appears to have reached only about 192 million pairs instead of 240 million. The output of cotton cloth was considerable, but that of wool cloth, which is so necessary for the Russian winter, was wholly inadequate. The Fourth Five-Year Plan did, however, effect considerable improvement in the housing situation. Before 1950 all those who had been rendered homeless by the war were moved from caves, barns, and other makeshift buildings into houses, but the floor space per capita was still very small, with whole families still living in one room and four or five families sharing a bathroom. Living standards were still far below those of France and Great Britain. Only in China and India, of the larger nations, were they lower. In December, 1948, the *New York Times* made a comparison of United States and Soviet retail prices on an average income of workers in both countries. According to this comparison, a United States worker had to work seven minutes for one pound of white bread, the Soviet worker thirty-one minutes for an equal amount of rye bread. A pound of butter cost forty-eight minutes of labor in the United States and ten hours and forty-two minutes in the Soviet Union.

In August, 1952, after nearly twenty months of the new plan had elapsed, the Soviet government published details of the Fifth Five-Year Plan. The accent was again on heavy industry. The goal set for the production of pig iron calls for an increase of 70 per cent by 1955 over the 1950 output, steel 62 per cent, oil 85 per cent, electric power 80 per cent, synthetic rubber 82 per cent. Consumer goods, however, were not neglected. Thus the plan sets such goals as the increase of cotton goods production over 1950 by no less than 61 per cent. The output of woolen fabrics is to be 54 per cent higher in 1955 than it was in 1950, footwear 55 per cent. The general level of industrial production is to be increased during the five-year period by approximately 70 per cent. In the directives provisions for the improvement of production and manufacturing processes are also laid down. One of the goals is described as "to mechanize mining and labor consuming operations, to automatize and intensify production processes, . . . to considerably extend and improve the utilization of the operating plants and to build new ones."

High goals were also set for agricultural production. "The main task in the sphere of agriculture," the directive states, "still is to insure an increase in harvest yields of all agricultural crops." The goal of the period 1950–1955 is an increase of 45 per cent in the production of grain, with the goal for wheat 55 to 65 per cent higher. The increase in the production of sugar beets is set at 65–70 per cent, potatoes 40–45 per cent, tobacco 65–70 per cent, high-quality green tea leaf 75 per cent, butter 72 per cent, and vegetable oil 77 per cent. Attention is also given to the increase and improvement of livestock. The number of pigs is to be increased by 45 to 50 per cent, sheep by 60 to 62 per cent, and large horned cattle by 18 to 20 per cent. A further goal was greater mechanization of agriculture. "To bring the level of mechanization by 1955," the directive states, "in ploughing, sowing of grain, technique, and fodder crops up to 90 to 95 per cent, in harvesting of grain crops and sunflowers by combines up to 80 to 90 per cent, . . . in planting, interfurrow cultivation, and digging of potatoes up to 55 to 60 per cent, haymaking and ensilaging up to 70 to 80 per cent."

Despite the tremendous projected increase of production and productive capacity, the goals of the Fifth Five-Year Plan still fall far short of the level of the United States economy in 1951. If the goals set forth in the plan are attained, the Soviet Union will in 1955 produce only about half as much in industrial goods as the United States did in 1951. Since the Soviet Union has a much larger population (about 215 millions against about 155 millions) the Soviet per capita production in 1955 will be only about one third as great as that in the United States. In the production of certain commodities the plan calls for an output that is two thirds or more as great as the 1951 output in the United States, but for other products the projected production is only about 10 per cent. The nearest approach of the Soviet economy to that of the United States is in the output of coal. The Soviet goal of 377.5 million metric tons is more than two thirds as great as the United States output of 523 million metric tons in 1951. The following figures may convey some idea of the comparative production in the two countries:

	U.S.S.R. PLAN FOR 1955			U.S. 1951		
Pig iron	34.3	million metric tons*		64	million metric tons	
Steel	44.7	"	" "	95.5	"	" "
Oil	69.4	"	" "	307.5	"	" "
Electricity	162.5	billion kilowatt hours		432.3	billion kilowatt hours	
Cattle	68.1	million		88.1	million	
Hogs	35.5	"		63.9	"	

* A metric ton equals 1.1 short tons.

5

RELIGION AND FAMILY LIFE IN SOVIET RUSSIA

One of the important changes which took place during the war was the official reestablishment of the Orthodox Church. This took place after twenty-five years of persecution of the church. During the early years of the Bolshevik regime it had been easy to direct hatred against a church which had been the upholder of tsarist autocracy, a church of which Count Witte, the last able minister of the tsars, had said: "Our church has unfortunately long since become a dead bureaucratic institution." The new education instilled atheism in the minds of Russian youth, but the closing of chapels, the liquidation of monasteries, the confiscation of the real estate and funds of the church, and the arrest of priests, monks, and pious laymen did not effect much change in the ingrained faith of Russia's believers. The fact that those who attended worship might be deprived of their ration tickets, lose their jobs, or be transported to Siberia did not put an end to attendance at worship. Many braved the wrath of the government. When the government census of 1937 was taken the people were asked one question about their religious faith. The figures showed that after twenty years of repression no less than one third of Russia's urban and two thirds of the rural population were still professing Christians. At least they had the courage to tell the representatives of an antireligious government that they were Christians. In 1940 there were, according to the *Statesman's Year-Book,* over 30,000 independent religious communities of every kind, over 8,000 churches, and about 60,000 priests and ministers of religion in the Soviet Union.

Although the Communist Party moderated its attacks on religion during the years preceding the Nazi invasion, there was no indication that the government would ever legalize the Orthodox Church. The change came after Russia was invaded. As part of a carefully planned campaign to win the favor of the Russian people the Nazi armies opened the churches as they advanced into Russia. The rejoicing of the believers forced the Soviet government to take notice. Stalin himself undoubtedly saw in the situation an opportunity to gain wider support among the Russian masses and to influence Western opinion in favor of the Soviet regime. Whatever the motives, the same Stalin who had said, "The Party cannot be neutral in regard to religion; communists who hinder the broadest development of antireligious propaganda have no place in the ranks," reversed his policy to the extent of reestablishing the legal status of the Orthodox Church. On September 5, 1943, he officially received Acting Patriarch Sergei

and other leaders of the Orthodox Church and approved their petition to call a congress for the election of a patriarch. Stalin's approval
was not only published on the front pages of the Soviet press but was
also broadcast to the people. The announcement over the Moscow
radio stated in part: "Comrade Stalin favorably considered these suggestions and stated that there would be no obstacle on the part of the
government."

The congress was held and after Acting Patriarch Sergei was
chosen patriarch he was enthroned in his packed cathedral with rit-
ualistic pomp not seen in Russia since the Bolshevik Revolution.
But the new patriarch was hardly an enemy of the Soviet regime. As
far back as 1925, while he was Metropolitan of Moscow, he had assured the government of his loyalty and also of that of his followers.
He regarded Stalin as a "genius" and after the coronation blessed
him in these words, "May God bless you with success, and with glory
your great deeds, for the sake of our country." Thus the Orthodox
Church returned to the same status it had before the revolution of
1917. It again became a church that is actually an arm of the state as
it was under the tsars. While the church is dependent upon the state
for its legal existence, it in turn bestows upon the autocratic institutions of the Soviet state the sanction of its supernatural power.
Through the official restoration of the Orthodox Church the Soviet
government made Moscow again the religious capital of a hundred
million Christians. It is possible that Stalin in doing so may have had
his eye on the Orthodox Balkans. At any rate the Kremlin later made
it clear that in the satellite Balkans there would be churches, but
that their allegiance must be to the government-approved patriarch
in Moscow.

After the enthronement of the patriarch the Soviet government
permitted a number of other changes regarding religion. For one
thing, it permitted the church to open a seminary for the training of
priests. The acute shortage which existed had been caused by government interdiction of the training of priests. Nor did the government stop at permitting the opening of a theological school. With its
sanction the Bible was printed for the first time since the revolution.
This also alleviated a great shortage. Another official change toward
religion was indicated when President Kalinin of the Soviet Union
asked antireligious citizens not to scoff at soldiers wearing religious
medals. The antireligious museums were soft-pedaled or closed and
pictures of religious services and processions were circulated abroad
to show how "free" religion is in Russia. When a new patriarch was
enthroned on February 4, 1945, after the death of Sergei, the government released official movies of the event.

Another important change was that regarding divorce. During the years after the revolution a Russian couple could get a divorce simply by registering at the proper bureau and paying a small fee. The marital instability which resulted from this procedure caused the government to abolish easy divorces. A law of 1944 decreed that divorces can be obtained only after a decision of the courts based on serious and valid reasons presented by the petitioners. Judges were instructed to bring about a reconciliation whenever possible and the fees for obtaining a divorce were raised considerably. The new divorce legislation is probably the greatest step taken by the Soviet government to establish stronger family ties and to strengthen the home. According to its own preamble, the law is a step toward "consolidation of the Soviet family." The Moscow press went so far as to call it the "charter of the Soviet family." In 1949 the Soviet Supreme Court tightened the marriage bonds further by ordering the lower courts to refuse divorces for "temporary divergencies of opinion or unwillingness of one side to continue the marriage." But the Supreme Court also ruled that when a marriage jeopardizes "the principles of communist morality" it constitutes "serious and well founded" grounds for a divorce. Since the new divorce law of 1944 loyal comradeship and marriage have been the recognized relationships of the heroes and heroines in Soviet literature.

At the same time that the Soviet government made divorce more difficult in 1944 it also took steps to encourage larger families. The policy was not a new one. Previously the government had granted a sum for the baby's layette and a food allowance during the infant's first year. Moreover, mothers of more than six children were entitled to an annual bonus for a period of five years. Further bonuses were paid for each additional child. Many thousands of Soviet families had received such payments. In 1944 the government introduced new scales of family allowances. According to the new plan the sum for the layette was greatly increased and the payment of monetary awards begins with the birth of the third child. Thereafter the payments increase for each further child born to the family. In addition to monetary awards mothers of large families also receive medals. Mothers of five or six children are accorded prestige by the bestowal of the Motherhood Medal, mothers of seven to nine children are given the Order of Glory, and for ten or more children the Order of Mother Heroine is bestowed. Pregnancy leave with pay was extended to 77 days and new rest homes and also centers for children were opened. On the other hand, the law of 1944 imposed a tax of 6 per cent on the income of all childless couples. Families with only one child were required to pay a tax of 1 per cent and parents of two children .5 per cent.

🌀

CHANGES AND DEVELOPMENTS

On September 4, 1945, the State Committee for Defense which had exercised complete governmental authority since the German invasion of 1941 was dissolved and its political functions were restored to the agencies of the Supreme Soviet and the Communist Party. During the war many able non-Communists had been given key posts in the government and had contributed much toward the war effort. Some of the ablest generals of the Red Army, for example, were non-Communists. All these were now unostentatiously retired with pensions and other rewards. The Communist Party became again the sole directing force in Soviet life.[2]

In October, 1945, the government fixed February 10, 1946, as the day for the election of a Supreme Soviet to replace the existing one which had been elected in 1937. The election regulations which the government issued changed the provisions of the constitution of 1936 in that they raised the minimum age of deputies from eighteen to twenty-three. The voting age remained at eighteen. A gesture was also made toward nominating more than one candidate for each post. Before the balloting, however, all candidates but one for each office withdrew, leaving the voters no choice. Thus only one aspirant for each post appeared on the ballot. After the election it was reported that more than 98 per cent of the eligible voters went to the polls and that 99 per cent of those who voted cast an affirmative vote for the list of candidates presented.

Both the Soviet government and the Communist Party emerged from the war in a strong position. Stalin himself said in February, 1946: "After this war no one dares any more to deny the vitality of the Soviet state system. Now it is no longer a question of the vitality of the Soviet state system since there can be no doubt of its vitality any more." As for the party, it had experienced considerable inflation during the war. After the German invasion the party had liberalized the admission requirements with the result that many new members flocked in. The party membership including candidates for admission increased from 2.4 million in 1939 to an all-time high of 5.7 million in 1945. Even these figures give no true indication of the

2 On August 20, 1952, *Pravda* announced that the first congress of the Russian Communist Party since 1939 would be held October 5, 1952. One of the items on the program was the adoption of a set of statutes which, among other things, would abolish the Politburo and the Orgburo, their present functions in the future to be exercised by the Presidium of the Supreme Soviet. At the same time the party changed its name from "the All-Union Communist Party" to "the Communist Party of the Soviet Union."

turnover of the party membership during the war years. Many party members had also been killed in the fight against the Germans and their places had been filled with new members. It is estimated that about two thirds of the membership had less than five years' experience in the party. Thus at the end of the war the party was "long" in membership but "short" in experience. The stresses of war had also led to a relaxation of discipline which opened the way for many members to deviate from the party line both in regard to conduct and doctrine.

The Communist Party as it was constituted in 1945 was not the kind of party Lenin had prescribed, one with a small, firmly indoctrinated and enthusiastic membership. The leaders of the party therefore decided to reduce the number of members and reindoctrinate the remainder. Such a purge of the party membership— *chistka* (cleansing), as the Russians called it—was nothing new. It is a feature of the Communist Party dating back to 1920. At that time the cleansing took place to rid the party of the many undesirables who had entered the party during the civil war. Lenin demanded not only belief in Marxist doctrines and performance of party duties but also a personal life that was so scrupulously correct as not to damage the name of the party. Serious dereliction in regard to any one of the three points was sufficient for expulsion. In 1946 examiners appointed by the Central Committee visited the various cells or units of the party and interrogated the members. All those who did not give satisfactory answers or against whom complaints or accusations were substantiated were promptly expelled. In this way the membership of the party was greatly reduced. An announcement of August 23, 1946, stated that in the Ukraine more than half of the party leaders and government appointees had been replaced since V-E Day.

The purge of the party membership was, however, only a phase of a wider purge. The purge after World War II was not as bloody as the great purge of the 1930's had been, but it did extend to all phases of Soviet life. *Pravda* claimed for the purge "political significance of the first importance." One of its phases was an intense drive to eliminate untrustworthy and incompetent persons from both industry and agriculture. In June, 1946, for example, the ministry of state control announced the dismissal of a large number of incompetent and untrustworthy managers and engineers; also accountants who were guilty of falsifying the records regarding funds or production figures. In September, 1946, a long, grim decree bearing the signature of Stalin for the Soviet government and of A. Zhdanov for the Communist Party was issued regarding irregularities in agriculture.

The decree condemned undemocratic methods of management and "swollen administrative staffs" on collective farms. But the major charge was that collective farm officials were "encouraging the seizure of communal lands by individual economic elements" who were endeavoring to "introduce the principles of private property." It was stated that in the Kuibyshev region a check on "by no means all" of the collective farms had led to the uncovering of 19,367 cases of individuals turning land "into sources of private income." Punishment of the guilty ones followed at once.

THOUGHT CONTROL IN THE SOVIET UNION

Since the revolution of 1917 it has been the aim of the Communist Party to organize, integrate, and dominate every form of human activity and to enlist it as a means of strengthening and perpetuating the communist regime. At various times, however, the control of the Communist Party has not been as strict as at other times. Such a time was World War II. While the Soviet government was occupied with the struggle for survival it had, as a means of gaining the general support of the Russian people, permitted digressions from the party line. But no sooner had the war ended than the Communist Party launched a campaign to enforce unflinching orthodoxy. It set up a rigid and all-inclusive system of thought control that leaves no room for divergence of opinion or free play of ideas.

The primary means employed to achieve uniformity of thought are education, radio, and the press. These are as much weapons of the Communist Party, and hence of the Kremlin, as the Soviet army, navy, and air force. Ever since the communists rose to power, educational policy in the Soviet Union has been dictated by the interests of the Soviet state. After World War II the communists decided to subordinate education absolutely to the aims of their party. As it was stated in *Pravda* (October 24, 1946) : "It must never be forgotten that every science and its teaching cannot be separated from the policy of the party which forms the vital basis of the Soviet State." During the succeeding months and years the idea that Marxist indoctrination is the primary function of education was restated again and again. "It is in the school, at the desk, in the first class," the *Literary Gazette* stated (September 3, 1949), "that the foundations of a communist outlook are laid in future Soviet citizens. The country entrusts the school with its most treasured possessions—its children— and no one should be allowed to indulge in the slightest deviation from the principles of communist materialistic upbringing of the new generation." Two days earlier *Pravda* had defined the task of Soviet education as being: "To bring up active fighters for the cause of communism, well-rounded, educated persons, possessing thorough and firmly based knowledge—such is the main task of our schools, such is the law of its life. All must be subordinated to this task."

Besides indoctrinating the children with the teachings of Marx and Lenin, the schools were asked to excite in them a feeling of Russian nationalism and Soviet patriotism. The Communist Party demanded that the children be taught that the Soviet way of life is superior to all others and that Russian achievements have outstripped those of the capitalist world. The claim of superiority was not made in the schools alone. The Soviet propaganda machine also used, and still uses, the press, radio, and the cinema to tell the Russian people that the Soviet Union has by far the most advanced form of society, the finest literature, and the best scientists. In an effort to prove the "best scientists" statement the propaganda has claimed for Russian inventors many inventions that were actually the work of Western inventors. It has, for example, claimed that a Russian named Aleksander Popov, and not Marconi, is the real inventor of radio. While Popov's contribution was important it was a good deal less than the invention of radio. Another example of Soviet propaganda is the claim that the Russian Lodygin, and not Thomas Edison, invented the electric incandescent lamp. The newspaper *Izvestia* went so far as to claim that a Russian sailor had taken a model of Lodygin's lamp to the United States and that Edison had stolen the idea. Other inventions claimed for the Russians are the steam engine, radar, and jet propulsion. Practically the height of absurdity was *Pravda's* assertion that the Russians had really discovered penicillin in 1871 but were prevented from developing it before the Bolshevik Revolution by the lack of proper scientific equipment.

Of paramount importance in the educational process is the glorification of the Soviet leaders, and particularly of Stalin. Teachers are trained to speak of Stalin with reverent awe. The cold-blooded politician is pictured as a mellow, uncle-like person to whom the Soviet system owes its success. Teachers are requested to use the characterization of Stalin which reads in part: "Everyone knows the irresistible, shattering power of Stalin's logic, the crystal clearness of his intellect, his iron will, devotion to the party, his modesty, artlessness, his solicitude for the people and mercilessness to enemies of the people." Nor is this glorification of Stalin restricted to the schools. Over and over again one may read the phrase, "Stalin is the Lenin of today."

In its campaign to achieve uniformity of thought the Communist Party has also enlisted radio. There is in the U.S.S.R. strict supervision over everything that is broadcast to the people. A high percentage of the programs are propagandist. The number of radios in the Soviet Union was estimated in 1950 at four million. In addition there were about eight million loud-speakers over which the Communist Party or the government broadcast propaganda.

Strict control, too, was established over the cinema. In 1946 the Central Committee of the Communist Party prepared a list of subjects, twenty in number, on which producers could base their films. The entire industry was warned to raise the ideological content of its films. Films, it was specified, must stress Soviet patriotism and in some way promote the new Five-Year Plan. "The cinema," film producers were told, "is a sharp, ideological party weapon, and departure from contemporary life would mean the loss of its principal valuable qualities." A number of films were at once withdrawn because they did not depict Soviet life in the proper terms. Of the films planned for 1946–1947 only eighteen of forty were released after the Central Committee launched its attack. The problem of meeting the ideological demands of the party increased the difficulties of production greatly during the succeeding years. Whereas forty to forty-five feature films were annually produced in the U.S.S.R. before World War II, the number scheduled for 1950 dropped to twenty, of which only eleven were released to the public.

The great propaganda instrument, however, which the Communist Party uses to condition the thinking of the masses in the U.S.S.R. is the press. In Stalin's words, "it is the only implement which helps the party to speak daily, hourly, with the working class." On another occasion he defined the function of the Russian press as the "transmission belt between the masses and the party." It is the duty of the press to emphasize the superiority of the Russian communist system and to insure a chorus of unanimous acclaim of the Soviet leaders and their policies. In short, every periodical becomes a house organ of the one-party system. An editorial in *Pravda* stated in May, 1947:

Now, in the face of the enormous tasks of the postwar Stalinist Five-Year Plan the people demand that newspapers, magazines, publishers, newspapermen, and writers elevate their activities to a new, higher ideological level. The press is a powerful instrument of communist education of the masses, of strengthening the socialist consciousness, of quickening of socialist society. . . . The main task of the press consists in intensifying the propaganda of Bolshevik ideology. . . . and inculcating in the people a feeling of Soviet national pride, unbending strength of spirit, and firm, unshaking faith in the triumph of our great cause.

Undoubtedly the most influential periodical in the Soviet Union is *Pravda* (Truth), the official organ of the Central Committee of the Communist Party. In discussing the functions of the press in the Soviet state Stalin held up *Pravda* as a model. *"Pravda,"* he said, "fulfills the dictum. It makes no pretense to objectivity." It was founded by Lenin himself in 1912 and directed by him from his place of exile, but it was actually put out by Stalin with the help of his friend Molotov. During the period before the revolution the issues were frequently confiscated, forcing the staff to publish it under various names. Its daily circulation in 1914 was about 40,000. Since the revolution it has set the tone for other Russian newspapers. Many newspapers reprint the *Pravda* editorials verbatim. It is published in eight cities besides Moscow and has a circulation of about three million. The *Pravda* staff includes seventy editors of whom twelve, appointed by the Party's Central Committee, form an inner circle called the Editorial Collegium. The second newspaper in Russia is *Izvestia* which means "news." It is the official government organ and as such is printed in the sixteen constituent languages of the U.S.S.R. Its circulation is about a million and a half. As a government organ it naturally stresses government news. The competition between *Pravda* and *Izvestia* is keen. One of the oldest Soviet jokes reads, "I see there is no *Izvestia* [news] in *Pravda,* and no *Pravda* [truth] in *Izvestia."*

Not only are the newspapers as such under a system of tight control, but the editors are carefully indoctrinated and the news collecting agency is also under strict supervision. Editors are carefully trained so that the news is censored in their own minds before they publish it. The chance that any news that is detrimental to the Communist Party might reach any newspaper through a news agency is slim. Tass (Telegraph Agency of the Soviet Union), which holds a monopoly on supplying foreign news to the newspapers of Russia, is also carefully controlled. The control, in fact, extends even to *Krokodil,* Russia's humorous magazine. It, too, must serve the purposes of the government and the Communist Party. Its purpose is to satirize or hold up to ridicule the existing abuses and inefficiency in the hope that this will effect improvement. An example of such humor is the following: Mr. A, who is slightly inebriated, boasts: "We have saved 462,593 loads of bricks, 843 tons of cement, 143 tons of sand, and 7,555 cubic feet of lumber." "And how many houses have you built?" Mr. B asks. "Not one!" is the reply. "That's another way we have economized."

Whatever newspaper or literary periodical a Russian buys, he is certain to find the same unvarying repetition of certain themes. So far as the Western nations are concerned, the perpetual refrain is the degeneracy and depravity of the Western world. "Soviet patriotism is indissolubly connected with hatred toward the enemies of the Socialist Fatherland," the brief *Soviet Encyclopedia* states. The special targets of press and radio attacks have been Britain and the United States. In the Soviet press, Uncle Sam has frequently been pictured as Uncle Shylock and the Statue of Liberty as the kept woman of Wall Street. According to the *New Times* the following conditions prevail in the United States: "A handful of plutocrats wallow in wealth and enjoy unlimited power, while tens of millions of ordinary people suffer privation and oppression and live in constant fear of the morrow. . . . Anyone who dares to give expression to thoughts which do not happen to be to the liking of the omnipotent monopolies and their agents is subjected to persecution." A few of the constantly recurring themes are: "The United States is reactionary and imperialistic," "The United States with Britain's assistance is seeking world domination," "The United States and Britain are obstructing the efforts to get peace treaties with Germany and Austria." Instructions issued by the Kremlin to the Soviet press read in part: "It is known that imperialist circles of Britain and the United States are stretching their tentacles across the seas and oceans and striving to subjugate entire countries and seize areas and bases. We are dealing with a new form of imperialist expansion, dangerous for peace. The Soviet press has not shown sufficient vigilance in unmasking these new intrigues of monopoly capitalism. It behooves the press resolutely to brand the imperialist policy and practice carried out under the semblance of showing care for democracy and order."

A favorite theme of press and radio has been the claim that the Russians won the war practically singlehanded. Stalin said to the Russian people on the first anniversary of V-J Day: "Today we celebrate the day of victory over imperialist Japan. A year ago the Soviet people and its armed forces victoriously concluded the war against imperialist Japan. Japan signed the act of unconditional surrender. The Soviet people and their armed forces won the victory." Without mentioning the Allied landing in Normandy and the campaign that followed, the Russian historian Eugene Tarlé wrote in *Trud* (May, 1947): "The Soviet Army bore nearly the entire brunt of the war without receiving any appreciable aid at the fronts during the most dangerous and most critical days of the deadly struggle."

The myths the Soviet propaganda machine has been circulating would be dispelled if the Russians were permitted contact with the outside world. But the Soviet government has blocked almost entirely the channels of communication between eastern and western Europe.

Few foreign films are shown in Russia and only such books as support Marxist teachings or proclaim the decadence of the West are translated into Russian. Every attempt to establish a cultural exchange of students and professors between the Soviet Union and the West has been blocked by the Kremlin. In 1950 even the requirement that courses in foreign history and literature are necessary for a secondary school diploma was abolished. An American who visited Russia in 1949 wrote:

> The extent to which the regime has gone in isolating the Russians from any foreign contacts and in keeping from them any news from abroad is beyond the imagination of any American who has not actually witnessed the situation with his own eyes. No Soviet citizen is permitted to travel abroad. No Soviet citizen is allowed to marry a foreigner. Few foreigners are permitted to enter the country: those who are permitted to enter are either foreign officials or communist stooges. The foreign officials are restricted in their movements and constantly spied upon. Even the foreign communists are kept well in hand. It is against the law for Russians to have any dealings with foreigners. A Russian practically never sees a foreign publication.[3]

By these and other means the Soviet government has endeavored to protect "a perfect Soviet society and a superior Soviet man" from contamination. The fact is, however, that the Soviet government is afraid the Russian masses might discover that the people in the Western democracies enjoy not only freedom but also a higher standard of living. The so-called "Iron Curtain" which the Russians have set up between their sphere of influence and Western Europe serves the double purpose of keeping the peoples of the Soviet Union ignorant about conditions in the outside world and of concealing unpleasant Soviet realities from the peoples of other lands. Red army troops who gained firsthand knowledge of the higher standards of living to the west of the Iron Curtain were subjected to a course of Marxist reindoctrination upon their return to Russia. Those who were brash enough to talk about the differences in the living standards were promptly sent to Siberian labor camps.

§

THE NEW EMPHASIS ON ORTHODOXY IN THE ARTS

The Soviet government did not stop at tightening the controls over press, radio, and the cinema. Literature and the other fine arts, too, were included in the government's program to reestablish Marx-

3 F. D. Kohler in *U.S. Department of State Bulletin,* vol. 22 (March 20, 1950), p. 430.

ist-Leninist orthodoxy. Literature, the drama, music, and painting had been absorbed into the service of the state soon after the Revolution of 1917. But the insistence on Marxist orthodoxy was more or less spasmodic. When the insistence subsided "bourgeois deviations and perversions" took place. Such a period was World War II. The high degree of freedom which the government permitted in the fine arts caused writers, dramatists, musicians, and artists who had been silent for some time to publish their works. But the freedom was short-lived. Soon after the end of the war the Communist Party terminated its liberal attitude. A thorough housecleaning of the arts was inaugurated to cleanse them of bourgeois capitalist tendencies. The severity of the postwar purges eclipsed all previous cultural purifications. They affected every branch of the arts. As a result the range of permissible subjects and techniques was greatly narrowed and the prohibited areas were greatly expanded.

The Soviet leaders, it appears, were convinced that the Fourth Five-Year Plan needed the services of the artists as well as the technicians. Consequently writers, dramatists, musicians, and artists—"engineers of the human soul," as Stalin called them—were ordered to devote their energies to the task of raising the ideological level and of exposing "survivals of capitalism." They were expected to be at the forefront of the psychological mobilization of the Soviet people. The philosophy of "art for art's sake," they were told, must be discarded in favor of art devoted to the state and its aims. The arts must have no other interests than those of the state. The basic principle was "whatever is not for the state is against it." Although the Soviet Union came into being as a result of revolution, its main interest soon became the defense of the status quo. In tsarist Russia such distinguished minds as Tolstoy, Dostoievsky, Chekhov, and Gorky raised their voices in protest against things as they were. In Soviet Russia such voices are silenced. Stringent measures are taken against all those who do not use their art to inculcate patriotism or to support the Marxist-Leninist philosophy.

The drive to reconvert the arts into weapons for the dissemination of communist teachings began in earnest on August 14, 1946, when the Central Committee of the Communist Party passed a resolution regarding two Leningrad literary journals. During the succeeding period resolutions on such other cultural activities as the drama, the cinema, and music were made public. Taken together these resolutions are known in the Soviet Union as the "Ideological Decrees." On August 17, 1946, in a speech before the first Congress of Soviet Writers at Moscow, Andrei Zhdanov, Secretary of the Central Committee, elaborated and interpreted the first resolution of the committee. This speech of Zhdanov and several others that followed were accepted as an authoritative guide in establishing the policy in the various phases of the arts. The mission of the arts in Soviet Russia, Zhdanov said in effect, is to inculcate Soviet patriotism, glorify the Soviet man, and expose the remnants of bourgeois culture. The arts cannot divorce themselves from the fate of the Soviet people and Soviet society. Any claim of the arts to ideological independence is a reflection of bourgeois thought. It discredits "the representatives of progressive Soviet culture, Soviet patriots, to adopt the attitude of admirers of bourgeois culture, or the attitudes of apprentices toward it."

In the campaign to reorient Soviet culture special emphasis was placed on the task of the Soviet writer. Zhdanov said pointedly: "Many writers, including those who work in the capacity of responsible editors or occupy important posts in the Writers' Union, think that politics is the business of the government and the Central Committee. As for writers, it is not their business to occupy themselves with politics. . . . We demand that our comrades, both those who give leadership in the literary field and those who write, be guided by that without which the Soviet order cannot live, that is, by politics." In support of his stand Zhdanov quoted from an article entitled "Party Organization and Party Literature" which Lenin wrote in 1905: "Literature must be partisan. To counterbalance bourgeois mores, to counterbalance the bourgeois entrepreneurial, commercial press . . . the socialist proletariat must put forward the principle of party literature, develop this principle and bring it to life in the most complete and integral form possible. . . . Down with nonpartisan writers! Down with supermen writers! The literary cause must become part of the general proletarian cause."

The first result of Zhdanov's speech was that the Union of Soviet Writers was reorganized and a new head was appointed; then the Union took up Zhdanov's refrain. Soviet literati were told that they "must expose . . . the nature of capitalist encirclement, struggle against its corrupting influence, and reveal the character of contemporary imperialism." During the years after Zhdanov's first speech and the directive of the Writers' Union the themes they sounded were repeated again and again. The *Literary Gazette*, for example, stated: "The writer cannot trudge along at the tail of events; he must march in the front ranks of the people, pointing out to them the road of their development. . . . This means that our literature and journals must not stand aside from the tasks of contemporary life, but must assist the party and the people in the education of the young in the spirit of supreme service to the interests of the people."

Writers whose works did not carry out the prescriptions of the Central Committee were taken to task. Two of these were the satirist Mikhail Zoshchenko and the poetess Anna Akhmatova. The former was soundly flayed by Zhdanov. "Zoshchenko," he said, "takes absolutely no interest in the labor of the Soviet people, their exertions and heroism, their high social and moral qualities. With him this theme is always absent. . . . They say that Zoshchenko's story, 'Adventures of a Monkey,' went the rounds of the Leningrad platforms. How greatly must the leadership of ideological work in Leningrad have weakened for such things to have taken place!" As an aside he hurled the following barb at the Writers' Union: "Why have the party activists of Leningrad, its writers' organization, permitted these shameful things?" The attack on the poetess was equally vitriolic. "Anna Akhmatova," Zhdanov said, "is one of the representatives of the ideologiless reactionary literary swamp. She is one of the bearers of empty, ideologiless aristocratic-salon poetry, absolutely alien to Soviet literature." He denounced her as belonging to a literary group which preaches "the theory of 'art for art's sake,' 'beauty for beauty's sake.' " Both were for a time barred from publishing further works. Only in 1950 after she had decided to espouse the party line were Soviet magazines permitted to publish further poems by Akhmatova.

Even works that had conformed to the party line when they were written were denounced because they were not in accord with the stricter interpretations of the "new social order." Alexander Fadeyev's novel, *The Young Guard,* for example, was first awarded the Stalin prize and lauded by the critics, but after selling more than a million copies it was attacked in *Pravda* for picturing the Soviet population as fleeing before the German advance. Early in 1950 *For the Power of the Soviets,* a book by V. Katayev, a prominent Soviet writer, was first highly praised, then sharply scored by *Pravda* within a week. The chief criticism of the work was that the writer had not drawn the hero as a Soviet man of the new order. Katayev at once prepared the following recantation which was also published in *Pravda:* "I agree with the just and principled criticism of my new novel *For the Power of the Soviets.* I promise my readers that I shall make a fundamental revision of the novel. I consider this a matter of honor as a writer."

The prescriptions of the Central Committee for literature also applied to music. Like the other phases of the arts, the committee stated, it must reflect Marxist-Leninist principles. Thus Muradeli's opera, *Great Friendship,* was denounced because it "reeked of contemporary modernistic bourgeois music of Europe and America." The same charge was flung at the music of Shostakovich, Prokofieff, Khachaturian, and others. At its premiere Shostakovich's *Ninth Symphony* was hailed as "a triumph of our great victory," but later *Culture and Life,* the periodical of the Central Committee, described it as a "playful and fanciful trifle" hopelessly lacking in "warm, ideological conviction." Shostakovich did penance by declaring in a signed article: "I know that the party is right, that the party wishes me well, and that I must search for and find creative paths which lead me to Soviet realistic popular art." Then he proceeded to write works crammed with ideology. An oratorio by him, dedicated to the Soviet reforestation program, was awarded a Stalin prize in 1950.

The other two distinguished Soviet composers were also flayed for creating music "which reflects the miasmas of bourgeois culture." Khachaturian was specifically condemned for writing music that was "alien to the Soviet people and its artistic taste." Moreover, he was replaced as chairman of the Union of Soviet Composers. In an effort to save his career he stated in a published article: "I have followed a formalistic path alien to the Soviet artists." The composer whose works were denounced most frequently was Prokofieff. While the others were products of the Soviet order, he had left Russia at the time of the Bolshevik Revolution in 1917, and had only returned to the land of his birth in 1933 after gaining a world reputation. After his compositions were criticized in February, 1948, because they did not properly express the ideology of the Soviet state, he wrote: "I am now working on a new opera, *The Tale of a Real Man.* It is dedicated to a heroic Soviet pilot." But even this did not satisfy the Soviet critics. They still discovered "formalistic trends" in it. Prokofieff responded by stating that he was sorry that there were still traces of "bourgeois formalism" in his music. In 1949 the newspaper *Soviet Art* stated that recent compositions were better, but that there was still much room for improvement. What it called for was a composition presenting "a full-scale image of the great Lenin and Stalin."

In regimenting Soviet art the Central Committee did not overlook the theater. Dramatists were told "to battle on the ideological front." The complaint against them was that they were trying "to poison the consciousness of the Soviet people with a world outlook hostile to Soviet society." A further complaint of the Central Committee was that only a few of the many plays being presented in the Soviet theater dealt with life in the Soviet Union and that those which did portrayed the Russians as primitive and uncultured. So that they can be instrumental in creating faith in the victory of the communist cause, the committee insisted, dramas must depict Russian life as dynamic and progressive. On the other hand, they must also expose the decadence of bourgeois culture. One of the most successful plays during the period since World War II has been Konstantin Simonov's *Russian Question,* which besides being performed in five hundred Soviet theaters has also been staged in some of the satellite countries and in the Soviet zone of Germany. The play is built on one of the favorite Soviet themes, corruption in American business, politics, and the press.

Soviet painters, too, are under pressure to carry out Marxist-Leninist teachings in their work. While the Central Committee has not denounced the work of any single painter, it has included painters among those who must express Marxist-Leninist teachings in their work. More specifically painters were warned against being influenced by such "formalists" as Picasso, Matisse, and the Cubists.

Consideration of the communist propaganda efforts might well lead to the conclusion that all Soviet citizens are being converted into unthinking and unquestioning puppets. But the known facts do not bear out this conclusion. During the Bolshevik Revolution and the succeeding years it was comparatively easy to stir the imagination of those who had suffered under the tsarist regime. The generation that has grown up since that time appears, however, to lack the crusading spirit. It is conscious of the weaknesses of the Soviet regime rather than of those of the tsarist government. There are many things, such as shortages and low living standards, to raise doubts in the mind of the average citizen regarding the Soviet regime. One historian has written:

There is a widespread assumption in the non-Soviet world that, since the Soviet regime controls all the instruments of indoctrination which shape the minds of youth, its hold on their loyalty is practically complete. Conversations with young ex-Soviet citizens, schoolteachers, and others who have had extensive contact with young people in Russia cast some doubt on that assumption. One schoolteacher who had taught for nearly twenty-five years in Soviet schools said that the attraction of communist ideology for Soviet youth is greatly exaggerated in the West. She pointed out that there was a great difference between a revolutionary ideology which appealed to youth's idealistic and utopian instincts, and an official ideology which insisted on conformity. Communism in its present state had become such an official ideology. It was dinned into the children day after day. But, she asserted, a number, instead of becoming imbued with it, became bored with it.[4]

4 Merle Fainsod, "Controls and Tensions in the Soviet System," *American Political Science Review,* vol. 44 (June, 1950), p. 266 et seq.

The New Soviet Imperialism

THE NATURE OF SOVIET IMPERIALISM TSARIST Russia was one of the great imperialist powers of the nineteenth century. During the period from 1853 to 1914 it acquired a total of 953,400 square miles of territory, an area almost equal to that of Western Europe. As a result of the 1917 Revolution, however, Russia lost a considerable portion of her territorial domain, the losses aggregating more than 450,000 square miles. Because of internal disorders the Soviet government found it necessary to relinquish its western border territories. Finland, Estonia, Latvia, and Lithuania became independent states, Bessarabia was returned to Rumania, and a large area was lost to the newly reconstituted Poland.

Such loss of territory appeared to be in harmony with communist teachings. Lenin had repeatedly denounced imperialism and imperialist nations. Before the Revolution of 1917 he had written *Imperialism: the Highest Stage of Capitalism,* an extensive attack on the imperialism of the "decadent capitalist nations." In the communist press of the first decades of the Soviet regime the tsarist colonial expansion was condemned as a search for colonial plunder. Anti-imperialism was, in fact, one of the most powerful weapons in the propaganda arsenal of the Russian Communist Party. Many supporters were won for communism by the denunciation of imperialist exploitation. Moreover, in creating anti-imperialist sentiment the Communist Party helped to undermine the colonial empires of the Western nations. Not all communists, however, appear to have shared Lenin's opposition to imperialism. In 1925 a group of Soviet spokesmen protested the repudiation of imperialism on Russia's behalf stating that Lenin had acted hastily. This group advocated a return to an imperialist foreign policy as a means of establishing spheres of influence. But Stalin believed that such a policy would spell the doom of international communism. "This," he said, "would be the road to nationalism and degeneration, the road to the full liquidation of the international policy of the proletariat." Stalin at that time saw no need for imperialism. He believed in the imminence of social revolution in other countries. He was still convinced that Marxism would inevitably expand without the use of force to embrace the whole globe. Soviet Russia would be the core of the hoped-for socialist world. "The entry into the Soviet Union," he said, "is free to all Socialist Soviet Republics, whether they already exist or will emerge in the future."

Several decades later, however, while continuing to hurl accusations of imperialist exploitation against the Western nations, the Kremlin embarked on a program of expansion which quickly dwarfed the imperialist expansion of the tsars; in fact, Soviet expansion since 1939 has not been equaled or even approached by any other country. While pretending to be anti-annexationist, the Kremlin has included in its empire all the territories which the Russian tsars believed should be part of a great Russian empire. While other empires were shrinking rapidly the Soviet government turned an idea into an empire that rules more than a quarter of the world's population and about a fifth of the world's area. The new Soviet empire includes over ten million square miles and extends from central Germany to the China Sea. "The only conclusion possible," one observer wrote, "is that Soviet Russia is actually the world's ranking present-day imperialist, its leading expansionist, and undisputed unilateral acquisitor of other people's lands.[1]

The first question that suggests itself in considering the new Soviet imperialism is, "How does it differ from the old colonial imperialism which the communists denounced so vigorously over a long period?" First, the technique employed by the communists differs from that used by the old empire builders. The Western nations and also the tsarist government established their empires by force. A nation would simply send a force equipped with modern weapons to occupy territory inhabited by peoples who were unable to offer effective resistance. In 1939 the Soviet Union used military force to occupy half of Poland and to annex Latvia, Lithuania, and Estonia. It also acquired the Isthmus of Karelia after defeating the Finns by military force. But after World War II the Russians employed different

[1] Neal Stanford in *American Mercury*, vol. 65 (1947), p. 684.

tactics to establish control over the satellite states which form the western rim of the Soviet empire. They first sent in fifth columns and later used the local communist parties as a means of gaining control of the state. The force employed was usually the police to compel noncommunists to accept a communist government. Second, the new Soviet imperialism differs from the old colonial imperialism in the scope of its aims. Britain, France, the Netherlands, and even tsarist Russia always had limited objectives. Thus the tsars aimed at including specific territories in the Russian Empire, but the new Soviet empire has no such restricted aim. The communist goal is nothing less than world empire.

The Soviet expansionist program was launched just before the outbreak of World War II. The way for its execution was opened by the Nazi-Kremlin pact of August 24, 1939. Thereafter in quick succession the Soviet government made its annexations of Poland, Karelia, Latvia, Lithuania, and Estonia. After the Nazi attack the Russians were busy defending themselves and driving back the German armies. But toward the end of the war they turned again to empire building. At Yalta and Potsdam the Soviet Union was awarded various areas with the provision that final possession was to await confirmation in the peace treaties with Germany and Japan; however, the Kremlin at once incorporated the territories in the Soviet empire without waiting for the peace treaties. After World War II Poland, Hungary, Rumania, Bulgaria, Yugoslavia, Albania, and Czechoslovakia slid swiftly into the grasp of the Kremlin. In Western Europe a strong resistance, sparked by Marshall Plan aid, administered setbacks to the communist movements in some nations and slowed them down in others. Meanwhile, however, the Soviet empire was expanding in another direction. Before the end of 1949 the communists were in control of China.

Although the communists varied their tactics according to the situation, the general technique was much the same in all the countries of eastern Europe. Soviet troops were present in these countries, and by their presence exercised a powerful indirect influence, but the Soviet military authorities did not endeavor to establish Soviet rule through the direct use of the Red army. The technique was more subtle. The principal instrument employed to establish communist rule was the communist parties of the respective countries. When the so-called popular front parties were formed in the various countries at the end of the war, the communist parties joined in the coalitions. Once in the government they made the most of every opportunity to strengthen their position. The primary aim was to gain control of the police, the press, and radio, a technique the Nazis employed in 1933. Consequently they demanded the cabinet posts which gave them this control. Upon achieving this aim they were in a position to propagandize the masses and to attack the opposition.

A favorite tactic was to arrest opposition leaders and to press false charges against them to discredit them. This is commonly known as the tactic of the "Big Lie" which was originated by Hitler. The Führer posed the theory that if a propagandist will not tire of repeating an assertion, no matter how preposterous, he can make it stick in many minds. The communists used this tactic with considerable success. After the democratic opposition had been "discredited" or liquidated, the communists would force a merger of weak parties with the Communist Party. The culmination of the process to gain control was an election in which both terror and fraud were employed to assure a communist victory. Thus a communist minority, backed by Russian force, became the dominating element in the states of eastern Europe.

Having gained control over the states of eastern Europe, the Kremlin devised means of retaining and strengthening this control. In September, 1947, representatives of the communist parties in the Russian sphere of control (the Soviet Union, Poland, Hungary, Rumania, Bulgaria, Czechoslovakia, and Yugoslavia) and of the two most powerful communist parties of Western Europe, the Italian and French, joined in setting up the Communist Information Bureau, more commonly known as the Cominform. Belgrade was not only chosen as the headquarters of the new bureau, but the Yugoslav Communist Party was also entrusted with the task of editing the official periodical of the Cominform.

The tasks assigned to the Cominform, according to the announcement, consisted in the "organization and exchange of experience between parties and, if necessary, the coordination of the activities of the communist parties on the basis of mutual agreement." At the time of its organization the activities of the bureau appeared harmless, but it gradually became evident that the new bureau was a means of exerting pressure upon any of the other communist parties that dared to offer resistance to the policies dictated by the Moscow Communist Party. *Pravda* went to some pains to insist that the creation of the Cominform was not a revival of the Third International or Comintern. But the Cominform is nevertheless a smaller edition of the old Comintern. Although the immediate purpose of the Cominform was to establish a firm control over the satellite states of eastern Europe and to counteract the influence of the Marshall

Plan, which had drawn the nations of Western Europe together, its broader purpose is to further the expansionist policy of the U.S.S.R. in the direction of world revolution.

∽

POLAND AND HUNGARY

Poland, where anti-Soviet feeling appeared to be particularly strong, was the first state to be drawn into the Soviet empire. The story of the subjugation of Poland begins with the Hitler-Stalin agreement of August, 1939. Within a week the Nazi armies invaded Poland, and sixteen days later the Red armies followed suit. Russia appropriated all the territory east of the Molotov-Ribbentrop line and Germany took the rest. Caught in the Nazi-Soviet vise, the Polish government fled to London. The Soviet press at once announced that "Poland has ceased to exist" and began making arrangements for the annexation of eastern Poland. In an effort to convince the world that the inhabitants of eastern Poland were eager to join the Soviet Union the Kremlin staged an election in which only one list of candidates appeared. It was then announced that 90 per cent of the people had voted to send delegates to the People's Assembly and that these delegates had voted for annexation. All Poles who did not vote in the affirmative became subject to the Russian deportation order. The number of those sent to Siberia and Kazakstan, including women and children, has been estimated at more than a million.

When the Polish government fled to London in 1939 it was recognized by the British and French, but the Russians refused recognition. The invasion of Russia by the Nazis, however, caused the Soviet government to shift and to accord recognition to it. This relationship lasted until the fortunes of the Russians began to improve. After the turn of the tide at Stalingrad the Kremlin changed its policy again. On April 25, 1943, it announced that it was severing relations with the London government. Upon entering Poland in its drive toward Berlin the Red army set up in western Poland its own government, which became known as the Lublin government. Thus the control of Poland by the Soviet Union was an accomplished fact when President Roosevelt and Mr. Churchill went to Yalta. Many hailed with relief the declaration of the Big Three after the Yalta Conference that the Provisional (Lublin) Government would be reorganized to include democratic leaders from Poland and from the London government. This new government was to hold free elections as soon as possible. But the pledge which Stalin made at Yalta was not carried out. First, the Kremlin made certain that the new government was controlled by communists and their sympathizers. Second, fearing that a popular vote would not support the communist elements in the government, the Kremlin postponed the elections. At Potsdam (August, 1945) the area of satellite Poland was greatly increased by the decision which placed German lands as far as the Oder River under Polish administration subject to a final decision in the peace treaty with Germany. Thus Poland gained 40,000 square miles as compensation for the 70,000 Russia had annexed.

Meanwhile the communists in the Polish government were not inactive. One of the first things they did was to organize a Polish secret police called *Urzad Bezpieczenstwa,* more familiarly known as UB. Not only was the UB modeled after the Russian secret police (NKVD, later MVD), but it was supervised by Poles who had been trained in Russia. By 1947 the UB had no less than 100,000 trained agents who turned their cunning against all noncommunists, and particularly against the leaders of opposition parties. Soon the Polish prisons were filled to capacity. Before risking an election the communists decided to test public opinion in a preliminary referendum in which the people were asked whether Poland should have a unicameral government, whether industry should be nationalized, and whether Poland's permanent frontiers should remain on the Oder. Despite the terror which the secret police inspired and despite the fraud in the counting of the ballots, the results were such that the government itself acknowledged that 80 per cent of the votes were against it. Later the government reversed itself and announced that 68 per cent of the votes were in its favor.

What the communists did learn from the preliminary referendum was where the principal centers of opposition to the puppet government were. Upon being told by Stalin that the "election must be won before the election," the government enlarged the secret police to 230,000 agents and launched a more determined drive against the opposition. The special target of the drive was the Peasant Party, which was offering stubborn opposition. After the election was finally scheduled for January 19, 1947, a time which made it impossible for many peasants to travel to the polling places, about 100,000 leading members of the party were arrested and the names of Peasant Party candidates were in many instances simply stricken from the ballots. The voting procedure was also made complex as a means of confusing the peasants. Despite all this the vote was anti-communist in some districts. The over-all result, as announced by the government, was a defeat for the Peasant Party and a victory for the government. Foreign observers have stated that they are convinced the Peasant Party polled 60 per cent of the votes. Objections by the British and United States governments against the failure to carry out the promise of "free and unfettered elections" were received with shrugs indicating "so what?" After December, 1948, at which time a merger of Socialists and Communists took place, the latter dropped all pretense of sharing authority with any other party. The final result of the Nazi-Soviet deal was that 40 per cent of Poland was part of the U.S.S.R. and the remainder a satellite state.

After the communist control of the government was assured, the pattern continued to unfold itself. Poland was quickly sovietized. One of the first things the communist government did was to confiscate the larger industrial establishments, freeze workers in their jobs, and outlaw strikes. All youth groups were merged in one communist-controlled organization, the Union of Polish Youth. Communist control was established at once over education, so that it could be used to indoctrinate the youth of Poland. The communist government divided up some of the large estates, but the parcels peasants received were so small that they could not sustain a peasant family. To make certain that individual ownership would not be a success, the taxes on individual farmers were increased 300 per cent. The aim of the communist leaders in Poland was, of course, collectivization. Peasants on collective farms can be controlled much more easily than individual owners. Steps were also taken to limit the power and influence of the Roman Catholic Church. The excuse for such a move was that the clergy were meddling in politics. In their attacks against the church in the press and over the radio the communist propaganda machine even denounced the Vatican as "a capitalist state." The Six-Year Reconstruction Plan, inaugurated in 1949, called for an annual increase in industrial production of 11 to 12 per cent. In other words, it means a minimum increase of 66 per cent by 1955.

Another state which became an Axis satellite was Hungary. At Yalta the Big Three decided to help not only the peoples that had been liberated from Nazi occupation but also the "people of the former Axis satellite states." They agreed upon joint supervision of the ex-satellite states. Although an Allied Control Commission for Hungary composed of representatives of the three nations was set up, the Russians acted without consulting the other members. Actually the Soviet army of occupation and the Hungarian Communist Party were the principal and all-powerful agencies in the conquered country. The communists were a small group at first, but their number was soon increased by Moscow-trained Hungarian communists, some of whom had been in Russia since the collapse of Bela Kun's rule after World War I. This small minority missed no opportunity to strengthen its position. The members of the party concentrated at first on the relatively easy task of gaining control of the local administrations—provincial, county, and municipal. They were not ready to attempt national control. Hence when the governments of Britain and the United States asked after V-E Day for the reconstruction of the government on a more representative basis in conformity with the Yalta agreement, the Kremlin took its time in setting a date for the elections. It wished more time to consolidate its hold on the political and economic life of Hungary. When the elections were held (November 4, 1945) the communists, much to the disappointment of the Kremlin, got only 800,000 of the 4.7 million votes that were cast.

The new government was still a popular front coalition, but the communists managed to have one of their number chosen minister of the interior, which gave them control of the police. This enabled them to tighten the screws on the opposition. Every possible means— bribery and intimidation, favors and threats—were used to intimidate the opposition or to cause dissension in its ranks. Opposition leaders were arrested on trumped-up charges and sentenced to imprisonment or exile. A favorite accusation was that of "Fascist," after which an anti-communist government official or army officer was discharged and a communist was appointed to fill his place. Opposition newspapers were harried and hampered in every way. Since the ministry of the interior had charge of the distribution of newsprint, it could dole out the newsprint in meager portions to unfriendly newspapers.

On the eve of the next general elections the communists did everything possible to terrorize the opposition, even to accusing members of the opposition parties of plotting to overthrow the republic by force.[2] When the election lists were published about two weeks before the election many of those who were unfriendly to the communists found that their names had been stricken from them, while the names of others who had passed away months and even years before that time were still on it. Despite all this the communists received only 22 per cent of the votes (August 31, 1947). They did, however, manage to get a third of the cabinet posts. This and the support of the left-wing Social Democrats enabled them gradually to stamp out all effective opposition. Finally on June 12, 1948, the Communist Party became the dominant party through a merger with the Social Democrats. During the months that followed the Soviet Union tightened its grip not only on the political and economic but

[2] A republic had been proclaimed in Hungary in January, 1946.

also on the religious and cultural life of Hungary. In other words, Hungary was reduced to the status of a Soviet colony.

ᛈ

RUMANIA, BULGARIA, AND ALBANIA

In December, 1944, King Michael of Rumania requested General Radescu to form a cabinet in which all major parties were represented. The communists, too, participated in it. During the cabinet meetings they attacked the policies of the Radescu government in the most intemperate terms, but the democratic parties offered stiff opposition and were able to hold their own. Having observed how the power of the Communist Party in Greece was broken and a right-wing regime was established, the Kremlin decided to make certain that this would not happen in Rumania. It, therefore, sent Andrei Vishinsky, at the time Soviet deputy foreign minister, to Rumania to install a puppet Soviet regime. Vishinsky browbeat King Michael by a threat of force into accepting a panel of ministers of Vishinsky's choosing, composed entirely of left-wing elements.

According to the set pattern, a communist was given the post of minister of the interior. This minister had charge of the police, of the elections, and of the appointment of local officials. Within a few days this government, known as the Groza government after its prime minister, began to make arrests for political purposes. A concentration camp was opened and many Rumanian leaders of opposing political views were consigned to it. Because it was the center of opposition the National Peasant Party was the primary target of the communist attack. Although Iuliu Maniu, the leader of the Peasant Party, made no secret of the fact that he was unalterably opposed to communist domination, the communists did not dare lay hands on him because of the affection in which he was held by his followers. He was, however, denounced as a "Fascist" and a "Nazi collaborator." Actually he had been the leader of the group which was instrumental in getting Rumania to join the Allies.

As in Poland and Hungary, the communists did everything possible to discredit and weaken the opposition. An innovation in Rumania was the appointment of a propaganda minister who prescribed the line newspapers were expected to follow. Each day all newspapers received a bundle of propaganda material with orders that it be printed in a prominent place. Declarations by the United States and Great Britain that the Groza government was not representative of the people within the meaning and intention of the Yalta agreement encouraged King Michael to try to effect a change of government. He conferred with Groza (August, 1945) and demanded his resignation, but the latter refused to surrender his mandate. Michael then appealed to the United States, Britain, and the Soviet Union to intervene under the terms of the Yalta agreement. No discussion of the problem by the Big Three ever took place. The Soviet government settled the issue to all intents and purposes by stating that the Groza government as it was constituted was democratic and met the requirements of the Yalta agreement in every way. At subsequent conferences the British and United States delegates raised the problem without achieving anything.

Finally the government set November 19, 1946, as the date for the elections. During the weeks preceding it the communists resorted to the same terroristic practices which were being used in the other countries of eastern Europe. Armed communist gangs broke up political rallies held by the Peasant and Liberal parties. Opposition leaders were threatened or beaten. Moreover, a new electoral law was passed which disfranchised thousands of Rumanians who might have voted against the communists. After the election the government claimed an overwhelming victory. It was announced that the government bloc had won 348 seats and the opposition only 64. During the months that followed every vestige of opposition was wiped out. In 1947 the Peasant Party was officially dissolved and its leaders, including Maniu, were sentenced to solitary confinement for life. In November, 1947, King Michael himself was asked to resign. There was no other recourse for him but to comply. Rumania was proclaimed a "people's republic" with a constitution modeled after that of the Soviet Union.

Developments in Bulgaria took much the same course. In September, 1944, a popular front government (Fatherland Front) was organized. It is again the old story of a communist obtaining the cabinet post of minister of the interior. The control of the police enabled the communists to take over other key posts and to harry the opposition. After the government set a date for holding elections in the summer of 1945 the same old technique was employed—the opposition was denounced, threatened, terrorized. The result was that the new parliament contained no representatives of the opposition. The next aim of the communists was to abolish the monarchy. After the communist propaganda machine had done everything possible to discredit the monarchy, the question was put before the people. By an overwhelming vote they decided in favor of a republic (September, 1946). The next month delegates were elected to a Grand National Assembly which was to draw up a constitution. Most of the opposition candidates were in prison or concentration camps when election day dawned. The results of the voting, as announced by the government, were 277 seats for the communists, 87 for the other parties of the Fatherland Front, and 101 for the opposition. The last step was the liquidation of the opposition by various means. Before the end of 1947 the communists were in complete control. The constitution which the Bulgarian parliament ratified in December, 1947, was much like that of the other satellite states.

In the meantime Nikola Petkov, leader of the Agrarian Party, who had dared to oppose communist control, had been executed and his party dissolved. During the summer of 1948 all other noncommunist parties were gradually strangled, so that by the beginning of 1949 the Bulgarian government virtually became a one-party system. Steps were also taken to collectivize agriculture. According to the five-year plan adopted in 1949 no less than 75 per cent of the holdings are to be collectivized. Five per cent is to revert to the state and the rest to be left to individual owners. Before long, however, pressure was put on the individual owners to join collectives. Bulgarian youth was carefully indoctrinated. Non-Marxist students were expelled from the universities. Religious instruction was banned in the schools and many priests of the Orthodox Church were arrested because they disapproved of the communist regime. In general, during the years 1949 and 1950 trials of anti-Marxists and non-Marxists followed each other in rapid succession. Many were sentenced to prison terms and more to the twenty known penal labor camps.

The poorest and smallest of the Soviet satellites is Albania. The communist leader of that country is Enver Hoxha (pronounced Hodja), who delights, as Göring once did, in wearing ornate military uniforms. He was one of the founders of the Albanian Communist Party (1941) and quickly rose to the position of secretary of the party and editor of its paper, the *Voice of the People*. He was also the leader of the National Liberation Front, a communist resistance movement against Italian rule in Albania. When Albania was cleared of Hitler's troops in 1944, the National Liberation Front was in control of the whole country. Hoxha emerged from his mountain hideout and established a provisional government in Tirana with himself as prime minister. A general election which took place in December, 1945, gave the National Front an overwhelming majority and six days later the Constituent Assembly proclaimed Albania a "people's democracy," a euphemism to cover a totalitarian regime. Once Hoxha was established in his control of the government he set about making Albania a one-party state. To achieve this he resorted to the now familiar methods of purge, arrests, and terrorization.

᠗

YUGOSLAVIA AND TITOISM

In Yugoslavia the Communist Party was already in control before the fighting in World War II ceased. Its leading spirit was Josip Broz, better known as Marshal Tito. Taken prisoner by the Russians in World War I, he spent several years in Russia and when he returned home it was as an enthusiastic communist. Gradually he became the leader of the communist underground in Yugoslavia. The origin of the name "Tito" is explained as follows. As underground leader he would give orders to the members of his group, saying "You will do this; and you that." In Serbo-Croat the order was "Ti, to; ti, to." He used these words so often that his friends began to call him "Tito," a name which gradually replaced his real name. A good organizer, a resourceful leader, and an orthodox communist, he organized a communist anti-Nazi resistance. Upon entering the field he found another resistance movement, the Chetniks under General Mihailovich. The two groups were soon at each other's throats. While the Chetniks were intent on preserving the old order, Tito's Partisans were determined to destroy it and set up a communist regime. Soon a civil war was in progress simultaneously with the war of resistance against the Nazis. The civil war did not end until the spring of 1946 when Mihailovich was captured and executed.

After the Germans were driven out, a people's front government was established with Tito as prime minister. In November, 1945, this government proclaimed Yugoslavia a republic and several months later adopted a constitution modeled after that of Soviet Russia. Thereafter the Yugoslav communists proceeded to employ the same ruthless methods to stamp out the opposition that were being used in the other satellite states. All those who did not adhere to the Marxist line were promptly purged. Yugoslavia appeared so firmly fixed under the control of the Kremlin that the Russian troops were withdrawn. After their withdrawal Tito continued his program of sovietization. One phase of this program was the collectivization of agriculture. By the end of 1949 there were no less than 4250 collectives in Yugoslavia.

What distinguishes the developments in Yugoslavia from those in the other satellite states is that the Soviet Communist Party did not retain its control over Yugoslavia. Tito and the other leaders of the Yugoslav Communist Party refused to be mere puppets. High-spirited Tito was not ready to limit his own independence and that of his country in the interests of the Kremlin or the Cominform. The Kremlin leaders discovered as early as 1945 that he was not as docile as they had hoped. In that year Tito complained that the Kremlin was not supporting his claim to Trieste. The Yugoslav leader felt that the Soviet Union was favoring the Italian claim as a means of strengthening the Italian Communist Party. In a speech of May, 1945, Tito warned the Kremlin that the interests of Yugoslavia must not be used in Soviet bargaining. "We demand," he said, "that everyone shall be master in his own house. We do not want to pay for others. We do not want to get involved in spheres of influence." This speech excited Stalin's wrath and the Kremlin at once informed Tito that such things "could not be tolerated." The Soviet ambassador at Belgrade was also given the following instructions: "Tell Comrade Tito that if he should once again permit such an attack on the Soviet Union we shall be forced to reply with open criticism in the press and disavow him." What the Kremlin expected was the type of obedience expressed by Maurice Thorez, leader of the French Communist Party: "Our confidence in the Communist Party of the Soviet Union, in Stalin, is absolute and unreserved."

Further friction developed because Tito refused to accept the role of Kremlin stooge and to subordinate the interests of his country to those of the Soviet Union. What he and his followers demanded was the right to run their own country in their own way. This vexed the Russian communists greatly. On March 27, 1948, the Central Committee of the Soviet Communist Party complained to Tito about the existence of an anti-Soviet sentiment in Yugoslavia. The complaint stated in part:

Leading comrades in Yugoslavia are saying things like "The (Soviet) All-Union Communist Party is degenerate" and "the Cominform is a means of controlling other parties by the All-Union Communist Party." The anti-Soviet phrases are usually covered up by leftist phrases such as "Socialism in the Soviet Union has ceased to be revolutionary." We are disturbed by the present condition of the Yugoslav Communist Party. It is being put to sleep by rotten opportunistic theories of peaceful absorption of capitalist elements.

The big question was, "Would Tito confess his sins and repent?" He gave some indication as to what his answer might be when he had his police arrest two pro-Stalin comrades. Then, after a silence of more than two weeks, he wrote to Comrade J. V. Stalin and Comrade V. M. Molotov:

We are terribly surprised by the tone and content of your letter. . . . We study and take as an example the Soviet system, but we are developing socialism in our country in somewhat different forms. We do this . . . because it is forced on us by conditions in our daily life. . . . We have proof that certain members of Soviet Intelligence in recruiting our party members have cast doubts on our leaders, harmed their reputation. . . . These activities by Soviet Intelligence continue today. We cannot allow their spread.

In its answer the Central Committee stated (May 4, 1948): "Your tone can only be described as unboundedly pretentious. Yugoslav comrades do not accept criticism in the Marxist manner, but in a bourgeois manner." It was still not too late for Tito to confess his sins and be restored to good standing. He chose the other course and wrote (May 17, 1948): "It would be too much to write of the depressing effect [your letter] created. It has convinced us all explanations are in vain." A few weeks later Tito, his associates, and the Yugoslav Communist Party were officially expelled from the Cominform. In its denunciation of Tito and his associates the Cominform said:

The Cominform finds that the leadership of the Yugoslav Communist Party creates a hateful policy in relation to the Soviet Union and to the All-Communist Union of Bolsheviks. The leading persons of the Communist Party of Yugoslavia take a standpoint unworthy of Communists . . . and they treat the Soviet Union in the same manner as they treat the bourgeois states. . . . The Cominform condemns these anti-Soviet conceptions of leading members of the Yugoslav Communist Party as incompatible with Marxism-Leninism and as suitable for nationalists. The leading members of the Yugoslav Communist Party are slipping off the Marx-Lenin path to the nationalist, kulak road.

The communist world shuddered at Tito's brazen stand and said it would be of short duration. One communist dispatch read: "Forty-eight hours have passed and Tito has not crawled to Moscow on his belly—he must do it in the next few days." Radio Moscow declared the Tito regime in Yugoslavia "an enemy of the Soviet Union," and *Pravda* asserted that Tito was Russia's "most dangerous enemy." In Bucharest the *Cominform Journal* under the headline "The Fascist Beast Runs Amok" called on Tito's party comrades in Yugoslavia to oust him and to "raise from below a new international leadership." If all this disturbed Tito he gave no indication of it. He was confident that the Yugoslav Communist Party would refuse to bow to the pressure of the Kremlin and the Cominform. The Yugoslav communists, in fact, flatly rejected the Cominform charges as "slanders and fabrications" and countered by accusing the Cominform of "conspiracy" to impair the prestige of the Yugoslav Communist Party. Tito's excommunication by the Cominform did not mean, however, that he and his government would turn from the Marxist-Leninist path. He continued to insist that he was a hundred-per-cent communist. The basic ideological difference between Stalin and himself, he said, was "between centralized power in a monolithic communist world organization and decentralized power which recognizes the autonomy of various segments of the communist world." Tito's government remained totalitarian and he continued to carry out a program of industrialization and agricultural collectivization in essence not dissimilar from the Russian pattern.

When Tito refused to recant, the Kremlin became apprehensive that the revolt against the Soviet Communist Party might spread. On instructions from Moscow a general purge of the communist parties in all the satellite states was inaugurated. Many of the local leaders who might possibly follow Tito's example were replaced with Moscow-trained communists. The Kremlin leaders also reverted to greater reliance on armed force, for they believed that no rebellion would have taken place in Yugoslavia if the army had been loyal to Moscow. Consequently Russian officers were sent to some of the satellite states to take over the command of the local armies. The precautions which the Soviet government took do not seem, however, to have been sufficient. On May 10, 1952, the Cominform admitted in its official weekly that despite a thoroughgoing purge during which 17,466 full and probationary members of the Bulgarian Communist Party had been expelled, the party has been penetrated by "avowed enemies" of the regime, some of whom have managed to work their way into "responsible posts." It is frankly admitted that "how the avowed enemies succeeded in worming their way into the party and even to responsible posts" is a "task which remains to be solved."

_☞

THE SOVIETIZATION OF CZECHOSLOVAKIA

Czechoslovakia was the last nation of eastern Europe to become a Soviet satellite. On the eve of World War II it had been the only democratic state in eastern Europe and even at the end of the war it appeared as if the Czechoslovaks would maintain their democratic liberties and national independence. Because Stalin had agreed at Yalta not to interfere in the affairs of the countries of eastern Europe, the noncommunists of Czechoslovakia believed that there could be equal cooperation of all parties in a popular front. In the elections of 1946, which were still fairly free, the noncommunist parties did

gain a majority, but when the new cabinet was formed the communists managed to get control of the ministry of the interior, the ministry of agriculture, and the ministry of information. Through the
first they gained control of the police. The ministry of agriculture
put them in charge of the distribution of the lands which had been
confiscated from the Sudeten Germans. The ministry of information
put radio under their control. Moreover, the prime minister, Klement
Gottwald, was a communist. In addition the communists were increasing in numbers. First, many opportunists hurried to join the
party. Second, many soldiers who had been trained in Russia had also
been indoctrinated and upon their return to Czechoslovakia swelled
the ranks of the communists.

The hopes of the noncommunists were centered on President
Beneš and foreign minister Masaryk, both of whom were not communists. Then, too, there were many noncommunists in Parliament
who courageously opposed the communists. For a time, although
there was some friction, the coalition in the Popular Front worked
fairly well. The communists even boasted that they were staunch up-
holders of parliamentary government. Thus Premier Gottwald said:
"With regard to parliamentary institutions, they will have no more
vigilant guardians than the Communist Party when they are written
into the new constitution." The turning point came in the summer
of 1947 after the Czech cabinet accepted the invitation to attend the
Marshall Plan conference in Paris and later refused it under pressure
from the Kremlin. This was followed shortly by the creation of the
Cominform, which prescribed for the communist parties the task of
gaining complete control. Thereafter without renouncing adherence
to parliamentary principles the communists worked single-mindedly
to gain a majority in Parliament. During the succeeding months
there was a permanent political crisis in Czechoslovakia. Communist
"action committees" were organized in all important organizations.
As was later revealed, there were secret communist committees even
in the opposition political parties. The police were active arresting
opposition leaders on trumped-up charges, strikes were called to paralyze industry, and the "workers' militia" used force against stubborn
opposition. On the night of February 20, 1948, the "action committees" by a bold stroke dismissed from most organizations chairmen,
managers, directors, and others who were not sympathetic with communist aims. Before the opposition could raise a hand most phases of
political and economic life in Czechoslovakia had passed under communist control.

Two men still held out. President Beneš and foreign minister

Masaryk. It was, however, a losing fight. On February 25, 1948, Beneš gave way and accepted a cabinet composed largely of communists and communist collaborators. Masaryk retained the post of foreign minister, but upon realizing that collaboration with the communists was impossible committed suicide on February 10. The death of Beneš in September of the same year marked the end of effective resistance to communist control. Systematically every phase of life was sovietized. Libraries were purged of all books that were not pro-Marxist, teachers were ordered under threat of dismissal to teach the children the Marxist-Leninist way of life, and all known anti-communist professors were expelled from the universities. In the meantime the nationalization of the larger industries, of export and import firms, department stores, wholesale agencies, spas, and hotels had been completed. It has been estimated that by the end of 1949 nearly 95 per cent of the nation's industrial enterprises were under state control. In the rural districts all farms of more than 125 acres were confiscated and pressure was put on peasants who owned less to join collectives. In November, 1949, laws were passed which classified the clergy as civil servants and gave the government control of church appointments, finances, and administration. Thus inch by inch the sovietization of Czechoslovakia proceeded. At the beginning of 1950 the communist paper *Rude Pravo* published the following directive which was almost on the humorous side: "All employees are to ask their patrons to cease giving them tips because it is a dishonorable means of rewarding service." Tipping, the paper asserted, was a "degrading reminder of the obsolete capitalist era." Curiously enough, tipping is still expected in the better Russian hotels and restaurants.

Meanwhile a new election had been held at the end of May, 1949. A single list, without opposition candidates, was presented to the voters. According to the official report 90 per cent of the Czechs voted for the list and 86 per cent in Slovakia. On May 8 a new constitution modeled on that of the U.S.S.R. had been proclaimed. Like its model it is liberal in appearance, but illiberal in reality. All the provisions regarding individual freedom or independence of the judiciary are hedged with restrictions which dilute or eliminate these rights.

CHINA BECOMES A SOVIET APPENDAGE

When the Japanese launched their major attack against China in 1937 the communists and nationalists (Kuomintang) who had been fighting each other joined forces against the enemy. Chiang Kai-shek even supplied the communists with arms and ammunition for the fight against the Japanese. The communists were successful both in their guerrilla warfare and in organizing popular resistance to the Japanese. While they were fighting the Japanese, the communists made the most of the opportunity to strengthen their own position. They were particularly intent on ingratiating themselves with the peasants. In their instructions from central headquarters the guerrilla fighters were told not to steal from the peasants and never to abuse them, but to help them in every possible way. This they did, for example, by working in the fields of the peasants during lulls between battles. The result was that besides creating much good will they also gained many peasant recruits.

At the end of the war China was ranked as one of the great powers, but it soon became evident that this designation was a fallacy. First, China was economically prostrate. Such progress as Chiang Kai-shek had made in reorganizing the economic life during the years from 1928 to 1937 was wiped out by the long war that followed. Second, the country was divided into two hostile camps. Throughout the war various attempts had been made to bring about full cooperation between the communists and nationalists and by the middle of 1944 negotiations for a coalition government were well under way. Any real compromise solution was, however, obstructed by extremists on both sides.

Late in 1945 President Truman dispatched General George Marshall to China to see what he could do toward establishing a "coalition" government. When he arrived there a draft had already been prepared for the inclusion of the communists in a constitutional government. In January, 1946, Generalissimo Chiang Kai-shek signed an armistice with the communists and for a brief time prospects for cooperation seemed bright. Actually, however, the chasm between the two parties was too wide to be bridged. In the final showdown Chiang refused to accept the communists' proposals and they, in turn, rejected his counterproposals. Neither side appears to have been sincere in trying to reach a compromise. While the communists had no intention of abandoning their efforts to extend their control over the whole of China, Generalissimo Chiang was convinced that he could suppress the communists by force and thereby eliminate them from competition in the government. All attempts of General Marshall to dissuade Chiang from adopting this course failed.

In April, 1946, the communists broke the truce by an attack on Changchun and the civil war was resumed. For the fighting Chiang had an army of thirty-nine divisions and an air force to go with them, but the generals who led the armies were largely incompetent, having been appointed for political reasons. Moreover, the general staff of the Kuomintang armies appears to have had no real plans for military action and the armies generally were defensive-minded. One observer styled Chiang's military leaders as "unsurpassed in incompetence." On the other hand, the equipment of the Nationalist armies could have been better. At the end of the war the U.S. Navy and Marines left much equipment and ammunition for Chiang's armies. But from the fall of 1946 to March, 1948, not a single combat plane or bomber was sent to the armies of Chiang Kai-shek. General Marshall himself told the Committee on Foreign Affairs of the House of Representatives (February, 1948) that "it was in effect an embargo on military supplies." It is very doubtful, however, whether the sending of supplies and equipment would have done more than prolong the war.

While the United States Department of State was curtailing supplies to Chiang's armies, the communists were receiving vast quantities of military supplies from the Russians. President Roosevelt made this possible at Yalta (February, 1945) when he restored to the Soviet Union the imperialistic rights which the Japanese had taken from Russia in 1905. Although the Russians only entered the war after the atom bombs had been dropped on Hiroshima and Nagasaki and although their participation amounted to very little, the Yalta terms were carried out. Thus all the Japanese arms, equipment, and arsenals of Manchuria came under Russian control. The Russians at once turned the arms and equipment over to the Chinese communists, thereby equipping them to fight against Chiang's armies. It has been stated that the Russians did not turn the arms over to the communists directly; they only permitted the latter to "find" them in Manchuria. At first the communists fought guerrilla style against the armies and government of Chiang, but gradually larger armies were trained and equipped with the arms the Russians had turned over to the communists.

With their armies the communists succeeded in gaining control in 1947 of all of Manchuria except a few large cities along the southern border and by the end of 1948 they had extended their sway over the whole of the northern provinces. During the early months of 1949 the People's Liberation Army of the communists made rapid advances toward the south as the resistance of the Kuomintang forces grew less and less effective. On January 15 the communists occupied Tientsin, a week later they took Peiping (Peking), and in April they crossed the Yangtze and captured Nanking. The following month saw the fall of both Hangchow and Shanghai under the communist at-

tack. The communists were now well on the way to the conquest of
the whole of China.

The question is often asked, How did it come about that the communist army was able to conquer China? The reasons are not easy to
find. The deeper one penetrates into the situation the more complex
it becomes. Many observers are of the opinion that the success of the
communists was less cause than effect, that they would not have succeeded if the Nationalist government had not been on the verge of
collapse. In a general way one can, therefore, say that the weaknesses
of the Nationalist government opened the way for the communist success and such strength as the communists had carried them on to their
goal. As for the weaknesses of the nationalists, they were many.

The major weakness of the Kuomintang government was that it
did not have the support of the Chinese people. This accounts for the
fact that on a number of occasions whole divisions went over to the
communists without firing a shot. Others simply deserted. The divisions which joined the communists took their equipment with them.
The communists also acquired equipment from Chiang's armies
through bribery. This helps explain the fact that the transportation
facilities of the communists consisted mainly of trucks and jeeps
which the United States had originally given to Chiang's armies. The
same was true regarding tanks and artillery. Secretary of State Acheson
said in 1949: "The Nationalist armies did not lose a single battle
during the crucial year of 1948 through lack of arms or ammunition. . . . The Nationalist armies did not have to be defeated; they
disintegrated." The Chinese communists did not stop at acquiring
United States equipment from Chiang's armies; they were also quick
to announce the fact that Chiang was receiving arms and equipment
from the United States, thereby exposing him to the charge that he
was a "running dog" of foreign imperialism.

A second major weakness of the Nationalist government was its
failure to carry out land reforms. It was the great need of China since
75 to 85 per cent of the population obtained a living from the soil.
In 1938 the estimated income per capita of the Chinese farmer was
the lowest in the world. The difficulties caused by overpopulation
and exhaustion of the soil were further intensified by high taxes,
usurious interest rates, and exorbitant rents. High rents and low income prevented the average farmer from accumulating a surplus;
hence economic crises put him at the mercy of moneylenders charging rates of 20 to 85 per cent. An enlightened program of land distribution, reorganization of the tax structure, and low-cost farm credits
would have earned the Nationalist government the support of a large

portion of the Chinese peasantry. Originally such a program was part of the Kuomintang platform, but those who desired to carry out this program were not strong enough to overcome the opposition of the reactionary elements that were determined to perpetuate the old land-owning system.

A third major weakness of the Kuomintang government was the fact that it was honeycombed with greed, corruption, and nepotism. Observers have gone so far as to style it "one of the most corrupt governments of modern times" and "the government which has set a new low in corruption and mismanagement." Chiang Kai-shek himself said in his message to the people at the end of 1946: "Honesty is regarded as pedantic and self-respect as backward. The practice of speculation and trickery has spread from business circles to the community as a whole. Officials and gentry, in seeking gratification of their selfish purposes, resort to manipulation and other ill practices in total disregard of the country as well as of the people." United States General Joseph W. Stilwell had reported in 1944 that the Kuomintang "was once the expression of genuine nationalistic feeling, but is now an uncertain equilibrium of decadent, competing factions, with neither dynamic principles nor a popular base."

If the nationalists failed to gain popular support, this was not true of the communists. The man who made Chinese communism a dynamic movement based on the support of the masses was Mao Tse-tung. Mao, who had already displayed revolutionary tendencies as a youth, was a member of the group that founded the Chinese Communist Party in 1921. During the early years of the party's existence he was not, however, the leading spirit in the party. This role was played by Moscow-trained communists who hoped to build the strength of the party on the urban proletariat. According to the orthodox Marxism of the period, the peasantry were not regarded as being capable of successfully promoting a communist revolution. So long as the communists based their hopes on the urban proletariat the party was not an important factor in China. But Mao Tse-tung had other ideas. He advocated a program with the peasantry rather than the urban proletariat as the driving force. For his heretical views Mao was for a time dropped from the Central Committee. Only after the policy based on the urban proletariat failed did Mao get his opportunity; then the Chinese Communist Party modified its Marxist creed to fit the idea of a revolution based on the peasants, and Mao was credited with furthering the development of Marxism-Leninism.

The three factors that gave Chinese communism its momentum were nationalism, Marxism, and agrarian reform. During World

War II many students, intellectuals, and members of the middle classes were attracted to the communist banners by the heavy emphasis which the communists placed on nationalism. In the north of China a large section of the youth believed that it was the communists alone who were really fighting the Japanese. The communist propaganda also accused the Kuomintang of "selling" China to "United States imperialists." Many young Chinese were drawn into the Communist Party by promises of a "new democracy." Just what the words "new democracy" meant no one was able to say, but the idea did offer a change, an alternative to the Kuomintang dictatorship. The intellectuals were made to feel that their specialized skills were needed in the new order. In general, the communists convinced many that Marxism was the cure-all for the ills of the Chinese people. Their fervor for the cause was a striking contrast to the apathy of the Kuomintang Party.

Important as nationalism and Marxism were to the success of the Chinese communist movement, it was the explosive force of the agrarian revolt which provided the main motive power. As a peasant's son, Mao had early in his life resented the treatment accorded the peasants and had been the leader of a number of minor peasant revolts. Thus it was natural that he should become the champion of agrarian reform after he helped to found the Communist Party. His friendliness toward the peasants gave support to the promises of "land reform," promises that were carried out in the newly occupied territories as soon as the communist civilian organizers arrived. What appealed to the landless peasants above all was the fact that the communists distributed the land in plots instead of collectivizing it. When this is contrasted with the lack of any positive Kuomintang achievement it is easy to see why the Chinese peasant masses should be attracted to the communist movement. The mobilization of the peasants was the key to communist military power.

As the communists pressed southward the resistance of the Nationalist armies grew less and less. In April, 1949, the communist armies crossed the Yangtze and captured Nanking. The following month saw them take both Hangchow and Shanghai. In the meantime Chiang Kai-shek and the Nationalist government had left the mainland to establish headquarters on the island of Formosa off China's eastern coast. Thereafter the communist armies met with little effective resistance as they moved southward and eastward. By the end of 1949 most of the Chinese mainland was under their control. On September 22, 1949, they had proclaimed the "Chinese Peoples' Republic" with Peiping as the capital. Mao Tse-tung, secretary general of the Chinese Communist Party, was named chairman of the Central Committee. In this he paralleled the rise of Stalin. The Soviet Union at once accorded the new government recognition and Britain later followed suit. The United States, however, withheld recognition. In the Western democracies many hoped that Mao Tse-tung would be another Tito who would soon jettison his association with the Kremlin. There were, however, no indications that he would do so. On the contrary, on a number of occasions he has repeated the sentiments he expressed on the twenty-eighth anniversary of the founding of the Chinese Communist Party (July 1, 1949) when he proclaimed his allegiance to the Soviet Union and stated that China's course was "to ally with the Soviet Union." The Chinese Communist Party is unquestionably a party of the Leninist-Stalinist variety and like other parties of its type believes that "the Kremlin can do no wrong."

CHAPTER THIRTY-TWO

Recent Developments in the Soviet Sphere

THE NEW SOVIET LEADERS   WHEN Georgi Malenkov assumed Stalin's mantle after the latter's death on March 5, 1953, it was widely assumed abroad that the heir apparent, as he had been during the lifetime of Stalin, would be another powerful dictator and that his rule would be a long one. In both respects the conjecture proved incorrect. It soon became apparent that he did not possess the absolute power wielded by Stalin. This led foreign writers to conclude that the authority was now vested in a directory type of administration. It seemed as if some of Malenkov's rivals, remembering the frequent purges of the Stalin period, had entered into a combination to prevent him from becoming too overwhelmingly strong. Neither was Malenkov's tenure of power of long duration. Only nine days after Stalin's death he resigned the post of First Secretary of the Central Committee of the Communist Party, a post which had enabled Stalin to rise to power after Lenin's death and to control the machinery of the Communist Party, and thereby the Soviet Union, for almost thirty years. Most observers felt that Malenkov had lost little power or prestige in stepping down from the party secretariat. Thus one correspondent wrote, "Experts here are sure Malenkov has not relinquished any of his power." Nevertheless, it was the turning point in the fortunes of Malenkov. Before many months passed Nikita Khrushchev, his successor as First Secretary, was, to all appearances, the most powerful figure in the Kremlin circle.

The next step downward came on February 8, 1955, when Malenkov relinquished his post as premier of the Soviet Union. His resignation statement, read to a joint meeting of both houses of the Supreme Soviet, ascribed the step to "the necessity of strengthening the leadership of the Council of Ministers and the need to have at the post of the chairman of the Council of Ministers another comrade with greater experience in state work." In the statement Malenkov assumes the blame for the poor showing of Soviet agriculture. "I see particularly clearly," the statement asserts, " my guilt and responsibility for the unsatisfactory state of affairs which has arisen in agriculture." In other words, the statement makes Malenkov the scapegoat for the disappointing agricultural output. Many observers have expressed doubt regarding Malenkov's personal guilt. The poor showing of Soviet agriculture was the obvious result of faulty Soviet planning, not of Malenkov's management. The resignation statement also implies that the emphasis Malenkov put on the production of consumer goods was a mistake. "The only correct foundation," it avers, is "the further development, by every means, of heavy industry." In his speech of August 8, 1953, Malenkov had said, "At the present time we are able to insure—and therefore we must—a more rapid increase in the material and cultural levels of the life of the people, force by every means the development of our light industry." Anastas Mikoyan, the Minister of Trade, had gone into detail, promising the production of watches, bicycles, stoves, washing machines, electric irons, blankets—all the necessities of modern living that the Soviet citizens had been denied. "We shall," he declared, "make up for lost time." If the other Kremlin leaders had originally supported this policy, they had experienced a change of heart, for top priority was once again accorded heavy industry and expansion of armaments. It was a return to Stalin's emphasis on the production of capital goods.

How much personal rivalries within the Kremlin had to do with Malenkov's resignation has not been revealed. It is generally believed by those foreign observers occupying the best vantage point that Malenkov was acting under duress when he resigned. Contrary, however, to purge procedures in the Stalinist era Malenkov was not "liquidated." He was named a deputy premier and given the post of Minister of Electric Power Stations for the time being. Marshal Nikolai Bulganin succeeded him as premier.

But the person who emerged as the major figure in the Soviet ruling body is Nikita S. Khrushchev. He seems to be in no sense a classical dictator or supreme ruler, but he does appear to be the single individual who is able to speak with authority on Soviet policy and attitudes. He is the principal representative of Soviet Russia to the outside world. The power he wields seems to be with the advice and the consent of the other members of the collective ruling body. Born of peasant stock in 1894, Khrushchev attended school for only three years before he went to work. Among the various jobs he held were those of shepherd, miner, and factory worker. He joined the Communist Party in 1918 and fought in the civil war in the Ukraine. Later he attended a technical school in Moscow, after which he returned to the Ukraine as a communist official, gradually making his way upward in the ranks of the party until he became party boss of the Ukraine. In 1937 Khrushchev staged a series of purges that claimed the lives of the majority of the Ukrainian communist leaders. As a reward he was named alternate member of the Politburo, becoming a full member the following year. Khrushchev was very fortunate in that he himself managed to escape the various purges Stalin launched periodically. On many occasions Khrushchev's voice rang out loud and clear in praise of the "Great Master," styling him "the beacon which guides progressive mankind."

Khrushchev started his real rise to power nine days after Stalin's death when he took over the title of First Secretary relinquished by Malenkov. At that time he was generally ranked number five in the communist hierarchy, with Malenkov, Beria, Molotov, and Voroshilov ahead of him. But it did not take him long to move to the top rank. Malenkov had already given ground when he stepped down as First Secretary. Molotov and Voroshilov were no real obstacles to Khrushchev's advancement since they had no personal political machines. The one man who was a particular threat to Khrushchev was Lavrenti Beria, the head of the Secret Police (MVD). A month after Stalin's death Beria's MVD exposed the so-called "Doctors' Plot," supposedly a plot by nine Soviet physicians, acting on the orders of American Intelligence agencies and the Jewish Joint Distribution Committee, to kill high Soviet officials by improper treatment. The announcement of this plot in 1952, during Stalin's lifetime, had been accompanied by a denunciation of Jews and Zionism because six or seven of the accused physicians were Jewish. The unfortunate physicians had already "confessed" and a medical commission had formally confirmed the allegations of mistreatment of the distinguished patients. In April, 1953, the MVD officially stated that the accusations were without foundation in fact and that the innocent victims had been framed. The MVD also announced that the confessions had been obtained "through the use of methods of investigation which are inadmissible and most strictly forbidden by Soviet law." But Beria's triumph was short-lived. In July of the same year he was arrested and in the following December his execution was announced. Khrushchev was now the dominant figure.

As the dominant figure in the Soviet system Khrushchev soon demonstrated that he differed from his Georgian master in many respects. While Stalin was an introvert who was virtually inaccessible to foreigners, Khrushchev adopted an attitude toward the foreign press that is exceedingly free by Soviet standards. He made himself more accessible to visiting journalists than any other Soviet leader before him. He attended many social affairs, particularly in foreign embassies, and often attracted the spotlight through his volubility and hard drinking. Correspondents who attended these functions have variously described him as boasting of his power, showing off, playing the fool, exuding confidence. In appearance he is "chunky as a juke box" with a glistening bald head, two glittering gold teeth, small widely-set eyes, and an extrovertish and genial smile. However, behind the effervescent peasant exterior and the seeming friendliness there is a driving ambition and a cool, calculating shrewdness coupled with a ruthlessness developed in the Stalinist school of statesmanship.

THE DOWNGRADING OF STALIN

The most sensational development of the new regime was the carefully planned campaign to destroy the myth of Stalin's greatness. After his accession to power Stalin had gradually become the great Soviet ikon. A web of myths and lies were employed to build him into a godlike figure. He was represented to the people of the Soviet Union as being the all-wise, all-knowing, all-benevolent, all-powerful father and was accepted as such. For example, the million and a half inhabitants of the Karabakh territory hailed him in verse as the "wisest and best-beloved father." A message to Stalin from two million White Russian workers read in part:

> Oh wise master, genius of geniuses!
> Sun of the workers! Sun of the peasants! Sun of the world!
> Power of rivers! Glory and pride of labor!

Religious imagery was even used to extol the "Great Master" as is evidenced by the following from *Pravda* (August 28, 1936):

> Then I say, STALIN, and everything is said;
> O, thou great leader of peoples, who hast called man to life,
> Who hast ordered earth to bear fruit,
> Who hast sentenced centuries to be forever young,
> Who hast called upon springs to flower,
> Strings to sing, hearts to love, and factories to produce.

Wherever we look, we see clearly thy hand everywhere.
Thou art the spring of my life, the sunshine
That finds its reflection in millions of human hearts.

The new leaders decided to revoke Stalin's deification, to smash the hollow plaster image of the godlike figure, and to dance on the fragments. The initiative came from Khrushchev and his colleagues. There was no observable demand for the downgrading of Stalin among the masses. On the contrary, the hold of the Stalin myth on the popular imagination was such that the new leaders moved cautiously. Eighteen days after Stalin's death *Pravda* ceased calling the Communist Party "the party of Lenin and Stalin." Next came the exposure of the notorious "Doctors' Plot." During this time it was the abuses, such as the "cult of the individual," that were denounced rather than Stalin himself. For a time Lavrenti Beria, who had been the head of the MVD for fourteen years, was blamed for many of Stalin's misdeeds. The first direct attack on Stalin appears to have been made by Marshal Nikolai Bulganin, then Defense Minister, in the midsummer of 1953. His comments about the dead dictator were so caustic that Moscow was startled. But the new leaders still waited for about two and a half years before discharging their big guns at Stalin, meanwhile consolidating their strength. When the time seemed right it was Khrushchev himself who attacked the memory of the "Great Master." At the Nineteenth Congress of the Soviet Communist Party in 1952, this same Khrushchev had ended his speech with the customary cry, "Long live the wise leader of the party and the people, the inspirer and organizer of all our victories, Comrade Stalin!" At the Twentieth Congress, which met in February, 1956, it was another story. This time he painted a picture of Stalin which is so black that no anti-communist survivor of a Soviet concentration camp could have painted a darker one.

Khrushchev's picture of Stalin is one which irresistibly recalls the psychopathic Tsar Ivan the Terrible. He depicted Stalin as a suspicious, cruel, and brutal tyrant who demanded absolute submission to his opinion. "Stalin," he stated, "was a very distrustful man, sickly suspicious. We know this from our work with him. . . . Everywhere, and in everything, he saw 'enemies,' 'two-facers,' and 'spies.'" He described Stalin as a man who took a sadistic delight in the infliction of pain and suffering, as a paranoid murderer who repeatedly condemned innocent persons to death. Stalin, he stated, "practised brutal violence, not only toward everything which opposed him, but also toward that which seemed to his capricious and despotic character contrary to his concepts." Stalin's mass arrests and deportations, and executions without trial, he said, created insecurity, fear, and terror.

This terror was actually directed not at the remnants of the defeated exploiting classes, but against the honest workers of the party and of the Soviet state; against them were made lying, slanderous and absurd accusations concerning 'two-facedness,' 'espionage,' 'sabotage,' preparation of fictitious 'plots,' etc. . . . Now when the cases of some of these so-called 'spies' and 'saboteurs' were examined it was found that all their cases were fabricated. Confessions of guilt of many arrested and charged with enemy activity were gained with the help of cruel and inhuman torture. . . . Many thousands of honest and innocent Communists have died as a result of this monstrous falsification of such 'cases.'

Khrushchev pointed out especially how Stalin had treated the members of the Central Committee:

It was determined that of the 139 members and candidates of the party's Central Committee who were elected at the Seventeenth Congress, ninety-eight persons, i.e., 70 per cent, were arrested and shot (mostly in 1937–1938) . . . . Of 1966 delegates with either voting or advisory rights, 1108 persons were arrested on charges of anti-revolutionary crimes, i.e., decidedly more than a majority. This very fact shows how absurd, wild, and contrary to common sense were the charges of counter-revolutionary crimes.

In his indictment of Stalin, Khrushchev also provided an answer to the question which had long puzzled many in the free world, "Why did the old Bolsheviks confess to crimes they had not committed?" "And how," he said, "is it possible that a person confesses to crimes he has not committed? Only in one way—because of application of physical methods of pressuring him, tortures, bringing him to a state of unconsciousness, deprivation of his judgment, taking away of his human dignity." He quotes Stalin as saying to one minister, "If you do not obtain confessions we will shorten you by a head." Khrushchev also cited excerpts from the final statements made by old Bolsheviks just before they were shot. For example, Robert I. Eikhe, a member of the Politburo, made a final appeal to Stalin in which he asserted that the only crime of which he was guilty was that of having confessed crimes he had not committed "by not being able to suffer the tortures to which I was submitted."

According to Khrushchev, Stalin became more irritable, suspicious, and brutal toward the end of his life. "His persecution mania reached unbelievable dimensions." A new blood bath, Khrushchev indicated, was brewing at the time Stalin died. Among those Stalin planned "to finish off" were a number of high-ranking officials, including Molotov and Mikoyan. Khrushchev also quoted a remark attributed to Nikolai Bulganin, "It has happened sometimes that a man goes to Stalin on his invitation as a friend. And when he sits with Stalin, he does not know where he will be sent next—home or jail."

Khrushchev also scoffed at the "military genius" of his one-time master and benefactor, pouring contemptuous scorn on Stalin's claim to be "the genius strategist of all ages." He evoked loud laughter from the members of the Supreme Soviet by poking fun at the master strategist who planned his campaigns on a globe rather than a military map. Khrushchev sought, above all, to dispel the legend that it was Stalin who saved Russia in the war with Nazi Germany. He pictured Stalin as the blundering tyrant whose incompetence, stupidity, and obstinacy almost destroyed the Soviet Union. First, Khrushchev asserted that although Stalin was informed as early as April 3, 1941, by Sir Winston Churchill that the Germans were regrouping their armed units with the intent of attacking the Soviet Union he paid no heed; in fact "Stalin ordered that no credence be given to information of this sort, in order not to provoke the initiation of military operations. . . . Despite these particular grave warnings, the necessary steps were not taken to prepare the country properly for defense and to prevent it from being caught unawares. . . . Had our industry been mobilized properly and in time to support the army with the necessary material, our wartime losses could have been decidedly smaller." Second, Khrushchev charged that Stalin had liquidated most of the Soviet officers who had gained combat experience in Spain and in the Far East. Third, Khrushchev asserted that although Stalin could not read a military map, he had ordered operations which resulted in enormous losses for the Red Army. Fourth, Khrushchev stated that Stalin had created for himself the reputation of being a master of military strategy "not in his role as a strategist, but as an author-editor, as one of the main creators of his self-adulatory biography."

Time and again Khrushchev deplored "the cult of the hero" and extolled "collective leadership." He contrasted Stalin's "cult of the individual" with Lenin's principle of "collective leadership." With bitter sarcasm he denounced Stalin's absolute one-man rule, stating that Stalin "never acknowledged to anyone that he made a mistake, large or small, despite the fact that he made not a few mistakes in the matter of theory and in his practical activity." In commenting on the speech *Pravda* stated, "As time went on the cult of the individual assumed ever more monstrous forms, and did serious harm to the cause." Speakers who followed Khrushchev were even less restrained than he. First deputy premier Anastas Mikoyan, for example, referred with open contempt to the former dictator.

To the free world, the story of Stalin's crimes was no revelation. There it had long been known that he disregarded warnings of Hitler's attack, that he sent many Soviet officials to their deaths without fair trials, and that he was guilty of other crimes. To the Soviet people, to whom a slave press had systematically lied, these things were not revealed. Even Khrushchev's speech was not published in the newspapers, but its contents did filter down to the masses. What they heard shocked the people, particularly those who had been brought up in the Stalin cult. An American correspondent reported from Moscow that "a severe disorientation of public opinion has been caused" and "searching debate and discussion are going on in thousands of homes and enterprises." In Georgia, Stalin's native land, the drive against his name caused some counter-demonstrations on the part of students. Among the communists outside the Soviet Union, where the contents of the speech were soon made known, the impact was no less severe. Many supporters of Stalin were stunned as they began to realize that free-world reports about Stalin, which every communist leader had denounced as slander, were the unvarnished truth. Many communist leaders were hard pressed to justify their record of ardent Stalinism.

It is noteworthy that Khrushchev's indictment, devastating as it is, is very selective. He makes no mention of Stalin's greatest crimes: his liquidation of the kulaks as a class, his mass starvation of the peasants to compel them to submit to collective farming, his institution of a vast network of slave labor camps. Nor does Khrushchev take up the question as to what he and his colleagues, who held key posts in the administration, did to restrain Stalin's lust for mass murder. The truth is that Khrushchev himself employed drastic means to establish collective farming and was himself a ruthless purger of suspected dissidents in the Ukraine.

When Khrushchev opened the dossier of Stalin's crimes he inevitably posed the question as to how far the criticism of the Soviet system was to go. His denunciation of Stalin's autocracy, of his demand that all persons must think as he did, indirectly legalized a plurality of views and differences of opinion. Some made the most of what they regarded as the "new license" in order to attack certain government policies. *Pravda* soon stated that "rotten elements" within the

Communist Party were using the campaign against Stalin as a cover for "slanderous speeches directed against the party's policy." Denunciation of some of the evils of Stalin's government also encouraged satellite countries to demand some degree of autonomy. The result was that the new oligarchy first sought to confine the tide of criticism within certain limits and then called a halt to the attacks on Stalin. It again became fashionable to stress Stalin's alleged merits rather than his crimes. Thus on the fourth anniversary of Stalin's death (March, 1957) *Pravda* called him "an outstanding revolutionary, a devoted Marxist-Leninist theoretician, and a great organizer." Even Khrushchev has been speaking of the dead dictator in milder accents. In September, 1957, he said, as quoted in the *New York Times,* "Stalin made many mistakes in the latter period of his activity, but he also did much that was beneficial to our country, to our party and the whole international workers' movement." Some statues and many pictures of Stalin, it is true, have been removed, but no steps have been taken to remove his embalmed corpse from its place of honor beside that of Lenin in Red Square. Neither have towns, such as the Stalingrads, the Stalinabads, and Stalinos, which assumed variants of the dictator's name been renamed. To the Russian masses Stalin remains a figure of imposing majesty, the embodiment of his country's new-found might and world-wide prestige.

There has been much conjecture as to the motives of Khrushchev and his colleagues in making so sensational an attack on the man the people had been taught to revere as a demigod. A number of motives undoubtedly contributed toward bringing about the denunciation. Among these the need for a scapegoat certainly ranked high. The new leaders needed a scapegoat upon which they could put the blame for the crimes of the Stalin period. By ascribing the blame for the terroristic acts and purges to Stalin they hoped to exculpate themselves. Khrushchev repeatedly sought to prove in his speech that he and his colleagues had no part in Stalin's crimes, that Stalin was solely and alone responsible for them. Stalin was equally useful as a scapegoat in foreign affairs. Any unpleasantness in the relations with other nations could be charged to his account. It was a means of repudiating the most repugnant aspects of Soviet rule so as to make communism more palatable to the non-communist countries.

Khrushchev's self-defense does not, however, carry conviction. The best case he can make out for himself is that he was an accomplice under duress. His defense applies as well to the executed Beria as it does to himself. Again and again in the speech Khrushchev stressed the idea of the "wilfulness of one man." He failed to add, however, that Stalin had so much wilfulness because Khrushchev and his like acknowledged him as their leader and accepted his will, because he and the members of the Communist Party had puffed up Stalin's authority sky high.

THE NEW LOOK

Since Stalin's demise, and particularly since Malenkov stepped down as premier, the ruling oligarchy has inaugurated a series of changes which have been summed up in the term "the New Look." Among the changes which aimed to improve the lot of the workers was the reduction of working hours for the average work week from 48 to 46 hours. Another decree removed some of the arbitrary compulsion from labor by permitting a worker to leave his job on two weeks' notice. In doing so he loses his social security benefits, but he does have the "freedom" to change jobs. Undoubtedly the most popular recent measure was that providing for an improved system of old-age pensions. It provided for the payment of a minimum of 300 rubles per month at retirement to each industrial worker and of 270 rubles per month to agricultural workers after January 1, 1957. This was an important step in improving the well-being of the lowest income classes.

Other changes have tended to loosen the irritating controls imposed on all phases of life and to relax the tensions under which the people lived. Under Stalin the Soviet Union was a state which was run largely by fear and force. Life was filled with fear of the secret police, of the Siberian camps, of informers—in general, of the brutal and remorseless power of the state. Workers did their jobs because if they did not they would be sent to a labor camp. Peasants tilled their fields after a fashion because if they did not do at least a minimum of work they might be transported to Siberia. Even sacrifices were enforced by a constant resort to police methods and by an instilled fear of foreign invasion. Under the new oligarchy the whole police apparatus has been subjected to a revision in order to safeguard individuals against police persecution. In line with this the special power of the MVD to sentence workers up to five years of forced labor merely on review of their dossiers has been abolished. Some of the worst features of labor camps have also been changed, and various amnesties have permitted thousands of inmates of labor camps to return to their homes. In general, under the new leaders the whole domestic program has been shifting from fear and compulsion to persuasion and rewards. One of the purposes of the lessening of the terrorist pressure seems to be to stimulate a new burst of creative activity—one that may achieve industrial and technical progress surpassing all previous progress of the Soviet Union.

In 1957 Khrushchev presented a comprehensive plan for the reorganization of the entire Soviet industry, a plan which was adopted by the Supreme Soviet in May. The essence of the plan, which represents another break with the Stalin era, is decentralization. Under Stalin, Soviet industry was directed exclusively from Moscow down to the last detail. A steel producer could not, for example, buy his coal from a coal producer in his neighborhood. He could buy his coal and sell his steel only through the proper ministry in Moscow. During the early years of the Soviet regime there had been regional economic councils, but they were abolished because Stalin regarded them as potential organs of economic autonomy. Thereafter Stalin reserved for Moscow the power of decision on all economic matters. The machinery needed for this was so vast that it became cumbersome and inefficient. The new plan divided the country into ninety-two regions, each with its own regional council. The regional councils have jurisdiction over all state-owned concerns (some few are run by municipalities) in their respective regions. Consequently the producers in each region are able to deal with each other without consulting Moscow.

The changes introduced by the new oligarchy, together with the downgrading of Stalin, stirred hopes in the western world that more fundamental changes in the direction of democracy might be in the offing. But the hopes were not fulfilled. The changes that were made were not designed to remove communism, but to make it work better. They were maneuvers to achieve the old goals faster and more easily. The changes did not basically alter the structure of dictatorship. Instead of being exercised by one man, authority is now wielded by an oligarchy. In other words, the vital decisions are still made at the top of the Soviet power pyramid and then imposed on the populace. Whatever sacrifices the people must make are still exacted from them without their consent. The present government may permit some debate on secondary matters, but free public debate is still conspicuously absent. It has been made sufficiently clear that deviations from the party line will not be tolerated in the future any more than they were under Stalin. The new leaders have warned that violence is still necessary where "bourgeois resistance" is encountered. Even in economic matters local officials decide only how the orders from Moscow are to be implemented. Economic policies are still formulated in Moscow. In industry the accent is still on the production of capital goods as it was under Stalin, and in agriculture Stalin's policies are being carried to greater extremes than he dared to carry them. A new campaign has been launched to eliminate the peasant's private garden and the family cow, the last vestiges of productive private property on the collective farms.

In the intellectual world the basic demand that all literature, all art, and all science must not deviate from ideological purity is as binding as ever. The government still decides what the citizens may read and instructs the writers what to write. By and large the policy is the same as that promulgated by the Central Committee on August 14, 1946: "The force of Soviet literature lies in the fact that it neither has nor can have any other interests than those of the people and the State. Its task is to help the State to educate the youth." Khrushchev himself has restated the purpose of the arts in the Soviet Union a number of times. "The party's decisions on ideological questions," he said, "defined the major tasks and basic principles of the party's policy in the sphere of art and literature, and they retain their force at the present time. One of the major principles is that Soviet literature and art must be inseverably linked with the policy of the Communist Party which constitutes the vital foundation of the Soviet system." The arts can never be neutral in the "severe struggle that is proceeding between two ideologies, the socialist and the bourgeois. . . . We would not have been Marxist-Leninists if we held aloof, if we were indifferent and passive to the attempts to infiltrate into our literature and art bourgeois views which are alien to the spirit of the Soviet people. . . . Literary and art workers are active fighters for communism. Millions of people learn from their best works."

It must be stated, however, that in practice the official censors have recently been more liberal than they were under Stalin. A large group of poets, playwrights, and novelists whose books were banned have been "rehabilitated" and much of the "forbidden literature" of the Stalin era has been republished. Unfortunately many of those whose reputations have been cleared perished in the concentration camps to which they were sent in the thirties. Two notable victims of the postwar purge of Soviet arts, the poetess Mme. Anna Akhmatova and the satirist Mikhail Zoshchenko, have received a qualified re-reprieve in that some of their works have been republished.

Another noteworthy change is the "new look" in faces about the Kremlin. To convince the world that Stalin's methods are passé, a number of old Stalinists who were too closely associated with the old dictator have been "purged." But whereas Stalin "liquidated" those he wished to be rid of, Khrushchev and associates have employed the bloodless method. Their technique is a reversion to that of the tsars, who sent their political enemies to far-off places. Accordingly they have demoted undesirables and sent them to some remote part of the Soviet Union. In 1957 Malenkov, who after losing his premiership in 1955 had become Minister of Electric Power Stations, was demoted to superintendent of a single power station in the remote province of Kazakhstan in Eastern Russia. This further demotion followed the announcement that Malenkov had helped to plot some of Stalin's purges. Previously, in June, 1956, Radio Moscow had announced that V. M. Molotov had resigned as foreign minister and that Dmitri T. Shepilov, a protégé of Khrushchev, had been chosen to succeed him. Molotov, whom Sir Winston Churchill described as "a man of cold-blooded ruthlessness," had been so closely associated with Stalin that many regarded him as Stalin's rubber stamp. He was also closely identified with certain aspects of foreign policy the Soviet oligarchy would like the world to forget. Probably the most notorious thing he did was to conclude the Nazi-Soviet pact which touched off World War II. For a time after his "resignation" as foreign minister Molotov held the position of deputy premier, but in 1957 he was banished from the Kremlin circle by being commissioned Soviet ambassador to the isolated puppet state of Outer Mongolia. A third associate of Stalin who was exiled from Moscow was Lazar Kaganovich, who had been a deputy premier for twenty years and also tsar of the Soviet construction industry. Kaganovich was assigned to run a cement factory at Sverdlovsk in Western Siberia. In October of 1957 General Zhukov was ousted as Defense Minister for encouraging a "personality cult." Thus Premier Bulganin remained as the only major figure beside Khrushchev in the Soviet hierarchy.

But Bulganin's days as Premier were also numbered. On March 27, 1958, he "resigned" his premiership and the Supreme Soviet dutifully and unanimously elected Nikita Khrushchev as his successor. With Khrushchev's accession to the premiership the struggle among Stalin's heirs came to a formal conclusion. Khrushchev was now the undisputed leader and chief spokesman of Soviet Russia in name as well as in fact. Like Stalin, he now stood at the summit of both the Soviet Government and the Communist Party.

A further change inaugurated by the new administration was the dissolution in April, 1956, of the Communist Information Bureau, better known as Cominform, which had been set up in 1947. The Cominform was the successor to the old Communist International or Comintern, the international revolutionary arm of communism dissolved by Stalin in 1943 as a gesture to his World War II allies. The official declaration stated that the Cominform had been established as a means of "bridging the gap among communist parties." As for its achievements the declaration states, "It has contributed notably by its reinforcement of the international proletariat and by better linking the working class and all the workers in the struggle for a stable peace, for democracy, and for socialism." The Cominform's major act was the expulsion of the Yugoslav party in May, 1948. Thereafter it fell into disuse. In the years before its dissolution its only apparent function was the publication of a weekly journal. One reason for its liquidation was undoubtedly the desire of Khrushchev and his associates to establish better relations with Yugoslavia. The announcement that the Cominform had gone the way of its founder was greeted with unrestrained delight by the Yugoslavs.

SOVIET ECONOMIC PROGRESS

In January, 1956, the Soviet government announced a new Five-Year Plan, its sixth, covering the years 1956–1960. The official text of the new plan begins with the announcement that the goals set for the previous plan were attained. It states that between 1951 and 1955 industrial production rose 85 per cent with heavy industry rising 91 per cent and consumer output 76 per cent. The text then presents detailed directives for the Sixth Five-Year Plan. The Five-Year Plans, in effect since 1929, embrace every aspect of the Soviet economy from sunflower seeds to dynamos. When the First Five-Year Plan was inaugurated Soviet production was only a fraction of U.S. output. Each successive plan (*piatiletka*) was another milestone in a rapid development which now finds the Soviet Union second only to the United States in industrial power. Not only did the Soviet Union outdistance each of the other European nations, in some respects it produced more than the combined output of Britain and West Germany, the two most highly developed industrial nations of Western Europe. Thus, for example, while Britain and West Germany together produced 41 million tons of crude steel in 1955, the U.S.S.R. turned out 45 million tons. Again, whereas Britain and the Federal Republic of Germany mined 360 million tons of coal in 1955, the Soviet Union produced 390 million tons. Finally, whereas the Soviet Union generated 166 billion kilowatt-hours of electricity, Britain and West Germany produced only 155 billion. The declared Soviet aim now is to close the gap between its production and that of the United States. "The Soviet land now has all necessary conditions," the new plan asserts, "to equal and exceed the most developed capitalist countries in the volume of production per capita."

The Sixth Plan shows the same intention to advance with seven-league strides that characterized previous plans; in some respects it calls for even larger increases than previous plans did. For example, the increase planned in the production of electricity—154 billion kilowatt-hours—is more than Russia's total production for 1954. A feature of the plan for the production of electricity is the construction of a group of atomic power stations with a total capacity of about two and a half million kilowatt-hours or the equivalent of four or five hydroelectric stations. The increase in steel production called for by 1960 is 51 per cent over 1955, an increase of twenty-three million metric tons or roughly the total Soviet steel production in 1949. During the five years, 1956–1960, the production of coal is scheduled to increase 49 per cent, that of oil 100 per cent, and that of consumer goods 60 per cent. In more general terms the plan looks to a 65 per cent over-all increase in industrial output, with heavy industry itself rising by 70 per cent. According to the plan wages are to rise 30 per cent by 1960, and the system of norms under which wage payments are made will be subjected to a drastic revision. In the industrial development which the plan outlines special attention is to be paid to developing the eastern part of the country, particularly the Don Basin, the Kuznetsk Basin, and the South Yakutsk coal basin.

In education the new plan calls for an extension of ten-year schooling to the entire country by 1960. At the end of the Fifth Five-Year Plan many Soviet children attended only seven-year elementary school. To provide the necessary facilities the Soviet government plans to construct twice as many schools as under the preceding plan. Furthermore, beginning with the school year 1956–1957 all tuition fees were abolished. As fees were previously charged for secondary and academic education, only the sons and daughters of members of the bureaucracy and labor aristocracy could afford more than primary education. Higher education was largely a privilege for the children of the privileged and tended to deepen the stratification of society. A further feature of the plan is the provision for the training of more technicians. The number of technicians and specialists trained each year is to increase 50 per cent, reaching two and a half million annually by 1960. This is considerably above the rate of increase in technical personnel in the United States, Britain or other Western countries. As regards housing, the plan is somewhat vague. Housing in the industrial centers continues to be exceedingly bad despite the number of apartment houses that have been constructed. Overcrowding is still appalling and the lack of maintenance causes much of the new housing to deteriorate rapidly.

An important feature of the new plan is the attention it gives to agricultural production. The reason for this becomes clear if one keeps in mind the fact that the goals of the Fifth Five-Year Plan in agriculture were not reached. The production of food has, in fact, been the weakest link in the Soviet economy. The collective farms have in many cases not produced as much as the government hoped they would. According to United States standards the production per agricultural worker on Soviet collective and state farms is very small. Meat and dairy produce have lagged behind production quotas even more seriously than grain. As regards the per capita meat consumption the people of Russia are little if any better off than they were when the First Five-Year Plan was launched.

In general, the discrepancy between the spectacular rise of industrial production and the slow increase of agricultural production troubled Stalin greatly and appears to worry Khrushchev and his colleagues no less. In the years they have been at the summit the new leaders have initiated a whole series of measures to increase farm output. A greater agricultural production is necessary not only to provide a better diet for the Russian people but also to obtain the agricultural raw materials needed for the expanding industrial production. If, for example, the goal for the increase in wool production is achieved, more clothing will be available. For the production of cereals the old 1950 quota, which was not reached in 1955, has been set up as the goal for 1960. Khrushchev and his colleagues hope to attain it by opening to cultivation new lands which are larger than the total area sown in wheat in the United States. The plan also calls for an impressive increase in farm machinery and a wider use of fertilizers. If the plan can be carried out it may solve Russia's food problem.

The most striking feature of the plan is the continued emphasis on heavy industry. It shows that the further increase of Soviet military and economic power remains the Kremlin's primary goal. Soviet proponents of the development of heavy industry argue that if they had emphasized the production of consumer goods the Soviet Union would today be the fifth or sixth, not the second industrial power of the world. The accent on heavy industry means that the production of consumer goods will again not be spectacular. Despite the projected increase of 60 per cent, the actual increase per person will be small because the production of these goods was previously completely subordinated to the production of heavy industry. There will be no great increase in textiles, and only two pairs of shoes a year per capita as against one and a half pairs in 1955. Most of the increase will be in such "luxury" goods as automobiles, television sets, radios, refrigerators, and washing machines. The living standard will rise more slowly than it would have under the plan of former premier Georgi Malenkov, who in 1953 declared, "A task that cannot be postponed is to increase sharply in two or three years the population's supply of food and manufactures." But even under Malenkov's premiership the argument in the Presidium turned not on the question of cutting back heavy industry but on the more subtle question of slowing the rate of development of heavy industry somewhat in order to permit the production of more consumer goods. "Heavy industry," Malenkov said, "is the fundamental basis of our socialist economy, for without its growth it is impossible to assure the further growth of light industry, the growth of the productive forces of agriculture, and to strengthen the defense capacity of our country."

As regards the Soviet Union's ability to challenge the economic supremacy of the United States, the new plan, if fulfilled, will leave Russia with a productive capacity in 1960 of about two thirds of the capacity of the United States. Hence there will as yet be no question of surpassing the United States. The one exception is the production of coal. The Soviet target for 1960 is 593 million tons as against the 447 million tons mined in the United States in 1955. In the production of steel, electric power, and oil Soviet Russia will still be far behind the United States in 1960. The threat to the United States lies in the Soviet rate of increase. For example, if the plan is carried out, the U.S.S.R. will in 1960 have more than doubled its steel output in 10 years, an increase it took the United States 30 years to achieve (1910–1948). The annual rate of growth projected for the national income in the Sixth Five-Year Plan is 12 per cent or about three times the rate of increase for the United States in the period 1950 to 1955. If the industry of the United States continues to expand, the task of surpassing it will take longer, but a recession might help the Russians overtake the United States in 10 to 15 years. The Kremlin confidently expects the Soviet Union to outproduce the United States before 1970. In the area of trade the Soviet Union might become a serious competitor to United States exports, one who would not be bound by the need for a profit.

🜚

THE CONQUEST OF SPACE

October 4, 1957, will be remembered as a milestone in the story of man's efforts to conquer space. On that day an artificial satellite was launched from Soviet Russia into the outer fringes of the earth's atmosphere. As the satellite was fitted with radio transmitters emitting signals continuously, short-wave radio receivers in various countries soon began picking up the beeping signals. The satellite could at times be seen from various parts of the globe. The Russians called the satellite "Sputnik," which is short for Iskustvennyi Sputnik Zemli (Artificial Fellow Traveler around the Earth). According to information broadcast by Radio Moscow, the Sputnik was made of aluminum alloys, was spherical in shape, and weighed 184 pounds. Calculations suggested that it was traveling along an elliptical orbit about 170 miles from the earth at its closest point, 580 miles at its most distant. It traveled at a speed of about 18,000 miles an hour, circling the globe every 96.2 minutes. To propel the satellite into the outer regions the Soviet government, it is generally assumed, used a three-stage rocket. The first-stage rocket carried the satellite up through the lower atmosphere to a distance of 50 or 60 miles. When its fuel was spent the first-stage shell with its fuel tank and machinery dropped off and the second-stage rocket assumed the task of propulsion, turning the satellite in a somewhat horizontal direction. When the fuel of the second stage was used up, its shell dropped off and the third stage took over. According to a law of physics a body, once set in motion, remains in that state unless some force changes it. Consequently it remains at a relatively constant distance from the earth.

The first step in the conquest of outer space was taken by the Wright brothers when they succeeded in making an airplane flight which lasted only 12 seconds at Kitty Hawk, North Carolina, in 1903. Soon men were flying propeller planes, and later jet-driven planes, which attained heights of eight to ten miles over the earth. But the conquest of outer space posed two problems, the rarity of oxygen in the upper levels and the earth's gravitational pull. Scientists calculated that if a body could travel 18,000 miles per hour or faster it could reach the upper atmosphere, where gravitational force diminishes, before earth's gravity could pull it back. The means of achieving this was the rocket. In the United States a two-stage rocket composed of a captured German V-2 with a smaller rocket attached to its nose attained a height of between 200 and 300 miles as early as 1949. But it was the Russians who first achieved intermediate and long-range missiles.

The launching of the Sputnik represented an achievement of great scientific significance for all mankind. Opening as it did a whole new frontier of outer space for exploration, it gave to the dream of contact with the moon and other planets at least the outlines of reality. The space ships of science fiction became a possibility in the not-too-distant future. Hence the launching of the Sputnik should have been an occasion for great rejoicing even for the citizens of the free world. Unfortunately it had ominous implications. The disquieting feature was the military potential of the rocket. The success of the Sputnik gave strong support to the Soviet claim of having during the preceding August successfully test-fired a "super-long-distance intercontinental" missile which proved "that it is possible to direct rockets into any part of the world." The rocket which carried the Sputnik to outer space was probably a revamped intercontinental ballistic missile.

The Sputnik and guided missiles gave hints of future conflicts that would make World War II as outdated as the Civil War. Nikita Khrushchev himself stressed the military implications when he said that the Soviet possession of the intercontinental ballistic missile had made piloted bombers obsolete. The fact that the Russians have stolen a march on the nations of the free world by being the first to send up a satellite gave them a propaganda tool of great leverage. They were not slow to make political capital of the Sputnik by declaring it to be an achievement of "the new socialist society." Khrushchev himself, confident that Russia had a military and scientific advantage, was trying to exploit the advantage to the utmost. Rattling rockets, he insisted that peace must be made on Russian terms. The alternative, he declared, might be war and the end of capitalism.

On November 3, 1957, the Soviet government announced that a second and larger Sputnik had been projected into space. Sputnik II was about three and a half feet in diameter and weighed 1120 pounds, or about as much as a Volkswagen automobile. Moving slightly slower than its predecessor, it circled the earth once every 103.6 minutes in an elliptical orbit about 300 miles at its closest to the earth and 923 miles at its farthest. The most novel feature of Sputnik II was that it contained a live female dog, named Kudryavka (Curly, in English) encased in a tiny pressurized and heated cabin containing oxygen and liquid food. Because of this some wit was not slow in nicknaming the second satellite "Muttnik." In addition to the regular radio transmitters which supposedly sent coded signals to Moscow, Sputnik II carried instruments which recorded the dog's breathing, heart beat, and blood pressure. After about ten days Soviet scientists announced that the dog had probably died.

Early in January, 1958, Sputnik I dropped toward the earth and disintegrated in the earth's atmosphere, but Sputnik II continued to circle the earth. On the last day of January the United States entered the contest for the conquest of space by launching a small satellite, called Explorer. The U.S. satellite, weighing 30.8 pounds and tubular in shape, cruised through space in an elliptical orbit which at its farthest point was about 1700 miles from the earth. The instruments in the Explorer included two radio transmitters and devices for measuring temperature, cosmic rays, and the frequency of meteorite particles.

UNREST AND REVOLT IN THE SATELLITES

In the satellite states the period following the death of Stalin was one of unrest. More than a decade of communist indoctrination had not changed the satellite peoples into robots. In some of the countries ruled by the Kremlin, anti-imperialism was just as powerful a force as in the Asiatic and African lands which had been or still are under foreign rule. The Poles and the Hungarians demonstrated that they resent being governed from Moscow no less than the Indians, the Indonesians, and Vietnamese resented British, Dutch, and French rule. In Poland the unrest expressed itself in demands for a degree of self-government, and in Hungary the desire for freedom and national emancipation flared into armed revolt.

A number of factors were immediately responsible for the demands for greater freedom. The first of these was Marshal Tito's success in developing "national communism" in Yugoslavia. Tito not only insisted in the face of Stalin's opposition on the right of Yugoslavia to map its own road to communism, and to decide the tempo for proceeding on the chosen way; he also managed to survive against the massed attacks of the Cominform. The result was that communism was no longer a monolith, but was split into two factions: one composed of those who favored centralization of power in the Kremlin and the other of the "Titoists" who favored decentralization and independence. After Stalin's death his successors, previously numbered among those who had denounced Tito as a "Fascist beast," decided to make a major effort to entice the Yugoslav ruler back into the Soviet fold. After a period of persistent wooing of Tito, a delegation of Soviet leaders went to Belgrade in May, 1955. The importance attached by the Kremlin to the meeting with Tito is indicated by the fact that the Soviet delegation was headed by party chief Khrushchev, Premier Bulganin, First Deputy Premier Mikoyan, and Deputy Foreign Minister Gromyko. Foreign Minister Molotov was probably excluded because he had been most vociferous in denouncing Tito as a "Judas" to communism and "to all progressive mankind." The obeisance of this select group of communists before Marshal Tito took the sting out of his heresy. More than this, in readmitting the "heretic" to the company of sanctified communists, Khrushchev and his colleagues appeared to accept the "heresy of national communism" as good communist doctrine. In general, the meeting, which was a great personal triumph for Tito, left the impression that Tito was being permitted, even encouraged, to maintain his independent stand. This gave hope to those leaders in the satellite states who resented the imposed Russian communism and hoped to develop their own brand.

A second factor was the downgrading of Stalin. When Khrushchev told the Soviet assembly that the Stalin legends were deliberately fabricated, his statements started a chain reaction in the satellites. It brought into the open the pent-up grievances against the police rulers and the hatred of the occupation power. Under Stalin the communist parties had been ruled from Moscow with a rod of iron. So firm was the grip in which Stalin held the satellites that often a few words over the telephone were enough to bring about a change of cabinet, to shape and reshape satellite policies. During the months after the denunciation satellite governments proceeded to apply the principles of "de-Stalinization" to a number of ruling political cliques. In the shake-ups many of the old-style Stalinists with the best lines to Moscow were "purged." At the same time communist leaders who had once been cast out because Stalin regarded them with disfavor were restored to national favor. Many of the rehabilitated were "Titoists."

A third factor was the failure of Soviet communism "to deliver the goods." Many who had labored and sacrificed for the cause of communism discovered that their dreams of better conditions were empty ones. Some who had lived better before the advent of communism resented an economic policy that sacrificed their consumer interests to heavy industry and armaments. While West Germany was prospering under a capitalist economy, conditions among the satellite peoples were well-nigh hopeless for all but the ruling classes. More and more the satellite peoples were realizing that Russia was exploiting them.

In part the discontent was also generated by a hope for better things. When Khrushchev and his colleagues relaxed the totalitarian grip on the satellites slightly, they gave the satellite peoples a taste of freedom. The taste generated a desire for more. In his studies of French society before the revolution of 1789 Alexis de Tocqueville found that "a people which had supported the most crushing laws without complaint, and apparently as if they were unfelt, throws them off with violence as soon as the burden begins to be diminished." In other words, he was convinced that an uprising is less likely when oppression is crushing than when it is somewhat relaxed. It was thus as a result of the demands for more freedom that serious trouble developed in Poland and Hungary. The demands for more freedom were common to all classes. They were voiced by workers, civil servants, and army officers, but they found their most vigorous expression in the intellectual strata, that is, among university students, writers, playwrights, and artists.

THE SHIFT TO NATIONAL LEADERSHIP IN POLAND

It was in Poland that the demands for a shift to national leadership first became insistent. On June 28, 1956, the workers of the Stalin Locomotive Works at Poznan staged a demonstration when their demands for enough pay to live on were not answered. Other workers joined in the demonstrations, shouting, "We want bread," "We want freedom," and "Down with the Soviet occupation." The Soviet regime had to resort to troops and heavy artillery to quell the uprising. According to the official report no less than 53 persons were killed and more than 300 wounded. During the succeeding months discontent and unrest seethed throughout the country with national feeling running high. The desire to be more independent of Russian rule was evident everywhere.

Poland, the largest and most populous of the Soviet satellites, had a tradition of hostility toward Russia. Over the years Poland had again and again been invaded, subdued, and plundered by the Russians. Hence there smouldered in the heart of the Pole a distrust of the colossus on its eastern frontier. A new impetus was given to the nationalist demands through the readmission to the Communist Party of Wladislaw Gomulka, a leading advocate of "national communism" who at Stalin's insistence had been forced out of the government as a "Titoist." Happy over the return of Gomulka, the Poles now demanded the removal of Marshal Konstantin Rokossovsky, a Russian war hero whom Stalin had sent to Poland to insulate the Poles against Titoism and who in 1949 was installed as Polish defense minister. To the Poles Rokossovsky had become a symbol of Russian domination; hence the demand for his removal. During the months after the Poznan uprisings the Kremlin had warned the Poles against excesses, but beyond that had done nothing. It had been closing one eye toward the de-Stalinization proceedings. But the new leaders became alarmed over the demand that Rokossovsky be removed. De-Stalinization was one thing, but the move to oust Rokossovsky was tantamount to de-Russification.

The ruling circle in the Kremlin undoubtedly discussed ways and means of checking Poland's rush toward "national communism," and it was decided that Khrushchev and a party of top-ranking leaders would go to Poland to survey the situation. Khrushchev himself would address the Central Committee of the Polish Workers party and point out to it the error of its ways. In addition to Khrushchev the group included Molotov, Mikoyan, and Kaganovich; also a number of leading Soviet generals. At the airport this group was met by a delegation from the Central Committee which included Gomulka. Khrushchev greeted the delegation with the remark, "We have come to prevent you from handing Poland over to the Americans and the Zionists." His efforts, however, to be permitted to address the Central Committee proved unavailing. Edward Ochab, who was the leading Polish spokesman, and the delegation stood firm in their refusal despite Khrushchev's ranting and raving, and threats to use force. When Khrushchev accused the Poles of "blindly following the Yugoslav model of independent communism," Gomulka replied, "We are not following any models; we are following our own Polish way." The Polish delegation remained adamant even when it was informed that Soviet troops were converging on Warsaw. Khrushchev did not, however, use the troops to enforce his demands. He knew that the result would be a bloody war which would have made a mockery of his proud boast of communist solidarity. He also knew that civil war in Poland would endanger Russia's vital communications with Soviet East Germany. Informed by the Polish delegation that the Central Committee would not convene until after they had departed, Khrushchev and his party left the next morning, after Gomulka has assured them he would personally come to Moscow for consultations.

Several hours after the departure of the Russian party the Polish Central Committee met and voted Rokossovsky and his pro-Soviet henchmen out of the Politburo. It also chose Gomulka as first secretary and party boss. In a speech to the Committee Gomulka denounced the Soviet misrule of the preceding twelve years and declared that "there is more than one road to socialism. There is the Soviet way. There is the Yugoslav way. And there are other ways." Over Radio Warsaw he told the Poles, "Each people has a right to independence. . . . This is how it always should have been—and now it is beginning to come that way." But he was also careful not to irritate the Kremlin leaders any more than necessary. When students and workers staged demonstrations in which Russian flags were torn down and there was rhythmic chanting of "Long live free Poland" and "Rokossovsky to Siberia," Gomulka in a speech to a large outdoor gathering scored the anti-Russian sentiment displayed by the trampling of Russian flags and the chanting. He even went so far as to say that Soviet troops would remain in Poland so long as NATO bases were maintained in West Germany. Thus Gomulka was navigating a tricky course between the demands of his people for greater national independence and the possibility of inviting reprisals by pushing the demands for freedom too far.

In his efforts to calm Khrushchev and his colleagues, Gomulka received support from the Polish communist newspaper, *Tribuna Ludu*. In an editorial the paper stated, "Our alliance and friendship with the Soviet Union, based on ideological unity of our parties, complete equality of our states, and full solidarity between our peoples, was, is, and will remain the cornerstone of our party." This, added to Gomulka's speech, reassured Khrushchev that the Poles did not aim at a complete break with Russia. On November 13 Rokossovsky resigned as Polish defense minister and returned to the Soviet Union. Two days later Gomulka and other top Polish leaders arrived in Moscow. After four days of hard bargaining this delegation returned to Warsaw with concessions that brought Poland considerably closer to national independence.

REVOLT IN HUNGARY

When the Soviet police terror was eased a little in Hungary after Stalin's death, Hungarians began to discuss their grievances more openly. Previously fear of the secret police had been so great that few Hungarians had dared to express their feelings even in a guarded manner. The real center of ferment was the Communist Party itself. A group of young intellectuals in the communist-led Youth Association organized a weekly discussion forum, inviting outstanding writers, scientists, teachers, and philosophers as guest speakers. Each week the discussions became more and more free, and more and more critical of communist leaders. Many of the thousands who attended these meetings were university students.

After Khrushchev's denunciation of Stalin, an effort was made to apply the principles of "de-Stalinization" to Stalinist cliques and to exonerate those who had been victims of Stalin's regime. Among the latter was Laszlo Rajk, who had been hanged in 1949 on the trumped-up charge that he was a Titoist and secret agent of the United States.

Later Rajk's body was exhumed and he was reburied with honor and nation-wide homage, with more than 200,000 people passing the catafalque. Another who was publicly "rehabilitated" was Bela Kun, the communist pioneer in Hungary, who was probably executed as a "Trotskyite" in Russia during one of Stalin's purges in the decade of the Thirties. During the Stalin regime Bela Kun's name had not appeared in the Hungarian textbooks, although much was made of the "proletarian dictatorship" of 1919, of which he was the leader.

In the de-Stalinization proceedings the contrast was between Marxist-Leninist communism and Stalin's "cult of personality," but many used the opportunity to ventilate their grievances and even to express "heretical views." Among the things that the "party intellectuals," who were the pampered pets of the regime, denounced were the low quality of industrial production, the collectivization of agriculture, and the lack of artistic value in Soviet propaganda plays and books. At the same time a number of demands were also voiced. They included the abolition of the secret police, the establishment of freedom of speech, and the organization of free elections. In short, by the fall of 1956 the Hungarian atmosphere was charged with revolutionary ideas.

Hence it was not surprising that the demand of the Poles for more freedom kindled the fires of revolt in Hungary. The seeds of discontent sown in the spring by the "party intelligentsia" had fallen on fertile ground in the minds of the university students. By the fall when the universities reopened the students were in a rebellious mood. On October 21, 1956, thousands of students at three Hungarian universities in Budapest issued an ultimatum declaring that they would start street demonstrations unless they were given greater freedom and better living conditions. They also demanded the return to power of Imre Nagy who had been ousted from the Communist Party because he put the interests of the Hungarian people above the interests of the Kremlin.

On October 23 thousands of students, including some from the Lenin-Marx Institute, staged what was to have been a peaceful demonstration. They decided to march to Radio Budapest to broadcast their demands, which included withdrawal of Soviet occupation troops; freedom of speech, press, and elections; and ouster and punishment of Stalinist leaders. Marching in orderly fashion, some of the students chanted "Long live Gomulka," and "Long live Nagy." Some even shouted "Russkies go home." As the crowd moved toward the Radio Building it was gradually swelled by the addition of workers. At the radio station the Hungarian secret police (AVO) barred the way into the building and asked the demonstrators to disperse. But they refused. Then the AVO brought out tear gas and fire hoses, but the crowd still would not move. Finally the AVO commander gave the order to fire on the crowd. Three students and a little girl fell dead, while many were wounded. Becoming infuriated, the crowd stormed the building and literally tore the AVO members who had fired the shots limb from limb. Contingents of Hungarian soldiers, summoned to disperse the mob, fraternized with the rioters and shared their weapons with them. From the Radio Building groups fanned out in all directions, storming public buildings, pillaging food shops, and taking possession of Soviet-controlled factories. On the west bank of the Danube a crowd toppled the huge statue of Stalin, thrusting Hungarian flags into its twisted legs and spitting on the statue's face.

Hungary's Politburo sought to placate the rioters by quickly installing Imre Nagy as premier in the early morning hours of October 24. Nagy made a radio speech that sounded much like the one Gomulka had made in Poland. He spoke of the "grave political and economic mistakes of the past" and vowed to correct them. He promised free and secret elections, and abolition of the secret police. He even assured his listeners that he would demand the withdrawal of Soviet troops from Hungary. In short, he promised the Hungarians "national independence," but was careful to add that it would be "on the basis of Hungarian-Soviet friendship." Even these promises failed to curb the fury of the Hungarian patriots. They did not feel any friendship for Russia. A resurgence of nationalism had made them anti-Russian. Moreover, they were tired of communism. The protest movement which had started within the Communist Party as a demand for a better kind of communism was now directed against communism itself. Demands for more freedom under communism had suddenly turned into demands for freedom from communism. In Poland the people were ready to continue with communism provided it was their own brand, but in Hungary the people wanted no part of a communist dictatorship whether foreign or home-grown. In his efforts to calm the people Nagy even went so far as to announce the formation of a new popular-front government in which noncommunists were to be included. Even this did not stop the fighting. By November 3 the Hungarians roundly defeated the three Soviet divisions stationed in Hungary.

Meanwhile the revolt had spread from Budapest to other parts of Hungary. Large blocks of territory between Budapest and the Austro-Hungarian border, and also about 160 miles of the border,

were soon under the control of the Hungarian patriots. About
175,000 Hungarians made the most of the opportunity to cross the
border and become fugitives in other lands. The few days of freedom enjoyed by the Hungarian people provided abundant evidence
of the popular nature of the uprising. A free press and radio came to
life all over Hungary and the disbanding of the Soviet-controlled
secret police caused general rejoicing.

When the Kremlin and its supporters in Hungary realized that
the three Soviet divisions had been thoroughly defeated, they decided
that the uprising had to be checked in order to prevent it from
spreading to the other satellites. The Kremlin leaders feared that
the nationalist contagion might spell the end of the satellite empire.
Hence they sent forces to quell the revolt. Soon armored cars and
tanks, artillery and Soviet troops were rolling into Hungary. In
Budapest Nagy succeeded in stopping the fighting for a time by stating that he would negotiate with the Kremlin for the withdrawal
of the Soviet troops. But for some unknown reason a Soviet tank
started firing on the crowd in Parliament Square. A bloody massacre
followed. Hundreds were cut down by the murderous fire of tanks
and armored cars and their bodies were dumped into the Danube.
Although the patriots were in a hopeless situation, without adequate
arms and ammunition, they fought on with matchless courage. Those
who did not have guns fought with stones and clubs, while some few
managed to hurl Molotov cocktails — bottles of flaming gasoline—
at armored cars and tanks. They battled the Russians from square to
square in the face of certain death. Older residents of Budapest compared the fighting with that of 1944 when Russian troops drove out
the Nazis street by street.

The Hungarians continued their stubborn resistance despite the
fact that more and more Soviet troops and tanks were moving into
Hungary. Premier Nagy sent out pathetic appeals for help to the
United Nations, evoking sympathy but no action. Finally he himself
escaped arrest only by taking refuge in the Yugoslav embassy. Soviet
agents set up a new ministry with Janos Kadar as premier. Kadar
sought to appease the insurgents, but many preferred to continue the
resistance and to die at their posts. By mid-November most of the
resistance had been suppressed. No exact calculation has been made
of the cost in human lives. One estimate has it that 25,000 Hungarians and 7,000 Russians died. Thus the Hungarian uprising was suffocated in blood. It was clearly the ghastly handiwork of reborn Stalinism. It dispelled any illusion that the brutality and duplicity of
Stalinism were dead. By smashing a helpless Hungary with its mailed

fist the Kremlin regained a satellite but lost all claim to morality. The resort to tanks and machine guns cost the communist parties heavily in terms of membership. Thousands of rank and file members as well as some leaders in the communist parties of Italy, France, England, Holland and Austria tore up their membership cards in disgust.

✍

THE RECONCILIATION WITH TITO

Meanwhile Marshal Tito, the author of the doctrine of "separate roads to socialism," had managed to remain beyond reach of the Kremlin's military might. After being one of Stalin's favorites for a time because of his zeal for communism, Tito had suddenly fallen from grace when he refused to be a puppet who moved only as Stalin pulled the strings. His insistence on going his own way irritated Stalin to the extent that he had Yugoslavia expelled from the Cominform in 1948. When this did not bring Tito to his knees, Stalin became so infuriated that he threatened to destroy Tito's regime. He once said in a fit of rage, as quoted by Khrushchev, "I will shake my little finger and there will be no more Tito. He will fall." No matter how much Stalin shook his little finger, and everything else he could shake, Tito did not fall. His appeals to the Yugoslav Communist Party to replace Tito with a new leader fell on deaf ears. Other Soviet leaders, among them Foreign Minister Molotov, also predicted the downfall of "Tito's traitorous Fascist regime," and during the remainder of Stalin's life the Soviet government resorted to every means short of outright military intervention to overthrow the recalcitrant Tito. Even a severe economic boycott was clamped on rebellious Yugoslavia. But Tito managed not only to weather the storm; he also became a larger figure on the world stage.

To maintain his nation's independence after his fallout with Stalin, Tito performed a delicate balancing act between the Soviet and Western blocs. Previously somewhat hostile toward the Western states, he now adopted a friendly attitude toward them. This maneuver was dictated by the necessity of survival. His state needed financial aid if his regime was to survive. The strategy was so successful that between 1949 and 1956 he received from the Western powers, mainly from the United States, grants, gifts, loans and long-term credits of more than a billion dollars to bolster Yugoslav's shaky economy.

After the visit of Secretary Khrushchev and Premier Bulganin to Tito in 1955 for purposes of reconciliation, Tito's sympathies seemed to shift in the direction of the Kremlin. His rapprochement with Khrushchev brought him the promise of a quarter of a billion dollars in economic assistance. In a communiqué issued at the conclusion of his meeting with Khrushchev in Rumania (August, 1957) Tito promised to support Soviet policy on Germany and Hungary. The promise was carried out in part when he extended recognition to the Soviet East German puppet regime in October, 1957. Before that, Tito had undoubtedly sacrificed some of his moral leadership of anti-Stalinism when he came close to justifying Soviet military intervention to save Hungary for communism. During the debate of the Hungarian question in the United Nations Assembly Yugoslavia was the only nation outside the Soviet bloc to vote with the Soviet Union against the resolution calling for the withdrawal of the Soviet forces.

Although Tito has evinced a desire to please the Kremlin, this does not necessarily mean that Yugoslavia will move back into the Soviet bloc. Tito is too shrewd and resourceful to give up his independent leadership. His brand of communism has little hope of survival unless he maintains his ties with the West. So it is unlikely that he will put his head into the bear's mouth. What will happen after his death is another matter. In this connection one must remember that mistrust of Russia is strong in Yugoslavia. The Yugoslavs have not forgotten the prolonged attempt to crush Yugoslavia by all means short of war. This is true also of the Yugoslav communists who were once enthusiastic devotees of the Kremlin. Now they seem convinced that an independent Yugoslavia can get along equally well with the East and the West.

His reconciliation with Khrushchev notwithstanding, Tito is still a very disturbing influence to the Soviet bloc. The fact that his example fired the revolutionary ardor of the Poles and the Hungarians is a proof of this. Despite Khrushchev's denunciation of the "cult of personality," it still flourishes in Yugoslavia. Not that the Tito cult and the Stalin cult are identical. Although pictures and busts of Tito adorn public places in Yugoslavia in much the same manner as those of Stalin did in Soviet Russia, Tito has not forced all thought into the straightjacket of conformity. Tito does not, for example, prescribe the type of music Yugoslav composers are permitted to write. Nor does he forbid Yugoslav painters to follow the impressionists or abstractionists of the West if they so desire. There is also no jamming of foreign broadcasts, and Western periodicals and newspapers are available in Belgrade to those who wish to read them. Yugoslav communism also differs in other respects from that of Soviet Russia.

Some years ago Tito and his associates discarded the policy of using force to compel collectivization of agriculture. The control of a large part of industry is in the hands of Workers' Councils. In general, People's Committees have much more authority in Yugoslavia than in Russia. Moreover, a number of features of the competitive market still exist. But if the communism of Yugoslavia differs from Soviet communism, it is none the less communism. Tito has repeatedly asserted that he is a communist and expects to remain one. His state is a one-party state, and the communists are determined that it shall remain so. After the Khrushchev-Bulganin visit, Tito said in referring to the visitors, "They saw . . . that we have not betrayed the ideology of Marx-Engels-Lenin, that we are building up in our own way our internal socialist life." On June 6, 1955, on a visit to Russia, he said in a speech in Leningrad, "We will do everything to make our cooperation useful for both sides and for the construction of socialism and communism."

THE CONTINUING STRUGGLE FOR PEACE

Soon after World War II a hostility of such intensity developed between the Soviet bloc and the Western allies that the relations between the two groups of nations were soon described as "the cold war." Not that the hostility was constant. Whenever it suited their purposes to create a crisis the Russian leaders would hurl threats and imprecations; again when they believed it to be to their advantage they would speak friendly words. If such tactics were successful in solving problems within the Soviet Union, they created a state of almost constant tension in foreign affairs. It was all a part of the grand strategy of communism conceived on a global scale. As a result the policies of the Western allies and those of the Kremlin were in conflict in almost every part of the world. Prominent among the specific questions on which there was disagreement were those of disarmament and German reunification. Although both sides were agreed "in principle" on the need for disarmament and German reunification, they differed widely on the ways and means of achieving them. In the discussion of disarmament, for example, the Western allies insisted on the establishment of a system of mutual inspection as a prerequisite, while the Kremlin demanded a ban on atomic weapons as a preliminary to any accord. Neither side was able to evolve a compromise formula that was acceptable to the other. Negotiations appeared to have reached a stalemate.

After Stalin's death in March, 1953, Georgi Malenkov, his successor, shelved the "tough line" which had been characteristic of Soviet diplomacy in favor of a more friendly spirit. He believed that a showdown by arms between East and West would destroy civilization on both sides of the Iron Curtain. In a speech before the Supreme Soviet (August 8, 1953) he said: "We firmly maintain that at the present moment there is no disputable or outstanding issue that could not be settled in a peaceful way on the basis of mutual agreement between the countries concerned. This refers also to those issues under dispute that exist between the U.S.A. and the U.S.S.R. We stood and stand for a peaceful coexistence of two systems." In short, he saw "no objective grounds for a collision." When Malenkov stepped down from the premiership it was feared that the new leaders would revert to Stalin's "tough policy." It was, therefore, a great relief when Khrushchev and Bulganin turned on their smiles.

After the gloominess of the Stalin era the attitude of the new leaders appeared friendly indeed. In foreign affairs the new friendliness showed itself in a change of attitude toward Austria. The question of a treaty with Austria had been left open since 1945, with the Soviet government insisting that no treaty could be signed until an agreement had been reached on a treaty with Germany. Suddenly early in 1955 the Kremlin announced that it was ready to conclude the Austrian treaty separately from the German problem. Comments in the Soviet press about the French and British were less severe than during the Stalin era, and at times surprisingly friendly. Toward the United States the new friendliness expressed itself in the hailing of President Eisenhower as a man of peace in the Soviet press; also in offering apologies after the Bering Sea incident in which a U.S. plane had been shot down by Soviet planes. Furthermore, Soviet delegations of various kinds rambled all over the five continents in a friendly spirit. At the same time more correspondents were admitted to Russia, the censorship was made less strict, and restrictions on travel were relaxed somewhat. Chinks were also opened in the Iron Curtain to admit various economic, cultural, and political delegations from Europe and America. Above all, Khrushchev and Bulganin, the two smiling salesmen, not only appeared at many functions at home but also traveled to other countries where they were always careful to stress the idea of "peaceful coexistence."

All this stimulated the hope that the "cold war" might give way to an era of international friendship and cooperation. Every smile was interpreted as a peace offensive, as a desire on the part of the Russians to translate the idea of "peaceful coexistence" into practice. Some were even convinced that the Soviet leaders were ready to sacrifice the goals of world communism to the cause of national security and welfare. More and more citizens of the Western states became convinced that some kind of settlement could be reached if only the responsible heads of the governments, often referred to as the Big Four, could get together for a frank discussion. No such conference had been held since the meeting at Potsdam in 1945. British Prime Minister Winston Churchill had in 1953 suggested such a conference "at the summit" as the only alternative to co-annihilation. At that time, however, his suggestion evoked little favorable response. But in 1955 opinion was much more in favor of such a meeting. President Eisenhower, who had been opposed to such a meeting because he felt it would achieve little unless the ground had been thoroughly prepared by prior meetings of the foreign ministers, now gave way before the pressure of opinion. "We stand ready," he said, "to do anything, to meet with anyone, anywhere, so long as we may do so with self-respect . . . and there is the slightest chance of furthering the great cause of peace." Early in May, Washington, Paris, and London sent identical notes to the Kremlin inviting the Soviet leaders to participate in a "summit" conference. Before the end of the month the Kremlin accepted the invitation, though rejecting the suggestion of Secretary Dulles that the question of the liberation of the Soviet satellites be discussed. After some further discussion Geneva, Switzerland, was accepted as the meeting place.

Most conferences are known by the names of the places at which they were held, as, for example, Potsdam and Yalta, but the Swiss city has been host to so many international assemblies that the name "Geneva" no longer implies a distinctive label. Consequently some writers refer to the conference as the Summit Conference, a name taken from Winston Churchill's phrase "at the summit," which he used in proposing it. The conference opened on July 18 in the Palace of Nations, former headquarters of the League of Nations, with President Eisenhower, British Prime Minister Eden, and French Premier Faure at the head of the delegation from their respective countries. Although Premier Bulganin was the Soviet "summit" by title, it was Nikita Khrushchev, First Secretary of the Communist Party, who led the conversation in important matters. The general atmosphere was one of tolerance and was characterized by an absence of acrimony. In the opening speech President Eisenhower suggested the issues that should be discussed, and elaborated on his plan for mutual inspection of each other's defense installations. "In the matter of disarmament," he said, "the American government believes that an effective disarmament system can be reached only if at its base there is an effective reciprocal inspection and over-all supervision system, one in which we can have confidence and each side can know that the other side is carrying out its commitments." Sir Anthony Eden then presented the Western plan for German reunification through free elections and was followed by Premier Faure who spoke on the reduction of expenditures for armaments. Premier Bulganin was careful to create the impression that the Soviet leaders were eager to lessen world tension. He, too, did not go beyond stating the position of his government. Every attempt to get the Soviet negotiators to bargain or discuss a series of new proposals failed.

The meeting concluded on July 23 in an atmosphere of cordiality. Everything was sweetness and light. After a round of parties, hand-shaking, and back-slapping the delegations departed. In East Germany, where he stopped on his way home, Khrushchev pronounced the Summit Conference a success because "both sides won the conviction that neither side wants war." During the succeeding weeks much was said about the "spirit of Geneva" as the basis for a happier future. Wide gaps still separated the two blocs, but it was hoped that negotiators animated by the "spirit of Geneva" would soon bridge the gap. R. A. Butler, British Chancellor of the Exchequer, said, "There is in the international scene today a feeling of spring after a long winter of discontent." But the fact that the Kremlin stopped growling like a bear and began cooing like a dove did not disarm all non-Russians. British newspapers, for example, sounded a warning against too much optimism, reminding their readers that Russia had at Geneva given up nothing and settled nothing.

Before the Summit Conference disbanded it had issued a directive to the foreign ministers of the Big Four to meet at Geneva in October to discuss points of disagreement further. The meeting opened on October 27 and lasted until November 16. Present were U.S. Secretary of State Dulles, British Foreign Minister Harold Macmillan, French Foreign Minister Antoine Pinay, and Soviet Foreign Minister V. M. Molotov. Again speeches were made which reiterated the views of the two blocs. Both sides made proposals which effected no changes. The first subject of discussion was the reunification of Germany. When Molotov stated with finality on November 8 that the question of German reunification could not be solved on the terms proposed by the Western powers, the foreign ministers turned to the question of disarmament the next day. No progress was made in solving this problem. All were agreed on the need for disarmament, but there was no agreement on the means for achieving it. After Molotov stated that President Eisenhower's plan, which called for mutual inspection of defense installations, was not acceptable to the Soviet Union, Secretary Dulles tried to offer compromises, but all were rejected. Having reached an impasse the conference broke up on November 16 without making arrangements for further discussions.

The "spirit of Geneva" did for a short time lessen international tensions. Moreover, the Geneva Conference gave both sides the opportunity to state that they did not want war. "President Eisenhower," the *Manchester Guardian* stated, "has had an opportunity to state frankly to the Russians that the U.S. will not make war. . . . Russia's propagandists will find it harder to print such a black picture of Western intentions as they have done in recent years." But to those who believed that peace can be achieved through negotiation the Geneva conferences were a bitter disappointment. Despite the fact that the Soviet Union had insisted so strongly on reaching a settlement, it had not modified its position on vital issues; nor did it change its objectives. There was no putting aside of the communist hope of world hegemony, no abandonment of the Marxist-Leninist idea of world revolution. This, as Secretary Khrushchev told the East Germans, will happen only "when the lobsters in the sea learn to whistle." The Soviet "new look" in foreign affairs was a change of strategy, not a change of doctrine or a change of heart. In scrapping the Stalinist technique the new leaders removed a hindrance to the more effective prosecution of the Stalinist goals. Stalin's successors may trample his image and denounce his methods, but they still pursue his goals. The new technique is merely a new means of strengthening the Kremlin's apparatus of world-wide power. Foreign Minister Molotov's blunt rejection of free German elections in a manner reminiscent of the cold war's darkest days dealt the coup de grâce to the "spirit of Geneva." It revealed the real purpose of the Kremlin: the scrapping of NATO and the sovietization of the whole of Germany.

Recent Developments in Central and Western Europe

CRISES IN FRANCE

IN France the years since 1952 have been a period of perpetual crisis. There has been revolt and unrest in the colonies, economic trouble at home, and confusion in the National Assembly. While the politicians argued, governments were made and unmade with confusing rapidity. Thus France offers a striking example of the failure of democracy to produce a government as stable and effective as those it has produced in the United States, Britain, the Low Countries, and Scandinavia. Government instability is a political disease which is sapping the strength of French democracy and may in time kill the Fourth Republic. Few cabinets are able to hold together long enough to formulate a policy and see it through to the end. It has been said that the one way in which France is "stable" is in the instability of its government. Because of the built-in constitutional instability in the French governmental system, the cabinet can be overthrown by an opposition composed of a hodgepodge of elements from both the extreme Left and Right. Consequently government crisis has become a tradition in France. The bickering democratic parties cannot furnish the competent and vigorous leadership that is necessary to solve urgent problems. Indochina, for example, was lost while the parties of the National Assembly continued their debate into the eighth year without being able to decide whether to grant independence to Vietnam. Agreement was reached only when it was too late. The handling of the situation in the protectorates of Morocco and Tunisia was no better. After the policy of arbitrary and bloody repression failed, minor reforms which aroused no one's enthusiasm were finally voted, leaving the Assembly no alternative but to recognize the independence of the protectorates. The

864

Saar voted to sever its connections with France because the Assembly could not agree on uniting Europe. The handling of internal problems, too, has been characterized by political ineptitude. Among the problems urgently in need of solution are those of housing, rising prices, and increased production.

When a number of French parties join temporarily in overthrowing a cabinet such groups usually have no common program and are incapable of forming a new government. This was demonstrated on September 30, 1957, when an adverse vote of the National Assembly forced the resignation of the cabinet of Premier Maurice Bourgès-Maunoury. This cabinet was a minority coalition of Socialists and Radical Socialists which could stay in office only with the support of half a dozen other parties. It could retain power only so long as each major proposal was modified to fit the conflicting views of the supporting parties. Otherwise the quicksand of French politics would shift and the cabinet would fall. The immediate cause of the fall of the Bourgès-Maunoury cabinet was the inability to agree on a policy for Algeria. Premier Bourgès-Maunoury's solution was a new basic law which would create six autonomous administrative departments in Algeria, set up on ethnic lines. The plan would have given the 1.2 million Algerians of French extraction control of the rich coastal regions, while the nine million Arabs would have dominated the interior. The plan further provided that the six departments would eventually elect a central executive council for the whole of Algeria, but that France would retain control of defense, diplomacy, and currency. The plan, however, pleased few in France and fell far short of meeting the demands of either the Arabs or the French settlers in Algeria. In the National Assembly the difference of opinion regarding Algeria was so sharp that under the circumstances no resolution would have gained a majority support. In Algeria the Arabs vowed not to be satisfied with anything less than independence, while the French settlers, fearful of losing their privileged position, opposed any concessions whatsoever. The latter were strongly in favor of continuing the policy of repression.

The Algerian question that caused the overthrow of the Bourgès-Maunoury cabinet was not a new one. It had been urgent since the Algerian Arabs sounded the call to "independence and action" in November of 1954. In 1955 it had caused the fall of the government of Mendès-France, and in the spring of 1957 it had been an underlying factor in the economic and social questions that brought about the fall of Premier Guy Mollet. While the National Assembly was endeavoring to find a solution, the French had to deal with an active war in Algeria which took a large toll in human lives. The estimated weekly loss during 1956 and 1957, according to one estimate, was 200 Frenchmen and 600 Algerians. The fighting tied down more than 400,000 French troops at a cost, according to the official estimate, of a billion francs a day. This not only put a heavy drain on the French treasury but also stimulated the growth of inflation. Besides consuming a large share of French production, it withdrew tens of thousands of young Frenchmen from their jobs in industry, thereby reducing the supply of goods for export and aggravating the trade deficit caused by increased imports.

In October, 1957, the Algerian nationalists asked the UN General Assembly to intervene on the ground that the French were incapable of resolving the conflict. France countered with a warning to the UN to stay out of a dispute that is a "domestic" affair. Officially the French do not recognize the existence of "Algeria." Under the French constitution the territory known as Algeria is an integral part of France. It forms five departments which like all other departments of France are administered by prefects appointed by the Minister of the Interior in Paris. Until 1956 these departments sent representatives to the French National Assembly. Neither is there in France legal recognition of the term "Algerians." In parliamentary parlance the Algerians are referred to as "French Moslems." Thus if Algeria gains independence, France will lose not a colony, but French citizens and an integral part of the French Republic. This view is, however, not accepted by the Algerians and their Arab neighbors. In the fall of 1957 the Tunisian delegate to the UN General Assembly stated that the French contention that Algeria is a part of France and Algerians are Frenchmen is "pure fiction."

Another problem pressing for solution is the need for modernization in French industry and agriculture. Until 1914 France had an economy that was balanced between industry and agriculture, one that was envied by other nations. But during and after World War I France fell behind. The much-lauded economy soon meant a backward industry balanced by a backward agriculture. The outstanding weakness of both is low productivity according to present-day standards. A number of steps have already been taken to remedy this. With the help of financial aid from the United States after World War II, France constructed modern steel mills, raised the efficiency of its coal mines to the highest level, greatly improved its railroads, and introduced other improvements. But much more remains to be done. While consumer appetites are whetted for assembly-line goods, mass production is still in its first stages. Moreover, there is still much re-

sistance to change. Many Frenchmen still regard such mass production as that of the United States as dangerous to French individualism. In addition, many French manufacturers are reluctant to
assume the risks involved in supplying a mass market with high-
volume, low-priced goods. They prefer what they regard as a safer
method, a low volume with high profits on each item for a market
that is protected by high tariffs. It is, in fact, only by virtue of artificial protection that many industries survive. Modernization of
French industry requires a comprehensive long-term plan. But looking at the record it is apparent that a short-lived government is unable to push long-range plans. Such plans have usually gone down
to defeat before National Assemblies with short-range views. There
is, however, a favorable factor in the unfavorable economic situation. Since 1952 French production has increased at the rate of 10
per cent each year. Based on 1952 as 100, the official production
index reached 152 in October of 1957.

In agriculture, modernization would entail the merging of small
plots into large farms, for the majority of French farms are too small
and fragmented to make mechanization of agriculture practical. Antiquated agricultural techniques result in low yields which keep
prices high. A further remedy to bring down the high prices of food
would be curtailment of the production of such crops as grapes and
sugar beets in favor of products that are in greater demand. A step
in this direction has been taken in the greatly reduced production
of wine in 1957.

Measures have also been adopted to raise the standard of living
for the French workman. He is the forgotten man of the economic
order. While prices have skyrocketed since World War II wages
have not gone up commensurately. Despite his militancy the French
worker has not been as successful in improving his lot as the wage-
earner of Britain. The wage level is, in fact, so low in France that
many workers would be unable to make ends meet if it were not for
extra family allowances, bonuses, and other supplementary benefits.
Such measures as have been taken have not sufficed to improve the
worker's lot greatly. Wage increases have been offset by the rise in
the cost of living. During the period from the summer of 1956 to
the fall of 1957 the 10 per cent rise in wages just about equaled the
rate of increase of the official cost of living index for the same period.
The most important item in the workman's budget is food. Because
the prices of food are so high, and food is a primary concern of the
French worker, it consumes about two thirds of his income. This
leaves little for housing, which is notoriously bad. Overcrowding is

far from being the exception. Frequently whole families live in small dilapidated apartments which lack both water and electricity. About one third of the town and city dwellings have neither water nor electricity. Even in Paris only 17 per cent of the apartments have bathtubs. Although France was two million housing units short, only 205,000 new units were built in 1955, and many of these were in the luxury class.

Furthermore, the inequitable tax system bears heavily on the working classes. Since the government has been unable to derive sufficient revenue from the direct levies, it has fallen back on indirect taxes with the result that almost every consumer product and service is taxed. These taxes are, of course, reflected in the high prices which wreak havoc on the meager income of the worker. Income tax as a means of increasing the government's revenues has not been as productive as it should be because evasion is tolerated as being completely normal. Since many members of the moneyed classes refuse to pay taxes on their income, the burden of providing revenue falls almost exclusively on the consumer. A Frenchman wrote in 1956, "The French tax system is as inequitable as any system with which a civilized nation has been saddled: there are, for instance, only 700,000 Frenchmen who pay income taxes. Such tax revenues are derived from small incomes which are impossible to conceal; many categories, such as the liberal professions, business, and farming, virtually escape income taxes altogether, thanks to fraud." [1] Recently, it is true, new taxes have been levied on incomes, motor cars, alcoholic beverages, and luxury goods to raise the pensions of the aged, but the government income is still insufficient to meet other expenses. In 1956 the customary annual deficit in the national budget reached a new high.

Such conditions help to explain why so many of the French industrial workers vote with the Communist Party. Very few of these would-be communists are true communists in the sense that they know or accept Marxist teachings. Most of them do not carry a party membership card; neither do they read the communist press or attend party meetings. Voting for the Communist Party is a means of protesting against their lot. They are convinced that the existing political and social structure is devoted primarily to the support of the vested interests and therefore holds no future for them. In such an atmosphere the communists can obviously make excellent propaganda inroads. The basic argument of the communists is "embrace communism so that things will change." They encourage the masses

[1] Robert Barrat in *The Commonweal*, September 21, 1956, p. 607.

to believe that they will carry out the fundamental changes that millions of Frenchmen think are necessary and which the present government appears either unable or unwilling to make. Each show of irresponsibility on the part of the government distinctly aids the communist cause. If the government would set about doing more for the industrial worker, he would be less easily induced to see "pie in the communist sky." Capitalism as practised in France has few defenders in the working class. Even in the ranks of noncommunist labor there is little feeling of identity of interests between the workingman and those who govern the country.

As it is, general conditions are such that many Frenchmen propose to end the political, economic, and social chaos by ending the Fourth Republic. In the national elections of 1956 more than 40 per cent of the votes supported parties opposed to the Republic. Although the Republic has managed to survive despite the chaos and the hostile vote, it is, to use the phrase of the French statesman Paul Reynaud, "the sick man of Europe." Economic difficulties, political paralysis, low standard of living for the masses, further disintegration of the French colonial empire, military impotence of the erstwhile Grand Nation—it all adds up to a melancholy malaise. Only through the inauguration of drastic political, economic, and social reforms can the patient's health be restored.

The man who assumed the task of restoring the health of France was M. Félix Gaillard. After the fall, on September 30, 1957, of the Bourgès-Maunoury government, the twenty-second government since World War II, President René Coty experienced considerable difficulty in finding a man who was willing to try to form a new government. Thus when former premier Guy Mollet was asked to try, he replied, "Nothing leads me to think that the task will be possible." Four other outstanding French leaders failed to find enough support in the 600-member Assembly to form a cabinet. Finally M. Gaillard was successful and was installed as premier on November 6, 1957, just thirty-seven days after the fall of his predecessor, ending France's longest postwar cabinet crisis. At thirty-eight he is the youngest French premier since 1817. His support in addition to that of his own party, the moderate Radicals, ranges from the Socialists on the left to the Independents on the right. It is not a firm coalition because of the diversity of views held by the supporting parties. How insecure the position of Gaillard's cabinet is was demonstrated on January 16, 1958, when the Assembly reluctantly voted its confidence in the premier by 253 votes to 233. As one observer put it, the Assembly gave M. Gaillard "a suspended sentence."

Realizing his tenure as precarious, M. Gaillard lost no time coming to grips with the problems confronting him. The first of these was the financial crisis. Since the nation had been spending more for imports than it received for exports, the reserves of France's foreign exchange were virtually exhausted. Furthermore, food prices were rising. During the three months before M. Gaillard became premier they increased at an annual rate of almost 15 per cent, evoking pressure from the unions for wage increases. Previously the government had been able to ward off the threat of inflation to a large degree by using its monetary reserves to purchase goods outside France. This became impossible in 1957 since there were no longer any monetary reserves to use for this purpose. A further problem was the lack of funds in the national treasury. The expensive Algerian war and the extra cost of such reforms as higher pensions were not offset by larger revenues. Consequently they depleted the treasury and carried the nation to the verge of bankruptcy. In 1956 expenditures had exceeded receipts by $2.8 billion. Moreover, the government had no funds with which it could pay its bills.

These problems were not new to M. Gaillard. He had wrestled with them as finance minister in the cabinet of M. Bourgès-Maunoury. In an effort to stop inflation he had sought to freeze prices while devaluing the franc 20 per cent without once mentioning the dreaded word "devaluation." He had even advised the housewives over the radio which foods to buy, recommending the purchase of those that were cheap and plentiful as a means of holding down the cost of living and of reducing the need for imports. In these addresses he bluntly told the housewives that they were buying too much meat, thereby creating a need for importing more meat. To discourage imports he imposed a tax of 20 per cent on nonessential imported items. These moves marked him as the boldest minister since Pierre Mendès-France.

During the period of more than a month while France was drifting without a government the financial situation had grown steadily worse. This did not, however, discourage M. Gaillard. He was not able to suggest any spectacular remedies, but he did tackle the problems with determination. His first move was to request the Assembly's approval for a $595 million loan from the Bank of France so that the government would be able to pay its bills through 1957. Next he requested special financial powers to raise at least $248 million in new taxes, to impose rigid price controls, and possibly to devaluate the franc further. He also warned that France "should now learn to live without foreign aid, and learn quickly." Foreign leaders also suggested that the French follow the lead of Britain in cutting down their domestic and overseas commitments to a point where they would fit within the limits of the nation's financial resources. Drastic measures are necessary to achieve this. If M. Gaillard does not find a quick and acceptable solution for France's economic problems, they could become the shoals on which the government might founder at any time.

Since the Algerian war alone accounted for well over half of the deficit, both in the budget and in the foreign-trade balance, it was imperative that a settlement be reached with the Algerian rebels. On November 26, 1957, he offered the Assembly essentially the same bill (calling for the establishment of six departments in Algeria along ethnic lines with limited home rule) which had toppled the cabinet of M. Bourgès-Maunoury. After heated debate it was passed on November 29 by a vote of 269 to 200. It was not that the members of the National Assembly liked M. Gaillard's bill any better than they did that of his predecessor. A major reason for its passing was the fact that the Assembly wished to avoid another cabinet crisis. A second bill was also passed to give Arabs equal voting rights with Europeans in Algeria. Both laws reaffirmed the determination of the French to keep Algeria. But the Algerians vigorously denounced them. Soon after the bills were passed the question was again brought before the UN General Assembly. This started the search for a compromise that would be acceptable to the Algerian Arabs as well as to the French. Finally, early in December after several statements proved to be unacceptable to one or another of the parties, the Assembly passed by a vote of 80 to 0 a resolution whose wording was sufficiently general to be acceptable to both the French and the Algerian Arabs. "The Assembly," the resolution stated, "expresses the wish that in a spirit of effective cooperation pourparlers will be entered into and other appropriate means utilized, with a view to a solution in conformity with the principles of the Charter of the United Nations." The terms of the resolution are so vague that they convey little definite meaning; nevertheless, the statement did excite some hope in the French and the Algerian Arabs that the costly fighting might soon be terminated.

THE RESURGENCE OF WEST GERMANY

One of the most impressive facts about recent German history is the spectacular economic boom. This is all the more amazing when one remembers that at the end of World War II Germany was flat on its back, with its industry a bomb-ravished shambles. West Germany had not only been shorn of the East German territory but had also lost the mining region of Silesia. Moreover, the Ruhr, the heart of industrialized Germany, had suffered severely from the systematic bombing of the war years. Forty per cent of Duesseldorf, for example, had been destroyed. After the war many of the factories and plants that had survived the bombings were dismantled and the equipment was taken as reparations by one of the victors. Since the role of the Ruhr industrialists in aiding Hitler's rise to power, and in keeping him there, had been grossly exaggerated, the Ruhr industries also bore the brunt of an allied drive for deconcentration and the break-up of large combinations of industry. The Vereinigte Stahlwerke (United Steelworks) was broken up into seventeen small companies. West Germany was also under the control of four occupying powers who regulated production and cut Germany off from the world. The German reputation had in many parts of the world dropped to an all-time low. In summary, it appeared as if West Germany would not make a comeback for a long time, if ever. As late as 1948 West Germany looked down and out. Its industry was still largely prostrate and its exports were negligible.

The change came in 1948 and the progress in subsequent years was phenomenal. Within a few years a war-ruined, demoralized nation was transformed into a vast, humming industrial machine. Various factors were responsible for the change. One of these was the freeing of the West German economy. In 1948 the controlled economy of fixed prices and ration books was terminated in favor of free competition in a free market. A second factor was the establishment of a new currency. The old reichsmarks were replaced by Deutsche marks which were at first accepted on faith, but later became the soundest currency of Europe. A third factor was the flow of Marshall Plan funds which permitted the industries to tool up for large-scale production. Chancellor Adenauer himself said, "A high level of economic efficiency has been attained in the Federal Republic of Germany—thanks to the generous help of the United States in time of need and to the German people's tireless industry and vitality." A further important factor was the fact that the Germans did not have to carry the burden of defense. Sir Anthony Eden gave this as one of the primary reasons why Germany surpassed Great Britain in the manufacture of peacetime commodities. Shortly after the German export drive began to hurt the British he said, "She has not to carry the rearmament burden under which her Western neighbors stagger." A final contributing factor was the movement of entire industries from East Germany to West Germany in order to escape communist rule. An outstanding example is the famous optical firm, the Carl Zeiss Company, which not many years after it moved from Jena in Soviet Germany to the Western zone was employing more than 5000 workers. In the same way other industries moved. The toy industry formerly located in East Germany was gradually transferred to Bavaria. West German cities also took over the book-publishing and printing trades for which Leipzig had been famous.

The production of coal and steel soon set new records. In the basic steel industry West Germany soon passed France and in 1955 moved ahead of Britain to become the leading steel producer of Europe outside the Soviet Union. In August of 1956 the monthly steel production passed the two-million-ton mark and has since increased. While the steel industry was growing, the coal industry was keeping pace; so were other industries, such as the machine and the automobile industries. Some were expanding by leaps and bounds. In the expanding industries the ten million refugees and expellees from Eastern Europe, who for some years had been a liability, were a welcome addition to the labor force. Many even brought special skills with them to enrich German industry. As the industries grew, unemployment in general decreased. Soon the unemployed were down almost to the unemployables. In 1955 a shortage of skilled workers was reported in the Ruhr. With the expansion of industry, wages were increased. It is estimated that at the end of 1955 the wages of German workers were 25 per cent above the prewar level. According to U.S. standards the wages are modest, but the cost of living is also lower in Germany.

The upsurge in industry was accompanied by a tremendous boom in West German foreign trade. After 1948 German trade missions visited various parts of the globe in their efforts to rebuild prewar trade and to win new customers. The harvest of orders which they, and the sales forces maintained abroad by German firms, garnered was a rich one. Their success in the undeveloped lands of Asia and Africa was particularly impressive. In 1955, for example, the great Krupp firm was building a large steel mill in India, bridges over the Nile in Egypt, and factories for processing vegetable oils in the Sudan and in Iran. Both Turkey and Egypt in the Middle East became good customers of West Germany. In South America sales and purchases in Argentina and Brazil helped considerably to swell the total of West German foreign trade. Even in the markets of highly industrialized Western Europe the West Germans found outlets for their products. Thus West German sales of electric equipment, for example, have increased in France, Switzerland, Italy, Denmark, Sweden, and the Benelux countries. In 1955 about one-fifth of the imports of machinery into the United States came from West Germany. The West Germans did not even overlook Russia and the Soviet satellites. A trade pact was, for example, negotiated with Czechoslovakia which called for trade amounting to $74 million in 1956. In 1949 the value of imports into West Germany had been twice that of exports. But the exports were soon running ahead of imports, despite the fact that imports, too, continued to increase. In 1955 the surplus of exports over imports was $450 million and in 1956 $600 million. As a result the German stock of gold has risen from practically nothing to the largest in Europe.

Many factors help to explain why West Germany has outstripped its neighbors in the volume of its exports. A very important reason is undoubtedly the quality of the products produced in West Germany. In most parts of the globe the reputation of German machinery, in fact, German products generally, is high. A second reason is that the West Germans are in many cases able to offer better credit terms than their competitors. Their ability to manufacture quickly and deliver promptly is also a factor of importance. A further reason is the energy with which the representatives of West German industry contend for business, even for relatively small deals. They have again and again outbargained and outmaneuvered the agents of other nations. Then there is also the willingness of the West German industries to change their products in order to please their customers. Another reason which must not be overlooked is that in the countries which have recently acquired independence the German exporters and importers enjoy a psychological advantage over the agents of other nations. The West Germans are free from the taint of "colonialism," they are not deeply involved in the game of power politics, and have no political ambitions that are suspect. Consequently such former colonies as India, Indonesia, Burma, and Egypt are particularly friendly.

Prospects for a further expansion of the West German economy were strengthened by the return to Germany of the Saar, a small area rich in coal and iron at the French-German border. The French succeeded in detaching it from Germany after World War I, but in 1935 the Saarlanders, the majority of whom are German by language, culture, and tradition, voted nine to one to return to Germany. After World War II the Saar again came under French control and in 1955 it again voted for a return to Germany. In 1956 French and German representatives reached an agreement according to which the Saar was to be incorporated into West Germany. Later in the same year the French National Assembly sanctioned the agreement and on January 1, 1957, after eleven years of French political control, the Saar became a part of West Germany. Not until 1960 will it, however, fall completely within the West German economic orbit. West Germany, for its part, agreed to pay France 24 million tons of coal and to permit the French to mine some of the coal that lies under the Saar but is extracted from pitheads in France. In addition, West Germany agreed to help build a canal from the Rhine River across to France's Moselle River in order to give France cheaper water transportation for the German coke it needs to fire its steel mills.

PROGRESS IN EAST GERMANY

In East Germany economic development was also impressive, but not as phenomenal as in West Germany. At the end of World War II the immediate objective of the Kremlin appeared to be the exploitation of East Germany in order to recover war damages. Hence East Germany suffered far more than West Germany from the dismantling of industrial machinery in the immediate postwar period. Salvage crews with strings of empty freight cars moved in and proceeded to ship to Russia everything they regarded as being of value. They sent to the U.S.S.R. not only factories and goods worth $12 billion, but also aircraft designers, atom scientists, rocket experts, engineers, and men of various skills. By 1950, however, the Russians decided to rebuild the economy of East Germany rather than to continue taking out what little there was left. The new policy was so successful that the German Democratic Republic soon became the most prosperous of the Russian satellites. During the First East German Five-Year Plan, which was completed in 1955, everything else was subordinated to the aim of giving the new state a basis of heavy industry which it had lacked before, since East Germany had been the agricultural section of prewar Germany. The result was that a considerable steel industry was created out of virtually nothing. Steel production which was less than half a million tons in 1950 increased to two and a half million in 1955, or about as much as Sweden produced in the same year. The output of electricity was increased to 29 billion kilowatt-hours, which was double the 1936 output. Vast strides were made in the production of coal. The annual output of soft coal was expanded from 137 million tons in 1950 to 200 million in 1955. Since East Germany has only meager hard coal deposits, the production of hard coal was less than three million tons, with little prospect of increasing the annual output.

In 1956 the Second Five-Year Plan went into effect. It was a less ambitious plan than the first one had been. The accent was on consolidation and quality rather than on quantity. The goal of the second plan was an over-all increase in production of 55 per cent as against an increase of 100 per cent planned and 92 per cent achieved in the first plan. In the production of steel, for example, the goal of the second plan was set at three and a half million tons, only a million tons above the production achieved in 1955. The concentration of all available means on the development of heavy industry in the first plan left consumer-goods industries far behind and living standards far lower than they were in West Germany. In 1956 automobiles were in East Germany still restricted to physicians, technicians, and the communist elite, while in West Germany one person out of twenty-five owned a car. During the period of the first plan wages increased 100 per cent in West Germany, but they rose only 50 per cent in East Germany. Whereas West Germany finished more than two million dwellings in the period, East Germany completed only 215,000. In the second plan more attention is given to the production of consumer goods. It calls, for example, for increased manufacture of such things as refrigerators and television sets, but many of these products may be for export. During the period of the first plan 80 per cent of the export trade of East Germany was with the Soviet bloc, Russia alone taking 47 per cent of the East German exports of machinery, electrical equipment, and optical instruments, probably at prices set by the Russians. More recently, however, vigorous efforts have been made to expand trade with noncommunist countries, notably the uncommitted and underdeveloped. It is reported that by the end of 1955 East Germany had signed trade agreements with some thirty noncommunist countries.

The weakest link in the East German economy, as in that of Soviet Russia, is the production of food. Although in the prewar days the territory now included in East Germany produced much of the food for all Germany, shortages of meat, potatoes, vegetables, and beet sugar have necessitated rationing and the importation of large quantities of food. Important factors in the shortages are the lack of seeds, feeds, fertilizers, and adequate machinery. The harsh delivery quotas set by the government are a further factor. Since 1953 the Soviet leaders have no longer forced the establishment of collectives in East Germany. Consequently only 19 per cent of the arable land is included in the 6000 "agricultural cooperatives."

Conditions improved so greatly during the months preceding October, 1956, that the citizens of East Germany were not in a rebellious mood when Poland demanded a national administration and the Hungarian revolt began. To nip any incipient uprising in the bud, the Soviet authorities in East Germany had alerted the police, the military forces, and the factory guards. No uprising took place, but the example of the Hungarian students did make the East German students restive. Encouraged by certain of their professors, they demanded the abolition of the compulsory study of the Russian language and of the compulsory courses in communist philosophy, the right to form their own organizations, and more academic freedom generally. They even planned to stage a protest march down Unter den Linden on November 2, the same kind the Hungarian students had staged in Budapest ten days earlier. The authorities, however, convinced them by a display of force to call off the march. Next the authorities took steps to repress the intellectuals. Some of the professors and student leaders were arrested, others reprimanded, and the students generally were warned. Toward the masses the Soviet officials adopted a policy of appeasement. The 48-hour week was reduced to 45, old-age pensions were increased, some limited authority was given to elected Workers' Committees in the factories, and promises were made to end food rationing.

Early in 1957 the East German economy was confronted by serious difficulties because of a shortage of hard coal. Since East Germany mines only between 2.5 and 3 million tons annually, it has to depend on imports for the necessary supply. The primary source of these imports was Poland. After the establishment of the new regime in Poland (October, 1956), coal exports from Poland stopped almost completely. For a time there was a resumption of shipments, but early in 1957 the Poles notified the East Germans that in the future Poland will produce less coal and keep more for itself. Whereas Polish coal imports into East Germany had previously been about 4 million tons per year, the Poles promised only 1.5 million tons for 1957. Consequently the available supply is far too small for East Germany's expanded economy. Unless the problem is solved it will necessitate a downward revision of the Second Five-Year Plan. In the words of Bruno Leuschner, head of the State Planning Commission in East Germany, "The development of our coal industry and our power economy determines the extent of our whole further economic development; for we must face the fact that we must now, by and large, solve the fuel and power problem within our own country." Since there is a limit to what can be done with soft coal, some other way out of the difficulty must be found if industrial output is not to drop sharply.

ら

THE PROBLEM OF GERMAN REUNIFICATION

The one respect in which the Germans have made no progress is German reunification; in fact, recent negotiations have dimmed their hopes. The question of German reunification is, like Banquo's ghost, always present at the diplomatic table. It is a ghost with prodigious haunting talents. But, like Banquo's ghost, it has little chance of materializing in the foreseeable future. In early 1958 the views of the Russians and the Western allies on the question were still poles apart and there were no indications that the gap would be bridged. As Chancellor Adenauer recently put it, "Nobody in the world can say how long it will take." West Germany under his leadership insists on being united with East Germany under a government that would be freely elected and free to hold membership in NATO. For this stand he had the support of the other NATO nations. Such terms are anything but acceptable to the Kremlin. It could hardly permit a free election in one of its satellites without creating demands for the same in the others. As for NATO, the Russians are intent upon disrupting, not upon strengthening it. Some years ago they stated their price. A Germany reunified with Russia's consent must be a neutralized Germany, unarmed and free of alliances. Since the neutralization of Germany would mean the withdrawal of West Germany from NATO, Soviet diplomacy has been singing siren songs in praise of neutrality. At various times Soviet representatives have made statements which carried the suggestion that the Kremlin was willing to accept German unification at any price. Such statements were, however, only psychological maneuvers staged for the purpose of implanting in the minds of the West Germans the idea that they would fare better if they withdrew from the Western alliance.

Negotiations did not narrow the gap between the Western allies and the Russians on the reunification question. The Summit Conference of 1955 extinguished any hope of an immediate reunification or any hope that Germany would ever be reunified on the conditions laid down by the West German government. While in East Germany on his way home from Geneva Nikita Khrushchev said, "The German question cannot be solved at the cost of [East Germany]." The realization was bitter, but Dr. Adenauer consoled himself with the fact that he had an invitation to Moscow to discuss the question (September, 1955). He and his supporters were hopeful that some progress might be made through direct negotiations. But during the negotiations it quickly became apparent that the Kremlin leaders were not ready to concede anything on the reunification question, that they had invited the German chancellor only as the head of one of the two Germanies, both of which would continue to exist.

After three days of exhausting bargaining Chancellor Adenauer succeeded only in getting a verbal promise from Premier Bulganin that the last German war prisoners, about 10,000 in number, would be repatriated. The price demanded for the promise was the establishment of diplomatic relations between Bonn and Moscow. By opening a direct channel of communication with Bonn, the Kremlin built a mechanism for bypassing the Western powers on German matters. When Chancellor Adenauer later stated that "the establishment of diplomatic relations . . . constitutes no recognition of the present territorial situation," Moscow bluntly rejected this assertion with an official statement which read in part: "The Soviet government considers the German Federal Republic a part of Germany. Another part of Germany is the Democratic Republic . . . The question of the borders of Germany has been settled by the Potsdam agreement." The Soviet leaders brusquely informed the West German chancellor that "in our opinion, the [East] German Democratic Republic is the future." The Kremlin leaders will consent to the union of East and West Germany only if the Germans are ready to accept the policy of "neutralization," if the prospects are good for the sovietization of the whole of Germany, or if Russia's satellite empire becomes a greater liability than an asset. As the situation stands, even the West Germans have shown a willingness to reconcile themselves to continued partition. Meanwhile the Western allies have the consolation that half a pie is better than none.

CHANGES IN BRITAIN

On April 5, 1955, Britain came to the threshold of a new era as Sir Winston Churchill drove to Buckingham Palace to tender his resignation to the Queen. Then came the announcement: "The Right Honorable Sir Winston Churchill had an audience of the Queen this evening and tendered his resignation as Prime Minister and First Lord of the Treasury, which Her Majesty was graciously pleased to accept." This announcement rang down the curtain on the political career of one of the great statesmen of the century. After forty years of public service he had become prime minister in May, 1940, after the Nazis had breached the Maginot Line, and Denmark and Norway had fallen. Thenceforth he was the voice of the British people in their, and his, finest hour. All that preceded it had been merely prologue. Undaunted he led the British through dark days to victory. Despite his personal popularity Churchill was voted out of office a few weeks after V-E Day because the voters were not convinced that the Conservative Party would inaugurate the social reforms they felt were badly needed. But Churchill was far from being through. When the new parliament opened he was back as the leader of His Majesty's Loyal Opposition. During the war and the succeeding period he gradually assumed a position in the esteem of his countrymen enjoyed by no other Englishman since the first Duke of Wellington early in the nineteenth century. He was regarded as a national rather than a party leader. His return to the helm in 1951 was but an epilogue. His greatest work had been achieved earlier.

The day after Churchill's resignation the Queen summoned Sir Anthony Eden to the palace and offered him the post of prime minister. Eden had, as Disraeli put it, reached "the top of the greasy pole." Having spent thirty-two years in the House of Commons and served as foreign secretary under three different governments for twelve years, Sir Anthony was certainly no amateur at politics. He had won considerable acclaim by walking out of the cabinet in February, 1938, when Neville Chamberlain insisted on testing Mussolini's good faith by meeting his demands. He commanded wide respect as a diplomat. At Yalta he had urged Churchill not to sign the agreements on the Far East without the approval of the cabinet. Churchill had hailed him as "the one fresh figure of the first magnitude arising out of a generation ravaged by the war." Only on domestic policy was he an unknown quantity. But he had about him the same men who had surrounded Sir Winston; hence he was expected to adhere to the policies of his predecessor. In 1951 when it was returned to power the Conservative Party had actually received fewer popular votes than the Labor Party. But in 1955 the Conservatives polled about a million more votes than the Laborites. Consequently they had a comfortable 59-man majority in the House of Commons. In general everything seemed tranquil on the national scene. The people were prosperous, and unemployment figures were low. Some were becoming apprehensive over inflation and an unfavorable turn in trade, but it was hoped that the Conservatives would be able to cope successfully with these problems. There was every indication that Sir Anthony would fare well as prime minister.

The first months of Eden's tenure of office were reasonably calm. But it was the calm before the storm. Unfortunately he was handicapped by the fact that he was Churchill's successor. Not only was Churchill a national hero; he also had a flair for the dramatic, and never failed to make the most of the dramatic elements in every situation. It was, therefore, difficult for the British people to accustom themselves to the prosaic methods and uninspired sentences of Sir Anthony Eden. But it was the Anglo-French invasion of Egypt which contributed most to undermining his popularity. From October 31, 1956, on the day the Egyptian airfields were bombed, his downfall was prophesied with increasing frequency.[2]

Although the House of Commons had endorsed this program by a majority of 62, the surprise move into Egypt was far from popular with the Laborites. The Labor Party was loud and vehement in its denunciation of the resort to arms. Mr. Hugh Gaitskell, the leader of the Laborites, said emphatically in the House of Commons, regarding the invasion of Egypt: "An act of disastrous folly . . . we shall regret for years . . . a positive assault upon the three principles which have governed British foreign policy for at any rate the last ten years— solidarity with the Commonwealth, the Anglo-American alliance, and adherence to the Charter of the United Nations." The Archbishop of Canterbury said, "World opinion on the whole—almost entirely—is convinced we made a grave error." The press turned loose a heavy barrage of criticism. The *Manchester Guardian,* for example, stated that the prime minister was guilty of "a disaster of the first magnitude. It is wrong on every count—moral, military and political." In London thousands, led by London University students, marched to Trafalgar Square chanting, "Eden must go!" The Labor Party scheduled monster rallies in many cities to denounce the military action, and unions launched a "Stop the War" campaign.

The succeeding weeks saw the opposition to Sir Anthony continue to grow. With the Suez Canal blocked, Britain ran short of gasoline and oil by mid-November, with the result that gasoline rationing was inaugurated December 17. Even more important as a source of opposition was Britain's unsatisfactory economic picture. Since Eden had become prime minister there had been an increase of 8 per cent in the cost of living and 10 per cent in food prices. Toward the end of December the big guns of Fleet Street began to lay down a terrific barrage of criticism. The Conservative *Daily Telegraph* said bluntly, "The present Government has lost both decisiveness and prestige." The Labor press was even more emphatic. While the *Daily Herald* said, "Sir Anthony Eden has no grip," the front page of the *Daily Mirror* stated in large headlines, "Even the Tories are saying it now: Eden is a Flop." Not only had Eden's position been greatly damaged, but his health was also failing. An old abdominal illness began

2 See p. 904.

to recur. On January 9, 1957, he drove the mile from No. 10 Downing Street to Buckingham Palace to tender his resignation. It was not only the end of his premiership but of his political career as well.

To many Englishmen the debacle of the Anglo-French intervention and the ignominious cease-fire that followed drove home the realization that Britain's once paramount power had passed. Never had the diminished proportions of British power been more nakedly apparent. Hitherto the passing of British power had been veiled in generalities, but Suez had underlined the fact with a heavy line. Now it was no longer possible to evade the issue. It became clear that Britain could no longer maintain an independent policy, that it could not try again to "go it alone" or with other weak nations in the face of such united opposition as that of the British Commonwealth, NATO, or the United Nations. In the words of the editor of Punch, "The days of GREAT Britain are over." Another British editor wrote, "Britain is no longer a super-Power." It is necessary, he stated, for Britain and France "to realize the extent to which they have become dependent on the U.S. and to accommodate themselves to this fact." Another fact which Suez bared was the utter dependence of Britain and Western Europe on Middle Eastern oil. All Britain's plans for future industrial development and for appreciably raising the standard of living must take this into consideration until such time as nuclear energy creates sufficient power.

The day after Sir Anthony Eden resigned Queen Elizabeth asked Mr. Harold Macmillan, who had been chancellor of the exchequer in the Eden cabinet, to form a new government. Whereas Sir Anthony's basic interest was foreign affairs, the new prime minister had a wide experience in many phases of government. He had been a member of parliament almost continuously since 1924, and through the years had held a number of ministries. He had been minister of housing, secretary of defense, foreign secretary, and chancellor of the exchequer. Thus his training for his post as prime minister was unique. In international affairs he gave top priority to revitalizing the alliance between Britain and the United States, which had been badly damaged by the Suez adventure. He also had the background for this. In 1942 he had been resident minister at Allied headquarters in Algeria and there had met General Eisenhower, with the result that a firm friendship developed between the two. In a friendly discussion with President Eisenhower at the Bermuda Conference in mid-March, 1957, he was able to clear away the diplomatic debris of Suez and renew the feelings of friendship between the two nations.

Later, in the fall of 1957, the visit of Queen Elizabeth to the United States helped to restore much of the old luster to the relations between the two countries.

More challenging were Britain's internal problems for which the new prime minister was expected to provide solutions. His forceful actions and decisions as he tackled the various problems surprised his friends in the Conservative Party as well as the Labor Party critics and made the British feel that a steady hand was once again at the controls. Mr. Macmillan's approach was dictated by a firm conviction that Britain's future strength depends on economic stability; hence he endeavored to put new muscle into Britain's economic system. The Suez crisis, which had cost Britain at least $1 billion, had stretched the British economy almost to the snapping point. After the country's economy had skirted disaster at various times during the preceding decade, the Suez crisis sounded the warning that the economic strain had to be eased if the country was to remain solvent. The obvious remedy was a drastic cut-back in expenditures. Under the Laborite Clement Attlee Britain had become a welfare state distributing welfare to its citizens from the cradle to the grave. After receiving free prenatal care and delivery into this world, the citizen receives a gentle rain of benefits on the way to maturity, including a "toddlers' clinic," free milk, vaccinations, medical and dental care, and education. For the rest of a citizen's life medical care is free, except for a nominal charge for such things as glasses, false teeth, and abdominal belts. Upon retirement the Briton receives a pension, and when he leaves this world the state pays the survivors a "death grant" so that they can properly bury the deceased. Only one seventeenth of the cost of this welfare program is paid by individual contributions; the rest is defrayed by the government. The total annual bill for this program increased from $490 million in 1948 to almost $2 billion in 1957. Hence the government of Prime Minister Macmillan decided that the individual must increase his contribution slightly. In this way the government hoped to decrease its share by $160 million.

Reducing the cost of the welfare state was, however, only one small phase of the economy program. Suez, in driving home the fact that the small island kingdom could no longer afford the huge defense budget of $4.5 billion, caused the new prime minister to take the boldest economy measure, namely a sharp cutback in defense expenditures. Not long after becoming prime minister Mr. Macmillan announced a gradual reduction of the three armed services from the existing 690,000 to 375,000 men by the end of 1962. He further announced that Britain would stop work on the development of advanced fighters and bombers, both of which were to be replaced by guided missiles with atomic warheads. The battleships, too, were to be scrapped in favor of a task-force navy equipped with guided missiles. The draft was to give way to a system of selective service, with the quota filled by lot. In addition, Mr. Macmillan executed what has been called the "great pullback," that is, he recalled British troops from the world-wide network of garrisons to which the British had committed themselves. Thus the government announced the withdrawal of its troops from Jordan and from Korea. Other garrisons were to be reduced. Another move involved the withdrawal of 13,000 of the 77,000 troops Britain contributed to NATO on the German front. By these and other expedients Mr. Macmillan hoped to slash the defense budget by a third. The release of large numbers of young men from military service would also relieve the shortage of manpower for the production of exports. The need, in particular, for scientists and technicians had been crying.

Another drain on the nation's finances was the mounting trade deficit caused by the fact that the British were buying more abroad than they were exporting. The situation was not new, for Britain had been falling behind in the race for production and exports since 1950. But in 1957 a balanced trade was more vital to Britain's future than ever before. All the old headlines and slogans which had had such a vogue in 1947 began to reappear, among them "export or die," "close the trade gap," and "Britain must sell abroad in order to pay for her imports." Although the volume of production had fallen 2 per cent in 1956, the reason for the trade deficit was not only a scarcity of goods, but also a lack of markets, many markets having been taken over by the revived export industries of West Germany. Rarely in modern commercial history has a nation had the opportunity to gain a lasting trade advantage as the British had during the years after World War II while Germany was prostrate. But they failed to make the most of the opportunity. Many of the markets they did capture they failed to hold against the new West German competition. In Argentina, for example, the British sold six times as much in 1950 as the West Germans did, but by 1952 the latter had reversed the situation to the extent that they were selling 60 per cent more than the British. The story was similar in Ecuador. There the British sold almost twice as much as the West Germans in 1950, but by 1952 the West Germans were selling slightly more than the British. The story was much the same in other parts of the world. In 1956 alone Britain's share of world trade fell from 15 to 11 per cent.

The Macmillan government immediately launched a drive to

close the gap between exports and imports. On the home front the immediate aim was to goad industry into new expansion programs. One of the expedients was a modest tax cut heavily weighted in favor of the middle and upper income brackets. The tax relief provided a slight decrease in the purchase tax on household goods, reductions in entertainment taxes, and an increase in the allowances for families with children of high-school age, but the bulk of the largesse was for the middle class whose activities, in the words of the chancellor of the exchequer, "determine the rate of our expansion." To end Britain's reliance on Middle Eastern oil, the government laid plans for the construction by 1965 of 20 atomic power stations. Shipbuilding firms were given a 100 per cent increase in the deductible allowance on newly built ships as a move to stimulate shipbuilding, in which the Japanese had surpassed the British. The government also set aside $350 million for the construction of new steel plants. British industry was also encouraged to develop new products which might attract foreign buyers. Thus the textile industry, for example, produced some exciting new fabrics to replace the old staples. Above all, efforts were made to instil in the British public the spirit of "do or die." One result was that British salesmen went out determined to obtain what they regarded as Britain's rightful share of the world trade.

The results were surprisingly good. Although for much of 1957 the picture of Britain's foreign trade was not an encouraging one, it did show improvement later in the year. Exports to Canada during the first eleven months of the year were $9\frac{1}{2}$ per cent higher than they had been during the same period of 1956. Exports to the United States were $6\frac{1}{2}$ per cent higher during the same period of 1957, and there were also increases in the British exports to Europe, to the Commonwealth, and to Soviet Russia. British shipyards, determined to regain first place from Japan, reported nearly $2 billion in orders on their books. Total British exports in the first eleven months of 1957 were $4\frac{1}{2}$ per cent higher than in the same period of 1956. With exports rising and imports dropping, the trade deficit for November, 1957, was the smallest in seven years, if we except October, 1954, and November, 1956, when a dock strike and the Suez situation caused shipping delays. All this encouraged the British to believe they have a good chance of regaining some of the markets they lost. But the task is enormously complicated. Not only is competition getting more fierce; the British economy is so delicately balanced, so dependent on imported raw materials and overseas markets, that economic changes in other countries can cripple it. Over against this is the urgent necessity of succeeding. Peter Thorneycroft, former chancellor of the exchequer, put it this way: "If we fail to solve this problem, there is no government that can stand between us and drab decline."

In the period during which Mr. Macmillan has been prime minister inflation has been a serious problem in Britain as well as in most of the rest of Europe. In July, 1957, the chancellor of the exchequer described it as one of the most difficult problems facing Britain. "This nation," he said, "must either squarely face the problem of inflation and accept the policies necessary to check and curtail it, or else it must face a continual decline in the value of its currency." One of the causes was that wages were climbing faster than production. Higher wages not only boost production costs, making it difficult for British goods to compete in overseas markets, but also increase domestic buying power. The danger lies in the fact that the greater domestic purchasing power will drain off too large a portion of the manufactured goods to domestic consumers and thus permit imports increasingly to outpace exports. Since Britain's economy depends upon her ability to export sufficient goods to pay for the food and raw materials it has to import, any increase in the demand for goods in the home market correspondingly reduces the exports.

To curb this danger both the Labor and the Conservative governments maintained the highest tax rate in the world, i.e., 29.5 per cent of the national product as against 24 per cent in the United States. Before Mr. Macmillan became prime minister, the Conservatives had started tightening credit by successively raising interest on bank loans from 3 to $3\frac{1}{2}$ per cent, then to $4\frac{1}{2}$ per cent, and finally to $5\frac{1}{2}$ per cent. Down payments for installment buying were raised to 50 per cent on such items as autos, TV sets, and washing machines. The sales tax was also raised on some items to 20 per cent. But these and other measures did not check the inflationary pressures sufficiently, so that the Macmillan government found it necessary to take further steps. Among these was the freezing of wages for a year. Even more dramatic was the increase of the interest on bank loans to 7 per cent (September, 1957), the highest level since the early 1920's. At the end of 1957 it seemed as if the government was winning its fight against the inflationary pressure. But a series of wage and price increases could restore the threat of inflation at any time.

In his efforts to shore up Britain's sagging economy, Mr. Macmillan's primary interest was the welfare of Britain. He did not stop to count the cost to his own popularity. For example, the Rent Act which removed rent restrictions from nearly five million homes either wholly or in part alienated many working-class voters. The high interest rates angered the commercial middle class, which found it-self in a credit squeeze. The curbs which the government placed on retail buying were anything but popular with the workers, who found that many luxuries they might otherwise have been able to afford were now beyond their reach. Consequently Mr. Macmillan, never a popular figure with his countrymen, lost much of the popularity he did enjoy. Asked in a recent poll to name the politician they trust most, 51 per cent of the British citizens asked named Sir Winston Churchill. Harold Macmillan was in sixth place, with only 2 per cent stating that they trusted him most. The lack of enthusiasm for the prime minister was confirmed by the latest Gallup poll, according to which only 39 per cent of the electorate is satisfied with his leadership as opposed to 51 per cent in May, 1957. But all this has left him unshaken in his determination to eliminate the recurrent financial crisis and to improve the English economy on a long range basis. If he should succeed, he may well be the most popular figure in Britain by the time the next general election rolls around.

🖎

ITALY MOVES AHEAD

The years since 1952 have been a period of expansion and increased production for both industry and agriculture in Italy. In some sectors of the economy the improvement assumed the proportions of a boom. Each year has seen production increase over the preceding one. By the middle of 1956 industrial production was more than double the volume produced just before World War II and was still increasing. The annual steel output was five million tons compared to 2.3 million when Benito Mussolini's Fascist regime boasted loudly of Italy's industrial power. The production of cement increased from an average of less than five million tons a year before World War II to more than ten million tons in 1956. The increase in steel and cement production furnished materials for the construction of housing for a growing population. In 1955 the Italian government and private contractors completed apartment buildings and housing developments totaling a million and a half rooms, or more than the total number of room units constructed in the six years following V-E Day. In 1956 Italian plants turned out more than 300,-000 cars as compared to 59,000 in the year before World War II. The production of electric power rose from 15 billion kilowatt-hours per year in the prewar period to 38 billion by 1956. Although there was appreciable progress in the years 1956 and 1957, the general advance moved at a slower pace than it had in 1955. Thus whereas the gross national production increased 7.2 per cent in 1955, the increase was less than five per cent in 1956. During the first nine months of 1957 the production pace quickened but slowed appreciably during the last three months, particularly in building, in iron, and in steel. In the iron and steel industry progress was less rapid because the maximum productivity of some of the existing plants had been reached. Plant expansion is expected to increase production again in 1958 if the demand remains at high levels.

During the same period equal progress was made in agriculture. In 1955, for example, the wheat crop reached a total of 9.5 million tons, which was about 2 per cent larger than the previous high set in 1953 and almost 20 per cent above the best prewar levels. Other crops were also produced in greater quantities during the period since 1952. Corn production, for example, was boosted to three million tons, or twice the prewar output. Marked progress was also made in the mechanization of agriculture. By the end of 1955 tractors and harvesting units numbered 170,000, an increase of 30,000 during one year. In general, farm output rose so high by the end of 1955 that Italy, once heavily dependent on food imports, was well on the way to becoming self-supporting in this respect. Unfortunately during 1956 and 1957 agricultural production showed a drop in comparison with 1955. Because of less favorable weather the 1956 wheat crop was 10 per cent less. In 1957 the grape as well as the wheat harvest was bad because of unfavorable weather. Furthermore, voluntary or compulsory limitation of the production of rice, sugar beets, and hemp, of which the supply had previously exceeded the demand, further reduced the over-all production. It has been calculated that in 1956 and 1957 the total farm income was between 2 and 3 per cent less than it had been in 1955. Much has also been done since 1952 to improve rural housing and to reclaim waste lands by means of irrigation. Even in southern Italy many families who once lived in hovels are now housed in new homes and are farming land reclaimed by irrigation.

Most Italians agree that what has made the patient so vigorous has been a series of financial blood transfusions by the United States. Without this treatment there would have been progress, but no boom. Over a period of ten years gifts and loans to Italy by the United States totaled $4.5 billion. Some of these funds helped to finance the construction in Rome of a new railroad station, of which many Romans are more proud than of the ancient ruins of the Coliseum or the Forum. Funds from the United States also financed the machinery for the great Fiat automobile plant in Turin, one of the finest in Europe. Forty million dollars of U.S. funds were used to build the new steel plant at Cornigliano, which is now Italy's largest steel plant. U.S. aid was also an important factor in the expansion of power facilities. As the existing hydro-electric power was inadequate for the needs of Italian industry, a chain of steam power plants stretching from Genoa in the North to Palermo on the island of Sicily was constructed with U.S. financial aid.

The expanded industrial activity and increased agricultural production raised the national income considerably. In 1955 alone the increase was 7 per cent. Wages also rose apace. Although the cost of living increased 5.2 per cent during the year ending September 1, 1956, wages and salaries rose 7.8 per cent, so that the real wage showed a margin of 2.6 per cent in favor of the Italian worker. For most of the other peoples of Europe the postwar boom brought a return of the good times they had known before; for the Italians it brought, by and large, a new way of life. In Italy a little prosperity effected more changes. It has been estimated that in 1956 the average Italian family had a purchasing power that was 50 per cent greater than it had been in the best year before World War II. Hence the Italians had more money for better food, better clothes, luxuries, and cars. In 1956 they ate more meat, eggs, vegetables, fruit, and sugar, but less rice, potatoes, and pasta. More money has permitted them to buy more radios, telephones, refrigerators, and television sets. The number of radios and telephones has more than doubled since 1950, and refrigerators, a novelty just a few years ago, are now commonplace. In the three years from 1953 to the end of 1956 the number of television sets increased from a very few to half a million. The number of vehicles on Italian roads has more than quadrupled since 1950. Whereas most Italians formerly walked to where they were going, many have now equipped themselves with automobiles, motorcycles, or motor scooters. Prosperity has "Americanized" Italy in certain respects through the importation of juke boxes, hamburger bars, blue jeans, and even a few drive-in movies and supermarkets. It has also effected changes in the social structure. A decade ago woman's accepted place was in the home; now the career woman is no longer the exception. In general, prosperity has brought more social freedom for both young and old.

The improvement of economic conditions has not, however, eliminated all of Italy's problems. One of these is unemployment. In some large segments of the population, particularly in the agrarian South, unemployment is still chronic, and there is much under-employment. The year 1957, however, showed the most substantial drop in the number of jobless since World War II. At the end of August, 1957, there were in Italy 170,000 fewer unemployed than in the previous year. For the first time in the postwar era the number of idle dropped to 1.6 per cent. Increased emigration as well as increased industrial activity were among the factors responsible for the decrease. During the first eight months of 1957, the net emigration from Italy was 244,000, or 111,000 above that of the same period of 1956. The problem of unemployment has been scientifically studied by the government, but the development of a final solution may take some time. Senator Ezio Vanoni devoted years to elaborating a ten-year plan which would eliminate unemployment by creating four million new jobs through massive investments in various enterprises. The Vanoni plan is now the basis of the government's financial and economic policy.

There have been no abrupt or striking changes in the over-all political picture of Italy. Since 1948 Italian voting has followed a fairly consistent pattern. Political parties have been grouped in three camps. About one third of the voters have supported the Communists and their allies, the right-wing Socialists led by Pietro Nenni. A smaller fraction, about 12 per cent, have backed the two parties of the Right, the Monarchists and the Neo-Fascists. Most of the rest of the Italians have voted for the four middle-of-the-road parties which, as a coalition, have held the political reins in Italy since 1946. The coalition is dominated by the Christian Democrats, a mass Catholic party backed unofficially by the Church. Since this party is not large enough to command a parliamentary majority, it needs the support of the three splinter parties, the right-wing Socialists, the Liberals, and the Republicans. This alliance between the Christian Democrats had been the keystone of Alcide de Gasperi's domestic policies, but after his death in 1954 the coalition was shaken by conflicting currents within the parties and by personal and political feuding. For a time rumors of a breakup even abounded. But the coalition received a new lease on life when it more than held its own in the municipal elections of May, 1956. Its support increased from 51.5 per cent in the 1951–1952 period to 53.4 per cent of the total vote. In these elections the right-wing parties drew less support, their share of the votes dropping from 12.3 per cent in the 1951–1952 period to 11.2 per cent.

In these elections the Italian Communist Party, the largest communist party outside the Iron Curtain, suffered a setback. Even in those districts of southern Italy where grinding poverty is still the lot of many, the determined efforts of the communists failed to achieve the desired results. Because of the fact that many who had previously voted for the communists cast their votes for the Nenni Socialists in this election, the left-wing parties held steady on a percentage basis, Italy being the only country of the West in which the socialists are allied with the communists. The decline of communist strength was ascribed largely to two factors, the downgrading of Stalin and improved economic conditions. On the one hand, Moscow's denunciation of Stalin greatly damaged the prestige of the Italian communist leaders who had long followed the Stalin line; on the other, many of those affected by the improved economic conditions turned from the communists to other parties. The rise of the standard of living combined with the anti-Stalin campaign also tended to loosen the hold of the communist-dominated General Confederation of Italian Labor on the industrial worker. This was true even in Turin where the Communist Party was born. In a vote taken in the great Fiat plant employing over 50,000 workers (March, 1956) the support of the Confederation of Labor fell from 36.7 per cent to 28.8 per cent, while the vote for the Catholic trade union representatives increased from 40.5 to 47.2 per cent. Communist support also declined in other plants.

An important event in the political scene was the election by the joint vote of the Senate and Chamber in August, 1955, of Giovanni Gronchi as president of the republic to succeed Luigi Einaudi whose seven-year term expired. Gronchi, a left-winger of the ruling Christian Democratic Party and president of the Chamber at the time he was elected, is an enthusiastic supporter of social progress. He has been described as a man who "sees far without being a visionary." Although under the Italian constitution the presidency is a ceremonial job, Gronchi has campaigned vigorously for more and better housing and for land and other reforms, thereby earning a wide popularity among the Italian masses.

In international affairs negotiations were renewed in the spring of 1954 over the vexing issue of Trieste, a territory of 293 square miles at the northern end of the Adriatic Sea between Italy and Yugoslavia. Finally in the fall of 1954 a "memorandum of understanding" was signed which allotted most of Zone A with the city of Trieste to Italy and Zone B with a small section of Zone A to Yugoslavia. The two zones were accordingly incorporated into Italy and Yugoslavia. The Yugoslavs incorporated Zone B into the republic of Slovenia, thereby giving it access to the sea for the first time in history.

ɕ

PROGRESS IN FRANCO'S SPAIN

During recent years the regime of Generalissimo Francisco Franco has eliminated many of the remaining scars of the civil war and taken long strides in the development of industry and agriculture. Among the key sectors of the Spanish economy in which vast improvements have been made are the production of steel and electric power. In 1953 Spanish mills, for example, turned out less than 900,000 tons of steel. In 1954 production rose to 1.1 million tons and in 1955 to 1.25 million, with a further increase in 1956. A more dramatic spurt should result from the opening in 1957 of the new steel plant at Aviles in northern Spain which has an annual capacity of 750,000 tons. Power output has also been increased each year. In the middle of 1957 the production of electricity was 18 per cent higher than in mid-1956. This increase permitted the modernization of many plants which, in turn, paid dividends in greater production. Thus the automobile output showed an increase of about 50 per cent in two years. At the same time the Franco regime pushed its program of railway modernization by spending large sums on new equipment, in addition to several millions supplied by the United States for the repair of the Madrid-Seville line. Many highways were regraded, resurfaced, and generally improved. Steps were also taken to improve agricultural techniques and to solve the perennial problem of water shortage by the construction of new reservoirs and irrigation facilities. In recent years some 70,000 acres of land have been reclaimed annually by irrigation.

Many of the improvements made since 1953 have been financed with funds provided by the United States. In September, 1953, United States-Spanish defense and economic agreements were signed, the United States promising to provide economic assistance in return for the use of five Spanish air and naval bases. The defense of these bases was entrusted to the Spanish army, which the United States promised to re-equip. During the years since the signing of the agreements the United States has sent Spain more than $200 million in military equipment. The United States has further sold Spain $200 million worth of surplus food for pesetas, which were then reloaned to Spain on easy terms. In addition, through Roman Catholic charities in the United States, $80 million worth of food has been donated to Spain. Most stimulating, however, has been the $300 million provided by the United States to bolster Spain's flagging economy. This and the other forms of help have created an effect that has been felt in every corner of the Spanish economy. Nearly 35 per cent of the $300 million was allocated to the expansion and improvement of the steel and electric power industries. Much of the remainder was used to purchase badly needed capital equipment for other industries. Friendly relations with the United States have helped to increase tourism in Spain. In 1955 more than a quarter of a million Americans visited Spain as compared to 4,500 in 1947. In 1956 and 1957 the number was even larger. The total number of foreign tourists who visited Spain in 1957 was 2.7 million. These visitors set a new high for tourist spending.

Although considerable progress has been made, Spain is still the least mechanized of Western European nations. Much more remains to be done before the country can emerge from its serious economic predicament. The roads are still far below the standards of France, Britain, Germany, and Italy. Housing has not kept pace with the increasing population, despite the fact that much public and private capital has been devoted to housing. Many Spaniards are still living in hovels, and some in caves, as tourists will testify. Spain's per capita national production is only about half that of the other Western European countries and about one seventh of that of the United States. Not only is there a real shortage of consumer goods; the equipment also is lacking to increase the production of such goods. Outmoded agricultural techniques are another problem calling for solution. During the last six years agricultural production has increased very little. This can be ascribed in part to drought and bad weather, but the continued shortage of tractors and up-to-date farming implements and machinery is also a factor. Much of the ploughing is still done with oxen, and grain is still harvested with the sickle and scythe. Early in 1956 the United States ambassador to Spain stated. "One need only travel a few miles outside of Madrid into the Castilian countryside during the time of wheat harvesting to believe oneself back in Biblical times. In village after village the grain has been spread out on circular stone threshing floors over which a kind of sled is drawn by a patient mule. Later, when the grain has been sufficiently separated, it is pitchforked into the air so that the wind will blow the straw and husks to one side." [3] Since nature has never supplied an abundance of water to some parts of Spain, the need for irrigation projects remains acute. Such funds as the government has been able to devote to this purpose are grossly inadequate. The agricultural backwardness of Spain is still such that much of the food for its growing population has to be imported. This need for foreign

[3] Ambassador John Lodge in *U.S. Department of State Bulletin*, January 9, 1956, p. 44.

food continues to upset the balance of trade and to drain the nation of capital.

The great problem of the Spanish economy is still inflation. Prices are still rising faster than wages. The result is that many workers are worse off than they were under the Second Republic. *Pueblo*, a pro-labor daily, asks, "Our workers are poorer than workers in other countries, but our rich are as rich or richer than the rich elsewhere—why?" A recent survey of the Banco Central in Madrid produced the information that "the distribution of income is more unequal now than before the civil war." It has been calculated that 83 per cent of the Spanish people still account for less than a third of the national income. The average income of the workers in 1956 was, according to one report, in the vicinity of $260, almost the lowest in Europe. In 1956 a pastoral letter issued by the Spanish cardinals and archbishops stated, "It is not fair to establish wages so miserable that they are not sufficient to feed a family." Since it requires more to feed a family of three than the average worker receives, a large part of the Spanish population lives on the bare subsistence level. Unrest among the masses jolted the government into granting large wage increases in 1956, but these increases set off another round of inflation. Employers, forced to pay more for labor, quickly boosted prices. Wholesalers, retailers, purveyors, exporters, importers, and others immediately followed suit, thereby nullifying to a large extent the benefits of the wage increases. In an effort to stop the price rise the government reimposed price controls on fruit, eggs, vegetables, beer, and wine in August, 1957.

During recent years signs of discontent with the Franco government have been widespread. In a poll conducted at the University of Madrid in 1956 a great majority of the students were opposed to Franco's totalitarian regime, some because they disliked totalitarian forms of government and others because they found the Franco regime to be incompetent. On a number of occasions student discontent expressed itself in open demonstrations. Student riots broke out at the University of Madrid in February, 1956, during which shots were fired and a number of policemen and students were injured. Sympathy demonstrations were staged in other universities. In the fall of 1956 a Barcelona student rally in support of the Hungarian revolutionists turned into an anti-Franco demonstration accompanied by shouts of "Liberty for Spain! Down with Franco!" Despite the fact that strikes are forbidden in Spain, a strike broke out in a shoe factory in Pamplona in April, 1956, over the inadequacy of the wages and quickly spread to other factories. Workers also left their jobs in Barcelona and San Sebastián. The strikers returned to work several days later after the government announced the dismissal of the strikers and the cancellation of their various benefits. But the order was never enforced. Instead the government sought to allay some of the discontent by granting pay increases. In Barcelona the people staged a ten-day boycott of the subways, streetcars, and buses against a rise in fares. Even some of the monarchists who supported the Franco regime because they saw in it a transition to monarchy have become bitter and resentful. Although Generalissimo Franco pledged himself in the Law of Succession of 1947 to restore the monarchy, he has consistently refused to designate his successor.

The fact that the Franco regime is not popular in Spain has caused some observers to predict its collapse or overthrow in the near future. At the present time the facts do not support such a prediction. First, many Spaniards who do not like the Franco regime nevertheless accept it as a guarantee against the renewal of the holocaust of 1936–1939. Second, if there is opposition, there is no concrete sign of any serious organized political opposition to the Franco dictatorship. Opposition the Caudillo (leader) has tolerated, but he will not brook the slightest organized effort at opposing him. He has in the past demonstrated his ability to keep the opposition divided. Moreover, his police have more than twenty years of experience in countering dangerous subversion. Observers who have lived in Spain report that such "opposition groups" as exist both inside and outside Spain are completely penetrated by Franco's agents. General Franco did, it is true, bow before the storm of criticism to the extent that he reshuffled his cabinet in February, 1957. The ousting of eleven members was the most drastic change in the machinery of government since he seized power in 1936. A group of inefficient primadonna ministers were replaced by more serious and more capable ministers. Beyond this nothing was changed. Dictator Franco remains the Caudillo of thirty million Spaniards, the central figure of a totalitarian regime. Neither has the stifling censorship of virtually all thought and public speech been eased. There was never a question of his giving up one iota of his personal authority. His survival as the dictator of Spain for twenty-two years is in itself a remarkable achievement.

DUSK OF EMPIRE

An issue that has been in the forefront of international politics in recent years is colonialism. The struggle for independence of the colonies ruled by Western powers has continued unabated and produced a large measure of success. Large areas of Asia and Africa which had long been under Western rule have gained their independence. Since 1946 more than a score of nations in Asia and Africa have achieved self-determination. During this period Britain alone has given independence to more than 500 million people. Moreover, the hold of the Western nations on the remaining colonies has become precarious. Belief in the rightness of empire has been shattered beyond repair. Everywhere the colonial peoples are demanding freedom in terms which cannot be refuted. They refuse to accept any longer the status of inferiority which is the core of the old imperialism. Such benefits as hospitals, towns, roads, education and modern equipment notwithstanding, they want to decide their own affairs. Thus, for example, M. O. M. Maduagwu, a leader in the Nigerian independence movement, wrote, "Colonialism is evil. Not liking evil, we do not choose to remain colonials forever and be forever exploited, overtly or covertly. We want liberty." The colonial peoples are in no mood to wait. The question of whether they are ready for self-government has no relevancy so far as they are concerned. Their great desideratum is to be rid of foreign rule. The very presence of the alien master is to them the source of all evil. They are convinced that, having achieved freedom, they will find ways and means of solving all their problems.

The communists have not been slow in making the most of the situation for the advancement of their cause. In the fertile soil created by the conflict between the colonial peoples and their Western rulers the communists have ploughed deep and hard. It was Lenin who first saw what a fruitful harvest communism could reap by supporting the colonies in their struggle for self-determination. In 1922 he said, "The Communist International . . . must establish relations with these revolutionary forces that are working for the overthrow of imperialism in the countries subjected politically and economically."

The communists achieved their first conspicuous success in China. Soon after World War I they went into China with promises of aid in the Chinese struggle for deliverance from the foreign yoke. At first the accent was on Chinese independence, and little was said about Marxist ideology and program. Only later, when they felt strong enough to do so, did they proclaim their real purpose and strive to establish a communist order. The same tactics were employed with varying success in other countries. They were, however, less successful in countries such as India, Burma, and Ceylon to which Britain voluntarily granted independence. They were more successful when fighting broke out between the colony and a Western country, as in Indo-China. Such aid as they gave was accompanied by propaganda which held up communism as the best means for achieving speedy progress and national prestige. As proof they could point to the rise of Russia to almost overweening power; also to China's recovery of power and prestige. All this electrified many colonial peoples with hope. Unfortunately many, blinded by their nationalist desires, failed to see that the Russia which was promising to help them attain freedom is the greatest and most ruthless imperial power in the world. They were oblivious to the fact that while most of the colonies of Western Europe were gaining their freedom, a hundred million people in Eastern and Central Europe were losing theirs to the Soviet Union.

The march of colonial lands toward independence has been especially apparent in the British Empire in recent years. Despite Sir Winston Churchill's assertion that he had not become prime minister in order to preside over the liquidation of the British Empire, the process has continued. His successor, Clement Attlee, signed agreements giving independence to a vast area of Southern Asia—India, Pakistan, Ceylon, and Burma. Later neither Churchill, upon his return to power, nor his successor, Sir Anthony Eden, was able to stem the tide of nationalism. All of Britain's overseas possessions are on the march toward independence in one degree or another. There are many indications that the British Empire by the end of this century will be a memory. The fact that the colonial governments are locally organized, with a minimum of British supervision, provides in each case the personnel basis for eventual self-government. Taxes and revenues are raised locally; budgets are decided locally; courts and government services are all organized locally. Consequently local people are qualified to take over the responsibility of government when the time comes. In this way Britain has speeded the march of her colonies toward independence. The friendly relations between Britain and the colonies have borne fruit in the decisions of many of the freed colonies to join the British Commonwealth of Nations, a voluntary association which is replacing the old British Empire.

Two such independent states which joined the British Commonwealth are Ghana and the Federation of Malaya. After 112 years of British rule, the African colony known as the Gold Coast in March, 1957, became the sovereign state of Ghana, named after an ancient African empire which flourished there between the second and tenth centuries. Just before the British Union Jack was lowered and the new national flag of Ghana was raised over the National Assembly building, Prime Minister Kwame Nkrumah, who had been the leader of Ghana's bloodless liberation movement, stated in a ringing speech that the "chains of imperialism and colonialism which have hitherto bound us to Britain" have fallen away. He asserted that his country aimed to "promote the interests and advancement of all African peoples in their pursuit of freedom and social progress." These were ominous words for the European powers who still have colonies in Africa. But the new nation did remain friendly with Britain as a member of the British Commonwealth of Nations, becoming the first Negro nation in the Commonwealth. A few months later the historical spotlight was turned on Asia. There, in August, 1957, the nine Malay states and the former British colonies of Malacca and Penang, comprising an area rich in tin and rubber, became an independent nation within the British Commonwealth of Nations as the Free and United Federation of Malaya, thereby terminating eighty-three years of British rule.

Previously in Northern Africa, the Sudan, which had been ruled jointly by Britain and Egypt, but mainly by Britain, declared its independence in December, 1955. This was not wholly unexpected, since in 1953 Britain and Egypt had agreed that within three years the Sudanese might hold a plebiscite to choose independence or some form of association with London or Cairo. But the demand for independence was so overwhelming that the Sudanese parliament unanimously adopted an independence resolution without holding a plebiscite.

Just to the north of the Sudan, in Egypt, the British had previously bowed to the growing nationalist pressure and in October, 1954, had signed an agreement to leave. In June, 1956, Britain quietly ended her seventy-four-year occupation of the Suez Canal Zone as the last British forces sailed out of Port Said. A week before the event Premier Gamal Abdul Nasser told the Egyptians that the departure of the British would usher in "a bright new era" in which "Egypt would no longer be under the domination of the imperialists."

The British hoped that after the loss of the Suez Canal Zone, which had been Britain's principal military base in the Mediterranean, Jordan and Cyprus might serve as substitute bases. But a fanatical Arab nationalism, inflamed by embittered refugees from Palestine, caused young King Hussein of Jordan, in an effort to bolster his somewhat shaky throne, abruptly to dismiss the celebrated commander of his Arab Legion, Lieutenant General Sir John Bagot Glubb (March, 1956). Although Jordan had legally been independent, it had spiritually been a British protectorate, with all key posts in the army held by British officers and with Britain footing the bill for the army, the cost of which was nearly half of the total Jordanian budget. The expulsion of Glubb Pasha, as he was affectionately called by the Arabs, resulted in the termination of the Anglo-Jordanian alliance. Moreover, it dealt British power and prestige in Jordan a sickening blow, frustrating the British hopes in that direction.

This left the British only Cyprus as their last bastion in the Middle East. Lying athwart the sea routes of the Eastern Mediterranean, the island is 50 miles from Turkey and 650 miles from the nearest point in Greece. The British received occupation and administration rights from Turkey in 1878 so that they could use the island as a base from which to defend the Ottoman Empire against agression by tsarist Russia. The island was formally annexed by the British in 1914, and in 1923 the annexation was approved by the treaty of Lausanne, a treaty signed by both Greece and Turkey. The British hold on Cyprus, however, is anything but secure. Although the island has never been a part of the modern state of Greece, the Greek Cypriotes, who number about 400,000 or four fifths of the population, are determined on *enosis,* or union with Greece. The nationalist desires were raised to fever heat by the Cypriot communists and by Bishop Makarios, head of the Greek Orthodox Church in Cyprus. Both have actively fostered terrorism against the British as a means of promoting their aims. Shootings, bombings, riots, and ambushes have not only kept the island in a state of turmoil but have also taken a heavy toll of lives. While the British government is prepared to offer the island a constitution providing for an assembly with an "elected majority," the Greek Cypriotes demand self-government now and self-determination later. These demands have been supported to the hilt by the government of Greece. On the other hand, the Turks of Cyprus, numbering about 100,000, are opposed to self-government, which would put them under the majority rule of the Greeks. The government of Turkey, too, opposes self-government for the island or union of the island with Greece. It fears not only that the Greeks would oppress the Turkish minority but also that the island would, in the possession of the Greeks, be "a dagger pointed at the heart of Turkey." Meanwhile the British, determined to keep Cyprus as a vital military base, are trying to suppress the uprising of the Greek Cypriotes by the use of drastic measures. The real peril is the friction the Cyprus affair is generating between Britain and Greece, and between Greece and Turkey.

Meanwhile France, too, was losing more and more of her colonies. After years of bloody fighting, which was a terrific drain on the French finances as well as on French lives, the war in Indo-China finally came to an end in 1954. Previously, in 1953, France had given full independence to the state of Laos, but the fighting continued in Vietnam until after the dramatic episode of Dien Bien Phu, where a small French garrison repelled the determined attacks of the Viet Minh (communist) forces for fifty-five days, a heroic defense which was hailed in many parts of the world. On July 21, 1954, a cease-fire was signed in Geneva, Switzerland, and Indo-China was divided into four parts. North Vietnam was assigned to the Viet Minh communists, who established the Democratic Republic of Viet Minh with Ho-Chi-Minh as president. South Vietnam, Cambodia, and Laos were recognized as independent states associated with the French Union.

In 1954 France also lost the last settlements in India, which had served as trading posts for nearly three centuries. The five settlements—Pondicherry, Karikal, Chandernagore, Mahe, and Yanam—embraced an area of 196 square miles with a population of 325,000. These colonies were retained by France after its defeat by the British in the eighteenth-century struggle for supremacy over the old Indian empire. Indian leaders had during the years since India achieved independence been pressing the French to give up the enclaves. Finally France and India decided that the future of the settlements should be decided by their inhabitants. After elected representatives of the districts voted for merger, France assisted in the transfer of sovereignty to the Indian Union.

The gradual shrinking of the colonial empires left Central or Middle Africa as the last stronghold of colonialism. The vast area south of the Sahara has only three fully independent nations, the Union of South Africa, Liberia, and Ghana. Most of the rest of the area is still governed by white foreigners who, outside the Union of South Africa, are outnumbered ninety to one. The four Western colonial powers who still have considerable control over the area are Britain, France, Portugal, and Belgium. But the African giant is stirring uneasily. The some 130 million natives of Middle Africa, who speak more than 300 languages and dialects, want the techniques and the standard of living of the Western colonial powers. But more than this they want the right to determine their future.

Millions of the natives are still primitive and backward, with tribal ways that do not fit into twentieth-century civilization. About 90 per cent are still illiterate. Thus they undoubtedly need further tutelage. But the pace of change is accelerating. In many ways the seeds of liberty are being planted in the minds of the natives. Many are learning about Western civilization and Western ideas of liberty through their contact with the civilization of the white man, through their work in mines and factories, in cities and towns, in the shops and homes of Europeans. A select few are even being educated in the schools of Europe and the United States to assume the leadership in the march toward freedom. An outstanding example of a leader educated in foreign countries is Kwame Nkrumah of Ghana.

The Central African peoples are achieving self-determination at a pace that would have been thought impossible a generation ago. Vice President Richard M. Nixon reported, after an extended tour of Middle Africa, "Africa is the most rapidly changing area in the world today." Some of this change can be ascribed to the fact that the colonial powers are in some ways helping to prepare the great mass of Africans for self-government. Thus the British are preparing their colonies for independence and membership in the British Commonwealth. Of this the new state of Ghana is a good example. Nigeria, the largest of the British colonies in Africa, with a population of about 32 millions, is well on the way to independence. Alhaji Balewa, installed as the first prime minister of the Nigerian Federation (September, 1957), told the Nigerian House of Representatives that he is aiming for the end of Nigeria's status as a British colony by 1960. British authorities assured the Nigerians they would support these efforts toward independence. The Federation of Rhodesia and Nyasaland, which already has a large measure of self-government, is also looking forward to complete independence. Uganda, a British protectorate in the heart of Africa, petitioned the London government to develop a government policy which would insure self-government at a fixed date.

France's policy, in the great sweep of Central African territory under French rule, has been to grant French citizenship to some of the natives. The reasoning seems to be that once the natives are French citizens they will remain French. Both the Portuguese and the Belgians have offered the natives the possibility of achieving some degree of social equality with the white man by announcing that any native of Portuguese Mozambique and Angola, and of the Belgian Congo, who demonstrates certain educational qualifications and attains certain economic levels may enjoy the same rights of citizenship as the Portuguese and the Belgians. It is doubtful, however, that this device will stem the surging tide of nationalism for very long. In some of the colonies progress may be slow, but the march of events clearly presages the end of white domination in Africa before the year 2000.

Ƨ

THE SUEZ AFFAIR

In 1952 a military junta staged a bloodless coup in Egypt, forcing out the corrupt King Farouk. "Corruption and bribery," the junta announced, "are the main reasons for troubles in Egypt's political and economic life. Our aim is reform." Until 1954 General Mohammed Naguib exercised dictatorial powers, but in that year Colonel Gamal Abdel Nasser replaced him as the dominant figure in Egypt. One of Premier Nasser's first important moves was to issue a new constitution which declared Egypt an Islamic Arab republic headed by a president elected for a term of six years. The elections were held on June 23, and the next day it was announced that Nasser had been elected president by an overwhelming vote, with no less than 99 per cent of the voters casting their vote for him. At first the Western allies had high hopes for the Nasser government. Colonel Nasser was young, personable, and dynamic, and he appeared to be sincerely interested in political reform. Moreover, he gave no evidence of the fanatical nationalism he was to display later. On the contrary, he appeared ready and willing to live at peace with all nations, including Israel. Thus he told representatives of the Western nations that he was hoping for peace talks to end the hostilities with Israel.

But the smiles of the Western allies soon turned to frowns as all hopes of cooperation with Nasser were shattered. The first objective of the rising Egyptian nationalism was to end British occupation of the Canal Zone. In July, 1954, Britain, in response to some pressure from the United States, finally bowed to the demands of Nasser and the Egyptian nationalists by signing an agreement to evacuate the Suez Canal Zone. Both London and Washington hoped that with Egyptian nationalism placated a period of friendly relations would be ushered in. Nasser himself spoke glowingly of the opening of "a new era of friendly relations based on mutual trust, confidence, and cooperation between Egypt and Britain and the Western countries."

Nasser, however, soon showed that he had other things in mind by making a strong bid to unite the Arab world under his leadership. To achieve this he missed no opportunity to excite the Arabs' resentment of Western colonialism. Not only did he support the rising Arab nationalism in North Africa; he also denounced the British for moving their Middle East military headquarters to Cyprus. Furthermore, he made a bid for Soviet friendship by extending diplomatic recognition to Communist China. In the hope that they could still win his cooperation the Western allies showed an interest in Nasser's domestic program by offering him funds to help finance the construction across the Nile of the Aswan Dam which was expected to increase Egypt's area of irrigated land by one third and to multiply the output of electrical current. Washington offered a grant of $56 million and Britain one of $14 million, with a promise of more at a later time. But Nasser toyed with the offers for months, meanwhile angling for a better offer from Moscow. What Nasser wanted in addition to help in building the dam was arms. When the Western allies refused to sell them to him, he negotiated a deal with the Soviet bloc (September, 1955), mortgaging half the Egyptian cotton crop for years to come in order to pay for them. These arms were to be used, first of all, for war against Israel. In 1948–1949 Egypt and other Arab nations had tried to overwhelm the Israelis, but had suffered a defeat. They still refused, however, to give legal recognition to Israel. Fighting had continued intermittently on Israel's borders through the years.

The Western allies decided that something would have to be done to curb Nasser's ambitions and to keep the peace in the Middle East. Washington took the lead on July 19, 1956, by withdrawing the proffered loan for the Aswan Dam, and the next day Britain followed suit. On July 26 Nasser struck back by proclaiming the nationalization of the Suez Canal Company, although the internationally owned company had a concession which was not to expire until 1968. Nasser also announced that Egypt would operate the canal and use the profits from it to build the Aswan Dam. "The Suez Canal belongs to us," he said, ". . . and will be run by Egyptians! Egyptians! Egyptians!" Britain and France at once sharply protested the nationalization as a flagrant violation of the 1888 convention which assured to all nations the right to send their ships through the canal, and Britain went so far as to freeze all Egyptian accounts. But Nasser rejected the protests and asserted that Egypt would fight "to the last drop of blood" to hold the canal. He was encouraged in his stand by the announcement of the Kremlin that it approved Egypt's nationalization of the canal. Consequently he even rejected an eighteen-nation proposal that he accept international control of the canal. This caused Britain and France not only to announce that they were ready to use force if necessary to protect their rights but also to strengthen their naval and land forces in the Mediterranean.

While various efforts were being made to persuade Nasser to accept international control of the canal, border clashes between Israel and Egypt, and Israel and Jordan, were continuing. During the previous months, as a result of arms shipments by the Soviet bloc to Egypt, the border incidents had manifested a particularly ominous quality. Israel believed that Egypt was girding for a full-scale war and that a "preventive war" was necessary before Egyptian strength increased any further. On October 17, 1956, Israel's prime minister stated that an attack by Egypt was the gravest peril facing his nation. In defending his country before the UN General Assembly a week later against a complaint by Jordan, Israel's representative charged that the tempo of Arab attacks was increasing and that Egypt was sending suicide squads across the Israeli border. Several days later Israel announced partial mobilization of its military forces, giving as reasons the conclusion of a military alliance against Israel by Egypt, Jordan, and Syria, more frequent raids into Israel by Arab guerrillas, and the mobilization of Syrian troops on the border of Jordan in readiness for an attack on Israel. The situation erupted into an explosion on October 29 when Israeli forces invaded the Sinai Peninsula of Egypt. A communiqué issued by Israel army headquarters gave the following reason for the invasion of Egyptian territory: "This operation was necessitated by the continuing Egyptian military attacks on citizens and on Israel land and sea communications, the purpose of which was to cause destruction and to deprive the people of Israel of the possibility of peaceful existence." As the Egyptian troops were no match for the better-trained and better-equipped Israeli soldiers, the latter quickly drove to within a few miles of the Canal Zone, capturing vast quantities of arms and ammunition on the way. On October 31 a second Israeli force moved into Egypt for the purpose of cutting off the Gaza Strip.

On the day preceding the Israeli invasion of the Gaza Strip, Britain and France, over the objections of the United States and the Soviet Union, delivered an ultimatum demanding within twelve hours a "cease-fire" to safeguard freedom of passage through the Suez Canal. Israel accepted, but when Egypt did not answer, Anglo-French planes from Cyprus began bombing Egyptian airfields, destroying much of the military equipment Nasser had purchased from the Soviet bloc. The next day the Egyptian government announced that the Suez Canal was blocked by two ships sunk by the Anglo-French planes. On November 2 the UN General Assembly passed a resolution by a vote of 64 to 5 calling for an immediate cease-fire. But the British and French, rejecting the UN demand, continued their attacks on Egypt. When the General Assembly voted on November 4 to set up an international "police force" both France and Britain voted for the proposal. On the next day, however, Anglo-French paratroops seized Port Said and the northern twenty-five miles of the Suez Canal. In the brief fighting Nasser's Soviet-equipped force lost half its planes, two thirds of its navy, and one fifth of its 80,000-man army, together with tanks and guns. Nasser did succeed in effectively blocking the canal by scuttling many ships in the channel. The aim of Britain and France, according to Britain's prime minister Eden, was to occupy the Suez Canal Zone "temporarily" in order to stop the fighting and protect the canal. Not to have acted, he said, would for Britain "have meant being slowly strangled." At best it was a wild gamble which jeopardized the Western alliance and doomed Eden's government.

The fighting stopped as suddenly as it had started. On November 6, in response to United States warnings, Soviet threats "to crush the aggressors," and UN condemnation of aggression, the British and French announced a cease-fire, which was also observed by the Israelis and Egyptians. Upon receiving the news of the cease-fire the UN General Assembly voted immediately to set up its international "police force" before Soviet and Chinese "volunteers" and other adventurers could reach Egypt in numbers. The answer of Britain, France, and Israel was that they would withdraw their troops from the Canal Zone as soon as the UN forces were ready to take effective control. Twenty-three nations volunteered to send men to the United Nations Emergency Force (UNEF), eight of them dispatching contingents at once. The Great Powers were excluded from sending troops. With the arrival of UNEF contingents in Egypt, the Soviet threats to turn the Suez and Arab-Israeli conflicts into a new Korea abated. The British, French, and Israelis, though still concerned over how the Suez Canal would be reopened and the Israeli borders would be secured, announced on December 4 that they would withdraw their forces from Egypt within two or three weeks. By December 22 all their troops had evacuated Egyptian soil. While the evacuation was going on the UN troops helped to maintain order.

The man who emerged as the victor was, of course, President Nasser. The irony of the situation is that he achieved victory despite Egypt's military debacle. When the crisis ended he was the sovereign master of the Suez Canal. By his stand he not only asserted Egypt's territorial sovereignty over the canal area, which had never been contested, but he also imposed his own absolute control on the canal, including canal operations, tolls, and all other conditions under which he would permit the ships of other nations to use the waterway. More than this, when he defied the Western nations he assumed heroic stature in the eyes of the Egyptians, and his stand was also widely acclaimed throughout the Arab world. However, in antagonizing the Western powers by assuming control of the shipping lifeline that keeps Europe's economy going, he found it necessary to seek financial help from the Soviet bloc. In doing so he vowed that he would resist all foreign ideologies, including Marxism. "I will not," he said, "become the stooge or satellite . . . or hireling of anybody."

In Britain and France the bitterness over the loss of the canal, and the frustration of the efforts to hold it, were coupled with fears of the disastrous economic aftermath. It has been estimated that the cost to Britain and France was about $2.4 billion. This burden was imposed on economies already badly strained. Added to this were the immeasurable costs of general business declines, weakened currencies, fuel shortages, and unemployment caused by the closing of the canal. Shortages of rubber, tin, manganese, jute, sugar, and other supplies which had formerly reached Britain and France by way of the Suez Canal developed very quickly. But the greatest shortage was in oil, the commodity on which postwar Europe had built its recovery. The use of oil in industry had increased to the extent that Great Britain was consuming twice as much as it had in 1946, France four times as much, Italy six times as much, and West Germany eight times as much. Since Europe had normally received a third of its oil via the Suez Canal, gasoline and oil shortages developed by mid-November. The situation became particularly critical in Britain and France so that rationing had to be inaugurated. Europe's big hope was for the speedy reopening of the canal.

When Britain, France, and Israel announced the withdrawal of their troops, the Egyptian government asked the UN for help in clearing the canal. Before the end of December, 1956, UN salvage crews started the work of removing forty-nine obstacles, mostly ships scuttled by the Egyptians in the canal and entrance harbors at both ends. By the beginning of March, 1957, this work had progressed to the extent that the canal was reopened for daylight use by small vessels of up to 500 tons. It required another month, however, to complete the removal of the major obstacles. On April 8 the canal was reopened to vessels up to 20,000 tons. At the beginning of June traffic through the canal was again near normal, with an average of thirty-one ships passing through it daily.

ऊ

THE CHANGING UN

Despite its recent successes there is still in some circles a prevailing uneasiness about the future usefulness of the United Nations Organization. Thus, for example, Lord Cherwell, in a speech before the British House of Lords on December 11, 1956, said, "And though, like everyone else, I wish the U.N.O. could work, I have come reluctantly to the view that, in its present form, it cannot." Its resolutions, he stated, have no effective way of being enforced. "I cannot help feeling," he said, "that people tend to overestimate its power for good and to underrate its potentialities for evil." In other words, he is inclined to regard the UN as a useless debating society whose decisions are largely controlled by regional blocs motivated by self-interest, not by judicial impartiality. The UN, it is true, is in a broad sense a debating society, a public forum where the problems which disrupt the world are discussed and debated. Since the charter does not endow the UN with the attributes of a super-state, it has authority only to discuss and make recommendations. It cannot command action and can act only when the sovereign states of which it is composed agree to act. It is effective only when nations are responsive to world opinion. But the UN is certainly not a useless debating society. It can and does exercise immense influence. It can get attention and bring the weight of world opinion to bear on problems and injustices. Consequently it is a major force in keeping the peace and in removing causes of war. Even when the UN fails to solve a problem, justice and morality are at least heard if not heeded. Moreover, it is the only world forum where nations can discuss, debate, and mediate conflicts arising among them. The UN is, as Secretary-General Dag Hammarskjold put it, "an admittedly imperfect but indispensable instrument of nations in working for a peaceful evolution toward a more just and secure world order."

Because of the nature of the UN it cannot always serve the functions it was intended to serve. If nations are not responsive to world opinion they can, and do, flout the resolutions of the UN. This is exemplified by the Kashmir question. When both India and Pakistan occupied Kashmir the UN called for both sides to withdraw so that Kashmir could decide its own future by means of a plebiscite. Although the shooting stopped, India and Pakistan could not agree on terms for joint withdrawal. The plebiscite, too, was postponed indefinitely. In 1957 India openly defied the UN by announcing the annexation of Kashmir. For many years the UN has also been trying to establish peace between the Arab states and Israel. In 1949 the UN called for a cease-fire between the Arabs and Israelis, urged them to make Jerusalem a neutral city, to repay and resettle the 900,000 Arab refugees expelled from Israel, and to lift the Egyptian embargo on Israeli goods through the Suez Canal. The cease-fire was agreed to, but the firing did not stop. The Arabs and Israelis continue to engage in constant shooting at each other in disregard of the numerous UN resolutions. Furthermore, Egypt refused to lift the Suez embargo on Israeli goods, Jerusalem remains divided, and the refugees are unpaid and have not been resettled. The UN also failed in its efforts to stop the bloodshed and vengeance in Hungary. When it called for cessation of the armed attacks on the Hungarians by Soviet Russia, the withdrawal of all Soviet troops from Hungary, and the holding of free elections in Hungary under UN supervision, the Kremlin either ignored or rejected the pleas and sent in more troops to crush the Hungarian uprising.

Although the UN has failed to solve some problems, it nevertheless has a record of solid accomplishment. It has fought disease, hunger, poverty and ignorance in many lands, it has increased the world's food through the dissemination of information and the conquest of plant diseases, and it has helped underdeveloped areas become self-sustaining. Furthermore, the UN also helped in the creation of an International Atomic Energy Agency for the peaceful development of the atom. Although it was unsuccessful in stopping the bloody repression of the Hungarian uprising by the Soviet forces, it did center world opinion on the event, reveal the brutality of the methods employed, and make it less likely that such brutal methods will be employed again. Any attempt at on-the-spot efforts by UN representatives was ruled out because the UN Charter bars the peace organization from moving into a country unless that country agrees. In Hungary the puppet government refused entry to the UN observers. Later, when Britain, France, and Israel invaded Egypt, the UN helped to prevent the conflict from developing into a major war by calling for a quick end to hostilities. After a cease-fire was agreed upon it took the unprecedented step of creating an Emergency Force (UNEF) to police the troubled areas during the withdrawal of the invasion forces. Then, after the withdrawal of the British, French, and Israelis, it assumed the task of clearing the canal at the bidding of the Egyptian government. Like UNEF the clearing of the canal was also without a precedent for the UN. The UN General Assembly also threw the weight of its influence into the Algerian crisis. Although it failed in its efforts to stop the fighting, it did succeed

(December, 1957) in adopting a basis for discussion which was acceptable to both the Paris government and the Algerian rebels.

The major limitation on the actions of the UN is still the veto by the five permanent members in the Security Council. This veto has been exercised most frequently by the Soviet Union. The Soviet Union has, in fact, resorted to the veto some 80-odd times. No resolution can be adopted which would in any way obstruct the march of Soviet imperialism. Unfortunately the founders in setting up the machinery of the UN did not foresee the clash between the ideologies of Marxist communism and democratic liberalism. When the Charter was drawn up the great powers, with the exception of Germany, were allies and it was hoped that they would remain in agreement on major problems concerning world peace. The harmony was short-lived. Soon the nations which had permanent seats in the Security Council, particularly Soviet Russia, resorted to the veto whenever controversial questions arose. Because obstructionist tactics were so frequently employed in the Security Council, there has been a diversion of activity from the Security Council to the General Assembly where the veto does not apply. Since resolutions in the General Assembly are passed either by a simple majority or by a two-thirds majority vote, it is somewhat more difficult to obstruct adoption. A tendency has, however, developed in the voting to vote by blocs. Among the blocs there are the Soviet or Iron Curtain bloc, the NATO bloc, the South American bloc, and the Afro-Asian bloc. The members of these blocs tend to vote together on the basis of sectional interests, ideologies, prejudices or likes and dislikes. In most cases there is not even a pretense of judicial impartiality. Such voting could well paralyze the General Assembly in the same way as the veto virtually stalemated the functions of the Security Council. Sir Winston Churchill called attention to the danger in a speech in London (1957) when he said, "It is certain that if the Assembly continues to take its decisions on grounds of enmity, opportunism, or merely jealousy and petulance, the whole structure may be brought to nothing."

In addition to other changes the UN has grown in size, increasing its membership by more than a third in three years. As recently as 1954 it had only 60 members, but when the General Assembly ended its twelfth session in December, 1957, the number had increased to 82. No less than 16 members were added in 1955, 4 in 1956, and 2 in 1957. As a result of the increase in membership the UN has become more universal, more of a world forum. With the exception of the two Germanies and Switzerland, who have not applied for membership, all of the European states are now members as well as all of the states of the American continent. Most of the recently admitted members are Afro-Asian states and the number is constantly increasing. With the admission of Ghana and Malaya in 1957 the Afro-Asian group increased its votes to 28. If all its members vote together this group now has enough votes to block any resolution which must be passed by a two-thirds majority. Moreover, as the Afro-Asian bloc continues to grow in numbers, the numerical influence of Europe and the New World will continue to diminish. One must be careful, however, not to overemphasize the cohesion of the Afro-Asian bloc. Whereas the members have voted together at times, the opposite has been true at other times. The group is divided by differences of language, tradition, and culture, by conflicting ambitions and ideological incompatibilities. On the other hand, a common feeling against colonialism is a strong cohesive force which can wield its influence on the voting of the bloc when the opportunity presents itself.

A number of observers have pointed out that a majority of the votes in the General Assembly do not necessarily represent a majority of the world's population. While 77 delegates represent one half of the population represented in the UN, the other 5 delegates represent the other half. In other words, the vote of a delegate is not weighted in accordance with population. Irrespective of its population each member nation has an equal vote. The vote of India is equated by the vote of Iceland, although the population of the former is almost 4000 times greater than that of the latter. Consequently the power of making vital decisions is, in the words of an American historian, "in the hands of the small powers, most of which are weak, newly independent, internally unstable, not highly developed, and reflecting not a corporate conscience or wisdom but merely a spectrum of all the passions, interests, and prejudices that bless and curse mankind." [4] Sir Winston Churchill warned that this development constitutes a real danger to the effectiveness, even to the existence, of the UN. "We wish these new nations well," he said in 1957. "Indeed we created many of them, and have done our best since to ensure their integrity and prosperity. But it is anomalous that the vote or prejudice of any small country should affect events involving populations many times its own numbers, and affect them as momentary self-advantage may direct. This should be changed."

[4] Vernon V. Aspaturian, "The Metamorphosis of the United Nations," *Yale Review,* vol. 46 (1956–57), p. 559.

As the West's most formidable reply to the communist threat, NATO has been "a thorn in the side" of the Kremlin. The Western European states, however, have been so eager to curtail their military expenditures and to end the "cold war" that they have been ready to grasp at any straw. Hence when the new Soviet leaders shifted their tactics from military pressure to diplomatic enticement, from harsh words to soft words, some of the leaders of the NATO nations concluded that the Russians were sincere in their peaceful avowals. The effect on NATO was a softening of the determination to hold the line against the communist bloc. The French withdrew more than three of their five NATO divisions for action in North Africa. West Germany, which had pledged to build up its military strength "as rapidly as possible," was not only slow in mustering troops for Western defense but also scaled down its commitments drastically. Britain, absorbed in the struggle to maintain its ascendancy in the Middle East, was soon at odds with Greece, a fellow member of NATO, over Cyprus. In March, 1956, Iceland requested the withdrawal of United States troops because the improved relations between East and West made their presence in that country unnecessary. Some Western leaders even expressed the idea that NATO was in some respects outdated. One of these was President Giovanni Gronchi of Italy, who told the Congress of the United States in February, 1956, that NATO should be reorganized in line with existing conditions. Another was Sir Winston Churchill, who said, "It may well be that the great issues that perplex us . . . today can be solved more easily than they can by rival blocs confronting each other with suspicion and hostility."

But the hopes of those who had accepted the Kremlin's soft words at face value were gradually dispelled. Grave doubts as to the peaceful intentions of the Kremlin were created by the Red Army's bloody suppression of the Hungarian uprising. It made many realize that the Kremlin leaders will not hesitate to use their military forces if they can derive benefit from doing so. Then in the fall of 1957 a new threat developed. This time it was not the massive Red Army, but the intercontinental missile. After the Sputniks demonstrated Russia's capacity to fire long-range missiles, Nikita Khrushchev and his colleagues played Russia's military and psychological advantage to the hilt. Khrushchev, in particular, adopted a tougher policy toward the West. He did not miss an opportunity to play on the fears of the NATO peoples by threatening not only to turn Western Europe into a cemetery if war broke out but also to rain missiles on the United States. The reaction in the West was mixed. Some NATO leaders, particularly those of the smaller states, urged that disarmament talks be resumed with the Kremlin in the hope of reaching some kind of reasonable settlement. They feared that a rigid military program might make a nuclear war with its frightful consequences inevitable. A refusal to negotiate, they held, would only help the Soviet leaders convince the uncommitted peoples that the West is interested only in starting World War III. Others held that the West should first build an arsenal of intercontinental missiles so it can negotiate from a position of strength. As British Foreign Minister Harold Macmillan summarized it in a phrase borrowed from Sir Winston Churchill, "We arm to parley." "We shall not parley successfully," he said, "unless we arm effectively." The supporters of this view argued that history has demonstrated that the Kremlin respects strength. Being strong, NATO can negotiate with Russia when negotiations offer promise. Only in this way can NATO defend peace and protect the liberty of free peoples.

Thus opinion was divided when the NATO conference opened in Paris in December, 1957. Although the final declaration affirmed NATO's determination to resist aggression and subversion, the decisions of the conference were in the nature of a compromise between those who favored the armaments plan and those who urged negotiations with the Kremlin to see if the arms race could be checked. First, it was decided in principle to establish missile bases in the NATO states that were willing to accept them and to stock them with intermediate-range missiles from the United States. Second, it was decided "to promote, preferably within the framework of the United Nations," negotiations with the Kremlin on the deadlocked issue of disarmament. This was a direct and concrete bid for East-West talks. The NATO members made plain that they wanted to test once more the Kremlin's readiness to ease tensions at the conference table. Regarding the establishment of missile bases in Europe, some differences of approach became apparent. The premiers of Norway and Denmark stated at once that their countries did not want missile bases, and West German Defense Minister Strauss announced that his country was not ready to commit itself to having missile bases on its soil. On the other hand, the British Parliament quickly approved the establishment of nuclear missile sites on British soil, and the Turkish representative stated that his country would welcome such bases. Other NATO nations were expected to follow the example of Britain and Turkey.

While some of the NATO leaders, including President Eisenhower, were trying to revitalize NATO and to create a deeper sense
of unity, some progress was being made outside NATO. In March,
1957, two treaties were signed in Rome by representatives of France,
West Germany, Italy, the Netherlands, Belgium, and Luxemburg,
the six countries which were already cooperating in the six-year-old
European Coal and Steel Community. Whereas the European Coal
and Steel Community provides a tariff-free market for coal, iron, and
steel, the first of the new treaties aimed to set up over a period of
years a common external tariff for all goods, and common policies for
agriculture, transport, labor and other sectors of the economy. The
new community is to be known as the European Economic Community. The second treaty laid down provisions for a European Atomic
Energy Community, having as its basic purpose the pooling of the
resources of the six participating nations for the peaceful uses of
nuclear power. After the parliaments of all six signatories had ratified the treaties, they went into effect January 1, 1958. Many Europeans hailed the joining of the six nations into a vast economic bloc
as the first step in a development that would enable Western Europe
to compete on an equal economic footing with the United States and
Soviet Russia. Some even hoped that the communities would work
so well they would eventually lead to a full political union of the
participants. The big question mark is France which is so deeply
involved in economic troubles as to find it necessary to increase trade
restrictions.

Bibliography

THE number of books on European history since 1914 is so large that a mere listing of them would fill a volume. Various periodicals publish lists of the books they receive, among them the *American Historical Review* and the *Journal of Modern History*. An exceptionally full list can be found in *Foreign Affairs*. For books on the earlier years of the period the student can consult *A Guide to Historical Literature*, edited by W. H. Allison, Sidney B. Fay, A. H. Shearer, and H. R. Shipman (1931). A more recent bibliography is L. J. Ragatz' *A Bibliography for the Study of European History* (1942), with supplements. Other important volumes are *Foreign Affairs Bibliography* (1933, 1945, and 1955), which cover international affairs from 1922–1932, 1932–1942, and 1942–1952, respectively.

For more recent material not included in this volume the student can consult such periodicals as the *Journal of Modern History, Current History, Foreign Affairs, Political Science Quarterly, Contemporary Review, Facts on File*, or any of the better periodicals which include discussions of current events. Other good sources of information are *The American Year Book, The Annual Register, The New International Yearbook, The Statesman's Year Book, The New Standard Year Book*, and a number of other summaries which are published annually.

As supplements to this volume there are a number of collections of documents such as *Documents and Readings in the History of Europe since 1918*, edited by Walter C. Langsam (1951); *Readings in European International Relations since 1879*, edited by W. H. Cooke and E. P. Stickney (1939); *Modern Constitutions since 1787*, edited by J. A. Hawgood (1938); and *Documents on International Affairs*, edited by J. W. Wheeler-Bennett (1928, *et seq.*).

CHAPTERS 1, 2, 3. *World War* I

Causes of the war. Outstanding among the detailed, scholarly treatments of the causes of World War I are Sidney B. Fay's *The Origins of the World War* (2 vols. in one, rev. ed., 1930) and Bernadotte E. Schmitt's *The Coming of the War: 1914* (2 vols., 1930). H. E. Barnes' *The Genesis of the World War* (1928) attempts to lay the blame at the door of France and Russia. J. S. Ewart's *The Roots and Causes of the War, 1914–1918* (2 vols., 1925) is a scholarly work. A good shorter work is H. W. Wilson's *The War Guilt* (1928). The best defense of Germany and Austria-Hungary is Count M. Montgelas' *The Case for the Central Powers* (1925). An important book by a Frenchman is C. Bloch's *The Causes of the World War* (1935). Ross J. Hoffman's *Great Britain and the German Trade Rivalry, 1875–1914* (1933) throws considerable light on the economic causes of the war. A notable study of one phase of Germany's *Drang nach Osten* is E. M. Earle's *Turkey, the Great Powers, and the Bagdad Railway* (1923).

Events preceding the war. Noteworthy among the accounts of events immediately preceding the declaration of war are E. F. Benson's *The Outbreak of War, 1914* (1934), R. W. Seton-Watson's *Sarajevo: A Study in the Origins of the Great War* (1928), and M. E. Durham's *The Sarajevo Crime* (1925). B. E. Schmitt's "July, 1914: Thirty Years After," *Journal of Modern History*, vol. 16 (1944), pp. 169–204, discusses the new evidence that has been brought to light.

Diplomatic history. Among the discussions of European diplomacy on the eve of World War I, W. L. Langer's *European Alliances and Alignments* (1931) is one of the best. This work was continued in the same author's *The Diplomacy of Imperialism* (2 vols., 1935). G. P. Gooch's *Studies in Statecraft and Diplomacy* (1936 and 1942) throws considerable light on the diplomatic background of the war. A good short summary is C. Seymour's *The Diplomatic Background of the War, 1870–1914* (1916); also R. B. Mowat's *The Concert of Europe* (1931). The first half of R. J. Sontag's *European Diplomatic History, 1871–1932* (1933) presents an excellent summary of the years from 1871 to 1914. T. Wolff's *The Eve of 1914* (1934) is a good study by a German with a thorough knowledge of European diplomacy. Discussions of various phases of diplomacy are numerous. Eugene N. Anderson's *The First Moroccan Crisis, 1904–1906* (1930) is the most thorough study of the subject. Professor Schmitt has written three scholarly books on various phases of diplomatic history: *England and Germany, 1790–1914* (1916), *Triple Alliance and Triple Entente* (1934), and *The Annexation of Bosnia, 1908–1909* (1937). Other important books are O. H. Wedel's *Austro-German Diplomatic Relations, 1908–1914* (1932), E. Malcolm Carroll's *Germany and the Great Powers, 1866–1914* (1938), W. C. Askew's *Europe and Italy's Acquisition of Libya, 1911–1912* (1942), and E. C. Helmreich's *The Diplomacy of the Balkan Wars, 1912–1913* (1938). British foreign policy is exhaustively treated in A. W. Ward and G. P. Gooch's *Cambridge History of British Foreign Policy, 1783–1919* (3 vols., 1922–1923). G. P. Gooch's *Franco-German Relations, 1871–1914* (1923) is an excellent short survey. Another excellent brief study is A. C. Coolidge's *The Origins of the Triple Alliance* (1926). E. Brandenburg's *From Bismarck to the World War* (1927) is an interesting book by a German writer.

Bibliographical studies. Professor Schmitt has published a short critical survey of published source and secondary materials entitled "The Origins of the War," in *Journal* *of Modern History,* vol. 6 (1934), pp. 160–174. This study is supplemented by the same author's later articles in the same periodical, vol. 13 (1941), pp. 225–236, and vol. 16 (1944), pp. 169–204. O. H. Wedel has published a critical discussion of Austro-Hungarian documents (1908–1914) in *Journal of Modern History,* vol. 3 (1931), pp. 84–107. Another noteworthy review article is R. J. Sontag's "British Policy in 1913–1914," *Journal of Modern History,* vol. 10 (1938), pp. 542–553. Philip E. Mosely's "Russian Policy in 1911–1912," *Journal of Modern History,* vol. 12 (1940), pp. 69–86, is an excellent critical discussion of printed documents and secondary works on Russian foreign policy.

Short histories. Among the many short histories of the First World War C. R. M. Cruttwell's *A History of the Great War, 1914–1918* (1935) is one of the best; written in non-technical language and based on the best authorities. More concerned with the strategical and tactical side is Captain Liddell Hart's *A History of the World War, 1914–1918* (1934). Another good military history is G. L. McEntee's *Military History of the World War* (1937). An excellent short account for the general reader is C. J. H. Hayes' *A Brief History of the Great War* (1926). T. G. Frothingham's *A Guide to the Military History of the World War* (1920) is a useful synopsis. Sir G. G. Aston wrote a good brief survey for the Home University Library under the title, *The Great War of 1914–1918* (1930). A. F. Pollard's *A Short History of the Great War* (1928) is a good account by a British historian. Two other useful books are W. L. McPherson's *The Strategy of the Great War* (1919) and *A Short History of the Great War* (1920). J. Buchan's *A History of the Great War* (4 vols., 1922) and F. H. Simonds' *A History of the World War* (5 vols., 1917–1920) are good longer accounts. There is an excellent discussion by A. L. P. Johnson of the military histories that appeared up to 1931, in *Journal of Modern History,* vol. 3 (1931), pp. 266–286. A history of the war as seen by a camera is *The First World War: A Photographic History* (1933), edited by L. Stallings. For those who are interested in mistakes there is W. S. Woods' *Colossal Blunders of the War* (1930).

Special operations. Books on operations in special areas are so numerous that only a few can be listed. On the drive of 1914 S. Tyng's *The Campaign of the Marne, 1914* (1935) throws considerable light. General A. von Kluck's *The March on Paris, 1914* (1920) is an account by a German general. There are two good books on the campaign in East Prussia: N. N. Golovine's *The Russian Campaign of 1914* (1933) and Sir E. Ironside's *Tannenberg: The First Thirty Days in East Prussia* (1925). Winston Churchill's *The Unknown War* (1931) is a brilliant account of the fighting on the eastern front. L. Villari's *The War on the Italian Front* (1932) and O. L. McEntee's *Italy's Part in Winning the World War* (1934) are good discussions of Italy's war effort. R. W. Seton-Watson's *Roumania and the Great War* (1915) is a good account. E. Ashmead-Bartlett's *The Uncensored Dardanelles* (1928) is an authoritative discussion. On the question of the Straits in general there is the excellent article by R. J. Kerner, "Russia, the Straits, and Constantinople," *Journal of Modern History,* vol. 1 (1929), pp. 400–415. H. Kannengiesser's *The Campaign in Gallipoli* (1928) is an account by a general who fought on the side of the Central Powers. G. Gordon-Smith's *From Serbia to Jugo-Slavia* (1920) is an informative account of the Serbian military campaigns. Among the many books on the Arabian adventure the following are outstanding: R. Graves' *Lawrence and the Arabian Adventure* (1928), C. T. E. Edmonds' *Law-*

rence of Arabia (1935), and Captain Liddell Hart's *Colonel Lawrence: The Man Behind the Legend* (1935). Lowell Thomas' *With Lawrence in Arabia* (1924) is an interesting account. Not to be overlooked, of course, is T. E. Lawrence's *Revolt in the Desert* (1927). For the operations in Palestine the student should consult Major-General M. G. E. Bowman-Manifold's *Outline of the Egyptian and Palestine Campaigns, 1914 to 1918* (1922) and Colonel A. P. Wavell's *The Palestine Campaigns* (1928). There is much interesting information in the two books by W. T. Massey, *How Jerusalem Was Won* (1920) and *Allenby's Final Triumph* (1920).

Naval warfare. A good treatment of Anglo-German naval competition between 1900 and 1914 can be found in E. L. Woodward's *Great Britain and the German Navy* (1935). Sir H. Newbolt's *A Naval History of the War, 1914–1918* (1920) is an excellent survey of British operations. One of the most important books in the field of naval history is Sir Julian Corbett's *History of the Great War: Naval Operations*, 5 vols. (1920–1931), based on the British Admiralty Papers. J. R. Jellicoe's *The Grand Fleet, 1914–1916* (1919) is an account by the man who commanded the Grand Fleet. The commander of the German fleet at the battle of Jutland, Admiral R. Scheer, has also written an account which is entitled *Germany's High Seas Fleet in the World War* (1920). Another interesting work by a German naval officer is Admiral A. von Tirpitz' *My Memoirs* (2 vols., 1919). J. E. T. Harper's *The Truth about Jutland* (1927) and *The Riddle of Jutland* (1934) by the same author in collaboration with L. Gibson are two of the best books on the famous battle.

The submarine. Two careful and fair-minded studies on submarine activities are R. H. Gibson and Maurice Prendergast's *The German Submarine War, 1914–1918* (1931) and David Masters' *The Submarine War* (1935). Louis Guichard's *The Naval Blockade* (1930) is a good scholarly account. W. G. Carr's *By Guess and by God* (1930) and L. Thomas' *Raiders of the Deep* (1928) tell the story of submarine activities in interesting fashion. J. R. Jellicoe's *The Submarine Peril* (1934) is a record of British policy during the early years of the war.

Propaganda and secret service. Ralph H. Lutz's "Studies of World War Propaganda," *Journal of Modern History,* vol. 5 (1935), pp. 496–516, offers an excellent critical discussion of the various books on war propaganda during World War I. Harold D. Lasswell's *Propaganda Technique in the World War* (1927) is a definitive book based on exhaustive study of the sources. Another important work is George Bruntz's *Allied Propaganda and the Collapse of the German Empire in 1918* (1938). James M. Read's *Atrocity Propaganda, 1914–1919* (1941) is a careful study of the causes and consequences of atrocity propaganda. Arthur Ponsonby's *Falsehood in Wartime* (1928) discusses an assortment of lies "considered necessary to maintain the morale of soldiers and civilians." On espionage during World War I there are a number of interesting books including W. Nicolai's *The German Secret Service* (1924), H. R. Berndorff's *Espionage* (1930), and Sir B. Thomson's *The Allied Secret Service in Greece* (1931).

Biographies, memoirs, and reminiscences. Four outstanding biographies of military men are Captain B. H. Liddell Hart's *Foch, the Man of Orleans* (1932), Sir G. G. Aston's *Biography of the Late Marshal Foch* (1929), Karl Tschuppik's *Ludendorff: The Tragedy of a Military Mind,* translated by W. H. Johnston (1932), and Sir Archibald Wavell's illuminating biography of his former commander, *Allenby: A Study in Great-*

ness (1941). Other important biographies are E. J. Galet's *Albert, King of the Belgians, in the Great War* (1931), R. Recouly's *Joffre* (1931), and H. A. Gibbons' *Venizelos* (1923). Memoirs and reminiscences of men who played leading roles during the period are so numerous that only a few can be listed. Important British memoirs include Winston Churchill's *The World Crisis, 1911–1918* (4 vols., 1923–1927), D. Lloyd George's *War Memoirs* (6 vols., 1933–1937), Viscount Grey's *Twenty-Five Years, 1892–1916* (2 vols., 1925), and Viscount Haldane's *Before the War* (1920), Sir G. Buchanan's *Mission to Russia* (2 vols., 1923) and H. H. Asquith's *Genesis of the War* (1924) contain much important information. Memoirs by prominent Frenchmen are R. Poincaré's *The Origins of the War* (1922) and *The Memoirs of Raymond Poincaré* (2 vols., 1926–1928); also G. M. Paléologue's *An Ambassador's Memoirs* (3 vols., 1924–1926), F. Foch's *Memoirs* (1931), and J. J. C. Joffre's *Personal Memoirs* (2 vols., 1932). Notable memoirs by prominent Germans include Wilhelm II's *The Kaiser's Memoirs, 1887–1918* (1922), Th. von Bethmann-Hollweg's *Reflections on the World War* (1920), Prince Lichnowsky's *Heading for the Abyss* (1928), B. von Bülow's *Memoirs* (4 vols., 1931–1932), E. Ludendorff's *Ludendorff's Own Story* (2 vols., 1920), and P. von Hindenburg's *Out of My Life* (2 vols., 1921). Important memoirs by Americans include Brand Whitlock's *Belgium: A Personal Narrative* (2 vols., 1919) and J. J. Pershing's *My Experiences in the World War* (2 vols., 1931).

Miscellaneous. Frank P. Chambers' *The War Behind the War, 1914–1918* (1939) shows what took place in civil life during the war years. Leon W. Fuller's "The War of 1914 as Interpreted by German Intellectuals," *Journal of Modern History,* vol. 14 (1942), pp. 145–160, is an interesting study of a neglected phase. The development of the tank and its use in the First World War is presented in detail in J. F. C. Fuller's *Tanks in the Great War, 1914–1918* (1920) and Sir Murray Sueter's *The Evolution of the Tank* (1937). Edwin Campbell's *Zeppelins: The Past and the Future* (1918) contains an interesting brief account of the part Zeppelins played in World War I. For a more detailed treatment see Ernst A. Lehmann and Howard Mingos' *The Zeppelins* (1927). Treusch von Buttlar-Brandenfels' *Zeppelins over England* (1932) is an account by a German Zeppelin expert. On the use of gas the student will find an interesting discussion in C. H. Foulkes' *Gas! The Story of the Special Brigade* (1934). H. W. Miller's *The Paris Gun* (1930) tells the story of the gun which dropped shells into Paris from a distance of seventy miles.

Russian Revolution of 1917. M. M. Karpovich's *Imperial Russia, 1801–1917* (1932) is a good brief outline of a century of Tsarist rule. A more comprehensive survey can be found in Sir Bernard Pares' *History of Russia* (1926). Sir George Buchanan's *My Mission to Russia* (1923) contains some interesting observations on Russian conditions. Gleb Botkin's *The Real Romanovs* (1931) presents a picture of the Romanovs as seen by the court physician. William Gerhardi's *The Romanovs* (1940) tells the story of the Russian imperial family. *Letters of the Tsaritsa to the Tsar, 1914–1916* (1923) and *The Letters of the Tsar to the Tsaritsa, 1914–1917* (1929) afford a real insight into the character of both. An excellent scholarly account of conditions among the peasants is to be found in Geroid T. Robinson's *Rural Russia under the Old Regime* (1932). René Fülop-Miller's *Rasputin: The Holy Devil* (1928) is a sensational biography of the Russian "holy man," but not always authentic. For further information on the influence of Rasputin the student may consult Prince F. F. Iusupov's *Rasputin* (1927) by one of Rasputin's assassins and M. V. Rodzyanko's *The Reign of Rasputin* (1927) by the president of the Duma to whom Rasputin became an obsession. G. G. Tellberg and R. Wilton's *Last Days of the Romanovs* (1920) offer a good account of the murder of the tsar and his family. Sir John Hanbury-Williams' *The Emperor Nicholas II as I Knew Him* (1922) is a picture of the tsar as seen by an Englishman. M. T. Florinsky's *The End of the Russian Empire* (1931) is an excellent study of Russia during the early years of the war. Victor Chernov's *The Great Russian Revolution* (1936) tells the story largely in terms of the prominent persons involved. Alexander Kerensky's *The Catastrophe* (1927) is his own story of the Russian Revolution. Anton I. Denikin's *The White Army* (1930) and George Stewart's *The White Armies of Russia* (1933) record the counterrevolutionary efforts.

For critical discussion of books on the Russian Revolution up to 1930 the student may consult Michael Karpovich's bibliographical article, "The Russian Revolution of 1917," *Journal of Modern History*, vol. 2 (1930), pp. 258–280. An excellent brief survey is to be found in George Vernadsky's *The Russian Revolution, 1917–1931* (1932). James Mavor's *The Russian Revolution* (1928), Lancelot Lawton's *The Russian Revolution, 1917–1926* (1927), and Louis P. Kirby's *The Russian Revolution* (1940) are good short accounts. A good longer work is William H. Chamberlin's *History of the Russian Revolution* (2 vols., 1935). G. R. Treviranus' *Revolutions in Russia: Their Lessons for the Western World* (1944) is a historical interpretation of revolutionary politics. Sir Bernard Pares' *The Fall of the Russian Monarchy* (1939) is one of the better accounts of the causes and outbreak of the revolution. E. A. Walsh's *Fall of the Russian Empire* (1928) is successful in dealing with the Romanovs, but not with the revolution. Documentary materials are to be found in *Documents of Russian History, 1914–1917*, edited by F. A. Golder (1927); *The Bolshevik Revolution, 1917–1918*, edited by J. Bunyan and H. H. Fisher (1934); and *The Red Archives*, edited by C. E. Vulliamy (1929). For an account by one of the key figures see Leon Trotsky's *History of the Russian Revolution* (1934). Morris G. Hindus' *The Russian Peasant and the Revolution* (1920) is a vivid account of the effect of the revolution on rural life. For other books on Russia and the Russian Revolution consult the bibliography for Chapter 7.

United States enters the war. An excellent discussion of works on the gradual drift of the United States into the war is to be found in B. E. Schmitt's "American Neutrality, 1914–1917," in *Journal of Modern History*, vol. 8 (1936), pp. 200–211. Charles Seymour's *American Neutrality, 1914–1917* (1935) is a series of revealing essays. The most detailed discussion of American neutrality is C. C. Tansill's *America Goes to War* (1938). Other important discussions include C. F. Gauss' *Why We Went to War* (1919), Newton D. Baker's *Why We Went to War* (1936), and H. Gratton's *Why We Fought* (1929). T. A. Bailey's "German Documents Relating to the 'Lusitania,," *Journal of Modern History*, vol. 8 (1936), pp. 320–337, throws much light on the *Lusitania* controversy. Walter Millis' *Road to War: America, 1914–1917* (1935) is an interesting study which presents novel viewpoints. The most adequate general account of the United States war effort is Frederic L. Paxson's *American Democracy and the World War* (2 vols., 1939). Other informative volumes are S. T. Moore's *America and the World War* (1937), H. J. Reilly's *America's Part* (1928), and F. Palmer's *Our Gallant Madness* (1937). Among the interesting recollections one must include J. W. Gerard's *My Four Years in*

Germany (1917) by the United States Ambassador to Germany; R. Lansing's *War Memoirs* (1935) by the United States Secretary of State; and J. von Bernstorff's *My Three Years in America* (1920) by the German ambassador to the United States. Of special interest are the memoirs of the commander-in-chief of the A. E. F., General J. J. Pershing's *My Experiences in the World War* (2 vols., 1931).

United States in the war. On the military participation of the United States, General James G. Harbord has written two good books: *America in the World War* (1933) and *The American Army in France* (1936). A brief popular account of American operations can be found in A. W. Page's *Our 110 Days Fighting* (1920). Other informative accounts are S. Thomas' *History of the A. E. F.* (1920), H. Liggett's *A. E. F.* (1928), D. Van Every's *The A. E. F. in Battle* (1928), and F. Palmer's *Our Greatest Battle*. For naval operations there is an excellent book by W. S. Sims, the commander of the United States naval forces that operated in European waters, entitled *The American Navy in the War* (1920). Another good account by the same author in collaboration with B. J. Hendrick is *The Victory at Sea* (1920). For an account of aerial operations the student may consult M. M. Patrick's *The United States in the Air* (1928). The problem of recruiting the A. E. F. and shipping it across the ocean is ably discussed in T. G. Frothingham's *The American Reinforcement in the World War* (1927), A. Gleaves' *A History of the Transport Service* (1921), and E. N. Hurley's *The Bridge to France* (1927).

End of the war. Harry M. Rudin's *Armistice, 1918* (1944) offers a dispassionate day-by-day account of events leading to the armistice. Sir Frederick Maurice's *The Armistices of 1918* (1943) is a well documented study. Another good book by the same author is *The Last Four Months* (1919) which describes the last military campaign. The documents regarding the armistice are to be found in *Preliminary History of the Armistice,* edited by J. B. Scott (1924). Karl F. Nowak's *The Collapse of Central Europe* (1924) is a sound informative volume. Stephen M. Bouton's *And the Kaiser Abdicates* (1920) is an account by an American who was in Germany at the time. M. Baumont's *The Fall of the Kaiser* (1931) is the best treatment of the subject. For information on the costs of the war the student can consult H. Folks' *The Human Costs of the War* (1920), E. L. Bogart's *Direct and Indirect Costs of the Great World War* (1919), and J. M. Clark's *The Costs of the World War to the American People* (1931).

CHAPTER 4. *The Paris Peace Conference*

Making the peace. There are three interesting brief accounts, all written by journalists: H. Wilson Harris' *The Peace in the Making* (1919), Sisley Huddleston's *Peace-Making at Paris* (1919), and E. J. Dillon's *The Inside Story of the Peace Conference* (1920). C. T. Thompson's *The Peace Conference Day by Day* (1920) contains some interesting sidelights. Frank H. Simonds' *How Europe Made Peace without America* (1920) is a good popular account. D. H. Miller's *The Drafting of the Covenant* (2 vols., 1928) is a good account by a leading American jurist on the Commission. Edward M. House and Charles Seymour's *What Really Happened at Paris* (1921) is a series of lectures by leading members of the American delegation. Harold Nicolson's *Peacemaking, 1919* (1933) contains vivid excerpts from the diary of a liberal Englishman. *History of the Peace Conference* (6 vols., 1920–1924), edited by H. Temperley, offers a detailed account by experts attached to the British and American delegations. James

T. Shotwell's *At the Paris Peace Conference* (1937) is a day-to-day record of what a distinguished historian saw. Critical discussions of all the important books that appeared on the Peace Conference from 1919 to 1944 can be found in Robert E. Binkley's "Ten Years of Peace Conference History," *Journal of Modern History,* vol. 1 (1929), pp. 607–629; Paul Birdsall's "The Second Decade of Peace Conference History," *ibid.,* vol. 11 (1939), pp. 362–378; and Bernadotte E. Schmitt's "The Peace Conference of 1919," *ibid.,* vol. 16 (1944), pp. 49–59. The text of the treaties is to be found in *The Treaties of Peace, 1919–1923* (2 vols., 1924) issued by the Carnegie Endowment for International Peace.

Specific countries. Alma M. Luckau's *The German Delegation at the Paris Peace Conference* (1941) is a detailed treatment of the subject. Victor Schiff's *The Germans at Versailles* (1919) presents the observations of a socialist journalist. A detailed and impartial study of the treaty as it affected the relations between Germany and Poland is to be found in Ian Morrow's *The Peace Settlement in the German-Polish Borderlands* (1936). G. E. R. Gedye's *The Revolver Republic: France's Bid for the Rhine* (1930) tells the story of the efforts to separate the Rhineland from Germany. René Albrecht-Carrié's *Italy at the Paris Peace Conference* (1938) is a clear, scholarly account of the negotiations regarding Italy. Francesco Nitti's *Peaceless Europe* (1922) denounces the treaty. For Hungary there is Francis Deák's *Hungary at the Paris Peace Conference* (1942), a painstaking collection of materials, but somewhat onesided. Count Albert Apponyi, head of the Hungarian delegation, discusses the making of the Treaty of Trianon in a chapter of his *Memoirs* (1936). *The Treaty of St. Germain,* edited by Nina Almond and Ralph H. Lutz (1934), is a valuable study which sets forth by means of documents the evolution of the territorial and political clauses of the treaty.

Discussions of the treaties. Paul Birdsall's *Versailles Twenty Years After* (1941) is an excellent piece of historical writing. A. P. Scott's *An Introduction to the Peace Treaties* (1920) is a good analysis of the treaty of Versailles. Another good analysis is H. Stegeman's *The Mirage of Versailles* (1928). G. Adam's *The Tiger: Georges Clemenceau* (1930) and Geoffrey Bruun's *Clemenceau* (1943) are two good brief biographies. A. Tardieu's *The Truth about the Treaty* (1921) is an account by Clemenceau's right-hand man. G. M. Gathorne-Hardy's *The Fourteen Points and the Treaty of Versailles* (1939) is an interesting brief discussion. Clemenceau's attitude toward the treaties is to be found in his *Grandeur and Misery of Victory* (1930). W. H. Dawson's *Germany under the Treaty* (1933) is an eloquent demand for a revision of the treaty by a British historian. R. B. McCallum's *Public Opinion and the Last Peace* (1945) is a scholarly and interesting study which refutes some popular misconceptions about the Versailles treaty. William O. Molony's *Nationality and the Peace Treaties* (1934) is a penetrating discussion by an official of the League. George B. Noble's *Policies and Opinions at Paris, 1919* (1935) makes a striking comparison between the diplomacy at Paris and earlier diplomacy. Bernard M. Baruch's *The Making of the Reparation and Economic Sections of the Treaty* (1920) is a good discussion by the economic adviser to the American Peace Commission.

Woodrow Wilson and the peace. Thomas A. Bailey's *Woodrow Wilson and the Lost Peace* (1944) is an interesting study of the struggle over the treaties. Ray S. Baker's *What Wilson Did at Paris* (1919) is a defense of Wilson. Karl F. Nowak's *Versailles* (1928) is based on information from members of the German delegation and, therefore, unsympathetic to Wilson. Robert Lansing's *The Peace Negotiations* (1921) and *The Big Four and Others at the Peace Conference* (1921) are angry attacks on Wilson's methods and policies. A detailed defense of Wilson's efforts can be found in R. S. Baker's *Woodrow Wilson and World Settlement* (3 vols., 1923). Another sympathetic work is W. E. Dodd's *Woodrow Wilson and His Work* (1932). Stephen Bonsal's *Unfinished Business* (1944) is a simple and straightforward study of Wilson's idealism and the postwar ferment. Important for the study of United States diplomacy in the peace efforts are *The Intimate Papers of Colonel House* (4 vols., 1928), edited by Charles Seymour.

The League of Nations. R. Jones and S. S. Sherman's *The League of Nations: From Idea to Reality* (1927) traces the growth of the idea of a League. A more detailed account is to be found in T. Marburg's *Development of the League of Nations Idea* (2 vols., 1932). W. E. Rappard's *United Europe* (1930) is a good short account by a distinguished student of international relations. A good penetrating discussion of the Covenant is at hand in F. Wilson's *The Origins of the League Covenant* (1928). C. Howard Ellis' *The Origin, Structure and Working of the League of Nations* (1928) is an excellent introduction. In a more popular vein there is P. J. N. Baker's *The League of Nations at Work* (1926). J. S. Bassett's *The League of Nations* (1928) is a careful and fair-minded account. Woodrow Wilson's *Case for the League of Nations* (1923) contains a collection of President Wilson's speeches in behalf of the League idea. M. O. Hudson's *The Permanent Court of International Justice* (1934), E. Lindsey's *The International Court* (1931), and J. W. Wheeler-Bennett's *Information on the World Court, 1918–1928* (1929) are three good books on the World Court.

CHAPTER 5. *The Weimar Republic*

Founding of the Republic. *Fall of the German Empire, 1914–1918* (2 vols., 1932), edited by Ralph H. Lutz, is a valuable collection of documents. A. Rosenberg's *The Birth of the German Republic, 1871–1918* (1931) is a good objective narrative of events. H. G. Daniels' *The Rise of the German Republic* (1927) is a slow-moving survey. Ralph H. Lutz's *The German Revolution, 1918–1919* (1922) is an excellent account of the first year of the republic. G. Young's *The New Germany* (1920) and H. Stroebel's *The German Revolution and After* (1923) are two good surveys of conditions in Germany at the close of the war. *The Making of New Germany: The Memoirs of Philipp Scheidemann* (2 vols., 1929) are reminiscences by one of the founders of the republic. *The Memoirs of Prince Max of Baden* (2 vols., 1928) are interesting revelations by the last German chancellor. G. P. Gooch's *Germany* (1925) is an excellent short survey of Germany after World War I. R. Brunet's *The New German Constitution* (1922) and H. Oppenheimer's *The Constitution of the German Republic* (1923) are invaluable for an understanding of the constitution. J. F. Coar's *The Old and New Germany* (1924) offers an interesting comparison between the Germany before and after 1917.

Books on the Republic. One of the best accounts of the first years of the Weimar Republic is to be found in Elmer Luehr's *The New German Republic* (1929). J. W. Angell's *The Recovery of Germany* (rev. ed., 1932) is an excellent survey of German economic conditions. A. Rosenberg's *History of the German Republic* (1936) is fair. H. Quigley and R. Clark's *Republican Germany* (1928) is a well-written survey of the first years of the republic. Paul Kosok's *Modern Germany: A Study in Conflicting*

Loyalties (1933) contains some penetrating discussions on various phases of German life. E. Jaeckh's *The New Germany* (1927) is a survey by a German professor. Rupert Emerson's *State and Sovereignty in Modern Germany, 1871–1928* (1928) is an excellent discussion of political theory.

Reparations and inflation. Karl Bergmann's *History of Reparations* (1927) is a good detailed account by a German expert. Sir A. McFadyean's *Reparation Reviewed* (1930) is a clear treatment up to the acceptance of the Young Plan. J. W. Wheeler-Bennett's *Wreck of Reparations* (1933) tells the story of the failure to extract reparations from Germany. J. M. Keynes' *The Economic Consequences of Peace* (1919) is a determined attack on the reparation agreement. C. Bresciani-Turroni's *The Economics of Inflation* (1927) and Frank D. Graham's *Exchange, Prices and Production in Hyperinflation: Germany, 1920–1923* (1930) are two informative books. Hjalmar Schacht's *Stabilization of the Mark* (1927) is an account by the man who played a large part in stabilizing it.

Biographical works. Rudolf Olden's *Stresemann,* translated by R. T. Clark (1930), is a sound, informative biography. The most intimate biography of the German statesman is *Stresemann* (1931) by A. Vallentin, his devoted secretary. There is also an intimate record of Stresemann and his diplomacy in E. Stern-Rubarth's *Three Men Tried* (1939). There are two well-chosen collections of documents on Stresemann's life, *Stresemann's Papers* (3 vols., 1936) edited by Henry Bernhard, and *Gustav Stresemann: His Diaries, Letters, and Papers* (2 vols., 1935–1937). The best biography of Hindenburg in English is J. W. Wheeler-Bennett's *Hindenburg, the Wooden Titan* (1936). M. L. Goldsmith and F. Voigt's *Hindenburg, the Man and the Legend* (1930) is a popular account. Emil Ludwig's *Hindenburg and the Saga of the German Republic* (1935) is an attempt to explode the Hindenburg myth. T. R. Ybarra's *Hindenburg, the Man with Three Lives* (1932) stresses the changes in his career.

CHAPTER 6. *Battered and Bleeding France*

General. Paul Vaucher's *Post-War France* (1934) is an admirable brief survey. For the years immediately after the war William MacDonald's *Reconstruction in France* (1922) contains a good account. D. W. Brogan's *The Development of Modern France, 1870–1939* (1940) and Richard W. Hale's *Democratic France; The Third Republic from Sedan to Vichy* (1941) are good surveys of a wider period of French history. Gordon Wright's *Raymond Poincaré and the French Presidency* (1942) is a work of painstaking and thorough research. H. G. Daniels' *The Framework of France* (1937) and Walter R. Sharp's *The Government of the French Republic* (1938) are good introductions. A good brief account of the political confusion is to be found in R. H. Soltau's *French Parties and Politics* (1930). André Siegfried's *France: A Study in Nationality* (1930) offers a brief analysis of French character, parties, and politics. There are several interesting books on the political confusion in France by Alexander Werth whose sympathies are with the left: *France in Ferment* (1934) and *Destiny of France* (1937). C. J. H. Hayes' *France: A Nation of Patriots* (1930) is a penetrating study of patriotism in French education. D. J. Saposs' *The Labor Movement in Post-War France* (1931) is a thoroughgoing analysis. Sisley Huddleston has written two interesting popular books: *France and the French* (1925) and *France* (1927).

Economic conditions. Economic conditions in France during the first decade after World War I are expertly described by William F. Ogburn and William Jaffé in

The Economic Development of Post-War France (1929). Shepard B. Clough's *France: A History of National Economics, 1789–1939* (1939) is an excellent survey. There are two good books on French economic history by George Peel: *The Financial Crisis of France* (1925) and *The Economic Policy of France* (1937). R. M. Haig's *The Public Finances of Post-War France* (1929) is a clear discussion of a complex subject. Two other informative books on finances are E. Dulles' *The French Franc, 1914–1928* (1929) and J. H. Rogers' *The Process of Inflation in France, 1914–1927* (1929). An enlightening discussion on the population problem in France is to be found in J. J. Spengler's *France Faces Depopulation* (1938).

Empire and foreign affairs. H. I. Priestley's *France Overseas* (1938) is an excellent survey of French colonialism. C. Southworth's *The French Colonial Adventure* (1931) is a well-done authoritative treatment. A detailed scholarly discussion is to be found in S. Roberts' *History of French Colonial Policy* (2 vols., 1929). W. A. Roberts' *The French in the West Indies* (1931) is a timely, interesting, and carefully done book. Melvin M. Knight's *Morocco as a French Economic Venture* (1937) is a penetrating study of one of the French colonies. V. D'Ormesson's *France* (1939) is an excellent survey of French foreign policy in the period between the two World Wars. Arnold Wolfer's *Britain and France Between Two Wars: Conflicting Strategies of Peace Since Versailles* (1940) is a well written, authoritative analysis.

CHAPTER 7. *Soviet Russia*

General. For books on the Russian Revolution of 1917 see the bibliography for Chapters 1, 2, and 3. There is a plethora of books on the Soviet experiment. One of the best introductions is *U.S.S.R.: A Concise Handbook* (1947), edited by Ernest J. Simmons; it contains a series of well-written articles by nineteen writers. William Mandel has written a good factual description in his *A Guide to the Soviet Union* (1946). *Understanding the Russians*, edited by Bernhard J. Stern and Samuel Smith (1947), is a collection of fifty-two articles which previously appeared in various periodicals; uneven in character. Among the better introductions to Soviet Russia which appeared before World War II one must include Michael T. Florinsky's *Toward an Understanding of the U.S.S.R.* (1939), Ethan T. Colton's *The XYZ of Communism* (1931), Albert R. Williams' *The Soviets* (1937), Arthur Feiler's *The Russian Experiment* (1930), Waldemar Gurian's *Bolshevism: Theory and Practice* (1932), and René Fülop-Miller's *The Mind and the Face of Bolshevism* (1928). N. de Basily's *Russia under Soviet Rule* (1938) and Victor Serge's *Russia: Twenty Years After* (1937) are acute appraisals of twenty years of Bolshevik rule. Samuel N. Harper's *The Government of the Soviet Union* (1938) deals with the structure and functioning of the Soviet agencies. Hans Kohn's *Nationalism in the Soviet Union* (1933) is a well written, scholarly book. Victor Serge's *From Lenin to Stalin*, translated from the French by Ralph Manheim (1937), is unsympathetic. Nicholas Berdyaev's *The Origin of Russian Communism* (1938) traces the roots of Leninism. F. W. Halle's *Women in Soviet Russia* (1933) discusses the position of women in the communist state. W. P. and Zelda Coates' *From Tsardom to the Stalin Constitution* (1938) is a sympathetic account. David J. Dallin's *The Real Soviet Russia* (1945) is a dispassionate indictment of the Russian regime by a Russian socialist who is an anti-Bolshevik.

Russia as seen by visitors. W. Duranty's *I Write as I Please* (1935) and *Duranty Reports Russia* (1934) paint a vivid picture of life in Russia. Morris G. Hindus' *Broken Earth* (1926) depicts village life during the early years of the Soviet regime. William H. Chamberlin's *Soviet Russia: A Living Record and a History* (1931) is a competent and interesting account by an American journalist. Eugene Lyons' *Assignment in Utopia* (1937) records the author's disappointment over what he found in Russia. J. E. Davies' *Mission to Moscow* (1941) is a record of the experiences of the United States ambassador to the Soviet Union. Walter Citrine's *I Search for the Truth in Russia* (1937) contains the diary kept by the general secretary of the British Trades Union Congress during his travels in Russia. Sidney and Beatrice Webb's *The Truth about Soviet Russia* (1942) depicts life in Russia as a superior civilization. N. S. Timasheff's *Religion in Soviet Russia, 1917–1942* (1942) describes the resistance of the believers to the efforts to stamp out religion.

Biographical works. There is no really good biography of Lenin. Informative biographies are F. J. P. Veale's *The Man from the Volga* (1932), Isaac D. Levine's *The Man Lenin* (1924), and M. A. Landau-Aldanov's *Lenin* (1922). *Lenin: Toward the Seizure of Power* (2 vols., 1932) is a collection of Lenin's articles and papers edited by A. Trachtenberg. N. K. Krupskaia's *Memories of Lenin* (1930) is a volume by Lenin's widow. Eugene Lyon's *Stalin: Czar of All the Russias* (1940) is a brief but well-rounded story of Stalin's life written in a critical vein. Stephen Graham's *Stalin* (1939) is slow moving and unsympathetic. Leon Trotsky's *Stalin: An Appraisal of the Man and His Influence* (1946) is an appraisal by an avowed enemy. Isaac D. Levine's *Stalin* (1931) tells the story of Stalin's rise to power. Boris Souvarine's *Stalin: A Critical Study of Bolshevism* (1939) is a long scholarly and well-documented study. Stalin's *Leninism* (1941) is an authorized translation of Stalin's papers and addresses. *Stalin's Kampf: Joseph Stalin's Credo, Written by Himself,* edited by M. R. Werner (1940), contains excerpts from his speeches, interviews, articles, and books. For Trotsky there is an early life by R. Levy (1920). Trotsky himself left an interesting autobiography entitled *My Life* (1930).

Economic history. Lancelot Lawton's *An Economic History of Soviet Russia* (2 vols., 1932) is a very important study. Two good surveys are L. E. Hubbard's *Soviet Labor and Industry* (1942) and A. Yugow's *Russia's Economic Front for War and Peace* (1942). William H. Chamberlin's *Soviet Planned Economic Order* (1931) is a competent book by a trained observer. The same author's *Russia's Iron Age* (1935) is less sympathetic. Calvin B. Hoover's *The Economic Life of Soviet Russia* (1931) is a good survey by an able American historian. Maurice Dobb's *Russian Economic Development since the Revolution* (1928) is a keen analysis. G. F. Gringko's *The Five Year Plan of the Soviet Union* (1930) is a discussion by a Soviet official. M. Farbman's *Piatiletka: Russia's Five Year Plan* (1931) is a good discussion. W. P. and Zelda Coates' *The Second Five Year Plan of Development of the U.S.S.R.* (1934) is a sympathetic account. J. Beauchamp's *Agriculture in Soviet Russia* (1931) discusses the state farms. M. G. Hindus' *The Russian Peasant and the Revolution* (1920) and *Humanity Uprooted* (rev. ed., 1930) are two interesting accounts of rural changes. A more up-to-date survey of Soviet agriculture can be found in L. E. Hubbard's *The Economics of Soviet Agriculture* (1939). Manya Gordon's *Workers Before and After Lenin* (1941) is an interesting comparison of conditions under the tsars with those under the Bolsheviks.

Secret police and labor camps. The story of the dreaded Russian secret police is told in G. K. Popov's *The Tcheka: The Red Inquisition* (1925) and S. Melgunov's *The Red Terror in Russia* (1925). Studies of the secret police at a later period are to be found in G. Agabekov's *Ogpu* (1931). The story of the labor camps is told in David J. Dallin and Boris I. Nicholaevsky's *Forced Labor in Soviet Russia* (1947), a book buttressed by careful scholarship. T. Tchernavin's *Escape from the Soviets* (1934) is a record of personal experiences at the hands of the police. W. G. Krivitsky's *In Stalin's Secret Service* (1939) recounts the experiences of the former chief of the Soviet Intelligence.

Education and culture. Beatrice King's *Changing Man: The Education System in the U.S.S.R.* (1936) tells the story of the educational changes under Soviet rule. Scott Nearing's *Education in Soviet Russia* (1926) is a sympathetic discussion of the early years by an American socialist. A. P. Pinkevich's *The New Education in the Soviet Republic* (1929) is an account by a Russian educator. S. N. Harper's *Making Bolsheviks* (1931) is an interesting study by an expert on Russian history. Gleb Struve's *Soviet Russian Literature* (1935) is an excellent discussion of the new literature to 1935. G. Reavey and M. Slonim's *Soviet Literature: An Anthology* (1934) has an introductory chapter on "The New Spirit in Russian Literature." Paul Miliukov's *Outlines of Russian Culture* (3 vols., 1942) contains some excellent brief summaries of culture under the Soviets. R. J. Cooke's *Religion in Russia under the Soviets* (1924) and W. C. Emhardt's *Religion in Soviet Russia* (1929) are two accounts by American clergymen. J. F. Hecker's *Religion under the Soviets* (1927) is a defense of the Soviet policy toward religion. M. Spinka's *The Church and the Russian Revolution* (1927) discusses the effects of the revolution on the Orthodox Church.

Foreign policy. Louis Fischer's *The Soviets in World Affairs* (2 vols., 1930) is a full account by an American who at the time had leftist sympathies. A good brief account can be found in R. P. Arnot's *Soviet Russia and Her Neighbors* (1927). Two other well founded studies are Alfred L. P. Dennis' *The Foreign Policies of Soviet Russia* (1924) and S. N. Harper's *The Soviet Union and World Problems* (1935). William P. and Zelda Coates' *World Affairs and the U.S.S.R.* (1939) is an interesting defense of Russian foreign policy. John T. Murphy's *Russia on the March: A Study of Soviet Foreign Policy* (1941) is a good brief account by a socialist. F. Borkenau's *The Communist International* (1938) is a good account of the evolution and activities of the Comintern. K. W. Davis' *The Soviets at Geneva: The U.S.S.R. and the League of Nations, 1919–1933* (1934) is an interesting account of Russia's attitude toward the League.

CHAPTER 8. *British Economic and Imperial Problems*

General. For the effects of World War I on Britain the student may consult Frank Dilnot's *England after the War* (1920), A. L. Bowley's *Some Economic Consequences of the Great War* (1930), Francis W. Hirst's *The Consequences of the War to Great Britain* (1934), and C. F. G. Masterman's *England after War* (1922). On the coal mines there are three informative volumes: I. Lubin and H. Everett's *The British Coal Dilemma* (1927), J. P. Dickie's *The Coal Problem, 1910–1936* (1936), and G. D. H.

Cole's *Labour in the Coal Mining Industry, 1914–1921* (1923). The latter has also
written an interesting volume entitled *A Short History of the British Working Class
Movement* (1927). A. Hutt's *The Post-War History of the British Working Class*
(1938) is another important book. There is a good account of British protectionism
in F. Benham's *Great Britain under Protection* (1941). Ramsay Muir's *How Britain
Is Governed* (3rd ed., 1933) is an excellent introduction to the study of Britain.

British Empire. Paul Knaplund's *The British Empire 1815–1939* (1942) is an excellent
scholarly and dispassionate survey. Albert Viton's *Great Britain: An Empire in Tran-
sition* (1940) is a keen analysis of British imperialism. Stephen Leacock's *The British
Empire* (1940) is a combination of entertainment and history. W. K. Hancock's
Survey of British Commonwealth Affairs (2 vols., 1937 and 1942) is a good survey
of a complicated period, 1918–1939. Ramsay Muir's *The British Commonwealth: How
It Grew and How It Works* (1941) is a lucid treatise by a noted British historian.
Ernest Barker's *The Ideas and Ideals of the British Empire* (1941) is a good discussion.
Other good books are William Y. Elliott's *The New British Empire* (1932) and
Ralph W. Fox's *The Colonial Policy of British Imperialism* (1933). R. H. Murray and
H. Law's *Ireland* (1924) is a good brief outline. A good account of a short period of
Irish history can be found in D. R. Gwynn's *The Irish Free State, 1922–1927* (1928).
B. O. Briain's *The Irish Constitution* (1929), W. Moss' *Political Parties in the Irish
Free State* (1933), and J. G. MacNeill's *Studies in the Constitution of the Irish Free
State* (1925) are informative discussions of parties and political organization. D. Gwynn's
De Valera (1933) is a good biography of the Irish leader. L. Paul Dubois and
T. P. Gill's *The Irish Struggle and Its Results* (1934) puts special emphasis on the
period after 1914. Among the books on Palestine there are but few dispassionate ac-
counts. N. Bentwich's *England in Palestine* (1932) and *Fulfillment in the Promised
Land, 1917–1937* (1938), T. R. Feiwel's *No Ease in Zion* (1939), E. Main's *Palestine
at the Crossroads* (1937), and F. F. Andrews' *The Holy Land under Mandate* (2 vols.,
1931) are outstanding for their moderate viewpoints. A. Granovsky's *A Land Policy in
Palestine* (1940) is interesting. J. M. N. Jeffries' *Palestine: The Reality* (1939) is not
sympathetic with Zionism. L. Farago's *Palestine at the Cross-Roads* (1937) is an account
of a trip in 1936. Other works are listed in the bibliography for Chapter 21.

Biographical. Philip Guedalla's *A Gallery* (1924) offers brief incisive studies of
British political leaders. Short biographies of George V and Edward VIII can be found
in E. Acland and E. H. Bartlett's *Long Live the King!* (1936). For a longer biography
of George V the student may consult J. Gore's *King George V* (1941). C. E. Mallet's
Mr. Lloyd George: A Study (1930) is critical, while E. A. Thompson's *Mr. Lloyd George*
(1922) is sympathetic. Iconoclast's *James Ramsay MacDonald* (1931) and H. H. Tilt-
man's *Ramsay MacDonald: Labor's Man of Destiny* (1929) are good biographies.
H. W. Steed's *The Real Stanley Baldwin* (1930) is a sympathetic study. Robert Sencourt's *Winston Churchill* (1940) is a picture of the British leader as seen through
"right wing" eyes.

CHAPTER 9. *Fascist Italy*

Democracy and the dictatorships. J. F. Coar's *Democracy and the War* (1922) discusses the influence of World War I on the development of democracy. Alan F. Hatters-
ley's *Short History of Democracy* (1930) is a good brief survey. F. W. Coker's *Recent*

Political Thought (1934) and A. Zimmern's *Modern Political Doctrines* (1939) contain illuminating discussions. A. D. Lindsay's *The Modern Democratic State* (1943) is an analysis of the essence and functions of the modern democratic state. J. A. Leighton's *Social Philosophies in Conflict: Fascism and Nazism, Communism, Liberal Democracy* (1937) is a careful, provocative volume. Michael Oakeshott's *The Social and Political Doctrines of Contemporary Europe* (1939) is a good analysis. F. A. Voight's *Unto Caesar* (new ed., 1939) is a searching analysis of the ideology of the three European dictatorships. Francesco Nitti's *Bolshevism, Fascism, and Democracy* (1927) is a discussion by an exiled Italian statesman. Albert Carr's *Juggernaut: The Path of Dictatorship* (1939) is a good exposition.

Rise of Fascism. For a general survey of modern Italian history the student can consult Margot Hentze's *Pre-Fascist Italy* (1939). Cecil J. S. Sprigge's *The Development of Modern Italy* (1944) is a survey by a correspondent of the *Manchester Guardian* who spent twenty years in Italy. Count Carlo Sforza's *Contemporary Italy: Its Intellectual and Moral Origins* (1944) is a book of essays dealing with the political, cultural, and historical aspects of Italian history. George D. Herron's *The Revival of Italy* (1922) is a survey of economic conditions after World War I. One of the best accounts of the rise of Fascism to power is Angelo Rossi's *The Rise of Fascism: Italy from 1918 to 1922* (1938). Paul Einzig's *The Economic Foundations of Fascism* (1933) is an illuminating study. Gaudens Megaro's *Mussolini in the Making* (1938) is a revealing reconstruction of the early years of Mussolini's career; reveals the opportunist in Mussolini. Giorgio Pini's *The Official Life of Benito Mussolini* (1939) does not adequately trace the development of Mussolini's mind and thought. V. E. De Fiori's *Mussolini: The Man of Destiny* (1928) is marred by a pro-Mussolini bias. Among Mussolini's own writings that had a wide circulation are his *Fascism: Doctrine and Institutions* (1935), *Four Speeches on the Corporate State* (1935), and *My Autobiography* (1928). There is a good brief life of Mussolini in J. A. R. Marriott's *Makers of Modern Italy* (1937). Gilbert Seldes' *Sawdust Caesar* (1935) is a popular biography.

Fascism in action. One of the best short introductions to Fascism is Bolton King's *Fascism in Italy* (1931). William Ebenstein's *Fascist Italy* (1939) is a well written, scholarly account based on the best authorities. One of the most thorough investigations of Fascism as a political, economic, and social system is to be found in Herman Finer's *Mussolini's Italy* (1935). Stephen Rauschenbush's *The March of Fascism* (1939) is a critical analysis of Fascism "with a sobriety of style and an absence of vituperation." Max Ascoli and Arthur Feiler's *Fascism for Whom?* (1938) is an analysis of both German and Italian Fascism. G. A. Borgese's *Goliath: The March of Fascism* (1937) is written in a brilliant style, but its treatment of the various phases of Fascism is not always adequate. Gaetano Salvemini's *Under the Axe of Fascism* (1936) is a devastating analysis of Italian Fascism. Michael T. Florinsky's *Fascism and National Socialism* (1936) is a comparison of the social and economic policies of the two "isms" in action. Herbert W. Schneider's *Making the Fascist State* (1928) and *The Fascist Government of Italy* (1936) are good scholarly studies. *Making Fascists* (1929) by the same author in collaboration with Shepard B. Clough tells the story of the propaganda techniques of Fascism.

Economic history. For the economic history of Italy under Fascism the student may consult William G. Welk's *Fascist Economic Policy* (1938), Giuseppe Gaddi's *The Workers in Fascist Italy* (1939), and Henry S. Miller's *Price Control in Fascist Italy* (1938). Carl T. Schmidt's *The Plough and the Sword* (1938) is an excellent account of rural Italy under Fascism. The efforts of the Fascists to increase the population are discussed in a chapter of D. V. Glass' *The Struggle for Population* (1936). William S. Halperin's *Italy and the Vatican at War* (1939) is a scholarly study of the relations between the Vatican and the Italian state from 1870 to the death of Pius X. T. E. Moore's *Peter's City* (1930) and B. Williamson's *The Treaty of the Lateran* (1929) tell how the Lateran agreements were concluded. W. Parsons' *The Pope and Italy* (1929) is a brief discussion by a Catholic. Luigi Villari's *The Expansion of Italy* (1930) is sympathetic with the Italian idea of empire. An excellent brief discussion of the Ethiopian question is to be found in E. P. McCallum's *Rivalries in Ethiopia* (1935). For a longer account see E. Work's *Ethiopia: A Pawn in European Diplomacy* (1935). Carl T. Schmidt's *The Corporate State in Action* (1939) and Herbert L. Matthews' *The Fruits of Fascism* (1943) are interesting attempts to evaluate the achievements and weaknesses of Fascism.

CHAPTER 10. *The Succession States of the Habsburg Empire*

General. Oscar Jaszi's *The Dissolution of the Habsburg Monarchy* (1929) is a good account of the collapse of the Dual Monarchy. S. Burian von Rajecz's *Austria in Dissolution* (1925) and E. von Glaise-Horstenau's *The Collapse of the Austro-Hungarian Empire* (1930) are two accounts by officials of the old empire. K. Werkmann von Hohensalzburg's *The Tragedy of Charles of Habsburg* (1924) tells the story of the ill-starred monarch. M. G. Graham's *The New Governments of Central Europe* (1926) has good chapters on the organization of new governments in Austria, Hungary, and Czechoslovakia. G. E. R. Gedye's *Heirs to the Hapsburgs* (1932) presents a picture drawn by a British correspondent. L. Pasvolsky's *Economic Nationalism of the Danubian States* (1929) is an enlightening scholarly study. Arnold J. Zurcher's *The Experiment with Democracy in Central Europe* (1933) is a sound and interesting survey. The background of the collapse of the Dual Monarchy is interestingly treated in K. Tschuppik's *Francis Joseph I: The Downfall of an Empire* (1930) and A. Margutti's *The Emperor Francis Joseph and His Times* (1921).

Austria. David F. Strong's *Austria (October, 1918–March, 1919): Transition from Empire to Republic* (1939) contributes much to a fuller understanding of the problem. Otto Bauer's *The Austrian Revolution* (1925) is a worthwhile account. For a short account of Austria during the years immediately after World War I the student may consult M. H. Macartney's *Five Years of European Chaos* (1923). O. Bauer's *The Austrian Revolution* (1925) is a good book by a Social Democrat. An excellent account of the social changes can be found in C. A. Macartney's *The Social Revolution in Austria* (1926). There is a good survey of Austrian history to 1935 in C. Hamilton's *Modern Austria* (1935). Mary MacDonald's *The Republic of Austria: A Study in the Failure of Democratic Government* (1947) is a good brief account. M. Bullock's *Austria, 1918–1938: A Study in Failure* (new ed., 1941) is a good survey of Austria between the two wars. For Dollfuss there is John D. Gregory's *Dollfuss and His Times* (1935). The last days and the *Anschluss* are treated in Franz Borkenau's *Austria and After* (1938) and Ernst Klein's *Road to Disaster,* translated by D. Weaver (1940). Kurt von Schuschnigg's *Austrian Requiem* (1947) is the confession of an honest, naive chancellor who appeased Hitler.

Hungary. C. A. Macartney's *Hungary* (1934) and *Hungary and Her Successors: The Treaty of Trianon and Its Consequences* (1937) are two good accounts of the modern period. F. Eckhart's *Short History of the Hungarian People* (1931) offers a brief background of Hungarian history. For the Béla Kun period there is Albert Kaas and F. Lazarovics' *Bolshevism in Hungary* (1931), a series of documents. Oscar Jaszi's *Revolution and Counterrevolution in Hungary* (1924) is excellent. Dominic G. Kosáry's *Hungary* (1941) lacks fluency of expression, but is, nevertheless, a book of solid worth. On the Treaty of Trianon and the demand for revision there are *Justice for Hungary* by A. Apponyi and others (1928), E. Ashmead-Bartlett's *The Tragedy of Central Europe* (1923), R. Donald's *The Tragedy of Trianon* (1928), and R. W. Seton-Watson's *Treaty Revision and the Hungarian Frontiers* (1934). On the question of minorities the student may consult R. Gower's *The Hungarian Minorities in the Succession States* (1937). Hungarian agriculture is discussed in *Agricultural Systems of Middle Europe: A Symposium,* edited by O. S. Morgan (1933).

Czechoslovakia. *Czechoslovakia: Twenty Years of Independence,* edited by Robert J. Kerner (1940), is a comprehensive and thoroughly objective study of the various phases of internal and external life. S. Harrison Thomson's *Czechoslovakia in European History* (1941) is a good general discussion. *Slovakia, Then and Now,* edited by R. W. Seton-Watson (1931), is a careful and interesting survey. Thomas Capek's *The Origins of the Czechoslovak State* (1926) is a good account by a Bohemian historian. Robert Birley's *Czechoslovakia* (1939) is a sound and readable short account in the series, Oxford Pamphlets on World Affairs. E. P. Young's *Czechoslovakia: Keystone of Peace and Democracy* (1938) is dispassionate. Kamil Krofta's *Short History of Czechoslovakia* (1935) is a good survey by a Czech historian. L. E. Textor's *Land Reform in Czecho-Slovakia* (1923) is a sound analysis. Paul Selver's *Masaryk* (1940) is an authorized biography of the father of the Czechoslovak Republic. Edward B. Hitchcock's *Beneš: The Man and the Statesman* (1940) is a good biography.

Poland. Raymond L. Buell's *Poland: Key to Europe* (1939) is one of the best books available in English. A good general survey is Oscar Halecki's *History of Poland* (1943), written in scholarly language. R. Dyboski's *Outlines of Polish History* (1931) is a sound and interesting popular survey. *Poland,* edited by Bernadotte E. Schmitt (1945), is a collective work of twenty-three scholars; an objective and comprehensive guide. *Poland's Progress, 1919-1939,* edited by Michael Murray (1944), is another handy guide on Poland. R. Machray's *Poland, 1914-1931* (1933) is a sober narrative of facts. The same author has also written *The Poland of Pilsudski* (1936). Probably the best life of Pilsudski in English is W. F. Reddaway's *Marshal Pilsudski* (1939). There is also a well written biography of Pilsudski by his wife Alexandra (1941) as a tribute to her husband. Roman Gorecki's *Poland and Her Economic Development* (1935) is an enlightening study. For a more detailed account of Polish history the student may consult *The Cam-*

bridge History of Poland, edited by W. F. Reddaway, J. H. Penson, O. Halecki, and R. Dyboski (1940). The question of the minority groups is discussed in A. L. Goodhart's *Poland, the Minority Races* (1922). Two thoroughgoing scholarly studies on the Jewish question are O. I. Janowsky's *The Jews and Minority Rights, 1898–1919* (1933) and the same author's *People at Bay: The Jewish Problem in East-Central Europe* (1938).

CHAPTER 11. *Turkey Faces toward the West*

General. Lord Eversley's *The Turkish Empire: Its Growth and Decay* (1923) is probably the best known brief account to 1922 of the Turks in English. T. W. Arnold's *The Caliphate* (1924) is the best account of the subject in English. William Miller's *The Ottoman Empire and Its Successors* (3rd ed., 1927) has been a standard survey for many years. This is true also of W. S. Davis' *Short History of the Near East (330 A.D. to 1922)* (1937). Ahmet E. Bey's *Turkey in the World War* (1930) is an account by a Turkish writer. Harry N. Howard's *Partition of Turkey: A Diplomatic History, 1913–1923* (1931) is a careful scholarly study. Halidé Edib's *Turkey Faces West: A Turkish View of Recent Changes and Their Origin* (1930) is an account by an ardent Turkish feminist and reform leader. Hans Kohn's *Western Civilization in the Near East* (1936) describes the Europeanization of the Near East and its place in modern civilization. Donald E. Webster's *The Turkey of Atatürk* (1939) is a scholarly and comprehensive study of the transformation of Turkey. Another excellent volume is H. E. Allen's *The Turkish Transformation* (1935). Probably the best brief account of the changes that took place in Turkey is Barbara Ward's *Turkey* (1942).

Ruth F. Woodsmall's *Moslem Women Enter a New World* (1936) is interesting. The most prominent Turkish woman of the period throws much light on the changes that took place in *The Memoirs of Halidé Edib* (1926). *Unveiled: The Autobiography of a Turkish Girl,* by Selma Ekrem (1930), is the story of a girl who grew up in the midst of the changes. A more recent account of the changes can be found in Ernest Jackh's *The Rising Crescent* (1944) which deflates many legends about the Turks. On the man who inaugurated the changes there are a number of interesting books. One of the best though somewhat critical is H. C. Armstrong's *Gray Wolf, Mustafa Kemal* (1933). Other interesting biographies are H. E. Wortham's *Mustapha Kemal of Turkey* (1931) and H. Froembgen's *Kemal Atatürk* (1937). J. T. Shotwell and Francis Deak's *Turkey at the Straits* (1940) is a short history of the struggle for possession of the straits connecting the Black Sea and the Mediterranean.

CHAPTER 12. *Nazi Germany*

Rise of nazism. Robert T. Clark's *The Fall of the German Republic* (1935) sharply criticizes the errors of the Weimar statesmen. Calvin B. Hoover's *Germany Enters the Third Reich* (1933) offers an objective analysis of the forces and events leading to the Nazi Revolution. Louis L. Snyder's *Hitlerism: The Iron Fist in Germany* (1932) is one of the best of the earlier accounts of the development of nazism. The same author has also written a good scholarly analysis of German nationalism under the title, *From Bismarck to Hitler: The Background of Modern German Nationalism* (1935). Ernst Cassirer's *The Myth of the State* (1947) reveals the deep roots of nazism. Rohan D. Butler's *The Roots of National Socialism* (1942) is one of the most thorough books in English on the ideas of German origin that contributed to National Socialist beliefs.

William M. McGovern's *From Luther to Hitler: The History of Fascist Nazi Political Philosophy* (1941) traces the totalitarian tradition into the dimmest recesses of the past. One of the fullest accounts of the rise and victory of nazism is Konrad Heiden's *History of National Socialism* (1934); at times hostile, but often fair and objective. Less openly hostile than Konrad Heiden is H. Powys Greenwood's *The German Revolution* (1934). Peter Viereck's *Metapolitics: From the Romantics to Hitler* (1941) is a valuable book. On the question of race there are two excellent general discussions: Louis L. Snyder's *Race: A History of Modern Ethnic Theories* (1939) and Jacques Barzun's *Race: A Study in Modern Superstition* (1938).

Hitler. Konrad Heiden's *Der Fuehrer: Hitler's Rise to Power* (1944) is the most authoritative account that has appeared in English. Emil Lengyel's *Hitler* (1932) and Ludwig Wagner's *Hitler: Man of Strife* (1942) also tell effectively and convincingly the story of the intrigue that raised Hitler to the dictatorship. Theodore Abel's *Why Hitler Came into Power* (1938) is a judicious and readable account. Frank Owen's *The Three Dictators: Mussolini, Stalin, Hitler* (1936) contains a good brief biography of Hitler. Rudolf Olden's *Hitler* (1936) is a biography by a German journalist. Hitler's own story is, of course, recorded in large part in *Mein Kampf*, of which there are a number of translations. A vivid record of the struggle for power is also to be found in *Dr. Goebbels' Diary* (1938). Adolf Hitler's *My New Order*, edited by Raoul de Sales (1941), is a revealing collection of Hitler's speeches. There is a more complete collection in *The Speeches of Adolf Hitler, April, 1922–August, 1939,* edited by N. H. Baynes (2 vols., 1943). Herman Rauschning's *Hitler Speaks* (1939) is a record of conversations the author heard in Hitler's circle by a former high Nazi official. *The Voice of Destruction* (1940) reproduces conversations with Hitler. Oswald Dutch's *The Errant Diplomat* (1940) is a competent biography of a Nazi diplomatist who aided Hitler in his rise to power. Otto Strasser's *Hitler and I* (1940) contains reminiscences by a man who was Hitler's intimate friend but became his enemy. Fritz Thyssen's *I Paid Hitler* (1941) is the amazing story of the relations of a powerful German industrialist with Hitler and the Nazis. K. G. W. Lüdecke's *I Knew Hitler* (1937) offers recollections by a former friend of Hitler.

The Nazis in power. Franz L. Neumann's *Behemoth: The Structure and Practice of National Socialism* (1942) is one of the most important books on the Third Reich in English. Albert Carr's *Juggernaut: The Path of Dictatorship* (1939) offers an interesting survey. Frederick Schumann's *Hitler and the Nazi Dictatorship* (1936) presents a record of Nazi achievements and a critical analysis. William Ebenstein's *The Nazi State* (1943) is a work of painstaking research, shows real insight into the facts. Albert C. Grzesinski's *Inside Germany* (1939) is an interesting account by a former German trade union leader. Henri Lichtenberger's *The Third Reich: Germany under National Socialism* (1937) is still one of the best books on the subject. H. Rauschning's *The Revolution of Nihilism* (1939) is an exposé of Nazi methods by a former Nazi leader. Stephen Roberts' *The House that Hitler Built* (1938) is a penetrating analysis of the man, the system, and the movement. Robert A. Brady's *The Spirit and Structure of German Fascism* (1937) is a detailed, well documented account. On the Nazi government there are two careful studies: Fritz M. Marx's *Government in the Third Reich* (1936) and Fritz Ermarth's *The New Germany: National Socialist Government in*

Theory and Practice (1936). Wallace R. Deuel's *People under Hitler* (1942) is a richly informative volume by a United States correspondent.

Nazi economics. C. W. Guillebaud's *The Social Policy of Nazi Germany* (1941) is a valuable discussion. The same author had also written *The Economic Recovery of Germany, 1933–1938* (1939), which discusses Nazi economics. Antonin Basch's *The New Economic Warfare* (1941) discusses the methods employed by the Nazis to expand their trade. D. Miller's *You Can't Do Business with Hitler* (1941) is an interesting revelation of Nazi business methods. Vaso Trivanovitch's *Economic Development of Germany under National Socialism* (1937) is a dispassionate survey which neglects agriculture. Otto Nathan and Milton Fried's *The Nazi Economic System: Germany's Mobilization for War* (1944) is an excellent analysis. E. Banse's *Germany Prepares for War* (new ed., 1941) is a solid treatise. Ralph E. Bischoff's *Nazi Conquest through German Culture* (1943) is a valuable addition to the literature on German nationalism. Clifford Kirkpatrick's *Nazi Germany: Its Women and Family Life* (1938) is an able and interesting survey. James T. Shotwell's *What Germany Forgot* (1940) is a group of illuminating essays on the relationship of Germany with the rest of the world between 1919 and 1939.

Jews in Germany. G. Warburg's *Six Years of Hitler: The Jews under the Nazi Regime* (1939) is a grim record of man's inhumanity to man. *Nazi Germany's War against the Jews* (1947) is a collection of documents on anti-Semitism in Nazi Germany collected by Seymour Krieger. There is also a discussion of the German Jews in Oscar I. Janowsky's *People at Bay: The Jewish Problem in East-Central Europe* (1938). The same author in collaboration with M. M. Fagen published a collection of documents under the title, *International Aspects of German Racial Policies* (1937). M. Lowenthal's *The Jews of Germany* (1936) is a good account.

Education and culture. Edward Y. Hartshorne's *The German Universities and National Socialism* (1937) is a record of the changes that took place in higher education. Gregor A. Ziemer's *Education for Death: The Making of the Nazi* (1941) is a unique account of an educator's experiences in Germany. Erika Mann's *School for Barbarians* (1938) is an interesting brief discussion of Nazi educational methods. Isaac L. Kandel's *The Making of Nazis* (1935) is an informative account of Nazi educational and propaganda technique. George F. Kneller's *The Educational Philosophy of National Socialism* (1941) is a careful analysis. Oscar J. Hammen's "German Historians and the Advent of the National Socialist State," *Journal of Modern History*, vol. 13 (1941), pp. 161–188, is an interesting study of a neglected subject. Mario Bendiscioli's *Nazism versus Christianity* (1938) is a careful survey of the position of Roman Catholics and Protestants under nazism. Nathaniel Micklem's *National Socialism and the Roman Catholic Church* (1939) is a fair-minded account of the conflict between the Nazis and the Roman Catholic Church. A. S. Duncan-Jones' *The Struggle for Religious Freedom in Germany* (1938) is a chronological account by a British clergyman. C. S. MacFarland's *The New Church and the New Germany* (1934) is scholarly and fair minded.

CHAPTER 13. *The Balkans*

General. Bernard Newman's *Balkan Background* (1945) is an important book, packed with solid information and well balanced. H. F. Armstrong's *The New Balkans* (1926) is a sane and careful study by the editor of *Foreign Affairs*. Frederic W. L. Kovacs'

The Untamed Balkans (1941) contains summaries of the history of each Balkan state; stresses exploitation of the peasants by the dynasties. L. S. Stavrianos' *Balkan Federation: A History of the Movement toward Balkan Unity in Modern Times* (1944) deals with the problem of Balkan union from the late eighteenth century to the present. R. Machray's *Little Entente* (1929) traces its beginnings and development to 1928. J. O. Crane's *The Little Entente* (1931) is an informative survey from the Czech viewpoint. Oscar I. Janowsky's *Nationalities and National Minorities* (1941) is a scholarly analysis of the problems of the nationalities of eastern Europe. Joseph S. Rouček's *Central-Eastern Europe* (1946) and *The Politics of the Balkans* (1939) are two surveys by a recognized authority.

Rumania. Joseph S. Rouček's *Contemporary Roumania and Her Problems* (1932) is one of the best accounts in English. Another good source of information is N. L. Forter and D. B. Rostovsky's *Roumanian Handbook* (1931). R. W. Seton-Watson's *History of the Roumanians* (1934) is a sympathetic study by a distinguished historian. N. A. Jorga's *History of Rumania* (1925) is a good survey. V. Madgearu's *Roumania's New Economic Policy* (1930) is based on official statements. On the peasant problem there are two careful studies: Ifor L. Evans' *The Agrarian Revolution in Roumania* (1924) and D. Mitrany's *The Land and the Peasant in Rumania* (1930). Hector Bolitho's *Roumania under King Carol* (1939) is a spirited account. Derek Patmore's *Balkan Correspondent* (1941) contains revealing sketches of Rumanian high advisers. Baroness Helena von der Hoven's *King Carol of Romania* (1940) is an "official biography." George Gay's *King Carol of Rumania* (1940) gives a clear account of the domestic and foreign policies of King Carol's government. On the Bessarabian question the student can consult A. Popovici's *The Political Status of Bessarabia* (1925), which supports the claims of Rumania, and C. G. Rakovsky's *Roumania and Bessarabia* (1925), which expounds the Russian claims. J. M. Cabot's *The Racial Conflict in Transylvania* (1926) is a clear statement of the problem.

Yugoslavia. Henry Baerlein's *The Birth of Yugo-Slavia* (2 vols., 1922) is a valuable account of the welding of the Serbians, Montenegrins, and other Southern Slavs into the new kingdom. Robert D. Hogg's *Yugoslavia* (1944) is a good survey of Yugoslav history from World War I to 1941. *Yugoslavia*, edited by John Buchan (1923), is a good account of the early years. For the government and administration of Yugoslavia the student can consult Charles Beard and G. Radin's *The Balkan Pivot: Yugoslavia* (1929). Eric J. Patterson's *Yugoslavia* (1936) and R. G. D. Laffan's *Yugoslavia since 1918* (1929) are good surveys. Grace Ellison's *Yugoslavia: A New Country and Its People* (1935) is a popular description. Louis Adamic's *My Native Land* (1934) records the impressions of a United States citizen upon his return to the land of his birth. Nora Alexander's *Wanderings in Yugoslavia* (1936) and Lovett F. Edwards' *Profane Pilgrimage* (1938) are two interesting travelogues.

Greece. William Miller's *History of the Greek People, 1821–1921* (1922) is an excellent account by a student of the Near East. E. G. Mears' *Greece Today: The Aftermath of the Refugee Impact* (1929) is a survey which gives considerable attention to economic factors. C. B. Eddy's *Greece and the Greek Refugees* (1931) is a sound and well done study. A. J. Toynbee's *The Western Question in Greece and Turkey: A Study* *in the Contact of Civilizations* (new ed., 1923) is a stimulating book. J. Mavrogordato's *Modern Greece* (1931) is an informative survey. C. A. Macartney's *Refugees* (1931) tells the story of the exchange of population between Greece and Bulgaria. There is a more detailed account in S. P. Ladas' *The Exchange of Minorities* (1932). H. A. Gibbons' *Venizelos* (2nd ed., 1923) is a good biography of the Greek leader. P. Hibben's *Constantine I and the Greek People* (1920) is sympathetic to the king. Demetrius Caclamanos' *Greece: A Panorama* (1944) is an account by the editor of the *Athenian Daily,* who possesses a wide knowledge of Greek statesmen and affairs.

Bulgaria. Philip E. Mosely's "The Post-War Historiography of Modern Bulgaria," *Journal of Modern History,* vol. 9 (1937), pp. 348–366, is an excellent critical discussion of works that have appeared on Bulgaria. G. C. Logio's *Bulgaria: Past and Present* (1936) is a judicious survey. C. E. Black's *The Establishment of Constitutional Government in Bulgaria* (1944) is a valuable scholarly study. L. Pasvolsky's *Bulgaria's Economic Position* (1930) is an able analysis. H. Leslie's *Where East Is West: Life in Bulgaria* (1933) endeavors to analyze the Bulgarians. L. Buxton's *The Black Sheep of the Balkans* (1920) is a pointed criticism of the treatment of Bulgaria and Turkey after World War I. On the movement for Macedonian independence the student can consult S. Christowe's *Heroes and Assassins* (1935) or C. Anastasoff's *The Tragic Peninsula* (1938).

Albania. J. Swire's *Albania: The Rise of a Kingdom* (1929) is probably the best account in English. Two good earlier accounts are: C. A. Chekrezi's *Albania, Past and Present* (1919) and *Albania and the Albanians* (1920) by B. Bareilles and others.

CHAPTER 14. *Spain and Portugal*

General. J. B. Trend's *The Civilization of Spain* (1944) is a clear and unified story of a peculiar but fascinating civilization. R. Altamira's *A History of Spanish Civilization* (1930) is a first-rate survey. W. C. Atkinson's *Spain: A Brief History* (1934) is a clear and well planned survey. H. D. Sedgwick's *Spain: A Short History of Its Politics, Literature and Art* (1925) is a good brief survey. Salvador de Madariaga's *Spain* (1943) condenses a lifetime of meditation on Spain's character and destiny by a Spanish republican.

Modern Spain. J. A. Brandt's *Toward the New Spain* (1932) traces the development of republicanism in Spain from 1873 to 1931. G. Young's *The New Spain* (1933) is an interesting portrayal. The early postwar years are also analyzed in F. B. Deakin's *Spain Today* (1924). R. Sencourt's *The Spanish Crown, 1808–1931* (1932) is a survey with rightist sympathies. E. Stewart's *Twenty-nine Years* (1931) is an interesting biography of Alfonso XIII. W. B. Wells' *The Last King* (1934) is a severe indictment. V. Blasco Ibánez' *Alfonso XIII Unmasked: The Military Terror in Spain* (1924) is a bitter attack. Princess Pilar and D. Chapman-Huston's *Every Inch a King* (1931) is a sympathetic account. F. E. Manuel's *The Politics of Modern Spain* (1938) is a well documented interpretation of the period of the republic: sympathy leftist. Gil Robles' *Spain in Chains* (1937) is a sharp attack on the leftist republic. J. McCabe's *Spain in Revolt, 1814–1931* (1931), is a survey that is unsympathetic to the Church. There is a first-rate discussion of the Church in E. A. Peers' *The Church in Spain, 1737–1937* (1938), by a noted British historian. On the constitution of 1931 the student may consult R. M.

Smith's *The Day of the Liber...s in Spain* (1939) or *Manual of Spanish Constitutions, 1808–1931,* compiled by A. R. Verduin (1941).

Dictatorship and civil war. Emmet J. Hughes' *Report from Spain* (1947) is a stern picture of Spain and its dictator by an American Roman Catholic. Sir Samuel Hoare's *Complacent Dictator* (1947) is an unsympathetic account of the Franco regime. Gerald Brenan's *The Spanish Labyrinth* (1943) and T. J. Hamilton's *Appeasement's Child, The Franco Regime in Spain* (1943) offer two careful analyses of the causes that precipitated the civil war. F. Borkenau's *The Spanish Cockpit* (1937) is an interesting study of the social elements in Spain. G. M. Godden's *Conflict in Spain, 1920–1937* (1937) and E. A. Peers' *The Spanish Tragedy, 1930–1936* (1937) are two carefully documented accounts. R. Sender's *Counter-Attack in Spain* (1937), is by one of Loyalist persuasion. E. White's *War in Spain* (1937) and A. L. Strong's *Spain in Arms* (1937) are two readable volumes. For Italian participation the student may consult *The Spanish White Book: The Italian Invasion of Spain. Official Documents and Papers Seized from Italian Units in Action at Guadalajara* (1937).

Portugal. V. de Braganza-Cunha's *Revolutionary Portugal, 1910–1936* (1937) is a well done and readable volume. M. Derrick's *The Portugal of Salazar* (1938) is an analysis of government policies under the dictatorship. F. Cotta's *Economic Planning in Corporative Portugal* (1937) is sympathetic to Salazar's regime. S. West's *The New Corporative State of Portugal* (1937) is the official introduction to Salazar's government. The dictator himself has laid down the principles of his government in *Doctrine and Action* (1939).

CHAPTER 15. *The Small States of Europe*

Belgium. *Belgium,* edited by John Epstein (1944), is an up-to-date brief account in the *British Survey Handbook Series.* For a longer account the student may consult Claude E. A. Andrews' *Belgium* (1932). *Belgium,* edited by Jan-Albert Goris (1945), is an excellent introduction to all aspects of Belgian life and achievement. T. H. Reed's *Government and Politics in Belgium* (1924) is a good analysis. H. L. Shepherd's *The Monetary Experience of Belgium, 1914–1936* (1936) is an illuminating study. King Albert and his house are the subjects of two sympathetic studies by Emil Cammaerts: *Albert of Belgium* (1935) and *The Keystone of Europe: A History of the Belgian Dynasty* (1939). Shepard B. Clough's *The Flemish Movement* (1930) is a first-rate analysis of the subject.

Netherlands. A J Barnouw's *The Making of Modern Holland* (1944) is an excellent survey. Bernhard H. M. Vlekke's *Evolution of the Dutch Nation* (1945) and Hendrik Riemens' *The Netherlands* (1944) are good accounts. *The Netherlands,* edited by B. Landheer (1944), is a series of essays on various phases of Dutch history. *Contribution of Holland to the Sciences,* edited by A. J. Barnouw and B. Landheer (1943), is a much-needed addition to the historical literature on the Netherlands. Philip Paneth's *Queen Wilhelmina* (1943) is an appreciation. L. J. Power's *The Royal Ladies of the Netherlands* (1939) offers an interesting story. Albert Hyma's *The Dutch in the Far East* (1942) is an admirable brief treatment of the subject. E. S. de Klerck's *History of the Netherlands East Indies* (2 vols., 1938) is the work of a competent historian. B. H. M. Vlekke's *Nusantara: A History of the East Indian Archipelago* (1943) is the most up-to-date history of the East Indian archipelago in English. Two other important books are A. Vandenbosch's *The Dutch East Indies* (4th ed., 1943) and J. S. Furnivall's *Netherlands India* (1939). Albert Hyma's "Recent Literature on the Netherlands," *Journal of Modern History,* vol. 16 (1944), pp. 299–305, offers a critical discussion of a number of works on various phases of Dutch history.

Norway. *Sweden, Norway, Denmark and Iceland in the World War* (1930), by E. F. Heckscher and others, tells the story of Scandinavia in World War I. Paul G. Vigness' *The Neutrality of Norway in the World War* (1932) is a sound and informative discussion of the effect of World War I on Norway. For the historical background of Norwegian history the student may consult Knut Gjerset's *History of the Norwegian People* (1927), G. M. Gathorne-Hardy's *Norway* (1925), S. C. Hammer's *Norway* (1928), or Jacob Vidnes' *Norway* (1935). *Norway Today,* edited by Karl Fischer (1933), gives the reader glimpses of the many facets of Norwegian life. O. B. Grimley's *The New Norway* (1939) is an instructive volume. Harold Larson's *Björnstjerne Björnson: A Study in Norwegian Nationalism* (1944) is a careful scholarly study of one of the most picturesque figures of modern Norway. Oscar J. Falnes' *Norway and the Nobel Peace Prize* (1938) is a painstaking and scholarly history.

Denmark and Sweden. J. H. S. Birch's *Denmark in History* (1938) is a useful survey. Josephine Goldmark's *Democracy in Denmark* (1936) is a good brief analysis of the Danish government. Andrew A. Stromberg's *History of Sweden* (1931) is a well proportioned analysis of the political, social, and cultural development of the Swedish people. C. Hallendorf and A. Schück's *History of Sweden* (1929) and R. Svanström and C. F. Palmstierna's *Short History of Sweden* (1934) are two good surveys. Other brief surveys can be found in Carl Grimberg's *Sweden* (1935) and Dudley Heathcote's *Sweden* (1927). Marquis Childs' *Sweden: The Middle Way* (1936) is a widely circulated popular account of the Swedish cooperatives. M. Blomstedt and F. Böök's *Sweden of Today: A Survey of Its Intellectual and Material Culture* (1930) is an informative study. M. Cole and C. Smith's *Democratic Sweden* (1938) is a careful analysis of the structure of Sweden's government. Agnes Rothery's *Sweden: The Land and the People* (1934) is a good work of description. An earlier work of the same nature is Robert M. Medill's *Sweden and Its People* (1924).

Finland. Kay Gilmour's *Finland* (1931), Frank Fox's *Finland Today* (1926), and Agnes Rothery's *Finland: The New Nation* (1936) are good descriptive works. Eugene Van Cleef's *Finland: The Republic Farthest North* (1929) is a good account of the earlier years of the new nation. J. H. Jackson's *Finland* (1938) is one of the best surveys in English. John H. Wuorinen's *Nationalism in Modern Finland* (1931) is a careful scholarly study of the rise of nationalism in Finland. There are a number of good biographies of Sibelius, including Elliott Arnold's *Finlandia: The Story of Sibelius* (1941), Karl Ekman's *Jean Sibelius: His Life and Personality* (1936), and Rosa H. Newmarch's *Jean Sibelius* (1939).

Switzerland. R. C. Brooks' *Government and Politics of Switzerland* (1927) is a good introduction. The same author's *Civic Training in Switzerland* (1930) is an interesting account of many phases of Swiss political life. D. de Rougemont and C. Muret's *The Heart of Europe* (1941) is a readable discussion of Swiss life and character. W. E. Rappard's *The Government of Switzerland* (1936) is an excellent analysis by a distinguished Swiss historian. There is a translation of the Swiss constitution in C. E. Martin and W. H. George's *Representative Modern Constitutions* (1923).

CHAPTER 16. *Revolt of the East against Western Imperialism*

General. George M. Dutcher's *Political Awakening of the East* (1925) shows how the Western political ideas stimulated the awakening. Upton Close's (Josef W. Hall) *Revolt of Asia* (1927) is one of the earliest popular accounts to discuss the revolt. Nathaniel Peffer's *The White Man's Dilemma* (1927) is a first-rate analysis of the conflict between the Orient and Occident. J. A. Spender's *The Changing East* (1926) puts the emphasis principally on Egypt and India. M. M. Hyndman's *Awakening of Asia* (1939) is also an informative account. Philip Jaffe's *New Frontiers in Asia: A Challenge to the West* (1943) is a good analysis of the interrelationship of the Western powers with Asia. Moritz Bonn's *The Crumbling of an Empire: The Disintegration of World Economy* (1938) is an informative volume. Hans Kohn's *Orient and Occident* (1934) points out some interesting differences. The same author's *History of Nationalism in the East* (1929) is an excellent study which analyzes the Near East and India. *Government and Nationalism in Southeast Asia,* by Rupert Emerson and others (1942), is a rich source of information. G. Antonius' *The Arab Awakening* (1939) tells the story of the awakening of political consciousness among the Arabs. A well documented and reliable book on Egypt is M. T. Symons' *Britain and Egypt: The Rise of Egyptian Nationalism* (1925). A treatment of the growth of Egyptian nationalism which deserves careful attention is George Young's *Egypt* (1927), written by a man who had long and varied experiences in Egypt. Three fine studies on various phases of Far Eastern history, issued by the Institute of Pacific Affairs, are: Ian F. G. Milner's *New Zealand's Interests and Policies in the Far East* (1940), Jack Shepherd's *Australia's Interests and Policies in the Far East* (1940), and R. Levy and others' *French and Italian Interests in the Far East* (1940). B. Emeny's *The Strategy of Raw Materials* (1936), Clark Grover's *The Balance Sheets of Imperialism* (1934) and F. V. Field's *Economic Handbook of the Pacific Area* (1934) are rich sources of information on the economic phases of imperialism. P. J. Treat's *The Far East* (1928), H. M. Vinacke's *A History of the Far East in Modern Times* (1933) and G. Nye Steiger's *A History of the Far East* (1929) are excellent general surveys. E. Dennery's *Asia's Teeming Millions* (1931) is an interesting discussion of the population problem. *Northeastern Asia,* collected and edited by Robert J. Kerner (2 vols., 1939), is a selected bibliography of works in Oriental and European languages.

India. Peter Muir's *This Is India* (1943) and F. R. Moraes and Robert Stimson's *Introduction to India* (1943) are designed as introductions, but are not always clear and unbiased. For the period immediately after World War I there is an excellent account in C. H. Van Tyne's *India in Ferment* (1923). Sir F. E. Younghusband's *Dawn in India* (1931) is a good account of the rise of Indian nationalism. Bruce T. McCully's "The Origins of Indian Nationalism According to Native Writers," *Journal of Modern History,* vol. 7 (1935), is a first-rate discussion of the origins of Indian nationalism as indicated in the works of native writers. E. Thompson and G. T. Garratt's *Rise and Fulfillment of British Rule in India* (1934) is a sound fair-minded survey. E. A. Horne's *The Political System of British India* (1922) is a good introduction for the period immediately after World War I. A. Duncan's *India in Crisis* (1931) is a good survey of Indian affairs during the two decades before 1931. J. Beauchamp's *British Imperialism in India* (1934) and Kate L. Mitchell's *India without Fable* (1942) score British imperialism. R. Palme Dutt's *The Problem of India* (1943) is a veritable arsenal of argument for India's freedom. M. Read's *The Indian Peasant Uprooted: A Study of the Human Machine* (1931) paints a black picture based on official documents. L. M. Schiff's *The Present Condition of India* (1939) is good reporting. W. R. Smith's *Nationalism and Reform in India, 1900–1937* (1938) is a first-rate survey. H. G. Rawlinson's *India: A Short Cultural History* (1938) is well organized and authoritative. *Mahatma Gandhi: His Own Story*, edited by his friend, C. F. Andrews (1930), with a continuation in 1931 are autobiographical. M. K. Gandhi's *The Story of My Experiments with Truth* (2 vols., 1927–1929) is a longer autobiography.

China. Thomas E. LaFargue's *China and the World War* (1937) is an account of the main events in China during the period of World War I, based on a careful use of the sources. Paul Monroe's *China: A Nation in Evolution* (1928) is a good survey by an American. Another good survey is Paul Hutchinson's *What and Why in China* (1927). One of the best surveys in English is Kenneth S. Latourette's *The Development of China* (4th rev. ed., 1929). The same author has written a monumental work entitled *The Chinese: Their History and Culture* (2 vols., rev. ed., 1934). A third important work by the same author is his *History of Christian Missions in China* (1929). *China*, edited by Harley F. MacNair (1947), is a comprehensive survey by a notable group of scholars. Owen and Eleanor Lattimore's *The Making of Modern China* (1944) is a skillful primer written by a couple who have a wide knowledge of their subject. H. B. Restarick's *Sun Yat-sen: Liberator of China* (1931) and L. Sharman's *Sun Yat-sen: His Life and Its Meaning* (1934) are two good biographies. There is also a compilation of Sun Yat-sen's writings under the title, *Sun Yat-sen: His Political and Social Ideals*, edited by L. S. Hsu (1933). Arthur N. Holcombe's *The Spirit of the Chinese Revolution* (1930) is an interesting account. H. F. MacNair's *China in Revolution* (1931) is a first-rate presentation. The same author's *China's New Nationalism* (1925) is also a good study. G. W. Keeton's *The Development of Extraterritoriality in China* (2 vols., 1928) is a sound scholarly study. H. A. Van Dorn's *Twenty Years of the Chinese Republic* (1932) is a mine of information. W. W. Willoughby's *Foreign Rights and Interests in China* (2 vols., 1927) is a solid study by a keen student of Chinese affairs. Robert Berkov's *Strong Man of China: The Story of Chiang Kai-shek* (1938) and Sven A. Hedin's *Chiang Kai-shek: Marshal of China* (1940) are two informative biographies. Hollington K. Tong's *Chiang Kai-shek: Soldier and Statesman* (2 vols., 1937) is an authorized biography. *China's Destiny and Chinese Economic Theory* by Chiang Kai-shek, with notes and commentary by Philip Jaffe (1947), and *China's Destiny* by Chiang Kai-shek, with an introduction by Lin Yutang (1947), are two competing editions of a book giving access to the Generalissimo's mind. Paul M. Linebarger's *The China of Chiang Kai-shek* (1941) and William F. Bainbridge's *Rising China* (1943) are two recent surveys that throw light on a complex situation.

Japan. A. J. Brown's *Japan in the World of Today* (1928) and Arthur M. Young's *Imperial Japan, 1926–1938* (1938) are two good surveys which together cover the period between the two wars. Norman E. Herbert's *Japan's Emergence as a Modern State*

(1940) is an excellent introductory volume for the study of Japanese history. There are a number of good discussions of the Japanese government, among them Charles B. Fahs' *Government in Japan* (1940), Naokichi Kitazawa's *The Government of Japan* (1929), Robert K. Reischauer's *Japan: Government and Politics* (1939), and Harold S. Quigley's *Japanese Government and Politics* (1932). Kenneth S. Latourette's *The Development of Japan* (1938) is a readable volume. Other good discussions of Japan between two wars include Hugh Borton's *Japan since 1931* (1940), M. D. Kennedy's *The Changing Fabric of Japan* (1930), Morgan Young's *Imperial Japan, 1926–1938* (1938), Wilfrid Fleisher's *Volcanic Isle* (1941), and William H. Chamberlin's *Modern Japan* (1942). William H. Chamberlin has also written one of the best accounts of the Japanese invasion of China, under the title *Japan in China* (1940). An excellent earlier volume by the same author is entitled *Japan over Asia* (1937). A. E. Hindmarsh's *The Basis of Japanese Foreign Policy* (1936) is an informative volume. O. D. Rasmussen's *The Reconquest of Asia* (1934) discusses Japan's designs to dominate Asia. O. Lattimore's *Manchuria: Cradle of Conflict* (rev. ed., 1935) is a standard treatise. H. F. MacNair's *The Real Conflict between China and Japan* (1938) is a first-rate book. D. C. Holton's *Modern Japan and Shinto Nationalism* (1941) is a revealing study by an outstanding scholar on Shinto. O. Tanin and E. Yohan's *Militarism and Fascism in Japan* (1934) is a well-founded account. W. R. Crocker's *The Japanese Population Problem* (1931) is a technical discussion of the subject.

Economic history. John E. Orchard's *Japan's Economic Position: The Progress of Industrialization* (1930) is a careful appraisal of Japan's position in terms of industrial development. G. C. Allen's *Japanese Industry: Its Recent Development and Present Condition* (1940) is an interesting analysis of the technical efficiency of Japanese industry during the period between the two wars. D. R. Nugent and R. Bell's *The Pacific Area and Its Problems* (1936) includes a discussion of Japan. C. Lowe's *Japan's Economic Offensive in China* (1939) is an interesting discussion of Japanese imperialism. Harold M. Vinacke's "Japanese Imperialism," *Journal of Modern History*, vol. 5 (1935), pp. 366–380, is an excellent critical discussion of the books which appeared up to 1934. G. Stein's *Made in Japan* (1935) is a short discussion of Japanese economic expansion. *The Industrialization of Japan and Manchukuo, 1930–1940*, edited by Elizabeth B. Schumpeter (1940), discusses the problem of population, raw materials, and industry. Oland D. Russel's *The House of Mitsui* (1939) is an enlightening account of one of the powerful houses that controlled so large a part of Japanese economic life. For further titles see bibliography for chapters 19, 20, and 21.

CHAPTER 17. *The Background of World War* II

Decline of security. Robert Dell's *The Rise and Fall of the League of Nations* (1943) records the impressions of one who had ample opportunity to observe the workings of the League. There is an excellent discussion of the League in Lord Robert Cecil's autobiography, *A Great Experiment* (1941). Edward H. Carr's *The Twenty Years' Crisis, 1919–1939* (1940) develops the thesis that the League was an instrument for the preservation of the *status quo*. J. W. Wheeler-Bennett's *The Disarmament Deadlock* (1934) and *The Pipe Dream of Peace* (1935) are two good accounts of the failure of disarmament efforts. *War in the Twentieth Century*, edited by Willard Waller (1940), is an excellent series of essays by United States historians on the background of the war. E. Stanley's *Raw Materials in War and Peace* (1937) discusses the effects of unequal distribution. *The World Economic Crisis,* by Sir Arthur Salzer and others (1932), is a discussion of the great depression. Margaret S. Gordon's *Barriers to World Trade* (1941) discusses the question of tariffs. H. Liepmann's *Tariff Levels and the Economic Unity of Europe* (1938) is a careful study. On the Treaty of Versailles there is Paul Birdsall's excellent *Versailles Twenty Years After* (1941).

International relations. G. M. Gathorne-Hardy's *Short History of International Affairs* (1938) is a good survey. Count Carlo Sforza's *Diplomatic History of Europe Since the Treaty of Versailles* (1928) is a picture as seen by an Italian statesman. A. C. Coolidge's *Ten Years of War and Peace* (1927) and F. Alexander's *From Paris to Locarno* (1928) survey the years immediately after Versailles. W. E. Rappard's *The Quest for Peace* (1940) is an important contribution by a student of international affairs. Frederick L. Schumann's *Europe on the Eve: The Crises of Diplomacy, 1933–1939* (1939) is a spirited analysis. Bernadotte E. Schmitt's *From Versailles to Munich* (1938) is a brief, lucid treatment. Two other revealing accounts are C. Golding's *From Versailles to Danzig* (1941) and M. Foote's *Armistice, 1919–1939* (1940). Sumner Welles' *The Time for Decision* (1944) presents the first-hand knowledge and experience of an American diplomat, Arnold Wolfers' *Britain and France Between Two Wars; Conflicting Strategies of Peace since Versailles* (1940) is a work of careful scholarly research and high literary excellence.

Britain. R. W. Seton-Watson's *Britain and the Dictators* (1938) is a good analysis. Paul Einzig's *Appeasement Before, During and After the War* (1942) is one of the best accounts in English. In this connection the student must not overlook Neville Chamberlain's *In Search of Peace* (1939), a collection of speeches. Winston Churchill's *While England Slept* (1938) and *Step by Step, 1936–1939* (1938) vigorously attack the policy of appeasement. The foreign relations of Britain are competently and comprehensively surveyed in Edward H. Carr's *Great Britain: A Study of Foreign Policy from the Versailles Treaty to the Outbreak of War* (1939) and W. M. Medlicott's *British Foreign Policy since Versailles* (1940). C. Scarfoglio's *England and the Continent* (1939) is critical of British foreign policy. An excellent account of British foreign policy is to be found in G. P. Gooch's *Studies in Diplomacy and Statecraft* (1942). John F. Kennedy's *Why England Slept* (1940) shows how and why Britain slept while Germany whetted her sword.

Nazi Germany. Peter de Mendelssohn's *Design for Aggression: The Inside Story of Hitler's War Plans* (1946) reveals the inside story of Hitler's war plans on the basis of newly discovered documents. Karl Loewenstein's *Hitler's Germany: The Nazi Background to War* (rev. ed., 1944) shows how the Nazi government was a war government from its inception. Gerhard Thomée's *Der Wiederaufstieg des Deutschen Heeres, 1918–1938* (1939) tells the story of the rebuilding of the German army in preparation for war. *Ambassador Dodd's Diary, 1933–1938* (1941), edited by William E. Dodd and Martha Dodd, contains not a few tart and juicy comments on prominent Nazis. Otto D. Fraser's *Germany Between Two Wars: A Study of Propaganda and War-Guilt* (1945) shows how Germany sabotaged the Peace of Versailles and prepared for the next war. Margaret M. Ball's *Post-War German-Austrian Relations, 1918–1936* (1937) is a careful account of the historical development of the *Anschluss* movement. For a more detailed account of the *Anschluss* the student may consult Oswald Dutch's *Thus Died Austria* (1938), G. E. R. Gedye's *Betrayal in Central Europe* (1939), or Martin Fuchs' *Showdown in Vienna: The Death of Austria* (1938). Gerhard Schacher's *Germany Pushes South-East* (1938) tells one phase of the *Drang nach Osten* story.

General accounts of the causes. C. Grove Haines and Ross J. S. Hoffman's *The Origins and Background of the Second World War* (1943) is a work of mature historical scholarship. Dwight E. Lee's *Ten Years: The World on Its Way to War, 1930–1940* (1942) is a first-rate survey of the decade before the war. Walter Millis' *Why Europe Fights* (1940) is a broad interpretation by an American writer of the factors which made for war. *The Deeper Causes of the War and Its Issues,* edited by Sydney E. Hooper (1940), is a discussion of the causes by a group of British writers. Another work by a group of Englishmen is *The Background and Issues of the War,* by G. Murray and others (1940). Frederick T. Birchall's *The Storm Breaks: A Panorama of Europe and the Forces That Have Wrecked Its Peace* (1940) is a picture of Europe on the eve of World War II, by a correspondent. J. Mackintosh's *The Paths That Led to War* (1940) is an analysis by a British author. Kurt London's *Backgrounds of Conflict* (1945) is designed to give the student a grasp of the basic ideas dominant in world politics at the time the war broke out.

Munich. Vera M. Dean's *Europe in Retreat* (1939) provides an interesting background of the Munich crisis. There are also good accounts in Hamilton F. Armstrong's *When There Is No Peace* (1939) and R. W. Seton-Watson's *Munich and the Dictators* (1939). Alexander Werth's *France and Munich: Before and After Surrender* (1939) recounts the rise and decline of appeasement in France. R. W. Seton-Watson's *From Munich to Danzig* (1939), which is a revision of his *Munich and the Dictators,* tells how Czechoslovakia was finally dismembered. Maurice Hindus' *We Shall Live Again* (1939) is an eye-witness story of the German occupation. Another vivid account is V. Beneš and R. Ginsburg's *Ten Million Prisoners* (1940). Felix J. Vondráček's *The Foreign Policy of Czechoslovakia, 1918–1935* (1937) is a scholarly account of the diplomatic background. Kamil Krofta's *Germany and Czechoslovakia* (2 vols., 1937) is a competent scholarly study of the relations between the two countries.

After Munich. G. Hutton's *Survey After Munich* (1939) is a clear, well-organized discussion. Frederick L. Schumann's *Europe on the Eve: The Crises of Diplomacy, 1933–1939* (1939) is a detailed record of the events preceding the outbreak of war. Most of the nations involved in the war have published pertinent documents. The principal publications are: *British War Blue Book* (1939), *The French Yellow Book* (1940), *The German White Book* (1940), *The Polish Official Documents Concerning Polish-German and Polish-Soviet Relations, 1933–1939* (1940), and *The Finnish Blue Book* (1940). Raymond Swing's *How War Came* (1939) is a news analyst's interpretation of the events that led to the outbreak of hostilities. Nevile Henderson's *Failure of a Mission: Berlin, 1937–1939* (1940) contains the observations of the last British ambassador before the war.

CHAPTERS 18, 19, 20. *World War* II

General. *The Background of Our War,* by the Bureau of Public Relations of the United States War Department (1942), written by Colonel Herman Beukema and others, is an excellent brief survey of the early period of the war. J. H. Varwell's *The War up to Date* (1942) is a brief account by a British author. For a brief survey of the entire war the student may consult *The Pocket History of the Second World War* (1945), edited by Henry Steele Commager. Roger W. Shugg and Major H. A. De Weerd's *World War II: A Concise History* (1946) is a sound survey devoted largely to military affairs. A more detailed survey may be found in Francis T. Miller's *History of World War II* (1945). Edgar McInnis' *The War* (5 vols., 1940–1947) coordinates a bewildering amount of material in a sound, readable account. Adrian van Sinderen's *The Story of the Six Years of Global War* (1946) is a chronicle of the war by months through the surrender of Japan. Walter P. Hall's *Iron Out of Calvary: An Interpretative History of the Second World War* (1946) offers an emphatic interpretation of events. Waverly L. Root's *The Secret History of the War* (3 vols., 1945–1946) purports to reveal little-known actions, diplomatic transactions, and personalities; informative but not always sound. For a photographic record of action in all theaters the student may consult *Pictorial History of the Second World War* (2 vols., 1944). A more complete record of the war in pictures may be found in Walter Hutchinson's *Pictorial History of the War* (26 vols., 1939–1945). Rudolf Modley's *History of the War in Maps, in Pictographs, in Words* (rev. ed., 1944) is a useful volume. More inclusive is James F. Horrabin's *Atlas History of the Second Great War* (9 vols., 1941–1945).

Military background. For the military background of the war there is *Makers of Modern Strategy: From Machiavelli to Hitler* (1943), an authoritative group of essays edited by Edward M. Earle. Thomas H. Wintringham's *The Story of Weapon and Tactics: From Troy to Stalingrad* (1943) is a vivid though not always accurate survey. Two books by Harvey A. De Weerd portray the outstanding military leaders, *Great Soldiers of the Two World Wars* (1941) and *Great Soldiers of World War II* (1944). Brief sketches of United States generals may be found in *These Are the Generals* (1943), by a group of writers with a foreword by Walter Millis. Other informative volumes are Don Cook's *Fighting Americans of Today* (1944), Johannes Steel's *Men Behind the War* (1942), and Donald H. Stokes' *Men Behind Victory* (1944). A discussion of the German military leaders may be found in W. E. Hart's *Hitler's Generals* (1944). British leaders are portrayed in the *Leaders of Britain* series, which includes Edward K. Chatterton's *Leaders of the Royal Navy* (1940), Henry Karslake's *Leaders of the Army* (1940), and A. O. Pollard's *Leaders of the Royal Air Force* (1940). Max Werner (pseudonym for Aleksandr Shifrin) published three interesting books: *The Military Strength of the Powers* (1940), *The Battle for the World* (1941), and *The Great Offensive* (1942). Alfred H. Burne's *Strategy in World War II* (1947) is a brief analysis of land operations.

Early campaigns. F. O. Miksche's *Attack: A Study of Blitzkrieg Tactics* (1942) is an outstanding exposition by a military officer of the methods of warfare practised by the Germans. A somewhat briefer survey, though equally well informed, is to be found in W. E. Hart's *Landmarks of Modern Strategy* (1942). Other informative volumes are Major Paul C. Raborg's *Mechanized Might: The Story of Mechanized Warfare* (1944),

Paul W. Thompson's *Modern Battle* (1941), and H. Foertsch's *The Art of Modern Warfare* (1940). *The Axis Grand Strategy: Blueprints for the Total War*, compiled and edited by Ladislas Farago (1942), analyzes German military literature dealing with the aims, methods, and conduct of total war. How a Polish general foresaw the German attack on Poland and warned his countrymen is related in General Wladyslaw Sikorski's *Modern Warfare* (1944). Josef Hanč's *Tornado Across Europe; The Path of Nazi Destruction from Poland to Greece* (1942) is based on a thorough knowledge of the subject matter. Ann Su Cardwell's *Poland and Russia: The Last Quarter Century* (1944) traces Soviet-Polish relations from 1917 to 1943. Cedric Salter's *Flight from Poland* (1940) relates the experiences of a British correspondent. Simon Segal's *The New Order in Poland* (1942) is a picture of Poland under Nazi rule. On the Polish resistance movement there is Jan Karski's *Story of a Secret State* (1943). *The Black Book of Polish Jewry*, edited by Jacob Apenszlak (1944), shows how the Nazis tried to exterminate the Polish Jews. In Irena Oska's *Silent Is the Vistula* (1946) a Polish patriot describes her experiences during the tragic and futile Warsaw uprising of 1944.

John Langdon-Davies' *Invasion in the Snow* (1941) discusses the strategy and tactics of the Finnish war. There is a graphic eyewitness account of the Russian attack in H. B. Elliston's *Finland Fights* (1940). Hudson Strode's *Finland Forever* (1941) is based on the author's experiences during a visit to Finland. *The Finnish Blue Book,* issued by the Finnish Ministry for Foreign Affairs (1940), traces the development of Finnish-Soviet relations and includes the official documents and the peace treaty of 1940. There is an interesting biography of *Field-Marshal Mannerheim,* who designed the Mannerheim Line, by Tancred Borenius (1940). Halvdan Koht's *Norway: Neutral and Invaded* (1941) paints a picture of Norway's futile efforts to preserve her neutrality, by the former foreign minister of Norway. Carl J. Hambro's *I Saw It Happen in Norway* (1940) is a vivid eyewitness account. *Norway and the War: September, 1939–December, 1940* (1941), edited by Monica Curtis, is a collection of documents on the invasion of Norway. J. S. Worm-Müller's *Norway Revolts Against the Nazis* (1942) offers an account of the first nine months of German occupation. A similar book on Denmark is Paul Paulmer's *Denmark in Nazi Chains* (1942). The invasion of Holland is aptly described in Elco N. van Kleffen's *Juggernaut over Holland* (1941). L. de Jong and W. F. Stoppleman's *The Lion Rampant: The Story of Holland's Resistance to the Nazis* (1943) is a revealing book. On the Belgian campaign there is *The Official Account of What Happened, 1939–1940* (1942), by the Belgian Ministry of Foreign Affairs. There is also a brief account by a group of writers entitled *The Belgian Army* (1940), published by the Belgian-American Educational Foundation. On the Belgian resistance to the Nazis there are two graphic books: Lars Moéns' *Under the Iron Heel* (1941) and Jan-Albert Garis' *Belgium in Bondage* (1944). A. D. Divine's *Dunkirk* (1945) tells the story of the withdrawal. Douglas Williams' *Retreat from Dunkirk* (1941) contains ten short narrative sketches by British soldiers who participated in the withdrawal.

The Fall of France. There are many books which try to explain the causes of the French collapse. Among the more notable are André Maurois' *Why France Fell*, translated from the French by Denver Lindley (1941), Alexander Werth's *The Twilight of France, 1933–1940* (1942), and Elie J. Bois' *Truth on the Tragedy of France* (1941). Albert L. Guérard's *The France of Tomorrow* (1942) offers an historian's diagnosis of the causes of the French collapse. Daniel Vilfroy's *War in the West: The Battle of France, May–June, 1940* (1942) is an enlightening brief description of the French débâcle. Pierre Mailland's *France* (1942) is perhaps the best and most compact appraisement of the factors making for the capitulation of June, 1940. *The Grave-Diggers of France* (Gamelin, Daladier, Reynaud, Pétain) by Pertinax (1943) is an indictment of the French leaders. Robert de Saint Jean's *France Speaking* (1941) is a French journalist's record of the French republic's fall. Heinz Pol's *The Suicide of Democracy* (1940) is a journalist's account of what happened and why. Alexander Werth's *The Last Days of Paris* (1940) is an interesting record. Hamilton F. Armstrong's *Chronology of Failure* (1940) is a factual account of the collapse. Stanton B. Leeds' *These Rule France* (1940) contains impressions of a number of French leaders. René de Chambrun's *I Saw France Fall* (1940) is a more or less legendary account by the son-in-law of Pierre Laval. Charles A. Micaud's *The French Right and Nazi Germany, 1933–1939; A Study of Public Opinion* (1943) is a useful and valuable contribution to the literature on the French crisis of 1940. For the Vichy regime Paul Tissier's *The Government of Vichy* (1942) is an excellent introduction. Janet Flanner's *Pétain: The Old Man of France* (1945) offers a brief incisive sketch, clearly and simply written. Henry Torres' *Pierre Laval* (1941) is a highly critical biography of the arch-appeaser of Germany. One phase of the resistance movement is discussed in George R. Millar's *Maquis* (1945). Noteworthy also is Fred L. Hadsel's "Some Sources on the Resistance Movement in France During the Nazi Occupation," *Journal of Modern History*, vol. 18 (1946), pp. 333–340. Raoul Aglion's *The Fighting French* (1943) gives an account of the Free French movement from its birth in June, 1940, to the invasion of North Africa in November, 1942. Philip Barrès' *Charles de Gaulle* (1941) presents a somewhat superficial sketch of the general and his associates. Irving M. Gibson's "The Maginot Line," *Journal of Modern History*, vol. 7 (1945), is an interesting short study of the line which the French believed insured their safety against invasion.

Italy's entrance. Reynolds and Eleanor Packard's *Balcony Empire* (1942) and Richard G. Massock's *Italy from Within* (1943) are the work of veteran correspondents who remained in Italy until Mussolini declared war on the United States. *Twilight of the Gladiators* (1944), by Frank Heller (pseudonym of Gunnar Serner), recapitulates events in Italy from 1939 to 1943. *The Ciano Diaries, 1939–1943*, by Count Ciano, edited by Hugh Gibson (1946), contain invaluable information about Italy and Mussolini.

The Battle of Britain. *The Battle of Britain: An Air Ministry Record of the Great Days from August 8th to October 31st, 1940*, by H. A. Saunders (1941), is the official account of the British Air Ministry. On the Royal Air Force there are two informative books: *The Royal Air Force at War*, edited by William Buchan (4th rev. ed., 1940), and *The Sky's the Limit; A Study of British Air Power*, by James M. Spaight (1940). Hector Bolitho's *Combat Report; The Story of a Fighter Pilot* (1943) is an interesting record. Allan Nevins' *This Is England Today* (1941) is an American's readable account of the reorganization in economic, political, and cultural life caused by wartime conditions. René Kraus' *The Men Around Churchill* (1941) is an interesting discussion of British leaders. The same author has also written a sympathetic biography of the British prime minister entitled *Winston Churchill* (1940). Philip Guedalla's *Mr. Churchill* (1942) is a biography by a brilliant British writer. *The Lives of*

Winston Churchill (1945), by Charles Davenport and Charles J. V. Murphy, is a brief anecdotal biography devoted largely to the war years. Two books by Mr. Churchill himself on this period are *Blood, Sweat and Tears* (1941) and *The Unrelenting Struggle* (1942). *The British Commonwealth at War* (1943), edited by W. Y. Elliott and H. Duncan Hall, is a symposium on the empire's role in the war. W. E. Murphy's *The British War Economy, 1939–1943* (1943) is an informative study.

War at sea. On the war at sea there is a monumental fourteen-volume history in preparation, edited by Samuel E. Morison. Volume 2, entitled *Operations in North African Waters, October 1942–June 1943*, was published early in 1947. Volume 1, which bears the title, *The Battle of the Atlantic, 1939–1943*, is scheduled for publication late in 1947. The Atlantic war is also treated in Volume 2 of *Battle Report*, prepared from official naval sources by Commander Walter Karig and others (1946). Captain W. D. Puleston's *The Influence of Sea Power in World War II* (1947) assesses sea power in the light of new weapons. Another revealing account is Bernard Brodie's *Seapower in the Machine Age* (1943). A. M. Low's *The Submarine at War* (1942) and Herbert S. Zim's *Submarines* (1942) are two general discussions of submarine warfare. Warren Armstrong's *Battle of the Oceans* (1944) is an account of the British merchant marine in World War II. Ivor Halstead's *Heroes of the Atlantic* (1942) offers a description of the activities of British seamen during the early part of the war.

Air war in Europe. *Target Germany* (1943) is the official story of the Eighth Bomber Command's first year over Europe. Allan A. Michie's *The Air Offensive Against Germany* (1943) is a plea to substitute night bombing for the daytime "precision" bombing. *Air Force Diary*, edited by James H. Straubel (1947), is a terse, first-hand account of the vital part played by the United States Air Force. The air fighting during the early part of the war is surveyed in David Garnett's *War in the Air, September, 1939–May, 1941* (1941). Keith Ayling's *Bombers* (1944) and Charles G. Grey's *Bombers* (1942) describe the chief characteristics of the principal types of American and British bombers. Eric Friedheim's *Fighters Up* (1945) tells the story of American fighter pilots in the battle of Europe. Asher Lee's *The German Air Force* (1946) is a critical history of the *Luftwaffe*. Hauptmann Hermann's *The Luftwaffe: Its Rise and Fall* (1943) is an account of the growth and development of the German aircraft industry. Ferdinand O. Miksche's *Paratroops* (1943) discusses the part of air-borne troops in modern warfare. James M. Spaight's *Blockade by Air* (1942) is an account of the campaign against Axis shipping.

Greece and the Balkans. Stephen Lavra's *The Greek Miracle* (1943) is a study of the political and diplomatic background of the invasion of Greece. Stanley Casson's *Greece Against the Axis* (1943) gives a general outline of the campaign in Greece. Betty Wason's *Miracle in Hellas: The Greeks Fight On* (1943) describes conditions in Greece under Axis occupation. *Italy's Aggression Against Greece* (1940) and *The Greek White Book* (1942) contain the official documents published by the Greek government. David Martin's *Ally Betrayed: The Uncensored Story of Tito and Mihailovich* (1946) is an attempt to explain the situation in Yugoslavia. Michael Padev's *Marshal Tito* (1944) is a good biography by a Bulgarian journalist. Ruth Mitchell's *The Serbs Choose War* (1943) relates the author's experiences in Albania and Yugoslavia. Howard M. Coffin's *Malta Story* (1943) is a record of the experiences of an American pilot who joined the RAF. Major General Sir Francis De Guingand's *Operation Victory* (1947) is a defense of General Montgomery's tactics. There is also a good biography of Montgomery by Alan Moorehead (1946).

Invasion of Russia. Among the various books on the Russian army Walter Kerr's *The Russian Army: Its Men, Its Leaders and Its Battles* (1944) is outstanding for its objectivity and readability. Other informative books on the Russian army are: I. Minz' *The Red Army* (1943), D. Fedotoff White's *The Growth of the Red Army* (1944), Sergi N. Kournakoff's *Russia's Fighting Forces* (1942), Michel Berchin and E. Ben-Horin's *The Red Army* (1942), Alexander Poliakov's *Russians Don't Surrender* (1942), and Nikolaus Basseches' *The Unknown Army* (1943). John Scott's *Duel for Europe* (1942) tells how Hitler and Stalin came to blows. David J. Dallin's *Soviet Russia's Foreign Policy* (1943) is a careful and thorough account. Alexander Werth has written two interesting books on the fighting in Russia: *Moscow War Diary* (1942) and *The Year of Stalingrad* (1947). William H. Chamberlin's *The Ukraine: A Submerged Nation* (1944), W. E. D. Allen's *The Ukraine: A History* (1940), and Michael Hrushevsky's *A History of the Ukraine,* edited by O. J. Frederiksen (1941), are good accounts of the Ukraine. On the relations between the Soviet Union and Japan, Maurice Hindus has written a book under the title *Russia and Japan* (1942). Two stirring pictures of the Russian war are to be found in Boris Voyetekhov's *The Last Days of Sevastopol* (1943) and Boris Skomorovsky and E. G. Morris' *The Siege of Leningrad* (1944).

Inside Germany. William L. Shirer's *Berlin Diary, 1934–1941* (1942) is an informal but penetrating record of the way the war affected the German people. Harry W. Flannery's *Assignment to Berlin* (1942) carries on from where the "Berlin Diary" leaves off. Howard K. Smith's *The Last Train from Berlin* (1942) makes clear what it was like to live in Germany. Max Seydewitz's *Civil Life in Wartime Germany* (1945) describes the experiences of the German people and attempts to defend them against the charge of willingly supporting the Nazi rule. Joseph C. Harsh's *Germany at War* (1942) and Wallace Deuel's *People under Hitler* (1942) contain interesting revelations of life in wartime Germany. One of the best books on the Third Reich at war is *This Is the Enemy,* by F. C. Oechsner and other correspondents (1942). *The Von Hassell Diaries, 1938–1944,* by Ulrich von Hassell (1947), is a valuable and informing record kept by a member of the underground. Other good accounts of the German underground in the war years are Allen W. Dulles' *Germany's Underground* (1947); F. von Schlabrendorff's *They Almost Killed Hitler,* edited by Gero V. S. Gaevernitz (1947); and Ruth Andreas-Friedrich's *Berlin Underground* (1947). *Pens Under the Swastika,* by William W. Schuetz (1946), is an analysis of recent German writing.

United States and the war. An excellent series of essays on various phases of United States foreign policy are to be found in *The United States and Its Place in World Affairs, 1918–1943* (1943), edited by Allan Nevins and Louis M. Hacker. Denys Smith's *America and the Axis War* (1942) is a smoothly running account of United States foreign policy during the two decades before the war. One of the best records of United States policy before Pearl Harbor is Forrest Davis and Ernest K. Lindley's *How War Came* (1942). A brief official summary may be found in *Peace and War: United States Foreign Policy, 1931–1941* (1943), issued by the United States Department of State. Joseph Alsop and Robert Kintner's *American White Paper* (1940) offers a summary of the United States policies before 1940. George Morgenstern's *Pearl Harbor: The Story of the Secret*

War (1947) presents a bitter and highly biased view; charges that Roosevelt plotted to get the United States into the war. Walter Millis' *This Is Pearl! The United States and Japan—1941* (1947) contains much new material on the period before Pearl Harbor. S. K. Hornbeck's *The United States and the Far East: Certain Fundamentals of Policy* (1942) is an authoritative discussion. W. C. Johnstone's *The United States and Japan's New Order* (1941) is an exposition of Japanese aims. An excellent summary may be found in *The United States at War* (1947) prepared under the auspices of the Committee of Records of War Administration. Francis L. Bacon's *The War and America* (1942) is a good brief summary. Francis T. Miller's *Eisenhower, Man and Soldier* (1944) contains much human interest material but no real evaluation of the soldier. The same author has also written a brief popular biography under the title *General Douglas MacArthur, Fighter for Freedom* (1942). *Yank—The GI Story of the War* by the staff of *Yank,* the army weekly (1947), is a grim record in photography and prose. John R. Deane's *The Strange Alliance: The Story of Our Efforts at Wartime Cooperation with Russia* (1947) is a semiofficial account of our not always successful efforts to cooperate with the Soviet Union. De Witt Mackenzie's *Men Without Arms* (1946) tells the story of the United States Medical Department in World War II. On lend-lease there is *Lend-Lease: Weapon for Victory* by Edward R. Stettinius, Jr. (1944), a volume packed with information.

Japan. Hugh Byas' *The Japanese Enemy: His Power and His Vulnerability* (1942) is an excellent brief survey. Carl Crow's *Japan's Dream of World Empire* (1942) outlines the Japanese plan of conquest on the basis of the Tanaka Memorial. John Goette's *Japan Fights for Asia* (1943) gives the inside story of Japan's attempt to dominate the Far East. Kate L. Mitchell's *Japan's Industrial Strength* (1942) gives an outline of Japan's industrial development during the preceding decade. *Japan: Its Resources and Industries,* by Clayton D. Carus and Charles L. McNichols (1944), is an excellent compilation of factual information. How Japan coiled to strike is related in Otto D. Tolischus' *Tokyo Record* (1943). The same author's *Through Japanese Eyes* (1945) lets the Japanese speak for themselves regarding their aims, plans, and ideas. Willard Price's *Japan Rides the Tiger* (1942) presents a close-up view of the Japanese and their country. John F. Embree's *The Japanese Nation* (1945) is primarily a study of the Japanese social organization. Hillis Lory's *Japan's Military Masters* (1943) discusses the organization, psychology, and training of the Japanese army. Edwin A. Falk's *From Perry to Pearl Harbor* (1943) outlines the story of the rise of the Japanese navy. Mark J. Gayn's *The Fight for the Pacific* (1941) is a competent survey. Joseph C. Grew's *Ten Years in Japan* (1944) is the interesting diary of the United States Ambassador to Japan. Hubertus J. van Mook's *The Netherlands Indies and Japan: Battle on Paper, 1940–1941* (1944) is a concrete account of Japanese machinations, by the Netherlands Minister for the Colonies.

China. Lawrence K. Rosinger's *China's Wartime Politics, 1937–1944* (1944) is a brief but clear and well-balanced narrative. Edgar Snow's *The Battle of Asia* (1941) is a terse, authentic report of the Japanese terror in China. David N. Rowe's *China Among the Powers* (1945) presents an interesting summary of China's position. Harold S. Quigley's *The Far Eastern War, 1937–1941* (1942) is a comprehensive account of the struggle up to the time the United States became involved. Carl Crow's *China Takes*

Her Place (1944) is an informally written survey of Chinese politics from 1911 to 1944. Mme. Mei-ling Chiang's *China Shall Rise Again* (1941) is a discussion of China's plight by the wife of Chiang Kai-shek.

Pacific area. *Government and Nationalism in South-East Asia,* by Rupert Emerson and others (1942), is an excellent brief survey of the problems arising from the war in the Far East. Roger Levy's *French Interests and Policies in the Far East* (1942) is a good survey of the French Far Eastern relations. Lenox A. Mills' *British Rule in Eastern Asia* (1942) is a valuable study of British colonial administration in Malaya and Hong Kong. Bruno Lasker's *Peoples of South East Asia* (1943) contains much interesting information. John L. Christian's *Modern Burma* (1942) surveys the political and economic development of modern Burma. Sir Richard Winstedt's *Britain and Malaya* (1945) is a good brief discussion. Robert T. Oliver's *Korea: Forgotten Nation* (1944), Andrew J. Grajdanzev's *Modern Korea* (1944), and M. Frederick Nelson's *Korea and the Old Order in Eastern Asia* (1945) are good accounts.

The United States in the Pacific. Frank O. Hough's *The Island War: The United States Marine Corps in the Pacific* (1947) tells the story of the fighting from one grim island to another. *Semper Fidelis: The U. S. Marines in the Pacific, 1942–1945,* by U.S.M.C. combat correspondents, edited by Captain Patrick O'Sheel and Staff Sergeant Gene Cook (1947), is a vivid account by men who were eyewitnesses of the fighting. Keith Ayling's *Semper Fidelis: The U. S. Marines in Action* (1943) presents a description of Marine exploits in Guadalcanal, Wake, and Midway. *Betio Beachhead: The U. S. Marines' Own Story of the Battle for Tarawa,* by Marine combat correspondents with a summary by Lieutenant-General A. A. Vandegrift (1945), tells the story of the first seaborne assault on a defended atoll. Laura Thompson's *Guam and Its People* (1947) is interesting descriptive writing. D. N. Leff's *Uncle Sam's Pacific Islets* (1940) is a brief survey. Richard Tregaskis' *Guadalcanal Diary* (1943) is an unforgettable record of the Pacific war.

Philippines. Joseph R. Hayden's *The Philippines: A Study in National Development* (1942) is a solid, detailed, and factual presentation of the political situation in 1941. *I Saw the Fall of the Philippines* by Carlos P. Romulo (1942) is an excellent piece of reporting on the fighting. William L. White's *They Were Expendable* (1942) is a chronicle of Bataan. Juanita Redmond's *I Served on Bataan* (1943) is a simple story of the nurses' heroic part in the Manila war. *The Dyess Story,* by William E. Dyess (1944), is an eyewitness account of the death march from Bataan and a narrative of experiences in Japanese prison camps. John Hersey's *Men on Bataan* (1943) is one of the first full accounts of the fighting on Bataan. *Bataan: The Judgment Seat,* by Allison Ind (1944), is one of the most complete records of the Philippine campaign. *General Wainwright's Story,* by Jonathan M. Wainwright (1946), is, as the subtitle states, "the account of four years of humiliating defeat, surrender, and captivity."

Sea and air war in the Pacific. Three books by Gilbert Cant cover American naval action in the Pacific: *The War at Sea* (1942), *America's Navy in World War II* (1943), and *The Great Pacific Victory: From the Solomons to Tokyo* (1946). Fletcher Pratt's *The Navy's War* (1944) is a factual account of the major engagements of the United States Navy to 1944. Another interesting book is Oliver Jensen's *Carrier War* (1945). C. Vann Woodward's *The Battle for Leyte Gulf* (1947) is an authentic account of the greatest naval battle of the war. *Admiral Halsey's Story*, by William F. Halsey and J. Bryan, 3rd (1947), covers the period from Guadalcanal to Tokyo. Richard G. Hubler's *Flying Leathernecks* (1944) surveys the Pacific war during the years 1941 to 1944 from the viewpoint of the Marine Air Corps. *The Brereton Diaries*, by Lewis H. Brereton (1946), is the personal record of General Brereton in the air war of the Pacific, the Middle East, and Europe. *Mission Beyond Darkness*, by Joseph Bryan and Philip Reed (1945), is a thrilling account of an attack on a Japanese fleet by an air group from the U.S.S. *Lexington*. *The Flying Guns: Cockpit Record of a Naval Pilot from Pearl Harbor to Midway*, by Clarence E. Dickinson and Boyden Sparkes (1942), re-lates the experiences of an American naval pilot during the first six months of the Pacific war.

The end of the war in Europe. Richard Tregaskis' *Invasion Diary* (1944) is an unadorned account by a soldier who participated in the invasion of Italy. *Invasion*, by Charles C. Wertenbaker (1944), tells the story of D-Day and after in words and pictures. Colonel Robert S. Allen's *Lucky Forward* (1947) relates the story of General Patton's Third United States Army. *Dark December: The Full Account of the Battle of the Bulge*, by Robert E. Merriam (1947), gives a factual account of the famous battle. Leo Heaps' *Escape from Arnheim* (1945) records the personal experiences of a para-trooper. H. R. Trevor-Roper's *The Last Days of Hitler* (1947) develops the idea that Adolf shot himself while Eva gulped poison.

The end of the war in Japan. Ted W. Lawson's *Thirty Seconds Over Tokio* (1943) is the personal narrative of one of the pilots who bombed Tokyo on the Doolittle raid. *The Lost War*, by Masuo Kato (1946), is a Japanese reporter's story of the events lead-ing to the defeat of Japan. John W. Campbell's *The Atomic Story* (1947) is a primer of the atom. Two other simply written introductory volumes are Selig Hecht's *Explain-ing the Atom* (1947) and O. R. Frisch's *Meet the Atoms* (1947). *One World or None: A Report to the Public on the Full Meaning of the Atomic Bomb*, edited by Dexter Masters and Katherine Way (1946), is the story of the atom bomb versus the human race.

Miscellaneous. Raphael Lemkin's *Axis Rule in Occupied Europe* (1944) is a scholarly study of the laws of occupation in occupied Europe. *The Hidden Weapon: A Story of Economic Warfare*, by David L. Gordon and Royden Dangerfield (1947), presents a panoramic view of economic warfare in World War II. David Rousset's *The Other Kingdom* (1947) is a revealing book on concentration camps. Kurt D. Singer's *Spies and Traitors of World War II* (1945) contains stories of spies of all types the world over. Richard W. Rowan's *Terror in Our Time* (1941) gives a detailed account of the sen-sational methods developed by secret agents in the underground combat of modern times. *Total Espionage* by Curt Riess (1941) tells how the enormous espionage organ-ization of the Third Reich was started. Interesting books on the Fifth Column and espionage in the United States include *Sabotage: The Secret War Against America*, by Michael Sayres and Albert E. Kahn (1942), Alan Hynd's *Passport to Treason* (1943) and *Betrayal from the East* (1943), and Roy Carlson's (pseudonym of Arthur Derou-nian) *Under Cover* (1943). *Medicine and the War*, edited by William H. Taliaferro (1944), is an enlightening study.

CHAPTER 21. *The Preliminary Peace Conferences*

Peace principles. During World War II a considerable number of books laid down principles for a lasting peace. Among the best of these are two books by Herbert C. Hoover and Hugh Gibson, *The Problems of Lasting Peace* (1942) and *The Basis of Lasting Peace* (1945). Two other important books of this kind are *An Intelligent American's Guide to the Peace*, edited by Sumner Welles (1945), and Robert M. Mac-Iver's *Toward an Abiding Peace* (1943). W. L. Neumann's *Making the Peace, 1941–1945; the Diplomacy of the Wartime Conferences* (1950) offers a brief survey of the negotiations toward peace during the war. Invaluable for the Yalta Conference is Edward R. Stettinius' *Roosevelt and the Russians; the Yalta Conference*, edited by Walter Johnson (1947). *The Four Cornerstones of Peace*, by Vera M. Dean (1946), discusses the Dumbarton Oaks, Yalta, Mexico City, San Francisco, and Potsdam conferences.

CHAPTER 22. *The Struggle for Peace*

Conferences. Important sources for the various conferences and meetings are the memoirs of participants. Outstanding among these are James F. Byrnes' *Speaking Frankly* (1947) and Admiral W. D. Leahy's *I Was There* (1950). Much information is to be found in R. E. Sherwood's *Roosevelt and Hopkins: an Intimate History* (1948) based on the Hopkins documents. The complete text of the Italian treaty is to be found in *Current History*, n.s. vol. 12 (April, 1947), pp. 376–425. For an enlightening discussion see R. Albrecht-Carrie's "Peace with Italy; an Appraisal," *Political Science Quarterly*, vol. 62 (December, 1947), pp. 481–503. David J. Dallin's *The Big Three: The United States, Britain, and Russia* (1945) is a well-organized summary of the interests and policies of the Big Three. The early treaties are ably discussed in *Peace Settlements of World War II*, edited by T. V. Kalijarvi (1948).

CHAPTER 23. *The United Nations*

General. S. S. Fenichall and P. Andrews' *United Nations: Blueprint for Peace* (1952) is a concise study of the history, purpose, and activity of the UN. A searching brief diagnosis of the UN is to be found in H. V. Evatt's *The United Nations* (1948). Another valuable study of the work of the UN is *The Task of the Nations* (1949) by the same author. E. P. Chase's *United Nations in Action* (1951) is a valuable and comprehensive study. H. Kelsen's *Law of the United Nations* (1951) is a somewhat technical discussion of the fundamental problems of the UN. Norman D. Bentwich's *From Geneva to San Francisco* (1946) tells how the new international organization was set up. J. Mac Laurin's *United Nations and Power Politics* (1952) is a skillful polemic against the failure of the powers to live up to their obligations. Useful among the older books are Louis Dolivet's *The United Nations; A Handbook on the New World Organization* (1946), E. M. Patterson's *Making the United Nations Work* (1946), W. G. Carr's *One World in the Making* (1946), and A. K. Boyd's *The United Nations Organization Handbook* (1946). *The Political Role of the General Assembly*, by H. F. Haviland (1951), surveys the work of the General Assembly. L. M. Goodrich and Edward Hambro's *Charter of the United Nations: Commentary and Document* (1947) is an informative volume. S. M. Schwebel's *The Secretary-General of the United Nations* (1952) is an enlightening discussion of the powers and activities of the Secretary-General.

Korea. A. W. Green's *Epic of Korea* (1951) offers a brief introduction to the Korean conflict. G. M. McCune and A. L. Grey's *Korea Today* (1950) is an objective, penetrating, and scholarly study of both North and South Korea. *Why War Came in Korea* (1950) by R. T. Oliver favors South Korea. Marguerite Higgins' *War in Korea* (1951) is the vivid and readable report of a woman combat correspondent. E. G. Meade's *American Military Government in Korea* (1951) is a worthwhile analysis of the American Occupation Administration in Korea during 1945 and 1946. R. B. Rigg's *Red China's Fighting Hordes* (1951) is a realistic account of the Chinese Communist Army by a U.S. Army officer. *The General and the President,* by R. H. Rovere and A. M. Schlesinger (1952), is a controversial book on the MacArthur controversy.

CHAPTER 24. *Western Europe after World War II*

European recovery. William H. Chamberlin's *The European Cockpit* (1947) records the author's impressions of Europe in the summer and early fall of 1946. Karl Loewenstein's *Political Reconstruction* (1947) offers proposals for the political reconstruction. There is a treasure trove of material in *Voices of History, 1945–1946,* edited by Nathan Ausubel (1946), which includes state papers and important speeches by leading figures. *UNRRA,* edited by G. Woodbridge (3 vols., 1951), is the official history of the United Nations Relief and Rehabilitation Administration. *The European Recovery Program,* edited by Seymour Harris (1949), is a group of twenty-four essays concerned almost exclusively with the role of the United States in the Marshall Plan. *Economic Survey of Europe,* issued annually by the Department of Economic Affairs of the United Nations, is invaluable for an understanding of the economic conditions. See also *Documents on European Recovery and Defense—March, 1947–April, 1949* (1949). *The State of Europe,* by Howard K. Smith (1949), is an interesting survey. G. D. H. Cole's *World in Transition; a Guide to the Shifting Political and Economic Forces of Our Time* (1949) is an important book by an English economist. F. A. Hermens' *Europe between Democracy and Anarchy* (1951) offers a survey of representative government in Europe. *The West at Bay,* by Barbara Ward (1948), is a provocative book on the postwar problems of Western Europe. J. S. Schapiro's *World in Crisis* (1951) sketches the pattern of political development in the twentieth century. *Defense of Western Europe,* edited by W. M. Daniels (1951), is a reprint of articles bearing on various problems affecting the U.S.A. and Europe. Drew Middleton's *The Defense of Western Europe* (1952) is a discussion of NATO by the chief German correspondent of the *New York Times.* There is an enlightening short discussion of the North Atlantic Pact by Marina Salvin in *International Conciliaton,* no. 451 (May, 1949), pp. 373–456.

CHAPTER 25. *Postwar Germany*

General. Philip E. Mosely's "The Occupation of Germany," *Foreign Affairs,* vol. 28 (1950), pp. 580–604, offers "new light on how the zones were drawn." J. K. Pollock and J. H. Meisel's *Germany under Occupation: Illustrative Materials and Documents* (1947) is a useful collection of documents and papers. *American Military Government in Germany,* by Harold Zink (1947), is a well-written account. *The Dilemma of Postwar*

Germany, compiled by Julia E. Johnsen (1948), is a series of articles selected to represent various points of view. Carl Landauer, "The Allies and Germany's Future," *Journal of Modern History,* vol. 18 (1946), pp. 251–260, is an excellent discussion of pertinent books. Donald F. Lach, "What They Would Do about Germany," *ibid.,* vol. 17 (1945), pp. 227–243, offers an interesting critical discussion of the literature on the subject of Germany's future. Saul K. Padover's *Experiment in Germany: the Story of an American Intelligence Officer* (1946) presents a colorful description of some phases of German life. Invaluable for a knowledge of postwar Germany is Lucius D. Clay's *Decision in Germany* (1950), a lengthy chronicle by a top official. *German Faces* by Ann Stringer and H. Ries (1950) is a report on interviews with postwar Germans.

Nuremberg trials.   V. H. Bernstein's *Final Judgment: the Story of Nuremberg* (1947) is a well-written account of the trial by a newspaper correspondent. *Nuremberg Diary,* by G. M. Gilbert (1947), contains notes from the diary of an observer. *Moral Aspects of Nuremberg,* by J. P. Kenny (1949), is an evaluation of the philosophic basis underlying the trials. *The Nurnberg Case,* as presented by Robert H. Jackson, Chief Counsel for the United States (1947), is an important contribution to the literature on the trial. *The Case of Rudolph Hess,* edited by J. R. Rees (1948), contains a series of discussions by eight British and U.S. psychiatrists. C. P. Calvocoressi's *Nuremberg, the Facts, the Law and the Consequences* (1948) is a brief survey by a British lawyer.

German problems.   C. J. Friedrich, "Rebuilding the German Constitution," *American Political Science Review,* vol. 43 (1949), pp. 461–482, 704–720, presents a detailed analysis of the new West German constitution. *The Struggle for Democracy in Germany,* edited by G. A. Almond (1949), is a well-balanced discussion by a group of able historians. *This Is Germany,* edited by A. Settel (1950), is a report on economic and social aspects of contemporary Germany. Karl Brandt's *Germany: Key to Peace in Europe* (1950) is an informing series of lectures. *Struggle for Germany,* by Drew Middleton (1949), is an honest, balanced report about Germany and her problems since 1945. Russell Hill's volume under the same title (1947) is useful but somewhat older. An important little volume is F. Meinecke's *The German Catastrophe,* translated by Sidney B. Fay (1949), containing the reflections and recollections of a distinguished German historian. *Postwar Reconstruction in Western Germany,* edited by A. Schönke (1948), contains much interesting information. Wilhelm Röpke's *The Solution of the German Problem,* translated by E. W. Dickes (1947), offers a solution of the German problem by a German. G. Stolper's *German Realities* (1948) contains a wealth of information but is not always trustworthy. W. L. White's *Report on the Germans* (1947) presents the postwar observations of a U.S. journalist. Three useful books on East Germany are J. P. Nettl's *The Eastern Zone and Soviet Policy in Germany* (1951), G. Schaffer's *The Russian Zone of Germany* (1948), and F. Lowenthal's *News from Soviet Germany* (1950). E. H. Buschbeck's *Austria* (1950) is a survey of postwar conditions.

CHAPTER 26. *Socialist Britain*

General.   *The Cautious Revolution,* by E. S. Watkins (1951), is a well-informed, well-tempered study of the Labor government. Francis Williams' *Socialist Britain* (1949) surveys the policies and personalities of the Labor Party. *A History of the Labour Party from 1914*, by G. D. H. Cole (1948), is a study by a distinguished British historian. C. L. Mowat, "Some Recent Books on the British Labor Movement," *Journal of Modern History*, vol. 17 (1945), pp. 356–366, is a useful discussion of pertinent literature. *Britain Today*, by C. F. O. Clarke (1951), offers a review of current trends in Britain. J. Jewkes' *Ordeal by Planning* (1949) discusses British economic policy and suggests a remedy. *Assignment to Austerity: an American Family in Britain*, by Herbert and Nancie Matthews (1950), offers an interesting commentary on life in Socialist Britain. Herbert Morrison's *The Peaceful Revolution* (1949) is a series of addresses by one of the leaders of the Labor Party. *The English Middle Classes*, by Roy Lewis and Angus Maude (1950), is an interesting discussion of the middle classes under socialism. Robert A. Brady's *Crisis in Britain* (1950) is a keen analysis of the first four years of Labor government. *British Trade Unions*, by N. Barou (1947), offers an analysis of the trade-union movement. E. Estorick's *Stafford Cripps: Master Statesman* (1949) is a sympathetic biography. Keith Hutchinson's *The Rise and Fall of British Capitalism* (1950) is a stimulating survey of British economic history in the twentieth century. E. Lipson's *Growth of English Society* (1951) is a brief survey embodying the fruits of forty years of study.

CHAPTER 27. *The French Dilemma*

General. *France between the Republics*, by Dorothy M. Pickles (1946), gives an informed, though often simplified, account of the French background of 1940–1945. Fred S. Hadsell, "Some Sources on the Resistance Movement in France during the Nazi Occupation," *Journal of Modern History*, vol. 18 (1946), pp. 333–340, is an excellent bibliographical discussion. *Our Vichy Gamble*, by W. L. Langer (1947), is a notable scholarly account of the relationship of the United States and France, June, 1940–December, 1942. Henry W. Ehrmann, "Recent Writings on the French Labor Movement," *Journal of Modern History*, vol. 22 (1950), pp. 151–158, offers a critical discussion of recent books. *French Labor from the Popular Front to the Liberation*, by the same author (1947), is invaluable for an understanding of the period. A good brief survey of postwar France is to be found in Saul K. Padover's *France: Setting or Rising Star* (Foreign Policy Association Headline Series, 1950). Gordon Wright's *The Reshaping of French Democracy* (1948), with an introduction by Paul Birdsall, is the best book on the early years of the Fourth Republic. *Modern France: Problems of the Third and Fourth Republics*, edited by E. M. Earle (1951), is an indispensable analysis of the problems of contemporary France by twenty-eight contributors. O. R. Taylor's *The Fourth Republic of France* (1951) offers a good discussion of the new French constitution and of the French political parties. *Communist Party in Action*, by A. Rossi, translated by W. Kendall (1950), is an analytical study of communism in France. L. G. Cowan's *France and the Saar, 1680–1948* (1951) discusses the claims of France and Germany to the Saar Basin. The *Monetary Problem of France*, by P. Dieterlen and C. Rist (1949), reviews briefly the monetary situation inherited by liberated France in 1944. D. C. MacKay's *The United States and France* (1951) offers an illuminating account of the sociological, economic, and political aspects of French life.

CHAPTER 28. *Franco's Spain and Republican Italy*

Spain. *Report from Spain,* by Emmet J. Hughes (1947), is a readable, penetrating analysis of Franco's regime. Sir Samuel Hoare's *Complacent Dictator* (1947) relates his experiences as wartime ambassador to Franco. C. J. H. Hayes' *Wartime Mission in Spain, 1942–1945* (1945) is an interesting record of the experiences of a U.S. ambassador to Spain. *The Face of Spain,* by Gerald Brenan (1951), is a report on Spain after its years under Franco. In 1947 John E. Hughes published his useful *Report from Spain.* An account of Franco's relations with the belligerent states from 1939 to 1945 can be found in Herbert Feis' *The Spanish Story: Franco and the Nations at War* (1948). *The Masquerade in Spain,* by Charles Foltz (1948), is a competent and revealing reporter's report on conditions in Spain. C. J. H. Hayes' *United States and Spain* (1952) argues for the admission of Spain as a member in good standing of the European family. Sheila M. O'Callaghan's *Cinderella of Europe* (1951) is a defense of the Franco regime. In *The Last Optimist,* by J. Alvarez del Vayo (1950), a Spanish democrat tells his story. The documents portraying the relations between Franco and the Axis were published by the U.S. Department of State in 1946.

Italy. *The New Italy,* by Muriel Grindrod (1949), presents the factual highlights of Italy's transition from war to peace. Count Carlo Sforza's *Contemporary Italy* (1944) is a survey of two centuries of Italian life. *The King and the Allies,* translated by Sylvia Sprigge (1951), consists of extracts from the diary of Benedetto Croce for the period from July, 1943–June, 1944; valuable for its account of the political struggle to get rid of Victor Emmanuel III, but to save the monarchy. Among the better articles on post-war Italy are the following: Colston E. Warne, "Italy: Pauper or Convalescent?" *Current History,* November, 1948; F. A. Hermens, "Troubled Italian Politics," *ibid.,* May, 1951; M. Einaudi, "The Constitution of the Italian Republic," *American Political Science Review,* August, 1948; L. Matthews, "Italian Colonies: Politics and Realities," *American Perspective,* October, 1948.

CHAPTER 29. *The Passing of the Old Colonial Imperialism*

Asia. So many works have been published on Asia since World War II that only a few can be listed. *Ferment in the Far East: an Historical Interpretation,* by Mary A. Nourse (1949), is an interesting study which puts the emphasis largely on China. Paul H. Clyde's *The Far East: a History of the Impact of the West on Eastern Asia* (1948) is a lucid, interesting, and authoritative study. A lively and revealing survey of the Far East is to be found in Paul E. Eckel's *The Far East since 1500* (1947). Robert Payne's *The Revolt of Asia* (1947) analyzes the men and forces behind the upheaval in the East. *The Future of Freedom in the Orient,* by Ralph Coniston (1947), develops the idea that after the collapse of Western imperialism the Asiatic natives will be ruled by oppressors from their midst. *New Forces in Asia,* by Bruno Lasker (1950), offers a brief survey of the Asiatic rising. Osgood Hardy and Glenn S. Dumke's *A History of the Pacific Area in Modern Times* (1949) is a good general survey. *The Voice* of *Asia*, by J. A. Michener (1952), is a report on what the author saw and heard in Asia. *Southeast Asia in the World Today*, edited by Phillips Talbot (1950), is a volume of lectures and summaries of discussions. K. P. Landon's *Southeast Asia: Crossroad of Religions* (1949) is a lucid discussion of the religious factor in southeast Asia. *Agrarian Unrest in Southeast Asia*, by E. H. Jacoby (1949), provides a well-organized picture. *New Cycle in Asia*, with notes by H. R. Isaacs (1947), is a selection of documents on major developments in the Far East, 1943–1947. Valuable for the political life is *Postwar Governments in the Far East*, edited by Taylor Cole and J. H. Hallowell (1947). *Modern Far Eastern International Relations*, by Harley MacNair and Donald Lach (1950), is a good survey. H. J. Van Mook's *The Stakes of Democracy in Southeastern Asia* (1950) is an enlightening account by a Dutch historian. R. Payne's *Red Storm over Asia* (1951) is a timely analysis of the march of communism in Asia. *The State of Asia*, by L. K. Rosinger and Associates (1951), treats the major developments in the Asiatic states since World War II in a somewhat uneven way. *Collision of East and West*, by H. Maurer (1951), is a series of essays on the collision of cultures.

Individual countries. *British Rule in Burma, 1824–1942*, by G. E. Harvey (1946), is a brief survey by a member of the British Civil Service. Roy McKelvie's *The War in Burma* (1948) is an informing volume. *The Birth of Indonesia*, by David Wehl (1948), is a well-informed, objective presentation of the facts.

India. T. W. Wallbank's *India in the New Era* (1951) is an able account of the origin and development of the Indian Union and Pakistan. *The Awakening of India*, by W. A. Stanton (1950), is a popular account by a Baptist missionary. A. R. Desai's *Social Background of Indian Nationalism* (1950) is an important contribution to the history of Indian nationalism. *Independence and After*, by Jawaharlal Nehru (1950), is a series of speeches by the first prime minister of India. Richard Symonds' *The Making of Pakistan* (1950) is a valuable study. *India, Pakistan, and the West*, by P. Speer (1949), discusses the relationship of cultures.

British Empire. *The British Empire*, edited by Hector Bolitho (1948), is a collection of essays on all parts of the empire. M. Mansergh's *Commonwealth and the Nations* (1949) discusses the attitudes of the dominions. The effects of Britain's imperial preference on trade is ably discussed in F. V. Meyer's *Britain's Colonies in World Trade* (1949). Paul McGuire's *Experiment in World Order* (1948) is an interesting popular account of the development of the Commonwealth. *Changing Empire: Churchill to Nehru*, by Eric Estorick (1950), presents a fascinating survey of the process of recent change.

Middle East. George E. Kirk's *Short History of the Middle East* (1949) surveys the period from the seventh century to the present. *Blood, Oil, and Sand*, by Ray Brock (1952), presents a picture of the Near East as seen by a correspondent. *The Near East and the Great Powers*, edited by R. N. Frye (1951), is a group of papers by specialists in Near Eastern history. R. Bullard's *Britain and the Middle East from the Earliest Times to 1950* (1951) is a brief, readable survey. *The Struggle for Palestine*, by J. C. Hurewitz (1951), is scholarly and objective. J. J. Smertenko's *Palestine in Revolt* (1947) sketches a brief background of events. *Palestine and the United Nations: Prelude to Solution* (1947) presents an account of the discussions and negotiations in the UN. J. W.

Parke's *History of Palestine* (1949) is an objective survey from the second century to
1948. J. Dunner's *Republic of Israel: Its History and Its Promise* (1950) examines the
new republic and its problems.

CHAPTER 30. *The Soviet Union since World War II*

General. For a critical discussion of books on the Soviet Union published during the
years immediately after World War II, see F. C. Barghoorn, "Some Recent Books on
Russia and the Soviet Union," *Journal of Modern History*, vol. 21 (1949), pp. 115–120.
W. Kirchner's *Russia: an Outline History*, 2nd edition (1950), is a helpful little volume.
Stalin and Co., by Walter Duranty (1949), tells about the men in the Kremlin who run
the Soviet Union. For careful analysis of the governmental system of the Soviet Union,
see *Soviet Politics—The Dilemma of Power; a Study of the Role of Ideas in Social
Change*, by Barrington Moore, Jr. (1950). W. B. Smith's *My Three Years in Moscow*
(1950) presents a detailed and interesting appraisal of the Soviet scene. N. C. Leites'
Operational Code of the Politburo (1951) is a brief, careful study. *Soviet Attitudes toward Authority*, by Margaret Mead (1951), is a revealing book on the nature of Soviet
leadership. Anatole G. Mazour's *Russia, Past and Present* (1951) offers a sound historical background arranged under topical headings. *The Soviet Union: Background, Ideology, Reality*, edited by W. Gurian (1951), is a useful collection of essays by distinguished scholars. *The People of Great Russia: A Psychological Study*, by Geoffrey Gorer
and John Rickman (1950), discusses the relationship of the Russian people to their
rulers. Boris Shub's *The Choice* (1950) is based on the thesis that mass dissatisfaction
is the Achilles' heel of the Kremlin. *This Is Russia—Uncensored*, by Edmund Stevens
(1950), paints a picture of the Soviet Union in the postwar period which is neither all
black nor all white. The same author's *Russia Is No Riddle* (1945) throws light on the
Soviet Union at war and the conclusion of hostilities. Julian Towster's *Political Power
in the USSR, 1917–1947* (1947) is a solid account of the dynamics of political power in
the Soviet Union. *Cracks in the Kremlin Wall*, by Edward Crankshaw (1951), points
out what he regards as the weaknesses of the Soviet regime.

Economic History. *Russia's Soviet Economy*, by Harry Schwartz (1951), is an informed
account of the economic development of the Soviet Union as regards its strength and
weaknesses. *The Economy of the USSR during World War II*, by N. K. Voznesensky
(1948), is a brief account of the Soviet industrial war effort by a Soviet writer. Alexander
Baykov's *The Development of the Soviet Economic System* (1947) is the product of a
lifetime of study. *Management in Russian Industry and Agriculture*, by G. Brenstock,
S. M. Schwarz, and A. Yugow (1947), shows how the Russian economic system works.
For an excellent brief discussion of the Fourth Five-Year Plan see A. Bergson's "The
Fourth Five-Year Plan, *Political Science Quarterly*, vol. 62 (1947) pp. 195–227.

Miscellaneous. *Stalin: an Appraisal of the Man and His Influence*, by Leon Trotsky,
translated from the Russian by Charles Malamuth (1946), is an uncompleted biography
left by Trotsky when he was assassinated. Isaac Deutscher's *Stalin* (1949) is a readable
authoritative biography. *The Accused; a Personal Story of Imprisonment in Russia*, by
A. Weissberg, translated from the German by E. Fitzgerald (1950), is a rare, exciting
record. Michael Koriakov's *I'll Never Go Back* (1948) is an interesting account of a

Russian expatriate. *Tell the West*, by Jerzy Gliksman (1948), is an unforgettable picture of life in a Soviet labor camp. Elinor Lipper's *11 Years in Soviet Labor Camps*
(1951) is a personal human story. *The Jews in the Soviet Union*, by S. M. Schwarz
(1951), is a work of solid scholarship which contributes much to our knowledge of one
phase of life in the USSR. R. N. Carew Hunt's *The Theory and Practice of Communism* (1951) is a compact account and analysis of Marxism. In *The Rise of Modern
Communism* (1952) Massimo Salvadori surveys the rise of communism in a hundred
pages. Martin Ebon's *World Communism Today* (1948) is a good survey of communism
in every country in which it is a political factor.

International relations. Harold H. Fisher's *America and Russia in the World Community* (1947) is an honest, objective account. *Russia and Britain*, by Edward Crankshaw
(1951), covers the period from Muscovy to the present time. E. H. Carr's *The Soviet
Impact on the Western World* (1947) briefly sketches the outlines of the interaction.
American-Russian Relations in the Far East, by Pauline Tompkins (1950), is a work
of careful research. Thomas A. Bailey's *America Faces Russia: Russian-American Relations from Early Times to Our Day* (1950) is lucid and well-documented. *Russia and
the West in Iran, 1918–1948: A Study in Big-Power Rivalry*, by George Lenczowski
(1949), is the fullest and most informative study on the subject.

Soviet culture. *Soviet Literature of Today*, by George Reavey (1948), presents a series
of separate studies covering Soviet literature during World War II. For a more general
survey, see Marc Slonim's *The Epic of Russian Literature* (1950). *The Country of the
Blind: the Soviet System of Mind Control*, by George S. Counts and Nucia Lodge (1949),
shows how the Communist Party controls every phase of culture. Zhdanov's *Essays on
Literature, Philosophy, and Music* were published in a translation in 1950 as a small
volume. The first essay was published earlier in *Political Affairs*, December, 1946. For
an excellent discussion of the Soviet techniques of "persuasion," see Alex Inkeles' *Public
Opinion in Soviet Russia* (1950).

CHAPTER 31. *The New Soviet Imperialism*

General. *The East European Revolution*, by Hugh Seton-Watson (1951), combines
broad scholarship with firsthand observation. Leland Stowe's *Conquest by Terror*
(1952) is a readable report on the sovietization of eastern Europe. *Russia Astride the
Balkans*, by R. Bishop and E. S. Crayfield (1950), presents a behind-the-scenes report.
John Gunther's *Behind the Iron Curtain* (1949) is a journalistic travelogue covering
the Soviet satellites and other countries. *East of the Iron Curtain*, by Vernon Bartlett
(1950), is the record of a visit to the iron curtain countries; information now somewhat dated. J. C. Harsch's *The Curtain Isn't Iron* (1950) is a correspondent's quick
view of what is going on in eastern Europe. *Soviet Expansion and the West*, by Anthony
Bouscaren (1949), and *Soviet Imperialism: Russia's Drive toward World Domination*
(1950), by E. D. Carman, present brief discussions of Soviet imperialism. Samuel L.
Sharp's *New Constitutions in the Soviet Sphere* (1950) is a useful little book. *The Soviet
Slave Empire*, by Albert K. Herling (1951), offers a report on slave labor in the USSR
and satellite nations. Joseph S. Roucek's *Balkan Politics: International Relations in No
Man's Land* (1948) reviews the history of the Balkan countries and brings it up to date.

...land and Hungary. The story of the struggle to maintain an independent Poland is told in Stanislaw Mikolajeczk's *The Rape of Poland* (1948) and Arthur B. Lane's *I Saw Poland Betrayed* (1949). Z. F. Stypulkowski's *Invitation to Moscow* (1951) is a macabre book on the Polish underground toward the end of World War II. *Poland's Place in History*, by S. Wojciechowski (1947), is a collection of well-done essays presenting the Polish point of view. Ferenc Nagy's *The Struggle Behind the Iron Curtain* (1948) is an account of the revolutionary changes by a man who was prime minister of Hungary from January, 1946, to June, 1947. John Flournoy's *Hungary: the Unwilling Satellite* (1947) contains much interesting information. For an excellent short survey, see H. F. A. Schoenfeld, "Soviet Imperialism in Hungary," *Foreign Affairs*, April, 1948. *I Was Stalin's Prisoner*, by Robert A. Vogeler (1952), relates the story of the author's imprisonment in communist Hungary.

Yugoslavia. *Yugoslavia*, edited by Robert J. Kerner (1949), a symposium by fifteen historians, is a good introduction for the general reader. H. F. Armstrong's *Tito and Goliath* (1951) is an informative, detailed account of the background of Yugoslavia's break with the Kremlin. *Tito's Communism*, by J. Korbel (1951), is a worthwhile study by a former Czech ambassador to Yugoslavia. Leigh White's *Balkan Caesar: Tito versus Stalin* (1951) is both anti-Stalin and anti-Tito. *Whirlwind: an Account of Marshal Tito's Rise to Power*, by Stephen Clissold (1950), records the momentous events which culminated in the communist revolution in Yugoslavia. G. Bilaikin's *Tito* (1950) is an outstanding example of hero worship. *Tito's Republic*, by M. Radulovic (1948), is an informative study. R. H. Markham's *Tito's Imperial Communism* (1947) sharply condemns the Yugoslav regime; a lively account. *Titoism and the Cominform*, by Adam B. Ulam (1952), shows how the rift developed. *The War We Lost: Yugoslavia's Tragedy and the Failure of the West*, by Constantin Fotitch (1948), is a lively but partisan account by a former ambassador to Washington. M. S. Handler, "Communist Dogma and Jugoslav Practice," *Foreign Affairs*, April, 1952, is a good brief discussion.

Other countries. *Rumania under the Soviet Yoke*, by R. H. Markham (1949), is a report by an American correspondent. H. L. Roberts' *Rumania: Political Problems of an Agrarian State* (1951) presents a scholarly discussion of the depressed state of the Rumanian peasantry. For a good brief account of the sovietization of Rumania, see B. Brannen, "The Soviet Conquest of Rumania," *Foreign Affairs*, April, 1952. *East Wind over Prague*, by J. Stransky (1951), vividly depicts the cold-blooded methods employed by the communists to subjugate Czechoslovakia. *Czechoslovakia Enslaved: the Story of the Communist Coup d'Etat*, by Hubert Ripka (1951), is an account by a former cabinet minister of Czechoslovakia. For a revealing short discussion, see W. S. Vucinich, "Czechoslovakia: Three Communist Years," *Current History*, n.s. vol. 20 (May, 1951), pp. 266–271. See also "Bulgaria: A Balkan Soviet," *ibid.*, pp. 129–135, by the same author.

Russia in Asia. D. J. Dallin's *Soviet Russia and the Far East* (1949) is based on a thorough acquaintance with the sources. *The New Soviet Empire*, by the same author (1951), is a thoroughgoing and reliable discussion of the Russian system as such rather than of the empire. *Red Banners over Asia*, by O. O. Trullinger (1951), is based on the thesis that the communist conquest of Asia is the object of a skillful Kremlin-directed conspiracy.

China. *Chinese Communism and the Rise of Mao,* by B. I. Schwartz (1951), presents the background of communism's success in China. *The Government and Politics of China,* by Ch'ien Tuan-sheng (1950), presents a readable account of the rise and decline of Nationalist China. Jack Belden's *China Shakes the World* (1949) depicts graphically the progressive moral degeneration of the Nationalist ruling group. *Peking Diary: A Year of Revolution,* by Derk Bodde (1950), presents the diary of an eye-witness. The man who more than any other was instrumental in bringing about the revolution is described in R. Payne's *Mao Tse-tung: Ruler of Red China* (1950). *China's Economic Stabilization and Reconstruction,* by D. K. Lieu (1948), is a balanced study of China's postwar economic problem. *Chinese-Russian Relations,* by M. N. Pavlovsky (1949), presents the history of the relations between the two countries over a period of three hundred years. P. Chang's *Agriculture and Industrialization* (1949) discusses the relationship between the two in China. *Russia's Race for Asia,* by George Creel (1949), attempts to show that Chinese communism is controlled from the Kremlin. R. S. Elegant's *China's Red Masters* (1951) contains a collection of biographical sketches about the leading figures in the Chinese communist government. Freda Utley's *The China Story* (1951) is a documented account of the errors of U.S. policy in China. *Mao's China: Party Reform Documents, 1942–44,* translated with an introduction by Boyd Compton (1950), is invaluable for an understanding of Chinese communism.

CHAPTER 32. *Recent Developments in the Soviet Sphere*
Soviet Russia. M. Ebon's *Malenkov* (1956) is a revealing study. E. Crankshaw's *Russia without Stalin* (1956) is a good report on post-Stalin Russia. W. W. Kulski's *The Soviet Regime* (1954) shows how communism is used to mold Russian life. I. Deutscher's *Russia in Transition* (1957) contains some incisive essays on the post-Stalin period. D. J. Dallin's *The Changing World of Soviet Russia* (1956) presents a vivid analysis of the same period. M. Djilas' *New Class* (1957) is an unsparing analysis of the communist system. *Soviet Russia Today,* edited by J. L. Stipp (1957), is an excellent collection of excerpts from histories and documents.

Poland, Hungary, and Yugoslavia. *National Communism and Popular Revolt in Eastern Europe,* edited by P. E. Zinner (1957), is a collection of documents on the events in Poland and Hungary. F. Fetjo's *Behind the Rape of Hungary,* translated by N. Guterman (1957), is a readable survey of the 1956 uprising. *Hungarian Revolution,* edited by M. J. Lasky (1957), presents the story in excerpts from documents. *National Communism* by D. A. Tomasic (1957) gives a detailed account of the development of Titoism. C. P. McVickers' *Titoism* (1957) is a well-informed study. *Tito's Yugoslavia* by E. L. Pridonoff (1956) is very critical of Tito's regime. M. Dedijer's *Tito* (1953) and F. H. McLean's *The Heretic* (1957) are useful biographies.

CHAPTER 33. *Recent Developments in Central and Western Europe*
France, Germany, and Britain. H. Luethy's *France Against Herself* (1955) is an excel-

lent study of the unending crises. D. Schoenbrun's *As France Goes* (1957) and P. M. Williams' *Politics in Post-War France* (1954) are useful accounts. Other valuable studies are H. W. Ehrmann's *Organized Business in France* (1957), L. A. Dale's *Marxism and French Labor* (1957), and V. R. Lorwin's *The French Labor Movement* (1955). *The Culture of France in Our Time*, edited by J. Park (1954), is an illuminating symposium. E. Alexander's *Adenauer and the New Germany* (1957) is an invaluable analysis of the German situation. H. C. Wallich's *Mainsprings of the German Revival* (1955) is a clear and lively exposition. Other useful accounts are L. Erhard's *Germany's Comeback in the World Market* (1955) and A. Grosser's *The Colossus Again*, translated by R. Rees (1955). *Soviet Economic Policy in Postwar Germany*, edited by R. Slusser (1954), is a collection of papers by Soviet officials. *German Democracy at Work*, edited by J. K. Pollock (1955), is a valuable symposium. G. D. H. Cole's *Post-War Condition of Britain* (1957) contains much vital information. *British Economy*, edited by G. D. N. Worswick and P. H. Ady (1953), is a comprehensive study of the economic problems of postwar Britain. A. Campbell-Johnson's *Eden* (1955) and D. Bardens' *Portrait of a Statesman* (1957) are two useful biographies. C. Furth's *Life since 1900* (1956) is a lively short account of the social changes in Britain.

Italy and Spain. M. Carlyle's *Modern Italy* (1957) contains a good brief survey of present-day Italy and her problems. M. Grindrod's *Rebuilding of Italy* (1955) is compact, well documented and clearly written. R. E. Dickinson's *Population Problem of Southern Italy* (1956) is a well-informed treatise. J. La Palombara's *Italian Labor Movement* (1956) is a careful study. H. L. Matthews' *Yoke and the Arrows* (1957) is a good factual report on present-day Spain. J. Cleugh's *Spain in the Modern World* (1953) and A. Castro's *Structure of Spanish History* (1954) are important contributions to our understanding of present-day Spain.

Colonialism. K. M. Stahl's *British and Soviet Colonial System* (1952) offers a brief analysis of the two systems. E. J. Hammer's *The Struggle for Indochina* (1954) is a rich mine of information. T. W. Wallbank's *Contemporary Africa; Continent in Transition* (Anvil Books, 1956) is a good short survey. B. Davidson's *African Awakening* (1955) is an illuminating study of Belgian and Portuguese Africa. T. L. Hodgkin's *Nationalism in Colonial Africa* (1957) is a valuable short analysis. B. Timothy's *Kwame Nkrumah* (1957) and K. Nkrumah's *Ghana* (1957) are timely and revealing. V. Bartlett's *Struggle for Africa* (1954) is readable, but no longer up-to-date. E. Stevens' *North African Powder Keg* (1955) blames France for the troubles in North Africa. P. Johnson's *Suez War* (1957) presents the British side of the story. W. F. Longgood's *Suez Story* (1957) is a useful history of the canal. H. B. Ellis' *Israel and the Middle East* (1957) is a painstaking defense of Israeli policies.

NATO and the UN M. Salvadori's *NATO* (Anvil Books, 1957) is a good short discussion with much attention to the background. J. D. Warne's *N.A.T.O. and Its Prospects* (1954) is a useful study. J. H. Joyce's *Revolution on East River* (1957) is a highly partisan view of the UN. *The United Nations and Economic and Social Cooperation* by R. E. Asher and others (1957) is a penetrating study.

Supplementary Bibliography

Europe. The journalist Blair Bolles has written a lively survey of present-day Europe under the title *The Big Change in Europe* (1958) based on a sojourn of five years in Europe. *The Temper of Western Europe* by Crane Brinton (1953) is a lively, informed report on the problems and prospects of Western Europe. *The Diplomats, 1919–1930*, edited by G. A. Craig and F. Gilbert (1953), is an impressive discussion of diplomats and diplomacy. A. J. Zurcher's *The Struggle to Unite Europe, 1940–1958* (1958) is a concise factual account of the development of European unity. Another important volume on the same subject is *European Integration*, edited by C. G. Haines (1957), a series of papers read at a conference in Bologna, Italy, in 1956. F. C. Northrup's *The Taming of the Nations* (1952) is a scholarly examination of the spiritual and philosophic foundations on which modern civilizations base their values. *The World and the West* by A. J. Toynbee (1953) is a series of interesting lectures on the impact of Western civilization on the rest of the world.

Germany and Great Britain. Important among the recent books on West Germany is James B. Conant's *Germany and Freedom* (1958), a personal appraisal of Germany's attitude toward Nazism, unification, rearmament, and democracy by our former Ambassador to the Federal Republic. K. S. Pinson's *Modern Germany; Its History and Civilization* (1955) is well-written, well organized, and thoroughly documented. *German Nationalism: the Tragedy of a People* by Louis L. Snyder (1952) ably discusses the influence of extreme nationalism on German history; lucid and well-written. H. W. Gatzke's *Stresemann and the Rearmament of Germany* (1954) is a timely and carefully argued revision of the Stresemann portrait. A. Bullock's *Hitler* (1953) is comprehensive, well written, and authoritative. *German History: Some New German Views* (1954), edited by Hans Kohn (1954), presents the views of nine liberal German historians; interesting and revealing. On the recent economic history of West Germany there are two books by the Minister of Economics of the Bonn Government, L. Erhard: *Germany's Comeback in the World Market* (1955) and *Prosperity Through Competition* (1958). Three useful books on East Germany are: J. P. Nettl, *The Eastern Zone and Soviet Policy in Germany, 1945–1950* (1951); *Soviet Economic Policy in Postwar Germany* (1953), edited by Robert Slusser; and G. Schaffer, *The Russian Zone of Germany* (1948). N. J. G. Pounds' *The Ruhr* (1953) discusses the meaning of the

Ruhr to the German and European economy. J. W. Wheeler-Bennett's *Nemesis of Power: the German Army in Politics, 1918–1945* (1954) is well-written, carefully documented, and well-organized. On Great Britain there is a recent interesting survey by R. B. Eckles and R. W. Hale titled *Britain, Her Peoples, and the Commonwealth* (1953). W. S. Reid's *Economic History of Great Britain* (1954) is a useful survey from prehistoric times to 1951. *British Economy, 1945–1950*, edited by G. D. N. Worswick and P. H. Ady (1953), is a comprehensive study by a group of Oxford professors, with special emphasis on the economic problems facing postwar Britain. *Problems of Nationalized Industry* (1952), edited by W. A. Robson, is a discussion of British economic problems by fourteen outstanding historians. F. Owen's *Tempestuous Journey: Lloyd George, His Life and Times* (1955) is a comprehensive study of the Welshman's public and private life based on careful research. *Churchill by His Contemporaries* (1954), edited by C. Eade, is a discussion of various aspects of Churchill by forty writers. C. L. Broad's *Winston Churchill* (1952) is a revised edition of a comprehensive story of Sir Winston; sound and readable. *Winston Churchill* by E. Hughes (1955) takes a look at the contradictions and inconsistencies of Churchill. *The Foreign Policy of the British Labour Government, 1945–1951* (1953) is a careful analysis of Britain's foreign policy under the Labor Government.

France, Italy, and Spain. *French Politics: the First Years of the Fourth Republic* by Dorothy M. Pickles (1953) is a competent study of the formative years of the Fourth Republic. R. Matthews' *Death of the Fourth Republic* (1954) surveys postwar politics in France; journalistic, but lucid and readable. *French Institutions* by S. K. Padover and others (1953) is a brief interesting discussion of the basic values of French civilization. P. Farmer's *Vichy, Political Dilemma* (1955) is a sane and judicious study of one of the most controversial phases of French history. *Christian Democracy in Italy and France* by M. Einaudi and F. Goguel-Nyegaard (1952) offers an authentic account of the Italian Christian Democratic Party and the French Mouvement Republicain Populaire. H. S. Hughes' *The United States and Italy* (1953) is a concise and informative study of the political development of modern Italy, with special emphasis on the contacts between Italy and the United States. Among the new books on the Spanish Civil War D. T. Cattell's *Communism and the Spanish Civil War* (1956) and his *Soviet Diplomacy and the Spanish Civil War* (1957) throw much light on Russia's part in the Spanish struggle. F. J. Taylor's *The United States and the Spanish Civil War* (1957) is based on firsthand study of the sources.

Russia. *Inside Russia Today* by John Gunther (1958) is an eminently successful attempt to bring Russian history down to the level of the average reader; interesting and revealing. J. N. Hazard's *Soviet System of Government* (1957) is an able and authoritative discussion. *How Russia Is Ruled* by M. Fainsod (1953) is a comprehensive and well-written analysis of the Soviet system. A third important book on the Soviet system is *How the Soviet System Works* by R. A. Bauer and others (1956) which assesses the social and psychological strength and weakness of this system. B. D. Wolfe's *Six Keys to the Soviet System* (1956) discusses the basic source of stress in the Soviet Union. The same author's *Khrushchev and Stalin's Ghost* (1956) contains Khrushchev's speech denouncing Stalin and a discussion of the speech. F. C. Barghoorn's *Soviet Russian Nationalism* (1956) is a thoughtful analysis of the content and significance of

Soviet nationalism. *Soviet Economic Growth,* edited by A. Bergson (1953), presents the results of the research of a dozen American scholars on the subject of Soviet economy. Other important books on Soviet economic history include M. G. Clarke's *The Economics of Soviet Steel* (1956); W. Galenson's *Labor Productivity in Soviet and American Industry* (1955); and N. Spulber's *The Economics of Communist Europe* (1957). A. Yarmolinsky's *Road to Revolution* (1956) traces the development of radicalism during the century before the Revolution of 1917. H. Seton-Watson's *The Decline of Imperial Russia, 1855–1914* (1952) is a scholarly account of an important period; lucid and well-organized. Another publication of outstanding importance is the fourth volume of E. H. Carr's *History of Soviet Russia* (1954) covering the years 1923–1924. For a graphic narrative of the Revolution of 1917 there is N. N. Sukhanov's *Russian Revolution* (1955) which offers personal reminiscences of the revolution written down shortly after the events took place. Another important work is Volume One of G. F. Kennan's *Soviet-American Relations, 1917–1920.* This volume, titled *Russia Leaves the War* (1957), is based on many hitherto unused primary sources; lucid, comprehensive, and absorbing. L. B. Schapiro's *Origin of the Communist Autocracy* (1955) is the first systematic study of the opposition to communist rule. *The Mind of Russia,* edited by Hans Kohn (1955), offers a group of well-chosen selections from little-known Russian works. I. Deutscher's *Prophet Armed: Trotsky, 1879–1921* (1954) is the first of two volumes on the life of Trotsky; well-informed, well-organized, and well-written. *The Soviet Secret Police,* edited by S. Wolin and R. M. Slusser (1957), is the most detailed history of the Soviet secret police published thus far; interesting and informative. B. Moore's *Terror and Progress USSR* (1954) discusses the tensions operating in the Soviet Union; stimulating and revealing. *The Permanent Purge* by Z. K. Brzezinski (1956) presents an invaluable picture and a philosophy of purges as a permanent part of the Soviet system. *Russia: a History and an Interpretation* by M. T. Florinsky (2 vols., 1953) is a comprehensive and enlightening guide to the development of the Russian people and state. A. Dallin's *German Rule in Russia, 1941–1945* (1957) is a skillful and detailed study of the Nazi occupation policies.

Communism. E. H. Carr's *Studies in Revolution* (1950) is a pleasing but sketchy primer of the march of revolutionary theory in the last century and a half. *Marxism, Past and Present* by R. N. C. Hunt (1954) presents a revaluation of the central theories of Marxism. F. Borkenau's *European Communism* (1953) is a book about the political policies of the leaders of the communist world movement by a former communist. *German Marxism and Russian Communism* by J. V. Plamenatz (1954) is a controversial discussion of Marx and German Marxism. *Communism in Western Europe* by M. Einaudi and others (1951) discusses the political, economic, and constitutional problems of postwar France and Italy, with special emphasis on French and Italian communism.

The East and Middle East. *South-East Asia* by B. Harrison (1954) is an introductory survey by a professor at the University of Malaya; sound and readable. Herbert Feis' *China Tangle* (1953) is a thorough review of American policy in China from 1941 to 1946; a valuable study. *Prospects for Communist China* by W. W. Rostow and others (1954) is an interesting analysis of the communist regime by a team of American scholars. Ellen J. Hammer's *Struggle for Indochina* (1954) is a well-written account of the struggle between France and the communist Viet Minh, with an anti-colonial bias. *The Middle East: Problem Area in World Politics* by H. L. Hoskins (1954) is a sound, detailed study of present-day problems in the Near East. R. N. Frye's *Iran* (1953) is an excellent concise survey in the Berkshire Series. *The History of Israel* by M. Noth, translated from the German by S. Godman (1958), is a scholarly, interpretative volume. J. Marlowe's *History of Modern Egypt and Anglo-Egyptian Relations, 1800–1953* (1954) is one of the few books available on the subject.

Miscellaneous.   Sir Winston Churchill's *Second World War* (6 vols., 1948–1953) is a monumental work which in some parts is superficial and ponderous and in others brilliant and interesting; an important contribution to the history of the war. *The Struggle for Europe* by C. Wilmot (1952) is an important revaluation of some of the main events of World War II; interesting but controversial. H. Feis' *Churchill, Roosevelt, Stalin* (1957) is a lucid and stimulating account of the wartime relations between Britain, Russia, and the United States, with special emphasis on the stresses and strains to which the coalition was exposed. Boyd C. Shafer's *Nationalism: Myth and Reality* (1955) is a succinct and well-written analysis of modern nationalism; an indispensable guide to the subject. Two recent books on the causes of World War I, N. Mansergh's *The Coming of the First World War* (1949) and L. Albertini's *The Origins of the War of 1914* (vol. 1, 1952), are detailed and objective, but add little, if anything, to the findings of Professors Fay and Schmidt. The story of the Korean armistice negotiations is authoritatively and interestingly related in *Panmunjom* by W. H. Vatcher, Jr. (1958). *Rockets, Missiles, and Space Travel* by Willy Ley (1958) presents the history, advances, problems, and prospects of rocketry and space exploration; one of the best of the books that have appeared. A. C. Clarke's *The Making of a Moon* (rev. ed., 1958) contains a brief history of rockets and satellite research. *Rockets, Missiles, and Moons* by C. I. Coombs (1957) is a simple account of the history and theory of rockets, missiles, and earth satellites.

Index

Abd-el-Krim, 380
Abyssinia, *see* Ethiopia
Acheson, Dean, 661, 664, 679–680, 696, 703, 826
Addis Ababa, 257, 536
Adenauer, Konrad, 684, 699, 703
Adowa, battle of (1896), 257
Agriculture: in Russia, 174, 181, 185–186, 784–785; in Germany, 340–341; in the Balkans, 353; in Denmark, 420–421; in Norway, 421–422; in Britain, 706, 710; in Spain, 743–744; in Italy, 754–755
Aircraft: in World War I, 44; in the Pacific, 162, 567; in World War II, 500, 509; in battle of Britain, 523–527; over Europe, 579 583; over Japan, 606–607
Albania, 373–375; 534, 817–818
Albert, king of Belgians, 404, 407
Aleutian Islands, 566
Alexander, king of Greece, 367–369
Alexander, king of Yugoslavia, 362
Alexander II, tsar of Russia, 63
Alfonso XIII, king of Spain, 378
Algeciras Conference, 14
Alsace-Lorraine, 4, 103; loss cripples German industry, 138; loss to France, 148
Amritsar massacre, 439
Anarcho-syndicalists, in Spain, 378, 387
Anschluss, see Austria
Anti-semitism, in Germany, 321–322, 327, 336, 346
Arabs, in Palestine, 223–226, 776
Armistice: Allied-German (1918), 85; Franco-German (1940), 518; Allied-German (1945), 598–599; Allied-Japanese (1945), 608
Ataturk, Kemal, 298; death of, 312
Atlantic Charter, 645–646
Atomic bomb, 607–608, 612, 631
Attlee, Clement R., 622, 769–770
Australia, and World War II, 566
Austria, republic of: treaty of St. Germain, 109–110; between two wars, 262–270; *Anschluss*, 263, 266, 487
Austro-Hungarian Empire, 3, 5, 11, 16, 17, 18, 21, 31; collapse of, 77, 84, 259–262
Autarchy, in Germany, 339–346
Azaña, Manuel, 386

Baden, Prince Max of, 79, 118, 119
Balfour Declaration, 223
Balkans, 11; Balkan Wars, 16; unrest in, 350–355; in World War II, 533–535, 537–539, 593–594; after World War II, 811–820
Baruch Plan, 657–658
Bataan, 564–565, 605
Belgium, 9; invasion of (1914), 22–25; between two wars, 404–409; war damage in, 405; invasion by Nazis, 513–516
Beneš, Edvard, 275, 495, 822–823
Bengazi, 535, 536, 572
Berchtesgaden, 489
Berlin blockade (1949), 695–698
Bevin, Ernest, 629, 631, 634, 639, 674, 769
Bidault, Georges, 629, 632, 635, 639–641, 674
Birth rate: in Italy, 253–254; in Germany, 333–334
Bismarck, Count Otto von, 4, 5, 10, 22
Bismarck Sea, battle of, 600
Blitzkrieg, 499–501, 513, 538–539, 543, 571
Blockade, naval (World War I), 49–50
Blum, Léon, 152–154, 725, 729
Bolsheviks: origin of, 64; stage revolution, 74, 167; theory of, 166; Red Terror, 170–172; in Hungary, 271–272
Bonn government, 698–700
Boris III, tsar of Bulgaria, 371
Bosnia-Herzegovina, 14–15
Bougainville Island, 601
Braun, Eva, "wife of Hitler," 598
Brest-Litovsk, treaty of, 75, 104
Briand, Aristide, 138, 155, 467–468
Britain: *see* Great Britain
Bulgaria, 16, 33; collapse of (1918), 77, 79; treaty of Neuilly, 111–112; between two wars, 371–373; in World War II, 533, 537, 593; treaty after World War

967

II, 636; becomes Soviet satellite, 816–817
Bulge, battle of the, 593
Bülow, Prince Bernhard von, 13, 14
Burma, 564, 771
Byrnes, James F., 627–634 *passim*, 729

Caliphate, abolition of, 304
Cape Matapan, battle of, 537
Carol, king of Rumania, 358–360, 533
Cassino, 587
Catalonia, separation movement, 378, 381, 385, 397
Central Powers, 31, 90
Chamberlain, Neville, 489, 512
Charles, Habsburg emperor, 84, 261–262, 272
Château-Thierry, battle of, 78, 517
Cherbourg, Allied capture of, 589–591
Chiang Kai-shek, 449, 823–828
China: imperialism in, 443–447; republican movement in, 447–449; between two wars, 449–452; Japanese invasion of, 451–452, 458–462; after World War II, 823–827
Churchill, Winston, 18, 31, 360, 513, 516, 573, 577, 587, 593, 612–619, 645, 709–710, 715–719, 759, 769
Clemenceau, Georges, 88, 91, 93, 98, 633
Colonies: German, 9–10, 104–105; French, 157–164, 573–575, 761–766; British, 217–220, 769–779; Belgian, 405–408; Netherlands, 415–416, 766–769
Cominform, 810, 820, 821
Comintern, 202–204
Commonwealth of Nations, British, 217–226; after World War II, 769–779
Communism: theory of, 165–166, 192–195; in Hungary, 271–272; in China, 449, 823–829; in Russia, 782–806
Communist International, *see* Comintern
Communist Party: in France, 152, 724–725; in Russia, 190, 794–796, 799–806; in Germany, 323–324; in Italy, 751–752
Constitution, Weimar, 124
Coral Sea, battle of, 49
Corregidor, 564–565, 605
Council of Foreign Ministers, 627–628; in London (1945), 629; in Moscow (1945), 630–631; in Paris (1946), 631–632; in New York (1946), 634–635; in Moscow (1947), 639; in London (1947), 640–641
Court of International Justice (The Hague), 103
Crete, battle for, 539–540
Czechoslovakia, 274–284, 636; rape of, 487–493; becomes Soviet satellite, 821–823

Daladier, Edouard, 154, 490, 493
D'Annunzio, Gabriele, 31, 97
Danzig, Free City of, 140, 286, 481
Dawes Plan, 132, 139

de Gasperi, Alcide, 634, 747, 748–753 *passim*, 756
de Gaulle, General Charles, 721–724
Delcassé, Théophile, 13, 14
Democracy, growth of, 227–228
Denmark: during and after World War I, 16, 103, 417–419; between two wars, 419–420; invasion by the Nazis, 509–511
Depression, world (1929), 141; in Germany, 141, 313; in Britain, 212; in Austria, 266; in Belgium, 407; in Netherlands, 413–414; in Japan, 458–459; in Europe, 469–470
de Valera, Eamon, 222
Dictatorship, resurgence of, 228–232; in Italy, 233–258; in Hungary, 272–273; in Poland, 285; in Germany, 313–339; in Yugoslavia, 363–365; in Greece, 369–370; in Spain, 378–382, 396, 399, 737–746; in Portugal, 399–402
Disarmament, failure of, 475–476, 659–663
Dnepropetrovsk, 181, 546
Dodecanese Islands, 31, 779
Dollfuss, Chancellor Engelbert, 266–269
Drang nach Osten, 16, 532, 543
Dual Alliance, 4–5
Duma, Russian, 64
Dumbarton Oaks, 646, 647
Dunkirk, battle of, 516

East Prussia, 29, 300
Ebert, President Friedrich, 98, 99, 119, 121, 123, 135
Education: in Russia 200–202; in Italy, 251–252; in Germany, 344–347
Edward VIII, king of England, 215–216
Egypt, 13, 777–778
Eire, 222
Eisenhower, General Dwight D., 574, 585, 586, 588–589, 591, 594, 599, 628, 679, 681, 684–685, 689, 691
El Agheila, 535, 573
El Alamein, 572–573
Elizabeth II, queen of Britain, 718
Entente Cordiale, 5, 6
European Coal and Steel Community, 678–679
Estonia, 502
Ethiopia: conquest of, by Italian armies, 255–258; freed from Italian rule, 536, 779, 780
Evatt, Herbert V., 633

Falkenhayn, General Erich von, 33–34, 36
Falkland Islands, battle of, 49
Fascio di Combattimento, 237, 245
Fascism: in Italy, 235–253; in Rumania, 360; in Spain, 396–399. *See also* Dictatorship
Ferdinand, king of Rumania, 354–358
Finland: between two wars, 427–429; invaded by Russia, 502–506; joins in the

fight against the Axis, 593; treaty after World War II, 636
Fiume, 96
Five-Year Plans, Soviet, 177–178, 785–790
Foch, Marshal Ferdinand, 78, 79, 85, 99
Fort Capuzzo, 532, 535
Four-Year Plans, in Germany, 340–343
Fourteen Points, 80, 88, 93, 98, 105
France, 4, 5, 9, 16, 22, 23, 29, 31; between two wars, 145–164; war damage, 145–147; recovery of, 147–149; political picture, 149–150; Fascist groups, 150; foreign policy (1919–1939), 154–157; colonial empire, 157–164; on the eve of World War II, 465–498; German invasion of, 516–522; occupation of French North Africa, 573–575; Allied invasion of, 588–593; after World War II, 718–731; war damage, 726–727; and Korean war, 730–731; revolt in French empire, 761–765
Francis Ferdinand, assassination of, 17
Franco, Francisco, 388; dictatorship of, 396–399, 737–746; and the Axis, 732–737; and the UN, 738–739

Gallipoli peninsula, 31
Gamelin, General Maurice, 485
Gandhi, Mohandas K., 439–442, 771, 774
Gas, in warfare, 39, 42
George II, king of Greece, 369, 540
George V, king of Britain, 215
George VI, king of Britain, 217, 717–718
Germany, before 1914, 4, 6–10, 13, 14, 21, 23; industry, 9–10; in World War I, 24. *See also* Weimar Republic
Germany, Nazi, 313–349; and Poland, 294–295, 481–482, 496–498; and Spanish civil war, 394–395, 485–486; foreign policy, 481–498; introduces conscription, 483; invades Russia, 531–541, 568–571, 576–579
Germany, post-World War II: in defeat, 616–689; war damage, 687–689; divided, 689–691; Soviet zone of, 690–691; reparations, 693–695; Berlin blockade, 695–698; West German republic, 698–700; Soviet East Germany, 700–702
Gilbert Islands, 601
Goebbels, Joseph, 320, 325, 326, 348, 542, 549, 692
Göring, Hermann, 316, 322, 325, 341, 343, 347, 524, 631, 693
Graziani, Marshal Rodolfo, 532, 535
Great Britain, 4–9, 16, 22, 29, 31; government after World War I, 206–208; industrial decline, 208–212; cabinets and governments, 212–214; colonies, 217–220; air strength, 483; battle of Britain, 522–531; Anglo-American occupation of North Africa, 573–575; Anglo-American landings in Italy, 583–588; after World War II, 705–709; Labor government in,

709–714; return of Conservatives, 714–717; change of rulers, 717–718
Greece, 16; and Smyrna, 298–300; between two wars, 367–370; in World War II, 534–535, 537, 539
Grey, Sir Edward, 8, 21, 22
Grieg, Edvard, 422
Guadalcanal, 567
Guam, 562
Gustav V, king of Sweden, 422–423

Haakon VII, king of Denmark, 421
Hacha, President Emil (Czechoslovakia), 495
Hague conferences, 7
Henlein, Konrad, 283–284
Herriot, Edouard, 133
Hindenburg, Paul von, 29, 30, 58, 61, 77, 79, 135, 143, 322, 324, 328
Hirohito, emperor of Japan, 608
Hitler, Adolf, 314; *Mein Kampf*, 205, 316; anti-Semitism, 315, 321, 327; idea of *Lebensraum*, 318–319; as demagogue, 320–321; accession to power, 321–323; as Führer, 328; rapprochement with Mussolini, 485–486; on the invasion of Russia, 542–543; death, 597–598; and Franco, 732–737
Ho Chi-minh, 759, 764, 765
Holy See, 249–250
Hong Kong, 562–563
Hopkins, Harry, 622, 649
Horthy, Admiral Miklós, 272
Hull, Cordell, 556–560, 617
Humbert II, king of Italy, 588, 747
Hungary: treaty of Trianon (1919), 111; between two wars, 270–274; in World War II, 533, 594; treaty (1947), 636

Imperialism: economic, 9; German, 10–11; revolt against, 432–435; in China, 443–447; as cause of World War II, 469–473; passing of old colonial, 758–781; new Soviet, 807–829
India: struggle for independence, 435–443; achieves independence, 771–775
Indies, Netherlands, revolt of, 766–769
Indo-China, revolt in, 761–766
Indonesia, *see* Indies, Netherlands
Inflation, in Germany, 127–129
Inönü, Ismet, 305, 312
Ireland, 220–223
Irish Free State, establishment of, 222–223
Irredentism: Hungarian, 270–274; in the Balkans, 352–353
Italy, 4, 31; after World War I, 232–235; genesis of Fascism, 235–238; Fascism in action, 238–253; quest for empire, 254–258; conquest of Albania, 374–375; and Spanish civil war, 394–395, 485–486; preparation for war, 483; rapprochement with Germany, 485; in World War II, 518; loss of empire, 531–532; Al-

lied landings in, 583–586; loss of colonies, 629, 779–781; reparations, 629; treaty after World War II, 635–636; after World War II, 746–749; establishment of republic, 749–753; war damage, 753–756
Iwo Jima, 605

Japan, 6, 11, 22; government of, 452–454; development of imperialist idea, 454–456, 556–558; during World War I, 456–458; between two wars, 458–462; invasion of China, 458; attack on Pearl Harbor, 558–561; conquests in the Pacific, 561–568; defeat of, 600–608; treaty after World War II, 641–644
Java, 363–364
Jews: in Palestine, 223–226, 776–777; in Poland, 293–294; in Germany, 321–322, 327, 336
Joffre, Marshal Joseph, 26, 33
Jutland, battle of, 52, 53

Kapp Putsch, 125–126
Karolyi, Count Mihály, 270–271
Kellogg—Briand Peace Pact, 467–468
Kerensky, Alexander, 73
Kharkov, 546, 577, 578
Kiev, 578
Kolchak, Admiral Aleksandr, 173
Kolkhozi, 181, 185–186
Korea, 455, 456, 630; background of war (1950), 665–667; republic of, 666–667; war in, 667–671; truce talks in, 671; influence of war on Europe, 729–730
Kulaks, 177, 182, 185–186
Kun, Béla, 271–272
Kuomintang, 448, 824–828
Kurile Islands, 618, 643
Kurusu, Saburo, 556–558

Labor Front, in Germany, 330–333
Labor Party, British, 213–214, 709–714
Lagerlöf, Selma, 425
Lansing, Robert, Secretary of State, 89
Lateran Treaty, 249–250
Latvia, 502
Laval, Pierre, 517, 719, 721
League of Nations, 94, 99–103; failure of, 473–478, 645; and UN, 651–652
Lemberg, 29, 30
Lend-Lease, 527–532, 554, 576
Lenin, Nikolai, 64, 75, 166, 175, 807
Leningrad, 543, 544
Leopold III, king of Belgians, 404–408, 515
Lie, Trygve, 652, 662, 668
Liebknecht, Karl, 118–121
Liége, 25
Literature: in Soviet Russia, 198–200, 801–805; in Nazi Germany, 347–349; in Norway, 422; in Sweden, 425
Lithuania, 287, 502

Lloyd George, David, 37, 88, 93, 109, 208, 212–213, 437, 476, 477
Locarno treaties, 137, 156, 467, 485
Ludendorff, General Erich, 29, 37, 58, 61, 77, 79, 117, 125, 316
Luftwaffe, 500, 509, 513, 523, 580
Lusitania, sinking of, 52, 57
Luxemburg, 24, 25; invasion of, by Nazis, 515
Luxemburg, Rosa, 118, 121

Malaya, self-government in, 770
MacArthur, General Douglas, 564–565, 567, 604–605, 606, 608, 642, 668, 670
MacDonald, Ramsay, 213–214
Maginot Line, 505–506, 517, 520
Malay peninsula, 563
Manchukuo, *see* Manchuria
Manchuria: Japanese invasion of, 451–452, 458–462; in World War II, 614
Mao-Tse-tung, 827–829
Mariana Islands, 604, 643
Marne, battle of, 26, 40, 77
Marshall, General George, 639–641, 672–674, 824, 825
Marshall Islands, 603, 643
Marshall Plan, 673–676, 756
Masaryk, Thomas, 275, 822–823
Mein Kampf, 205, 316, 345, 543
Mersa Matruh, 532, 535, 572, 573
Metaxas Line, 539
Michael, king of Rumania, 360, 533, 593, 621, 815–816
Midway Island, 562; battle of, 566
Mines: in World War I, 49, 76; in World War II, 508
Minorities: in the Balkans, 352–353; in Rumania, 357–358; in Yugoslavia, 361–362; problem of, 477–478
Molotov, Vyacheslav, 541, 542, 629, 632, 633, 634, 639, 640–641
Mons, battle of, 26, 44
Montgomery, General Sir Bernard, 573–599
Morocco, crises over, 13–16
Moscow, 543, 546, 547
Moslem League of India, 438, 771–775
Munich, conference at, 490–492
Mussolini, Benito, 31, 236–242; as absolute ruler of Italy, 242–258; and the Roman Catholic Church, 249–250; quest for empire, 255–258; at the Munich conference, 490–492; loss of African empire, 531–532; attempts to conquer Greece, 534–535; dismissal of, 586; death of, 597; and Franco, 733–734, 737

NATO, *see* North Atlantic Treaty Organization
Nagasaki, 608
Namur, 25
Nationalism: as cause of World War I, 11; economic, 469–473; as cause of World

War II, 479–480; resurgence of, in Asia, 758–761

Naval warfare (1914–1918), 48, 76; in World War II, 506–509, 562

Navy: British, 23, 49, 506–509; French, 521–522; German, 23, 49, 107, 506–509; U.S., 558, 566–568

Nazis: in Germany, 313–349; propaganda technique, 319; consolidate their power, 322–328; make Germany strong, 324; problem of population, 333–335; prepare for war, 336–344; agricultural policy, 340–341; education and culture under the, 344–349; concentration camps, 688–689; punishment of, 691–692; Nuremberg trials, 692–693

Nazism: in Austria, 266–270; in Rumania, 360; in Belgium, 407–408; in the Netherlands, 414–415; in Sweden, 424; in Switzerland, 430–431

Nehru, Pandit, 442, 771, 775

NEP, 174, 184

Neuilly, treaty of, 111–112, 371–372

Nicholas II, tsar of Russia, 7, 21, 64, 66, 68, 73, 173

Nimitz, Admiral Chester, 603, 604

Nobel, Alfred, 425–426

Nomura, Kichisaburo, 556–558

Normandy landings, 589

North Africa: campaign in, 531–532, 535–537, 571–573; Anglo-American occupation of, 573–575

North Atlantic Treaty Organization, 679–685, 702, 704

Norway, 420–422; invasion of, by Nazis, 511–512

Nuremberg trials, 692–693

Okinawa, 605–606, 643

Orient, awakening of, 432–435

Orlando, Vittorio, 93, 109, 748

Orthodox church, in Russia, 63, 195–198, 791–792

Ottoman Empire, 11; end of, 296–298

Paderewski, Ignace, 289

Pakistan, 772–775

Palau Islands, 105, 604

Palestine, 298–???; after World War II, 776–777

Paris Peace Conferences (1919), 87–98; (1946), 632–634

Patton, General George S., 591

Peace: efforts to make (1915), 31; (1916), 39; (1945), 611–625

Pearl Harbor, attack on, 558–561

Pershing, General John J., 78, 79

Pétain, Marshal Henri, 517, 574, 719–721

Peter II, king of Yugoslavia, 364

Philippines: war in, 564–565; reconquest of, 604–605, 606

Pilsudski, Josef, 285

Pius XI, 250

Poincaré, President Raymond, 90, 92, 128, 132, 151

Poland, 30, 33, 284–295; government of, 289–290, 292–293; agriculture in, 290–292; and Germany, 294–295, 481–482; and Russia, 294–295, 481–482, 496–498; conquest of, 499–505; post-World War II boundaries, 615, 621; becomes Soviet satellite, 811–813

Polish Corridor, 104, 286, 481

Popular Front: in France, 151–154; in Spain, 387–388

Port Arthur, 455, 456

Portsmouth, treaty of, 456

Portugal: in World War I, 399–401; between two wars, 401–402

Potsdam Conference, 607, 622–626

Pravda, 795–799 *passim*

Primo de Rivera, Jose, 378–382

Propaganda in World War I, 56–58

Race, in Nazi Germany, 322, 327, 336, 345, 346

Rasputin, Grigori, 67, 68, 72

Raw materials, contest for, 469–473

"Red Sunday," 65

Red Terror, 170, 196

Reichstag fire, 323

Reichswehr, 105–106, 327–328, 336–338

Reinsurance treaty, 5

Religion: in Soviet Russia, 195, 791–792; in Italy, 749–750

Reparations: after World War I, 108, 109, 127; after World War II, 627–638 *passim*

Reynaud, Premier Paul, 517, 725

Ribbentrop, Joachim von, 533, 542, 693

Roman Catholic Church: in Italy, 249–251, 749–750; in Spain, 383, 397, 741

Rommel, General Erwin, 535, 572–573, 575, 583, 585

Roosevelt, President Franklin D., 518, 527, 551, 560, 573, 588, 645, 663, 689, 759; at Yalta, 612–619

Roosevelt, President Theodore, 54, 78

Rosenberg, Alfred, 316, 541

Ruhr, invasion of, 127

Rumania: in World War I, 31, 36, 37, 76; between two wars, 353–361; loss of territory, 533; joins Allies, 593–594; treaty (1946), 696; becomes Soviet satellite, 815–816

Russia, Soviet: revolution, 73, 167; New Economic Policy (NEP), 174; five-year plans, 177–178, 785–790; collectivization of agriculture, 181–186; government of, 189–191; religion and culture, 195–200; foreign policy, 202–205; invasion of Poland, 501–502; invasion of Estonia, Latvia, Lithuania, and Finland, 501–506; invaded by Nazis, 541–551, 568–571, 576–579; drive into Germany, 593; and Japan, 607–608; after World War II, 782–806; religion and family life in, 791–

793; enforcement of orthodoxy, 793–806; thought control in, 796–801; imperialism of, 807–829
Russo-Japanese War, 6, 15, 65, 456
Russo-Polish War (1920), 287

St. Germain, treaty of, 109, 263, 276–277, 287
Saipan, 604
Salazar, Oliveira, 401–402
San Francisco UN Conference, 646–647
Sarajevo, 17, 18
Scandinavia, 416–426
Schlieffen, General Alfred von, 24
Schuman, Robert, 677
Schuman Plan, 677–679
Schuschnigg, Kurt, 269–270, 486–487
Serbia, 14, 16–18, 21, 22
Sèvres, treaty of, 109; revolt against, 298–302, 368
Shimonoseki, treaty of, 455
Sholokhov, Michael, 199–200
Shostakovich, Dmitri, 805
Sibelius, Jan, 428–429
Sicily, Allied landings in, 585–586
Siegfried Line, 506, 591, 594
Singapore, 563
Sinn Fein, 220
Sitzkrieg, 505–506
Smolensk, 544
Socialism: in Germany, 118; in Italy, 234–235; in Scandinavia, 416–426; in Britain, 632–634. *See also* Russia, Soviet
Solomon Islands, 566–567, 600–601
Somme, battle of, 36, 43
Soviet Union, *see* Russia, Soviet
Spain: during World War I, 376; between two wars, 377; dictatorship of Primo de Rivera, 378–382; republic in, 382–388; civil war in, 388–396; Franco dictatorship, 396–399; after World War II, 737–746
Spartacists, 118
Stakhanovism, 184–185
Stalin, Josef, 168, 175, 178, 189, 622, 639, 785, 791, 792, 794, 797, 809, 812; at Yalta, 612–619
Stalingrad, 570–571, 576
Stambolisky, 371–372
Stettinius, Edward R., 617, 647
Strait of Constantinople, 11, 31, 49
Strength through Joy (*Kraft durch Freude*), 330–331
Stresemann, Gustav, 131, 136, 140, 295
Sturzo, Don, 234
Submarines: in World War I, 49, 52, 58, 59, 61; in World War II, 506–509, 526–531, 574–575, 583
Sudeten Germans, 277, 283–284, 487–489
Sumatra, 563
Sun Yat-sen, 447–449
Sweden, 422–426
Switzerland, 9, 16, 429–431

Tangier incident, 14
Tanks, in World War I, 42–44
Tannenberg, battle of, 30
Tarawa, 601
Tirpitz, Admiral Alfred von, 7
Tito, Marshal (Josip Broz), 818–821
Tobruk, 535, 536, 572
Tojo, Premier Hideki, 604
Tokyo, bombing of, 568
Totalitarianism, 231–232. *See also* Fascism; Germany, Nazi
Transylvania, transfer to Rumania, 111
Treaties, secret (1915), 30–31, 88
Trianon, treaty of, 111, 273–274
Trieste, 629, 634–635, 819
Tripartite Pact (1940), 462, 555–556
Triple Alliance, 4, 11, 18, 22
Triple Entente, 6, 11
Trotsky, Leon, 74, 168, 175, 176
Truman, President Harry S., 599, 600, 607, 612, 622, 627, 641–642, 647, 657, 661, 668, 679, 680, 824
Turkey: and Germany, 16; in World War I, 31, 77; treaty with, 109; between two wars, 296–312; westernization of, 302–309; education in, 305–306; economic development, 309–311; nationalism in, 311–312

U.S.S.R., *see* Russia, Soviet
Undset, Sigrid, 422
United Nations: founding of, 645–647; organs of, 647–652; and the League, 651–652; achievements of, 653–657; and atomic energy, 657–659; and disarmament, 659–663; veto in the Security Council, 663–665; and Korea, 665–671
United States: neutrality of (1914–1917), 53–62; declaration of war (1917), 62; expeditionary force, 78; rejects treaty of Versailles, 108–109; isolationism after World War I, 466–467; and invasion of Russia, 548–549; and World War II (1939–1941), 551–556; and Japan (1941), 556–558; Pearl Harbor and after, 558–560; declaration of war, 560; in the Philippines, 564–565; in Pacific, 566–568; bombing of Tokyo, 568; Anglo-American occupation of North Africa, 573–575; invasion of Italy, 583–588; invasion of France, 588–593; victory over Germany, 593–600; victory over Japan, 600–608; treaty with Japan, 641–644
Universal Declaration of the Rights of Man, 655–657

V-bombs, 582–583
Venizelos, Eleutherios, 367–369
Verdun, battle of, 34–36
Versailles, treaty of, 97; reception of, in Germany, 125; and Poland, 287–288; and Nazis, 313, 315, 321, 337; and Belgium,

406; resentment against, 478–479; repudiation of, by Hitler, 486
Vichy regime, 719–721
Victor Emmanuel III, king of Italy, 238, 257, 586, 588, 747
Viet Minh, 764–766
Viet Nam, 764–766
Voroshilov, Marshal Kliment, 544

Wainwright, General Jonathan, 565
Wake Island, 562
Warsaw, 33, 500, 501
Washington Conference (1921), 448, 458, 476
Wavell, General Sir Archibald, 532, 535
Weimar Assembly, 122
Weimar Republic: at the Paris Peace Conference, 98; reparations, 108–127; early period, 117–136; at its height, 137–140; decline of, 140–144
White armies, in Russia, 172
Wilhelmina, queen of the Netherlands, 410–416
William II, German emperor, 5, 8, 13, 21, 55, 83
Wilson, President Woodrow, 3, 39, 53, 54, 56, 57, 61, 62, 78, 88, 98, 108–109, 117, 118, 367, 403, 479
Women, emancipation of, in Turkey, 306–309
World War I: causes, 3–20; outbreak of, 21–24; early campaigns, 24–53; second phase, 54–85; end of, 86

World War II: background of, 465; basic causes, 468–480; the road to, 484–498; invasion of Poland, 499–505; invasion of Denmark and Norway, 509–512; invasion of Netherlands, Belgium, and Luxemburg, 513–516; fall of France, 516–522; the Battle of Britain, 522–529; war in the Mediterranean area, 531–540; invasion of Russia, 541–551; U.S. neutrality, 551–556; Japan and the U.S., 556–558; Pearl Harbor and after, 558–561; Japanese conquests, 561–568; Anglo-American occupation of North Africa, 573–575; bombers over Europe, 579–583; invasion of Italy, 583–588; Allied invasion of France, 588–593; defeat of Germany, 593–600; defeat of Japan, 600–609

Yalta Conference, 612–619, 646, 649
Young Plan, 139–140
"Young Turks," 14
Youth organizations: in Italy, 245–246, 252–253; in Germany, 345–346
Yugoslavia: between two wars, 361–367; and World War II, 533, 537–539; becomes Axis satellite, 818; revolt against Soviet domination, 819–821

Zamora, Alcala, 382
Zeppelins, 44
Zionists, 223–226, 776–777
Zog I, king of the Albanians, 374–375